Almanac of Business and Industrial Financial Ratios

2010 EDITION

LEO TROY, Ph.D.

.CCH
a Wolters Kluwer business

Editorial Staff

Production..Christopher Zwirek
Design .... Craig Arritola

This publication is designed to provide accurate and authoritative information in regard to the subject matter covered. It is sold with the understanding that the publisher is not engaged in rendering legal, accounting, or other professional service and that the author is not offering such advice in this publication. If legal advice or other professional assistance is required, the services of a competent professional person should be sought.

ISBN: 978-0-8080-2245-9

© 2009, CCH. All Rights Reserved.
4025 W. Peterson Avenue
Chicago, IL 60646-6085
1 800 248 3248
www.CCHGroup.com

Printed in the United States of America

Dedicated

To Alexander, Suzannah, Dale, Ariel Sarah Troy, Abigayle Hannah Troy, and Rachel Ilana Troy

Preface

Now in its 41st Edition, the *Almanac of Business and Industrial Financial Ratios* provides a precise benchmark for evaluating an individual company's financial performance. The performance data is derived from the latest available IRS figures on U.S. and international companies, and tracks 50 operating and financial factors in nearly 200 industries. The *Almanac* provides competitive norms in actual dollar amounts for revenue and capital factors, as well as important average operating costs in percent of net sales. It also provides other critical financial factors in percentage, including debt ratio, return on assets, return on equity, profit margin, and more. Beyond its reliable insights into corporate behavior, the *Almanac* can be used by other countries looking to model their economies on American performance.

Also included with the text, in a special pocket provided in the inside cover of the book, is a CD-ROM that contains all the materials found in the book including the explanatory discussion, the data tables, and the supporting index. Also included on the CD, but not in the book itself, is a special template that allows the reader to add individual company data of interest to compare and contrast with data from the book.

2010 Edition Highlights

The 2010 Edition of the *Almanac of Business and Industrial Financial Ratios* has been updated to include the following:

- **Broad scope:** *2010 Almanac* features the North American Industry Classification System (NAICS), so you can benchmark or analyze results consistently with corporations in the United States, Canada, and Mexico.

- **Most industry types:** *2010 Almanac* highlights most industry types, including industries with advanced technologies and newly emerging industries such as paging and wireless communications.

- **A truer picture** of corporate financial performance, since the data isn't based on a mixed bag of averages that might include partnerships or sole proprietors. *2010 Almanac* features a homogeneous universe of American corporate financial performance.

- **Many classifications:** *2010 Almanac* analyzes 197 industries with 50 financial performance items.

- **Benchmarks:** *2010 Almanac* provides 13 benchmarks, including such critical measures as Receipts to Cash Flow, Debt to Total Assets, and Return on Equity both before and after taxes.

- **Analytical tables:** *Table I, Corporations with and without Net Income (All Corporations), and Table II, Corporations with Net Income.*

- **Easier apples-to-apples comparisons:** Each table is divided into 13 asset sizes.

- **More comprehensive:** Total receipts of all corporations covered by *2010 Almanac* is $27.4 trillion, making the *Almanac* the Anatomy of American Corporate Capitalism.

Leo Troy, Ph. D.

October 2009

About the Author

Dr. Leo Troy is Professor of Economics at Rutgers University. He has been a faculty member of Rutgers for 50 years. In addition to authoring the widely praised *Almanac*, he has written many other books and articles published in leading journals. Professor Troy has been the recipient of numerous awards including two from the National Science Foundation, and two Fulbright grants. In addition, he has received numerous awards from private foundations. Dr. Troy received his Ph.D. from Columbia University and is a member of Phi Beta Kappa. He is a veteran of World War II with three battle stars and the combat infantry badge. He is the father of two children and is also a grandfather of three girls, including twins.

Acknowledgments

I wish to acknowledge the contributions of five people in particular for the development of the 41st Edition of the *Almanac:* Phil Wilson, Alan Kovar of Brighton Best, Lawrence R. Chodor, CPA, CVA, Wiss & Company, Marvin Sunshine, and Karen Kane.

Philip is responsible for the programming, which dealt with a very large amount of data, covering both the current and trend information. Alan, drawing upon his knowledge and experience as a CPA and Partner of Wiss and Company of Livingston, N.J., contributed significantly to the new content of the book. To Marvin Sunshine, Esq, my appreciation for actions and support that helped make the *Almanac* a continuing publication. Karen Kane is acknowledged for her contributions to the graphics of this issue.

Special acknowledgement is due my late friends and colleagues, Stan Katz, CPA, and Professor Emeritus of Accounting, Rutgers University, John Gilmour. I thank, too, Professor of Accounting, Rutgers University, David Zaumeyer, Ph.D., CPA, for recommending several ratios that continue to be included in the *Almanac*. I thank Mr. Ka-Neng Au, Business Librarian, Rutgers University, for significant contributions to the *Almanac*.

I wish to recognize, too, the cooperation of members of the Statistics of Income Division of the Internal Revenue Service—in particular, Ken Szeflinksi, Martha A. Harris, and Phyllis J. Whiles of the Corporation Returns Analysis Section. Without their data and its reliability, the Almanac would not be possible. Responsibility for the use of their facts and figures is, of course, solely my own. In this regard, I recall the valuable assistance I received from Barry Rosenstein, MBA, CPA, in checking procedures, in earlier editions, and which have continued into the current one. Finally, I wish to recognize the help of Suzannah B. Troy in bringing about the 41st annual edition of the *Almanac*. I anticipate continuation of her valuable assistance in subsequent editions.

INTRODUCTION

QUESTIONS, ANSWERS AND COMMENTS ON THE ALMANAC
Some users have requested further information on the use of the Almanac's ratios and statistics. This Q & A addition to the Almanac is in response to that demand.

1. What are the general purposes of the Almanac?

The goal of the Almanac is to provide users with a reliable and comprehensive source of standard financial ratios and financial statistics on all corporations, public and private, including those filing 1120S returns in the United States. Excluded are all individual proprietorships and partnerships. The Almanac makes available key business and financial statistics, which are consistent and neutral (unbiased by any commercial publisher or trade association).

2. What is the source and reliability of the Almanac's results?

The Almanac's results are computed from the Department of the Treasury, Internal Revenue Service's statistical sampling of the tax returns of all corporations. Dividends received from foreign corporations are included in total receipts of those corporations affected. The statistics apply to the company rather than the establishment.

3. Are international comparisons available?

Yes. Because of the adoption of a common system of industrial classification by the U.S., Canada and Mexico, known as the North American Industrial Classification System of industries (NAICS), under the North American Free Trade Agreement, users in Canada and Mexico can compare and contrast their results with those corporations in the United States.

4. What about comparisons within the U.S?

These are the most important applications of the Almanac. Results are available for each and every corporation within the U.S., whether public or private, and include small business corporations, those which file the 1120S tax return. Therefore, users can compare their corporate performance with that of their industry and asset size group of corporate enterprise in the United States.

5. How many corporations are covered in the Almanac?

The Almanac's results are derived from more than 5.8 million corporation tax returns. Furthermore, the user can easily determine the number of enterprises for the total of each industry and by each of the 12 asset size groups. This makes for a total of 13 asset size comparisons.

6. What about differences in the size of corporations?

In addition to the results for each industry, the Almanac displays 12 columns of performance by the size of assets. Again, this makes for a total of 13 asset size comparisons.

7. Does the Almanac distinguish between the profitability of corporations?

In a word, yes. Each industry is divided between two tables: Table I reports the results of all corporations in an industry, that is, those with and without net income. It is followed by a second table for the same industry, Table II, which reports only those corporations with net income.

8. How many items of information are there for each industry?

There are 50 indicators of corporate performance in each table and each industry and for all asset size groups, except where the IRS' data sample is too small, or it does not supply the necessary information.

9. Who are the users of the Almanac?

Accountants, corporate managers, business consultants, investors evaluating a corporate takeover, entrepreneurs considering new businesses, lawyers, and students of accounting, business, and management.

10. What accounting time period is covered?

The Internal Revenue Service provides the most recent statistics publicly available for the Almanac. For the 2010 Almanac, these statistics apply to the accounting period from July 2006 through June 2007.

WHAT'S NEW IN THIS EDITION

Beginning with the year 2002, the *Almanac of Business and Industrial Financial Ratios* began using the North American Industry Classification System (NAICS). NAICS replaces the Internal Revenue Service's own system, which it had used for many years, an adaptation of Standard Industrial Classification (SIC); all previous *Almanacs* had used that adaptation.

The new industrial classification system is the product of the North American Free Trade Agreement (NAFTA), and it replaces the existing classification systems not only of the United States but also of Canada and Mexico. Hence, the new system applies uniformly to the three countries, and users of the *Almanac 2010*, utilizing the new international industrial classification system, can now compare their results with corporations in all three nations.

In the United States, the new manual was created by the Office of Management and Budget (OMB). The NAICS system gives special attention to industries producing and furnishing advanced technologies, new and emerging industries, as well as service industries in general. NAICS divides the economy into 21 sectors, five in the predominantly goods-producing area, and 16 in the service producing area.

INDUSTRY SECTORS

Particularly noteworthy is NAICS's introduction of an Information sector. This sector assembles the industries from Newspaper Publishers (511110) to Internet Service Providers, Web Portals, and Data Processing Services (518115). Within this span, NAICS and therefore the *Almanac* include such important industries as software publishing, database and directory publishing, satellite telecommunications, paging and cellular, and other wireless communications. NAICS and the *Almanac* also provide a category of industries on Professional, Scientific, and Technical Services, industries in which human capital is the major input. The sector includes Legal Services (541115) and Scientific Research and Development Services (541700), as well as Management, Scientific, and Technical Services (541600) and Computer Systems Design and Related Services (541515).

Other important sectors are the Arts, Entertainment, and Recreation including Amusement, Gambling, and Recreation (713105), and the Health Care and Social Assistance including

Offices of Physicians (621115), Hospitals, Nursing, and Residential Care Facilities (622005). Within Manufacturing, the key goods sector industry, there is now a category embracing Computer and Electronic Product Manufacturing. It spans industries such as Computer and Peripheral Equipment (334110) to Navigational, Measuring, Electromedical, and Control Instruments (334500).

The source of the IRS's data are the tax returns of all *active* public and private corporations. Because the *Almanac's* data are derived only from corporate tax returns, there is a mixture of corporate with the financial performance of partnerships and individual proprietorships; the *Almanac's* information constitutes a **homogeneous universe**. The tax returns are classified by the IRS on the basis of the business activity which accounts for a corporation's largest percentage of total receipts. Large corporations with dissimilar business activities are included in only one industry, despite operations that are unrelated to the industry in which they are grouped.

The data developed by the IRS are derived from a stratified probability sample of corporation income tax returns. Where the sample data from the sample are small and should those numbers be used in a denominator, the result is reported as a dot (·) in the *Almanac*. Returns of the largest corporations are generally in the sample from year to year, but comparability can be affected by consolidations and mergers, changes in the law and the tax forms, and changes in the industrial classification system used over the years.

REPRESENTATIVE INDUSTRIES

The *Almanac* reports on nearly 200 industries. Minor industries are denoted by a six-digit code; major industries are designated by a three-digit industry code; industrial sectors by a two-digit code; and industrial divisions by a two-digit code. When the data are the same for minor, major, sector, and industrial division, the IRS reports only the industrial division, and similarly for other identities applicable to the major and sectoral industries; the *Almanac* follows this procedure.

Almanac 2010 continues the previous coverage of reporting information: for all industries, **Table I, Corporations with and without Net Income** (that is, the entire universe of active reporting corporations), and **Table II, Corporations with Net Income**, a subset of the universe. In the *Almanac 2010*, Table I covers over 5.8 million enterprises (corporations), and Table II covers 3.4 million corporations with net income. This implies that 2.4 million corporations reported deficits. The IRS defines net income (or deficit) as the companies' net profit or loss from taxable sources of income reduced by allowable deductions. Total receipts of the 5.8 million corporations reported in *Almanac 2010* was $27.4 trillion, up by $1.9 trillion.

The *Almanac* continues to report performance results not only by the total for each industry, but by 12 other asset size groups (a total of 13 asset size groups), providing 50 items of data and/or ratios on corporate performance:

Total

Zero
$1 to $500,000
$500,001 to $1,000,000
$1,000,001 to $5,000,000
$5,000,001 to $10,000,000
$10,000,001 to $25,000,000
$25,000,001 to $50,000,000
$50,000,001 to $100,000,000
$100,000,001 to $250,000,000
$250,000,001 to $500,000,000
$500,000,001 to $2,500,000,000
$2,500,000,001 or more

All data in Tables I and II cover an accounting period identified on all tables and are the most recent information available from the IRS. For the *Almanac 2010*, the accounting period is July 2006 through June 2007. The dating of the data is counterbalanced by the most extensive industrial coverage available in any report on financial performance, the number of items of corporate performance, and their availability in thirteen asset size groups. Moreover, the timing of the data are also counterbalanced by the stability of the *Almanac's* values as past trends have indicated. Therefore, the *Almanac's* financial results are reliable in assessing current corporate performance.

Beyond its reliable insights into corporate behavior on a micro basis, its comprehensive and detailed coverage make the *Almanac* the **Anatomy of American Corporate Capitalism**. In this macro sense, it constitutes **the** example to those countries desirous of modeling their economies on the American performance.

How to Use the Almanac

On the micro level, the *Almanac* multiplies manyfold the power of financial analysis to evaluate an individual company's financial performance: In contrast to many standard reports, the *Almanac* gives management, and analysts independent of any company, more of the fundamental analytical tools needed to compare their company with companies in the same industry and of the same asset size. The *Almanac* can enhance the value of any company's annual report because it affords the analyst and the stockholder detailed background of financial information for comparison.

All items and ratios are listed in Both Table I and Table II. No figures are reported in the *Almanac* when the IRS has either suppressed the underlying data, or the sample size, or other reasons affecting a calculated result, and where the ratio/item was not applicable to an industry. The 50 tax-based items that provide that financial analysis are as follows:

1. Number of Enterprises

These are the count of corporate tax returns filed by active corporations on one of the Form 1120-series returns.

> **Special Note:** Net Sales is used to compute the percentage of items 3 to 7 to Net Sales for all industries, except Finance, Insurance, and Real Estate (FIRE). For the FIRE industries, Total Receipts are used to compute the percentage of items 3 to 7.

Revenues ($ in thousands), Items 2 to 9

2. Operating Income (Net Sales)

This is the IRS item Business Receipts, the gross operating receipts reduced by the cost of returned goods and allowances.

3. Interest

Taxable interest includes interest on U.S. Government obligations, loans, notes, mortgages, arbitrage bonds, nonexempt private activity bonds, corporate bonds, bank deposits, and tax refunds; interest received from tax-exempt state or local municipal bonds and ESOP loans are not included in this item.

4. Rents

These are the gross amounts received from the use or occupancy of property by corporations whose principal activities did not involve operating rental properties.

5. Royalties

These are gross payments received for the use of property rights before taking deductions.

6. Other Portfolio Income

These consist of cash, notes, and accounts receivable, less allowance for bad debts and inventories.

7. Other Receipts

These receipts include such items as income from minor operations, cash discounts, claims, license rights, judgments, and joint ventures.

8. Total Receipts

Total receipts are the sum of ten items: 1. Business receipts; 2. Interest; 3. Interest on government obligations: state and local; 4. Rents; 5. Royalties; 6. Net capital gains (excluding long-term gains from regulated investment companies); 7. Net gain, noncapital assets; 8. Dividends received from domestic corporations; 9. Dividends received from foreign corporations; 10. Other receipts.

9. Average Total Receipts

Total receipts divided by the number of enterprises.

OPERATING COSTS/OPERATING INCOME, ITEMS 10 TO 22

10. Cost of Operations

This is the IRS's Costs of Goods Sold; it consists of the costs incurred in producing the goods or furnishing the services that generated the corporations' business receipts.

11. Salaries and Wages

These include the amount of salaries and wages paid as well as bonuses and director's fees, but no contributions to pension plans (see item 16) nor compensation of officers (see item 20).

12. Taxes Paid

Excludes Federal Income Taxes; they are the amounts paid for ordinary state and local taxes, social security, payroll taxes, unemployment insurance taxes, excise taxes, import and tariff duties, and business license and privilege taxes.

13. Interest Paid

These amounts consist of interest paid on all business indebtedness.

14. Depreciation

The charges allowed are governed principally by the IRS rules in effect in 1997, basically enacted in 1986, but also include other modifications. Hence, depreciation could represent amounts computed by different sets of rules.

15. Amortization and Depletion

Most amortization is calculated on a straight-line basis. Depletion is allowed for the exhaustion of natural deposits and timber.

16. Pensions, Profit-Sharing, Stock Bonus, and Annuity Plans

These are amounts deducted during the current year for qualified pension, profit-sharing, or other funded deferred compensation plans.

17. Employee Benefits

These are employer contributions to death benefit, insurance, health, accident, and sickness, and other welfare plans.

18. Advertising

Amounts include promotion and publicity expenses.

19. Other Expenses

These include expenses for repairs, bad debts, rent paid on business property, domestic production activities, contributions and gifts, and expenses not allocable to specific deductible items.

20. Officers' Compensation

Salaries, wages, stock bonuses, bonds, and other forms of compensation are included in this item.

21. Operating Margin

This is the net income after all operating costs have been deducted.

22. Operating Margin Before Officers' Compensation

This measure takes into account the effect of Officers' Compensation on the operating margin.

Selected Average Balance Sheet Items ($ in thousands) Items 23 to 29

23. Average Net Receivables

The total of Notes and Accounts Receivable, less Allowance for Bad Debts, divided by the number of enterprises. Notes and Accounts Receivable are the gross amounts arising from business sales or services to customers on credit in the course of ordinary trade or business. This includes commercial paper, charge accounts, current intercompany receivables, property investment loans, and trade acceptances.

24. Average Inventories

Total inventories are divided by the number of enterprises. Inventories include finished goods, partially finished goods, new materials and supplies acquired for sale, merchandise on hand or in transit, and growing crops reported as assets by agricultural enterprises.

25. Average Net Property, Plant and Equipment

This includes depreciable assets less accumulated depreciation, depletable assets less accumulated depletion, and land; the sum is divided by the number of enterprises. Depreciable assets consist of end-of-year balance sheet tangible property, such as buildings and equipment used in trade or business, or held for the production of income, and that has a useful life of one year or more. The amount of accumulated depreciation represents the portion written off in the current year, as well as in prior years. Depletable assets represent the end-of-year value of mineral property, oil and gas wells, and other natural resources; standing timber; intangible development and drilling costs capitalized; and leases and leaseholds, subject to depletion. Accumulated depletion represents the cumulative adjustment of these assets.

26. Average Total Assets

Total Assets (and Total Liabilities) are amounts reported in the end-of-year balance sheet. Total Assets are net amounts after reduction from accumulated depreciation, accumulated amortization, accumulated depletion, and the reserve for bad debts. Total Liabilities include the claims of creditors and stockholders' equity, and were net after reduction by the cost of treasury stock. The average of total assets was obtained by dividing it by the number of enterprises.

27. Average of Notes and Loans Payable, and Mortgages

These liabilities were separated on the balance sheet according to the time to maturity of the obligations. Time to maturity was based on the date of the balance sheet, rather than the date of issue of the obligations. The total was divided by the number of enterprises.

28. Average of All Other Liabilities

These included accounts payable, and other liabilities including other current liabilities. The total was divided by the number of enterprises.

29. Average Net Worth

Net Worth represents the stockholders' equity in the corporation (total assets minus the claims of creditors). It consists of Capital Stock, Paid-In Capital Surplus, Retained Earnings Appropriated, Retained Earnings Unappropriated, less cost of treasury stock.

SELECTED FINANCIAL RATIOS, NUMBER OF TIMES TO ONE, RATIOS 30 TO 44

30. Current Ratio

The items that used Current Assets for this ratio are Cash; Notes and Accounts Receivable, Less: Allowance for Bad Debts; Inventories; Government Obligations; Tax-Exempt Securities; and Other Current Assets. For Current Liabilities, the following items were included: Accounts Payable; Mortgages and Notes Maturing in Less than 1 Year; and Other Current Liabilities.

This ratio, rated highest by CPAs as a measure of liquidity, gauges the ability of a company to meet its short-term financial obligations should it be compelled to liquidate its assets. However, it is not an absolute measure of the company's ability to meet its obligations. It is obtained by dividing current assets by current liabilities. The standard guideline has been a ratio of 2 to 1; however, some companies have found that in their experience, a ratio less than 2 to 1 is adequate, while others consider a larger one to be necessary. The ratio is affected by the method of valuation of inventory (LIFO or FIFO) and by inflation. The *Almanac* provides measures that can be treated as standards by size of asset.

31. Quick Ratio

This ratio is also known as the "Acid Test Ratio" because it is often used to estimate a company's general liquidity. There is some disagreement about the inclusion of inventory in the numerator because it may be slow moving, obsolete, or pledged to specific creditors, and, therefore, not be readily convertible into cash. The *Almanac* adopts a conservative approach and does not include the item in calculating the ratio. Excluding inventories and other current assets, the numerator is the same as that used in determining current assets. The denominator, current liabilities, is unchanged. The ratio of 1 to 1 has been considered a reasonable standard, but it is jeopardized because accounts and notes receivable may not be convertible into cash at face value and at short notice. The *Almanac* provides measures that can be treated as standards by size of asset.

32. Net Sales to Working Capital

This is an efficiency, or turnover, ratio that measures the rate at which current assets less current liabilities (Working Capital) is used in making sales. (In industries in Finance, Insurance, and Real Estate, total receipts rather than net sales is used.) A low ratio indicates a less efficient (profitable) use of working capital in making sales. The *Almanac* provides measures that can be treated as standards by size of asset. Working Capital is the difference between current assets and current liabilities.

33. Coverage Ratio

This ratio measures the number of times all interest paid by the company is covered by earnings before interest charges and taxes (EBIT). For that reason, the ratio is also known as the "times interest earned ratio." The ratio indicates the company's ability to service its debt based on its income.

34. Total Asset Turnover

The ratio is an efficiency ratio because it indicates the effectiveness of the company's use of its total assets in generating sales. It is measured by dividing net sales by total assets.

35. Inventory Turnover

Inventory turnover measures the liquidity of the inventory. It is computed by dividing the cost of goods sold by the average inventory. The result shows the number of times that the average inventory can be converted into receivables or cash. The ratio reflects both on the quality of the inventory and the efficiency of management. Typically, the higher the turnover rate, the more likely profits will be higher.

SPECIAL NOTE: Inventory turnover is not computed for industries in Finance, Insurance, and Real Estate.

36. Receivables Turnover

This ratio measures the liquidity of accounts receivable. It indicates the average collection period throughout the year. It is obtained by dividing sales average by net receivables. It is not computed in the Finance, Insurance, and Real Estate industries (although it is calculated for all other industries even though conventional analysis typically omits it) for many of the industries in the *Almanac*.

37. Total Liabilities to Net Worth

This ratio indicates the extent to which the company's funds are supplied by short- and long-term creditors compared to its owners. It is an indicator of the company's long-term debt paying ability. The ratio is one of the most important bearing on the company's capital structure. Net worth is defined in ratio 29.

38. Current Assets to Working Capital

The dependence of Working Capital in part on current assets is important to understanding this part of the source of Working Capital. Current Assets are defined in ratio 30 and Working Capital is defined in ratio 32.

39. Current Liabilities to Working Capital

The dependence of Working Capital in part on current liabilities is important to understanding this part of the source of Working Capital. Current Liabilities are defined in ratio 30 and Working Capital is defined in ratio 32.

40. Working Capital to Net Sales or Total Receipts

The purpose of this ratio is to determine the working capital needed in relation to projected sales or receipts. Working Capital is defined in ratio 32.

41. Inventory to Working Capital

This ratio, by showing the proportion of Working Capital invested in Inventory, indicates the part of Current Assets that are least liquid. Inventories which exceed working capital indicate that current liabilities exceed liquid current assets. Working Capital is defined in ratio 32.

42. Total Receipts to Cash Flow

Cash Flow is the difference between cash receipts and cash disbursements. The ratio of total receipts to cash flow could suggest steps which management might take to improve the company's cash position.

43. Cost of Goods to Cash Flow

This ratio can be the basis for projections of cash requirements needed to fund projected costs of production. Cash flow is defined in ratio 42.

44. Cash Flow to Total Debt

This ratio indicates the extent to which a company could service its total debt from cash flow. It is analogous to the coverage ratio; refer to ratio 33. Cash flow is defined in ratio 42.

SELECTED FINANCIAL FACTORS (IN PERCENTAGES), ITEMS 45 TO 50

45. Debt Ratio (Total Liabilities to Total Assets)

This ratio indicates the company's ability to pay all its debts. It measures the creditors' and owners' of the company's ability to withstand losses. It is an indicator of the long-run solvency of the firm.

46. Return on Total Assets

The ratio combines the turnover and profit ratios (Sales/Total Assets x [times] Profit/Sales) and yields the return on investment (Total Assets). The result is the end product of the DuPont System of financial analysis. The system takes into account both operating income and operating assets. In Table I of each industry, the Return on Investment (ROI) is net income less deficit before income taxes divided by total assets. In Table II of each industry, the ROI is net income before income taxes divided by Total Assets. Total Assets are used because management has discretion in the investment of the resources provided by both the creditors and owners.

47. Return on Equity Before Income Taxes

This ratio measures the profitability of the company's operations to owners, before income taxes. For Table I this is net income, less deficit before income taxes and before credits. For Table II this is net income minus income tax before credits.

48. Return on Equity After Income Taxes

This ratio measures the profitability of the company's operations to owners, after income taxes. For Table I this is net income, less deficit and minus income tax before credits. For Table II this is net income minus income tax and before credits.

49. Profit Margin (Before Income Tax)

This is net income before income tax divided by net sales (or total receipts) and indicates the contribution of sales to the profitability of the company. Competition, capital structure, and operating characteristics cause the margin to vary within and among industries. For Table I, net income less deficit and before income taxes is the numerator; for Table II it is net income before tax.

50. Profit Margin (After Income Tax)

This ratio is the same as ratio 49 except that income taxes are taken into account.

Table of Contents

Page references to tables for industries with net income are in italic

PRINCIPAL BUSINESS ACTIVITY (BASED ON NAICS)

ALMANAC
of Business and Industrial
FINANCIAL RATIOS

41st ANNUAL EDITION
2010

Table I

Corporations with and without Net Income

AGRICULTURAL PRODUCTION

MONEY AMOUNTS AND SIZE OF ASSETS IN THOUSANDS OF DOLLARS

Item Description for Accounting Period 7/06 Through 6/07	Total	Zero Assets	Under 500	500 to 1,000	1,000 to 5,000	5,000 to 10,000	10,000 to 25,000	25,000 to 50,000	50,000 to 100,000	100,000 to 250,000	250,000 to 500,000	500,000 to 2,500,000	2,500,000 and over
Number of Enterprises **1**	100992	9946	60219	15129	13779	1095	547	110	93	49	16	9	0
Revenues ($ in Thousands)													
Net Sales **2**	89453717	851369	11727346	8670173	17674552	7740263	9556037	2569258	6872132	8013015	4060934	11718637	0
Interest **3**	360996	5387	44039	39107	83385	25541	27694	13990	28247	37288	10317	46001	0
Rents **4**	888695	1834	204064	170036	296181	72428	19005	12100	34583	46976	14299	17189	0
Royalties **5**	130892	0	7511	9941	20087	6193	11487	522	6042	22335	15011	31763	0
Other Portfolio Income **6**	1767062	34548	321526	193334	327875	109327	117686	72997	33514	80488	51285	424483	0
Other Receipts **7**	9103067	156185	3008945	1309742	2929398	686520	173972	125150	170014	218255	182075	142810	0
Total Receipts **8**	101704429	1049323	15313431	10392333	21331478	8640272	9905881	2794017	7144532	8418357	4333921	12380883	0
Average Total Receipts **9**	1007	106	254	687	1548	7891	18109	25400	76823	171803	270870	1375654	•
Operating Costs/Operating Income (%)													
Cost of Operations **10**	51.9	25.9	18.5	30.9	36.1	49.1	67.0	60.2	75.5	65.5	83.0	80.7	•
Salaries and Wages **11**	8.2	5.2	10.1	10.0	12.1	9.1	5.7	7.3	5.9	5.9	2.7	5.9	•
Taxes Paid **12**	2.3	2.1	3.1	3.5	3.5	2.2	1.6	2.2	1.4	1.8	1.6	0.9	•
Interest Paid **13**	3.0	3.5	3.7	3.7	3.7	3.4	2.5	3.4	2.2	2.0	1.6	2.3	•
Depreciation **14**	5.5	7.7	8.5	7.9	7.8	5.9	3.3	5.3	3.0	3.6	4.1	1.9	•
Amortization and Depletion **15**	0.3	0.4	0.1	0.0	0.1	0.2	0.3	0.6	0.4	0.5	1.2	0.3	•
Pensions and Other Deferred Comp. **16**	0.3	0.0	0.1	0.5	0.3	0.1	0.2	0.1	0.3	0.1	0.5	0.3	•
Employee Benefits **17**	1.1	0.7	1.1	1.4	1.2	0.9	0.8	0.8	0.7	0.9	0.9	1.9	•
Advertising **18**	0.4	0.2	0.3	0.4	0.3	0.3	0.4	0.4	0.3	0.3	0.2	0.6	•
Other Expenses **19**	36.9	62.9	80.7	55.5	51.5	40.3	19.4	23.1	12.4	20.1	8.1	6.2	•
Officers' Compensation **20**	2.2	1.5	4.4	4.5	3.2	1.7	1.5	1.2	1.0	0.9	0.6	0.6	•
Operating Margin **21**	•	•	•	•	•	•	•	•	•	•	•	•	•
Operating Margin Before Officers' Comp. **22**	•	•	•	•	•	•	•	•	•	•	•	•	•

Selected Average Balance Sheet ($ in Thousands)

Net Receivables 23	71	0	4	28	49	348	1538	4958	11007	19563	31307	170715
Inventories 24	98	0	9	45	149	1002	2330	5899	10396	16268	36477	94826
Net Property, Plant and Equipment 25	454	0	93	422	1062	3923	5879	14765	26596	59804	126886	292517
Total Assets 26	980	0	171	707	1867	6793	15731	34265	69668	148250	308193	1521476
Notes and Loans Payable 27	515	0	163	320	1060	4357	8590	15620	29767	46680	71711	600052
All Other Liabilities 28	166	0	8	48	148	832	2665	4499	14174	30194	67898	753677
Net Worth 29	298	0	0	339	659	1604	4476	14146	25727	71376	168584	167747

Selected Financial Ratios (Times to 1)

Current Ratio 30	1.4	•	1.5	1.6	1.4	1.1	1.5	1.5	1.4	1.6	1.9	1.1
Quick Ratio 31	0.7	•	1.0	1.0	0.7	0.5	0.7	0.8	0.7	0.9	0.7	0.6
Net Sales to Working Capital 32	10.3	•	14.2	9.1	10.2	37.8	7.6	4.8	7.8	8.3	4.8	23.5
Coverage Ratio 33	1.5	4.7	1.0	1.4	1.2	0.5	1.4	2.3	1.4	2.7	2.2	3.1
Total Asset Turnover 34	0.9	•	1.1	0.8	0.7	1.0	1.1	0.7	1.1	1.1	0.8	0.9
Inventory Turnover 35	4.7	•	3.9	3.9	3.1	3.5	5.0	2.4	5.4	6.6	5.8	11.1
Receivables Turnover 36	10.6	•	55.8	22.8	18.2	22.4	11.5	4.3	7.6	8.3	11.0	13.5
Total Liabilities to Net Worth 37	2.3	•	347.0	1.1	1.8	3.2	2.5	1.4	1.7	1.1	0.8	8.1
Current Assets to Working Capital 38	3.5	•	3.1	2.6	3.6	10.8	3.0	3.0	3.2	2.8	2.1	8.4
Current Liabilities to Working Capital 39	2.5	•	2.1	1.6	2.6	9.8	2.0	2.0	2.2	1.8	1.1	7.4
Working Capital to Net Sales 40	0.1	•	0.1	0.1	0.1	0.0	0.1	0.2	0.1	0.1	0.2	0.0
Inventory to Working Capital 41	1.2	•	0.6	0.8	1.2	4.7	1.2	1.2	1.2	0.8	0.7	3.1
Total Receipts to Cash Flow 42	3.6	1.6	1.9	2.5	2.6	3.2	6.5	4.8	9.4	4.8	13.5	15.1
Cost of Goods to Cash Flow 43	1.9	0.4	0.3	0.8	0.9	1.6	4.3	2.9	7.1	3.1	11.2	12.2
Cash Flow to Total Debt 44	0.4	•	0.6	0.6	0.4	0.4	0.2	0.2	0.2	0.4	0.1	0.1

Selected Financial Factors (in Percentages)

Debt Ratio 45	69.6	•	99.7	52.0	64.7	76.4	71.5	58.7	63.1	51.9	45.3	89.0
Return on Total Assets 46	4.2	•	4.1	4.1	3.2	1.9	3.9	5.2	3.4	6.0	2.9	5.9
Return on Equity Before Income Taxes 47	4.8	•	•	2.4	1.8	•	3.9	7.0	2.7	8.0	2.9	36.2
Return on Equity After Income Taxes 48	2.8	•	•	1.6	0.8	•	2.4	5.7	1.5	5.3	1.0	26.7
Profit Margin (Before Income Tax) 49	1.6	13.0	•	1.4	0.9	•	1.0	4.2	1.0	3.5	1.9	4.7
Profit Margin (After Income Tax) 50	0.9	12.4	•	1.0	0.4	•	0.6	3.5	0.5	2.3	0.7	3.4

Table II

Corporations with Net Income

AGRICULTURAL PRODUCTION

MONEY AMOUNTS AND SIZE OF ASSETS IN THOUSANDS OF DOLLARS

Item Description for Accounting Period 7/06 Through 6/07	Total	Zero Assets	Under 500	500 to 1000	251 to 500	501 to 1,000	1,001 to 5,000	5,001 to 10,000	10,001 to 25,000	25,001 to 50,000	50,001 to 100,000	100,001 to 250,000	250,001 and over
Number of Enterprises 1	51838	4047	29874	8928	7930	•	294	67	•	34	9	•	0
Revenues ($ in Thousands)													
Net Sales 2	58726220	461155	6923653	5961026	10539200	•	6080107	1676171	•	6325607	2371993	•	0
Interest 3	282312	3583	33931	31807	68031	•	19792	11026	•	30091	10102	•	0
Rents 4	610517	1709	88637	131378	218852	•	14025	11603	•	37242	13197	•	0
Royalties 5	94021	0	1769	910	15035	•	11487	522	•	16396	15011	•	0
Other Portfolio Income 6	1460185	32089	214630	172985	283502	•	91257	64767	•	45402	35315	•	0
Other Receipts 7	6444764	149972	1955690	834605	2378348	•	88849	67241	•	192835	108688	•	0
Total Receipts 8	67618019	648508	9218310	7132711	13502768	•	6305517	1831330	•	6647573	2554306	•	0
Average Total Receipts 9	1304	160	309	799	1703	•	21447	27333	•	195517	283812	•	•
Operating Costs/Operating Income (%)													
Cost of Operations 10	51.7	6.9	16.6	34.1	32.7	•	68.6	61.6	•	63.7	80.6	•	•
Salaries and Wages 11	7.9	5.6	9.5	7.3	13.4	•	4.5	7.8	•	5.8	1.7	•	•
Taxes Paid 12	2.2	2.2	2.8	3.2	3.5	•	1.3	2.2	•	1.7	1.9	•	•
Interest Paid 13	2.2	4.6	2.8	2.1	3.3	•	1.7	3.1	•	1.3	1.6	•	•
Depreciation 14	4.8	9.4	7.2	6.6	7.9	•	2.5	5.0	•	2.7	3.5	•	•
Amortization and Depletion 15	0.3	0.7	0.1	0.1	0.1	•	0.3	0.1	•	0.4	1.9	•	•
Pensions and Other Deferred Comp. 16	0.3	0.0	0.1	0.8	0.5	•	0.1	0.2	•	0.1	0.5	•	•
Employee Benefits 17	1.0	0.7	0.8	1.2	0.8	•	0.5	0.9	•	0.9	1.0	•	•
Advertising 18	0.3	0.0	0.3	0.3	0.2	•	0.5	0.3	•	0.2	0.3	•	•
Other Expenses 19	32.3	59.6	69.5	48.7	50.5	•	15.0	16.1	•	20.6	5.6	•	•
Officers' Compensation 20	2.3	2.4	4.3	4.9	3.9	•	1.2	1.2	•	0.7	0.9	•	•
Operating Margin 21	•	7.8	•	•	•	•	3.6	1.5	•	1.8	0.5	•	•
Operating Margin Before Officers' Comp. 22	•	10.3	•	•	•	•	4.9	2.7	•	2.5	1.4	•	•

Selected Average Balance Sheet ($ in Thousands)

Net Receivables 23	82	0	6	31	44	•	2120	5998	•	23750	24657
Inventories 24	129	0	9	39	181	•	2530	6309	•	13709	44533
Net Property, Plant and Equipment 25	472	0	79	371	1012	•	4345	13922	•	56329	129580
Total Assets 26	1119	0	179	703	1874	•	15306	35563	•	146922	309819
Notes and Loans Payable 27	424	0	106	218	743	•	6443	12797	•	36416	82384
All Other Liabilities 28	195	0	6	49	125	•	2791	5622	•	31266	79581
Net Worth 29	499	0	66	437	1005	•	6072	17144	•	79240	147854

Selected Financial Ratios (Times to 1)

Current Ratio 30	1.7	•	2.1	2.9	1.8	•	1.5	1.8	•	1.5	1.7
Quick Ratio 31	0.9	•	1.6	1.9	1.0	•	0.8	1.1	•	0.9	0.6
Net Sales to Working Capital 32	7.3	•	7.6	5.4	6.6	•	7.3	3.5	•	10.5	6.4
Coverage Ratio 33	5.4	11.5	7.8	6.0	4.5	•	5.2	4.5	•	6.3	6.1
Total Asset Turnover 34	1.0	•	1.3	0.9	0.7	•	1.4	0.7	•	1.3	0.9
Inventory Turnover 35	4.6	•	4.3	5.8	2.4	•	5.6	2.4	•	8.6	4.8
Receivables Turnover 36	9.7	•	45.1	22.6	16.9	•	11.1	3.8	•	•	•
Total Liabilities to Net Worth 37	1.2	•	1.7	0.6	0.9	•	1.5	1.1	•	0.9	1.1
Current Assets to Working Capital 38	2.4	•	1.9	1.5	2.3	•	3.0	2.2	•	3.1	2.4
Current Liabilities to Working Capital 39	1.4	•	0.9	0.5	1.3	•	2.0	1.2	•	2.1	1.4
Working Capital to Net Sales 40	0.1	•	0.1	0.2	0.2	•	0.1	0.3	•	0.1	0.2
Inventory to Working Capital 41	0.8	•	0.2	0.3	0.8	•	1.2	0.7	•	0.8	1.1
Total Receipts to Cash Flow 42	3.1	1.0	1.6	2.4	2.1	•	5.7	4.7	•	4.0	9.8
Cost of Goods to Cash Flow 43	1.6	0.1	0.3	0.8	0.7	•	3.9	2.9	•	2.5	7.9
Cash Flow to Total Debt 44	0.6	•	1.3	1.0	0.7	•	0.4	0.3	•	0.7	0.2

Selected Financial Factors (in Percentages)

Debt Ratio 45	55.4	•	63.0	37.9	46.4	•	60.3	51.8	•	46.1	52.3
Return on Total Assets 46	12.1	•	28.4	11.9	10.3	•	12.1	9.7	•	10.1	8.3
Return on Equity Before Income Taxes 47	22.1	•	66.9	15.9	15.0	•	24.6	15.6	•	15.7	14.5
Return on Equity After Income Taxes 48	19.8	•	64.4	14.8	13.9	•	22.5	14.0	•	12.4	10.8
Profit Margin (Before Income Tax) 49	9.8	48.5	19.1	10.4	11.3	•	7.2	10.7	•	6.7	8.1
Profit Margin (After Income Tax) 50	8.7	47.2	18.4	9.7	10.5	•	6.6	9.6	•	5.3	6.0

2

Table I

Corporations with and without Net Income

FORESTRY AND LOGGING

MONEY AMOUNTS AND SIZE OF ASSETS IN THOUSANDS OF DOLLARS

Item Description for Accounting Period 7/06 Through 6/07	Total	Zero Assets	Under 500	500 to 1,000	1,000 to 5,000	5,000 to 10,000	10,000 to 25,000	25,000 to 50,000	50,000 to 100,000	100,000 to 250,000	250,000 to 500,000	500,000 to 2,500,000	2,500,000 and over
Number of Enterprises **1**	10850	1267	6758	1037	1541	67	122	35	7	3	3	7	0
Revenues ($ in Thousands)													
Net Sales **2**	14807922	495721	3106523	2545145	3925910	139488	1705383	1041539	495057	503569	227081	622506	0
Interest **3**	122096	142	2414	723	6091	4231	4422	5891	1028	1417	9934	85804	0
Rents **4**	77293	382	8065	747	5901	569	3986	22027	203	0	1583	33829	0
Royalties **5**	4008	0	0	2886	0	0	917	0	0	0	0	206	0
Other Portfolio Income **6**	431591	82665	97021	33119	95851	32189	42934	12700	931	2053	31724	400	0
Other Receipts **7**	208851	1124	5899	11582	48258	-22155	25173	-967	4448	10422	13796	111274	0
Total Receipts **8**	15651761	580034	3219922	2594202	4082011	154322	1782815	1081190	501667	517461	284118	854019	0
Average Total Receipts **9**	1443	458	476	2502	2649	2303	14613	30891	71667	172487	94706	122003	•
Operating Costs/Operating Income (%)													
Cost of Operations **10**	66.1	7.8	64.0	66.8	59.1	73.6	71.7	86.1	88.9	75.5	75.6	85.1	•
Salaries and Wages **11**	6.5	2.2	5.1	8.4	8.6	4.3	8.8	1.7	3.1	5.1	4.4	3.0	•
Taxes Paid **12**	2.0	1.0	1.8	1.6	2.6	10.2	1.6	2.5	0.9	1.4	1.7	2.3	•
Interest Paid **13**	3.5	5.9	2.0	1.6	2.0	2.8	2.0	2.1	1.6	1.9	5.4	35.0	•
Depreciation **14**	5.3	0.1	6.3	5.1	7.9	14.1	2.9	2.7	3.0	0.6	5.0	4.4	•
Amortization and Depletion **15**	0.5	0.1	0.0	0.0	0.0	0.0	0.1	0.4	0.0	0.4	16.4	3.7	•
Pensions and Other Deferred Comp. **16**	0.2	•	•	0.0	0.2	0.7	0.4	0.3	0.2	0.5	0.3	0.7	•
Employee Benefits **17**	1.1	0.3	1.3	1.0	1.4	0.7	1.2	0.7	0.3	2.2	1.1	0.1	•
Advertising **18**	0.1	0.0	0.1	0.1	0.2	0.1	0.2	0.0	0.1	0.1	0.1	0.2	•
Other Expenses **19**	16.6	90.1	17.0	11.1	17.8	16.5	9.8	6.0	3.3	10.8	17.5	23.1	•
Officers' Compensation **20**	2.4	•	3.8	2.1	2.8	2.5	2.2	0.9	0.9	1.2	1.7	0.8	•
Operating Margin **21**	•	•	•	2.2	•	•	•	•	•	0.3	•	•	•
Operating Margin Before Officers' Comp. **22**	•	•	2.4	4.3	0.2	1.2	1.2	•	1.5	•	•	•	•

Selected Average Balance Sheet ($ in Thousands)

Net Receivables 23	66	0	1	68	97	133	804	1687	5444	28641	37746	12051	•
Inventories 24	75	0	5	11	119	22	2860	2654	6810	253	6124	11289	•
Net Property, Plant and Equipment 25	890	0	76	312	1049	1570	6446	14260	29364	76779	57157	743265	•
Total Assets 26	1947	0	108	706	1763	9099	15265	33952	70680	159833	288730	1635305	•
Notes and Loans Payable 27	1051	0	113	551	1122	810	6073	12899	15809	53740	137079	915601	•
All Other Liabilities 28	196	0	9	23	147	248	1598	584	6503	26241	16922	201210	•
Net Worth 29	700	0	-14	132	495	8041	7594	20469	48368	79852	134729	518494	•

Selected Financial Ratios (Times to 1)

Current Ratio 30	3.2	•	1.9	1.1	1.4	3.9	1.4	2.3	1.8	1.0	4.3	11.2	•
Quick Ratio 31	2.4	•	1.5	0.8	0.7	1.2	0.4	1.1	1.3	0.9	2.8	10.4	•
Net Sales to Working Capital 32	3.2	•	52.6	84.4	20.8	1.7	8.2	5.3	6.9	•	1.5	0.2	•
Coverage Ratio 33	1.4	2.6	2.2	3.5	1.7	•	2.8	1.1	0.4	2.6	0.2	0.4	•
Total Asset Turnover 34	0.7	•	4.3	3.5	1.4	0.2	0.9	0.9	1.0	1.1	0.3	0.1	•
Inventory Turnover 35	12.0	•	58.5	151.7	12.6	70.2	3.5	9.7	9.2	501.5	9.3	6.7	•
Receivables Turnover 36	20.4	•	111.7	46.9	24.1	18.4	15.2	20.0	6.2	11.7	3.4	5.2	•
Total Liabilities to Net Worth 37	1.8	•	•	4.3	2.6	0.1	1.0	0.7	0.5	1.0	1.1	2.2	•
Current Assets to Working Capital 38	1.5	•	2.1	10.7	3.8	1.3	3.3	1.8	2.2	•	1.3	1.1	•
Current Liabilities to Working Capital 39	0.5	•	1.1	9.7	2.8	0.3	2.3	0.8	1.2	•	0.3	0.1	•
Working Capital to Net Sales 40	0.3	•	0.0	0.0	0.0	0.6	0.1	0.2	0.1	•	0.7	5.8	•
Inventory to Working Capital 41	0.2	•	0.3	0.7	1.2	0.0	2.1	0.7	0.6	•	0.1	0.0	•
Total Receipts to Cash Flow 42	7.6	1.2	6.4	8.3	7.7	•	10.7	20.0	63.4	8.1	•	83.2	•
Cost of Goods to Cash Flow 43	5.0	0.1	4.1	5.6	4.6	•	7.7	17.2	56.4	6.1	•	70.8	•
Cash Flow to Total Debt 44	0.1	•	0.6	0.5	0.3	•	0.2	0.1	0.1	0.3	•	0.0	•

Selected Financial Factors (in Percentages)

Debt Ratio 45	64.0	•	112.8	81.3	71.9	11.6	50.2	39.7	31.6	50.0	53.3	68.3	•
Return on Total Assets 46	3.3	•	18.0	20.0	4.9	•	5.1	2.0	0.6	5.2	0.3	0.7	•
Return on Equity Before Income Taxes 47	2.4	•	•	76.5	7.1	•	6.5	0.3	•	6.4	•	•	•
Return on Equity After Income Taxes 48	1.2	•	•	76.1	6.2	•	3.7	•	•	6.2	•	•	•
Profit Margin (Before Income Tax) 49	1.3	9.4	2.3	4.1	1.4	•	3.5	0.2	•	3.0	•	•	•
Profit Margin (After Income Tax) 50	0.6	7.3	2.3	4.1	1.2	•	2.0	•	•	2.9	•	•	•

3

Table II

Corporations with Net Income

FORESTRY AND LOGGING

MONEY AMOUNTS AND SIZE OF ASSETS IN THOUSANDS OF DOLLARS

Item Description for Accounting Period 7/06 Through 6/07	Total	Zero Assets	Under 500	500 to 1,000	1,000 to 5,000	5,000 to 10,000	10,000 to 25,000	25,000 to 50,000	50,000 to 100,000	100,000 to 250,000	250,000 to 500,000	500,000 to 2,500,000	2,500,000 and over
Number of Enterprises 1	5397	519	3182	650	956	•	54	16	0	0	•	•	0

Revenues ($ in Thousands)

	Total	Zero Assets	Under 500	500 to 1,000	1,000 to 5,000	5,000 to 10,000	10,000 to 25,000	25,000 to 50,000	50,000 to 100,000	100,000 to 250,000	250,000 to 500,000	500,000 to 2,500,000	2,500,000 and over
Net Sales 2	8897973	492375	1359067	1041673	3025138	•	1292767	1227943	0	0	•	•	0
Interest 3	76415	40	1690	708	5136	•	4128	7266	0	0	•	•	0
Rents 4	45547	50	8065	747	2420	•	3180	22027	0	0	•	•	0
Royalties 5	3727	0	0	2886	0	•	642	0	0	0	•	•	0
Other Portfolio Income 6	366919	76729	76153	17030	83286	•	41225	12537	0	0	•	•	0
Other Receipts 7	209728	971	313	11440	43251	•	6529	12788	0	0	•	•	0
Total Receipts 8	9600309	570165	1445288	1074484	3159231	•	1348471	1282561	0	0	•	•	0
Average Total Receipts 9	1779	1099	454	1653	3305	•	24972	80160	•	•	•	•	•

Operating Costs/Operating Income (%)

	Total	Zero Assets	Under 500	500 to 1,000	1,000 to 5,000	5,000 to 10,000	10,000 to 25,000	25,000 to 50,000	50,000 to 100,000	100,000 to 250,000	250,000 to 500,000	500,000 to 2,500,000	2,500,000 and over
Cost of Operations 10	56.5	7.4	58.4	32.7	53.7	•	73.9	79.8	•	•	•	•	•
Salaries and Wages 11	8.3	2.3	5.9	17.9	10.4	•	7.9	2.9	•	•	•	•	•
Taxes Paid 12	2.1	0.9	2.1	2.2	2.3	•	1.4	1.7	•	•	•	•	•
Interest Paid 13	2.8	6.0	1.2	1.4	2.1	•	0.8	1.2	•	•	•	•	•
Depreciation 14	4.9	0.1	4.2	6.2	7.9	•	1.8	1.5	•	•	•	•	•
Amortization and Depletion 15	0.5	0.0	0.0	•	0.0	•	0.0	0.1	•	•	•	•	•
Pensions and Other Deferred Comp. 16	0.2	•	•	0.0	0.0	•	0.5	0.3	•	•	•	•	•
Employee Benefits 17	1.0	0.3	0.0	2.2	0.9	•	1.5	1.4	•	•	•	•	•
Advertising 18	0.2	0.0	0.1	0.2	0.2	•	0.3	0.1	•	•	•	•	•
Other Expenses 19	20.1	83.1	22.9	21.8	19.0	•	6.7	6.4	•	•	•	•	•
Officers' Compensation 20	1.7	•	1.7	2.6	2.0	•	2.4	0.8	•	•	•	•	•
Operating Margin 21	1.6	•	3.5	12.8	1.2	•	2.8	3.9	•	•	•	•	•
Operating Margin Before Officers' Comp. 22	3.4	•	5.1	15.4	3.1	•	5.2	4.7	•	•	•	•	•

Selected Average Balance Sheet ($ in Thousands)

Net Receivables 23	88	0	1	63	127	•	1363	7444
Inventories 24	98	0	8	3	150	•	3662	4929
Net Property, Plant and Equipment 25	425	0	72	322	980	•	4508	12612
Total Assets 26	1282	0	119	647	1702	•	13714	48802
Notes and Loans Payable 27	489	0	104	370	1086	•	3490	17985
All Other Liabilities 28	300	0	6	7	147	•	2031	6221
Net Worth 29	493	0	10	270	469	•	8193	24595

Selected Financial Ratios (Times to 1)

Current Ratio 30	1.9	•	2.7	1.4	1.5	•	1.9	2.1
Quick Ratio 31	1.0	•	2.1	0.9	0.8	•	0.7	1.3
Net Sales to Working Capital 32	11.4	•	28.8	23.9	17.4	•	7.5	6.8
Coverage Ratio 33	4.4	3.6	9.4	12.7	3.6	•	9.5	7.7
Total Asset Turnover 34	1.3	•	3.6	2.5	1.9	•	1.7	1.6
Inventory Turnover 35	9.5	•	30.9	180.6	11.3	•	4.8	12.4
Receivables Turnover 36	17.7	•	57.7	27.5	27.6	•	14.1	19.4
Total Liabilities to Net Worth 37	1.6	•	10.6	1.4	2.6	•	0.7	1.0
Current Assets to Working Capital 38	2.2	•	1.6	3.5	3.0	•	2.1	2.0
Current Liabilities to Working Capital 39	1.2	•	0.6	2.5	2.0	•	1.1	1.0
Working Capital to Net Sales 40	0.1	•	0.0	0.0	0.1	•	0.1	0.1
Inventory to Working Capital 41	0.7	•	0.3	0.1	1.1	•	1.2	0.7
Total Receipts to Cash Flow 42	4.3	1.2	3.5	3.2	5.5	•	10.5	7.6
Cost of Goods to Cash Flow 43	2.4	0.1	2.0	1.1	2.9	•	7.8	6.0
Cash Flow to Total Debt 44	0.5	•	1.1	1.3	0.5	•	0.4	0.4

Selected Financial Factors (in Percentages)

Debt Ratio 45	61.5	•	91.4	58.3	72.5	•	40.3	49.6
Return on Total Assets 46	15.9	•	39.3	42.8	14.3	•	13.9	14.8
Return on Equity Before Income Taxes 47	31.8	•	405.5	94.4	37.6	•	20.9	25.6
Return on Equity After Income Taxes 48	28.3	•	404.9	94.1	36.1	•	15.1	21.7
Profit Margin (Before Income Tax) 49	9.5	15.7	9.8	15.9	5.6	•	7.1	8.2
Profit Margin (After Income Tax) 50	8.5	13.6	9.8	15.9	5.3	•	5.2	7.0

4

SUPPORT ACTIVITIES AND FISHING, HUNTING AND TRAPPING

Table I

Corporations with and without Net Income

MONEY AMOUNTS AND SIZE OF ASSETS IN THOUSANDS OF DOLLARS

Item Description for Accounting Period 7/06 Through 6/07	Total	Zero Assets	Under 500	500 to 1,000	1,000 to 5,000	5,000 to 10,000	10,000 to 25,000	25,000 to 50,000	50,000 to 100,000	100,000 to 250,000	250,000 to 500,000	500,000 to 2,500,000	2,500,000 and over
Number of Enterprises 1	28683	6471	17709	2570	1462	301	123	36	6	5	0	0	0
Revenues ($ in Thousands)													
Net Sales 2	23467304	905893	6729729	2930828	5273540	2554999	2015486	1142883	455685	1458260	0	0	0
Interest 3	31583	470	2094	961	14232	3121	5154	1130	1291	3131	0	0	0
Rents 4	24915	0	581	7973	8545	6968	826	0	0	22	0	0	0
Royalties 5	425	0	0	0	0	0	0	0	0	425	0	0	0
Other Portfolio Income 6	291600	62650	28091	35184	48886	8573	18167	7778	976	81296	0	0	0
Other Receipts 7	939031	-2592	211159	188063	210000	113164	103845	61956	23210	30226	0	0	0
Total Receipts 8	24754858	966421	6971654	3163009	5555203	2688825	2143478	1213747	481162	1573360	0	0	0
Average Total Receipts 9	863	149	394	1231	3800	8926	17427	33715	80194	314672	•	•	•
Operating Costs/Operating Income (%)													
Cost of Operations 10	55.1	5.9	47.5	32.5	66.0	60.2	70.2	78.6	65.1	75.3	•	•	•
Salaries and Wages 11	9.3	26.8	9.0	9.4	8.9	11.2	7.1	2.7	12.6	5.1	•	•	•
Taxes Paid 12	2.1	4.7	2.0	2.1	2.0	1.7	2.0	1.1	3.1	2.2	•	•	•
Interest Paid 13	1.3	1.4	1.1	1.5	0.9	1.2	1.8	2.5	1.3	2.2	•	•	•
Depreciation 14	3.1	1.9	2.6	4.8	2.5	4.8	2.9	2.2	3.1	2.0	•	•	•
Amortization and Depletion 15	0.1	0.0	0.1	0.1	0.2	0.0	0.2	0.1	0.3	0.3	•	•	•
Pensions and Other Deferred Comp. 16	0.2	0.4	0.2	0.1	0.1	0.6	0.4	0.3	0.3	0.1	•	•	•
Employee Benefits 17	0.6	0.3	0.6	0.5	0.6	1.0	0.7	0.7	1.8	0.4	•	•	•
Advertising 18	0.4	0.1	0.5	0.1	0.2	1.8	0.2	0.1	0.9	0.3	•	•	•
Other Expenses 19	24.5	57.0	27.8	46.7	19.5	14.1	15.2	13.5	6.9	8.1	•	•	•
Officers' Compensation 20	3.1	1.5	4.6	5.8	2.1	2.9	1.3	1.1	1.0	0.6	•	•	•
Operating Margin 21	0.0	0.1	4.1	•	•	0.4	•	•	3.5	3.4	•	•	•
Operating Margin Before Officers' Comp. 22	3.1	1.6	8.6	2.1	•	3.3	•	•	4.5	4.0	•	•	•

Selected Average Balance Sheet ($ in Thousands)

Net Receivables 23	57	0	9	29	209	1043	2555	5254	14370	35894
Inventories 24	48	0	5	21	147	534	2189	5707	9832	63707
Net Property, Plant and Equipment 25	168	0	36	328	794	3419	4223	7779	14276	54513
Total Assets 26	463	0	110	693	1842	7072	14083	35462	66892	263914
Notes and Loans Payable 27	240	0	113	365	947	2367	5537	13882	16211	114048
All Other Liabilities 28	77	0	9	63	265	986	3753	11215	13094	48259
Net Worth 29	146	0	-13	265	629	3719	4793	10365	37587	101607

Selected Financial Ratios (Times to 1)

Current Ratio 30	1.7	•	2.1	1.8	1.4	1.2	1.4		1.8	2.7
Quick Ratio 31	1.1	•	1.6	1.4	1.3	1.1	0.7	0.7	1.0	1.2
Net Sales to Working Capital 32	10.2	•	17.7	8.5	12.8	9.8	11.8	5.9	5.2	3.3
Coverage Ratio 33	5.2	5.7	8.0	3.8	3.6	5.8	3.4	2.3	7.8	6.4
Total Asset Turnover 34	1.8	•	3.5	1.6	2.0	1.2	1.2	0.9	1.1	1.1
Inventory Turnover 35	9.4	•	35.2	17.4	16.2	9.6	5.3	4.4	5.0	3.4
Receivables Turnover 36	13.6	•	42.3	28.1	13.3	8.4	5.9	6.5	5.5	8.7
Total Liabilities to Net Worth 37	2.2	•	•	1.6	1.9	0.9	1.9	2.4	0.8	1.6
Current Assets to Working Capital 38	2.5	•	1.9	1.9	2.2	3.5	5.1	3.8	2.3	1.6
Current Liabilities to Working Capital 39	1.5	•	0.9	0.9	1.2	2.5	4.1	2.8	1.3	0.6
Working Capital to Net Sales 40	0.1	•	0.1	0.1	0.1	0.1	0.1	0.2	0.2	0.3
Inventory to Working Capital 41	0.7	•	0.3	0.5	0.6	1.8	1.3	0.8	0.8	
Total Receipts to Cash Flow 42	4.1	2.0	3.7	2.2	5.4	5.9	6.1	6.7	7.1	6.6
Cost of Goods to Cash Flow 43	2.2	0.1	1.8	0.7	3.6	3.5	4.3	5.3	4.6	5.0
Cash Flow to Total Debt 44	0.6	•	0.8	1.2	0.5	0.4	0.3	0.2	0.4	0.3

Selected Financial Factors (in Percentages)

Debt Ratio 45	68.5	•	111.9	61.7	65.8	47.4	66.0	70.8	43.8	61.5
Return on Total Assets 46	12.1	•	30.3	9.4	6.2	8.1	7.0	5.2	11.7	15.6
Return on Equity Before Income Taxes 47	31.1	•	•	18.1	13.1	12.8	14.5	10.1	18.2	34.1
Return on Equity After Income Taxes 48	29.8	•	•	17.8	11.3	12.4	13.0	9.6	14.9	34.0
Profit Margin (Before Income Tax) 49	5.5	6.8	7.7	4.2	2.3	5.6	4.2	3.3	9.0	11.9
Profit Margin (After Income Tax) 50	5.3	6.1	7.6	4.1	2.0	5.4	3.8	3.1	7.4	11.9

Table II
Corporations with Net Income

AGRICULTURE, FORESTRY, FISHING AND HUNTING 114005

SUPPORT ACTIVITIES AND FISHING, HUNTING AND TRAPPING

MONEY AMOUNTS AND SIZE OF ASSETS IN THOUSANDS OF DOLLARS

Item Description for Accounting Period 7/06 Through 6/07	Total	Zero Assets	Under 500	500 to 1,000	1,000 to 5,000	5,000 to 10,000	10,000 to 25,000	25,000 to 50,000	50,000 to 100,000	100,000 to 250,000	250,000 to 500,000	500,000 to 2,500,000	2,500,000 and over
Number of Enterprises **1**	14306	2808	8401	1638	1117	•	90	19	•	5	0	0	0
Revenues ($ in Thousands)													
Net Sales **2**	18964069	225257	4923649	2627023	4541171	•	1661286	852680	•	1458260	0	0	0
Interest **3**	25564	0	463	369	13458	•	3070	1130	•	3131	0	0	0
Rents **4**	18012	0	461	7422	2716	•	826	0	•	22	0	0	0
Royalties **5**	425	0	0	0	0	•	0	0	•	425	0	0	0
Other Portfolio Income **6**	260280	62650	22892	30246	38148	•	18078	391	•	81296	0	0	0
Other Receipts **7**	567683	1329	143520	35129	69656	•	101835	56295	•	30226	0	0	0
Total Receipts **8**	19836033	289236	5090985	2700189	4665149	•	1785095	910496	•	1573360	0	0	0
Average Total Receipts **9**	1387	103	606	1648	4176	•	19834	47921	•	314672	•	•	•
Operating Costs/Operating Income (%)													
Cost of Operations **10**	56.2	19.4	46.5	32.5	65.3	•	68.1	77.4	•	75.3	•	•	•
Salaries and Wages **11**	7.7	0.0	7.0	7.0	8.4	•	8.3	2.1	•	5.1	•	•	•
Taxes Paid **12**	1.9	2.7	1.9	1.5	1.9	•	2.0	0.9	•	2.2	•	•	•
Interest Paid **13**	1.0	0.6	0.7	1.0	0.6	•	1.6	1.7	•	2.2	•	•	•
Depreciation **14**	2.5	4.1	2.2	3.5	2.2	•	2.7	0.9	•	2.0	•	•	•
Amortization and Depletion **15**	0.1	0.0	0.0	0.2	0.2	•	0.0	0.0	•	0.3	•	•	•
Pensions and Other Deferred Comp. **16**	0.3	1.4	0.2	0.1	0.1	•	0.4	0.3	•	0.1	•	•	•
Employee Benefits **17**	0.6	•	0.6	0.2	0.5	•	0.8	0.9	•	0.4	•	•	•
Advertising **18**	0.5	0.1	0.5	0.0	0.1	•	0.2	0.0	•	0.3	•	•	•
Other Expenses **19**	21.2	45.4	24.9	43.6	16.1	•	14.9	13.8	•	8.1	•	•	•
Officers' Compensation **20**	3.2	5.9	5.0	4.8	2.3	•	1.6	1.2	•	0.6	•	•	•
Operating Margin **21**	4.9	20.5	10.4	5.5	2.2	•	•	0.7	•	3.4	•	•	•
Operating Margin Before Officers' Comp. **22**	8.1	26.3	15.4	10.3	4.4	•	1.0	2.0	•	4.0	•	•	•

Selected Average Balance Sheet ($ in Thousands)

Net Receivables 23	98	0	16	25	226	3094	6818	35894
Inventories 24	76	0	6	24	117	2014	9074	66784
Net Property, Plant and Equipment 25	204	0	42	294	674	3578	5296	54513
Total Assets 26	661	0	139	728	1722	13670	38089	263914
Notes and Loans Payable 27	248	0	90	287	499	5024	9141	114048
All Other Liabilities 28	119	0	13	53	251	3503	18179	48259
Net Worth 29	294	0	36	388	972	5142	10769	101607

Selected Financial Ratios (Times to 1)

Current Ratio 30	1.8	•	2.5	2.7	1.8	1.5	1.1	2.7
Quick Ratio 31	1.2	•	2.0	2.1	1.6	0.9	0.6	1.2
Net Sales to Working Capital 32	9.4	•	15.1	8.1	15.0	7.3	21.8	3.3
Coverage Ratio 33	10.9	83.2	19.7	9.1	8.9	5.4	5.5	6.4
Total Asset Turnover 34	2.0	•	4.2	2.2	2.4	1.4	1.2	1.1
Inventory Turnover 35	9.8	•	45.2	22.1	22.8	6.2	3.8	3.3
Receivables Turnover 36	13.6	•	41.9	33.6	16.5	5.7	6.2	•
Total Liabilities to Net Worth 37	1.3	•	2.9	0.9	0.8	1.7	2.5	1.6
Current Assets to Working Capital 38	2.3	•	1.7	1.6	2.2	3.1	11.8	1.6
Current Liabilities to Working Capital 39	1.3	•	0.7	0.6	1.2	2.1	10.8	0.6
Working Capital to Net Sales 40	0.1	•	0.1	0.1	0.1	0.1	0.0	0.3
Inventory to Working Capital 41	0.6	•	0.3	0.1	0.2	0.9	5.1	0.8
Total Receipts to Cash Flow 42	3.8	1.3	3.2	2.1	5.6	5.5	5.0	6.6
Cost of Goods to Cash Flow 43	2.1	0.2	1.5	0.7	3.6	3.7	3.9	5.0
Cash Flow to Total Debt 44	0.9	•	1.8	2.2	1.0	0.4	0.3	0.3

Selected Financial Factors (in Percentages)

Debt Ratio 45	55.6	•	74.3	46.7	43.6	62.4	71.7	61.5
Return on Total Assets 46	21.1	•	61.5	20.5	13.0	11.3	10.8	15.6
Return on Equity Before Income Taxes 47	43.2	•	226.7	34.3	20.5	24.5	31.3	34.1
Return on Equity After Income Taxes 48	41.9	•	225.1	34.0	19.0	22.5	30.4	34.0
Profit Margin (Before Income Tax) 49	9.6	48.9	13.8	8.3	4.9	6.8	7.5	11.9
Profit Margin (After Income Tax) 50	9.3	45.8	13.8	8.2	4.5	6.3	7.3	11.9

Table I

Corporations with and without Net Income

OIL AND GAS EXTRACTION

MONEY AMOUNTS AND SIZE OF ASSETS IN THOUSANDS OF DOLLARS

Item Description for Accounting Period 7/06 Through 6/07	Total	Zero Assets	Under 500	500 to 1,000	1,000 to 5,000	5,000 to 10,000	10,000 to 25,000	25,000 to 50,000	50,000 to 100,000	100,000 to 250,000	250,000 to 500,000	500,000 to 2,500,000	2,500,000 and over
Number of Enterprises 1	18630	3588	9946	1577	2028	611	368	183	116	98	42	51	22
Revenues ($ in Thousands)													
Net Sales 2	152711273	6027037	3063628	1874500	3723553	3618409	3368476	3224440	3439943	5814910	5765333	20035860	92755183
Interest 3	2444175	18077	4859	5426	20595	17147	25023	35848	46887	103398	86835	305827	1774253
Rents 4	126598	3771	0	2016	26234	1960	6652	15120	5127	26129	2567	5680	31342
Royalties 5	721532	53728	12542	23600	36117	50044	113788	1906	72605	66708	16066	93861	180566
Other Portfolio Income 6	8521609	317111	61807	101774	241670	175373	187863	256528	643180	460449	134314	2187830	3753710
Other Receipts 7	12575133	-274653	154257	67607	431714	249829	304502	272503	455792	481842	362410	851762	9217569
Total Receipts 8	177100320	6145071	3297093	2074923	4479883	4112762	4006304	3806345	4663534	6953436	6367525	23480820	107712623
Average Total Receipts 9	9506	1713	331	1316	2209	6731	10887	20800	40203	70953	151608	460408	4896028
Operating Costs/Operating Income (%)													
Cost of Operations 10	48.6	18.6	17.7	22.3	18.0	45.0	34.0	41.7	26.7	43.3	38.3	23.7	61.4
Salaries and Wages 11	4.7	9.7	2.7	3.7	13.0	8.5	8.4	6.0	10.1	5.3	4.9	3.9	3.7
Taxes Paid 12	3.8	2.9	3.6	3.3	5.7	2.6	3.9	4.7	4.4	3.0	3.9	3.8	3.8
Interest Paid 13	4.2	6.6	1.3	0.5	1.9	1.0	1.9	1.9	4.0	3.9	3.1	6.0	4.4
Depreciation 14	4.2	8.7	3.4	2.0	4.2	3.2	4.8	4.5	6.7	5.5	7.2	7.4	3.0
Amortization and Depletion 15	4.2	4.1	1.1	1.3	3.6	2.2	4.7	5.3	7.2	8.2	7.2	10.3	2.6
Pensions and Other Deferred Comp. 16	0.3	0.1	1.1	1.1	0.2	0.3	0.6	0.3	0.8	0.3	0.4	0.2	0.3
Employee Benefits 17	0.5	0.5	0.5	0.4	1.2	0.7	0.8	0.5	0.7	0.4	0.8	0.9	0.3
Advertising 18	0.0	0.0	0.1	0.2	0.2	0.1	0.1	0.2	0.3	0.0	0.0	0.0	0.0
Other Expenses 19	26.9	31.0	42.9	41.4	29.0	20.4	27.9	36.2	39.3	34.3	26.9	43.0	21.2
Officers' Compensation 20	1.7	5.2	10.2	4.0	5.3	3.0	3.6	3.8	3.1	1.9	1.3	1.1	0.9
Operating Margin 21	0.9	12.5	15.3	19.8	17.6	13.1	9.3	•	•	•	5.8	•	•
Operating Margin Before Officers' Comp. 22	2.6	17.8	25.5	23.8	23.0	16.1	12.9	•	•	•	•	7.2	0.8

Selected Average Balance Sheet ($ in Thousands)

Net Receivables 23	1844	0	27	84	194	1070	2398	3953	6236	20997	39019	111342	963474
Inventories 24	141	0	0	1	15	35	151	212	1198	2385	2547	13012	60367
Net Property, Plant and Equipment 25	9598	0	64	69	749	1285	4664	12550	32170	72131	189248	854987	4972790
Total Assets 26	18691	0	156	645	2213	7516	15805	36064	70405	154379	352418	1326842	9926831
Notes and Loans Payable 27	5453	0	110	144	625	1404	2790	7872	19236	44932	87193	370107	3023234
All Other Liabilities 28	4617	0	13	178	519	1260	4609	7411	12678	28776	80500	310526	2600709
Net Worth 29	8622	0	34	323	1069	4851	8406	20781	38491	80670	184724	646208	4302887

Selected Financial Ratios (Times to 1)

Current Ratio 30	1.1	•	2.3	2.6	1.7	2.4	1.5	1.6	1.7	2.2	1.6	1.3	0.8
Quick Ratio 31	0.9	•	2.2	2.4	1.4	1.8	1.3	1.3	1.2	1.6	1.2	1.0	0.6
Net Sales to Working Capital 32	37.4	•	7.5	5.0	5.2	2.7	3.5	3.6	3.4	2.2	4.5	8.9	•
Coverage Ratio 33	5.1	3.2	18.3	65.2	21.0	28.1	15.9	7.9	9.1	4.4	6.2	3.9	4.5
Total Asset Turnover 34	0.4	•	2.0	1.8	0.8	0.8	0.6	0.5	0.4	0.4	0.4	0.3	0.4
Inventory Turnover 35	28.3	•	723.0	449.9	22.2	76.2	20.6	34.6	6.6	10.8	20.7	7.1	42.9
Receivables Turnover 36	4.4	•	9.8	26.3	7.8	7.6	3.7	4.5	4.2	3.2	3.2	3.8	4.3
Total Liabilities to Net Worth 37	1.2	•	3.6	1.0	1.1	0.5	0.9	0.7	0.8	0.9	0.9	1.1	1.3
Current Assets to Working Capital 38	15.3	•	1.8	1.6	2.4	1.7	2.9	2.6	2.5	1.9	2.7	5.0	•
Current Liabilities to Working Capital 39	14.3	•	0.8	0.6	1.4	0.7	1.9	1.6	1.5	0.9	1.7	4.0	•
Working Capital to Net Sales 40	0.0	•	0.1	0.2	0.2	0.4	0.3	0.3	0.3	0.5	0.2	0.1	•
Inventory to Working Capital 41	0.6	•	•	0.0	0.0	0.0	0.1	0.1	0.2	0.1	0.1	0.3	•
Total Receipts to Cash Flow 42	2.6	2.5	1.8	1.6	1.7	2.4	2.0	2.4	1.5	2.4	2.6	1.9	3.2
Cost of Goods to Cash Flow 43	1.3	0.5	0.3	0.4	0.3	1.1	0.7	1.0	0.4	1.0	1.0	0.4	2.0
Cash Flow to Total Debt 44	0.3	•	1.4	2.3	0.9	0.9	0.6	0.5	0.6	0.3	0.3	0.3	0.2

Selected Financial Factors (in Percentages)

Debt Ratio 45	53.9	•	78.5	49.9	51.7	35.4	46.8	42.4	45.3	47.7	47.6	51.3	56.7
Return on Total Assets 46	9.4	•	47.9	57.1	32.9	21.5	17.3	7.3	15.2	6.6	7.5	6.9	8.3
Return on Equity Before Income Taxes 47	16.3	•	210.6	112.2	64.9	32.1	30.5	11.0	24.7	9.7	12.0	10.4	14.9
Return on Equity After Income Taxes 48	12.1	•	205.6	107.0	62.8	30.6	28.0	8.8	21.1	5.8	7.5	7.9	9.8
Profit Margin (Before Income Tax) 49	17.2	14.5	22.9	30.5	37.7	26.3	28.0	13.0	32.1	13.2	16.2	17.2	15.2
Profit Margin (After Income Tax) 50	12.7	14.0	22.4	29.1	36.6	25.0	25.7	10.4	27.3	7.9	10.1	13.0	10.0

Table II

Corporations with Net Income

OIL AND GAS EXTRACTION

MONEY AMOUNTS AND SIZE OF ASSETS IN THOUSANDS OF DOLLARS

Item Description for Accounting Period 7/06 Through 6/07		Total	Zero Assets	Under 500	500 to 1,000	1,000 to 5,000	5,000 to 10,000	10,000 to 25,000	25,000 to 50,000	50,000 to 100,000	100,000 to 250,000	250,000 to 500,000	500,000 to 2,500,000	2,500,000 and over
Number of Enterprises	1	12151	1463	6521	1420	1604	552	294	105	69	55	17	34	16
Revenues ($ in Thousands)														
Net Sales	2	136168226	1852020	2825442	1850367	3508118	3567336	3108517	2892847	2766504	4653240	4114334	15463770	89565731
Interest	3	2114344	7801	4675	5221	18774	13201	18562	20227	33246	65425	50335	199786	1677092
Rents	4	98147	3713	0	2013	10926	1935	6563	13237	4715	18512	325	4927	31281
Royalties	5	644029	1411	12507	23599	34253	50044	113761	1815	72045	60951	12309	80766	180566
Other Portfolio Income	6	8102370	210431	61807	101383	236423	154617	177650	244695	627667	380329	103637	2122499	3681231
Other Receipts	7	12092413	137198	158476	60526	427318	291298	291992	251792	448800	440461	243360	546675	8794519
Total Receipts	8	159219529	2212574	3062907	2043109	4235812	4078431	3717045	3424613	3952977	5618918	4524300	18418423	103930420
Average Total Receipts	9	13103	1512	470	1439	2641	7388	12643	32615	57290	102162	266135	541718	6495651
Operating Costs/Operating Income (%)														
Cost of Operations	10	52.0	20.4	18.7	22.6	18.2	45.5	33.3	44.1	24.0	48.2	43.7	23.8	63.2
Salaries and Wages	11	4.2	2.7	1.9	3.4	13.0	7.4	8.3	5.1	10.3	3.9	3.0	3.8	3.7
Taxes Paid	12	3.8	1.1	3.4	3.1	5.5	2.5	3.9	4.5	4.4	2.8	3.8	4.1	3.8
Interest Paid	13	3.6	6.3	0.5	0.5	1.5	0.9	1.2	0.9	2.6	2.0	0.8	4.0	4.2
Depreciation	14	3.7	14.9	2.5	2.0	3.6	3.2	4.7	3.9	6.3	3.7	6.2	6.7	2.8
Amortization and Depletion	15	3.0	0.4	1.2	1.3	2.9	1.9	3.8	3.5	5.4	4.8	2.4	8.9	2.0
Pensions and Other Deferred Comp.	16	0.3	0.0	1.2	1.1	0.2	0.3	0.7	0.2	0.9	0.2	0.1	0.2	0.3
Employee Benefits	17	0.4	0.1	0.5	0.4	1.1	0.6	0.7	0.4	0.7	0.4	0.6	1.1	0.3
Advertising	18	0.0	0.0	0.1	0.2	0.2	0.1	0.1	0.2	0.1	0.0	0.0	0.0	0.0
Other Expenses	19	22.0	8.7	32.3	40.8	24.1	18.1	23.1	24.5	30.7	22.5	11.2	37.8	19.0
Officers' Compensation	20	1.5	0.2	10.7	3.8	4.7	2.9	3.3	2.6	2.9	1.5	0.7	1.1	0.9
Operating Margin	21	5.4	45.0	26.9	20.8	25.1	16.6	16.8	10.1	11.6	10.0	27.4	8.5	•
Operating Margin Before Officers' Comp.	22	6.9	45.2	37.7	24.7	29.8	19.5	20.1	12.8	14.6	11.5	28.1	9.5	0.8

Selected Average Balance Sheet ($ in Thousands)

Net Receivables 23	2411	0	31	84	207	1054	2496	4149	7477	26726	52647	118921	1248110
Inventories 24	169	0	0	1	14	37	174	333	1162	3073	3326	9028	81543
Net Property, Plant and Equipment 25	11388	0	57	75	757	1273	4108	10774	27563	56227	176640	836090	6076036
Total Assets 26	23172	0	172	648	2336	7495	15440	35800	71939	154154	362788	1338547	12388740
Notes and Loans Payable 27	6353	0	79	159	406	684	2014	3562	11215	29314	54681	296368	3816535
All Other Liabilities 28	5782	0	12	159	524	1070	3673	7007	12323	30620	77857	310549	3268402
Net Worth 29	11037	0	81	330	1406	5741	9753	25231	48401	94220	230250	731630	5303803

Selected Financial Ratios (Times to 1)

Current Ratio 30	1.1	•	2.7	2.6	2.0	2.7	1.9	2.3	2.5	2.6	2.0	1.7	0.8
Quick Ratio 31	0.9	•	2.6	2.4	1.7	2.1	1.5	1.8	1.8	2.0	1.7	1.4	0.6
Net Sales to Working Capital 32	28.7	•	7.1	5.5	4.4	2.7	2.9	3.4	2.6	2.2	4.7	4.7	•
Coverage Ratio 33	7.4	11.3	74.1	66.6	31.3	34.4	31.0	32.1	21.8	16.2	48.2	7.9	4.9
Total Asset Turnover 34	0.5	•	2.5	2.0	0.9	0.9	0.7	0.8	0.6	0.5	0.7	0.3	0.5
Inventory Turnover 35	34.6	•	•	449.9	27.7	78.9	20.2	36.4	8.3	13.3	31.8	12.0	43.4
Receivables Turnover 36	4.5	•	11.0	30.5	9.1	8.3	4.2	6.0	4.5	3.5	3.1	4.1	4.3
Total Liabilities to Net Worth 37	1.1	•	1.1	1.0	0.7	0.3	0.6	0.4	0.5	0.6	0.8	0.8	1.3
Current Assets to Working Capital 38	10.9	•	1.6	1.6	2.0	1.6	2.1	1.8	1.7	1.6	2.0	2.5	•
Current Liabilities to Working Capital 39	9.9	•	0.6	0.6	1.0	0.6	1.1	0.8	0.7	0.6	1.0	1.5	•
Working Capital to Net Sales 40	0.0	•	0.1	0.2	0.2	0.4	0.3	0.3	0.4	0.5	0.2	0.2	•
Inventory to Working Capital 41	0.4	•	•	0.0	0.0	0.0	0.0	0.0	0.1	0.1	0.1	0.1	•
Total Receipts to Cash Flow 42	2.6	1.4	1.8	1.6	1.6	2.2	1.9	2.2	1.3	2.1	2.3	1.8	3.3
Cost of Goods to Cash Flow 43	1.3	0.3	0.3	0.4	0.3	1.0	0.6	1.0	0.3	1.0	1.0	0.4	2.1
Cash Flow to Total Debt 44	0.4	•	2.7	2.5	1.5	1.6	1.0	1.2	1.3	0.7	0.8	0.4	0.2

Selected Financial Factors (in Percentages)

Debt Ratio 45	52.4	•	53.0	49.1	39.8	23.4	36.8	29.5	32.7	38.9	36.5	45.3	57.2
Return on Total Assets 46	12.7	•	90.3	63.7	44.1	27.1	25.6	22.6	31.8	17.8	25.4	10.8	9.3
Return on Equity Before Income Taxes 47	23.0	•	189.4	123.3	71.0	34.4	39.3	31.1	45.0	27.4	39.1	17.3	17.4
Return on Equity After Income Taxes 48	17.9	•	186.3	117.6	69.0	32.9	36.5	27.9	40.2	21.5	30.2	13.9	11.6
Profit Margin (Before Income Tax) 49	22.7	64.4	35.3	31.2	45.6	30.5	36.2	28.4	54.4	30.5	37.2	27.8	16.5
Profit Margin (After Income Tax) 50	17.7	62.9	34.7	29.8	44.4	29.2	33.7	25.5	48.5	24.0	28.7	22.3	11.0

Table I

Corporations with and without Net Income

COAL MINING

MONEY AMOUNTS AND SIZE OF ASSETS IN THOUSANDS OF DOLLARS

Item Description for Accounting Period 7/06 Through 6/07		Total	Zero Assets	Under 500	500 to 1,000	1,000 to 5,000	5,000 to 10,000	10,000 to 25,000	25,000 to 50,000	50,000 to 100,000	100,000 to 250,000	250,000 to 500,000	500,000 to 2,500,000	2,500,000 and over
Number of Enterprises	1	939	9	539	0	191	91	47	21	18	6	3	11	3
Revenues ($ in Thousands)														
Net Sales	2	26238743	36842	119045	0	1496635	1041549	2209549	973148	1868334	1084249	635567	7511893	9261932
Interest	3	218895	0	30	0	2232	1586	3039	0	4229	3077	5973	53234	145495
Rents	4	17561	0	0	0	0	134	1456	0	534	1212	0	3789	10436
Royalties	5	255389	0	0	0	2510	5473	9139	0	1039	313	9899	104302	122715
Other Portfolio Income	6	458107	21093	0	0	2159	20685	37873	856	21123	3461	102	134603	216154
Other Receipts	7	1307178	341	1	0	2449	10993	10150	19962	18935	11790	17205	823027	392322
Total Receipts	8	28495873	58276	119076	0	1505985	1080420	2271206	993966	1914194	1104102	668746	8630848	10149054
Average Total Receipts	9	30347	6475	221	•	7885	11873	48324	47332	106344	184017	222915	784623	3383018
Operating Costs/Operating Income (%)														
Cost of Operations	10	68.6	45.9	45.3	•	43.4	63.6	88.9	44.1	63.8	79.9	70.4	80.3	61.6
Salaries and Wages	11	3.1	10.8	•	•	11.0	5.3	1.3	10.9	4.1	1.3	3.5	1.9	2.1
Taxes Paid	12	6.1	10.1	16.5	•	5.3	6.5	1.4	6.3	4.3	2.2	5.0	5.5	8.4
Interest Paid	13	3.5	0.9	0.3	•	0.8	0.9	0.9	1.6	1.7	3.7	3.6	5.7	3.8
Depreciation	14	4.6	3.1	5.7	•	1.7	8.0	1.7	6.4	4.4	3.4	9.2	4.4	5.2
Amortization and Depletion	15	5.4	•	•	•	0.1	2.7	1.3	2.8	2.9	3.2	2.9	5.4	8.8
Pensions and Other Deferred Comp.	16	0.8	•	•	•	0.0	0.1	0.1	0.1	0.3	0.6	1.3	0.7	1.4
Employee Benefits	17	3.0	0.0	4.4	•	4.1	0.9	0.3	2.5	2.3	1.4	4.8	2.3	4.4
Advertising	18	0.0	•	•	•	0.0	0.0	0.0	0.0	0.0	0.1	0.0	0.1	0.1
Other Expenses	19	12.7	117.3	9.5	•	29.2	24.6	5.4	25.8	19.6	5.4	20.2	8.9	10.9
Officers' Compensation	20	0.5	0.2	23.6	•	0.5	0.2	0.3	0.5	0.6	0.2	0.7	0.6	0.3
Operating Margin	21	•	•	•	•	3.9	•	•	•	•	•	•	•	•
Operating Margin Before Officers' Comp.	22	•	•	18.4	•	4.4	•	•	•	•	•	•	•	•

Selected Average Balance Sheet ($ in Thousands)

Net Receivables 23	4812	0	0	452	740	3046	6960	11356	12020	63518	128467	731662
Inventories 24	1148	0	0	15	80	1223	966	1920	8524	4740	22767	215533
Net Property, Plant and Equipment 25	18167	0	32	596	2881	4992	14204	33122	54460	109465	529297	3019576
Total Assets 26	40992	0	148	1922	8023	15548	34980	69226	143998	336635	1085448	6929686
Notes and Loans Payable 27	12517	0	13	975	1784	4185	12847	23421	66552	99308	334408	2044530
All Other Liabilities 28	14889	0	58	733	2170	5845	9572	30008	22698	98287	470052	2331528
Net Worth 29	13586	0	77	214	4069	5518	12561	15798	54748	139040	280988	2553629

Selected Financial Ratios (Times to 1)

Current Ratio 30	1.6	1.2	•	1.2	1.0	1.2	1.3	0.7	1.2	1.7	1.3	2.7
Quick Ratio 31	1.2	1.0	•	1.1	0.8	0.9	1.2	0.5	0.8	1.5	1.0	2.0
Net Sales to Working Capital 32	8.2	16.0	•	56.9	244.0	50.6	14.3	•	33.6	4.0	15.6	3.6
Coverage Ratio 33	1.1	•	•	6.8	•	2.4	1.7	0.1	1.1	•	0.9	1.7
Total Asset Turnover 34	0.7	1.5	•	4.1	1.4	3.0	1.3	1.5	1.3	0.6	0.6	0.4
Inventory Turnover 35	16.7	•	•	221.0	90.7	34.2	21.1	34.5	16.9	31.5	24.1	8.8
Receivables Turnover 36	3.6	20.9	•	21.4	15.5	18.2	7.5	11.9	9.8	6.7	6.7	1.7
Total Liabilities to Net Worth 37	2.0	0.9	•	8.0	1.0	1.8	1.8	3.4	1.6	1.4	2.9	1.7
Current Assets to Working Capital 38	2.7	5.2	•	7.6	49.2	7.4	4.2	•	5.7	2.5	4.8	1.6
Current Liabilities to Working Capital 39	1.7	4.2	•	6.6	48.2	6.4	3.2	•	4.7	1.5	3.8	0.6
Working Capital to Net Sales 40	0.1	0.1	•	0.0	0.0	0.0	0.1	•	0.0	0.3	0.1	0.3
Inventory to Working Capital 41	0.3	•	•	0.1	1.7	1.5	0.2	•	1.2	0.1	0.6	0.2
Total Receipts to Cash Flow 42	11.4	23.3	1.3	3.5	20.9	18.4	5.0	9.2	22.1	31.6	21.4	10.8
Cost of Goods to Cash Flow 43	7.8	10.5	0.6	1.5	13.3	16.4	2.2	5.9	17.7	22.2	17.2	6.7
Cash Flow to Total Debt 44	0.1	•	•	1.3	0.1	0.3	0.4	0.2	0.1	0.0	0.0	0.1

Selected Financial Factors (in Percentages)

Debt Ratio 45	66.9	48.2	•	88.9	49.3	64.5	64.1	77.2	62.0	58.7	74.1	63.1
Return on Total Assets 46	2.6	•	•	21.5	•	6.2	3.5	0.2	5.2	•	3.1	2.9
Return on Equity Before Income Taxes 47	0.5	•	•	164.9	•	10.1	4.0	•	1.4	•	•	3.3
Return on Equity After Income Taxes 48	•	•	•	148.3	•	8.7	4.0	•	0.7	•	•	2.0
Profit Margin (Before Income Tax) 49	0.2	•	•	4.5	•	1.2	1.1	•	0.4	0.6	•	2.7
Profit Margin (After Income Tax) 50	•	•	•	4.1	•	1.0	1.1	•	0.2	0.0	•	1.7

Table II

Corporations with Net Income

COAL MINING

MONEY AMOUNTS AND SIZE OF ASSETS IN THOUSANDS OF DOLLARS

Item Description for Accounting Period 7/06 Through 6/07	Total	Zero Assets	Under 500	500 to 1,000	1,000 to 5,000	5,000 to 10,000	10,000 to 25,000	25,000 to 50,000	50,000 to 100,000	100,000 to 250,000	250,000 to 500,000	500,000 to 2,500,000	2,500,000 and over
Number of Enterprises **1**	245	•	•	0	•	20	34	11	11	0	0	5	0
Revenues ($ in Thousands)													
Net Sales **2**	15946932	•	•	•	•	301459	1686734	615377	2055804	0	0	10106303	0
Interest **3**	139314	•	•	•	•	868	2927	0	3185	0	0	130329	0
Rents **4**	14418	•	•	•	•	0	1294	0	1676	0	0	11448	0
Royalties **5**	84135	•	•	•	•	0	9139	0	922	0	0	74075	0
Other Portfolio Income **6**	277095	•	•	•	•	11011	29558	529	24170	0	0	190446	0
Other Receipts **7**	543054	•	•	•	•	722	10017	2916	34755	0	0	484655	0
Total Receipts **8**	17004948	•	•	•	•	314060	1739669	618822	2120512	0	0	10997256	0
Average Total Receipts **9**	69408	•	•	•	•	15703	51167	56257	192774	•	•	2199451	•
Operating Costs/Operating Income (%)													
Cost of Operations **10**	62.6	•	•	•	•	60.6	88.9	23.4	73.1	•	•	61.6	•
Salaries and Wages **11**	3.6	•	•	•	•	6.2	1.6	13.7	2.8	•	•	2.4	•
Taxes Paid **12**	6.6	•	•	•	•	2.0	0.5	8.1	2.8	•	•	8.8	•
Interest Paid **13**	2.7	•	•	•	•	1.4	0.7	1.8	1.1	•	•	3.7	•
Depreciation **14**	3.8	•	•	•	•	7.7	1.1	8.2	3.0	•	•	4.3	•
Amortization and Depletion **15**	5.9	•	•	•	•	1.5	1.5	3.8	2.5	•	•	8.2	•
Pensions and Other Deferred Comp. **16**	1.0	•	•	•	•	0.1	0.1	0.1	0.4	•	•	1.4	•
Employee Benefits **17**	3.0	•	•	•	•	•	0.3	1.3	1.7	•	•	3.9	•
Advertising **18**	0.1	•	•	•	•	•	0.0	0.0	0.0	•	•	0.1	•
Other Expenses **19**	12.1	•	•	•	•	21.7	5.4	34.5	11.6	•	•	9.6	•
Officers' Compensation **20**	0.2	•	•	•	•	0.4	0.4	0.5	0.2	•	•	0.2	•
Operating Margin **21**	•	•	•	•	•	•	•	4.7	0.8	•	•	•	•
Operating Margin Before Officers' Comp. **22**	•	•	•	•	•	•	•	5.2	1.0	•	•	•	•

Selected Average Balance Sheet ($ in Thousands)

Net Receivables 23	11465	1161	3496	2691	19258	476396
Inventories 24	1841	224	1615	959	3116	73278
Net Property, Plant and Equipment 25	43422	4358	4977	22983	36430	1931331
Total Assets 26	96833	7846	16117	37508	90684	4273185
Notes and Loans Payable 27	28876	3581	3393	13681	27604	1277278
All Other Liabilities 28	32978	1597	6184	13109	25511	1468997
Net Worth 29	34979	2668	6541	10718	37570	1526911

Selected Financial Ratios (Times to 1)

Current Ratio 30	2.0	1.2	1.2	0.5	1.3	2.4
Quick Ratio 31	1.6	1.1	0.9	0.4	1.0	2.0
Net Sales to Working Capital 32	6.6	32.6	33.7	•	20.2	4.4
Coverage Ratio 33	2.9	2.9	4.8	4.0	4.7	2.3
Total Asset Turnover 34	0.7	1.9	3.1	1.5	2.1	0.5
Inventory Turnover 35	22.1	40.9	27.3	13.7	43.8	17.0
Receivables Turnover 36	5.7	11.8	17.0	10.7	15.4	•
Total Liabilities to Net Worth 37	1.8	1.9	1.5	2.5	1.4	1.8
Current Assets to Working Capital 38	2.0	5.1	5.6	3.9	1.7	
Current Liabilities to Working Capital 39	1.0	4.1	4.6	•	2.9	0.7
Working Capital to Net Sales 40	0.2	0.0	0.0	•	0.0	0.2
Inventory to Working Capital 41	0.2	0.4	1.2	•	0.5	0.2
Total Receipts to Cash Flow 42	7.6	5.1	14.4	3.3	9.2	9.5
Cost of Goods to Cash Flow 43	4.7	3.1	12.8	0.8	6.7	5.9
Cash Flow to Total Debt 44	0.1	0.6	0.4	0.6	0.4	0.1

Selected Financial Factors (in Percentages)

Debt Ratio 45	63.9	66.0	59.4	71.4	58.6	64.3
Return on Total Assets 46	5.2	7.6	10.2	10.5	10.4	4.0
Return on Equity Before Income Taxes 47	9.4	14.6	19.9	27.5	19.7	6.3
Return on Equity After Income Taxes 48	7.6	11.8	18.4	27.5	19.1	4.3
Profit Margin (Before Income Tax) 49	5.1	2.6	2.6	5.3	4.0	4.7
Profit Margin (After Income Tax) 50	4.1	2.1	2.4	5.3	3.8	3.3

10

Table I

Corporations with and without Net Income

METAL ORE MINING

MONEY AMOUNTS AND SIZE OF ASSETS IN THOUSANDS OF DOLLARS

Item Description for Accounting Period 7/06 Through 6/07	Total	Zero Assets	Under 500	500 to 1,000	1,000 to 5,000	5,000 to 10,000	10,000 to 25,000	25,000 to 50,000	50,000 to 100,000	100,000 to 250,000	250,000 to 500,000	500,000 to 2,500,000	2,500,000 and over
Number of Enterprises **1**	1985	11	1661	103	73	21	50	25	11	5	9	8	8
Revenues ($ in Thousands)													
Net Sales **2**	40501806	489	44663	29854	6354	4036	280575	86833	237532	274381	2173589	4328448	33035052
Interest **3**	988630	341	726	481	1950	88	5244	4837	11290	4433	30141	97943	831155
Rents **4**	24028	0	6844	0	0	0	86	0	491	194	194	0	16219
Royalties **5**	199540	0	0	0	0	0	0	0	390	61	43141	2258	153689
Other Portfolio Income **6**	2874772	23	624	0	38431	1881	11823	11269	35709	24059	36913	143689	2570354
Other Receipts **7**	1855397	3596	29339	3	941	69453	24783	27372	221253	3126	3025	104772	1367731
Total Receipts **8**	46444173	4449	82196	30338	47676	75458	322511	130311	506665	306254	2287003	4677110	37974200
Average Total Receipts **9**	23398	404	49	295	653	3593	6450	5212	46060	61251	254111	584639	4746775
Operating Costs/Operating Income (%)													
Cost of Operations **10**	45.7	•	11.6	•	77.5	•	87.4	42.5	107.7	65.0	60.8	51.4	43.1
Salaries and Wages **11**	1.9	139.5	18.2	17.0	218.5	799.8	3.5	15.3	2.1	9.6	0.5	0.5	1.9
Taxes Paid **12**	4.4	42.9	12.6	2.6	25.4	25.7	1.6	2.2	1.7	1.3	0.6	4.7	4.6
Interest Paid **13**	1.8	127.0	3.8	0.4	95.8	288.8	2.5	2.4	1.1	7.2	1.4	3.2	1.6
Depreciation **14**	3.5	2.0	3.8	1.9	48.4	23.5	3.5	8.6	3.1	9.2	3.3	4.1	3.4
Amortization and Depletion **15**	9.3	45.4	7.7	1.9	14.0	20.1	2.9	16.8	7.5	16.3	8.0	12.8	8.9
Pensions and Other Deferred Comp. **16**	0.5	18.8	9.4	•	•	•	•	0.0	0.2	•	0.0	0.9	0.4
Employee Benefits **17**	0.7	•	3.2	•	2.3	•	0.2	0.1	0.3	0.1	1.4	0.4	0.7
Advertising **18**	0.0	•	0.8	•	1.0	2.4	0.1	0.0	0.0	0.0	0.0	0.0	0.0
Other Expenses **19**	13.3	32.9	206.1	46.2	481.9	641.0	18.4	121.9	24.4	21.3	17.8	6.6	13.0
Officers' Compensation **20**	0.4	554.0	64.2	8.0	31.7	•	1.1	4.7	4.5	3.8	0.3	0.2	0.3
Operating Margin **21**	18.4	•	•	22.1	•	•	•	•	•	•	5.7	15.2	22.1
Operating Margin Before Officers' Comp. **22**	18.9	•	•	30.1	•	•	•	•	•	•	6.0	15.4	22.4

Selected Average Balance Sheet ($ in Thousands)

Net Receivables 23	10331	0	0	8	7	146	2861	390	1724	4158	20268	94737	2421112
Inventories 24	1635	0	0	0	5	61	147	915	1459	5656	23180	81285	288691
Net Property, Plant and Equipment 25	11083	0	5	361	802	2856	5154	12180	12834	54822	201795	359984	2020359
Total Assets 26	52088	0	110	731	1938	5734	16553	33341	66131	130490	327387	1146539	10964343
Notes and Loans Payable 27	4124	0	162	5	518	2660	5694	12796	7237	55681	56307	144082	650137
All Other Liabilities 28	17451	0	45	45	385	3442	3968	8105	19320	69208	102602	357282	3714831
Net Worth 29	30513	0	-97	681	1035	-368	6890	12439	39574	5602	168478	645175	6599376

Selected Financial Ratios (Times to 1)

Current Ratio 30	1.6	•	4.1	3.0	2.3	0.1	2.7	0.9	1.7	0.6	1.2	2.0	1.6
Quick Ratio 31	1.3	•	4.1	2.9	2.2	0.1	2.3	0.7	1.5	0.4	0.8	1.4	1.3
Net Sales to Working Capital 32	3.0	•	0.9	3.0	0.2	•	1.5	•	2.3	•	15.1	2.5	2.9
Coverage Ratio 33	19.5	0.6	•	64.3	•	1.2	•	•	57.1	•	8.7	8.4	25.1
Total Asset Turnover 34	0.4	•	0.2	0.4	0.0	0.0	0.3	0.1	0.3	0.4	0.7	0.5	0.4
Inventory Turnover 35	5.7	•	•	•	13.5	•	33.3	1.6	15.9	6.3	6.3	3.4	6.2
Receivables Turnover 36	2.3	•	•	57.2	25.1	2.6	2.0	3.5	19.4	10.1	13.1	6.0	2.0
Total Liabilities to Net Worth 37	0.7	•	•	0.1	0.9	•	1.4	1.7	0.7	22.3	0.9	0.8	0.7
Current Assets to Working Capital 38	2.7	•	1.3	1.5	1.8	•	1.6	•	2.5	•	5.2	2.0	2.7
Current Liabilities to Working Capital 39	1.7	•	0.3	0.5	0.8	•	0.6	•	1.5	•	4.2	1.0	1.7
Working Capital to Net Sales 40	0.3	•	1.1	0.3	4.4	•	0.7	•	0.4	•	0.1	0.4	0.3
Inventory to Working Capital 41	0.3	•	•	•	0.0	•	0.1	•	0.3	•	1.0	0.5	0.2
Total Receipts to Cash Flow 42	2.3	•	2.9	1.5	•	0.2	14.7	2.4	1.4	•	5.0	3.4	2.1
Cost of Goods to Cash Flow 43	1.0	•	0.3	•	•	•	12.9	1.0	1.5	•	3.1	1.8	0.9
Cash Flow to Total Debt 44	0.4	•	0.0	3.9	•	0.2	0.0	0.1	0.6	•	0.3	0.3	0.5

Selected Financial Factors (in Percentages)

Debt Ratio 45	41.4	•	188.7	6.9	46.6	106.4	58.4	62.7	40.2	95.7	48.5	43.7	39.8
Return on Total Assets 46	14.1	•	•	9.6	•	12.0	•	•	20.3	•	9.1	12.8	15.0
Return on Equity Before Income Taxes 47	22.8	•	43.8	10.1	•	•	•	•	33.3	•	15.7	20.1	23.9
Return on Equity After Income Taxes 48	15.6	•	43.8	10.1	•	•	•	•	32.5	•	12.9	13.8	16.3
Profit Margin (Before Income Tax) 49	34.2	•	•	23.7	68.3	•	•	•	61.0	•	11.0	24.0	38.2
Profit Margin (After Income Tax) 50	23.3	•	•	23.6	68.3	•	59.6	•	•	•	9.0	16.5	26.1

Table II

Corporations with Net Income

METAL ORE MINING

MONEY AMOUNTS AND SIZE OF ASSETS IN THOUSANDS OF DOLLARS

Item Description for Accounting Period 7/06 Through 6/07		Total	Zero Assets	Under 500	500 to 1,000	1,000 to 5,000	5,000 to 10,000	10,000 to 25,000	25,000 to 50,000	50,000 to 100,000	100,000 to 250,000	250,000 to 500,000	500,000 to 2,500,000	2,500,000 and over
Number of Enterprises	1	670	•	•	62	•	10	10	11	4	0	0	5	8
Revenues ($ in Thousands)														
Net Sales	2	38723802	•	•	29854	•	4036	94469	76273	80465	0	•	3220163	33035052
Interest	3	954650	•	•	0	•	59	1706	2682	6037	0	•	81156	831155
Rents	4	16488	•	•	0	•	0	0	0	75	0	•	0	16219
Royalties	5	197421	•	•	0	•	0	0	0	0	0	•	591	153689
Other Portfolio Income	6	2825044	•	•	0	•	1881	46	10567	30295	0	•	136529	2570354
Other Receipts	7	1663371	•	•	3	•	69453	23039	24090	171442	0	•	-27944	1367731
Total Receipts	8	44380776	•	•	29857	•	75429	119260	113612	288314	0	•	3410495	37974200
Average Total Receipts	9	66240	•	•	482	•	7543	11926	10328	72078	•	•	682099	4746775
Operating Costs/Operating Income (%)														
Cost of Operations	10	44.2	•	•	•	•	•	85.4	17.0	59.2	•	•	44.6	43.1
Salaries and Wages	11	1.8	•	•	1.9	•	797.8	•	4.8	1.8	•	•	0.4	1.9
Taxes Paid	12	4.5	•	•	0.9	•	19.7	0.1	1.3	2.4	•	•	5.5	4.6
Interest Paid	13	1.7	•	•	0.4	•	288.8	0.0	0.6	2.4	•	•	2.5	1.6
Depreciation	14	3.4	•	•	1.1	•	23.5	0.0	6.1	3.7	•	•	3.5	3.4
Amortization and Depletion	15	9.1	•	•	0.0	•	0.1	0.0	9.0	15.5	•	•	11.9	8.9
Pensions and Other Deferred Comp.	16	0.5	•	•	•	•	•	•	•	0.1	•	•	1.3	0.4
Employee Benefits	17	0.7	•	•	•	•	0.1	•	•	0.1	•	•	0.1	0.7
Advertising	18	0.0	•	•	•	•	2.4	0.1	0.0	•	•	•	•	0.0
Other Expenses	19	12.7	•	•	11.9	•	627.8	6.4	90.1	12.8	•	•	3.8	13.0
Officers' Compensation	20	0.3	•	•	1.8	•	•	0.3	0.0	0.1	•	•	0.0	0.3
Operating Margin	21	21.2	•	•	82.1	•	•	7.6	•	1.9	•	•	26.5	22.1
Operating Margin Before Officers' Comp.	22	21.6	•	•	83.9	•	•	7.9	•	2.0	•	•	26.6	22.4

Selected Average Balance Sheet ($ in Thousands)

Net Receivables 23	30030	13	306	2183	527	2314	•	105688	2421112
Inventories 24	4094	0	18	58	1888	2955	•	73519	340835
Net Property, Plant and Equipment 25	28813	528	640	3287	10745	15381	•	404702	2020359
Total Assets 26	144127	687	5274	12200	30950	68361	•	1180958	10964343
Notes and Loans Payable 27	10499	9	3028	3990	20553	17409	•	182057	650137
All Other Liabilities 28	48457	6	6437	2935	3669	15835	•	357023	3714831
Net Worth 29	85172	672	-4192	5276	6728	35116	•	641879	6599376

Selected Financial Ratios (Times to 1)

Current Ratio 30	1.6	2.2	0.3	3.0	2.8	1.9	•	2.9	1.6
Quick Ratio 31	1.4	2.2	0.2	2.4	1.5	1.3	•	2.1	1.3
Net Sales to Working Capital 32	2.9	36.8	•	1.6	3.5	2.7	•	2.0	2.9
Coverage Ratio 33	23.1	219.8	1.4	7997.0	31.8	108.6	•	14.1	25.1
Total Asset Turnover 34	0.4	0.7	0.1	0.8	0.2	0.3	•	0.5	0.4
Inventory Turnover 35	6.2	•	•	138.8	0.6	4.0	•	3.9	5.2
Receivables Turnover 36	2.3	•	2.6	1.2	21.1	7.4	•	6.8	•
Total Liabilities to Net Worth 37	0.7	0.0	•	1.3	3.6	0.9	•	0.8	0.7
Current Assets to Working Capital 38	2.5	1.8	•	1.5	1.5	2.1	•	1.5	2.7
Current Liabilities to Working Capital 39	1.5	0.8	•	0.5	0.5	1.1	•	0.5	1.7
Working Capital to Net Sales 40	0.3	0.0	•	0.6	0.3	0.4	•	0.5	0.3
Inventory to Working Capital 41	0.3	•	•	•	0.6	0.7	•	0.3	0.2
Total Receipts to Cash Flow 42	2.2	1.1	0.2	2.5	1.0	0.4	•	2.8	2.1
Cost of Goods to Cash Flow 43	1.0	•	•	2.1	0.2	0.3	•	1.3	0.9
Cash Flow to Total Debt 44	0.4	30.3	0.2	0.5	0.3	1.4	•	0.4	0.5

Selected Financial Factors (in Percentages)

Debt Ratio 45	40.9	2.2	179.5	56.8	78.3	48.6	•	45.6	39.8
Return on Total Assets 46	15.5	57.8	30.4	26.2	4.6	77.0	•	19.6	15.0
Return on Equity Before Income Taxes 47	25.1	58.8	•	60.6	20.5	148.6	•	33.5	23.9
Return on Equity After Income Taxes 48	17.4	58.7	•	46.8	14.8	146.2	•	23.4	16.3
Profit Margin (Before Income Tax) 49	37.0	82.1	108.7	33.9	19.9	259.4	•	33.4	38.2
Profit Margin (After Income Tax) 50	25.6	82.0	108.7	26.2	14.4	255.3	•	23.3	26.1

Table I

Corporations with and without Net Income

NONMETALLIC MINERAL MINING AND QUARRYING

MONEY AMOUNTS AND SIZE OF ASSETS IN THOUSANDS OF DOLLARS

Item Description for Accounting Period 7/06 Through 6/07

Item	Total	Zero Assets	Under 500	500 to 1,000	1,000 to 5,000	5,000 to 10,000	10,000 to 25,000	25,000 to 50,000	50,000 to 100,000	100,000 to 250,000	250,000 to 500,000	500,000 to 2,500,000	2,500,000 and over
Number of Enterprises 1	6333	506	3811	643	913	150	176	63	31	25	6	7	0

Revenues ($ in Thousands)

Item	Total	Zero Assets	Under 500	500 to 1,000	1,000 to 5,000	5,000 to 10,000	10,000 to 25,000	25,000 to 50,000	50,000 to 100,000	100,000 to 250,000	250,000 to 500,000	500,000 to 2,500,000	2,500,000 and over
Net Sales 2	28760104	7872	630890	1254363	3718354	1169444	3191841	1812496	2416379	3488332	2249423	8820711	0
Interest 3	89028	0	1058	992	1960	5207	4621	10068	8218	9658	3757	43490	0
Rents 4	40654	70	0	0	882	355	1338	2439	7189	8059	641	19679	0
Royalties 5	24927	0	399	0	0	1228	293	1125	0	2178	657	19047	0
Other Portfolio Income 6	442230	0	5308	10981	10739	37320	22237	26891	22651	19021	10293	276789	0
Other Receipts 7	641891	43	291	34871	40777	8693	36362	46964	24481	49949	18683	380777	0
Total Receipts 8	29998834	7985	637946	1301207	3772712	1222247	3256692	1899983	2478918	3577197	2283454	9560493	0
Average Total Receipts 9	4737	16	167	2024	4132	8148	18504	30158	79965	143088	380576	1365785	•

Operating Costs/Operating Income (%)

Item	Total	Zero Assets	Under 500	500 to 1,000	1,000 to 5,000	5,000 to 10,000	10,000 to 25,000	25,000 to 50,000	50,000 to 100,000	100,000 to 250,000	250,000 to 500,000	500,000 to 2,500,000	2,500,000 and over
Cost of Operations 10	62.4	45.8	35.7	69.6	57.3	58.8	63.8	67.3	66.9	67.2	69.0	59.5	•
Salaries and Wages 11	4.6	1.9	11.8	1.6	4.3	5.8	3.8	3.1	4.8	4.1	3.7	5.4	•
Taxes Paid 12	2.5	1.7	4.3	3.8	3.1	2.4	2.7	2.2	2.0	1.5	1.8	2.7	•
Interest Paid 13	2.1	•	3.2	1.4	1.4	3.0	1.8	1.5	1.6	2.4	1.7	2.5	•
Depreciation 14	5.2	1.7	7.5	4.6	4.1	4.0	6.6	4.0	4.7	5.9	4.7	5.4	•
Amortization and Depletion 15	2.5	•	1.6	0.4	1.1	1.2	2.5	2.1	2.2	2.5	2.4	3.8	•
Pensions and Other Deferred Comp. 16	0.7	•	0.4	0.0	0.6	0.8	0.4	0.7	0.5	0.9	0.8	0.9	•
Employee Benefits 17	1.9	2.9	1.1	1.2	1.2	2.1	1.6	1.6	1.5	2.7	2.1	2.2	•
Advertising 18	0.2	0.0	1.2	0.5	0.2	1.2	0.2	0.1	0.1	0.1	0.2	0.1	•
Other Expenses 19	12.4	49.7	39.0	11.9	15.8	11.8	9.5	8.7	11.4	9.0	8.6	13.5	•
Officers' Compensation 20	1.5	11.7	1.6	2.6	2.3	2.7	2.0	2.4	1.0	1.0	1.2	0.9	•
Operating Margin 21	4.0	•	•	2.3	8.6	6.4	5.0	6.3	3.4	2.7	3.6	2.9	•
Operating Margin Before Officers' Comp. 22	5.6	•	•	4.9	10.9	9.0	7.0	8.8	4.4	3.7	4.9	3.8	•

Selected Average Balance Sheet ($ in Thousands)

Item													
Net Receivables 23	565	0	1	96	488	857	2476	3944	10641	21869	43875	158761	•
Inventories 24	400	0	6	41	123	635	1491	2627	6250	18213	27451	82388	•
Net Property, Plant and Equipment 25	2000	0	50	363	1167	2163	7648	12134	33970	66139	184986	703645	•
Total Assets 26	4827		84	807	2434	6762	16418	36784	73404	159565	353888	1842435	•
Notes and Loans Payable 27	1570	0	101	355	716		3449	8786	21694	46348	146322	579743	•
All Other Liabilities 28	1034	0	7	240	407	1202	2269	4509	18639	34150	54428	482260	•
Net Worth 29	2222	0	-23	212	1311	2111	9365	23490	33072	79066	153138	780432	•

Selected Financial Ratios (Times to 1)

Item													
Current Ratio 30	1.6	•	1.5	1.1	2.5	2.3	2.5	3.1	1.6	2.1	1.1	1.1	•
Quick Ratio 31	1.0	•	0.9	0.9	2.2	1.2	1.6	2.3	1.0	1.0	0.5	0.5	•
Net Sales to Working Capital 32	7.6	•	18.6	58.5	5.6	4.6	4.4	3.4	7.2	4.2	43.7	25.1	•
Coverage Ratio 33	5.0	•	•	5.4	8.2	4.7	4.8	8.3	4.8	3.1	4.1	5.5	•
Total Asset Turnover 34	0.9	•	2.0	2.4	1.7	1.2	1.1	0.8	1.1	0.9	1.1	0.7	•
Inventory Turnover 35	7.1	•	10.1	33.5	18.9	7.2	7.8	7.4	8.3	5.2	9.4	9.1	•
Receivables Turnover 36	8.0	•	49.0	24.1	10.7	11.9	7.9	7.0	8.0	6.6	11.1	11.4	•
Total Liabilities to Net Worth 37	1.2	•	•	2.8	0.9	2.2	0.8	0.6	1.2	1.0	1.3	1.4	•
Current Assets to Working Capital 38	2.6	•	3.2	8.7	1.7	1.8	1.7	1.5	2.7	1.9	11.8	8.1	•
Current Liabilities to Working Capital 39	1.6	•	2.2	7.7	0.7	0.8	0.7	0.5	1.7	0.9	10.8	7.1	•
Working Capital to Net Sales 40	0.1	•	0.1	0.0	0.2	0.2	0.2	0.3	0.1	0.2	0.0	0.0	•
Inventory to Working Capital 41	0.7	•	0.7	1.4	0.2	0.5	0.4	0.3	0.6	0.6	4.1	2.4	•
Total Receipts to Cash Flow 42	6.6	2.8	4.5	6.4	6.2	5.3	8.4	5.8	7.5	8.6	10.2	5.7	•
Cost of Goods to Cash Flow 43	4.1	1.3	1.6	4.5	3.6	3.1	5.4	3.9	5.0	5.8	7.0	3.4	•
Cash Flow to Total Debt 44	0.3	•	0.3	0.5	0.6	0.3	0.3	0.4	0.3	0.2	0.2	0.2	•

Selected Financial Factors (in Percentages)

Item													
Debt Ratio 45	54.0	•	127.7	73.7	46.1	68.8	43.0	36.1	54.9	50.4	56.7	57.6	•
Return on Total Assets 46	9.8	•	•	17.9	19.1	15.9	9.7	9.7	8.0	6.6	7.2	9.6	•
Return on Equity Before Income Taxes 47	17.1	•	45.1	55.6	31.1	40.1	13.5	13.4	14.0	9.1	12.5	18.4	•
Return on Equity After Income Taxes 48	13.8	•	45.2	55.2	30.9	38.4	12.1	12.1	10.8	6.7	10.7	12.7	•
Profit Margin (Before Income Tax) 49	8.3	•	•	6.0	10.9	10.0	7.0	11.0	5.9	5.2	5.1	11.4	•
Profit Margin (After Income Tax) 50	6.7	•	•	6.0	9.9	10.4	6.2	9.9	4.6	3.8	4.4	7.9	•

13

Table II

Corporations with Net Income

NONMETALLIC MINERAL MINING AND QUARRYING

MONEY AMOUNTS AND SIZE OF ASSETS IN THOUSANDS OF DOLLARS

Item Description for Accounting Period 7/06 Through 6/07	Total	Zero Assets	Under 500	500 to 1,000	1,000 to 5,000	5,000 to 10,000	10,000 to 25,000	25,000 to 50,000	50,000 to 100,000	100,000 to 250,000	250,000 to 500,000	500,000 to 2,500,000	2,500,000 and over
Number of Enterprises 1	3285	0	1479	612	•	97	148	56	22	19	•	7	0
Revenues ($ in Thousands)													
Net Sales 2	26319531	0	282744	1223181	•	882280	2941409	1655592	1933593	2799881	•	8820711	0
Interest 3	75560	0	1057	904	•	162	3713	9743	5475	6162	•	43490	0
Rents 4	32454	0	0	0	•	0	1040	2229	604	7736	•	19679	0
Royalties 5	23294	0	399	0	•	0	293	1125	0	1773	•	19047	0
Other Portfolio Income 6	421752	0	5308	10981	•	32256	20518	25030	20574	10543	•	276789	0
Other Receipts 7	603516	0	262	34857	•	2982	32675	41145	20126	32389	•	380777	0
Total Receipts 8	27476107	0	289770	1269923	•	917680	2999648	1734864	1980372	2858484	•	9560493	0
Average Total Receipts 9	8364	•	196	2075	•	9461	20268	30980	90017	150447	•	1365785	•
Operating Costs/Operating Income (%)													
Cost of Operations 10	62.5	•	49.4	71.4	•	53.1	63.9	67.2	65.3	66.7	•	59.5	•
Salaries and Wages 11	4.3	•	2.5	0.9	•	5.3	3.5	2.9	4.7	4.0	•	5.4	•
Taxes Paid 12	2.5	•	3.5	3.8	•	2.4	2.6	2.1	1.8	1.4	•	2.7	•
Interest Paid 13	1.9	•	1.0	1.3	•	3.3	1.4	1.5	1.4	1.7	•	2.5	•
Depreciation 14	4.9	•	6.7	4.4	•	2.9	6.3	3.8	4.2	5.1	•	5.4	•
Amortization and Depletion 15	2.5	•	0.0	0.4	•	1.5	2.5	2.0	2.3	2.5	•	3.8	•
Pensions and Other Deferred Comp. 16	0.7	•	0.9	0.0	•	0.9	0.4	0.6	0.4	0.9	•	0.9	•
Employee Benefits 17	1.8	•	•	1.3	•	2.0	1.6	1.7	1.2	2.3	•	2.2	•
Advertising 18	0.2	•	0.5	0.6	•	1.4	0.2	0.1	0.2	0.1	•	0.1	•
Other Expenses 19	11.7	•	20.4	10.1	•	12.1	8.2	8.6	11.2	8.6	•	13.5	•
Officers' Compensation 20	1.5	•	3.5	2.7	•	2.3	2.0	1.9	0.9	0.8	•	0.9	•
Operating Margin 21	5.6	•	11.5	3.2	•	12.8	7.4	7.5	6.5	5.8	•	2.9	•
Operating Margin Before Officers' Comp. 22	7.1	•	15.0	5.8	•	15.1	9.4	9.4	7.4	6.6	•	3.8	•

Selected Average Balance Sheet ($ in Thousands)

Net Receivables 23	1007	•	1	96	•	1025	2640	4065	12471	23328	•	158761
Inventories 24	672	•	6	46	•	516	1374	2554	6375	21282	•	120356
Net Property, Plant and Equipment 25	3389	•	36	347	•	2052	7675	12059	33463	62811	•	703645
Total Assets 26	8269	•	104	804	•	6686	16915	35548	72302	161380	•	1842435
Notes and Loans Payable 27	2489	•	36	339	•	3964	4106	9116	17965	32935	•	579743
All Other Liabilities 28	1789	•	9	249	•	1101	2117	4622	17453	32717	•	482260
Net Worth 29	3990	•	59	216	•	1621	10691	21810	36884	95727	•	780432

Selected Financial Ratios (Times to 1)

Current Ratio 30	1.7	•	5.7	1.1	•	2.4	2.8	2.9	1.5	2.7	•	1.1
Quick Ratio 31	1.0	•	4.2	0.9	•	1.5	1.9	2.2	0.9	1.3	•	0.5
Net Sales to Working Capital 32	7.6	•	4.1	71.5	•	5.5	4.3	3.9	8.3	3.5	•	25.1
Coverage Ratio 33	6.3	•	14.6	6.5	•	6.0	7.5	9.1	7.6	5.6	•	5.5
Total Asset Turnover 34	1.0	•	1.8	2.5	•	1.4	1.2	0.8	1.2	0.9	•	0.7
Inventory Turnover 35	7.4	•	15.9	31.1	•	9.4	9.2	7.8	9.0	4.6	•	6.2
Receivables Turnover 36	8.1	•	71.8	•	•	13.3	8.4	7.0	7.9	5.9	•	•
Total Liabilities to Net Worth 37	1.1	•	0.8	2.7	•	3.1	0.6	0.6	1.0	0.7	•	1.4
Current Assets to Working Capital 38	2.5	•	1.2	10.5	•	1.7	1.5	1.5	2.9	1.6	•	8.1
Current Liabilities to Working Capital 39	1.5	•	0.2	9.5	•	0.7	0.5	0.5	1.9	0.6	•	7.1
Working Capital to Net Sales 40	0.1	•	0.2	0.0	•	0.2	0.2	0.3	0.1	0.3	•	0.0
Inventory to Working Capital 41	0.6	•	0.1	1.6	•	0.6	0.3	0.3	0.6	0.5	•	2.4
Total Receipts to Cash Flow 42	6.2	•	3.3	6.7	•	3.9	7.3	5.5	5.7	7.1	•	5.7
Cost of Goods to Cash Flow 43	3.8	•	1.6	4.8	•	2.1	4.7	3.7	3.7	4.7	•	3.4
Cash Flow to Total Debt 44	0.3	•	1.3	0.5	•	0.5	0.4	0.4	0.4	0.3	•	0.2

Selected Financial Factors (in Percentages)

Debt Ratio 45	51.7	•	43.2	73.1	•	75.8	36.8	38.6	49.0	40.7	•	57.6
Return on Total Assets 46	11.6	•	27.6	20.5	•	27.4	12.6	11.4	12.5	8.7	•	9.6
Return on Equity Before Income Taxes 47	20.1	•	45.3	64.7	•	94.3	17.3	16.5	21.2	12.1	•	18.4
Return on Equity After Income Taxes 48	16.6	•	45.1	64.3	•	90.9	15.8	15.0	17.1	9.4	•	12.7
Profit Margin (Before Income Tax) 49	10.0	•	14.0	7.0	•	16.8	9.3	12.2	8.9	7.8	•	11.4
Profit Margin (After Income Tax) 50	8.3	•	14.0	6.9	•	16.2	8.5	11.0	7.2	6.1	•	7.9

14

Table I

Corporations with and without Net Income

SUPPORT ACTIVITIES FOR MINING

MONEY AMOUNTS AND SIZE OF ASSETS IN THOUSANDS OF DOLLARS

Item Description for Accounting Period 7/06 Through 6/07	Total	Zero Assets	Under 500	500 to 1,000	1,000 to 5,000	5,000 to 10,000	10,000 to 25,000	25,000 to 50,000	50,000 to 100,000	100,000 to 250,000	250,000 to 500,000	500,000 to 2,500,000	2,500,000 and over
Number of Enterprises **1**	9059	2215	4653	866	923	187	99	29	19	18	13	24	12
Revenues ($ in Thousands)													
Net Sales **2**	79060261	1081211	3139758	1245574	4051213	2287128	2479320	1203493	1093179	2442703	2521015	19215139	38300527
Interest **3**	1258674	2369	1835	652	7689	5015	2724	2792	7684	5847	33092	182541	1006434
Rents **4**	347033	803	226	0	690	4299	1786	379	36	51025	95970	121863	69956
Royalties **5**	235970	0	111	418	19937	824	0	66	504	107	5245	8556	200204
Other Portfolio Income **6**	1261755	7011	18179	16745	67647	18767	42598	2097	36139	18260	30730	330616	672965
Other Receipts **7**	2310895	631	17814	2267	30275	39886	47018	38461	60893	35603	36272	236297	1765478
Total Receipts **8**	84474588	1092025	3177923	1265656	4177451	2355919	2573446	1247288	1198435	2553545	2722324	20095012	42015564
Average Total Receipts **9**	9325	493	683	1461	4526	12598	25994	43010	63076	141864	209410	837292	3501297
Operating Costs/Operating Income (%)													
Cost of Operations **10**	44.8	48.7	25.1	27.0	33.6	48.2	57.1	36.5	36.7	53.4	37.5	38.5	50.6
Salaries and Wages **11**	10.2	10.3	15.8	12.9	15.9	7.3	11.6	17.1	15.4	15.6	11.3	7.4	9.6
Taxes Paid **12**	2.2	0.8	3.4	5.7	3.6	2.5	2.3	3.1	2.8	1.6	2.8	2.3	1.7
Interest Paid **13**	3.1	0.8	0.6	1.0	0.7	0.9	0.7	2.0	2.6	2.2	2.3	2.7	4.3
Depreciation **14**	6.0	3.9	4.0	4.2	4.4	5.2	3.6	7.4	10.1	6.3	12.2	8.8	4.7
Amortization and Depletion **15**	0.5	0.3	0.2	0.1	0.2	0.0	0.3	0.4	0.5	0.5	0.3	0.9	0.4
Pensions and Other Deferred Comp. **16**	0.9	0.8	1.3	0.8	0.5	0.1	0.3	0.5	0.4	0.2	0.4	0.3	1.4
Employee Benefits **17**	1.8	1.0	1.4	0.6	1.2	0.8	0.4	2.2	1.5	1.1	0.5	1.6	2.2
Advertising **18**	0.1	0.3	0.2	0.2	0.2	0.2	0.1	0.3	0.1	0.1	0.1	0.1	0.1
Other Expenses **19**	15.5	16.7	26.6	21.4	24.0	21.4	11.5	21.7	27.2	14.5	21.4	17.9	11.4
Officers' Compensation **20**	1.6	3.4	9.6	7.6	5.5	1.8	1.5	1.4	0.8	2.1	0.9	1.1	0.6
Operating Margin **21**	13.4	12.9	11.7	18.5	10.1	11.6	10.5	7.6	1.8	2.5	10.3	18.5	12.8
Operating Margin Before Officers' Comp. **22**	15.0	16.3	21.3	26.0	15.7	13.4	12.0	8.9	2.6	4.5	11.2	19.6	13.4

Selected Average Balance Sheet ($ in Thousands)

Net Receivables 23	2168	0	15	75	533	1468	4944	9500	19641	34469	105549	217386	866185
Inventories 24	357	0	2	19	51	184	674	1347	1463	5068	5190	40384	155294
Net Property, Plant and Equipment 25	4215	0	83	204	651	3025	3557	11814	29455	55078	131073	623385	1462026
Total Assets 26	12099	0	145	659	1904	7153	13853	35381	70716	141752	367907	1263243	5322756
Notes and Loans Payable 27	3331	0	71	293	379	2522	2922	10425	35920	55705	71271	328259	1473958
All Other Liabilities 28	2852	0	20	63	294	1449	3265	10317	21771	37581	79944	286741	1292359
Net Worth 29	5917	0	54	303	1231	3182	7666	14639	13025	48466	216693	648242	2556439

Selected Financial Ratios (Times to 1)

Current Ratio 30	2.0	•	2.4	2.1	3.5	2.5	2.4	1.7	1.1	1.4	1.9	2.2	2.1
Quick Ratio 31	1.6	•	2.1	1.2	3.1	1.8	2.1	1.4	0.9	1.0	1.8	1.7	1.6
Net Sales to Working Capital 32	4.4	•	20.1	10.5	5.2	6.0	5.1	6.0	35.2	9.0	3.1	4.4	3.6
Coverage Ratio 33	7.7	17.7	22.5	20.2	20.3	16.5	20.3	6.7	5.3	4.2	9.2	9.7	6.4
Total Asset Turnover 34	0.7	•	4.7	2.2	2.3	1.7	1.8	1.2	0.8	1.0	0.5	0.6	0.6
Inventory Turnover 35	11.0	•	96.3	20.0	29.0	32.0	21.2	11.3	14.4	14.3	14.0	7.6	10.4
Receivables Turnover 36	4.9	•	63.8	15.0	9.2	12.1	6.5	5.0	3.1	4.6	2.0	4.1	4.9
Total Liabilities to Net Worth 37	1.0	•	1.7	1.2	0.5	1.2	0.8	1.4	4.4	1.9	0.7	0.9	1.1
Current Assets to Working Capital 38	2.0	•	1.7	1.9	1.4	1.6	1.7	2.4	19.0	3.6	2.1	1.9	1.9
Current Liabilities to Working Capital 39	1.0	•	0.7	0.9	0.4	0.6	0.7	1.4	18.0	2.6	1.1	0.9	0.9
Working Capital to Net Sales 40	0.2	•	0.0	0.1	0.2	0.2	0.2	0.2	0.0	0.1	0.3	0.2	0.3
Inventory to Working Capital 41	0.2	•	0.1	0.1	0.1	0.1	0.2	0.3	1.1	0.4	0.0	0.2	0.2
Total Receipts to Cash Flow 42	3.2	3.8	3.0	2.7	3.6	3.3	4.5	3.8	3.0	5.5	3.0	2.9	3.3
Cost of Goods to Cash Flow 43	1.4	1.8	0.7	0.7	1.2	1.6	2.5	1.4	1.1	2.9	1.1	1.1	1.7
Cash Flow to Total Debt 44	0.4	•	2.5	1.5	1.8	0.9	0.9	0.5	0.3	0.3	0.4	0.5	0.3

Selected Financial Factors (in Percentages)

Debt Ratio 45	51.1	•	62.7	54.0	35.3	55.5	44.7	58.6	81.6	65.8	41.1	48.7	52.0
Return on Total Assets 46	17.1	•	63.3	46.1	32.1	26.5	27.1	15.5	11.5	8.7	11.0	16.3	16.6
Return on Equity Before Income Taxes 47	30.4	•	162.1	95.3	47.2	56.0	46.5	31.8	50.7	19.4	16.7	28.5	29.1
Return on Equity After Income Taxes 48	23.4	•	158.3	89.8	41.7	46.8	40.4	28.4	39.3	13.2	10.5	20.0	22.8
Profit Margin (Before Income Tax) 49	20.6	13.9	13.0	20.1	13.2	14.6	14.2	11.2	11.2	6.9	18.6	23.1	23.3
Profit Margin (After Income Tax) 50	15.9	12.6	12.7	18.9	11.7	12.2	12.4	10.0	8.9	4.7	11.8	16.2	18.3

15

Table II
Corporations with Net Income

SUPPORT ACTIVITIES FOR MINING

MONEY AMOUNTS AND SIZE OF ASSETS IN THOUSANDS OF DOLLARS

Item Description for Accounting Period 7/06 Through 6/07		Total	Zero Assets	Under 500	500 to 1,000	1,000 to 5,000	5,000 to 10,000	10,000 to 25,000	25,000 to 50,000	50,000 to 100,000	100,000 to 250,000	250,000 to 500,000	500,000 to 2,500,000	2,500,000 and over
Number of Enterprises	1	7275	1766	3623	808	753	138	95	23	10	13	10	24	12
Revenues ($ in Thousands)														
Net Sales	2	76038429	662049	2829408	1169427	3378407	2082556	2391840	1122968	744018	2014390	2127701	19215139	38300527
Interest	3	1239726	1318	1821	652	6970	1929	2724	2480	1958	2813	28085	182541	1006434
Rents	4	341173	0	0	0	156	3436	1786	0	0	50989	92987	121863	69956
Royalties	5	235330	0	111	418	19356	764	0	66	504	107	5245	8556	200204
Other Portfolio Income	6	1233470	4878	18179	16745	67564	17561	42507	2097	15703	15819	28837	330616	672965
Other Receipts	7	2268029	523	17309	2267	26110	29803	47116	25729	51924	28329	37141	236297	1765478
Total Receipts	8	81356157	668768	2866828	1189509	3498563	2136049	2485973	1153340	814107	2112447	2319996	20095012	42015564
Average Total Receipts	9	11183	379	791	1472	4646	15479	26168	50145	81411	162496	232000	837292	3501297
Operating Costs/Operating Income (%)														
Cost of Operations	10	45.2	25.5	24.0	28.8	34.7	49.2	59.2	36.1	37.8	61.2	40.0	38.5	50.6
Salaries and Wages	11	9.9	14.2	16.5	10.5	16.6	7.9	10.7	17.1	18.0	10.8	10.8	7.4	9.6
Taxes Paid	12	2.1	0.9	3.3	5.8	3.4	2.5	2.1	3.2	3.3	1.4	2.7	2.3	1.7
Interest Paid	13	3.1	1.0	0.6	1.0	0.4	0.5	0.6	1.8	1.6	1.6	1.7	2.7	4.3
Depreciation	14	5.8	3.9	3.9	4.4	4.3	4.3	3.3	5.7	10.8	4.2	10.0	8.8	4.7
Amortization and Depletion	15	0.5	0.4	0.3	0.1	0.2	0.0	0.3	0.4	0.4	0.3	0.2	0.9	0.4
Pensions and Other Deferred Comp.	16	0.9	1.2	1.5	0.9	0.4	0.1	0.3	0.4	0.2	0.3	0.5	0.3	1.4
Employee Benefits	17	1.8	1.1	1.4	0.6	1.4	0.7	0.4	2.2	0.8	1.0	0.5	1.6	2.2
Advertising	18	0.1	0.5	0.2	0.2	0.3	0.2	0.1	0.3	0.1	0.1	0.1	0.1	0.1
Other Expenses	19	14.5	20.3	24.1	20.2	18.6	18.0	9.8	17.7	15.5	11.2	18.2	17.9	11.4
Officers' Compensation	20	1.6	5.1	8.4	7.6	6.4	1.8	1.4	0.9	0.7	2.0	1.0	1.1	0.6
Operating Margin	21	14.5	25.8	16.0	20.1	13.5	14.8	11.6	14.3	10.9	5.9	14.3	18.5	12.8
Operating Margin Before Officers' Comp.	22	16.0	30.9	24.4	27.6	19.9	16.6	13.1	15.2	11.6	7.9	15.3	19.6	13.4

Selected Average Balance Sheet ($ in Thousands)

Net Receivables 23	2580	0	3	52	396	1780	5152	11334	14887	39817	114498	217386	866185
Inventories 24	380	0	1	21	38	129	702	1428	1575	7901	5774	32067	208371
Net Property, Plant and Equipment 25	4993	0	87	201	621	3068	3348	10233	33937	41478	102008	623385	1462026
Total Assets 26	14557	0	145	661	1802	7439	13965	34706	69953	143244	358480	1263243	5322756
Notes and Loans Payable 27	3903	0	52	284	282	2276	2405	12693	20244	54215	45548	328259	1473958
All Other Liabilities 28	3417	0	18	62	227	1545	3354	6249	17334	40763	80204	286741	1292359
Net Worth 29	7238	0	75	315	1293	3619	8206	15764	32375	48267	232727	648242	2556439

Selected Financial Ratios (Times to 1)

Current Ratio 30	2.1	•	2.5	2.2	4.2	2.6	2.5	3.2	1.4	1.4	2.0	2.2	2.1
Quick Ratio 31	1.7	•	2.0	1.2	3.8	1.9	2.2	2.6	1.3	1.0	1.8	1.7	1.6
Net Sales to Working Capital 32	4.3	•	24.4	10.7	5.4	6.3	4.8	3.7	8.2	9.2	3.0	4.4	3.6
Coverage Ratio 33	8.1	27.2	29.3	22.6	42.3	36.4	25.7	10.3	13.5	7.8	15.3	9.7	6.4
Total Asset Turnover 34	0.7	•	5.4	2.2	2.5	2.0	1.8	1.4	1.1	1.1	0.6	0.6	0.6
Inventory Turnover 35	12.4	•	125.1	20.0	40.5	57.8	21.2	12.3	17.9	12.0	14.7	9.6	7.8
Receivables Turnover 36	5.4	•	165.1	16.3	10.0	12.6	6.4	5.6	3.8	•	2.4	•	•
Total Liabilities to Net Worth 37	1.0	•	0.9	1.1	0.4	1.1	0.7	1.2	1.2	2.0	0.5	0.9	1.1
Current Assets to Working Capital 38	1.9	•	1.7	1.9	1.3	1.6	1.7	1.5	3.3	3.7	2.0	1.9	1.9
Current Liabilities to Working Capital 39	0.9	•	0.7	0.9	0.3	0.6	0.7	0.5	2.3	2.7	1.0	0.9	0.9
Working Capital to Net Sales 40	0.2	•	0.0	0.1	0.2	0.2	0.2	0.3	0.1	0.1	0.3	0.2	0.3
Inventory to Working Capital 41	0.2	•	0.0	0.1	0.0	0.0	0.2	0.2	0.2	0.5	0.1	0.2	0.2
Total Receipts to Cash Flow 42	3.2	2.4	2.7	2.7	3.4	3.3	4.5	3.5	3.3	5.4	2.8	2.9	3.3
Cost of Goods to Cash Flow 43	1.4	0.6	0.7	0.8	1.2	1.6	2.7	1.3	1.2	3.3	1.1	1.1	1.7
Cash Flow to Total Debt 44	0.4	•	4.1	1.6	2.6	1.2	1.0	0.7	0.6	0.3	0.6	0.5	0.3

Selected Financial Factors (in Percentages)

Debt Ratio 45	50.3	•	48.3	52.4	28.2	51.4	41.2	54.6	53.7	66.3	35.1	48.7	52.0
Return on Total Assets 46	17.9	•	96.7	49.9	43.5	36.2	29.1	26.4	23.3	13.2	15.0	16.3	16.6
Return on Equity Before Income Taxes 47	31.6	•	180.5	100.2	59.2	72.3	47.6	52.5	46.7	34.3	21.6	28.5	29.1
Return on Equity After Income Taxes 48	24.6	•	177.0	94.5	52.7	61.3	41.6	48.6	37.9	25.6	14.2	20.0	22.8
Profit Margin (Before Income Tax) 49	21.9	26.8	17.3	21.8	17.1	17.3	15.5	17.0	20.3	10.7	23.7	23.1	23.3
Profit Margin (After Income Tax) 50	17.0	24.7	17.0	20.5	15.2	14.7	13.6	15.7	16.5	8.0	15.5	16.2	18.3

Table I

Corporations with and without Net Income

ELECTRIC POWER GENERATION, TRANSMISSION AND DISTRIBUTION

MONEY AMOUNTS AND SIZE OF ASSETS IN THOUSANDS OF DOLLARS

Item Description for Accounting Period 7/06 Through 6/07	Total	Zero Assets	Under 500	500 to 1,000	1,000 to 5,000	5,000 to 10,000	10,000 to 25,000	25,000 to 50,000	50,000 to 100,000	100,000 to 250,000	250,000 to 500,000	500,000 to 2,500,000	2,500,000 and over
Number of Enterprises 1	1272	67	678	190	88	54	45	16	22	25	16	30	40
Revenues ($ in Thousands)													
Net Sales 2	290534311	179250	8202	92532	99641	471575	1169316	824829	1538403	2542744	2981151	14636866	265989802
Interest 3	5782483	298006	0	0	4148	1956	8456	10818	42334	44982	61582	477061	4833140
Rents 4	1730142	247	0	0	0	2276	0	32	137	1757	1093	47695	1676904
Royalties 5	36227	0	0	0	0	0	598	0	0	0	0	21364	14265
Other Portfolio Income 6	5934726	715	0	0	6580	16633	116452	2667	23729	60492	34663	102560	5570236
Other Receipts 7	3033001	58352	0	4	1017	10316	14055	14604	53293	82049	144432	487600	2167280
Total Receipts 8	307050890	536570	8202	92536	111386	502756	1308877	852950	1657896	2732024	3222921	15773146	280251627
Average Total Receipts 9	241392	8009	12	487	1266	9310	29086	53309	75359	109281	201433	525772	7006291
Operating Costs/Operating Income (%)													
Cost of Operations 10	60.5	34.2	37.1	9.2	•	63.7	85.7	72.9	82.1	27.0	58.8	63.8	60.4
Salaries and Wages 11	3.6	3.5	5.9	5.9	22.9	5.0	3.3	12.6	1.9	3.5	4.9	3.5	3.6
Taxes Paid 12	3.7	5.7	5.4	10.5	2.7	3.0	1.8	1.4	1.2	1.2	2.3	2.5	3.8
Interest Paid 13	6.7	184.9	•	1.3	5.6	4.6	2.3	0.9	3.3	3.7	4.7	7.3	6.7
Depreciation 14	6.1	29.7	•	0.0	11.0	3.5	2.8	1.8	1.4	3.1	4.8	7.0	6.2
Amortization and Depletion 15	0.9	3.8	4.5	0.1	1.7	0.4	0.4	0.0	1.1	0.4	0.6	0.9	0.9
Pensions and Other Deferred Comp. 16	1.1	0.3	•	•	2.4	0.2	0.4	0.3	0.1	0.3	0.5	0.8	1.1
Employee Benefits 17	1.0	0.8	•	0.5	2.7	0.5	0.4	4.2	0.2	0.5	1.2	0.7	1.0
Advertising 18	0.1	0.0	19.9	1.3	0.3	0.0	0.1	0.4	0.4	0.1	0.3	0.1	0.1
Other Expenses 19	16.7	42.1	14.7	52.5	66.5	23.4	7.7	8.2	11.6	65.7	18.2	19.8	16.1
Officers' Compensation 20	0.3	2.3	23.9	23.9	2.7	0.1	2.5	0.9	0.9	0.3	1.0	0.4	0.3
Operating Margin 21	•	18.4	18.4	•	•	•	•	•	•	•	2.8	•	•
Operating Margin Before Officers' Comp. 22	•	•	18.6	•	•	•	•	•	•	•	3.8	•	0.3

Selected Average Balance Sheet ($ in Thousands)

Net Receivables 23	35761	0	19	12	1	263	3136	3532	23145	14476	16662	113475	1017988
Inventories 24	7649	0	5	0	15	129	407	941	556	1735	13419	24089	217292
Net Property, Plant and Equipment 25	293919	0	2	3	282	3824	6807	6460	19840	63212	169610	721563	8671123
Total Assets 26	610913	0	31	565	2011	7586	19201	38230	74010	158279	380544	1338248	18076721
Notes and Loans Payable 27	224262	0	1	25	238	4504	5619	21642	25678	91449	167683	693854	6451067
All Other Liabilities 28	208842	0	14	185	246	1916	6798	43005	22892	43570	150944	387179	6221478
Net Worth 29	177809	0	16	354	1526	1166	6784	-26418	25440	23260	61917	257216	5404176

Selected Financial Ratios (Times to 1)

Current Ratio 30	0.9	•	3.8	2.7	24.8	1.1	1.0	0.6	1.8	1.2	1.2	1.1	0.9
Quick Ratio 31	0.5	•	2.7	2.7	3.3	0.7	0.8	0.2	1.7	0.9	0.7	0.7	0.4
Net Sales to Working Capital 32	•	1.0	0.6	1.4	0.8	67.2	75.1	•	5.0	16.0	9.0	25.3	•
Coverage Ratio 33	1.8	•	•	•	0.2	1.5	2.9	0.4	2.1	1.4	3.3	1.1	1.8
Total Asset Turnover 34	0.4	•	0.4	0.9	0.6	1.2	1.4	1.3	0.9	0.6	0.5	0.4	0.4
Inventory Turnover 35	18.1	•	0.9	•	•	43.1	54.7	40.0	103.2	15.8	8.2	12.9	18.5
Receivables Turnover 36	5.6	•	1.3	81.6	28.1	22.5	9.4	8.7	3.2	8.0	11.4	5.0	5.6
Total Liabilities to Net Worth 37	2.4	•	0.9	0.6	0.3	5.5	1.8	•	1.9	5.8	5.1	4.2	2.3
Current Assets to Working Capital 38	•	•	1.4	1.6	1.0	11.5	23.1	•	2.3	5.7	5.7	15.3	•
Current Liabilities to Working Capital 39	•	•	0.4	0.6	0.0	10.5	22.1	•	1.3	4.7	4.7	14.3	•
Working Capital to Net Sales 40	•	•	1.8	0.7	1.2	0.0	0.0	•	0.2	0.1	0.1	0.0	•
Inventory to Working Capital 41	•	•	0.2	•	•	0.7	1.7	•	0.0	0.2	1.1	1.5	•
Total Receipts to Cash Flow 42	6.1	3.2	3.0	3.4	2.1	8.1	61.2	13.5	8.6	1.6	3.8	6.9	6.2
Cost of Goods to Cash Flow 43	3.7	1.1	1.1	0.3	•	5.2	52.4	9.8	7.1	0.4	2.2	4.4	3.7
Cash Flow to Total Debt 44	0.1	•	0.3	0.7	1.1	0.2	0.0	0.1	0.2	0.5	0.2	0.1	0.1

Selected Financial Factors (in Percentages)

Debt Ratio 45	70.9	•	48.5	37.3	24.1	84.6	64.7	169.1	65.6	85.3	83.7	80.8	70.1
Return on Total Assets 46	4.4	•	7.2	•	0.7	7.8	9.2	0.5	6.4	3.5	7.6	2.9	4.4
Return on Equity Before Income Taxes 47	6.6	•	13.9	•	•	15.9	17.2	0.9	9.8	7.2	32.8	1.5	6.6
Return on Equity After Income Taxes 48	4.3	•	13.9	•	•	12.9	11.8	2.3	8.4	2.8	22.8	•	4.4
Profit Margin (Before Income Tax) 49	5.1	•	18.4	•	•	2.1	4.5	•	3.6	1.6	10.9	0.8	5.4
Profit Margin (After Income Tax) 50	3.4	•	18.4	•	•	1.7	3.1	•	3.0	0.7	7.6	•	3.6

Table II

Corporations with Net Income

ELECTRIC POWER GENERATION, TRANSMISSION AND DISTRIBUTION

MONEY AMOUNTS AND SIZE OF ASSETS IN THOUSANDS OF DOLLARS

Item Description for Accounting Period 7/06 Through 6/07	Total	Zero Assets	Under 500	500 to 1,000	1,000 to 5,000	5,000 to 10,000	10,000 to 25,000	25,000 to 50,000	50,000 to 100,000	100,000 to 250,000	250,000 to 500,000	500,000 to 2,500,000	2,500,000 and over
Number of Enterprises **1**	862	36	425	186	66	25	25	11	13	16	12	16	29
Revenues ($ in Thousands)													
Net Sales **2**	239920345	86407	6599	79006	41023	85564	719531	761959	943121	1942717	2659899	9279678	223314841
Interest **3**	4500121	296541	0	0	3598	1058	5023	3569	25991	31392	49277	207501	3876170
Rents **4**	1711010	21	0	0	0	0	0	32	5	1471	940	40019	1668523
Royalties **5**	36053	0	0	0	0	0	598	0	0	0	0	21295	14160
Other Portfolio Income **6**	4199901	0	0	0	6580	16633	116452	0	20541	59330	9507	29283	3941574
Other Receipts **7**	4424546	56946	0	0	5	9808	9421	7863	27492	69436	139437	277617	3826522
Total Receipts **8**	254791976	439915	6599	79006	51206	113063	851025	773423	1017150	2104346	2859060	9855393	236641790
Average Total Receipts **9**	295582	12220	16	425	776	4523	34041	70311	78242	131522	238255	615962	8160062
Operating Costs/Operating Income (%)													
Cost of Operations **10**	59.0	2.7	22.5	•	•	•	83.7	73.5	82.5	22.2	61.3	61.7	59.0
Salaries and Wages **11**	3.6	3.2	•	2.4	•	24.2	3.9	12.0	1.3	2.7	4.4	4.2	3.5
Taxes Paid **12**	4.0	6.3	•	11.4	2.3	1.9	1.2	1.3	1.2	1.0	2.0	3.1	4.1
Interest Paid **13**	6.0	357.8	•	0.7	4.0	11.8	1.4	0.4	2.3	2.7	3.5	5.7	6.0
Depreciation **14**	6.2	42.2	•	0.0	18.1	7.8	3.8	0.9	1.5	2.0	4.2	5.5	6.3
Amortization and Depletion **15**	0.8	6.2	5.6	•	0.3	2.4	0.2	•	1.2	0.5	0.6	0.9	0.8
Pensions and Other Deferred Comp. **16**	1.1	0.7	•	•	•	0.1	0.5	0.3	0.2	0.2	0.4	1.0	1.2
Employee Benefits **17**	1.0	1.3	1.3	•	•	1.0	0.2	4.4	0.1	0.3	1.2	0.6	1.1
Advertising **18**	0.1	•	24.7	•	•	0.2	0.0	0.3	0.0	0.0	0.3	0.1	0.1
Other Expenses **19**	16.5	46.4	0.0	51.3	77.0	35.1	6.1	5.0	9.4	72.0	15.3	15.4	16.1
Officers' Compensation **20**	0.3	•	•	26.1	•	0.4	3.6	0.9	0.5	0.2	1.0	0.6	0.3
Operating Margin **21**	1.3	•	47.1	8.0	•	15.1	•	0.9	•	•	5.8	1.1	1.5
Operating Margin Before Officers' Comp. **22**	1.7	•	47.1	34.1	•	15.5	•	1.7	0.3	•	6.7	1.8	1.8

Selected Average Balance Sheet ($ in Thousands)

	1	2	3	4	5	6	7	8	9	10	11	12
Net Receivables 23	42420	0	0	0	0	3018	4495	29786	14386	18985	83303	1181471
Inventories 24	9368	0	0	0	0	218	1241	770	1914	9825	27089	257201
Net Property, Plant and Equipment 25	359253	0	2	34	3905	7692	3473	19312	53336	138464	706645	1018826
Total Assets 26	721598	8	558	1700	7771	17873	37155	72893	150833	376164	1342804	20392695
Notes and Loans Payable 27	251145	1	0	31	4306	3972	22904	17650	78207	147720	563390	7026144
All Other Liabilities 28	244480	0	152	-2	1092	4392	60649	19847	40232	160208	387246	6927215
Net Worth 29	225972	7	406	1670	2373	9509	-46398	35395	32393	68236	392169	6439335

Selected Financial Ratios (Times to 1)

	1	2	3	4	5	6	7	8	9	10	11	12
Current Ratio 30	0.9	•	3.7	92.7	0.5	1.4	0.5	2.4	1.1	1.4	1.2	0.9
Quick Ratio 31	0.4	•	3.7	3.5	0.5	1.1	0.1	2.3	0.8	0.7	0.7	0.4
Net Sales to Working Capital 32	•	1.9	1.1	0.4	•	13.1	•	3.5	38.8	7.1	15.1	•
Coverage Ratio 33	2.2	1.1	12.0	8.1	5.0	11.1	6.3	4.4	2.7	4.7	2.3	2.2
Total Asset Turnover 34	0.4	•	1.9	0.8	0.4	1.6	1.9	1.0	0.8	0.6	0.4	0.4
Inventory Turnover 35	17.5	12.1	•	•	•	110.7	41.0	77.8	14.1	13.8	13.2	17.7
Receivables Turnover 36	5.8	•	•	12.7	•	14.1	9.5	•	9.5	14.3	6.6	5.7
Total Liabilities to Net Worth 37	2.2	0.1	0.4	0.0	2.3	0.9	9.5	1.1	3.7	4.5	2.4	2.2
Current Assets to Working Capital 38	•	1.0	1.4	1.0	•	3.3	•	1.7	12.8	3.8	6.4	•
Current Liabilities to Working Capital 39	•	•	0.4	0.0	•	2.3	•	0.7	11.8	2.8	5.4	•
Working Capital to Net Sales 40	•	0.5	1.0	2.5	•	0.1	•	0.3	0.0	0.1	0.1	•
Inventory to Working Capital 41	•	0.0	•	•	•	0.1	•	0.0	0.6	0.6	0.9	•
Total Receipts to Cash Flow 42	5.3	1.2	2.1	2.5	1.6	33.4	14.1	6.8	1.4	3.7	5.2	5.5
Cost of Goods to Cash Flow 43	3.1	0.0	0.5	•	•	28.0	10.4	5.7	0.3	2.3	3.2	3.2
Cash Flow to Total Debt 44	0.1	•	6.8	1.1	20.5	0.4	0.1	0.1	0.3	0.7	0.2	0.1

Selected Financial Factors (in Percentages)

	1	2	3	4	5	6	7	8	9	10	11	12
Debt Ratio 45	68.7	•	12.8	27.2	1.7	46.8	224.9	51.4	78.5	81.9	70.8	68.4
Return on Total Assets 46	5.2	•	6.6	12.0	5.3	24.3	•	9.9	5.8	9.9	5.6	5.1
Return on Equity Before Income Taxes 47	9.2	•	100.0	8.4	10.7	41.6	68.1	15.7	17.2	43.0	10.7	8.9
Return on Equity After Income Taxes 48	6.6	•	100.0	8.4	7.9	34.7	64.9	13.9	12.3	30.9	8.3	6.3
Profit Margin (Before Income Tax) 49	7.5	42.4	47.1	8.0	28.8	13.7	47.2	2.4	13.9	13.2	7.2	7.4
Profit Margin (After Income Tax) 50	5.4	32.0	47.1	8.0	21.1	11.5	45.0	1.6	6.8	3.3	5.6	5.3

18

Table II
Corporations with Net Income

NATURAL GAS DISTRIBUTION

MONEY AMOUNTS AND SIZE OF ASSETS IN THOUSANDS OF DOLLARS

Item Description for Accounting Period 7/06 Through 6/07	Total	Zero Assets	Under 500	500 to 1,000	1,000 to 5,000	5,000 to 10,000	10,000 to 25,000	25,000 to 50,000	50,000 to 100,000	100,000 to 250,000	250,000 to 500,000	500,000 to 2,500,000	2,500,000 and over
Number of Enterprises **1**	•	•	0	122	168	28	9	10	•	•	•	4	•
Revenues ($ in Thousands)													
Net Sales **2**	•	•	0	148160	842583	616189	1469545	840133	•	•	•	8201121	•
Interest **3**	•	•	0	856	3129	1227	0	3420	•	•	•	33955	•
Rents **4**	•	•	0	1986	0	0	0	0	•	•	•	1168	•
Royalties **5**	•	•	0	21	0	0	0	0	•	•	•	0	•
Other Portfolio Income **6**	•	•	0	0	50327	1640	0	18856	•	•	•	1896	•
Other Receipts **7**	•	•	0	4376	3461	1036	113	4798	•	•	•	139669	•
Total Receipts **8**	•	•	0	155399	899500	620092	1469658	867207	•	•	•	8377809	•
Average Total Receipts **9**	•	•	•	1274	5354	22146	163295	86721	•	•	•	2094452	•
Operating Costs/Operating Income (%)													
Cost of Operations **10**	•	•	•	70.6	67.7	84.3	96.3	90.5	•	•	•	87.8	•
Salaries and Wages **11**	•	•	•	•	3.3	0.9	0.9	2.8	•	•	•	2.1	•
Taxes Paid **12**	•	•	•	0.3	1.5	0.8	0.1	0.6	•	•	•	1.7	•
Interest Paid **13**	•	•	•	•	0.6	0.5	0.2	0.3	•	•	•	1.1	•
Depreciation **14**	•	•	•	•	2.3	1.9	0.3	0.3	•	•	•	2.1	•
Amortization and Depletion **15**	•	•	•	0.0	0.0	0.6	0.0	•	•	•	•	0.0	•
Pensions and Other Deferred Comp. **16**	•	•	•	•	1.6	0.2	0.0	0.0	•	•	•	0.2	•
Employee Benefits **17**	•	•	•	•	1.4	0.2	0.1	0.2	•	•	•	0.4	•
Advertising **18**	•	•	•	0.0	0.3	0.0	0.0	0.0	•	•	•	0.0	•
Other Expenses **19**	•	•	•	23.2	6.1	4.0	0.9	2.3	•	•	•	2.8	•
Officers' Compensation **20**	•	•	•	9.3	6.0	2.1	0.2	1.3	•	•	•	0.2	•
Operating Margin **21**	•	•	•	•	9.3	4.3	0.9	1.7	•	•	•	1.5	•
Operating Margin Before Officers' Comp. **22**	•	•	•	5.9	15.2	6.4	1.1	3.1	•	•	•	1.7	•

Selected Average Balance Sheet ($ in Thousands)

Net Receivables 23	202	357	519	9020	17202	101083
Inventories 24	0	122	449	1838	2962	181745
Net Property, Plant and Equipment 25	29	1171	3055	6859	4893	961288
Total Assets 26	583	2706	7825	18988	32922	1882988
Notes and Loans Payable 27	149	378	1755	3996	1919	852004
All Other Liabilities 28	363	391	1516	8541	18487	603350
Net Worth 29	71	1937	4554	6451	12516	427634

Selected Financial Ratios (Times to 1)

Current Ratio 30	1.5	2.0	3.1	1.9	1.3	0.9
Quick Ratio 31	1.5	1.6	2.0	1.6	1.1	0.2
Net Sales to Working Capital 32	6.3	10.2	11.5	29.3	13.2	•
Coverage Ratio 33	•	28.7	10.0	4.7	19.6	4.4
Total Asset Turnover 34	2.1	1.9	2.8	8.6	2.6	1.1
Inventory Turnover 35	•	27.9	41.4	85.5	25.7	9.9
Receivables Turnover 36	9.5	13.7	•	14.8	•	•
Total Liabilities to Net Worth 37	7.2	0.4	0.7	1.9	1.6	3.4
Current Assets to Working Capital 38	2.9	2.0	1.5	2.2	3.9	•
Current Liabilities to Working Capital 39	1.9	1.0	0.5	1.2	2.9	•
Working Capital to Net Sales 40	0.2	0.1	0.1	0.0	0.1	•
Inventory to Working Capital 41	•	0.2	0.2	0.3	0.5	•
Total Receipts to Cash Flow 42	5.1	4.8	11.5	60.0	22.4	17.6
Cost of Goods to Cash Flow 43	3.6	3.3	9.7	57.7	20.3	15.5
Cash Flow to Total Debt 44	0.5	1.4	0.6	0.2	0.2	0.1

Selected Financial Factors (in Percentages)

Debt Ratio 45	87.8	28.4	41.8	66.0	62.0	77.3
Return on Total Assets 46	3.1	30.7	15.1	9.8	13.4	5.2
Return on Equity Before Income Taxes 47	25.3	41.5	23.3	22.7	33.4	17.7
Return on Equity After Income Taxes 48	21.5	39.0	16.0	18.9	30.1	11.5
Profit Margin (Before Income Tax) 49	1.5	16.0	4.8	0.9	5.0	3.7
Profit Margin (After Income Tax) 50	1.3	15.1	3.3	0.7	4.5	2.4

Table I

Corporations with and without Net Income

WATER, SEWAGE AND OTHER SYSTEMS

MONEY AMOUNTS AND SIZE OF ASSETS IN THOUSANDS OF DOLLARS

Item Description for Accounting Period 7/06 Through 6/07		Total	Zero Assets	Under 500	500 to 1,000	1,000 to 5,000	5,000 to 10,000	10,000 to 25,000	25,000 to 50,000	50,000 to 100,000	100,000 to 250,000	250,000 to 500,000	500,000 to 2,500,000	2,500,000 and over
Number of Enterprises	1	5882	554	4319	305	520	70	58	27	8	7	5	7	3
Revenues ($ in Thousands)														
Net Sales	2	8469609	40354	721422	175315	1026226	176204	578864	228027	101362	193906	450089	1411752	3366088
Interest	3	234394	430	1919	726	1354	4961	833	6953	1288	6165	2420	9451	197894
Rents	4	19546	0	425	712	7	50	313	2933	10	995	483	9008	4610
Royalties	5	66	0	0	0	0	0	0	65	0	0	0	0	0
Other Portfolio Income	6	61466	17491	14055	486	76	1244	15205	4104	105	1478	2624	2635	1964
Other Receipts	7	180345	10	7919	5547	21589	3698	3409	15449	228	6810	24144	35388	56153
Total Receipts	8	8965426	58285	745740	182786	1049252	186157	598624	257531	102993	209354	479760	1468234	3626709
Average Total Receipts	9	1524	105	173	599	2018	2659	10321	9538	12874	29908	95952	209748	1208903
Operating Costs/Operating Income (%)														
Cost of Operations	10	37.4	17.8	14.9	26.0	68.2	44.3	29.4	41.5	27.3	21.2	35.9	51.5	29.9
Salaries and Wages	11	7.7	1.1	8.6	6.1	4.3	5.8	27.1	5.3	7.5	8.6	17.6	3.3	6.2
Taxes Paid	12	6.1	1.2	3.3	4.4	1.7	6.7	4.1	10.1	12.3	6.7	6.0	5.4	8.3
Interest Paid	13	10.9	0.2	0.5	1.4	3.4	3.4	2.9	5.8	7.2	12.4	7.7	8.3	19.7
Depreciation	14	10.2	2.1	3.5	6.6	5.5	3.9	3.2	10.8	11.5	18.7	10.2	11.5	13.7
Amortization and Depletion	15	0.7	•	0.0	•	0.2	0.2	0.2	0.5	0.8	0.6	0.5	0.4	1.2
Pensions and Other Deferred Comp.	16	1.4	•	1.1	0.5	0.2	0.1	0.5	0.5	1.8	2.5	0.7	1.4	2.1
Employee Benefits	17	3.6	0.2	1.5	0.0	0.6	2.1	13.8	2.4	3.5	2.5	4.2	2.6	3.9
Advertising	18	0.3	•	0.7	0.1	0.6	1.2	0.1	0.1	0.0	0.0	0.7	0.0	0.2
Other Expenses	19	20.9	114.6	45.7	47.3	15.2	36.5	14.4	23.3	22.4	19.7	17.2	10.5	19.8
Officers' Compensation	20	2.2	0.3	11.8	5.6	1.8	0.7	2.3	1.4	1.9	4.1	2.0	1.2	0.4
Operating Margin	21	•	•	8.3	1.8	•	•	1.9	•	3.9	3.1	•	3.9	•
Operating Margin Before Officers' Comp.	22	0.9	•	20.1	7.4	0.2	•	4.2	•	5.8	7.2	5.1	•	•

Selected Average Balance Sheet ($ in Thousands)

Net Receivables 23	205	0	14	33	284	420	1573	1546	1348	3266	14655	50369	121784
Inventories 24	39	0	0	100	7	22	65	91	279	536	23550	6768	5511
Net Property, Plant and Equipment 25	3758	0	55	490	1416	4827	10082	19648	45380	140794	249617	577167	4296895
Total Assets 26	5937	0	116	702	2336	6782	15106	30674	67573	170282	359479	859119	7089964
Notes and Loans Payable 27	1895	0	28	204	1002	2220	5296	5559	24866	50852	138888	267510	2235524
All Other Liabilities 28	2021	0	20	112	1190	1733	7367	10975	24300	65716	115987	274231	2384524
Net Worth 29	2021	0	68	385	145	2829	2443	14139	18406	53714	104605	317378	2469916

Selected Financial Ratios (Times to 1)

Current Ratio 30	1.0	•	1.7	2.6	1.6	1.2	1.1	2.0	1.9	0.8	1.8	1.9	0.6
Quick Ratio 31	0.6	•	1.7	1.3	1.6	1.1	1.0	1.7	1.2	0.6	0.6	1.3	0.3
Net Sales to Working Capital 32	•	•	8.7	4.4	6.8	15.7	27.6	3.9	2.6	•	4.0	3.8	•
Coverage Ratio 33	1.4	38.7	25.4	5.3	1.2	1.2	2.8	2.9	1.8	1.9	1.5	2.0	1.1
Total Asset Turnover 34	0.2	•	1.4	0.8	0.8	0.4	0.7	0.3	0.2	0.2	0.3	0.2	0.2
Inventory Turnover 35	13.8	•	•	1.5	197.4	51.1	44.9	38.3	12.4	11.0	1.4	15.3	60.8
Receivables Turnover 36	7.5	•	11.5	10.3	11.0	3.7	8.4	5.8	9.3	6.9	3.8	5.6	8.5
Total Liabilities to Net Worth 37	1.9	•	0.7	0.8	15.2	1.4	5.2	1.2	2.7	2.2	2.4	1.7	1.9
Current Assets to Working Capital 38	•	•	2.3	1.6	2.6	6.8	7.9	2.0	2.2	•	2.3	2.1	•
Current Liabilities to Working Capital 39	•	•	1.3	0.6	1.6	5.8	6.9	1.0	1.2	•	1.3	1.1	•
Working Capital to Net Sales 40	•	•	0.1	0.2	0.1	0.1	0.0	0.3	0.4	•	0.2	0.3	•
Inventory to Working Capital 41	•	•	•	0.8	0.0	0.1	0.2	0.0	0.1	•	1.3	0.1	•
Total Receipts to Cash Flow 42	4.5	•	2.0	2.1	7.0	3.1	6.3	3.3	4.0	3.8	5.7	6.7	4.9
Cost of Goods to Cash Flow 43	1.7	1.1	•	0.6	4.8	1.4	1.9	1.4	1.1	0.8	2.0	3.5	1.5
Cash Flow to Total Debt 44	0.1	0.2	1.8	0.8	0.1	0.2	0.1	0.2	0.1	0.1	0.1	0.1	0.0

Selected Financial Factors (in Percentages)

Debt Ratio 45	66.0	•	41.1	45.1	93.8	58.3	83.8	53.9	72.8	68.5	70.9	63.1	65.2
Return on Total Assets 46	3.8	•	17.4	6.1	3.4	1.5	5.4	4.7	2.4	3.8	2.9	3.8	3.5
Return on Equity Before Income Taxes 47	3.3	•	28.4	9.0	7.7	0.5	21.6	6.7	3.8	5.5	3.3	5.0	1.0
Return on Equity After Income Taxes 48	2.1	•	27.3	5.8	•	•	14.5	4.3	2.2	3.4	2.1	2.6	0.6
Profit Margin (Before Income Tax) 49	4.6	6.9	11.6	6.1	0.6	0.6	5.3	11.2	5.5	10.7	3.8	7.9	2.2
Profit Margin (After Income Tax) 50	2.9	•	11.2	3.9	•	•	3.6	7.2	3.2	6.7	2.5	4.1	1.2

21

Table II

Corporations with Net Income

WATER, SEWAGE AND OTHER SYSTEMS

MONEY AMOUNTS AND SIZE OF ASSETS IN THOUSANDS OF DOLLARS

Item Description for Accounting Period 7/06 Through 6/07	Total	Zero Assets	Under 500	500 to 1,000	1,000 to 5,000	5,000 to 10,000	10,000 to 25,000	25,000 to 50,000	50,000 to 100,000	100,000 to 250,000	250,000 to 500,000	500,000 to 2,500,000	2,500,000 and over
Number of Enterprises 1	3597	•	3049	61	364	31	36	23	•	•	•	7	0
Revenues ($ in Thousands)													
Net Sales 2	4741820	•	564467	73110	874550	145845	332410	181722	•	•	•	2097542	0
Interest 3	38176	•	1308	493	1007	4003	716	6765	•	•	•	16777	0
Rents 4	13382	•	0	0	7	50	313	2722	•	•	•	8907	0
Royalties 5	0	•	0	0	0	0	0	0	•	•	•	0	0
Other Portfolio Income 6	56364	•	13960	486	56	1244	15205	1897	•	•	•	3070	0
Other Receipts 7	121650	•	6691	114	7441	2366	2894	14917	•	•	•	64433	0
Total Receipts 8	4971392	•	586426	74203	883061	153508	351538	208023	•	•	•	2190729	0
Average Total Receipts 9	1382	•	192	1216	2426	4952	9765	9044	•	•	•	312961	•
Operating Costs/Operating Income (%)													
Cost of Operations 10	42.6	•	14.8	52.8	69.9	53.5	51.3	28.0	•	•	•	41.1	•
Salaries and Wages 11	5.3	•	5.9	5.7	3.6	3.5	7.0	4.6	•	•	•	5.3	•
Taxes Paid 12	5.8	•	2.5	1.2	1.2	5.1	3.3	12.6	•	•	•	7.9	•
Interest Paid 13	5.9	•	0.3	0.2	2.9	0.6	3.2	7.1	•	•	•	8.4	•
Depreciation 14	9.1	•	2.9	1.0	3.8	1.9	3.9	13.0	•	•	•	12.8	•
Amortization and Depletion 15	0.5	•	0.0	•	0.0	0.2	0.3	0.2	•	•	•	0.9	•
Pensions and Other Deferred Comp. 16	1.0	•	0.7	•	0.2	0.1	0.7	0.7	•	•	•	1.5	•
Employee Benefits 17	2.0	•	0.0	0.0	0.4	2.2	3.4	3.0	•	•	•	2.7	•
Advertising 18	0.3	•	1.0	0.2	0.0	1.5	0.1	•	•	•	•	0.0	•
Other Expenses 19	17.7	•	45.6	21.1	11.7	33.2	16.5	26.8	•	•	•	10.8	•
Officers' Compensation 20	2.4	•	9.1	3.6	1.5	0.6	3.6	1.7	•	•	•	0.8	•
Operating Margin 21	7.5	•	17.2	14.1	4.9	•	6.8	2.4	•	•	•	7.8	•
Operating Margin Before Officers' Comp. 22	9.9	•	26.3	17.7	6.4	•	10.4	4.1	•	•	•	8.6	•

Selected Average Balance Sheet ($ in Thousands)

Net Receivables 23	171	14	111	334	879	1581	1367	39366
Inventories 24	59	0	496	8	49	102	107	7701
Net Property, Plant and Equipment 25	3048	51	20	1034	3339	9622	22743	1076598
Total Assets 26	4582	120	649	2207	6949	15033	31055	1597885
Notes and Loans Payable 27	1369	17	413	968	588	6384	6526	443557
All Other Liabilities 28	1740	9	307	1019	3611	4370	12593	631047
Net Worth 29	1473	93	-72	221	2750	4279	11936	523281

Selected Financial Ratios (Times to 1)

Current Ratio 30	1.3	7.9	2.0	2.2	4.3	1.4	1.8	0.9
Quick Ratio 31	1.0	7.9	0.4	2.1	4.1	1.2	1.6	0.6
Net Sales to Working Capital 32	9.4	4.1	3.8	4.7	2.9	8.8	4.0	•
Coverage Ratio 33	3.1	74.9	81.3	3.0	6.3	5.0	3.4	2.5
Total Asset Turnover 34	0.3	1.5	1.8	1.1	0.7	0.6	0.3	0.2
Inventory Turnover 35	9.6	•	1.3	213.7	51.1	46.6	20.6	16.0
Receivables Turnover 36	6.4	13.4	4.7	12.7	3.5	6.6	5.4	•
Total Liabilities to Net Worth 37	2.1	0.3	•	9.0	1.5	2.5	1.6	2.1
Current Assets to Working Capital 38	3.9	1.1	2.0	1.8	1.3	3.3	2.2	•
Current Liabilities to Working Capital 39	2.9	0.1	1.0	0.8	0.3	2.3	1.2	•
Working Capital to Net Sales 40	0.1	0.2	0.3	0.2	0.3	0.1	0.3	•
Inventory to Working Capital 41	0.5	•	1.6	0.0	0.0	0.1	0.1	•
Total Receipts to Cash Flow 42	3.8	1.7	3.3	6.2	3.0	4.4	2.6	5.0
Cost of Goods to Cash Flow 43	1.6	0.2	1.7	4.3	1.6	2.2	0.7	2.0
Cash Flow to Total Debt 44	0.1	4.1	0.5	0.2	0.4	0.2	0.2	0.1

Selected Financial Factors (in Percentages)

Debt Ratio 45	67.8	22.5	111.1	90.0	60.4	71.5	61.6	67.3
Return on Total Assets 46	5.2	33.1	29.2	9.6	2.5	9.7	6.1	3.9
Return on Equity Before Income Taxes 47	11.1	42.2	•	64.1	5.2	27.1	11.2	7.0
Return on Equity After Income Taxes 48	8.4	41.0	•	55.2	3.8	20.6	7.8	4.7
Profit Margin (Before Income Tax) 49	12.4	21.1	15.6	5.9	3.0	12.6	16.9	12.2
Profit Margin (After Income Tax) 50	9.4	20.5	10.3	5.1	2.2	9.5	11.9	8.1

22

Table I

Corporations with and without Net Income

COMBINATION GAS AND ELECTRIC

MONEY AMOUNTS AND SIZE OF ASSETS IN THOUSANDS OF DOLLARS

Item Description for Accounting Period 7/06 Through 6/07		Total	Zero Assets	Under 500	500 to 1,000	1,000 to 5,000	5,000 to 10,000	10,000 to 25,000	25,000 to 50,000	50,000 to 100,000	100,000 to 250,000	250,000 to 500,000	500,000 to 2,500,000	2,500,000 and over
Number of Enterprises	1	34	•	0	0	0	0	•	0	0	0	0	•	26

Revenues ($ in Thousands)

		Total	Zero Assets	Under 500	500 to 1,000	1,000 to 5,000	5,000 to 10,000	10,000 to 25,000	25,000 to 50,000	50,000 to 100,000	100,000 to 250,000	250,000 to 500,000	500,000 to 2,500,000	2,500,000 and over
Net Sales	2	183162513	•	0	0	0	0	•	0	0	0	0	•	176282366
Interest	3	2794986	•	0	0	0	0	•	0	0	0	0	•	2660227
Rents	4	929201	•	0	0	0	0	•	0	0	0	0	•	889734
Royalties	5	6247	•	0	0	0	0	•	0	0	0	0	•	6247
Other Portfolio Income	6	2523487	•	0	0	0	0	•	0	0	0	0	•	2397553
Other Receipts	7	8143625	•	0	0	0	0	•	0	0	0	0	•	7976708
Total Receipts	8	197560059	•	0	0	0	0	•	0	0	0	0	•	190212835
Average Total Receipts	9	5810590	•	•	•	•	•	•	•	•	•	•	•	7315878

Operating Costs/Operating Income (%)

		Total	Zero Assets	Under 500	500 to 1,000	1,000 to 5,000	5,000 to 10,000	10,000 to 25,000	25,000 to 50,000	50,000 to 100,000	100,000 to 250,000	250,000 to 500,000	500,000 to 2,500,000	2,500,000 and over
Cost of Operations	10	50.8	•	•	•	•	•	•	•	•	•	•	•	50.4
Salaries and Wages	11	4.9	•	•	•	•	•	•	•	•	•	•	•	4.9
Taxes Paid	12	4.5	•	•	•	•	•	•	•	•	•	•	•	4.6
Interest Paid	13	5.5	•	•	•	•	•	•	•	•	•	•	•	5.6
Depreciation	14	6.7	•	•	•	•	•	•	•	•	•	•	•	6.8
Amortization and Depletion	15	2.9	•	•	•	•	•	•	•	•	•	•	•	3.0
Pensions and Other Deferred Comp.	16	1.1	•	•	•	•	•	•	•	•	•	•	•	1.1
Employee Benefits	17	1.4	•	•	•	•	•	•	•	•	•	•	•	1.4
Advertising	18	0.1	•	•	•	•	•	•	•	•	•	•	•	0.1
Other Expenses	19	19.6	•	•	•	•	•	•	•	•	•	•	•	19.8
Officers' Compensation	20	0.3	•	•	•	•	•	•	•	•	•	•	•	0.3
Operating Margin	21	1.9	•	•	•	•	•	•	•	•	•	•	•	2.0
Operating Margin Before Officers' Comp.	22	2.2	•	•	•	•	•	•	•	•	•	•	•	2.3

Selected Average Balance Sheet ($ in Thousands)

Net Receivables 23	731754	934301
Inventories 24	315821	403786
Net Property, Plant and Equipment 25	6299502	8037087
Total Assets 26	11894843	15209946
Notes and Loans Payable 27	4010111	5135061
All Other Liabilities 28	4715543	6051252
Net Worth 29	3169189	4023633

Selected Financial Ratios (Times to 1)

Current Ratio 30	1.0	1.0
Quick Ratio 31	0.5	0.5
Net Sales to Working Capital 32	•	•
Coverage Ratio 33	2.8	2.8
Total Asset Turnover 34	0.5	0.4
Inventory Turnover 35	8.7	8.5
Receivables Turnover 36	5.1	5.0
Total Liabilities to Net Worth 37	2.8	2.8
Current Assets to Working Capital 38	•	•
Current Liabilities to Working Capital 39	•	•
Working Capital to Net Sales 40	•	•
Inventory to Working Capital 41	•	•
Total Receipts to Cash Flow 42	3.9	3.9
Cost of Goods to Cash Flow 43	2.0	2.0
Cash Flow to Total Debt 44	0.2	0.2

Selected Financial Factors (in Percentages)

Debt Ratio 45	73.4	73.5
Return on Total Assets 46	7.0	6.9
Return on Equity Before Income Taxes 47	16.7	16.7
Return on Equity After Income Taxes 48	12.1	12.2
Profit Margin (Before Income Tax) 49	9.8	9.9
Profit Margin (After Income Tax) 50	7.1	7.2

Table II

Corporations with Net Income

COMBINATION GAS AND ELECTRIC

MONEY AMOUNTS AND SIZE OF ASSETS IN THOUSANDS OF DOLLARS

Item Description for Accounting Period 7/06 Through 6/07	Total	Zero Assets	Under 500	500 to 1,000	1,000 to 5,000	5,000 to 10,000	10,000 to 25,000	25,000 to 50,000	50,000 to 100,000	100,000 to 250,000	250,000 to 500,000	500,000 to 2,500,000	2,500,000 and over
Number of Enterprises 1	•	0	0	0	0	0	3	0	0	0	0	4	•

Revenues ($ in Thousands)

Item	Total	Zero Assets	Under 500	500 to 1,000	1,000 to 5,000	5,000 to 10,000	10,000 to 25,000	25,000 to 50,000	50,000 to 100,000	100,000 to 250,000	250,000 to 500,000	500,000 to 2,500,000	2,500,000 and over
Net Sales 2	•	•	0	0	0	0	546602	0	0	0	0	4770494	•
Interest 3	•	•	0	0	0	0	3554	0	0	0	0	110725	•
Rents 4	•	•	0	0	0	0	2197	0	0	0	0	34970	•
Royalties 5	•	•	0	0	0	0	0	0	0	0	0	0	•
Other Portfolio Income 6	•	•	0	0	0	0	896	0	0	0	0	115221	•
Other Receipts 7	•	•	0	0	0	0	-9691	0	0	0	0	182892	•
Total Receipts 8	•	•	0	0	0	0	543558	0	0	0	0	5214302	•
Average Total Receipts 9	•	•	•	•	•	•	181186	•	•	•	•	1303576	•

Operating Costs/Operating Income (%)

Item	Total	Zero Assets	Under 500	500 to 1,000	1,000 to 5,000	5,000 to 10,000	10,000 to 25,000	25,000 to 50,000	50,000 to 100,000	100,000 to 250,000	250,000 to 500,000	500,000 to 2,500,000	2,500,000 and over
Cost of Operations 10	•	•	•	•	•	•	67.9	•	•	•	•	66.3	•
Salaries and Wages 11	•	•	•	•	•	•	6.4	•	•	•	•	4.8	•
Taxes Paid 12	•	•	•	•	•	•	3.0	•	•	•	•	3.6	•
Interest Paid 13	•	•	•	•	•	•	3.1	•	•	•	•	5.1	•
Depreciation 14	•	•	•	•	•	•	3.6	•	•	•	•	5.8	•
Amortization and Depletion 15	•	•	•	•	•	•	0.5	•	•	•	•	0.9	•
Pensions and Other Deferred Comp. 16	•	•	•	•	•	•	1.2	•	•	•	•	0.7	•
Employee Benefits 17	•	•	•	•	•	•	1.2	•	•	•	•	1.2	•
Advertising 18	•	•	•	•	•	•	0.7	•	•	•	•	0.1	•
Other Expenses 19	•	•	•	•	•	•	5.2	•	•	•	•	12.7	•
Officers' Compensation 20	•	•	•	•	•	•	1.0	•	•	•	•	0.6	•
Operating Margin 21	•	•	•	•	•	•	6.2	•	•	•	•	•	•
Operating Margin Before Officers' Comp. 22	•	•	•	•	•	•	7.2	•	•	•	•	•	•

Selected Average Balance Sheet ($ in Thousands)

Net Receivables 23	16072	134901
Inventories 24	1375	100717
Net Property, Plant and Equipment 25	120424	1214385
Total Assets 26	228205	2070361
Notes and Loans Payable 27	73683	652783
All Other Liabilities 28	95656	677234
Net Worth 29	58866	740345

Selected Financial Ratios (Times to 1)

Current Ratio 30	1.2	1.0
Quick Ratio 31	0.8	0.5
Net Sales to Working Capital 32	44.2	44.2
Coverage Ratio 33	2.8	2.6
Total Asset Turnover 34	0.8	0.6
Inventory Turnover 35	90.0	7.8
Receivables Turnover 36	22.7	17.7
Total Liabilities to Net Worth 37	2.9	1.8
Current Assets to Working Capital 38	7.6	
Current Liabilities to Working Capital 39	6.6	
Working Capital to Net Sales 40	0.0	
Inventory to Working Capital 41	0.3	
Total Receipts to Cash Flow 42	10.9	6.1
Cost of Goods to Cash Flow 43	7.4	4.0
Cash Flow to Total Debt 44	0.1	0.1

Selected Financial Factors (in Percentages)

Debt Ratio 45	74.2	64.2
Return on Total Assets 46	6.8	7.7
Return on Equity Before Income Taxes 47	17.1	13.3
Return on Equity After Income Taxes 48	14.1	9.1
Profit Margin (Before Income Tax) 49	5.5	8.3
Profit Margin (After Income Tax) 50	4.6	5.7

24

Table I

Corporations with and without Net Income

CONSTRUCTION OF BUILDINGS

MONEY AMOUNTS AND SIZE OF ASSETS IN THOUSANDS OF DOLLARS

Item Description for Accounting Period 7/06 Through 6/07	Total	Zero Assets	Under 500	500 to 1,000	1,000 to 5,000	5,000 to 10,000	10,000 to 25,000	25,000 to 50,000	50,000 to 100,000	100,000 to 250,000	250,000 to 500,000	500,000 to 2,500,000	2,500,000 and over
Number of Enterprises 1	235572	39969	139469	19755	27765	4431	2894	729	310	154	40	42	13
Revenues ($ in Thousands)													
Net Sales 2	693085320	8551529	79359077	36191313	117336902	56402165	82966652	45539531	37438770	41752452	20438897	63503836	103604197
Interest 3	1948282	16597	29633	22950	122203	52579	76913	37615	37858	41234	44279	231168	1235252
Rents 4	550392	2386	31007	35300	62757	35154	19267	24368	28620	37148	55870	153958	64557
Royalties 5	134546	503	0	0	318	0	0	0	6632	0	0	4680	122413
Other Portfolio Income 6	1880639	85043	90497	118437	146449	44981	110796	89924	28174	73525	57254	448481	587076
Other Receipts 7	8975018	45551	503227	206919	933976	508114	518692	330519	415515	639458	415154	1326346	3131549
Total Receipts 8	706574197	8701609	80013441	36574919	118602605	57042993	83692320	46021957	37955569	42543817	21011454	65668469	108745044
Average Total Receipts 9	2999	218	574	1851	4272	12874	28919	63130	122437	276259	525286	1563535	8365003
Operating Costs/Operating Income (%)													
Cost of Operations 10	80.9	65.1	67.9	82.2	82.9	85.9	87.9	89.7	88.6	89.9	89.0	83.9	67.6
Salaries and Wages 11	3.5	5.6	5.8	3.5	3.0	2.5	2.5	2.3	2.6	2.4	3.6	3.9	4.3
Taxes Paid 12	1.1	1.7	1.9	1.3	1.0	0.8	0.7	0.6	0.7	0.6	0.7	0.9	1.4
Interest Paid 13	0.9	1.0	0.6	1.0	0.7	0.5	0.6	0.6	0.6	0.6	1.0	1.0	1.7
Depreciation 14	0.5	1.3	0.9	0.7	0.6	0.5	0.3	0.3	0.3	0.3	0.4	0.5	0.2
Amortization and Depletion 15	0.1	0.1	0.0	0.0	0.0	0.0	0.0	0.0	0.0	0.0	0.0	0.1	0.2
Pensions and Other Deferred Comp. 16	0.2	0.4	0.2	0.2	0.2	0.2	0.2	0.2	0.2	0.2	0.2	0.3	0.1
Employee Benefits 17	0.5	0.9	1.0	0.5	0.5	0.5	0.6	0.3	0.4	0.3	0.3	0.4	0.3
Advertising 18	0.3	0.2	0.5	0.3	0.2	0.2	0.2	0.2	0.3	0.3	0.3	0.4	0.7
Other Expenses 19	7.7	19.3	14.0	6.2	6.7	3.8	3.0	2.4	2.6	2.5	3.0	4.0	19.0
Officers' Compensation 20	1.9	2.9	4.7	2.6	2.7	2.3	1.6	1.2	1.1	0.8	0.7	0.8	0.4
Operating Margin 21	2.5	1.5	2.5	1.5	1.5	2.6	2.4	2.2	2.6	2.1	0.8	3.7	4.2
Operating Margin Before Officers' Comp. 22	4.4	4.4	7.2	4.0	4.3	4.9	4.0	3.4	3.6	2.9	1.5	4.5	4.6

Selected Average Balance Sheet ($ in Thousands)

Net Receivables 23	315	0	10	96	361	1585	4057	8696	19692	43801	83458	218061	811608
Inventories 24	475	0	14	159	575	1811	3348	7519	15500	35666	97028	248653	3302879
Net Property, Plant and Equipment 25	170	0	23	104	265	632	1329	3988	5929	12022	35418	207527	307458
Total Assets 26	1664	0	97	714	2170	7032	15080	34279	70986	152486	357127	1143989	7412432
Notes and Loans Payable 27	646	0	65	408	1046	2991	5517	12899	25662	45129	114009	290542	2753852
All Other Liabilities 28	564	0	19	169	729	2792	6708	14279	29330	68311	136485	445972	1585372
Net Worth 29	453	0	13	137	395	1249	2855	7101	15994	39046	106634	407475	3073208

Selected Financial Ratios (Times to 1)

Current Ratio 30	1.7	•	1.6	1.7	1.5	1.4	1.4	1.4	1.4	1.5	1.7	1.4	3.0
Quick Ratio 31	0.7	•	0.9	0.7	0.5	0.6	0.7	0.7	0.7	0.8	0.8	0.8	0.7
Net Sales to Working Capital 32	6.1	•	24.8	8.8	7.8	7.5	8.6	8.9	7.7	6.5	4.8	8.0	2.2
Coverage Ratio 33	6.2	4.2	6.2	3.4	4.5	8.2	6.8	6.5	7.3	7.4	4.6	8.0	6.6
Total Asset Turnover 34	1.8	•	5.8	2.6	1.9	1.8	1.9	1.8	1.7	1.8	1.4	1.3	1.1
Inventory Turnover 35	5.0	•	26.7	9.5	6.1	6.0	7.5	7.5	6.9	6.8	4.7	5.1	1.6
Receivables Turnover 36	9.9	•	51.0	21.2	12.3	8.1	7.8	7.2	6.4	7.3	6.9	7.5	10.0
Total Liabilities to Net Worth 37	2.7	•	6.3	4.2	4.5	4.6	4.3	3.8	3.4	2.9	2.3	1.8	1.4
Current Assets to Working Capital 38	2.5	•	2.6	2.5	3.2	3.4	3.7	3.8	3.5	3.0	2.4	3.3	1.5
Current Liabilities to Working Capital 39	1.5	•	1.6	1.5	2.2	2.4	2.7	2.8	2.5	2.0	1.4	2.3	0.5
Working Capital to Net Sales 40	0.2	•	0.0	0.1	0.1	0.1	0.1	0.1	0.1	0.2	0.2	0.1	0.4
Inventory to Working Capital 41	1.0	•	0.6	0.9	1.1	1.2	1.1	1.2	1.1	1.0	1.0	1.2	1.0
Total Receipts to Cash Flow 42	9.1	5.0	6.5	13.8	12.1	15.2	19.1	20.2	17.2	17.1	16.8	10.5	3.8
Cost of Goods to Cash Flow 43	7.4	3.3	4.4	11.3	10.1	13.0	16.7	18.1	15.2	15.4	14.9	8.8	2.6
Cash Flow to Total Debt 44	0.3	•	1.0	0.2	0.2	0.1	0.1	0.1	0.1	0.1	0.1	0.2	0.5

Selected Financial Factors (in Percentages)

Debt Ratio 45	72.7	•	86.2	80.8	81.8	82.2	81.1	79.3	77.5	74.4	70.1	64.4	58.5
Return on Total Assets 46	9.4	•	23.2	9.1	6.5	7.7	7.2	7.0	7.8	8.1	6.5	10.7	11.7
Return on Equity Before Income Taxes 47	29.1	•	141.1	33.6	27.8	38.1	32.5	28.5	29.9	27.5	17.1	26.3	23.9
Return on Equity After Income Taxes 48	24.2	•	138.0	32.6	26.5	36.1	31.0	27.1	28.2	26.0	15.6	20.3	15.5
Profit Margin (Before Income Tax) 49	4.5	3.3	3.3	2.5	2.6	3.7	3.2	3.2	4.0	4.0	3.6	7.1	9.2
Profit Margin (After Income Tax) 50	3.7	3.0	3.3	2.4	2.5	3.5	3.1	3.7	3.7	3.7	3.2	5.5	6.0

Table II
Corporations with Net Income

CONSTRUCTION OF BUILDINGS

MONEY AMOUNTS AND SIZE OF ASSETS IN THOUSANDS OF DOLLARS

Item Description for Accounting Period 7/06 Through 6/07	Total	Zero Assets	Under 500	500 to 1,000	1,000 to 5,000	5,000 to 10,000	10,000 to 25,000	25,000 to 50,000	50,000 to 100,000	100,000 to 250,000	250,000 to 500,000	500,000 to 2,500,000	2,500,000 and over
Number of Enterprises **1**	141339	20920	•	11774	18206	3251	2127	549	235	128	31	•	13
Revenues ($ in Thousands)													
Net Sales **2**	603116229	6375098	•	•26023577	97916384	48939927	71641021	40564875	33503367	37122771	18110480	•	•103604197
Interest **3**	1828862	10947	•	16816	94027	47627	61567	32169	23781	32344	32327	•	1235252
Rents **4**	415107	2158	•	26949	41802	16778	12899	7996	20191	20314	55723	•	64557
Royalties **5**	127617	503	•	0	0	0	0	0	21	0	0	•	122413
Other Portfolio Income **6**	1711236	79175	•	111331	118385	37401	85942	77681	24677	53202	44420	•	587076
Other Receipts **7**	8518398	51441	•	191083	738465	474793	458328	287482	394414	674145	376914	•	3131549
Total Receipts **8**	615717449	6519322	•	•26369756	98909063	49516526	72259757	40970203	33966451	37902776	18619864	•	•108745044
Average Total Receipts **9**	4356	312	•	2240	5433	15231	33973	74627	144538	296115	600641	•	8365003
Operating Costs/Operating Income (%)													
Cost of Operations **10**	80.4	61.2	•	80.8	81.7	85.5	87.2	89.3	88.3	89.7	89.6	•	67.6
Salaries and Wages **11**	3.3	5.5	•	2.6	2.8	2.4	2.4	2.3	2.4	2.4	3.2	•	4.3
Taxes Paid **12**	1.0	1.4	•	1.2	0.9	0.8	0.7	0.5	0.6	0.6	0.6	•	1.4
Interest Paid **13**	0.8	0.9	•	1.1	0.6	0.4	0.4	0.5	0.5	0.5	0.7	•	1.7
Depreciation **14**	0.4	0.9	•	0.7	0.5	0.5	0.3	0.3	0.3	0.3	0.3	•	0.2
Amortization and Depletion **15**	0.0	0.0	•	0.0	0.0	0.0	0.0	0.0	0.0	0.0	0.0	•	0.2
Pensions and Other Deferred Comp. **16**	0.2	0.0	•	0.1	0.2	0.3	0.2	0.2	0.2	0.2	0.2	•	0.1
Employee Benefits **17**	0.5	1.0	•	0.5	0.4	0.5	0.6	0.3	0.3	0.3	0.3	•	0.3
Advertising **18**	0.3	0.2	•	0.4	0.2	0.2	0.2	0.2	0.2	0.3	0.2	•	0.7
Other Expenses **19**	7.5	19.0	•	5.9	6.4	3.5	2.7	2.1	2.3	2.1	1.9	•	19.0
Officers' Compensation **20**	1.7	2.4	•	2.7	2.7	2.1	1.6	1.2	1.0	0.8	0.7	•	0.4
Operating Margin **21**	4.0	7.4	•	4.1	3.4	3.9	3.6	3.3	3.8	2.9	2.3	•	4.2
Operating Margin Before Officers' Comp. **22**	5.7	9.8	•	6.8	6.1	5.9	5.2	4.5	4.8	3.7	3.0	•	4.6

Selected Average Balance Sheet ($ in Thousands)

Net Receivables 23	463	0	•	107	451	1754	4729	10351	22061	46894	93371	•	811608
Inventories 24	677	0	•	149	596	1817	3284	7469	16003	36698	92061	•	3302879
Net Property, Plant and Equipment 25	196	0	•	112	225	533	1047	3157	5170	10609	32589	•	307458
Total Assets 26	2273	0	•	735	2243	7186	15178	33755	70480	154335	355340	•	7412432
Notes and Loans Payable 27	762	0	•	361	892	2514	4582	9992	20997	40590	106287	•	2753852
All Other Liabilities 28	793	0	•	162	813	3008	7231	15464	32031	71275	139776	•	1585372
Net Worth 29	718	0	•	212	538	1664	3366	8300	17452	42470	109276	•	3073208

Selected Financial Ratios (Times to 1)

Current Ratio 30	1.7	•	1.7	1.5	1.4	1.4	1.3	1.5	1.6	•	3.0
Quick Ratio 31	0.7	•	0.8	0.6	0.7	0.8	0.7	0.8	0.8	•	0.7
Net Sales to Working Capital 32	6.0	•	10.3	8.2	9.5	9.8	9.8	7.0	6.2	•	2.2
Coverage Ratio 33	9.0	11.8	6.2	8.9	12.3	10.3	11.8	10.5	8.1	•	6.6
Total Asset Turnover 34	1.9	•	3.0	2.4	2.2	2.2	2.0	1.9	1.6	•	1.1
Inventory Turnover 35	5.1	•	12.0	7.4	8.9	8.8	7.9	7.1	5.7	•	1.6
Receivables Turnover 36	9.9	•	21.6	13.0	8.0	7.4	6.7	7.2	•	•	10.0
Total Liabilities to Net Worth 37	2.2	•	2.5	3.2	3.5	3.1	3.0	2.6	2.3	•	1.4
Current Assets to Working Capital 38	2.4	•	2.5	2.8	3.7	3.7	4.0	3.1	2.8	•	1.5
Current Liabilities to Working Capital 39	1.4	•	1.5	1.8	2.7	2.7	3.0	2.1	1.8	•	0.5
Working Capital to Net Sales 40	0.2	•	0.1	0.1	0.1	0.1	0.1	0.1	0.2	•	0.4
Inventory to Working Capital 41	1.0	•	0.8	0.9	0.9	1.0	1.1	1.0	1.0	•	1.0
Total Receipts to Cash Flow 42	8.1	3.8	10.2	10.1	16.1	17.7	14.8	15.5	15.7	•	3.8
Cost of Goods to Cash Flow 43	6.5	2.4	8.3	8.2	14.0	15.8	13.0	13.9	14.0	•	2.6
Cash Flow to Total Debt 44	0.3	•	0.4	0.3	0.2	0.2	0.2	0.2	0.2	•	0.5

Selected Financial Factors (in Percentages)

Debt Ratio 45	68.4	•	71.2	76.0	77.8	75.4	75.2	72.5	69.2	•	58.5
Return on Total Assets 46	12.8	•	19.5	12.0	10.8	10.3	11.5	10.3	9.5	•	11.7
Return on Equity Before Income Taxes 47	36.0	•	56.6	44.3	44.8	37.8	42.5	33.9	27.0	•	23.9
Return on Equity After Income Taxes 48	30.9	•	55.5	42.8	43.1	36.2	40.4	32.3	25.1	•	15.5
Profit Margin (Before Income Tax) 49	6.1	9.7	5.4	4.4	4.5	4.2	5.2	5.0	5.0	•	9.2
Profit Margin (After Income Tax) 50	5.2	9.4	5.3	4.3	4.3	4.1	4.9	4.7	4.7	•	6.0

Table I

Corporations with and without Net Income

HEAVY AND CIVIL ENGINEERING CONSTRUCTION

MONEY AMOUNTS AND SIZE OF ASSETS IN THOUSANDS OF DOLLARS

Item Description for Accounting Period 7/06 Through 6/07		Total	Zero Assets	Under 500	500 to 1,000	1,000 to 5,000	5,000 to 10,000	10,000 to 25,000	25,000 to 50,000	50,000 to 100,000	100,000 to 250,000	250,000 to 500,000	500,000 to 2,500,000	2,500,000 and over
Number of Enterprises	1	26441	2570	12052	3044	5673	1643	958	283	126	62	11	16	3
Revenues ($ in Thousands)														
Net Sales	2	206293770	834463	9793010	8230763	27602628	27051691	32095873	20602562	15298595	14635052	8455693	25136599	16556842
Interest	3	384202	1959	12190	4051	35616	32093	38476	22604	26469	26228	12938	132421	39156
Rents	4	108999	1006	390	5805	11024	4908	24439	20676	10683	13750	700	12004	3613
Royalties	5	97862	0	0	0	0	0	2491	21473	176	7806	0	7340	58576
Other Portfolio Income	6	885668	33348	25085	54028	195612	120753	106701	89838	62568	59895	28686	80462	28692
Other Receipts	7	2190880	76512	58960	2751	-25796	232826	183353	119161	195754	233986	8783	263932	840659
Total Receipts	8	209961381	947288	9889635	8297398	27819084	27442271	32451333	20876314	15594245	14976717	8506800	25632758	17527538
Average Total Receipts	9	7941	369	821	2726	4904	16703	33874	73768	123764	241560	773345	1602047	5842513
Operating Costs/Operating Income (%)														
Cost of Operations	10	75.7	63.4	50.8	58.5	64.1	76.4	77.8	80.0	80.8	81.5	85.4	81.5	84.5
Salaries and Wages	11	4.2	4.2	10.5	9.6	6.4	2.8	3.0	2.6	3.0	3.0	1.8	3.8	5.3
Taxes Paid	12	1.7	2.9	2.5	2.4	2.5	1.6	1.7	1.2	1.5	1.0	0.8	2.0	0.5
Interest Paid	13	0.8	3.7	0.7	0.6	0.9	0.6	0.6	0.5	0.6	1.4	0.5	0.7	1.0
Depreciation	14	2.7	4.3	2.5	3.5	4.4	2.7	2.6	2.4	2.8	3.0	1.9	1.6	1.4
Amortization and Depletion	15	0.2	11.6	0.0	0.0	0.0	0.0	0.0	0.1	0.1	0.2	0.3	0.8	0.4
Pensions and Other Deferred Comp.	16	0.4	0.4	0.7	0.5	0.5	0.7	0.4	0.4	0.3	0.4	0.6	0.3	0.2
Employee Benefits	17	0.9	0.9	0.9	0.7	1.0	1.5	1.0	1.2	0.9	0.8	0.8	0.8	0.1
Advertising	18	0.1	0.2	0.4	0.3	0.1	0.1	0.1	0.1	0.1	0.1	0.0	0.1	0.0
Other Expenses	19	7.6	27.1	18.9	17.4	12.1	5.6	6.1	5.2	5.2	5.2	2.1	6.3	6.1
Officers' Compensation	20	2.5	1.4	10.5	3.1	4.1	2.9	1.9	1.7	1.0	1.0	1.1	0.8	2.0
Operating Margin	21	3.2	•	1.6	3.2	3.8	5.1	4.7	4.7	3.7	2.5	4.6	1.5	•
Operating Margin Before Officers' Comp.	22	5.7	•	12.1	6.3	7.9	7.9	6.6	6.3	4.7	3.5	5.7	2.3	0.5

Selected Average Balance Sheet ($ in Thousands)

Net Receivables 23	1234	0	14	163	565	2355	5762	12547	23692	41678	109137	221649	1832050
Inventories 24	108	0	4	8	52	312	452	825	2158	5870	16426	22182	86501
Net Property, Plant and Equipment 25	1036	0	66	313	817	1809	3927	8775	17259	36977	94535	173110	1168074
Total Assets 26	4074	0	156	697	2111	7002	15519	34703	70148	152913	334300	896968	6400450
Notes and Loans Payable 27	853	0	114	229	703	1642	3466	5761	13569	44458	65220	116112	599026
All Other Liabilities 28	1707	0	23	109	532	2408	5599	14703	26999	64933	115303	388923	4373746
Net Worth 29	1514	0	19	360	877	2952	6454	14238	29580	43522	153777	391933	1427678

Selected Financial Ratios (Times to 1)

Current Ratio 30	1.4	•	1.5	1.8	1.7	1.6	1.6	1.6	1.6	1.4	1.6	1.5	0.8
Quick Ratio 31	1.1	•	1.1	1.6	1.5	1.4	1.4	1.2	1.3	1.0	1.3	0.9	0.7
Net Sales to Working Capital 32	11.5	•	34.6	17.5	9.7	8.0	8.3	8.5	7.7	8.8	9.9	9.6	•
Coverage Ratio 33	7.5	•	4.5	7.3	5.9	11.9	10.3	12.4	10.5	4.4	11.9	6.0	5.1
Total Asset Turnover 34	1.9	•	5.2	3.9	2.3	2.4	2.2	2.1	1.7	1.5	2.3	1.8	0.9
Inventory Turnover 35	54.8	•	94.3	205.1	60.2	40.3	57.7	70.6	45.5	32.8	40.0	57.7	53.9
Receivables Turnover 36	6.9	•	46.5	14.2	7.9	8.4	6.1	6.3	5.4	6.4	7.0	5.4	6.0
Total Liabilities to Net Worth 37	1.7	•	7.2	0.9	1.4	1.4	1.4	1.4	1.4	2.5	1.2	1.3	3.5
Current Assets to Working Capital 38	3.5	•	2.9	2.2	2.3	2.3	2.6	2.8	2.7	3.2	2.6	2.9	•
Current Liabilities to Working Capital 39	2.5	•	1.9	1.2	1.3	1.3	1.6	1.8	1.7	2.2	1.6	1.9	•
Working Capital to Net Sales 40	0.1	•	0.0	0.1	0.1	0.1	0.1	0.1	0.1	0.1	0.1	0.1	•
Inventory to Working Capital 41	0.2	•	0.2	0.0	0.1	0.1	0.1	0.1	0.1	0.3	0.2	0.1	•
Total Receipts to Cash Flow 42	10.4	7.3	5.7	6.7	8.3	10.8	11.8	11.5	12.4	12.6	15.7	13.5	10.6
Cost of Goods to Cash Flow 43	7.9	4.6	2.9	3.9	5.3	8.3	9.2	9.2	10.0	10.3	13.4	11.0	9.0
Cash Flow to Total Debt 44	0.3	•	1.0	1.2	0.5	0.4	0.3	0.3	0.2	0.2	0.3	0.2	0.1

Selected Financial Factors (in Percentages)

Debt Ratio 45	62.8	•	87.8	48.4	58.5	57.8	58.4	59.0	57.8	71.5	54.0	56.3	77.7
Return on Total Assets 46	10.9	•	17.1	18.1	12.6	16.7	13.8	13.7	10.7	9.6	13.0	7.2	4.6
Return on Equity Before Income Taxes 47	25.5	•	108.8	30.3	25.2	36.3	29.9	30.6	23.0	26.2	25.8	13.7	16.7
Return on Equity After Income Taxes 48	22.8	•	107.9	29.0	22.9	33.8	27.6	27.7	21.3	23.8	23.8	8.9	14.3
Profit Margin (Before Income Tax) 49	4.9	•	2.5	4.0	4.5	6.5	5.8	6.0	5.6	4.8	5.2	3.4	4.3
Profit Margin (After Income Tax) 50	4.4	•	2.5	3.9	4.1	6.1	5.3	5.4	5.2	4.4	4.8	2.2	3.7

Table II
Corporations with Net Income

HEAVY AND CIVIL ENGINEERING CONSTRUCTION

Money Amounts and Size of Assets in Thousands of Dollars

Item Description for Accounting Period 7/06 Through 6/07		Total	Zero Assets	Under 500	500 to 1,000	1,000 to 5,000	5,000 to 10,000	10,000 to 25,000	25,000 to 50,000	50,000 to 100,000	100,000 to 250,000	250,000 to 500,000	500,000 to 2,500,000	2,500,000 and over
Number of Enterprises	1	17602	1059	•	2195	4460	1475	881	268	103	51	•	13	0

Revenues ($ in Thousands)

Net Sales	2	181347056	585311	•	7492597	23277217	25713604	30454152	19923266	13393612	12401923	•	33494635	0
Interest	3	303454	570	•	2940	28992	26521	33775	21357	19506	20003	•	134383	0
Rents	4	74212	1004	•	1470	8993	3248	20608	19755	1767	3223	•	14051	0
Royalties	5	97804	0	•	0	0	0	2468	21473	176	7806	•	65881	0
Other Portfolio Income	6	698385	32114	•	33940	143249	111518	96516	69873	39443	44377	•	88330	0
Other Receipts	7	2101815	3144	•	2440	95314	229798	156547	118824	179303	231136	•	1023076	0
Total Receipts	8	184622726	622143	•	7533387	23553765	26084689	30764066	20174548	13633807	12708468	•	34820356	0
Average Total Receipts	9	10489	587	•	3432	5281	17685	34919	75278	132367	249186	•	2678489	•

Operating Costs/Operating Income (%)

Cost of Operations	10	75.3	62.1	•	58.5	63.9	76.1	77.3	79.7	79.9	80.4	•	81.9	•
Salaries and Wages	11	4.1	4.2	•	9.1	6.4	2.7	2.9	2.5	3.0	2.9	•	4.2	•
Taxes Paid	12	1.6	1.6	•	2.3	2.4	1.6	1.7	1.2	1.4	0.8	•	1.6	•
Interest Paid	13	0.6	4.8	•	0.6	0.8	0.5	0.6	0.5	0.5	0.6	•	0.8	•
Depreciation	14	2.6	5.6	•	3.4	4.0	2.7	2.6	2.4	2.7	2.9	•	1.6	•
Amortization and Depletion	15	0.1	•	•	0.0	0.0	0.0	0.0	0.1	0.1	0.1	•	0.4	•
Pensions and Other Deferred Comp.	16	0.4	0.6	•	0.5	0.5	0.7	0.4	0.3	0.3	0.4	•	0.2	•
Employee Benefits	17	0.9	0.5	•	0.6	1.0	1.6	1.0	1.2	0.9	0.6	•	0.3	•
Advertising	18	0.1	0.1	•	0.2	0.1	0.1	0.1	0.1	0.1	0.1	•	0.1	•
Other Expenses	19	7.1	17.6	•	17.2	10.9	5.4	6.1	5.2	4.9	5.1	•	6.1	•
Officers' Compensation	20	2.4	1.9	•	3.1	4.3	2.9	1.9	1.7	1.0	1.0	•	1.4	•
Operating Margin	21	4.6	0.9	•	4.6	5.6	5.7	5.3	5.2	5.3	5.0	•	1.2	•
Operating Margin Before Officers' Comp.	22	7.0	2.8	•	7.6	9.9	8.6	7.2	6.9	6.3	6.0	•	2.6	•

Selected Average Balance Sheet ($ in Thousands)

Item										
Net Receivables 23	1480	0	160	573	2489	5807	12740	23379	40048	406096
Inventories 24	121	0	10	57	160	411	691	2157	5264	31886
Net Property, Plant and Equipment 25	1335	0	318	775	1784	3982	8852	17150	38853	430932
Total Assets 26	4918	0	717	2130	7016	15620	34719	69261	150575	1741781
Notes and Loans Payable 27	949	0	244	607	1587	3405	5822	11376	26504	214483
All Other Liabilities 28	1908	0	127	550	2345	5599	14789	26102	49567	918511
Net Worth 29	2062	0	346	973	3084	6616	14108	31784	74505	608786

Selected Financial Ratios (Times to 1)

Item										
Current Ratio 30	1.5	•	1.7	1.9	1.8	1.6	1.5	1.6	1.7	1.1
Quick Ratio 31	1.2	•	1.6	1.5	1.6	1.4	1.2	1.3	1.2	0.9
Net Sales to Working Capital 32	10.3	•	23.1	9.4	7.9	8.4	8.9	7.9	6.6	33.3
Coverage Ratio 33	10.9	2.5	10.1	9.3	14.9	11.6	13.6	15.9	12.5	7.4
Total Asset Turnover 34	2.1	•	4.8	2.4	2.5	2.2	2.1	1.9	1.6	1.5
Inventory Turnover 35	64.0	•	198.8	58.9	82.7	65.0	85.8	48.2	37.2	66.2
Receivables Turnover 36	7.4	•	17.0	7.9	8.8	6.5	6.5	5.8	•	•
Total Liabilities to Net Worth 37	1.4	•	1.1	1.2	1.3	1.4	1.5	1.2	1.0	1.9
Current Assets to Working Capital 38	2.9	•	2.4	2.2	2.2	2.5	2.8	2.6	2.4	11.1
Current Liabilities to Working Capital 39	1.9	•	1.4	1.2	1.2	1.5	1.8	1.6	1.4	10.1
Working Capital to Net Sales 40	0.1	•	0.0	0.1	0.1	0.1	0.1	0.1	0.2	0.0
Inventory to Working Capital 41	0.1	•	0.1	0.1	0.0	0.1	0.1	0.1	0.1	0.4
Total Receipts to Cash Flow 42	9.3	5.3	6.3	7.3	10.3	11.2	10.9	10.7	9.3	10.2
Cost of Goods to Cash Flow 43	7.0	3.3	3.7	4.7	7.9	8.7	8.7	8.5	7.5	8.4
Cash Flow to Total Debt 44	0.4	•	1.5	0.6	0.4	0.3	0.3	0.3	0.3	0.2

Selected Financial Factors (in Percentages)

Item										
Debt Ratio 45	58.1	•	51.7	54.3	56.0	57.6	59.4	54.1	50.5	65.0
Return on Total Assets 46	14.7	•	27.0	18.7	19.0	15.3	14.9	14.1	13.0	8.8
Return on Equity Before Income Taxes 47	32.0	•	50.4	36.6	40.3	33.0	34.0	28.8	24.2	21.8
Return on Equity After Income Taxes 48	29.0	•	48.6	34.0	37.7	30.5	31.0	26.9	22.6	16.7
Profit Margin (Before Income Tax) 49	6.4	7.2	5.1	6.8	7.1	6.3	6.5	7.0	7.4	5.2
Profit Margin (After Income Tax) 50	5.8	5.5	4.9	6.3	6.7	5.8	5.9	6.6	6.9	3.9

28

Table I
Corporations with and without Net Income

LAND SUBDIVISION

MONEY AMOUNTS AND SIZE OF ASSETS IN THOUSANDS OF DOLLARS

Item Description for Accounting Period 7/06 Through 6/07	Total	Zero Assets	Under 500	500 to 1,000	1,000 to 5,000	5,000 to 10,000	10,000 to 25,000	25,000 to 50,000	50,000 to 100,000	100,000 to 250,000	250,000 to 500,000	500,000 to 2,500,000	2,500,000 and over
Number of Enterprises 1	47342	5267	24442	4892	9818	1496	936	252	129	73	16	20	0
Revenues ($ in Thousands)													
Net Sales 2	48683096	410883	2745682	1863499	13174739	3582382	5503524	3737679	3973121	3211281	1752872	8722433	0
Interest 3	347201	10504	4516	4739	38555	16837	14435	14695	31665	42685	33239	135331	0
Rents 4	492906	6503	9677	14478	33138	19450	45328	27375	84084	76290	14740	161843	0
Royalties 5	5484	0	0	0	99	2986	321	701	69	1267	0	41	0
Other Portfolio Income 6	544449	14207	22	133	52115	43154	51962	29563	50839	73098	45364	183991	0
Other Receipts 7	2242184	76624	28289	81825	470569	88054	305687	199079	237787	253401	81642	419230	0
Total Receipts 8	52315320	518721	2788186	1964674	13769215	3752863	5921257	4009092	4377565	3658022	1927857	9627869	0
Average Total Receipts 9	1105	98	114	402	1402	2509	6326	15909	33935	50110	120491	481393	•
Operating Costs/Operating Income (%)													
Cost of Operations 10	72.9	103.0	50.0	67.5	77.5	74.4	78.1	73.6	78.4	65.6	70.4	69.4	•
Salaries and Wages 11	5.3	7.2	13.5	4.6	2.6	2.3	4.6	7.5	4.9	8.0	10.5	5.7	•
Taxes Paid 12	1.9	4.6	3.3	3.3	1.3	1.3	1.4	1.8	1.5	2.3	1.6	2.9	•
Interest Paid 13	4.0	4.1	2.3	3.7	2.7	4.4	3.6	4.5	3.8	7.1	4.3	5.6	•
Depreciation 14	1.4	4.9	2.0	1.4	0.8	0.7	1.4	1.8	1.4	3.2	2.4	1.1	•
Amortization and Depletion 15	0.2	0.0	0.1	0.0	0.0	0.3	0.1	0.1	0.1	0.3	0.2	0.3	•
Pensions and Other Deferred Comp. 16	0.3	0.6	0.4	0.5	0.4	0.3	0.1	0.2	0.1	0.2	0.8	0.1	•
Employee Benefits 17	0.6	0.5	3.1	0.1	0.2	0.3	0.3	0.3	0.3	0.9	0.7	0.9	•
Advertising 18	0.8	1.8	1.2	0.1	0.6	0.5	0.6	1.4	1.0	1.4	1.0	0.8	•
Other Expenses 19	10.9	15.0	20.7	15.7	10.5	8.2	10.2	10.4	8.8	12.4	11.0	9.1	•
Officers' Compensation 20	2.2	1.1	9.6	4.8	1.6	1.7	1.6	1.3	1.6	4.3	1.2	1.0	•
Operating Margin 21	•	•	•	•	1.8	5.5	•	•	•	•	•	3.1	•
Operating Margin Before Officers' Comp. 22	1.8	•	3.4	3.1	3.4	7.2	•	•	•	•	•	4.1	•

Net Receivables 23	183	0	109	10	196	99	797	3171	5037	8192	59527	102517	•
Inventories 24	563	0	167	33	561	1917	3780	8731	19881	24273	97874	250570	•
Net Property, Plant and Equipment 25	550	0	185	35	521	1787	4188	11384	12268	41046	67507	201092	•
Total Assets 26	2263	0	725	132	2138	6888	14955	34826	68810	150167	369365	1027783	•
Notes and Loans Payable 27	1334	0	460	148	1241	4664	9962	21666	39719	77981	163180	494025	•
All Other Liabilities 28	341	0	124	69	268	827	2479	7869	11560	-16435	79934	205850	•
Net Worth 29	588	0	140	-86	628	1397	2514	5290	17530	88621	126251	327909	•

Selected Financial Ratios (Times to 1)

Current Ratio 30	2.2	•	1.1	2.5	2.6	2.3	2.0	2.0	2.7	1.9	2.8	2.4	•
Quick Ratio 31	0.6	•	0.4	0.8	0.8	0.2	0.4	0.6	0.6	0.5	1.1	0.7	•
Net Sales to Working Capital 32	1.5	•	19.1	1.4	1.9	1.0	1.4	1.7	1.1	1.5	0.9	1.4	•
Coverage Ratio 33	2.7	•	•	2.0	3.4	3.3	2.6	1.9	3.2	2.1	2.4	3.4	•
Total Asset Turnover 34	0.5	•	0.9	0.5	0.6	0.3	0.4	0.4	0.4	0.3	0.3	0.4	•
Inventory Turnover 35	1.3	•	1.7	1.5	1.9	0.9	1.2	1.3	1.2	1.2	0.8	1.2	•
Receivables Turnover 36	5.9	•	11.5	4.5	7.0	11.7	7.4	4.9	8.4	4.7	1.9	4.8	•
Total Liabilities to Net Worth 37	2.8	•	•	4.2	2.4	3.9	4.9	5.6	2.9	0.7	1.9	2.1	•
Current Assets to Working Capital 38	1.8	•	12.4	1.7	1.6	1.7	2.0	2.0	1.6	2.1	1.6	1.7	•
Current Liabilities to Working Capital 39	0.8	•	11.4	0.7	0.6	0.7	1.0	1.0	0.6	1.1	0.6	0.7	•
Working Capital to Net Sales 40	0.7	•	0.1	0.7	0.5	1.0	0.7	0.6	0.9	0.7	1.1	0.7	•
Inventory to Working Capital 41	0.9	•	5.2	0.6	0.8	1.1	1.0	1.0	0.9	0.9	0.8	1.0	•
Total Receipts to Cash Flow 42	6.5	•	7.6	6.1	6.5	6.2	7.4	8.2	7.1	6.1	6.6	5.3	•
Cost of Goods to Cash Flow 43	4.8	•	3.8	4.1	5.1	4.6	5.8	6.0	5.6	4.0	4.6	3.7	•
Cash Flow to Total Debt 44	0.1	•	0.1	0.1	0.1	0.1	0.1	0.1	0.1	0.1	0.1	0.1	•

Selected Financial Factors (in Percentages)

Debt Ratio 45	74.0	•	165.1	80.7	70.6	79.7	83.2	84.8	74.5	41.0	65.8	68.1	•
Return on Total Assets 46	5.0	•	•	3.9	5.6	5.1	3.6	3.7	5.3	4.5	3.0	8.1	•
Return on Equity Before Income Taxes 47	12.2	•	6.1	10.0	13.4	17.6	13.3	11.8	14.4	4.0	5.0	17.9	•
Return on Equity After Income Taxes 48	10.0	•	6.3	9.5	12.7	16.3	12.2	10.7	12.4	3.3	4.5	11.9	•
Profit Margin (Before Income Tax) 49	7.0	•	•	3.7	6.3	10.3	5.7	4.2	8.2	8.1	5.8	13.5	•
Profit Margin (After Income Tax) 50	5.7	•	3.5	•	6.0	9.5	5.2	3.8	7.0	6.6	5.2	8.9	•

Table II
Corporations with Net Income

LAND SUBDIVISION

MONEY AMOUNTS AND SIZE OF ASSETS IN THOUSANDS OF DOLLARS

Item Description for Accounting Period 7/06 Through 6/07	Total	Zero Assets	Under 500	500 to 1,000	1,000 to 5,000	5,000 to 10,000	10,000 to 25,000	25,000 to 50,000	50,000 to 100,000	100,000 to 250,000	250,000 to 500,000	500,000 to 2,500,000	2,500,000 and over
Number of Enterprises 1	14866	861	•	2594	4395	586	448	134	76	42	•	15	0
Revenues ($ in Thousands)													
Net Sales 2	37247702	139773	•	1488223	10383666	2667287	3995474	3120224	2708262	2110122	•	7987721	0
Interest 3	223841	9089	•	3211	25996	14877	6094	11238	21590	21784	•	101793	0
Rents 4	385309	6324	•	12571	18911	10695	22616	12993	80743	42228	•	159601	0
Royalties 5	5438	0	•	0	55	2986	321	701	69	1267	•	40	0
Other Portfolio Income 6	490773	13087	•	87	43057	36867	45657	15198	43248	68707	•	182225	0
Other Receipts 7	1917953	79419	•	76167	338412	83261	289968	164950	186704	211899	•	403458	0
Total Receipts 8	40271016	247692	•	1580259	10810097	2815973	4360130	3325304	3040616	2456007	•	8834838	0
Average Total Receipts 9	2709	288	•	609	2460	4805	9732	24816	40008	58476	•	588989	•
Operating Costs/Operating Income (%)													
Cost of Operations 10	73.7	61.2	•	68.6	79.5	70.1	73.4	74.0	75.6	67.7	•	72.7	•
Salaries and Wages 11	3.7	5.0	•	0.8	1.6	1.7	4.7	6.1	4.5	5.1	•	4.9	•
Taxes Paid 12	1.4	6.0	•	1.4	0.9	1.1	1.1	1.6	1.4	1.9	•	1.7	•
Interest Paid 13	2.8	2.9	•	2.1	1.9	1.8	2.3	2.1	2.7	4.3	•	4.9	•
Depreciation 14	0.9	1.7	•	0.8	0.5	0.4	0.9	1.1	1.2	3.4	•	0.7	•
Amortization and Depletion 15	0.1	0.0	•	0.0	0.0	0.0	0.0	0.1	0.1	0.1	•	0.3	•
Pensions and Other Deferred Comp. 16	0.2	•	•	0.6	0.1	0.4	0.1	0.2	0.1	0.1	•	0.1	•
Employee Benefits 17	0.3	0.2	•	0.1	0.1	0.3	0.3	0.2	0.1	0.4	•	0.7	•
Advertising 18	0.6	5.2	•	0.1	0.5	0.5	0.3	1.2	0.9	0.9	•	0.7	•
Other Expenses 19	7.1	19.2	•	9.1	5.3	5.5	8.6	7.2	7.9	9.2	•	7.6	•
Officers' Compensation 20	1.8	1.7	•	4.9	1.3	1.9	1.7	1.1	1.2	1.9	•	1.1	•
Operating Margin 21	7.4	•	•	11.5	8.2	16.4	6.6	5.1	4.2	4.8	•	4.6	•
Operating Margin Before Officers' Comp. 22	9.2	•	•	16.4	9.5	18.3	8.2	6.1	5.4	6.8	•	5.7	•

Selected Average Balance Sheet ($ in Thousands)

	•	•	•	•	•	•	•	•	•	•
Net Receivables 23	366	0	119	202	163	918	4058	5512	4702	117327
Inventories 24	1203	0	156	769	2306	4412	8859	24707	31739	313815
Net Property, Plant and Equipment 25	862	0	178	450	1607	3481	10117	10630	35619	234883
Total Assets 26	4054	0	725	2334	6871	15057	34582	69778	148606	1101303
Notes and Loans Payable 27	2011	0	346	1214	4445	8419	18618	33785	72280	497020
All Other Liabilities 28	481	0	125	317	605	2902	7409	11775	-52472	204215
Net Worth 29	1562	0	253	803	1820	3736	8555	24218	128799	400068

Selected Financial Ratios (Times to 1)

	•	•	•	•	•	•	•	•	•	•
Current Ratio 30	2.6		2.4	2.5	2.7	2.3	2.6	3.0	2.3	2.5
Quick Ratio 31	0.7		1.0	0.8	0.4	0.5	0.9	0.8	0.5	0.7
Net Sales to Working Capital 32	1.8		2.6	2.7	1.9	1.8	2.0	1.2	1.4	1.5
Coverage Ratio 33	6.5	26.1	9.6	7.3	13.2	7.8	6.6	7.2	5.9	4.1
Total Asset Turnover 34	0.6		0.8	1.0	0.7	0.6	0.7	0.5	0.3	0.5
Inventory Turnover 35	1.5		2.5	2.4	1.4	1.5	1.9	1.1	1.1	1.2
Receivables Turnover 36	6.5		5.9	10.3	10.0	9.7	6.3	8.4	5.0	4.8
Total Liabilities to Net Worth 37	1.6		1.9	1.9	2.8	3.0	3.0	1.9	0.2	1.8
Current Assets to Working Capital 38	1.6		1.7	1.6	1.6	1.8	1.6	1.5	1.8	1.7
Current Liabilities to Working Capital 39	0.6		0.7	0.6	0.6	0.8	0.6	0.5	0.8	0.7
Working Capital to Net Sales 40	0.6		0.4	0.4	0.5	0.6	0.5	0.8	0.7	0.7
Inventory to Working Capital 41	0.9		0.6	0.7	1.0	0.9	0.7	0.8	0.8	1.1
Total Receipts to Cash Flow 42	4.9	1.2	4.2	6.1	4.0	4.5	6.0	4.8	3.8	5.2
Cost of Goods to Cash Flow 43	3.6	0.7	2.9	4.8	2.8	3.3	4.4	3.6	2.6	3.8
Cash Flow to Total Debt 44	0.2		0.3	0.3	0.2	0.2	0.1	0.2	0.7	0.1

Selected Financial Factors (in Percentages)

	•	•	•	•	•	•	•	•	•	•
Debt Ratio 45	61.5		65.0	65.6	73.5	75.2	75.3	65.3	13.3	63.7
Return on Total Assets 46	11.3		15.7	14.4	15.8	10.6	9.2	9.7	8.6	9.8
Return on Equity Before Income Taxes 47	24.9		40.1	36.2	55.0	37.3	31.5	24.1	8.3	20.4
Return on Equity After Income Taxes 48	22.2		39.7	35.1	52.5	35.8	30.1	21.8	7.4	13.7
Profit Margin (Before Income Tax) 49	15.5	74.0	17.7	12.3	22.0	15.6	11.6	16.4	21.2	15.3
Profit Margin (After Income Tax) 50	13.8	69.0	17.5	11.9	21.0	15.0	11.1	14.8	19.0	10.3

Table I

Corporations with and without Net Income

ELECTRICAL CONTRACTORS

MONEY AMOUNTS AND SIZE OF ASSETS IN THOUSANDS OF DOLLARS

Item Description for Accounting Period 7/06 Through 6/07		Total	Zero Assets	Under 500	500 to 1,000	1,000 to 5,000	5,000 to 10,000	10,000 to 25,000	25,000 to 50,000	50,000 to 100,000	100,000 to 250,000	250,000 to 500,000	500,000 to 2,500,000	2,500,000 and over
Number of Enterprises	1	54863	9637	36758	4285	3063	739	283	64	20	15	0	0	0
Revenues ($ in Thousands)														
Net Sales	2	86792214	1192177	20033122	10301013	17838168	13418732	11104550	4822969	3437537	4643947	0	0	0
Interest	3	81780	855	7806	9847	19715	7855	6220	5217	11992	12271	0	0	0
Rents	4	16121	6	7053	4	3809	320	422	1580	355	2572	0	0	0
Royalties	5	0	0	0	0	0	0	0	0	0	0	0	0	0
Other Portfolio Income	6	177506	17157	32177	1700	73586	14907	7970	2123	8504	19381	0	0	0
Other Receipts	7	666483	7700	9329	15868	56496	34446	38711	32786	23143	448006	0	0	0
Total Receipts	8	87734104	1217895	20089487	10328432	17991774	13476260	11157873	4864675	3481531	5126177	•	•	•
Average Total Receipts	9	1599	126	547	2410	5874	18236	39427	76011	174077	341745	•	•	•
Operating Costs/Operating Income (%)														
Cost of Operations	10	67.0	40.0	50.0	61.7	70.7	77.3	76.2	75.9	78.2	75.5	•	•	•
Salaries and Wages	11	7.4	7.1	11.7	8.3	6.1	5.0	4.7	4.8	5.0	9.7	•	•	•
Taxes Paid	12	2.6	3.0	3.3	2.7	2.9	2.1	2.1	2.3	1.8	2.6	•	•	•
Interest Paid	13	0.7	2.2	0.6	0.7	0.5	0.6	0.4	0.4	0.9	3.1	•	•	•
Depreciation	14	1.2	1.5	1.7	1.3	1.1	0.8	0.7	1.1	0.9	1.6	•	•	•
Amortization and Depletion	15	0.1	0.0	0.0	0.1	0.0	0.0	0.0	0.0	0.2	1.2	•	•	•
Pensions and Other Deferred Comp.	16	0.5	2.3	0.3	0.6	0.4	0.4	0.5	0.2	0.6	0.9	•	•	•
Employee Benefits	17	2.6	1.4	1.4	2.3	3.2	2.2	4.0	4.3	2.4	2.9	•	•	•
Advertising	18	0.3	0.7	0.4	0.4	0.4	0.1	0.1	0.2	0.1	0.1	•	•	•
Other Expenses	19	9.7	23.0	17.0	10.3	7.6	6.0	4.7	4.3	5.1	12.9	•	•	•
Officers' Compensation	20	4.4	9.7	7.7	4.7	4.2	2.6	2.9	2.9	1.2	1.3	•	•	•
Operating Margin	21	3.5	9.0	5.9	6.9	3.0	2.9	3.7	3.5	3.6	•	•	•	•
Operating Margin Before Officers' Comp.	22	7.9	18.7	13.6	11.6	7.2	5.5	6.6	6.4	4.8	•	•	•	•

Selected Average Balance Sheet ($ in Thousands)

Net Receivables 23	255	0	18	288	1020	4198	9374	17000	36803	93241	•
Inventories 24	27	0	8	53	147	245	432	1780	1295	5149	•
Net Property, Plant and Equipment 25	74	0	31	133	260	475	1224	3899	7179	30779	•
Total Assets 26	553	0	99	741	2207	6974	15269	32965	65751	257751	•
Notes and Loans Payable 27	124	0	44	249	424	1077	2638	3952	11872	53349	•
All Other Liabilities 28	246	0	26	211	969	4126	7325	17722	35272	111504	•
Net Worth 29	184	0	29	282	814	1771	5306	11291	18607	92899	•

Selected Financial Ratios (Times to 1)

Current Ratio 30	1.6	•	1.7	2.0	1.6	1.3	1.6	1.6	1.5	1.8	•
Quick Ratio 31	1.3	•	1.3	1.8	1.3	1.1	1.4	1.3	1.2	1.4	•
Net Sales to Working Capital 32	9.9	•	22.6	9.0	8.8	12.3	7.8	7.8	9.2	4.0	•
Coverage Ratio 33	7.5	6.0	12.1	11.6	8.8	7.0	10.5	10.8	6.4	0.5	•
Total Asset Turnover 34	2.9	•	5.5	3.2	2.6	2.6	2.6	2.3	2.6	1.2	•
Inventory Turnover 35	38.6	•	32.4	27.9	28.0	57.3	69.1	32.1	103.9	45.4	•
Receivables Turnover 36	6.5	•	29.2	9.4	5.6	4.6	4.6	4.4	4.7	4.0	•
Total Liabilities to Net Worth 37	2.0	•	2.4	1.6	1.7	2.9	1.9	1.9	2.5	1.8	•
Current Assets to Working Capital 38	2.7	•	2.5	2.0	2.6	4.1	2.6	2.8	2.9	2.3	•
Current Liabilities to Working Capital 39	1.7	•	1.5	1.0	1.6	3.1	1.6	1.8	1.9	1.3	•
Working Capital to Net Sales 40	0.1	•	0.0	0.1	0.1	0.1	0.1	0.1	0.1	0.3	•
Inventory to Working Capital 41	0.2	•	0.4	0.2	0.3	0.2	0.1	0.3	0.1	0.1	•
Total Receipts to Cash Flow 42	8.2	3.3	4.9	6.5	10.8	12.7	13.2	14.6	12.3	12.2	•
Cost of Goods to Cash Flow 43	5.5	1.3	2.4	4.0	7.6	9.8	10.1	11.1	9.6	9.2	•
Cash Flow to Total Debt 44	0.5	•	1.6	0.8	0.4	0.3	0.3	0.2	0.3	0.2	•

Selected Financial Factors (in Percentages)

Debt Ratio 45	66.8	•	70.7	62.0	63.1	74.6	65.3	65.7	71.7	64.0	•
Return on Total Assets 46	15.2	•	36.8	25.4	11.5	10.0	11.8	10.9	15.0	1.8	•
Return on Equity Before Income Taxes 47	39.6	•	114.9	61.0	27.6	33.8	30.7	28.8	44.7	•	•
Return on Equity After Income Taxes 48	36.9	•	113.1	59.7	24.7	31.2	27.7	26.8	38.9	•	•
Profit Margin (Before Income Tax) 49	4.6	11.1	6.1	7.2	3.9	3.3	4.2	4.3	4.8	•	•
Profit Margin (After Income Tax) 50	4.3	11.1	6.0	7.0	3.5	3.0	3.7	4.0	4.2	•	•

Table II

Corporations with Net Income

ELECTRICAL CONTRACTORS

MONEY AMOUNTS AND SIZE OF ASSETS IN THOUSANDS OF DOLLARS

Item Description for Accounting Period 7/06 Through 6/07	Total	Zero Assets	Under 500	500 to 1,000	1,000 to 5,000	5,000 to 10,000	10,000 to 25,000	25,000 to 50,000	50,000 to 100,000	100,000 to 250,000	250,000 to 500,000	500,000 to 2,500,000	2,500,000 and over
Number of Enterprises **1**	37517	5194	•	3022	2240	679	270	55	•	•	0	0	0
Revenues ($ in Thousands)													
Net Sales **2**	72139898	860297	•	7883124	13809217	12781595	10596091	4275847	•	•	0	0	0
Interest **3**	59220	705	•	8213	14736	7712	6060	3711	•	•	0	0	0
Rents **4**	9679	6	•	4	3782	320	422	1580	•	•	0	0	0
Royalties **5**	0	0	•	0	0	0	0	0	•	•	0	0	0
Other Portfolio Income **6**	161736	16239	•	1485	67272	12024	7936	1968	•	•	0	0	0
Other Receipts **7**	586868	7252	•	9198	27563	34228	36127	31822	•	•	0	0	0
Total Receipts **8**	72957401	884499	•	7902024	13922570	12835879	10646636	4314928	•	•	0	0	0
Average Total Receipts **9**	1945	170	•	2615	6215	18904	39432	78453	•	•	•	•	•
Operating Costs/Operating Income (%)													
Cost of Operations **10**	66.9	35.3	•	61.6	68.4	77.1	75.9	76.0	•	•	•	•	•
Salaries and Wages **11**	6.7	7.9	•	6.7	6.6	5.1	4.6	5.2	•	•	•	•	•
Taxes Paid **12**	2.6	2.7	•	2.9	2.9	2.1	2.1	2.1	•	•	•	•	•
Interest Paid **13**	0.5	2.1	•	0.4	0.4	0.5	0.4	0.3	•	•	•	•	•
Depreciation **14**	1.1	1.6	•	1.2	1.1	0.7	0.6	0.8	•	•	•	•	•
Amortization and Depletion **15**	0.1	0.0	•	0.1	0.0	0.0	0.1	0.0	•	•	•	•	•
Pensions and Other Deferred Comp. **16**	0.5	0.0	•	0.7	0.4	0.4	0.5	0.2	•	•	•	•	•
Employee Benefits **17**	2.5	1.7	•	1.8	2.2	1.9	4.1	4.2	•	•	•	•	•
Advertising **18**	0.3	0.6	•	0.3	0.5	0.1	0.1	0.2	•	•	•	•	•
Other Expenses **19**	8.6	20.6	•	9.4	7.3	6.0	4.6	3.5	•	•	•	•	•
Officers' Compensation **20**	4.5	12.2	•	4.5	4.7	2.7	3.0	3.2	•	•	•	•	•
Operating Margin **21**	5.7	15.2	•	10.4	5.5	3.2	4.0	4.3	•	•	•	•	•
Operating Margin Before Officers' Comp. **22**	10.2	27.4	•	14.9	10.2	5.9	7.0	7.5	•	•	•	•	•

Selected Average Balance Sheet ($ in Thousands)

Item							
Net Receivables 23	313	0	•	288	1016	4317	9437	17935
Inventories 24	30	0	•	56	160	189	358	2761
Net Property, Plant and Equipment 25	76	0	•	85	267	468	1140	3338
Total Assets 26	657	0	•	759	2201	7053	15281	33298
Notes and Loans Payable 27	111	0	•	170	305	852	2606	2942
All Other Liabilities 28	295	0	•	191	1016	4206	7362	17895
Net Worth 29	250	0	•	398	881	1995	5313	12461

Selected Financial Ratios (Times to 1)

Item							
Current Ratio 30	1.7	•	2.4	1.7	1.4	1.6	1.6
Quick Ratio 31	1.4	•	2.1	1.4	1.2	1.4	1.3
Net Sales to Working Capital 32	8.8	•	7.6	7.9	11.2	7.7	7.0
Coverage Ratio 33	15.2	9.6	27.6	15.9	8.9	11.4	17.0
Total Asset Turnover 34	2.9	•	3.4	2.8	2.7	2.6	2.3
Inventory Turnover 35	43.1	•	28.8	26.3	76.7	83.3	21.4
Receivables Turnover 36	6.6	•	10.0	5.8	4.7	4.7	•
Total Liabilities to Net Worth 37	1.6	•	0.9	1.5	2.5	1.9	1.7
Current Assets to Working Capital 38	2.4	•	1.7	2.3	3.7	2.6	2.5
Current Liabilities to Working Capital 39	1.4	•	0.7	1.3	2.7	1.6	1.5
Working Capital to Net Sales 40	0.1	•	0.1	0.1	0.1	0.1	0.1
Inventory to Working Capital 41	0.2	•	0.1	0.2	0.1	0.1	0.2
Total Receipts to Cash Flow 42	7.4	2.9	5.5	8.7	12.1	12.9	13.6
Cost of Goods to Cash Flow 43	4.9	1.0	3.4	6.0	9.4	9.8	10.3
Cash Flow to Total Debt 44	0.6	•	1.3	0.5	0.3	0.3	0.3

Selected Financial Factors (in Percentages)

Item							
Debt Ratio 45	61.8	•	47.5	60.0	71.7	65.2	62.6
Return on Total Assets 46	21.5	•	38.0	18.9	10.9	12.5	12.9
Return on Equity Before Income Taxes 47	52.6	•	69.7	44.3	-34.1	32.8	32.6
Return on Equity After Income Taxes 48	49.6	•	68.4	40.7	31.6	29.6	30.4
Profit Margin (Before Income Tax) 49	6.9	18.0	10.6	6.3	3.6	4.4	5.2
Profit Margin (After Income Tax) 50	6.5	18.0	10.5	5.8	3.4	4.0	4.9

Table I

Corporations with and without Net Income

PLUMBING, HEATING, AND AIR-CONDITIONING CONTRACTORS

MONEY AMOUNTS AND SIZE OF ASSETS IN THOUSANDS OF DOLLARS

Item Description for Accounting Period 7/06 Through 6/07	Total	Zero Assets	Under 500	500 to 1,000	1,000 to 5,000	5,000 to 10,000	10,000 to 25,000	25,000 to 50,000	50,000 to 100,000	100,000 to 250,000	250,000 to 500,000	500,000 to 2,500,000	2,500,000 and over
Number of Enterprises 1	75812	5013	61113	4580	4098	581	334	69	18	5	0	0	0
Revenues ($ in Thousands)													
Net Sales 2	125164143	1590724	40308642	11724709	30646464	11481160	13928298	6139768	3149187	6195190	0	0	0
Interest 3	78373	1277	11334	11888	25737	10373	9004	3001	726	5032	0	0	0
Rents 4	9658	0	713	2306	2355	2046	1555	187	193	302	0	0	0
Royalties 5	0	0	0	0	0	0	0	0	0	0	0	0	0
Other Portfolio Income 6	171049	263	93714	18130	17352	16143	19539	1523	748	3638	0	0	0
Other Receipts 7	467914	857	98845	31096	99009	122995	24214	27504	36085	27311	0	0	0
Total Receipts 8	125891137	1593121	40513248	11788129	30790917	11632717	13982610	6171983	3186939	6231473	0	0	0
Average Total Receipts 9	1661	318	663	2574	7514	20022	41864	89449	177052	1246295	•	•	•
Operating Costs/Operating Income (%)													
Cost of Operations 10	66.0	56.2	51.7	59.8	71.0	74.4	78.6	82.4	78.7	83.0	•	•	•
Salaries and Wages 11	7.9	7.3	12.3	7.2	6.2	6.4	4.3	4.5	6.5	4.8	•	•	•
Taxes Paid 12	2.6	4.7	3.0	3.1	2.5	2.3	2.2	1.9	1.7	2.1	•	•	•
Interest Paid 13	0.4	0.8	0.5	0.4	0.4	0.4	0.4	0.3	0.2	0.2	•	•	•
Depreciation 14	1.1	0.4	1.6	1.6	0.9	0.8	0.5	0.4	0.5	0.3	•	•	•
Amortization and Depletion 15	0.1	0.9	0.0	0.0	0.0	0.0	0.0	0.1	0.1	0.4	•	•	•
Pensions and Other Deferred Comp. 16	0.5	0.6	0.4	0.5	0.6	0.6	0.8	0.8	0.3	0.2	•	•	•
Employee Benefits 17	1.7	3.3	1.4	2.0	1.7	2.4	2.6	1.5	1.6	0.5	•	•	•
Advertising 18	0.6	2.1	0.8	1.2	0.7	0.3	0.1	0.1	0.1	0.1	•	•	•
Other Expenses 19	10.7	19.8	16.6	13.4	9.1	6.0	4.2	3.3	6.0	5.5	•	•	•
Officers' Compensation 20	5.0	2.3	7.9	6.0	4.4	3.6	2.3	1.5	1.3	1.4	•	•	•
Operating Margin 21	3.3	1.5	3.7	4.7	2.6	2.9	4.0	3.3	3.0	1.5	•	•	•
Operating Margin Before Officers' Comp. 22	8.3	3.8	11.6	10.7	6.9	6.4	6.3	4.8	4.3	2.9	•	•	•

Selected Average Balance Sheet ($ in Thousands)

Net Receivables 23	213	0	25	238	1088	3669	8864	21795	37455	361627
Inventories 24	25	0	8	44	155	395	433	1319	1957	5437
Net Property, Plant and Equipment 25	65	0	31	155	263	767	1151	2205	7000	22966
Total Assets 26	456	0	104	686	2242	6974	15222	36005	65016	618523
Notes and Loans Payable 27	106	0	55	179	488	942	2126	3510	5394	39052
All Other Liabilities 28	217	0	34	244	1006	3459	9165	22824	35196	371243
Net Worth 29	134	0	15	264	748	2573	3930	9670	24426	208229

Selected Financial Ratios (Times to 1)

Current Ratio 30	1.5	•	1.5	1.9	1.6	1.6	1.5	1.3	1.6	1.4
Quick Ratio 31	1.3	•	1.2	1.6	1.3	1.3	1.2	1.1	1.4	1.3
Net Sales to Working Capital 32	13.2	•	33.2	10.5	11.3	8.8	9.5	11.9	8.7	8.0
Coverage Ratio 33	10.1	2.9	9.0	13.2	9.3	10.6	11.7	12.4	20.6	9.8
Total Asset Turnover 34	3.6	•	6.3	3.7	3.3	2.8	2.7	2.5	2.7	2.0
Inventory Turnover 35	44.4	•	42.0	34.6	34.4	37.2	75.7	55.6	70.4	189.1
Receivables Turnover 36	8.2	•	26.7	10.8	6.9	5.2	5.4	5.5	5.2	3.6
Total Liabilities to Net Worth 37	2.4	•	6.1	1.6	2.0	1.7	2.9	2.7	1.7	2.0
Current Assets to Working Capital 38	2.8	•	3.1	2.1	2.7	2.6	3.0	4.1	2.7	3.2
Current Liabilities to Working Capital 39	1.8	•	2.1	1.1	1.7	1.6	2.0	3.1	1.7	2.2
Working Capital to Net Sales 40	0.1	•	0.0	0.1	0.1	0.1	0.1	0.1	0.1	0.1
Inventory to Working Capital 41	0.2	•	0.4	0.2	0.3	0.2	0.1	0.3	0.1	0.0
Total Receipts to Cash Flow 42	8.1	5.9	5.4	6.2	10.4	12.0	13.8	16.8	10.8	17.7
Cost of Goods to Cash Flow 43	5.3	3.3	2.8	3.7	7.4	8.9	10.8	13.9	8.5	14.7
Cash Flow to Total Debt 44	0.6	•	1.4	1.0	0.5	0.4	0.3	0.2	0.4	0.2

Selected Financial Factors (in Percentages)

Debt Ratio 45	70.7	•	85.9	61.5	66.6	63.1	74.2	73.1	62.4	66.3
Return on Total Assets 46	15.6	•	30.2	21.1	11.4	13.0	13.1	10.2	11.8	4.7
Return on Equity Before Income Taxes 47	48.0	•	190.5	50.6	30.4	32.0	46.3	34.8	30.0	12.6
Return on Equity After Income Taxes 48	45.5	•	188.2	49.5	28.2	29.8	43.4	31.5	28.6	7.6
Profit Margin (Before Income Tax) 49	3.9	1.6	4.2	5.2	3.0	4.2	4.4	3.8	4.2	2.1
Profit Margin (After Income Tax) 50	3.7	1.6	4.2	5.1	2.8	3.9	4.1	3.4	4.0	1.3

Table II
Corporations with Net Income

PLUMBING, HEATING, AND AIR-CONDITIONING CONTRACTORS

MONEY AMOUNTS AND SIZE OF ASSETS IN THOUSANDS OF DOLLARS

Item Description for Accounting Period 7/06 Through 6/07	Total	Zero Assets	Under 500	500 to 1,000	1,000 to 5,000	5,000 to 10,000	10,000 to 25,000	25,000 to 50,000	50,000 to 100,000	100,000 to 250,000	250,000 to 500,000	500,000 to 2,500,000	2,500,000 and over
Number of Enterprises 1	50294	2078	40541	3578	3191	513	307	66	•	•	0	0	0
Revenues ($ in Thousands)													
Net Sales 2	103756933	450390	29823811	9103031	26350664	10251122	13242770	5914259	•	•	0	0	0
Interest 3	58901	0	3646	9611	19381	10229	7787	3001	•	•	0	0	0
Rents 4	8954	0	713	2278	1786	1940	1555	187	•	•	0	0	0
Royalties 5	0	0	0	0	0	0	0	0	•	•	0	0	0
Other Portfolio Income 6	104360	66	33862	14299	16060	15831	19271	1504	•	•	0	0	0
Other Receipts 7	295973	412	77995	26647	70184	24813	22054	27302	•	•	0	0	0
Total Receipts 8	104225121	450868	29940027	9155866	26458075	10303935	13293437	5946253	•	•	0	0	0
Average Total Receipts 9	2072	217	739	2559	8291	20086	43301	90095	•	•	•	•	•
Operating Costs/Operating Income (%)													
Cost of Operations 10	66.1	53.5	49.7	57.8	70.1	73.0	78.4	82.6	•	•	•	•	•
Salaries and Wages 11	7.6	5.7	12.0	7.1	6.4	6.5	4.3	4.6	•	•	•	•	•
Taxes Paid 12	2.5	1.8	2.8	2.9	2.4	2.3	2.2	1.9	•	•	•	•	•
Interest Paid 13	0.3	0.1	0.4	0.3	0.3	0.4	0.4	0.3	•	•	•	•	•
Depreciation 14	1.0	1.0	1.5	1.4	0.9	0.8	0.5	0.4	•	•	•	•	•
Amortization and Depletion 15	0.0	0.0	0.0	0.0	0.0	0.0	0.0	0.1	•	•	•	•	•
Pensions and Other Deferred Comp. 16	0.5	1.3	0.4	0.5	0.6	0.6	0.9	0.8	•	•	•	•	•
Employee Benefits 17	1.7	3.0	1.3	1.9	1.7	2.0	2.5	1.5	•	•	•	•	•
Advertising 18	0.6	0.4	0.8	1.3	0.8	0.3	0.1	0.1	•	•	•	•	•
Other Expenses 19	10.1	14.8	16.7	14.0	8.9	5.8	4.1	2.8	•	•	•	•	•
Officers' Compensation 20	4.6	7.2	7.3	6.0	4.3	3.8	2.3	1.5	•	•	•	•	•
Operating Margin 21	5.0	11.2	7.1	6.8	3.5	4.6	4.3	3.5	•	•	•	•	•
Operating Margin Before Officers' Comp. 22	9.6	18.4	14.4	12.7	7.9	8.4	6.6	5.0	•	•	•	•	•

Selected Average Balance Sheet ($ in Thousands)

Net Receivables 23	274	0	24	209	1148	3703	9157	21350
Inventories 24	30	0	8	43	168	397	435	1258
Net Property, Plant and Equipment 25	71	0	28	142	265	710	1166	1973
Total Assets 26	571	0	104	667	2328	7033	15508	35390
Notes and Loans Payable 27	105	0	44	154	443	816	2184	3466
All Other Liabilities 28	263	0	26	213	1023	3414	8385	22847
Net Worth 29	203	0	35	300	861	2802	4938	9077

Selected Financial Ratios (Times to 1)

Current Ratio 30	1.6	•	2.0	2.2	1.6	1.7	1.5	1.3
Quick Ratio 31	1.3	•	1.7	1.8	1.3	1.4	1.2	1.1
Net Sales to Working Capital 32	12.0	•	23.5	9.5	11.3	8.3	9.8	12.6
Coverage Ratio 33	16.8	95.1	19.2	22.6	14.3	14.6	12.3	12.9
Total Asset Turnover 34	3.6	•	7.1	3.8	3.5	2.8	2.8	2.5
Inventory Turnover 35	45.9	•	45.1	34.0	34.4	36.8	77.8	58.9
Receivables Turnover 36	8.0	•	30.2	11.4	7.3	5.1	5.7	5.5
Total Liabilities to Net Worth 37	1.8	•	2.0	1.2	1.7	1.5	2.1	2.9
Current Assets to Working Capital 38	2.6	•	2.0	1.8	2.6	2.5	3.1	4.3
Current Liabilities to Working Capital 39	1.6	•	1.0	0.8	1.6	1.5	2.1	3.3
Working Capital to Net Sales 40	0.1	•	0.0	0.1	0.1	0.1	0.1	0.1
Inventory to Working Capital 41	0.2	•	0.2	0.2	0.3	0.2	0.1	0.3
Total Receipts to Cash Flow 42	7.5	4.6	4.6	5.3	9.7	10.7	13.4	17.5
Cost of Goods to Cash Flow 43	4.9	2.4	2.3	3.1	6.8	7.8	10.5	14.4
Cash Flow to Total Debt 44	0.8	•	2.3	1.3	0.6	0.4	0.3	0.2

Selected Financial Factors (in Percentages)

Debt Ratio 45	64.5	•	66.7	55.0	63.0	60.2	68.2	74.4
Return on Total Assets 46	21.0	•	56.1	29.3	15.0	15.5	14.2	11.0
Return on Equity Before Income Taxes 47	55.5	•	159.8	62.2	37.8	36.2	40.9	39.6
Return on Equity After Income Taxes 48	53.0	•	158.3	60.9	35.3	33.9	38.4	36.0
Profit Margin (Before Income Tax) 49	5.5	11.3	7.5	7.3	3.9	5.1	4.7	4.0
Profit Margin (After Income Tax) 50	5.2	11.3	7.4	7.2	3.7	4.7	4.4	3.6

Table II

Corporations with Net Income

OTHER SPECIALTY TRADE CONTRACTORS

MONEY AMOUNTS AND SIZE OF ASSETS IN THOUSANDS OF DOLLARS

Item Description for Accounting Period 7/06 Through 6/07	Total	Zero Assets	Under 500	500 to 1,000	1,000 to 5,000	5,000 to 10,000	10,000 to 25,000	25,000 to 50,000	50,000 to 100,000	100,000 to 250,000	250,000 to 500,000	500,000 to 2,500,000	2,500,000 and over
Number of Enterprises **1**	227552	36007	161334	13361	13719	1840	924	245	75	•	9	•	0
Revenues ($ in Thousands)													
Net Sales **2**	342261573	6143311	101111483	37462421	86139923	31065612	32535408	20051528	10956850	•	4224194	•	0
Interest **3**	241433	608	33710	19131	58211	21497	23882	21063	17618	•	32566	•	0
Rents **4**	252528	1	19769	5544	23444	7097	24716	19144	828	•	10162	•	0
Royalties **5**	7871	0	254	0	0	10	0	5287	17	•	79	•	0
Other Portfolio Income **6**	874733	48819	203594	161471	147843	50989	99429	76382	25794	•	3287	•	0
Other Receipts **7**	1326386	19743	240339	94148	349809	147480	185493	126352	75838	•	32303	•	0
Total Receipts **8**	344964524	6212482	101609149	37742715	86719230	31292685	32868928	20299756	11076945	•	4302591	•	0
Average Total Receipts **9**	1516	173	630	2825	6321	17007	35572	82856	147693	•	478066	•	•
Operating Costs/Operating Income (%)													
Cost of Operations **10**	65.2	46.4	53.1	61.9	69.1	72.2	75.8	78.4	76.0	•	75.5	•	•
Salaries and Wages **11**	6.7	5.6	9.4	8.0	5.8	4.8	4.1	3.6	5.0	•	5.4	•	•
Taxes Paid **12**	2.1	1.5	2.6	2.3	2.2	1.8	1.7	1.6	1.5	•	0.8	•	•
Interest Paid **13**	0.6	0.6	0.5	0.6	0.5	0.5	0.5	0.4	0.5	•	2.7	•	•
Depreciation **14**	1.7	1.9	1.6	2.0	1.8	1.3	1.5	1.6	1.6	•	1.6	•	•
Amortization and Depletion **15**	0.0	0.0	0.0	0.0	0.0	0.0	0.0	0.1	0.0	•	1.1	•	•
Pensions and Other Deferred Comp. **16**	0.4	0.2	0.3	0.3	0.5	0.6	0.6	0.4	0.4	•	0.3	•	•
Employee Benefits **17**	1.2	0.7	0.8	1.0	1.6	1.7	1.5	1.2	1.4	•	0.9	•	•
Advertising **18**	0.3	0.5	0.5	0.4	0.3	0.2	0.1	0.2	0.2	•	0.1	•	•
Other Expenses **19**	11.4	22.6	16.8	14.2	9.3	7.4	5.8	6.9	6.8	•	5.3	•	•
Officers' Compensation **20**	4.0	7.0	6.4	4.4	3.5	2.8	2.0	1.3	1.6	•	1.2	•	•
Operating Margin **21**	6.4	13.1	7.9	4.9	5.6	6.8	6.3	4.4	5.2	•	5.2	•	•
Operating Margin Before Officers' Comp. **22**	10.4	20.1	14.3	9.3	9.0	9.6	8.3	5.7	6.7	•	6.3	•	•

Selected Average Balance Sheet ($ in Thousands)

	C1	C2	C3	C4	C5	C6	C7	C8	C9	C10	
Net Receivables 23	172	0	14	182	853	3305	7400	15433	32652	84853	•
Inventories 24	20	0	5	43	109	300	527	1288	1895	5451	•
Net Property, Plant and Equipment 25	100	0	30	221	468	989	2529	6442	10807	44706	•
Total Assets 26	460	0	91	702	2089	6872	15083	33842	70189	367140	•
Notes and Loans Payable 27	126	0	45	218	543	1099	2800	7457	10280	155351	•
All Other Liabilities 28	160	0	17	157	670	3041	6607	14593	34245	152022	•
Net Worth 29	174	0	30	327	876	2732	5676	11793	25663	59767	•

Selected Financial Ratios (Times to 1)

	C1	C2	C3	C4	C5	C6	C7	C8	C9	C10	
Current Ratio 30	1.6	•	1.9	1.8	1.6	1.5	1.5	1.5	1.3	1.3	•
Quick Ratio 31	1.3	•	1.5	1.5	1.3	1.2	1.3	1.2	1.2	0.7	•
Net Sales to Working Capital 32	12.5	•	29.0	15.4	9.6	8.2	8.8	10.8	8.9	9.9	•
Coverage Ratio 33	13.9	26.3	17.3	11.0	13.7	17.6	16.4	13.5	14.5	3.6	•
Total Asset Turnover 34	3.3	•	6.9	4.0	3.0	2.5	2.3	2.4	2.1	1.3	•
Inventory Turnover 35	48.1	•	66.4	40.8	39.8	40.6	50.7	49.8	58.6	65.0	•
Receivables Turnover 36	9.1	•	45.4	17.4	7.4	5.2	4.9	•	4.9	•	•
Total Liabilities to Net Worth 37	1.6	•	2.1	1.1	1.4	1.5	1.7	1.9	1.7	5.1	•
Current Assets to Working Capital 38	2.6	•	2.1	2.2	2.2	2.6	2.9	3.2	3.1	4.3	•
Current Liabilities to Working Capital 39	1.6	•	1.1	1.2	1.2	1.6	1.9	2.2	2.1	3.3	•
Working Capital to Net Sales 40	0.1	•	0.0	0.1	0.1	0.1	0.1	0.1	0.1	0.1	•
Inventory to Working Capital 41	0.2	•	0.2	0.2	0.1	0.2	0.1	0.2	0.1	0.1	•
Total Receipts to Cash Flow 42	6.4	3.0	4.6	6.3	7.9	8.5	9.3	10.5	9.4	9.1	•
Cost of Goods to Cash Flow 43	4.2	1.4	2.4	3.9	5.5	6.1	7.1	8.2	7.2	6.9	•
Cash Flow to Total Debt 44	0.8	•	2.2	1.2	0.7	0.5	0.4	0.4	0.3	0.2	•

Selected Financial Factors (in Percentages)

	C1	C2	C3	C4	C5	C6	C7	C8	C9	C10	
Debt Ratio 45	62.2	•	67.5	53.4	58.1	60.2	62.4	65.2	63.4	83.7	•
Return on Total Assets 46	25.2	•	61.0	24.7	20.3	19.6	18.2	14.7	14.0	12.4	•
Return on Equity Before Income Taxes 47	61.9	176.8	48.2	44.9	46.6	45.5	39.1	35.7	55.2		•
Return on Equity After Income Taxes 48	59.2	175.1	46.7	42.7	43.1	42.6	36.0	30.9	49.1		•
Profit Margin (Before Income Tax) 49	7.2	14.2	8.4	5.6	6.3	7.5	7.3	5.6	6.3	7.0	•
Profit Margin (After Income Tax) 50	6.9	14.0	8.3	5.5	6.0	7.0	6.9	5.2	5.4	6.2	•

Table I

Corporations with and without Net Income

ANIMAL FOOD AND GRAIN AND OILSEED MILLING

Money Amounts and Size of Assets in Thousands of Dollars

Item Description for Accounting Period 7/06 Through 6/07	Total	Zero Assets	Under 500	500 to 1,000	1,000 to 5,000	5,000 to 10,000	10,000 to 25,000	25,000 to 50,000	50,000 to 100,000	100,000 to 250,000	250,000 to 500,000	500,000 to 2,500,000	2,500,000 and over
Number of Enterprises **1**	2015	499	891	0	396	39	91	47	18	22	4	4	4
Revenues ($ in Thousands)													
Net Sales **2**	82507710	1146274	180493	0	2267344	467317	2840943	5070267	2641763	5265981	1652645	2633706	58340977
Interest **3**	608532	4475	222	0	4366	654	2789	4079	3485	8820	14668	21424	543550
Rents **4**	188094	0	228	0	262	0	143	1513	425	196	1	702	184624
Royalties **5**	257014	0	0	0	0	0	57	0	0	1136	2	45558	210261
Other Portfolio Income **6**	389926	20169	2903	0	2782	471	2333	1083	986	30442	1400	152188	175169
Other Receipts **7**	1148525	8504	7691	0	6856	19958	1471	34568	24964	27532	27380	20749	968851
Total Receipts **8**	85099801	1179422	191537	0	2281610	488400	2847736	5111510	2671623	5334107	1696096	2874327	60423432
Average Total Receipts **9**	42233	2364	215	•	5762	12523	31294	108756	148424	242459	424024	718582	15105858
Operating Costs/Operating Income (%)													
Cost of Operations **10**	76.2	65.5	71.0	•	82.1	71.5	78.1	81.3	84.4	80.2	68.6	75.6	75.1
Salaries and Wages **11**	3.3	4.2	18.8	•	5.2	7.2	3.9	4.2	3.1	3.4	5.0	3.1	3.0
Taxes Paid **12**	0.8	1.3	6.5	•	0.6	1.6	1.1	0.8	0.7	1.1	1.0	0.9	0.8
Interest Paid **13**	2.5	4.7	1.6	•	0.9	1.5	0.8	0.7	0.9	1.2	4.9	3.8	2.8
Depreciation **14**	1.7	2.1	1.4	•	1.2	3.0	2.1	1.6	1.7	2.3	3.4	2.9	1.5
Amortization and Depletion **15**	0.2	0.9	0.4	•	0.0	0.1	0.1	0.1	0.0	0.4	1.4	2.4	0.1
Pensions and Other Deferred Comp. **16**	0.4	0.1	0.0	•	0.0	0.6	0.2	0.3	0.2	0.2	1.0	0.6	0.5
Employee Benefits **17**	0.8	0.4	6.4	•	0.3	0.6	0.5	0.7	0.8	1.0	0.5	2.2	0.8
Advertising **18**	5.8	9.4	0.3	•	0.7	1.5	0.4	0.3	0.3	0.3	1.4	0.7	7.8
Other Expenses **19**	6.2	10.0	23.4	•	6.8	12.5	7.1	6.5	6.5	6.2	12.7	5.8	5.7
Officers' Compensation **20**	0.6	2.9	1.9	•	1.6	1.0	1.3	0.7	0.5	0.9	0.9	1.2	0.4
Operating Margin **21**	1.5	•	•	•	0.7	•	4.3	2.8	0.8	2.7	•	0.8	1.5
Operating Margin Before Officers' Comp. **22**	2.0	1.4	•	•	2.2	•	5.5	3.5	1.3	3.6	0.1	2.0	1.8

Selected Average Balance Sheet ($ in Thousands)

Net Receivables 23	2710	0	11	•	465	594	3711	7929	14974	21888	46947	55726	842866
Inventories 24	3375	0	22	•	589	2176	2302	7883	16958	22600	45874	54004	1166105
Net Property, Plant and Equipment 25	6632	0	20	•	655	3447	5971	11165	23084	55360	153690	237792	2171057
Total Assets 26	34322	0	76	•	2088	7293	14443	34729	70531	150051	396320	1101041	13618294
Notes and Loans Payable 27	13503	0	87	•	777	2149	5456	10465	23550	46187	191562	495661	5390384
All Other Liabilities 28	10044	0	51	•	672	2886	2987	10244	14949	34913	89695	184760	4231426
Net Worth 29	10776	0	-62	•	639	2258	6001	14020	32032	68952	115063	420620	3996485

Selected Financial Ratios (Times to 1)

Current Ratio 30	1.0	•	0.8	•	1.7	1.0	1.5	1.6	1.6	1.7	1.7	1.1	0.9
Quick Ratio 31	0.4	•	0.3	•	0.8	0.4	1.0	0.8	0.8	0.7	0.9	0.5	0.3
Net Sales to Working Capital 32	161.5	•	•	•	9.8	868.6	12.1	14.2	11.3	9.1	8.2	37.0	•
Coverage Ratio 33	3.0	1.3	•	•	2.5	3.2	6.3	6.1	3.0	4.3	1.4	4.2	2.9
Total Asset Turnover 34	1.2	•	2.7	•	2.7	1.6	2.2	3.1	2.1	1.6	1.0	0.6	1.1
Inventory Turnover 35	9.2	•	6.4	•	8.0	3.9	10.6	11.1	7.3	8.5	6.2	9.2	9.4
Receivables Turnover 36	15.9	•	13.5	•	14.1	4.8	9.9	16.4	9.5	12.7	10.7	5.0	19.9
Total Liabilities to Net Worth 37	2.2	•	•	•	2.3	2.2	1.4	1.5	1.2	2.4	2.4	1.6	2.4
Current Assets to Working Capital 38	38.1	•	•	•	2.3	217.9	2.9	2.7	2.8	2.4	2.4	15.4	•
Current Liabilities to Working Capital 39	37.1	•	•	•	1.3	216.9	1.9	1.7	1.8	1.4	1.4	14.4	•
Working Capital to Net Sales 40	0.0	•	•	•	0.1	0.0	0.1	0.1	0.1	0.1	0.1	0.0	•
Inventory to Working Capital 41	15.2	•	•	•	1.2	108.0	0.9	1.3	1.3	1.0	1.0	3.0	•
Total Receipts to Cash Flow 42	11.3	10.5	•	•	15.3	8.3	9.6	11.4	13.8	11.2	7.6	7.1	11.6
Cost of Goods to Cash Flow 43	8.6	6.9	•	•	12.5	5.9	7.5	9.3	11.7	8.9	5.2	5.4	8.7
Cash Flow to Total Debt 44	0.2	•	•	•	0.3	0.3	0.4	0.5	0.3	0.3	0.2	0.1	0.1

Selected Financial Factors (in Percentages)

Debt Ratio 45	68.6	•	181.2	•	69.4	69.0	58.5	59.6	54.6	54.0	71.0	61.8	70.7
Return on Total Assets 46	8.9	•	•	•	6.0	8.1	11.5	13.3	6.0	8.3	7.1	9.6	8.9
Return on Equity Before Income Taxes 47	18.9	•	83.5	•	11.7	18.1	23.3	27.6	8.8	13.8	6.8	19.2	19.9
Return on Equity After Income Taxes 48	12.9	•	83.5	•	10.8	17.6	21.2	26.4	6.3	10.1	6.8	11.8	13.2
Profit Margin (Before Income Tax) 49	5.0	1.4	•	•	1.3	3.4	4.5	3.6	1.9	4.0	1.9	12.2	5.4
Profit Margin (After Income Tax) 50	3.4	•	•	•	1.2	3.3	4.1	3.4	1.4	2.9	1.9	7.5	3.6

Table II
Corporations with Net Income

ANIMAL FOOD AND GRAIN AND OILSEED MILLING

MONEY AMOUNTS AND SIZE OF ASSETS IN THOUSANDS OF DOLLARS

Item Description for Accounting Period 7/06 Through 6/07	Total	Zero Assets	Under 500	500 to 1,000	1,000 to 5,000	5,000 to 10,000	10,000 to 25,000	25,000 to 50,000	50,000 to 100,000	100,000 to 250,000	250,000 to 500,000	500,000 to 2,500,000	2,500,000 and over
Number of Enterprises **1**	1079	197	•	0	286	21	78	43	•	19	0	•	4
Revenues ($ in Thousands)													
Net Sales **2**	77287086	688629	•	0	1718068	336189	2763432	4216943	•	5180197	0	•	58340977
Interest **3**	585742	0	•	0	4232	616	2532	4079	•	6857	0	•	543550
Rents **4**	187855	0	•	0	262	0	140	1513	•	196	0	•	184624
Royalties **5**	257012	0	•	0	0	0	57	0	•	1136	0	•	210261
Other Portfolio Income **6**	380411	17882	•	0	2184	471	2261	1083	•	28295	0	•	175169
Other Receipts **7**	1106697	841	•	0	2754	19889	3498	33730	•	25809	0	•	968851
Total Receipts **8**	79804803	707352	•	0	1727500	357165	2771920	4257348	•	5242490	0	•	60423432
Average Total Receipts **9**	73962	3591	•	•	6040	17008	35537	99008	•	275921	•	•	15105858
Operating Costs/Operating Income (%)													
Cost of Operations **10**	75.9	56.6	•	•	83.4	72.1	78.0	79.2	•	76.3	•	•	75.1
Salaries and Wages **11**	3.2	5.2	•	•	4.2	7.0	3.9	4.6	•	3.7	•	•	3.0
Taxes Paid **12**	0.8	1.6	•	•	0.6	1.2	1.1	0.9	•	1.1	•	•	0.8
Interest Paid **13**	2.4	4.6	•	•	0.8	0.7	0.6	0.5	•	1.1	•	•	2.8
Depreciation **14**	1.7	1.3	•	•	1.1	2.9	1.9	1.7	•	2.9	•	•	1.5
Amortization and Depletion **15**	0.1	0.6	•	•	0.0	0.1	0.1	0.1	•	0.4	•	•	0.1
Pensions and Other Deferred Comp. **16**	0.4	0.2	•	•	0.1	0.8	0.2	0.4	•	0.5	•	•	0.5
Employee Benefits **17**	0.8	0.3	•	•	0.3	0.8	0.5	0.8	•	1.0	•	•	0.8
Advertising **18**	6.1	15.7	•	•	0.7	0.4	0.4	0.4	•	0.6	•	•	7.8
Other Expenses **19**	5.9	7.0	•	•	5.3	12.8	6.4	7.0	•	7.0	•	•	5.7
Officers' Compensation **20**	0.5	1.6	•	•	1.6	1.0	1.2	0.8	•	0.8	•	•	0.4
Operating Margin **21**	2.0	5.3	•	•	1.8	0.2	5.6	3.6	•	4.7	•	•	1.5
Operating Margin Before Officers' Comp. **22**	2.5	6.9	•	•	3.5	1.2	6.8	4.4	•	5.4	•	•	1.8

Selected Average Balance Sheet ($ in Thousands)

Net Receivables	23	4628	0	•	400	684	3927	7812	•	25214	•	842866
Inventories	24	5899	0	•	768	3310	2379	7493	•	21430	•	1166105
Net Property, Plant and Equipment	25	11638	0	•	648	2512	5918	11371	•	82288	•	2171057
Total Assets	26	61141	0	•	2299	7498	14665	35347	•	181663	•	13618294
Notes and Loans Payable	27	23206	0	•	838	1316	3818	9043	•	54923	•	5390384
All Other Liabilities	28	18022	0	•	721	997	3168	10212	•	42183	•	4231426
Net Worth	29	19913	0	•	741	5185	7680	16092	•	84557	•	3996485

Selected Financial Ratios (Times to 1)

Current Ratio	30	1.0	•	•	1.8	4.2	2.0	1.6	•	1.8	•	0.9
Quick Ratio	31	0.4	•	•	0.7	2.3	1.3	0.8	•	0.8	•	0.3
Net Sales to Working Capital	32	219.5	•	•	8.4	6.0	9.2	12.1	•	8.4	•	•
Coverage Ratio	33	3.3	2.8	•	3.9	10.1	11.3	9.6	•	6.1	•	2.9
Total Asset Turnover	34	1.2	•	•	2.6	2.1	2.4	2.8	•	1.5	•	1.1
Inventory Turnover	35	9.2	•	•	6.5	3.5	11.6	10.4	•	9.7	•	9.4
Receivables Turnover	36	16.3	•	•	14.2	3.6	10.9	15.5	•	14.8	•	19.9
Total Liabilities to Net Worth	37	2.1	•	•	2.1	0.4	0.9	1.2	•	1.1	•	2.4
Current Assets to Working Capital	38	52.0	•	•	2.2	1.3	2.0	2.6	•	2.3	•	•
Current Liabilities to Working Capital	39	51.0	•	•	1.2	0.3	1.0	1.6	•	1.3	•	•
Working Capital to Net Sales	40	0.0	•	•	0.1	0.2	0.1	0.1	•	0.1	•	•
Inventory to Working Capital	41	20.7	•	•	1.2	0.5	0.7	1.3	•	0.9	•	•
Total Receipts to Cash Flow	42	10.9	8.0	•	16.4	7.1	8.9	9.8	•	8.7	•	11.6
Cost of Goods to Cash Flow	43	8.2	4.5	•	13.6	5.1	6.9	7.8	•	6.6	•	8.7
Cash Flow to Total Debt	44	0.2	•	•	0.2	1.0	0.6	0.5	•	0.3	•	0.1

Selected Financial Factors (in Percentages)

Debt Ratio	45	67.4	•	•	67.8	30.8	47.6	54.5	•	53.5	•	70.7
Return on Total Assets	46	9.5	•	•	8.3	15.2	15.6	14.2	•	10.5	•	8.9
Return on Equity Before Income Taxes	47	20.4	•	•	19.2	19.9	27.2	28.0	•	18.9	•	19.9
Return on Equity After Income Taxes	48	14.3	•	•	18.2	19.5	25.3	26.9	•	15.3	•	13.2
Profit Margin (Before Income Tax)	49	5.7	8.0	•	2.4	6.4	5.9	4.6	•	5.9	•	5.4
Profit Margin (After Income Tax)	50	4.0	5.0	•	2.2	6.3	5.5	4.4	•	4.8	•	3.6

Table I

Corporations with and without Net Income

SUGAR AND CONFECTIONERY PRODUCT

MONEY AMOUNTS AND SIZE OF ASSETS IN THOUSANDS OF DOLLARS

Item Description for Accounting Period 7/06 Through 6/07		Total	Zero Assets	Under 500	500 to 1,000	1,000 to 5,000	5,000 to 10,000	10,000 to 25,000	25,000 to 50,000	50,000 to 100,000	100,000 to 250,000	250,000 to 500,000	500,000 to 2,500,000	2,500,000 and over
Number of Enterprises	1	1150	11	750	185	81	38	34	21	15	0	6	5	4
Revenues ($ in Thousands)														
Net Sales	2	42868933	14457	1008299	497470	256563	744213	1706650	1006523	1853313	0	1929200	2167611	31684634
Interest	3	363573	303	0	17	917	386	721	844	896	0	14545	31832	313112
Rents	4	56601	0	0	0	0	403	1	2905	1595	0	179	20998	30519
Royalties	5	224124	0	0	0	0	0	67	2565	2	0	7821	2613	211055
Other Portfolio Income	6	1438354	835	174	1	0	303	9966	1755	966	0	1117	16453	1406785
Other Receipts	7	567416	773	1148	2214	7	1736	10942	1925	8807	0	119455	56647	363764
Total Receipts	8	45519001	16368	1009621	499702	257487	747041	1728347	1016517	1865579	0	2072317	2296154	34009869
Average Total Receipts	9	39582	1488	1346	2701	3179	19659	50834	48406	124372	•	345386	459231	8502467
Operating Costs/Operating Income (%)														
Cost of Operations	10	52.4	77.1	68.0	58.6	55.1	66.4	82.3	76.3	68.2	•	68.1	74.3	45.7
Salaries and Wages	11	6.3	10.0	5.2	12.8	10.3	5.3	2.6	4.7	6.2	•	6.2	3.6	6.7
Taxes Paid	12	1.4	0.9	3.5	1.9	4.1	1.5	1.3	1.3	1.4	•	1.2	0.9	1.4
Interest Paid	13	3.8	1.3	0.2	1.8	0.8	1.3	0.7	2.3	1.3	•	6.9	2.8	4.3
Depreciation	14	2.3	0.9	0.8	1.7	2.1	1.4	1.4	5.1	2.2	•	3.0	4.3	2.2
Amortization and Depletion	15	1.0	8.7	0.0	1.2	•	0.0	0.1	0.3	0.3	•	1.5	0.5	1.1
Pensions and Other Deferred Comp.	16	1.0	0.4	•	1.8	1.6	0.5	0.2	0.2	0.8	•	0.7	0.6	1.1
Employee Benefits	17	1.2	0.3	•	0.6	1.9	0.4	0.3	0.9	2.0	•	1.6	0.9	1.3
Advertising	18	5.8	0.1	1.6	0.2	1.8	1.8	0.4	0.6	2.3	•	2.5	0.3	7.4
Other Expenses	19	21.9	133.4	12.9	19.5	10.1	13.0	7.6	8.0	12.8	•	14.4	14.6	25.2
Officers' Compensation	20	0.8	10.6	0.7	4.0	9.0	3.4	1.8	1.3	1.2	•	1.4	0.9	0.5
Operating Margin	21	2.1	•	7.1	•	3.2	5.2	1.1	•	1.2	•	•	•	3.1
Operating Margin Before Officers' Comp.	22	2.8	•	7.8	•	12.2	8.6	2.9	0.2	2.4	•	•	•	3.6

Selected Average Balance Sheet ($ in Thousands)

	1	2	3	4	5	6	7	8	9	10	11	12	13
Net Receivables 23	7278	0	51	391	342	1412	4157	4553	14435	•	46957	165860	1653326
Inventories 24	3405	0	29	272	570	1641	4785	5766	22279	•	52234	69660	594567
Net Property, Plant and Equipment 25	8191	0	14	161	385	2844	5583	15506	20915	•	87278	281114	1620443
Total Assets 26	48741	220	894	1907	8170	18402	33541	74362	349958	•		883922	11573042
Notes and Loans Payable 27	21011	0	4	830	299	2970	4306	15305	20973	•	243606	179941	5181266
All Other Liabilities 28	14753	0	87	382	167	1656	5935	6182	19188	•	10448	237223	3721282
Net Worth 29	12978	0	129	-319	1441	3544	8161	12054	34201	•	95903	466759	2670495

Selected Financial Ratios (Times to 1)

	1	2	3	4	5	6	7	8	9	10	11	12	13
Current Ratio 30	0.8	•	2.4	1.3	4.3	1.8	1.6	1.3	1.7	•	1.2	1.6	0.7
Quick Ratio 31	0.5	•	2.1	0.8	2.5	1.0	0.9	0.6	0.7	•	0.6	0.8	0.4
Net Sales to Working Capital 32	•	•	11.3	16.1	3.4	11.2	12.0	14.3	7.0	•	11.9	3.4	•
Coverage Ratio 33	3.5	•	44.0	•	5.3	5.4	4.3	1.0	2.4	•	1.1	1.8	3.8
Total Asset Turnover 34	0.8	•	6.1	3.0	1.7	2.4	2.7	1.4	1.7	•	0.9	0.5	0.7
Inventory Turnover 35	5.7	•	31.1	5.8	3.1	7.9	8.6	6.3	3.8	•	4.2	4.6	6.1
Receivables Turnover 36	5.3	•	17.0	6.9	6.6	14.3	11.8	11.2	8.8	•	7.5	2.6	5.0
Total Liabilities to Net Worth 37	2.8	•	0.7	•	0.3	1.3	1.3	1.8	1.2	•	2.6	0.9	3.3
Current Assets to Working Capital 38	•	•	1.7	4.3	1.3	2.2	2.7	4.6	2.4	•	5.6	2.7	•
Current Liabilities to Working Capital 39	•	•	0.7	3.3	0.3	1.2	1.7	3.6	1.4	•	4.6	1.7	•
Working Capital to Net Sales 40	•	•	0.1	0.1	0.3	0.1	0.1	0.1	0.1	•	0.1	0.3	•
Inventory to Working Capital 41	•	•	0.2	1.6	0.5	0.9	1.1	2.1	1.2	•	2.4	0.6	•
Total Receipts to Cash Flow 42	3.8	•	7.2	9.5	11.6	5.8	11.8	16.4	7.8	•	8.1	6.7	3.2
Cost of Goods to Cash Flow 43	2.0	•	4.9	5.6	6.4	3.8	9.7	12.5	5.3	•	5.5	5.0	1.4
Cash Flow to Total Debt 44	0.3	•	2.1	0.2	0.6	0.7	0.4	0.1	0.4	•	0.2	0.2	0.3

Selected Financial Factors (in Percentages)

	1	2	3	4	5	6	7	8	9	10	11	12	13
Debt Ratio 45	73.4	•	41.2	135.6	24.4	56.6	55.7	64.1	54.0	•	72.6	47.2	76.9
Return on Total Assets 46	10.2	•	45.3	•	7.4	16.4	8.4	3.2	5.4	•	6.8	2.5	11.2
Return on Equity Before Income Taxes 47	27.3	•	75.3	31.1	7.9	30.8	14.6	•	6.8	•	1.8	2.1	36.1
Return on Equity After Income Taxes 48	19.1	•	75.3	33.6	4.5	25.2	12.6	•	6.6	•	0.1	0.8	25.2
Profit Margin (Before Income Tax) 49	9.5	•	7.2	•	3.6	5.6	2.4	•	1.9	•	0.5	2.3	12.2
Profit Margin (After Income Tax) 50	6.6	•	7.2	•	2.1	4.6	2.0	•	1.8	•	0.0	0.8	8.5

Table II
Corporations with Net Income

SUGAR AND CONFECTIONERY PRODUCT

MONEY AMOUNTS AND SIZE OF ASSETS IN THOUSANDS OF DOLLARS

Item Description for Accounting Period 7/06 Through 6/07	Total	Zero Assets	Under 500	500 to 1,000	1,000 to 5,000	5,000 to 10,000	10,000 to 25,000	25,000 to 50,000	50,000 to 100,000	100,000 to 250,000	250,000 to 500,000	500,000 to 2,500,000	2,500,000 and over
Number of Enterprises **1**	976	•	750	108	19	38	26	12	12	0	•	•	4
Revenues ($ in Thousands)													
Net Sales **2**	40133651	•	1008299	312331	147629	744213	1567292	676284	1588858	0	•	•	31684634
Interest **3**	355558	•	0	0	812	386	186	327	708	0	•	•	313112
Rents **4**	56258	•	0	0	0	403	1	2905	1595	0	•	•	30519
Royalties **5**	224124	•	0	0	0	0	67	2565	2	0	•	•	211055
Other Portfolio Income **6**	1432967	•	174	0	0	303	5716	1755	682	0	•	•	1406785
Other Receipts **7**	531111	•	1148	2212	7	1736	10684	1103	7811	0	•	•	363764
Total Receipts **8**	42733669	•	1009621	314543	148448	747041	1583946	684939	1599656	0	•	•	34009869
Average Total Receipts **9**	43784	•	1346	2912	7813	19659	60921	57078	133305	•	•	•	8502467
Operating Costs/Operating Income (%)													
Cost of Operations **10**	50.8	•	68.0	67.9	49.1	66.4	82.0	77.6	67.5	•	•	•	45.7
Salaries and Wages **11**	6.4	•	5.2	8.3	17.8	5.3	2.4	5.3	6.3	•	•	•	6.7
Taxes Paid **12**	1.5	•	3.5	1.0	4.2	1.5	1.2	1.2	1.4	•	•	•	1.4
Interest Paid **13**	3.7	•	0.2	0.2	0.3	1.3	0.6	1.8	0.9	•	•	•	4.3
Depreciation **14**	2.2	•	0.8	0.5	2.6	1.4	0.9	2.5	2.2	•	•	•	2.2
Amortization and Depletion **15**	0.9	•	0.0	0.1	•	0.0	0.0	0.3	0.1	•	•	•	1.1
Pensions and Other Deferred Comp. **16**	1.0	•	•	2.9	1.1	0.5	0.2	0.2	0.9	•	•	•	1.1
Employee Benefits **17**	1.3	•	•	1.0	2.2	0.4	0.2	1.0	2.2	•	•	•	1.3
Advertising **18**	6.1	•	1.6	0.1	2.4	1.8	0.4	0.5	1.7	•	•	•	7.4
Other Expenses **19**	22.6	•	12.9	12.0	10.2	13.0	7.0	6.9	13.2	•	•	•	25.2
Officers' Compensation **20**	0.7	•	0.7	4.4	2.6	3.4	1.7	0.9	1.2	•	•	•	0.5
Operating Margin **21**	3.0	•	7.1	1.6	7.3	5.2	3.3	1.7	2.5	•	•	•	3.1
Operating Margin Before Officers' Comp. **22**	3.7	•	7.8	6.0	9.9	8.6	5.0	2.6	3.7	•	•	•	3.6

Selected Average Balance Sheet ($ in Thousands)

Net Receivables 23	7705	•	51	629	582	1412	4482	5318	14720	•	1653326
Inventories 24	3521	•	29	214	1705	5794	7049	20799		•	594567
Net Property, Plant and Equipment 25	8389	•	14	44	668	2844	5694	13812	22871	•	1620443
Total Assets 26	53624	•	220	965	4594	8170	20200	33434	76578	•	11573042
Notes and Loans Payable 27	22676	•	4	175	385	2970	3924	13386	15479	•	5181266
All Other Liabilities 28	16012	•	87	331	247	1656	6775	6913	19894	•	3721282
Net Worth 29	14936	•	129	459	3963	3544	9501	13135	41205	•	2670495

Selected Financial Ratios (Times to 1)

Current Ratio 30	0.8	•	2.4	2.5	13.0	1.8	1.6	1.3	1.8	•	0.7
Quick Ratio 31	0.5	•	2.1	1.9	7.5	1.0	0.8	0.5	0.7	•	0.4
Net Sales to Working Capital 32	•	•	11.3	5.4	3.2	11.2	12.9	14.6	6.7	•	3.8
Coverage Ratio 33	3.9	•	44.0	11.2	23.9	5.4	8.4	2.7	4.6	•	3.8
Total Asset Turnover 34	0.8	•	6.1	3.0	1.7	2.4	3.0	1.7	1.7	•	0.7
Inventory Turnover 35	5.9	•	31.1	9.2	2.2	8.2	8.5	6.2	4.3	•	6.1
Receivables Turnover 36	5.6	•	17.0	•	6.8	14.4	12.5	10.2	10.5	•	5.0
Total Liabilities to Net Worth 37	2.6	•	0.7	1.1	0.2	1.3	1.1	1.5	0.9	•	3.3
Current Assets to Working Capital 38	•	•	1.7	1.7	1.1	2.2	2.7	4.2	2.3	•	•
Current Liabilities to Working Capital 39	0.7	•	0.7	0.7	0.1	1.2	1.7	3.2	1.3	•	•
Working Capital to Net Sales 40	•	•	0.1	0.2	0.3	0.1	0.1	0.1	0.2	•	•
Inventory to Working Capital 41	•	•	0.2	0.4	0.5	0.9	1.2	2.2	1.2	•	•
Total Receipts to Cash Flow 42	3.5	•	7.2	8.3	7.8	5.8	9.9	12.6	6.9	•	3.2
Cost of Goods to Cash Flow 43	1.8	•	4.9	5.6	3.8	3.8	8.1	9.7	4.7	•	1.4
Cash Flow to Total Debt 44	0.3	•	2.1	0.7	1.6	0.7	0.6	0.2	0.5	•	0.3

Selected Financial Factors (in Percentages)

Debt Ratio 45	72.1	•	41.2	52.4	13.7	56.6	53.0	60.7	46.2	•	76.9
Return on Total Assets 46	11.1	•	45.3	7.4	13.9	16.4	14.7	7.9	7.0	•	11.2
Return on Equity Before Income Taxes 47	29.7	•	75.3	14.3	15.4	30.8	27.6	12.6	10.2	•	36.1
Return on Equity After Income Taxes 48	21.3	•	75.3	11.3	10.2	25.2	25.3	11.7	9.9	•	25.2
Profit Margin (Before Income Tax) 49	10.8	•	7.2	2.3	7.9	5.6	4.3	2.9	3.2	•	12.2
Profit Margin (After Income Tax) 50	7.7	•	7.2	1.8	5.2	4.6	4.0	2.7	3.1	•	8.5

40

Table I

Corporations with and without Net Income

FRUIT AND VEGETABLE PRESERVING AND SPECIALITY FOOD

MONEY AMOUNTS AND SIZE OF ASSETS IN THOUSANDS OF DOLLARS

Item Description for Accounting Period 7/06 Through 6/07	Total	Zero Assets	Under 500	500 to 1,000	1,000 to 5,000	5,000 to 10,000	10,000 to 25,000	25,000 to 50,000	50,000 to 100,000	100,000 to 250,000	250,000 to 500,000	500,000 to 2,500,000	2,500,000 and over
Number of Enterprises 1	1097	458	270	0	181	20	86	25	26	16	4	7	4
Revenues ($ in Thousands)													
Net Sales 2	37795122	125699	92956	0	954179	242474	2672061	1452495	3155366	4437823	1918867	10556830	12186573
Interest 3	129015	289	178	0	532	179	1033	3948	3650	7597	3516	34175	73918
Rents 4	21632	0	1	0	2924	0	1101	181	4630	6003	404	5566	821
Royalties 5	261756	0	0	0	0	0	0	0	101	0	0	52139	209516
Other Portfolio Income 6	2056347	6	6153	0	0	0	1923	35566	613	43885	4089	74144	1889969
Other Receipts 7	606036	278	297	0	2866	284	7926	18063	27407	27203	27777	102159	391775
Total Receipts 8	40869908	126272	99585	0	960501	242937	2684044	1510253	3191767	4522511	1954453	10825013	14752572
Average Total Receipts 9	37256	276	369	•	5307	12147	31210	60410	122760	282657	488613	1546430	3688143
Operating Costs/Operating Income (%)													
Cost of Operations 10	66.8	78.5	38.6	•	79.4	81.7	74.2	76.5	76.5	77.6	69.3	68.6	54.6
Salaries and Wages 11	5.6	17.1	25.9	•	0.8	4.1	5.4	3.3	3.2	3.2	4.1	8.4	5.2
Taxes Paid 12	1.2	2.1	2.5	•	2.1	1.4	1.0	1.9	1.1	1.9	0.9	1.7	0.5
Interest Paid 13	2.7	6.4	1.0	•	0.9	0.7	1.3	1.8	2.1	1.3	1.4	2.4	4.3
Depreciation 14	2.3	0.9	6.4	•	2.0	0.8	2.0	1.6	1.8	2.1	3.3	2.6	2.2
Amortization and Depletion 15	1.1	0.1	0.2	•	0.7	2.0	0.3	0.3	0.4	0.1	0.5	1.7	1.7
Pensions and Other Deferred Comp. 16	0.5	0.0	0.1	•	0.7	0.0	0.3	0.2	0.5	0.3	0.1	0.7	0.5
Employee Benefits 17	1.2	0.6	0.3	•	1.5	1.1	0.8	1.1	1.4	0.7	1.5	1.7	0.8
Advertising 18	2.6	2.0	0.0	•	0.5	1.3	2.2	0.7	0.7	0.5	3.2	3.7	3.3
Other Expenses 19	14.5	15.2	49.6	•	4.0	14.1	9.3	9.6	9.5	10.2	11.8	9.8	24.3
Officers' Compensation 20	0.8	0.4	2.4	•	4.4	3.4	1.3	1.4	0.8	0.8	0.5	0.2	0.7
Operating Margin 21	0.8	•	•	•	3.0	•	1.9	1.6	2.0	1.4	3.4	•	2.0
Operating Margin Before Officers' Comp. 22	1.6	•	•	•	7.4	•	3.2	3.0	2.8	2.2	3.9	•	2.7

Selected Average Balance Sheet ($ in Thousands)

Net Receivables 23	3896	0	1	•	299	1211	3331	6830	12614	22204	36759	95913	559001
Inventories 24	5340	0	0	•	558	2267	6368	10052	27779	65113	56628	199528	381352
Net Property, Plant and Equipment 25	6570	0	1	•	652	393	4124	10393	19090	57550	124411	314837	587014
Total Assets 26	40198	0	239	•	2195	6083	16567	36928	71146	163966	338245	1282367	6590652
Notes and Loans Payable 27	10985	0	220	•	543	5081	5493	14594	30821	52316	92086	510243	1344023
All Other Liabilities 28	8867	0	1	•	377	2031	6404	8068	17772	44144	89642	280981	1342877
Net Worth 29	20345	0	18	•	1275	-1030	4671	14267	22553	67506	156517	491143	3903752

Selected Financial Ratios (Times to 1)

Current Ratio 30	1.4	14.4	•	1.9	1.3	1.3	1.7	1.5	1.8	1.3	2.1	1.0
Quick Ratio 31	0.6	13.2	•	0.9	0.4	0.5	0.7	0.5	0.5	0.5	0.8	0.6
Net Sales to Working Capital 32	12.0	17.7	•	11.3	13.3	14.5	7.1	8.0	6.7	13.8	7.3	422.3
Coverage Ratio 33	5.0	•	•	5.1	•	2.7	4.1	2.5	3.5	4.8	1.5	7.6
Total Asset Turnover 34	0.9	1.4	•	2.4	2.0	1.9	1.6	1.7	1.7	1.4	1.2	0.5
Inventory Turnover 35	4.3	1355.5	•	7.5	4.4	3.6	4.4	3.3	3.3	5.9	5.2	4.4
Receivables Turnover 36	8.6	25.6	•	17.0	11.6	8.2	9.1	9.3	12.4	15.7	17.7	5.1
Total Liabilities to Net Worth 37	1.0	12.2	•	0.7	•	2.5	1.6	2.2	1.4	1.2	1.6	0.7
Current Assets to Working Capital 38	3.8	1.1	•	2.1	4.3	5.0	2.5	2.8	2.3	4.2	1.9	152.8
Current Liabilities to Working Capital 39	2.8	0.1	•	1.1	3.3	4.0	1.5	1.8	1.3	3.2	0.9	151.8
Working Capital to Net Sales 40	0.1	0.1	•	0.1	0.1	0.1	0.1	0.1	0.1	0.1	0.1	0.0
Inventory to Working Capital 41	1.9	0.0	•	1.1	2.7	2.8	1.3	1.8	1.5	2.2	1.0	53.3
Total Receipts to Cash Flow 42	4.7	4.1	•	18.8	122.2	10.2	9.1	9.2	9.4	6.2	12.5	2.2
Cost of Goods to Cash Flow 43	3.1	1.6	•	14.9	99.8	7.5	6.9	7.0	7.3	4.3	8.6	1.2
Cash Flow to Total Debt 44	0.4	0.4	•	0.3	0.0	0.3	0.3	0.3	0.3	0.4	0.2	0.5

Selected Financial Factors (in Percentages)

Debt Ratio 45	49.4	92.4	•	41.9	116.9	71.8	61.4	68.3	58.8	53.7	61.7	40.8
Return on Total Assets 46	11.3	•	•	11.0	•	6.9	11.6	9.1	7.9	9.3	4.2	14.9
Return on Equity Before Income Taxes 47	17.9	•	•	15.3	122.7	15.6	22.6	17.1	13.7	15.9	3.5	21.9
Return on Equity After Income Taxes 48	14.4	•	•	15.1	123.4	14.1	16.2	14.5	10.6	10.7	2.2	18.0
Profit Margin (Before Income Tax) 49	10.6	3.7	•	3.7	•	2.3	5.5	3.2	3.3	5.2	1.1	28.1
Profit Margin (After Income Tax) 50	8.5	3.7	•	3.7	•	2.1	4.0	2.7	2.6	3.5	0.7	23.0

41

Table II
Corporations with Net Income

FRUIT AND VEGETABLE PRESERVING AND SPECIALTY FOOD

Money Amounts and Size of Assets in Thousands of Dollars

Item Description for Accounting Period 7/06 Through 6/07	Total	Zero Assets	Under 500	500 to 1,000	1,000 to 5,000	5,000 to 10,000	10,000 to 25,000	25,000 to 50,000	50,000 to 100,000	100,000 to 250,000	250,000 to 500,000	500,000 to 2,500,000	2,500,000 and over
Number of Enterprises **1**	311	•	•	0	148	9	50	16	20	13	4	•	4
Revenues ($ in Thousands)													
Net Sales **2**	32494954	•	•	0	818298	148298	1710202	873442	2343678	3679616	1918667	•	12186573
Interest **3**	119446	•	•	0	532	172	690	2471	1266	3919	3516	•	73918
Rents **4**	16665	•	•	0	2924	0	39	147	761	6003	404	•	821
Royalties **5**	261445	•	•	0	0	0	0	0	0	0	0	•	209516
Other Portfolio Income **6**	2048309	•	•	0	0	0	198	35551	586	43774	4089	•	1889969
Other Receipts **7**	582074	•	•	0	2866	0	5259	14295	12245	25659	27777	•	391775
Total Receipts **8**	35522893	•	•	0	824620	148470	1716388	925906	2358536	3758971	1954453	•	14752572
Average Total Receipts **9**	114222	•	•	•	5572	16497	34328	57869	117927	289152	488613	•	3688143
Operating Costs/Operating Income (%)													
Cost of Operations **10**	65.1	•	•	•	79.9	81.0	70.9	73.4	75.7	76.9	69.3	•	54.6
Salaries and Wages **11**	5.8	•	•	•	0.6	0.8	6.2	2.9	2.2	3.6	4.1	•	5.2
Taxes Paid **12**	1.3	•	•	•	2.0	1.4	1.0	2.5	1.0	2.1	0.9	•	0.5
Interest Paid **13**	2.4	•	•	•	0.8	0.8	0.9	0.8	1.7	1.0	1.4	•	4.3
Depreciation **14**	2.3	•	•	•	1.9	0.3	2.5	1.6	2.0	2.0	3.3	•	2.2
Amortization and Depletion **15**	0.9	•	•	•	0.8	•	0.1	0.0	0.3	0.1	0.5	•	1.7
Pensions and Other Deferred Comp. **16**	0.5	•	•	•	0.9	0.0	0.4	0.3	0.7	0.3	0.1	•	0.5
Employee Benefits **17**	1.2	•	•	•	1.4	1.0	0.8	1.4	1.4	0.7	1.5	•	0.8
Advertising **18**	2.8	•	•	•	0.3	•	2.8	0.8	0.6	0.5	3.2	•	3.3
Other Expenses **19**	15.2	•	•	•	2.7	10.5	8.0	9.7	9.2	9.9	11.8	•	24.3
Officers' Compensation **20**	0.8	•	•	•	5.1	4.0	1.3	1.8	0.8	0.9	0.5	•	0.7
Operating Margin **21**	1.7	•	•	•	3.7	0.3	5.1	4.7	4.3	2.1	3.4	•	2.0
Operating Margin Before Officers' Comp. **22**	2.4	•	•	•	8.9	4.3	6.4	6.5	5.1	2.9	3.9	•	2.7

Selected Average Balance Sheet ($ in Thousands)

Net Receivables 23	12204	285	1563	3103	7520	12319	21399	36759	559001
Inventories 24	15681	485	4243	8447	11116	28545	63346	56628	384800
Net Property, Plant and Equipment 25	20595	625	248	4718	10296	20729	56815	124411	587014
Total Assets 26	127477	2232	6123	17791	34419	71713	160908	338245	6590652
Notes and Loans Payable 27	31029	467	2967	4729	9921	25893	51651	92086	1344023
All Other Liabilities 28	27575	400	2026	6391	8441	16632	42681	89642	1342877
Net Worth 29	68873	1366	1130	6671	16056	29188	66576	156517	3903752

Selected Financial Ratios (Times to 1)

Current Ratio 30	1.3	2.3	1.4	1.4	1.7	1.6	1.6	1.3	1.0
Quick Ratio 31	0.6	1.2	0.4	0.5	0.9	0.5	0.4	0.5	0.6
Net Sales to Working Capital 32	12.5	10.4	9.4	9.7	6.3	7.3	8.0	13.8	422.3
Coverage Ratio 33	6.4	6.9	1.5	6.8	13.9	3.9	5.3	4.8	7.6
Total Asset Turnover 34	0.8	2.5	2.7	1.9	1.6	1.6	1.8	1.4	0.5
Inventory Turnover 35	4.3	9.1	3.1	2.9	3.6	3.1	3.4	5.9	4.3
Receivables Turnover 36	8.5	22.5	•	7.0	6.9	9.4	13.0	15.7	•
Total Liabilities to Net Worth 37	0.9	0.6	4.4	1.7	1.1	1.5	1.4	1.2	0.7
Current Assets to Working Capital 38	4.0	1.8	3.3	3.4	2.4	2.7	2.6	4.2	152.8
Current Liabilities to Working Capital 39	3.0	0.8	2.3	2.4	1.4	1.7	1.6	3.2	151.8
Working Capital to Net Sales 40	0.1	0.1	0.1	0.1	0.2	0.1	0.1	0.1	0.0
Inventory to Working Capital 41	1.9	0.9	2.4	2.0	1.1	1.7	1.6	2.2	53.3
Total Receipts to Cash Flow 42	4.2	18.2	14.1	8.6	6.9	7.9	9.1	6.2	2.2
Cost of Goods to Cash Flow 43	2.7	14.5	11.4	6.1	5.1	6.0	7.0	4.3	1.2
Cash Flow to Total Debt 44	0.4	0.4	0.2	0.4	0.4	0.4	0.3	0.4	0.5

Selected Financial Factors (in Percentages)

Debt Ratio 45	46.0	38.8	81.5	62.5	53.4	59.3	58.6	53.7	40.8
Return on Total Assets 46	12.5	13.0	3.1	12.3	18.2	10.9	9.2	9.3	14.9
Return on Equity Before Income Taxes 47	19.5	18.3	5.9	28.0	36.3	20.0	18.0	15.9	21.9
Return on Equity After Income Taxes 48	16.0	18.0	4.3	26.3	27.3	17.3	14.1	10.7	18.0
Profit Margin (Before Income Tax) 49	12.9	4.5	0.4	5.5	10.7	5.0	4.2	5.2	28.1
Profit Margin (After Income Tax) 50	10.5	4.5	0.3	5.1	8.0	4.3	3.3	3.5	23.0

Table I

Corporations with and without Net Income

DAIRY PRODUCT

MONEY AMOUNTS AND SIZE OF ASSETS IN THOUSANDS OF DOLLARS

Item Description for Accounting Period 7/06 Through 6/07		Total	Zero Assets	Under 500	500 to 1,000	1,000 to 5,000	5,000 to 10,000	10,000 to 25,000	25,000 to 50,000	50,000 to 100,000	100,000 to 250,000	250,000 to 500,000	500,000 to 2,500,000	2,500,000 and over
Number of Enterprises	1	640	93	277	5	89	80	38	22	17	7	6	6	0
Revenues ($ in Thousands)														
Net Sales	2	30075528	17320	130581	105562	1135626	2012334	1385814	2120630	2444600	2179073	3687564	14856424	0
Interest	3	65064	1	0	0	831	1681	512	1726	7375	7549	20256	25133	0
Rents	4	4593	0	0	0	0	1254	762	45	515	127	0	1891	0
Royalties	5	13331	0	0	0	0	0	0	0	2941	0	0	10390	0
Other Portfolio Income	6	53712	0	2570	124	4258	1028	3246	6158	1348	1238	19757	13987	0
Other Receipts	7	226171	289	0	0	779	2200	2578	33134	8841	11658	25684	141006	0
Total Receipts	8	30438399	17610	133151	105686	1141494	2018497	1392912	2161693	2465620	2199645	3753261	15048831	0
Average Total Receipts	9	47560	189	481	21137	12826	25231	36656	98259	145036	314235	625544	2508138	•
Operating Costs/Operating Income (%)														
Cost of Operations	10	77.1	•	42.4	85.4	85.5	78.6	72.3	75.2	74.2	80.2	81.2	76.4	•
Salaries and Wages	11	5.0	•	18.7	8.2	3.6	3.3	7.2	7.0	6.0	3.6	2.8	5.2	•
Taxes Paid	12	1.1	0.0	6.9	0.3	1.4	1.3	1.7	1.4	1.0	1.0	0.8	0.9	•
Interest Paid	13	1.5	•	0.4	1.7	0.9	0.3	1.1	0.7	1.3	0.2	1.9	2.0	•
Depreciation	14	1.6	32.0	1.3	0.9	1.6	1.4	1.5	1.9	2.1	1.3	2.4	1.4	•
Amortization and Depletion	15	0.4	•	•	0.1	•	0.0	0.1	0.1	0.1	0.0	0.1	0.8	•
Pensions and Other Deferred Comp.	16	0.4	•	1.9	•	0.2	0.2	0.4	0.9	0.4	0.4	0.3	0.4	•
Employee Benefits	17	0.9	•	2.4	•	1.0	0.8	0.7	1.1	1.0	1.3	1.0	0.8	•
Advertising	18	1.5	•	1.7	0.9	0.1	0.8	0.8	0.7	1.2	1.0	1.8	2.0	•
Other Expenses	19	8.0	133.3	21.9	5.2	4.9	7.0	10.7	9.7	7.1	5.2	9.4	7.8	•
Officers' Compensation	20	1.0	•	5.5	0.1	1.2	2.4	1.9	0.6	0.7	0.6	0.3	0.9	•
Operating Margin	21	1.5	•	•	•	•	3.9	1.5	0.7	5.0	5.3	•	1.3	•
Operating Margin Before Officers' Comp.	22	2.4	•	2.5	•	0.8	6.2	3.4	1.3	5.7	5.9	•	2.2	•

Selected Average Balance Sheet ($ in Thousands)

		1	2	3	4	5	6	7	8	9	10	11	12
Net Receivables	23	3782	0	18	67	863	1910	3168	8278	11959	21121	50998	204390
Inventories	24	3310	0	3	105	763	1270	4877	5824	12984	28807	38457	163567
Net Property, Plant and Equipment	25	9724	0	52	0	1002	2367	6675	16961	23482	37047	118091	656134
Total Assets	26	33789	0	146	614	3195	6581	18341	36664	75660	162479	336648	2470541
Notes and Loans Payable	27	15306	0	97	0	1204	1002	6927	9032	22605	39546	161919	1247873
All Other Liabilities	28	9023	0	14	3	799	2083	4347	9711	15024	32638	102284	676080
Net Worth	29	9460	0	35	611	1192	3496	7067	17921	38031	90296	72446	546588

Selected Financial Ratios (Times to 1)

		1	2	3	4	5	6	7	8	9	10	11	12
Current Ratio	30	1.4	•	0.9	219.1	1.6	1.9	1.9	1.2	2.1	2.6	1.5	1.2
Quick Ratio	31	0.7	•	0.9	180.8	0.9	1.1	0.7	0.8	1.1	1.7	0.7	0.6
Net Sales to Working Capital	32	15.8	•	•	34.6	17.7	13.3	7.2	37.5	7.9	6.2	14.4	28.3
Coverage Ratio	33	2.8	•	•	•	1.2	17.3	2.7	4.9	5.7	33.5	0.9	2.2
Total Asset Turnover	34	1.4	•	3.2	34.4	4.0	3.8	2.0	2.6	1.9	1.9	1.8	1.0
Inventory Turnover	35	10.9	•	65.2	171.5	14.3	15.6	5.4	12.4	8.2	8.7	13.0	11.6
Receivables Turnover	36	11.8	•	29.2	630.2	14.3	13.2	9.9	10.2	10.8	11.2	14.4	11.4
Total Liabilities to Net Worth	37	2.6	•	3.2	0.0	1.7	0.9	1.6	1.0	1.0	0.8	3.6	3.5
Current Assets to Working Capital	38	3.4	•	•	1.0	2.8	2.2	2.1	5.6	1.9	1.6	3.1	6.2
Current Liabilities to Working Capital	39	2.4	•	•	0.0	1.8	1.2	1.1	4.6	0.9	0.6	2.1	5.2
Working Capital to Net Sales	40	0.1	•	0.0	0.0	0.1	0.1	0.1	0.0	0.1	0.2	0.1	0.0
Inventory to Working Capital	41	1.1	•	•	0.2	1.0	0.8	1.0	1.5	0.7	0.5	1.0	1.8
Total Receipts to Cash Flow	42	11.2	4.1	6.6	41.5	29.5	10.3	9.4	9.2	8.7	9.4	13.2	11.8
Cost of Goods to Cash Flow	43	8.6	•	2.8	35.4	25.2	8.1	6.8	6.9	6.5	7.5	10.7	9.0
Cash Flow to Total Debt	44	0.2	•	0.6	181.9	0.2	0.8	0.3	0.6	0.4	0.5	0.2	0.1

Selected Financial Factors (in Percentages)

		1	2	3	4	5	6	7	8	9	10	11
Debt Ratio	45	72.0	76.1	0.5	62.7	46.9	61.5	51.1	49.7	44.4	78.5	77.9
Return on Total Assets	46	5.8	•	•	4.0	16.9	6.0	8.8	13.5	12.3	3.1	4.5
Return on Equity Before Income Taxes	47	13.1	•	•	1.6	29.9	9.9	14.3	22.1	21.5	•	11.2
Return on Equity After Income Taxes	48	9.8	•	•	0.8	22.8	9.1	11.3	17.7	20.1	•	7.4
Profit Margin (Before Income Tax)	49	2.6	•	•	0.1	4.2	1.9	2.7	5.8	6.2	•	2.5
Profit Margin (After Income Tax)	50	2.0	•	•	0.1	3.2	1.8	2.1	4.7	5.8	•	1.6

Table II

Corporations with Net Income

DAIRY PRODUCT

MONEY AMOUNTS AND SIZE OF ASSETS IN THOUSANDS OF DOLLARS

Item Description for Accounting Period 7/06 Through 6/07	Total	Zero Assets	Under 500	500 to 1,000	1,000 to 5,000	5,000 to 10,000	10,000 to 25,000	25,000 to 50,000	50,000 to 100,000	100,000 to 250,000	250,000 to 500,000	500,000 to 2,500,000	2,500,000 and over
Number of Enterprises **1**	218	0	0	0	71	70	33	14	•	•	3	•	0
Revenues ($ in Thousands)													
Net Sales **2**	23380228	0	0	0	788512	1864519	1104760	1590959	•	•	1495357	•	0
Interest **3**	63021	0	0	0	775	1473	190	1571	•	•	19132	•	0
Rents **4**	3881	0	0	0	0	1254	303	45	•	•	0	•	0
Royalties **5**	13320	0	0	0	0	0	0	0	•	•	0	•	0
Other Portfolio Income **6**	25733	0	0	0	3248	937	3205	1712	•	•	58	•	0
Other Receipts **7**	200059	0	0	0	620	2134	2366	31590	•	•	11834	•	0
Total Receipts **8**	23686242	0	0	0	793155	1870317	1110824	1625877	•	•	1526381	•	0
Average Total Receipts **9**	108652	•	•	•	11171	26719	33661	116134	•	•	508794	•	•
Operating Costs/Operating Income (%)													
Cost of Operations **10**	75.5	•	•	•	82.3	77.8	72.6	73.9	•	•	84.1	•	•
Salaries and Wages **11**	5.2	•	•	•	4.3	3.2	6.3	6.9	•	•	1.6	•	•
Taxes Paid **12**	1.1	•	•	•	1.5	1.4	1.6	1.4	•	•	0.6	•	•
Interest Paid **13**	1.6	•	•	•	0.8	0.3	1.0	0.4	•	•	1.7	•	•
Depreciation **14**	1.5	•	•	•	1.9	1.4	1.3	1.9	•	•	2.0	•	•
Amortization and Depletion **15**	0.5	•	•	•	•	0.0	0.0	0.1	•	•	0.2	•	•
Pensions and Other Deferred Comp. **16**	0.4	•	•	•	0.4	0.2	0.1	0.9	•	•	0.2	•	•
Employee Benefits **17**	0.9	•	•	•	1.4	0.8	0.4	0.8	•	•	0.8	•	•
Advertising **18**	1.7	•	•	•	0.1	0.8	0.7	0.6	•	•	1.5	•	•
Other Expenses **19**	8.1	•	•	•	5.7	7.3	10.8	10.3	•	•	7.1	•	•
Officers' Compensation **20**	0.9	•	•	•	1.5	2.6	2.3	0.6	•	•	0.4	•	•
Operating Margin **21**	2.6	•	•	•	0.0	4.3	2.9	2.3	•	•	2.9	•	•
Operating Margin Before Officers' Comp. **22**	3.5	•	•	•	1.5	6.8	5.2	2.9	•	•	0.4	•	•

Selected Average Balance Sheet ($ in Thousands)

Net Receivables 23	8522	801	1956	3092	9078	44832
Inventories 24	7417	883	1137	5068	6347	54648
Net Property, Plant and Equipment 25	20118	825	2236	6578	16033	82980
Total Assets 26	66646	3039	6491	17674	35525	346257
Notes and Loans Payable 27	23516	768	1144	6651	6517	138268
All Other Liabilities 28	19339	768	2187	4614	8982	94187
Net Worth 29	23791	1503	3161	6409	20027	113803

Selected Financial Ratios (Times to 1)

Current Ratio 30	1.6	2.1	1.7	2.0	1.3	1.4
Quick Ratio 31	0.8	1.2	1.1	0.7	0.9	0.6
Net Sales to Working Capital 32	12.8	10.2	15.4	6.0	27.1	13.0
Coverage Ratio 33	3.5	1.7	17.7	4.4	13.4	2.2
Total Asset Turnover 34	1.6	3.7	4.1	1.9	3.2	1.4
Inventory Turnover 35	10.9	10.4	18.2	4.8	13.2	7.7
Receivables Turnover 36	11.2	11.3	13.5	9.2	11.1	8.8
Total Liabilities to Net Worth 37	1.8	1.0	1.1	1.8	0.8	2.0
Current Assets to Working Capital 38	2.8	1.9	2.4	2.0	3.9	3.5
Current Liabilities to Working Capital 39	1.8	0.9	1.4	1.0	2.9	2.5
Working Capital to Net Sales 40	0.1	0.1	0.1	0.2	0.0	0.1
Inventory to Working Capital 41	0.8	0.7	0.8	1.0	1.1	1.0
Total Receipts to Cash Flow 42	9.7	21.4	9.7	8.3	7.5	12.1
Cost of Goods to Cash Flow 43	7.3	17.6	7.6	6.0	5.5	10.2
Cash Flow to Total Debt 44	0.3	0.3	0.8	0.4	1.0	0.2

Selected Financial Factors (in Percentages)

Debt Ratio 45	64.3	50.5	51.3	63.7	43.6	67.1
Return on Total Assets 46	8.7	5.2	19.8	8.3	15.6	5.3
Return on Equity Before Income Taxes 47	17.5	4.5	38.4	17.5	25.6	8.7
Return on Equity After Income Taxes 48	13.6	3.7	29.4	16.5	21.4	8.2
Profit Margin (Before Income Tax) 49	3.9	0.6	4.6	3.4	4.5	2.0
Profit Margin (After Income Tax) 50	3.0	0.5	3.5	3.2	3.8	1.9

Table I

Corporations with and without Net Income

MEAT AND SEAFOOD PROCESSING

MONEY AMOUNTS AND SIZE OF ASSETS IN THOUSANDS OF DOLLARS

Item Description for Accounting Period 7/06 Through 6/07	Total	Zero Assets	Under 500	500 to 1,000	1,000 to 5,000	5,000 to 10,000	10,000 to 25,000	25,000 to 50,000	50,000 to 100,000	100,000 to 250,000	250,000 to 500,000	500,000 to 2,500,000	2,500,000 and over
Number of Enterprises **1**	2257	401	1153	121	178	149	121	54	35	25	9	9	3
Revenues ($ in Thousands)													
Net Sales **2**	99799205	1001844	603045	214254	1217639	3385979	7067072	5912152	6502164	10118925	5828363	17334895	40612872
Interest **3**	198873	1583	86	671	1139	630	5341	4253	1208	26355	11634	65815	80157
Rents **4**	33310	489	0	320	872	644	1847	429	102	938	3857	3976	19835
Royalties **5**	30845	0	0	0	0	0	0	0	0	0	37	26344	4463
Other Portfolio Income **6**	187752	1081	226	2339	4919	4403	5093	3249	31002	9960	28236	78352	18892
Other Receipts **7**	1075882	1044	488	14	148917	23407	30855	22095	27786	47883	53552	283507	436338
Total Receipts **8**	101325867	1006041	603845	217598	1373486	3415063	7110208	5942178	6562262	10204061	5925679	17792889	41172557
Average Total Receipts **9**	44894	2509	524	1798	7716	22920	58762	110040	187493	408162	658409	1976988	13724186
Operating Costs/Operating Income (%)													
Cost of Operations **10**	83.1	65.7	59.6	69.0	73.0	78.0	83.2	84.6	84.2	83.9	81.4	82.8	84.5
Salaries and Wages **11**	3.9	15.3	11.7	5.2	6.9	5.0	3.6	3.8	3.0	3.0	2.3	7.1	2.7
Taxes Paid **12**	1.1	1.6	3.4	3.0	2.0	1.1	0.9	1.0	0.9	0.8	1.1	0.9	1.2
Interest Paid **13**	1.0	0.8	0.1	0.1	0.9	0.6	0.7	0.7	0.9	0.8	1.0	1.3	1.2
Depreciation **14**	1.4	2.0	1.4	0.9	2.7	1.3	1.1	1.4	1.8	1.8	2.3	1.4	1.2
Amortization and Depletion **15**	•	0.0	0.0	•	0.1	0.1	0.1	0.2	0.1	0.1	0.2	0.2	•
Pensions and Other Deferred Comp. **16**	0.2	0.1	•	0.1	0.1	0.2	0.1	0.2	0.1	0.1	0.2	0.2	0.3
Employee Benefits **17**	0.7	0.2	0.2	1.2	1.1	0.6	0.8	0.7	0.9	1.0	1.6	1.0	0.4
Advertising **18**	0.7	0.2	0.3	3.2	0.3	0.1	0.6	0.6	2.2	0.4	1.5	0.4	0.7
Other Expenses **19**	7.3	15.8	18.9	11.9	15.8	9.6	5.8	6.0	4.5	5.7	7.1	6.9	8.0
Officers' Compensation **20**	0.5	0.7	6.8	5.3	4.0	2.2	1.2	0.6	0.5	0.3	0.5	0.3	0.2
Operating Margin **21**	•	•	•	0.1	•	1.4	1.8	0.2	0.8	2.0	0.8	•	•
Operating Margin Before Officers' Comp. **22**	0.5	•	•	5.4	•	3.6	3.1	0.9	1.3	2.3	1.3	•	0.1

Selected Average Balance Sheet ($ in Thousands)

Net Receivables 23	2524	0	30	116	401	1628	3641	7810	13980	29734	45743	82827	693938
Inventories 24	3951	0	2	107	187	552	3335	7584	16624	41834	61801	204874	1315335
Net Property, Plant and Equipment 25	6168	0	61	52	1488	1745	5291	11526	26065	62610	138820	224376	2103464
Total Assets 26	20091	0	103	767	2588	6729	15495	34078	73200	171776	341121	1050705	6857248
Notes and Loans Payable 27	6827	0	38	21	2759	2756	5894	15309	24344	47691	97459	315530	2386455
All Other Liabilities 28	5348	0	10	50	666	2080	2510	10692	17910	39414	99078	251013	1993398
Net Worth 29	7916	0	56	696	-837	1893	7090	8077	30946	84671	144584	484162	2477395

Selected Financial Ratios (Times to 1)

Current Ratio 30	1.4	•	1.3	4.1	1.0	1.3	2.1	1.4	1.4	1.7	1.3	1.8	1.2
Quick Ratio 31	0.5	•	1.2	2.6	0.7	0.6	1.1	0.8	0.7	0.8	0.5	0.6	0.4
Net Sales to Working Capital 32	17.9	•	60.8	8.1	•	27.9	13.2	19.7	17.8	10.8	18.6	11.9	27.0
Coverage Ratio 33	2.4	•	•	19.4	7.5	4.9	4.7	2.1	2.8	4.5	3.6	1.1	2.1
Total Asset Turnover 34	2.2	•	5.1	2.3	2.6	3.4	3.8	3.2	2.5	2.4	1.9	1.8	2.0
Inventory Turnover 35	9.3	•	169.1	11.5	26.6	32.1	14.6	12.2	9.4	8.1	8.5	7.8	8.7
Receivables Turnover 36	16.3	•	20.5	14.8	11.8	14.2	13.9	15.4	14.3	13.6	16.1	13.4	20.6
Total Liabilities to Net Worth 37	1.5	•	0.9	0.1	•	2.6	1.2	3.2	1.4	1.0	1.4	1.2	1.8
Current Assets to Working Capital 38	3.3	•	4.6	1.3	•	4.8	1.9	3.5	3.4	2.3	4.2	2.2	5.2
Current Liabilities to Working Capital 39	2.3	•	3.6	0.3	•	3.8	0.9	2.5	2.4	1.3	3.2	1.2	4.2
Working Capital to Net Sales 40	0.1	•	0.0	0.1	•	0.0	0.1	0.1	0.1	0.1	0.1	0.1	0.0
Inventory to Working Capital 41	1.6	•	0.1	0.4	•	0.8	0.6	1.4	1.6	1.1	2.0	1.2	2.7
Total Receipts to Cash Flow 42	13.5	10.1	7.5	10.9	5.3	10.7	14.0	19.2	18.5	13.9	11.5	20.1	12.0
Cost of Goods to Cash Flow 43	11.2	6.6	4.5	7.5	3.9	8.3	11.7	16.2	15.5	11.7	9.4	16.7	10.1
Cash Flow to Total Debt 44	0.3	•	1.5	2.3	0.4	0.4	0.5	0.2	0.2	0.3	0.3	0.2	0.3

Selected Financial Factors (in Percentages)

Debt Ratio 45	60.6	•	46.0	9.3	132.4	71.9	54.2	76.3	57.7	50.7	57.6	53.9	63.9
Return on Total Assets 46	5.5	•	•	3.6	18.4	9.5	11.8	4.5	6.8	8.5	6.9	2.7	4.9
Return on Equity Before Income Taxes 47	8.1	•	•	3.8	•	26.8	20.3	10.1	10.4	13.4	11.8	0.7	7.2
Return on Equity After Income Taxes 48	5.9	•	•	3.5	•	19.7	17.2	8.9	9.1	12.1	8.9	•	4.5
Profit Margin (Before Income Tax) 49	1.5	•	•	1.5	6.0	2.2	2.5	0.7	1.7	2.8	2.6	0.2	1.3
Profit Margin (After Income Tax) 50	1.0	•	•	1.4	6.0	1.6	2.1	0.7	1.5	2.5	2.0	•	0.8

Table II

Corporations with Net Income

MEAT AND SEAFOOD PROCESSING

MONEY AMOUNTS AND SIZE OF ASSETS IN THOUSANDS OF DOLLARS

Item Description for Accounting Period 7/06 Through 6/07	Total	Zero Assets	Under 500	500 to 1,000	1,000 to 5,000	5,000 to 10,000	10,000 to 25,000	25,000 to 50,000	50,000 to 100,000	100,000 to 250,000	250,000 to 500,000	500,000 to 2,500,000	2,500,000 and over
Number of Enterprises **1**	1159	398	•	121	146	121	95	33	21	•	•	6	0
Revenues ($ in Thousands)													
Net Sales **2**	48416634	377214	•	214254	973087	3000639	5517765	3753787	4639067	•	•	17971081	0
Interest **3**	132870	136	•	671	1128	293	4834	2973	652	•	•	88773	0
Rents **4**	27128	15	•	320	238	421	1837	393	81	•	•	19027	0
Royalties **5**	4276	0	•	0	0	0	0	0	0	•	•	4238	0
Other Portfolio Income **6**	139381	24	•	2339	4537	3110	2564	3185	27557	•	•	57827	0
Other Receipts **7**	738028	93	•	14	147772	21565	30687	11754	20970	•	•	439220	0
Total Receipts **8**	49458317	377482	•	217598	1126762	3026028	5157687	3772092	4668327	•	•	18580166	0
Average Total Receipts **9**	42673	948	•	1798	7718	25008	54291	114306	223254	•	•	3096694	•
Operating Costs/Operating Income (%)													
Cost of Operations **10**	81.8	71.6	•	69.0	71.9	80.6	82.4	84.3	83.0	•	•	82.9	•
Salaries and Wages **11**	3.2	10.6	•	5.2	7.1	3.8	3.0	3.5	2.9	•	•	2.7	•
Taxes Paid **12**	1.1	1.2	•	3.0	1.6	1.0	0.8	0.9	0.8	•	•	1.3	•
Interest Paid **13**	1.0	0.8	•	0.1	0.9	0.4	0.5	0.5	0.7	•	•	1.6	•
Depreciation **14**	1.4	1.3	•	0.9	2.5	1.1	1.2	1.3	1.5	•	•	0.9	•
Amortization and Depletion **15**	•	•	•	•	0.1	0.0	0.2	0.0	0.0	•	•	•	•
Pensions and Other Deferred Comp. **16**	0.4	0.0	•	0.1	0.1	0.2	0.1	0.2	0.2	•	•	0.8	•
Employee Benefits **17**	0.9	•	•	1.2	0.4	0.5	0.6	0.9	1.1	•	•	1.0	•
Advertising **18**	1.0	0.3	•	3.2	0.3	0.0	0.8	0.6	2.3	•	•	1.0	•
Other Expenses **19**	6.7	9.4	•	11.9	16.9	7.7	5.6	4.5	4.2	•	•	7.2	•
Officers' Compensation **20**	0.8	0.8	•	5.3	4.6	2.4	1.5	0.7	0.5	•	•	0.5	•
Operating Margin **21**	2.0	4.0	•	0.1	•	2.3	3.2	2.7	2.9	•	•	1.0	•
Operating Margin Before Officers' Comp. **22**	2.8	4.8	•	5.4	4.7	4.7	4.7	3.4	3.4	•	•	1.5	•

Selected Average Balance Sheet ($ in Thousands)

Item											
Net Receivables 23	2767	0	•	116	425	1753	3426	8810	14273	•	175332
Inventories 24	5228	0	•	98	187	668	3193	8535	20790	•	299262
Net Property, Plant and Equipment 25	6080	0	•	52	1456	1076	5195	11175	25606	•	514547
Total Assets 26	20616	0	•	767	2526	6221	14691	34019	76121	•	2113521
Notes and Loans Payable 27	5808	0	•	21	2863	2345	4781	8208	19253	•	566263
All Other Liabilities 28	5297	0	•	50	654	1787	2178	1015	17158	•	582021
Net Worth 29	9511	0	•	696	-991	2088	7732	15696	39709	•	965236

Selected Financial Ratios (Times to 1)

Item										
Current Ratio 30	1.7	•	4.1	1.1	1.7	2.8	1.5	1.6	•	1.7
Quick Ratio 31	0.7	•	2.6	0.8	0.8	1.5	0.8	0.7	•	0.6
Net Sales to Working Capital 32	11.7	•	8.1	183.7	14.0	10.9	17.8	14.9	•	10.0
Coverage Ratio 33	5.1	6.2	19.4	11.8	8.7	8.5	7.8	7.0	•	3.7
Total Asset Turnover 34	2.0	•	2.3	2.6	4.0	3.7	3.3	2.9	•	1.4
Inventory Turnover 35	6.5	•	12.4	25.7	29.9	13.9	11.2	8.8	•	8.3
Receivables Turnover 36	12.6	•	13.1	•	•	13.0	13.2	14.7	•	25.6
Total Liabilities to Net Worth 37	1.2	•	0.1	•	2.0	0.9	1.2	0.9	•	1.2
Current Assets to Working Capital 38	2.4	•	1.3	18.9	2.4	1.6	3.1	2.7	•	2.4
Current Liabilities to Working Capital 39	1.4	•	0.3	17.9	1.4	0.6	2.1	1.7	•	1.4
Working Capital to Net Sales 40	0.1	•	0.1	0.0	0.1	0.1	0.1	0.1	•	0.1
Inventory to Working Capital 41	1.1	•	0.4	4.2	0.4	0.5	1.2	1.3	•	1.4
Total Receipts to Cash Flow 42	10.3	8.5	10.9	4.2	11.4	11.6	15.0	13.6	•	9.5
Cost of Goods to Cash Flow 43	8.4	6.1	7.5	3.0	9.2	9.6	12.7	11.3	•	7.9
Cash Flow to Total Debt 44	0.4	•	2.3	0.4	0.5	0.7	0.4	0.4	•	0.3

Selected Financial Factors (in Percentages)

Item										
Debt Ratio 45	53.9	•	9.3	139.2	66.4	47.4	53.9	47.8	•	54.3
Return on Total Assets 46	10.5	•	3.6	27.3	14.0	16.6	12.3	13.4	•	8.5
Return on Equity Before Income Taxes 47	18.3	•	3.8	•	37.0	27.8	23.2	22.0	•	13.6
Return on Equity After Income Taxes 48	14.6	•	3.5	•	29.1	24.5	22.2	20.4	•	8.9
Profit Margin (Before Income Tax) 49	4.2	4.1	1.5	9.5	3.1	4.0	3.2	4.0	•	4.4
Profit Margin (After Income Tax) 50	3.3	4.0	1.4	9.5	2.4	3.5	3.1	3.7	•	2.9

Table I

Corporations with and without Net Income

BAKERIES AND TORTILLA

MONEY AMOUNTS AND SIZE OF ASSETS IN THOUSANDS OF DOLLARS

Item Description for Accounting Period 7/06 Through 6/07	Total	Zero Assets	Under 500	500 to 1,000	1,000 to 5,000	5,000 to 10,000	10,000 to 25,000	25,000 to 50,000	50,000 to 100,000	100,000 to 250,000	250,000 to 500,000	500,000 to 2,500,000	2,500,000 and over
Number of Enterprises **1**	4727	421	3672	256	164	39	105	21	21	10	7	11	0
Revenues ($ in Thousands)													
Net Sales **2**	82129266	441858	2043548	147123	667509	523612	3033858	1712936	3307702	1956477	4086923	64207721	0
Interest **3**	503442	331	10	1	272	576	2591	1201	1417	6268	4456	486318	0
Rents **4**	1795297	0	16	0	3310	0	0	239	4854	0	250	1786628	0
Royalties **5**	276355	368	0	0	0	0	158	0	674	0	28917	246238	0
Other Portfolio Income **6**	2789995	6500	4	1	203	94	765	1681	7463	20995	4818	2747471	0
Other Receipts **7**	3917433	9	4211	42	8524	527	17574	2908	14549	10312	11408	3847367	0
Total Receipts **8**	91411788	449066	2047789	147167	679818	524809	3054946	1718965	3336659	1994052	4136772	73321743	0
Average Total Receipts **9**	19338	1067	558	575	4145	13457	29095	81855	158889	199405	590967	6665613	•
Operating Costs/Operating Income (%)													
Cost of Operations **10**	55.6	53.4	45.7	46.3	54.7	69.2	68.3	61.1	65.4	68.7	69.2	53.3	•
Salaries and Wages **11**	7.6	9.9	11.3	7.9	11.8	7.5	5.9	9.5	11.0	5.2	9.1	7.2	•
Taxes Paid **12**	6.8	1.5	1.8	3.4	3.3	2.6	2.1	1.7	1.8	1.8	1.9	8.1	•
Interest Paid **13**	3.1	4.9	0.8	•	0.7	1.4	0.9	1.5	0.9	1.5	1.7	3.6	•
Depreciation **14**	2.7	3.2	4.7	1.3	2.1	4.0	2.9	2.6	2.8	4.3	2.6	2.6	•
Amortization and Depletion **15**	0.5	0.5	0.1	0.0	0.0	0.0	0.1	0.6	0.1	0.7	1.3	0.5	•
Pensions and Other Deferred Comp. **16**	1.6	2.6	0.0	0.2	0.4	0.1	0.3	0.9	1.9	0.5	0.6	1.8	•
Employee Benefits **17**	3.0	1.7	3.6	0.9	1.2	1.6	1.6	2.6	3.4	2.6	2.2	3.1	•
Advertising **18**	1.9	0.5	1.3	1.1	0.7	0.3	0.5	1.5	0.7	1.3	0.6	2.2	•
Other Expenses **19**	13.3	23.7	29.9	18.4	18.2	9.8	11.2	14.9	9.8	13.9	10.6	13.1	•
Officers' Compensation **20**	0.9	5.9	5.3	5.8	6.6	3.2	2.3	1.5	1.2	0.9	0.7	0.5	•
Operating Margin **21**	3.1	•	•	14.5	0.4	0.3	3.8	1.6	0.9	•	•	4.0	•
Operating Margin Before Officers' Comp. **22**	4.0	•	•	20.3	7.0	3.4	6.0	3.1	2.0	•	0.2	4.5	•

Selected Average Balance Sheet ($ in Thousands)

Net Receivables 23	1477	0	10	29	236	826	2863	6361	13217	26940	59522	497119
Inventories 24	1272	0	9	43	211	2427	1556	4096	5976	16299	34705	459778
Net Property, Plant and Equipment 25	3543	0	60	105	859	4110	7044	18059	34327	55101	117420	1180573
Total Assets 26	25312	0	114	647	2489	6669	15364	37269	69782	142175	372958	10045814
Notes and Loans Payable 27	5675	0	113	34	456	3297	5266	18562	15161	20407	90170	2190966
All Other Liabilities 28	9240	0	21	22	237	1200	3524	11477	26346	64858	99484	3727230
Net Worth 29	10397	0	-20	592	1796	2173	6574	7229	28274	56910	183304	4127618

Selected Financial Ratios (Times to 1)

Current Ratio 30	0.7	•	1.4	25.0	5.4	1.5	1.5	0.8	1.1	0.9	1.5	0.6
Quick Ratio 31	0.4	•	1.0	23.3	1.8	1.0	1.0	0.5	0.7	0.6	1.0	0.3
Net Sales to Working Capital 32	•	•	46.2	1.1	3.4	17.4	14.0	•	57.8	•	12.9	•
Coverage Ratio 33	7.1	•	•	•	4.3	1.3	5.8	2.3	2.8	1.4	1.4	7.7
Total Asset Turnover 34	0.7	•	4.9	0.9	1.6	2.0	1.9	2.2	2.3	1.4	1.6	0.6
Inventory Turnover 35	7.6	•	27.2	6.2	10.5	3.8	12.7	12.2	17.2	8.3	11.6	6.8
Receivables Turnover 36	12.3	•	55.7	20.6	12.7	5.0	10.3	11.2	12.9	6.6	10.9	12.6
Total Liabilities to Net Worth 37	1.4	•	•	0.1	0.4	2.1	1.3	4.2	1.5	1.5	1.0	1.4
Current Assets to Working Capital 38	•	•	3.7	1.0	1.2	3.2	3.1	•	9.9	•	3.1	•
Current Liabilities to Working Capital 39	•	•	2.7	0.0	0.2	2.2	2.1	•	8.9	•	2.1	•
Working Capital to Net Sales 40	•	•	0.0	0.9	0.3	0.1	0.1	•	0.0	•	0.1	•
Inventory to Working Capital 41	•	•	0.7	0.1	0.1	0.9	0.7	•	2.4	•	0.8	•
Total Receipts to Cash Flow 42	4.1	11.6	6.6	3.7	6.4	12.9	7.5	7.7	10.9	8.9	11.4	3.6
Cost of Goods to Cash Flow 43	2.3	6.2	3.0	1.7	3.5	8.9	5.2	4.7	7.1	6.1	7.9	1.9
Cash Flow to Total Debt 44	0.3	•	0.6	2.8	0.9	0.2	0.4	0.4	0.3	0.3	0.3	0.3

Selected Financial Factors (in Percentages)

Debt Ratio 45	58.9	•	117.6	8.6	27.9	67.4	57.2	80.6	59.5	60.0	50.9	58.9
Return on Total Assets 46	14.9	•	•	12.9	4.9	3.8	10.1	7.6	5.9	2.8	3.8	15.8
Return on Equity Before Income Taxes 47	31.3	•	119.3	14.1	5.2	3.0	19.5	22.0	9.5	2.1	2.4	33.4
Return on Equity After Income Taxes 48	20.2	•	122.1	14.0	4.8	•	18.2	19.1	8.0	2.1	•	21.6
Profit Margin (Before Income Tax) 49	18.7	•	•	14.6	2.3	0.5	4.4	1.9	1.7	0.6	0.7	23.6
Profit Margin (After Income Tax) 50	12.1	•	•	14.4	2.1	•	4.1	1.7	1.4	0.6	•	15.3

47

Table II

Corporations with Net Income

BAKERIES AND TORTILLA

MONEY AMOUNTS AND SIZE OF ASSETS IN THOUSANDS OF DOLLARS

Item Description for Accounting Period 7/06 Through 6/07	Total	Zero Assets	Under 500	500 to 1,000	1,000 to 5,000	5,000 to 10,000	10,000 to 25,000	25,000 to 50,000	50,000 to 100,000	100,000 to 250,000	250,000 to 500,000	500,000 to 2,500,000	2,500,000 and over
Number of Enterprises **1**	1977	0	•	•	60	23	83	13	17	6	4	7	0
Revenues ($ in Thousands)													
Net Sales **2**	71014918	0	•	•	390048	410976	2529188	1021632	2768115	1288790	2923476	58994692	0
Interest **3**	484908	0	•	•	207	576	2422	609	1009	1342	2384	476360	0
Rents **4**	1794749	0	•	•	3310	0	0	239	4498	0	66	1786619	0
Royalties **5**	248521	0	•	•	0	0	158	0	500	0	4346	243517	0
Other Portfolio Income **6**	2753359	0	•	•	36	94	701	1477	3627	2016	4589	2740821	0
Other Receipts **7**	3900724	0	•	•	563	140	13019	1561	12894	9413	4937	3855134	0
Total Receipts **8**	80197179	0	•	•	394164	411786	2545488	1025518	2790643	1301561	2939798	68097143	0
Average Total Receipts **9**	40565	•	•	•	6569	17904	30669	78886	164155	216927	734950	9728163	•
Operating Costs/Operating Income (%)													
Cost of Operations **10**	55.2	•	•	•	60.7	62.3	67.5	60.3	64.7	70.7	68.6	53.1	•
Salaries and Wages **11**	6.9	•	•	•	6.9	7.2	5.9	9.9	10.9	4.4	10.6	6.6	•
Taxes Paid **12**	7.5	•	•	•	2.6	2.3	2.1	1.8	1.9	2.1	2.0	8.6	•
Interest Paid **13**	3.2	•	•	•	1.0	0.9	0.7	0.9	0.6	1.3	0.4	3.7	•
Depreciation **14**	2.7	•	•	•	2.4	3.4	2.6	2.5	2.6	4.1	2.4	2.7	•
Amortization and Depletion **15**	0.4	•	•	•	0.0	0.0	0.0	0.1	0.1	0.5	0.6	0.4	•
Pensions and Other Deferred Comp. **16**	1.5	•	•	•	0.4	0.1	0.4	0.8	2.1	0.5	0.7	1.7	•
Employee Benefits **17**	2.7	•	•	•	1.0	1.7	1.7	2.5	3.3	3.1	2.4	2.8	•
Advertising **18**	2.0	•	•	•	0.9	0.4	0.5	1.5	0.8	1.7	0.5	2.2	•
Other Expenses **19**	12.5	•	•	•	16.1	11.1	9.4	12.8	8.5	8.6	7.3	13.1	•
Officers' Compensation **20**	0.8	•	•	•	3.9	4.0	2.5	2.0	1.3	0.9	0.5	0.5	•
Operating Margin **21**	4.6	•	•	•	4.1	6.7	6.7	4.8	3.2	2.2	4.2	4.6	•
Operating Margin Before Officers' Comp. **22**	5.4	•	•	•	8.0	10.7	9.2	6.9	4.5	3.1	4.6	5.1	•

Selected Average Balance Sheet ($ in Thousands)

Net Receivables 23	3108	414	1107	2746	6312	11051	25004	80598	730080
Inventories 24	2805	421	2590	1563	4202	5940	11324	46658	697060
Net Property, Plant and Equipment 25	7307	1265	3615	6954	21167	35934	70050	113834	1694360
Total Assets 26	57295	2719	7354	14797	38742	69767	139072	378492	15341794
Notes and Loans Payable 27	12301	971	2054	4191	16067	15097	21115	63020	3278736
All Other Liabilities 28	20905	429	1493	2833	9372	20200	56445	103232	5685539
Net Worth 29	24089	1319	3806	7773	13303	34470	61511	212240	6377519

Selected Financial Ratios (Times to 1)

Current Ratio 30	0.7	2.1	2.2	1.8	0.8	1.3	0.9	1.6	0.7
Quick Ratio 31	0.4	1.3	1.6	1.3	0.6	0.8	0.5	1.1	0.3
Net Sales to Working Capital 32	•	10.8	9.3	10.4	•	27.9	•	11.7	•
Coverage Ratio 33	8.0	5.9	8.6	11.4	6.5	7.5	3.5	12.9	8.0
Total Asset Turnover 34	0.6	2.4	2.4	2.1	2.0	2.3	1.5	1.9	0.5
Inventory Turnover 35	7.1	9.4	4.3	13.2	11.3	17.7	13.4	10.7	6.4
Receivables Turnover 36	12.5	11.4	7.1	10.6	10.8	13.8	12.0	•	12.8
Total Liabilities to Net Worth 37	1.4	1.1	0.9	0.9	1.9	1.0	1.3	0.8	1.4
Current Assets to Working Capital 38	•	1.9	1.8	2.2	4.3	•	•	2.7	•
Current Liabilities to Working Capital 39	•	0.9	0.8	1.2	3.3	•	•	1.7	•
Working Capital to Net Sales 40	•	0.1	0.1	0.1	0.0	•	•	0.1	•
Inventory to Working Capital 41	•	0.6	0.4	0.5	1.0	•	•	0.7	•
Total Receipts to Cash Flow 42	3.7	6.0	6.6	6.9	6.7	9.7	9.7	9.9	3.4
Cost of Goods to Cash Flow 43	2.1	3.7	4.1	4.6	4.0	6.3	6.9	6.8	1.8
Cash Flow to Total Debt 44	0.3	0.8	0.8	0.6	0.5	0.5	0.3	0.4	0.3

Selected Financial Factors (in Percentages)

Debt Ratio 45	58.0	51.5	48.2	47.5	65.7	50.6	55.8	43.9	58.4
Return on Total Assets 46	16.1	14.7	18.8	16.5	12.5	10.6	7.0	9.8	16.3
Return on Equity Before Income Taxes 47	33.5	25.2	32.1	28.7	30.9	18.6	11.2	16.2	34.3
Return on Equity After Income Taxes 48	22.1	23.7	26.7	27.3	28.4	17.0	11.2	12.3	22.3
Profit Margin (Before Income Tax) 49	22.5	5.1	6.8	7.3	5.2	3.9	3.2	4.7	26.0
Profit Margin (After Income Tax) 50	14.8	4.8	5.7	7.0	4.8	3.6	3.2	3.6	16.9

Table I

Corporations with and without Net Income

OTHER FOOD

MONEY AMOUNTS AND SIZE OF ASSETS IN THOUSANDS OF DOLLARS

Item Description for Accounting Period 7/06 Through 6/07	Total	Zero Assets	Under 500	500 to 1,000	1,000 to 5,000	5,000 to 10,000	10,000 to 25,000	25,000 to 50,000	50,000 to 100,000	100,000 to 250,000	250,000 to 500,000	500,000 to 2,500,000	2,500,000 and over
Number of Enterprises **1**	4259	756	2214	389	391	169	179	71	34	30	13	9	3
Revenues ($ in Thousands)													
Net Sales **2**	84708899	64968	265931	1109140	1563212	2554590	5842558	4493426	3834237	6732420	5152176	10213355	42882886
Interest **3**	2443061	306	1	579	3088	2676	3412	3966	5964	11449	38161	66100	2307360
Rents **4**	106643	0	0	604	1055	948	3414	1217	2919	1447	9920	4443	80675
Royalties **5**	776473	0	0	0	0	498	0	3984	22915	29849	4061	34911	680255
Other Portfolio Income **6**	401264	21151	0	0	5	662	38541	42402	8296	26213	24734	46777	176418
Other Receipts **7**	1092214	480	1	906	898	28912	18704	31002	29393	118745	52742	151950	658482
Total Receipts **8**	89528554	86905	265933	1127292	1568258	2588286	5906629	4575997	3903724	6920123	5281794	10517536	46786076
Average Total Receipts **9**	21021	115	120	2898	4011	15315	32998	64451	114815	230671	406292	1168615	15595359
Operating Costs/Operating Income (%)													
Cost of Operations **10**	72.2	82.0	57.5	63.6	67.3	70.6	71.9	75.4	70.9	67.7	70.1	68.1	74.6
Salaries and Wages **11**	4.9	6.2	•	13.8	6.1	7.3	6.6	6.0	6.0	6.9	6.7	5.5	3.4
Taxes Paid **12**	1.4	1.3	2.8	1.9	2.1	1.8	1.3	1.0	1.3	1.3	1.3	1.7	1.3
Interest Paid **13**	4.4	2.7	0.1	1.3	1.7	0.8	1.1	1.2	1.5	2.1	2.3	3.8	6.5
Depreciation **14**	1.7	1.5	3.2	0.8	3.0	1.5	2.2	1.6	2.7	2.2	2.6	2.2	1.3
Amortization and Depletion **15**	0.5	•	0.0	0.1	0.2	0.0	0.5	0.4	0.8	0.9	0.5	1.2	0.3
Pensions and Other Deferred Comp. **16**	0.3	0.8	•	•	0.6	0.3	0.2	0.2	0.5	0.4	0.4	1.1	0.1
Employee Benefits **17**	1.0	0.5	•	•	0.8	0.9	1.2	1.6	1.4	1.4	1.3	1.6	0.6
Advertising **18**	4.3	1.9	6.4	0.7	0.5	0.5	0.7	1.8	2.2	3.5	2.8	1.0	6.7
Other Expenses **19**	9.6	9.6	31.5	8.6	12.8	8.4	9.3	9.2	10.5	11.0	11.3	11.3	8.7
Officers' Compensation **20**	0.7	2.9	5.3	4.3	5.6	3.7	1.5	1.1	1.2	1.1	0.5	0.5	0.1
Operating Margin **21**	•	•	•	5.0	•	4.1	3.4	0.6	1.1	1.3	0.3	2.1	•
Operating Margin Before Officers' Comp. **22**	•	•	•	9.2	4.9	7.8	4.9	1.7	2.3	2.4	0.8	2.6	•

Selected Average Balance Sheet ($ in Thousands)

Net Receivables 23	57328	0	106	255	1750	3157	6415	9336	26455	38990	105474	80044760
Inventories 24	1467	0	83	455	1282	2924	9183	15217	24043	42116	219872	585283
Net Property, Plant and Equipment 25	3044	22	248	865	1955	5814	9084	21024	40246	104977	248192	1647570
Total Assets 26	89835	36	859	1975	7106	15155	34457	71060	151315	333616	1207221	117633838
Notes and Loans Payable 27	5004	27	222	1000	2932	5528	13060	21685	69131	116938	607995	2853943
All Other Liabilities 28	62037	12	235	284	2216	3498	9508	18959	37468	86348	308018	85548933
Net Worth 29	22794	-2	402	692	1958	6129	11889	30415	44716	130330	291208	29230963

Selected Financial Ratios (Times to 1)

Current Ratio 30	1.0	•	1.0	2.6	1.5	1.8	1.6	1.5	1.8	1.8	1.4	1.0
Quick Ratio 31	1.0	•	1.0	1.4	0.8	1.0	0.7	0.7	0.9	0.7	0.6	1.0
Net Sales to Working Capital 32	•	213.8	25.5	6.7	10.7	8.6	8.3	10.3	7.3	6.1	12.9	•
Coverage Ratio 33	2.2	9.8	6.2	0.8	8.1	5.1	3.1	3.0	2.9	2.2	2.5	2.0
Total Asset Turnover 34	0.2	•	3.3	2.0	2.1	2.2	1.8	1.6	1.5	1.2	0.9	0.1
Inventory Turnover 35	9.8	158.8	21.8	5.9	8.3	8.0	5.2	5.3	6.3	6.6	3.5	18.2
Receivables Turnover 36	0.4	550.6	38.5	9.2	10.1	11.3	9.6	11.8	9.2	13.3	0.1	0.4
Total Liabilities to Net Worth 37	2.9	•	1.1	1.9	2.6	1.5	1.9	1.3	2.4	1.6	3.1	3.0
Current Assets to Working Capital 38	•	21.6	3.3	1.6	3.0	2.2	2.6	2.9	2.3	2.2	3.5	•
Current Liabilities to Working Capital 39	•	20.6	2.3	0.6	2.0	1.2	1.6	1.9	1.3	1.2	2.5	•
Working Capital to Net Sales 40	•	0.0	0.0	0.1	0.1	0.1	0.1	0.1	0.1	0.2	0.1	•
Inventory to Working Capital 41	•	0.8	1.2	0.7	1.0	0.9	1.2	1.4	0.8	0.7	1.6	•
Total Receipts to Cash Flow 42	7.9	3.1	9.1	11.9	8.3	9.0	9.8	8.8	7.4	9.1	6.8	7.7
Cost of Goods to Cash Flow 43	5.7	2.5	5.8	8.0	5.8	6.5	7.4	6.2	5.0	6.4	4.6	5.8
Cash Flow to Total Debt 44	0.0	•	0.7	0.3	0.4	0.4	0.3	0.3	0.2	0.2	0.2	0.0

Selected Financial Factors (in Percentages)

Debt Ratio 45	74.6	105.7	53.2	65.0	72.4	59.6	65.5	57.2	70.4	60.9	75.9	75.2
Return on Total Assets 46	2.1	•	26.0	2.9	13.3	12.1	6.8	6.9	9.2	6.0	8.8	1.6
Return on Equity Before Income Taxes 47	4.5	397.0	46.7	•	42.2	24.0	13.4	10.6	20.5	8.4	21.9	3.1
Return on Equity After Income Taxes 48	3.1	397.0	46.1	•	37.5	21.5	10.2	6.3	17.0	5.2	13.5	2.1
Profit Margin (Before Income Tax) 49	5.2	24.0	6.6	•	5.5	4.5	2.5	2.9	4.1	2.8	5.6	6.3
Profit Margin (After Income Tax) 50	3.6	24.0	6.5	•	4.9	4.0	1.9	1.7	2.8	1.7	3.5	4.2

Table II
Corporations with Net Income

OTHER FOOD

MONEY AMOUNTS AND SIZE OF ASSETS IN THOUSANDS OF DOLLARS

Item Description for Accounting Period 7/06 Through 6/07	Total	Zero Assets	Under 500	500 to 1,000	1,000 to 5,000	5,000 to 10,000	10,000 to 25,000	25,000 to 50,000	50,000 to 100,000	100,000 to 250,000	250,000 to 500,000	500,000 to 2,500,000	2,500,000 and over
Number of Enterprises **1**	1612	483	170	•	201	132	120	49	23	24	9	•	3
Revenues ($ in Thousands)													
Net Sales **2**	76072377	5520	238685	•	1149494	2241111	4159411	3684852	2688243	5441908	3564631	•	42882886
Interest **3**	2431810	306	0	•	2440	2296	2996	2630	3656	8261	36383	•	2307360
Rents **4**	103648	0	0	•	1055	862	3414	467	1644	1416	9458	•	80675
Royalties **5**	752657	0	0	•	0	334	0	3984	1392	29849	1933	•	680255
Other Portfolio Income **6**	389636	21018	0	•	5	0	38345	42323	7479	25341	15863	•	176418
Other Receipts **7**	897931	0	0	•	532	26670	13822	26649	13674	18054	33853	•	658482
Total Receipts **8**	80648059	26844	238685	•	1153526	2271273	4217988	3760905	2716088	5524829	3662121	•	46786076
Average Total Receipts **9**	50030	56	1404	•	5739	17207	35150	76753	118091	230201	406902	•	15595359
Operating Costs/Operating Income (%)													
Cost of Operations **10**	71.8	75.7	59.8	•	69.0	71.2	68.9	74.1	68.0	64.7	70.0	•	74.6
Salaries and Wages **11**	4.7	•	•	•	5.1	6.5	7.5	5.9	6.2	6.8	6.8	•	3.4
Taxes Paid **12**	1.3	•	3.0	•	2.1	1.8	1.3	1.1	1.3	1.4	1.0	•	1.3
Interest Paid **13**	4.5	6.7	0.1	•	0.8	0.8	0.8	1.0	1.3	1.9	1.4	•	6.5
Depreciation **14**	1.6	0.5	2.8	•	2.0	1.6	1.9	1.2	2.7	2.1	2.2	•	1.3
Amortization and Depletion **15**	0.4	•	•	•	0.1	0.0	0.7	0.4	0.6	0.8	0.5	•	0.3
Pensions and Other Deferred Comp. **16**	0.3	•	•	•	0.7	0.3	0.3	0.2	0.5	0.5	0.4	•	0.1
Employee Benefits **17**	0.8	•	•	•	0.4	0.7	1.1	1.5	1.3	1.1	0.7	•	0.6
Advertising **18**	4.6	•	7.0	•	0.4	0.4	0.7	1.9	2.4	4.1	2.1	•	6.7
Other Expenses **19**	9.5	37.7	19.7	•	10.5	8.0	9.3	9.0	9.8	10.6	11.9	•	8.7
Officers' Compensation **20**	0.7	•	5.9	•	6.2	3.4	1.6	1.2	1.4	1.3	0.3	•	0.1
Operating Margin **21**	•	•	1.8	•	2.6	5.2	5.9	2.6	4.6	4.8	2.7	•	•
Operating Margin Before Officers' Comp. **22**	0.4	•	7.7	•	8.8	8.7	7.5	3.8	6.0	6.1	3.0	•	•

Selected Average Balance Sheet ($ in Thousands)

Net Receivables 23	150881	0	0	•	324	1554	3124	7199	9473	29335	34186	• 80044760
Inventories 24	3160	0	3	•	629	1388	3275	9472	17212	26060	25421	• 585283
Net Property, Plant and Equipment 25	6685	0	211	•	955	2172	5454	8668	21293	39685	85147	• 1647570
Total Assets 26	233127	0	368	•	2340	7120	15438	35314	72251	151828	304022	• 117633838
Notes and Loans Payable 27	11072	0	20	•	762	2665	4031	13422	22191	72080	60597	• 2853943
All Other Liabilities 28	162801	0	4	•	358	1998	3169	9238	17465	40503	79859	• 85548933
Net Worth 29	59254	0	•	345	1219	2457	8238	12654	32596	39244	163566	• 29230963

Selected Financial Ratios (Times to 1)

Current Ratio 30	1.0	•	39.0	•	2.8	1.4	2.0	1.8	1.6	1.7	2.3	• 1.0
Quick Ratio 31	1.0	•	36.5	•	1.5	0.8	1.1	0.9	0.6	0.9	1.1	• 1.0
Net Sales to Working Capital 32	•	•	10.5	•	7.4	16.3	7.5	7.6	8.9	7.6	5.9	• •
Coverage Ratio 33	2.4	55.3	29.2	•	4.6	8.8	10.0	5.8	5.3	4.2	4.8	• 2.0
Total Asset Turnover 34	0.2	•	3.8	•	2.4	2.4	2.2	2.1	1.6	1.5	1.3	• 0.1
Inventory Turnover 35	10.7	•	275.0	•	6.3	8.7	7.3	5.9	4.6	5.6	10.9	• 18.2
Receivables Turnover 36	0.4	•	17680.4	•	8.1	11.1	11.2	11.0	12.0	8.1	14.2	• 0.4
Total Liabilities to Net Worth 37	2.9	•	0.1	•	0.9	1.9	0.9	1.8	1.2	2.9	0.9	• 3.0
Current Assets to Working Capital 38	•	•	1.0	•	1.6	3.6	2.0	2.2	2.6	2.4	1.8	• •
Current Liabilities to Working Capital 39	•	•	0.0	•	0.6	2.6	1.0	1.2	1.6	1.4	0.8	• •
Working Capital to Net Sales 40	•	•	0.1	•	0.1	0.1	0.1	0.1	0.1	0.1	0.2	• •
Inventory to Working Capital 41	•	•	0.0	•	0.6	1.4	0.8	1.0	1.4	0.8	0.5	• •
Total Receipts to Cash Flow 42	7.4	0.3	6.9	•	11.0	7.8	7.4	8.2	7.4	6.6	7.0	• 7.7
Cost of Goods to Cash Flow 43	5.3	0.2	4.2	•	7.6	5.5	5.1	6.1	5.0	4.3	4.9	• 5.8
Cash Flow to Total Debt 44	0.0	•	8.8	•	0.5	0.5	0.7	0.4	0.4	0.3	0.4	• 0.0

Selected Financial Factors (in Percentages)

Debt Ratio 45	74.6	•	6.3	•	47.9	65.5	46.6	64.2	54.9	74.2	46.2	• 75.2
Return on Total Assets 46	2.2	•	7.2	•	9.3	17.7	18.2	12.1	11.2	12.3	8.9	• 1.6
Return on Equity Before Income Taxes 47	5.0	•	7.4	•	13.9	45.5	30.7	28.0	20.2	36.4	13.1	• 3.1
Return on Equity After Income Taxes 48	3.6	•	7.4	•	9.8	40.7	28.0	23.7	14.3	31.5	9.4	• 2.1
Profit Margin (Before Income Tax) 49	6.3	365.7	1.8	•	3.0	6.6	7.3	4.7	5.6	6.3	5.4	• 6.3
Profit Margin (After Income Tax) 50	4.5	365.7	1.8	•	2.1	5.9	6.7	4.0	4.0	5.4	3.9	• 4.2

Table I

Corporations with and without Net Income

SOFT DRINK AND ICE

MONEY AMOUNTS AND SIZE OF ASSETS IN THOUSANDS OF DOLLARS

Item Description for Accounting Period 7/06 Through 6/07	Total	Zero Assets	Under 500	500 to 1,000	1,000 to 5,000	5,000 to 10,000	10,000 to 25,000	25,000 to 50,000	50,000 to 100,000	100,000 to 250,000	250,000 to 500,000	500,000 to 2,500,000	2,500,000 and over
Number of Enterprises **1**	695	245	69	91	159	21	37	31	13	11	9	3	6
Revenues ($ in Thousands)													
Net Sales **2**	52627229	62339	31401	182585	1068860	253723	1449671	2859859	1520331	2718131	3615486	2925322	35939521
Interest **3**	1254216	170	872	123	1481	492	2525	4439	2927	8593	29990	1330	1201273
Rents **4**	84181	0	0	644	2253	652	4984	417	611	1340	1184	5019	67076
Royalties **5**	1214776	0	0	0	0	0	0	0	0	0	0	121	1214654
Other Portfolio Income **6**	1362530	0	27744	21070	52871	33416	3052	5583	2539	6179	10132	1834	1198111
Other Receipts **7**	2095636	0	178	2	6507	28938	13513	15758	43171	89543	100479	58871	1738678
Total Receipts **8**	58638568	62509	60195	204424	1131972	317221	1473745	2886056	1569579	2823786	3757271	2992497	41359313
Average Total Receipts **9**	84372	255	872	2246	7119	15106	39831	93099	120737	256708	417475	997499	6893219
Operating Costs/Operating Income (%)													
Cost of Operations **10**	52.3	70.8	82.4	55.7	75.6	77.2	76.3	65.2	67.9	70.8	52.2	59.4	46.8
Salaries and Wages **11**	11.8	23.9	18.6	4.9	9.6	10.1	6.5	10.2	9.6	9.7	17.0	10.8	12.0
Taxes Paid **12**	2.0	3.6	10.3	3.6	2.1	2.8	1.2	1.2	2.0	1.5	2.5	1.8	2.1
Interest Paid **13**	4.3	0.3	0.7	1.0	0.9	0.7	0.6	1.0	1.6	1.0	2.9	3.0	5.5
Depreciation **14**	3.2	0.0	1.9	3.5	1.6	2.1	1.8	1.9	3.5	2.7	4.7	3.0	3.4
Amortization and Depletion **15**	0.9	•	0.2	0.4	0.0	0.3	0.1	0.3	0.4	0.5	1.0	0.6	1.1
Pensions and Other Deferred Comp. **16**	1.2	•	•	2.5	0.6	0.6	0.1	0.3	0.2	0.6	0.8	0.4	1.5
Employee Benefits **17**	2.0	•	•	1.3	1.9	1.6	1.2	2.3	1.7	2.5	2.0	3.0	1.9
Advertising **18**	7.8	2.8	1.5	1.4	0.9	2.8	1.2	6.0	1.6	0.6	3.0	0.3	10.3
Other Expenses **19**	14.2	137.7	51.6	19.5	4.9	18.6	8.5	7.0	9.3	7.4	11.1	17.8	15.6
Officers' Compensation **20**	0.6	7.4	5.8	6.5	5.3	1.2	1.1	1.4	0.8	0.6	0.9	0.9	0.2
Operating Margin **21**	•	•	•	•	•	•	1.2	3.0	1.5	2.0	2.3	•	•
Operating Margin Before Officers' Comp. **22**	0.3	•	•	6.2	1.9	•	2.4	4.4	2.3	2.6	2.9	•	•

Selected Average Balance Sheet ($ in Thousands)

	1	2	3	4	5	6	7	8	9	10	11	12	13
Net Receivables 23	15640	0	0	113	985	909	2844	8082	14154	17630	46575	217366	1479815
Inventories 24	3718	0	0	216	94	744	2480	4957	5643	16886	16896	108268	258713
Net Property, Plant and Equipment 25	19234	0	0	208	668	2394	5403	10014	29589	42643	105923	246054	1689485
Total Assets 26	112861	0	192	693	2081	7318	15635	39654	72186	151440	359305	944763	11232936
Notes and Loans Payable 27	39916	0	0	176	784	184	3899	14502	24118	25844	120615	467289	3986392
All Other Liabilities 28	42702	0	0	174	721	1160	3882	12958	16176	33321	125929	348633	4370302
Net Worth 29	30243	0	192	343	576	5974	7855	12194	31892	92275	112761	128841	2876242

Selected Financial Ratios (Times to 1)

	1	2	3	4	5	6	7	8	9	10	11	12	13
Current Ratio 30	1.4	•	•	2.6	1.1	2.3	1.5	1.7	1.7	2.0	1.5	1.3	1.4
Quick Ratio 31	0.9	•	•	1.4	1.0	1.7	1.0	1.1	1.2	1.1	1.0	1.1	0.9
Net Sales to Working Capital 32	9.6	•	22.0	7.3	64.5	8.1	16.2	11.5	9.9	8.6	10.3	11.9	8.9
Coverage Ratio 33	3.8	•	26.2	12.8	3.8	10.8	5.6	4.9	3.9	6.9	3.1	1.4	3.9
Total Asset Turnover 34	0.7	•	2.4	2.9	3.2	1.7	2.5	2.3	1.6	1.6	1.1	1.0	0.5
Inventory Turnover 35	10.7	•	•	5.2	54.2	12.5	12.1	12.1	14.1	10.4	12.4	5.3	10.8
Receivables Turnover 36	5.0	•	•	17.9	5.4	11.0	10.0	11.5	7.1	11.7	9.7	3.1	4.4
Total Liabilities to Net Worth 37	2.7	•	•	1.0	2.6	0.2	1.0	2.3	1.3	0.6	2.2	6.3	2.9
Current Assets to Working Capital 38	3.5	•	1.0	1.6	12.3	1.7	2.9	2.5	2.4	2.0	2.8	3.9	3.8
Current Liabilities to Working Capital 39	2.5	•	•	0.6	11.3	0.7	1.9	1.5	1.4	1.0	1.8	2.9	2.8
Working Capital to Net Sales 40	0.1	0.0	•	0.1	0.0	0.1	0.1	0.1	0.1	0.1	0.1	0.1	0.1
Inventory to Working Capital 41	0.5	•	•	0.7	0.8	0.4	0.8	0.6	0.5	0.5	0.7	0.6	0.4
Total Receipts to Cash Flow 42	4.4	•	12.9	4.7	25.1	6.6	11.0	11.5	8.5	8.3	7.2	6.5	3.6
Cost of Goods to Cash Flow 43	2.3	•	10.7	2.6	18.9	5.1	8.4	7.5	5.8	5.9	3.7	3.8	1.7
Cash Flow to Total Debt 44	0.2	•	•	1.2	0.2	1.4	0.5	0.3	0.3	0.5	0.2	0.2	0.2

Selected Financial Factors (in Percentages)

	1	2	3	4	5	6	7	8	9	10	11	12	13
Debt Ratio 45	73.2	•	•	50.5	72.3	18.4	49.8	69.2	55.8	39.1	68.6	86.4	74.4
Return on Total Assets 46	11.0	•	46.0	36.7	11.0	12.6	8.9	11.2	10.3	11.1	10.2	4.5	11.4
Return on Equity Before Income Taxes 47	30.2	•	44.3	68.3	29.4	14.0	14.5	29.0	17.4	15.5	22.0	10.0	33.2
Return on Equity After Income Taxes 48	20.6	•	18.7	47.3	25.6	9.0	12.3	26.8	14.9	13.2	14.2	5.2	22.5
Profit Margin (Before Income Tax) 49	12.1	•	18.7	11.7	2.5	6.9	2.9	3.8	4.7	5.8	6.2	1.3	16.0
Profit Margin (After Income Tax) 50	8.2	•	7.9	8.1	2.2	4.5	2.5	3.5	4.1	4.9	5.8	0.7	10.8

Table II

Corporations with Net Income

SOFT DRINK AND ICE

MONEY AMOUNTS AND SIZE OF ASSETS IN THOUSANDS OF DOLLARS

Revenues ($ in Thousands)

Item Description for Accounting Period 7/06 Through 6/07	Total	Zero Assets	Under 500	500 to 1000	251 to 500	501 to 1,000	1,001 to 5,000	5,001 to 10,000	10,001 to 25,000	25,001 to 50,000	50,001 to 100,000	100,001 to 250,000	250,001 and over
Number of Enterprises 1	248	0	10	91	36	18	31	26	•	•	•	0	6
Net Sales 2	48977353	0	0	182585	315813	240111	1254979	2512623	•	•	•	0	35939521
Interest 3	1250729	0	872	123	1182	411	2525	4223	•	•	•	0	1201273
Rents 4	81916	0	0	644	63	601	4984	417	•	•	•	0	67076
Royalties 5	1214776	0	0	0	0	0	0	0	•	•	•	0	1214654
Other Portfolio Income 6	1341442	0	13009	21070	48847	33416	3052	5265	•	•	•	0	1198111
Other Receipts 7	2060745	0	178	2	6184	28775	10325	15583	•	•	•	0	1738678
Total Receipts 8	54926961	0	14059	204424	372089	303314	1275865	2538111	•	•	•	0	41359313
Average Total Receipts 9	221480	•	1406	2246	10336	16851	41157	97620	•	•	•	•	6893219

Operating Costs/Operating Income (%)

Item Description for Accounting Period 7/06 Through 6/07	Total	Zero Assets	Under 500	500 to 1000	251 to 500	501 to 1,000	1,001 to 5,000	5,001 to 10,000	10,001 to 25,000	25,001 to 50,000	50,001 to 100,000	100,001 to 250,000	250,001 and over
Cost of Operations 10	50.3	•	•	55.7	62.8	78.5	74.9	63.0	•	•	•	•	46.8
Salaries and Wages 11	12.2	•	•	4.9	8.8	9.3	6.9	10.9	•	•	•	•	12.0
Taxes Paid 12	2.1	•	•	3.6	2.1	2.8	1.2	1.2	•	•	•	•	2.1
Interest Paid 13	4.5	•	•	1.0	1.4	0.6	0.4	0.8	•	•	•	•	5.5
Depreciation 14	3.3	•	•	3.5	4.1	2.0	1.7	1.7	•	•	•	•	3.4
Amortization and Depletion 15	0.9	•	•	0.4	0.0	0.2	0.1	0.1	•	•	•	•	1.1
Pensions and Other Deferred Comp. 16	1.2	•	•	2.5	0.5	0.6	0.1	0.3	•	•	•	•	1.5
Employee Benefits 17	2.0	•	•	1.3	1.5	1.6	0.8	2.4	•	•	•	•	1.9
Advertising 18	8.3	•	•	1.4	1.1	0.4	1.3	6.6	•	•	•	•	10.3
Other Expenses 19	14.4	•	•	19.5	12.3	17.1	8.6	6.8	•	•	•	•	15.6
Officers' Compensation 20	0.5	•	•	6.5	4.6	0.9	1.1	1.6	•	•	•	•	0.2
Operating Margin 21	0.3	•	•	•	0.6	•	3.1	4.6	•	•	•	•	•
Operating Margin Before Officers' Comp. 22	0.8	•	•	6.2	5.3	•	4.2	6.2	•	•	•	•	•

Selected Average Balance Sheet ($ in Thousands)

Net Receivables 23	42507	0	113	391	917	2938	8072	1479815
Inventories 24	9702	0	187	63	407	2764	5066	258713
Net Property, Plant and Equipment 25	51284	0	208	1020	2512	4680	9265	1689485
Total Assets 26	308436	142	693	2877	6956	15987	40220	11232936
Notes and Loans Payable 27	107839	0	176	772	0	2877	10352	3986392
All Other Liabilities 28	117225	0	174	690	1054	3577	10835	4370302
Net Worth 29	83371	142	343	1415	5902	9532	19033	2876242

Selected Financial Ratios (Times to 1)

Current Ratio 30	1.4	•	2.6	1.3	2.1	1.9	2.3	1.4
Quick Ratio 31	0.9	•	1.4	1.2	1.6	1.2	1.5	0.9
Net Sales to Working Capital 32	9.0	•	7.3	30.3	11.7	11.4	8.1	8.9
Coverage Ratio 33	4.0	103.9	12.8	13.9	22.1	13.2	8.2	3.9
Total Asset Turnover 34	0.6	•	2.9	3.0	1.9	2.5	2.4	0.5
Inventory Turnover 35	10.2	•	6.0	88.1	25.7	11.0	12.0	10.8
Receivables Turnover 36	4.8	•	20.7	25.3	•	9.2	12.0	4.4
Total Liabilities to Net Worth 37	2.7	•	1.0	1.0	0.2	0.7	1.1	2.9
Current Assets to Working Capital 38	3.4	1.0	1.6	4.1	1.9	2.1	1.7	3.8
Current Liabilities to Working Capital 39	2.4	•	0.6	3.1	0.9	1.1	0.7	2.8
Working Capital to Net Sales 40	0.1	•	0.1	0.0	0.1	0.1	0.1	0.1
Inventory to Working Capital 41	0.4	•	0.7	0.2	0.4	0.6	0.4	0.4
Total Receipts to Cash Flow 42	4.1	•	4.7	4.9	5.3	9.0	9.6	3.6
Cost of Goods to Cash Flow 43	2.1	•	2.6	3.1	4.2	6.7	6.0	1.7
Cash Flow to Total Debt 44	0.2	•	1.2	1.2	2.4	0.7	0.5	0.2

Selected Financial Factors (in Percentages)

Debt Ratio 45	73.0	•	50.5	50.8	15.1	40.4	52.7	74.4
Return on Total Assets 46	11.5	710.1	36.7	60.5	24.9	13.0	15.1	11.4
Return on Equity Before Income Taxes 47	31.9	703.2	68.3	114.2	28.0	20.1	28.0	33.2
Return on Equity After Income Taxes 48	22.1	464.1	47.3	107.5	22.1	17.9	26.4	22.5
Profit Margin (Before Income Tax) 49	13.5	•	11.7	18.4	12.4	4.7	5.5	16.0
Profit Margin (After Income Tax) 50	9.3	•	8.1	17.3	9.8	4.2	5.2	10.8

Table I

Corporations with and without Net Income

BREWERIES

MONEY AMOUNTS AND SIZE OF ASSETS IN THOUSANDS OF DOLLARS

Item Description for Accounting Period 7/06 Through 6/07	Total	Zero Assets	Under 500	500 to 1,000	1,000 to 5,000	5,000 to 10,000	10,000 to 25,000	25,000 to 50,000	50,000 to 100,000	100,000 to 250,000	250,000 to 500,000	500,000 to 2,500,000	2,500,000 and over
Number of Enterprises **1**	112	0	59	0	30	0	11	6	0	3	0	0	3
Revenues ($ in Thousands)													
Net Sales **2**	25416746	0	27546	0	227544	0	142729	244305	0	649932	0	0	24124690
Interest **3**	69121	0	500	0	0	0	31	297	0	2227	0	0	66066
Rents **4**	30042	0	0	0	55	0	0	0	0	670	0	0	29317
Royalties **5**	408065	0	0	0	0	0	0	0	0	0	0	0	408065
Other Portfolio Income **6**	327157	0	0	0	35647	0	58	323	0	68138	0	0	222991
Other Receipts **7**	65658	0	0	0	608	0	1016	6234	0	5018	0	0	52781
Total Receipts **8**	26316789	0	28046	0	263854	0	143834	251159	0	725985	0	0	24903910
Average Total Receipts **9**	234971	•	475	•	8795	•	13076	41860	•	241995	•	•	8301303
Operating Costs/Operating Income (%)													
Cost of Operations **10**	44.0	•	54.1	•	78.0	•	51.3	52.0	•	52.5	•	•	43.4
Salaries and Wages **11**	8.5	•	•	•	4.7	•	7.2	10.0	•	5.4	•	•	8.6
Taxes Paid **12**	14.3	•	2.7	•	2.5	•	6.3	8.9	•	3.5	•	•	14.8
Interest Paid **13**	3.2	•	•	•	0.9	•	3.7	2.2	•	0.0	•	•	3.3
Depreciation **14**	3.7	•	•	•	1.7	•	7.7	5.6	•	1.5	•	•	3.7
Amortization and Depletion **15**	0.4	•	0.1	•	0.2	•	0.1	0.1	•	0.1	•	•	0.4
Pensions and Other Deferred Comp. **16**	1.8	•	•	•	0.3	•	0.1	1.1	•	0.5	•	•	1.8
Employee Benefits **17**	1.3	•	•	•	1.4	•	1.8	2.1	•	0.5	•	•	1.3
Advertising **18**	7.3	•	•	•	2.6	•	3.2	4.1	•	4.5	•	•	7.5
Other Expenses **19**	8.4	•	44.6	•	9.8	•	11.0	9.8	•	17.1	•	•	8.1
Officers' Compensation **20**	0.5	•	•	•	1.0	•	4.4	0.9	•	0.6	•	•	0.4
Operating Margin **21**	6.6	•	•	•	•	•	3.1	3.3	•	13.8	•	•	6.6
Operating Margin Before Officers' Comp. **22**	7.1	•	•	•	•	•	7.5	4.3	•	14.4	•	•	7.0

Selected Average Balance Sheet ($ in Thousands)

Net Receivables 23	12946	40	2637	1026	2570	14768	432490
Inventories 24	8071	248	422	1104	3054	7679	273865
Net Property, Plant and Equipment 25	95596	180	713	9811	31064	28952	3431210
Total Assets 26	266264	418	3904	13326	38826	155589	961163
Notes and Loans Payable 27	132344	0	5488	6413	15072	0	4832308
All Other Liabilities 28	72083	162	-1271	2236	4043	16164	2668188
Net Worth 29	61836	256	-313	4676	19711	139425	2110667

Selected Financial Ratios (Times to 1)

Current Ratio 30	0.9	1.5	4.1	1.0	1.6	4.3	0.9
Quick Ratio 31	0.6	0.8	3.5	0.5	0.9	3.8	0.5
Net Sales to Working Capital 32	•	6.1	2.8	97.8	13.9	3.5	•
Coverage Ratio 33	4.3	•	15.7	2.0	3.8	7144.5	4.1
Total Asset Turnover 34	0.9	1.1	1.9	1.0	1.0	1.4	0.8
Inventory Turnover 35	12.4	1.0	14.0	6.0	6.9	14.8	12.7
Receivables Turnover 36	15.3	6.1	5.1	12.8	31.7	29.3	15.8
Total Liabilities to Net Worth 37	3.3	0.6	•	1.8	1.0	0.1	3.6
Current Assets to Working Capital 38	•	3.1	1.3	21.4	2.6	1.3	•
Current Liabilities to Working Capital 39	•	2.1	0.3	20.4	1.6	0.3	•
Working Capital to Net Sales 40	•	0.2	0.4	0.0	0.1	0.3	•
Inventory to Working Capital 41	•	0.9	0.2	8.4	1.0	0.1	•
Total Receipts to Cash Flow 42	6.2	59.5	4.7	8.4	6.5	2.4	6.5
Cost of Goods to Cash Flow 43	2.7	32.2	3.7	4.3	3.4	1.3	2.8
Cash Flow to Total Debt 44	0.2	0.0	0.4	0.2	0.3	5.6	0.2

Selected Financial Factors (in Percentages)

Debt Ratio 45	76.8	38.8	108.0	64.9	49.2	10.4	78.0
Return on Total Assets 46	11.9	0.3	26.8	7.4	8.6	35.2	11.5
Return on Equity Before Income Taxes 47	39.3	0.5	•	10.7	12.4	39.3	39.6
Return on Equity After Income Taxes 48	26.5	0.4	•	6.1	12.4	37.2	25.8
Profit Margin (Before Income Tax) 49	10.7	0.3	12.9	3.8	6.0	25.3	10.4
Profit Margin (After Income Tax) 50	7.2	0.2	12.8	2.2	6.0	23.9	6.8

Table II

Corporations with Net Income

BREWERIES

MONEY AMOUNTS AND SIZE OF ASSETS IN THOUSANDS OF DOLLARS

Item Description for Accounting Period 7/06 Through 6/07	Total	Zero Assets	Under 500	500 to 1,000	1,000 to 5,000	5,000 to 10,000	10,000 to 25,000	25,000 to 50,000	50,000 to 100,000	100,000 to 250,000	250,000 to 500,000	500,000 to 2,500,000	2,500,000 and over
Number of Enterprises **1**	90	0	59	0	12	0	7	6	0	3	0	0	3
Revenues ($ in Thousands)													
Net Sales **2**	25289550	0	27546	0	146832	0	96246	244305	0	649932	0	0	24124690
Interest **3**	69121	0	500	0	0	0	31	297	0	2227	0	0	66066
Rents **4**	30042	0	0	0	55	0	0	0	0	670	0	0	29317
Royalties **5**	408065	0	0	0	0	0	0	0	0	0	0	0	408065
Other Portfolio Income **6**	327157	0	0	0	35647	0	58	323	0	68138	0	0	222991
Other Receipts **7**	65001	0	0	0	608	0	359	6234	0	5018	0	0	52781
Total Receipts **8**	26188936	0	28046	0	183142	0	96694	251159	0	725985	0	0	24903910
Average Total Receipts **9**	290988	•	475	•	15262	•	13813	41860	•	241995	•	•	8301303
Operating Costs/Operating Income (%)													
Cost of Operations **10**	43.9	•	54.1	•	71.5	•	45.9	52.0	•	52.5	•	•	43.4
Salaries and Wages **11**	8.5	•	•	•	5.2	•	6.2	10.0	•	5.4	•	•	8.6
Taxes Paid **12**	14.4	•	2.7	•	3.9	•	7.7	8.9	•	3.5	•	•	14.8
Interest Paid **13**	3.2	•	•	•	1.3	•	2.2	2.2	•	0.0	•	•	3.3
Depreciation **14**	3.7	•	•	•	2.7	•	7.4	5.6	•	1.5	•	•	3.7
Amortization and Depletion **15**	0.4	•	0.1	•	0.2	•	0.1	0.1	•	0.1	•	•	0.4
Pensions and Other Deferred Comp. **16**	1.8	•	•	•	0.4	•	0.2	1.1	•	0.5	•	•	1.8
Employee Benefits **17**	1.3	•	•	•	2.1	•	1.0	2.1	•	0.5	•	•	1.3
Advertising **18**	7.3	•	•	•	2.8	•	4.8	4.1	•	4.5	•	•	7.5
Other Expenses **19**	8.4	•	44.6	•	12.4	•	12.2	9.8	•	17.1	•	•	8.1
Officers' Compensation **20**	0.4	•	•	•	1.6	•	5.3	0.9	•	0.6	•	•	0.4
Operating Margin **21**	6.7	•	•	•	•	•	7.1	3.3	•	13.8	•	•	6.6
Operating Margin Before Officers' Comp. **22**	7.1	•	•	•	•	•	12.4	4.3	•	14.4	•	•	7.0

Selected Average Balance Sheet ($ in Thousands)

Net Receivables 23	16028	40	6211	1213	2570	14768	432490
Inventories 24	9651	72	505	1064	3054	7679	273865
Net Property, Plant and Equipment 25	118475	180	1783	9130	31064	28952	3431210
Total Assets 26	329999	418	4529	12525	38826	155589	9611163
Notes and Loans Payable 27	163672	0	8774	5400	15072	0	4832308
All Other Liabilities 28	89585	162	-3461	2470	4043	16164	2668188
Net Worth 29	76742	256	-784	4655	19711	139425	2110667

Selected Financial Ratios (Times to 1)

Current Ratio 30	0.9	1.5	3.5	1.4	1.6	4.3	0.9
Quick Ratio 31	0.6	0.8	3.2	0.8	0.9	3.8	0.5
Net Sales to Working Capital 32		6.1	2.5	16.0	13.9	3.5	
Coverage Ratio 33	4.4		16.5	4.4	3.8	7144.5	4.1
Total Asset Turnover 34	0.9	1.1	2.7	1.1	1.0	1.4	0.8
Inventory Turnover 35	12.8	3.5	17.3	5.9	6.9	14.8	12.7
Receivables Turnover 36	15.4	23.4	3.9	13.4	31.7	29.3	15.8
Total Liabilities to Net Worth 37	3.3	0.6		1.7	1.0	0.1	3.6
Current Assets to Working Capital 38		3.1	1.4	3.7	2.6	1.3	
Current Liabilities to Working Capital 39		2.1	0.4	2.7	1.6	0.3	
Working Capital to Net Sales 40		0.2	0.4	0.1	0.1	0.3	
Inventory to Working Capital 41		0.9	0.1	1.2	1.0	0.1	
Total Receipts to Cash Flow 42	6.2	59.5	3.3	6.2	6.5	2.4	6.5
Cost of Goods to Cash Flow 43	2.7	32.2	2.3	2.9	3.4	1.3	2.8
Cash Flow to Total Debt 44	0.2	0.0	0.7	0.3	0.3	5.6	0.2

Selected Financial Factors (in Percentages)

Debt Ratio 45	76.7	38.8	117.3	62.8	49.2	10.4	78.0
Return on Total Assets 46	11.9	0.3	59.0	10.8	8.6	35.2	11.5
Return on Equity Before Income Taxes 47	39.4	0.5		22.4	12.4	39.3	39.6
Return on Equity After Income Taxes 48	26.6	0.4		15.2	12.4	37.2	25.8
Profit Margin (Before Income Tax) 49	10.8	0.3	20.5	7.6	6.0	25.3	10.4
Profit Margin (After Income Tax) 50	7.3	0.2	20.3	5.1	6.0	23.9	6.8

Table I

Corporations with and without Net Income

WINERIES AND DISTILLERIES

MONEY AMOUNTS AND SIZE OF ASSETS IN THOUSANDS OF DOLLARS

Item Description for Accounting Period 7/06 Through 6/07	Total	Zero Assets	Under 500	500 to 1,000	1,000 to 5,000	5,000 to 10,000	10,000 to 25,000	25,000 to 50,000	50,000 to 100,000	100,000 to 250,000	250,000 to 500,000	500,000 to 2,500,000	2,500,000 and over
Number of Enterprises **1**	1422	4	332	254	565	176	17	35	22	6	7	0	4
Revenues ($ in Thousands)													
Net Sales **2**	22405056	58735	17090	209368	752926	674717	155853	682335	1189762	536331	5277882	0	12850058
Interest **3**	249942	2118	0	0	3635	1335	198	1501	3549	356	21796	0	215453
Rents **4**	12919	0	0	0	437	0	0	158	450	0	1014	0	1761
Royalties **5**	541561	0	0	0	36415	0	0	2312	0	0	163	0	502671
Other Portfolio Income **6**	255122	3	0	720	711	282	4455	2810	3604	1579	200822	0	40139
Other Receipts **7**	304879	2230	0	1963	15714	14758	4421	1052	17810	9731	85650	0	151545
Total Receipts **8**	23769479	63086	17090	212051	809838	691092	164927	690168	1215175	547997	5596427	0	13761627
Average Total Receipts **9**	16716	15772	51	835	1433	3927	9702	19719	55235	91333	799490	•	3440407
Operating Costs/Operating Income (%)													
Cost of Operations **10**	56.6	68.1	48.1	61.1	44.6	49.8	38.6	43.8	62.8	53.4	62.7	•	55.6
Salaries and Wages **11**	6.5	10.2	13.6	•	10.4	11.8	13.0	10.6	6.2	7.3	6.9	•	5.7
Taxes Paid **12**	10.4	11.7	9.5	5.2	4.0	4.5	5.6	3.3	6.7	11.3	13.5	•	10.7
Interest Paid **13**	5.7	3.4	4.8	3.1	2.7	4.0	5.1	1.6	3.1	3.1	1.1	•	8.5
Depreciation **14**	2.6	3.6	8.6	2.1	11.1	5.2	9.5	6.6	3.2	2.8	3.0	•	1.5
Amortization and Depletion **15**	1.5	1.4	2.4	•	0.6	0.1	1.8	0.2	0.7	2.8	0.3	•	2.3
Pensions and Other Deferred Comp. **16**	0.5	1.1	•	•	0.6	0.2	0.3	0.6	0.5	0.4	0.5	•	0.6
Employee Benefits **17**	1.2	2.1	•	0.5	3.6	1.1	2.0	1.3	0.5	1.2	0.8	•	1.3
Advertising **18**	4.8	3.5	7.2	2.9	2.0	0.8	2.4	1.3	2.6	4.4	2.6	•	6.5
Other Expenses **19**	8.6	20.6	75.8	6.4	28.0	14.0	23.5	15.1	9.4	7.4	6.8	•	7.3
Officers' Compensation **20**	1.1	8.2	27.1	17.5	4.8	1.1	2.1	2.3	1.3	1.6	0.5	•	0.7
Operating Margin **21**	0.2	•	•	1.3	•	7.4	•	13.4	2.7	4.4	1.2	•	•
Operating Margin Before Officers' Comp. **22**	1.3	•	•	18.9	•	8.5	•	15.7	4.1	5.9	1.7	•	0.1

Selected Average Balance Sheet ($ in Thousands)

Net Receivables 23	3404	0	0	22	142	356	1109	2497	7879	13441	105411	898537
Inventories 24	4790	0	6	384	838	1806	7102	8374	19293	63399	232948	746872
Net Property, Plant and Equipment 25	4161	0	35	187	896	2377	10177	14213	24360	37570	163094	589818
Total Assets 26	24541	0	68	630	2119	6844	20297	31181	71224	150702	701465	5873932
Notes and Loans Payable 27	11738	0	98	424	914	3505	8066	5645	24204	39620	196881	3233724
All Other Liabilities 28	4337	0	5	13	77	1252	1410	5749	13241	29518	131280	1071376
Net Worth 29	8467	0	-34	193	1128	2087	10821	19787	33779	81565	373304	1568833

Selected Financial Ratios (Times to 1)

Current Ratio 30	2.3	•	3.8	6.1	2.3	6.0	2.4	2.2	1.8	2.3	2.5	2.2
Quick Ratio 31	1.0	•	1.8	1.0	1.4	0.5	0.5	0.7	0.5	0.8	0.8	1.1
Net Sales to Working Capital 32	2.9	•	3.8	2.3	1.4	2.2	1.7	2.5	3.6	1.8	3.0	3.2
Coverage Ratio 33	2.2	•	•	1.8	•	3.5	1.4	10.1	2.5	3.1	7.6	1.8
Total Asset Turnover 34	0.6	•	0.8	1.3	0.6	0.6	0.5	0.6	0.8	0.6	1.1	0.5
Inventory Turnover 35	1.9	•	4.3	1.3	0.7	1.1	0.5	1.0	1.8	0.8	2.0	2.4
Receivables Turnover 36	5.0	•	•	42.9	9.0	16.4	•	7.8	7.3	4.7	7.1	4.0
Total Liabilities to Net Worth 37	1.9	•	•	2.3	0.9	2.3	0.9	0.6	1.1	0.8	0.9	2.7
Current Assets to Working Capital 38	1.7	•	1.4	1.2	1.2	1.8	1.7	1.8	2.2	1.8	1.7	1.8
Current Liabilities to Working Capital 39	0.7	•	0.4	0.2	0.2	0.8	0.7	0.8	1.2	0.8	0.7	0.8
Working Capital to Net Sales 40	0.3	•	0.3	0.4	0.7	0.5	0.6	0.4	0.3	0.6	0.3	0.3
Inventory to Working Capital 41	0.9	•	0.7	1.0	0.9	1.2	1.3	1.2	1.4	1.1	1.0	0.8
Total Receipts to Cash Flow 42	7.6	•	23.7	6.2	4.7	4.7	5.3	3.7	8.0	8.1	7.9	8.1
Cost of Goods to Cash Flow 43	4.3	•	14.5	2.8	2.3	2.3	2.0	1.6	5.0	4.3	4.9	4.5
Cash Flow to Total Debt 44	0.1	•	•	0.2	0.2	0.2	0.2	0.5	0.2	0.2	0.3	0.1

Selected Financial Factors (in Percentages)

Debt Ratio 45	65.5	•	150.7	69.4	46.8	69.5	46.7	36.5	52.6	45.9	46.8	73.3
Return on Total Assets 46	7.9	•	•	7.4	•	7.7	3.2	10.0	6.0	5.7	9.1	8.5
Return on Equity Before Income Taxes 47	12.4	•	145.1	11.0	145.1	18.1	1.8	14.2	7.7	7.2	14.8	14.5
Return on Equity After Income Taxes 48	8.8	•	145.1	10.5	•	14.2	•	13.2	5.7	6.8	12.2	9.4
Profit Margin (Before Income Tax) 49	6.7	•	2.6	2.6	•	9.8	2.1	14.4	4.8	6.5	7.3	7.1
Profit Margin (After Income Tax) 50	4.7	•	2.4	2.4	•	7.7	•	13.4	3.6	6.2	6.0	4.6

Table II

Corporations with Net Income

WINERIES AND DISTILLERIES

MONEY AMOUNTS AND SIZE OF ASSETS IN THOUSANDS OF DOLLARS

Item Description for Accounting Period 7/06 Through 6/07	Total	Zero Assets	Under 500	500 to 1,000	1,000 to 5,000	5,000 to 10,000	10,000 to 25,000	25,000 to 50,000	50,000 to 100,000	100,000 to 250,000	250,000 to 500,000	500,000 to 2,500,000	2,500,000 and over
Number of Enterprises 1	610	0	0	254	126	166	•	28	14	•	7	0	•
Revenues ($ in Thousands)													
Net Sales 2	20310423	0	0	209368	284971	647841	•	534865	965310	•	5277882	0	•
Interest 3	236933	0	0	0	3635	1335	•	1099	1589	•	21796	0	•
Rents 4	12519	0	0	0	437	0	•	17	272	•	10114	0	•
Royalties 5	541561	0	0	0	36415	0	•	2312	0	•	163	0	•
Other Portfolio Income 6	248644	0	0	720	711	282	•	1310	3162	•	200822	0	•
Other Receipts 7	299452	0	0	1963	4746	14072	•	344	17507	•	85650	0	•
Total Receipts 8	21649532	0	0	212051	330915	663530	•	539947	987840	•	5596427	0	•
Average Total Receipts 9	35491	•	•	835	2626	3997	•	19284	70560	•	799490	•	•
Operating Costs/Operating Income (%)													
Cost of Operations 10	55.9	•	•	61.1	31.2	49.3	•	38.4	58.0	•	62.7	•	•
Salaries and Wages 11	6.5	•	•	•	16.7	11.2	•	10.3	6.8	•	6.9	•	•
Taxes Paid 12	11.1	•	•	5.2	3.2	4.5	•	3.6	8.0	•	13.5	•	•
Interest Paid 13	5.9	•	•	3.1	2.4	3.7	•	1.6	2.6	•	1.1	•	•
Depreciation 14	2.2	•	•	2.1	4.9	5.0	•	7.0	2.4	•	3.0	•	•
Amortization and Depletion 15	1.6	•	•	•	0.1	0.1	•	0.2	0.5	•	0.3	•	•
Pensions and Other Deferred Comp. 16	0.6	•	•	•	1.6	0.2	•	0.3	0.5	•	0.5	•	•
Employee Benefits 17	1.1	•	•	0.5	3.4	1.0	•	1.1	0.6	•	0.8	•	•
Advertising 18	4.8	•	•	2.9	2.6	0.8	•	1.7	3.2	•	2.6	•	•
Other Expenses 19	7.9	•	•	6.4	31.9	14.6	•	14.8	8.8	•	6.8	•	•
Officers' Compensation 20	1.1	•	•	17.5	6.8	1.1	•	2.3	1.4	•	0.5	•	•
Operating Margin 21	1.3	•	•	1.3	•	8.5	•	18.6	7.1	•	1.2	•	•
Operating Margin Before Officers' Comp. 22	2.3	•	•	18.9	2.0	9.7	•	21.0	8.5	•	1.7	•	•

Selected Average Balance Sheet ($ in Thousands)

Net Receivables 23	7159	22	117	356	2194	10538	105411
Inventories 24	9767	349	960	2037	9277	23138	232948
Net Property, Plant and Equipment 25	6991	187	419	2212	13520	16857	163094
Total Assets 26	48493	630	2132	6690	30599	70642	701465
Notes and Loans Payable 27	24616	424	766	3461	5666	22203	196881
All Other Liabilities 28	8922	13	277	1318	6017	17051	131280
Net Worth 29	14955	193	1089	1911	18915	31389	373304

Selected Financial Ratios (Times to 1)

Current Ratio 30	2.2	6.1	4.2	2.2	2.2	1.7	2.5
Quick Ratio 31	0.9	1.0	1.0	0.5	0.6	0.5	0.8
Net Sales to Working Capital 32	3.1	2.3	2.2	2.4	2.5	4.2	3.0
Coverage Ratio 33	2.4	1.8	5.8	4.0	12.8	4.6	7.6
Total Asset Turnover 34	0.7	1.3	1.1	0.6	0.6	1.0	1.1
Inventory Turnover 35	1.9	1.4	0.7	0.9	0.8	1.7	2.0
Receivables Turnover 36	4.9	49.0	14.0	•	•	7.4	7.1
Total Liabilities to Net Worth 37	2.2	2.3	1.0	2.5	0.6	1.3	0.9
Current Assets to Working Capital 38	1.8	1.2	1.3	1.9	1.9	2.4	1.7
Current Liabilities to Working Capital 39	0.8	0.2	0.3	0.9	0.9	1.4	0.7
Working Capital to Net Sales 40	0.3	0.4	0.5	0.4	0.4	0.2	0.3
Inventory to Working Capital 41	0.9	1.0	1.0	1.3	1.2	1.5	1.0
Total Receipts to Cash Flow 42	7.1	23.7	3.1	4.3	3.1	6.1	7.9
Cost of Goods to Cash Flow 43	3.9	14.5	1.0	2.1	1.2	3.6	4.9
Cash Flow to Total Debt 44	0.1	0.1	0.7	0.2	0.5	0.3	0.3

Selected Financial Factors (in Percentages)

Debt Ratio 45	69.2	69.4	48.9	71.4	38.2	55.6	46.8
Return on Total Assets 46	9.8	7.4	14.5	8.6	13.2	11.8	9.1
Return on Equity Before Income Taxes 47	18.4	11.0	23.5	22.4	19.7	20.8	14.8
Return on Equity After Income Taxes 48	13.6	10.5	20.4	17.9	18.3	17.4	12.2
Profit Margin (Before Income Tax) 49	8.3	2.6	11.3	11.0	19.5	9.5	7.3
Profit Margin (After Income Tax) 50	6.1	2.4	9.8	8.8	18.1	7.9	6.0

Table I

Corporations with and without Net Income

TOBACCO MANUFACTURING

MONEY AMOUNTS AND SIZE OF ASSETS IN THOUSANDS OF DOLLARS

Item Description for Accounting Period 7/06 Through 6/07	Total	Zero Assets	Under 500	500 to 1,000	1,000 to 5,000	5,000 to 10,000	10,000 to 25,000	25,000 to 50,000	50,000 to 100,000	100,000 to 250,000	250,000 to 500,000	500,000 to 2,500,000	2,500,000 and over
Number of Enterprises **1**	35	0	0	0	0	10	9	6	5	0	0	6	0
Revenues ($ in Thousands)													
Net Sales **2**	18612457	0	0	0	0	276778	297952	568224	803550	0	0	16665953	0
Interest **3**	278896	0	0	0	0	7015	0	0	21891	0	0	249991	0
Rents **4**	3026	0	0	0	0	0	0	0	392	0	0	2634	0
Royalties **5**	128269	0	0	0	0	0	0	0	4990	0	0	123279	0
Other Portfolio Income **6**	436255	0	0	0	0	0	261	327	22033	0	0	413632	0
Other Receipts **7**	37831	0	0	0	0	79	37028	2638	12114	0	0	-14027	0
Total Receipts **8**	19496734	0	0	0	0	283872	335241	571189	864970	0	0	17441462	0
Average Total Receipts **9**	557050	•	•	•	•	28387	37249	95198	172994	•	•	2906910	•
Operating Costs/Operating Income (%)													
Cost of Operations **10**	44.4	•	•	•	•	41.9	61.2	69.2	51.1	•	•	43.0	•
Salaries and Wages **11**	5.1	•	•	•	•	0.6	6.6	4.1	5.7	•	•	5.2	•
Taxes Paid **12**	15.4	•	•	•	•	38.7	22.9	15.4	10.2	•	•	15.1	•
Interest Paid **13**	3.2	•	•	•	•	0.3	1.4	0.3	2.8	•	•	3.4	•
Depreciation **14**	0.7	•	•	•	•	1.0	0.3	0.8	1.0	•	•	0.7	•
Amortization and Depletion **15**	0.3	•	•	•	•	0.0	0.0	0.1	0.4	•	•	0.3	•
Pensions and Other Deferred Comp. **16**	1.6	•	•	•	•	•	0.5	0.1	0.3	•	•	1.7	•
Employee Benefits **17**	1.8	•	•	•	•	0.9	0.5	0.3	0.8	•	•	2.0	•
Advertising **18**	4.3	•	•	•	•	0.4	1.4	0.7	1.1	•	•	4.7	•
Other Expenses **19**	9.8	•	•	•	•	1.3	14.6	4.2	13.8	•	•	9.9	•
Officers' Compensation **20**	0.9	•	•	•	•	12.6	2.5	1.5	1.7	•	•	0.6	•
Operating Margin **21**	12.6	•	•	•	•	2.2	•	3.4	11.1	•	•	13.6	•
Operating Margin Before Officers' Comp. **22**	13.5	•	•	•	•	14.9	•	4.9	12.8	•	•	14.2	•

Selected Average Balance Sheet ($ in Thousands)

Net Receivables 23	11716	385	4213	2140	13093	48332
Inventories 24	65803	2669	4900	9812	20203	348752
Net Property, Plant and Equipment 25	53023	1028	489	2611	9812	296068
Total Assets 26	776390	5897	17666	27098	193664	4304131
Notes and Loans Payable 27	226710	173	6880	4255	42526	1272171
All Other Liabilities 28	260287	2514	11003	7026	38017	1458937
Net Worth 29	289394	3209	-217	15817	113120	1573022

Selected Financial Ratios (Times to 1)

Current Ratio 30	1.4	1.6	1.5	2.1	2.9	1.3
Quick Ratio 31	0.5	0.6	0.6	0.7	2.3	0.4
Net Sales to Working Capital 32	9.3	16.7	6.3	8.7	2.0	11.3
Coverage Ratio 33	6.5	19.4	1.4	14.1	7.8	6.4
Total Asset Turnover 34	0.7	4.7	1.9	3.5	0.8	0.6
Inventory Turnover 35	3.6	4.3	4.1	6.7	4.1	3.4
Receivables Turnover 36	39.6	143.7	•	35.6	24.5	45.3
Total Liabilities to Net Worth 37	1.7	0.8	•	0.7	0.7	1.7
Current Assets to Working Capital 38	3.3	2.6	3.1	1.9	1.5	3.9
Current Liabilities to Working Capital 39	2.3	1.6	2.1	0.9	0.5	2.9
Working Capital to Net Sales 40	0.1	0.1	0.2	0.1	0.5	0.1
Inventory to Working Capital 41	1.2	1.6	0.9	0.7	0.3	1.4
Total Receipts to Cash Flow 42	3.9	16.9	8.6	13.9	3.4	3.8
Cost of Goods to Cash Flow 43	1.7	7.1	5.3	9.6	1.7	1.6
Cash Flow to Total Debt 44	0.3	0.6	0.2	0.6	0.6	0.3

Selected Financial Factors (in Percentages)

Debt Ratio 45	62.7	45.6	101.2	41.6	41.6	63.5
Return on Total Assets 46	14.0	23.8	3.7	14.8	17.8	13.9
Return on Equity Before Income Taxes 47	31.8	41.5	•	23.6	26.6	32.1
Return on Equity After Income Taxes 48	22.7	27.4	•	23.6	24.3	22.5
Profit Margin (Before Income Tax) 49	17.3	4.8	0.6	3.9	18.7	18.2
Profit Margin (After Income Tax) 50	12.3	3.2	0.6	3.9	17.1	12.8

Table II

Corporations with Net Income

TOBACCO MANUFACTURING

MONEY AMOUNTS AND SIZE OF ASSETS IN THOUSANDS OF DOLLARS

Item Description for Accounting Period 7/06 Through 6/07	Total	Zero Assets	Under 500	500 to 1,000	1,000 to 5,000	5,000 to 10,000	10,000 to 25,000	25,000 to 50,000	50,000 to 100,000	100,000 to 250,000	250,000 to 500,000	500,000 to 2,500,000	2,500,000 and over
Number of Enterprises 1	27	0	0	0	0	10	•	0	•	0	0	6	0
Revenues ($ in Thousands)													
Net Sales 2	18013073	0	0	0	0	276778	•	0	•	0	0	16665953	0
Interest 3	276948	0	0	0	0	7015	•	0	•	0	0	249991	0
Rents 4	3026	0	0	0	0	0	•	0	•	0	0	2634	0
Royalties 5	128269	0	0	0	0	0	•	0	•	0	0	123279	0
Other Portfolio Income 6	435666	0	0	0	0	0	•	0	•	0	0	413632	0
Other Receipts 7	30646	0	0	0	0	79	•	0	•	0	0	-14027	0
Total Receipts 8	18887628	0	0	0	0	283872	•	0	•	0	0	17441462	0
Average Total Receipts 9	699542	•	•	•	•	28387	•	•	•	•	•	2906910	•
Operating Costs/Operating Income (%)													
Cost of Operations 10	43.4	•	•	•	•	41.9	•	•	•	•	•	43.0	•
Salaries and Wages 11	5.2	•	•	•	•	0.6	•	•	•	•	•	5.2	•
Taxes Paid 12	15.4	•	•	•	•	38.7	•	•	•	•	•	15.1	•
Interest Paid 13	3.2	•	•	•	•	0.3	•	•	•	•	•	3.4	•
Depreciation 14	0.7	•	•	•	•	1.0	•	•	•	•	•	0.7	•
Amortization and Depletion 15	0.3	•	•	•	•	0.0	•	•	•	•	•	0.3	•
Pensions and Other Deferred Comp. 16	1.6	•	•	•	•	•	•	•	•	•	•	1.7	•
Employee Benefits 17	1.9	•	•	•	•	0.9	•	•	•	•	•	2.0	•
Advertising 18	4.4	•	•	•	•	0.4	•	•	•	•	•	4.7	•
Other Expenses 19	9.9	•	•	•	•	1.3	•	•	•	•	•	9.9	•
Officers' Compensation 20	0.9	•	•	•	•	12.6	•	•	•	•	•	0.6	•
Operating Margin 21	13.2	•	•	•	•	2.2	•	•	•	•	•	13.6	•
Operating Margin Before Officers' Comp. 22	14.0	•	•	•	•	14.9	•	•	•	•	•	14.2	•

Selected Average Balance Sheet ($ in Thousands)

Net Receivables 23	13936	385	48332
Inventories 24	84534	2669	352354
Net Property, Plant and Equipment 25	67920	1028	296068
Total Assets 26	996985	5897	4304131
Notes and Loans Payable 27	290530	173	1272171
All Other Liabilities 28	332994	2514	1458937
Net Worth 29	373462	3209	1573022

Selected Financial Ratios (Times to 1)

Current Ratio 30	1.4	1.6	1.3
Quick Ratio 31	0.5	0.6	0.4
Net Sales to Working Capital 32	9.3	16.7	11.3
Coverage Ratio 33	6.6	19.4	6.4
Total Asset Turnover 34	0.7	4.7	0.6
Inventory Turnover 35	3.4	4.3	3.4
Receivables Turnover 36	39.9	143.7	•
Total Liabilities to Net Worth 37	1.7	0.8	1.7
Current Assets to Working Capital 38	3.3	2.6	3.9
Current Liabilities to Working Capital 39	2.3	1.6	2.9
Working Capital to Net Sales 40	0.1	0.1	0.1
Inventory to Working Capital 41	1.2	1.6	1.4
Total Receipts to Cash Flow 42	3.8	16.9	3.8
Cost of Goods to Cash Flow 43	1.6	7.1	1.6
Cash Flow to Total Debt 44	0.3	0.3	0.3

Selected Financial Factors (in Percentages)

Debt Ratio 45	62.5	45.6	63.5
Return on Total Assets 46	14.2	23.8	13.9
Return on Equity Before Income Taxes 47	32.1	41.5	32.1
Return on Equity After Income Taxes 48	23.0	27.4	22.5
Profit Margin (Before Income Tax) 49	18.0	4.8	18.2
Profit Margin (After Income Tax) 50	12.9	3.2	12.8

Table I

Corporations with and without Net Income

TEXTILE MILLS

MONEY AMOUNTS AND SIZE OF ASSETS IN THOUSANDS OF DOLLARS

Item Description for Accounting Period 7/06 Through 6/07	Total	Zero Assets	Under 500	500 to 1,000	1,000 to 5,000	5,000 to 10,000	10,000 to 25,000	25,000 to 50,000	50,000 to 100,000	100,000 to 250,000	250,000 to 500,000	500,000 to 2,500,000	2,500,000 and over
Number of Enterprises **1**	1892	•	•	•	326	46	68	15	17	15	5	5	0
Revenues ($ in Thousands)													
Net Sales **2**	14817891	•	•	•	1244472	639334	2006448	691075	1500645	3279785	1897239	2383349	0
Interest **3**	86739	•	•	•	3172	1170	5345	1697	4859	8986	9740	51460	0
Rents **4**	6299	•	•	•	1555	247	384	721	748	323	2126	194	0
Royalties **5**	39396	•	•	•	0	0	168	0	15	327	446	38146	0
Other Portfolio Income **6**	88122	•	•	•	8996	1	1880	2051	2106	35594	1325	33320	0
Other Receipts **7**	170825	•	•	•	1703	333	6036	1060	43878	57906	10622	32922	0
Total Receipts **8**	15209272	•	•	•	1259898	641085	2020261	696604	1552251	3382921	1921498	2539391	0
Average Total Receipts **9**	8039	•	•	•	3865	13937	29710	46440	91309	225528	384300	507878	•
Operating Costs/Operating Income (%)													
Cost of Operations **10**	75.0	•	•	•	57.9	75.8	81.7	88.4	78.3	77.5	74.2	73.7	•
Salaries and Wages **11**	5.7	•	•	•	5.6	4.5	6.3	3.2	5.2	5.7	5.2	6.7	•
Taxes Paid **12**	1.9	•	•	•	2.7	1.3	1.3	2.2	2.2	1.2	2.1	2.2	•
Interest Paid **13**	2.6	•	•	•	0.2	1.6	1.9	2.3	2.0	2.5	1.7	5.6	•
Depreciation **14**	2.8	•	•	•	2.4	1.0	2.1	3.5	2.8	3.2	4.1	3.2	•
Amortization and Depletion **15**	0.4	•	•	•	0.0	0.3	0.1	0.1	0.3	0.7	0.3	0.8	•
Pensions and Other Deferred Comp. **16**	0.9	•	•	•	1.9	0.2	0.0	0.2	0.7	1.0	0.7	2.2	•
Employee Benefits **17**	1.1	•	•	•	1.3	0.5	1.0	1.0	1.2	1.3	0.9	1.8	•
Advertising **18**	0.5	•	•	•	3.5	0.0	0.2	0.0	0.8	0.2	0.4	0.1	•
Other Expenses **19**	9.8	•	•	•	16.5	9.0	5.9	3.8	11.0	8.7	8.1	10.2	•
Officers' Compensation **20**	2.3	•	•	•	10.5	1.0	1.1	0.7	1.0	0.9	1.5	1.1	•
Operating Margin **21**	•	•	•	•	•	4.7	•	•	•	•	0.6	•	•
Operating Margin Before Officers' Comp. **22**	•	•	•	•	8.0	5.7	•	•	•	•	•	2.1	•

Selected Average Balance Sheet ($ in Thousands)

Item									
Net Receivables 23	1092	511	1637	3344	5962	9121	26427	55214	114171
Inventories 24	1068	414	1833	4220	9133	15362	27019	76526	62540
Net Property, Plant and Equipment 25	1535	260	680	5161	11609	26199	46973	101487	107453
Total Assets 26	6477	1786	6497	17335	33280	71658	153599	356520	802208
Notes and Loans Payable 27	2350	650	2660	6357	13373	26639	51816	76152	351916
All Other Liabilities 28	1371	442	1515	3560	8841	14851	45311	51918	141391
Net Worth 29	2756	694	2322	7418	11065	30168	56472	228450	308901

Selected Financial Ratios (Times to 1)

Item									
Current Ratio 30	1.8	3.1	1.7	1.7	1.2	1.9	1.7	1.8	1.7
Quick Ratio 31	0.9	1.9	0.8	0.7	0.6	0.8	0.9	0.8	1.0
Net Sales to Working Capital 32	6.3	4.0	6.9	7.0	18.0	5.6	7.4	6.8	4.8
Coverage Ratio 33	0.9	•	4.1	0.6	•	•	1.1	2.1	0.9
Total Asset Turnover 34	1.2	2.1	2.1	1.7	1.4	1.2	1.4	1.1	0.6
Inventory Turnover 35	5.5	5.3	5.7	5.7	4.5	4.5	6.3	3.7	5.6
Receivables Turnover 36	7.3	7.9	8.4	8.0	6.4	8.3	9.1	5.4	5.3
Total Liabilities to Net Worth 37	1.4	1.6	1.8	1.3	2.0	1.4	1.7	0.6	1.6
Current Assets to Working Capital 38	2.3	1.5	2.3	2.5	7.0	2.1	2.4	2.3	2.4
Current Liabilities to Working Capital 39	1.3	0.5	1.3	1.5	6.0	1.1	1.4	1.3	1.4
Working Capital to Net Sales 40	0.2	0.2	0.1	0.1	0.1	0.2	0.1	0.1	0.2
Inventory to Working Capital 41	0.9	0.4	1.1	1.1	3.0	0.9	0.9	1.2	0.8
Total Receipts to Cash Flow 42	15.3	11.3	9.0	29.5	•	20.7	15.5	11.3	16.3
Cost of Goods to Cash Flow 43	11.5	6.5	6.8	24.1	•	16.2	12.0	8.4	12.0
Cash Flow to Total Debt 44	0.1	0.3	0.4	0.1	•	0.1	0.1	0.3	0.1

Selected Financial Factors (in Percentages)

Item									
Debt Ratio 45	57.5	61.1	64.3	57.2	66.8	57.9	63.2	35.9	61.5
Return on Total Assets 46	2.8	•	14.1	1.8	•	3.8	3.8	3.0	•
Return on Equity Before Income Taxes 47	•	•	29.7	•	•	1.0	3.1	•	•
Return on Equity After Income Taxes 48	•	•	22.3	•	•	•	1.8	•	•
Profit Margin (Before Income Tax) 49	•	•	5.0	•	•	0.2	0.2	1.9	•
Profit Margin (After Income Tax) 50	•	•	3.7	•	•	•	1.1	•	•

Table II
Corporations with Net Income

TEXTILE MILLS

MONEY AMOUNTS AND SIZE OF ASSETS IN THOUSANDS OF DOLLARS

Item Description for Accounting Period 7/06 Through 6/07	Total	Zero Assets	Under 500	500 to 1,000	1,000 to 5,000	5,000 to 10,000	10,000 to 25,000	25,000 to 50,000	50,000 to 100,000	100,000 to 250,000	250,000 to 500,000	500,000 to 2,500,000	2,500,000 and over
Number of Enterprises **1**	1014	•	709	94	107	•	41	3	•	7	•	0	0
Revenues ($ in Thousands)													
Net Sales **2**	8158271	•	360486	281468	452037	•	1436543	79912	•	1811393	•	0	0
Interest **3**	66857	•	0	10	1646	•	5284	1	•	1246	•	0	0
Rents **4**	4426	•	0	0	1555	•	384	0	•	57	•	0	0
Royalties **5**	10511	•	0	0	0	•	0	0	•	0	•	0	0
Other Portfolio Income **6**	58411	•	0	0	8996	•	830	683	•	22300	•	0	0
Other Receipts **7**	95128	•	0	39	1087	•	4568	466	•	54145	•	0	0
Total Receipts **8**	8393604	•	360486	281517	465321	•	1447609	81062	•	1889141	•	0	0
Average Total Receipts **9**	8278	•	508	2995	4349	•	35308	27021	•	269877	•	•	•
Operating Costs/Operating Income (%)													
Cost of Operations **10**	71.3	•	40.1	70.7	70.4	•	78.5	76.4	•	77.1	•	•	•
Salaries and Wages **11**	6.7	•	13.3	3.7	2.6	•	7.5	4.6	•	5.4	•	•	•
Taxes Paid **12**	1.9	•	3.8	3.2	2.0	•	1.5	1.8	•	1.3	•	•	•
Interest Paid **13**	2.4	•	1.7	0.4	0.4	•	1.6	1.3	•	2.4	•	•	•
Depreciation **14**	2.3	•	0.8	0.6	2.4	•	0.8	3.1	•	3.7	•	•	•
Amortization and Depletion **15**	0.2	•	0.0	0.0	0.0	•	0.0	•	•	0.1	•	•	•
Pensions and Other Deferred Comp. **16**	0.6	•	•	0.0	0.0	•	0.0	0.3	•	0.9	•	•	•
Employee Benefits **17**	1.3	•	0.0	0.0	2.9	•	0.6	1.9	•	1.3	•	•	•
Advertising **18**	0.3	•	0.1	0.1	0.1	•	0.2	0.0	•	0.1	•	•	•
Other Expenses **19**	9.1	•	28.2	11.2	10.6	•	4.3	6.7	•	6.1	•	•	•
Officers' Compensation **20**	1.8	•	8.3	9.5	3.1	•	1.3	0.9	•	0.8	•	•	•
Operating Margin **21**	2.3	•	3.6	0.6	5.4	•	3.7	3.0	•	0.8	•	•	•
Operating Margin Before Officers' Comp. **22**	4.0	•	11.9	10.1	8.5	•	5.0	3.9	•	1.5	•	•	•

Selected Average Balance Sheet ($ in Thousands)

Net Receivables 23	1103	50	222	455	3972	3338	29849
Inventories 24	1086	11	142	753	5344	14390	26074
Net Property, Plant and Equipment 25	1406	22	202	488	3341	13508	62429
Total Assets 26	6257	118	639	2406	18690	35382	170937
Notes and Loans Payable 27	1887	95	121	234	3063	9052	58365
All Other Liabilities 28	1093	19	193	229	4796	1341	40900
Net Worth 29	3278	4	326	1944	10831	24989	71672

Selected Financial Ratios (Times to 1)

Current Ratio 30	2.0	2.8	1.6	5.5	2.2	1.5	2.0
Quick Ratio 31	1.1	2.3	1.0	2.8	0.8	0.6	1.2
Net Sales to Working Capital 32	5.5	11.7	19.5	2.9	4.9	5.4	7.0
Coverage Ratio 33	3.2	3.2	2.6	21.6	3.8	3.8	3.1
Total Asset Turnover 34	1.3	4.3	4.7	1.8	1.9	0.8	1.5
Inventory Turnover 35	5.3	18.9	14.9	3.9	5.1	1.4	7.6
Receivables Turnover 36	7.4	8.3	•	5.6	7.6	2.9	10.8
Total Liabilities to Net Worth 37	0.9	26.9	1.0	0.2	0.7	0.4	1.4
Current Assets to Working Capital 38	2.0	1.6	2.5	1.2	1.8	3.0	2.0
Current Liabilities to Working Capital 39	1.0	0.6	1.5	0.2	0.8	2.0	1.0
Working Capital to Net Sales 40	0.2	0.1	0.1	0.3	0.2	0.2	0.1
Inventory to Working Capital 41	0.7	0.2	0.9	0.4	0.9	1.5	0.7
Total Receipts to Cash Flow 42	8.7	5.1	11.9	6.6	12.8	12.1	11.5
Cost of Goods to Cash Flow 43	6.2	2.1	8.4	4.7	10.1	9.2	8.8
Cash Flow to Total Debt 44	0.3	0.9	0.8	1.4	0.3	0.2	0.2

Selected Financial Factors (in Percentages)

Debt Ratio 45	47.6	96.4	49.0	19.2	42.0	29.4	58.1
Return on Total Assets 46	9.7	22.8	4.5	15.3	11.3	3.7	11.3
Return on Equity Before Income Taxes 47	12.7	435.4	5.4	18.1	14.4	3.9	18.2
Return on Equity After Income Taxes 48	10.9	435.4	4.6	17.2	13.8	3.8	16.1
Profit Margin (Before Income Tax) 49	5.2	3.6	0.6	8.3	4.5	3.6	5.0
Profit Margin (After Income Tax) 50	4.5	3.6	0.5	7.9	4.3	3.6	4.5

Table I
Corporations with and without Net Income

TEXTILE PRODUCT MILLS

MONEY AMOUNTS AND SIZE OF ASSETS IN THOUSANDS OF DOLLARS

Item Description for Accounting Period 7/06 Through 6/07	Total	Zero Assets	Under 500	500 to 1,000	1,000 to 5,000	5,000 to 10,000	10,000 to 25,000	25,000 to 50,000	50,000 to 100,000	100,000 to 250,000	250,000 to 500,000	500,000 to 2,500,000	2,500,000 and over
Number of Enterprises **1**	3006	•	•	•	275	29	68	49	11	15	5	7	0
Revenues ($ in Thousands)													
Net Sales **2**	27159803	•	•	•	1493425	568100	2244640	3005720	1305119	3083657	1842171	12019775	0
Interest **3**	95271	•	•	•	1183	276	2226	1809	690	11713	9323	66477	0
Rents **4**	6129	•	•	•	0	0	854	300	571	2518	175	619	0
Royalties **5**	35747	•	•	•	0	0	0	0	19	403	843	33333	0
Other Portfolio Income **6**	87795	•	•	•	11	6	0	2623	5670	15384	19524	32566	0
Other Receipts **7**	102125	•	•	•	15546	861	14537	11412	3232	19444	6307	15673	0
Total Receipts **8**	27486870	•	•	•	1510165	569243	2268566	3021864	1315301	3133119	1878343	12168443	0
Average Total Receipts **9**	9144	•	•	•	5492	19629	33361	61671	119573	208875	375669	1738349	•
Operating Costs/Operating Income (%)													
Cost of Operations **10**	69.3	•	•	•	57.9	69.6	81.7	77.3	74.5	79.4	66.6	65.2	•
Salaries and Wages **11**	9.8	•	•	•	10.6	4.7	4.4	7.1	6.0	5.5	3.5	14.4	•
Taxes Paid **12**	2.0	•	•	•	2.6	1.5	1.2	1.7	1.4	1.5	3.8	1.9	•
Interest Paid **13**	1.9	•	•	•	0.6	1.4	1.1	1.3	1.4	2.4	3.3	2.1	•
Depreciation **14**	2.1	•	•	•	1.6	0.5	1.4	1.6	1.8	2.3	2.1	2.4	•
Amortization and Depletion **15**	0.3	•	•	•	0.0	0.0	0.2	0.1	0.5	0.2	0.7	0.2	•
Pensions and Other Deferred Comp. **16**	0.6	•	•	•	0.8	0.6	0.1	0.5	0.5	0.9	1.2	0.6	•
Employee Benefits **17**	1.8	•	•	•	1.2	0.9	1.0	1.1	1.8	1.8	1.5	2.5	•
Advertising **18**	0.8	•	•	•	0.3	0.8	0.6	0.4	0.8	0.8	0.7	1.0	•
Other Expenses **19**	9.0	•	•	•	18.0	5.9	5.9	6.6	6.5	6.9	16.1	8.0	•
Officers' Compensation **20**	1.8	•	•	•	3.2	5.7	2.1	1.8	0.7	1.6	1.0	0.6	•
Operating Margin **21**	0.8	•	•	•	3.1	8.5	0.4	0.4	4.1	•	•	1.1	•
Operating Margin Before Officers' Comp. **22**	2.6	•	•	•	6.3	14.1	2.5	2.2	4.8	•	0.5	1.7	•

Selected Average Balance Sheet ($ in Thousands)

	•	•	•	•	•	•	•	•	•
Net Receivables 23	776	571	2474	3507	6681	16322	26313	36968	97889
Inventories 24	1480	702	2110	7594	10830	20201	34898	50396	289720
Net Property, Plant and Equipment 25	1292	320	956	2547	7796	18438	34818	69000	281230
Total Assets 26	7485	2291	6861	15913	36185	77745	152134	373580	1886133
Notes and Loans Payable 27	2333	892	2638	4766	10314	22704	41063	151962	559682
All Other Liabilities 28	1441	475	1041	4668	9900	19696	57169	113565	233728
Net Worth 29	3712	925	3182	6478	15970	35345	53902	108053	1092723

Selected Financial Ratios (Times to 1)

	•	•	•	•	•	•	•	•	•
Current Ratio 30	1.9	2.4	3.1	1.7	1.6	2.5	1.8	1.5	2.1
Quick Ratio 31	0.9	1.5	1.5	0.7	0.6	1.3	0.8	0.6	1.0
Net Sales to Working Capital 32	6.0	5.2	4.9	7.0	6.6	4.6	6.1	10.7	5.4
Coverage Ratio 33	2.0	7.5	7.2	2.4	1.7	4.5	0.2	1.5	2.1
Total Asset Turnover 34	1.2	2.4	2.9	2.1	1.7	1.5	1.4	1.0	0.9
Inventory Turnover 35	4.2	4.5	6.5	3.6	4.4	4.4	4.7	4.9	3.9
Receivables Turnover 36	9.6	9.6	11.9	7.7	9.0	6.2	8.3	10.3	10.5
Total Liabilities to Net Worth 37	1.0	1.5	1.2	1.5	1.3	1.2	1.8	2.5	0.7
Current Assets to Working Capital 38	2.1	1.7	1.5	2.5	2.6	1.7	2.3	3.1	1.9
Current Liabilities to Working Capital 39	1.1	0.7	0.5	1.5	1.6	0.7	1.3	2.1	0.9
Working Capital to Net Sales 40	0.2	0.2	0.2	0.1	0.2	0.2	0.2	0.1	0.2
Inventory to Working Capital 41	1.0	0.6	0.7	1.4	1.3	0.8	1.1	1.6	0.9
Total Receipts to Cash Flow 42	11.6	5.1	7.4	18.8	16.3	10.2	28.1	7.1	12.6
Cost of Goods to Cash Flow 43	8.0	3.0	5.1	15.4	12.6	7.6	22.3	4.7	8.2
Cash Flow to Total Debt 44	0.2	0.8	0.7	0.2	0.2	0.3	0.1	0.2	0.2

Selected Financial Factors (in Percentages)

	•	•	•	•	•	•	•	•	•
Debt Ratio 45	50.4	59.6	53.6	59.3	55.9	54.5	64.6	71.1	42.1
Return on Total Assets 46	4.6	11.5	28.7	5.3	3.8	9.5	0.6	4.7	4.0
Return on Equity Before Income Taxes 47	4.7	24.7	53.3	7.6	3.7	16.2	•	5.1	3.7
Return on Equity After Income Taxes 48	2.6	21.8	44.6	5.4	3.0	14.2	•	2.5	1.6
Profit Margin (Before Income Tax) 49	1.9	4.2	8.7	1.5	1.0	4.8	•	1.5	2.3
Profit Margin (After Income Tax) 50	1.1	3.7	7.3	1.1	0.8	4.2	•	0.7	1.0

61

Table II
Corporations with Net Income

TEXTILE PRODUCT MILLS

MONEY AMOUNTS AND SIZE OF ASSETS IN THOUSANDS OF DOLLARS

Item Description for Accounting Period 7/06 Through 6/07		Total	Zero Assets	Under 500	500 to 1,000	1,000 to 5,000	5,000 to 10,000	10,000 to 25,000	25,000 to 50,000	50,000 to 100,000	100,000 to 250,000	250,000 to 500,000	500,000 to 2,500,000	2,500,000 and over
Number of Enterprises	1	2045	•	880	467	127	•	48	23	•	8	•	3	0
Revenues ($ in Thousands)														
Net Sales	2	19206228	•	470909	804800	856829	•	1726633	1588833	•	2159331	•	8595478	0
Interest	3	79092	•	5	53	164	•	1729	1274	•	8090	•	56772	0
Rents	4	2967	•	39	0	0	•	0	113	•	585	•	450	0
Royalties	5	27711	•	0	0	0	•	0	0	•	403	•	26061	0
Other Portfolio Income	6	62216	•	0	5198	11	•	1965	1265	•	7655	•	20732	0
Other Receipts	7	64996	•	0	188	12448	•	11958	8557	•	5218	•	2316	0
Total Receipts	8	19443210	•	470953	810239	869452	•	1742285	1600042	•	2181282	•	8701809	0
Average Total Receipts	9	9508	•	535	1735	6846	•	36298	69567	•	272660	•	2900603	•
Operating Costs/Operating Income (%)														
Cost of Operations	10	64.6	•	44.9	62.1	49.6	•	80.9	72.9	•	75.7	•	58.4	•
Salaries and Wages	11	10.8	•	10.3	5.5	13.1	•	3.9	6.3	•	4.8	•	16.9	•
Taxes Paid	12	2.1	•	5.8	2.3	2.6	•	1.2	2.1	•	1.4	•	1.9	•
Interest Paid	13	1.7	•	0.1	1.3	0.4	•	1.1	1.5	•	1.5	•	2.2	•
Depreciation	14	1.8	•	0.9	0.4	1.0	•	1.5	1.4	•	1.8	•	2.1	•
Amortization and Depletion	15	0.2	•	•	0.0	0.0	•	0.1	0.2	•	0.1	•	0.3	•
Pensions and Other Deferred Comp.	16	0.6	•	0.0	0.1	0.9	•	0.1	0.5	•	0.3	•	0.7	•
Employee Benefits	17	1.9	•	0.0	0.9	0.9	•	1.3	1.1	•	1.6	•	2.7	•
Advertising	18	0.7	•	0.3	0.4	0.5	•	0.1	0.4	•	1.0	•	1.0	•
Other Expenses	19	9.3	•	13.3	17.3	20.0	•	4.7	6.7	•	6.4	•	9.2	•
Officers' Compensation	20	1.8	•	19.9	6.1	2.4	•	2.4	1.9	•	1.4	•	0.3	•
Operating Margin	21	4.4	•	4.5	3.6	8.5	•	2.8	5.2	•	4.0	•	4.4	•
Operating Margin Before Officers' Comp.	22	6.2	•	24.4	9.7	11.0	•	5.2	7.1	•	5.3	•	4.7	•

Selected Average Balance Sheet ($ in Thousands)

Net Receivables 23	631	0	155	739	3941	5830	35664	58493
Inventories 24	1393	6	217	775	7055	13422	43905	407891
Net Property, Plant and Equipment 25	1278	36	62	293	2909	8149	34849	467551
Total Assets 26	7714	32	806	2890	16439	37299	152994	3215656
Notes and Loans Payable 27	2496	18	258	1022	3946	11785	36735	1097940
All Other Liabilities 28	1447	0	171	654	5682	9202	41104	447193
Net Worth 29	3771	14	377	1215	6811	16312	75156	1670523

Selected Financial Ratios (Times to 1)

Current Ratio 30	1.9	3.8	3.3	2.0	1.4	2.2	2.0	1.9
Quick Ratio 31	0.9	3.5	1.2	1.3	0.6	0.8	1.0	0.9
Net Sales to Working Capital 32	6.4	1105.4	3.7	6.0	9.8	5.0	5.9	6.5
Coverage Ratio 33	4.2	63.9	4.2	26.3	4.4	4.8	4.3	3.5
Total Asset Turnover 34	1.2	16.6	2.1	2.3	2.2	1.9	1.8	0.9
Inventory Turnover 35	4.4	38.4	4.9	4.3	4.1	3.7	4.7	4.1
Receivables Turnover 36	15.3	65.2		8.7	8.6	8.6		58.6
Total Liabilities to Net Worth 37	1.0	1.3	1.1	1.4	1.4	1.3	1.0	0.9
Current Assets to Working Capital 38	2.1	1.4	1.4	2.0	3.3	1.9	2.0	2.1
Current Liabilities to Working Capital 39	1.1	0.4	0.4	1.0	2.3	0.9	1.0	1.1
Working Capital to Net Sales 40	0.2	0.0	0.3	0.2	0.1	0.2	0.2	0.2
Inventory to Working Capital 41	0.9	0.1	0.5	0.6	1.8	0.8	1.0	0.9
Total Receipts to Cash Flow 42	7.9	6.0	6.2	3.8	14.5	8.9	10.2	8.1
Cost of Goods to Cash Flow 43	5.1	2.7	3.9	1.9	11.7	6.5	7.7	4.7
Cash Flow to Total Debt 44	0.3	4.9	0.6	1.1	0.3	0.4	0.3	0.2

Selected Financial Factors (in Percentages)

Debt Ratio 45	51.1	56.8	53.2	58.0	58.6	56.3	50.9	48.1
Return on Total Assets 46	9.0	75.7	11.9	24.3	10.4	13.8	11.4	6.9
Return on Equity Before Income Taxes 47	14.0	172.5	19.4	55.6	19.4	25.0	17.8	9.5
Return on Equity After Income Taxes 48	11.0	172.5	18.7	50.9	16.5	23.5	15.2	6.3
Profit Margin (Before Income Tax) 49	5.6	4.5	4.3	10.0	3.7	5.9	5.0	5.5
Profit Margin (After Income Tax) 50	4.4	4.5	4.1	9.2	3.1	5.6	4.2	3.7

Table I

Corporations with and without Net Income

APPAREL KNITTING MILLS

MONEY AMOUNTS AND SIZE OF ASSETS IN THOUSANDS OF DOLLARS

Item Description for Accounting Period 7/06 Through 6/07	Total	Zero Assets	Under 500	500 to 1,000	1,000 to 5,000	5,000 to 10,000	10,000 to 25,000	25,000 to 50,000	50,000 to 100,000	100,000 to 250,000	250,000 to 500,000	500,000 to 2,500,000	2,500,000 and over
Number of Enterprises 1	131	4	0	0	68	24	13	10	4	4	4	0	0
Revenues ($ in Thousands)													
Net Sales 2	5419567	262480	0	0	271333	594242	175403	924624	229936	767923	2193627	0	0
Interest 3	6419	0	0	0	1385	432	1906	2	16	401	2278	0	0
Rents 4	105	0	0	0	0	0	15	90	0	1	0	0	0
Royalties 5	27780	0	0	0	0	0	0	0	101	12703	14977	0	0
Other Portfolio Income 6	11271	1718	0	0	0	0	1003	1800	324	2445	3981	0	0
Other Receipts 7	32341	269	0	0	2732	387	19389	1460	144	3861	4096	0	0
Total Receipts 8	5497483	264467	0	0	275450	595061	197716	927976	230521	787334	2218959	0	0
Average Total Receipts 9	41966	66117	•	•	4051	24794	15209	92798	57630	196834	554740	•	•
Operating Costs/Operating Income (%)													
Cost of Operations 10	76.7	89.7	•	•	74.5	74.8	77.9	81.6	88.3	69.4	75.2	•	•
Salaries and Wages 11	5.0	3.9	•	•	3.2	5.3	10.8	4.3	3.9	6.9	4.6	•	•
Taxes Paid 12	1.7	2.7	•	•	4.4	2.5	1.2	1.9	1.6	2.1	0.8	•	•
Interest Paid 13	2.6	2.0	•	•	1.3	0.7	1.8	1.6	4.1	1.3	4.3	•	•
Depreciation 14	1.2	0.7	•	•	0.4	0.8	0.5	1.2	1.5	2.3	1.1	•	•
Amortization and Depletion 15	0.4	0.3	•	•	0.1	0.0	0.0	0.3	1.1	0.8	0.3	•	•
Pensions and Other Deferred Comp. 16	2.0	2.5	•	•	0.0	0.0	0.2	0.2	0.0	0.6	4.4	•	•
Employee Benefits 17	1.5	•	•	•	0.7	0.8	0.2	0.5	0.4	1.5	2.7	•	•
Advertising 18	2.4	•	•	•	2.2	0.1	1.0	0.5	0.1	4.0	4.0	•	•
Other Expenses 19	7.2	6.0	•	•	10.6	8.2	8.9	5.0	8.1	8.8	6.8	•	•
Officers' Compensation 20	1.9	1.1	•	•	5.4	3.6	3.3	0.7	0.7	0.8	2.0	•	•
Operating Margin 21	•	•	•	•	•	3.3	•	2.1	•	1.7	•	•	•
Operating Margin Before Officers' Comp. 22	•	•	•	•	2.6	6.9	•	2.8	•	2.5	•	•	•

Selected Average Balance Sheet ($ in Thousands)

Net Receivables 23	6664	0	439	2714	698	8272	14171	32926	124468
Inventories 24	9603	0	666	2179	4603	18250	21242	66128	284287
Net Property, Plant and Equipment 25	5677	0	325	625	619	6312	16780	34021	108048
Total Assets 26	48038	0	2317	6891	15195	44449	74320	156688	1100996
Notes and Loans Payable 27	26359	0	404	739	3161	4383	35183	31349	764195
All Other Liabilities 28	13694	0	560	1855	2294	23274	12644	39544	309997
Net Worth 29	7985	0	1353	4297	9741	16792	26492	85794	26804

Selected Financial Ratios (Times to 1)

Current Ratio 30	2.1	•	1.5	2.9	1.7	1.5	2.3	3.1	2.1
Quick Ratio 31	0.7	•	0.7	1.4	0.8	0.5	0.9	1.2	0.6
Net Sales to Working Capital 32	3.2	•	9.9	6.3	4.7	7.4	2.2	2.9	2.1
Coverage Ratio 33	0.7	•	0.0	5.8	4.9	2.6	•	4.4	0.1
Total Asset Turnover 34	0.9	•	1.7	3.6	0.9	2.1	0.8	1.2	0.5
Inventory Turnover 35	3.3	•	4.5	8.5	2.3	4.1	2.4	2.0	1.5
Receivables Turnover 36	8.4	•	7.6	16.8	4.0	11.7	4.2	5.1	8.8
Total Liabilities to Net Worth 37	5.0	•	0.7	0.6	0.6	1.6	1.8	0.8	40.1
Current Assets to Working Capital 38	1.9	•	3.1	1.5	2.4	2.9	1.8	1.5	1.9
Current Liabilities to Working Capital 39	0.9	•	2.1	0.5	1.4	1.9	0.8	0.5	0.9
Working Capital to Net Sales 40	0.3	•	0.1	0.2	0.2	0.1	0.5	0.3	0.5
Inventory to Working Capital 41	1.1	•	1.6	0.6	0.8	1.8	1.0	0.9	1.1
Total Receipts to Cash Flow 42	22.5	•	15.8	10.3	7.5	16.8	•	8.7	129.7
Cost of Goods to Cash Flow 43	17.2	•	11.8	7.7	5.9	13.7	•	6.0	97.6
Cash Flow to Total Debt 44	0.0	•	0.3	0.9	0.3	0.2	•	0.3	0.0

Selected Financial Factors (in Percentages)

Debt Ratio 45	83.4	•	41.6	37.6	35.9	62.2	64.4	45.2	97.6
Return on Total Assets 46	1.6	•	0.1	15.1	7.8	8.4	•	6.7	0.2
Return on Equity Before Income Taxes 47	•	•	•	20.0	9.7	13.6	•	9.4	•
Return on Equity After Income Taxes 48	•	•	•	20.0	9.1	11.7	•	8.4	•
Profit Margin (Before Income Tax) 49	•	•	•	3.5	7.0	2.5	•	4.2	•
Profit Margin (After Income Tax) 50	•	•	•	3.5	6.6	2.1	•	3.8	•

Table II

Corporations with Net Income

APPAREL KNITTING MILLS

MONEY AMOUNTS AND SIZE OF ASSETS IN THOUSANDS OF DOLLARS

Item Description for Accounting Period 7/06 Through 6/07	Total	Zero Assets	Under 500	500 to 1,000	1,000 to 5,000	5,000 to 10,000	10,000 to 25,000	25,000 to 50,000	50,000 to 100,000	100,000 to 250,000	250,000 to 500,000	500,000 to 2,500,000	2,500,000 and over
Number of Enterprises **1**	60	0	0	0	20	13	•	10	0	•	0	0	0
Revenues ($ in Thousands)													
Net Sales **2**	2685071	0	0	0	53900	460969	•	841890	0	•	0	0	0
Interest **3**	4091	0	0	0	1385	432	•	2	0	•	0	0	0
Rents **4**	105	0	0	0	0	0	•	90	0	•	0	0	0
Royalties **5**	12703	0	0	0	0	0	•	0	0	•	0	0	0
Other Portfolio Income **6**	4473	0	0	0	0	0	•	1800	0	•	0	0	0
Other Receipts **7**	22591	0	0	0	0	234	•	1492	0	•	0	0	0
Total Receipts **8**	2729034	0	0	0	55285	461635	•	845274	0	•	0	0	•
Average Total Receipts **9**	45484	•	•	•	2764	35510	•	84527	•	•	•	•	•
Operating Costs/Operating Income (%)													
Cost of Operations **10**	74.8	•	•	•	54.6	74.5	•	80.6	•	•	•	•	•
Salaries and Wages **11**	5.6	•	•	•	1.7	5.9	•	4.8	•	•	•	•	•
Taxes Paid **12**	1.9	•	•	•	5.6	2.4	•	1.9	•	•	•	•	•
Interest Paid **13**	1.3	•	•	•	0.9	0.3	•	1.7	•	•	•	•	•
Depreciation **14**	1.4	•	•	•	0.5	0.1	•	1.3	•	•	•	•	•
Amortization and Depletion **15**	0.4	•	•	•	•	0.0	•	0.3	•	•	•	•	•
Pensions and Other Deferred Comp. **16**	0.4	•	•	•	0.1	0.0	•	0.3	•	•	•	•	•
Employee Benefits **17**	1.1	•	•	•	0.4	0.5	•	0.6	•	•	•	•	•
Advertising **18**	1.7	•	•	•	10.0	0.1	•	0.6	•	•	•	•	•
Other Expenses **19**	6.9	•	•	•	14.9	8.0	•	4.7	•	•	•	•	•
Officers' Compensation **20**	1.8	•	•	•	3.0	3.8	•	0.7	•	•	•	•	•
Operating Margin **21**	2.8	•	•	•	8.3	4.4	•	2.4	•	•	•	•	•
Operating Margin Before Officers' Comp. **22**	4.7	•	•	•	11.4	8.2	•	3.1	•	•	•	•	•

Selected Average Balance Sheet ($ in Thousands)

Net Receivables 23	5217	258	4729	7431
Inventories 24	9035	132	1266	21481
Net Property, Plant and Equipment 25	5042	132	220	8825
Total Assets 26	36652	2567	8648	47832
Notes and Loans Payable 27	5591	0	34	4545
All Other Liabilities 28	8658	402	2621	22889
Net Worth 29	22403	2164	5993	20399

Selected Financial Ratios (Times to 1)

Current Ratio 30	2.2	1.5	3.1	1.5
Quick Ratio 31	0.9	1.1	2.0	0.6
Net Sales to Working Capital 32	4.6	13.7	6.4	6.9
Coverage Ratio 33	4.5	13.6	16.3	2.7
Total Asset Turnover 34	1.2	1.1	4.1	1.8
Inventory Turnover 35	3.7	11.1	20.9	3.2
Receivables Turnover 36	8.5	7.4	14.9	•
Total Liabilities to Net Worth 37	0.6	0.2	0.4	1.3
Current Assets to Working Capital 38	1.8	3.0	1.5	2.9
Current Liabilities to Working Capital 39	0.8	2.0	0.5	1.9
Working Capital to Net Sales 40	0.2	0.1	0.2	0.1
Inventory to Working Capital 41	1.0	0.7	0.3	1.8
Total Receipts to Cash Flow 42	10.5	6.6	9.0	16.7
Cost of Goods to Cash Flow 43	7.8	3.6	6.7	13.5
Cash Flow to Total Debt 44	0.3	1.0	1.5	0.2

Selected Financial Factors (in Percentages)

Debt Ratio 45	38.9	15.7	30.7	57.4
Return on Total Assets 46	7.2	12.4	19.7	8.0
Return on Equity Before Income Taxes 47	9.1	13.6	26.7	11.7
Return on Equity After Income Taxes 48	7.9	9.3	26.7	10.2
Profit Margin (Before Income Tax) 49	4.6	10.9	4.5	2.8
Profit Margin (After Income Tax) 50	3.9	7.5	4.5	2.5

Table I

Corporations with and without Net Income

CUT AND SEW APPAREL CONTRACTORS AND MFRS.

MONEY AMOUNTS AND SIZE OF ASSETS IN THOUSANDS OF DOLLARS

Item Description for Accounting Period 7/06 Through 6/07	Total	Zero Assets	Under 500	500 to 1,000	1,000 to 5,000	5,000 to 10,000	10,000 to 25,000	25,000 to 50,000	50,000 to 100,000	100,000 to 250,000	250,000 to 500,000	500,000 to 2,500,000	2,500,000 and over
Number of Enterprises 1	6258	1084	3681	331	785	163	129	40	20	12	8	0	4
Revenues ($ in Thousands)													
Net Sales 2	45940893	1011198	2025864	611209	5487217	3245683	4931981	2925224	2420355	2581581	4758653	0	15941928
Interest 3	222763	552	6	39	6358	212	2544	2014	1013	12788	3324	0	193914
Rents 4	20676	129	0	0	540	0	0	1980	106	29	1043	0	16849
Royalties 5	920486	5103	0	0	2302	115	5230	34501	458	710	47507	0	824559
Other Portfolio Income 6	208436	9727	9314	0	121	10476	7983	949	28612	29439	11493	0	100320
Other Receipts 7	1067198	17629	1542	0	41434	21323	70948	16342	45617	34608	180241	0	637517
Total Receipts 8	48380452	1044338	2036726	611248	5537972	3277809	5018686	2981010	2496161	2659155	5002261	0	17715087
Average Total Receipts 9	7731	963	553	1847	7055	20109	38905	74525	124808	221596	625283	•	4428772
Operating Costs/Operating Income (%)													
Cost of Operations 10	64.4	78.2	34.0	63.3	68.6	66.1	75.6	71.8	67.3	67.1	59.0	•	61.7
Salaries and Wages 11	9.9	7.2	14.3	12.3	9.1	9.7	5.6	8.9	10.7	9.7	11.6	•	10.8
Taxes Paid 12	1.9	1.9	3.4	2.4	1.4	2.9	2.1	1.2	2.1	1.7	1.8	•	1.6
Interest Paid 13	2.1	2.8	0.5	1.0	1.2	1.2	1.3	1.6	1.1	3.5	1.1	•	3.5
Depreciation 14	0.8	1.5	0.8	1.5	0.6	0.2	0.4	0.7	0.9	0.9	1.1	•	1.1
Amortization and Depletion 15	0.5	0.5	0.3	0.0	0.1	0.1	0.1	0.5	0.2	0.6	0.3	•	1.1
Pensions and Other Deferred Comp. 16	0.3	0.0	0.0	•	0.3	0.1	0.1	0.2	0.3	0.3	0.4	•	0.5
Employee Benefits 17	1.1	0.5	0.6	0.6	0.9	0.3	0.4	0.5	1.3	1.3	1.5	•	1.6
Advertising 18	2.4	3.0	0.1	0.9	1.2	1.9	0.4	1.4	1.8	1.8	3.3	•	3.9
Other Expenses 19	13.7	18.9	37.8	15.2	11.5	9.8	7.4	10.1	8.2	7.4	14.0	•	16.1
Officers' Compensation 20	2.4	0.5	4.9	3.1	3.5	3.5	3.9	2.8	1.7	1.3	1.3	•	1.7
Operating Margin 21	0.3	•	3.3	•	1.6	4.3	2.7	0.4	4.6	4.3	4.7	•	•
Operating Margin Before Officers' Comp. 22	2.7	•	8.2	2.8	5.1	7.8	6.6	3.2	6.2	5.6	5.9	•	•

Selected Average Balance Sheet ($ in Thousands)

Net Receivables 23	934	0	10	92	628	1554	5242	6475	15879	29797	122018	611755
Inventories 24	1037	0	23	97	958	2329	4583	15420	24040	33115	70744	527136
Net Property, Plant and Equipment 25	515	0	11	167	203	1390	1699	3443	8385	15874	66329	373388
Total Assets 26	5372	0	82	615	2543	6830	16633	35876	75169	153246	471395	4826915
Notes and Loans Payable 27	1157	0	20	228	744	2186	5024	9153	17202	63413	79735	848967
All Other Liabilities 28	1916	0	29	180	820	2261	5052	11309	12548	34466	137987	1984786
Net Worth 29	2299	0	33	207	978	2383	6557	15414	45420	55368	253673	1993161

Selected Financial Ratios (Times to 1)

Current Ratio 30	1.4	•	2.3	1.0	2.2	1.6	1.5	1.7	2.5	2.0	2.4	1.0
Quick Ratio 31	0.7	•	1.4	0.5	1.0	0.7	0.8	0.5	1.0	1.0	1.4	0.5
Net Sales to Working Capital 32	9.5	•	15.3	314.1	6.0	11.0	8.7	6.5	3.8	5.0	3.6	2898.0
Coverage Ratio 33	3.7	•	8.5	0.7	3.0	5.5	4.3	2.5	8.1	3.1	9.9	3.4
Total Asset Turnover 34	1.4	•	6.7	3.0	2.7	2.9	2.3	2.0	1.6	1.4	1.3	0.8
Inventory Turnover 35	4.6	•	8.1	12.0	5.0	5.6	6.3	3.4	3.4	4.4	5.0	4.7
Receivables Turnover 36	7.5	•	43.7	20.3	13.3	13.3	8.3	11.1	8.8	7.3	6.2	5.9
Total Liabilities to Net Worth 37	1.3	•	1.5	2.0	1.6	1.9	1.5	1.3	0.7	1.8	0.9	1.4
Current Assets to Working Capital 38	3.2	•	1.8	48.3	1.9	2.6	2.8	2.5	1.7	2.0	1.7	1066.5
Current Liabilities to Working Capital 39	2.2	•	0.8	47.3	0.9	1.6	1.8	1.5	0.7	1.0	0.7	1065.5
Working Capital to Net Sales 40	0.1	•	0.1	0.0	0.2	0.1	0.1	0.2	0.3	0.2	0.3	0.0
Inventory to Working Capital 41	1.3	•	0.6	24.3	0.9	1.1	1.1	1.5	0.9	0.8	0.6	383.7
Total Receipts to Cash Flow 42	6.1	217.1	2.8	10.1	8.7	7.5	9.6	10.0	7.3	9.2	5.0	4.9
Cost of Goods to Cash Flow 43	4.0	169.7	1.0	6.4	6.0	5.0	7.3	7.2	4.9	6.2	3.0	3.0
Cash Flow to Total Debt 44	0.4	•	4.0	0.4	0.5	0.6	0.4	0.4	0.6	0.2	0.5	0.3

Selected Financial Factors (in Percentages)

Debt Ratio 45	57.2	•	59.5	66.3	65.1	61.5	60.6	57.0	39.6	63.9	46.2	58.7
Return on Total Assets 46	11.0	•	29.2	2.1	19.0	10.3	13.2	8.0	14.2	15.2	13.7	9.7
Return on Equity Before Income Taxes 47	18.8	•	63.5	•	44.6	17.9	25.8	11.1	20.7	28.5	22.9	16.6
Return on Equity After Income Taxes 48	15.0	•	63.2	•	43.2	17.2	24.5	10.5	18.6	25.2	18.4	11.7
Profit Margin (Before Income Tax) 49	5.9	•	3.8	•	5.3	2.5	4.4	2.3	7.8	7.3	9.8	8.3
Profit Margin (After Income Tax) 50	4.7	•	3.8	•	5.2	2.4	4.2	2.2	7.0	6.5	7.9	5.9

Table II

Corporations with Net Income

CUT AND SEW APPAREL CONTRACTORS AND MFRS.

MONEY AMOUNTS AND SIZE OF ASSETS IN THOUSANDS OF DOLLARS

Item Description for Accounting Period 7/06 Through 6/07		Total	Zero Assets	Under 500	500 to 1,000	1,000 to 5,000	5,000 to 10,000	10,000 to 25,000	25,000 to 50,000	50,000 to 100,000	100,000 to 250,000	250,000 to 500,000	500,000 to 2,500,000	2,500,000 and over
Number of Enterprises	1	3727	•	2471	320	550	114	109	26	•	•	8	0	4
Revenues ($ in Thousands)														
Net Sales	2	42011733	•	1785281	611209	4746699	3035194	4316001	2047785	•	•	4758653	0	15941928
Interest	3	220655	•	0	39	5951	76	2275	1194	•	•	3324	0	193914
Rents	4	20353	•	0	0	345	0	0	1980	•	•	1043	0	16849
Royalties	5	915289	•	0	0	464	115	5230	34501	•	•	47507	0	824559
Other Portfolio Income	6	190206	•	9314	0	1	10476	512	916	•	•	11493	0	100320
Other Receipts	7	1003582	•	1	-1	5711	20493	62541	8195	•	•	180241	0	637517
Total Receipts	8	44361818	•	1794596	611247	4759171	3066354	4386559	2094571	•	•	5002261	0	17715087
Average Total Receipts	9	11903	•	726	1910	8653	26898	40244	80560	•	•	625283	•	4428772
Operating Costs/Operating Income (%)														
Cost of Operations	10	63.7	•	32.8	61.9	69.0	66.4	74.1	72.7	•	•	59.0	•	61.7
Salaries and Wages	11	9.9	•	12.7	12.1	8.3	9.5	5.8	8.9	•	•	11.6	•	10.8
Taxes Paid	12	1.9	•	3.4	2.4	1.4	2.8	2.2	1.3	•	•	1.8	•	1.6
Interest Paid	13	2.1	•	0.3	1.0	0.8	1.1	1.3	1.3	•	•	1.1	•	3.5
Depreciation	14	0.8	•	0.7	1.2	0.5	0.2	0.3	0.8	•	•	1.1	•	1.1
Amortization and Depletion	15	0.5	•	0.3	0.0	0.0	0.0	0.1	0.2	•	•	0.3	•	1.1
Pensions and Other Deferred Comp.	16	0.3	•	0.0	•	0.2	0.1	0.1	0.2	•	•	0.4	•	0.5
Employee Benefits	17	1.2	•	0.6	0.6	0.9	0.3	0.4	0.6	•	•	1.5	•	1.6
Advertising	18	2.4	•	0.0	0.9	1.1	1.9	0.4	1.0	•	•	3.3	•	3.9
Other Expenses	19	13.3	•	39.3	14.1	9.9	9.3	6.8	7.1	•	•	14.0	•	16.1
Officers' Compensation	20	2.4	•	5.0	3.1	3.4	3.6	4.3	2.4	•	•	1.3	•	1.7
Operating Margin	21	1.4	•	4.8	2.6	4.5	4.8	4.3	3.7	•	•	4.7	•	•
Operating Margin Before Officers' Comp.	22	3.8	•	9.8	5.8	7.9	8.4	8.5	6.1	•	•	5.9	•	•

Selected Average Balance Sheet ($ in Thousands)

Net Receivables 23	1483	15	95	716	2023	5401	7952	122018	611755
Inventories 24	1511	26	100	1072	2440	4331	16462	70744	527683
Net Property, Plant and Equipment 25	764	15	162	228	313	1290	4235	66329	373388
Total Assets 26	8476	101	618	2725	7145	16678	35417	471395	4826915
Notes and Loans Payable 27	1716	10	235	485	2581	5230	9067	79735	848967
All Other Liabilities 28	3060	34	186	959	2462	4772	11640	137987	1984786
Net Worth 29	3700	58	197	1281	2102	6677	14711	253673	1993161

Selected Financial Ratios (Times to 1)

Current Ratio 30	1.4	2.5	1.0	1.9	1.9	1.5	1.7	2.4	1.0
Quick Ratio 31	0.7	1.6	0.5	0.9	0.9	0.7	0.6	1.4	0.5
Net Sales to Working Capital 32	9.7	15.1	•	7.7	9.2	8.8	6.5	3.6	2898.0
Coverage Ratio 33	4.5	19.3	3.6	6.7	6.5	5.5	5.7	9.9	3.4
Total Asset Turnover 34	1.3	7.1	3.1	3.2	3.7	2.4	2.2	1.3	0.8
Inventory Turnover 35	4.7	9.2	11.9	5.6	7.2	6.8	3.5	5.0	4.7
Receivables Turnover 36	7.6	46.9	20.3	13.2	15.3	8.6	9.6	6.2	•
Total Liabilities to Net Worth 37	1.3	0.7	2.1	1.1	2.4	1.5	1.4	0.9	1.4
Current Assets to Working Capital 38	3.3	1.7	•	2.1	2.1	2.9	2.4	1.7	1066.5
Current Liabilities to Working Capital 39	2.3	0.7	•	1.1	1.1	1.9	1.4	0.7	1065.5
Working Capital to Net Sales 40	0.1	0.1	•	0.1	0.1	0.1	0.2	0.3	0.0
Inventory to Working Capital 41	1.3	0.6	•	1.0	0.9	1.1	1.3	0.6	383.7
Total Receipts to Cash Flow 42	5.7	2.5	8.2	7.9	7.3	8.9	9.3	5.0	4.9
Cost of Goods to Cash Flow 43	3.6	0.8	5.1	5.5	4.8	6.6	6.8	3.0	3.0
Cash Flow to Total Debt 44	0.4	6.6	0.6	0.8	0.7	0.4	0.4	0.5	0.3

Selected Financial Factors (in Percentages)

Debt Ratio 45	56.3	42.9	68.2	53.0	70.6	60.0	58.5	46.2	58.7
Return on Total Assets 46	12.5	39.8	11.3	17.8	25.6	17.1	16.1	13.7	9.7
Return on Equity Before Income Taxes 47	22.3	66.1	25.8	32.2	73.6	34.9	32.0	22.9	16.6
Return on Equity After Income Taxes 48	18.3	65.8	21.8	31.3	71.3	33.3	31.1	18.4	11.7
Profit Margin (Before Income Tax) 49	7.3	5.3	2.7	4.8	5.8	5.9	6.0	9.8	8.3
Profit Margin (After Income Tax) 50	6.0	5.3	2.2	4.7	5.6	5.6	5.8	7.9	5.9

Table I

Corporations with and without Net Income

APPAREL ACCESSORIES AND OTHER APPAREL

MONEY AMOUNTS AND SIZE OF ASSETS IN THOUSANDS OF DOLLARS

Item Description for Accounting Period 7/06 Through 6/07		Total	Zero Assets	Under 500	500 to 1,000	1,000 to 5,000	5,000 to 10,000	10,000 to 25,000	25,000 to 50,000	50,000 to 100,000	100,000 to 250,000	250,000 to 500,000	500,000 to 2,500,000	2,500,000 and over
Number of Enterprises	1	3014	708	1386	449	375	0	60	22	10	4	0	0	0
Revenues ($ in Thousands)														
Net Sales	2	8557367	37603	1138993	543689	1976243	0	1736034	1009765	916408	1198632	0	0	0
Interest	3	10264	9	12	55	2296	0	4506	1034	944	1408	0	0	0
Rents	4	344	0	0	0	0	0	111	0	219	14	0	0	0
Royalties	5	17243	0	0	0	0	0	41	0	117	17085	0	0	0
Other Portfolio Income	6	46581	0	2	0	1140	0	26511	17579	1261	88	0	0	0
Other Receipts	7	147324	4	12306	11662	8581	0	7605	56569	-1606	52203	0	0	0
Total Receipts	8	8779123	37616	1151313	555406	1988260	0	1774808	1084947	917343	1269430	0	0	0
Average Total Receipts	9	2913	53	831	1237	5302	•	29580	49316	91734	317358	•	•	•
Operating Costs/Operating Income (%)														
Cost of Operations	10	64.1	35.0	66.6	64.0	67.4	•	69.5	70.9	66.0	42.3	•	•	•
Salaries and Wages	11	11.3	12.3	9.8	7.3	13.8	•	9.6	8.3	9.5	16.9	•	•	•
Taxes Paid	12	2.8	4.7	1.1	3.0	1.7	•	2.0	2.3	1.7	8.7	•	•	•
Interest Paid	13	2.0	7.5	0.2	1.5	1.6	•	1.8	2.1	3.1	3.7	•	•	•
Depreciation	14	1.0	0.9	0.9	1.2	0.7	•	0.9	1.1	1.3	1.5	•	•	•
Amortization and Depletion	15	0.2	0.0	•	0.2	0.0	•	0.2	0.1	0.5	0.5	•	•	•
Pensions and Other Deferred Comp.	16	0.3	0.1	0.5	0.0	0.4	•	0.6	0.1	0.2	0.1	•	•	•
Employee Benefits	17	1.1	1.3	0.4	0.2	1.1	•	1.9	1.4	1.0	1.3	•	•	•
Advertising	18	1.7	0.5	0.7	0.4	1.1	•	1.6	2.0	1.2	4.6	•	•	•
Other Expenses	19	14.3	22.1	10.4	21.9	10.5	•	14.6	12.3	14.0	22.3	•	•	•
Officers' Compensation	20	1.9	8.0	2.6	4.2	1.5	•	1.9	1.9	2.0	0.6	•	•	•
Operating Margin	21	•	7.6	6.8	•	0.2	•	•	•	•	•	•	•	•
Operating Margin Before Officers' Comp.	22	1.0	15.6	9.3	0.3	1.7	•	•	•	1.5	•	•	•	•

Selected Average Balance Sheet ($ in Thousands)

Net Receivables 23	372	0	66	119	555	•	3571	9428	18101	41062
Inventories 24	531	0	30	339	968	•	5209	9596	22244	67119
Net Property, Plant and Equipment 25	172	0	12	94	157	•	1673	2806	7810	40278
Total Assets 26	1642	0	192	711	2179	•	14552	33895	69232	309096
Notes and Loans Payable 27	841	0	30	357	584	•	14134	11824	21656	196829
All Other Liabilities 28	558	0	54	344	887	•	4831	10824	25000	85476
Net Worth 29	244	0	108	9	708	•	-4413	11247	22576	26790

Selected Financial Ratios (Times to 1)

Current Ratio 30	1.9	•	3.3	1.9	1.7	•	1.9	1.9	2.1	1.6
Quick Ratio 31	0.8	•	2.3	0.8	0.8	•	0.8	0.8	1.0	0.6
Net Sales to Working Capital 32	5.2	•	6.5	4.6	8.2	•	5.4	3.5	3.4	5.3
Coverage Ratio 33	1.9	2.0	44.5	•	1.5	•	•	3.3	0.9	2.1
Total Asset Turnover 34	1.7	•	4.3	1.7	2.4	•	2.0	1.4	1.3	1.0
Inventory Turnover 35	3.4	•	18.4	2.3	3.7	•	3.9	3.4	2.7	1.9
Receivables Turnover 36	7.4	•	15.1	6.3	9.1	•	7.8	6.0	5.0	7.0
Total Liabilities to Net Worth 37	5.7	•	0.8	76.8	2.1	•	•	2.0	2.1	10.5
Current Assets to Working Capital 38	2.1	•	1.4	2.1	2.4	•	2.1	2.1	1.9	2.6
Current Liabilities to Working Capital 39	1.1	•	0.4	1.1	1.4	•	1.1	1.1	0.9	1.6
Working Capital to Net Sales 40	0.2	•	0.2	0.2	0.1	•	0.2	0.3	0.3	0.2
Inventory to Working Capital 41	1.0	•	0.5	1.2	1.3	•	1.0	0.7	0.7	1.3
Total Receipts to Cash Flow 42	8.1	4.5	6.6	6.3	11.4	•	12.4	8.0	8.2	5.1
Cost of Goods to Cash Flow 43	5.2	1.6	4.4	4.1	7.7	•	8.6	5.7	5.4	2.2
Cash Flow to Total Debt 44	0.2	•	1.5	0.3	0.3	•	0.1	0.3	0.2	0.2

Selected Financial Factors (in Percentages)

Debt Ratio 45	85.2	•	43.8	98.7	67.5	•	130.3	66.8	67.4	91.3
Return on Total Assets 46	6.5	•	34.3	•	5.9	•	•	9.6	3.5	7.4
Return on Equity Before Income Taxes 47	20.7	•	59.7	•	6.1	•	15.3	20.3	•	44.1
Return on Equity After Income Taxes 48	14.1	•	59.6	•	3.5	•	20.0	19.5	•	34.3
Profit Margin (Before Income Tax) 49	1.8	7.6	7.8	•	0.8	•	5.0	5.0	•	3.9
Profit Margin (After Income Tax) 50	1.2	7.6	7.8	•	0.5	•	4.8	4.8	•	3.1

Table II

Corporations with Net Income

APPAREL ACCESSORIES AND OTHER APPAREL

MONEY AMOUNTS AND SIZE OF ASSETS IN THOUSANDS OF DOLLARS

Item Description for Accounting Period 7/06 Through 6/07		Total	Zero Assets	Under 500	500 to 1,000	1,000 to 5,000	5,000 to 10,000	10,000 to 25,000	25,000 to 50,000	50,000 to 100,000	100,000 to 250,000	250,000 to 500,000	500,000 to 2,500,000	2,500,000 and over
Number of Enterprises	1	2431	•	1227	123	323	0	•	18	4	•	0	0	0
Revenues ($ in Thousands)														
Net Sales	2	5856746	•	993454	160835	1788024	0	•	994740	458579	•	0	0	0
Interest	3	4742	•	12	55	2238	0	•	95	404	•	0	0	0
Rents	4	312	•	0	0	0	0	•	0	200	•	0	0	0
Royalties	5	17119	•	0	0	0	0	•	0	34	•	0	0	0
Other Portfolio Income	6	2707	•	2	0	1140	0	•	80	502	•	0	0	0
Other Receipts	7	119477	•	12273	7373	8414	0	•	56567	528	•	0	0	0
Total Receipts	8	6001103	•	1005741	168263	1799816	0	•	1051482	460247	•	0	0	0
Average Total Receipts	9	2469	•	820	1368	5572	•	•	58416	115062	•	•	•	•
Operating Costs/Operating Income (%)														
Cost of Operations	10	64.6	•	65.3	54.6	66.7	•	•	70.1	64.8	•	•	•	•
Salaries and Wages	11	10.5	•	10.0	6.0	14.5	•	•	8.3	7.8	•	•	•	•
Taxes Paid	12	2.5	•	1.1	1.9	1.6	•	•	2.2	1.4	•	•	•	•
Interest Paid	13	1.5	•	0.1	1.6	1.4	•	•	1.9	0.9	•	•	•	•
Depreciation	14	0.7	•	0.0	2.2	0.7	•	•	1.1	0.6	•	•	•	•
Amortization and Depletion	15	0.1	•	•	•	0.0	•	•	0.1	0.0	•	•	•	•
Pensions and Other Deferred Comp.	16	0.3	•	0.6	•	0.4	•	•	0.1	•	•	•	•	•
Employee Benefits	17	1.0	•	0.4	0.5	1.0	•	•	1.4	0.6	•	•	•	•
Advertising	18	1.7	•	0.8	0.0	1.2	•	•	2.0	0.8	•	•	•	•
Other Expenses	19	11.1	•	9.5	26.4	9.4	•	•	9.7	10.3	•	•	•	•
Officers' Compensation	20	1.7	•	2.8	•	1.1	•	•	2.0	3.1	•	•	•	•
Operating Margin	21	4.4	•	9.3	6.7	2.0	•	•	1.1	9.6	•	•	•	•
Operating Margin Before Officers' Comp.	22	6.1	•	12.1	6.7	3.1	•	•	3.1	12.7	•	•	•	•

Selected Average Balance Sheet ($ in Thousands)

Net Receivables 23	297	75	132	588	•	11295	14213
Inventories 24	443	32	329	1060	•	9819	28753
Net Property, Plant and Equipment 25	91	1	74	163	•	3418	5108
Total Assets 26	1183	203	823	2327	•	34165	74079
Notes and Loans Payable 27	403	23	171	460	•	14407	16038
All Other Liabilities 28	326	60	684	934	•	6438	11564
Net Worth 29	455	119	-33	932	•	13321	46478

Selected Financial Ratios (Times to 1)

Current Ratio 30	2.2	3.3	5.7	1.7	•	2.7	2.4
Quick Ratio 31	1.0	2.3	3.2	0.8	•	1.2	1.0
Net Sales to Working Capital 32	5.0	5.7	2.1	8.3	•	3.1	3.1
Coverage Ratio 33	5.6	95.0	8.0	2.9	•	4.6	11.6
Total Asset Turnover 34	2.0	4.0	1.6	2.4	•	1.6	1.5
Inventory Turnover 35	3.5	16.3	2.2	3.5	•	3.9	2.6
Receivables Turnover 36	7.1	13.2	3.3	9.0	•	6.7	6.8
Total Liabilities to Net Worth 37	1.6	0.7	•	1.5	•	1.6	0.6
Current Assets to Working Capital 38	1.8	1.4	1.2	2.4	•	1.6	1.7
Current Liabilities to Working Capital 39	0.8	0.4	0.2	1.4	•	0.6	0.7
Working Capital to Net Sales 40	0.2	0.2	0.5	0.1	•	0.3	0.3
Inventory to Working Capital 41	0.8	0.5	0.5	1.3	•	0.6	0.6
Total Receipts to Cash Flow 42	6.4	5.8	2.9	10.5	•	6.9	5.2
Cost of Goods to Cash Flow 43	4.1	3.8	1.6	7.0	•	4.8	3.4
Cash Flow to Total Debt 44	0.5	1.7	0.5	0.4	•	0.4	0.8

Selected Financial Factors (in Percentages)

Debt Ratio 45	61.6	41.2	104.0	59.9	•	61.0	37.3
Return on Total Assets 46	17.2	42.5	20.6	9.5	•	14.1	16.7
Return on Equity Before Income Taxes 47	36.7	71.5	•	15.5	•	28.2	24.3
Return on Equity After Income Taxes 48	32.4	71.5	•	13.3	•	27.3	17.1
Profit Margin (Before Income Tax) 49	6.9	10.5	11.3	2.6	•	6.8	9.9
Profit Margin (After Income Tax) 50	6.1	10.5	9.7	2.2	•	6.6	6.9

Table I

Corporations with and without Net Income

LEATHER AND ALLIED PRODUCT MANUFACTURING

MONEY AMOUNTS AND SIZE OF ASSETS IN THOUSANDS OF DOLLARS

Item Description for Accounting Period 7/06 Through 6/07	Total	Zero Assets	Under 500	500 to 1,000	1,000 to 5,000	5,000 to 10,000	10,000 to 25,000	25,000 to 50,000	50,000 to 100,000	100,000 to 250,000	250,000 to 500,000	500,000 to 2,500,000	2,500,000 and over
Number of Enterprises **1**	2141	824	1100	0	152	7	24	15	6	7	0	5	0
Revenues ($ in Thousands)													
Net Sales **2**	8832457	145717	207960	0	568063	102658	685818	985932	862773	1367536	0	3906001	0
Interest **3**	25167	89	5	0	688	293	353	1051	985	857	0	20845	0
Rents **4**	1440	233	0	0	0	0	0	12	263	652	0	280	0
Royalties **5**	113847	1	0	0	0	0	0	0	2369	810	0	110667	0
Other Portfolio Income **6**	36305	0	0	0	1275	2	510	217	1009	30845	0	2444	0
Other Receipts **7**	90066	996	31	0	59	216	1483	4389	918	42331	0	39646	0
Total Receipts **8**	9099282	147036	207996	0	570085	103169	688164	991601	868317	1443031	0	4079883	0
Average Total Receipts **9**	4250	178	189	•	3751	14738	28674	66107	144720	206147	•	815977	•
Operating Costs/Operating Income (%)													
Cost of Operations **10**	64.3	90.2	37.6	•	62.0	63.2	62.0	74.7	63.4	56.0	•	65.9	•
Salaries and Wages **11**	9.6	12.7	12.5	•	8.4	11.5	11.0	6.6	10.4	10.0	•	9.7	•
Taxes Paid **12**	2.2	2.5	2.2	•	2.4	2.8	1.6	2.1	2.1	2.5	•	2.2	•
Interest Paid **13**	1.3	2.5	0.4	•	0.0	1.3	0.9	0.8	2.4	1.1	•	1.5	•
Depreciation **14**	1.4	5.9	3.9	•	0.4	0.7	0.9	1.9	0.6	1.1	•	1.5	•
Amortization and Depletion **15**	0.4	0.1	0.5	•	0.0	0.0	0.8	0.2	0.2	0.3	•	0.7	•
Pensions and Other Deferred Comp. **16**	0.4	0.1	0.2	•	0.3	0.1	0.3	0.1	0.4	0.7	•	0.4	•
Employee Benefits **17**	1.0	4.7	0.6	•	0.3	1.8	1.0	1.7	0.7	0.8	•	0.9	•
Advertising **18**	2.7	0.3	1.8	•	0.7	1.8	4.0	1.0	2.7	2.9	•	3.2	•
Other Expenses **19**	12.2	40.2	35.3	•	20.3	11.7	13.2	7.7	12.8	12.8	•	9.5	•
Officers' Compensation **20**	2.2	5.4	8.3	•	3.3	2.9	2.1	1.0	0.7	4.3	•	1.4	•
Operating Margin **21**	2.3	•	•	•	1.9	2.2	2.2	2.2	3.5	7.4	•	3.1	•
Operating Margin Before Officers' Comp. **22**	4.5	•	5.1	•	5.3	5.2	4.3	3.2	4.2	11.7	•	4.6	•

Selected Average Balance Sheet ($ in Thousands)

Net Receivables 23	616	0	18	•	76	1550	3382	9301	18732	31543	•	144423
Inventories 24	716	0	49	•	427	3910	6897	9347	40174	46329	•	118712
Net Property, Plant and Equipment 25	309	0	9	•	190	1229	1252	6532	5833	13748	•	70928
Total Assets 26	3083	0	102	•	1605	8088	15595	30922	77607	203968	•	691464
Notes and Loans Payable 27	648	0	202	•	47	1383	2473	6700	20178	34488	•	124980
All Other Liabilities 28	1118	0	11	•	769	2846	4260	6542	19762	128083	•	205945
Net Worth 29	1318	0	-111	•	790	3858	8861	17680	37666	41397	•	360539

Selected Financial Ratios (Times to 1)

Current Ratio 30	1.9	•	17.2	•	1.5	2.2	2.3	2.7	3.6	1.2	•	2.1
Quick Ratio 31	0.9	•	7.1	•	0.5	0.7	1.2	1.5	1.9	0.4	•	1.1
Net Sales to Working Capital 32	4.3	•	2.3	•	8.4	4.1	4.4	5.1	3.6	8.8	•	3.4
Coverage Ratio 33	5.4	•		•	46.6	3.2	3.9	4.5	2.7	13.9	•	6.4
Total Asset Turnover 34	1.3	•	1.9	•	2.3	1.8	1.8	2.1	1.9	1.0	•	1.1
Inventory Turnover 35	3.7	•	1.5	•	5.4	2.4	2.6	5.3	2.3	2.4	•	4.3
Receivables Turnover 36	6.1	•	9.5	•	59.9	18.9	4.5	7.2	2.8	12.4	•	6.5
Total Liabilities to Net Worth 37	1.3	•		•	1.0	1.1	0.8	0.7	1.1	3.9	•	0.9
Current Assets to Working Capital 38	2.2	•	1.1	•	2.8	1.8	1.8	1.6	1.4	7.0	•	1.9
Current Liabilities to Working Capital 39	1.2	•	0.1	•	1.8	0.8	0.8	0.6	0.4	6.0	•	0.9
Working Capital to Net Sales 40	0.2	•	0.4	•	0.1	0.2	0.2	0.2	0.3	0.1	•	0.3
Inventory to Working Capital 41	0.7	•	0.6	•	1.0	1.1	0.6	0.6	0.6	2.1	•	0.5
Total Receipts to Cash Flow 42	6.5	•	3.4	•	5.8	8.5	7.1	10.7	6.8	4.3	•	6.5
Cost of Goods to Cash Flow 43	4.2	•	1.3	•	3.6	5.3	4.4	8.0	4.3	2.4	•	4.3
Cash Flow to Total Debt 44	0.4	•	0.3	•	0.8	0.4	0.6	0.5	0.5	0.3	•	0.4

Selected Financial Factors (in Percentages)

Debt Ratio 45	57.3	•	209.2	•	50.8	52.3	43.2	42.8	51.5	79.7	•	47.9
Return on Total Assets 46	9.2	•		•	5.0	7.3	6.2	7.5	12.2	14.3	•	10.7
Return on Equity Before Income Taxes 47	17.6	•	5.5	•	9.8	10.4	8.2	10.2	15.8	65.5	•	17.3
Return on Equity After Income Taxes 48	13.1	•	6.0	•	9.8	9.8	8.0	9.0	13.1	49.9	•	13.3
Profit Margin (Before Income Tax) 49	5.6	•		•	2.1	2.7	2.5	2.7	4.1	13.9	•	8.0
Profit Margin (After Income Tax) 50	4.2	•		•	2.1	2.6	2.5	2.4	3.4	10.6	•	6.1

Table II

Corporations with Net Income

LEATHER AND ALLIED PRODUCT MANUFACTURING

MONEY AMOUNTS AND SIZE OF ASSETS IN THOUSANDS OF DOLLARS

Item Description for Accounting Period 7/06 Through 6/07	Total	Zero Assets	Under 500	500 to 1,000	1,000 to 5,000	5,000 to 10,000	10,000 to 25,000	25,000 to 50,000	50,000 to 100,000	100,000 to 250,000	250,000 to 500,000	500,000 to 2,500,000	2,500,000 and over
Number of Enterprises **1**	1266	350	749	0	121	0	20	11	•	•	0	•	0
Revenues ($ in Thousands)													
Net Sales **2**	7374627	1890	194378	0	303033	0	558443	798840	•	•	0	•	0
Interest **3**	19747	0	0	0	156	0	353	27	•	•	0	•	0
Rents **4**	1186	0	0	0	0	0	0	0	•	•	0	•	0
Royalties **5**	111539	0	0	0	0	0	0	0	•	•	0	•	0
Other Portfolio Income **6**	35936	0	0	0	1277	0	270	217	•	•	0	•	0
Other Receipts **7**	85879	0	0	0	59	0	846	2143	•	•	0	•	0
Total Receipts **8**	7628914	1890	194378	0	304525	0	559912	801227	•	•	0	•	0
Average Total Receipts **9**	6026	5	260	•	2517	•	27996	72839	•	•	0	•	•
Operating Costs/Operating Income (%)													
Cost of Operations **10**	62.7	17.3	36.6	•	47.5	•	58.2	76.6	•	•	•	•	•
Salaries and Wages **11**	9.4	•	11.0	•	7.7	•	9.9	4.5	•	•	•	•	•
Taxes Paid **12**	2.2	•	1.8	•	3.1	•	1.5	2.0	•	•	•	•	•
Interest Paid **13**	0.7	•	•	•	0.1	•	0.5	0.6	•	•	•	•	•
Depreciation **14**	1.1	•	0.2	•	0.5	•	0.8	1.2	•	•	•	•	•
Amortization and Depletion **15**	0.4	•	0.3	•	0.0	•	0.2	0.2	•	•	•	•	•
Pensions and Other Deferred Comp. **16**	0.3	•	0.2	•	0.1	•	0.4	0.1	•	•	•	•	•
Employee Benefits **17**	0.7	•	•	•	0.3	•	0.7	0.7	•	•	•	•	•
Advertising **18**	2.9	•	1.3	•	0.7	•	4.0	0.5	•	•	•	•	•
Other Expenses **19**	11.5	10.8	28.3	•	30.8	•	9.7	6.4	•	•	•	•	•
Officers' Compensation **20**	2.3	•	8.9	•	4.2	•	2.4	1.2	•	•	•	•	•
Operating Margin **21**	5.7	71.9	11.4	•	5.1	•	11.7	6.2	•	•	•	•	•
Operating Margin Before Officers' Comp. **22**	8.1	71.9	20.3	•	9.3	•	14.0	7.3	•	•	•	•	•

Selected Average Balance Sheet ($ in Thousands)

Net Receivables 23	961	0	26	•	126	•	3873	10903
Inventories 24	970	0	8	•	308	•	5794	8784
Net Property, Plant and Equipment 25	405	0	0	•	168	•	1198	4551
Total Assets 26	4231	0	66	•	1459	•	14727	29910
Notes and Loans Payable 27	458	0	0	•	82	•	2298	5985
All Other Liabilities 28	1704	0	1	•	730	•	2599	6880
Net Worth 29	2069	0	65	•	648	•	9829	17045

Selected Financial Ratios (Times to 1)

Current Ratio 30	1.8	•	129.2	1.4	•	3.5	2.8
Quick Ratio 31	0.9	•	99.8	0.4	•	2.1	1.5
Net Sales to Working Capital 32	4.0	•	4.0	7.0	•	3.3	5.3
Coverage Ratio 33	14.5	•	•	62.7	•	24.2	12.5
Total Asset Turnover 34	1.4	•	4.0	1.7	•	1.9	2.4
Inventory Turnover 35	3.8	•	12.1	3.9	•	2.8	6.3
Receivables Turnover 36	5.8	•	19.3	36.6	•	4.7	•
Total Liabilities to Net Worth 37	1.0	•	0.0	1.3	•	0.5	0.8
Current Assets to Working Capital 38	2.2	•	1.0	3.3	•	1.4	1.6
Current Liabilities to Working Capital 39	1.2	•	0.0	2.3	•	0.4	0.6
Working Capital to Net Sales 40	0.2	•	0.2	0.1	•	0.3	0.2
Inventory to Working Capital 41	0.6	•	0.2	0.9	•	0.5	0.6
Total Receipts to Cash Flow 42	5.4	1.2	2.6	3.4	•	4.8	8.4
Cost of Goods to Cash Flow 43	3.4	0.2	0.9	1.6	•	2.8	6.4
Cash Flow to Total Debt 44	0.5	•	200.6	0.9	•	1.2	0.7

Selected Financial Factors (in Percentages)

Debt Ratio 45	51.1	•	0.8	55.6	•	33.3	43.0
Return on Total Assets 46	14.1	•	45.2	9.1	•	23.5	17.0
Return on Equity Before Income Taxes 47	26.8	•	45.5	20.1	•	33.7	27.5
Return on Equity After Income Taxes 48	21.9	•	44.2	19.7	•	33.6	25.8
Profit Margin (Before Income Tax) 49	9.5	71.9	11.4	5.2	•	11.9	6.5
Profit Margin (After Income Tax) 50	7.8	71.9	11.1	5.1	•	11.8	6.1

Table I

Corporations with and without Net Income

WOOD PRODUCT MANUFACTURING

MONEY AMOUNTS AND SIZE OF ASSETS IN THOUSANDS OF DOLLARS

Item Description for Accounting Period 7/06 Through 6/07		Total	Zero Assets	Under 500	500 to 1,000	1,000 to 5,000	5,000 to 10,000	10,000 to 25,000	25,000 to 50,000	50,000 to 100,000	100,000 to 250,000	250,000 to 500,000	500,000 to 2,500,000	2,500,000 and over
Number of Enterprises	1	12537	503	7537	859	2797	288	312	124	58	37	7	15	0
Revenues ($ in Thousands)														
Net Sales	2	82525311	695418	4737556	1969342	16911340	5092095	9714321	9048418	6119960	8373975	4137091	15725793	0
Interest	3	298184	1257	1594	1547	23903	5012	4225	10702	14409	22656	10720	202158	0
Rents	4	39001	242	2392	360	6676	1590	9869	2937	8190	2069	1194	3481	0
Royalties	5	14228	0	231	0	0	0	191	1536	17	9150	0	3103	0
Other Portfolio Income	6	345898	2455	15874	12901	49837	18210	26642	40880	37467	42645	8650	90336	0
Other Receipts	7	716228	3454	56907	8851	61700	16910	57493	45170	78829	112746	62924	211248	0
Total Receipts	8	83938850	702826	4814554	1993001	17053456	5133817	9812741	9149643	6258872	8563241	4220579	16236119	0
Average Total Receipts	9	6695	1397	639	2320	6097	17826	31451	73787	107912	231439	602940	1082408	•
Operating Costs/Operating Income (%)														
Cost of Operations	10	74.4	105.6	56.8	57.5	70.4	77.2	76.3	81.9	80.8	80.7	77.1	71.8	•
Salaries and Wages	11	6.1	2.3	11.0	10.1	7.5	4.9	5.2	3.6	4.6	3.7	5.0	7.4	•
Taxes Paid	12	1.8	0.5	2.6	3.1	2.3	1.7	1.8	1.7	1.6	1.5	1.4	1.6	•
Interest Paid	13	1.5	5.7	1.0	1.0	0.9	0.7	1.3	0.9	1.6	1.8	1.4	2.7	•
Depreciation	14	2.4	12.3	2.4	1.6	1.6	2.1	2.6	1.9	2.4	2.7	3.5	2.8	•
Amortization and Depletion	15	0.4	0.5	0.0	0.1	0.0	0.0	0.0	0.1	0.4	0.4	0.3	1.2	•
Pensions and Other Deferred Comp.	16	0.4	0.5	0.1	0.0	0.2	0.2	0.2	0.5	0.3	0.2	0.3	1.0	•
Employee Benefits	17	1.1	0.7	1.4	1.6	0.9	1.3	1.3	1.0	1.1	0.9	0.8	1.6	•
Advertising	18	0.5	0.0	0.5	0.2	0.2	0.3	0.4	0.4	0.7	0.5	1.1	0.8	•
Other Expenses	19	9.0	7.8	15.5	12.5	10.5	6.1	8.0	4.4	5.6	6.1	8.1	12.4	•
Officers' Compensation	20	1.8	2.9	5.4	6.2	2.8	2.0	1.4	1.3	0.9	0.7	0.5	0.5	•
Operating Margin	21	0.6	•	3.4	6.1	2.7	3.4	1.7	2.4	0.1	0.8	0.6	•	•
Operating Margin Before Officers' Comp.	22	2.4	•	8.7	12.3	5.5	5.4	3.1	3.7	1.0	1.5	1.1	•	•

Selected Average Balance Sheet ($ in Thousands)

	•	•	•	•	•	•	•	•	•	•	•	•
Net Receivables 23	516	0	32	152	506	1256	2523	5737	8632	20046	62803	76478
Inventories 24	801	0	23	276	569	2911	4314	7930	17235	23296	82004	161802
Net Property, Plant and Equipment 25	1361	0	45	114	492	2333	5443	11742	23816	61457	144892	450671
Total Assets 26	4064	0	133	770	2157	7491	14521	33445	69791	151930	363066	1346948
Notes and Loans Payable 27	1361	0	70	284	823	1622	5581	9778	25564	54094	83096	433334
All Other Liabilities 28	910	0	23	170	532	1175	2798	5749	12847	36457	82097	334222
Net Worth 29	1793	0	40	317	802	4694	6141	17918	31379	61378	197873	579392

Selected Financial Ratios (Times to 1)

Current Ratio 30	1.9	•	2.2	2.2	1.9	2.7	1.6	2.0	1.6	2.0	2.0	1.8
Quick Ratio 31	0.9	•	1.3	1.2	1.0	1.2	0.7	0.9	0.7	1.0	0.9	1.0
Net Sales to Working Capital 32	8.0	•	15.0	7.3	8.8	6.2	10.4	7.8	9.0	6.9	7.5	6.4
Coverage Ratio 33	2.5	•	6.0	8.3	5.0	6.8	3.1	4.7	2.4	2.6	2.9	0.8
Total Asset Turnover 34	1.6	•	4.7	3.0	2.8	2.4	2.1	2.2	1.5	1.5	1.6	0.8
Inventory Turnover 35	6.1	•	15.2	4.8	7.5	4.7	5.5	7.5	4.9	7.8	5.6	4.6
Receivables Turnover 36	4.1	•	16.8	13.8	11.2	9.1	11.3	13.9	11.3	10.8	8.1	1.1
Total Liabilities to Net Worth 37	1.3	•	2.3	1.4	1.7	0.6	1.4	0.9	1.2	1.5	0.8	1.3
Current Assets to Working Capital 38	2.1	•	1.8	1.9	2.1	1.6	2.7	2.0	2.6	2.0	2.0	2.2
Current Liabilities to Working Capital 39	1.1	•	0.8	0.9	1.1	0.6	1.7	1.0	1.6	1.0	1.0	1.2
Working Capital to Net Sales 40	0.1	•	0.1	0.1	0.1	0.2	0.1	0.1	0.1	0.1	0.1	0.2
Inventory to Working Capital 41	0.9	•	0.5	0.8	0.9	0.8	1.4	0.9	1.3	0.8	0.9	0.8
Total Receipts to Cash Flow 42	11.1	•	6.4	6.7	9.3	12.2	11.3	15.2	16.1	12.5	11.4	10.6
Cost of Goods to Cash Flow 43	8.3	•	3.6	3.8	6.5	9.4	8.6	12.5	13.0	10.1	8.8	7.6
Cash Flow to Total Debt 44	0.3	•	1.1	0.8	0.5	0.5	0.3	0.3	0.2	0.2	0.3	0.1

Selected Financial Factors (in Percentages)

Debt Ratio 45	55.9	•	69.7	58.9	62.8	37.3	57.7	46.4	55.0	59.6	45.5	57.0
Return on Total Assets 46	6.2	•	28.3	24.6	12.3	11.7	8.6	9.7	5.9	7.2	6.4	1.6
Return on Equity Before Income Taxes 47	8.5	•	77.8	52.6	26.6	15.9	13.7	14.3	7.8	11.1	7.7	•
Return on Equity After Income Taxes 48	6.4	•	76.6	51.6	24.4	14.8	12.3	12.0	6.2	8.0	6.0	•
Profit Margin (Before Income Tax) 49	2.3	•	5.0	7.3	3.5	4.2	2.7	3.5	2.3	3.0	2.6	•
Profit Margin (After Income Tax) 50	1.7	•	4.9	7.1	3.2	3.9	2.4	3.0	1.9	2.2	2.0	•

71

Table II
Corporations with Net Income

WOOD PRODUCT MANUFACTURING

MONEY AMOUNTS AND SIZE OF ASSETS IN THOUSANDS OF DOLLARS

Item Description for Accounting Period 7/06 Through 6/07	Total	Zero Assets	Under 500	500 to 1,000	1,000 to 5,000	5,000 to 10,000	10,000 to 25,000	25,000 to 50,000	50,000 to 100,000	100,000 to 250,000	250,000 to 500,000	500,000 to 2,500,000	2,500,000 and over
Number of Enterprises 1	7818	41	4187	852	2102	262	201	103	•	21	•	7	0
Revenues ($ in Thousands)													
Net Sales 2	62828049	307835	3897392	1960632	13285894	4786491	6643525	7999391	•	5261091	•	11463514	0
Interest 3	195591	1219	925	1547	22869	4867	3292	8495	•	11822	•	122893	0
Rents 4	27670	85	2392	360	6523	1590	3091	2620	•	1176	•	3379	0
Royalties 5	7613	0	0	0	0	0	191	1536	•	5047	•	839	0
Other Portfolio Income 6	291228	2454	6824	11703	49153	17176	22268	32631	•	35884	•	79436	0
Other Receipts 7	494645	1939	58164	8320	49616	15451	39794	29216	•	93253	•	94973	0
Total Receipts 8	63844796	313532	3965697	1982562	13414055	4825575	6712161	8073889	•	5408273	•	11765034	0
Average Total Receipts 9	8166	7647	947	2327	6382	18418	33394	78387	•	257537	•	1680719	•
Operating Costs/Operating Income (%)													
Cost of Operations 10	73.4	72.7	59.1	57.4	71.6	77.6	77.1	81.3	•	76.4	•	69.0	•
Salaries and Wages 11	5.8	1.9	10.7	10.1	6.1	4.4	4.4	3.5	•	4.4	•	7.8	•
Taxes Paid 12	1.8	0.9	2.3	3.1	2.1	1.7	1.5	1.6	•	1.7	•	1.8	•
Interest Paid 13	1.2	2.2	0.6	1.0	0.7	0.6	1.0	0.8	•	1.5	•	2.4	•
Depreciation 14	2.1	5.7	1.9	1.6	1.5	2.1	2.0	1.7	•	2.3	•	2.7	•
Amortization and Depletion 15	0.2	0.6	0.0	0.1	0.0	0.0	0.0	0.1	•	0.2	•	0.7	•
Pensions and Other Deferred Comp. 16	0.4	0.0	0.1	0.0	0.2	0.2	0.2	0.5	•	0.2	•	1.0	•
Employee Benefits 17	1.2	0.5	1.3	1.0	0.9	1.3	1.0	1.0	•	1.0	•	1.8	•
Advertising 18	0.4	0.0	0.3	0.2	0.2	0.2	0.3	0.3	•	0.4	•	0.8	•
Other Expenses 19	7.3	7.5	13.5	12.3	9.4	5.1	5.9	4.2	•	6.3	•	7.3	•
Officers' Compensation 20	1.8	6.6	3.4	6.3	2.7	2.1	1.5	1.4	•	0.9	•	0.5	•
Operating Margin 21	4.4	1.3	6.9	6.9	4.5	4.6	5.0	3.5	•	4.7	•	4.4	•
Operating Margin Before Officers' Comp. 22	6.2	7.9	10.3	13.1	7.2	6.6	6.5	4.9	•	5.6	•	4.8	•

Selected Average Balance Sheet ($ in Thousands)

Net Receivables 23	634	0	•	49	153	557	1229	2990	6225	•	20391	•	109385
Inventories 24	943	0	•	22	183	520	2526	4991	8157	•	24147	•	259712
Net Property, Plant and Equipment 25	1204	0	•	57	112	507	2327	4599	10475	•	61144	•	361472
Total Assets 26	4077	0	•	178	770	2130	7455	14093	33120	•	157802	•	1457014
Notes and Loans Payable 27	1385	0	•	80	284	709	1440	4091	9743	•	45707	•	627172
All Other Liabilities 28	893	0	•	22	170	488	1059	2760	5480	•	44228	•	345539
Net Worth 29	1798	0	•	75	316	933	4956	7243	17898	•	67867	•	484303

Selected Financial Ratios (Times to 1)

Current Ratio 30	2.1	•	3.3	2.2	2.1	3.1	2.0	2.1	2.1	•	2.0	•	2.0
Quick Ratio 31	1.1	•	2.1	1.2	1.2	1.4	0.9	0.9	0.9	•	1.2	•	1.3
Net Sales to Working Capital 32	7.7	•	12.1	7.3	8.2	5.8	7.8	7.7	7.7	•	7.5	•	7.2
Coverage Ratio 33	6.1	2.4	16.4	9.2	8.5	9.6	7.1	6.4	6.4	•	5.8	•	3.9
Total Asset Turnover 34	2.0	•	5.2	3.0	3.0	2.5	2.3	2.3	1.6	•	1.6	•	1.1
Inventory Turnover 35	6.3	•	25.4	7.2	8.7	5.6	5.1	7.7	7.9	•	7.9	•	4.4
Receivables Turnover 36	3.4	•	18.9	14.7	10.2	10.8	9.2	13.7	9.2	•	9.2	•	0.8
Total Liabilities to Net Worth 37	1.3	•	1.4	1.4	1.3	0.5	0.9	0.9	1.3	•	1.3	•	2.0
Current Assets to Working Capital 38	1.9	•	1.4	1.9	1.9	1.5	2.0	1.9	2.0	•	2.0	•	2.0
Current Liabilities to Working Capital 39	0.9	•	0.4	0.9	0.9	0.5	1.0	0.9	1.0	•	1.0	•	1.0
Working Capital to Net Sales 40	0.1	•	0.1	0.1	0.1	0.2	0.1	0.1	0.1	•	0.1	•	0.1
Inventory to Working Capital 41	0.8	•	0.3	0.8	0.7	0.8	1.0	1.0	0.9	•	0.6	•	0.6
Total Receipts to Cash Flow 42	9.1	13.0	5.6	6.4	8.5	11.7	9.8	13.4	8.0	•	8.0	•	8.5
Cost of Goods to Cash Flow 43	6.6	9.4	3.3	3.7	6.1	9.1	7.5	10.9	6.1	•	6.1	•	5.9
Cash Flow to Total Debt 44	0.4	•	1.6	0.8	0.6	0.6	0.5	0.4	0.6	•	0.3	•	0.2

Selected Financial Factors (in Percentages)

Debt Ratio 45	55.9	•	57.6	59.0	56.2	33.5	48.6	46.0	57.0	•	57.0	•	66.8
Return on Total Assets 46	14.2	•	48.0	26.9	18.2	14.7	16.5	12.4	14.3	•	14.3	•	10.6
Return on Equity Before Income Taxes 47	26.9	•	106.3	58.4	36.8	19.8	27.6	19.3	27.5	•	27.5	•	23.6
Return on Equity After Income Taxes 48	23.5	•	105.1	57.5	34.3	18.6	25.8	16.7	22.6	•	22.6	•	17.5
Profit Margin (Before Income Tax) 49	6.0	3.1	8.6	8.0	5.4	5.4	6.0	4.5	7.5	•	7.5	•	7.0
Profit Margin (After Income Tax) 50	5.3	2.7	8.5	7.9	5.1	5.1	5.7	3.8	6.1	•	6.1	•	5.2

Table I

Corporations with and without Net Income

PULP, PAPER, AND PAPERBOARD MILLS

MONEY AMOUNTS AND SIZE OF ASSETS IN THOUSANDS OF DOLLARS

Item Description for Accounting Period 7/06 Through 6/07	Total	Zero Assets	Under 500	500 to 1,000	1,000 to 5,000	5,000 to 10,000	10,000 to 25,000	25,000 to 50,000	50,000 to 100,000	100,000 to 250,000	250,000 to 500,000	500,000 to 2,500,000	2,500,000 and over
Number of Enterprises **1**	200	4	0	•	72	•	27	24	13	18	8	20	8
Revenues ($ in Thousands)													
Net Sales **2**	101525493	191148	0	•	958436	•	854269	1297874	945759	3088290	3142653	25783851	65022506
Interest **3**	1233023	1007	0	•	40	•	178	1000	1566	33648	7250	239742	947142
Rents **4**	55363	20	0	•	0	•	382	233	358	394	2582	11331	40063
Royalties **5**	172381	0	0	•	0	•	0	0	0	0	0	69232	103149
Other Portfolio Income **6**	3234163	783	0	•	1151	•	1020	619	23474	235799	46152	121271	2803863
Other Receipts **7**	1729099	3997	0	•	135	•	3635	2724	16396	54397	35058	287552	1322703
Total Receipts **8**	107949522	196955	0	•	959762	•	859484	1302450	987553	3412528	3233695	26512979	70239426
Average Total Receipts **9**	539748	49239	•	•	13330	•	31833	54269	75966	189585	404212	1325649	8779928
Operating Costs/Operating Income (%)													
Cost of Operations **10**	76.8	67.7	•	•	86.4	•	66.2	86.6	79.0	81.7	75.4	78.3	75.9
Salaries and Wages **11**	4.6	7.7	•	•	1.5	•	6.5	3.7	3.9	2.8	7.8	3.9	4.9
Taxes Paid **12**	1.4	1.1	•	•	0.4	•	1.4	1.0	1.0	0.7	1.1	1.4	1.5
Interest Paid **13**	3.7	5.3	•	•	0.7	•	1.0	0.7	2.7	3.1	2.1	3.5	4.0
Depreciation **14**	3.0	6.0	•	•	0.1	•	2.9	1.8	4.2	4.0	3.6	4.5	2.3
Amortization and Depletion **15**	0.4	0.5	•	•	•	•	0.1	0.0	0.3	0.2	0.7	0.4	0.3
Pensions and Other Deferred Comp. **16**	1.6	3.3	•	•	0.2	•	0.2	0.9	1.4	0.6	1.7	0.4	2.2
Employee Benefits **17**	1.8	1.7	•	•	0.0	•	1.2	1.2	1.5	2.1	3.4	1.5	1.8
Advertising **18**	0.3	0.0	•	•	0.0	•	0.0	0.0	0.2	0.4	0.2	0.4	0.2
Other Expenses **19**	8.2	9.0	•	•	7.0	•	15.8	4.3	4.8	7.7	8.8	7.6	8.5
Officers' Compensation **20**	0.3	0.4	•	•	3.1	•	0.8	0.9	0.8	0.6	0.4	0.3	0.1
Operating Margin **21**	•	•	•	•	0.6	•	3.8	•	0.2	•	•	•	•
Operating Margin Before Officers' Comp. **22**	•	•	•	•	3.6	•	4.7	•	0.9	•	•	•	•

Net Receivables 23	65379	0	947	2502	6167	8918	21502	38873	176555	1054660
Inventories 24	44277	0	104	2740	4431	6950	20152	38819	140609	636150
Net Property, Plant and Equipment 25	236070	0	87	6644	9085	26916	57569	176400	568501	4078469
Total Assets 26	739314	0	1612	14187	32660	61733	163232	315074	1203220	14525724
Notes and Loans Payable 27	296910	0	1577	5224	11128	43783	62194	141314	413980	5970034
All Other Liabilities 28	188947	0	40	3100	19026	14897	51314	86371	351874	3548662
Net Worth 29	253457	0	-4	5863	2506	3052	49723	87389	437366	5007028

Selected Financial Ratios (Times to 1)

Current Ratio 30	1.1	•	36.3	1.3	1.1	1.2	2.2	1.8	0.9
Quick Ratio 31	0.6	•	33.7	0.7	0.5	0.8	0.6	0.8	1.0	0.5
Net Sales to Working Capital 32	31.0	•	9.5	19.5	29.0	17.9	21.5	5.4	7.5	•
Coverage Ratio 33	2.2	1.1	1.8	5.4	0.0	2.7	3.5	•	1.1	2.6
Total Asset Turnover 34	0.7	•	8.3	2.2	1.7	1.2	1.1	1.2	1.1	0.6
Inventory Turnover 35	8.8	•	110.1	7.6	10.6	8.3	7.0	7.6	7.2	9.7
Receivables Turnover 36	8.5	•	18.0	12.0	10.2	6.7	8.2	13.5	8.4	8.3
Total Liabilities to Net Worth 37	1.9	•	•	1.4	12.0	19.2	2.3	2.6	1.8	1.9
Current Assets to Working Capital 38	8.9	•	1.0	3.9	10.0	5.4	6.5	1.8	2.2	•
Current Liabilities to Working Capital 39	7.9	•	0.0	2.9	9.0	4.4	5.5	0.8	1.2	•
Working Capital to Net Sales 40	0.0	•	0.1	0.1	0.0	0.1	0.0	0.2	0.1	•
Inventory to Working Capital 41	2.7	•	0.1	1.9	2.9	1.6	2.5	0.5	0.8	•
Total Receipts to Cash Flow 42	11.0	12.1	14.8	5.6	11.9	35.4	8.5	•	17.0	9.3
Cost of Goods to Cash Flow 43	8.5	8.2	12.8	3.7	9.4	30.7	7.0	•	13.3	7.0
Cash Flow to Total Debt 44	0.1	•	0.6	0.7	0.1	0.1	0.2	•	0.1	0.1

Selected Financial Factors (in Percentages)

Debt Ratio 45	65.7	•	100.2	58.7	95.1	92.3	69.5	72.3	63.7	65.5
Return on Total Assets 46	5.6	•	11.1	12.2	8.6	0.0	11.6	•	4.3	5.8
Return on Equity Before Income Taxes 47	8.8	•	•	24.0	109.6	•	27.2	•	1.5	10.2
Return on Equity After Income Taxes 48	6.9	•	•	23.1	79.6	•	21.0	•	0.1	8.4
Profit Margin (Before Income Tax) 49	4.4	0.4	0.6	4.4	4.6	•	7.9	•	0.5	6.3
Profit Margin (After Income Tax) 50	3.4	0.4	0.6	4.3	3.3	•	6.1	•	0.0	5.2

Table II

Corporations with Net Income

PULP, PAPER, AND PAPERBOARD MILLS

MONEY AMOUNTS AND SIZE OF ASSETS IN THOUSANDS OF DOLLARS

Item Description for Accounting Period 7/06 Through 6/07	Total	Zero Assets	Under 500	500 to 1,000	1,000 to 5,000	5,000 to 10,000	10,000 to 25,000	25,000 to 50,000	50,000 to 100,000	100,000 to 250,000	250,000 to 500,000	500,000 to 2,500,000	2,500,000 and over
Number of Enterprises **1**	154	•	0	•	72	•	21	12	8	11	5	12	•
Revenues ($ in Thousands)													
Net Sales **2**	84809377	•	0	•	958436	•	778595	744246	658069	2008277	1660008	14906531	•
Interest **3**	1113590	•	0	•	40	•	0	545	1139	30092	6625	127479	•
Rents **4**	39621	•	0	•	0	•	0	125	162	394	2582	2923	•
Royalties **5**	166196	•	0	•	0	•	0	0	0	0	0	69212	•
Other Portfolio Income **6**	3161871	•	0	•	1151	•	510	619	23470	225659	46139	62982	•
Other Receipts **7**	1614536	•	0	•	135	•	3242	1835	14797	33143	32500	214895	•
Total Receipts **8**	90905191	•	0	•	959762	•	782347	747370	697637	2297565	1747854	15384022	•
Average Total Receipts **9**	590293	•	•	•	13330	•	37255	62281	87205	208870	349571	1282002	•
Operating Costs/Operating Income (%)													
Cost of Operations **10**	76.5	•	•	•	86.4	•	66.0	80.0	75.4	78.3	62.7	80.0	•
Salaries and Wages **11**	4.8	•	•	•	1.5	•	6.6	4.6	4.8	2.8	11.0	4.1	•
Taxes Paid **12**	1.4	•	•	•	0.4	•	1.2	1.2	1.2	0.5	1.6	1.2	•
Interest Paid **13**	3.5	•	•	•	0.7	•	0.8	0.3	2.5	2.8	2.4	2.3	•
Depreciation **14**	2.4	•	•	•	0.1	•	2.6	1.3	1.8	3.2	4.4	3.4	•
Amortization and Depletion **15**	0.2	•	•	•	•	•	0.1	0.0	0.3	0.2	1.0	0.1	•
Pensions and Other Deferred Comp. **16**	1.8	•	•	•	0.2	•	0.2	1.4	2.0	0.5	3.1	0.4	•
Employee Benefits **17**	1.7	•	•	•	0.0	•	1.1	1.4	2.1	1.4	3.8	0.8	•
Advertising **18**	0.3	•	•	•	0.0	•	0.1	0.1	0.1	0.5	0.4	0.3	•
Other Expenses **19**	8.1	•	•	•	7.0	•	13.7	6.0	4.8	8.8	9.8	6.0	•
Officers' Compensation **20**	0.2	•	•	•	3.1	•	0.8	1.0	1.0	0.7	0.5	0.3	•
Operating Margin **21**	•	•	•	•	0.6	•	6.8	2.8	3.9	0.4	•	0.9	•
Operating Margin Before Officers' Comp. **22**	•	•	•	•	3.6	•	7.6	3.9	4.8	1.1	•	1.3	•

Selected Average Balance Sheet ($ in Thousands)

Net Receivables 23	73550	947	2688	6646	10081	24398	45860	187676
Inventories 24	42723	104	2650	4308	8430	20980	30874	94313
Net Property, Plant and Equipment 25	253029	87	6165	8267	17705	46051	173482	496657
Total Assets 26	847799	1612	14320	34197	57980	170053	328998	1086652
Notes and Loans Payable 27	334083	1577	4660	4827	31748	59129	151422	303330
All Other Liabilities 28	200291	40	3092	9724	13955	43558	66755	251283
Net Worth 29	313426	-4	6568	19646	12277	67366	110821	532038

Selected Financial Ratios (Times to 1)

Current Ratio 30	1.1	36.3	1.4	1.7	1.3	1.7	2.8	1.7
Quick Ratio 31	0.6	33.7	0.8	0.8	0.9	0.9	1.2	1.0
Net Sales to Working Capital 32	56.2	9.5	17.9	7.8	14.7	7.6	3.7	8.8
Coverage Ratio 33	2.8	1.8	10.0	12.6	4.9	7.1	3.0	2.8
Total Asset Turnover 34	0.6	8.3	2.6	1.8	1.4	1.1	1.0	1.1
Inventory Turnover 35	9.9	110.1	9.2	11.5	7.4	6.8	6.7	10.5
Receivables Turnover 36	8.5	28.1	13.0	9.9	6.8	8.8	•	8.7
Total Liabilities to Net Worth 37	1.7	•	1.2	0.7	3.7	1.5	2.0	1.0
Current Assets to Working Capital 38	16.2	1.0	3.2	2.4	4.5	2.4	1.5	2.5
Current Liabilities to Working Capital 39	15.2	0.0	2.2	1.4	3.5	1.4	0.5	1.5
Working Capital to Net Sales 40	0.0	0.1	0.1	0.1	0.1	0.1	0.3	0.1
Inventory to Working Capital 41	4.5	0.1	1.5	0.7	1.2	0.9	0.3	0.8
Total Receipts to Cash Flow 42	9.3	14.8	5.2	12.0	7.3	4.9	11.5	12.9
Cost of Goods to Cash Flow 43	7.1	12.8	3.5	9.6	5.5	3.8	7.2	10.3
Cash Flow to Total Debt 44	0.1	0.6	0.9	0.4	0.2	0.4	0.1	0.2

Selected Financial Factors (in Percentages)

Debt Ratio 45	63.0	100.2	54.1	42.6	78.8	60.4	66.3	51.0
Return on Total Assets 46	6.4	11.1	21.0	6.3	17.6	21.4	7.1	7.4
Return on Equity Before Income Taxes 47	11.2	•	41.3	10.1	66.1	46.4	13.9	9.6
Return on Equity After Income Taxes 48	9.2	•	40.3	10.1	54.0	38.9	9.4	7.6
Profit Margin (Before Income Tax) 49	6.4	0.6	7.3	3.2	9.9	17.1	4.7	4.1
Profit Margin (After Income Tax) 50	5.2	0.6	7.1	3.2	8.1	14.4	3.1	3.3

Table I
Corporations with and without Net Income

CONVERTED PAPER PRODUCT

MONEY AMOUNTS AND SIZE OF ASSETS IN THOUSANDS OF DOLLARS

Item Description for Accounting Period 7/06 Through 6/07	Total	Zero Assets	Under 500	500 to 1,000	1,000 to 5,000	5,000 to 10,000	10,000 to 25,000	25,000 to 50,000	50,000 to 100,000	100,000 to 250,000	250,000 to 500,000	500,000 to 2,500,000	2,500,000 and over
Number of Enterprises **1**	3210	225	1241	•	1139	•	178	96	35	21	10	14	4
Revenues ($ in Thousands)													
Net Sales **2**	80561176	401415	1821341	•	6351656	•	6155114	6334409	3358609	4676181	4002391	15740719	29086567
Interest **3**	2076947	0	1097	•	277	•	6771	3946	4911	3241	20771	110258	1923431
Rents **4**	68192	0	0	•	1106	•	525	1973	1818	174	681	3529	53733
Royalties **5**	938845	0	0	•	0	•	11	0	0	2067	3161	23867	909739
Other Portfolio Income **6**	2300669	65532	762	•	13537	•	8570	26200	1888	21791	18348	399747	1719724
Other Receipts **7**	2194944	-19958	7292	•	19754	•	16167	41717	23355	23033	81613	146176	1839493
Total Receipts **8**	88140773	446989	1830492	•	6386330	•	6187158	6408245	3390581	4726487	4126965	16424296	35532687
Average Total Receipts **9**	27458	1987	1475	•	5607	•	34759	66753	96874	225071	412696	1173164	8883172
Operating Costs/Operating Income (%)													
Cost of Operations **10**	68.0	75.6	78.5	•	66.2	•	75.2	75.5	74.9	72.9	71.7	73.2	59.4
Salaries and Wages **11**	9.5	9.8	4.1	•	10.1	•	5.2	6.0	6.0	5.3	6.9	5.6	15.3
Taxes Paid **12**	1.6	1.5	2.0	•	2.3	•	1.9	1.5	1.5	1.3	1.8	1.5	1.5
Interest Paid **13**	3.9	1.2	1.1	•	1.5	•	1.6	1.3	1.9	1.8	1.8	3.5	7.2
Depreciation **14**	3.0	3.2	0.8	•	2.1	•	2.1	2.8	3.2	1.9	3.2	3.3	3.6
Amortization and Depletion **15**	0.6	0.5	0.0	•	0.2	•	0.1	0.1	0.3	0.3	0.4	1.3	0.7
Pensions and Other Deferred Comp. **16**	1.0	0.2	0.1	•	0.4	•	0.2	0.5	0.4	0.5	1.2	0.6	2.0
Employee Benefits **17**	2.1	1.5	0.9	•	2.3	•	1.3	1.7	1.7	1.4	1.8	2.5	2.4
Advertising **18**	0.7	0.2	0.1	•	0.3	•	0.1	0.2	0.3	0.7	1.0	0.2	1.5
Other Expenses **19**	8.2	6.5	10.0	•	8.7	•	8.1	6.5	6.8	10.7	8.6	7.1	8.6
Officers' Compensation **20**	1.0	1.0	3.2	•	3.2	•	1.7	1.3	1.1	0.7	0.9	0.4	0.4
Operating Margin **21**	0.2	•	•	•	2.7	•	2.4	2.5	2.0	2.3	0.6	0.7	•
Operating Margin Before Officers' Comp. **22**	1.2	•	2.3	•	5.9	•	4.1	3.8	3.1	3.0	1.5	1.1	•

Selected Average Balance Sheet ($ in Thousands)

Net Receivables **23**	4498	0	80	683	•	4328	8879	13288	25996	51342	159037	1970192
Inventories **24**	2142	0	31	288	•	3172	5759	12519	21837	38734	95900	636131
Net Property, Plant and Equipment **25**	7018	0	41	775	•	5509	13928	24092	36785	114725	396882	2625956
Total Assets **26**	36507	0	209	2123	•	15578	36640	69583	132334	353875	1123156	20596159
Notes and Loans Payable **27**	10961	0	498	1051	•	7244	12131	25330	45944	56057	518936	5192163
All Other Liabilities **28**	12098	0	71	568	•	5005	8513	15567	39664	110868	276745	7431717
Net Worth **29**	13448	0	-360	504	•	3329	15997	28686	46726	186950	327474	7972279

Selected Financial Ratios (Times to 1)

Current Ratio **30**	0.7	2.1	1.4	•	1.2	1.6	1.5	1.8	1.3	1.3	0.5
Quick Ratio **31**	0.4	1.5	1.0	•	0.7	0.9	0.7	0.9	0.7	0.7	0.3
Net Sales to Working Capital **32**	•	•	16.3	15.6	24.2	9.6	9.1	8.3	13.0	13.7	•
Coverage Ratio **33**	3.8	9.6	0.6	3.2	2.9	3.9	2.6	2.8	3.1	2.4	4.3
Total Asset Turnover **34**	0.7	•	7.0	2.6	2.2	1.8	1.4	1.7	1.1	1.0	0.4
Inventory Turnover **35**	8.0	•	37.1	12.8	8.2	8.6	5.7	7.4	7.4	8.6	6.8
Receivables Turnover **36**	6.7	•	•	8.8	8.1	8.5	8.5	9.0	10.0	8.6	4.7
Total Liabilities to Net Worth **37**	1.7	•	•	3.2	3.7	1.3	1.4	1.8	0.9	2.4	1.6
Current Assets to Working Capital **38**	•	1.9	•	3.4	6.1	2.7	3.1	2.3	4.5	3.9	•
Current Liabilities to Working Capital **39**	•	0.9	•	2.4	5.1	1.7	2.1	1.3	3.5	2.9	•
Working Capital to Net Sales **40**	•	0.1	•	0.1	0.0	0.1	0.1	0.1	0.1	0.1	•
Inventory to Working Capital **41**	•	0.3	•	0.9	2.3	0.9	1.4	0.9	1.4	1.4	•
Total Receipts to Cash Flow **42**	7.3	25.9	12.3	12.1	13.4	12.3	8.3	9.4	11.8	4.5	
Cost of Goods to Cash Flow **43**	5.5	20.3	8.2	9.1	10.1	9.3	6.1	6.7	8.6	2.7	
Cash Flow to Total Debt **44**	0.1	•	0.3	0.2	0.2	0.3	0.3	0.3	0.1	0.1	

Selected Financial Factors (in Percentages)

Debt Ratio **45**	63.2	272.0	76.3	•	78.6	56.3	58.8	64.7	47.2	70.8	61.3
Return on Total Assets **46**	10.4	4.5	12.3	•	10.0	8.8	6.6	8.7	6.5	8.6	11.0
Return on Equity Before Income Taxes **47**	20.8	2.0	35.8	•	30.5	15.1	9.8	15.8	8.3	17.5	21.9
Return on Equity After Income Taxes **48**	14.4	2.0	35.4	•	25.7	13.9	7.5	14.2	5.8	13.4	14.2
Profit Margin (Before Income Tax) **49**	11.1	10.3	3.2	•	2.9	3.7	2.9	3.3	3.9	5.1	24.0
Profit Margin (After Income Tax) **50**	7.7	10.3	3.2	•	2.5	3.4	2.2	3.0	2.7	3.9	15.6

Table II
Corporations with Net Income

CONVERTED PAPER PRODUCT

MONEY AMOUNTS AND SIZE OF ASSETS IN THOUSANDS OF DOLLARS

Item Description for Accounting Period 7/06 Through 6/07		Total	Zero Assets	Under 500	500 to 1,000	1,000 to 5,000	5,000 to 10,000	10,000 to 25,000	25,000 to 50,000	50,000 to 100,000	100,000 to 250,000	250,000 to 500,000	500,000 to 2,500,000	2,500,000 and over
Number of Enterprises	1	2126	•	628	•	847	•	142	82	24	14	7	10	4
Revenues ($ in Thousands)														
Net Sales	2	70044289	•	1048447	•	4924297	•	5203629	5445006	2437960	2957634	2530606	13742928	29086567
Interest	3	1971461	•	1092	•	275	•	6180	3234	2574	1325	12770	18341	1923431
Rents	4	62001	•	0	•	140	•	525	66	12	173	681	3527	53733
Royalties	5	936653	•	0	•	0	•	11	0	0	1110	2611	23183	909739
Other Portfolio Income	6	2283698	•	762	•	13261	•	8165	23493	1108	21552	18334	399747	1719724
Other Receipts	7	2107552	•	7293	•	18762	•	13849	34752	8831	4590	75547	92362	1839493
Total Receipts	8	77405654	•	1057594	•	4956735	•	5232359	5506551	2450485	2986384	2640549	14280088	35532687
Average Total Receipts	9	36409	•	1684	•	5852	•	36848	67153	102104	213313	377221	1428009	8883172
Operating Costs/Operating Income (%)														
Cost of Operations	10	66.8	•	80.9	•	64.8	•	74.2	74.3	72.8	75.3	67.7	72.7	59.4
Salaries and Wages	11	9.9	•	0.9	•	10.4	•	5.2	6.3	5.9	4.8	8.4	5.3	15.3
Taxes Paid	12	1.6	•	1.4	•	2.1	•	2.0	1.7	1.4	1.3	1.7	1.5	1.5
Interest Paid	13	4.0	•	0.3	•	1.4	•	1.5	1.0	1.7	1.3	1.1	2.8	7.2
Depreciation	14	3.0	•	0.7	•	1.9	•	2.0	2.7	3.4	1.6	3.3	3.3	3.6
Amortization and Depletion	15	0.6	•	0.0	•	0.2	•	0.1	0.1	0.1	0.2	0.5	1.2	0.7
Pensions and Other Deferred Comp.	16	1.1	•	0.3	•	0.5	•	0.2	0.6	0.4	0.4	0.7	0.7	2.0
Employee Benefits	17	2.1	•	0.3	•	2.4	•	1.3	1.6	1.8	0.6	1.3	2.4	2.4
Advertising	18	0.8	•	0.2	•	0.3	•	0.1	0.2	0.1	0.2	1.2	0.2	1.5
Other Expenses	19	7.9	•	9.8	•	7.0	•	8.2	6.2	7.0	8.3	8.7	7.2	8.6
Officers' Compensation	20	0.9	•	0.9	•	2.7	•	1.7	1.3	1.1	0.9	1.1	0.4	0.4
Operating Margin	21	1.2	•	4.3	•	6.3	•	3.5	4.0	4.1	5.1	4.3	2.2	•
Operating Margin Before Officers' Comp.	22	2.1	•	5.2	•	9.0	•	5.2	5.3	5.2	6.0	5.4	2.7	•

Selected Average Balance Sheet ($ in Thousands)

Net Receivables 23	6002	142	614	4337	9250	13556	25039	45228	162831	1970192
Inventories 24	2760	56	296	3295	5415	13208	24636	34969	101397	636131
Net Property, Plant and Equipment 25	9290	52	736	5269	13195	26045	31158	99474	463034	2625956
Total Assets 26	51329	361	2061	15541	36119	69582	121439	327071	1279580	20596159
Notes and Loans Payable 27	14449	52	965	6946	10059	27302	35370	47745	544111	5192163
All Other Liabilities 28	17060	128	535	4421	8246	16112	34538	60883	316694	7431717
Net Worth 29	19820	181	562	4174	17814	26167	51532	218442	418775	7972279

Selected Financial Ratios (Times to 1)

Current Ratio 30	0.7	2.3	1.6	1.3	1.7	1.5	2.1	2.2	1.4	0.5
Quick Ratio 31	0.4	1.6	1.1	0.7	1.1	0.7	1.2	1.3	0.7	0.3
Net Sales to Working Capital 32	•	9.4	12.7	16.9	8.5	8.9	6.6	4.9	14.1	•
Coverage Ratio 33	4.4	16.5	6.1	3.7	6.4	3.7	5.6	8.9	3.2	4.3
Total Asset Turnover 34	0.6	4.6	2.8	2.4	1.8	1.5	1.7	1.1	1.1	0.4
Inventory Turnover 35	8.0	23.9	12.7	8.3	9.1	5.6	6.5	7.0	9.9	6.8
Receivables Turnover 36	6.6	11.2	9.9	8.4	8.5	8.6	•	•	10.8	4.7
Total Liabilities to Net Worth 37	1.6	1.0	2.7	2.7	1.0	1.7	1.4	0.5	2.1	1.6
Current Assets to Working Capital 38	•	1.8	2.6	4.1	2.4	2.9	1.9	1.8	3.5	•
Current Liabilities to Working Capital 39	•	0.8	1.6	3.1	1.4	1.9	0.9	0.8	2.5	•
Working Capital to Net Sales 40	•	0.1	0.1	0.1	0.1	0.1	0.2	0.2	0.1	•
Inventory to Working Capital 41	•	0.3	0.7	1.6	0.7	1.3	0.8	0.5	1.3	•
Total Receipts to Cash Flow 42	6.5	12.8	9.4	10.4	10.8	10.7	8.1	6.5	10.6	4.5
Cost of Goods to Cash Flow 43	4.4	10.4	6.1	7.7	8.1	7.8	6.1	4.4	7.7	2.7
Cash Flow to Total Debt 44	0.2	0.7	0.4	0.3	0.3	0.2	0.4	0.5	0.2	0.1

Selected Financial Factors (in Percentages)

Debt Ratio 45	61.4	49.9	72.7	73.1	50.7	62.4	57.6	33.2	67.3	61.3
Return on Total Assets 46	11.2	25.4	23.4	13.2	11.2	9.2	12.6	11.1	9.7	11.0
Return on Equity Before Income Taxes 47	22.4	47.7	71.9	35.8	19.2	17.9	24.3	14.8	20.4	21.9
Return on Equity After Income Taxes 48	15.9	47.7	71.4	31.0	17.9	14.2	22.2	11.7	15.9	14.2
Profit Margin (Before Income Tax) 49	13.5	5.2	6.9	4.1	5.1	4.6	5.9	8.9	6.2	24.0
Profit Margin (After Income Tax) 50	9.5	5.2	6.9	3.5	4.8	3.7	5.4	7.0	4.8	15.6

Table I

Corporations with and without Net Income

PRINTING AND RELATED SUPPORT ACTIVITIES

MONEY AMOUNTS AND SIZE OF ASSETS IN THOUSANDS OF DOLLARS

Item Description for Accounting Period 7/06 Through 6/07		Total	Zero Assets	Under 500	500 to 1,000	1,000 to 5,000	5,000 to 10,000	10,000 to 25,000	25,000 to 50,000	50,000 to 100,000	100,000 to 250,000	250,000 to 500,000	500,000 to 2,500,000	2,500,000 and over
Number of Enterprises	1	34408	5103	21825	3357	3109	458	361	112	35	25	7	13	4
Revenues ($ in Thousands)														
Net Sales	2	91596845	1618928	10777371	6980884	14817181	6044369	9856631	5626230	2845413	4534757	3175397	13446179	11873505
Interest	3	215018	13365	3497	5751	12030	3013	7086	4898	5007	7568	21596	81799	49408
Rents	4	106850	4857	84	7028	5144	4005	3219	606	1125	4296	190	74582	1713
Royalties	5	340093	28985	10477	0	0	1	5025	2026	368	17977	35582	227348	12305
Other Portfolio Income	6	400560	45254	18097	17430	9249	66964	28701	15453	22441	6197	9951	137690	23133
Other Receipts	7	857444	8223	-16046	79382	89980	49763	58924	144185	22728	16563	89930	156147	157666
Total Receipts	8	93516810	1719612	10793480	7090475	14933584	6168115	9959586	5793398	2897082	4587358	3332646	14123745	12117730
Average Total Receipts	9	2718	337	495	2112	4803	13468	27589	51727	82774	183494	476092	1086442	3029432
Operating Costs/Operating Income (%)														
Cost of Operations	10	60.2	46.9	47.0	50.4	58.8	64.8	67.8	71.8	67.6	63.9	59.5	55.0	70.6
Salaries and Wages	11	10.7	18.5	11.7	13.8	11.5	9.7	8.9	8.3	7.2	7.7	11.4	14.1	7.1
Taxes Paid	12	2.5	3.6	3.0	2.7	2.9	2.6	2.2	2.2	2.1	2.1	2.4	2.3	2.2
Interest Paid	13	2.1	2.3	1.1	1.2	1.5	1.7	1.4	2.0	2.2	4.1	2.7	3.2	3.3
Depreciation	14	3.1	3.8	2.1	2.8	3.2	3.1	3.5	3.2	3.2	3.7	3.1	2.9	3.7
Amortization and Depletion	15	0.5	0.6	0.2	0.1	0.2	0.2	0.3	0.4	0.7	1.1	1.5	1.0	0.5
Pensions and Other Deferred Comp.	16	0.4	0.3	0.2	0.6	0.4	0.3	0.5	0.5	0.5	0.5	0.4	0.4	0.4
Employee Benefits	17	1.6	3.0	1.2	0.9	1.4	1.3	1.3	1.7	2.2	1.8	3.3	2.7	0.8
Advertising	18	0.9	0.8	0.8	0.4	0.5	0.2	0.4	0.3	0.6	1.8	0.3	2.9	0.2
Other Expenses	19	12.3	23.9	21.4	18.2	11.1	12.1	8.2	6.6	8.5	10.8	18.2	11.8	7.2
Officers' Compensation	20	3.4	7.2	9.0	5.4	5.2	3.6	2.4	2.5	2.1	1.0	0.6	0.6	0.4
Operating Margin	21	2.3	•	2.5	3.3	3.4	0.4	3.1	0.6	3.1	1.5	•	3.1	3.8
Operating Margin Before Officers' Comp.	22	5.6	•	11.5	8.7	8.6	4.0	5.5	3.1	5.1	2.5	•	3.6	4.2

Selected Average Balance Sheet ($ in Thousands)

Net Receivables 23	353	0	26	194	576	1896	4174	7850	12563	25251	56945	203418	446498
Inventories 24	135	0	6	41	202	1020	1645	4626	8620	13922	30117	75508	153808
Net Property, Plant and Equipment 25	501	0	35	278	815	2421	5882	9267	16912	44469	81197	253825	788313
Total Assets 26	1862	0	107	723	2147	6863	15171	34116	66848	163720	393142	1070108	4273014
Notes and Loans Payable 27	732	0	101	423	960	2559	5490	12254	22699	89626	127520	436950	1114512
All Other Liabilities 28	566	0	36	197	460	1778	3938	9911	14861	36539	105314	256885	1937016
Net Worth 29	564	0	-30	103	728	2526	5743	11951	29287	37554	160309	376273	1221486

Selected Financial Ratios (Times to 1)

Current Ratio 30	1.4	•	1.2	1.8	1.8	1.6	1.6	1.8	1.6	1.0	1.6	1.4	1.1
Quick Ratio 31	0.9	•	1.0	1.5	1.1	1.2	1.1	1.2	1.0	0.6	1.0	1.1	0.5
Net Sales to Working Capital 32	13.0	•	43.4	12.8	7.4	11.3	9.7	6.7	7.6	236.7	10.7	10.2	43.6
Coverage Ratio 33	3.0	•	3.5	5.2	2.5	3.8	3.9	2.8	3.1	1.6	1.2	3.5	2.8
Total Asset Turnover 34	1.4	•	4.6	2.9	1.9	2.2	1.8	1.5	1.2	1.1	1.2	1.0	0.7
Inventory Turnover 35	11.9	•	35.8	25.7	8.4	13.9	11.3	7.8	6.4	8.3	9.0	7.5	13.6
Receivables Turnover 36	7.6	•	20.4	11.2	6.6	7.8	7.0	6.2	6.0	7.5	7.7	3.9	13.3
Total Liabilities to Net Worth 37	2.3	•	•	6.0	1.7	2.0	1.6	1.9	1.3	3.4	1.5	1.8	2.5
Current Assets to Working Capital 38	3.4	•	5.1	2.3	2.3	2.6	2.6	2.3	2.8	68.0	2.6	3.3	15.2
Current Liabilities to Working Capital 39	2.4	•	4.1	1.3	1.3	1.6	1.6	1.3	1.8	67.0	1.6	2.3	14.2
Working Capital to Net Sales 40	0.1	•	0.0	0.1	0.1	0.1	0.1	0.1	0.1	0.0	0.1	0.1	0.0
Inventory to Working Capital 41	0.7	•	0.7	0.2	0.5	0.5	0.6	0.6	0.7	19.2	0.6	0.5	2.3
Total Receipts to Cash Flow 42	7.9	8.5	6.0	5.9	8.5	10.5	10.6	13.1	9.1	9.2	7.5	6.0	9.0
Cost of Goods to Cash Flow 43	4.7	4.0	2.8	3.0	5.0	6.8	7.2	9.4	6.2	5.9	4.5	3.3	6.4
Cash Flow to Total Debt 44	0.3	•	0.6	0.6	0.4	0.3	0.3	0.2	0.2	0.2	0.3	0.2	0.1

Selected Financial Factors (in Percentages)

Debt Ratio 45	69.7	•	127.7	85.7	66.1	63.2	62.1	65.0	56.2	77.1	59.2	64.8	71.4
Return on Total Assets 46	9.3	•	17.0	17.5	12.6	8.1	10.0	8.2	8.4	7.4	3.7	10.8	6.5
Return on Equity Before Income Taxes 47	20.6	•	•	98.3	27.5	13.3	19.7	15.0	13.0	12.4	1.4	22.1	14.6
Return on Equity After Income Taxes 48	17.2	•	•	96.9	26.6	11.9	17.7	12.8	10.3	8.5	•	16.4	10.9
Profit Margin (Before Income Tax) 49	4.4	•	2.6	4.9	4.2	2.5	4.1	3.6	4.7	2.6	0.5	8.0	6.0
Profit Margin (After Income Tax) 50	3.6	•	2.6	4.8	4.1	2.3	3.7	3.0	3.7	1.8	•	6.0	4.5

Table II
Corporations with Net Income

PRINTING AND RELATED SUPPORT ACTIVITIES

MONEY AMOUNTS AND SIZE OF ASSETS IN THOUSANDS OF DOLLARS

Item Description for Accounting Period 7/06 Through 6/07	Total	Zero Assets	Under 500	500 to 1,000	1,000 to 5,000	5,000 to 10,000	10,000 to 25,000	25,000 to 50,000	50,000 to 100,000	100,000 to 250,000	250,000 to 500,000	500,000 to 2,500,000	2,500,000 and over
Number of Enterprises 1	18396	2746	10250	•	2174	376	289	77	25	17	3	•	4
Revenues ($ in Thousands)													
Net Sales 2	73519128	512760	7106130	•	11422378	5064739	8221917	3959483	2314290	3310524	1000986	•	11873505
Interest 3	136595	20	2846	•	8888	1782	5235	3990	3038	7185	338	•	49408
Rents 4	99472	0	84	•	3739	4005	2581	261	1077	4286	114	•	1713
Royalties 5	263729	0	0	•	0	1	4054	2008	37	17977	0	•	12305
Other Portfolio Income 6	346370	38431	3455	•	3681	65822	27974	10887	20169	4757	7679	•	23133
Other Receipts 7	709199	-615	9745	•	58258	29290	64533	129944	24568	13423	2269	•	157666
Total Receipts 8	75074493	550596	7122260	•	11496944	5165639	8326294	4106573	2363179	3358152	1011386	•	12117730
Average Total Receipts 9	4081	201	695	•	5288	13738	28811	53332	94527	197538	337129	•	3029432
Operating Costs/Operating Income (%)													
Cost of Operations 10	60.3	30.4	45.1	•	58.1	62.7	67.7	71.5	65.9	60.0	69.6	•	70.6
Salaries and Wages 11	10.4	7.8	11.2	•	11.2	10.2	8.2	7.5	7.6	8.5	5.7	•	7.1
Taxes Paid 12	2.4	2.7	2.6	•	2.5	2.6	2.2	1.9	2.2	2.0	2.9	•	2.2
Interest Paid 13	1.9	1.1	0.6	•	1.3	1.3	1.3	1.3	1.7	3.0	2.6	•	3.3
Depreciation 14	3.0	5.3	2.1	•	2.8	2.7	3.4	3.0	3.1	3.4	3.0	•	3.7
Amortization and Depletion 15	0.4	0.0	0.1	•	0.2	0.0	0.3	0.3	0.3	1.0	0.7	•	0.5
Pensions and Other Deferred Comp. 16	0.4	0.0	0.2	•	0.4	0.4	0.4	0.6	0.5	0.4	0.8	•	0.4
Employee Benefits 17	1.5	0.4	1.0	•	1.2	1.3	1.3	1.6	2.4	2.0	2.3	•	0.8
Advertising 18	0.9	0.8	0.5	•	0.5	0.2	0.4	0.3	0.7	2.4	0.1	•	0.2
Other Expenses 19	10.9	30.8	20.1	•	10.2	11.9	7.6	5.7	8.0	12.1	5.0	•	7.2
Officers' Compensation 20	3.1	11.4	8.6	•	5.5	3.9	2.4	2.7	2.2	1.0	1.0	•	0.4
Operating Margin 21	4.8	9.4	7.9	•	5.9	2.7	4.7	3.4	5.3	4.0	6.1	•	3.8
Operating Margin Before Officers' Comp. 22	8.0	20.8	16.5	•	11.4	6.7	7.1	6.1	7.5	5.0	7.1	•	4.2

Selected Average Balance Sheet ($ in Thousands)

Net Receivables 23	543	0	28	•	598	1919	4451	7455	14181	23253	30422	•	446498
Inventories 24	192	0	6	•	199	894	1645	4677	9910	15532	36725	•	153808
Net Property, Plant and Equipment 25	768	0	52	•	867	2441	6003	8869	18465	41307	71812	•	788313
Total Assets 26	2907	0	136	•	2296	6862	15479	34501	66231	164346	347593	•	4273014
Notes and Loans Payable 27	977	0	68	•	960	1940	5279	7985	20677	76529	92373	•	1114512
All Other Liabilities 28	887	0	33	•	473	1601	3585	9550	16635	34570	52584	•	1937016
Net Worth 29	1042	0	35	•	863	3321	6616	16967	28920	53247	202635	•	1221486

Selected Financial Ratios (Times to 1)

Current Ratio 30	1.5	1.9	•	1.7	1.9	1.6	1.7	1.4	1.5	2.1	•	1.1
Quick Ratio 31	1.0	1.7	•	1.3	1.3	1.2	1.2	1.0	0.8	0.9	•	0.5
Net Sales to Working Capital 32	11.5	21.7	•	10.7	7.0	9.3	7.3	9.4	10.9	8.1	•	43.6
Coverage Ratio 33	4.6	13.6	16.2	5.9	4.7	5.5	6.4	5.2	2.8	3.8	•	2.8
Total Asset Turnover 34	1.4	5.1	•	2.3	2.0	1.8	1.5	1.4	1.2	1.0	•	0.7
Inventory Turnover 35	12.6	52.4	•	15.3	9.4	11.7	7.9	6.2	7.5	6.3	•	13.6
Receivables Turnover 36	7.7	23.1	•	8.9	7.1	7.0	6.4	5.8	9.3	•	•	13.3
Total Liabilities to Net Worth 37	1.8	2.9	•	1.7	1.1	1.3	1.0	1.3	2.1	0.7	•	2.5
Current Assets to Working Capital 38	3.1	2.2	•	2.4	2.1	2.5	2.3	3.2	3.1	1.9	•	15.2
Current Liabilities to Working Capital 39	2.1	1.2	•	1.4	1.1	1.5	1.3	2.2	2.1	0.9	•	14.2
Working Capital to Net Sales 40	0.1	0.0	•	0.1	0.1	0.1	0.1	0.1	0.1	0.1	•	0.0
Inventory to Working Capital 41	0.6	0.2	•	0.4	0.5	0.6	0.7	0.8	1.0	0.9	•	2.3
Total Receipts to Cash Flow 42	7.1	4.7	3.1	7.5	8.7	9.5	9.7	7.8	6.7	9.5	•	9.0
Cost of Goods to Cash Flow 43	4.3	2.1	1.0	4.3	5.5	6.4	6.9	5.2	4.0	6.6	•	6.4
Cash Flow to Total Debt 44	0.3	1.5	•	0.5	0.4	0.3	0.3	0.3	0.3	0.2	•	0.1

Selected Financial Factors (in Percentages)

Debt Ratio 45	64.1	74.1	•	62.4	51.6	57.3	50.8	56.3	67.6	41.7	•	71.4
Return on Total Assets 46	12.2	44.4	•	18.2	11.8	13.3	12.6	12.4	9.9	9.4	•	6.5
Return on Equity Before Income Taxes 47	26.6	158.9	•	40.2	19.2	25.4	21.6	22.8	19.5	11.9	•	14.6
Return on Equity After Income Taxes 48	23.2	158.1	•	39.1	17.9	23.3	19.3	19.1	15.4	8.2	•	10.9
Profit Margin (Before Income Tax) 49	6.9	16.8	8.1	6.6	4.7	5.9	7.1	7.1	5.3	7.2	•	6.0
Profit Margin (After Income Tax) 50	6.0	16.7	8.1	6.4	4.4	5.4	6.4	6.0	4.2	5.0	•	4.5

Table I

Corporations with and without Net Income

PETROLEUM REFINERIES (INCLUDING INTEGRATED)

MONEY AMOUNTS AND SIZE OF ASSETS IN THOUSANDS OF DOLLARS

Item Description for Accounting Period 7/06 Through 6/07	Total	Zero Assets	Under 500	500 to 1,000	1,000 to 5,000	5,000 to 10,000	10,000 to 25,000	25,000 to 50,000	50,000 to 100,000	100,000 to 250,000	250,000 to 500,000	500,000 to 2,500,000	2,500,000 and over
Number of Enterprises 1	928	•	•	•	111	0	21	9	9	8	0	12	17
Revenues ($ in Thousands)													
Net Sales 2	1682736166	•	•	•	0	0	330242	1311837	2123197	2384290	0	344634161	1634475369
Interest 3	21412583	•	•	•	181	0	842	3100	988	16333	0	130835	21259750
Rents 4	1422005	•	•	•	0	0	290	0	0	6904	0	37881	1376720
Royalties 5	817799	•	•	•	0	0	0	0	0	10800	0	32	806967
Other Portfolio Income 6	27004997	•	•	•	0	0	6418	7868	2982	27901	0	96417	26863412
Other Receipts 7	39279227	•	•	•	86269	0	3931	413	25097	87319	0	431291	37971593
Total Receipts 8	1772672777	•	•	•	86450	0	341723	1323218	2152264	2533547	0	351598721	1722753811
Average Total Receipts 9	1910208	•	•	•	779	•	16273	147024	239140	316693	•	2929989	101338459
Operating Costs/Operating Income (%)													
Cost of Operations 10	88.1	•	•	•	•	•	55.5	93.2	87.7	89.5	•	86.3	88.1
Salaries and Wages 11	1.3	•	•	•	•	•	10.4	1.5	1.8	1.0	•	1.9	1.3
Taxes Paid 12	1.6	•	•	•	•	•	1.6	0.2	0.5	0.5	•	1.6	1.6
Interest Paid 13	1.6	•	•	•	•	•	1.6	0.8	0.4	1.1	•	0.7	1.6
Depreciation 14	0.9	•	•	•	•	•	1.8	1.0	0.7	1.3	•	1.3	0.8
Amortization and Depletion 15	0.3	•	•	•	•	•	0.2	0.5	0.1	1.9	•	0.8	0.3
Pensions and Other Deferred Comp. 16	0.4	•	•	•	•	•	0.5	0.0	0.1	0.1	•	0.1	0.4
Employee Benefits 17	0.1	•	•	•	•	•	0.7	0.0	0.2	0.4	•	0.2	0.1
Advertising 18	0.1	•	•	•	•	•	0.0	0.0	0.0	0.1	•	0.0	0.1
Other Expenses 19	3.7	•	•	•	•	•	19.6	1.9	2.7	4.5	•	3.7	3.7
Officers' Compensation 20	0.1	•	•	•	•	•	4.6	0.2	0.3	0.5	•	0.3	0.0
Operating Margin 21	2.0	•	•	•	•	•	3.5	0.5	5.3	•	•	3.1	2.0
Operating Margin Before Officers' Comp. 22	2.0	•	•	•	•	•	8.1	0.7	5.7	•	•	3.4	2.0

Selected Average Balance Sheet ($ in Thousands)

	1	2	3	4	5	6	7	8
Net Receivables 23	895083	4	2500	7836	21609	23492	150482	48725012
Inventories 24	31508	0	1251	1344	13097	31136	147991	1591547
Net Property, Plant and Equipment 25	230366	90	2929	7519	22297	20792	396469	12265631
Total Assets 26	2064835	1663	12552	39682	79518	202279	1018750	111807098
Notes and Loans Payable 27	258722	115	5045	13384	12540	24220	202609	13943329
All Other Liabilities 28	1049810	16	2845	12530	26929	83745	374584	56978024
Net Worth 29	756302	1532	4662	13768	40048	94314	441556	40085746

Selected Financial Ratios (Times to 1)

	1	2	3	4	5	6	7	8
Current Ratio 30	1.0	4.8	1.8	1.3	1.8	1.0	1.5	1.0
Quick Ratio 31	0.9	4.7	1.3	1.1	1.1	0.6	0.8	0.9
Net Sales to Working Capital 32	79.3		5.2	36.8	10.9	389.5	16.9	86.7
Coverage Ratio 33	6.4	142.9	5.4	2.6	16.7	6.0	8.7	6.4
Total Asset Turnover 34	0.9		1.3	3.7	3.0	1.5	2.8	0.9
Inventory Turnover 35	50.7		7.0	101.1	15.8	8.6	16.7	53.2
Receivables Turnover 36	1.8		6.6	16.3	11.7	7.7	20.9	1.8
Total Liabilities to Net Worth 37	1.7	0.1	1.7	1.9	1.0	1.1	1.3	1.7
Current Assets to Working Capital 38	43.5	1.3	2.2	4.3	2.3	107.3	2.8	48.6
Current Liabilities to Working Capital 39	42.5	0.3	1.2	3.3	1.3	106.3	1.8	47.6
Working Capital to Net Sales 40	0.0	0.0	0.2	0.0	0.1	0.0	0.1	0.0
Inventory to Working Capital 41	1.5		0.4	0.3	0.8	20.0	1.1	1.5
Total Receipts to Cash Flow 42	9.8		4.2	45.0	11.5	11.4	12.8	9.8
Cost of Goods to Cash Flow 43	8.7		2.4	41.9	10.1	10.2	11.1	8.6
Cash Flow to Total Debt 44	0.1	5.4	0.5	0.1	0.5	0.2	0.4	0.1

Selected Financial Factors (in Percentages)

	1	2	3	4	5	6	7	8
Debt Ratio 45	63.4	7.9	62.9	65.3	49.6	53.4	56.7	63.4
Return on Total Assets 46	8.8	37.4	10.7	8.0	21.2	9.4	16.3	8.7
Return on Equity Before Income Taxes 47	20.2	40.3	23.5	14.1	39.5	16.9	33.2	20.0
Return on Equity After Income Taxes 48	13.2	37.1	22.4	6.8	37.5	11.2	22.1	13.0
Profit Margin (Before Income Tax) 49	8.4		7.0	1.3	6.7	5.3	5.1	8.5
Profit Margin (After Income Tax) 50	5.5		6.6	0.6	6.4	3.5	3.4	5.5

Table II

Corporations with Net Income

PETROLEUM REFINERIES (INCLUDING INTEGRATED)

MONEY AMOUNTS AND SIZE OF ASSETS IN THOUSANDS OF DOLLARS

Item Description for Accounting Period 7/06 Through 6/07		Total	Zero Assets	Under 500	500 to 1,000	1,000 to 5,000	5,000 to 10,000	10,000 to 25,000	25,000 to 50,000	50,000 to 100,000	100,000 to 250,000	250,000 to 500,000	500,000 to 2,500,000	2,500,000 and over
Number of Enterprises	1	171	•	0	0	•	0	15	•	•	•	0	•	•
Revenues ($ in Thousands)														
Net Sales	2	1672180762	•	0	0	•	0	249408	•	•	•	0	•	•
Interest	3	20937732	•	0	0	•	0	189	•	•	•	0	•	•
Rents	4	1395484	•	0	0	•	0	290	•	•	•	0	•	•
Royalties	5	817799	•	0	0	•	0	0	•	•	•	0	•	•
Other Portfolio Income	6	26677410	•	0	0	•	0	990	•	•	•	0	•	•
Other Receipts	7	38195895	•	0	0	•	0	3575	•	•	•	0	•	•
Total Receipts	8	1760205082	•	0	0	•	0	254452	•	•	•	0	•	•
Average Total Receipts	9	10293597	•	•	•	•	•	16963	•	•	•	•	•	•
Operating Costs/Operating Income (%)														
Cost of Operations	10	88.2	•	•	•	•	•	43.5	•	•	•	•	•	•
Salaries and Wages	11	1.3	•	•	•	•	•	11.9	•	•	•	•	•	•
Taxes Paid	12	1.6	•	•	•	•	•	1.7	•	•	•	•	•	•
Interest Paid	13	1.5	•	•	•	•	•	1.2	•	•	•	•	•	•
Depreciation	14	0.8	•	•	•	•	•	1.3	•	•	•	•	•	•
Amortization and Depletion	15	0.3	•	•	•	•	•	•	•	•	•	•	•	•
Pensions and Other Deferred Comp.	16	0.4	•	•	•	•	•	0.6	•	•	•	•	•	•
Employee Benefits	17	0.1	•	•	•	•	•	0.8	•	•	•	•	•	•
Advertising	18	0.1	•	•	•	•	•	0.0	•	•	•	•	•	•
Other Expenses	19	3.6	•	•	•	•	•	21.3	•	•	•	•	•	•
Officers' Compensation	20	0.1	•	•	•	•	•	5.5	•	•	•	•	•	•
Operating Margin	21	2.1	•	•	•	•	•	12.2	•	•	•	•	•	•
Operating Margin Before Officers' Comp.	22	2.2	•	•	•	•	•	17.7	•	•	•	•	•	•

Selected Average Balance Sheet ($ in Thousands)

Net Receivables 23	4828222	3279
Inventories 24	169064	917
Net Property, Plant and Equipment 25	1173923	2306
Total Assets 26	11026211	12079
Notes and Loans Payable 27	1291126	3403
All Other Liabilities 28	5561010	3371
Net Worth 29	4074074	5305

Selected Financial Ratios (Times to 1)

Current Ratio 30	1.0	1.5
Quick Ratio 31	0.9	1.1
Net Sales to Working Capital 32	79.2	7.2
Coverage Ratio 33	6.8	13.1
Total Asset Turnover 34	0.9	1.4
Inventory Turnover 35	51.0	7.9
Receivables Turnover 36	1.8	7.9
Total Liabilities to Net Worth 37	1.7	1.3
Current Assets to Working Capital 38	43.4	3.0
Current Liabilities to Working Capital 39	42.4	2.0
Working Capital to Net Sales 40	0.0	0.1
Inventory to Working Capital 41	1.4	0.5
Total Receipts to Cash Flow 42	9.8	3.0
Cost of Goods to Cash Flow 43	8.7	1.3
Cash Flow to Total Debt 44	0.1	0.8

Selected Financial Factors (in Percentages)

Debt Ratio 45	63.1	56.1
Return on Total Assets 46	8.8	21.2
Return on Equity Before Income Taxes 47	20.4	44.5
Return on Equity After Income Taxes 48	13.3	43.2
Profit Margin (Before Income Tax) 49	8.5	14.2
Profit Margin (After Income Tax) 50	5.5	13.8

80

Table I
Corporations with and without Net Income

ASPHALT PAVING, ROOFING, OTHER PETROLEUM AND COAL PRODUCTS

MONEY AMOUNTS AND SIZE OF ASSETS IN THOUSANDS OF DOLLARS

Item Description for Accounting Period 7/06 Through 6/07	Total	Zero Assets	Under 500	500 to 1,000	1,000 to 5,000	5,000 to 10,000	10,000 to 25,000	25,000 to 50,000	50,000 to 100,000	100,000 to 250,000	250,000 to 500,000	500,000 to 2,500,000	2,500,000 and over
Number of Enterprises 1	716	•	•	•	211	73	77	16	13	10	3	5	0
Revenues ($ in Thousands)													
Net Sales 2	17026083	•	•	•	693635	1127577	2421992	1198392	1588113	1872633	998428	5614247	0
Interest 3	94430	•	•	•	82	28	5367	4664	873	4311	843	77423	0
Rents 4	9070	•	•	•	203	245	7016	0	190	0	700	554	0
Royalties 5	9671	•	•	•	0	5	0	640	3	313	6211	2223	0
Other Portfolio Income 6	121790	•	•	•	169	1786	20253	2457	946	20138	25149	50528	0
Other Receipts 7	227376	•	•	•	12683	738	9294	5798	18060	71435	12928	92937	0
Total Receipts 8	17488420	•	•	•	706772	1130379	2463922	1211951	1606185	1968830	1044259	5837912	0
Average Total Receipts 9	24425	•	•	•	3350	15485	31999	75747	123553	196883	348086	1167582	•
Operating Costs/Operating Income (%)													
Cost of Operations 10	76.5	•	•	•	35.9	83.3	76.1	79.1	82.0	76.9	76.1	76.6	•
Salaries and Wages 11	4.5	•	•	•	25.4	3.8	3.9	3.1	3.2	5.0	3.0	3.9	•
Taxes Paid 12	1.1	•	•	•	3.1	0.9	1.4	1.1	0.8	1.0	1.6	0.8	•
Interest Paid 13	2.6	•	•	•	4.6	1.7	1.3	0.8	1.2	1.0	9.5	3.6	•
Depreciation 14	2.2	•	•	•	5.6	2.1	1.9	1.8	1.9	1.3	2.0	2.5	•
Amortization and Depletion 15	0.3	•	•	•	0.2	0.2	0.1	0.1	0.3	0.7	0.5	0.3	•
Pensions and Other Deferred Comp. 16	0.3	•	•	•	0.2	0.1	0.2	0.3	0.2	0.3	0.4	0.3	•
Employee Benefits 17	1.1	•	•	•	1.0	0.7	1.0	1.2	0.4	0.6	0.6	1.5	•
Advertising 18	0.7	•	•	•	0.8	2.1	0.5	0.4	1.7	0.3	0.1	0.6	•
Other Expenses 19	9.1	•	•	•	35.8	•	7.8	8.7	4.5	5.7	8.6	11.5	•
Officers' Compensation 20	1.7	•	•	•	1.7	1.9	5.1	2.0	0.7	0.9	0.7	0.5	•
Operating Margin 21	•	•	•	•	•	4.6	0.7	1.5	3.0	6.4	•	•	•
Operating Margin Before Officers' Comp. 22	1.6	•	•	•	•	6.5	5.8	3.4	3.7	7.3	•	•	•

Selected Average Balance Sheet ($ in Thousands)

Net Receivables 23	2814	511	2089	3683	6546	21080	25240	54902	132072
Inventories 24	1967	97	526	2681	6569	12890	14072	73904	101628
Net Property, Plant and Equipment 25	4473	1284	3166	4929	9745	16959	32995	92327	256945
Total Assets 26	14370	2200	7622	16406	39461	70890	145629	369204	752536
Notes and Loans Payable 27	5680	2326	3425	3666	5694	19182	31832	281978	297654
All Other Liabilities 28	4434	1177	1823	4379	11850	21406	33909	100126	263972
Net Worth 29	4255	-1304	2374	8360	21917	30302	79888	-12899	190910

Selected Financial Ratios (Times to 1)

Current Ratio 30	1.8	0.5	1.4	1.9	2.3	2.1	2.1	2.3	2.1
Quick Ratio 31	1.0	0.4	1.1	1.2	1.2	1.3	1.0	1.0	1.0
Net Sales to Working Capital 32	7.9	•	16.3	7.2	5.3	5.3	5.2	4.0	7.1
Coverage Ratio 33	2.0	•	3.8	2.9	4.0	4.4	12.2	1.1	1.6
Total Asset Turnover 34	1.7	1.5	2.0	1.9	1.9	1.7	1.3	0.9	1.5
Inventory Turnover 35	9.2	12.2	24.5	8.9	9.0	7.8	10.2	3.4	8.5
Receivables Turnover 36	8.3	5.9	8.7	8.1	11.9	6.2	6.7	4.4	8.8
Total Liabilities to Net Worth 37	2.4	•	2.2	1.0	0.8	1.3	0.8	•	2.9
Current Assets to Working Capital 38	2.2	•	3.7	2.2	1.8	1.9	1.9	1.7	1.9
Current Liabilities to Working Capital 39	1.2	•	2.7	1.2	0.8	0.9	0.9	0.7	0.9
Working Capital to Net Sales 40	0.1	•	0.1	0.1	0.2	0.2	0.2	0.2	0.1
Inventory to Working Capital 41	0.7	•	0.7	0.7	0.5	0.7	0.4	0.8	0.8
Total Receipts to Cash Flow 42	10.2	7.4	35.5	11.5	10.6	13.0	6.4	11.4	8.9
Cost of Goods to Cash Flow 43	7.8	2.7	29.6	8.7	8.4	10.7	4.9	8.7	6.8
Cash Flow to Total Debt 44	0.2	0.1	0.1	0.3	0.4	0.2	0.4	0.1	0.2

Selected Financial Factors (in Percentages)

Debt Ratio 45	70.4	159.3	68.9	49.0	44.5	57.3	45.1	103.5	74.6
Return on Total Assets 46	8.8	•	13.3	7.1	6.4	9.4	16.2	9.8	8.7
Return on Equity Before Income Taxes 47	14.9	31.3	31.5	9.1	8.6	16.9	27.2	•	12.8
Return on Equity After Income Taxes 48	11.8	31.8	31.0	7.8	3.4	14.5	22.9	•	11.2
Profit Margin (Before Income Tax) 49	2.7	•	4.8	2.4	2.5	4.2	11.6	1.4	2.2
Profit Margin (After Income Tax) 50	2.1	•	4.8	2.1	1.0	3.6	9.8	1.4	1.9

Table II

Corporations with Net Income

ASPHALT PAVING, ROOFING, OTHER PETROLEUM AND COAL PRODUCTS

MONEY AMOUNTS AND SIZE OF ASSETS IN THOUSANDS OF DOLLARS

Item Description for Accounting Period 7/06 Through 6/07	Total	Zero Assets	Under 500	500 to 1,000	1,000 to 5,000	5,000 to 10,000	10,000 to 25,000	25,000 to 50,000	50,000 to 100,000	100,000 to 250,000	250,000 to 500,000	500,000 to 2,500,000	2,500,000 and over
Number of Enterprises 1	387	•	0	164	•	73	48	•	•	10	0	•	0
Revenues ($ in Thousands)													
Net Sales 2	13692014	•	0	874050	•	1127577	1588145	•	•	2225515	0	•	0
Interest 3	60787	•	0	83	•	28	901	•	•	4095	0	•	0
Rents 4	8219	•	0	0	•	245	6172	•	•	700	0	•	0
Royalties 5	7652	•	0	0	•	5	0	•	•	4505	0	•	0
Other Portfolio Income 6	108454	•	0	0	•	1786	7342	•	•	45045	0	•	0
Other Receipts 7	185525	•	0	228	•	738	6454	•	•	84015	0	•	0
Total Receipts 8	14062651	•	0	874361	•	1130379	1609014	•	•	2363875	0	•	0
Average Total Receipts 9	36338	•	•	5331	•	15485	33521	•	•	236388	•	•	•
Operating Costs/Operating Income (%)													
Cost of Operations 10	76.6	•	•	73.8	•	83.3	76.7	•	•	75.0	•	•	•
Salaries and Wages 11	3.9	•	•	1.4	•	3.8	4.2	•	•	4.6	•	•	•
Taxes Paid 12	1.1	•	•	2.1	•	0.9	1.7	•	•	1.3	•	•	•
Interest Paid 13	2.3	•	•	0.2	•	1.7	0.6	•	•	4.1	•	•	•
Depreciation 14	2.1	•	•	3.1	•	2.1	2.1	•	•	1.5	•	•	•
Amortization and Depletion 15	0.3	•	•	•	•	0.2	0.2	•	•	0.6	•	•	•
Pensions and Other Deferred Comp. 16	0.2	•	•	0.0	•	0.1	0.2	•	•	0.4	•	•	•
Employee Benefits 17	1.2	•	•	2.5	•	0.7	1.4	•	•	0.5	•	•	•
Advertising 18	0.8	•	•	0.2	•	2.1	0.5	•	•	0.3	•	•	•
Other Expenses 19	7.4	•	•	4.9	•	•	6.6	•	•	5.7	•	•	•
Officers' Compensation 20	1.3	•	•	5.2	•	1.9	1.9	•	•	1.0	•	•	•
Operating Margin 21	2.7	•	•	6.6	•	4.6	4.0	•	•	5.0	•	•	•
Operating Margin Before Officers' Comp. 22	4.0	•	•	11.8	•	6.5	5.9	•	•	6.0	•	•	•

Selected Average Balance Sheet ($ in Thousands)

Item								
Net Receivables 23	4021	•	89	•	2089	3207	•	35936
Inventories 24	2900	•	0	•	459	3145	•	29105
Net Property, Plant and Equipment 25	6109	•	288	•	3166	5305	•	51658
Total Assets 26	20302	•	626	•	7622	16152	•	200430
Notes and Loans Payable 27	7523	•	279	•	3425	2766	•	90394
All Other Liabilities 28	5945	•	168	•	1823	3012	•	46619
Net Worth 29	6834	•	179	•	2374	10374	•	63417

Selected Financial Ratios (Times to 1)

Item								
Current Ratio 30	2.0	•	1.8	•	1.4	2.4	•	2.2
Quick Ratio 31	1.1	•	1.8	•	1.1	1.5	•	1.1
Net Sales to Working Capital 32	7.7	•	37.4	•	16.3	6.9	•	4.7
Coverage Ratio 33	3.4	•	30.4	•	3.8	9.5	•	3.7
Total Asset Turnover 34	1.7	•	8.5	•	2.0	2.0	•	1.1
Inventory Turnover 35	9.3	•	•	•	28.1	8.1	•	5.7
Receivables Turnover 36	8.2	•	60.3	•	9.4	8.1	•	•
Total Liabilities to Net Worth 37	2.0	•	2.5	•	2.2	0.6	•	2.2
Current Assets to Working Capital 38	2.0	•	2.2	•	3.7	1.7	•	1.8
Current Liabilities to Working Capital 39	1.0	•	1.2	•	2.7	0.7	•	0.8
Working Capital to Net Sales 40	0.1	•	0.0	•	0.1	0.1	•	0.2
Inventory to Working Capital 41	0.7	•	•	•	0.7	0.6	•	0.6
Total Receipts to Cash Flow 42	9.0	•	9.2	•	35.5	9.8	•	6.6
Cost of Goods to Cash Flow 43	6.9	•	6.8	•	29.6	7.5	•	4.9
Cash Flow to Total Debt 44	0.3	•	1.3	•	0.1	0.6	•	0.2

Selected Financial Factors (in Percentages)

Item								
Debt Ratio 45	66.3	•	71.3	•	68.9	35.8	•	68.4
Return on Total Assets 46	13.6	•	58.0	•	13.3	12.1	•	17.1
Return on Equity Before Income Taxes 47	28.4	•	195.7	•	31.5	16.9	•	39.5
Return on Equity After Income Taxes 48	24.8	•	194.7	•	31.0	15.2	•	34.0
Profit Margin (Before Income Tax) 49	5.5	•	6.6	•	4.8	5.3	•	11.2
Profit Margin (After Income Tax) 50	4.8	•	6.6	•	4.8	4.8	•	9.7

Table I

Corporations with and without Net Income

BASIC CHEMICAL

MONEY AMOUNTS AND SIZE OF ASSETS IN THOUSANDS OF DOLLARS

Item Description for Accounting Period 7/06 Through 6/07	Total	Zero Assets	Under 500	500 to 1,000	1,000 to 5,000	5,000 to 10,000	10,000 to 25,000	25,000 to 50,000	50,000 to 100,000	100,000 to 250,000	250,000 to 500,000	500,000 to 2,500,000	2,500,000 and over
Number of Enterprises 1	1221	27	354	279	178	98	110	53	24	26	17	32	23
Revenues ($ in Thousands)													
Net Sales 2	170474535	1974684	131529	720158	623288	1412044	3772168	2799474	2244034	3930831	6378815	30857349	115630162
Interest 3	3946223	14991	0	188	2672	3022	6133	2463	4042	29513	64166	545489	3273544
Rents 4	227943	0	0	0	0	6	3599	2774	221	15861	1362	11209	192910
Royalties 5	3556315	1921	0	0	1139	0	1071	0	1147	17279	27403	199556	3306798
Other Portfolio Income 6	4033483	19362	0	824	16967	3	4184	4602	10565	35550	349529	710563	2881338
Other Receipts 7	5106534	5912	3	14275	3949	26555	47035	13053	16524	100578	196259	604640	4077749
Total Receipts 8	187345033	2016870	131532	735445	648015	1441630	3834190	2822366	2276533	4129612	7017534	32928806	129362501
Average Total Receipts 9	153436	74699	372	2636	3641	14711	34856	53252	94856	158831	412796	1029025	5624457
Operating Costs/Operating Income (%)													
Cost of Operations 10	76.9	79.1	73.5	64.6	68.5	73.3	76.3	70.5	78.6	69.2	79.1	71.9	78.6
Salaries and Wages 11	4.7	3.6	3.1	8.5	8.2	4.9	4.8	6.9	4.8	7.1	3.1	6.0	4.3
Taxes Paid 12	1.1	0.7	3.1	0.9	2.2	1.9	1.4	1.6	1.4	1.3	0.8	1.1	1.1
Interest Paid 13	4.8	1.6	1.5	0.3	1.5	0.7	1.1	1.0	1.6	2.7	1.7	4.0	5.7
Depreciation 14	3.2	5.8	0.2	0.6	3.2	1.2	2.6	2.2	1.9	3.2	2.8	3.7	3.1
Amortization and Depletion 15	0.7	0.8	1.7	•	0.1	0.2	0.1	0.2	0.8	0.9	0.5	1.0	0.7
Pensions and Other Deferred Comp. 16	1.2	0.0	0.0	•	0.5	0.4	0.3	0.7	0.2	0.8	0.4	1.6	1.3
Employee Benefits 17	2.0	1.3	3.7	0.7	1.2	1.5	1.0	1.2	1.2	1.4	1.2	2.5	2.0
Advertising 18	0.5	0.1	0.0	0.1	0.5	0.3	0.1	0.2	0.1	0.2	0.1	0.2	0.7
Other Expenses 19	8.7	7.2	13.1	9.1	15.6	5.2	7.3	7.2	5.9	13.3	7.5	11.2	8.0
Officers' Compensation 20	0.6	0.8	9.3	7.1	6.0	2.7	1.8	1.9	1.2	1.1	0.8	0.7	0.4
Operating Margin 21	•	•	•	8.1	•	7.7	3.0	6.5	2.2	•	2.1	•	•
Operating Margin Before Officers' Comp. 22	•	•	0.1	15.2	•	10.4	4.9	8.4	3.4	2.9	•	•	•

Selected Average Balance Sheet ($ in Thousands)

Net Receivables 23 49418	0	25	281	810	2327	3871	7508	15845	25876	64446	169444	2238497
Inventories 24 14125	0	35	108	279	1801	2750	5551	13041	15888	37431	154844	437548
Net Property, Plant and Equipment 25 38900	0	2	37	312	2525	5805	9760	19287	45894	106455	336432	1382381
Total Assets 26 230903		85	634	2185	8413	16848	33410	71812	161650	402712	1178861	9843414
Notes and Loans Payable 27 91143	0	84	118	930	1979	5331	8106	30337	53208	93354	354589	4121832
All Other Liabilities 28 63380	0	13	192	832	1683	4337	6224	16324	40834	98023	418066	2596103
Net Worth 29 76380	-13	325	422	4751	7179	19080	25151	67609	211335	406005	3125480	

Selected Financial Ratios (Times to 1)

Current Ratio 30 1.0	•	2.5	2.2	1.3	3.3	1.9	2.0	1.8	1.8	2.3	1.5	0.9
Quick Ratio 31 0.8	•	1.2	1.3	0.9	1.8	1.1	1.1	1.0	1.2	1.5	0.8	0.7
Net Sales to Working Capital 32 61.6	•	8.0	8.0	9.2	3.7	8.5	6.2	6.1	5.0	4.1	6.6	•
Coverage Ratio 33 2.3	1.7	•	32.0	•	16.0	5.1	8.3	3.3	2.5	8.5	1.8	2.3
Total Asset Turnover 34 0.6	•	4.4	4.1	1.6	1.7	2.0	1.6	1.3	0.9	0.9	0.8	0.5
Inventory Turnover 35 7.6	7.7	15.4	8.6	5.9	9.5	6.7	5.6	6.6	7.9	4.5	9.0	
Receivables Turnover 36 2.8	13.0	9.7	4.9	7.0	10.6	8.3	5.7	6.1	6.7	5.8	2.2	
Total Liabilities to Net Worth 37 2.0	•	1.0	1.0	4.2	0.8	1.3	0.8	1.9	1.4	0.9	1.9	2.1
Current Assets to Working Capital 38 34.3	1.7	1.8	3.9	1.4	2.2	2.0	2.3	2.3	1.7	2.9	•	
Current Liabilities to Working Capital 39 33.3	0.7	0.8	2.9	0.4	1.2	1.0	1.3	1.3	0.7	1.9	•	
Working Capital to Net Sales 40 0.0	0.1	0.1	0.1	0.3	0.4	0.2	0.2	0.2	0.2	0.5	•	
Inventory to Working Capital 41 6.3	0.8	0.4	0.8	0.5	0.8	0.9	0.5	0.4	1.0	•		
Total Receipts to Cash Flow 42 8.8	15.7	5.4	18.7	7.1	9.6	7.9	13.4	6.7	7.4	9.8	8.6	
Cost of Goods to Cash Flow 43 6.7	12.5	3.5	12.8	5.2	7.3	5.6	10.5	4.7	5.8	7.1	6.8	
Cash Flow to Total Debt 44 0.1	•	1.5	0.1	0.6	0.4	0.5	0.1	0.2	0.3	0.1		

Selected Financial Factors (in Percentages)

Debt Ratio 45 66.9	•	115.1	48.8	80.7	43.5	57.4	42.9	65.0	58.2	47.5	65.6	68.2
Return on Total Assets 46 6.8	•	•	42.9	18.1	11.8	13.2	6.8	6.3	13.2	5.9	6.6	
Return on Equity Before Income Taxes 47 11.7	•	268.3	81.1	30.0	22.3	20.3	13.7	9.1	22.1	7.7	11.5	
Return on Equity After Income Taxes 48 8.3	•	268.3	80.7	27.2	17.1	17.8	10.7	6.1	15.0	4.4	8.3	
Profit Margin (Before Income Tax) 49 6.4	1.2	10.2	9.9	4.7	7.3	3.7	4.1	3.3	7.2			
Profit Margin (After Income Tax) 50 4.5	0.1	10.2	9.0	3.6	6.4	2.9	2.7	1.9	5.2			

Table II

Corporations with Net Income

BASIC CHEMICAL

MONEY AMOUNTS AND SIZE OF ASSETS IN THOUSANDS OF DOLLARS

Item Description for Accounting Period 7/06 Through 6/07	Total	Zero Assets	Under 500	500 to 1,000	1,000 to 5,000	5,000 to 10,000	10,000 to 25,000	25,000 to 50,000	50,000 to 100,000	100,000 to 250,000	250,000 to 500,000	500,000 to 2,500,000	2,500,000 and over
Number of Enterprises **1**	987	18	247	279	129	93	92	41	15	17	14	24	19
Revenues ($ in Thousands)													
Net Sales **2**	153321137	1355192	28063	720158	450093	1228199	3431552	2459890	1587324	3001138	5104090	23560460	110394980
Interest **3**	3728932	14722	0	188	2530	3022	5518	1826	2162	21595	58530	503696	3115143
Rents **4**	211011	0	0	0	0	6	3599	2774	209	15861	1342	6785	180434
Royalties **5**	3272676	1921	0	0	1139	0	1071	0	1147	14657	9999	91442	3151299
Other Portfolio Income **6**	3862897	19362	0	824	16967	3	4107	4602	10524	13831	346060	646757	2799864
Other Receipts **7**	4831299	5912	0	14275	2411	26543	46701	4994	14897	93023	190858	476040	3955642
Total Receipts **8**	169227952	1397109	28063	735445	473140	1257773	3492548	2474086	1616263	3160105	5710879	25285180	123597362
Average Total Receipts **9**	171457	77617	114	2636	3668	13524	37962	60344	107751	185889	407920	1053549	6505124
Operating Costs/Operating Income (%)													
Cost of Operations **10**	77.1	75.3	57.1	64.6	57.8	70.6	75.5	70.1	75.6	67.1	78.6	70.8	79.1
Salaries and Wages **11**	4.4	4.0	0.2	8.5	8.1	5.3	4.6	6.3	4.7	7.9	2.8	5.8	4.0
Taxes Paid **12**	1.1	0.8	5.1	0.9	2.1	2.0	1.4	1.6	1.6	1.3	0.8	1.1	1.1
Interest Paid **13**	4.7	1.4	5.3	0.3	1.1	0.7	1.0	0.9	1.4	0.9	2.0	3.8	5.4
Depreciation **14**	3.1	3.1	0.0	0.6	2.7	1.4	1.8	2.1	1.6	2.1	2.4	3.6	3.2
Amortization and Depletion **15**	0.7	0.6	0.4	*	*	0.0	0.1	0.1	0.8	0.4	0.6	1.1	0.6
Pensions and Other Deferred Comp. **16**	1.0	0.0	0.0	*	0.6	0.4	0.3	0.7	0.2	1.1	0.5	1.0	1.1
Employee Benefits **17**	1.9	1.5	4.8	0.7	1.4	1.7	1.0	1.1	1.2	1.5	0.8	2.2	2.0
Advertising **18**	0.6	0.1	0.0	0.1	0.4	0.4	0.1	0.1	0.2	0.2	0.1	0.2	0.7
Other Expenses **19**	8.4	8.0	22.7	9.1	16.8	5.4	6.7	6.5	7.0	12.5	7.1	11.0	7.8
Officers' Compensation **20**	0.6	1.1	0.2	7.1	7.8	3.1	1.8	2.1	1.3	1.2	0.8	0.7	0.3
Operating Margin **21**	*	4.2	4.1	8.1	1.1	9.0	5.8	8.4	4.4	3.9	3.7	*	*
Operating Margin Before Officers' Comp. **22**	*	5.3	4.3	15.2	8.9	12.1	7.6	10.4	5.6	5.1	4.5	*	*

Selected Average Balance Sheet ($ in Thousands)

Net Receivables 23	58245	0	0	281	880	2426	4134	7973	16801	28092	67962	173747	2658540
Inventories 24	13925	0	1	108	226	1669	2986	5798	12353	16569	35792	156860	438470
Net Property, Plant and Equipment 25	42596	0	0	37	270	2654	4862	9824	18347	41202	98587	325753	1617158
Total Assets 26	251791	0	1	634	2226	8465	16276	34372	69062	153286	400339	1141730	10932206
Notes and Loans Payable 27	100654	0	0	118	524	1967	4038	7993	29001	32373	82918	297768	4687924
All Other Liabilities 28	64352	0	0	192	404	1529	3891	7143	16586	42390	96930	382267	2690336
Net Worth 29	86784	0	0	325	1298	4968	8347	19236	23475	78523	220491	461694	3553946

Selected Financial Ratios (Times to 1)

Current Ratio 30	1.0	•	14.8	2.2	2.2	3.7	2.4	1.8	1.7	1.9	2.2	1.9	0.9
Quick Ratio 31	0.8	•	2.5	1.3	1.8	2.1	1.4	1.1	0.9	1.2	1.5	1.0	0.7
Net Sales to Working Capital 32	66.0	•	170.1	8.0	4.5	3.2	6.9	7.7	7.1	4.9	4.1	4.9	•
Coverage Ratio 33	2.7	6.1	1.8	32.0	6.4	17.7	8.7	11.4	5.3	11.8	9.0	2.7	2.4
Total Asset Turnover 34	0.6	•	146.9	4.1	1.6	1.6	2.3	1.7	1.5	1.2	0.9	0.9	0.5
Inventory Turnover 35	8.6	•	109.1	15.4	8.9	5.6	9.4	7.3	6.5	7.2	8.0	4.4	10.5
Receivables Turnover 36	2.8	•	•	9.7	4.6	6.2	10.9	8.8	6.5	•	6.2	•	2.3
Total Liabilities to Net Worth 37	1.9	•	2.1	1.0	0.7	0.7	0.9	0.8	1.9	1.0	0.8	1.5	2.1
Current Assets to Working Capital 38	37.7	•	1.1	1.8	1.8	1.4	1.7	2.2	2.4	2.1	1.8	2.2	•
Current Liabilities to Working Capital 39	36.7	•	0.1	0.8	0.8	0.4	0.7	1.2	1.4	1.1	0.8	1.2	•
Working Capital to Net Sales 40	0.0	•	0.0	0.1	0.2	0.3	0.1	0.1	0.1	0.2	0.2	0.2	•
Inventory to Working Capital 41	6.7	•	0.9	0.4	0.2	0.5	0.6	0.8	1.0	0.5	0.4	0.8	•
Total Receipts to Cash Flow 42	8.0	7.8	6.2	5.4	6.9	6.3	7.8	7.3	9.0	5.1	6.5	7.7	8.4
Cost of Goods to Cash Flow 43	6.2	5.9	3.5	3.5	4.0	4.4	5.9	5.1	6.8	3.4	5.1	5.5	6.7
Cash Flow to Total Debt 44	0.1	•	35.3	1.5	0.5	0.6	0.6	0.5	0.3	0.5	0.3	0.2	0.1

Selected Financial Factors (in Percentages)

Debt Ratio 45	65.5	•	67.5	48.8	41.7	41.3	48.7	44.0	66.0	48.8	44.9	59.6	67.5
Return on Total Assets 46	7.7	•	1377.5	42.9	11.5	19.0	19.6	17.1	11.7	11.8	16.4	8.9	7.0
Return on Equity Before Income Taxes 47	14.0	•	1864.5	81.1	16.6	30.5	33.8	27.9	27.9	21.1	26.5	13.8	12.5
Return on Equity After Income Taxes 48	10.3	•	1864.5	80.7	11.6	27.8	28.4	24.7	22.9	17.1	18.2	9.9	9.1
Profit Margin (Before Income Tax) 49	7.8	7.3	4.1	10.2	6.2	11.5	7.6	8.9	6.2	9.4	16.0	6.5	7.6
Profit Margin (After Income Tax) 50	5.7	5.7	4.1	10.2	4.3	10.4	6.4	7.9	5.1	7.6	11.0	4.7	5.6

Table I

Corporations with and without Net Income

RESIN, SYNTHETIC RUBBER AND FIBERS AND FILAMENTS

MONEY AMOUNTS AND SIZE OF ASSETS IN THOUSANDS OF DOLLARS

Item Description for Accounting Period 7/06 Through 6/07	Total	Zero Assets	Under 500	500 to 1,000	1,000 to 5,000	5,000 to 10,000	10,000 to 25,000	25,000 to 50,000	50,000 to 100,000	100,000 to 250,000	250,000 to 500,000	500,000 to 2,500,000	2,500,000 and over
Number of Enterprises **1**	886	5	451	120	161	45	52	15	12	11	5	7	3
Revenues ($ in Thousands)													
Net Sales **2**	40069949	207904	56909	318897	944099	861382	1522115	606904	1096129	2138324	1855345	8197666	22264276
Interest **3**	1856573	1977	0	0	31	0	1607	2472	2234	16602	14224	49000	1768426
Rents **4**	65775	0	0	0	0	0	92	58	175	809	0	1242	63399
Royalties **5**	676070	0	0	0	0	0	0	1132	0	4588	2051	8559	659739
Other Portfolio Income **6**	447477	896	0	0	1	0	10987	248	3577	12765	192544	106474	119984
Other Receipts **7**	1685209	126	51	0	1709	58	8082	20888	-261	10600	9446	142258	1492253
Total Receipts **8**	44801053	210903	56960	318897	945840	861440	1542883	631702	1101854	2183688	2073610	8505199	26368077
Average Total Receipts **9**	50566	42181	126	2657	5875	19143	29671	42113	91821	198517	414722	1215028	8789359
Operating Costs/Operating Income (%)													
Cost of Operations **10**	70.7	55.8	91.3	45.8	61.3	67.0	74.9	68.2	79.1	79.4	83.0	82.9	64.8
Salaries and Wages **11**	2.4	10.2	8.5	8.5	5.4	11.4	3.6	4.7	3.9	4.3	4.0	3.8	0.7
Taxes Paid **12**	0.8	2.3	5.8	1.2	2.7	1.7	1.6	1.7	1.4	1.2	0.9	0.7	0.5
Interest Paid **13**	6.0	1.5	•	0.2	1.3	0.8	1.8	3.4	0.4	2.1	2.2	3.1	9.0
Depreciation **14**	3.9	0.5	6.4	•	2.8	0.3	2.8	3.0	1.9	2.3	1.4	3.5	5.0
Amortization and Depletion **15**	0.3	0.1	•	•	0.0	•	0.1	•	0.1	0.2	0.5	0.4	0.3
Pensions and Other Deferred Comp. **16**	0.6	0.5	•	•	1.5	0.2	0.2	0.4	0.6	0.2	0.7	0.6	0.6
Employee Benefits **17**	2.8	0.4	4.0	•	3.5	0.4	1.7	1.8	0.8	1.3	1.2	0.6	4.2
Advertising **18**	0.3	0.5	2.4	0.1	0.5	0.3	0.4	0.7	0.3	0.2	0.1	0.1	0.4
Other Expenses **19**	15.2	17.1	45.4	20.2	10.5	11.7	7.7	9.8	8.3	5.9	4.6	4.3	22.2
Officers' Compensation **20**	0.5	1.9	2.2	3.0	3.8	4.1	1.9	1.5	0.5	0.9	1.0	0.3	0.0
Operating Margin **21**	•	9.3	•	20.9	6.5	2.1	3.5	5.2	2.8	2.0	0.3	•	•
Operating Margin Before Officers' Comp. **22**	•	11.2	•	23.9	10.3	6.2	5.4	6.7	3.3	2.9	1.3	0.2	•

Selected Average Balance Sheet ($ in Thousands)

Net Receivables 23	10559	0	11	292	639	1980	4419	5719	12661	25125	115664	143530	2265546
Inventories 24	5443	0	8	74	523	2583	2340	4470	11888	15215	53518	339189	980611
Net Property, Plant and Equipment 25	15864	0	29	0	554	883	4904	11573	23972	45134	99123	356884	3235472
Total Assets 26	117216	0	225	546	2533	5392	14903	36886	68022	143411	360758	948913	30289103
Notes and Loans Payable 27	14113	0	344	36	153	1807	5327	12862	11738	35169	140991	477009	2399050
All Other Liabilities 28	42917	0	73	230	260	2227	5867	9456	16995	40135	98189	252922	11489421
Net Worth 29	60185	0	-193	280	2120	1358	3710	14569	39289	68106	121578	218982	16400633

Selected Financial Ratios (Times to 1)

Current Ratio 30	2.0	•	3.5	2.3	4.9	1.1	1.5	1.7	1.9	1.7	2.3	1.6	2.2
Quick Ratio 31	1.2	•	0.6	1.9	3.0	0.5	0.9	1.1	1.1	0.8	1.6	0.8	1.4
Net Sales to Working Capital 32	4.2	•	0.9	8.5	4.6	40.3	9.1	6.9	5.9	6.9	3.3	9.4	3.1
Coverage Ratio 33	2.5	8.4	•	98.0	6.0	3.6	3.8	3.9	9.4	2.9	8.7	2.2	2.2
Total Asset Turnover 34	0.4	•	0.6	4.9	2.3	3.6	2.0	1.1	1.3	1.4	1.0	1.2	0.2
Inventory Turnover 35	5.9	•	14.3	16.3	6.9	5.0	9.4	6.2	6.1	10.1	5.8	2.9	4.9
Receivables Turnover 36	4.4	•	22.6	17.8	10.8	6.5	9.6	6.4	6.6	11.5	4.3	1.8	6.6
Total Liabilities to Net Worth 37	0.9	•	•	1.0	0.2	3.0	3.0	1.5	0.7	1.1	2.0	3.3	0.8
Current Assets to Working Capital 38	2.0	•	1.4	1.7	1.3	9.5	3.0	2.5	2.1	2.4	1.8	2.7	1.8
Current Liabilities to Working Capital 39	1.0	•	0.4	0.7	0.3	8.5	2.0	1.5	1.1	1.4	0.8	1.7	0.8
Working Capital to Net Sales 40	0.2	•	1.1	0.1	0.2	0.0	0.1	0.1	0.2	0.1	0.3	0.1	0.3
Inventory to Working Capital 41	0.5	•	0.1	0.3	0.4	4.9	0.9	0.8	0.7	0.7	0.5	0.9	0.4
Total Receipts to Cash Flow 42	4.8	3.7	•	2.6	7.9	8.3	10.7	5.7	9.2	11.0	6.3	15.7	3.4
Cost of Goods to Cash Flow 43	3.4	2.1	•	1.2	4.9	5.6	8.0	3.9	7.3	8.7	5.2	13.0	2.2
Cash Flow to Total Debt 44	0.2	•	•	3.9	1.8	0.6	0.2	0.3	0.3	0.2	0.2	0.1	0.2

Selected Financial Factors (in Percentages)

Debt Ratio 45	48.7	•	185.7	48.8	16.3	74.8	75.1	60.5	42.2	52.5	66.3	76.9	45.9
Return on Total Assets 46	5.7	•	•	102.7	18.6	10.4	13.0	14.3	5.0	8.5	20.1	8.3	5.0
Return on Equity Before Income Taxes 47	6.6	•	43.2	198.5	18.5	29.7	38.5	26.8	7.7	11.9	52.7	19.6	5.1
Return on Equity After Income Taxes 48	4.6	•	43.2	198.5	18.5	29.7	34.1	20.6	4.8	10.0	34.1	15.2	3.4
Profit Margin (Before Income Tax) 49	8.8	10.7	•	20.9	6.7	2.1	4.9	9.6	3.3	4.2	17.3	3.7	11.2
Profit Margin (After Income Tax) 50	6.1	10.7	•	20.9	6.7	2.1	4.3	7.4	2.1	3.5	11.2	2.8	7.4

Table II
Corporations with Net Income

RESIN, SYNTHETIC RUBBER AND FIBERS AND FILAMENTS

MONEY AMOUNTS AND SIZE OF ASSETS IN THOUSANDS OF DOLLARS

Item Description for Accounting Period 7/06 Through 6/07	Total	Zero Assets	Under 500	500 to 1,000	1,000 to 5,000	5,000 to 10,000	10,000 to 25,000	25,000 to 50,000	50,000 to 100,000	100,000 to 250,000	250,000 to 500,000	500,000 to 2,500,000	2,500,000 and over
Number of Enterprises **1**	403	•	0	120	161	45	33	11	8	7	•	•	3
Revenues ($ in Thousands)													
Net Sales **2**	37071535	•	0	318897	944099	861382	1037963	569073	844262	1459471	•	•	22264276
Interest **3**	1852685	•	0	0	31	0	1388	1801	1709	16105	•	•	1768426
Rents **4**	65567	•	0	0	0	0	0	58	175	693	•	•	63399
Royalties **5**	671481	•	0	0	0	0	0	1132	0	0	•	•	659739
Other Portfolio Income **6**	432872	•	0	0	1	0	44	248	2602	10285	•	•	119984
Other Receipts **7**	1674752	•	0	0	1709	58	7429	20886	415	5342	•	•	1492253
Total Receipts **8**	41768892	•	0	318897	945840	861440	1046824	593198	849163	1491896	•	•	26368077
Average Total Receipts **9**	103645	•	•	2657	5875	19143	31722	53927	106145	213128	•	•	8789359
Operating Costs/Operating Income (%)													
Cost of Operations **10**	69.4	•	•	45.8	61.3	67.0	71.7	67.7	79.8	74.6	•	•	64.8
Salaries and Wages **11**	2.4	•	•	8.5	5.4	11.4	3.6	4.5	3.4	5.9	•	•	0.7
Taxes Paid **12**	0.8	•	•	1.2	2.7	1.7	1.7	1.7	1.4	1.3	•	•	0.5
Interest Paid **13**	6.2	•	•	0.2	1.3	0.8	1.0	1.6	0.1	2.1	•	•	9.0
Depreciation **14**	4.1	•	•	•	2.8	0.3	2.0	3.1	2.1	2.1	•	•	5.0
Amortization and Depletion **15**	0.3	•	•	•	0.0	•	0.0	•	0.0	0.2	•	•	0.3
Pensions and Other Deferred Comp. **16**	0.6	•	•	•	1.5	0.2	0.2	0.4	0.7	0.3	•	•	0.6
Employee Benefits **17**	2.9	•	•	•	3.5	0.4	1.8	1.8	0.8	1.1	•	•	4.2
Advertising **18**	0.3	•	•	0.1	0.5	0.3	0.4	0.7	0.2	0.2	•	•	0.4
Other Expenses **19**	15.8	•	•	20.2	10.5	11.7	7.5	9.5	2.6	5.9	•	•	22.2
Officers' Compensation **20**	0.5	•	•	3.0	3.8	4.1	2.2	1.3	0.6	1.2	•	•	0.0
Operating Margin **21**	•	•	•	20.9	6.5	2.1	7.8	8.3	8.2	4.9	•	•	•
Operating Margin Before Officers' Comp. **22**	•	•	•	23.9	10.3	6.2	10.0	9.6	8.8	6.2	•	•	•

Selected Average Balance Sheet ($ in Thousands)

		•								•	
Net Receivables	23	•	21706	292	639	7261	5617	1980	14904	29728	•	2265546
Inventories	24	•	11261	99	523	5745	2652	2583	14412	21412	•	980611
Net Property, Plant and Equipment	25	•	32464	0	554	15305	3692	883	28094	48134	•	3235472
Total Assets	26	•	250250	546	2533	38763	15274	5392	73108	153029	•	30289103
Notes and Loans Payable	27	•	25977	36	153	10071	2830	1807	6084	18034	•	2399050
All Other Liabilities	28	•	92898	230	260	13395	6589	2227	20014	36119	•	11489421
Net Worth	29	•	131376	280	2120	15297	5856	1358	47010	98876	•	16400633

Selected Financial Ratios (Times to 1)

		•									•	
Current Ratio	30	•	2.1	2.3	4.9	1.4	1.8	1.1	2.1	2.6	•	2.2
Quick Ratio	31	•	1.2	1.9	3.0	0.8	1.1	0.5	1.3	1.3	•	1.4
Net Sales to Working Capital	32	•	4.1	8.5	4.6	11.8	6.4	40.3	5.2	4.5	•	3.1
Coverage Ratio	33	•	2.6	98.0	6.0	8.8	10.1	3.6	63.0	4.3	•	2.2
Total Asset Turnover	34	•	0.4	4.9	2.3	1.3	2.1	3.6	1.4	1.4	•	0.2
Inventory Turnover	35	•	5.7	12.2	6.9	6.1	8.5	5.0	5.8	7.3	•	4.9
Receivables Turnover	36	•	4.3	18.2	10.8	•	8.1	6.5	6.4	•	•	6.6
Total Liabilities to Net Worth	37	•	0.9	1.0	0.2	1.5	1.6	3.0	0.6	0.5	•	0.8
Current Assets to Working Capital	38	•	2.0	1.7	1.3	3.6	2.3	9.5	1.9	1.6	•	1.8
Current Liabilities to Working Capital	39	•	1.0	0.7	0.3	2.6	1.3	8.5	0.9	0.6	•	0.8
Working Capital to Net Sales	40	•	0.2	0.1	0.2	0.1	0.2	0.0	0.2	0.2	•	0.3
Inventory to Working Capital	41	•	0.5	0.3	0.4	1.3	0.7	4.9	0.6	0.5	•	0.4
Total Receipts to Cash Flow	42	•	4.4	2.6	7.9	4.9	7.5	8.3	9.2	8.4	•	3.4
Cost of Goods to Cash Flow	43	•	3.1	1.2	4.9	3.3	5.4	5.6	7.4	6.3	•	2.2
Cash Flow to Total Debt	44	•	0.2	3.9	1.8	0.5	0.4	0.6	0.4	0.5	•	0.2

Selected Financial Factors (in Percentages)

		•									•	
Debt Ratio	45	•	47.5	48.8	16.3	60.5	61.7	74.8	35.7	35.4	•	45.9
Return on Total Assets	46	•	6.0	102.7	18.6	18.9	19.9	10.4	12.9	12.6	•	5.0
Return on Equity Before Income Taxes	47	•	7.0	198.5	18.5	42.4	46.7	29.7	19.7	15.0	•	5.1
Return on Equity After Income Taxes	48	•	5.0	198.5	18.5	34.4	42.2	29.7	16.0	13.1	•	3.4
Profit Margin (Before Income Tax)	49	•	10.0	20.9	6.7	12.5	8.7	2.1	8.8	7.1	•	11.2
Profit Margin (After Income Tax)	50	•	7.1	20.9	6.7	10.2	7.9	2.1	7.1	6.2	•	7.4

Table I

Corporations with and without Net Income

PHARMACEUTICAL AND MEDICINE

MONEY AMOUNTS AND SIZE OF ASSETS IN THOUSANDS OF DOLLARS

Item Description for Accounting Period 7/06 Through 6/07	Total	Zero Assets	Under 500	500 to 1,000	1,000 to 5,000	5,000 to 10,000	10,000 to 25,000	25,000 to 50,000	50,000 to 100,000	100,000 to 250,000	250,000 to 500,000	500,000 to 2,500,000	2,500,000 and over
Number of Enterprises 1	1678	287	532	160	197	147	126	50	51	47	17	32	31
Revenues ($ in Thousands)													
Net Sales 2	304120391	476337	129571	416491	353662	1767252	2539538	1669527	1991029	5455956	3354610	28029370	257933048
Interest 3	10529436	164424	59	12	3291	5076	25857	18480	48986	76995	68662	470247	9647347
Rents 4	149158	193	808	0	311	786	954	94	332	2504	3094	10970	129111
Royalties 5	20327045	296020	0	0	0	1003	16222	0	52750	101587	246351	316199	19296913
Other Portfolio Income 6	10325601	1086	0	0	24303	1713	3961	28386	27819	136339	11948	373005	9717043
Other Receipts 7	22488722	674802	27918	236	742	8018	47519	22848	90280	136281	84857	2275974	19119247
Total Receipts 8	367940353	1612862	158356	416739	382309	1783848	2634051	1739335	2211196	5913662	3769522	31475765	315842709
Average Total Receipts 9	219273	5620	298	2605	1941	12135	20905	34787	43357	125823	221737	983618	10188474
Operating Costs/Operating Income (%)													
Cost of Operations 10	49.7	35.5	69.0	68.5	46.1	65.0	55.6	65.1	51.5	43.3	35.5	45.2	50.3
Salaries and Wages 11	13.9	26.3	8.6	11.2	17.9	6.9	10.7	10.5	18.3	11.9	17.1	13.0	14.1
Taxes Paid 12	1.7	8.4	0.5	2.5	4.7	1.8	2.9	2.2	2.6	1.9	2.3	1.9	1.6
Interest Paid 13	4.6	10.3	1.7	1.0	4.4	1.4	1.6	2.0	4.4	2.1	4.0	2.4	4.9
Depreciation 14	2.3	5.8	5.7	1.0	3.5	2.4	2.6	2.8	4.2	2.8	1.6	1.7	2.4
Amortization and Depletion 15	1.3	2.7	•	1.1	2.2	1.0	0.3	1.8	2.4	2.0	5.0	1.3	1.2
Pensions and Other Deferred Comp. 16	1.4	1.3	•	0.3	0.3	0.4	0.4	0.8	0.3	0.5	0.2	0.6	1.5
Employee Benefits 17	2.7	4.0	•	0.5	3.6	1.9	2.0	1.2	3.0	1.8	2.4	1.7	2.9
Advertising 18	5.0	0.9	10.1	0.0	0.4	0.5	1.6	2.7	4.0	2.3	4.5	3.4	5.4
Other Expenses 19	21.7	179.2	23.6	24.0	45.2	10.9	23.8	21.4	38.5	27.9	34.3	24.3	20.8
Officers' Compensation 20	0.6	5.9	0.2	1.8	10.9	6.4	4.4	2.5	3.3	1.9	2.3	1.6	0.3
Operating Margin 21	•	•	•	•	•	1.5	•	•	•	1.5	•	2.8	•
Operating Margin Before Officers' Comp. 22	•	•	•	•	•	7.9	•	•	•	3.4	•	4.5	•

Selected Average Balance Sheet ($ in Thousands)

Net Receivables 23	73466	0	18	169	569	1583	3412	4843	9226	20649	43244	280196	3583210
Inventories 24	21775	0	14	304	197	1539	2340	5832	5962	16841	28392	147294	946413
Net Property, Plant and Equipment 25	43706	0	82	114	458	2324	3768	7598	11970	22797	33429	141807	2103305
Total Assets 26	502429	0	139	880	2413	7813	18151	35025	69957	152843	344874	1206907	25224633
Notes and Loans Payable 27	149109	0	235	451	814	2077	6473	9969	21272	31183	103692	271962	7587478
All Other Liabilities 28	135125	0	12	420	728	2069	4091	8859	23139	40835	112444	313475	6781254
Net Worth 29	218195	0	-108	9	871	3667	7587	16198	25545	80825	128738	621470	10855901

Selected Financial Ratios (Times to 1)

Current Ratio 30	1.2	•	0.4	1.5	2.0	1.7	1.8	2.1	2.2	2.1	2.4	2.1	1.2
Quick Ratio 31	0.7	•	0.2	0.7	1.7	1.1	1.2	1.4	1.5	1.2	1.2	1.3	0.6
Net Sales to Working Capital 32	5.7	•	•	10.9	2.1	6.8	4.1	3.0	1.9	2.7	1.8	2.8	7.0
Coverage Ratio 33	4.8	6.6	2.7	•	•	2.7	•	•	•	5.8	1.7	7.3	4.8
Total Asset Turnover 34	0.4	•	1.8	3.0	0.7	1.5	1.1	1.0	0.6	0.8	0.6	0.7	0.3
Inventory Turnover 35	4.1	•	12.1	5.9	4.2	5.1	4.8	3.7	3.4	3.0	2.5	2.7	4.4
Receivables Turnover 36	1.7	•	17.6	21.9	3.8	6.4	7.3	6.7	4.2	5.7	4.1	3.6	1.5
Total Liabilities to Net Worth 37	1.3	•	98.0	•	1.8	1.1	1.4	1.2	1.7	0.9	1.7	0.9	1.3
Current Assets to Working Capital 38	5.1	•	•	3.2	2.0	2.4	2.3	1.9	1.8	1.9	1.7	1.9	6.5
Current Liabilities to Working Capital 39	4.1	•	•	2.2	1.0	1.4	1.3	0.9	0.8	0.9	0.7	0.9	5.5
Working Capital to Net Sales 40	0.2	•	•	0.1	0.5	0.1	0.2	0.3	0.5	0.4	0.6	0.4	0.1
Inventory to Working Capital 41	0.7	•	•	1.6	0.3	0.8	0.6	0.5	0.3	0.4	0.3	0.4	0.9
Total Receipts to Cash Flow 42	3.1	0.5	5.8	17.9	154.5	9.4	5.5	10.6	8.1	3.0	3.0	2.7	3.1
Cost of Goods to Cash Flow 43	1.5	0.2	4.0	12.3	71.3	6.1	3.0	6.9	4.2	1.3	1.1	1.2	1.6
Cash Flow to Total Debt 44	0.2	•	0.2	0.2	0.0	0.3	0.3	0.2	0.1	0.5	0.3	0.5	0.2

Selected Financial Factors (in Percentages)

Debt Ratio 45	56.6	•	178.0	99.0	63.9	53.1	58.2	53.8	63.5	47.1	62.7	48.5	57.0
Return on Total Assets 46	8.0	•	8.0	•	•	5.7	•	•	•	9.1	4.0	12.9	7.9
Return on Equity Before Income Taxes 47	14.6	•	•	•	•	7.7	•	•	•	14.3	4.5	21.7	14.5
Return on Equity After Income Taxes 48	9.4	•	•	•	•	4.6	•	•	•	8.2	•	14.1	9.6
Profit Margin (Before Income Tax) 49	17.5	58.1	2.9	•	2.3	•	•	•	•	9.9	2.9	15.4	18.9
Profit Margin (After Income Tax) 50	11.3	22.1	2.9	•	1.4	•	•	•	•	5.7	•	10.0	12.5

Table II
Corporations with Net Income

PHARMACEUTICAL AND MEDICINE

MONEY AMOUNTS AND SIZE OF ASSETS IN THOUSANDS OF DOLLARS

Item Description for Accounting Period 7/06 Through 6/07	Total	Zero Assets	Under 500	500 to 1,000	1,000 to 5,000	5,000 to 10,000	10,000 to 25,000	25,000 to 50,000	50,000 to 100,000	100,000 to 250,000	250,000 to 500,000	500,000 to 2,500,000	2,500,000 and over
Number of Enterprises 1	510	17	21	60	68	128	81	21	19	28	11	27	28
Revenues ($ in Thousands)													
Net Sales **2**	278662258	237547	10960	298550	216818	1696034	2101844	1222846	1186407	4485985	2366175	26440713	238398377
Interest **3**	9666320	158063	59	0	765	3218	7674	5688	14705	39341	34437	419304	8983066
Rents **4**	137564	88	0	0	0	786	892	15	0	1141	585	10924	123133
Royalties **5**	18079326	287609	0	0	0	0	16222	0	24930	31787	237454	227215	17254109
Other Portfolio Income **6**	10178200	1086	0	0	2	1709	2195	25292	8466	115179	11916	371425	9640933
Other Receipts **7**	19674772	667529	26270	0	588	6101	31145	13077	47467	64784	46613	2130038	16641159
Total Receipts **8**	336398440	1351922	37289	298550	218173	1707848	2159972	1266918	1281975	4738217	2697180	29599619	291040777
Average Total Receipts **9**	659605	79525	1776	4976	3208	13343	26666	60329	67472	169222	245198	1096282	10394313
Operating Costs/Operating Income (%)													
Cost of Operations **10**	50.1	33.7	4.1	70.0	43.5	66.0	55.4	60.8	50.1	40.1	36.2	46.6	50.6
Salaries and Wages **11**	13.3	14.8	•	6.7	4.1	5.2	8.7	7.1	11.5	9.8	13.7	11.6	13.6
Taxes Paid **12**	1.7	14.1	1.3	2.7	3.0	1.6	2.5	2.0	2.1	1.7	2.7	1.8	1.6
Interest Paid **13**	4.6	0.1	•	0.3	0.3	0.8	1.2	1.3	2.6	1.3	3.2	2.2	5.0
Depreciation **14**	2.3	2.8	0.4	0.2	1.3	2.1	2.4	1.5	2.7	1.8	1.7	1.7	2.3
Amortization and Depletion **15**	1.1	1.0	•	•	0.1	0.4	0.2	0.2	1.3	1.5	3.5	1.1	1.1
Pensions and Other Deferred Comp. **16**	1.4	0.4	•	•	0.3	0.4	0.4	0.9	0.4	0.6	0.3	0.6	1.6
Employee Benefits **17**	2.8	2.2	•	0.1	1.1	1.7	1.9	0.9	2.1	1.5	1.7	1.6	3.0
Advertising **18**	4.8	1.1	•	0.0	0.2	0.5	1.3	2.4	3.0	2.5	4.8	3.4	5.1
Other Expenses **19**	19.6	283.4	0.7	15.0	15.3	8.0	14.6	12.0	19.1	23.7	23.4	22.7	19.1
Officers' Compensation **20**	0.4	2.0	•	1.5	7.2	6.2	3.7	1.8	1.6	1.6	2.4	0.8	0.3
Operating Margin **21**	•	•	93.5	3.4	23.6	7.1	7.6	9.1	3.7	14.1	6.5	5.6	•
Operating Margin Before Officers' Comp. **22**	•	•	93.5	5.0	30.7	13.3	11.3	10.9	5.3	15.6	8.9	6.5	•

Selected Average Balance Sheet ($ in Thousands)

Net Receivables 23	200327	0	0	213	438	1717	4332	7296	11639	27225	48794	310888	3267361
Inventories 24	67928	0	6	555	160	1561	3134	8590	8643	22303	31670	159820	1073136
Net Property, Plant and Equipment 25	127550	0	1	20	615	2351	4534	6972	13400	22184	30186	157260	2097816
Total Assets 26	1494365	0	143	955	1923	7751	18631	35089	70130	156211	330004	1266550	25541567
Notes and Loans Payable 27	454763	0	3661	195	82	1608	6954	8794	19817	26938	71498	274565	7912524
All Other Liabilities 28	375425	0	0	397	686	1631	3786	8300	12714	45885	113036	333721	6390222
Net Worth 29	664177	-3517	0	364	1155	4511	7891	17995	37600	83388	145469	658264	11238821

Selected Financial Ratios (Times to 1)

Current Ratio 30	1.2	•	0.0	2.4	2.8	2.5	1.8	2.2	2.5	1.8	1.8	2.1	1.2
Quick Ratio 31	0.6	•	0.0	0.9	2.2	1.5	1.2	1.4	1.6	1.0	1.0	1.4	0.6
Net Sales to Working Capital 32	6.2	•	•	9.3	3.8	5.2	4.7	4.5	3.0	3.8	2.5	3.0	7.4
Coverage Ratio 33	5.4	1808.2	•	13.6	83.3	10.2	9.8	10.9	5.5	16.3	7.2	8.9	5.1
Total Asset Turnover 34	0.4	•	3.6	5.2	1.7	1.7	1.4	1.7	0.9	1.0	0.7	0.8	0.3
Inventory Turnover 35	4.0	•	3.9	6.3	8.7	5.6	4.6	4.1	3.6	2.9	2.5	2.9	4.0
Receivables Turnover 36	1.6	•	•	25.8	12.5	7.1	7.4	7.0	4.8	5.8	3.7	3.8	•
Total Liabilities to Net Worth 37	1.2	•	•	1.6	0.7	0.7	1.4	0.9	0.9	0.9	1.3	0.9	1.3
Current Assets to Working Capital 38	5.2	•	•	1.7	1.5	1.6	2.2	1.8	1.7	2.2	2.2	1.9	6.4
Current Liabilities to Working Capital 39	4.2	•	•	0.7	0.5	0.6	1.2	0.8	0.7	1.2	1.2	0.9	5.4
Working Capital to Net Sales 40	0.2	•	•	0.1	0.3	0.2	0.2	0.2	0.3	0.3	0.4	0.3	0.1
Inventory to Working Capital 41	0.8	•	•	1.0	0.3	0.6	0.7	0.6	0.4	0.5	0.4	0.5	0.9
Total Receipts to Cash Flow 42	3.0	0.2	0.3	8.0	2.7	7.3	4.5	4.5	3.6	2.5	2.4	2.7	3.1
Cost of Goods to Cash Flow 43	1.5	0.1	0.0	5.6	1.2	4.8	2.5	2.7	1.8	1.0	0.9	1.2	1.6
Cash Flow to Total Debt 44	0.2	•	0.5	1.1	1.5	0.6	0.5	0.8	0.5	0.9	0.5	0.6	0.2

Selected Financial Factors (in Percentages)

Debt Ratio 45	55.6	•	2558.1	61.9	39.9	41.8	57.6	48.7	46.4	46.6	55.9	48.0	56.0
Return on Total Assets 46	9.1	1217.1	•	19.4	40.6	14.7	16.1	23.1	12.6	21.6	15.2	15.5	8.6
Return on Equity Before Income Taxes 47	16.7	•	•	47.1	66.8	22.7	34.1	40.9	19.2	38.0	29.8	26.4	15.7
Return on Equity After Income Taxes 48	11.1	•	•	33.4	56.4	19.9	31.3	34.0	14.1	28.2	21.3	18.0	10.4
Profit Margin (Before Income Tax) 49	20.3	213.0	333.7	3.4	24.2	7.7	10.4	12.6	11.6	19.8	20.1	17.8	20.7
Profit Margin (After Income Tax) 50	13.5	140.7	333.7	2.4	20.4	6.8	9.5	10.5	8.5	14.7	14.4	12.1	13.7

Table I

Corporations with and without Net Income

PAINT, COATING, AND ADHESIVE

MONEY AMOUNTS AND SIZE OF ASSETS IN THOUSANDS OF DOLLARS

Item Description for Accounting Period 7/06 Through 6/07	Total	Zero Assets	Under 500	500 to 1,000	1,000 to 5,000	5,000 to 10,000	10,000 to 25,000	25,000 to 50,000	50,000 to 100,000	100,000 to 250,000	250,000 to 500,000	500,000 to 2,500,000	2,500,000 and over
Number of Enterprises **1**	1668	220	103	334	751	127	54	34	19	9	0	10	6
Revenues ($ in Thousands)													
Net Sales **2**	46535038	124250	84217	512036	3257323	2439441	1514795	1981041	1756943	2135120	0	7403296	25326576
Interest **3**	401862	0	0	1277	855	1519	750	1568	5527	10913	0	61035	318418
Rents **4**	14441	0	0	0	0	0	422	1906	117	1357	0	7020	3620
Royalties **5**	509732	0	0	0	0	0	0	542	1453	346	0	56244	451147
Other Portfolio Income **6**	557360	28430	0	0	1932	6767	2518	19146	6393	3104	0	125790	363283
Other Receipts **7**	383636	-105154	418	2168	12678	5383	4232	5795	7123	17166	0	66076	367746
Total Receipts **8**	48402069	47526	84635	515481	3272788	2453110	1522717	2009998	1777556	2168006	0	7719461	26830790
Average Total Receipts **9**	29018	216	822	1543	4358	19316	28198	59118	93556	240890	•	771946	4471798
Operating Costs/Operating Income (%)													
Cost of Operations **10**	64.9	64.1	65.7	61.0	65.7	64.0	65.8	67.5	69.5	69.2	•	66.9	63.5
Salaries and Wages **11**	9.8	10.1	5.5	8.1	9.0	6.5	11.8	9.0	7.0	9.1	•	10.0	10.3
Taxes Paid **12**	1.9	0.8	3.1	4.3	1.8	3.8	1.9	1.7	2.1	1.8	•	1.7	1.7
Interest Paid **13**	2.8	0.7	0.2	2.5	1.2	1.1	1.5	0.4	1.5	1.6	•	3.3	3.4
Depreciation **14**	1.3	0.8	0.2	2.8	0.8	1.7	1.4	1.3	2.2	1.8	•	2.2	1.0
Amortization and Depletion **15**	0.6	0.0	•	0.1	0.1	0.0	0.2	0.1	1.1	0.6	•	1.0	0.7
Pensions and Other Deferred Comp. **16**	1.5	0.1	•	0.0	0.8	0.5	0.6	0.5	0.9	2.4	•	1.5	1.9
Employee Benefits **17**	1.6	3.3	3.9	2.3	1.2	1.5	1.1	1.2	2.0	1.4	•	1.9	1.6
Advertising **18**	1.1	0.8	•	0.3	0.6	0.9	0.6	0.4	0.4	1.1	•	0.5	1.6
Other Expenses **19**	12.1	11.0	21.8	16.0	11.1	12.9	8.1	9.6	9.0	7.6	•	11.9	13.1
Officers' Compensation **20**	1.4	6.8	6.0	3.9	6.4	5.0	1.8	3.2	1.5	1.0	•	0.7	0.4
Operating Margin **21**	1.0	1.6	•	•	1.3	2.0	5.2	5.0	2.9	2.4	•	•	0.8
Operating Margin Before Officers' Comp. **22**	2.4	8.4	•	2.5	7.8	7.0	7.0	8.2	4.4	3.4	•	•	1.2

Selected Average Balance Sheet ($ in Thousands)

Item													
Net Receivables 23	4195	0	114	313	554	1998	3540	7378	13388	33087	•	158751	604866
Inventories 24	2718	0	117	152	407	1397	4402	6597	11352	28004	•	90260	359375
Net Property, Plant and Equipment 25	4468	0	25	227	332	1759	2860	4967	18010	38712	•	161260	712412
Total Assets 26	25627	0	254	797	1882	7244	14817	32599	71586	202355	•	949119	4256583
Notes and Loans Payable 27	6714	0	150	600	610	2585	4540	4071	15270	53010	•	269407	1058678
All Other Liabilities 28	10129	0	139	276	616	1952	3505	6691	15937	55239	•	253818	2053788
Net Worth 29	8784	0	-34	-80	655	2707	6771	21837	40379	94107	•	425895	1144118

Selected Financial Ratios (Times to 1)

Item													
Current Ratio 30	1.3	•	1.6	1.2	1.7	1.2	1.9	3.0	2.0	1.7	•	1.9	1.0
Quick Ratio 31	0.7	•	0.8	0.8	1.1	0.6	1.1	1.7	1.0	0.9	•	1.2	0.5
Net Sales to Working Capital 32	13.5	•	9.4	15.6	8.5	32.8	5.8	4.1	5.9	6.8	•	4.4	•
Coverage Ratio 33	2.9	•	•	0.7	2.5	3.3	4.9	17.5	3.8	3.4	•	2.0	3.1
Total Asset Turnover 34	1.1	•	3.2	1.9	2.3	2.7	1.9	1.8	1.3	1.2	•	0.8	1.0
Inventory Turnover 35	6.7	•	4.6	6.2	7.0	8.8	4.2	6.0	5.7	5.9	•	5.5	7.5
Receivables Turnover 36	6.8	•	9.1	8.5	8.1	10.0	7.2	7.7	7.4	6.1	•	4.6	7.3
Total Liabilities to Net Worth 37	1.9	•	1.9	•	1.9	1.7	1.2	0.5	0.8	1.2	•	1.2	2.7
Current Assets to Working Capital 38	4.6	•	2.6	5.3	2.5	7.4	2.1	1.5	2.0	2.4	•	2.2	•
Current Liabilities to Working Capital 39	3.6	•	1.6	4.3	1.5	6.4	1.1	0.5	1.0	1.4	•	1.2	•
Working Capital to Net Sales 40	0.1	•	0.1	0.1	0.1	0.0	0.2	0.2	0.2	0.1	•	0.2	•
Inventory to Working Capital 41	1.4	•	1.3	1.8	0.9	2.9	0.9	0.5	0.8	0.8	•	0.5	•
Total Receipts to Cash Flow 42	7.0	•	8.5	10.8	9.2	11.5	8.2	6.9	8.6	10.9	•	8.5	5.8
Cost of Goods to Cash Flow 43	4.5	•	5.6	6.6	6.1	7.3	5.4	4.6	6.0	7.6	•	5.7	3.7
Cash Flow to Total Debt 44	0.2	•	0.3	0.2	0.4	0.4	0.4	0.8	0.3	0.2	•	0.2	0.2

Selected Financial Factors (in Percentages)

Item													
Debt Ratio 45	65.7	•	113.5	110.0	65.2	62.6	54.3	33.0	43.6	53.5	•	55.1	73.1
Return on Total Assets 46	8.8	•	3.3	3.3	6.8	9.8	13.5	12.7	7.3	6.5	•	5.0	10.6
Return on Equity Before Income Taxes 47	16.9	•	137.3	14.7	11.7	18.1	23.5	17.9	9.5	9.9	•	5.4	26.7
Return on Equity After Income Taxes 48	11.3	•	137.3	14.7	10.9	16.9	22.8	13.8	7.1	7.3	•	3.4	17.1
Profit Margin (Before Income Tax) 49	5.3	•	•	•	1.8	2.6	5.7	6.7	4.2	3.9	•	3.1	7.2
Profit Margin (After Income Tax) 50	3.5	•	•	1.6	1.6	2.4	5.5	5.2	3.1	2.9	•	2.0	4.6

Table II
Corporations with Net Income

PAINT, COATING, AND ADHESIVE

MONEY AMOUNTS AND SIZE OF ASSETS IN THOUSANDS OF DOLLARS

Item Description for Accounting Period 7/06 Through 6/07	Total	Zero Assets	Under 500	500 to 1,000	1,000 to 5,000	5,000 to 10,000	10,000 to 25,000	25,000 to 50,000	50,000 to 100,000	100,000 to 250,000	250,000 to 500,000	500,000 to 2,500,000	2,500,000 and over
Number of Enterprises 1	1046	6	0	280	554	103	•	30	15	9	0	7	•
Revenues ($ in Thousands)													
Net Sales 2	39866614	124250	0	446495	2951845	1992665	•	1874595	1368943	2135120	0	4719026	•
Interest 3	383493	0	0	1277	583	1339	•	1568	3799	10913	0	47200	•
Rents 4	12391	0	0	0	0	0	•	1906	117	1357	0	5392	•
Royalties 5	490912	0	0	0	0	0	•	542	1453	346	0	53817	•
Other Portfolio Income 6	487329	28430	0	0	1474	6679	•	12063	6357	3104	0	115535	•
Other Receipts 7	311288	466	0	1926	11692	1179	•	3886	7365	17166	0	32560	•
Total Receipts 8	41552027	153146	0	449698	2965594	2001862	•	1894560	1388034	2168006	0	4973530	•
Average Total Receipts 9	39725	25524	•	1606	5353	19436	•	63152	92536	240890	•	710504	•
Operating Costs/Operating Income (%)													
Cost of Operations 10	63.7	64.1	•	62.3	64.3	62.7	•	67.6	67.3	69.2	•	66.2	•
Salaries and Wages 11	9.8	10.1	•	8.1	8.8	5.1	•	8.0	7.7	9.1	•	10.9	•
Taxes Paid 12	1.9	0.8	•	4.2	1.5	4.2	•	1.7	2.3	1.8	•	1.9	•
Interest Paid 13	2.0	0.7	•	2.6	0.4	1.3	•	0.3	1.5	1.6	•	3.2	•
Depreciation 14	1.1	0.8	•	3.1	0.3	1.7	•	1.2	2.0	1.8	•	1.3	•
Amortization and Depletion 15	0.6	0.0	•	0.0	0.0	0.0	•	0.1	0.6	0.6	•	1.1	•
Pensions and Other Deferred Comp. 16	1.6	0.1	•	0.0	0.8	0.6	•	0.5	0.9	2.4	•	1.4	•
Employee Benefits 17	1.7	3.3	•	2.4	1.0	1.7	•	0.9	1.5	1.4	•	2.3	•
Advertising 18	1.2	0.8	•	0.2	0.7	0.4	•	0.4	0.5	1.1	•	0.4	•
Other Expenses 19	12.0	11.0	•	10.9	9.9	12.9	•	9.8	9.5	7.6	•	10.8	•
Officers' Compensation 20	1.4	6.8	•	4.2	6.8	5.2	•	2.0	1.4	1.0	•	0.6	•
Operating Margin 21	3.0	1.6	•	2.0	5.3	4.2	•	7.5	4.9	2.4	•	2.4	•
Operating Margin Before Officers' Comp. 22	4.4	8.4	•	6.1	12.2	9.4	•	9.5	6.3	3.4	•	0.4	•

Selected Average Balance Sheet ($ in Thousands)

Net Receivables 23	5239	0	348	674	2036	•	7893	13146	33087	80436
Inventories 24	3376	0	133	405	1204	•	7706	10699	28004	46569
Net Property, Plant and Equipment 25	5429	0	264	168	2040	•	5457	16581	38712	120825
Total Assets 26	33565	0	831	1704	6897	•	32464	70299	202355	845374
Notes and Loans Payable 27	6826	0	578	415	2973	•	2515	15377	53010	264534
All Other Liabilities 28	14120	0	231	673	1655	•	6989	15381	55239	233896
Net Worth 29	12620	0	21	615	2268	•	22960	39541	94107	346943

Selected Financial Ratios (Times to 1)

Current Ratio 30	1.2	•	1.2	1.7	0.9	•	3.1	2.1	1.7	1.8
Quick Ratio 31	0.7	•	0.9	1.1	0.6	•	1.9	1.1	0.9	1.2
Net Sales to Working Capital 32	16.2	•	16.0	9.3	•	•	4.3	5.4	6.8	6.0
Coverage Ratio 33	4.8	34.7	2.0	15.1	4.7	•	27.6	5.3	3.4	2.8
Total Asset Turnover 34	1.1	•	1.9	3.1	2.8	•	1.9	1.3	1.2	0.8
Inventory Turnover 35	7.2	•	7.5	8.5	10.1	•	5.5	5.7	5.9	9.6
Receivables Turnover 36	7.5	•	9.2	9.6	9.1	•	•	7.5	6.1	10.4
Total Liabilities to Net Worth 37	1.7	•	38.4	1.8	2.0	•	0.4	0.8	1.2	1.4
Current Assets to Working Capital 38	5.1	•	5.1	2.4	•	•	1.5	1.9	2.4	2.3
Current Liabilities to Working Capital 39	4.1	•	4.1	1.4	•	•	0.5	0.9	1.4	1.3
Working Capital to Net Sales 40	0.1	•	0.1	0.1	•	•	0.2	0.2	0.1	0.2
Inventory to Working Capital 41	1.5	•	1.3	0.9	•	•	0.5	0.7	0.8	0.5
Total Receipts to Cash Flow 42	6.1	3.3	13.4	7.1	9.6	•	5.9	7.0	10.9	8.0
Cost of Goods to Cash Flow 43	3.9	2.1	8.4	4.6	6.0	•	4.0	4.7	7.6	5.3
Cash Flow to Total Debt 44	0.3	•	0.1	0.7	0.4	•	1.1	0.4	0.2	0.2

Selected Financial Factors (in Percentages)

Debt Ratio 45	62.4	•	97.5	63.9	67.1	•	29.3	43.8	53.5	59.0
Return on Total Assets 46	10.9	•	10.1	19.3	16.7	•	17.6	10.1	6.5	7.1
Return on Equity Before Income Taxes 47	22.9	•	202.6	49.8	39.9	•	24.0	14.5	9.9	11.1
Return on Equity After Income Taxes 48	16.6	•	202.5	48.7	38.1	•	20.0	11.4	7.3	7.6
Profit Margin (Before Income Tax) 49	7.6	24.9	2.7	5.8	4.7	•	8.8	6.3	3.9	5.7
Profit Margin (After Income Tax) 50	5.5	24.9	2.7	5.6	4.5	•	7.3	4.9	2.9	3.9

Table I

Corporations with and without Net Income

SOAP, CLEANING COMPOUND, AND TOILET PREPARATION

MONEY AMOUNTS AND SIZE OF ASSETS IN THOUSANDS OF DOLLARS

Item Description for Accounting Period 7/06 Through 6/07	Total	Zero Assets	Under 500	500 to 1,000	1,000 to 5,000	5,000 to 10,000	10,000 to 25,000	25,000 to 50,000	50,000 to 100,000	100,000 to 250,000	250,000 to 500,000	500,000 to 2,500,000	2,500,000 and over
Number of Enterprises 1	1385	3	647	264	245	96	56	28	10	12	5	9	9
Revenues ($ in Thousands)													
Net Sales 2	134472667	116415	704995	514335	1693213	844773	2212123	1260414	1048832	2613230	2981090	12726999	107756249
Interest 3	1184062	249	410	178	1136	308	1905	6908	1060	4836	4890	100327	1061857
Rents 4	71646	0	0	12	2199	890	2705	197	659	0	662	49446	14876
Royalties 5	3469008	0	0	0	7224	0	2310	1414	102	0	1052	469241	2977665
Other Portfolio Income 6	2744414	6001	0	433	4769	224	18973	1867	10558	9219	11554	755195	1925622
Other Receipts 7	2554656	3381	89629	603	2394	10720	12237	9170	49201	56217	17676	268777	2034648
Total Receipts 8	144496453	126046	795034	515561	1710935	856915	2250253	1279970	1110412	2683502	3026924	14369985	115770917
Average Total Receipts 9	104330	42015	1229	1953	6983	8926	40183	45713	111041	223625	605385	1596665	12863435
Operating Costs/Operating Income (%)													
Cost of Operations 10	60.9	77.7	80.1	47.2	61.2	59.0	69.0	61.2	65.3	50.0	67.2	47.0	62.4
Salaries and Wages 11	6.6	11.9	7.5	17.3	9.0	6.8	8.0	10.2	10.5	9.0	7.3	12.3	5.6
Taxes Paid 12	1.2	3.2	3.2	2.9	2.0	1.3	1.6	1.6	1.8	1.1	1.7	2.5	1.0
Interest Paid 13	3.0	0.4	1.3	0.8	0.7	0.6	0.9	1.7	1.0	2.7	1.0	3.6	3.2
Depreciation 14	1.6	0.6	1.1	1.6	0.5	1.3	1.4	1.5	1.3	1.9	2.4	1.4	1.6
Amortization and Depletion 15	1.0	0.0	0.0	0.0	0.0	0.0	0.1	1.0	0.5	0.8	0.6	0.8	1.2
Pensions and Other Deferred Comp. 16	0.9	0.1	0.1	0.0	1.0	0.1	0.3	0.2	0.5	0.7	1.8	1.0	0.9
Employee Benefits 17	1.2	0.2	0.5	2.2	0.9	0.9	2.0	1.2	1.4	0.9	1.6	2.5	1.0
Advertising 18	5.4	0.4	2.2	0.1	1.3	2.2	0.8	2.8	2.3	11.9	1.3	7.3	5.4
Other Expenses 19	15.6	7.9	16.5	21.7	14.2	11.2	10.2	13.3	15.5	15.2	11.4	24.7	14.9
Officers' Compensation 20	0.7	19.5	9.8	6.2	7.1	2.8	1.4	2.6	3.3	0.8	1.0	1.7	0.3
Operating Margin 21	1.8	•	•	•	2.0	13.9	4.3	2.9	•	4.9	2.8	•	2.6
Operating Margin Before Officers' Comp. 22	2.6	•	•	6.1	9.2	16.7	5.7	5.5	•	5.7	3.7	•	2.9

Selected Average Balance Sheet ($ in Thousands)

Item													
Net Receivables 23	26333	0	57	247	664	1566	3959	6956	16600	29930	80223	171731	3685297
Inventories 24	5740	0	79	304	439	635	3545	7112	14160	24145	76048	178712	536998
Net Property, Plant and Equipment 25	12549	0	19	67	256	1290	4522	5571	11747	29474	136929	159404	1573780
Total Assets 26	177155		408	667	2515	5907	15132	30825	63130	180846	443311	1555774	24778485
Notes and Loans Payable 27	44115	0	2	639	658	527	4116	10895	15325	60553	99660	602960	5930757
All Other Liabilities 28	39241	0	32	143	472	1993	4076	7283	16955	43269	131939	528158	5272181
Net Worth 29	93799	0	374	-114	1385	3386	6940	12647	30851	77024	211712	424656	13575547

Selected Financial Ratios (Times to 1)

Item													
Current Ratio 30	1.1	•	12.7	3.5	2.3	1.6	2.1	1.7	1.5	1.6	1.2	1.0	
Quick Ratio 31	0.7	•	7.9	2.1	1.1	0.9	1.2	0.9	0.8	0.9	0.5	0.7	
Net Sales to Working Capital 32	29.6	•	3.1	4.8	6.2	10.8	5.3	7.5	8.3	8.6	17.0	62.1	
Coverage Ratio 33	4.6	•	•	1.3	5.4	7.9	3.7	3.6	3.8	5.4	3.9	4.7	
Total Asset Turnover 34	0.5	•	2.7	2.9	2.7	1.5	2.6	1.5	1.7	1.2	1.3	0.9	0.5
Inventory Turnover 35	10.3	•	11.1	3.0	9.6	8.2	7.7	3.9	4.8	4.5	5.3	3.7	13.9
Receivables Turnover 36	4.5	•	19.2	7.2	10.7	9.4	10.2	6.2	5.7	8.0	7.2	8.5	4.1
Total Liabilities to Net Worth 37	0.9	•	0.1	•	0.8	0.7	1.2	1.4	1.0	1.3	1.1	2.7	0.8
Current Assets to Working Capital 38	12.4	•	1.1	1.4	1.8	2.6	1.9	2.4	3.0	2.6	6.0	27.3	
Current Liabilities to Working Capital 39	11.4	•	0.1	0.4	0.8	0.9	1.6	0.9	1.4	2.0	1.6	5.0	26.3
Working Capital to Net Sales 40	0.0	•	0.3	0.2	0.2	0.3	0.1	0.2	0.1	0.1	0.1	0.1	0.0
Inventory to Working Capital 41	1.8	•	0.2	0.3	0.4	0.4	1.0	0.7	1.0	1.1	1.1	2.1	2.9
Total Receipts to Cash Flow 42	4.3	•	19.7	5.5	6.8	4.1	7.0	6.3	6.1	4.8	7.1	3.5	4.3
Cost of Goods to Cash Flow 43	2.6	•	15.8	2.6	4.1	2.4	4.8	3.9	4.0	2.4	4.8	1.7	2.7
Cash Flow to Total Debt 44	0.3	•	1.6	0.4	0.9	0.9	0.7	0.4	0.5	0.4	0.4	0.4	0.2

Selected Financial Factors (in Percentages)

Item													
Debt Ratio 45	47.1	•	8.3	117.1	44.9	54.1	42.7	59.0	51.1	57.4	52.2	72.7	45.2
Return on Total Assets 46	7.6	•	•	2.8	9.7	18.1	9.0	6.2	12.4	7.1	12.6	7.2	
Return on Equity Before Income Taxes 47	11.2	•	•	•	14.4	39.8	34.5	16.1	9.2	21.4	12.2	34.1	10.4
Return on Equity After Income Taxes 48	7.4	•	•	•	12.3	37.8	29.9	12.9	7.8	17.0	7.9	20.5	6.8
Profit Margin (Before Income Tax) 49	10.9	•	0.2	2.9	15.3	6.1	4.5	2.7	7.6	4.3	10.3	11.8	
Profit Margin (After Income Tax) 50	7.2	•	0.1	2.5	14.5	5.2	3.6	2.3	6.0	2.8	6.1	7.7	

Table II
Corporations with Net Income

SOAP, CLEANING COMPOUND, AND TOILET PREPARATION

MONEY AMOUNTS AND SIZE OF ASSETS IN THOUSANDS OF DOLLARS

Item Description for Accounting Period 7/06 Through 6/07	Total	Zero Assets	Under 500	500 to 1,000	1,000 to 5,000	5,000 to 10,000	10,000 to 25,000	25,000 to 50,000	50,000 to 100,000	100,000 to 250,000	250,000 to 500,000	500,000 to 2,500,000	2,500,000 and over
Number of Enterprises **1**	584	•	103	65	221	84	•	21	5	9	•	•	9
Revenues ($ in Thousands)													
Net Sales **2**	129237858	•	103145	83273	1498742	752990	•	1026707	622426	2128542	•	•	107756249
Interest **3**	1174459	•	91	0	200	308	•	6401	100	4658	•	•	1061857
Rents **4**	68722	•	0	0	0	890	•	197	126	0	•	•	14876
Royalties **5**	3460973	•	0	0	7224	0	•	251	0	0	•	•	2977665
Other Portfolio Income **6**	2729387	•	0	0	4749	40	•	1636	6743	7519	•	•	1925622
Other Receipts **7**	2387895	•	0	116	1796	10719	•	9057	627	55058	•	•	2034648
Total Receipts **8**	139059294	•	103236	83389	1512711	764947	•	1044249	630022	2195777	•	•	115777917
Average Total Receipts **9**	238115	•	1002	1283	6845	9107	•	49726	126004	243975	•	•	12863435
Operating Costs/Operating Income (%)													
Cost of Operations **10**	60.8	•	73.9	54.4	59.0	59.6	•	59.1	60.2	49.7	•	•	62.4
Salaries and Wages **11**	6.5	•	5.4	19.3	8.8	5.8	•	10.4	8.9	7.0	•	•	5.6
Taxes Paid **12**	1.2	•	3.2	2.7	2.1	1.1	•	1.5	2.1	1.0	•	•	1.0
Interest Paid **13**	2.9	•	•	•	0.4	0.4	•	1.7	0.9	2.3	•	•	3.2
Depreciation **14**	1.6	•	0.0	1.2	0.5	1.1	•	1.6	1.0	1.8	•	•	1.6
Amortization and Depletion **15**	1.1	•	0.2	•	0.0	•	•	0.6	0.1	0.4	•	•	1.2
Pensions and Other Deferred Comp. **16**	0.9	•	1.0	•	1.1	0.1	•	0.2	0.7	0.7	•	•	0.9
Employee Benefits **17**	1.1	•	1.0	•	0.8	1.0	•	1.3	1.2	0.7	•	•	1.0
Advertising **18**	5.4	•	0.1	0.1	1.4	2.3	•	3.1	1.7	14.3	•	•	5.4
Other Expenses **19**	15.6	•	10.4	14.6	14.7	9.6	•	13.2	14.0	14.5	•	•	14.9
Officers' Compensation **20**	0.6	•	4.8	3.8	7.2	2.9	•	2.8	4.2	0.9	•	•	0.3
Operating Margin **21**	2.4	•	0.1	3.9	4.0	16.1	•	4.5	5.1	6.7	•	•	2.6
Operating Margin Before Officers' Comp. **22**	3.0	•	4.9	7.8	11.2	19.0	•	7.3	9.3	7.6	•	•	2.9

Selected Average Balance Sheet ($ in Thousands)

Net Receivables 23	61382	•	55	138	638	1628	•	8206	21173	33205	•	3685297
Inventories 24	12207	•	84	258	369	480	•	7142	19292	27716	•	565244
Net Property, Plant and Equipment 25	28488	•	0	158	250	1361	•	6159	9108	29093	•	1573780
Total Assets 26	410566	•	433	791	2381	6019	•	31068	63152	180347	•	24778485
Notes and Loans Payable 27	99492	•	0	0	531	323	•	9724	17279	53365	•	5930757
All Other Liabilities 28	90874	•	15	58	433	2021	•	7828	15524	40975	•	5272181
Net Worth 29	220200	•	418	733	1418	3675	•	13515	30349	86007	•	13575547

Selected Financial Ratios (Times to 1)

Current Ratio 30	1.1	•	82.1	9.7	2.7	2.0	•	1.9	1.8	2.3	•	1.0
Quick Ratio 31	0.7	•	65.9	8.3	1.3	1.6	•	1.1	1.0	1.3	•	0.7
Net Sales to Working Capital 32	33.2	•	2.4	2.5	5.5	4.1	•	5.9	6.7	4.9	•	62.1
Coverage Ratio 33	5.0	•	•	1.6	12.2	42.4	•	4.6	8.5	5.4	•	4.7
Total Asset Turnover 34	0.5	•	2.3	1.6	2.8	1.5	•	1.6	2.0	1.3	•	0.5
Inventory Turnover 35	11.0	•	8.8	2.7	10.8	11.1	•	4.0	3.9	4.2	•	13.2
Receivables Turnover 36	4.5	•	36.3	2.5	11.3	9.3	•	6.1	4.6	7.2	•	•
Total Liabilities to Net Worth 37	0.9	•	0.0	0.7	0.6	0.6	•	1.3	1.1	1.1	•	0.8
Current Assets to Working Capital 38	14.0	•	1.0	1.6	2.0	2.0	•	2.1	2.2	1.8	•	27.3
Current Liabilities to Working Capital 39	13.0	•	0.0	0.6	1.0	1.0	•	1.1	1.2	0.8	•	26.3
Working Capital to Net Sales 40	0.0	•	0.4	0.2	0.2	0.2	•	0.2	0.1	0.2	•	0.0
Inventory to Working Capital 41	1.9	•	0.2	0.3	0.3	0.3	•	0.8	0.9	0.6	•	2.9
Total Receipts to Cash Flow 42	4.2	•	14.5	7.1	6.0	3.9	•	5.7	5.3	4.4	•	4.3
Cost of Goods to Cash Flow 43	2.6	•	10.7	3.9	3.5	2.3	•	3.4	3.2	2.2	•	2.7
Cash Flow to Total Debt 44	0.3	•	4.5	3.1	1.2	1.0	•	0.5	0.7	0.6	•	0.2

Selected Financial Factors (in Percentages)

Debt Ratio 45	46.4	•	3.5	7.3	40.5	38.9	•	56.5	51.9	52.3	•	45.2
Return on Total Assets 46	7.8	•	0.4	6.6	14.7	27.0	•	12.5	15.5	15.9	•	7.2
Return on Equity Before Income Taxes 47	11.7	•	0.4	7.1	22.7	43.2	•	22.6	28.4	27.2	•	10.4
Return on Equity After Income Taxes 48	7.8	•	0.4	6.0	20.4	41.1	•	18.7	25.7	21.8	•	6.8
Profit Margin (Before Income Tax) 49	11.6	•	0.2	4.1	4.7	17.7	•	6.2	6.9	9.9	•	11.8
Profit Margin (After Income Tax) 50	7.8	•	0.2	3.4	4.3	16.8	•	5.2	6.3	7.9	•	7.7

Table I

Corporations with and without Net Income

CHEMICAL PRODUCT AND PREPARATION

MONEY AMOUNTS AND SIZE OF ASSETS IN THOUSANDS OF DOLLARS

Item Description for Accounting Period 7/06 Through 6/07	Total	Zero Assets	Under 500	500 to 1,000	1,000 to 5,000	5,000 to 10,000	10,000 to 25,000	25,000 to 50,000	50,000 to 100,000	100,000 to 250,000	250,000 to 500,000	500,000 to 2,500,000	2,500,000 and over
Number of Enterprises **1**	2745	619	739	493	464	115	148	62	40	25	17	17	6
Revenues ($ in Thousands)													
Net Sales **2**	77150085	9034743	584659	709645	1997588	1508685	3556167	3861413	3581185	4597369	5822959	17712328	24183342
Interest **3**	533743	23572	3	785	1668	1308	10454	4065	11500	21361	33817	198165	227046
Rents **4**	34021	6261	0	2221	514	6893	510	157	879	140	4352	10416	1677
Royalties **5**	373033	2171	0	0	169	0	27542	0	2038	22826	16157	194110	108018
Other Portfolio Income **6**	1250930	37453	10	3144	382	945	12684	9250	20360	197467	96981	352440	519817
Other Receipts **7**	1791806	-21776	4907	488	24114	7792	21309	57517	41374	131611	63051	572611	888810
Total Receipts **8**	81133618	9082424	589579	716283	2024435	1525623	3628666	3932402	3657336	4970774	6037317	19040070	25928710
Average Total Receipts **9**	29557	14673	798	1453	4363	13266	24518	63426	91433	198831	355136	1120004	4321452
Operating Costs/Operating Income (%)													
Cost of Operations **10**	75.6	92.9	47.6	51.8	55.6	58.0	69.0	68.4	73.5	68.3	75.0	72.1	79.7
Salaries and Wages **11**	5.8	3.6	0.1	12.6	9.4	12.5	6.3	7.9	6.6	8.8	6.4	5.5	4.7
Taxes Paid **12**	1.3	0.4	3.5	3.2	1.8	2.7	1.7	1.4	1.3	1.8	1.2	1.3	1.2
Interest Paid **13**	2.6	0.7	0.3	2.4	0.6	1.2	1.3	1.3	2.0	1.9	2.3	2.7	4.3
Depreciation **14**	2.9	1.0	0.6	4.4	2.5	2.3	2.2	1.6	2.0	1.9	3.0	3.1	4.0
Amortization and Depletion **15**	0.7	0.4	0.0	•	0.0	0.1	0.2	0.3	0.6	0.5	0.8	1.1	0.8
Pensions and Other Deferred Comp. **16**	0.5	0.1	1.3	0.4	0.3	0.5	0.4	0.3	0.5	0.8	0.8	0.7	0.3
Employee Benefits **17**	1.0	0.2	1.7	0.2	1.6	1.9	0.9	0.6	1.3	1.5	1.1	1.5	0.7
Advertising **18**	0.7	0.1	0.1	1.0	0.1	0.6	0.8	0.6	0.6	0.6	0.2	2.1	0.1
Other Expenses **19**	11.0	2.7	20.9	17.1	19.9	16.8	12.0	17.6	10.5	11.0	7.4	13.2	10.9
Officers' Compensation **20**	1.3	2.2	14.3	5.2	4.9	4.9	2.8	1.9	1.4	0.8	0.9	0.8	0.1
Operating Margin **21**	•	•	9.5	1.7	3.4	•	2.4	•	•	2.0	0.8	•	•
Operating Margin Before Officers' Comp. **22**	•	•	23.8	6.9	8.3	3.2	5.3	0.2	1.2	2.8	1.6	•	•

Selected Average Balance Sheet ($ in Thousands)

Net Receivables 23	3323	0	118	145	422	1815	3456	8588	15291	25300	69127	185408	323707
Inventories 24	2834	0	20	126	312	1432	2881	7122	13568	25574	37576	123492	434162
Net Property, Plant and Equipment 25	5914	0	15	186	622	2554	3853	8518	15410	33112	89627	273993	1137277
Total Assets 26	25671	0	162	689	1823	7393	15203	35613	72030	154509	352199	1171086	5202496
Notes and Loans Payable 27	8523	0	172	404	597	2043	3881	8219	20326	52167	120128	330868	1947920
All Other Liabilities 28	8192	0	52	161	299	1937	3659	11653	22275	46558	92676	383942	1764557
Net Worth 29	8957	0	-62	124	927	3413	7663	15741	29429	55784	139396	456275	1490018

Selected Financial Ratios (Times to 1)

Current Ratio 30	1.2	•	0.7	1.1	3.2	2.2	2.3	1.8	1.7	1.5	1.6	1.5	0.7
Quick Ratio 31	0.6	•	0.6	0.6	2.2	1.2	1.4	1.0	0.9	0.8	1.0	0.8	0.2
Net Sales to Working Capital 32	22.3	•	•	65.1	5.6	5.5	4.2	6.5	5.6	8.0	6.0	6.9	•
Coverage Ratio 33	1.9	•	33.0	2.1	9.6	0.5	4.4	1.4	2.0	6.3	2.9	2.3	1.3
Total Asset Turnover 34	1.1	•	4.9	2.1	2.4	1.8	1.6	1.7	1.2	1.2	1.0	0.9	0.8
Inventory Turnover 35	7.5	•	18.5	5.9	7.7	5.3	5.8	6.0	4.8	4.9	6.8	6.1	7.4
Receivables Turnover 36	7.9	•	6.1	11.9	11.2	8.6	7.2	9.0	6.1	5.7	4.8	5.7	9.1
Total Liabilities to Net Worth 37	1.9	•	•	4.5	1.0	1.2	1.0	1.3	1.4	1.8	1.5	1.6	2.5
Current Assets to Working Capital 38	7.5	•	•	14.0	1.4	1.8	1.8	2.3	2.5	3.0	2.7	3.1	•
Current Liabilities to Working Capital 39	6.5	•	•	13.0	0.4	0.8	0.8	1.3	1.5	2.0	1.7	2.1	•
Working Capital to Net Sales 40	0.0	•	•	0.0	0.2	0.2	0.2	0.2	0.2	0.1	0.2	0.1	•
Inventory to Working Capital 41	2.2	•	•	5.7	0.4	0.6	0.5	0.8	0.9	1.0	0.8	0.8	•
Total Receipts to Cash Flow 42	9.4	•	3.7	6.3	4.9	7.2	6.9	6.8	9.7	6.5	10.1	7.4	10.1
Cost of Goods to Cash Flow 43	7.1	•	1.8	3.3	2.7	4.2	4.7	4.6	7.1	4.4	7.6	5.4	8.0
Cash Flow to Total Debt 44	0.2	•	0.9	0.4	1.0	0.5	0.5	0.5	0.2	0.3	0.2	0.2	0.1

Selected Financial Factors (in Percentages)

Debt Ratio 45	65.1	•	138.5	82.0	49.2	53.8	49.6	55.8	59.1	63.9	60.4	61.0	71.4
Return on Total Assets 46	5.4	•	52.0	10.5	12.5	1.1	8.8	3.1	5.0	14.4	6.4	5.5	4.5
Return on Equity Before Income Taxes 47	7.3	•	•	30.3	22.0	•	13.5	2.0	6.0	33.6	10.5	8.1	4.0
Return on Equity After Income Taxes 48	4.6	•	•	27.2	20.4	•	9.6	•	1.9	23.9	7.5	6.1	2.7
Profit Margin (Before Income Tax) 49	2.3	•	10.3	2.6	4.7	4.3	•	0.5	2.0	10.2	4.3	3.6	1.5
Profit Margin (After Income Tax) 50	1.5	•	10.3	2.3	4.4	3.0	•	0.5	1.0	7.3	3.1	2.7	1.0

Table II

Corporations with Net Income

CHEMICAL PRODUCT AND PREPARATION

MONEY AMOUNTS AND SIZE OF ASSETS IN THOUSANDS OF DOLLARS

Item Description for Accounting Period 7/06 Through 6/07	Total	Zero Assets	Under 500	500 to 1,000	1,000 to 5,000	5,000 to 10,000	10,000 to 25,000	25,000 to 50,000	50,000 to 100,000	100,000 to 250,000	250,000 to 500,000	500,000 to 2,500,000	2,500,000 and over
Number of Enterprises 1	1805	22	736	493	248	77	107	41	30	18	13	•	•
Revenues ($ in Thousands)													
Net Sales 2	44660079	732967	581995	709645	1530310	1191808	3022229	2569644	3101209	3841203	4830782	•	•
Interest 3	344404	5160	0	785	1428	736	8526	1737	8499	12143	18871	•	•
Rents 4	28271	3914	0	2221	514	3696	510	157	865	16	4338	•	•
Royalties 5	332386	0	0	0	0	0	27542	0	1954	22461	4608	•	•
Other Portfolio Income 6	1181546	22320	0	3144	90	802	2911	1396	9469	196318	96772	•	•
Other Receipts 7	1328520	22243	4907	488	22996	6440	20415	36464	40875	96134	63449	•	•
Total Receipts 8	47875206	786604	586902	716283	1555338	1203482	3082133	2609398	3162871	4168275	5018820	•	•
Average Total Receipts 9	26524	35755	797	1453	6272	15630	28805	63644	105429	231571	386063	•	•
Operating Costs/Operating Income (%)													
Cost of Operations 10	68.0	78.3	47.6	51.8	55.0	57.7	67.9	62.6	73.9	64.7	75.2	•	•
Salaries and Wages 11	7.4	5.4	•	12.6	7.6	11.8	5.8	8.8	5.4	9.1	5.7	•	•
Taxes Paid 12	1.4	1.3	3.5	3.2	1.5	2.5	1.6	1.5	1.2	1.9	1.1	•	•
Interest Paid 13	2.5	2.8	0.3	2.4	0.5	0.9	0.7	0.9	1.7	1.2	2.0	•	•
Depreciation 14	2.5	0.5	0.6	4.4	1.1	2.0	2.0	1.7	1.5	1.7	2.2	•	•
Amortization and Depletion 15	0.6	0.4	•	•	•	0.1	0.1	0.1	0.4	0.4	1.0	•	•
Pensions and Other Deferred Comp. 16	0.6	0.5	1.3	0.4	0.4	0.7	0.3	0.3	0.5	0.9	0.8	•	•
Employee Benefits 17	1.4	0.4	1.2	0.2	1.7	2.0	1.0	0.6	1.1	1.6	0.9	•	•
Advertising 18	1.1	0.0	0.1	1.0	0.1	0.3	0.6	0.5	0.6	0.6	0.2	•	•
Other Expenses 19	13.5	8.1	21.1	17.1	20.0	13.6	10.3	18.4	8.9	11.0	7.2	•	•
Officers' Compensation 20	1.4	0.5	14.3	5.2	4.2	4.9	2.8	1.4	1.3	0.7	0.8	•	•
Operating Margin 21	•	1.9	9.9	1.7	8.0	3.7	6.8	3.1	3.6	6.2	2.8	•	•
Operating Margin Before Officers' Comp. 22	1.0	2.3	24.2	6.9	12.2	8.6	9.6	4.5	4.9	6.9	3.7	•	•

Selected Average Balance Sheet ($ in Thousands)

Net Receivables 23	3587	0	118	145	616	2160	4012	9058	16256	28020	68039
Inventories 24	3372	0	17	73	428	1648	3423	7291	13005	26120	37960
Net Property, Plant and Equipment 25	5089	0	15	186	321	2383	3785	8878	15007	37097	76101
Total Assets 26	23993	0	162	689	1843	7460	15371	35583	73395	154372	356962
Notes and Loans Payable 27	7167	0	47	404	331	1990	3615	7586	18377	44642	123304
All Other Liabilities 28	6882	0	45	161	364	2059	3898	8487	21031	35706	79863
Net Worth 29	9944	0	70	124	1149	3412	7858	19510	33986	74024	153794

Selected Financial Ratios (Times to 1)

Current Ratio 30	1.5	•	1.7	1.1	3.2	2.0	2.2	2.1	1.9	2.1	1.9
Quick Ratio 31	0.8	•	1.6	0.6	2.1	1.1	1.3	1.1	1.1	1.1	1.1
Net Sales to Working Capital 32	8.0	•	12.8	65.1	6.5	6.9	4.9	5.7	5.1	6.0	4.8
Coverage Ratio 33	3.9	4.3	34.6	2.1	18.7	6.3	13.4	6.9	4.3	13.6	4.2
Total Asset Turnover 34	1.0	•	4.9	2.1	3.3	2.1	1.8	1.8	1.4	1.4	1.0
Inventory Turnover 35	5.0	•	22.5	10.3	7.9	5.4	5.6	5.4	5.9	5.3	7.4
Receivables Turnover 36	5.9	•	6.4	18.5	11.7	8.6	7.2	8.1	7.0	6.1	5.4
Total Liabilities to Net Worth 37	1.4	•	1.3	4.5	0.6	1.2	1.0	0.8	1.2	1.1	1.3
Current Assets to Working Capital 38	3.0	•	2.3	14.0	1.5	2.0	1.8	1.9	2.1	1.9	2.1
Current Liabilities to Working Capital 39	2.0	•	1.3	13.0	0.5	1.0	0.8	0.9	1.1	0.9	1.1
Working Capital to Net Sales 40	0.1	•	0.1	0.0	0.2	0.1	0.2	0.2	0.2	0.2	0.2
Inventory to Working Capital 41	1.0	•	0.2	5.7	0.5	0.7	0.6	0.7	0.7	0.6	0.6
Total Receipts to Cash Flow 42	5.8	6.8	3.6	6.3	3.8	6.4	5.7	4.7	7.7	5.2	8.3
Cost of Goods to Cash Flow 43	3.9	5.3	1.7	3.3	2.1	3.7	3.9	2.9	5.7	3.4	6.3
Cash Flow to Total Debt 44	0.3	•	2.4	0.4	2.4	0.6	0.7	0.8	0.3	0.5	0.2

Selected Financial Factors (in Percentages)

Debt Ratio 45	58.6	•	56.8	82.0	37.7	54.3	48.9	45.2	53.7	52.0	56.9
Return on Total Assets 46	10.1	•	54.0	10.5	34.0	11.5	17.4	10.5	10.3	22.1	8.8
Return on Equity Before Income Taxes 47	18.2	•	121.6	30.3	51.6	21.1	31.4	16.4	17.1	42.6	15.7
Return on Equity After Income Taxes 48	14.6	•	121.6	27.2	49.1	17.5	26.1	13.5	12.3	32.5	12.1
Profit Margin (Before Income Tax) 49	7.3	9.2	10.7	2.6	9.6	4.7	8.7	5.1	5.6	14.8	6.5
Profit Margin (After Income Tax) 50	5.9	6.0	10.7	2.3	9.1	3.8	7.3	4.2	4.0	11.3	5.0

Table I
Corporations with and without Net Income

PLASTICS PRODUCT

MONEY AMOUNTS AND SIZE OF ASSETS IN THOUSANDS OF DOLLARS

Item Description for Accounting Period 7/06 Through 6/07	Total	Zero Assets	Under 500	500 to 1,000	1,000 to 5,000	5,000 to 10,000	10,000 to 25,000	25,000 to 50,000	50,000 to 100,000	100,000 to 250,000	250,000 to 500,000	500,000 to 2,500,000	2,500,000 and over
Number of Enterprises **1**	11331	•	•	•	2281	517	375	158	111	87	26	26	3
Revenues ($ in Thousands)													
Net Sales **2**	122831387	•	•	•	12191405	7119103	12012962	11479736	11650754	19625079	9271692	25111589	6474317
Interest **3**	515484	•	•	•	6330	4299	12342	20207	29013	58919	36091	195327	143520
Rents **4**	31993	•	•	•	387	2648	1206	1762	2226	6207	9641	6325	811
Royalties **5**	165718	•	•	•	0	48	4731	6600	6579	6666	24502	58071	53521
Other Portfolio Income **6**	902209	•	•	•	27108	4889	84921	31474	39439	49753	76249	79833	340085
Other Receipts **7**	1091741	•	•	•	81724	48261	56011	131391	64519	212309	-12809	158769	331314
Total Receipts **8**	125538532	•	•	•	12306954	7179248	12172173	11671170	11792530	19958933	9405366	25609914	7343568
Average Total Receipts **9**	11079	•	•	•	5395	13886	32459	73868	106239	229413	361745	984997	2447856
Operating Costs/Operating Income (%)													
Cost of Operations **10**	72.2	•	•	•	66.2	69.5	73.4	68.9	72.2	75.3	77.3	77.8	62.2
Salaries and Wages **11**	5.0	•	•	•	5.5	6.5	5.8	6.8	6.1	3.8	3.5	4.1	4.1
Taxes Paid **12**	1.6	•	•	•	2.3	1.8	1.9	1.8	1.7	1.6	1.1	1.1	0.9
Interest Paid **13**	2.7	•	•	•	0.8	1.0	1.6	1.3	1.9	2.1	3.8	4.1	9.2
Depreciation **14**	2.8	•	•	•	2.7	2.3	2.6	3.0	3.2	2.8	3.1	3.1	1.4
Amortization and Depletion **15**	0.4	•	•	•	0.1	0.2	0.3	0.2	0.6	0.5	0.5	0.7	0.3
Pensions and Other Deferred Comp. **16**	0.4	•	•	•	0.2	0.4	0.4	0.6	0.4	0.5	0.3	0.5	0.5
Employee Benefits **17**	1.6	•	•	•	1.4	1.1	1.7	1.7	1.8	1.5	2.1	1.2	3.1
Advertising **18**	0.4	•	•	•	0.4	0.8	0.3	1.1	0.5	0.4	0.1	0.3	0.3
Other Expenses **19**	11.3	•	•	•	11.1	9.3	8.7	27.7	8.8	7.8	7.0	6.8	19.7
Officers' Compensation **20**	1.6	•	•	•	3.9	3.4	1.6	1.4	1.0	0.8	0.4	0.3	1.4
Operating Margin **21**	•	•	•	•	5.5	3.7	1.7	•	1.8	2.9	0.7	0.0	•
Operating Margin Before Officers' Comp. **22**	1.5	•	•	•	9.4	7.1	3.3	•	2.8	3.7	1.1	0.3	•

Selected Average Balance Sheet ($ in Thousands)

Net Receivables 23	1373	•	616	1737	3939	8234	14053	26077	57754	146094	302995
Inventories 24	1089	•	459	1257	3754	6948	12033	26308	38844	91730	270726
Net Property, Plant and Equipment 25	1941	•	683	2082	4916	11919	20519	45705	79132	226087	369592
Total Assets 26	7662	•	2327	7175	15985	35630	68209	156272	327503	951534	3343022
Notes and Loans Payable 27	3483	•	869	2328	6053	12107	24783	52080	144942	477806	2629411
All Other Liabilities 28	2124	•	592	2032	4045	7478	17739	43282	117865	249823	1032616
Net Worth 29	2055	•	866	2815	5887	16045	25688	60909	64696	223905	-319004

Selected Financial Ratios (Times to 1)

Current Ratio 30	1.5	•	2.0	1.5	1.6	1.9	1.4	1.7	1.1	1.5	1.1
Quick Ratio 31	0.8	•	1.2	0.9	0.9	1.1	0.8	0.8	0.6	0.9	0.6
Net Sales to Working Capital 32	10.0	•	7.7	10.5	9.0	8.5	10.0	8.3	31.1	8.9	32.3
Coverage Ratio 33	1.8	•	8.8	5.5	3.0	•	2.6	3.2	1.5	1.5	2.3
Total Asset Turnover 34	1.4	•	2.3	1.9	2.0	2.0	1.5	1.4	1.1	1.0	0.6
Inventory Turnover 35	7.2	•	7.7	7.6	6.3	7.2	6.3	6.5	7.1	8.2	5.0
Receivables Turnover 36	7.4	•	8.9	9.0	7.8	8.0	7.3	8.3	6.1	7.6	2.8
Total Liabilities to Net Worth 37	2.7	•	1.7	1.5	1.7	1.2	1.7	1.6	4.1	3.2	•
Current Assets to Working Capital 38	3.0	•	2.0	3.0	2.7	2.2	3.3	2.5	10.9	3.0	10.8
Current Liabilities to Working Capital 39	2.0	•	1.0	2.0	1.7	1.2	2.3	1.5	9.9	2.0	9.8
Working Capital to Net Sales 40	0.1	•	0.1	0.1	0.1	0.1	0.1	0.1	0.0	0.1	0.0
Inventory to Working Capital 41	1.0	•	0.6	1.1	1.0	0.8	1.2	1.0	3.5	0.9	3.1
Total Receipts to Cash Flow 42	9.1	•	7.1	8.6	11.0	7.7	10.1	9.3	13.4	14.5	3.8
Cost of Goods to Cash Flow 43	6.6	•	4.7	6.0	8.1	5.3	7.3	7.0	10.4	11.3	2.4
Cash Flow to Total Debt 44	0.2	•	0.5	0.4	0.3	0.5	0.2	0.3	0.1	0.1	0.2

Selected Financial Factors (in Percentages)

Debt Ratio 45	73.2	•	62.8	60.8	63.2	55.0	62.3	61.0	80.2	76.5	109.5
Return on Total Assets 46	7.0	•	16.8	10.6	9.4	•	7.7	9.7	6.1	6.4	13.6
Return on Equity Before Income Taxes 47	11.7	•	39.9	22.1	17.0	•	12.6	17.0	10.0	9.4	•
Return on Equity After Income Taxes 48	7.9	•	38.6	20.7	13.1	•	9.9	13.1	8.0	6.9	•
Profit Margin (Before Income Tax) 49	2.2	•	6.5	4.5	3.1	•	3.1	4.6	1.8	2.2	11.8
Profit Margin (After Income Tax) 50	1.5	•	6.3	4.2	2.4	•	2.4	3.5	1.4	1.6	8.2

Table II

Corporations with Net Income

PLASTICS PRODUCT

MONEY AMOUNTS AND SIZE OF ASSETS IN THOUSANDS OF DOLLARS

Item Description for Accounting Period 7/06 Through 6/07		Total	Zero Assets	Under 500	500 to 1,000	1,000 to 5,000	5,000 to 10,000	10,000 to 25,000	25,000 to 50,000	50,000 to 100,000	100,000 to 250,000	250,000 to 500,000	500,000 to 2,500,000	2,500,000 and over
Number of Enterprises	1	6523	•	2025	•	1849	437	276	124	81	67	15	•	0
Revenues ($ in Thousands)														
Net Sales	2	89742774	•	1046483	•	10625373	6316930	8807666	7889484	8934978	16705209	5230319	•	0
Interest	3	424426	•	604	•	3131	3393	10479	9686	13725	40126	31006	•	0
Rents	4	27066	•	390	•	1	2648	282	1690	2184	3979	9571	•	0
Royalties	5	127950	•	0	•	0	0	2670	95	6410	2629	19847	•	0
Other Portfolio Income	6	757524	•	46965	•	26016	2990	39667	15997	36864	48710	39047	•	0
Other Receipts	7	954323	•	14477	•	79587	39359	47078	65037	44515	180588	34863	•	0
Total Receipts	8	92034063	•	1108919	•	10734108	6365320	8907842	7981989	9038676	16981241	5364653	•	0
Average Total Receipts	9	14109	•	548	•	5805	14566	32275	64371	111589	253451	357644	•	•
Operating Costs/Operating Income (%)														
Cost of Operations	10	70.2	•	52.8	•	65.3	68.0	71.3	68.2	69.8	75.5	73.1	•	•
Salaries and Wages	11	5.0	•	7.5	•	5.5	6.5	5.4	6.3	6.2	3.6	4.1	•	•
Taxes Paid	12	1.6	•	2.1	•	2.2	1.7	1.9	1.8	1.6	1.5	1.2	•	•
Interest Paid	13	2.2	•	1.1	•	0.7	0.9	0.9	1.2	1.3	1.7	3.0	•	•
Depreciation	14	2.5	•	0.7	•	2.4	2.1	2.1	2.9	2.9	2.6	3.3	•	•
Amortization and Depletion	15	0.3	•	0.0	•	0.1	0.0	0.2	0.1	0.3	0.3	0.3	•	•
Pensions and Other Deferred Comp.	16	0.4	•	0.0	•	0.2	0.4	0.4	0.5	0.5	0.4	0.5	•	•
Employee Benefits	17	1.5	•	1.2	•	1.3	0.9	1.4	1.6	1.9	1.2	2.7	•	•
Advertising	18	0.4	•	0.6	•	0.4	0.9	0.4	0.4	0.5	0.4	0.2	•	•
Other Expenses	19	9.2	•	18.6	•	10.6	9.3	7.5	8.0	9.0	7.2	7.4	•	•
Officers' Compensation	20	1.7	•	6.7	•	3.9	3.4	1.7	1.6	1.0	0.8	0.6	•	•
Operating Margin	21	4.9	•	8.6	•	7.3	5.9	6.8	7.3	4.9	4.8	3.7	•	•
Operating Margin Before Officers' Comp.	22	6.6	•	15.3	•	11.2	9.3	8.5	8.9	6.0	5.5	4.4	•	•

Selected Average Balance Sheet ($ in Thousands)

Net Receivables 23	1740	50	651	1852	3886	8388	14318	27808	43882
Inventories 24	1438	46	454	1182	3767	7173	12905	28804	46122
Net Property, Plant and Equipment 25	2349	6	678	2084	4815	12322	21071	47609	77323
Total Assets 26	9379	153	2405	7207	15970	35662	68311	156810	324665
Notes and Loans Payable 27	3756	76	774	2168	4872	10287	19472	48398	136213
All Other Liabilities 28	2373	70	591	1401	3297	6742	16104	41162	98568
Net Worth 29	3249	7	1040	3638	7800	18633	32735	67250	89883

Selected Financial Ratios (Times to 1)

Current Ratio 30	1.6	2.9	2.1	1.8	2.0	2.0	1.7	1.8	1.2
Quick Ratio 31	0.9	1.2	1.3	1.2	1.1	1.2	0.9	0.9	0.5
Net Sales to Working Capital 32	8.2	5.5	7.2	7.8	6.8	6.6	7.7	7.4	16.9
Coverage Ratio 33	4.4	13.7	13.1	8.7	10.0	8.0	5.8	4.7	3.1
Total Asset Turnover 34	1.5	3.4	2.4	2.0	2.0	1.8	1.6	1.6	1.1
Inventory Turnover 35	6.7	5.9	8.3	8.3	6.0	6.1	6.0	6.5	5.5
Receivables Turnover 36	7.7	14.6	9.3	9.4	7.6	6.9	7.3	8.4	2.6
Total Liabilities to Net Worth 37	1.9	22.4	1.3	1.0	1.0	0.9	1.1	1.3	2.6
Current Assets to Working Capital 38	2.6	1.5	1.9	2.2	2.0	2.0	2.5	2.3	6.2
Current Liabilities to Working Capital 39	1.6	0.5	0.9	1.2	1.0	1.0	1.5	1.3	5.2
Working Capital to Net Sales 40	0.1	0.2	0.1	0.1	0.1	0.2	0.1	0.1	0.1
Inventory to Working Capital 41	0.9	0.8	0.6	0.7	0.8	0.7	0.9	0.9	2.2
Total Receipts to Cash Flow 42	7.0	3.9	6.3	7.3	7.3	6.8	7.6	8.2	8.5
Cost of Goods to Cash Flow 43	4.9	2.0	4.1	5.0	5.2	4.6	5.3	6.2	6.2
Cash Flow to Total Debt 44	0.3	0.9	0.7	0.6	0.5	0.6	0.4	0.3	0.2

Selected Financial Factors (in Percentages)

Debt Ratio 45	65.4	95.7	56.7	49.5	51.2	47.8	52.1	57.1	72.3
Return on Total Assets 46	14.3	53.3	21.5	15.1	17.8	17.1	12.0	12.9	10.0
Return on Equity Before Income Taxes 47	32.0	1155.6	45.9	26.4	32.8	28.7	20.7	23.7	24.7
Return on Equity After Income Taxes 48	27.9	1133.8	44.5	25.2	28.8	27.0	17.8	19.1	22.2
Profit Margin (Before Income Tax) 49	7.6	14.6	8.3	6.6	8.0	8.4	6.1	6.4	6.4
Profit Margin (After Income Tax) 50	6.6	14.3	8.1	6.3	7.0	7.9	5.3	5.1	5.7

Table I

Corporations with and without Net Income

RUBBER PRODUCT

MONEY AMOUNTS AND SIZE OF ASSETS IN THOUSANDS OF DOLLARS

Item Description for Accounting Period 7/06 Through 6/07	Total	Zero Assets	Under 500	500 to 1,000	1,000 to 5,000	5,000 to 10,000	10,000 to 25,000	25,000 to 50,000	50,000 to 100,000	100,000 to 250,000	250,000 to 500,000	500,000 to 2,500,000	2,500,000 and over
Number of Enterprises 1	742	•	•	•	381	100	50	23	21	7	5	7	4
Revenues ($ in Thousands)													
Net Sales 2	53008610	•	•	•	2140724	2112422	1653847	1528933	2210980	1020616	2031183	8868044	30940121
Interest 3	369020	•	•	•	1619	2361	1470	785	4823	3711	7413	53644	292025
Rents 4	18500	•	•	•	0	0	0	444	1247	2888	849	2231	10564
Royalties 5	503153	•	•	•	0	0	0	160	4563	2647	1670	35960	456859
Other Portfolio Income 6	619570	•	•	•	2123	90	8015	18231	2239	13825	38142	112226	413025
Other Receipts 7	584167	•	•	•	1528	7330	2518	14026	10731	6661	73616	61996	402115
Total Receipts 8	55103020	•	•	•	2145994	2122203	1665850	1562579	2234583	1050348	2152873	9134101	32514709
Average Total Receipts 9	74263	•	•	•	5633	21222	33317	67938	106409	150050	430575	1304872	8128677
Operating Costs/Operating Income (%)													
Cost of Operations 10	71.5	•	•	•	67.5	75.8	73.3	72.2	75.0	76.9	71.2	74.8	70.0
Salaries and Wages 11	6.6	•	•	•	8.4	4.5	6.9	9.4	5.4	5.8	4.3	5.1	7.1
Taxes Paid 12	1.4	•	•	•	2.4	1.0	1.7	2.3	2.1	2.1	1.1	0.9	1.4
Interest Paid 13	2.1	•	•	•	1.2	0.7	0.6	1.6	2.2	1.8	3.4	2.0	2.3
Depreciation 14	2.3	•	•	•	1.2	2.0	1.9	2.7	2.6	2.9	1.5	3.2	2.2
Amortization and Depletion 15	0.7	•	•	•	0.0	0.0	0.1	0.4	0.7	0.6	0.9	0.5	1.0
Pensions and Other Deferred Comp. 16	2.1	•	•	•	0.4	0.2	0.6	0.5	0.5	0.9	1.3	1.2	3.0
Employee Benefits 17	3.5	•	•	•	1.8	0.6	1.9	1.9	2.7	3.2	1.3	4.5	4.0
Advertising 18	1.2	•	•	•	0.2	0.1	3.2	0.4	0.4	0.1	1.4	1.0	1.5
Other Expenses 19	10.9	•	•	•	11.3	6.1	6.2	7.1	6.4	7.6	11.4	6.1	13.4
Officers' Compensation 20	0.6	•	•	•	4.2	1.6	1.5	1.1	0.9	0.9	0.5	0.7	0.1
Operating Margin 21	•	•	•	•	1.4	7.5	2.2	0.4	1.2	•	1.7	0.3	•
Operating Margin Before Officers' Comp. 22	•	•	•	•	5.5	9.1	3.7	1.5	2.1	•	2.3	0.9	•

Selected Average Balance Sheet ($ in Thousands)

Net Receivables 23	9500	•	591	3411	2801	7796	14342	18891	65181	162010	1061062
Inventories 24	8711	•	450	933	3039	8742	12364	19526	68922	129743	1043703
Net Property, Plant and Equipment 25	12962	•	434	2674	4088	10215	20084	33428	52955	301120	1425426
Total Assets 26	56956	•	2210	8663	13570	32864	71481	155048	358082	1115232	6714524
Notes and Loans Payable 27	18459	•	688	2098	2386	14148	30741	41406	126202	257005	2339556
All Other Liabilities 28	26773	•	658	2852	3788	11788	18195	38568	132047	363573	3742331
Net Worth 29	11724	•	864	3714	7397	6928	22544	75075	99833	494653	632636

Selected Financial Ratios (Times to 1)

Current Ratio 30	1.7	•	1.8	1.9	1.8	1.3	1.5	1.4	1.6	2.0	1.7
Quick Ratio 31	1.0	•	1.1	1.4	1.0	0.7	0.8	0.7	0.8	1.1	1.0
Net Sales to Working Capital 32	6.6	•	8.2	7.6	8.8	14.0	10.5	9.8	6.6	6.0	6.1
Coverage Ratio 33	1.7	•	2.3	11.7	5.9	2.6	2.1	1.0	3.3	3.0	1.0
Total Asset Turnover 34	1.3	•	2.5	2.4	2.4	2.0	1.5	0.9	1.1	1.1	1.2
Inventory Turnover 35	5.9	•	8.4	17.2	8.0	5.5	6.4	5.7	4.2	7.3	5.2
Receivables Turnover 36	7.6	•	8.9	8.7	10.5	7.0	8.2	7.0	6.6	8.9	7.1
Total Liabilities to Net Worth 37	3.9	•	1.6	1.3	0.8	3.7	2.2	1.1	2.6	1.3	9.6
Current Assets to Working Capital 38	2.3	•	2.2	2.1	2.2	3.9	3.2	3.3	2.6	2.0	2.4
Current Liabilities to Working Capital 39	1.3	•	1.2	1.1	1.2	2.9	2.2	2.3	1.6	1.0	1.4
Working Capital to Net Sales 40	0.2	•	0.1	0.1	0.1	0.1	0.1	0.1	0.2	0.2	0.2
Inventory to Working Capital 41	0.8	•	0.8	0.5	0.8	1.6	1.4	1.1	1.1	0.7	0.8
Total Receipts to Cash Flow 42	11.0	•	9.5	8.1	14.6	14.0	14.1	18.8	5.6	12.3	11.2
Cost of Goods to Cash Flow 43	7.9	•	6.4	6.2	10.7	10.1	10.6	14.4	4.0	9.2	7.9
Cash Flow to Total Debt 44	0.1	•	0.4	0.5	0.4	0.2	0.2	0.1	0.3	0.2	0.1

Selected Financial Factors (in Percentages)

Debt Ratio 45	79.4	•	60.9	57.1	45.5	78.9	68.5	51.6	72.1	55.6	90.6
Return on Total Assets 46	4.5	•	7.2	21.1	8.6	8.4	6.6	1.7	12.6	6.7	2.6
Return on Equity Before Income Taxes 47	9.2	•	10.4	45.1	13.1	24.5	10.7	0.0	31.5	10.2	•
Return on Equity After Income Taxes 48	6.9	•	9.6	42.0	11.7	19.4	8.4	•	28.4	6.4	•
Profit Margin (Before Income Tax) 49	1.5	•	1.6	7.9	2.9	2.6	2.3	0.0	7.7	4.0	•
Profit Margin (After Income Tax) 50	1.1	•	1.5	7.4	2.6	2.0	1.8	•	7.0	2.5	•

Table II

Corporations with Net Income

RUBBER PRODUCT

MONEY AMOUNTS AND SIZE OF ASSETS IN THOUSANDS OF DOLLARS

Item Description for Accounting Period 7/06 Through 6/07	Total	Zero Assets	Under 500	500 to 1,000	1,000 to 5,000	5,000 to 10,000	10,000 to 25,000	25,000 to 50,000	50,000 to 100,000	100,000 to 250,000	250,000 to 500,000	500,000 to 2,500,000	2,500,000 and over
Number of Enterprises 1	448	•	0	•	229	92	33	12	14	3	5	•	0
Revenues ($ in Thousands)													
Net Sales 2	34647214	•	0	•	1903361	2049703	840349	844095	1586709	295186	2031183	•	0
Interest 3	176362	•	0	•	1521	2361	781	357	4563	2077	7413	•	0
Rents 4	17163	•	0	•	0	0	0	444	1049	2773	849	•	0
Royalties 5	77275	•	0	•	0	0	0	1	4563	1910	1670	•	0
Other Portfolio Income 6	340408	•	0	•	1858	90	1458	14597	2113	4225	38142	•	0
Other Receipts 7	285558	•	0	•	887	6580	2454	8153	8767	2180	73616	•	0
Total Receipts 8	35543980	•	0	•	1907627	2058734	845042	867647	1607764	308351	2152873	•	0
Average Total Receipts 9	79339	•	•	•	8330	22378	25607	72304	114840	102784	430575	•	•
Operating Costs/Operating Income (%)													
Cost of Operations 10	71.9	•	•	•	69.1	75.3	64.2	63.3	72.9	74.1	71.2	•	•
Salaries and Wages 11	6.1	•	•	•	8.0	4.4	6.7	13.8	5.2	5.6	4.3	•	•
Taxes Paid 12	1.4	•	•	•	2.5	1.0	2.4	2.7	2.2	2.1	1.1	•	•
Interest Paid 13	1.6	•	•	•	0.8	0.7	0.7	0.7	1.5	0.7	3.4	•	•
Depreciation 14	1.8	•	•	•	0.8	1.8	2.6	2.2	2.0	1.8	1.5	•	•
Amortization and Depletion 15	0.3	•	•	•	0.0	0.0	0.0	0.1	0.6	0.3	0.9	•	•
Pensions and Other Deferred Comp. 16	1.4	•	•	•	0.5	0.2	0.5	0.3	0.7	0.3	1.3	•	•
Employee Benefits 17	2.8	•	•	•	1.9	0.6	2.9	2.1	2.8	1.9	1.3	•	•
Advertising 18	1.2	•	•	•	0.1	0.1	0.7	0.5	0.6	0.4	1.4	•	•
Other Expenses 19	9.8	•	•	•	9.6	5.9	7.4	8.5	6.7	7.9	11.4	•	•
Officers' Compensation 20	0.7	•	•	•	3.9	1.7	1.9	1.1	1.0	1.3	0.5	•	•
Operating Margin 21	0.9	•	•	•	2.8	8.4	10.1	4.7	3.8	3.4	1.7	•	•
Operating Margin Before Officers' Comp. 22	1.6	•	•	•	6.7	10.1	12.0	5.8	4.8	3.4	2.3	•	•

Selected Average Balance Sheet ($ in Thousands)

Net Receivables 23	11961	•	829	3538	3521	8182	13795	14382	65181
Inventories 24	9609	•	664	945	3103	10075	14458	17756	69405
Net Property, Plant and Equipment 25	12638	•	497	2686	4035	9753	19172	17371	52955
Total Assets 26	56884	•	2524	8851	14370	34904	69913	107235	358082
Notes and Loans Payable 27	12134	•	815	1641	2340	9096	18756	5437	126202
All Other Liabilities 28	27001	•	850	2946	2657	9720	18995	31983	132047
Net Worth 29	17748	•	858	4265	9374	16088	32161	69815	99833

Selected Financial Ratios (Times to 1)

Current Ratio 30	1.6	•	1.7	1.9	3.2	1.4	1.9	2.6	1.6
Quick Ratio 31	0.9	•	1.0	1.4	1.8	0.7	0.9	1.3	0.8
Net Sales to Working Capital 32	8.1	•	10.8	7.9	4.1	12.3	7.1	3.7	6.6
Coverage Ratio 33	3.4	•	4.9	14.2	16.9	11.7	4.4	12.9	3.3
Total Asset Turnover 34	1.4	•	3.3	2.5	1.8	2.0	1.6	0.9	1.1
Inventory Turnover 35	5.8	•	8.7	17.7	5.3	4.4	5.7	4.1	4.2
Receivables Turnover 36	6.9	•	9.3	8.7	7.9	6.5	8.5	•	2.6
Total Liabilities to Net Worth 37	2.2	•	1.9	1.1	0.5	1.2	1.2	0.5	2.6
Current Assets to Working Capital 38	2.6	•	2.4	2.1	1.5	3.7	2.2	1.6	2.6
Current Liabilities to Working Capital 39	1.6	•	1.4	1.1	0.5	2.7	1.2	0.6	1.6
Working Capital to Net Sales 40	0.1	•	0.1	0.1	0.2	0.1	0.1	0.3	0.2
Inventory to Working Capital 41	1.1	•	1.0	0.5	0.5	1.5	1.0	0.7	1.1
Total Receipts to Cash Flow 42	9.1	•	9.6	7.7	6.5	8.2	9.8	7.1	5.6
Cost of Goods to Cash Flow 43	6.5	•	6.6	5.8	4.2	5.2	7.1	5.3	4.0
Cash Flow to Total Debt 44	0.2	•	0.5	0.6	0.8	0.5	0.3	0.4	0.3

Selected Financial Factors (in Percentages)

Debt Ratio 45	68.8	•	66.0	51.8	34.8	53.9	54.0	34.9	72.1
Return on Total Assets 46	7.2	•	12.5	23.9	20.0	16.4	10.8	7.9	12.6
Return on Equity Before Income Taxes 47	16.2	•	29.3	46.2	28.8	32.6	18.1	11.1	31.5
Return on Equity After Income Taxes 48	13.7	•	28.0	43.3	27.2	28.4	15.6	9.5	28.4
Profit Margin (Before Income Tax) 49	3.7	•	3.0	8.8	10.6	7.4	5.1	7.9	7.7
Profit Margin (After Income Tax) 50	3.1	•	2.9	8.3	10.0	6.5	4.4	6.8	7.0

Table I

Corporations with and without Net Income

CLAY, REFRACTORY AND OTHER NONMETALLIC MINERAL PRODUCT

MONEY AMOUNTS AND SIZE OF ASSETS IN THOUSANDS OF DOLLARS

Item Description for Accounting Period 7/06 Through 6/07	Total	Zero Assets	Under 500	500 to 1,000	1,000 to 5,000	5,000 to 10,000	10,000 to 25,000	25,000 to 50,000	50,000 to 100,000	100,000 to 250,000	250,000 to 500,000	500,000 to 2,500,000	2,500,000 and over
Number of Enterprises 1	2057	11	936	601	347	22	59	32	22	14	5	9	0
Revenues ($ in Thousands)													
Net Sales 2	24723260	459467	660827	1311955	1652863	212717	1581120	1674583	1891823	1932418	1435284	11910202	0
Interest 3	380788	6329	1169	946	864	190	383	2079	3080	8465	4178	353103	0
Rents 4	46273	0	0	467	0	43	134	28	1295	1009	1258	42040	0
Royalties 5	280871	0	0	0	0	5660	2675	0	407	2543	618	268969	0
Other Portfolio Income 6	163249	799	1940	5186	1404	110	558	3710	8923	4305	13769	122545	0
Other Receipts 7	386636	1523	455	8545	-10207	28554	4569	6683	83938	47303	7614	207660	0
Total Receipts 8	25981077	468118	664391	1327099	1644924	247274	1589439	1687083	1989466	1996043	1462721	12904519	0
Average Total Receipts 9	12631	42556	710	2208	4740	11240	26940	52721	90430	142574	292544	1433835	•
Operating Costs/Operating Income (%)													
Cost of Operations 10	68.1	56.6	54.0	61.8	67.3	79.1	68.4	71.5	71.4	64.3	53.1	71.4	•
Salaries and Wages 11	6.5	6.1	8.3	5.3	5.9	5.3	5.9	5.7	5.6	10.3	9.8	6.0	•
Taxes Paid 12	1.8	2.6	2.7	3.8	3.2	1.6	1.9	1.7	1.8	2.2	1.8	1.2	•
Interest Paid 13	5.2	0.9	0.2	0.5	0.7	1.3	1.3	1.2	2.0	1.7	1.4	9.5	•
Depreciation 14	2.6	5.6	2.1	1.1	2.0	3.1	2.4	2.9	3.0	3.3	3.8	2.5	•
Amortization and Depletion 15	0.6	0.2	0.0	0.2	0.7	0.2	0.6	0.1	1.0	0.4	0.6	0.6	•
Pensions and Other Deferred Comp. 16	1.2	1.6	•	0.4	0.2	0.3	0.4	0.3	0.8	1.1	0.3	2.0	•
Employee Benefits 17	1.7	1.6	0.6	3.0	0.2	1.3	1.2	1.8	0.9	2.5	1.9	1.8	•
Advertising 18	0.8	0.6	0.3	0.1	0.6	0.2	0.6	0.2	0.7	0.7	3.3	0.9	•
Other Expenses 19	17.0	11.1	14.1	11.9	12.2	19.6	8.9	6.8	9.4	9.5	13.5	24.0	•
Officers' Compensation 20	1.8	0.7	7.8	6.5	5.8	2.4	3.1	1.9	1.2	0.9	0.8	0.5	•
Operating Margin 21	•	12.5	10.0	5.4	1.4	•	5.2	5.9	2.1	3.1	9.6	•	•
Operating Margin Before Officers' Comp. 22	•	13.2	17.8	11.9	7.1	•	8.3	7.8	3.2	4.0	10.4	•	•

Selected Average Balance Sheet ($ in Thousands)

Net Receivables 23	3509	0	67	134	437	1287	3179	5996	10409	33618	41345	623200
Inventories 24	1314	0	37	76	385	1185	3650	7738	13307	27378	43189	121664
Net Property, Plant and Equipment 25	3092	0	56	185	441	1039	6231	13012	26508	55633	128939	358891
Total Assets 26	19696	0	270	755	1720	8501	14855	33829	70815	161122	370157	3489067
Notes and Loans Payable 27	7183	0	616	184	586	1144	5327	9861	24056	43527	94746	1290871
All Other Liabilities 28	3994	0	3	140	494	1369	3411	7417	16641	43534	79499	679601
Net Worth 29	8519	0	-349	431	640	5989	6118	16551	30117	74062	195912	1518595

Selected Financial Ratios (Times to 1)

Current Ratio 30	1.2	•	0.7	2.6	1.6	2.1	1.7	2.0	1.9	1.8	2.0	1.0
Quick Ratio 31	0.7	•	0.5	2.0	1.1	1.3	0.9	1.0	0.9	0.9	1.0	0.6
Net Sales to Working Capital 32	11.0	•	•	6.9	12.2	5.2	7.8	5.9	6.0	4.1	3.9	35.4
Coverage Ratio 33	0.6	17.7	48.9	15.1	2.3	2.4	5.3	6.6	4.5	4.9	9.4	•
Total Asset Turnover 34	0.6	•	2.6	2.9	2.8	1.1	1.8	1.5	1.2	0.9	0.8	0.4
Inventory Turnover 35	6.2	•	10.4	17.8	8.3	6.5	5.0	4.8	4.6	3.2	3.5	7.8
Receivables Turnover 36	3.0	•	9.6	16.5	14.4	•	8.6	8.4	8.0	4.7	8.1	1.8
Total Liabilities to Net Worth 37	1.3	•	•	0.8	1.7	0.4	1.4	1.0	1.4	1.2	0.9	1.3
Current Assets to Working Capital 38	6.6	•	•	1.6	2.6	1.9	2.3	2.0	2.1	2.3	2.0	31.2
Current Liabilities to Working Capital 39	5.6	•	•	0.6	1.6	0.9	1.3	1.0	1.1	1.3	1.0	30.2
Working Capital to Net Sales 40	0.1	•	•	0.1	0.1	0.2	0.1	0.2	0.2	0.2	0.3	0.0
Inventory to Working Capital 41	1.3	•	•	0.4	0.7	0.6	1.1	0.9	0.8	1.0	0.7	3.9
Total Receipts to Cash Flow 42	8.8	4.3	4.6	16.1	9.1	8.7	8.5	8.2	6.6	7.3	4.5	11.8
Cost of Goods to Cash Flow 43	6.0	2.4	2.5	9.9	6.1	6.9	5.8	5.9	4.7	4.7	2.4	8.4
Cash Flow to Total Debt 44	0.1	•	•	0.4	0.5	0.4	0.4	0.4	0.3	0.2	0.4	0.1

Selected Financial Factors (in Percentages)

Debt Ratio 45	56.7	•	229.4	42.9	62.8	29.6	58.8	51.1	57.5	54.0	47.1	56.5
Return on Total Assets 46	1.8	•	28.1	20.3	4.2	3.5	12.7	12.1	11.2	7.0	10.0	•
Return on Equity Before Income Taxes 47	•	•	•	33.2	6.5	2.9	25.1	20.9	20.6	12.1	16.9	•
Return on Equity After Income Taxes 48	•	•	•	32.1	6.4	2.0	22.2	16.3	17.0	8.3	12.5	•
Profit Margin (Before Income Tax) 49	•	14.2	10.5	6.6	0.9	1.8	5.7	6.6	7.2	6.5	11.5	•
Profit Margin (After Income Tax) 50	•	8.7	10.4	6.3	0.9	1.2	5.1	5.1	5.9	4.4	8.5	•

Table II

Corporations with Net Income

CLAY, REFRACTORY AND OTHER NONMETALLIC MINERAL PRODUCT

MONEY AMOUNTS AND SIZE OF ASSETS IN THOUSANDS OF DOLLARS

Item Description for Accounting Period 7/06 Through 6/07	Total	Zero Assets	Under 500	500 to 1,000	1,000 to 5,000	5,000 to 10,000	10,000 to 25,000	25,000 to 50,000	50,000 to 100,000	100,000 to 250,000	250,000 to 500,000	500,000 to 2,500,000	2,500,000 and over
Number of Enterprises **1**	1307	•	440	513	227	8	45	26	19	•	•	•	0
Revenues ($ in Thousands)													
Net Sales **2**	14843185	•	603121	1016054	1243720	149199	1313847	1492029	1628591	•	•	•	0
Interest **3**	128265	•	800	946	693	190	338	1970	2973	•	•	•	0
Rents **4**	4497	•	0	467	0	43	14	28	1295	•	•	•	0
Royalties **5**	13527	•	0	0	0	0	2675	0	247	•	•	•	0
Other Portfolio Income **6**	90130	•	1349	5186	1142	16	532	3710	8078	•	•	•	0
Other Receipts **7**	238110	•	173	8545	-10355	28821	1904	5729	82801	•	•	•	0
Total Receipts **8**	15317714	•	605443	1031198	1235200	178269	1319310	1503466	1723985	•	•	•	0
Average Total Receipts **9**	11720	•	1376	2010	5441	22284	29318	57826	90736	•	•	•	•
Operating Costs/Operating Income (%)													
Cost of Operations **10**	66.6	•	56.2	61.0	64.4	76.4	66.7	71.6	71.8	•	•	•	•
Salaries and Wages **11**	5.6	•	5.7	5.2	6.0	3.7	5.3	4.9	5.8	•	•	•	•
Taxes Paid **12**	2.0	•	2.5	3.1	3.3	1.7	2.1	1.6	1.6	•	•	•	•
Interest Paid **13**	2.3	•	0.2	0.6	0.5	0.3	1.0	1.1	2.0	•	•	•	•
Depreciation **14**	2.7	•	2.2	1.0	0.8	2.6	2.1	2.5	3.0	•	•	•	•
Amortization and Depletion **15**	0.6	•	•	0.2	0.8	0.2	0.6	0.1	1.1	•	•	•	•
Pensions and Other Deferred Comp. **16**	0.6	•	•	0.1	0.3	0.5	0.4	0.4	0.8	•	•	•	•
Employee Benefits **17**	1.5	•	0.6	0.4	0.2	1.1	1.3	1.8	1.0	•	•	•	•
Advertising **18**	0.4	•	0.3	0.2	0.4	0.2	0.6	0.2	0.4	•	•	•	•
Other Expenses **19**	8.6	•	12.5	10.6	12.2	15.7	6.4	5.7	7.4	•	•	•	•
Officers' Compensation **20**	2.4	•	8.1	7.1	6.2	0.9	3.4	1.9	1.4	•	•	•	•
Operating Margin **21**	6.8	•	11.7	10.5	4.9	•	10.2	8.2	3.7	•	•	•	•
Operating Margin Before Officers' Comp. **22**	9.1	•	19.8	17.6	11.1	•	13.5	10.1	5.1	•	•	•	•

Selected Average Balance Sheet ($ in Thousands)

Net Receivables 23	1539	131	149	472	2721	3579	6123	10022
Inventories 24	1344	70	36	380	2998	3948	7679	9717
Net Property, Plant and Equipment 25	2754	51	190	124	1799	6179	12696	25018
Total Assets 26	9503	470	718	1484	8483	15542	34132	69841
Notes and Loans Payable 27	3296	27	216	286	484	4501	8817	20581
All Other Liabilities 28	2396	4	98	564	1368	3043	7143	15073
Net Worth 29	3812	439	405	634	6632	7998	18172	34187

Selected Financial Ratios (Times to 1)

Current Ratio 30	2.2	181.1	2.9	1.6	4.7	2.0	2.4	2.2
Quick Ratio 31	1.2	141.0	2.6	1.3	3.2	1.1	1.2	1.1
Net Sales to Working Capital 32	5.2	3.5	6.7	13.8	3.6	6.8	5.5	5.2
Coverage Ratio 33	5.3	71.8	21.0	10.2	51.7	11.6	9.4	5.9
Total Asset Turnover 34	1.2	2.9	2.8	3.7	2.2	1.9	1.7	1.2
Inventory Turnover 35	5.6	10.9	33.5	9.3	4.8	4.9	5.4	6.3
Receivables Turnover 36	2.8	12.2	15.2	15.1	7.8	8.4	9.0	9.4
Total Liabilities to Net Worth 37	1.5	0.1	0.8	1.3	0.3	0.9	0.9	1.0
Current Assets to Working Capital 38	1.9	1.0	1.5	2.6	1.3	2.0	1.7	1.8
Current Liabilities to Working Capital 39	0.9	0.0	0.5	1.6	0.3	1.0	0.7	0.8
Working Capital to Net Sales 40	0.2	0.3	0.1	0.1	0.3	0.1	0.2	0.2
Inventory to Working Capital 41	0.6	0.2	0.1	0.5	0.4	0.9	0.7	0.6
Total Receipts to Cash Flow 42	6.0	4.7	5.3	7.0	5.1	6.6	7.4	6.4
Cost of Goods to Cash Flow 43	4.0	2.6	3.2	4.5	3.9	4.4	5.3	4.6
Cash Flow to Total Debt 44	0.3	9.5	1.2	0.9	2.0	0.6	0.5	0.4

Selected Financial Factors (in Percentages)

Debt Ratio 45	59.9	6.6	43.7	57.3	21.8	48.5	46.8	51.1
Return on Total Assets 46	14.7	35.8	34.7	17.2	36.4	21.7	16.7	14.2
Return on Equity Before Income Taxes 47	29.7	37.8	58.7	36.3	45.7	38.6	28.1	24.0
Return on Equity After Income Taxes 48	23.7	37.3	57.3	36.2	43.6	35.6	22.8	20.4
Profit Margin (Before Income Tax) 49	10.0	12.1	12.0	4.2	16.2	10.6	8.9	9.6
Profit Margin (After Income Tax) 50	8.0	12.0	11.7	4.2	15.5	9.8	7.2	8.1

Table I

Corporations with and without Net Income

GLASS AND GLASS PRODUCT

MONEY AMOUNTS AND SIZE OF ASSETS IN THOUSANDS OF DOLLARS

Item Description for Accounting Period 7/06 Through 6/07	Total	Zero Assets	Under 500	500 to 1,000	1,000 to 5,000	5,000 to 10,000	10,000 to 25,000	25,000 to 50,000	50,000 to 100,000	100,000 to 250,000	250,000 to 500,000	500,000 to 2,500,000	2,500,000 and over
Number of Enterprises 1	1992	25	1085	426	336	45	37	10	7	7	5	5	3
Revenues ($ in Thousands)													
Net Sales 2	25271073	0	622336	746234	1895812	641058	1105732	569153	416679	1505297	1589780	5769035	10409958
Interest 3	174185	0	164	278	1283	950	551	1117	186	8289	8826	22431	130109
Rents 4	13655	0	0	0	0	594	1137	240	275	1308	0	665	9436
Royalties 5	92542	0	0	0	0	31	0	0	100	15767	7	4603	72034
Other Portfolio Income 6	259913	0	2731	0	1177	770	9091	5929	3169	3095	25694	43323	164934
Other Receipts 7	275360	0	37	3232	2560	847	5673	3107	1844	39539	22806	69788	125927
Total Receipts 8	26086728	0	625268	749744	1900832	644250	1122184	579546	422253	1573295	1647113	5909845	10912398
Average Total Receipts 9	13096	0	576	1760	5657	14317	30329	57955	60322	224756	329423	1181969	3637466
Operating Costs/Operating Income (%)													
Cost of Operations 10	66.8	•	37.1	38.2	60.9	74.4	77.8	73.1	67.6	68.8	71.6	65.0	69.4
Salaries and Wages 11	6.9	•	20.9	19.8	7.6	6.7	4.1	4.0	4.9	8.2	4.8	6.9	5.7
Taxes Paid 12	2.3	•	3.1	2.2	2.5	2.0	1.2	2.2	2.3	3.3	2.2	2.2	2.3
Interest Paid 13	3.5	•	0.6	1.3	1.2	1.1	1.1	1.5	2.2	1.4	2.7	2.2	5.9
Depreciation 14	4.0	•	2.4	7.0	2.3	1.8	2.8	2.6	2.9	2.0	3.2	6.0	3.8
Amortization and Depletion 15	0.5	•	0.0	0.0	0.0	0.7	0.1	0.4	0.2	0.5	0.3	0.4	0.8
Pensions and Other Deferred Comp. 16	1.2	•	•	•	0.1	0.3	0.1	0.0	0.7	0.4	0.9	1.1	2.0
Employee Benefits 17	3.1	•	1.2	0.6	0.9	1.2	1.5	0.9	1.5	2.3	3.0	3.3	4.3
Advertising 18	0.5	•	1.6	1.1	0.4	1.7	0.1	0.5	0.1	2.0	0.3	0.3	0.3
Other Expenses 19	10.9	•	21.4	26.5	9.9	8.7	6.5	11.4	8.0	11.0	8.6	11.6	10.0
Officers' Compensation 20	1.6	•	10.8	5.1	8.5	3.6	1.3	0.9	1.7	0.6	1.8	0.4	0.2
Operating Margin 21	•	•	0.7	•	5.6	•	3.3	2.5	7.9	•	0.6	0.6	•
Operating Margin Before Officers' Comp. 22	0.4	•	11.5	3.3	14.1	1.5	4.6	3.4	9.6	0.2	2.4	1.0	•

Selected Average Balance Sheet ($ in Thousands)

Net Receivables 23	1479	0	43	86	646	1793	3247	7884	8839	22249	93326	193725	237415
Inventories 24	1501	0	48	311	450	875	2868	6628	11755	21597	45642	245376	478210
Net Property, Plant and Equipment 25	3786	0	24	159	785	1412	4991	9849	23931	35075	119937	514371	1083926
Total Assets 26	16672	0	199	730	2287	6578	15376	34973	70232	138322	406005	1300848	6901837
Notes and Loans Payable 27	5809	0	278	1308	1114	2296	5277	17994	23150	35201	137113	515053	2063505
All Other Liabilities 28	4026	0	35	113	380	1504	4809	6859	18437	39120	118588	369979	1548738
Net Worth 29	6836	0	-114	-691	794	2778	5290	10120	28645	64001	150305	415816	3289594

Selected Financial Ratios (Times to 1)

Current Ratio 30	1.1	•	6.7	2.2	2.9	2.0	1.3	1.4	1.6	1.8	1.6	0.9	0.8
Quick Ratio 31	0.5	•	3.7	1.0	1.9	1.3	0.8	0.8	0.8	0.9	1.0	0.6	0.2
Net Sales to Working Capital 32	39.2	•	3.9	7.2	6.1	7.4	15.7	10.6	6.5	7.2	5.1	•	•
Coverage Ratio 33	1.6	•	3.0	•	6.0	•	5.2	3.7	5.1	4.0	2.6	2.5	1.1
Total Asset Turnover 34	0.8	•	2.9	2.4	2.5	2.2	1.9	1.6	0.8	1.6	0.8	0.9	0.5
Inventory Turnover 35	5.6	•	4.4	2.2	7.6	12.1	8.1	6.3	3.4	6.8	5.0	3.1	5.0
Receivables Turnover 36	9.8	•	13.5	20.3	8.6	•	11.0	7.4	4.9	10.4	3.4	6.1	29.2
Total Liabilities to Net Worth 37	1.4	•	•	•	1.9	1.4	1.9	2.5	1.5	1.2	1.7	2.1	1.1
Current Assets to Working Capital 38	11.2	•	1.2	1.8	1.5	2.0	4.3	3.6	2.7	2.2	2.7	•	•
Current Liabilities to Working Capital 39	10.2	•	0.2	0.8	0.5	1.0	3.3	2.6	1.7	1.2	1.7	•	•
Working Capital to Net Sales 40	0.0	•	0.3	0.1	0.2	0.1	0.1	0.1	0.2	0.1	0.2	•	•
Inventory to Working Capital 41	4.7	•	0.5	1.0	0.5	0.5	1.5	1.3	1.0	0.7	0.6	•	•
Total Receipts to Cash Flow 42	11.4	•	6.2	6.1	7.6	18.5	11.3	7.7	6.8	7.9	10.1	8.5	22.2
Cost of Goods to Cash Flow 43	7.6	•	2.3	2.3	4.6	13.8	8.8	5.6	4.6	5.4	7.2	5.5	15.4
Cash Flow to Total Debt 44	0.1	•	0.3	0.2	0.5	0.2	0.3	0.3	0.2	0.4	0.1	0.2	0.0

Selected Financial Factors (in Percentages)

Debt Ratio 45	59.0	•	157.3	194.6	65.3	57.8	65.6	71.1	59.2	53.7	63.0	68.0	52.3
Return on Total Assets 46	4.3	•	5.0	•	17.4	•	11.4	9.3	9.7	8.5	5.5	4.9	3.2
Return on Equity Before Income Taxes 47	4.1	•	•	3.4	41.6	•	26.7	23.7	19.0	13.9	9.0	9.1	0.4
Return on Equity After Income Taxes 48	2.5	•	•	3.7	39.7	•	22.6	12.2	15.9	9.9	6.3	9.1	•
Profit Margin (Before Income Tax) 49	2.2	•	1.2	•	5.9	•	4.7	4.2	9.1	4.1	3.3	3.3	0.3
Profit Margin (After Income Tax) 50	1.4	•	1.2	•	5.6	•	4.0	2.2	7.6	2.9	3.3	3.3	•

Table II

Corporations with Net Income

GLASS AND GLASS PRODUCT

MONEY AMOUNTS AND SIZE OF ASSETS IN THOUSANDS OF DOLLARS

Item Description for Accounting Period 7/06 Through 6/07	Total	Zero Assets	Under 100	100 to 250	251 to 500	501 to 1,000	1,001 to 5,000	5,001 to 10,000	10,001 to 25,000	25,001 to 50,000	50,001 to 100,000	100,001 to 250,000	250,001 and over
Number of Enterprises **1**	1306	0	693	228	311	27	22	7	•	•	•	•	0

Revenues ($ in Thousands)

	Total	Zero Assets	Under 100	100 to 250	251 to 500	501 to 1,000	1,001 to 5,000	5,001 to 10,000	10,001 to 25,000	25,001 to 50,000	50,001 to 100,000	100,001 to 250,000	250,001 and over
Net Sales **2**	17330526	0	606633	425502	1812299	430213	742636	470987	•	•	•	•	0
Interest **3**	114730	0	164	278	1283	138	538	898	•	•	•	•	0
Rents **4**	4885	0	0	0	0	556	1137	240	•	•	•	•	0
Royalties **5**	28071	0	0	0	0	0	0	0	•	•	•	•	0
Other Portfolio Income **6**	252041	0	2422	0	1177	770	8317	5929	•	•	•	•	0
Other Receipts **7**	124177	0	26	623	1865	593	2545	1696	•	•	•	•	0
Total Receipts **8**	17854430	0	609245	426403	1816624	432270	755173	479750	•	•	•	•	0
Average Total Receipts **9**	13671	•	879	1870	5841	16010	34326	68536	•	•	•	•	•

Operating Costs/Operating Income (%)

	Total	Zero Assets	Under 100	100 to 250	251 to 500	501 to 1,000	1,001 to 5,000	5,001 to 10,000	10,001 to 25,000	25,001 to 50,000	50,001 to 100,000	100,001 to 250,000	250,001 and over
Cost of Operations **10**	63.9	•	34.2	39.9	60.7	75.3	78.1	68.6	•	•	•	•	•
Salaries and Wages **11**	7.4	•	21.5	6.4	7.5	4.7	3.1	3.7	•	•	•	•	•
Taxes Paid **12**	2.4	•	3.2	3.0	2.5	1.7	1.0	2.5	•	•	•	•	•
Interest Paid **13**	1.5	•	0.6	2.0	1.1	1.2	0.3	1.1	•	•	•	•	•
Depreciation **14**	3.8	•	2.3	6.8	2.4	1.5	1.7	2.2	•	•	•	•	•
Amortization and Depletion **15**	0.6	•	•	0.0	0.0	0.0	0.1	0.0	•	•	•	•	•
Pensions and Other Deferred Comp. **16**	1.5	•	•	•	0.1	0.4	0.1	0.1	•	•	•	•	•
Employee Benefits **17**	2.7	•	1.2	•	1.0	1.5	1.6	1.0	•	•	•	•	•
Advertising **18**	0.6	•	1.7	1.5	0.5	1.0	0.1	0.5	•	•	•	•	•
Other Expenses **19**	9.5	•	17.5	27.1	9.7	4.8	4.5	11.8	•	•	•	•	•
Officers' Compensation **20**	1.9	•	10.9	8.8	8.5	3.4	0.9	1.0	•	•	•	•	•
Operating Margin **21**	4.1	•	7.0	4.4	6.0	4.7	8.5	7.6	•	•	•	•	•
Operating Margin Before Officers' Comp. **22**	6.0	•	17.9	13.2	14.5	8.1	9.4	8.7	•	•	•	•	•

Selected Average Balance Sheet ($ in Thousands)

Net Receivables 23	1468	•	68	60	672	2121	4419	9331
Inventories 24	1543	•	15	333	474	2352	2546	7284
Net Property, Plant and Equipment 25	3535	•	33	223	792	1493	4128	9613
Total Assets 26	11324	•	215	795	2372	6374	15066	35808
Notes and Loans Payable 27	2788	•	116	483	1127	3004	2418	8829
All Other Liabilities 28	3182	•	55	105	366	1195	5632	6705
Net Worth 29	5353	•	44	207	879	2176	7016	20273

Selected Financial Ratios (Times to 1)

Current Ratio 30	1.3	•	4.4	2.0	3.0	2.4	1.9	2.1
Quick Ratio 31	0.6	•	3.7	0.7	2.0	1.6	1.4	1.3
Net Sales to Working Capital 32	17.5	•	6.3	7.4	5.8	6.6	7.2	5.9
Coverage Ratio 33	5.9	•	13.5	3.3	6.6	5.4	31.7	9.8
Total Asset Turnover 34	1.2	•	4.1	2.3	2.5	2.5	2.2	1.9
Inventory Turnover 35	5.5	•	20.1	2.2	7.5	5.1	10.3	6.3
Receivables Turnover 36	9.8	•	20.3	•	8.4	4.9	9.6	•
Total Liabilities to Net Worth 37	1.1	•	3.9	2.8	1.7	1.9	1.1	0.8
Current Assets to Working Capital 38	4.8	•	1.3	2.0	1.5	1.7	2.1	1.9
Current Liabilities to Working Capital 39	3.8	•	0.3	1.0	0.5	0.7	1.1	0.9
Working Capital to Net Sales 40	0.1	•	0.2	0.1	0.2	0.2	0.1	0.2
Inventory to Working Capital 41	1.9	•	0.2	1.3	0.5	0.3	0.5	0.6
Total Receipts to Cash Flow 42	8.0	•	5.5	4.5	7.5	11.3	7.8	5.5
Cost of Goods to Cash Flow 43	5.1	•	1.9	1.8	4.5	8.5	6.1	3.8
Cash Flow to Total Debt 44	0.3	•	0.9	0.7	0.5	0.3	0.5	0.8

Selected Financial Factors (in Percentages)

Debt Ratio 45	52.7	•	79.6	73.9	62.9	65.9	53.4	43.4
Return on Total Assets 46	10.3	•	32.7	15.4	18.2	15.8	23.6	19.6
Return on Equity Before Income Taxes 47	18.1	•	148.7	41.3	41.5	37.7	49.0	31.0
Return on Equity After Income Taxes 48	15.2	•	148.7	39.5	39.7	35.8	43.7	22.9
Profit Margin (Before Income Tax) 49	7.3	•	7.4	4.6	6.3	5.1	10.2	9.3
Profit Margin (After Income Tax) 50	6.1	•	7.4	4.4	6.0	4.9	9.1	6.9

Table I

Corporations with and without Net Income

CEMENT, CONCRETE, LIME AND GYPSUM PRODUCT

MONEY AMOUNTS AND SIZE OF ASSETS IN THOUSANDS OF DOLLARS

Item Description for Accounting Period 7/06 Through 6/07	Total	Zero Assets	Under 500	500 to 1,000	1,000 to 5,000	5,000 to 10,000	10,000 to 25,000	25,000 to 50,000	50,000 to 100,000	100,000 to 250,000	250,000 to 500,000	500,000 to 2,500,000	2,500,000 and over
Number of Enterprises 1	4670	7	2010	1131	921	297	152	60	30	25	8	17	11
Revenues ($ in Thousands)													
Net Sales 2	83596684	945898	1267170	1941562	5123739	4095335	4144599	3251127	3171895	4809505	3294496	13496796	38054563
Interest 3	862113	691	1706	2924	6661	4777	7099	2956	4573	12128	20445	128526	669626
Rents 4	53847	917	0	0	5152	910	4929	583	2057	694	8451	10645	19510
Royalties 5	62358	308	0	0	0	224	5	0	1966	855	15467	14787	28746
Other Portfolio Income 6	470232	2609	40420	9330	4843	6434	36594	8934	6700	9856	12528	58524	273458
Other Receipts 7	1233788	3287	5978	3276	72546	18897	42047	18415	9763	74162	123640	294601	567177
Total Receipts 8	86279022	953710	1315274	1957092	5212941	4126577	4235273	3282015	3196954	4907200	3475027	14003879	39613080
Average Total Receipts 9	18475	136244	654	1730	5660	13894	27864	54700	106565	196288	434378	823758	3601189
Operating Costs/Operating Income (%)													
Cost of Operations 10	64.0	63.5	53.9	52.2	65.8	67.0	68.9	70.4	70.5	68.3	68.9	62.1	62.4
Salaries and Wages 11	5.6	1.8	9.5	8.7	5.7	5.8	5.8	5.9	4.5	4.2	4.2	4.8	6.0
Taxes Paid 12	2.2	2.2	5.1	2.5	2.6	2.1	2.2	2.0	1.7	2.4	2.1	2.3	2.1
Interest Paid 13	3.9	2.9	1.1	3.4	1.6	1.7	1.3	1.0	0.9	1.9	1.3	2.8	6.2
Depreciation 14	4.0	6.1	3.5	3.8	3.8	4.0	3.4	3.9	4.0	4.6	4.6	4.9	3.6
Amortization and Depletion 15	1.1	0.4	0.2	0.1	0.1	0.0	0.2	0.2	0.3	0.9	1.0	2.0	1.5
Pensions and Other Deferred Comp. 16	0.7	0.6	*	0.5	0.4	0.4	0.6	0.6	0.7	0.7	0.4	0.9	0.9
Employee Benefits 17	1.7	1.9	0.4	1.0	1.8	1.0	1.3	1.3	1.5	2.5	1.1	1.7	1.8
Advertising 18	0.3	0.1	0.4	0.4	0.4	0.2	0.4	0.5	0.5	0.3	0.3	0.1	0.2
Other Expenses 19	14.4	7.2	22.5	22.6	12.4	10.2	8.9	8.0	6.0	5.2	8.8	6.3	21.0
Officers' Compensation 20	1.0	1.7	3.3	3.2	3.3	3.8	2.0	1.5	1.7	0.8	0.6	0.4	0.2
Operating Margin 21	1.1	11.6	*	1.5	2.2	3.8	5.1	4.8	7.8	8.2	6.7	11.7	*
Operating Margin Before Officers' Comp. 22	2.1	13.3	3.3	4.7	5.5	7.5	7.1	6.3	9.5	9.0	7.3	12.2	*

Selected Average Balance Sheet ($ in Thousands)

Net Receivables 23	3472	0	12	143	895	1873	3485	8274	16360	31598	50757	152421	849437
Inventories 24	1289	0	15	62	335	789	1659	4325	5979	13591	29139	65663	272505
Net Property, Plant and Equipment 25	8431	0	100	345	1050	3411	5606	15110	32585	64391	170742	494102	2062751
Total Assets 26	21781	0	189	691	2814	7272	14646	33513	70425	157696	376958	1065046	5853679
Notes and Loans Payable 27	6299	0	120	310	1323	4174	3782	10508	14732	48875	87457	258928	1672195
All Other Liabilities 28	7390	0	18	234	531	1728	3123	6010	19092	31083	85332	291036	2308242
Net Worth 29	8093	0	51	147	960	1370	7741	16994	36601	77737	204169	515081	1873242

Selected Financial Ratios (Times to 1)

Current Ratio 30	1.5	•	1.3	1.5	2.0	1.5	1.9	2.1	1.4	2.0	1.7	1.6	1.3
Quick Ratio 31	1.0	•	0.7	1.2	1.5	1.1	1.4	1.4	1.0	1.3	1.2	0.9	0.9
Net Sales to Working Capital 32	8.5	•	52.7	19.2	7.1	11.3	7.2	6.4	11.6	5.9	8.2	7.3	9.0
Coverage Ratio 33	2.1	5.3	4.3	1.7	3.5	3.6	6.5	6.7	10.0	6.3	10.1	6.5	0.7
Total Asset Turnover 34	0.8	•	3.3	2.5	2.0	1.9	1.9	1.6	1.5	1.2	1.1	0.7	0.6
Inventory Turnover 35	8.9	•	22.4	14.4	10.9	11.7	11.3	8.8	12.5	9.7	9.7	7.5	7.9
Receivables Turnover 36	5.7	•	34.3	11.1	6.1	8.0	7.9	6.4	7.3	6.9	6.5	5.6	4.8
Total Liabilities to Net Worth 37	1.7	•	2.7	3.7	1.9	4.3	0.9	1.0	0.9	1.0	0.8	1.1	2.1
Current Assets to Working Capital 38	3.1	•	4.1	3.2	2.0	2.9	2.1	1.9	3.5	2.0	2.4	2.7	3.9
Current Liabilities to Working Capital 39	2.1	•	3.1	2.2	1.0	1.9	1.1	0.9	2.5	1.0	1.4	1.7	2.9
Working Capital to Net Sales 40	0.1	•	0.0	0.1	0.1	0.1	0.1	0.2	0.1	0.2	0.1	0.1	0.1
Inventory to Working Capital 41	0.7	•	1.8	0.5	0.4	0.7	0.5	0.6	0.8	0.5	0.5	0.7	0.9
Total Receipts to Cash Flow 42	6.2	5.6	5.0	5.5	8.0	8.3	7.7	8.7	7.6	7.4	5.5	5.0	6.0
Cost of Goods to Cash Flow 43	3.9	3.6	2.7	2.9	5.3	5.6	5.3	6.1	5.4	5.1	3.8	3.1	3.7
Cash Flow to Total Debt 44	0.2	•	0.9	0.6	0.4	0.3	0.5	0.4	0.4	0.3	0.4	0.3	0.1

Selected Financial Factors (in Percentages)

Debt Ratio 45	62.8	•	73.2	78.7	65.9	81.2	47.1	49.3	48.0	50.7	45.8	51.6	68.0
Return on Total Assets 46	6.8	•	16.4	14.1	10.9	11.8	16.0	11.0	14.3	14.9	14.7	13.8	2.6
Return on Equity Before Income Taxes 47	9.7	•	46.9	26.3	22.6	45.5	25.6	18.5	24.7	25.3	24.4	24.1	•
Return on Equity After Income Taxes 48	4.0	•	44.4	23.3	21.3	42.0	22.5	15.9	22.2	20.3	16.0	16.1	•
Profit Margin (Before Income Tax) 49	4.4	12.5	3.8	2.3	3.9	4.5	7.3	5.8	8.5	10.2	12.1	15.7	•
Profit Margin (After Income Tax) 50	1.8	6.4	3.6	2.0	3.7	4.2	5.0	5.0	7.7	8.2	7.9	10.5	•

103

Table II

Corporations with Net Income

CEMENT, CONCRETE, LIME AND GYPSUM PRODUCT

MONEY AMOUNTS AND SIZE OF ASSETS IN THOUSANDS OF DOLLARS

Item Description for Accounting Period 7/06 Through 6/07	Total	Zero Assets	Under 500	500 to 1,000	1,000 to 5,000	5,000 to 10,000	10,000 to 25,000	25,000 to 50,000	50,000 to 100,000	100,000 to 250,000	250,000 to 500,000	500,000 to 2,500,000	2,500,000 and over
Number of Enterprises 1	3174	•	1135	758	816	198	136	48	•	20	8	17	•
Revenues ($ in Thousands)													
Net Sales 2	73069798	•	998874	1662780	4475005	3320136	3712826	2991671	•	3985271	3294496	13496796	•
Interest 3	766196		477	1730	4581	3928	6777	2947		11995	20445	128526	
Rents 4	52747		0	0	5152	823	4929	583		557	8451	10645	
Royalties 5	61100		0	0	0	224	5	0		757	15467	14787	
Other Portfolio Income 6	435063		40405	9329	4843	4771	36325	8354		6955	12528	58524	
Other Receipts 7	1200676		4539	1505	70643	13599	39952	17817		66259	123640	294601	
Total Receipts 8	75585580		1044295	1675344	4560224	3343481	3800814	3021372		4071794	3475027	14003879	
Average Total Receipts 9	23814		920	2210	5589	16886	27947	62945		203590	434378	823758	
Operating Costs/Operating Income (%)													
Cost of Operations 10	62.3	•	50.0	48.2	64.5	66.2	66.5	69.4	•	66.6	68.9	62.1	•
Salaries and Wages 11	5.8	•	10.6	8.9	5.8	5.5	6.2	6.0	•	4.1	4.2	4.8	•
Taxes Paid 12	2.3	•	5.8	2.1	2.7	1.9	2.3	1.9	•	2.4	2.1	2.3	•
Interest Paid 13	3.4	•	0.7	3.3	1.5	1.3	1.3	0.9	•	1.5	1.3	2.8	•
Depreciation 14	4.1	•	3.6	3.5	3.8	2.1	3.4	3.8	•	4.5	4.6	4.9	•
Amortization and Depletion 15	1.2	•	0.2	0.1	0.0	0.0	0.1	0.2	•	0.8	1.0	2.0	•
Pensions and Other Deferred Comp. 16	0.8	•	•	0.6	0.4	0.4	0.6	0.6	•	0.7	0.4	0.9	•
Employee Benefits 17	1.7	•	0.2	0.9	1.9	0.8	1.3	1.2	•	2.1	1.1	1.7	•
Advertising 18	0.2	•	0.5	0.5	0.4	0.2	0.3	0.5	•	0.3	0.3	0.1	•
Other Expenses 19	10.2	•	22.2	23.1	13.0	10.2	9.6	7.8	•	5.3	8.8	6.3	•
Officers' Compensation 20	0.9	•	2.8	3.3	3.0	4.4	2.2	1.6	•	0.6	0.6	0.4	•
Operating Margin 21	7.0	•	3.2	5.6	3.1	7.0	6.2	6.1	•	11.1	6.7	11.7	•
Operating Margin Before Officers' Comp. 22	8.0	•	6.0	8.9	6.2	11.3	8.4	7.7	•	11.7	7.3	12.2	•

Selected Average Balance Sheet ($ in Thousands)

Net Receivables 23	4773	•	2	167	943	2319	3598	9765	•	32101	50757	152421
Inventories 24	1703	•	16	67	211	1019	1622	4753	•	14786	29139	71789
Net Property, Plant and Equipment 25	10714	•	131	342	969	2525	5766	14239	•	65307	170742	494102
Total Assets 26	28425	•	224	727	2752	7270	14699	35100	•	158961	376958	1065046
Notes and Loans Payable 27	7964	•	139	225	1261	2894	3739	9631	•	39567	87457	258928
All Other Liabilities 28	9742	•	12	265	533	2077	2847	6538	•	31619	85332	291036
Net Worth 29	10719	•	73	237	957	2300	8113	18931	•	87775	204169	515081

Selected Financial Ratios (Times to 1)

Current Ratio 30	1.5	•	1.2	2.3	2.0	1.6	2.0	2.2	•	2.1	1.7	1.6
Quick Ratio 31	1.0	•	0.7	1.8	1.6	1.2	1.4	1.6	•	1.4	1.2	0.9
Net Sales to Working Capital 32	8.1	•	122.1	11.1	6.9	10.5	7.0	5.9	•	5.9	8.2	7.3
Coverage Ratio 33	4.1	•	11.3	2.9	4.4	7.0	7.5	8.8	•	9.6	10.1	6.5
Total Asset Turnover 34	0.8	•	3.9	3.0	2.0	2.3	1.9	1.8	•	1.3	1.1	0.7
Inventory Turnover 35	8.4	•	26.7	15.7	16.7	10.9	11.2	9.1	•	9.0	9.7	6.9
Receivables Turnover 36	5.4	•	47.3	•	7.1	7.4	7.8	6.1	•	•	6.5	•
Total Liabilities to Net Worth 37	1.7	•	2.1	2.1	1.9	2.2	0.8	0.9	•	0.8	0.8	1.1
Current Assets to Working Capital 38	3.0	•	6.5	1.8	2.0	2.7	2.0	1.8	•	1.9	2.4	2.7
Current Liabilities to Working Capital 39	2.0	•	5.5	0.8	1.0	1.7	1.0	0.8	•	0.9	1.4	1.7
Working Capital to Net Sales 40	0.1	•	0.0	0.1	0.1	0.1	0.1	0.2	•	0.2	0.1	0.1
Inventory to Working Capital 41	0.7	•	2.3	0.3	0.3	0.6	0.4	0.5	•	0.4	0.5	0.7
Total Receipts to Cash Flow 42	5.5	•	4.4	4.4	7.1	6.6	6.9	7.9	•	6.1	5.5	5.0
Cost of Goods to Cash Flow 43	3.5	•	2.2	2.1	4.6	4.4	4.6	5.5	•	4.0	3.8	3.1
Cash Flow to Total Debt 44	0.2	•	1.3	1.0	0.4	0.5	0.6	0.5	•	0.5	0.4	0.3

Selected Financial Factors (in Percentages)

Debt Ratio 45	62.3	•	67.4	67.4	65.2	68.4	44.8	46.1	•	44.8	45.8	51.6
Return on Total Assets 46	11.2	•	33.3	29.1	13.0	20.6	18.3	14.3	•	18.6	14.7	13.8
Return on Equity Before Income Taxes 47	22.6	•	93.2	58.2	28.9	55.9	28.8	23.5	•	30.2	24.4	24.1
Return on Equity After Income Taxes 48	16.3	•	90.1	55.4	27.4	52.8	25.4	20.6	•	24.6	16.0	16.1
Profit Margin (Before Income Tax) 49	10.5	•	7.7	6.3	5.0	7.7	8.5	7.1	•	13.3	12.1	15.7
Profit Margin (After Income Tax) 50	7.6	•	7.5	6.0	4.8	7.2	7.6	6.3	•	10.8	7.9	10.5

Table I

Corporations with and without Net Income

IRON, STEEL MILLS AND STEEL PRODUCT

MONEY AMOUNTS AND SIZE OF ASSETS IN THOUSANDS OF DOLLARS

Item Description for Accounting Period 7/06 Through 6/07	Total	Zero Assets	Under 500	500 to 1,000	1,000 to 5,000	5,000 to 10,000	10,000 to 25,000	25,000 to 50,000	50,000 to 100,000	100,000 to 250,000	250,000 to 500,000	500,000 to 2,500,000	2,500,000 and over
Number of Enterprises 1	4008	382	2203	164	608	294	167	56	48	44	12	21	8
Revenues ($ in Thousands)													
Net Sales 2	137379723	1328151	2066965	227350	3889653	3741427	5707495	3702927	4917225	11319710	7072961	38954206	54441653
Interest 3	766959	6051	0	827	1842	1601	3062	1428	17509	78653	32981	163180	459826
Rents 4	52274	8	0	138	0	3	2747	731	1720	10195	387	13546	22800
Royalties 5	436522	0	0	0	0	0	0	121	6186	21815	3249	260389	144763
Other Portfolio Income 6	1639255	10325	35116	1494	3949	24225	19530	2478	21763	9554	1108869	294419	107533
Other Receipts 7	1812990	5898	6114	247	22967	38005	25903	16967	55167	89635	54655	892457	604971
Total Receipts 8	142087723	1350433	2108195	230056	3928411	3805261	5758737	3724652	5019570	11529562	8273102	40578197	55781546
Average Total Receipts 9	35451	3535	957	1403	6461	12943	34483	66512	104574	262036	689425	1932295	6972693
Operating Costs/Operating Income (%)													
Cost of Operations 10	76.5	78.7	69.6	66.3	77.1	76.3	78.9	79.0	80.2	79.9	82.4	77.3	74.0
Salaries and Wages 11	2.9	1.6	10.0	1.3	4.9	4.3	3.7	2.8	3.1	3.3	2.1	3.3	2.1
Taxes Paid 12	1.3	1.2	2.2	3.2	1.3	1.6	1.3	1.1	1.4	1.4	0.8	1.1	1.4
Interest Paid 13	1.3	2.6	0.4	0.1	0.6	0.7	0.9	1.1	1.7	1.8	1.2	1.1	1.5
Depreciation 14	1.9	1.4	1.3	4.9	0.9	2.0	1.5	1.8	2.0	1.6	1.2	1.4	2.5
Amortization and Depletion 15	0.4	1.7	0.1	0.1	0.0	0.0	0.1	0.1	0.3	0.1	1.9	0.3	0.4
Pensions and Other Deferred Comp. 16	1.2	0.2	0.1	0.6	0.3	0.9	0.6	0.5	0.5	0.7	0.7	0.7	2.0
Employee Benefits 17	1.6	1.3	0.7	3.3	0.7	1.1	1.5	1.5	1.4	1.2	1.0	1.2	2.2
Advertising 18	0.1	0.0	0.2	0.3	0.2	0.2	0.1	0.3	0.1	0.2	0.0	0.1	0.0
Other Expenses 19	6.1	4.9	12.5	13.7	4.2	4.3	4.4	4.7	4.4	5.0	3.2	6.3	7.1
Officers' Compensation 20	0.7	1.1	2.1	6.6	4.9	2.0	2.0	1.7	1.0	0.7	0.4	0.3	0.4
Operating Margin 21	5.9	5.2	0.9	•	5.0	6.6	4.8	5.5	3.7	4.2	5.1	6.8	6.3
Operating Margin Before Officers' Comp. 22	6.6	6.3	3.0	6.2	10.0	8.7	6.8	7.2	4.8	4.8	5.5	7.1	6.7

Selected Average Balance Sheet ($ in Thousands)

Net Receivables **23**	3895	0	56	133	611	1602	4565	9289	12316	30299	72784	205334	778879
Inventories **24**	4398	0	18	197	586	1299	3650	8816	15829	42014	91700	271868	786776
Net Property, Plant and Equipment **25**	7292	0	33	136	272	1961	3637	10426	18356	41643	69723	339040	2066232
Total Assets **26**	24586	0	171	686	1998	6887	15764	34642	68318	162906	337330	1229510	6240528
Notes and Loans Payable **27**	5134	0	107	45	1193	1409	4276	12756	23815	51462	73479	198057	1164641
All Other Liabilities **28**	8820	0	56	96	481	1607	4900	9803	26999	41239	128256	438401	2403160
Net Worth **29**	10632	0	9	544	324	3871	6588	12083	17504	70206	135594	593052	2672727

Selected Financial Ratios (Times to 1)

Current Ratio **30**	2.0	•	2.0	3.8	2.4	2.2	1.7	1.3	1.4	2.0	2.1	2.1	2.0
Quick Ratio **31**	0.9	•	1.7	2.5	1.3	1.3	0.9	0.7	0.6	0.9	1.0	1.0	1.0
Net Sales to Working Capital **32**	5.9	•	14.6	5.0	6.5	5.0	8.2	15.2	9.7	5.2	5.4	5.6	5.5
Coverage Ratio **33**	8.0	3.7	7.3	6.3	10.8	13.1	7.0	6.4	4.4	4.4	19.2	10.6	6.8
Total Asset Turnover **34**	1.4	•	5.5	2.0	3.2	1.8	2.2	1.9	1.5	1.6	1.7	1.5	1.1
Inventory Turnover **35**	6.0	•	35.8	4.7	8.4	7.5	7.4	5.9	5.2	4.9	5.3	5.3	6.4
Receivables Turnover **36**	9.2	•	12.4	4.8	12.1	9.6	8.1	7.0	8.2	8.7	8.7	8.7	9.9
Total Liabilities to Net Worth **37**	1.3	•	18.6	0.3	5.2	0.8	1.4	1.9	2.9	1.3	1.5	1.1	1.3
Current Assets to Working Capital **38**	2.1	•	2.0	1.4	1.7	1.8	2.5	4.6	3.6	2.0	1.9	1.9	2.0
Current Liabilities to Working Capital **39**	1.1	•	1.0	0.4	0.7	0.8	1.5	3.6	2.6	1.0	0.9	0.9	1.0
Working Capital to Net Sales **40**	0.2	•	0.1	0.2	0.2	0.2	0.1	0.1	0.1	0.2	0.2	0.2	0.2
Inventory to Working Capital **41**	0.8	•	0.2	0.4	0.7	0.7	1.0	1.8	1.7	0.9	0.9	0.9	0.7
Total Receipts to Cash Flow **42**	7.5	9.1	9.4	10.3	12.3	9.2	11.9	10.3	10.9	10.1	4.1	6.3	7.9
Cost of Goods to Cash Flow **43**	5.7	7.2	6.6	6.8	9.5	7.0	9.4	8.2	8.8	8.0	3.4	4.9	5.8
Cash Flow to Total Debt **44**	0.3	•	0.6	1.0	0.3	0.5	0.3	0.3	0.2	0.3	0.7	0.5	0.2

Selected Financial Factors (in Percentages)

Debt Ratio **45**	56.8	•	94.9	20.7	83.8	43.8	58.2	65.1	74.4	56.9	59.8	51.8	57.2
Return on Total Assets **46**	14.8	•	18.1	1.7	20.4	16.7	14.4	13.8	11.0	12.3	40.6	18.2	11.1
Return on Equity Before Income Taxes **47**	29.9	•	306.2	1.9	114.1	27.4	29.6	33.5	33.0	22.1	95.7	34.1	22.1
Return on Equity After Income Taxes **48**	21.6	•	304.5	1.2	109.0	25.6	26.3	30.3	24.9	15.8	83.5	23.5	14.5
Profit Margin (Before Income Tax) **49**	9.3	6.9	2.9	0.7	5.8	8.3	5.7	6.1	5.6	6.0	22.0	10.9	8.7
Profit Margin (After Income Tax) **50**	6.7	4.5	2.8	0.5	5.5	7.8	5.1	5.5	4.2	4.3	19.2	7.5	5.7

Table II
Corporations with Net Income

IRON, STEEL MILLS AND STEEL PRODUCT

MONEY AMOUNTS AND SIZE OF ASSETS IN THOUSANDS OF DOLLARS

Item Description for Accounting Period 7/06 Through 6/07	Total	Zero Assets	Under 500	500 to 1,000	1,000 to 5,000	5,000 to 10,000	10,000 to 25,000	25,000 to 50,000	50,000 to 100,000	100,000 to 250,000	250,000 to 500,000	500,000 to 2,500,000	2,500,000 and over
1 Number of Enterprises	3048	7	1883	110	498	248	144	47	35	37	•	21	•
Revenues ($ in Thousands)													
2 Net Sales	126499700	1030118	1956247	115653	3479105	3672347	5286116	3143737	3842271	9948808	•	38954206	•
3 Interest	703878	6050	0	821	1712	1575	2941	1427	11404	66047	•	163180	•
4 Rents	51126	8	0	138	0	0	2747	731	1668	9273	•	13546	•
5 Royalties	433866	0	0	0	0	0	0	0	6186	21133	•	260389	•
6 Other Portfolio Income	1631131	10100	35116	1494	3876	24225	19489	2376	21070	7882	•	294419	•
7 Other Receipts	1834980	5036	6114	31	3799	37871	25461	16218	47566	84747	•	892457	•
8 Total Receipts	131154681	1051312	1997477	118137	3488492	3736018	5336754	3164489	3930165	10137890	•	40578197	•
9 Average Total Receipts	43030	150187	1061	1074	7005	15065	37061	67330	112290	273997	•	1932295	•
Operating Costs/Operating Income (%)													
10 Cost of Operations	75.8	79.9	69.1	61.5	76.2	76.4	78.6	76.7	79.6	79.7	•	77.3	•
11 Salaries and Wages	3.0	0.9	10.5	1.3	4.5	4.4	3.6	2.9	2.5	3.1	•	3.3	•
12 Taxes Paid	1.4	1.0	2.2	3.7	1.3	1.6	1.3	1.1	1.5	1.5	•	1.1	•
13 Interest Paid	1.2	1.8	0.3	0.2	0.6	0.6	0.7	1.2	1.4	1.4	•	1.1	•
14 Depreciation	1.8	0.9	1.2	8.5	0.6	1.3	1.4	1.7	1.8	1.5	•	1.4	•
15 Amortization and Depletion	0.4	2.0	0.1	0.1	0.0	0.0	0.0	0.1	0.2	0.1	•	0.3	•
16 Pensions and Other Deferred Comp.	1.0	0.0	0.1	0.6	0.3	0.9	0.6	0.5	0.5	0.5	•	0.7	•
17 Employee Benefits	1.5	0.6	0.6	3.6	0.6	1.1	1.3	1.5	1.4	1.0	•	1.2	•
18 Advertising	0.1	0.0	0.2	0.2	0.2	0.2	0.1	0.3	0.1	0.2	•	0.1	•
19 Other Expenses	6.3	2.9	12.2	13.6	3.9	3.9	4.2	5.1	3.6	4.3	•	6.3	•
20 Officers' Compensation	0.7	0.3	2.3	3.3	4.5	2.1	2.0	1.8	1.2	0.7	•	0.3	•
21 Operating Margin	6.8	9.7	1.2	3.3	7.2	7.6	6.1	7.0	6.4	5.9	•	6.8	•
22 Operating Margin Before Officers' Comp.	7.5	10.1	3.5	6.6	11.7	9.7	8.1	8.8	7.5	6.6	•	7.1	•

Selected Average Balance Sheet ($ in Thousands)

Net Receivables 23	4883	0	60	56	558	1806	4744	9089	13653	30973	205334	•
Inventories 24	5314	0	7	162	521	1326	3682	9721	18584	42796	259977	•
Net Property, Plant and Equipment 25	8547	0	37	190	233	1489	3791	10007	17806	42141	339040	•
Total Assets 26	29347	0	182	680	1901	6719	16120	34916	69879	161167	1229510	•
Notes and Loans Payable 27	5828	0	107	41	1221	1084	3942	12123	21337	47400	198057	•
All Other Liabilities 28	9854	0	65	38	454	1549	5028	10412	23301	37986	438401	•
Net Worth 29	13665	0	10	600	225	4085	7149	12382	25241	75780	593052	•

Selected Financial Ratios (Times to 1)

Current Ratio 30	2.0	•	1.8	6.6	2.7	2.9	1.7	1.5	1.7	2.1	2.1	•
Quick Ratio 31	1.0	•	1.7	5.2	1.3	1.8	1.0	0.8	0.7	1.0	1.0	•
Net Sales to Working Capital 32	5.7	•	17.5	4.8	6.9	4.6	7.9	9.6	6.6	5.1	5.6	•
Coverage Ratio 33	9.4	7.7	11.3	24.5	13.4	17.1	10.4	7.3	6.9	6.5	10.6	•
Total Asset Turnover 34	1.4	•	5.7	1.5	3.7	2.2	2.3	1.9	1.6	1.7	1.5	•
Inventory Turnover 35	5.9	•	98.9	4.0	10.2	8.5	7.8	5.3	4.7	5.0	5.5	•
Receivables Turnover 36	9.1	•	•	4.0	13.7	9.9	8.6	7.2	7.4	8.9	9.1	•
Total Liabilities to Net Worth 37	1.1	•	18.1	0.1	7.4	0.6	1.3	1.8	1.8	1.1	1.1	•
Current Assets to Working Capital 38	2.0	•	2.3	1.2	1.6	1.5	2.3	3.0	2.4	1.9	1.9	•
Current Liabilities to Working Capital 39	1.0	•	1.3	0.2	0.6	0.5	1.3	2.0	1.4	0.9	0.9	•
Working Capital to Net Sales 40	0.2	•	0.1	0.2	0.1	0.2	0.1	0.1	0.2	0.2	0.2	•
Inventory to Working Capital 41	0.8	•	0.1	0.2	0.7	0.5	0.9	1.3	1.2	0.8	0.9	•
Total Receipts to Cash Flow 42	6.9	7.0	9.2	6.8	10.3	8.5	10.5	8.6	8.9	9.1	6.3	•
Cost of Goods to Cash Flow 43	5.2	5.6	6.4	4.2	7.8	6.5	8.3	6.6	7.1	7.3	4.9	•
Cash Flow to Total Debt 44	0.4	•	0.7	1.9	0.4	0.7	0.4	0.3	0.3	0.3	0.5	•

Selected Financial Factors (in Percentages)

Debt Ratio 45	53.4	•	94.8	11.7	88.1	39.2	55.6	64.5	63.9	53.0	51.8	•
Return on Total Assets 46	16.4	•	21.0	8.7	29.6	21.8	17.7	17.1	15.4	15.4	18.2	•
Return on Equity Before Income Taxes 47	31.5	•	364.3	9.5	230.9	33.8	36.2	41.6	36.6	27.8	34.1	•
Return on Equity After Income Taxes 48	23.1	•	362.4	8.7	222.0	31.8	32.6	37.9	28.8	20.8	23.5	•
Profit Margin (Before Income Tax) 49	10.4	11.8	3.3	5.4	7.4	9.3	7.0	7.7	8.4	7.8	10.9	•
Profit Margin (After Income Tax) 50	7.6	8.7	3.3	4.9	7.2	8.8	6.4	7.0	6.6	5.9	7.5	•

Table I

Corporations with and without Net Income

NONFERROUS METAL PRODUCTION AND PROCESSING

MONEY AMOUNTS AND SIZE OF ASSETS IN THOUSANDS OF DOLLARS

Item Description for Accounting Period 7/06 Through 6/07		Total	Zero Assets	Under 500	500 to 1,000	1,000 to 5,000	5,000 to 10,000	10,000 to 25,000	25,000 to 50,000	50,000 to 100,000	100,000 to 250,000	250,000 to 500,000	500,000 to 2,500,000	2,500,000 and over
Number of Enterprises	1	1359	378	384	0	286	74	83	65	38	14	13	19	4
Revenues ($ in Thousands)														
Net Sales	2	103536005	1336925	544305	0	2155405	2155701	4089818	5686700	5252415	3978923	6565034	34461287	37309492
Interest	3	1755286	13232	1272	0	1698	92	687	3319	11479	8262	59536	189862	1465847
Rents	4	557988	17	0	0	6461	0	1987	341	278	30	40	18723	530112
Royalties	5	109680	149	0	0	0	0	316	5853	538	0	1317	25934	75573
Other Portfolio Income	6	1681604	39556	17744	0	3001	3	1529	23194	20282	1231	20080	169902	1385083
Other Receipts	7	1442339	10907	31	0	258	-29965	9186	42647	50181	357825	162180	241969	597119
Total Receipts	8	109082902	1400786	563352	0	2166823	2125831	4103523	5762054	5335173	4346271	6808187	35107677	41363226
Average Total Receipts	9	80267	3706	1467	•	7576	28727	49440	88647	140399	310448	523707	1847772	10340806
Operating Costs/Operating Income (%)														
Cost of Operations	10	83.7	87.8	54.6	•	80.1	88.8	86.2	81.2	83.7	80.8	89.1	84.6	82.5
Salaries and Wages	11	2.8	2.9	13.3	•	2.4	1.1	2.3	3.7	2.7	3.9	1.4	2.9	2.7
Taxes Paid	12	0.8	0.9	2.6	•	0.9	0.5	1.0	1.2	0.9	0.7	0.8	0.8	0.6
Interest Paid	13	2.9	3.1	0.2	•	0.2	0.8	0.7	1.2	1.2	1.9	1.7	1.7	5.3
Depreciation	14	1.5	1.3	0.7	•	1.9	0.6	0.8	1.6	1.3	2.0	1.1	1.3	1.8
Amortization and Depletion	15	0.7	0.5	0.0	•	0.0	0.1	0.0	0.2	0.1	0.1	0.2	0.2	1.6
Pensions and Other Deferred Comp.	16	0.9	0.2	0.1	•	0.4	0.3	0.3	0.4	0.4	0.1	0.3	2.2	0.3
Employee Benefits	17	0.9	0.7	1.0	•	0.5	0.4	1.1	1.1	0.8	2.3	1.0	0.8	1.0
Advertising	18	0.1	0.1	3.2	•	0.1	0.0	0.1	0.1	0.0	0.0	0.0	0.1	0.2
Other Expenses	19	5.0	8.9	14.2	•	6.0	1.7	3.0	4.9	4.7	9.3	3.7	4.3	5.5
Officers' Compensation	20	0.4	0.2	5.9	•	0.3	0.6	1.0	1.7	1.0	0.3	0.4	0.4	0.0
Operating Margin	21	0.3	•	4.3	•	7.1	5.1	3.5	2.8	3.0	•	0.2	0.8	•
Operating Margin Before Officers' Comp.	22	0.7	•	10.2	•	7.4	5.7	4.5	4.5	4.0	•	0.6	1.2	•

Selected Average Balance Sheet ($ in Thousands)

	C1	C2	C3	C4	C5	C6	C7	C8	C9	C10	C11	C12	C13
Net Receivables 23	34985	0	43	•	629	1925	6452	11027	18462	36572	70120	216703	9927888
Inventories 24	6159	0	2	•	765	1394	4403	9627	13509	30140	74706	148495	580874
Net Property, Plant and Equipment 25	13859	0	27	•	516	1324	3732	8795	14977	42514	100162	214502	2788718
Total Assets 26	111279	0	215	•	2209	6196	16585	37084	68838	159501	372264	1026881	29267118
Notes and Loans Payable 27	31575	0	68	•	1346	2680	4802	13419	21250	31207	111387	424240	7569442
All Other Liabilities 28	32292	0	55	•	591	2136	5834	12156	18039	56241	127769	283341	8436314
Net Worth 29	47411	0	92	•	273	1379	5949	11508	29548	72052	133108	319301	13261362

Selected Financial Ratios (Times to 1)

	C1	C2	C3	C4	C5	C6	C7	C8	C9	C10	C11	C12	C13
Current Ratio 30	1.1	•	2.4	•	2.1	1.4	1.8	1.5	1.9	1.7	1.4	1.8	1.0
Quick Ratio 31	0.9	•	2.3	•	1.2	0.7	1.1	0.8	1.1	0.9	0.6	1.0	0.9
Net Sales to Working Capital 32	13.3	•	13.8	•	8.8	22.7	9.1	9.8	6.9	8.4	10.8	8.6	65.1
Coverage Ratio 33	3.3	•	46.4	0.4	32.0	5.6	6.8	4.4	4.8	5.0	3.3	2.6	3.2
Total Asset Turnover 34	0.7	•	6.6	•	3.4	4.7	3.0	2.4	2.0	1.8	1.4	1.8	0.3
Inventory Turnover 35	10.4	•	372.5	•	7.9	18.6	9.6	7.4	8.6	7.6	6.0	10.3	13.2
Receivables Turnover 36	2.4	•	26.1	•	10.3	21.4	8.1	9.4	8.6	7.3	7.2	8.9	1.0
Total Liabilities to Net Worth 37	1.3	•	1.3	•	7.1	3.5	1.8	2.2	1.3	1.2	1.8	2.2	1.2
Current Assets to Working Capital 38	8.1	•	1.7	•	1.9	3.7	2.3	2.9	2.1	2.4	3.7	2.3	78.8
Current Liabilities to Working Capital 39	7.1	•	0.7	•	0.9	2.7	1.3	1.9	1.1	1.4	2.7	1.3	77.8
Working Capital to Net Sales 40	0.1	•	0.1	•	0.1	0.0	0.1	0.1	0.1	0.1	0.1	0.1	0.0
Inventory to Working Capital 41	1.2	•	0.0	•	0.7	1.7	0.8	1.3	0.8	0.8	1.7	0.8	4.7
Total Receipts to Cash Flow 42	11.1	•	5.7	223.5	8.7	20.7	16.6	13.0	12.1	6.4	14.6	16.8	8.1
Cost of Goods to Cash Flow 43	9.3	•	3.1	196.2	7.0	18.4	14.3	10.5	10.2	5.2	13.0	14.2	6.6
Cash Flow to Total Debt 44	0.1	•	2.0	•	0.4	0.3	0.3	0.3	0.3	0.5	0.1	0.2	0.1

Selected Financial Factors (in Percentages)

	C1	C2	C3	C4	C5	C6	C7	C8	C9	C10	C11	C12	C13
Debt Ratio 45	57.4	•	57.1	•	87.6	77.7	64.1	69.0	57.1	54.8	64.2	68.9	54.7
Return on Total Assets 46	6.4	•	52.6	•	26.8	21.5	13.3	12.7	11.7	17.4	7.7	8.0	5.4
Return on Equity Before Income Taxes 47	10.4	•	120.0	•	210.5	79.4	31.5	31.6	21.5	30.8	15.0	15.9	8.1
Return on Equity After Income Taxes 48	7.1	•	101.0	•	208.7	73.7	29.6	27.4	16.1	22.0	8.1	10.6	5.3
Profit Margin (Before Income Tax) 49	6.5	•	7.8	•	7.6	3.8	3.8	4.2	4.6	7.8	3.9	2.8	11.5
Profit Margin (After Income Tax) 50	4.4	•	6.6	•	7.6	3.5	3.6	3.6	3.4	5.6	2.1	1.9	7.6

Table II

Corporations with Net Income

NONFERROUS METAL PRODUCTION AND PROCESSING

MONEY AMOUNTS AND SIZE OF ASSETS IN THOUSANDS OF DOLLARS

Item Description for Accounting Period 7/06 Through 6/07	Total	Zero Assets	Under 500	500 to 1,000	1,000 to 5,000	5,000 to 10,000	10,000 to 25,000	25,000 to 50,000	50,000 to 100,000	100,000 to 250,000	250,000 to 500,000	500,000 to 2,500,000	2,500,000 and over
Number of Enterprises **1**	847	•	299	0	•	65	73	•	31	11	8	15	4

Revenues ($ in Thousands)

	Total	Zero Assets	Under 500	500 to 1,000	1,000 to 5,000	5,000 to 10,000	10,000 to 25,000	25,000 to 50,000	50,000 to 100,000	100,000 to 250,000	250,000 to 500,000	500,000 to 2,500,000	2,500,000 and over
Net Sales **2**	90241044	•	447600	0	•	2152806	3355919	•	4618599	3556236	5208513	25499677	37309492
Interest **3**	1693936	•	1271	0	•	64	487	•	9865	7733	58086	133494	1465847
Rents **4**	540785	•	0	0	•	0	0	•	273	30	39	3513	530112
Royalties **5**	109333	•	0	0	•	0	0	•	538	0	1317	25934	75573
Other Portfolio Income **6**	1653724	•	17744	0	•	3	263	•	19761	1132	8370	157733	1385083
Other Receipts **7**	924497	•	31	0	•	-30001	5467	•	39486	57045	147810	63672	597119
Total Receipts **8**	95163319	•	466646	0	•	2122872	3362136	•	4688522	3622176	5424135	25884023	41363226
Average Total Receipts **9**	112353	•	1561	•	•	32660	46057	•	151243	329289	678017	1725602	10340806

Operating Costs/Operating Income (%)

	Total	Zero Assets	Under 500	500 to 1,000	1,000 to 5,000	5,000 to 10,000	10,000 to 25,000	25,000 to 50,000	50,000 to 100,000	100,000 to 250,000	250,000 to 500,000	500,000 to 2,500,000	2,500,000 and over
Cost of Operations **10**	82.6	•	55.9	•	•	88.8	84.6	•	83.4	81.2	87.7	82.0	82.5
Salaries and Wages **11**	2.7	•	10.7	•	•	1.0	2.5	•	2.5	2.3	1.3	2.8	2.7
Taxes Paid **12**	0.8	•	3.1	•	•	0.5	1.0	•	0.8	0.6	0.8	0.9	0.6
Interest Paid **13**	3.0	•	0.1	•	•	0.8	0.6	•	1.2	1.6	1.5	1.7	5.3
Depreciation **14**	1.5	•	0.5	•	•	0.6	0.9	•	1.1	1.7	0.9	1.4	1.8
Amortization and Depletion **15**	0.8	•	0.0	•	•	0.1	0.0	•	0.1	0.1	0.1	0.2	1.6
Pensions and Other Deferred Comp. **16**	0.3	•	0.1	•	•	0.3	0.3	•	0.5	0.0	0.2	0.3	0.3
Employee Benefits **17**	0.9	•	1.2	•	•	0.4	0.9	•	0.6	1.4	1.0	0.9	1.0
Advertising **18**	0.1	•	3.5	•	•	0.0	0.1	•	0.0	0.0	0.0	0.1	0.2
Other Expenses **19**	4.5	•	9.9	•	•	1.6	3.1	•	3.8	3.7	2.9	3.7	5.5
Officers' Compensation **20**	0.4	•	7.2	•	•	0.5	1.0	•	1.1	0.3	0.3	0.4	0.0
Operating Margin **21**	2.5	•	7.9	•	•	5.5	5.1	•	5.0	7.1	3.3	5.6	•
Operating Margin Before Officers' Comp. **22**	2.9	•	15.0	•	•	6.0	6.0	•	6.0	7.4	3.6	6.0	•

Selected Average Balance Sheet ($ in Thousands)

Net Receivables 23	54488	31	2154	6431	19442	38982	81883	223120	9927888
Inventories 24	8524	3	1292	4049	16100	29420	94206	179705	580874
Net Property, Plant and Equipment 25	19856	18	1281	3798	13375	44542	96069	202403	2788718
Total Assets 26	170605	241	6207	16177	67560	157792	361988	1097141	2926718
Notes and Loans Payable 27	47219	31	2385	4691	20648	25553	91031	431976	7569442
All Other Liabilities 28	48315	46	2225	4525	17625	44442	134771	258622	8436314
Net Worth 29	75071	164	1596	6960	29287	87797	136185	406543	13261362

Selected Financial Ratios (Times to 1)

Current Ratio 30	1.1	4.3	1.3	2.2	2.0	2.1	1.3	2.2	1.0
Quick Ratio 31	0.9	4.3	0.7	1.4	1.2	1.2	0.6	1.2	0.9
Net Sales to Working Capital 32	11.7	9.6	31.9	7.1	6.6	7.1	14.1	6.2	65.1
Coverage Ratio 33	3.9	99.1	6.0	10.1	6.5	6.6	6.0	5.3	3.2
Total Asset Turnover 34	0.6	6.2	5.3	2.8	2.2	2.0	1.8	1.5	0.3
Inventory Turnover 35	10.3	310.7	22.8	9.6	7.7	8.9	6.1	7.8	13.2
Receivables Turnover 36	2.1	•	21.8	7.6	•	•	•	8.2	1.0
Total Liabilities to Net Worth 37	1.3	0.5	2.9	1.3	1.3	0.8	1.7	1.7	1.2
Current Assets to Working Capital 38	7.7	1.3	4.6	1.9	2.0	1.9	4.6	1.8	78.8
Current Liabilities to Working Capital 39	6.7	0.3	3.6	0.9	1.0	0.9	3.6	0.8	77.8
Working Capital to Net Sales 40	0.1	0.1	0.0	0.1	0.2	0.1	0.1	0.2	0.0
Inventory to Working Capital 41	1.1	0.0	1.9	0.6	0.7	0.6	2.1	0.7	4.7
Total Receipts to Cash Flow 42	9.3	5.5	19.6	13.4	10.9	8.4	10.4	10.4	8.1
Cost of Goods to Cash Flow 43	7.7	3.1	17.4	11.3	9.1	6.8	9.2	8.5	6.6
Cash Flow to Total Debt 44	0.1	3.5	0.4	0.4	0.4	0.6	0.3	0.2	0.1

Selected Financial Factors (in Percentages)

Debt Ratio 45	56.0	31.8	74.3	57.0	56.6	44.4	62.4	62.9	54.7
Return on Total Assets 46	7.4	76.1	26.1	16.5	16.8	21.7	16.1	13.7	5.4
Return on Equity Before Income Taxes 47	12.6	110.5	84.7	34.6	32.8	33.1	35.5	30.1	8.1
Return on Equity After Income Taxes 48	9.2	96.8	79.0	33.1	26.2	23.9	24.6	24.9	5.3
Profit Margin (Before Income Tax) 49	8.8	12.1	4.1	5.2	6.5	9.0	7.4	7.2	11.5
Profit Margin (After Income Tax) 50	6.5	10.6	3.8	5.0	5.1	6.5	5.1	6.0	7.6

Table I

Corporations with and without Net Income

FOUNDRIES

MONEY AMOUNTS AND SIZE OF ASSETS IN THOUSANDS OF DOLLARS

Item Description for Accounting Period 7/06 Through 6/07	Total	Zero Assets	Under 500	500 to 1,000	1,000 to 5,000	5,000 to 10,000	10,000 to 25,000	25,000 to 50,000	50,000 to 100,000	100,000 to 250,000	250,000 to 500,000	500,000 to 2,500,000	2,500,000 and over
Number of Enterprises **1**	1545	4	1073	0	265	108	45	17	14	4	9	5	0
Revenues ($ in Thousands)													
Net Sales **2**	27565768	160416	1073122	0	2142575	1492525	1139707	1155542	1631752	732772	5095458	12941899	0
Interest **3**	27066	23	68	0	1452	773	965	234	2242	1214	17787	2308	0
Rents **4**	3299	0	0	0	677	114	1252	14	209	0	197	836	0
Royalties **5**	20803	0	0	0	0	0	0	5	210	0	18160	2428	0
Other Portfolio Income **6**	94288	0	0	0	9221	100	388	7577	3530	1165	21865	50442	0
Other Receipts **7**	249716	649	-4585	0	53741	16183	4272	4519	7415	-183	65456	102250	0
Total Receipts **8**	27960940	161088	1068605	0	2207666	1509695	1146584	1167891	1645358	734968	5218923	13100163	0
Average Total Receipts **9**	18098	40272	996	•	8331	13979	25480	68699	117526	183742	579880	2620033	•
Operating Costs/Operating Income (%)													
Cost of Operations **10**	75.8	78.0	65.1	•	71.9	74.5	72.2	78.7	78.1	75.3	81.1	75.1	•
Salaries and Wages **11**	4.6	3.6	6.1	•	5.0	3.8	4.7	2.7	4.5	3.5	5.1	4.5	•
Taxes Paid **12**	1.6	1.4	2.4	•	2.6	2.4	2.2	1.7	1.7	1.3	1.3	1.3	•
Interest Paid **13**	2.0	4.0	0.6	•	0.6	1.4	1.0	1.4	1.8	4.2	2.4	2.3	•
Depreciation **14**	2.2	2.0	1.6	•	1.7	2.2	3.0	2.3	2.7	3.2	3.2	1.8	•
Amortization and Depletion **15**	0.2	0.0	0.2	•	0.0	0.1	0.0	0.0	0.1	0.4	0.5	0.2	•
Pensions and Other Deferred Comp. **16**	0.7	1.4	0.0	•	0.2	0.7	0.8	0.5	0.5	0.7	0.9	0.8	•
Employee Benefits **17**	2.1	1.4	0.5	•	2.8	2.3	1.7	1.5	0.8	2.2	2.6	2.1	•
Advertising **18**	0.1	0.0	0.1	•	0.1	0.2	0.1	0.0	0.3	0.0	0.1	0.1	•
Other Expenses **19**	4.8	5.9	9.3	•	11.8	4.2	5.2	2.8	5.5	3.8	3.5	3.9	•
Officers' Compensation **20**	1.6	0.7	4.9	•	5.1	1.8	2.5	1.7	1.0	0.2	0.4	1.2	•
Operating Margin **21**	4.4	1.4	9.0	•	•	6.4	6.6	6.7	2.9	5.1	•	6.7	•
Operating Margin Before Officers' Comp. **22**	6.0	2.1	14.0	•	3.3	8.2	9.1	8.4	3.9	5.4	•	8.0	•

Selected Average Balance Sheet ($ in Thousands)

Net Receivables **23**	2235	0	108	•	1194	2033	3420	9109	14174	28978	69021	311330
Inventories **24**	1837	0	40	•	664	1058	2120	7995	11878	18920	48168	319165
Net Property, Plant and Equipment **25**	3104	0	137	•	735	2499	5481	11639	27267	70108	103739	428798
Total Assets **26**	14352	0	335	1.4	3128	7010	14037	33200	73587	183524	363172	2799696
Notes and Loans Payable **27**	4489	0	157	•	621	3016	4149	10944	24063	81942	135317	804444
All Other Liabilities **28**	3454	0	65	•	1226	1811	3010	8719	19449	48042	100539	618621
Net Worth **29**	6408	0	114	•	1280	2183	6877	13537	30075	53539	127316	1376631

Selected Financial Ratios (Times to 1)

Current Ratio **30**	1.5	•	2.6	•	1.4	2.3	1.7	1.7	1.9	1.3	2.0	1.3
Quick Ratio **31**	0.8	•	2.0	•	0.8	1.5	1.0	0.9	1.1	0.7	1.3	0.6
Net Sales to Working Capital **32**	9.8	•	9.6	•	14.5	6.0	8.7	8.2	6.2	11.7	7.3	13.0
Coverage Ratio **33**	3.9	1.4	15.6	•	3.1	6.4	8.1	6.8	3.0	2.3	1.5	4.6
Total Asset Turnover **34**	1.2	•	3.0	•	2.6	2.0	1.8	2.0	1.6	1.0	1.6	0.9
Inventory Turnover **35**	7.4	•	16.2	•	8.8	9.7	8.6	6.7	7.7	7.3	9.5	6.1
Receivables Turnover **36**	8.3	•	10.9	•	7.1	8.8	7.4	6.8	9.5	6.8	7.6	8.9
Total Liabilities to Net Worth **37**	1.2	•	1.9	•	1.4	2.2	1.0	1.5	1.4	2.4	1.9	1.0
Current Assets to Working Capital **38**	2.9	•	1.6	•	3.8	1.8	2.5	2.4	2.1	4.0	2.0	4.0
Current Liabilities to Working Capital **39**	1.9	•	0.6	•	2.8	0.8	1.5	1.4	1.1	3.0	1.0	3.0
Working Capital to Net Sales **40**	0.1	•	0.1	•	0.1	0.2	0.1	0.1	0.2	0.1	0.1	0.1
Inventory to Working Capital **41**	1.1	•	0.3	•	1.4	0.5	0.8	1.0	0.8	1.5	0.6	1.8
Total Receipts to Cash Flow **42**	10.9	16.4	6.8	•	12.2	9.1	9.3	9.7	12.5	13.5	32.3	9.0
Cost of Goods to Cash Flow **43**	8.2	12.8	4.4	•	8.7	6.8	6.7	7.7	9.7	10.2	26.2	6.7
Cash Flow to Total Debt **44**	0.2	•	0.7	•	0.4	0.3	0.4	0.4	0.2	0.1	0.1	0.2

Selected Financial Factors (in Percentages)

Debt Ratio **45**	55.3	•	66.0	•	59.1	68.9	51.0	59.2	59.1	70.8	64.9	50.8
Return on Total Assets **46**	9.8	•	27.5	•	4.7	17.6	14.8	18.9	8.5	9.6	5.7	9.6
Return on Equity Before Income Taxes **47**	16.3	•	75.7	•	7.8	47.8	26.5	39.5	13.8	18.6	5.3	15.2
Return on Equity After Income Taxes **48**	12.9	•	75.7	•	6.8	44.7	20.8	38.7	10.4	12.7	0.8	11.9
Profit Margin (Before Income Tax) **49**	5.9	1.8	8.6	•	1.2	7.5	7.2	7.9	3.6	5.4	1.2	8.1
Profit Margin (After Income Tax) **50**	4.6	1.7	8.6	•	1.1	7.1	5.6	7.7	2.7	3.7	0.2	6.3

Table II

Corporations with Net Income

FOUNDRIES

MONEY AMOUNTS AND SIZE OF ASSETS IN THOUSANDS OF DOLLARS

Item Description for Accounting Period 7/06 Through 6/07	Total	Zero Assets	Under 500	500 to 1,000	1,000 to 5,000	5,000 to 10,000	10,000 to 25,000	25,000 to 50,000	50,000 to 100,000	100,000 to 250,000	250,000 to 500,000	500,000 to 2,500,000	2,500,000 and over
Number of Enterprises **1**	1009	•	600	0	•	94	41	•	10	4	•	5	0

Revenues ($ in Thousands)

Net Sales **2**	25002092	•	775099	0	•	1218565	1055866	•	993676	732772	•	12941899	0
Interest **3**	19677	•	0	0	•	764	965	•	2152	1214	•	2308	0
Rents **4**	3122	•	0	0	•	38	1252	•	108	0	•	836	0
Royalties **5**	20803	•	0	0	•	0	0	•	210	0	•	2428	0
Other Portfolio Income **6**	88657	•	0	0	•	84	245	•	2793	1165	•	50442	0
Other Receipts **7**	215591	•	0	0	•	3905	4271	•	674	-183	•	102250	0
Total Receipts **8**	25349942	•	775099	0	•	1223356	1062599	•	999613	734968	•	13100163	0
Average Total Receipts **9**	25124	•	1292	•	•	13014	25917	•	99961	183742	•	2620033	•

Operating Costs/Operating Income (%)

Cost of Operations **10**	74.9	•	64.0	•	•	72.4	71.8	•	72.4	75.3	•	75.1	•
Salaries and Wages **11**	4.6	•	4.1	•	•	3.8	4.6	•	4.8	3.5	•	4.5	•
Taxes Paid **12**	1.5	•	2.1	•	•	2.5	2.1	•	1.9	1.3	•	1.3	•
Interest Paid **13**	1.8	•	0.5	•	•	1.5	0.9	•	0.9	4.2	•	2.3	•
Depreciation **14**	2.0	•	1.3	•	•	2.2	2.6	•	2.6	3.2	•	1.8	•
Amortization and Depletion **15**	0.2	•	•	•	•	0.2	0.0	•	0.2	0.4	•	0.2	•
Pensions and Other Deferred Comp. **16**	0.8	•	0.0	•	•	0.8	0.9	•	0.7	0.7	•	0.8	•
Employee Benefits **17**	1.9	•	•	•	•	2.2	1.3	•	0.7	2.2	•	2.1	•
Advertising **18**	0.1	•	0.1	•	•	0.2	0.1	•	0.5	0.0	•	0.1	•
Other Expenses **19**	4.5	•	7.0	•	•	3.4	4.8	•	6.5	3.8	•	3.9	•
Officers' Compensation **20**	1.6	•	4.6	•	•	1.8	2.7	•	1.0	0.2	•	1.2	•
Operating Margin **21**	6.0	•	16.3	•	•	9.0	8.0	•	7.8	5.1	•	6.7	•
Operating Margin Before Officers' Comp. **22**	7.6	•	20.9	•	•	10.9	10.7	•	8.8	5.4	•	8.0	•

Selected Average Balance Sheet ($ in Thousands)

Net Receivables 23	3150	153	1953	3484	13116	28978	311330
Inventories 24	2561	37	780	2224	13463	23017	360346
Net Property, Plant and Equipment 25	4290	205	2322	5097	26698	70108	428798
Total Assets 26	20704	433	6698	13661	73126	183524	2799696
Notes and Loans Payable 27	6040	47	3210	3776	16099	81942	804444
All Other Liabilities 28	4812	63	1482	3002	16435	48042	618621
Net Worth 29	9853	323	2006	6883	40592	53539	1376631

Selected Financial Ratios (Times to 1)

Current Ratio 30	1.6	3.6	2.7	2.0	2.6	1.3	1.3
Quick Ratio 31	0.9	2.9	1.8	1.2	1.6	0.7	0.6
Net Sales to Working Capital 32	9.2	7.8	5.2	7.2	4.2	11.7	13.0
Coverage Ratio 33	5.1	35.4	7.4	10.3	9.8	2.3	4.6
Total Asset Turnover 34	1.2	3.0	1.9	1.9	1.4	1.0	0.9
Inventory Turnover 35	7.3	22.4	12.0	8.3	5.3	6.0	5.4
Receivables Turnover 36	8.4	10.3	9.3	7.4			
Total Liabilities to Net Worth 37	1.1	0.3	2.3	1.0	0.8	2.4	1.0
Current Assets to Working Capital 38	2.7	1.4	1.6	2.0	1.6	4.0	4.0
Current Liabilities to Working Capital 39	1.7	0.4	0.6	1.0	0.6	3.0	3.0
Working Capital to Net Sales 40	0.1	0.1	0.2	0.1	0.2	0.1	0.1
Inventory to Working Capital 41	1.1	0.2	0.4	0.7	0.6	1.5	1.8
Total Receipts to Cash Flow 42	9.5	4.8	8.4	8.5	7.2	13.5	9.0
Cost of Goods to Cash Flow 43	7.1	3.1	6.1	6.1	5.2	10.2	6.7
Cash Flow to Total Debt 44	0.2	2.4	0.3	0.4	0.4	0.1	0.2

Selected Financial Factors (in Percentages)

Debt Ratio 45	52.4	25.5	70.1	49.6	44.5	70.8	50.8
Return on Total Assets 46	11.1	50.0	21.1	18.0	12.4	9.6	9.6
Return on Equity Before Income Taxes 47	18.7	65.1	60.8	32.3	20.0	18.6	15.2
Return on Equity After Income Taxes 48	15.3	65.1	57.0	26.1	16.4	12.7	11.9
Profit Margin (Before Income Tax) 49	7.4	16.3	9.4	8.6	8.2	5.4	8.1
Profit Margin (After Income Tax) 50	6.1	16.3	8.8	7.0	6.7	3.7	6.3

Table I

Corporations with and without Net Income

FORGING AND STAMPING

MONEY AMOUNTS AND SIZE OF ASSETS IN THOUSANDS OF DOLLARS

Item Description for Accounting Period 7/06 Through 6/07	Total	Zero Assets	Under 500	500 to 1,000	1,000 to 5,000	5,000 to 10,000	10,000 to 25,000	25,000 to 50,000	50,000 to 100,000	100,000 to 250,000	250,000 to 500,000	500,000 to 2,500,000	2,500,000 and over
Number of Enterprises **1**	3208	29	1615	519	569	240	144	43	24	17	8	0	0
Revenues ($ in Thousands)													
Net Sales **2**	21571467	503675	316052	856434	2711084	2860130	4165123	2340003	2089193	2854195	2875578	0	0
Interest **3**	78164	18	675	257	1066	1914	1820	2185	3835	2215	64181	0	0
Rents **4**	2953	0	0	0	260	0	992	14	228	1010	448	0	0
Royalties **5**	12925	0	0	0	0	0	0	2	0	0	12923	0	0
Other Portfolio Income **6**	67707	14984	2163	1	14459	3733	1858	1411	5595	18011	5492	0	0
Other Receipts **7**	244559	12355	-69	134	7038	41775	43444	21372	12969	48630	56911	0	0
Total Receipts **8**	21977775	531032	318821	856826	2733907	2907552	4213237	2364987	2211820	2924061	3015533	0	•
Average Total Receipts **9**	6851	18311	197	1651	4805	12115	29259	55000	87992	172004	376942	•	•
Operating Costs/Operating Income (%)													
Cost of Operations **10**	73.1	85.1	45.1	61.0	70.1	68.4	77.5	76.8	76.2	74.9	72.1	•	•
Salaries and Wages **11**	4.5	1.9	10.1	1.8	4.8	8.3	3.3	4.4	3.8	4.2	3.6	•	•
Taxes Paid **12**	1.8	1.6	3.0	2.2	2.3	2.3	1.7	1.7	1.8	1.8	1.0	•	•
Interest Paid **13**	1.7	2.1	0.5	0.7	1.1	1.3	0.8	1.2	1.4	1.6	4.8	•	•
Depreciation **14**	2.6	1.9	3.4	1.2	2.8	1.4	2.4	2.3	3.4	2.4	4.4	•	•
Amortization and Depletion **15**	0.3	0.4	•	0.1	0.0	0.0	0.1	0.5	0.2	0.2	1.3	•	•
Pensions and Other Deferred Comp. **16**	0.6	0.0	0.3	0.3	1.0	0.2	0.8	0.4	0.6	0.4	1.1	•	•
Employee Benefits **17**	1.7	1.3	1.5	1.4	1.6	0.6	1.8	1.8	2.0	2.4	1.8	•	•
Advertising **18**	0.2	0.0	0.8	0.3	0.2	0.5	0.1	0.1	0.1	0.2	0.1	•	•
Other Expenses **19**	7.5	4.6	19.0	15.6	10.9	11.1	5.4	6.4	5.2	4.7	6.2	•	•
Officers' Compensation **20**	2.6	1.6	7.7	10.7	4.4	3.3	2.2	1.4	1.8	1.8	0.6	•	•
Operating Margin **21**	3.2	•	8.5	4.8	0.7	2.5	3.9	3.1	3.5	5.4	2.9	•	•
Operating Margin Before Officers' Comp. **22**	5.9	1.2	16.2	15.5	5.1	5.8	6.1	4.4	5.3	7.1	3.5	•	•

Selected Average Balance Sheet ($ in Thousands)

Net Receivables 23	1011	0	21	184	625	1948	4003	8613	13653	31593	60008	•
Inventories 24	823	0	8	146	546	1501	3053	7070	12479	24959	51976	•
Net Property, Plant and Equipment 25	1188	0	19	143	672	1538	3790	10208	23618	36074	98632	•
Total Assets 26	4722	0	102	752	2398	6769	14058	34872	69048	146017	492553	•
Notes and Loans Payable 27	1510	0	19	178	805	1889	3935	10035	18203	48402	193975	•
All Other Liabilities 28	1259	0	7	137	1491	2067	3052	8268	16113	37433	99348	•
Net Worth 29	1953	0	77	437	102	2813	7071	16569	34731	60182	199229	•

Selected Financial Ratios (Times to 1)

Current Ratio 30	1.7	•	10.9	3.2	1.6	1.7	2.1	1.7	1.8	2.0	1.0	•
Quick Ratio 31	1.0	•	8.5	2.3	1.0	0.9	1.2	1.0	1.0	1.0	0.5	•
Net Sales to Working Capital 32	7.0	•	3.0	4.1	8.0	6.9	6.3	7.0	5.7	4.7	90.0	•
Coverage Ratio 33	4.1	3.5	18.1	8.3	2.4	4.3	7.1	4.5	4.1	5.8	2.6	•
Total Asset Turnover 34	1.4	•	1.9	2.2	2.0	1.8	2.1	1.6	1.3	1.1	0.7	•
Inventory Turnover 35	6.0	•	11.4	6.9	6.1	5.4	7.3	5.9	5.3	5.0	5.0	•
Receivables Turnover 36	6.7	•	8.4	•	7.2	7.5	7.4	5.8	5.6	5.1	6.4	•
Total Liabilities to Net Worth 37	1.4	•	0.3	0.7	22.5	1.4	1.0	1.1	1.0	1.4	1.5	•
Current Assets to Working Capital 38	2.5	•	1.1	1.5	2.8	2.4	1.9	2.3	2.2	2.0	38.3	•
Current Liabilities to Working Capital 39	1.5	•	0.1	0.5	1.8	1.4	0.9	1.3	1.2	1.0	37.3	•
Working Capital to Net Sales 40	0.1	•	0.3	0.2	0.1	0.1	0.2	0.1	0.2	0.2	0.0	•
Inventory to Working Capital 41	0.9	•	0.1	0.4	0.8	0.9	0.7	0.8	0.7	0.8	13.9	•
Total Receipts to Cash Flow 42	9.9	11.5	4.4	6.4	13.8	9.0	12.5	11.8	12.0	8.9	7.6	•
Cost of Goods to Cash Flow 43	7.3	9.8	2.0	3.9	9.7	6.1	9.7	9.1	9.1	6.7	5.5	•
Cash Flow to Total Debt 44	0.2	•	1.8	0.8	0.2	0.3	0.3	0.3	0.2	0.2	0.2	•

Selected Financial Factors (in Percentages)

Debt Ratio 45	58.6	•	24.8	41.9	95.7	58.4	49.7	52.5	49.7	58.8	59.6	•
Return on Total Assets 46	9.7	•	19.0	12.1	5.3	9.5	12.1	8.2	7.4	10.8	9.3	•
Return on Equity Before Income Taxes 47	17.6	•	23.8	18.3	71.9	17.4	20.7	13.4	11.2	21.7	14.2	•
Return on Equity After Income Taxes 48	15.6	•	23.3	14.6	63.4	14.5	19.3	11.6	10.0	19.1	12.5	•
Profit Margin (Before Income Tax) 49	5.1	5.1	9.3	4.9	1.5	4.1	5.1	4.1	4.5	7.8	7.9	•
Profit Margin (After Income Tax) 50	4.5	5.1	9.1	3.9	1.4	3.4	4.7	3.5	4.0	6.8	6.9	•

111

Table II
Corporations with Net Income

FORGING AND STAMPING

MONEY AMOUNTS AND SIZE OF ASSETS IN THOUSANDS OF DOLLARS

Item Description for Accounting Period 7/06 Through 6/07	Total	Zero Assets	Under 500	500 to 1,000	1,000 to 5,000	5,000 to 10,000	10,000 to 25,000	25,000 to 50,000	50,000 to 100,000	100,000 to 250,000	250,000 to 500,000	500,000 to 2,500,000	2,500,000 and over
Number of Enterprises **1**	2715	23	1532	465	347	159	•	30	18	•	5	0	0
Revenues ($ in Thousands)													
Net Sales **2**	16725936	266751	268686	845814	2164658	1908030	•	1713483	1506626	•	1756606	0	0
Interest **3**	16499	16	212	257	786	1914	•	1597	3810	•	4234	0	0
Rents **4**	2634	0	0	0	0	0	•	14	225	•	446	0	0
Royalties **5**	136	0	0	0	0	0	•	2	0	•	134	0	0
Other Portfolio Income **6**	60974	14911	2163	1	14444	3625	•	835	5204	•	383	0	0
Other Receipts **7**	163278	12324	-121	134	1343	40849	•	-3256	9743	•	26591	0	0
Total Receipts **8**	16969457	294002	270940	846206	2181231	1954418	•	1712675	1525608	•	1788394	0	0
Average Total Receipts **9**	6250	12783	177	1820	6286	12292	•	57089	84756	•	357679	•	•
Operating Costs/Operating Income (%)													
Cost of Operations **10**	71.7	87.0	44.3	61.5	71.6	60.9	•	75.8	72.7	•	70.8	•	•
Salaries and Wages **11**	4.2	2.0	11.0	1.6	4.1	9.8	•	4.1	4.2	•	2.4	•	•
Taxes Paid **12**	1.8	0.7	2.4	2.2	2.4	2.4	•	1.5	1.7	•	0.9	•	•
Interest Paid **13**	1.1	0.5	0.6	0.7	1.0	1.1	•	1.0	1.2	•	1.9	•	•
Depreciation **14**	2.4	1.1	3.7	1.0	2.5	1.6	•	1.7	3.5	•	3.2	•	•
Amortization and Depletion **15**	0.1	0.0	•	0.1	0.0	0.0	•	0.3	0.1	•	0.2	•	•
Pensions and Other Deferred Comp. **16**	0.7	0.0	0.4	0.3	1.2	0.3	•	0.3	0.7	•	1.7	•	•
Employee Benefits **17**	1.6	0.5	0.5	1.4	1.3	1.0	•	1.7	1.5	•	1.7	•	•
Advertising **18**	0.2	0.1	0.9	0.3	0.1	0.8	•	0.1	0.0	•	0.0	•	•
Other Expenses **19**	6.7	5.5	18.0	15.3	8.7	11.4	•	5.1	5.5	•	4.5	•	•
Officers' Compensation **20**	2.9	2.2	6.1	10.8	4.0	4.5	•	1.6	2.2	•	0.4	•	•
Operating Margin **21**	6.5	0.3	12.2	5.0	3.3	6.1	•	6.9	6.8	•	12.2	•	•
Operating Margin Before Officers' Comp. **22**	9.4	2.5	18.3	15.7	7.2	10.7	•	8.5	9.0	•	12.6	•	•

Selected Average Balance Sheet ($ in Thousands)

Net Receivables 23	905	0	18	204	844	1563	8719	12066	62264
Inventories 24	779	0	7	156	692	1809	7094	10899	58069
Net Property, Plant and Equipment 25	1005	0	20	94	680	1243	8646	22899	101066
Total Assets 26	4036	0	87	767	2439	7046	35343	69365	459097
Notes and Loans Payable 27	1092	0	16	181	1002	1222	9334	13868	112995
All Other Liabilities 28	1029	0	7	149	839	2161	7957	13089	131112
Net Worth 29	1915	0	65	437	597	3662	18053	42407	214990

Selected Financial Ratios (Times to 1)

Current Ratio 30	1.9	•	8.5	3.5	1.3	1.9	1.8	2.4	1.5
Quick Ratio 31	1.1	•	6.5	2.5	0.8	0.9	1.1	1.3	0.8
Net Sales to Working Capital 32	5.9	•	3.5	3.9	17.8	5.9	6.3	4.1	6.3
Coverage Ratio 33	8.1	22.6	21.4	8.5	5.1	8.8	7.9	7.8	8.4
Total Asset Turnover 34	1.5	•	2.0	2.4	2.6	1.7	1.6	1.2	0.8
Inventory Turnover 35	5.7	•	10.9	7.2	6.4	4.0	6.1	5.6	4.3
Receivables Turnover 36	6.6	•	7.8	9.3	6.9	7.7	6.4	•	•
Total Liabilities to Net Worth 37	1.1	•	0.3	0.8	3.1	0.9	1.0	0.6	1.1
Current Assets to Working Capital 38	2.1	•	1.1	1.4	4.6	2.1	2.2	1.7	2.9
Current Liabilities to Working Capital 39	1.1	•	0.1	0.4	3.6	1.1	1.2	0.7	1.9
Working Capital to Net Sales 40	0.2	•	0.3	0.3	0.1	0.2	0.2	0.2	0.2
Inventory to Working Capital 41	0.7	•	0.1	0.4	1.6	0.9	0.7	0.5	1.0
Total Receipts to Cash Flow 42	8.0	6.5	3.7	6.5	11.8	6.0	9.7	8.3	5.6
Cost of Goods to Cash Flow 43	5.7	5.7	1.6	4.0	8.5	3.7	7.4	6.1	3.9
Cash Flow to Total Debt 44	0.4	•	2.1	0.9	0.3	0.6	0.3	0.4	0.3

Selected Financial Factors (in Percentages)

Debt Ratio 45	52.6	•	25.6	43.0	75.5	48.0	48.9	38.9	53.2
Return on Total Assets 46	13.9	•	27.6	13.5	12.8	16.5	12.6	11.0	12.2
Return on Equity Before Income Taxes 47	25.7	•	35.3	20.8	42.1	28.1	21.5	15.7	23.0
Return on Equity After Income Taxes 48	23.2	•	34.6	16.6	39.7	24.7	19.1	14.4	20.4
Profit Margin (Before Income Tax) 49	8.0	10.5	13.1	5.0	4.0	8.6	6.8	8.0	14.1
Profit Margin (After Income Tax) 50	7.2	10.5	12.8	4.0	3.8	7.5	6.0	7.3	12.5

Table I
Corporations with and without Net Income

CUTLERY, HARDWARE, SPRING AND WIRE MACHINE SHOPS, NUT, BOLT

MONEY AMOUNTS AND SIZE OF ASSETS IN THOUSANDS OF DOLLARS

Item Description for Accounting Period 7/06 Through 6/07	Total	Zero Assets	Under 500	500 to 1,000	1,000 to 5,000	5,000 to 10,000	10,000 to 25,000	25,000 to 50,000	50,000 to 100,000	100,000 to 250,000	250,000 to 500,000	500,000 to 2,500,000	2,500,000 and over
Number of Enterprises **1**	22078	2565	14325	1618	2578	510	332	72	30	23	12	12	0
Revenues ($ in Thousands)													
Net Sales **2**	69923205	489648	7121324	3212149	10941813	6452973	9007239	3833690	3093519	3924745	5834927	15311178	0
Interest **3**	1707130	101	2615	2201	16150	10036	6499	14846	4174	16974	23722	1609812	0
Rents **4**	31853	0	0	4488	8698	688	231	3861	1213	5828	875	5972	0
Royalties **5**	145311	0	34	0	7	0	15	213	846	8739	2236	133222	0
Other Portfolio Income **6**	696252	58356	69148	2389	47492	36002	18338	21744	15543	149713	50471	227054	0
Other Receipts **7**	966148	2030	22792	41014	128708	22755	64867	16191	18410	181500	20677	447205	0
Total Receipts **8**	72769899	550135	7215913	3262241	11142868	6522454	9097189	3890545	3133705	4287499	5932908	17734443	0
Average Total Receipts **9**	3296	214	504	2016	4322	12789	27401	54035	104457	186413	494409	1477870	•
Operating Costs/Operating Income (%)													
Cost of Operations **10**	64.6	54.4	55.0	64.8	61.8	67.4	69.2	70.5	73.1	70.3	70.0	60.5	•
Salaries and Wages **11**	7.0	10.9	9.6	4.0	6.9	4.2	5.4	5.2	5.5	7.4	7.1	9.2	•
Taxes Paid **12**	2.2	2.9	3.1	3.7	3.0	2.6	2.1	2.1	1.7	1.8	1.4	1.3	•
Interest Paid **13**	4.3	2.3	0.9	1.4	1.7	0.9	1.4	1.3	1.3	2.9	3.0	14.0	•
Depreciation **14**	2.6	3.0	3.3	3.8	3.5	2.9	2.5	3.4	2.7	2.8	1.7	1.4	•
Amortization and Depletion **15**	0.6	1.1	0.0	0.0	0.1	0.1	0.1	0.6	0.2	0.8	1.0	1.8	•
Pensions and Other Deferred Comp. **16**	0.5	0.3	0.5	0.4	0.5	0.8	0.8	0.4	0.5	0.8	0.5	0.2	•
Employee Benefits **17**	2.0	0.7	1.2	2.1	1.8	1.9	1.9	1.8	1.6	2.4	1.5	2.7	•
Advertising **18**	0.8	1.2	0.4	0.1	0.3	0.5	0.7	0.5	0.7	0.9	1.0	1.5	•
Other Expenses **19**	11.4	25.8	16.1	9.8	10.7	6.8	8.2	7.8	6.9	9.9	8.7	16.8	•
Officers' Compensation **20**	3.1	11.0	6.2	8.9	6.0	4.4	2.5	1.2	1.5	0.7	0.5	0.5	•
Operating Margin **21**	0.8	•	3.6	0.8	3.6	7.6	5.1	5.2	4.3	•	3.4	•	•
Operating Margin Before Officers' Comp. **22**	3.9	•	9.7	9.7	9.6	12.0	7.6	6.4	5.8	0.0	3.9	•	•

Selected Average Balance Sheet ($ in Thousands)

Net Receivables 23	423	0	31	219	441	1636	3444	7050	15123	28153	73744	245152	•
Inventories 24	346	0	19	108	397	1388	3522	8706	16634	27841	69535	141386	•
Net Property, Plant and Equipment 25	438	0	40	251	671	1957	4636	9040	18506	35924	61175	138378	•
Total Assets 26	2957	0	141	738	2257	7244	15315	34651	71584	164727	370211	2883508	•
Notes and Loans Payable 27	1083	0	83	463	979	1559	4901	10191	17145	50512	183925	1033671	•
All Other Liabilities 28	669	0	28	214	808	1596	3021	6676	18480	39840	87254	593582	•
Net Worth 29	1206	0	30	61	470	4089	7393	17784	35958	74375	99032	1256256	•

Selected Financial Ratios (Times to 1)

Current Ratio 30	1.6	•	2.4	1.6	1.2	2.3	2.0	2.3	2.0	1.9	2.1	1.3	•
Quick Ratio 31	0.9	•	1.7	1.1	0.8	1.2	1.0	1.1	1.0	1.1	1.0	0.7	•
Net Sales to Working Capital 32	7.8	•	10.3	12.6	20.5	4.9	6.1	5.1	5.2	4.7	5.6	11.3	•
Coverage Ratio 33	2.5	0.4	6.3	2.6	4.3	10.7	5.4	6.3	5.4	4.2	2.7	1.6	•
Total Asset Turnover 34	1.1	•	3.5	2.7	1.9	1.7	1.8	1.5	1.4	1.0	1.3	0.4	•
Inventory Turnover 35	5.8	•	14.3	11.9	6.6	6.1	5.3	4.3	4.5	4.3	4.9	5.5	•
Receivables Turnover 36	6.6	•	18.6	10.4	8.7	9.5	8.6	6.6	7.4	5.5	6.9	3.6	•
Total Liabilities to Net Worth 37	1.5	•	3.6	11.1	3.8	0.8	1.1	0.9	1.0	1.2	2.7	1.3	•
Current Assets to Working Capital 38	2.6	•	1.7	2.8	5.9	1.8	2.0	1.8	2.0	2.1	1.9	4.7	•
Current Liabilities to Working Capital 39	1.6	•	0.7	1.8	4.9	0.8	1.0	0.8	1.0	1.1	0.9	3.7	•
Working Capital to Net Sales 40	0.1	•	0.1	0.1	0.0	0.2	0.2	0.2	0.2	0.2	0.2	0.1	•
Inventory to Working Capital 41	0.9	•	0.4	0.6	1.9	0.7	0.9	0.8	0.9	0.7	0.9	1.4	•
Total Receipts to Cash Flow 42	6.8	8.0	6.1	11.1	8.4	8.0	8.0	7.9	8.9	6.5	8.5	4.7	•
Cost of Goods to Cash Flow 43	4.4	4.3	3.4	7.2	5.2	5.4	5.5	5.6	6.5	4.6	6.0	2.9	•
Cash Flow to Total Debt 44	0.3	•	0.7	0.3	0.3	0.5	0.4	0.4	0.3	0.3	0.2	0.2	•

Selected Financial Factors (in Percentages)

Debt Ratio 45	59.2	•	78.4	91.7	79.2	43.6	51.7	48.7	49.8	54.8	73.2	56.4	•
Return on Total Assets 46	11.4	•	20.5	10.3	13.4	16.7	13.2	12.2	9.9	12.7	10.7	9.7	•
Return on Equity Before Income Taxes 47	16.7	•	79.9	76.9	49.3	26.8	22.2	20.0	16.1	21.4	24.9	8.1	•
Return on Equity After Income Taxes 48	13.7	•	76.2	73.6	42.2	25.3	19.9	17.7	13.8	17.0	19.1	5.5	•
Profit Margin (Before Income Tax) 49	6.4	•	4.9	2.4	5.5	8.7	6.1	6.7	5.6	9.3	5.1	8.0	•
Profit Margin (After Income Tax) 50	5.3	•	4.7	2.3	4.7	8.2	5.4	5.9	4.8	7.4	3.9	5.4	•

Table II

Corporations with Net Income

CUTLERY, HARDWARE, SPRING AND WIRE MACHINE SHOPS, NUT, BOLT

MONEY AMOUNTS AND SIZE OF ASSETS IN THOUSANDS OF DOLLARS

Item Description for Accounting Period 7/06 Through 6/07	Total	Zero Assets	Under 500	500 to 1,000	1,000 to 5,000	5,000 to 10,000	10,000 to 25,000	25,000 to 50,000	50,000 to 100,000	100,000 to 250,000	250,000 to 500,000	500,000 to 2,500,000	2,500,000 and over
Number of Enterprises **1**	12485	914	7630	957	2105	469	296	•	23	20	8	•	0
Revenues ($ in Thousands)													
Net Sales **2**	57717149	309697	4534174	1746019	9711162	6006812	8062305	•	2531459	3495111	4596038	•	0
Interest **3**	1692538	0	2295	1289	15347	6977	6318	•	3584	16686	23405	•	0
Rents **4**	27072	0	0	4488	5791	133	231	•	1173	5554	875	•	0
Royalties **5**	142574	0	0	0	7	0	0	•	783	8739	737	•	0
Other Portfolio Income **6**	641610	46506	65342	1812	32351	28733	10851	•	13891	149347	48730	•	0
Other Receipts **7**	872662	1835	9180	4745	120980	21004	51901	•	12931	179182	12293	•	0
Total Receipts **8**	61093605	358038	4610991	1758353	9885638	6063659	8131606	•	2563821	3854619	4682078	•	0
Average Total Receipts **9**	4893	392	604	1837	4696	12929	27472	•	111470	192731	585260	•	•
Operating Costs/Operating Income (%)													
Cost of Operations **10**	63.9	56.5	53.6	62.1	61.7	66.8	68.1	•	71.7	68.8	70.3	•	•
Salaries and Wages **11**	6.9	13.2	8.1	1.5	6.9	3.9	5.5	•	5.8	7.8	7.5	•	•
Taxes Paid **12**	2.1	2.1	2.6	3.6	3.0	2.6	2.1	•	1.6	1.9	1.4	•	•
Interest Paid **13**	4.8	1.9	0.6	1.0	1.5	0.8	1.3	•	1.2	3.1	3.1	•	•
Depreciation **14**	2.4	1.1	3.2	3.9	3.3	2.8	2.4	•	2.1	2.6	1.3	•	•
Amortization and Depletion **15**	0.6	0.1	0.0	0.0	0.1	0.0	0.1	•	0.2	0.8	0.6	•	•
Pensions and Other Deferred Comp. **16**	0.5	0.5	0.5	0.3	0.5	0.8	0.6	•	0.5	0.9	0.3	•	•
Employee Benefits **17**	1.9	0.5	1.2	1.6	1.8	1.8	1.6	•	1.1	2.7	1.2	•	•
Advertising **18**	0.7	0.2	0.4	0.1	0.3	0.5	0.7	•	0.8	0.9	0.9	•	•
Other Expenses **19**	11.2	16.3	13.6	11.9	9.9	6.4	8.3	•	7.2	9.9	8.1	•	•
Officers' Compensation **20**	2.9	1.4	5.9	7.2	6.0	4.6	2.6	•	1.5	0.6	0.4	•	•
Operating Margin **21**	2.2	6.2	10.3	6.7	4.9	8.9	6.8	•	6.4	•	5.0	•	•
Operating Margin Before Officers' Comp. **22**	5.1	7.6	16.2	14.0	10.9	13.5	9.4	•	7.8	0.6	5.4	•	•

Selected Average Balance Sheet ($ in Thousands)

Net Receivables 23	645	0	35	241	454	1645	3458	16692	28156	94283
Inventories 24	495	0	16	134	416	1299	3447	17744	26405	72237
Net Property, Plant and Equipment 25	598	0	31	193	669	1919	4476	16556	31706	57673
Total Assets 26	4611	0	155	701	2260	7218	15365	70246	165418	368486
Notes and Loans Payable 27	1615	0	57	359	1005	1427	4655	16578	49418	169688
All Other Liabilities 28	1013	0	26	205	798	1581	2977	19312	40163	99017
Net Worth 29	1983	0	72	137	458	4210	7734	34356	75838	99780

Selected Financial Ratios (Times to 1)

Current Ratio 30	1.7	•	3.3	2.3	1.4	2.3	2.1	2.1	1.9	2.4
Quick Ratio 31	0.9	•	2.5	1.6	0.9	1.2	1.1	1.0	1.1	1.2
Net Sales to Working Capital 32	7.1	•	8.6	6.9	13.1	5.0	5.6	5.1	4.9	5.1
Coverage Ratio 33	2.8	12.2	21.4	8.5	5.4	12.9	7.0	7.5	4.6	3.2
Total Asset Turnover 34	1.0	•	3.8	2.6	2.0	1.8	1.8	1.6	1.1	1.6
Inventory Turnover 35	6.0	•	20.3	8.4	6.8	6.6	5.4	4.4	4.6	5.6
Receivables Turnover 36	6.5	•	20.0	9.2	9.7	10.3	8.8	7.5	•	6.8
Total Liabilities to Net Worth 37	1.3	•	1.2	4.1	3.9	0.7	1.0	1.0	1.2	2.7
Current Assets to Working Capital 38	2.4	•	1.4	1.8	3.7	1.8	1.9	1.9	2.1	1.7
Current Liabilities to Working Capital 39	1.4	•	0.4	0.8	2.7	0.8	0.9	0.9	1.1	0.7
Working Capital to Net Sales 40	0.1	•	0.1	0.1	0.1	0.2	0.2	0.2	0.2	0.2
Inventory to Working Capital 41	0.8	•	0.2	0.4	1.2	0.7	0.8	0.9	0.7	0.7
Total Receipts to Cash Flow 42	6.0	4.0	4.7	6.6	7.7	7.4	7.1	7.5	5.9	7.7
Cost of Goods to Cash Flow 43	3.8	2.3	2.5	4.1	4.7	5.0	4.8	5.4	4.1	5.4
Cash Flow to Total Debt 44	0.3	•	1.5	0.5	0.3	0.6	0.5	0.4	0.3	0.3

Selected Financial Factors (in Percentages)

Debt Ratio 45	57.0	•	53.5	80.5	79.8	41.7	49.7	51.1	54.2	72.9
Return on Total Assets 46	13.5	•	47.9	22.0	16.7	19.0	15.9	13.9	15.0	15.5
Return on Equity Before Income Taxes 47	20.2	•	98.3	99.3	67.2	30.1	27.1	24.6	25.5	39.5
Return on Equity After Income Taxes 48	17.1	•	95.5	96.8	58.3	28.5	24.6	21.5	20.5	30.9
Profit Margin (Before Income Tax) 49	8.7	21.8	11.9	7.4	6.7	9.9	7.7	7.7	11.1	6.9
Profit Margin (After Income Tax) 50	7.3	19.6	11.6	7.3	5.8	9.4	7.0	6.7	8.9	5.4

Table I

Corporations with and without Net Income

ARCHITECTURAL AND STRUCTURAL METALS

MONEY AMOUNTS AND SIZE OF ASSETS IN THOUSANDS OF DOLLARS

Item Description for Accounting Period 7/06 Through 6/07	Total	Zero Assets	Under 500	500 to 1,000	1,000 to 5,000	5,000 to 10,000	10,000 to 25,000	25,000 to 50,000	50,000 to 100,000	100,000 to 250,000	250,000 to 500,000	500,000 to 2,500,000	2,500,000 and over
Number of Enterprises **1**	7192	5	3592	987	1912	349	238	56	20	18	6	9	0
Revenues ($ in Thousands)													
Net Sales **2**	51205387	418510	2659756	2725215	10299597	4977365	6942538	3985644	2720261	4789745	2488815	9197940	0
Interest **3**	112086	233	4170	2081	6574	5245	6858	3454	1319	11264	11579	59309	0
Rents **4**	10713	54	0	0	228	891	2734	231	224	678	26	5645	0
Royalties **5**	11679	0	0	0	0	0	266	120	0	198	69	11027	0
Other Portfolio Income **6**	380937	73763	17751	286	10830	19835	11225	7258	5249	6994	3778	223971	0
Other Receipts **7**	439801	1180	1844	5318	19422	29088	47452	7725	23976	38984	18292	246519	0
Total Receipts **8**	52160603	493740	2683521	2732900	10336651	5032424	7011073	4004432	2751029	4847863	2522559	9744411	0
Average Total Receipts **9**	7253	98748	747	2769	5406	14420	29458	71508	137551	269326	420426	1082712	•
Operating Costs/Operating Income (%)													
Cost of Operations **10**	70.3	62.3	58.4	68.8	67.7	74.0	75.9	77.0	78.3	74.2	70.5	63.9	•
Salaries and Wages **11**	6.4	8.3	11.6	5.9	5.0	4.3	5.7	5.2	3.8	7.0	6.6	8.9	•
Taxes Paid **12**	2.0	4.5	2.4	2.2	2.4	1.9	1.8	1.7	1.6	1.6	2.3	2.1	•
Interest Paid **13**	1.6	0.3	0.9	0.3	0.7	0.9	1.1	0.9	1.2	1.4	3.4	4.2	•
Depreciation **14**	2.0	2.2	1.3	2.4	1.4	2.3	1.4	1.1	1.7	1.3	3.2	3.6	•
Amortization and Depletion **15**	0.2	•	0.0	•	0.0	0.1	0.1	0.1	0.3	0.3	1.1	0.5	•
Pensions and Other Deferred Comp. **16**	0.6	0.2	0.1	0.5	0.7	0.5	0.4	0.4	0.3	0.6	0.6	1.1	•
Employee Benefits **17**	1.8	2.1	1.1	1.8	2.6	0.9	1.6	1.4	1.1	1.5	1.4	2.2	•
Advertising **18**	0.6	1.8	0.3	0.4	0.3	0.3	0.3	0.3	0.5	0.7	0.5	1.4	•
Other Expenses **19**	8.7	11.6	18.2	12.0	9.4	7.3	6.4	5.1	5.7	6.9	6.1	10.5	•
Officers' Compensation **20**	2.3	1.3	5.0	4.5	3.8	3.2	2.0	1.4	0.9	0.8	2.0	0.8	•
Operating Margin **21**	3.5	5.4	0.7	1.1	5.9	4.3	3.4	5.5	4.7	3.8	2.4	0.9	•
Operating Margin Before Officers' Comp. **22**	5.8	6.7	5.7	5.6	9.7	7.5	5.4	6.9	5.6	4.7	4.4	1.7	•

Selected Average Balance Sheet ($ in Thousands)

Item												
	•	•	•	•	•	•	•	•	•	•	•	•
Net Receivables 23	1257	0	53	268	767	2257	5180	10922	19050	39859	58126	337590
Inventories 24	622	0	20	213	383	1448	2756	6786	15379	23962	55377	94317
Net Property, Plant and Equipment 25	1000	0	36	124	451	1948	2963	6295	16509	34815	95543	311869
Total Assets 26	4555	0	166	740	2144	7257	15012	34322	73730	160735	311442	1452219
Notes and Loans Payable 27	1450	0	85	173	634	2002	4814	8126	16799	35192	103152	538841
All Other Liabilities 28	1326	0	60	296	625	2171	5424	9634	21772	46027	85736	385162
Net Worth 29	1780	0	22	272	885	3085	4774	16562	35159	79515	122554	528216

Selected Financial Ratios (Times to 1)

Item												
	•	•	•	•	•	•	•	•	•	•	•	•
Current Ratio 30	1.9	•	1.6	1.9	2.2	1.9	1.5	1.9	1.8	1.8	2.0	2.2
Quick Ratio 31	1.2	•	1.2	1.2	1.5	1.1	0.9	1.1	1.0	1.1	1.0	1.5
Net Sales to Working Capital 32	6.2	•	17.6	9.8	6.5	6.2	8.5	6.2	7.1	7.3	5.7	3.6
Coverage Ratio 33	4.4	93.1	2.8	5.2	9.7	6.7	5.0	7.8	5.8	4.6	2.1	2.8
Total Asset Turnover 34	1.6	•	4.5	3.7	2.5	2.0	1.9	2.1	1.8	1.7	1.3	0.7
Inventory Turnover 35	8.0	•	21.8	8.9	9.5	7.3	8.0	8.1	6.9	8.2	5.3	6.9
Receivables Turnover 36	6.0	•	13.3	7.3	7.5	6.8	6.1	7.3	7.1	6.2	4.8	3.8
Total Liabilities to Net Worth 37	1.6	•	6.7	1.7	1.4	1.4	2.1	1.1	1.1	1.0	1.5	1.7
Current Assets to Working Capital 38	2.1	•	2.8	2.1	1.9	2.1	3.1	2.1	2.3	2.3	2.0	1.8
Current Liabilities to Working Capital 39	1.1	•	1.8	1.1	0.9	1.1	2.1	1.1	1.3	1.3	1.0	0.8
Working Capital to Net Sales 40	0.2	•	0.1	0.1	0.2	0.2	0.1	0.2	0.1	0.1	0.2	0.3
Inventory to Working Capital 41	0.6	•	0.5	0.7	0.5	0.7	0.9	0.7	0.9	0.7	0.7	0.4
Total Receipts to Cash Flow 42	8.8	3.2	6.7	10.2	7.8	9.1	10.9	10.6	9.4	9.6	12.2	7.7
Cost of Goods to Cash Flow 43	6.2	2.0	3.9	7.1	5.3	6.7	8.3	8.2	7.4	7.1	8.6	4.9
Cash Flow to Total Debt 44	0.3	•	0.8	0.6	0.5	0.4	0.3	0.4	0.4	0.3	0.2	0.1

Selected Financial Factors (in Percentages)

Item												
	•	•	•	•	•	•	•	•	•	•	•	•
Debt Ratio 45	60.9	•	87.1	63.3	58.7	57.5	68.2	51.7	52.3	50.5	60.6	63.6
Return on Total Assets 46	11.1	•	11.0	6.3	17.5	12.4	10.5	14.1	13.0	10.6	9.5	8.2
Return on Equity Before Income Taxes 47	21.9	•	54.1	13.8	38.1	24.8	26.5	25.5	22.6	16.7	12.6	14.4
Return on Equity After Income Taxes 48	18.1	•	53.5	12.8	35.6	21.9	24.0	22.7	21.0	12.5	8.9	9.1
Profit Margin (Before Income Tax) 49	5.5	23.1	1.6	1.4	6.3	5.4	4.3	5.9	5.8	5.0	3.7	7.4
Profit Margin (After Income Tax) 50	4.5	22.6	1.6	1.3	5.8	4.7	3.9	5.3	5.4	3.7	2.6	4.7

Table II
Corporations with Net Income

ARCHITECTURAL AND STRUCTURAL METALS

MONEY AMOUNTS AND SIZE OF ASSETS IN THOUSANDS OF DOLLARS

Item Description for Accounting Period 7/06 Through 6/07	Total	Zero Assets	Under 500	500 to 1,000	1,000 to 5,000	5,000 to 10,000	10,000 to 25,000	25,000 to 50,000	50,000 to 100,000	100,000 to 250,000	250,000 to 500,000	500,000 to 2,500,000	2,500,000 and over
Number of Enterprises **1**	4831	•	2114	555	1558	296	209	50	•	15	•	•	0
Revenues ($ in Thousands)													
Net Sales **2**	43557709	•	1865662	1634242	8406008	4466204	6228011	3739722	•	4371352	•	•	0
Interest **3**	103346	•	2734	1906	4988	5245	6336	3136	•	10178	•	•	0
Rents **4**	10709	•	0	0	228	891	2734	231	•	678	•	•	0
Royalties **5**	11612	•	0	0	0	0	266	120	•	198	•	•	0
Other Portfolio Income **6**	368561	•	8963	286	10113	19817	9253	7258	•	6965	•	•	0
Other Receipts **7**	348621	•	934	1897	18726	26711	44437	6486	•	36219	•	•	0
Total Receipts **8**	44400558	•	1878293	1638331	8440063	4518868	6291037	3756953	•	4425590	•	•	0
Average Total Receipts **9**	9191	•	889	2952	5417	15266	30101	75139	•	295039	•	•	•
Operating Costs/Operating Income (%)													
Cost of Operations **10**	70.4	•	61.1	66.1	67.4	73.3	74.3	77.2	•	74.9	•	•	•
Salaries and Wages **11**	5.8	•	7.7	6.2	4.5	3.9	5.8	5.1	•	6.5	•	•	•
Taxes Paid **12**	2.0	•	2.1	2.1	2.2	2.0	1.8	1.7	•	1.5	•	•	•
Interest Paid **13**	1.2	•	0.8	0.2	0.6	0.7	0.8	0.6	•	1.2	•	•	•
Depreciation **14**	1.9	•	1.3	2.5	1.4	2.1	1.3	1.1	•	1.2	•	•	•
Amortization and Depletion **15**	0.1	•	0.0	•	0.0	0.0	0.1	0.0	•	0.1	•	•	•
Pensions and Other Deferred Comp. **16**	0.6	•	0.1	0.2	0.8	0.5	0.4	0.4	•	0.6	•	•	•
Employee Benefits **17**	1.7	•	1.5	2.2	2.0	0.8	1.6	1.4	•	1.5	•	•	•
Advertising **18**	0.6	•	0.2	0.6	0.3	0.3	0.3	0.3	•	0.5	•	•	•
Other Expenses **19**	8.3	•	15.8	13.2	8.9	7.3	6.7	4.6	•	6.4	•	•	•
Officers' Compensation **20**	2.2	•	5.9	3.9	3.8	3.3	2.1	1.4	•	0.8	•	•	•
Operating Margin **21**	5.2	•	3.4	2.8	8.3	5.7	4.7	6.2	•	4.7	•	•	•
Operating Margin Before Officers' Comp. **22**	7.4	•	9.3	6.7	12.0	9.0	6.8	7.6	•	5.5	•	•	•

Selected Average Balance Sheet ($ in Thousands)

Net Receivables 23	1584	63	238	782	2313	5313	11552	43100
Inventories 24	753	24	270	297	1198	2745	8110	23604
Net Property, Plant and Equipment 25	1274	42	72	415	1759	2757	6589	38023
Total Assets 26	5674	187	773	1991	7089	14749	34688	168595
Notes and Loans Payable 27	1628	55	98	570	1592	3650	6853	32522
All Other Liabilities 28	1555	61	296	544	1843	4947	10112	49607
Net Worth 29	2491	72	379	877	3654	6153	17724	86466

Selected Financial Ratios (Times to 1)

Current Ratio 30	2.0	1.8	2.4	2.4	1.8	2.0	2.0	1.9
Quick Ratio 31	1.3	1.4	1.5	1.8	1.4	1.2	1.2	1.2
Net Sales to Working Capital 32	5.9	14.1	7.3	6.3	5.4	6.3	5.9	7.0
Coverage Ratio 33	6.9	6.0	18.7	15.8	11.0	8.5	12.1	6.0
Total Asset Turnover 34	1.6	4.7	3.8	2.7	2.1	2.0	2.2	1.7
Inventory Turnover 35	8.4	22.4	7.2	12.2	9.2	8.1	7.1	9.2
Receivables Turnover 36	6.1	11.8	6.2	7.4	7.2	6.2		6.8
Total Liabilities to Net Worth 37	1.3	1.6	1.0	1.3	0.9	1.4	1.0	0.9
Current Assets to Working Capital 38	2.0	2.3	1.7	1.7	1.7	2.3	2.0	2.1
Current Liabilities to Working Capital 39	1.0	1.3	0.7	0.7	0.7	1.3	1.0	1.1
Working Capital to Net Sales 40	0.2	0.1	0.1	0.2	0.2	0.2	0.2	0.1
Inventory to Working Capital 41	0.6	0.3	0.6	0.3	0.6	0.7	0.6	0.6
Total Receipts to Cash Flow 42	7.8	6.6	7.8	6.8	8.0	9.2	10.2	9.2
Cost of Goods to Cash Flow 43	5.5	4.0	5.2	4.6	5.9	6.8	7.9	6.9
Cash Flow to Total Debt 44	0.4	1.2	1.0	0.7	0.5	0.4	0.4	0.4

Selected Financial Factors (in Percentages)

Debt Ratio 45	56.1	61.8	51.0	56.0	48.5	58.3	48.9	48.7
Return on Total Assets 46	13.4	23.1	12.4	25.1	16.1	13.1	15.7	12.2
Return on Equity Before Income Taxes 47	26.1	50.3	24.0	53.3	28.5	27.7	28.1	19.9
Return on Equity After Income Taxes 48	22.1	50.0	22.7	50.1	25.6	25.5	25.3	15.2
Profit Margin (Before Income Tax) 49	7.2	4.1	3.1	8.7	6.9	5.7	6.7	5.9
Profit Margin (After Income Tax) 50	6.1	4.1	2.9	8.1	6.2	5.3	6.0	4.5

Table I

Corporations with and without Net Income

BOILER, TANK, AND SHIPPING CONTAINER

MONEY AMOUNTS AND SIZE OF ASSETS IN THOUSANDS OF DOLLARS

Item Description for Accounting Period 7/06 Through 6/07	Total	Zero Assets	Under 500	500 to 1,000	1,000 to 5,000	5,000 to 10,000	10,000 to 25,000	25,000 to 50,000	50,000 to 100,000	100,000 to 250,000	250,000 to 500,000	500,000 to 2,500,000	2,500,000 and over
Number of Enterprises **1**	533	9	0	190	187	32	63	25	11	4	4	4	4
Revenues ($ in Thousands)													
Net Sales **2**	24226870	257081	0	208177	822221	508177	1750332	1724408	1021619	745817	1146152	3578505	12464382
Interest **3**	106513	1	0	0	420	579	3618	1170	572	6812	12148	4592	76601
Rents **4**	23744	0	0	0	1924	1035	221	309	0	170	0	4302	15782
Royalties **5**	125690	67	0	0	0	0	0	0	319	57	0	17904	107342
Other Portfolio Income **6**	75301	12268	0	271	189	20	11480	2196	1696	1442	153	3678	41909
Other Receipts **7**	259245	8936	0	380	356	-89	18462	3866	3176	26614	2144	36524	158877
Total Receipts **8**	24817363	278353	0	208828	825110	509722	1784113	1731949	1027382	780912	1160597	3645505	12864893
Average Total Receipts **9**	46562	30928	•	1099	4412	15929	28319	69278	93398	195228	290149	911376	3216223
Operating Costs/Operating Income (%)													
Cost of Operations **10**	83.4	65.0	•	68.6	69.5	75.3	65.8	75.1	70.0	70.4	85.2	79.7	91.7
Salaries and Wages **11**	4.6	16.9	•	7.0	7.0	3.3	7.7	4.4	6.7	3.3	5.9	2.8	4.1
Taxes Paid **12**	1.3	1.8	•	2.2	2.9	1.3	2.0	1.4	1.5	1.4	1.5	1.7	0.8
Interest Paid **13**	2.4	0.9	•	4.8	0.0	1.1	0.7	0.7	2.3	4.9	2.2	3.6	2.7
Depreciation **14**	1.8	0.7	•	0.3	0.2	1.6	1.2	1.2	1.9	5.3	0.7	2.7	1.8
Amortization and Depletion **15**	0.3	0.6	•	•	•	0.3	0.1	0.1	1.8	0.2	0.1	0.4	0.3
Pensions and Other Deferred Comp. **16**	1.1	0.1	•	0.6	0.7	0.1	0.5	0.1	0.5	0.1	0.4	0.7	1.8
Employee Benefits **17**	2.0	0.5	•	0.9	2.5	0.8	1.4	2.7	1.6	0.5	1.1	1.4	2.4
Advertising **18**	0.2	0.3	•	0.5	0.6	0.2	1.1	0.2	0.4	0.4	0.1	0.1	0.0
Other Expenses **19**	4.1	11.9	•	8.8	5.0	6.3	7.5	7.3	9.2	11.0	0.4	3.9	2.5
Officers' Compensation **20**	1.1	5.0	•	6.2	4.9	1.3	2.1	1.5	4.1	0.8	1.0	0.6	0.5
Operating Margin **21**	•	•	•	0.1	6.6	8.5	9.9	5.6	0.0	1.6	1.6	2.3	•
Operating Margin Before Officers' Comp. **22**	•	1.3	•	6.3	11.5	9.7	12.0	7.1	4.1	2.4	2.5	2.9	•

Selected Average Balance Sheet ($ in Thousands)

Line Item													
Net Receivables 23	9363	0	•	325	518	3242	4840	10915	17136	26487	56963	84014	822975
Inventories 24	4163	0	•	115	543	980	3761	3407	11529	38251	75680	112282	232683
Net Property, Plant and Equipment 25	7288	0	•	127	78	1431	2380	4728	14145	59277	19880	197981	566901
Total Assets 26	47644	0	•	597	1606	7445	15882	29710	73070	173404	287963	877631	4209820
Notes and Loans Payable 27	15419	0	•	619	8	2599	2440	5766	27217	98532	90858	398124	1267217
All Other Liabilities 28	19896	0	•	420	338	2287	5478	12467	19481	42720	156389	233488	1946792
Net Worth 29	12328	0	•	-442	1260	2558	7963	11477	26372	32152	40717	246020	995812

Selected Financial Ratios (Times to 1)

Line Item													
Current Ratio 30	1.0	•	•	1.0	4.2	2.0	2.1	1.4	1.6	1.3	1.4	1.4	0.8
Quick Ratio 31	0.7	•	•	0.7	2.7	1.5	1.2	0.8	0.8	0.5	0.7	0.6	0.6
Net Sales to Working Capital 32	83.5	•	•	•	4.0	5.5	4.6	10.3	6.8	11.8	6.6	14.2	•
Coverage Ratio 33	1.1	6.3	•	1.1	181.5	8.7	17.5	9.8	1.5	2.3	2.3	2.2	•
Total Asset Turnover 34	1.0	•	•	1.8	2.7	2.1	1.7	2.3	1.3	1.1	1.0	1.0	0.7
Inventory Turnover 35	9.1	•	•	6.6	5.6	12.2	4.9	15.2	5.6	3.4	3.2	6.4	12.3
Receivables Turnover 36	5.4	•	•	•	7.2	7.6	6.1	7.5	5.1	5.6	4.5	21.3	4.2
Total Liabilities to Net Worth 37	2.9	•	•	•	0.3	1.9	1.0	1.6	1.8	4.4	6.1	2.6	3.2
Current Assets to Working Capital 38	32.6	•	•	•	1.3	2.0	1.9	3.3	2.7	4.7	3.8	3.8	•
Current Liabilities to Working Capital 39	31.6	•	•	•	0.3	1.0	0.9	2.3	1.7	3.7	2.8	2.8	•
Working Capital to Net Sales 40	0.0	•	•	•	0.4	0.2	0.2	0.1	0.1	0.1	0.2	0.1	•
Inventory to Working Capital 41	8.7	•	•	•	0.4	0.4	0.7	0.6	1.0	1.7	1.4	1.8	•
Total Receipts to Cash Flow 42	37.1	6.7	•	28.8	11.4	7.4	5.6	9.1	12.5	6.3	51.8	14.7	•
Cost of Goods to Cash Flow 43	31.0	4.3	•	19.7	7.9	5.6	3.7	6.8	8.7	4.5	44.1	11.7	•
Cash Flow to Total Debt 44	0.0	•	•	0.0	1.1	0.4	0.6	0.4	0.2	0.2	0.0	0.1	•

Selected Financial Factors (in Percentages)

Line Item													
Debt Ratio 45	74.1	•	•	174.2	21.5	65.6	49.9	61.4	63.9	81.5	85.9	72.0	76.3
Return on Total Assets 46	2.5	•	•	9.6	19.2	21.2	22.0	15.5	4.4	12.1	4.9	8.0	•
Return on Equity Before Income Taxes 47	0.6	•	•	•	24.4	54.5	41.4	36.0	4.3	36.7	19.8	15.5	•
Return on Equity After Income Taxes 48	•	•	•	•	24.0	42.9	37.4	32.3	0.4	19.6	13.8	10.1	•
Profit Margin (Before Income Tax) 49	0.2	4.6	•	0.4	7.0	8.8	11.9	6.0	1.2	6.3	2.8	4.3	•
Profit Margin (After Income Tax) 50	•	4.2	•	0.4	6.9	6.9	10.7	5.4	0.1	3.4	2.0	2.8	•

Table II
Corporations with Net Income

BOILER, TANK, AND SHIPPING CONTAINER

MONEY AMOUNTS AND SIZE OF ASSETS IN THOUSANDS OF DOLLARS

Item Description for Accounting Period 7/06 Through 6/07	Total	Zero Assets	Under 500	500 to 1,000	1,000 to 5,000	5,000 to 10,000	10,000 to 25,000	25,000 to 50,000	50,000 to 100,000	100,000 to 250,000	250,000 to 500,000	500,000 to 2,500,000	2,500,000 and over
Number of Enterprises **1**	479	•	0	175	158	•	•	•	•	•	4	•	4

Revenues ($ in Thousands)

Item Description for Accounting Period 7/06 Through 6/07	Total	Zero Assets	Under 500	500 to 1,000	1,000 to 5,000	5,000 to 10,000	10,000 to 25,000	25,000 to 50,000	50,000 to 100,000	100,000 to 250,000	250,000 to 500,000	500,000 to 2,500,000	2,500,000 and over
Net Sales **2**	20926512	•	0	182701	665367	•	•	•	•	•	1146152	•	3578505
Interest **3**	94947	•	0	0	420	•	•	•	•	•	12148	•	4592
Rents **4**	23298	•	0	0	1924	•	•	•	•	•	0	•	4302
Royalties **5**	109659	•	0	0	0	•	•	•	•	•	0	•	17904
Other Portfolio Income **6**	71079	•	0	271	189	•	•	•	•	•	153	•	3678
Other Receipts **7**	224119	•	0	381	342	•	•	•	•	•	2144	•	36524
Total Receipts **8**	21449614	•	0	183353	668242	•	•	•	•	•	1160597	•	3645505
Average Total Receipts **9**	44780	•	•	1048	4229	•	•	•	•	•	290149	•	911376

Operating Costs/Operating Income (%)

Item Description for Accounting Period 7/06 Through 6/07	Total	Zero Assets	Under 500	500 to 1,000	1,000 to 5,000	5,000 to 10,000	10,000 to 25,000	25,000 to 50,000	50,000 to 100,000	100,000 to 250,000	250,000 to 500,000	500,000 to 2,500,000	2,500,000 and over
Cost of Operations **10**	79.4	•	•	65.7	67.7	•	•	•	•	•	85.2	•	79.7
Salaries and Wages **11**	4.1	•	•	5.0	6.7	•	•	•	•	•	5.9	•	2.8
Taxes Paid **12**	1.3	•	•	2.3	3.0	•	•	•	•	•	1.5	•	1.7
Interest Paid **13**	2.5	•	•	•	0.0	•	•	•	•	•	2.2	•	3.6
Depreciation **14**	2.0	•	•	0.3	0.1	•	•	•	•	•	0.7	•	2.7
Amortization and Depletion **15**	0.3	•	•	•	•	•	•	•	•	•	0.1	•	0.4
Pensions and Other Deferred Comp. **16**	0.5	•	•	0.6	0.8	•	•	•	•	•	0.4	•	0.7
Employee Benefits **17**	2.1	•	•	0.3	2.4	•	•	•	•	•	1.1	•	1.4
Advertising **18**	0.2	•	•	0.5	0.7	•	•	•	•	•	0.1	•	0.1
Other Expenses **19**	4.0	•	•	6.3	5.2	•	•	•	•	•	0.4	•	3.9
Officers' Compensation **20**	1.0	•	•	7.1	4.5	•	•	•	•	•	1.0	•	0.6
Operating Margin **21**	2.6	•	•	11.9	8.7	•	•	•	•	•	1.6	•	2.3
Operating Margin Before Officers' Comp. **22**	3.6	•	•	19.0	13.2	•	•	•	•	•	2.5	•	2.9

Selected Average Balance Sheet ($ in Thousands)

Net Receivables 23	5215	•	332	501	•	•	56963	84014
Inventories 24	4130	•	104	560	•	•	75680	112282
Net Property, Plant and Equipment 25	7497	•	135	50	•	•	19880	197981
Total Assets 26	40472	•	591	1657	•	•	287963	877631
Notes and Loans Payable 27	15713	•	0	6	•	•	90858	398124
All Other Liabilities 28	11379	•	292	359	•	•	156389	233488
Net Worth 29	13379	•	299	1292	•	•	40717	246020

Selected Financial Ratios (Times to 1)

Current Ratio 30	1.5	•	1.6	4.2	•	•	1.4	1.4
Quick Ratio 31	0.7	•	1.2	2.7	•	•	0.7	0.6
Net Sales to Working Capital 32	10.5	•	6.4	3.7	•	•	6.6	14.2
Coverage Ratio 33	3.1	•	•	215.5	•	•	2.3	2.2
Total Asset Turnover 34	1.1	•	1.8	2.5	•	•	1.0	1.0
Inventory Turnover 35	8.4	•	6.6	5.1	•	•	3.2	6.4
Receivables Turnover 36	7.3	•	•	7.2	•	•	4.5	21.3
Total Liabilities to Net Worth 37	2.0	•	1.0	0.3	•	•	6.1	2.6
Current Assets to Working Capital 38	3.1	•	2.8	1.3	•	•	3.8	3.8
Current Liabilities to Working Capital 39	2.1	•	1.8	0.3	•	•	2.8	2.8
Working Capital to Net Sales 40	0.1	•	0.2	0.3	•	•	0.2	0.1
Inventory to Working Capital 41	1.2	•	0.6	0.4	•	•	1.4	1.8
Total Receipts to Cash Flow 42	13.2	•	7.4	9.3	•	•	51.8	14.7
Cost of Goods to Cash Flow 43	10.5	•	4.9	6.3	•	•	44.1	11.7
Cash Flow to Total Debt 44	0.1	•	0.5	1.2	•	•	0.0	0.1

Selected Financial Factors (in Percentages)

Debt Ratio 45	66.9	•	49.4	22.0	•	•	85.9	72.0
Return on Total Assets 46	8.4	•	21.6	23.3	•	•	4.9	8.0
Return on Equity Before Income Taxes 47	17.1	•	42.8	29.7	•	•	19.8	15.5
Return on Equity After Income Taxes 48	14.5	•	42.8	29.3	•	•	13.8	10.1
Profit Margin (Before Income Tax) 49	5.3	•	12.3	9.1	•	•	2.8	4.3
Profit Margin (After Income Tax) 50	4.4	•	12.3	9.0	•	•	2.0	2.8

Table I

Corporations with and without Net Income

COATING, ENGRAVING, HEAT TREATING, AND ALLIED ACTIVITIES

MONEY AMOUNTS AND SIZE OF ASSETS IN THOUSANDS OF DOLLARS

Item Description for Accounting Period 7/06 Through 6/07	Total	Zero Assets	Under 500	500 to 1,000	1,000 to 5,000	5,000 to 10,000	10,000 to 25,000	25,000 to 50,000	50,000 to 100,000	100,000 to 250,000	250,000 to 500,000	500,000 to 2,500,000	2,500,000 and over
Number of Enterprises 1	3917	418	2228	366	715	101	41	26	7	12	0	3	0
Revenues ($ in Thousands)													
Net Sales 2	16286130	91494	1472920	603503	3167433	1040811	893035	1502820	577703	2080545	0	4855867	0
Interest 3	57449	57	2518	102	2818	3359	2025	1552	775	9600	0	34644	0
Rents 4	11736	0	5178	236	3319	717	802	814	0	246	0	424	0
Royalties 5	55367	0	0	0	0	0	2469	0	0	16151	0	36747	0
Other Portfolio Income 6	97270	9544	10875	0	5979	4525	10909	41909	54	10831	0	2642	0
Other Receipts 7	244695	141288	1326	0	48240	4164	3936	13087	8395	1311	0	22947	0
Total Receipts 8	16752647	242383	1492817	603841	3227789	1053576	913176	1560182	586927	2118684	0	4953271	0
Average Total Receipts 9	4277	580	670	1650	4514	10431	22273	60007	83847	176557	•	1651090	•
Operating Costs/Operating Income (%)													
Cost of Operations 10	61.7	26.7	26.5	41.9	51.2	60.6	65.4	69.3	71.6	70.2	•	74.7	•
Salaries and Wages 11	7.4	6.2	13.8	3.2	10.3	3.6	7.5	5.6	6.4	5.0	•	6.4	•
Taxes Paid 12	2.6	2.1	4.2	4.5	3.9	3.5	2.9	2.4	1.8	2.1	•	1.2	•
Interest Paid 13	2.3	0.3	0.7	1.0	1.3	2.4	1.2	1.5	2.3	4.2	•	3.4	•
Depreciation 14	3.0	1.7	1.9	2.0	3.2	4.0	3.2	3.9	3.4	4.5	•	2.2	•
Amortization and Depletion 15	0.6	•	0.1	0.0	0.2	0.3	0.0	0.3	0.5	1.5	•	0.9	•
Pensions and Other Deferred Comp. 16	0.6	0.2	0.6	0.3	0.8	1.6	0.3	0.3	1.0	0.4	•	0.4	•
Employee Benefits 17	1.9	5.5	1.9	0.2	3.0	1.1	1.4	2.7	1.3	2.0	•	1.3	•
Advertising 18	0.4	0.1	0.2	0.2	0.1	0.3	0.2	0.1	0.3	0.1	•	1.1	•
Other Expenses 19	13.5	206.7	30.7	36.4	15.4	10.1	8.0	6.9	6.5	7.1	•	7.8	•
Officers' Compensation 20	4.2	1.1	16.4	4.4	8.6	4.4	3.4	1.8	1.2	0.9	•	0.3	•
Operating Margin 21	1.8	•	2.9	5.9	2.0	8.1	6.2	5.1	3.6	2.1	•	0.3	•
Operating Margin Before Officers' Comp. 22	6.0	•	19.3	10.3	10.6	12.5	9.6	7.0	4.8	3.0	•	0.6	•

Selected Average Balance Sheet ($ in Thousands)

Net Receivables 23	598	0	36	197	513	1270	3221	8018	12416	36280	277754	•
Inventories 24	322	0	14	62	139	337	1334	4267	10163	19984	198597	•
Net Property, Plant and Equipment 25	781	0	63	138	708	2562	5390	14376	25923	49914	242485	•
Total Assets 26	3223	0	164	632	1918	6424	16000	36175	63947	190654	1891550	•
Notes and Loans Payable 27	1208	0	140	263	614	2899	6390	13407	18017	87124	602947	•
All Other Liabilities 28	809	0	29	192	472	793	2634	8191	21436	39575	556258	•
Net Worth 29	1206	0	-5	178	832	2732	6975	14577	24494	63956	732345	•

Selected Financial Ratios (Times to 1)

Current Ratio 30	1.7	•	2.2	1.8	1.5	2.2	1.9	1.5	1.5	1.5	2.0	•
Quick Ratio 31	1.1	•	1.9	1.3	1.1	1.6	1.5	1.0	1.0	0.8	1.1	•
Net Sales to Working Capital 32	7.6	•	16.2	8.2	15.2	6.7	5.0	10.6	9.4	6.4	5.3	•
Coverage Ratio 33	3.0	45.0	6.8	7.1	4.1	4.9	7.9	6.9	3.2	1.9	1.7	•
Total Asset Turnover 34	1.3	•	4.0	2.6	2.3	1.6	1.4	1.6	1.3	0.9	0.9	•
Inventory Turnover 35	8.0	•	12.4	11.1	16.3	18.5	10.7	9.4	5.8	6.1	6.1	•
Receivables Turnover 36	7.5	•	12.9	11.4	9.0	9.1	6.1	8.1	6.3	6.5	6.1	•
Total Liabilities to Net Worth 37	1.7	•	•	2.6	1.3	1.4	1.3	1.5	1.6	2.0	1.6	•
Current Assets to Working Capital 38	2.3	•	1.8	2.3	3.1	1.8	2.1	2.9	3.1	2.9	2.0	•
Current Liabilities to Working Capital 39	1.3	•	0.8	1.3	2.1	0.8	1.1	1.9	2.1	1.9	1.0	•
Working Capital to Net Sales 40	0.1	•	0.1	0.1	0.1	0.1	0.2	0.1	0.1	0.2	0.2	•
Inventory to Working Capital 41	0.7	•	0.2	0.6	0.5	0.2	0.4	0.8	0.9	0.9	0.7	•
Total Receipts to Cash Flow 42	6.8	0.5	3.8	2.8	7.0	6.1	7.1	8.0	9.9	11.2	11.3	•
Cost of Goods to Cash Flow 43	4.2	0.1	1.0	1.2	3.6	3.7	4.7	5.6	7.1	7.8	8.4	•
Cash Flow to Total Debt 44	0.3	•	1.0	1.3	0.6	0.5	0.3	0.3	0.2	0.1	0.1	•

Selected Financial Factors (in Percentages)

Debt Ratio 45	62.6	•	103.3	71.8	56.6	57.5	56.4	59.7	61.7	66.5	61.3	•
Return on Total Assets 46	9.1	•	20.2	18.2	11.9	18.7	13.1	16.7	9.7	7.4	4.9	•
Return on Income Before Income Taxes 47	16.3	•	•	55.5	20.7	35.1	26.4	35.5	17.4	10.7	5.3	•
Return on Equity After Income Taxes 48	14.0	•	•	55.3	19.5	30.8	25.2	29.1	16.2	5.3	4.8	•
Profit Margin (Before Income Tax) 49	4.7	14.2	4.2	6.0	3.9	9.3	8.4	9.0	5.2	3.9	2.4	•
Profit Margin (After Income Tax) 50	4.1	9.7	4.1	6.0	3.7	8.2	8.1	7.3	4.8	2.0	2.2	•

119

Table II

Corporations with Net Income

COATING, ENGRAVING, HEAT TREATING, AND ALLIED ACTIVITIES

MONEY AMOUNTS AND SIZE OF ASSETS IN THOUSANDS OF DOLLARS

Item Description for Accounting Period 7/06 Through 6/07		Total	Zero Assets	Under 500	500 to 1,000	1,000 to 5,000	5,000 to 10,000	10,000 to 25,000	25,000 to 50,000	50,000 to 100,000	100,000 to 250,000	250,000 to 500,000	500,000 to 2,500,000	2,500,000 and over
Number of Enterprises	1	2725	116	1700	230	507	•	31	26	•	7	0	3	0
Revenues ($ in Thousands)														
Net Sales	2	13433627	40186	1091546	188419	2542486	•	766275	1502820	•	1057157	0	4855867	0
Interest	3	50261	57	1827	94	2714	•	1674	1552	•	3759	0	34644	0
Rents	4	10527	0	5178	236	2197	•	802	814	•	159	0	424	0
Royalties	5	55134	0	0	0	0	•	2469	0	•	15918	0	36747	0
Other Portfolio Income	6	95861	9544	10578	0	5979	•	10909	41909	•	9719	0	2642	0
Other Receipts	7	223904	141288	862	1	29451	•	3217	13087	•	1041	0	22947	0
Total Receipts	8	13869314	191075	1109991	188750	2582827	•	785346	1560182	•	1087753	0	4953271	0
Average Total Receipts	9	5090	1647	653	821	5094	•	25334	60007	•	155393	•	1651090	•
Operating Costs/Operating Income (%)														
Cost of Operations	10	62.3	40.5	23.5	50.6	51.5	•	63.5	69.3	•	62.6	•	74.7	•
Salaries and Wages	11	7.1	14.0	10.6	4.9	10.1	•	7.7	5.6	•	5.2	•	6.4	•
Taxes Paid	12	2.5	4.5	4.4	2.5	3.6	•	2.9	2.4	•	3.0	•	1.2	•
Interest Paid	13	2.0	0.6	0.6	1.1	0.7	•	0.9	1.5	•	2.6	•	3.4	•
Depreciation	14	2.8	3.6	2.3	4.8	2.8	•	2.5	3.9	•	3.6	•	2.2	•
Amortization and Depletion	15	0.5	•	0.0	0.1	0.3	•	0.0	0.3	•	1.4	•	0.9	•
Pensions and Other Deferred Comp.	16	0.7	0.5	0.8	1.0	1.0	•	0.3	0.3	•	0.4	•	0.4	•
Employee Benefits	17	1.9	2.3	2.3	0.6	2.6	•	1.5	2.7	•	2.8	•	1.3	•
Advertising	18	0.5	0.3	0.1	0.4	0.1	•	0.3	0.1	•	0.1	•	1.1	•
Other Expenses	19	11.4	364.0	29.3	5.1	12.7	•	7.3	6.9	•	7.3	•	7.8	•
Officers' Compensation	20	4.2	2.5	17.2	6.4	9.1	•	3.5	1.8	•	1.5	•	0.3	•
Operating Margin	21	4.1	•	8.9	22.6	5.4	•	9.6	5.1	•	9.5	•	0.3	•
Operating Margin Before Officers' Comp.	22	8.3	•	26.1	29.0	14.5	•	13.0	7.0	•	11.0	•	0.6	•

Selected Average Balance Sheet ($ in Thousands)

Net Receivables **23**	711	0	43	83	595	3354	8018	29824 • 277754
Inventories **24**	380	0	10	130	121	1563	4636	22462 • 216244
Net Property, Plant and Equipment **25**	896	0	63	159	755	4197	14376	43845 • 242485
Total Assets **26**	3942	0	176	555	2184	15932	36175	167778 • 1891550
Notes and Loans Payable **27**	1213	0	60	134	450	4907	13407	56954 • 602947
All Other Liabilities **28**	954	0	24	93	363	2885	8191	35396 • 556258
Net Worth **29**	1775	0	92	328	1371	8140	14577	75428 • 732345

Selected Financial Ratios (Times to 1)

Current Ratio **30**	2.1	•	3.1	3.6	2.1	2.2	1.5	2.2 • 2.0
Quick Ratio **31**	1.3	•	3.0	2.4	1.6	1.8	1.0	1.2 • 1.1
Net Sales to Working Capital **32**	6.1	•	11.5	2.9	9.2	4.4	10.6	3.7 • 5.3
Coverage Ratio **33**	4.8	67.2	18.0	21.5	10.9	13.9	6.9	5.7 • 1.7
Total Asset Turnover **34**	1.3	•	3.7	1.5	2.3	1.6	1.6	0.9 • 0.9
Inventory Turnover **35**	8.1	•	15.2	3.2	21.3	10.0	8.6	4.2 • 5.6
Receivables Turnover **36**	7.8	•	10.8	•	9.0	6.2	•	6.1 • 11.7
Total Liabilities to Net Worth **37**	1.2	•	0.9	0.7	0.6	1.0	1.5	1.2 • 1.6
Current Assets to Working Capital **38**	1.9	•	1.5	1.4	1.9	1.8	2.9	1.8 • 2.0
Current Liabilities to Working Capital **39**	0.9	•	0.5	0.4	0.9	0.8	1.9	0.8 • 1.0
Working Capital to Net Sales **40**	0.2	•	0.1	0.3	0.1	0.2	0.1	0.3 • 0.2
Inventory to Working Capital **41**	0.5	•	0.0	0.5	0.3	0.3	0.8	0.7 • 0.7
Total Receipts to Cash Flow **42**	6.4	0.3	3.2	3.8	6.8	5.8	8.0	5.9 • 11.3
Cost of Goods to Cash Flow **43**	4.0	0.1	0.7	1.9	3.5	3.7	5.6	3.7 • 8.4
Cash Flow to Total Debt **44**	0.4	•	2.4	0.9	0.9	0.5	0.3	0.5 • 0.1

Selected Financial Factors (in Percentages)

Debt Ratio **45**	55.0	•	47.7	41.0	37.2	48.9	59.7	55.0 • 61.3
Return on Total Assets **46**	11.7	•	41.0	35.3	17.8	20.1	16.7	13.5 • 4.9
Return on Equity Before Income Taxes **47**	20.6	•	74.1	57.0	25.7	36.5	35.5	24.8 • 5.3
Return on Equity After Income Taxes **48**	18.3	•	73.0	56.8	24.7	35.2	29.1	17.1 • 4.8
Profit Margin (Before Income Tax) **49**	7.4	42.5	10.6	22.8	7.0	12.0	9.0	12.4 • 2.4
Profit Margin (After Income Tax) **50**	6.6	32.3	10.4	22.7	6.8	11.6	7.3	8.5 • 2.2

Table I

Corporations with and without Net Income

OTHER FABRICATED METAL PRODUCT

MONEY AMOUNTS AND SIZE OF ASSETS IN THOUSANDS OF DOLLARS

Item Description for Accounting Period 7/06 Through 6/07		Total	Zero Assets	Under 500	500 to 1,000	1,000 to 5,000	5,000 to 10,000	10,000 to 25,000	25,000 to 50,000	50,000 to 100,000	100,000 to 250,000	250,000 to 500,000	500,000 to 2,500,000	2,500,000 and over
Number of Enterprises	1	17432	1821	9234	1740	3393	588	359	127	76	48	20	18	9
Revenues ($ in Thousands)														
Net Sales	2	137978597	1622829	6388551	3626958	19548946	7978972	10774407	8143250	7658490	8677657	8040768	17175763	38342005
Interest	3	1495918	35957	1791	3274	10885	4910	12644	9603	15686	26589	26435	326289	1021854
Rents	4	90341	812	11	50	4646	314	3332	966	2407	1711	6717	4577	64798
Royalties	5	672724	6057	0	0	0	0	857	1205	3937	15413	30877	27011	587367
Other Portfolio Income	6	1345658	108946	5866	1956	59448	43380	15572	19721	69919	42705	38558	150790	788799
Other Receipts	7	1872572	25537	41251	9019	156739	38915	62854	24822	53378	93509	100993	244275	1021279
Total Receipts	8	143455810	1800138	6437470	3641257	19780664	8066491	10869666	8199567	7803817	8857584	8244348	17928705	41826102
Average Total Receipts	9	8229	989	697	2093	5830	13719	30278	64564	102682	184533	412217	996039	4647345
Operating Costs/Operating Income (%)														
Cost of Operations	10	68.0	70.2	48.9	69.7	67.8	69.1	70.0	71.3	70.9	69.5	70.5	71.0	66.8
Salaries and Wages	11	6.8	8.5	14.4	6.9	6.5	5.8	6.6	6.0	6.2	7.6	6.2	6.4	6.2
Taxes Paid	12	2.1	2.0	3.9	2.2	2.7	2.1	1.9	1.6	1.6	1.7	2.0	1.6	2.0
Interest Paid	13	2.6	6.4	1.2	1.1	0.9	0.9	0.9	1.6	1.3	2.2	1.6	3.6	4.8
Depreciation	14	1.9	1.2	2.0	1.2	1.8	2.0	1.9	1.7	1.9	2.3	2.1	1.9	1.9
Amortization and Depletion	15	1.0	0.3	0.1	0.3	0.1	0.1	0.1	0.2	0.4	0.3	0.3	0.6	2.9
Pensions and Other Deferred Comp.	16	0.8	0.5	0.1	0.1	0.5	0.6	0.6	0.4	0.8	0.8	0.8	0.7	1.3
Employee Benefits	17	2.0	1.6	1.8	0.9	1.7	1.4	1.4	1.4	1.8	2.3	2.0	2.6	2.5
Advertising	18	0.8	0.8	0.2	0.3	0.4	0.3	0.5	0.7	0.5	0.8	0.7	0.4	1.6
Other Expenses	19	9.2	13.9	15.2	12.3	9.1	7.9	5.9	9.5	6.6	7.6	8.7	7.8	10.4
Officers' Compensation	20	2.2	7.9	9.2	4.0	4.5	3.6	2.8	1.5	1.5	1.3	0.9	0.6	0.4
Operating Margin	21	2.7	•	2.8	1.0	4.0	6.3	7.6	4.3	6.6	3.6	4.0	2.8	•
Operating Margin Before Officers' Comp.	22	4.9	•	12.1	5.0	8.6	9.9	10.3	5.8	8.1	4.9	5.0	3.4	•

Selected Average Balance Sheet ($ in Thousands)

Item	1	2	3	4	5	6	7	8	9	10	11	12	13
Net Receivables 23	1592	0	53	233	667	1764	4164	9447	15018	24980	61723	174557	1570810
Inventories 24	1016	0	27	170	561	1979	4197	10296	16184	29180	69954	154920	496714
Net Property, Plant and Equipment 25	1066	0	59	104	490	1703	3678	7273	15774	32607	64083	141660	706773
Total Assets 26	13225	205	692	2267	6900	15984	35039	69024	151462	313638	940970		18863838
Notes and Loans Payable 27	5452	0	132	334	703	1746	3885	11165	18208	46091	100368	286712	8471756
All Other Liabilities 28	1946	0	57	237	612	1801	3836	10029	16555	45847	78844	236221	1989712
Net Worth 29	5827	16	121	953	3353	8263	13844	34261	59524	134426	418037		8402371

Selected Financial Ratios (Times to 1)

Item	1	2	3	4	5	6	7	8	9	10	11	12	13
Current Ratio 30	1.8	•	1.5	1.6	2.1	2.0	1.9	2.2	1.9	1.8	1.9	2.1	1.6
Quick Ratio 31	1.1	•	1.0	1.0	1.3	1.1	1.0	1.2	1.0	0.8	0.8	1.1	1.1
Net Sales to Working Capital 32	5.2	•	15.8	11.5	6.8	5.7	5.7	5.0	5.2	5.1	5.6	4.0	4.3
Coverage Ratio 33	3.7	0.6	4.0	2.3	7.0	9.7	4.1	10.7	7.7	3.7	5.2	3.1	2.9
Total Asset Turnover 34	0.6	•	3.4	3.0	2.5	2.0	1.8	1.9	1.5	1.2	1.3	1.0	0.2
Inventory Turnover 35	5.3	•	12.4	8.5	7.0	4.7	4.4	5.0	4.4	4.3	4.1	4.4	5.7
Receivables Turnover 36	5.4	•	14.3	9.0	9.1	6.8	6.8	6.9	6.6	7.1	6.3	6.1	3.2
Total Liabilities to Net Worth 37	1.3	•	12.1	4.7	1.4	1.1	1.5	0.9	1.0	1.5	1.3	1.3	1.2
Current Assets to Working Capital 38	2.2	•	2.9	2.6	1.9	2.0	2.1	1.9	2.1	2.2	2.2	1.9	2.7
Current Liabilities to Working Capital 39	1.2	•	1.9	1.6	0.9	1.0	1.1	0.9	1.1	1.2	1.2	0.9	1.7
Working Capital to Net Sales 40	0.2	•	0.1	0.1	0.1	0.2	0.2	0.2	0.2	0.2	0.2	0.2	0.2
Inventory to Working Capital 41	0.7	•	0.7	0.9	0.7	0.8	0.9	0.7	0.9	0.9	0.9	0.7	0.5
Total Receipts to Cash Flow 42	7.3	29.3	7.0	10.6	9.0	7.7	8.4	7.8	7.4	8.7	7.3	7.4	5.9
Cost of Goods to Cash Flow 43	5.0	20.5	3.4	7.4	6.1	5.3	6.0	5.4	5.2	6.1	5.1	5.3	4.0
Cash Flow to Total Debt 44	0.1	•	0.5	0.3	0.5	0.5	0.4	0.5	0.4	0.2	0.3	0.2	0.1

Selected Financial Factors (in Percentages)

Item	1	2	3	4	5	6	7	8	9	10	11	12	13
Debt Ratio 45	55.9	•	92.4	82.5	58.0	51.4	60.5	48.3	50.4	60.7	57.1	55.6	55.5
Return on Total Assets 46	5.7	•	16.2	7.5	15.4	16.4	12.2	17.4	14.3	9.8	10.6	11.3	3.1
Return on Equity Before Income Taxes 47	9.5	•	160.0	24.3	31.5	30.2	23.4	30.5	25.0	18.2	20.0	17.1	4.6
Return on Equity After Income Taxes 48	7.2	•	153.6	23.0	29.5	28.4	19.1	28.0	21.2	13.3	15.0	11.2	3.0
Profit Margin (Before Income Tax) 49	7.0	•	3.6	1.4	5.2	7.5	5.0	8.4	8.5	6.0	6.7	7.5	9.0
Profit Margin (After Income Tax) 50	5.3	•	3.5	1.3	4.9	7.0	4.1	7.7	7.2	4.4	5.0	4.9	6.0

121

Table II
Corporations with Net Income

OTHER FABRICATED METAL PRODUCT

MONEY AMOUNTS AND SIZE OF ASSETS IN THOUSANDS OF DOLLARS

Item Description for Accounting Period 7/06 Through 6/07	Total	Zero Assets	Under 500	500 to 1,000	1,000 to 5,000	5,000 to 10,000	10,000 to 25,000	25,000 to 50,000	50,000 to 100,000	100,000 to 250,000	250,000 to 500,000	500,000 to 2,500,000	2,500,000 and over
Number of Enterprises **1**	11757	822	6006	1252	2593	493	335	109	64	38	•	•	9
Revenues ($ in Thousands)													
Net Sales **2**	123866902	711721	4361201	3004758	15768789	6886442	10182661	7180278	6498685	7219311	•	•	38342005
Interest **3**	1431568	2348	1453	1022	9111	4652	12374	8623	12550	19110	•	•	1021854
Rents **4**	88049	796	11	50	4646	212	3119	597	2067	1591	•	•	64798
Royalties **5**	644270	23	0	0	0	0	292	1155	3896	12701	•	•	587367
Other Portfolio Income **6**	1305505	108697	4757	1845	56754	22708	12298	18932	66008	41729	•	•	788799
Other Receipts **7**	1778310	14699	31873	4390	141421	30779	62131	18282	50183	77288	•	•	1021279
Total Receipts **8**	129117604	838284	4399295	3012065	15980721	6944793	10272875	7227867	6633389	7371730	•	•	41826102
Average Total Receipts **9**	10982	1020	732	2406	6163	14087	30665	66311	103647	193993	•	•	4647345
Operating Costs/Operating Income (%)													
Cost of Operations **10**	67.6	66.3	46.6	71.0	66.8	67.2	69.6	70.7	69.4	68.4	•	•	66.8
Salaries and Wages **11**	6.6	7.7	13.2	6.4	6.0	5.8	6.6	6.4	6.2	7.7	•	•	6.2
Taxes Paid **12**	2.0	2.0	3.6	2.0	2.5	2.2	1.8	1.5	1.5	1.6	•	•	2.0
Interest Paid **13**	2.5	1.4	1.1	0.7	0.8	0.9	0.8	1.2	1.2	1.4	•	•	4.8
Depreciation **14**	1.8	1.0	1.5	1.1	1.8	1.9	1.9	1.5	1.7	2.0	•	•	1.9
Amortization and Depletion **15**	1.0	0.2	0.1	0.2	0.0	0.0	0.1	0.1	0.3	0.2	•	•	2.9
Pensions and Other Deferred Comp. **16**	0.8	0.4	0.1	0.1	0.5	0.5	0.6	0.4	0.7	0.8	•	•	1.3
Employee Benefits **17**	2.0	1.4	1.8	0.8	1.6	1.6	1.3	1.4	1.6	2.0	•	•	2.5
Advertising **18**	0.8	0.5	0.3	0.3	0.4	0.3	0.4	0.7	0.4	0.6	•	•	1.6
Other Expenses **19**	8.7	7.1	14.2	11.0	8.0	7.2	5.7	8.7	6.5	6.8	•	•	10.4
Officers' Compensation **20**	2.1	14.2	9.9	3.5	4.9	3.7	2.8	1.5	1.7	1.4	•	•	0.4
Operating Margin **21**	4.0	•	7.5	2.8	6.5	8.8	8.4	6.1	8.6	7.0	•	•	•
Operating Margin Before Officers' Comp. **22**	6.1	12.2	17.3	6.4	11.4	12.5	11.2	7.6	10.3	8.4	•	•	•

Selected Average Balance Sheet ($ in Thousands)

Net Receivables 23	2175	0	52	270	674	1805	4254	9665	15265	26360	•	1570810
Inventories 24	1336	0	30	174	547	2028	4098	10252	16978	29745	•	479343
Net Property, Plant and Equipment 25	1420	0	51	111	531	1705	3729	6863	14772	31327	•	706773
Total Assets 26	18839	0	213	712	2289	6920	16066	35211	68702	146516	•	18863838
Notes and Loans Payable 27	7702	0	101	223	582	1804	3878	9759	15267	36562	•	8471756
All Other Liabilities 28	2620	0	52	225	579	1753	3712	9090	17488	37138	•	1989712
Net Worth 29	8516	0	60	264	1128	3363	8477	16362	35947	72816	•	8402371

Selected Financial Ratios (Times to 1)

Current Ratio 30	1.9	•	2.3	2.0	2.3	2.1	2.2	2.1	2.1	2.2	•	1.6
Quick Ratio 31	1.1	•	1.6	1.3	1.5	1.2	1.2	1.0	1.1	1.1	•	1.1
Net Sales to Working Capital 32	5.0	•	9.5	9.4	6.5	5.6	4.9	5.3	4.8	4.4	•	4.3
Coverage Ratio 33	4.4	12.4	8.3	5.2	11.2	12.3	12.0	6.7	10.1	7.7	•	2.9
Total Asset Turnover 34	0.6	•	3.4	3.4	2.7	2.0	1.9	1.9	1.5	1.3	•	0.2
Inventory Turnover 35	5.3	•	11.4	9.8	7.4	4.6	5.2	4.5	4.2	4.4	•	5.9
Receivables Turnover 36	5.4	•	12.5	9.5	9.2	6.6	7.3	7.1	6.4	7.1	•	•
Total Liabilities to Net Worth 37	1.2	•	2.5	1.7	1.0	1.1	0.9	1.2	0.9	1.0	•	1.2
Current Assets to Working Capital 38	2.2	•	1.8	2.0	1.8	1.9	1.8	1.9	1.9	1.8	•	2.7
Current Liabilities to Working Capital 39	1.2	•	0.8	1.0	0.8	0.9	0.8	0.9	0.9	0.8	•	1.7
Working Capital to Net Sales 40	0.2	•	0.1	0.1	0.2	0.2	0.2	0.2	0.2	0.2	•	0.2
Inventory to Working Capital 41	0.6	•	0.3	0.7	0.6	0.7	0.7	0.9	0.8	0.8	•	0.5
Total Receipts to Cash Flow 42	6.8	13.4	5.5	10.0	7.6	6.9	7.4	7.6	6.4	7.1	•	5.9
Cost of Goods to Cash Flow 43	4.6	8.9	2.6	7.1	5.1	4.7	5.1	5.4	4.5	4.9	•	4.0
Cash Flow to Total Debt 44	0.2	•	0.9	0.5	0.7	0.6	0.5	0.5	0.5	0.4	•	0.1

Selected Financial Factors (in Percentages)

Debt Ratio 45	54.8	•	71.8	62.9	50.7	51.4	47.2	53.5	47.7	50.3	•	55.5
Return on Total Assets 46	6.2	•	32.3	12.9	22.8	21.1	19.1	15.0	17.6	14.1	•	3.1
Return on Equity Before Income Taxes 47	10.6	•	100.6	28.1	42.1	40.0	33.1	27.4	30.3	24.6	•	4.6
Return on Equity After Income Taxes 48	8.3	•	98.1	27.2	39.9	37.8	30.5	23.2	25.9	19.6	•	3.0
Profit Margin (Before Income Tax) 49	8.5	15.8	8.4	3.1	7.8	9.6	9.2	6.8	10.7	9.4	•	9.0
Profit Margin (After Income Tax) 50	6.7	13.8	8.1	3.0	7.4	9.1	8.5	5.8	9.2	7.5	•	6.0

Table I

Corporations with and without Net Income

AGRICULTURE, CONSTRUCTION, AND MINING MACHINERY

MONEY AMOUNTS AND SIZE OF ASSETS IN THOUSANDS OF DOLLARS

Item Description for Accounting Period 7/06 Through 6/07	Total	Zero Assets	Under 500	500 to 1,000	1,000 to 5,000	5,000 to 10,000	10,000 to 25,000	25,000 to 50,000	50,000 to 100,000	100,000 to 250,000	250,000 to 500,000	500,000 to 2,500,000	2,500,000 and over
Number of Enterprises **1**	3353	290	1600	175	864	201	99	43	30	19	11	12	9
Revenues ($ in Thousands)													
Net Sales **2**	118126734	299592	340639	245144	5473384	2522510	2538406	2533653	3438867	3349230	4795662	16656643	75933205
Interest **3**	4640547	410	44	730	2899	2258	5069	5597	4784	12580	24611	121455	4460110
Rents **4**	1059707	4	1603	0	587	749	7806	4917	3205	333	2028	971	1037505
Royalties **5**	908153	0	0	0	0	0	0	0	589	0	3548	73943	830073
Other Portfolio Income **6**	2509799	3912	7824	0	4152	3424	18216	3992	16240	7820	3550	164964	2275706
Other Receipts **7**	2191553	234	4417	118	14550	14040	7112	8424	26765	93590	24533	258811	1738957
Total Receipts **8**	129436493	304152	354527	245992	5495572	2542981	2576609	2556583	3490250	3463553	4853932	17276787	86275556
Average Total Receipts **9**	38603	1049	222	1406	6361	12652	26026	59455	116342	182292	441267	1439732	9586173
Operating Costs/Operating Income (%)													
Cost of Operations **10**	72.1	62.4	68.8	64.2	74.8	62.2	68.4	67.9	74.2	69.9	74.5	75.4	71.7
Salaries and Wages **11**	6.1	2.9	5.1	7.8	4.7	11.4	6.9	7.3	6.4	7.7	7.8	5.0	6.1
Taxes Paid **12**	1.0	1.0	2.8	3.2	0.9	2.8	1.9	1.7	1.3	1.4	1.5	1.0	0.8
Interest Paid **13**	3.7	0.7	4.1	3.0	0.5	1.1	1.8	1.4	1.7	1.4	1.9	2.1	4.9
Depreciation **14**	2.1	0.9	1.8	2.0	0.9	2.0	1.6	1.3	1.3	1.6	1.6	1.4	2.4
Amortization and Depletion **15**	0.3	0.0	0.1	0.6	0.0	0.1	0.2	0.1	0.3	0.5	0.8	0.3	0.4
Pensions and Other Deferred Comp. **16**	0.6	0.1	0.2	0.1	0.5	0.1	0.7	0.5	0.4	0.7	0.5	1.0	0.6
Employee Benefits **17**	1.8	1.1	2.0	0.3	0.8	2.8	1.8	1.5	1.4	1.4	1.2	1.3	2.0
Advertising **18**	0.4	0.7	0.8	1.5	0.6	1.5	0.6	0.8	0.8	0.8	0.6	0.8	0.2
Other Expenses **19**	11.6	3.7	15.1	13.6	6.4	11.7	9.8	7.4	8.3	9.1	6.2	7.7	13.6
Officers' Compensation **20**	0.7	0.4	7.4	5.1	2.9	2.6	2.4	1.7	0.9	0.5	0.7	0.7	0.4
Operating Margin **21**	•	26.2	•	•	6.9	1.6	3.8	8.5	2.9	5.0	2.8	3.3	•
Operating Margin Before Officers' Comp. **22**	0.2	26.5	•	3.6	9.8	4.2	6.2	10.2	3.8	5.5	3.4	4.0	•

Selected Average Balance Sheet ($ in Thousands)

Net Receivables 23	15243	0	29	88	509	1396	3542	8198	15116	24727	57666	234493	5028172
Inventories 24	4667	0	18	247	880	2112	6241	11671	16374	42288	91680	202809	948340
Net Property, Plant and Equipment 25	4623	0	53	125	327	1400	3234	5754	10647	19875	57914	158441	1225296
Total Assets 26	48018	0	124	872	2365	6578	16039	33321	68552	147483	364226	1169092	14596818
Notes and Loans Payable 27	21200	0	164	542	618	1651	5690	9164	17171	36361	68692	341854	6982250
All Other Liabilities 28	14200	0	26	93	445	1855	4764	9273	25844	35424	129414	376686	4281548
Net Worth 29	12618	0	-66	237	1303	3072	5584	14884	25536	75698	166121	450552	3333019

Selected Financial Ratios (Times to 1)

Current Ratio 30	1.6	•	1.1	4.3	3.3	1.8	1.7	2.1	1.6	2.1	1.9	1.5	1.5
Quick Ratio 31	1.1	•	0.6	1.4	1.8	0.7	0.7	1.0	0.7	0.9	0.8	0.8	1.1
Net Sales to Working Capital 32	4.0	•	48.2	2.9	5.1	6.3	5.5	4.5	6.7	4.0	4.3	7.5	3.5
Coverage Ratio 33	3.8	40.5	•	0.6	14.7	3.1	4.0	7.8	3.5	7.0	3.2	4.8	3.5
Total Asset Turnover 34	0.7	•	1.7	1.6	2.7	1.9	1.6	1.8	1.7	1.2	1.2	1.2	0.6
Inventory Turnover 35	5.4	•	8.2	3.6	5.4	3.7	2.8	3.4	5.2	2.9	3.5	5.2	6.4
Receivables Turnover 36	2.3	•	7.7	23.8	10.8	10.0	6.5	7.0	9.0	6.5	6.6	5.3	1.7
Total Liabilities to Net Worth 37	2.8	•	•	2.7	0.8	1.1	1.9	1.2	1.7	0.9	1.2	1.6	3.4
Current Assets to Working Capital 38	2.8	•	14.9	1.3	1.4	2.3	2.4	1.9	2.5	1.9	2.2	3.0	3.0
Current Liabilities to Working Capital 39	1.8	•	13.9	0.3	0.4	1.3	1.4	0.9	1.5	0.9	1.2	2.0	2.0
Working Capital to Net Sales 40	0.2	•	0.0	0.3	0.2	0.2	0.2	0.2	0.1	0.2	0.2	0.1	0.3
Inventory to Working Capital 41	0.6	•	5.6	0.9	0.6	1.3	1.3	0.8	1.2	0.9	1.0	1.2	0.4
Total Receipts to Cash Flow 42	5.6	3.3	32.8	9.5	8.5	8.5	7.4	6.4	8.6	6.4	11.4	7.7	4.8
Cost of Goods to Cash Flow 43	4.0	2.1	22.6	6.1	6.4	5.3	5.1	4.4	6.4	4.5	8.5	5.8	3.4
Cash Flow to Total Debt 44	0.2	•	0.0	0.2	0.7	0.4	0.3	0.5	0.3	0.4	0.2	0.3	0.2

Selected Financial Factors (in Percentages)

Debt Ratio 45	73.7	•	153.0	72.8	44.9	53.3	65.2	55.3	62.7	48.7	54.4	61.5	77.2
Return on Total Assets 46	10.3	•	•	3.1	20.9	6.6	11.4	18.9	10.2	11.9	7.1	12.1	9.9
Return on Equity Before Income Taxes 47	28.9	•	13.8	•	35.4	9.7	24.4	36.9	19.7	19.9	10.6	24.9	31.2
Return on Equity After Income Taxes 48	20.2	•	14.5	•	34.1	6.6	15.7	31.1	15.2	15.2	6.7	16.6	21.4
Profit Margin (Before Income Tax) 49	10.3	27.7	•	•	7.3	2.4	5.3	9.3	4.4	8.6	4.0	8.1	12.3
Profit Margin (After Income Tax) 50	7.2	24.7	•	•	7.0	1.6	3.4	7.8	3.4	6.5	2.6	5.4	8.5

Table II
Corporations with Net Income

AGRICULTURE, CONSTRUCTION, AND MINING MACHINERY

MONEY AMOUNTS AND SIZE OF ASSETS IN THOUSANDS OF DOLLARS

Item Description for Accounting Period 7/06 Through 6/07		Total	Zero Assets	Under 500	500 to 1,000	1,000 to 5,000	5,000 to 10,000	10,000 to 25,000	25,000 to 50,000	50,000 to 100,000	100,000 to 250,000	250,000 to 500,000	500,000 to 2,500,000	2,500,000 and over
Number of Enterprises	1	2079	290	617	60	813	110	82	•	21	•	•	•	•
Revenues ($ in Thousands)														
Net Sales	2	112084566	299592	90050	76982	5243825	1425816	2177663	•	2684060	•	•	•	•
Interest	3	4613422	410	0	722	2854	2258	5008	•	4271	•	•	•	•
Rents	4	1058104	4	0	0	587	749	7806	•	3205	•	•	•	•
Royalties	5	898381	0	0	0	0	0	0	•	440	•	•	•	•
Other Portfolio Income	6	2500819	3912	0	0	4152	2749	18186	•	16204	•	•	•	•
Other Receipts	7	2032113	234	0	0	11223	12085	10999	•	14379	•	•	•	•
Total Receipts	8	123187405	304152	90050	77704	5262641	1443657	2219662	•	2722559	•	•	•	•
Average Total Receipts	9	59253	1049	146	1295	6473	13124	27069	•	129646	•	•	•	•
Operating Costs/Operating Income (%)														
Cost of Operations	10	71.9	62.4	46.2	64.7	74.2	61.4	67.5	•	75.3	•	•	•	•
Salaries and Wages	11	6.0	2.9	12.2	13.8	4.7	11.6	6.9	•	5.5	•	•	•	•
Taxes Paid	12	1.0	1.0	2.5	3.3	0.9	3.2	2.0	•	1.3	•	•	•	•
Interest Paid	13	3.7	0.7	3.7	0.0	0.4	1.3	1.7	•	1.6	•	•	•	•
Depreciation	14	2.0	0.9	2.3	0.2	0.9	2.5	1.3	•	1.2	•	•	•	•
Amortization and Depletion	15	0.3	0.0	0.5	•	0.0	0.2	0.2	•	0.2	•	•	•	•
Pensions and Other Deferred Comp.	16	0.6	0.1	0.2	0.4	0.5	0.2	0.8	•	0.4	•	•	•	•
Employee Benefits	17	1.8	1.1	0.7	1.0	0.7	3.5	1.6	•	1.2	•	•	•	•
Advertising	18	0.4	0.7	0.4	0.9	0.6	0.4	0.7	•	0.8	•	•	•	•
Other Expenses	19	11.7	3.7	19.3	7.7	6.4	9.5	8.0	•	6.8	•	•	•	•
Officers' Compensation	20	0.7	0.4	4.5	7.1	3.0	2.5	2.5	•	1.0	•	•	•	•
Operating Margin	21	•	26.2	7.5	0.9	7.7	4.0	6.8	•	4.7	•	•	•	•
Operating Margin Before Officers' Comp.	22	0.6	26.5	12.0	8.0	10.7	6.4	9.2	•	5.7	•	•	•	•

Selected Average Balance Sheet ($ in Thousands)

Net Receivables 23	23104	0	16	115	500	1381	3774	15066
Inventories 24	6760	0	7	209	806	1998	5876	19897
Net Property, Plant and Equipment 25	7039	0	68	40	335	1492	2997	12178
Total Assets 26	72958	0	112	650	2334	6243	15765	70661
Notes and Loans Payable 27	33061	0	79	0	552	2387	4582	14164
All Other Liabilities 28	20699	0	27	113	410	1476	4633	25406
Net Worth 29	19198	0	6	537	1372	2380	6550	31090

Selected Financial Ratios (Times to 1)

Current Ratio 30	1.6		0.8	5.4	3.7	1.8	1.9	1.9
Quick Ratio 31	1.1		0.6	3.7	2.1	0.7	0.9	0.8
Net Sales to Working Capital 32	3.9			2.6	5.1	6.4	4.9	5.7
Coverage Ratio 33	4.0	40.5	3.1	57.4	19.4	5.1	6.0	4.9
Total Asset Turnover 34	0.7		1.3	2.0	2.8	2.1	1.7	1.8
Inventory Turnover 35	5.7		10.3	4.0	5.9	4.0	3.1	4.8
Receivables Turnover 36	2.4		3.6	12.6	12.0	9.5	6.5	8.6
Total Liabilities to Net Worth 37	2.8		18.3	0.2	0.7	1.6	1.4	1.3
Current Assets to Working Capital 38	2.7			1.2	1.4	2.2	2.1	2.1
Current Liabilities to Working Capital 39	1.7			0.2	0.4	1.2	1.1	1.1
Working Capital to Net Sales 40	0.3			0.4	0.2	0.2	0.2	0.2
Inventory to Working Capital 41	0.5			0.4	0.6	1.3	1.0	1.0
Total Receipts to Cash Flow 42	5.4	3.3	4.0	10.7	7.9	8.1	6.6	8.4
Cost of Goods to Cash Flow 43	3.9	2.1	1.8	7.0	5.9	4.9	4.5	6.3
Cash Flow to Total Debt 44	0.2			1.1	0.8	0.4	0.4	0.4

Selected Financial Factors (in Percentages)

Debt Ratio 45	73.7		94.8	17.4	41.2	61.9	58.5	56.0
Return on Total Assets 46	11.0		14.5	3.7	23.4	13.5	17.5	14.0
Return on Equity Before Income Taxes 47	31.3		188.2	4.4	37.8	28.4	35.1	25.4
Return on Equity After Income Taxes 48	22.1		166.7	3.7	36.5	21.2	26.1	20.1
Profit Margin (Before Income Tax) 49	11.1	27.7	7.5	1.8	8.0	5.2	8.7	6.2
Profit Margin (After Income Tax) 50	7.9	24.7	6.6	1.6	7.8	3.9	6.4	4.9

Table I
Corporations with and without Net Income

INDUSTRIAL MACHINERY

MONEY AMOUNTS AND SIZE OF ASSETS IN THOUSANDS OF DOLLARS

Item Description for Accounting Period 7/06 Through 6/07		Total	Zero Assets	Under 500	500 to 1,000	1,000 to 5,000	5,000 to 10,000	10,000 to 25,000	25,000 to 50,000	50,000 to 100,000	100,000 to 250,000	250,000 to 500,000	500,000 to 2,500,000	2,500,000 and over
Number of Enterprises	1	3618	453	1493	186	852	329	128	78	44	27	14	10	4
Revenues ($ in Thousands)														
Net Sales	2	53814790	693493	909999	281753	3845715	3757446	3090034	3896841	3290848	4812249	5115191	6761917	17359305
Interest	3	459500	15086	237	14	4562	3430	8338	13857	29288	46796	30518	58586	248788
Rents	4	39097	36	0	1984	1833	425	1792	5985	2051	10761	3022	1780	9428
Royalties	5	279786	5724	0	0	83	0	5457	4828	1638	11994	26937	77045	146080
Other Portfolio Income	6	503299	9249	0	1	12203	680	7432	23362	40006	21367	31332	189528	168137
Other Receipts	7	499311	21313	10451	1412	65327	34253	13534	36277	43529	56100	95067	118491	3557
Total Receipts	8	55595783	744901	920687	285164	3929723	3796234	3126587	3981150	3407360	4959267	5302067	7207347	17935295
Average Total Receipts	9	15366	1644	617	1533	4612	11539	24426	51040	77440	183677	378719	720735	4483824
Operating Costs/Operating Income (%)														
Cost of Operations	10	64.7	62.4	68.6	64.7	64.4	68.6	66.3	69.4	70.0	68.1	68.7	60.7	60.9
Salaries and Wages	11	9.7	11.9	3.9	9.8	6.7	10.3	8.7	7.3	8.2	10.9	8.1	13.1	10.2
Taxes Paid	12	1.6	1.8	2.6	3.8	3.2	2.3	2.2	2.0	1.9	1.5	1.0	1.8	0.9
Interest Paid	13	1.9	4.4	1.5	1.3	1.2	1.0	0.9	1.0	1.7	2.0	2.8	3.2	1.7
Depreciation	14	2.0	4.0	1.5	2.0	1.8	1.2	1.6	1.8	2.2	2.1	1.5	2.5	2.1
Amortization and Depletion	15	0.7	1.1	•	0.2	0.1	0.3	0.2	0.2	0.8	0.9	0.6	1.7	0.6
Pensions and Other Deferred Comp.	16	0.8	1.5	•	0.1	0.9	0.5	0.7	1.1	1.1	1.0	1.0	1.4	0.4
Employee Benefits	17	2.0	2.6	3.1	0.2	3.2	2.3	1.8	1.7	1.9	2.6	2.3	1.9	1.6
Advertising	18	0.5	0.3	0.6	0.1	0.4	0.3	0.8	0.6	0.5	0.4	0.5	0.6	0.4
Other Expenses	19	8.9	16.1	12.0	11.3	10.4	7.0	9.9	8.4	9.0	9.1	7.1	10.1	8.5
Officers' Compensation	20	1.7	6.9	8.2	5.1	5.4	2.3	4.5	1.9	1.1	1.1	1.0	1.1	0.4
Operating Margin	21	5.6	•	•	1.4	2.4	3.9	2.5	4.5	1.5	0.3	5.6	1.9	12.3
Operating Margin Before Officers' Comp.	22	7.3	•	6.2	6.5	7.8	6.2	6.9	6.4	2.7	1.5	6.5	3.0	12.6

Selected Average Balance Sheet ($ in Thousands)

Net Receivables 23	3405	0	38	411	673	1592	3449	8781	15561	33059	84069	162172	1396863
Inventories 24	1936	0	62	34	637	1705	4384	9209	10330	33322	40234	81228	448780
Net Property, Plant and Equipment 25	1776	0	22	99	537	1407	2479	6460	11104	22501	41599	68196	567921
Total Assets 26	17414	0	156	628	2371	7621	15884	35448	71183	157703	394353	1174107	7169208
Notes and Loans Payable 27	3462	0	39	261	712	3284	2974	7836	18756	41374	109683	311827	785713
All Other Liabilities 28	5655	0	55	437	679	2007	4992	10231	22038	55892	129100	420740	2281324
Net Worth 29	8297	0	61	-70	980	2330	7919	17381	30389	60437	155569	441540	4102171

Selected Financial Ratios (Times to 1)

Current Ratio 30	1.6	•	2.5	1.0	2.1	1.7	1.9	2.1	1.5	1.7	1.9	1.2	1.6
Quick Ratio 31	1.0	•	1.5	0.8	1.2	0.8	1.1	1.2	0.9	0.9	1.1	0.7	1.1
Net Sales to Working Capital 32	4.8	•	7.8	•	5.1	6.2	4.6	3.9	5.6	4.2	4.2	12.4	3.8
Coverage Ratio 33	6.1	•	0.5	3.0	4.9	5.9	4.9	7.4	3.9	2.8	4.6	4.5	10.4
Total Asset Turnover 34	0.9	•	3.9	2.4	1.9	1.5	1.5	1.4	1.1	1.1	0.9	0.6	0.6
Inventory Turnover 35	5.0	•	6.8	28.7	4.6	4.6	3.6	3.8	5.1	3.6	6.2	5.1	5.9
Receivables Turnover 36	4.7	•	12.2	4.6	6.8	7.0	5.9	5.3	5.0	4.1	5.3	3.7	4.0
Total Liabilities to Net Worth 37	1.1	•	1.5	•	1.4	2.3	1.0	1.0	1.3	1.6	1.5	1.7	0.7
Current Assets to Working Capital 38	2.6	•	1.7	•	1.9	2.5	2.2	1.9	3.1	2.3	2.1	5.8	2.6
Current Liabilities to Working Capital 39	1.6	•	0.7	•	0.9	1.5	1.2	0.9	2.1	1.3	1.1	4.8	1.6
Working Capital to Net Sales 40	0.2	•	0.1	•	0.2	0.2	0.2	0.3	0.2	0.2	0.2	0.1	0.3
Inventory to Working Capital 41	0.7	•	0.7	•	0.7	1.1	0.8	0.7	0.8	0.7	0.6	1.6	0.4
Total Receipts to Cash Flow 42	6.4	10.5	12.8	9.3	8.5	9.9	8.5	7.5	8.8	9.2	6.6	6.0	4.6
Cost of Goods to Cash Flow 43	4.1	6.5	8.8	6.0	5.5	6.8	5.7	5.2	6.2	6.3	4.5	3.7	2.8
Cash Flow to Total Debt 44	0.3	•	0.5	0.2	0.4	0.2	0.4	0.4	0.2	0.2	0.6	0.2	0.3

Selected Financial Factors (in Percentages)

Debt Ratio 45	52.4	•	60.6	111.2	58.7	69.4	50.1	51.0	57.3	61.7	60.6	62.4	42.8
Return on Total Assets 46	9.7	•	2.8	9.5	10.9	8.9	6.9	10.9	7.1	6.2	12.0	8.3	10.8
Return on Equity Before Income Taxes 47	17.0	•	•	•	21.1	24.1	11.0	19.1	12.3	10.4	23.8	17.2	17.0
Return on Equity After Income Taxes 48	12.0	•	•	•	17.4	22.7	9.3	14.6	8.3	8.5	16.3	13.4	11.2
Profit Margin (Before Income Tax) 49	9.5	•	2.6	•	4.6	4.9	3.6	6.7	5.0	3.5	10.1	11.2	16.1
Profit Margin (After Income Tax) 50	6.7	•	2.5	•	3.8	4.6	3.0	5.1	3.4	2.9	6.9	8.7	10.5

Table II

Corporations with Net Income

INDUSTRIAL MACHINERY

MONEY AMOUNTS AND SIZE OF ASSETS IN THOUSANDS OF DOLLARS

Item Description for Accounting Period 7/06 Through 6/07	Total	Zero Assets	Under 500	500 to 1,000	1,000 to 5,000	5,000 to 10,000	10,000 to 25,000	25,000 to 50,000	50,000 to 100,000	100,000 to 250,000	250,000 to 500,000	500,000 to 2,500,000	2,500,000 and over
Number of Enterprises **1**	2316	447	490	124	706	307	97	63	36	20	•	•	4
Revenues ($ in Thousands)													
Net Sales **2**	48105799	26125	402408	217587	3232922	3604662	2534059	3183494	2733812	3803036	•	•	17359305
Interest **3**	427352	6582	108	14	4443	1586	7150	11063	26749	32339	•	•	248788
Rents **4**	31770	0	0	0	403	425	1584	4295	2051	8799	•	•	9428
Royalties **5**	269548	0	0	0	83	0	4863	4828	1593	8119	•	•	146080
Other Portfolio Income **6**	476756	5065	0	1	4285	515	5700	22699	39966	15676	•	•	168137
Other Receipts **7**	474591	7021	10452	7	65295	33520	12390	31042	43643	53216	•	•	3557
Total Receipts **8**	49785816	44793	412968	217609	3307431	3640708	2565746	3257421	2847814	3921185	•	•	17935295
Average Total Receipts **9**	21496	100	843	1755	4685	11859	26451	51705	79106	196059	•	•	4483824
Operating Costs/Operating Income (%)													
Cost of Operations **10**	63.8	46.0	69.4	62.1	61.4	69.0	64.9	66.2	71.2	67.9	•	•	60.9
Salaries and Wages **11**	9.8	8.0	4.6	11.3	6.6	10.3	8.5	7.5	7.4	10.1	•	•	10.2
Taxes Paid **12**	1.5	3.3	2.4	2.7	3.1	2.2	2.0	2.0	1.9	1.5	•	•	0.9
Interest Paid **13**	1.7	3.5	1.7	1.3	0.6	0.8	0.6	1.0	1.2	1.8	•	•	1.7
Depreciation **14**	1.9	2.1	2.8	2.4	1.9	1.1	1.2	2.0	1.6	1.8	•	•	2.1
Amortization and Depletion **15**	0.6	0.0	•	0.2	0.1	0.1	0.1	0.2	0.5	0.6	•	•	0.6
Pensions and Other Deferred Comp. **16**	0.7	0.1	•	0.1	1.1	0.4	0.7	1.1	1.1	1.1	•	•	0.4
Employee Benefits **17**	2.0	0.5	3.6	•	3.3	2.3	1.7	1.7	1.7	2.7	•	•	1.6
Advertising **18**	0.5	0.5	0.1	0.1	0.4	0.3	0.7	0.7	0.5	0.4	•	•	0.4
Other Expenses **19**	8.6	23.2	9.5	10.6	10.2	6.3	9.6	8.7	7.9	8.7	•	•	8.5
Officers' Compensation **20**	1.6	23.6	5.7	5.0	6.2	2.2	4.9	2.0	1.1	1.2	•	•	0.4
Operating Margin **21**	7.3	•	0.2	4.2	5.2	5.1	5.0	6.7	4.1	2.3	•	•	12.3
Operating Margin Before Officers' Comp. **22**	8.9	12.7	5.9	9.3	11.4	7.3	9.9	8.7	5.2	3.5	•	•	12.6

Selected Average Balance Sheet ($ in Thousands)

Line Item											
Net Receivables 23	4946	0	63	392	666	1615	3369	9130	15532	34343	1396863
Inventories 24	2455	0	33	44	486	1655	4631	9072	9196	25655	448780
Net Property, Plant and Equipment 25	2472	0	54	90	543	1419	2192	6417	10279	23347	567921
Total Assets 26	25238	0	185	624	2272	7590	15290	35230	68842	156884	7169208
Notes and Loans Payable 27	4589	0	58	285	463	3085	2365	8603	13028	39158	785713
All Other Liabilities 28	8218	0	154	372	569	1972	5140	10548	23650	56906	2281324
Net Worth 29	12430	0	-27	-33	1240	2533	7785	16079	32164	60820	4102171

Selected Financial Ratios (Times to 1)

Line Item											
Current Ratio 30	1.6	•	0.9	1.2	2.2	1.9	1.8	2.1	1.5	1.7	1.6
Quick Ratio 31	1.0	•	0.8	0.9	1.3	0.9	1.1	1.2	0.9	0.9	1.1
Net Sales to Working Capital 32	4.8	•	•	23.4	5.4	5.3	5.3	4.1	5.3	4.8	3.8
Coverage Ratio 33	7.7	18.2	2.7	4.3	12.7	8.5	10.8	9.9	7.8	4.1	10.4
Total Asset Turnover 34	0.8	•	4.4	2.8	2.0	1.5	1.7	1.4	1.1	1.2	0.6
Inventory Turnover 35	5.4	•	17.5	24.5	5.8	4.9	3.7	3.7	5.9	5.0	5.9
Receivables Turnover 36	4.9	•	11.4	4.6	8.8	7.3	6.2	5.0	5.2	5.1	4.0
Total Liabilities to Net Worth 37	1.0	•	•	•	0.8	2.0	1.0	1.2	1.1	1.6	0.7
Current Assets to Working Capital 38	2.6	•	•	7.1	1.9	2.1	2.2	1.9	2.9	2.5	2.6
Current Liabilities to Working Capital 39	1.6	•	•	6.1	0.9	1.1	1.2	0.9	1.9	1.5	1.6
Working Capital to Net Sales 40	0.2	•	•	0.0	0.2	0.2	0.2	0.2	0.2	0.2	0.3
Inventory to Working Capital 41	0.6	•	•	1.1	0.6	1.0	0.9	0.7	0.8	0.8	0.4
Total Receipts to Cash Flow 42	5.8	1.2	9.8	8.5	6.8	9.4	7.0	6.4	7.4	7.8	4.6
Cost of Goods to Cash Flow 43	3.7	0.6	6.8	5.3	4.2	6.5	4.5	4.2	5.3	5.3	2.8
Cash Flow to Total Debt 44	0.3	•	0.4	0.3	0.7	0.2	0.5	0.4	0.3	0.3	0.3

Selected Financial Factors (in Percentages)

Line Item											
Debt Ratio 45	50.7	•	114.7	105.3	45.4	66.6	49.1	54.4	53.3	61.2	42.8
Return on Total Assets 46	10.8	•	20.2	15.5	16.4	10.7	11.8	14.5	10.4	8.9	10.8
Return on Equity Before Income Taxes 47	19.1	•	•	•	27.6	28.2	21.0	28.5	19.3	17.4	17.0
Return on Equity After Income Taxes 48	13.9	•	•	•	24.1	26.9	18.7	22.4	14.6	14.8	11.2
Profit Margin (Before Income Tax) 49	11.5	60.6	2.8	4.2	7.5	6.1	6.3	9.1	8.2	5.6	16.1
Profit Margin (After Income Tax) 50	8.3	56.6	2.7	4.0	6.5	5.8	5.6	7.1	6.2	4.7	10.5

Table I
Corporations with and without Net Income

COMMERCIAL AND SERVICE INDUSTRY MACHINERY

MONEY AMOUNTS AND SIZE OF ASSETS IN THOUSANDS OF DOLLARS

Item Description for Accounting Period 7/06 Through 6/07	Total	Zero Assets	Under 500	500 to 1,000	1,000 to 5,000	5,000 to 10,000	10,000 to 25,000	25,000 to 50,000	50,000 to 100,000	100,000 to 250,000	250,000 to 500,000	500,000 to 2,500,000	2,500,000 and over
Number of Enterprises **1**	2436	457	1105	80	592	75	61	21	13	17	3	8	4
Revenues ($ in Thousands)													
Net Sales **2**	40712140	106396	1199998	37959	3579649	907598	1464645	821922	1267196	3178517	850074	4961645	22336541
Interest **3**	1301661	45	430	189	1823	1367	2662	3275	3603	19464	6192	33186	1229425
Rents **4**	167419	0	2364	0	3003	0	0	1360	553	3539	473	87066	69061
Royalties **5**	886239	0	0	0	0	0	0	0	232	7879	0	27535	850594
Other Portfolio Income **6**	2840399	229	743	0	4834	19623	866	15117	2974	32406	42068	74711	2646828
Other Receipts **7**	1396974	3780	2366	0	16481	13881	5135	9643	4761	66608	2737	40065	1231516
Total Receipts **8**	47304832	110450	1205901	38148	3605790	942469	1473308	851317	1279319	3308413	901544	5224208	28363965
Average Total Receipts **9**	19419	242	1091	477	6091	12566	24153	40539	98409	194613	300515	653026	7090991
Operating Costs/Operating Income (%)													
Cost of Operations **10**	56.9	85.4	72.2	86.6	59.0	65.6	67.1	70.9	59.6	66.6	57.8	66.4	50.4
Salaries and Wages **11**	15.7	5.5	5.9	28.2	17.7	8.0	9.4	10.7	9.5	11.5	4.6	9.8	19.5
Taxes Paid **12**	2.3	0.4	2.3	3.7	2.8	2.3	1.9	2.1	2.2	1.5	1.7	2.2	2.5
Interest Paid **13**	5.0	0.6	0.3	1.7	0.4	1.9	1.0	0.8	1.4	1.5	3.5	2.4	8.0
Depreciation **14**	4.4	0.2	0.6	2.8	0.8	3.3	1.8	1.8	1.6	1.6	6.6	3.5	6.2
Amortization and Depletion **15**	0.6	•	•	5.0	0.0	0.1	0.2	0.1	0.5	0.5	0.4	0.8	0.8
Pensions and Other Deferred Comp. **16**	1.6	1.4	0.4	0.6	1.0	0.1	0.4	0.6	1.1	0.6	0.4	1.0	2.2
Employee Benefits **17**	3.9	1.6	1.1	•	2.7	3.3	1.7	1.8	3.2	2.1	1.4	2.9	5.1
Advertising **18**	1.4	1.1	0.3	1.3	1.5	1.1	0.9	0.5	1.7	1.0	0.5	0.6	1.8
Other Expenses **19**	17.9	38.3	9.0	45.0	6.7	12.7	8.5	8.1	12.1	10.8	14.0	9.3	24.6
Officers' Compensation **20**	1.3	3.7	3.7	2.1	4.1	2.8	2.0	1.7	1.6	1.0	2.7	0.9	0.6
Operating Margin **21**	•	•	4.1	•	3.3	•	5.0	0.8	5.5	1.4	6.4	0.2	•
Operating Margin Before Officers' Comp. **22**	•	•	7.8	•	7.3	1.6	7.1	2.6	7.1	2.4	9.2	1.1	•

Selected Average Balance Sheet ($ in Thousands)

Net Receivables 23	5565	0	74	124	766	1704	2875	8039	16918	41722	42884	177472	2515392
Inventories 24	1619	0	46	531	820	1884	4140	9916	17079	28756	48072	68029	341086
Net Property, Plant and Equipment 25	2732	0	30	167	442	2039	3018	5176	11330	23535	44633	112373	1080412
Total Assets 26	24688	0	221	702	2886	7700	14659	33334	73385	175051	291584	764628	11259525
Notes and Loans Payable 27	10216	0	294	308	431	2334	3711	3930	16770	34847	162419	254474	5115833
All Other Liabilities 28	8870	0	52	1336	2403	4006	5062	15066	19622	54639	34870	352620	3746274
Net Worth 29	5603	0	-124	-942	52	1361	5887	14338	36993	85566	94295	157534	2397418

Selected Financial Ratios (Times to 1)

Current Ratio 30	1.1	•	2.1	0.4	0.9	1.4	1.5	1.9	1.8	1.8	1.1	1.7	1.0
Quick Ratio 31	0.7	•	1.2	0.2	0.5	0.6	0.7	1.0	1.0	1.0	0.4	1.0	0.7
Net Sales to Working Capital 32	13.8	•	11.9	•	•	10.4	8.0	3.2	5.1	4.4	28.4	4.3	59.2
Coverage Ratio 33	2.3	•	16.1	•	11.5	2.4	6.5	6.8	6.2	4.6	4.6	3.2	2.0
Total Asset Turnover 34	0.7	•	4.9	0.7	2.1	1.6	1.6	1.2	1.3	1.1	1.0	0.8	0.5
Inventory Turnover 35	5.9	•	16.9	0.8	4.4	4.2	3.9	2.8	3.4	4.3	3.4	6.1	8.3
Receivables Turnover 36	3.0	•	26.1	1.0	8.1	9.1	8.5	4.5	5.1	5.1	6.3	3.9	2.2
Total Liabilities to Net Worth 37	3.4	•	•	•	54.9	4.7	1.5	1.3	1.0	2.1	3.9	3.9	3.7
Current Assets to Working Capital 38	8.5	•	1.9	•	•	3.8	3.1	2.2	2.3	2.2	11.8	2.5	44.0
Current Liabilities to Working Capital 39	7.5	•	0.9	•	•	2.8	2.1	1.2	1.3	1.2	10.8	1.5	43.0
Working Capital to Net Sales 40	0.1	•	0.1	•	•	0.1	0.1	0.3	0.2	0.2	0.0	0.2	0.0
Inventory to Working Capital 41	1.4	•	0.7	•	•	1.9	1.5	0.8	0.7	0.8	4.5	0.5	3.8
Total Receipts to Cash Flow 42	5.2	21.3	8.3	•	13.0	8.1	7.8	8.7	6.0	6.9	4.1	9.0	4.0
Cost of Goods to Cash Flow 43	2.9	18.2	6.0	•	7.6	5.3	5.2	6.2	3.6	4.6	2.4	6.0	2.0
Cash Flow to Total Debt 44	0.2	•	0.4	•	0.2	0.2	0.4	0.2	0.4	0.3	0.3	0.1	0.2

Selected Financial Factors (in Percentages)

Debt Ratio 45	77.3	•	156.1	234.3	98.2	82.3	59.8	57.0	49.6	51.1	67.7	79.4	78.7
Return on Total Assets 46	7.8	•	23.8	•	9.2	7.1	10.9	6.0	11.3	7.5	15.7	6.3	7.8
Return on Equity Before Income Taxes 47	19.3	•	•	38.6	468.6	23.3	22.9	12.0	18.8	12.0	37.9	20.8	18.0
Return on Equity After Income Taxes 48	12.0	•	•	39.6	437.8	19.6	19.4	9.6	15.4	9.1	26.3	17.7	9.3
Profit Margin (Before Income Tax) 49	6.5	•	4.6	•	4.0	2.6	5.6	4.4	7.1	5.5	12.6	5.3	7.7
Profit Margin (After Income Tax) 50	4.0	•	4.5	•	3.7	2.2	4.8	3.5	5.8	4.2	8.8	4.5	4.0

127

Table II

Corporations with Net Income

COMMERCIAL AND SERVICE INDUSTRY MACHINERY

MONEY AMOUNTS AND SIZE OF ASSETS IN THOUSANDS OF DOLLARS

Item Description for Accounting Period 7/06 Through 6/07	Total	Zero Assets	Under 500	500 to 1,000	1,000 to 5,000	5,000 to 10,000	10,000 to 25,000	25,000 to 50,000	50,000 to 100,000	100,000 to 250,000	250,000 to 500,000	500,000 to 2,500,000	2,500,000 and over
Number of Enterprises 1	1681	8	1000	59	484	41	39	14	10	14	3	•	•
Revenues ($ in Thousands)													
Net Sales 2	28894973	0	993015	32432	2785990	433518	1015964	510381	1031576	2956787	850074	•	•
Interest 3	1207853	0	430	133	1306	345	1692	1188	2278	18655	6192	•	•
Rents 4	102958	0	2364	0	440	0	0	1360	193	3539	473	•	•
Royalties 5	452109	0	0	0	0	0	0	0	21	7879	0	•	•
Other Portfolio Income 6	2796091	0	743	0	4834	15666	128	1651	2948	31620	42068	•	•
Other Receipts 7	1112484	3643	2593	-1	11841	13711	3440	2304	4538	64927	2737	•	•
Total Receipts 8	34566468	3643	999145	32564	2804411	463240	1021224	516884	1041554	3083407	901544	•	•
Average Total Receipts 9	20563	455	999	552	5794	11299	26185	36920	104155	220243	300515	•	•
Operating Costs/Operating Income (%)													
Cost of Operations 10	50.8	•	63.7	72.0	58.7	62.3	63.8	66.7	59.4	64.8	57.8	•	•
Salaries and Wages 11	19.0	•	7.1	0.0	17.0	7.2	8.7	8.7	7.4	12.0	4.6	•	•
Taxes Paid 12	2.8	•	2.8	1.5	2.6	1.8	1.9	1.8	2.3	1.6	1.7	•	•
Interest Paid 13	5.9	•	0.3	•	0.3	2.9	0.6	0.5	1.3	1.6	3.5	•	•
Depreciation 14	5.0	•	0.7	0.1	0.8	2.9	1.7	0.8	1.7	1.7	6.6	•	•
Amortization and Depletion 15	0.5	•	•	•	0.1	0.3	0.1	0.2	0.4	0.5	0.4	•	•
Pensions and Other Deferred Comp. 16	1.0	•	0.5	•	0.8	0.2	0.5	0.4	1.3	0.5	0.4	•	•
Employee Benefits 17	4.3	•	1.3	•	2.6	1.2	2.0	1.4	3.2	2.1	1.4	•	•
Advertising 18	1.0	•	0.2	•	1.0	1.5	0.9	0.5	1.7	1.0	0.5	•	•
Other Expenses 19	17.1	•	8.6	13.8	6.0	12.5	7.6	6.9	10.6	11.3	14.0	•	•
Officers' Compensation 20	1.4	•	4.2	•	4.8	4.1	1.7	1.8	1.5	0.9	2.7	•	•
Operating Margin 21	•	•	10.6	12.6	5.4	2.9	10.4	10.4	9.4	2.1	6.4	•	•
Operating Margin Before Officers' Comp. 22	•	•	14.8	12.6	10.2	7.0	12.1	12.1	10.9	3.0	9.2	•	•

Selected Average Balance Sheet ($ in Thousands)

Net Receivables 23	6842	0	79	154	675	1735	3323	6148	16901	43482	42884
Inventories 24	1830	0	42	697	668	1780	4787	10978	16097	36788	44900
Net Property, Plant and Equipment 25	2612	0	33	0	435	1937	2702	2882	12729	26335	44633
Total Assets 26	25141	0	228	636	2731	7088	14737	28920	75527	178077	291584
Notes and Loans Payable 27	11008	0	39	0	393	2124	1633	3888	16001	40196	162419
All Other Liabilities 28	7248	0	50	234	818	2775	5640	15265	20048	50714	34870
Net Worth 29	6885	0	139	402	1520	2189	7465	9767	39478	87167	94295

Selected Financial Ratios (Times to 1)

Current Ratio 30	1.3	•	2.7	2.7	2.3	1.6	1.7	1.7	1.7	1.9	1.1
Quick Ratio 31	1.0	•	1.6	1.7	1.4	0.8	0.9	0.7	1.0	1.1	0.4
Net Sales to Working Capital 32	6.5	•	9.0	1.4	4.8	7.6	6.3	3.8	6.0	4.3	28.4
Coverage Ratio 33	3.1	1631.5	34.4	•	21.5	4.3	19.3	24.1	9.8	5.1	4.6
Total Asset Turnover 34	0.7	•	4.3	0.9	2.1	1.5	1.8	1.3	1.4	1.2	1.0
Inventory Turnover 35	4.8	•	15.1	0.6	5.1	3.7	3.5	2.2	3.8	3.7	3.6
Receivables Turnover 36	2.4	•	24.3	1.6	10.5	7.6	7.2	4.6	6.0	•	13.2
Total Liabilities to Net Worth 37	2.7	•	0.6	0.6	0.8	2.2	1.0	2.0	0.9	1.0	2.1
Current Assets to Working Capital 38	4.2	•	1.6	1.6	1.8	2.7	2.5	2.4	2.5	2.1	11.8
Current Liabilities to Working Capital 39	3.2	•	0.6	0.6	0.8	1.7	1.5	1.4	1.5	1.1	10.8
Working Capital to Net Sales 40	0.2	•	0.1	0.7	0.2	0.1	0.2	0.3	0.2	0.2	0.0
Inventory to Working Capital 41	0.7	•	0.5	0.6	0.6	1.2	1.1	1.2	0.9	0.7	4.5
Total Receipts to Cash Flow 42	4.3	•	5.5	3.7	10.9	5.2	5.9	5.8	5.2	6.4	4.1
Cost of Goods to Cash Flow 43	2.2	•	3.5	2.7	6.4	3.2	3.7	3.9	3.1	4.1	2.4
Cash Flow to Total Debt 44	0.2	•	2.0	0.6	0.4	0.4	0.6	0.3	0.6	0.4	0.3

Selected Financial Factors (in Percentages)

Debt Ratio 45	72.6	•	39.0	36.8	44.3	69.1	49.3	66.2	47.7	51.1	67.7
Return on Total Assets 46	12.5	•	50.3	11.3	13.5	19.0	20.3	15.2	17.0	9.4	15.7
Return on Equity Before Income Taxes 47	31.0	•	80.1	17.9	23.1	47.4	38.0	43.2	29.3	15.4	37.9
Return on Equity After Income Taxes 48	22.4	•	79.8	14.6	21.8	43.4	33.6	38.0	25.0	12.0	26.3
Profit Margin (Before Income Tax) 49	12.4	•	11.2	13.1	6.1	9.8	10.9	11.6	11.2	6.4	12.6
Profit Margin (After Income Tax) 50	9.0	•	11.2	10.7	5.8	9.0	9.6	10.2	9.6	5.0	8.8

Table I

Corporations with and without Net Income

VENTILATION, HEATING, A.C. & COMMERCIAL REFRIGERATION EQUIP.

MONEY AMOUNTS AND SIZE OF ASSETS IN THOUSANDS OF DOLLARS

Item Description for Accounting Period 7/06 Through 6/07	Total	Zero Assets	Under 500	500 to 1,000	1,000 to 5,000	5,000 to 10,000	10,000 to 25,000	25,000 to 50,000	50,000 to 100,000	100,000 to 250,000	250,000 to 500,000	500,000 to 2,500,000	2,500,000 and over
Number of Enterprises 1	907	3	310	•	155	•	68	46	27	11	5	6	3
Revenues ($ in Thousands)													
Net Sales 2	35816162	96646	331777	•	773793	•	1596706	2706056	2914711	2455420	879552	10808485	11416090
Interest 3	148588	87	577	•	1043	•	3221	7707	7195	3413	13155	29772	78100
Rents 4	18875	0	6123	•	1001	•	255	373	1117	958	78	2651	6319
Royalties 5	308860	0	0	•	0	•	1167	2972	7021	414	716	197244	99325
Other Portfolio Income 6	502682	12	0	•	19359	•	2934	2596	9191	6306	1946	21242	432576
Other Receipts 7	612606	43	1598	•	1379	•	23063	68740	4950	27553	6140	390965	83810
Total Receipts 8	37407773	96788	340075	•	796575	•	1627346	2788444	2944185	2494064	901587	11450359	12116220
Average Total Receipts 9	41243	32263	1097	•	5139	•	23932	60618	109044	226733	180317	1908393	4038740
Operating Costs/Operating Income (%)													
Cost of Operations 10	73.5	66.3	43.6	•	66.4	•	68.8	66.5	69.0	72.4	67.4	73.2	79.1
Salaries and Wages 11	6.7	6.8	12.2	•	9.0	•	8.3	9.5	7.3	6.6	7.6	6.1	6.1
Taxes Paid 12	1.1	3.2	1.6	•	2.9	•	2.1	1.8	1.5	1.6	1.2	1.1	0.4
Interest Paid 13	2.4	2.0	0.3	•	0.7	•	0.8	1.1	1.2	2.1	5.9	2.9	3.1
Depreciation 14	0.9	0.7	0.8	•	1.5	•	1.5	1.7	1.6	1.8	2.1	0.6	0.5
Amortization and Depletion 15	0.8	1.7	0.4	•	0.3	•	0.3	0.3	0.5	0.4	0.8	0.4	1.5
Pensions and Other Deferred Comp. 16	0.7	1.0	1.2	•	0.3	•	0.7	0.7	0.6	1.3	0.3	0.8	0.5
Employee Benefits 17	1.6	1.8	0.4	•	1.8	•	2.2	1.7	2.2	1.9	2.2	1.5	1.3
Advertising 18	0.9	0.2	0.1	•	0.8	•	0.4	0.6	0.6	0.8	1.2	1.2	1.1
Other Expenses 19	9.4	7.5	28.7	•	10.6	•	8.5	9.9	7.6	6.7	9.2	12.5	6.8
Officers' Compensation 20	1.4	1.8	4.0	•	6.8	•	3.0	1.2	1.2	0.7	0.8	1.4	0.3
Operating Margin 21	0.7	7.0	6.8	•	•	•	3.4	5.2	6.7	3.7	1.2	•	•
Operating Margin Before Officers' Comp. 22	2.1	8.8	10.7	•	5.9	•	6.4	6.3	7.9	4.4	2.0	•	•

Selected Average Balance Sheet ($ in Thousands)

Item											
Net Receivables **23**	5972	0	800	•	3553	10901	19383	29383	47896	174127	726264
Inventories **24**	3738	0	696	•	3673	6713	9277	31452	34531	154347	320283
Net Property, Plant and Equipment **25**	3831	0	344	•	2516	7186	12517	34407	28868	122587	373931
Total Assets **26**	41278	0	2384	•	14194	32732	69725	177626	369487	1649094	6033431
Notes and Loans Payable **27**	11517	0	760	•	3297	6336	17702	53552	137524	594025	1432934
All Other Liabilities **28**	16759	0	613	•	3525	10057	19091	56953	114036	475349	3163880
Net Worth **29**	13002	0	1011	•	7372	16339	32932	67121	117927	579720	1436617

Selected Financial Ratios (Times to 1)

Item											
Current Ratio **30**	1.2	1.0	2.6	•	1.8	1.9	1.9	1.5	1.0	1.5	0.9
Quick Ratio **31**	0.6	1.0	1.3	•	0.9	1.2	1.2	0.7	0.5	0.8	0.4
Net Sales to Working Capital **32**	14.7	•	4.5	•	5.5	5.9	5.4	9.1	109.2	11.5	•
Coverage Ratio **33**	3.3	4.6	4.1	•	7.3	8.7	7.4	3.5	1.7	2.5	3.0
Total Asset Turnover **34**	1.0	3.0	2.1	•	1.7	1.8	1.5	1.3	0.5	1.1	0.6
Inventory Turnover **35**	7.8	126.9	4.8	•	4.4	5.8	8.0	5.1	3.4	8.5	9.4
Receivables Turnover **36**	6.5	•	7.4	•	5.7	5.2	6.9	6.1	7.3	9.4	4.9
Total Liabilities to Net Worth **37**	2.2	1.9	1.4	•	0.9	1.0	1.1	1.6	2.1	1.8	3.2
Current Assets to Working Capital **38**	5.3	•	1.6	•	2.2	2.2	2.1	3.0	66.5	3.1	•
Current Liabilities to Working Capital **39**	4.3	•	0.6	•	1.2	1.2	1.1	2.0	65.5	2.1	•
Working Capital to Net Sales **40**	0.1	•	0.2	•	0.2	0.2	0.2	0.1	0.0	0.1	•
Inventory to Working Capital **41**	1.5	•	0.7	•	0.9	0.6	0.6	1.3	21.4	1.0	•
Total Receipts to Cash Flow **42**	7.6	3.0	10.9	•	8.1	6.2	7.1	9.9	8.3	6.5	8.8
Cost of Goods to Cash Flow **43**	5.6	1.3	7.2	•	5.6	4.1	4.9	7.2	5.6	4.8	7.0
Cash Flow to Total Debt **44**	0.2	•	0.3	•	0.4	0.6	0.4	0.2	0.1	0.3	0.1

Selected Financial Factors (in Percentages)

Item												
Debt Ratio **45**	68.5	65.8	57.6	•	48.1	50.1	52.8	62.2	68.1	64.8	76.2	
Return on Total Assets **46**	7.5	29.3	5.6	•	10.0	16.6	13.9	9.2	4.8	8.0	5.7	
Return on Equity Before Income Taxes **47**	16.5	82.6	9.9	•	16.6	29.4	25.5	17.4	6.1	13.7	16.0	
Return on Equity After Income Taxes **48**	12.5	82.3	6.8	•	13.9	23.5	19.8	14.4	4.7	9.1	12.3	
Profit Margin (Before Income Tax) **49**	5.4	7.2	9.3	2.0	•	5.2	8.2	7.8	5.2	4.1	4.4	6.0
Profit Margin (After Income Tax) **50**	4.1	4.7	9.3	1.4	•	4.4	6.5	6.0	4.3	3.2	2.9	4.6

Table II
Corporations with Net Income

VENTILATION, HEATING, A.C. & COMMERCIAL REFRIGERATION EQUIP.

MONEY AMOUNTS AND SIZE OF ASSETS IN THOUSANDS OF DOLLARS

Item Description for Accounting Period 7/06 Through 6/07	Total	Zero Assets	Under 500	500 to 1,000	1,000 to 5,000	5,000 to 10,000	10,000 to 25,000	25,000 to 50,000	50,000 to 100,000	100,000 to 250,000	250,000 to 500,000	500,000 to 2,500,000	2,500,000 and over
Number of Enterprises 1	788	3	292	123	143	88	53	40	23	•	5	•	0
Revenues ($ in Thousands)													
Net Sales 2	32551129	96646	315166	282332	760919	1339570	1263161	2430801	2499850	•	879552	•	0
Interest 3	84658	87	573	293	933	3705	2558	3256	6372	•	13155	•	0
Rents 4	18833	0	6123	0	1001	0	213	373	1117	•	78	•	0
Royalties 5	304535	0	0	0	0	0	1167	2969	6626	•	716	•	0
Other Portfolio Income 6	491903	12	0	0	18386	100	2153	2596	6585	•	1946	•	0
Other Receipts 7	545444	43	1599	447	1379	2836	14697	12501	5003	•	6140	•	0
Total Receipts 8	33996502	96788	323461	283072	782618	1346211	1283949	2452496	2525553	•	901587	•	0
Average Total Receipts 9	43143	32263	1108	2301	5473	15298	24225	61312	109807	•	180317	•	•
Operating Costs/Operating Income (%)													
Cost of Operations 10	72.9	66.3	42.2	66.2	66.3	75.0	66.3	64.4	66.7	•	67.4	•	•
Salaries and Wages 11	6.8	6.8	10.9	4.9	6.9	4.9	7.6	9.9	8.0	•	7.6	•	•
Taxes Paid 12	1.1	3.2	1.4	2.3	2.8	0.9	2.2	1.8	1.6	•	1.2	•	•
Interest Paid 13	1.9	2.0	0.0	0.8	0.5	0.7	0.8	0.7	1.0	•	5.9	•	•
Depreciation 14	0.9	0.7	0.8	2.6	1.3	0.4	1.4	1.6	1.5	•	2.1	•	•
Amortization and Depletion 15	0.4	1.7	•	•	0.3	0.0	0.4	0.1	0.4	•	0.8	•	•
Pensions and Other Deferred Comp. 16	0.7	1.0	1.2	0.3	0.3	0.4	0.8	0.7	0.6	•	0.3	•	•
Employee Benefits 17	1.6	1.8	0.3	1.7	1.7	0.5	2.1	1.7	2.2	•	2.2	•	•
Advertising 18	1.0	0.2	0.0	0.3	0.4	0.2	0.4	0.6	0.6	•	1.2	•	•
Other Expenses 19	9.3	7.5	26.1	9.4	9.2	7.9	7.6	8.3	7.8	•	9.2	•	•
Officers' Compensation 20	1.4	1.8	3.4	8.6	6.6	4.9	3.3	1.1	1.4	•	0.8	•	•
Operating Margin 21	2.0	7.0	13.7	3.0	3.7	4.1	7.2	8.9	8.3	•	1.2	•	•
Operating Margin Before Officers' Comp. 22	3.4	8.8	17.1	11.7	10.3	9.0	10.5	10.0	9.7	•	2.0	•	•

Selected Average Balance Sheet ($ in Thousands)

Net Receivables 23	•	6284	0	73	222	857	2080	3484	11121	20138	47896
Inventories 24	•	3792	0	0	151	703	1328	3981	6578	9065	34531
Net Property, Plant and Equipment 25	•	4021	0	158	32	342	1598	2456	7837	11161	28868
Total Assets 26	•	34558	0	344	627	2393	7234	14539	33498	69058	369487
Notes and Loans Payable 27	•	9744	0	0	138	714	1779	3067	6282	13939	137524
All Other Liabilities 28	•	15282	0	47	337	625	2595	3566	10551	17843	114036
Net Worth 29	•	9533	0	297	152	1055	2860	7907	16665	37276	117927

Selected Financial Ratios (Times to 1)

Current Ratio 30	•	1.2	•	4.0	1.4	2.7	2.0	1.8	2.1	2.2	1.0
Quick Ratio 31	•	0.6	•	3.9	1.0	1.3	1.3	0.9	1.4	1.5	0.5
Net Sales to Working Capital 32	•	16.9	•	7.8	13.2	4.5	5.4	5.7	5.2	4.6	109.2
Coverage Ratio 33	•	4.5	4.6	1073.6	5.3	14.4	7.2	11.9	14.4	10.8	1.7
Total Asset Turnover 34	•	1.2	•	3.1	3.7	2.2	2.1	1.6	1.8	1.6	0.5
Inventory Turnover 35	•	7.9	•	•	10.1	5.0	8.6	4.0	6.0	8.0	3.4
Receivables Turnover 36	•	6.4	•	22.4	11.6	7.6	9.8	5.1	•	6.8	7.3
Total Liabilities to Net Worth 37	•	2.6	•	0.2	3.1	1.3	1.5	0.8	1.0	0.9	2.1
Current Assets to Working Capital 38	•	6.1	•	1.3	3.3	1.6	2.0	2.2	1.9	1.8	66.5
Current Liabilities to Working Capital 39	•	5.1	•	0.3	2.3	0.6	1.0	1.2	0.9	0.8	65.5
Working Capital to Net Sales 40	•	0.1	•	0.1	0.1	0.2	0.2	0.2	0.2	0.2	0.0
Inventory to Working Capital 41	•	1.7	•	•	1.0	0.7	0.7	0.9	0.6	0.5	21.4
Total Receipts to Cash Flow 42	•	6.9	7.5	2.6	8.9	8.0	8.5	6.6	6.1	6.3	8.3
Cost of Goods to Cash Flow 43	•	5.1	5.0	1.1	5.9	5.3	6.4	4.4	3.9	4.2	5.6
Cash Flow to Total Debt 44	•	0.2	•	8.8	0.5	0.5	0.4	0.5	0.6	0.5	0.1

Selected Financial Factors (in Percentages)

Debt Ratio 45	•	72.4	•	13.6	75.7	55.9	60.5	45.6	50.2	46.0	68.1
Return on Total Assets 46	•	10.3	•	51.4	14.9	15.6	11.2	15.6	19.0	16.3	4.8
Return on Equity Before Income Taxes 47	•	29.2	•	59.4	49.9	32.9	24.4	26.3	35.5	27.5	6.1
Return on Equity After Income Taxes 48	•	22.9	•	59.3	44.9	29.7	22.9	23.1	28.9	21.5	4.7
Profit Margin (Before Income Tax) 49	•	6.7	7.2	16.3	3.3	6.5	4.6	8.7	9.7	9.4	4.1
Profit Margin (After Income Tax) 50	•	5.3	4.7	16.3	3.0	5.9	4.3	7.7	7.9	7.4	3.2

130

Table I

Corporations with and without Net Income

METALWORKING MACHINERY

MONEY AMOUNTS AND SIZE OF ASSETS IN THOUSANDS OF DOLLARS

Item Description for Accounting Period 7/06 Through 6/07	Total	Zero Assets	Under 500	500 to 1,000	1,000 to 5,000	5,000 to 10,000	10,000 to 25,000	25,000 to 50,000	50,000 to 100,000	100,000 to 250,000	250,000 to 500,000	500,000 to 2,500,000	2,500,000 and over
Number of Enterprises **1**	6918	250	3827	794	1728	155	92	39	16	9	3	4	0
Revenues ($ in Thousands)													
Net Sales **2**	24887749	107313	1674743	975635	6658007	1841791	1877140	1978191	1226946	1769030	792565	5986387	0
Interest **3**	222726	59	124	3003	8270	2178	4250	885	3817	5376	3105	191657	0
Rents **4**	7126	0	0	57	1535	881	918	9	603	934	1055	1133	0
Royalties **5**	14090	0	0	0	0	3597	99	203	1	4629	0	5561	0
Other Portfolio Income **6**	174026	8293	1952	412	24692	2127	13906	2859	3103	13568	1031	102083	0
Other Receipts **7**	286875	4395	15651	3974	79460	7703	55660	29161	7868	17351	401	65256	0
Total Receipts **8**	25592592	120060	1692470	983081	6771964	1858277	1951973	2011308	1242338	1810888	798157	6352077	0
Average Total Receipts **9**	3699	480	442	1238	3919	11989	21217	51572	77646	201210	266052	1588019	•
Operating Costs/Operating Income (%)													
Cost of Operations **10**	65.5	71.7	38.7	57.8	67.0	64.4	68.1	71.7	69.7	65.6	77.7	67.5	•
Salaries and Wages **11**	8.0	12.1	14.5	6.4	5.4	7.0	7.2	6.4	7.6	10.7	8.9	9.7	•
Taxes Paid **12**	2.5	2.6	4.7	4.7	3.2	3.1	2.7	2.4	2.1	2.2	1.5	1.1	•
Interest Paid **13**	1.3	0.6	1.6	1.2	1.0	1.0	1.7	1.1	0.9	2.2	1.2	1.4	•
Depreciation **14**	2.6	2.1	2.2	3.7	3.3	2.8	2.9	2.8	2.6	1.6	1.1	1.9	•
Amortization and Depletion **15**	0.3	0.0	0.0	0.0	0.0	0.0	0.0	0.1	0.3	0.3	0.1	1.0	•
Pensions and Other Deferred Comp. **16**	0.6	0.6	0.5	0.9	0.3	0.7	1.0	0.6	1.0	0.8	0.4	0.6	•
Employee Benefits **17**	2.6	0.9	2.9	3.1	1.9	2.0	3.1	2.3	1.8	1.7	0.8	3.8	•
Advertising **18**	0.4	0.1	0.1	0.1	0.2	0.2	0.5	0.3	0.6	0.6	0.4	0.6	•
Other Expenses **19**	10.7	16.0	29.9	14.9	8.8	8.1	10.0	8.4	8.2	11.3	3.4	10.0	•
Officers' Compensation **20**	3.1	1.4	10.6	8.5	4.4	3.0	2.1	2.2	1.3	1.4	0.4	0.5	•
Operating Margin **21**	2.4	•	•	•	4.4	7.7	0.7	1.8	4.0	1.6	4.2	1.9	•
Operating Margin Before Officers' Comp. **22**	5.4	4.9	•	7.1	8.8	10.7	2.8	4.0	5.3	3.0	4.5	2.4	•

Selected Average Balance Sheet ($ in Thousands)

Net Receivables 23	597	0	37	168	571	1679	3397	11079	12276	53167	50505	258492	•
Inventories 24	498	0	20	91	413	1364	4123	10845	13303	47170	97404	197274	•
Net Property, Plant and Equipment 25	552	0	29	210	666	2064	3741	8771	13622	22564	27808	218514	•
Total Assets 26	3162	0	111	651	2196	7095	14879	36331	66300	142159	304621	2499284	•
Notes and Loans Payable 27	912	0	135	353	781	1822	4417	8525	10861	51117	33904	602032	•
All Other Liabilities 28	983	0	42	92	534	1407	5202	10496	20998	44438	144192	841831	•
Net Worth 29	1267	0	-66	206	881	3866	5260	17309	34441	46604	126525	1055421	•

Selected Financial Ratios (Times to 1)

Current Ratio 30	1.6	•	1.2	3.4	1.8	2.1	1.2	1.9	1.8	1.8	1.6	1.3	•
Quick Ratio 31	0.9	•	0.9	2.6	1.1	1.3	0.6	1.2	1.0	1.1	0.6	0.6	•
Net Sales to Working Capital 32	6.9	•	35.4	4.4	6.4	5.3	14.3	4.5	4.6	4.5	4.1	10.9	•
Coverage Ratio 33	5.4	7.3	•	0.5	7.1	9.7	3.7	4.2	6.8	3.4	5.1	7.8	•
Total Asset Turnover 34	1.1	•	3.9	1.9	1.8	1.7	1.4	1.4	1.2	1.4	0.9	0.6	•
Inventory Turnover 35	4.7	•	8.6	7.8	6.3	5.6	3.4	3.4	4.0	2.7	2.1	5.1	•
Receivables Turnover 36	5.8	•	9.1	7.8	7.0	7.2	4.7	4.3	6.4	3.1	10.5	5.6	•
Total Liabilities to Net Worth 37	1.5	•	•	2.2	1.5	0.8	1.8	1.1	0.9	2.1	1.4	1.4	•
Current Assets to Working Capital 38	2.7	•	6.5	1.4	2.2	1.9	6.5	2.1	2.2	2.3	2.6	4.8	•
Current Liabilities to Working Capital 39	1.7	•	5.5	0.4	1.2	0.9	5.5	1.1	1.2	1.3	1.6	3.8	•
Working Capital to Net Sales 40	0.1	•	0.0	0.2	0.2	0.2	0.1	0.2	0.2	0.2	0.2	0.1	•
Inventory to Working Capital 41	0.9	•	1.3	0.3	0.7	0.6	2.5	0.8	0.8	0.7	1.5	1.5	•
Total Receipts to Cash Flow 42	7.4	5.7	4.9	12.0	8.4	7.1	9.1	9.6	8.0	7.3	12.6	6.0	•
Cost of Goods to Cash Flow 43	4.8	4.1	1.9	6.9	5.7	4.6	6.2	6.9	5.6	4.8	9.8	4.0	•
Cash Flow to Total Debt 44	0.3	•	0.5	0.2	0.3	0.5	0.2	0.3	0.3	0.3	0.1	0.2	•

Selected Financial Factors (in Percentages)

Debt Ratio 45	59.9	•	159.4	68.4	59.9	45.5	64.6	52.4	48.1	67.2	58.5	57.8	•
Return on Total Assets 46	8.0	•	•	1.0	12.4	16.0	8.6	6.3	7.3	10.4	5.2	6.7	•
Return on Equity Before Income Taxes 47	16.2	•	30.7	•	26.5	26.3	17.8	10.0	11.9	22.4	10.2	13.9	•
Return on Equity After Income Taxes 48	12.6	•	31.6	•	25.4	24.6	14.8	9.0	9.3	16.3	6.1	9.0	•
Profit Margin (Before Income Tax) 49	5.7	3.8	•	•	6.1	8.6	4.6	3.4	5.4	5.3	4.9	9.8	•
Profit Margin (After Income Tax) 50	4.4	3.2	•	•	5.8	8.0	3.8	3.1	4.2	3.9	2.9	6.3	•

Table II

Corporations with Net Income

METALWORKING MACHINERY

MONEY AMOUNTS AND SIZE OF ASSETS IN THOUSANDS OF DOLLARS

Item Description for Accounting Period 7/06 Through 6/07	Total	Zero Assets	Under 500	500 to 1,000	1,000 to 5,000	5,000 to 10,000	10,000 to 25,000	25,000 to 50,000	50,000 to 100,000	100,000 to 250,000	250,000 to 500,000	500,000 to 2,500,000	2,500,000 and over
Number of Enterprises 1	3572	246	1167	566	1335	136	69	27	13	•	0	0	0
Revenues ($ in Thousands)													
Net Sales 2	19699141	44468	222910	696714	5478992	1686124	1490848	1166172	1016019	•	0	0	0
Interest 3	213946	59	116	1481	6182	1065	2811	779	2537	•	0	0	0
Rents 4	5309	0	0	0	1535	881	816	9	0	•	0	0	0
Royalties 5	13855	0	0	0	0	3597	99	203	0	•	0	0	•
Other Portfolio Income 6	149804	8293	1952	176	20617	2066	6740	2529	1181	•	0	•	0
Other Receipts 7	230236	2302	1346	4341	60369	6914	51103	13696	7417	•	0	•	0
Total Receipts 8	20312291	55122	226324	702712	5567695	1700647	1552417	1183388	1027154	•	•	•	•
Average Total Receipts 9	5687	224	194	1242	4171	12505	22499	43829	79012	•	•	•	•
Operating Costs/Operating Income (%)													
Cost of Operations 10	66.2	40.3	64.5	53.1	65.4	63.7	66.2	63.9	66.7	•	•	•	•
Salaries and Wages 11	7.3	21.4	2.9	4.3	5.5	6.0	7.1	7.0	7.5	•	•	•	•
Taxes Paid 12	2.3	3.2	4.8	4.1	2.9	3.2	2.5	2.5	2.4	•	•	•	•
Interest Paid 13	1.1	•	2.3	1.3	0.9	1.0	1.4	1.1	1.1	•	•	•	•
Depreciation 14	2.5	2.4	2.8	4.6	3.0	2.9	3.1	3.3	2.6	•	•	•	•
Amortization and Depletion 15	0.3	0.0	•	0.0	0.0	0.0	0.0	0.1	0.4	•	•	•	•
Pensions and Other Deferred Comp. 16	0.6	1.4	0.2	0.8	0.4	0.8	1.1	0.3	0.7	•	•	•	•
Employee Benefits 17	2.5	2.1	3.5	2.3	1.8	1.8	2.4	2.1	1.9	•	•	•	•
Advertising 18	0.4	0.2	0.1	0.1	0.2	0.2	0.5	0.5	0.6	•	•	•	•
Other Expenses 19	9.2	30.8	10.5	17.0	8.0	8.0	9.6	9.4	9.1	•	•	•	•
Officers' Compensation 20	2.4	0.9	1.2	8.7	4.3	2.8	2.0	3.0	1.1	•	•	•	•
Operating Margin 21	5.2	•	7.3	3.7	7.6	9.6	4.1	6.8	5.8	•	•	•	•
Operating Margin Before Officers' Comp. 22	7.5	•	8.4	12.4	11.9	12.4	6.1	9.8	7.0	•	•	•	•

Selected Average Balance Sheet ($ in Thousands)

Net Receivables 23	931	0	14	157	567	1753	3591	10890	12848
Inventories 24	766	0	26	84	378	1210	4491	11237	13528
Net Property, Plant and Equipment 25	879	0	26	232	641	2238	4230	9204	14138
Total Assets 26	5163	0	106	644	2291	7150	14783	36206	63187
Notes and Loans Payable 27	1287	0	67	336	779	1790	2723	6652	12880
All Other Liabilities 28	1581	0	17	93	565	1313	3378	8758	17454
Net Worth 29	2295	0	22	215	946	4046	8683	20796	32853

Selected Financial Ratios (Times to 1)

Current Ratio 30	1.7	•	2.4	2.9	1.9	2.2	2.0	2.3	2.0
Quick Ratio 31	0.9	•	1.2	2.3	1.2	1.3	1.2	1.4	1.1
Net Sales to Working Capital 32	6.0	•	4.1	5.3	6.0	5.5	4.8	3.4	4.4
Coverage Ratio 33	8.8	•	4.8	4.5	11.1	11.7	6.6	8.2	7.6
Total Asset Turnover 34	1.1	•	1.8	1.9	1.8	1.7	1.5	1.2	1.2
Inventory Turnover 35	4.8	•	4.6	7.8	7.1	6.5	3.2	2.5	3.9
Receivables Turnover 36	5.6	•	2.2	7.8	7.8	7.1	4.4	3.5	•
Total Liabilities to Net Worth 37	1.2	•	3.7	2.0	1.4	0.8	0.7	0.7	0.9
Current Assets to Working Capital 38	2.5	•	1.7	1.5	2.1	1.9	2.0	1.8	2.0
Current Liabilities to Working Capital 39	1.5	•	0.7	0.5	1.1	0.9	1.0	0.8	1.0
Working Capital to Net Sales 40	0.2	•	0.2	0.2	0.2	0.2	0.2	0.3	0.2
Inventory to Working Capital 41	0.8	•	0.4	0.3	0.7	0.6	0.8	0.6	0.8
Total Receipts to Cash Flow 42	6.5	2.1	5.9	7.1	6.8	6.3	7.2	6.3	6.5
Cost of Goods to Cash Flow 43	4.3	0.8	3.8	3.8	4.4	4.0	4.8	4.0	4.4
Cash Flow to Total Debt 44	0.3	•	0.4	0.4	0.4	0.6	0.5	0.4	0.4

Selected Financial Factors (in Percentages)

Debt Ratio 45	55.5	•	78.9	66.6	58.7	43.4	41.3	42.6	48.0
Return on Total Assets 46	10.8	•	20.1	11.3	18.0	19.7	14.1	11.1	9.9
Return on Equity Before Income Taxes 47	21.4	•	75.4	26.3	39.7	31.8	20.3	17.0	16.5
Return on Equity After Income Taxes 48	17.6	•	66.9	22.2	38.4	29.9	18.0	15.9	13.1
Profit Margin (Before Income Tax) 49	8.9	21.2	8.8	4.6	9.2	10.4	8.2	8.2	6.9
Profit Margin (After Income Tax) 50	7.3	19.8	7.8	3.9	8.8	9.8	7.2	7.6	5.5

Table I

Corporations with and without Net Income

ENGINE, TURBINE AND POWER TRANSMISSION EQUIPMENT

MONEY AMOUNTS AND SIZE OF ASSETS IN THOUSANDS OF DOLLARS

Item Description for Accounting Period 7/06 Through 6/07	Total	Zero Assets	Under 500	500 to 1,000	1,000 to 5,000	5,000 to 10,000	10,000 to 25,000	25,000 to 50,000	50,000 to 100,000	100,000 to 250,000	250,000 to 500,000	500,000 to 2,500,000	2,500,000 and over
Number of Enterprises **1**	213	4	0	•	90	•	31	8	7	6	8	5	5
Revenues ($ in Thousands)													
Net Sales **2**	52317409	930384	0	•	415707	•	623605	297077	542387	959974	3647549	2718768	41793139
Interest **3**	1217235	34150	0	•	1436	•	3290	1784	3758	14964	15645	11429	1129316
Rents **4**	524817	446	0	•	0	•	0	0	322	442	448	1858	521301
Royalties **5**	485000	9430	0	•	0	•	0	0	0	16027	8569	22450	428524
Other Portfolio Income **6**	334141	11243	0	•	3131	•	198	114	30	6357	21689	5435	285852
Other Receipts **7**	517778	22292	0	•	1169	•	6829	255	2526	12163	45350	33034	393813
Total Receipts **8**	55396380	1007945	0	•	421443	•	633922	299230	549023	1009927	3739250	2792974	44551945
Average Total Receipts **9**	260077	251986	•	•	4683	•	20449	37404	78432	168321	467406	558595	8910389
Operating Costs/Operating Income (%)													
Cost of Operations **10**	73.8	65.0	•	•	62.4	•	71.4	70.3	82.8	61.6	77.7	68.2	74.4
Salaries and Wages **11**	13.0	8.5	•	•	6.3	•	5.2	6.1	7.5	8.3	5.3	10.9	14.4
Taxes Paid **12**	1.4	0.9	•	•	3.1	•	2.8	1.9	2.0	1.4	1.4	2.2	1.4
Interest Paid **13**	3.2	15.0	•	•	2.5	•	1.9	0.6	1.4	2.5	1.0	3.1	3.2
Depreciation **14**	2.5	3.4	•	•	2.2	•	2.6	2.1	2.5	2.5	1.4	3.0	2.5
Amortization and Depletion **15**	0.4	2.5	•	•	0.0	•	0.5	0.0	0.4	0.2	0.2	1.6	0.3
Pensions and Other Deferred Comp. **16**	3.1	3.0	•	•	2.2	•	0.2	0.3	0.2	0.7	0.4	2.4	3.6
Employee Benefits **17**	1.7	3.9	•	•	1.8	•	1.0	2.9	1.3	1.5	1.8	1.3	1.7
Advertising **18**	0.6	0.5	•	•	0.7	•	0.1	0.2	0.3	0.9	0.3	0.3	0.7
Other Expenses **19**	2.1	13.8	•	•	6.9	•	9.2	8.5	10.0	15.7	6.2	8.5	0.4
Officers' Compensation **20**	0.7	2.3	•	•	3.1	•	2.6	1.3	1.6	1.1	0.5	0.6	0.5
Operating Margin **21**	•	•	•	•	9.0	•	2.6	5.8	•	3.5	3.9	•	•
Operating Margin Before Officers' Comp. **22**	•	•	•	•	12.0	•	5.2	7.1	•	4.6	4.4	•	•

Selected Average Balance Sheet ($ in Thousands)

Item												
Net Receivables 23	43756	0	•	613	•	2537	6449	16600	38134	76773	234027	1390651
Inventories 24	29184	0	•	802	•	3842	15084	11841	52102	53582	206407	842718
Net Property, Plant and Equipment 25	33770	0	•	1460	•	2578	6449	14538	28995	45975	220711	1020972
Total Assets 26	249590	0	•	3467	•	14413	33934	69169	173623	322286	1147959	8390430
Notes and Loans Payable 27	28236	0	•	2619	•	5263	4138	18319	55314	56218	404704	513445
All Other Liabilities 28	136193	0	•	944	•	3195	10869	22099	39545	141890	503607	4917754
Net Worth 29	85162	0	•	-96	•	5954	18928	28751	78764	124178	239648	2959232

Selected Financial Ratios (Times to 1)

Item												
Current Ratio 30	1.5	•	•	1.2	•	1.6	2.4	1.5	2.0	1.5	1.3	1.5
Quick Ratio 31	0.8	•	•	0.6	•	0.8	1.0	1.0	1.2	0.8	0.8	0.7
Net Sales to Working Capital 32	7.5	•	•	15.2	•	5.2	2.4	4.4	3.7	6.6	5.6	8.1
Coverage Ratio 33	2.1	0.2	•	5.2	•	3.2	11.9	•	4.7	8.0	1.3	2.2
Total Asset Turnover 34	1.0	•	•	1.3	•	1.4	1.1	1.1	0.9	1.4	0.5	1.0
Inventory Turnover 35	6.2	•	•	3.6	•	3.7	1.7	5.4	1.9	6.6	1.8	7.4
Receivables Turnover 36	6.0	•	•	6.4	•	7.5	3.9	5.7	2.5	11.9	1.7	6.9
Total Liabilities to Net Worth 37	1.9	•	•	•	•	1.4	0.8	1.4	1.2	1.6	3.8	1.8
Current Assets to Working Capital 38	3.1	•	•	5.1	•	2.6	1.7	2.9	2.0	3.0	4.5	3.1
Current Liabilities to Working Capital 39	2.1	•	•	4.1	•	1.6	0.7	1.9	1.0	2.0	3.5	2.1
Working Capital to Net Sales 40	0.1	•	•	0.1	•	0.2	0.4	0.2	0.3	0.2	0.2	0.1
Inventory to Working Capital 41	0.9	•	•	2.2	•	1.0	0.9	1.0	0.7	0.8	1.5	0.9
Total Receipts to Cash Flow 42	28.8	71.0	•	6.4	•	8.8	7.2	•	4.3	9.3	13.5	53.8
Cost of Goods to Cash Flow 43	21.2	46.2	•	4.0	•	6.3	5.1	•	2.6	7.2	9.2	40.0
Cash Flow to Total Debt 44	0.1	•	•	0.2	•	0.3	0.3	•	0.4	0.2	0.0	0.0

Selected Financial Factors (in Percentages)

Item												
Debt Ratio 45	65.9	•	•	102.8	•	58.7	44.2	58.4	54.6	61.5	79.1	64.7
Return on Total Assets 46	6.7	•	•	17.0	•	8.6	7.8	•	10.8	10.8	1.9	6.9
Return on Equity Before Income Taxes 47	10.3	•	•	•	•	14.4	12.7	•	18.7	24.4	2.1	10.6
Return on Equity After Income Taxes 48	6.5	•	•	•	•	6.9	9.0	•	13.8	16.4	•	7.1
Profit Margin (Before Income Tax) 49	3.6	•	•	10.3	•	4.3	6.5	•	9.2	6.7	0.9	3.7
Profit Margin (After Income Tax) 50	2.3	•	•	7.1	•	2.0	4.6	•	6.8	4.5	•	2.5

Table II
Corporations with Net Income

ENGINE, TURBINE AND POWER TRANSMISSION EQUIPMENT

MONEY AMOUNTS AND SIZE OF ASSETS IN THOUSANDS OF DOLLARS

Item Description for Accounting Period 7/06 Through 6/07	Total	Zero Assets	Under 500	500 to 1,000	1,000 to 5,000	5,000 to 10,000	10,000 to 25,000	25,000 to 50,000	50,000 to 100,000	100,000 to 250,000	250,000 to 500,000	500,000 to 2,500,000	2,500,000 and over
Number of Enterprises 1	141	0	0	•	61	28	18	8	4	6	8	•	•
Revenues ($ in Thousands)													
Net Sales 2	48141948	0	0	•	380481	253093	473664	297077	443049	959974	3647549	•	•
Interest 3	1134870	0	0	•	1436	248	1404	1784	30	14964	15645	•	•
Rents 4	522006	0	0	•	0	0	0	0	0	442	448	•	•
Royalties 5	457216	0	0	•	0	0	0	0	0	16027	8569	•	•
Other Portfolio Income 6	317814	0	0	•	3131	92	6	114	30	6357	21689	•	•
Other Receipts 7	455204	0	0	•	614	-10	6193	255	564	12163	45350	•	•
Total Receipts 8	51029058	0	0	•	385662	253423	481267	299230	443673	1009927	3739250	•	•
Average Total Receipts 9	361908	•	•	•	6322	9051	26737	37404	110918	168321	467406	•	•
Operating Costs/Operating Income (%)													
Cost of Operations 10	74.8	•	•	•	58.5	65.2	71.6	70.3	81.2	61.6	77.7	•	•
Salaries and Wages 11	12.8	•	•	•	6.1	3.4	3.1	6.1	2.9	8.3	5.3	•	•
Taxes Paid 12	1.4	•	•	•	3.2	3.0	2.3	1.9	1.6	1.4	1.4	•	•
Interest Paid 13	3.1	•	•	•	1.1	0.4	1.7	0.6	1.3	2.5	1.0	•	•
Depreciation 14	2.5	•	•	•	2.3	2.9	1.4	2.1	1.9	2.5	1.4	•	•
Amortization and Depletion 15	0.3	•	•	•	0.0	0.1	0.0	0.0	0.2	0.2	0.2	•	•
Pensions and Other Deferred Comp. 16	3.2	•	•	•	2.4	0.7	0.2	0.3	0.1	0.7	0.4	•	•
Employee Benefits 17	1.5	•	•	•	1.9	2.7	1.2	2.9	1.4	1.5	1.8	•	•
Advertising 18	0.6	•	•	•	0.6	0.5	0.1	0.2	0.2	0.9	0.3	•	•
Other Expenses 19	0.8	•	•	•	5.4	4.9	8.2	8.5	6.0	15.7	6.2	•	•
Officers' Compensation 20	0.6	•	•	•	3.4	3.2	1.9	1.3	0.8	1.1	0.5	•	•
Operating Margin 21	•	•	•	•	14.9	13.0	8.4	5.8	2.3	3.5	3.9	•	•
Operating Margin Before Officers' Comp. 22	•	•	•	•	18.3	16.2	10.3	7.1	3.1	4.6	4.4	•	•

Selected Average Balance Sheet ($ in Thousands)

Net Receivables 23	57526	795	1104	3661	6449	20386	38134	76773
Inventories 24	40804	1144	1634	5391	14080	15689	32122	53582
Net Property, Plant and Equipment 25	47069	1686	2070	1966	6449	15860	28995	45975
Total Assets 26	337570	3749	7662	14246	33934	63866	173623	322286
Notes and Loans Payable 27	33048	2093	310	7073	4138	19550	55314	56218
All Other Liabilities 28	183458	695	1395	3559	10869	25538	39545	141890
Net Worth 29	121064	961	5957	3613	18928	18778	78764	124178

Selected Financial Ratios (Times to 1)

Current Ratio 30	1.6	2.0	2.7	1.5	2.4	1.2	2.0	1.5
Quick Ratio 31	0.8	1.0	1.2	0.6	1.0	0.7	1.2	0.8
Net Sales to Working Capital 32	6.6	6.1	4.0	7.2	2.4	13.7	3.7	6.6
Coverage Ratio 33	2.5	15.4	34.6	6.9	11.9	2.9	4.7	8.0
Total Asset Turnover 34	1.0	1.7	1.2	1.8	1.1	1.7	0.9	1.4
Inventory Turnover 35	6.3	3.2	3.6	3.5	1.9	5.7	3.1	6.6
Receivables Turnover 36	6.4	6.2	6.0	6.5	•	•	•	11.9
Total Liabilities to Net Worth 37	1.8	2.9	0.3	2.9	0.8	2.4	1.2	1.6
Current Assets to Working Capital 38	2.6	2.0	1.6	3.0	1.7	5.2	2.0	3.0
Current Liabilities to Working Capital 39	1.6	1.0	0.6	2.0	0.7	4.2	1.0	2.0
Working Capital to Net Sales 40	0.2	0.2	0.2	0.1	0.4	0.1	0.3	0.2
Inventory to Working Capital 41	0.8	0.9	0.8	1.4	0.9	1.9	0.7	0.8
Total Receipts to Cash Flow 42	31.3	5.0	6.0	6.1	7.2	12.7	4.3	9.3
Cost of Goods to Cash Flow 43	23.4	2.9	3.9	4.4	5.1	10.3	2.6	7.2
Cash Flow to Total Debt 44	0.1	0.4	0.9	0.4	0.3	0.2	0.4	0.2

Selected Financial Factors (in Percentages)

Debt Ratio 45	64.1	74.4	22.3	74.6	44.2	70.6	54.6	61.5
Return on Total Assets 46	7.7	28.9	17.4	21.5	7.8	6.4	10.8	10.8
Return on Equity Before Income Taxes 47	12.9	105.6	21.7	72.6	12.7	14.3	18.7	24.4
Return on Equity After Income Taxes 48	8.9	82.6	18.0	51.2	9.0	11.3	13.8	16.4
Profit Margin (Before Income Tax) 49	4.6	16.3	14.3	10.0	6.5	2.4	9.2	6.7
Profit Margin (After Income Tax) 50	3.1	12.7	11.8	7.0	4.6	1.9	6.8	4.5

Table I

Corporations with and without Net Income

OTHER GENERAL PURPOSE MACHINERY

MONEY AMOUNTS AND SIZE OF ASSETS IN THOUSANDS OF DOLLARS

Item Description for Accounting Period 7/06 Through 6/07	Total	Zero Assets	Under 500	500 to 1,000	1,000 to 5,000	5,000 to 10,000	10,000 to 25,000	25,000 to 50,000	50,000 to 100,000	100,000 to 250,000	250,000 to 500,000	500,000 to 2,500,000	2,500,000 and over
Number of Enterprises **1**	7937	890	5409	340	774	194	184	57	31	25	11	16	6
Revenues ($ in Thousands)													
Net Sales **2**	64630005	375183	1754471	509202	3740931	2605288	4981543	2332855	2641113	4893207	3622903	11718343	25454967
Interest **3**	1150859	1906	2707	467	6551	1084	2830	7157	7895	19003	17164	94548	989547
Rents **4**	12835	0	0	266	863	669	2203	51	685	1523	1314	1513	3749
Royalties **5**	684875	2678	0	0	3432	0	0	105	2303	15476	13263	110289	537329
Other Portfolio Income **6**	550282	0	694	4967	13234	1468	10945	63185	9532	24470	28262	247308	146215
Other Receipts **7**	598191	40860	1506	947	11025	12116	24500	22722	19105	36378	96730	115262	217037
Total Receipts **8**	67627047	420627	1759378	515849	3776036	2620625	5022021	2426075	2680633	4990057	3779636	12287263	27348844
Average Total Receipts **9**	8520	473	325	1517	4879	13508	27294	42563	86472	199602	343603	767954	4558141
Operating Costs/Operating Income (%)													
Cost of Operations **10**	66.4	74.2	41.0	69.8	61.9	62.4	69.7	69.0	69.3	69.5	65.2	62.9	69.0
Salaries and Wages **11**	8.7	13.8	15.0	8.6	10.8	8.3	8.1	7.5	7.8	9.1	11.3	9.0	7.8
Taxes Paid **12**	1.6	3.1	3.4	2.2	2.5	2.3	2.2	1.8	1.7	1.6	1.4	1.7	1.1
Interest Paid **13**	4.1	1.1	1.3	1.8	1.2	1.0	1.1	2.2	1.7	1.6	2.5	2.4	7.6
Depreciation **14**	2.3	1.4	4.3	1.0	1.6	2.0	1.5	1.7	1.8	1.5	2.4	1.5	3.2
Amortization and Depletion **15**	0.7	0.7	0.1	0.2	0.3	0.2	0.2	0.6	0.8	0.9	0.7	0.6	1.1
Pensions and Other Deferred Comp. **16**	0.9	0.8	0.4	0.3	0.4	0.8	0.6	0.4	0.8	0.8	0.6	1.2	1.0
Employee Benefits **17**	2.4	2.3	2.9	2.0	1.9	2.2	1.9	1.8	1.9	1.7	3.3	3.3	2.3
Advertising **18**	0.6	0.3	0.6	0.8	0.8	0.6	0.5	0.4	0.4	0.5	0.9	0.5	0.6
Other Expenses **19**	11.1	25.7	20.8	10.0	11.1	9.8	7.0	10.0	8.0	7.9	9.5	13.5	11.3
Officers' Compensation **20**	1.7	4.5	8.5	5.7	4.6	3.6	2.7	1.4	1.3	1.1	1.1	2.3	0.4
Operating Margin **21**	•	•	1.7	•	3.0	6.8	4.4	3.2	4.5	3.9	1.0	1.0	•
Operating Margin Before Officers' Comp. **22**	1.1	•	•	3.3	7.5	10.4	7.1	4.6	5.9	5.0	2.1	3.3	•

Selected Average Balance Sheet ($ in Thousands)

Item													
Net Receivables 23	1517	0	32	187	648	2120	3562	7363	14378	38243	62201	197197	762844
Inventories 24	1054	0	26	274	502	2117	3949	7888	13572	25679	46182	97324	504454
Net Property, Plant and Equipment 25	866	0	32	217	289	1514	2808	4868	11150	20554	55419	81393	424039
Total Assets 26	10180	0	122	750	2069	7847	15046	34926	67911	153483	393797	809670	8128763
Notes and Loans Payable 27	3155	0	113	303	842	1693	4486	9344	20932	39076	83446	195033	2721122
All Other Liabilities 28	3127	0	34	254	589	2602	4676	10469	24967	45634	67536	278459	2503611
Net Worth 29	3897	0	-25	193	638	3551	5884	15113	22012	68773	242815	336178	2904029

Selected Financial Ratios (Times to 1)

Item													
Current Ratio 30	1.5	•	2.1	1.8	1.9	1.8	1.7	1.8	1.7	1.7	1.5	1.8	1.2
Quick Ratio 31	0.8	•	1.4	0.9	1.2	0.9	0.9	0.9	0.9	1.0	0.9	1.1	0.6
Net Sales to Working Capital 32	7.1	•	7.9	6.5	6.8	5.5	6.1	4.3	5.3	5.6	7.5	4.4	13.4
Coverage Ratio 33	2.1	•	2.5	0.4	4.2	8.1	5.6	4.3	4.6	4.7	3.1	3.8	1.4
Total Asset Turnover 34	0.8	•	2.7	2.0	2.3	1.7	1.8	1.2	1.3	1.3	0.8	0.9	0.5
Inventory Turnover 35	5.1	•	5.2	3.8	6.0	4.0	4.8	3.6	4.3	5.3	4.7	4.7	5.8
Receivables Turnover 36	5.6	•	12.0	8.2	7.5	6.5	8.0	5.6	5.4	5.6	4.3	4.3	5.7
Total Liabilities to Net Worth 37	1.6	•	•	2.9	2.2	1.2	1.6	1.3	2.1	1.2	0.6	1.4	1.8
Current Assets to Working Capital 38	3.1	•	1.9	2.2	2.2	2.3	2.4	2.2	2.5	2.4	3.0	2.2	6.0
Current Liabilities to Working Capital 39	2.1	•	0.9	1.2	1.2	1.3	1.4	1.2	1.5	1.4	2.0	1.2	5.0
Working Capital to Net Sales 40	0.1	•	0.1	0.2	0.1	0.2	0.2	0.2	0.2	0.2	0.1	0.2	0.1
Inventory to Working Capital 41	0.9	•	0.5	1.1	0.7	0.9	1.0	0.8	0.9	0.8	0.7	0.6	1.5
Total Receipts to Cash Flow 42	7.9	15.2	6.4	18.3	7.7	6.9	9.7	8.0	7.8	8.5	7.6	5.6	9.4
Cost of Goods to Cash Flow 43	5.2	11.3	2.6	12.7	4.8	4.3	6.8	5.5	5.4	5.9	5.0	3.5	6.5
Cash Flow to Total Debt 44	0.2	•	0.3	0.1	0.4	0.5	0.3	0.3	0.2	0.3	0.3	0.3	0.1

Selected Financial Factors (in Percentages)

Item													
Debt Ratio 45	61.7	•	120.6	74.2	69.2	54.7	60.9	56.7	67.6	55.2	38.3	58.5	64.3
Return on Total Assets 46	6.9	•	8.9	1.5	12.0	14.3	11.4	10.9	9.8	9.6	6.6	8.0	5.6
Return on Equity Before Income Taxes 47	9.4	•	•	•	29.6	27.8	24.0	19.3	23.7	16.9	7.3	14.1	4.5
Return on Equity After Income Taxes 48	7.2	•	•	•	25.7	25.0	21.7	16.2	19.1	11.1	4.9	11.0	3.0
Profit Margin (Before Income Tax) 49	4.5	•	2.0	•	3.9	7.3	5.2	7.1	6.1	5.9	5.4	6.5	3.1
Profit Margin (After Income Tax) 50	3.4	•	2.0	•	3.4	6.6	4.7	6.0	4.9	3.9	3.6	5.0	2.1

Table II
Corporations with Net Income

OTHER GENERAL PURPOSE MACHINERY

Money Amounts and Size of Assets in Thousands of Dollars

Item Description for Accounting Period 7/06 Through 6/07	Total	Zero Assets	Under 500	500 to 1,000	1,000 to 5,000	5,000 to 10,000	10,000 to 25,000	25,000 to 50,000	50,000 to 100,000	100,000 to 250,000	250,000 to 500,000	500,000 to 2,500,000	2,500,000 and over
Number of Enterprises **1**	4747	9	3552	•	655	146	140	•	24	18	8	11	•
Revenues ($ in Thousands)													
Net Sales **2**	53157962	73682	1403757	•	3406853	2097689	4101846	•	2274436	3825562	3134299	9588314	•
Interest **3**	427087	546	1856	•	6251	934	1575	•	7380	15990	11422	81088	•
Rents **4**	11828	0	0	•	863	299	2203	•	649	1463	1314	1241	•
Royalties **5**	635980	0	0	•	3432	0	0	•	2255	417	3263	104094	•
Other Portfolio Income **6**	469113	0	694	•	13230	1423	5782	•	6585	22819	17827	224576	•
Other Receipts **7**	376103	1169	3	•	10534	9003	19212	•	17985	24232	90513	108235	•
Total Receipts **8**	55078073	75397	1406310	•	3441163	2109348	4130618	•	2309290	3890483	3258638	10107548	•
Average Total Receipts **9**	11603	8377	396	•	5254	14448	29504	•	96220	216138	407330	918868	•
Operating Costs/Operating Income (%)													
Cost of Operations **10**	64.4	84.4	40.2	•	61.0	60.4	66.8	•	68.8	68.4	65.9	60.6	•
Salaries and Wages **11**	8.7	3.5	15.1	•	11.1	8.5	8.1	•	8.1	8.3	10.1	8.9	•
Taxes Paid **12**	1.6	1.2	2.7	•	2.4	2.5	2.1	•	1.8	1.4	1.2	1.8	•
Interest Paid **13**	2.2	•	0.7	•	1.0	0.6	0.7	•	1.7	1.0	1.9	2.2	•
Depreciation **14**	2.3	0.8	1.7	•	1.5	2.2	1.3	•	1.6	1.5	2.0	1.6	•
Amortization and Depletion **15**	0.7	•	0.0	•	0.2	0.0	0.1	•	0.4	0.7	0.2	0.5	•
Pensions and Other Deferred Comp. **16**	1.0	•	0.3	•	0.4	1.0	0.6	•	0.9	0.8	0.7	1.2	•
Employee Benefits **17**	2.5	0.5	1.1	•	1.8	1.9	1.8	•	1.9	1.2	3.1	3.7	•
Advertising **18**	0.6	0.5	0.7	•	0.8	0.5	0.6	•	0.4	0.5	0.7	0.6	•
Other Expenses **19**	11.4	3.8	17.2	•	10.3	9.2	6.8	•	7.0	7.9	8.7	14.1	•
Officers' Compensation **20**	1.8	0.5	8.5	•	4.4	3.5	2.9	•	1.3	1.2	0.8	2.7	•
Operating Margin **21**	2.9	4.8	11.9	•	5.0	9.7	8.3	•	6.1	7.2	4.6	2.1	•
Operating Margin Before Officers' Comp. **22**	4.7	5.3	20.3	•	9.4	13.3	11.2	•	7.4	8.4	5.4	4.8	•

Selected Average Balance Sheet ($ in Thousands)

Net Receivables 23	2007	0	36	•	698	2227	3907	•	15205	38706	74941	157578	•
Inventories 24	1409	0	7	•	449	2159	3941	•	14332	27725	35708	105085	•
Net Property, Plant and Equipment 25	1163	0	21	•	261	1653	2690	•	12049	22669	64932	102908	•
Total Assets 26	10686	0	107	•	2059	8009	14828	•	67955	156010	379078	771732	•
Notes and Loans Payable 27	3180	0	39	•	590	1168	3364	•	15081	28928	62692	174504	•
All Other Liabilities 28	3446	0	23	•	528	2236	4189	•	25477	44825	71680	291767	•
Net Worth 29	4060	0	45	•	941	4605	7275	•	27397	82256	244706	305461	•

Selected Financial Ratios (Times to 1)

Current Ratio 30	1.6	•	2.7	•	2.3	2.2	2.0	•	1.8	1.8	1.6	1.9	•
Quick Ratio 31	0.9	•	2.1	•	1.5	1.2	1.1	•	1.0	1.0	1.0	1.0	•
Net Sales to Working Capital 32	6.6	•	8.5	•	5.9	4.5	5.5	•	5.1	5.4	7.3	5.2	•
Coverage Ratio 33	4.2	•	17.6	•	7.1	19.1	13.2	•	5.5	10.4	5.5	4.8	•
Total Asset Turnover 34	1.0	•	3.7	•	2.5	1.8	2.0	•	1.4	1.4	1.0	1.1	•
Inventory Turnover 35	5.1	•	21.8	•	7.1	4.0	5.0	•	4.5	5.2	7.2	5.0	•
Receivables Turnover 36	5.7	•	14.3	•	8.1	6.4	7.9	•	6.0	6.2	•	5.4	•
Total Liabilities to Net Worth 37	1.6	•	1.4	•	1.2	0.7	1.0	•	1.5	0.9	0.5	1.5	•
Current Assets to Working Capital 38	2.8	•	1.6	•	1.8	1.8	2.0	•	2.2	2.3	2.7	2.1	•
Current Liabilities to Working Capital 39	1.8	•	0.6	•	0.8	0.8	1.0	•	1.2	1.3	1.7	1.1	•
Working Capital to Net Sales 40	0.2	•	0.1	•	0.2	0.2	0.2	•	0.2	0.2	0.1	0.2	•
Inventory to Working Capital 41	0.8	•	0.2	•	0.5	0.7	0.8	•	0.8	0.8	0.7	0.7	•
Total Receipts to Cash Flow 42	6.5	9.7	4.6	•	6.8	6.0	7.2	•	7.5	6.7	6.2	5.0	•
Cost of Goods to Cash Flow 43	4.2	8.2	1.9	•	4.2	3.7	4.8	•	5.1	4.6	4.1	3.0	•
Cash Flow to Total Debt 44	0.3	•	1.4	•	0.7	0.7	0.5	•	0.3	0.4	0.5	0.4	•

Selected Financial Factors (in Percentages)

Debt Ratio 45	62.0	•	57.9	•	54.3	42.5	50.9	•	59.7	47.3	35.4	60.4	•
Return on Total Assets 46	9.7	•	47.0	•	17.7	19.5	19.2	•	13.2	13.5	10.8	12.0	•
Return on Equity Before Income Taxes 47	19.4	•	105.2	•	33.3	32.1	36.2	•	26.7	23.2	13.7	24.1	•
Return on Equity After Income Taxes 48	15.7	•	105.2	•	30.2	29.3	33.7	•	21.9	16.5	10.4	19.0	•
Profit Margin (Before Income Tax) 49	7.0	7.1	12.0	•	6.0	10.3	9.0	•	7.7	9.0	8.5	8.4	•
Profit Margin (After Income Tax) 50	5.7	5.8	12.0	•	5.5	9.4	8.4	•	6.3	6.4	6.5	6.7	•

COMPUTER AND PERIPHERAL EQUIPMENT

Table I

Corporations with and without Net Income

MONEY AMOUNTS AND SIZE OF ASSETS IN THOUSANDS OF DOLLARS

Item Description for Accounting Period 7/06 Through 6/07	Total	Zero Assets	Under 500	500 to 1,000	1,000 to 5,000	5,000 to 10,000	10,000 to 25,000	25,000 to 50,000	50,000 to 100,000	100,000 to 250,000	250,000 to 500,000	500,000 to 2,500,000	2,500,000 and over
Number of Enterprises **1**	2226	308	1110	0	429	127	101	57	28	25	10	22	8
Revenues ($ in Thousands)													
Net Sales **2**	176264727	195937	408075	0	1706956	1256036	1648635	2468031	2847313	4244895	2991095	24913236	133584517
Interest **3**	2809762	2755	18	0	6593	5384	22568	22093	22734	48423	49306	338892	2290995
Rents **4**	978437	0	0	0	0	0	2401	232	463	0	724	17142	957475
Royalties **5**	25734366	0	0	0	0	0	0	21541	2033	8156	33048	350557	25319031
Other Portfolio Income **6**	2529397	2	0	0	57	117	19798	13103	96542	53186	13404	137810	2195380
Other Receipts **7**	1870950	3735	5	0	2203	9190	33474	24534	9901	31299	14573	960504	781532
Total Receipts **8**	210187639	202429	408098	0	1715809	1270727	1726876	2549534	2978986	4385959	3102150	26718141	165128930
Average Total Receipts **9**	94424	657	368	•	4000	10006	17098	44729	106392	175438	310215	1214461	20641116
Operating Costs/Operating Income (%)													
Cost of Operations **10**	63.4	32.6	64.3	•	54.3	54.7	63.1	59.8	69.6	69.0	62.6	74.9	61.3
Salaries and Wages **11**	15.4	29.5	6.3	•	18.1	22.4	21.7	20.9	13.8	12.7	15.2	12.3	15.9
Taxes Paid **12**	1.7	2.2	2.3	•	2.9	2.9	2.2	1.9	1.4	1.5	1.5	1.3	1.8
Interest Paid **13**	1.3	3.5	0.5	•	0.5	1.6	2.6	1.7	1.4	1.8	1.5	1.0	1.3
Depreciation **14**	3.0	1.7	2.7	•	1.2	2.5	1.7	1.8	1.8	1.3	1.5	2.0	3.4
Amortization and Depletion **15**	1.2	1.7	0.2	•	1.9	1.0	1.3	0.4	1.0	2.0	0.6	1.0	1.2
Pensions and Other Deferred Comp. **16**	0.5	0.1	•	•	0.9	0.2	0.3	0.2	0.1	0.2	0.3	0.2	0.6
Employee Benefits **17**	1.8	2.3	0.1	•	1.5	1.3	2.2	1.5	1.4	1.9	1.1	1.2	2.0
Advertising **18**	1.9	1.7	0.1	•	0.6	1.1	1.1	1.7	0.9	1.4	1.9	2.5	1.8
Other Expenses **19**	21.9	31.1	26.4	•	14.0	16.0	12.2	18.0	14.1	16.0	12.4	7.3	25.5
Officers' Compensation **20**	0.8	3.0	8.8	•	7.0	2.2	3.0	2.3	1.3	0.9	2.1	0.6	0.6
Operating Margin **21**	•	•	•	•	•	•	•	•	•	•	•	•	•
Operating Margin Before Officers' Comp. **22**	•	•	•	•	4.2	•	•	•	•	•	1.3	•	•

Selected Average Balance Sheet ($ in Thousands)

Net Receivables 23	18839	44	0	•	509	1857	4494	8326	15344	36307	73438	233352	4162386
Inventories 24	4692	12	0	•	515	1119	2549	4639	10436	16991	47234	66340	860433
Net Property, Plant and Equipment 25	9162	34	0	•	144	1424	1079	2933	5788	10174	17793	94628	2145317
Total Assets 26	96577	95	0	•	2121	7878	15516	36339	73193	170538	358158	1206221	2161852
Notes and Loans Payable 27	18196	509	0	•	1934	2929	3576	7286	10468	33016	34886	199906	4011900
All Other Liabilities 28	41806	97	0	•	848	2162	6270	10469	44777	56786	108717	394336	9830884
Net Worth 29	36576	-511	0	•	-661	2788	5670	18584	17947	80737	214554	611978	7769068

Selected Financial Ratios (Times to 1)

Current Ratio 30	1.3	0.6	•	•	1.6	1.5	2.5	1.4	1.7	2.2	1.6	1.2
Quick Ratio 31	0.8	0.5	•	•	1.0	1.0	1.9	0.8	1.2	1.2	1.1	0.7
Net Sales to Working Capital 32	7.5	•	•	6.8	3.5	4.1	2.7	7.9	4.2	2.5	5.0	9.4
Coverage Ratio 33	7.0	•	•	•	•	•	•	0.3	•	2.8	4.3	8.7
Total Asset Turnover 34	0.8	3.9	•	1.9	1.3	1.1	1.2	1.4	1.0	0.8	0.9	0.8
Inventory Turnover 35	10.7	20.1	•	4.2	4.8	4.0	5.6	6.8	6.9	4.0	12.8	11.9
Receivables Turnover 36	4.6	8.4	•	6.9	5.9	4.0	6.3	8.0	4.9	3.6	5.6	4.4
Total Liabilities to Net Worth 37	1.6	•	•	•	1.8	1.7	1.0	3.1	1.1	0.7	1.0	1.8
Current Assets to Working Capital 38	4.4	•	•	2.8	1.9	2.9	1.6	3.6	2.4	1.8	2.7	5.6
Current Liabilities to Working Capital 39	3.4	•	•	1.8	0.9	1.9	0.6	2.6	1.4	0.8	1.7	4.6
Working Capital to Net Sales 40	0.1	•	•	0.1	0.3	0.2	0.4	0.1	0.2	0.4	0.2	0.1
Inventory to Working Capital 41	0.4	•	•	0.8	0.5	0.7	0.3	1.0	0.4	0.3	0.3	0.5
Total Receipts to Cash Flow 42	3.8	12.2	4.5	11.4	12.3	50.0	12.3	13.5	15.6	7.5	12.0	3.2
Cost of Goods to Cash Flow 43	2.4	7.9	1.5	6.2	6.7	31.6	7.4	9.4	10.8	4.7	9.0	1.9
Cash Flow to Total Debt 44	0.3	0.0	•	0.1	0.2	0.0	0.2	0.1	0.1	0.3	0.2	0.4

Selected Financial Factors (in Percentages)

Debt Ratio 45	62.1	635.4	•	131.2	64.6	63.5	48.9	75.5	52.7	40.1	49.3	64.1
Return on Total Assets 46	7.5	•	•	•	•	•	•	0.5	•	3.6	3.8	8.9
Return on Equity Before Income Taxes 47	17.0	8.4	•	13.9	•	•	•	•	•	3.9	5.7	22.0
Return on Equity After Income Taxes 48	11.6	8.5	•	15.7	•	•	•	•	•	1.9	3.9	15.5
Profit Margin (Before Income Tax) 49	7.8	•	•	•	•	•	•	•	•	2.8	3.1	10.2
Profit Margin (After Income Tax) 50	5.4	•	•	•	•	•	•	•	•	1.4	2.1	7.2

Table II
Corporations with Net Income

COMPUTER AND PERIPHERAL EQUIPMENT

MONEY AMOUNTS AND SIZE OF ASSETS IN THOUSANDS OF DOLLARS

Item Description for Accounting Period 7/06 Through 6/07	Total	Zero Assets	Under 500	500 to 1,000	1,000 to 5,000	5,000 to 10,000	10,000 to 25,000	25,000 to 50,000	50,000 to 100,000	100,000 to 250,000	250,000 to 500,000	500,000 to 2,500,000	2,500,000 and over
Number of Enterprises **1**	1187	17	•	0	294	83	44	31	16	12	7	14	•
Revenues ($ in Thousands)													
Net Sales **2**	167175133	114807	•	0	1177378	842276	918350	1797268	1969935	2256621	2081062	22024842	•
Interest **3**	2587987	399	•	0	3054	733	2831	6260	12894	14196	40424	216190	•
Rents **4**	975197	0	•	0	0	0	230	232	338	0	413	16509	•
Royalties **5**	25498296	0	•	0	0	0	0	21537	0	97	20722	136910	•
Other Portfolio Income **6**	2415712	1	•	0	0	3	2219	8794	95103	1410	8626	104177	•
Other Receipts **7**	1153279	3252	•	0	109	7090	7857	17422	9521	11180	53875	261437	•
Total Receipts **8**	199805604	118459	•	0	1180541	850102	931487	1851513	2087791	2283504	2205122	22760065	•
Average Total Receipts **9**	168328	6968	•	•	4015	10242	21170	59726	130487	190292	315017	1625719	•
Operating Costs/Operating Income (%)													
Cost of Operations **10**	63.2	13.6	•	•	52.3	51.8	57.6	62.2	78.3	68.2	63.7	74.4	•
Salaries and Wages **11**	14.7	19.8	•	•	14.0	12.8	14.0	13.4	7.0	13.3	14.9	9.0	•
Taxes Paid **12**	1.7	1.3	•	•	2.2	3.0	1.5	1.7	0.9	0.8	1.5	1.2	•
Interest Paid **13**	1.2	0.4	•	•	0.1	1.7	1.2	0.3	1.3	0.8	0.2	0.3	•
Depreciation **14**	3.0	1.4	•	•	1.0	2.6	0.7	1.2	1.4	1.2	1.2	1.6	•
Amortization and Depletion **15**	1.1	0.3	•	•	•	0.4	0.3	0.1	0.3	0.5	0.4	0.6	•
Pensions and Other Deferred Comp. **16**	0.6	0.0	•	•	1.0	0.1	0.3	0.2	0.1	0.2	0.3	0.2	•
Employee Benefits **17**	1.8	2.1	•	•	1.0	0.3	0.9	1.0	0.6	1.4	1.0	0.8	•
Advertising **18**	1.9	2.6	•	•	0.5	1.3	0.5	0.8	0.6	1.1	2.0	2.6	•
Other Expenses **19**	21.9	25.3	•	•	9.7	14.4	9.6	13.3	7.0	9.7	11.7	5.4	•
Officers' Compensation **20**	0.7	3.1	•	•	6.8	1.0	1.6	1.8	1.1	0.6	2.2	0.6	•
Operating Margin **21**	•	30.0	•	•	11.6	10.5	11.7	3.8	1.4	2.2	1.0	3.1	•
Operating Margin Before Officers' Comp. **22**	•	33.1	•	•	18.4	11.6	13.3	5.7	2.5	2.8	3.2	3.7	•

Selected Average Balance Sheet ($ in Thousands)

Net Receivables 23	33696	0	•	502	1996	5678	10442	15520	34105	73414	328392	•
Inventories 24	7984	0	•	537	1024	3107	6013	12563	21961	50272	85528	•
Net Property, Plant and Equipment 25	16532	0	•	76	1849	827	3239	6206	12215	12695	127334	•
Total Assets 26	168079	0	•	1683	7396	14841	35612	73794	155026	371374	1286751	•
Notes and Loans Payable 27	29207	0	•	325	3937	4236	4992	6930	28850	16567	86504	•
All Other Liabilities 28	74215	0	•	646	1806	8188	12559	45236	53617	87275	451910	•
Net Worth 29	64657	0	•	713	1653	2417	18061	21628	72560	267532	748338	•

Selected Financial Ratios (Times to 1)

Current Ratio 30	1.3	•	•	2.2	2.2	1.1	3.2	1.4	1.4	2.6	2.0	•
Quick Ratio 31	0.7	•	•	1.5	1.1	0.7	2.3	0.8	0.8	1.4	1.3	•
Net Sales to Working Capital 32	7.5	•	•	5.1	4.0	14.4	3.1	8.7	7.9	2.2	4.0	•
Coverage Ratio 33	9.3	84.3	•	106.2	7.6	11.6	22.0	7.7	5.4	36.4	19.9	•
Total Asset Turnover 34	0.8	•	•	2.4	1.4	1.4	1.6	1.7	1.2	0.8	1.2	•
Inventory Turnover 35	11.2	•	•	3.9	5.1	3.9	6.0	7.7	5.8	3.8	13.7	•
Receivables Turnover 36	4.6	•	•	6.7	7.9	4.5	6.7	10.3	5.2	3.3	5.5	•
Total Liabilities to Net Worth 37	1.6	•	•	1.4	3.5	5.1	1.0	2.4	1.1	0.4	0.7	•
Current Assets to Working Capital 38	4.3	•	•	1.8	1.8	8.3	1.5	3.3	3.6	1.6	2.0	•
Current Liabilities to Working Capital 39	3.3	•	•	0.8	0.8	7.3	0.5	2.3	2.6	0.6	1.0	•
Working Capital to Net Sales 40	0.1	•	•	0.2	0.3	0.1	0.3	0.1	0.1	0.4	0.3	•
Inventory to Working Capital 41	0.4	•	•	0.6	0.6	2.6	0.3	1.3	0.9	0.3	0.2	•
Total Receipts to Cash Flow 42	3.6	1.8	•	5.3	4.3	4.9	5.5	11.1	8.3	5.7	9.2	•
Cost of Goods to Cash Flow 43	2.3	0.2	•	2.8	2.2	2.8	3.4	8.7	5.7	3.6	6.9	•
Cash Flow to Total Debt 44	0.4	•	•	0.8	0.4	0.3	0.6	0.2	0.3	0.5	0.3	•

Selected Financial Factors (in Percentages)

Debt Ratio 45	61.5	•	•	57.6	77.6	83.7	49.3	70.7	53.2	28.0	41.8	•
Return on Total Assets 46	9.0	•	•	28.4	18.1	20.2	11.8	17.0	5.2	5.7	8.5	•
Return on Equity Before Income Taxes 47	20.9	•	•	66.5	70.3	113.5	22.1	50.5	9.1	7.6	13.8	•
Return on Equity After Income Taxes 48	15.2	•	•	64.1	64.0	102.1	18.5	43.4	6.7	5.4	11.4	•
Profit Margin (Before Income Tax) 49	9.6	33.1	•	11.8	11.5	13.1	6.9	8.9	3.5	6.9	6.6	•
Profit Margin (After Income Tax) 50	7.0	31.6	•	11.4	10.4	11.8	5.8	7.6	2.6	4.8	5.4	•

Table I

Corporations with and without Net Income

COMMUNICATIONS EQUIPMENT

MONEY AMOUNTS AND SIZE OF ASSETS IN THOUSANDS OF DOLLARS

Item Description for Accounting Period 7/06 Through 6/07		Total	Zero Assets	Under 500	500 to 1,000	1,000 to 5,000	5,000 to 10,000	10,000 to 25,000	25,000 to 50,000	50,000 to 100,000	100,000 to 250,000	250,000 to 500,000	500,000 to 2,500,000	2,500,000 and over
Number of Enterprises	1	1216	35	475	132	322	33	70	48	35	20	16	15	15
Revenues ($ in Thousands)														
Net Sales	2	134231580	929113	225005	61023	1366280	188114	1211311	2162649	2603176	2385646	4482962	15749412	102866888
Interest	3	2066953	54509	611	1522	7788	2433	8732	12617	29905	57820	78529	128489	1683997
Rents	4	231435	0	0	0	1408	0	13	143	1697	792	42	1190	226149
Royalties	5	5215345	264197	0	0	0	0	151	14	3015	26746	17691	39515	4864016
Other Portfolio Income	6	3654014	8162	5303	0	0	500	25232	11226	43974	32404	52826	340240	3134145
Other Receipts	7	1278711	216974	1878	60	9656	7127	4363	12732	41468	1152	313292	70636	589377
Total Receipts	8	146678038	1472955	232797	62605	1385132	198174	1249802	2199381	2723235	2514560	4945342	16329482	113364572
Average Total Receipts	9	120623	42084	490	474	4302	6005	17854	45820	77807	125728	309084	1088632	7557638
Operating Costs/Operating Income (%)														
Cost of Operations	10	69.4	83.6	49.5	37.1	48.0	70.3	62.0	66.1	56.1	58.9	67.4	75.9	69.5
Salaries and Wages	11	14.6	61.1	4.9	39.1	25.3	42.7	26.9	14.6	15.4	17.6	14.2	7.7	14.8
Taxes Paid	12	1.4	2.0	2.2	5.7	3.0	6.6	3.5	2.2	1.7	1.8	1.5	1.0	1.3
Interest Paid	13	1.7	9.2	0.2	1.0	1.3	2.1	4.1	0.8	2.7	1.6	1.4	1.2	1.7
Depreciation	14	1.9	3.5	0.2	1.9	1.6	5.8	2.5	1.8	1.9	1.8	2.1	1.6	2.0
Amortization and Depletion	15	1.4	7.3	0.0	1.7	2.4	8.0	2.1	2.2	1.8	1.1	1.3	0.9	1.3
Pensions and Other Deferred Comp.	16	1.1	0.2	•	3.6	0.3	0.1	0.4	0.2	0.2	0.3	0.2	0.3	1.4
Employee Benefits	17	2.0	61.9	•	5.2	2.5	3.3	3.3	1.5	2.1	2.2	1.7	1.7	1.5
Advertising	18	0.9	0.5	•	2.9	1.5	1.9	1.1	0.5	0.7	1.2	0.5	0.7	0.9
Other Expenses	19	8.1	24.5	•	19.9	24.6	38.5	18.7	14.7	19.7	13.5	9.1	9.7	7.2
Officers' Compensation	20	0.8	1.3	6.4	8.6	6.4	7.6	4.1	2.5	1.8	1.9	1.4	0.4	0.6
Operating Margin	21	•	•	12.0	•	•	•	•	•	•	0.0	•	•	•
Operating Margin Before Officers' Comp.	22	•	•	18.4	•	•	•	•	•	•	0.7	•	•	•

Selected Average Balance Sheet ($ in Thousands)

Net Receivables 23	20417	0	15	11	602	1233	2913	6169	13855	22586	56952	134309	1348103
Inventories 24	7920	0	82	138	709	1444	2922	6754	7304	21671	27232	92889	416745
Net Property, Plant and Equipment 25	10814	0	3	28	116	743	2044	3077	5791	8434	21430	86591	718554
Total Assets 26	163334	0	133	592	2510	7446	15118	34840	67770	147821	372999	1035277	11190889
Notes and Loans Payable 27	28621	0	46	131	798	1523	6691	4740	19297	14775	46166	183772	1952944
All Other Liabilities 28	55467	0	10	57	1099	1892	6536	15535	27209	37688	93828	306639	3867302
Net Worth 29	79246	0	77	405	612	4032	1890	14566	21264	95359	233005	544866	5370642

Selected Financial Ratios (Times to 1)

Current Ratio 30	1.7	•	2.3	4.7	1.5	2.2	2.0	1.5	1.8	2.4	2.4	1.6	1.7
Quick Ratio 31	1.0	•	1.7	2.8	0.9	1.5	1.0	0.9	1.2	1.5	1.5	1.0	1.0
Net Sales to Working Capital 32	4.0	•	6.6	1.1	5.6	2.2	2.9	5.4	3.8	2.7	2.4	6.3	3.9
Coverage Ratio 33	5.5	•	65.4	•	•	•	•	•	1.2	3.3	7.8	3.1	7.0
Total Asset Turnover 34	0.7	•	3.6	0.8	1.7	0.8	1.1	1.3	1.1	0.8	0.8	1.0	0.6
Inventory Turnover 35	9.7	•	2.9	1.2	2.9	2.8	3.7	4.4	5.7	3.2	6.9	8.6	11.4
Receivables Turnover 36	5.4	•	29.3	8.4	6.6	3.3	6.2	6.0	7.1	3.9	5.0	7.7	5.2
Total Liabilities to Net Worth 37	1.1	•	0.7	0.5	3.1	0.8	7.0	1.4	2.2	0.6	0.6	0.9	1.1
Current Assets to Working Capital 38	2.4	•	1.8	1.3	3.1	1.8	2.0	2.9	2.3	1.7	1.7	2.5	2.5
Current Liabilities to Working Capital 39	1.4	•	0.8	0.3	2.1	0.8	1.0	1.9	1.3	0.7	0.7	1.5	1.5
Working Capital to Net Sales 40	0.3	•	0.2	0.9	0.2	0.5	0.3	0.2	0.3	0.4	0.4	0.2	0.3
Inventory to Working Capital 41	0.3	•	0.5	0.5	1.1	0.4	0.5	0.8	0.5	0.3	0.3	0.6	0.2
Total Receipts to Cash Flow 42	8.7	•	2.7	•	20.7	•	•	14.4	5.9	7.1	6.3	9.8	8.0
Cost of Goods to Cash Flow 43	6.1	•	1.3	•	9.9	•	•	9.5	3.3	4.2	4.2	7.4	5.5
Cash Flow to Total Debt 44	0.2	•	3.2	•	0.1	•	•	0.2	0.3	0.3	0.3	0.2	0.1

Selected Financial Factors (in Percentages)

Debt Ratio 45	51.5	•	42.3	31.7	75.6	45.9	87.5	58.2	68.6	35.5	37.5	47.4	52.0
Return on Total Assets 46	6.2	•	56.0	•	•	•	•	•	3.6	4.2	8.4	3.8	7.2
Return on Equity Before Income Taxes 47	10.5	•	95.6	•	•	•	•	•	1.9	4.5	11.7	5.0	12.8
Return on Equity After Income Taxes 48	7.1	•	95.4	•	•	•	•	•	•	3.0	9.9	4.1	9.0
Profit Margin (Before Income Tax) 49	7.5	•	15.4	•	•	•	•	•	0.5	•	3.6	2.6	10.0
Profit Margin (After Income Tax) 50	5.1	•	15.4	•	•	•	•	•	•	•	2.4	2.1	7.1

139

Table II

Corporations with Net Income

COMMUNICATIONS EQUIPMENT

MONEY AMOUNTS AND SIZE OF ASSETS IN THOUSANDS OF DOLLARS

Item Description for Accounting Period 7/06 Through 6/07	Total	Zero Assets	Under 500	500 to 1,000	1,000 to 5,000	5,000 to 10,000	10,000 to 25,000	25,000 to 50,000	50,000 to 100,000	100,000 to 250,000	250,000 to 500,000	500,000 to 2,500,000	2,500,000 and over
Number of Enterprises **1**	725	7	377	62	163	0	24	25	19	15	11	12	11
Revenues ($ in Thousands)													
Net Sales **2**	117819863	107020	107762	26383	988700	0	550729	1423314	1661403	1953042	2684090	14745024	93572398
Interest **3**	1423491	1	557	181	2865	0	1023	4142	13972	20086	66838	70691	1243135
Rents **4**	227430	0	0	0	1408	0	13	124	834	792	30	11	224218
Royalties **5**	2971340	0	0	0	0	0	0	2	2617	26706	17691	39515	2884809
Other Portfolio Income **6**	3508329	14404	5303	0	0	0	24291	4065	42705	21269	40962	339998	3015330
Other Receipts **7**	752584	697	1681	61	284	0	4277	7129	24552	8116	311259	61969	332560
Total Receipts **8**	126703037	122122	115303	26625	993257	0	580333	1438776	1746083	2030011	3120870	15257208	101272450
Average Total Receipts **9**	174763	17446	306	429	6094	•	24181	57551	91899	135334	283715	1271434	9206586
Operating Costs/Operating Income (%)													
Cost of Operations **10**	69.4	58.1	60.8	50.7	49.3	•	66.2	69.0	57.6	57.7	59.1	76.5	69.3
Salaries and Wages **11**	12.9	5.2	•	14.4	14.9	•	9.5	8.3	12.2	16.8	15.1	6.9	13.8
Taxes Paid **12**	1.2	2.1	0.2	3.2	2.0	•	2.6	1.8	1.7	1.6	1.8	1.0	1.2
Interest Paid **13**	1.3	0.0	0.5	•	0.5	•	1.8	0.6	3.2	0.8	2.2	0.9	1.4
Depreciation **14**	1.8	0.3	•	1.3	1.2	•	1.5	1.1	1.4	1.6	2.1	1.4	1.9
Amortization and Depletion **15**	0.9	0.2	0.0	•	0.1	•	0.3	0.1	0.5	0.8	1.0	0.4	1.1
Pensions and Other Deferred Comp. **16**	1.0	1.6	•	0.8	0.5	•	0.1	0.3	0.3	0.3	0.3	0.4	1.2
Employee Benefits **17**	1.2	0.3	•	2.1	1.6	•	1.8	1.2	1.7	2.0	2.1	1.7	1.1
Advertising **18**	0.9	1.5	•	0.7	1.7	•	0.3	0.4	0.5	1.4	0.5	0.8	1.0
Other Expenses **19**	7.1	7.6	8.3	13.7	16.3	•	7.3	6.1	13.5	11.7	10.9	9.6	6.3
Officers' Compensation **20**	0.7	3.4	•	7.1	4.7	•	2.1	2.0	1.7	1.8	1.3	0.4	0.7
Operating Margin **21**	1.3	19.7	30.1	6.1	7.2	•	6.6	8.9	5.6	3.5	3.7	•	1.0
Operating Margin Before Officers' Comp. **22**	2.0	23.1	30.1	13.1	11.9	•	8.7	10.9	7.3	5.3	5.0	0.4	1.7

Selected Average Balance Sheet ($ in Thousands)

Net Receivables 23	29378	0	7	23	809	•	3866	6666	13984	23711	55600	150391	1624206
Inventories 24	10405	0	62	219	1067	•	2658	8819	6777	19357	28615	94313	492132
Net Property, Plant and Equipment 25	15463	0	0	25	134	•	2893	3538	6223	7714	22734	99203	850451
Total Assets 26	209382	0	84	504	3007	•	13376	32513	70744	148254	373768	946267	11916442
Notes and Loans Payable 27	37058	0	59	0	1227	•	4490	4331	28043	18348	52486	129765	2135128
All Other Liabilities 28	72204	0	0	20	1043	•	3012	13229	24325	36226	77180	334992	4172675
Net Worth 29	100120	0	25	484	737	•	5874	14953	18376	93679	244102	481509	5608639

Selected Financial Ratios (Times to 1)

Current Ratio 30	1.6	•	1.4	24.0	1.6	•	2.4	2.0	2.0	1.9	3.0	1.4	1.6
Quick Ratio 31	1.1	•	1.4	10.1	0.9	•	1.5	1.0	1.4	1.1	1.9	0.9	1.1
Net Sales to Working Capital 32	4.8	•	11.4	0.9	5.6	•	4.0	5.0	3.7	3.7	1.7	10.1	4.7
Coverage Ratio 33	8.9	1223.6	75.1	•	16.5	•	7.8	16.4	4.3	10.0	10.1	4.8	9.3
Total Asset Turnover 34	0.8	•	3.4	0.8	2.0	•	1.7	1.8	1.2	0.9	0.7	1.3	0.7
Inventory Turnover 35	10.8	•	2.8	1.0	2.8	•	5.7	4.5	7.4	3.9	5.0	10.0	12.0
Receivables Turnover 36	6.3	•	54.7	6.4	7.8	•	5.8	6.0	9.6	4.3	•	10.1	•
Total Liabilities to Net Worth 37	1.1	•	2.3	0.0	3.1	•	1.3	1.2	2.8	0.6	0.5	1.0	1.1
Current Assets to Working Capital 38	2.6	•	3.3	1.0	2.6	•	1.7	2.0	2.0	2.1	1.5	3.4	2.7
Current Liabilities to Working Capital 39	1.6	•	2.3	0.0	1.6	•	0.7	1.0	1.0	1.1	0.5	2.4	1.7
Working Capital to Net Sales 40	0.2	•	0.1	1.1	0.2	•	0.3	0.2	0.3	0.3	0.6	0.1	0.2
Inventory to Working Capital 41	0.3	•	0.1	0.6	1.1	•	0.3	0.7	0.4	0.4	0.2	0.9	0.3
Total Receipts to Cash Flow 42	7.5	3.6	2.2	7.7	4.7	•	7.4	6.8	4.8	6.1	3.7	8.8	7.7
Cost of Goods to Cash Flow 43	5.2	2.1	1.4	3.9	2.3	•	4.9	4.7	2.7	3.5	2.2	6.8	5.3
Cash Flow to Total Debt 44	0.2	•	2.2	2.8	0.6	•	0.4	0.5	0.4	0.4	0.5	0.3	0.2

Selected Financial Factors (in Percentages)

Debt Ratio 45	52.2	•	70.0	4.0	75.5	•	56.1	54.0	74.0	36.8	34.7	49.1	52.9
Return on Total Assets 46	9.3	•	128.5	5.9	16.5	•	23.6	18.6	17.3	7.3	14.5	5.7	9.2
Return on Equity Before Income Taxes 47	17.2	•	422.8	6.1	63.4	•	46.9	38.0	51.2	10.4	20.0	8.9	17.4
Return on Equity After Income Taxes 48	12.7	•	422.0	6.1	51.0	•	41.1	33.5	40.5	8.4	17.6	7.7	12.5
Profit Margin (Before Income Tax) 49	10.6	34.3	37.1	7.0	7.7	•	12.0	10.0	10.8	7.5	8.8	3.5	11.5
Profit Margin (After Income Tax) 50	7.8	33.7	37.0	7.0	6.2	•	10.5	8.5	6.0	6.0	3.0	17.6	8.2

Table I

Corporations with and without Net Income

AUDIO AND VIDEO EQUIP, REPRODUCING MAGNETIC & OPTICAL MEDIA

MONEY AMOUNTS AND SIZE OF ASSETS IN THOUSANDS OF DOLLARS

Item Description for Accounting Period 7/06 Through 6/07	Total	Zero Assets	Under 500	500 to 1,000	1,000 to 5,000	5,000 to 10,000	10,000 to 25,000	25,000 to 50,000	50,000 to 100,000	100,000 to 250,000	250,000 to 500,000	500,000 to 2,500,000	2,500,000 and over
Number of Enterprises **1**	1859	36	959	286	394	65	44	27	14	14	7	9	3
Revenues ($ in Thousands)													
Net Sales **2**	34764924	250250	23539	441164	1286988	670404	1071897	1111115	1125503	2542954	2762074	8309287	15516747
Interest **3**	220062	673	22	2	2085	9828	5957	4546	5618	19932	26967	55076	89356
Rents **4**	8734	0	0	0	0	0	343	189	214	1511	1730	866	3881
Royalties **5**	531891	0	0	0	0	0	3674	28	1181	640	76	394638	131654
Other Portfolio Income **6**	567145	7	0	0	37	7125	614	3639	5724	9760	13415	123841	402985
Other Receipts **7**	567144	977	-1	0	3396	5240	9541	32072	7481	27914	121119	19215	340189
Total Receipts **8**	36659900	251907	23560	441166	1292506	692597	1092026	1151589	1145721	2602711	2925381	8902923	16137812
Average Total Receipts **9**	19720	6997	25	1543	3280	10655	24819	42651	81837	185908	417912	989214	5379271
Operating Costs/Operating Income (%)													
Cost of Operations **10**	66.5	51.3	70.2	47.7	59.6	64.7	58.3	54.5	60.9	63.7	79.3	55.6	73.9
Salaries and Wages **11**	10.4	15.1	33.5	14.1	12.8	12.9	15.5	21.1	14.0	10.2	10.5	11.9	7.7
Taxes Paid **12**	1.0	0.6	3.0	1.8	2.4	2.1	1.7	2.2	1.6	1.5	0.9	0.9	0.7
Interest Paid **13**	1.4	0.9	0.7	1.0	0.8	2.2	2.1	1.9	2.6	1.3	1.2	1.7	1.3
Depreciation **14**	2.1	0.8	4.3	2.0	1.3	2.2	2.0	2.2	2.2	2.0	2.0	2.9	1.9
Amortization and Depletion **15**	1.1	4.1	7.4	0.6	0.9	0.4	0.5	1.1	1.0	0.3	0.7	0.9	1.5
Pensions and Other Deferred Comp. **16**	0.8	0.5	•	•	0.1	0.1	0.6	0.5	0.4	0.4	0.5	0.1	1.6
Employee Benefits **17**	1.7	2.1	1.8	0.4	1.0	1.4	2.9	1.6	3.5	1.6	1.1	2.4	1.3
Advertising **18**	2.0	1.8	1.4	10.0	1.4	0.2	1.0	1.5	1.6	2.3	0.6	2.8	1.9
Other Expenses **19**	14.5	39.4	74.0	25.5	19.6	20.2	15.0	20.6	13.1	15.4	8.9	20.7	10.0
Officers' Compensation **20**	0.9	0.4	•	4.0	4.6	3.3	3.0	1.7	1.6	0.9	0.7	0.7	0.2
Operating Margin **21**	•	•	•	•	•	•	•	•	•	0.3	•	•	•
Operating Margin Before Officers' Comp. **22**	•	•	•	•	0.0	•	0.6	•	•	1.2	•	•	0.2

Selected Average Balance Sheet ($ in Thousands)

Net Receivables 23	3558	0	0	234	392	2414	4924	11625	14857	28798	50693	183343	1029822
Inventories 24	1696	0	1	85	304	1048	4090	6235	14126	27345	44056	98409	544327
Net Property, Plant and Equipment 25	1738	0	2	45	137	1127	2193	2933	9987	16791	37314	107471	436673
Total Assets 26	21417	0	11	591	1950	7836	16342	34357	64010	153894	381535	1058066	7155373
Notes and Loans Payable 27	5507	0	17	466	650	2649	2975	11549	32070	36789	84891	171569	2037753
All Other Liabilities 28	5779	0	1	547	510	6154	6816	14444	13215	50830	126063	297939	1611593
Net Worth 29	10131	0	-7	-422	790	-967	6551	8364	18725	66275	170582	588558	3506027

Selected Financial Ratios (Times to 1)

Current Ratio 30	1.5	•	5.4	0.9	2.5	1.5	1.2	1.9	2.3	1.8	•	1.3	1.4
Quick Ratio 31	0.9	•	3.9	0.6	1.8	1.1	0.9	1.1	1.1	1.0	•	0.9	0.8
Net Sales to Working Capital 32	7.3	•	6.6	•	3.4	6.3	6.7	10.1	4.2	3.5	4.5	9.5	9.9
Coverage Ratio 33	3.1	•	•	•	•	•	0.8	•	0.8	2.9	0.7	5.0	4.6
Total Asset Turnover 34	0.9	•	2.2	2.6	1.7	1.3	1.5	1.2	1.3	1.2	1.0	0.9	0.7
Inventory Turnover 35	7.3	•	15.4	8.6	6.4	6.4	3.5	3.6	3.5	4.2	7.1	5.2	6.9
Receivables Turnover 36	6.1	•	33.1	11.7	9.8	4.2	4.3	3.6	5.0	6.4	7.3	3.7	9.8
Total Liabilities to Net Worth 37	1.1	•	1.2	•	1.5	1.5	1.5	3.1	2.4	1.3	1.2	0.8	1.0
Current Assets to Working Capital 38	3.2	•	1.2	•	1.6	3.1	3.2	5.5	2.2	1.8	2.2	4.6	3.7
Current Liabilities to Working Capital 39	2.2	•	0.2	•	0.6	2.1	2.2	4.5	1.2	0.8	1.2	3.6	2.7
Working Capital to Net Sales 40	0.1	•	0.2	•	0.3	0.2	0.2	0.1	0.2	0.3	0.2	0.1	0.1
Inventory to Working Capital 41	0.8	•	0.3	•	0.4	0.6	1.0	1.2	0.6	0.6	0.7	0.8	1.1
Total Receipts to Cash Flow 42	7.1	4.6	•	7.3	8.1	9.6	8.0	8.1	11.0	6.1	14.5	4.0	10.0
Cost of Goods to Cash Flow 43	4.7	2.4	•	3.5	4.8	6.2	4.7	4.4	6.7	3.9	11.5	2.2	7.4
Cash Flow to Total Debt 44	0.2	•	•	0.2	0.3	0.1	0.3	0.2	0.2	0.3	0.1	0.5	0.1

Selected Financial Factors (in Percentages)

Debt Ratio 45	52.7	•	161.1	171.4	59.5	112.3	75.7	59.9	70.7	56.9	55.3	44.4	51.0
Return on Total Assets 46	3.9	•	•	•	•	2.4	•	•	2.7	4.4	0.9	7.3	4.1
Return on Equity Before Income Taxes 47	5.5	•	348.7	26.3	•	68.1	•	•	6.7	4.4	6.7	10.6	6.5
Return on Equity After Income Taxes 48	4.0	•	354.6	26.3	•	75.4	•	•	3.1	•	3.1	7.7	5.9
Profit Margin (Before Income Tax) 49	3.0	•	•	•	•	•	•	•	•	•	2.5	6.7	4.5
Profit Margin (After Income Tax) 50	2.1	•	•	•	•	•	•	•	•	•	1.1	4.9	4.1

Table II

Corporations with Net Income

AUDIO AND VIDEO EQUIP., REPRODUCING MAGNETIC & OPTICAL MEDIA

MONEY AMOUNTS AND SIZE OF ASSETS IN THOUSANDS OF DOLLARS

Item Description for Accounting Period 7/06 Through 6/07	Total	Zero Assets	Under 500	500 to 1,000	1,000 to 5,000	5,000 to 10,000	10,000 to 25,000	25,000 to 50,000	50,000 to 100,000	100,000 to 250,000	250,000 to 500,000	500,000 to 2,500,000	2,500,000 and over
Number of Enterprises **1**	874	10	•	192	298	33	29	9	8	8	4	•	0
Revenues ($ in Thousands)													
Net Sales **2**	26530149	212655	•	287659	1002684	597446	820874	480184	681997	1936919	1511651	•	0
Interest **3**	160026	12	•	0	457	1056	1451	1319	1847	5577	7036	•	0
Rents **4**	6829	0	•	0	0	0	83	140	0	129	1730	•	0
Royalties **5**	456174	0	•	0	0	0	38	28	1094	640	76	•	0
Other Portfolio Income **6**	533287	0	•	0	0	7125	545	3575	119	4605	13212	•	0
Other Receipts **7**	393289	977	•	0	1466	391	4610	29887	4902	3797	15433	•	0
Total Receipts **8**	28079754	213644	•	287659	1004607	606018	827601	515133	689959	1951667	1549138	•	0
Average Total Receipts **9**	32128	21364	•	1498	3371	18364	28538	57237	86245	243958	387284	•	•
Operating Costs/Operating Income (%)													
Cost of Operations **10**	65.6	56.3	•	47.2	54.1	64.6	64.4	56.7	55.6	65.4	71.2	•	•
Salaries and Wages **11**	9.9	10.8	•	5.9	11.7	8.7	8.1	12.5	11.0	9.7	12.3	•	•
Taxes Paid **12**	0.9	•	•	1.0	2.4	1.9	1.4	1.6	1.6	1.4	1.2	•	•
Interest Paid **13**	1.3	0.9	•	•	0.1	0.8	2.0	0.9	3.0	1.1	1.2	•	•
Depreciation **14**	2.0	0.5	•	0.1	0.8	1.6	1.8	1.6	1.9	1.8	2.0	•	•
Amortization and Depletion **15**	0.8	2.0	•	•	0.1	0.2	0.4	0.2	0.5	0.3	0.8	•	•
Pensions and Other Deferred Comp. **16**	0.8	0.0	•	•	0.1	0.1	0.1	0.6	0.5	0.5	0.7	•	•
Employee Benefits **17**	1.8	0.1	•	0.7	0.6	1.0	2.6	1.2	4.9	1.5	1.7	•	•
Advertising **18**	2.4	2.0	•	15.3	1.5	0.2	0.2	2.0	0.6	2.2	0.8	•	•
Other Expenses **19**	11.8	24.5	•	20.7	12.9	11.7	9.5	15.5	9.8	10.6	5.7	•	•
Officers' Compensation **20**	0.8	0.1	•	6.2	4.4	2.7	2.7	1.5	1.2	0.5	0.8	•	•
Operating Margin **21**	1.8	2.8	•	2.9	11.3	6.5	6.9	5.7	9.4	5.0	1.7	•	•
Operating Margin Before Officers' Comp. **22**	2.6	2.9	•	9.1	15.7	9.2	9.5	7.2	10.6	5.5	2.4	•	•

Selected Average Balance Sheet ($ in Thousands)

Net Receivables 23	5481	0	•	256	355	4198	4427	10104	12904	30762	57530
Inventories 24	2566	0	•	204	330	923	4232	11836	13947	36679	49951
Net Property, Plant and Equipment 25	2824	0	•	2	63	887	2733	3867	7514	20863	43436
Total Assets 26	36526	0	•	560	1796	8738	16217	39593	64928	155845	362612
Notes and Loans Payable 27	7880	0	•	10	372	1048	3522	5498	37967	38336	97612
All Other Liabilities 28	8600	0	•	602	411	4537	5729	8698	12544	45829	118005
Net Worth 29	20046	0	•	-53	1013	3154	6966	25398	14416	71680	146995

Selected Financial Ratios (Times to 1)

Current Ratio 30	1.5	•	0.9	3.3	1.5	1.5	2.5	2.9	2.1	3.3	
Quick Ratio 31	0.9	•	0.6	2.3	1.2	0.9	1.6	1.4	1.0	1.7	
Net Sales to Working Capital 32	6.6	•	•	3.3	7.5	7.7	3.1	3.0	4.8	2.7	
Coverage Ratio 33	7.1	4.8	•	96.2	11.3	4.9	15.0	4.7	6.3	4.7	
Total Asset Turnover 34	0.8	•	2.7	1.9	2.1	1.7	1.3	1.3	1.6	1.0	
Inventory Turnover 35	7.8	•	3.5	5.5	12.7	4.3	2.6	3.4	4.3	5.4	
Receivables Turnover 36	7.8	•	11.7	10.4	5.7	5.8	3.6	6.8	7.3	8.7	
Total Liabilities to Net Worth 37	0.8	•	•	0.8	1.8	1.3	0.6	3.5	1.2	1.5	
Current Assets to Working Capital 38	2.8	•	•	1.4	2.9	3.1	1.7	1.5	1.9	1.4	
Current Liabilities to Working Capital 39	1.8	•	•	0.4	1.9	2.1	0.7	0.5	0.9	0.4	
Working Capital to Net Sales 40	0.2	•	•	0.3	0.1	0.1	0.3	0.3	0.2	0.4	
Inventory to Working Capital 41	0.8	•	•	0.4	0.5	1.2	0.5	0.5	0.8	0.5	
Total Receipts to Cash Flow 42	6.3	3.7	4.5	4.6	5.8	6.4	3.8	5.3	6.7	12.5	
Cost of Goods to Cash Flow 43	4.1	2.1	2.1	2.5	3.8	4.1	2.2	3.0	4.4	8.9	
Cash Flow to Total Debt 44	0.3	•	0.5	0.9	0.6	0.5	1.0	0.3	0.4	0.1	

Selected Financial Factors (in Percentages)

Debt Ratio 45	45.1	•	109.4	43.6	63.9	57.0	35.9	77.8	54.0	59.5	
Return on Total Assets 46	7.6	•	7.8	21.8	18.0	17.1	18.5	18.1	10.5	5.8	
Return on Equity Before Income Taxes 47	11.8	•	•	38.2	45.5	31.8	26.9	64.1	19.2	11.2	
Return on Equity After Income Taxes 48	10.1	•	•	36.5	41.1	26.0	21.8	62.9	13.3	9.4	
Profit Margin (Before Income Tax) 49	7.8	3.3	2.9	11.5	7.9	7.8	12.8	10.8	5.7	4.4	
Profit Margin (After Income Tax) 50	6.7	2.9	2.9	11.0	7.2	6.4	10.4	10.6	3.9	3.7	

142

Table I

Corporations with and without Net Income

SEMICONDUCTOR AND OTHER ELECTRONIC COMPONENT

MONEY AMOUNTS AND SIZE OF ASSETS IN THOUSANDS OF DOLLARS

Item Description for Accounting Period 7/06 Through 6/07	Total	Zero Assets	Under 500	500 to 1,000	1,000 to 5,000	5,000 to 10,000	10,000 to 25,000	25,000 to 50,000	50,000 to 100,000	100,000 to 250,000	250,000 to 500,000	500,000 to 2,500,000	2,500,000 and over
Number of Enterprises 1	6602	1571	2105	568	1451	424	179	81	53	56	37	54	23
Revenues ($ in Thousands)													
Net Sales 2	198355155	2297486	1346620	1126870	6895092	5175866	3771035	2951378	3300841	9570096	9608139	40882878	111428854
Interest 3	3396530	3365	3263	1619	10236	17902	28343	36654	44342	123103	166147	696710	2264847
Rents 4	52246	8780	0	0	471	2480	501	1103	5307	1851	5871	5997	19886
Royalties 5	5067540	1016	0	0	0	0	0	8759	23807	87372	45664	819556	4081366
Other Portfolio Income 6	3692246	57550	20579	1333	21033	778	37400	125340	41244	143117	173604	469600	2600669
Other Receipts 7	3948307	20083	26522	1576	22657	81677	23376	122914	69993	115215	87167	1517501	1859622
Total Receipts 8	214512024	2388280	1396984	1131398	6949489	5278703	3860655	3246148	3485534	10040754	10086592	44392242	122255244
Average Total Receipts 9	32492	1520	664	1992	4789	12450	21568	40076	65765	179299	272611	822079	5315445
Operating Costs/Operating Income (%)													
Cost of Operations 10	63.1	67.1	49.2	61.0	56.2	65.1	66.8	67.4	66.7	70.3	56.4	69.7	60.7
Salaries and Wages 11	12.4	7.7	18.6	9.7	14.9	11.2	11.1	12.2	15.2	9.6	14.8	12.5	12.3
Taxes Paid 12	1.3	3.6	4.7	2.2	3.3	2.2	2.3	1.9	1.7	1.5	1.7	1.1	1.0
Interest Paid 13	1.3	2.3	0.3	0.3	1.0	1.1	1.9	1.1	1.3	1.1	1.0	1.6	1.3
Depreciation 14	4.5	1.9	0.7	0.3	2.0	1.7	2.3	2.4	2.8	2.4	3.4	4.0	5.6
Amortization and Depletion 15	1.2	0.2	0.0	0.2	0.3	0.9	0.5	0.9	1.0	0.7	1.3	1.5	1.3
Pensions and Other Deferred Comp. 16	0.5	0.1	•	0.4	1.0	0.5	0.4	1.4	1.6	0.6	0.5	0.5	0.3
Employee Benefits 17	2.0	1.2	0.4	1.3	1.8	1.5	1.9	2.1	2.4	1.8	2.3	1.7	2.1
Advertising 18	1.9	0.3	0.1	0.0	0.6	0.5	0.5	0.6	0.9	0.7	0.4	0.2	3.0
Other Expenses 19	11.0	13.7	23.2	13.5	11.4	11.9	12.0	18.1	19.7	11.8	14.6	9.3	10.5
Officers' Compensation 20	1.2	4.7	3.6	8.8	5.6	2.9	3.4	2.1	1.9	1.3	1.1	0.9	0.7
Operating Margin 21	•	•	•	2.3	1.8	0.6	•	•	•	•	2.5	1.0	•
Operating Margin Before Officers' Comp. 22	0.8	1.9	2.8	11.1	7.5	3.5	0.3	•	•	•	3.6	1.8	•

Selected Average Balance Sheet ($ in Thousands)

Net Receivables 23	7505	0	16	204	580	1760	3766	6383	12892	32598	44309	166694	1455344
Inventories 24	2894	0	18	119	635	1389	3410	6225	8783	22994	28766	61541	445054
Net Property, Plant and Equipment 25	6596	0	16	56	542	1387	2499	4313	9425	19939	54758	165450	1249273
Total Assets 26	45373	0	115	697	2288	7165	16235	33265	68928	172033	386950	1073413	8755901
Notes and Loans Payable 27	7274	0	106	97	792	2672	5014	5967	12789	27893	68287	251112	1119809
All Other Liabilities 28	12679	0	26	295	608	2112	3748	9817	24483	42163	67151	274213	2577883
Net Worth 29	25420	0	-17	306	888	2381	7473	17481	31656	101978	251512	548087	5058209

Selected Financial Ratios (Times to 1)

Current Ratio 30	1.9	•	1.0	2.4	1.9	2.2	2.1	2.1	1.8	2.3	2.7	2.0	1.8
Quick Ratio 31	1.3	•	0.7	1.5	1.1	1.4	1.3	1.3	1.1	1.4	1.7	1.4	1.2
Net Sales to Working Capital 32	3.1	•	•	6.0	6.7	4.4	3.6	3.2	3.3	2.8	2.0	3.1	3.1
Coverage Ratio 33	7.6	1.5	10.7	10.3	3.5	3.3	0.6	0.6	•	4.0	8.8	5.2	10.4
Total Asset Turnover 34	0.7	•	5.5	2.8	2.1	1.7	1.3	1.1	0.9	1.0	0.7	0.7	0.6
Inventory Turnover 35	6.5	•	18.0	10.2	4.2	5.7	4.1	3.9	4.7	5.2	5.1	8.6	6.6
Receivables Turnover 36	3.9	•	45.6	12.0	6.6	8.2	5.9	4.7	4.8	4.9	5.4	5.4	3.2
Total Liabilities to Net Worth 37	0.8	•	•	1.3	1.6	2.0	1.2	0.9	1.2	0.7	0.5	1.0	0.7
Current Assets to Working Capital 38	2.1	•	•	1.7	2.1	1.8	1.9	1.9	2.3	1.8	1.6	2.0	2.2
Current Liabilities to Working Capital 39	1.1	•	•	0.7	1.1	0.8	0.9	0.9	1.3	0.8	0.6	1.0	1.2
Working Capital to Net Sales 40	0.3	•	•	0.2	0.2	0.2	0.3	0.3	0.3	0.4	0.5	0.3	0.3
Inventory to Working Capital 41	0.3	•	•	0.6	0.7	0.6	0.6	0.5	0.5	0.4	0.2	0.3	0.3
Total Receipts to Cash Flow 42	6.4	11.2	5.9	8.3	9.8	8.7	12.6	10.8	17.6	7.9	5.9	7.6	5.5
Cost of Goods to Cash Flow 43	4.0	7.5	2.9	5.0	5.5	5.6	8.4	7.3	11.8	5.6	3.3	5.3	3.3
Cash Flow to Total Debt 44	0.2	•	0.8	0.6	0.3	0.3	0.2	0.2	0.1	0.3	0.3	0.2	0.2

Selected Financial Factors (in Percentages)

Debt Ratio 45	44.0	•	114.4	56.2	61.2	66.8	54.0	47.4	54.1	40.7	35.0	48.9	42.2
Return on Total Assets 46	6.6	•	17.9	8.6	7.6	6.3	1.5	0.7	•	4.3	6.0	6.0	7.2
Return on Equity Before Income Taxes 47	10.2	•	•	17.6	14.1	13.2	•	•	•	5.5	8.2	9.4	11.3
Return on Equity After Income Taxes 48	6.7	•	•	16.9	10.8	12.0	•	•	•	3.1	6.4	6.3	7.4
Profit Margin (Before Income Tax) 49	8.6	1.1	2.9	2.7	2.6	2.6	•	•	•	3.3	7.9	6.8	11.8
Profit Margin (After Income Tax) 50	5.6	0.8	2.4	2.6	2.0	2.3	•	•	•	1.8	6.2	4.6	7.7

Table II

Corporations with Net Income

SEMICONDUCTOR AND OTHER ELECTRONIC COMPONENT

MONEY AMOUNTS AND SIZE OF ASSETS IN THOUSANDS OF DOLLARS

Item Description for Accounting Period 7/06 Through 6/07	Total	Zero Assets	Under 500	500 to 1,000	1,000 to 5,000	5,000 to 10,000	10,000 to 25,000	25,000 to 50,000	50,000 to 100,000	100,000 to 250,000	250,000 to 500,000	500,000 to 2,500,000	2,500,000 and over
Number of Enterprises **1**	3957	584	1168	455	1145	314	110	41	23	36	26	41	13
Revenues ($ in Thousands)													
Net Sales **2**	146007847	641512	851717	1058904	6188091	4338111	2827601	2147313	2018645	6910342	28133476	28133476	83987956
Interest **3**	2542349	119	2400	1000	5112	4326	10868	18001	16862	76410	125313	515816	1766123
Rents **4**	33135	0	0	0	406	2338	501	716	4820	1851	2431	5576	14496
Royalties **5**	4405401	0	0	0	0	0	0	75	23634	80163	38207	415331	3847991
Other Portfolio Income **6**	3347076	57473	20579	1056	20927	332	26706	124822	33218	129883	152850	424177	2355055
Other Receipts **7**	1909295	17902	17	1572	19414	72596	19442	106866	33279	86029	61312	627092	863771
Total Receipts **8**	158245103	717006	874713	1062532	6233950	4417703	2885118	2397793	2130458	7284678	7284292	30121468	92835392
Average Total Receipts **9**	39991	1228	749	2335	5444	14069	26228	58483	92629	202352	280165	734670	7141184
Operating Costs/Operating Income (%)													
Cost of Operations **10**	59.4	67.4	46.9	59.9	57.1	63.9	64.6	68.8	67.5	69.2	52.1	66.2	56.3
Salaries and Wages **11**	11.6	5.3	10.2	7.9	11.9	8.7	8.0	8.3	10.0	8.0	14.9	13.1	11.6
Taxes Paid **12**	1.3	4.0	3.9	2.1	3.1	1.9	1.9	1.5	1.5	1.3	1.8	1.2	1.0
Interest Paid **13**	1.1	0.6	0.4	0.2	0.9	0.6	1.1	0.9	1.2	0.9	0.8	1.6	1.1
Depreciation **14**	5.0	1.9	0.1	0.1	1.8	1.4	1.7	1.6	1.8	1.7	2.8	4.0	6.7
Amortization and Depletion **15**	0.8	0.1	•	0.1	0.3	0.1	0.4	0.4	0.2	0.5	0.9	0.8	1.0
Pensions and Other Deferred Comp. **16**	0.4	0.2	•	0.4	0.9	0.5	0.5	1.4	0.3	0.3	0.4	0.3	0.4
Employee Benefits **17**	2.0	2.4	0.6	1.1	1.4	1.2	1.7	1.7	1.7	1.9	2.5	1.6	2.2
Advertising **18**	2.4	0.3	0.1	0.0	0.6	0.6	0.3	0.3	0.5	0.9	0.4	0.3	3.9
Other Expenses **19**	9.3	9.0	21.4	11.3	9.4	9.2	8.0	15.2	10.4	11.2	13.9	6.4	9.5
Officers' Compensation **20**	1.2	6.0	4.5	8.7	5.3	2.4	3.1	1.9	1.3	1.2	1.0	1.0	0.6
Operating Margin **21**	5.4	2.9	11.9	8.2	7.3	9.5	8.7	•	3.6	2.9	8.5	3.6	5.7
Operating Margin Before Officers' Comp. **22**	6.6	9.0	16.4	16.8	12.6	12.0	11.8	•	4.9	4.1	9.6	4.6	6.3

Selected Average Balance Sheet ($ in Thousands)

Net Receivables 23	6991	0	24	243	645	1979	4507	9274	14565	33001	42478	158659	1242879
Inventories 24	3431	0	29	114	539	1419	3825	8591	11128	23322	30025	54708	579570
Net Property, Plant and Equipment 25	8574	0	16	48	545	1493	2552	3518	8868	19329	53221	151308	1837033
Total Assets 26	49500	0	150	705	2295	7139	16538	33547	69540	183437	379278	1018900	9805421
Notes and Loans Payable 27	6247	0	10	34	682	2214	3518	6311	14823	24326	34087	224519	866382
All Other Liabilities 28	12817	0	32	220	514	1678	4335	11433	17006	41188	61071	229309	2742682
Net Worth 29	30436	0	109	451	1099	3247	8684	15802	37712	117923	284120	565073	6196357

Selected Financial Ratios (Times to 1)

Current Ratio 30	2.3	•	3.2	2.6	2.2	2.7	2.4	2.2	2.0	2.3	3.3	2.4	2.1
Quick Ratio 31	1.4	•	2.1	1.8	1.3	1.6	1.5	1.4	1.3	1.5	2.2	1.7	1.2
Net Sales to Working Capital 32	3.0	•	11.3	6.6	6.4	4.2	3.7	3.9	4.1	2.9	1.9	2.4	3.2
Coverage Ratio 33	14.3	27.1	34.8	50.0	10.1	20.7	10.5	11.8	8.7	10.7	19.5	8.8	17.1
Total Asset Turnover 34	0.7	•	4.8	3.3	2.4	1.9	1.6	1.6	1.3	1.0	0.7	0.7	0.7
Inventory Turnover 35	6.4	•	11.8	12.2	5.7	6.2	4.3	4.2	5.3	5.7	4.6	8.3	6.3
Receivables Turnover 36	4.2	•	31.9	11.8	7.3	8.5	6.5	4.8	5.9	6.0	5.1	5.4	3.4
Total Liabilities to Net Worth 37	0.6	•	0.4	0.6	1.1	1.2	0.9	1.1	0.8	0.6	0.3	0.8	0.6
Current Assets to Working Capital 38	1.8	•	1.5	1.6	1.9	1.6	1.7	1.9	2.0	1.8	1.4	1.7	1.9
Current Liabilities to Working Capital 39	0.8	•	0.5	0.6	0.9	0.6	0.7	0.9	1.0	0.8	0.4	0.7	0.9
Working Capital to Net Sales 40	0.3	•	0.1	0.2	0.2	0.2	0.3	0.3	0.2	0.3	0.5	0.4	0.3
Inventory to Working Capital 41	0.3	•	0.5	0.5	0.7	0.5	0.6	0.5	0.5	0.4	0.2	0.2	0.3
Total Receipts to Cash Flow 42	5.0	5.7	3.6	6.4	7.3	5.4	6.3	7.0	5.7	5.7	4.1	6.5	4.5
Cost of Goods to Cash Flow 43	3.0	3.8	1.7	3.8	4.2	3.5	4.1	4.8	3.9	3.9	2.1	4.3	2.5
Cash Flow to Total Debt 44	0.4	•	4.9	1.4	0.6	0.7	0.5	0.4	0.5	0.5	0.7	0.2	0.4

Selected Financial Factors (in Percentages)

Debt Ratio 45	38.5	•	27.7	36.0	52.1	54.5	47.5	52.9	45.8	35.7	25.1	44.5	36.8
Return on Total Assets 46	11.8	•	72.7	28.7	20.9	23.1	18.5	16.2	13.1	9.7	10.7	9.2	12.1
Return on Equity Before Income Taxes 47	17.8	•	97.6	44.0	39.3	48.4	31.8	31.4	21.4	13.7	13.5	14.7	18.0
Return on Equity After Income Taxes 48	12.9	•	92.6	43.3	35.9	47.3	26.3	28.8	17.8	10.5	11.3	10.7	12.3
Profit Margin (Before Income Tax) 49	14.7	14.6	14.6	8.5	8.0	11.4	10.7	9.5	9.2	8.4	14.5	12.1	17.2
Profit Margin (After Income Tax) 50	10.6	13.6	13.8	7.3	7.3	11.1	8.9	8.7	7.7	6.4	12.1	8.9	11.8

Table I

Corporations with and without Net Income

NAVIGATIONAL, MEASURING, ELECTROMEDICAL, AND CONTROL

MONEY AMOUNTS AND SIZE OF ASSETS IN THOUSANDS OF DOLLARS

Item Description for Accounting Period 7/06 Through 6/07	Total	Zero Assets	Under 500	500 to 1,000	1,000 to 5,000	5,000 to 10,000	10,000 to 25,000	25,000 to 50,000	50,000 to 100,000	100,000 to 250,000	250,000 to 500,000	500,000 to 2,500,000	2,500,000 and over
Number of Enterprises **1**	2848	337	834	648	664	59	149	41	27	40	14	24	10
Revenues ($ in Thousands)													
Net Sales **2**	67073567	864500	210268	994926	3534555	878344	3347594	1979154	2275625	5587313	3369947	16647451	27383891
Interest **3**	1087803	6639	155	670	4622	2074	8531	8778	14697	56465	53438	226728	705005
Rents **4**	59288	0	0	1585	213	3830	233	1208	4986	972	2117	15686	28460
Royalties **5**	737684	4765	0	0	0	60	89	1525	351	10926	6421	214879	498667
Other Portfolio Income **6**	2504185	10766	0	26	681	18359	21752	19598	10584	31093	74472	165948	2150904
Other Receipts **7**	1792327	18514	0	3018	9178	18962	9121	31811	-83	39515	80021	419338	1162933
Total Receipts **8**	73254854	905184	210423	1000225	3549249	921629	3387320	2042074	2306160	5726284	3586416	17690030	31929860
Average Total Receipts **9**	25722	2686	252	1544	5345	15621	22734	49807	85413	143157	256173	737085	3192986
Operating Costs/Operating Income (%)													
Cost of Operations **10**	59.4	52.1	28.1	55.2	57.0	55.6	60.8	54.8	57.9	57.0	53.9	55.4	64.3
Salaries and Wages **11**	13.2	34.0	3.6	8.9	15.7	15.4	12.3	13.7	12.5	13.6	16.5	14.5	11.2
Taxes Paid **12**	2.1	2.3	3.7	3.3	3.0	2.0	2.4	2.1	2.1	1.9	2.3	1.4	2.3
Interest Paid **13**	3.3	1.0	3.6	0.7	1.0	0.6	1.0	1.6	0.9	1.8	2.3	2.2	5.5
Depreciation **14**	1.9	2.1	1.1	0.6	1.3	1.5	1.4	1.3	1.7	1.7	3.1	2.2	1.9
Amortization and Depletion **15**	1.9	3.7	•	•	0.2	0.2	0.2	1.1	0.6	1.0	0.6	3.4	2.0
Pensions and Other Deferred Comp. **16**	1.4	0.2	•	0.2	0.2	0.5	0.5	1.8	0.5	0.5	0.7	0.9	2.5
Employee Benefits **17**	2.8	3.1	•	1.5	2.8	3.1	1.7	2.7	2.1	2.8	2.7	2.2	3.4
Advertising **18**	0.8	1.2	0.9	0.9	1.0	1.5	1.4	0.8	1.2	1.4	1.6	0.7	0.5
Other Expenses **19**	13.2	25.4	47.0	13.8	14.8	15.2	10.9	14.5	14.0	15.3	16.5	12.8	11.7
Officers' Compensation **20**	1.6	7.3	20.1	10.7	4.5	1.6	3.4	2.9	1.9	1.8	1.0	1.4	0.4
Operating Margin **21**	•	•	•	4.1	•	3.0	3.9	2.8	4.6	1.1	•	2.9	•
Operating Margin Before Officers' Comp. **22**	0.1	•	12.1	14.8	3.2	4.6	7.3	5.6	6.5	2.9	•	4.3	•

Selected Average Balance Sheet ($ in Thousands)

Net Receivables 23	4756	0	12	179	784	2236	3658	8782	15878	29515	63656	176565	512216
Inventories 24	2630	0	9	144	651	3341	2586	5732	15166	19048	23884	81324	268142
Net Property, Plant and Equipment 25	2889	0	12	48	336	847	2449	4093	10823	16741	46990	94561	349154
Total Assets 26	38142	0	123	729	2676	7304	14482	34442	74506	168477	379662	1150525	6059610
Notes and Loans Payable 27	11320	0	79	159	773	899	3442	8648	8960	26092	74082	296691	2119453
All Other Liabilities 28	9075	0	57	113	835	1744	3377	10396	15001	39456	99490	241831	1495693
Net Worth 29	17747	0	-13	457	1068	4660	7663	15398	50544	102929	206090	612003	2244464

Selected Financial Ratios (Times to 1)

Current Ratio 30	1.3	•	0.9	5.8	2.2	3.0	2.0	1.7	2.3	2.1	2.6	1.8	0.8
Quick Ratio 31	0.9	•	0.7	4.2	1.1	1.7	1.2	1.0	1.3	1.2	1.7	1.3	0.5
Net Sales to Working Capital 32	8.0	•	•	2.8	5.0	3.9	4.7	6.3	3.2	3.1	2.1	3.6	•
Coverage Ratio 33	3.6	•	•	8.0	0.0	17.2	5.9	4.7	8.4	3.1	3.6	5.7	3.2
Total Asset Turnover 34	0.6	•	2.0	2.1	2.0	2.0	1.6	1.4	1.1	0.8	0.6	0.6	0.5
Inventory Turnover 35	5.3	•	7.7	5.9	4.7	2.5	5.3	4.6	3.2	4.2	5.4	4.7	6.6
Receivables Turnover 36	5.3	•	29.7	9.1	6.2	3.7	7.0	5.5	4.6	5.2	4.3	4.4	5.9
Total Liabilities to Net Worth 37	1.1	•	•	0.6	1.5	0.6	0.9	1.2	0.5	0.6	0.8	0.9	1.5
Current Assets to Working Capital 38	4.1	•	•	1.2	1.9	1.5	2.0	2.5	1.8	1.9	1.6	2.2	•
Current Liabilities to Working Capital 39	3.1	•	•	0.2	0.9	0.5	1.0	1.5	0.8	0.9	0.6	1.2	•
Working Capital to Net Sales 40	0.1	•	•	0.4	0.2	0.3	0.2	0.2	0.3	0.3	0.5	0.3	•
Inventory to Working Capital 41	0.9	•	•	0.3	0.6	0.5	0.6	0.7	0.5	0.5	0.2	0.4	•
Total Receipts to Cash Flow 42	6.0	•	2.9	7.1	9.2	5.2	7.2	5.7	5.6	6.1	5.2	5.0	6.4
Cost of Goods to Cash Flow 43	3.6	•	0.8	3.9	5.2	2.9	4.4	3.1	3.2	3.5	2.8	2.8	4.1
Cash Flow to Total Debt 44	0.2	•	0.6	0.8	0.4	1.1	0.5	0.4	0.6	0.4	0.3	0.3	0.1

Selected Financial Factors (in Percentages)

Debt Ratio 45	53.5	•	110.5	37.4	60.1	36.2	47.1	55.3	32.2	38.9	45.7	46.8	59.7
Return on Total Assets 46	7.3	•	•	11.2	0.0	20.4	9.6	10.9	8.6	4.5	5.3	7.7	7.8
Return on Equity Before Income Taxes 47	11.3	•	154.4	15.6	•	30.1	15.0	19.3	11.1	5.0	7.0	11.9	13.3
Return on Equity After Income Taxes 48	9.0	•	157.7	15.1	•	23.9	11.8	16.1	8.5	2.4	5.5	9.2	11.3
Profit Margin (Before Income Tax) 49	8.5	•	•	4.6	•	9.4	5.1	6.1	6.7	3.7	6.0	10.5	11.9
Profit Margin (After Income Tax) 50	6.8	•	•	4.5	•	7.5	4.0	5.1	1.8	3.7	4.7	8.1	10.1

Table II
Corporations with Net Income

Navigational, Measuring, Electromedical, and Control

Money Amounts and Size of Assets in Thousands of Dollars

Item Description for Accounting Period 7/06 Through 6/07	Total	Zero Assets	Under 500	500 to 1,000	1,000 to 5,000	5,000 to 10,000	10,000 to 25,000	25,000 to 50,000	50,000 to 100,000	100,000 to 250,000	250,000 to 500,000	500,000 to 2,500,000	2,500,000 and over
Number of Enterprises **1**	1571	9	•	556	451	34	114	34	22	26	10	•	•
Revenues ($ in Thousands)													
Net Sales **2**	58809852	3879	•	822774	2899638	552628	2708140	1908678	2049231	4244169	2507159	•	•
Interest **3**	520725	497	•	668	2071	714	4758	8643	11337	41714	43659	•	•
Rents **4**	57072	0	•	1135	213	3830	115	1208	4986	907	2117	•	•
Royalties **5**	705358	0	•	0	0	60	89	1525	351	10555	6421	•	•
Other Portfolio Income **6**	2420568	0	•	26	479	513	18073	9252	9276	26007	73808	•	•
Other Receipts **7**	1644114	0	•	534	5703	17625	6422	23382	-2140	19002	42676	•	•
Total Receipts **8**	64157689	4376	•	825137	2908104	575370	2737597	1952688	2073041	4342354	2675840	•	•
Average Total Receipts **9**	40839	486	•	1484	6448	16923	24014	57432	94229	167014	267584	•	•
Operating Costs/Operating Income (%)													
Cost of Operations **10**	59.7	14.3	•	54.5	57.3	55.9	60.1	54.7	59.3	58.4	50.2	•	•
Salaries and Wages **11**	12.4	3.7	•	7.8	14.1	16.1	11.0	13.4	11.5	11.2	15.7	•	•
Taxes Paid **12**	2.0	3.7	•	3.1	2.6	1.9	2.3	2.1	2.1	1.7	2.7	•	•
Interest Paid **13**	2.2	1.8	•	0.4	0.8	0.5	0.7	1.3	0.9	1.2	2.2	•	•
Depreciation **14**	1.8	3.0	•	0.6	1.1	1.3	1.4	1.2	1.6	1.6	2.6	•	•
Amortization and Depletion **15**	1.8	3.4	•	0.1	0.0	0.0	0.1	0.7	0.6	0.9	0.6	•	•
Pensions and Other Deferred Comp. **16**	1.6	•	•	0.1	0.2	0.3	0.5	1.7	0.5	0.6	0.9	•	•
Employee Benefits **17**	2.8	4.8	•	1.4	2.1	1.9	1.7	2.6	2.1	2.7	2.4	•	•
Advertising **18**	0.7	0.3	•	0.9	0.8	0.4	0.7	0.8	1.1	1.2	1.7	•	•
Other Expenses **19**	12.1	19.0	•	14.5	10.9	9.4	8.5	13.7	12.4	13.1	16.1	•	•
Officers' Compensation **20**	1.4	9.7	•	10.4	3.9	1.5	3.7	2.9	1.7	1.4	1.1	•	•
Operating Margin **21**	1.4	36.5	•	6.2	6.2	10.7	9.3	4.8	6.4	6.0	3.7	•	•
Operating Margin Before Officers' Comp. **22**	2.8	46.2	•	16.6	10.2	12.2	13.0	7.8	8.0	7.4	4.8	•	•

Selected Average Balance Sheet ($ in Thousands)

Net Receivables 23	7462	0	•	174	898	2358	3613	9723	16186	32678	65087
Inventories 24	4250	0	•	145	714	4594	2975	5967	15597	22191	27278
Net Property, Plant and Equipment 25	4519	0	•	22	333	924	2692	4809	11544	18930	49041
Total Assets 26	53157	0	•	723	2743	7048	14345	33922	73813	174436	382291
Notes and Loans Payable 27	14573	0	•	115	667	1004	2361	7731	9542	16441	41062
All Other Liabilities 28	12851	0	•	101	782	1564	2630	11474	16085	43346	106213
Net Worth 29	25733	0	•	507	1294	4481	9354	14717	48187	114649	235016

Selected Financial Ratios (Times to 1)

Current Ratio 30	1.4	•	•	7.4	2.4	2.7	2.8	1.7	2.4	2.7	3.1
Quick Ratio 31	0.9	•	•	5.7	1.3	1.6	1.7	1.0	1.3	1.5	1.9
Net Sales to Working Capital 32	7.5	•	•	2.5	5.4	4.5	3.8	6.5	3.4	2.8	1.9
Coverage Ratio 33	6.2	29.1	•	18.8	9.2	34.6	15.2	6.7	10.2	8.1	5.7
Total Asset Turnover 34	0.7	•	•	2.0	2.3	1.7	1.7	1.7	1.3	0.9	0.7
Inventory Turnover 35	5.3	•	•	5.5	5.2	2.0	4.8	5.1	3.5	4.3	4.6
Receivables Turnover 36	5.3	•	•	8.3	7.2	2.9	7.0	6.3	5.2	5.1	•
Total Liabilities to Net Worth 37	1.1	•	•	0.4	1.1	0.6	0.5	1.3	0.5	0.5	0.6
Current Assets to Working Capital 38	3.8	•	•	1.2	1.7	1.6	1.6	2.4	1.7	1.6	1.5
Current Liabilities to Working Capital 39	2.8	•	•	0.2	0.7	0.6	0.6	1.4	0.7	0.6	0.5
Working Capital to Net Sales 40	0.1	•	•	0.4	0.2	0.2	0.3	0.2	0.3	0.4	0.5
Inventory to Working Capital 41	0.9	•	•	0.3	0.5	0.5	0.5	0.7	0.6	0.3	0.2
Total Receipts to Cash Flow 42	5.5	1.6	•	6.3	7.0	4.6	5.9	5.3	5.6	5.2	4.2
Cost of Goods to Cash Flow 43	3.3	0.2	•	3.4	4.0	2.6	3.5	2.9	3.3	3.0	2.1
Cash Flow to Total Debt 44	0.2	•	•	1.1	0.6	1.4	0.8	0.6	0.6	0.5	0.4

Selected Financial Factors (in Percentages)

Debt Ratio 45	51.6	•	•	29.9	52.8	36.4	34.8	56.6	34.7	34.3	38.5
Return on Total Assets 46	9.5	•	•	14.0	17.2	40.8	18.4	14.3	11.6	9.0	8.4
Return on Equity Before Income Taxes 47	16.5	•	•	18.9	32.4	62.4	26.4	28.0	16.0	12.0	11.2
Return on Equity After Income Taxes 48	13.6	•	•	18.4	29.7	51.2	23.0	24.0	12.6	8.4	9.4
Profit Margin (Before Income Tax) 49	11.3	49.3	•	6.5	6.5	17.2	10.4	7.3	8.3	8.5	10.5
Profit Margin (After Income Tax) 50	9.4	49.3	•	6.3	6.0	14.1	9.0	6.3	6.5	5.9	8.8

Table I

Corporations with and without Net Income

ELECTRICAL LIGHTING EQUIPMENT AND HOUSEHOLD APPLIANCE

MONEY AMOUNTS AND SIZE OF ASSETS IN THOUSANDS OF DOLLARS

Item Description for Accounting Period 7/06 Through 6/07	Total	Zero Assets	Under 500	500 to 1,000	1,000 to 5,000	5,000 to 10,000	10,000 to 25,000	25,000 to 50,000	50,000 to 100,000	100,000 to 250,000	250,000 to 500,000	500,000 to 2,500,000	2,500,000 and over
Number of Enterprises **1**	1507	13	1059	0	145	126	99	24	4	21	7	5	3
Revenues ($ in Thousands)													
Net Sales **2**	145045605	703469	112815	0	385176	1353247	3504394	1250713	523015	4408745	3226328	11913597	117664106
Interest **3**	53734181	71	0	0	864	369	2346	499	157	13305	964	23496	53692110
Rents **4**	36064	0	0	0	0	0	5009	0	0	2301	234	21536	6984
Royalties **5**	2117370	0	0	0	0	0	0	1201	0	6728	532	31328	2077582
Other Portfolio Income **6**	12658187	1085	0	0	0	85	4216	884	5	57153	7056	87776	12499925
Other Receipts **7**	39598802	2343	26	0	59	5322	31200	-4061	1731	42361	12679	69962	39437182
Total Receipts **8**	253190209	706968	112841	0	386099	1359023	3547165	1249236	524908	4530593	3247793	12147695	225377889
Average Total Receipts **9**	168009	54382	107	•	2663	10786	35830	52052	131227	215743	463970	2429539	75125963
Operating Costs/Operating Income (%)													
Cost of Operations **10**	61.2	66.5	47.4	•	56.5	70.7	68.6	73.2	62.6	66.0	67.5	73.7	59.1
Salaries and Wages **11**	12.3	11.7	4.1	•	16.0	11.4	8.7	4.7	6.9	8.2	4.5	7.5	13.3
Taxes Paid **12**	0.9	0.5	2.9	•	1.9	2.3	1.9	1.5	1.3	1.5	1.4	1.2	0.8
Interest Paid **13**	42.2	2.4	0.8	•	3.1	1.5	1.0	1.3	1.1	1.8	1.3	1.4	51.6
Depreciation **14**	8.0	2.8	0.3	•	1.9	0.8	1.2	2.1	1.3	1.6	2.0	1.4	9.5
Amortization and Depletion **15**	1.2	7.1	•	•	0.4	0.5	0.1	0.1	0.8	0.7	0.4	0.4	1.3
Pensions and Other Deferred Comp. **16**	0.4	0.0	•	•	0.0	0.0	0.4	0.6	0.2	0.5	0.4	0.5	0.4
Employee Benefits **17**	2.0	0.1	0.0	•	0.8	1.4	1.7	1.6	2.5	1.3	1.8	1.4	2.1
Advertising **18**	1.0	1.1	0.4	•	1.8	0.8	0.9	0.8	3.8	2.4	6.2	1.0	0.8
Other Expenses **19**	41.3	9.9	33.0	•	26.7	13.3	11.2	10.0	12.1	10.0	8.9	10.2	48.4
Officers' Compensation **20**	0.4	0.3	10.0	•	4.7	0.5	1.3	2.7	0.8	0.9	2.5	0.2	0.3
Operating Margin **21**	•	•	1.0	•	•	•	2.9	1.6	6.5	5.1	3.2	1.1	•
Operating Margin Before Officers' Comp. **22**	•	•	11.0	•	•	•	4.2	4.3	7.3	5.9	5.8	1.3	•

Selected Average Balance Sheet

Item			
Net Receivables 23	118280	0	1
Inventories 24	7176	0	21
Net Property, Plant and Equipment 25	32281	0	1
Total Assets 26	538130	0	23
Notes and Loans Payable 27	316467	0	25
All Other Liabilities 28	104302	0	3
Net Worth 29	117360	0	-5

Selected Financial Ratios (Times to)

Item	Values (left to right)
Current Ratio 30	0.8, 1.3, 1.0, 1.9, 0.9, 1.6, 2.0, 0.7, 1.3, 2.0
Quick Ratio 31	0.6, 0.2, 0.3, 0.2, 0.2, 0.2, 0.1, 0.3, 0.2, 0.1
Net Sales to Working Capital 32	20.5, 3.1, 1.1, 1.3, 0.8, 1.1, 1.5, 0.6, 0.8, 1.0
Coverage Ratio 33	1.1, 0.2, 2.2
Total Asset Turnover 34	0.2, 4.6
Inventory Turnover 35	8.2, 2.4
Receivables Turnover 36	0.8, 28.7
Total Liabilities to Net Worth 37	3.6
Current Assets to Working Capital 38	4.0
Current Liabilities to Working Capital 39	3.0
Working Capital to Net Sales 40	0.0
Inventory to Working Capital 41	3.1
Total Receipts to Cash Flow 42	2.4, 16.4, 4.9, 9.2, 7.7, 11.1, 10.0, 6.3, 6.1, 8.9, 8.3, 2.1
Cost of Goods to Cash Flow 43	1.5, 10.9, 2.3, 5.2, 5.3, 7.9, 7.3, 4.0, 6.0, 6.1, 1.2
Cash Flow to Total Debt 44	0.2, 0.8, 0.2, 0.2, 0.5, 0.2, 0.5, 0.4, 0.3, 0.4, 0.1

Selected Financial Factors (in Percentages)

Item	Values (left to right)
Debt Ratio 45	78.2, 123.1, 79.9, 78.2, 50.5, 62.8, 66.6, 52.3, 60.9, 44.9, 78.7
Return on Total Assets 46	8.6, 8.5, 10.6, 4.2, 15.5, 12.3, 7.2, 7.1, 8.7
Return on Equity Before Income Taxes 47	5.0, 17.1, 6.2, 40.1, 21.0, 13.6, 8.9, 4.7
Return on Equity After Income Taxes 48	3.4, 15.1, 3.9, 37.2, 18.1, 11.3, 5.7, 3.1
Profit Margin (Before Income Tax) 49	6.1, 1.0, 4.1, 1.5, 6.9, 7.8, 3.7, 3.1, 6.7
Profit Margin (After Income Tax) 50	4.1, 1.0, 3.6, 1.0, 6.4, 6.7, 3.1, 2.0, 4.5

Table II

Corporations with Net Income

ELECTRICAL LIGHTING EQUIPMENT AND HOUSEHOLD APPLIANCE

MONEY AMOUNTS AND SIZE OF ASSETS IN THOUSANDS OF DOLLARS

Item Description for Accounting Period 7/06 Through 6/07	Total	Zero Assets	Under 500	500 to 1,000	1,000 to 5,000	5,000 to 10,000	10,000 to 25,000	25,000 to 50,000	50,000 to 100,000	100,000 to 250,000	250,000 to 500,000	500,000 to 2,500,000	2,500,000 and over
Number of Enterprises **1**	692	3	510	0	19	30	77	19	•	•	•	•	0
Revenues ($ in Thousands)													
Net Sales **2**	127693743	163494	108464	0	143694	623349	2865773	933486	•	•	•	•	0
Interest **3**	53694567	11	0	0	0	1	2086	364	•	•	•	•	0
Rents **4**	33025	0	0	0	0	0	5009	0	•	•	•	•	0
Royalties **5**	1451172	0	0	0	0	0	0	1201	•	•	•	•	0
Other Portfolio Income **6**	12646500	0	0	0	0	85	3799	753	•	•	•	•	0
Other Receipts **7**	39491054	423	0	0	20	1978	28534	1549	•	•	•	•	0
Total Receipts **8**	235010061	163928	108464	0	143714	625413	2905201	937353	•	•	•	•	0
Average Total Receipts **9**	339610	54643	213	•	7564	20847	37730	49334	•	•	•	•	•
Operating Costs/Operating Income (%)													
Cost of Operations **10**	60.0	70.0	45.8	•	66.9	70.5	70.2	69.3	•	•	•	•	•
Salaries and Wages **11**	12.7	3.3	4.3	•	4.6	7.3	7.6	5.1	•	•	•	•	•
Taxes Paid **12**	0.9	1.0	2.9	•	1.2	1.6	1.7	1.5	•	•	•	•	•
Interest Paid **13**	47.6	4.3	0.2	•	2.0	0.7	0.9	1.4	•	•	•	•	•
Depreciation **14**	8.8	0.7	0.3	•	1.7	0.5	1.1	1.9	•	•	•	•	•
Amortization and Depletion **15**	1.3	0.7	•	•	0.7	•	0.0	•	•	•	•	•	•
Pensions and Other Deferred Comp. **16**	0.4	•	•	•	0.0	0.0	0.5	0.8	•	•	•	•	•
Employee Benefits **17**	2.0	0.1	•	•	0.4	1.0	1.0	1.5	•	•	•	•	•
Advertising **18**	0.8	3.7	0.4	•	0.4	1.0	0.7	0.6	•	•	•	•	•
Other Expenses **19**	44.6	10.6	32.8	•	18.3	11.1	9.7	8.6	•	•	•	•	•
Officers' Compensation **20**	0.5	0.7	10.4	•	2.7	0.7	1.3	3.2	•	•	•	•	•
Operating Margin **21**	•	5.0	2.9	•	1.0	5.8	5.2	6.0	•	•	•	•	•
Operating Margin Before Officers' Comp. **22**	•	5.7	13.3	•	3.8	6.5	6.5	9.2	•	•	•	•	•

Selected Average Balance Sheet ($ in Thousands)

Net Receivables 23	240706	0	1	•	1207	2711	4684	7105
Inventories 24	13667	0	30	•	3092	4139	5205	8481
Net Property, Plant and Equipment 25	67530	0	1	•	354	565	2923	5030
Total Assets 26	1112649	0	40	•	4007	8205	17016	32551
Notes and Loans Payable 27	679631	0	8	•	713	2470	3535	9773
All Other Liabilities 28	207812	0	6	•	2313	3198	4221	9323
Net Worth 29	225206	0	25	•	981	2536	9259	13454

Selected Financial Ratios (Times to 1)

Current Ratio 30	0.8	•	1.1	1.3	1.5	2.4	1.9
Quick Ratio 31	0.6	•	0.2	0.5	0.6	1.3	0.8
Net Sales to Working Capital 32	•	•	55.7	11.3	7.9	4.9	4.5
Coverage Ratio 33	1.2	2.2	15.3	1.5	9.2	8.5	5.7
Total Asset Turnover 34	0.2	•	5.4	1.9	2.5	2.2	1.5
Inventory Turnover 35	8.1	•	3.2	1.6	3.5	5.0	4.0
Receivables Turnover 36	0.7	•	131.6	3.9	9.9	8.7	6.3
Total Liabilities to Net Worth 37	3.9	•	0.6	3.1	2.2	0.8	1.4
Current Assets to Working Capital 38	•	•	9.0	4.9	2.9	1.7	2.1
Current Liabilities to Working Capital 39	•	•	8.0	3.9	1.9	0.7	1.1
Working Capital to Net Sales 40	•	•	0.0	0.1	0.1	0.2	0.2
Inventory to Working Capital 41	•	•	6.9	2.8	1.6	0.7	0.9
Total Receipts to Cash Flow 42	2.2	7.0	4.6	5.7	6.4	7.0	7.4
Cost of Goods to Cash Flow 43	1.3	4.9	2.1	3.8	4.5	4.9	5.1
Cash Flow to Total Debt 44	0.1	•	3.2	0.4	0.6	0.7	0.3

Selected Financial Factors (in Percentages)

Debt Ratio 45	79.8	•	36.4	75.5	69.1	45.6	58.7
Return on Total Assets 46	9.1	•	16.5	5.8	17.3	16.3	11.8
Return on Equity Before Income Taxes 47	5.9	•	24.3	8.0	49.9	26.4	23.4
Return on Equity After Income Taxes 48	4.1	•	24.3	6.5	49.1	24.0	20.8
Profit Margin (Before Income Tax) 49	7.2	5.3	2.9	1.0	6.1	6.6	6.4
Profit Margin (After Income Tax) 50	5.0	3.5	2.9	0.8	6.0	6.0	5.7

Table I

Corporations with and without Net Income

ELECTRICAL EQUIPMENT

MONEY AMOUNTS AND SIZE OF ASSETS IN THOUSANDS OF DOLLARS

Item Description for Accounting Period 7/06 Through 6/07	Total	Zero Assets	Under 500	500 to 1,000	1,000 to 5,000	5,000 to 10,000	10,000 to 25,000	25,000 to 50,000	50,000 to 100,000	100,000 to 250,000	250,000 to 500,000	500,000 to 2,500,000	2,500,000 and over
Number of Enterprises **1**	1343	11	567	187	296	161	49	21	15	15	5	11	4
Revenues ($ in Thousands)													
Net Sales **2**	47976482	701790	235593	348763	1207048	2606545	1161687	1247983	1105275	3054041	2241424	7911714	26154618
Interest **3**	794654	29	0	177	627	1857	4664	461	14176	14529	17632	114860	625642
Rents **4**	80960	0	0	0	401	0	2101	170	393	15	145	710	77024
Royalties **5**	307267	0	0	0	0	0	0	63	2024	1235	6115	23786	274045
Other Portfolio Income **6**	356421	26794	0	23846	3009	174	1224	9017	11617	10720	27356	110572	132092
Other Receipts **7**	560582	-12	28	24	1978	17992	5324	5454	6108	35593	3884	58016	426194
Total Receipts **8**	50076366	728601	235621	372810	1213063	2626568	1175000	1263148	1139593	3116133	2296556	8219658	27689615
Average Total Receipts **9**	37287	66236	416	1994	4098	16314	23980	60150	75973	207742	459311	747242	6922404
Operating Costs/Operating Income (%)													
Cost of Operations **10**	69.9	60.1	71.8	56.2	69.5	68.1	68.2	76.3	68.7	65.3	69.7	67.3	71.7
Salaries and Wages **11**	7.9	26.2	2.2	6.0	6.5	8.4	8.4	5.2	7.7	9.6	7.6	10.9	6.5
Taxes Paid **12**	1.8	1.3	2.2	3.0	1.9	2.1	3.0	1.7	1.5	1.8	2.1	1.4	1.8
Interest Paid **13**	2.9	0.1	0.6	1.0	1.7	0.8	0.7	2.2	1.1	1.5	0.7	2.5	3.9
Depreciation **14**	1.5	0.8	0.7	1.1	1.0	0.7	1.6	1.5	1.6	2.3	1.9	2.0	1.4
Amortization and Depletion **15**	1.1	0.5	0.2	0.2	0.0	0.0	0.2	0.6	0.5	1.1	0.5	2.0	1.1
Pensions and Other Deferred Comp. **16**	1.0	0.2	•	0.2	0.4	0.6	0.7	0.4	0.4	1.3	1.1	0.8	1.3
Employee Benefits **17**	2.0	0.5	2.2	1.4	1.0	1.0	2.4	1.6	1.3	2.8	1.7	2.0	2.2
Advertising **18**	0.6	1.5	0.2	0.3	0.6	0.3	0.2	0.4	0.4	1.0	0.3	0.9	0.5
Other Expenses **19**	10.8	7.4	10.1	15.3	11.9	10.2	9.9	7.1	11.5	11.0	11.0	12.8	10.4
Officers' Compensation **20**	1.2	0.1	8.6	13.3	4.9	3.5	3.0	1.4	1.4	1.2	0.8	0.5	0.8
Operating Margin **21**	•	1.3	1.2	2.1	0.5	4.3	1.8	1.5	3.8	1.1	2.4	•	•
Operating Margin Before Officers' Comp. **22**	0.5	1.4	9.8	15.4	5.5	7.8	4.8	2.9	5.2	2.3	3.3	•	•

Selected Average Balance Sheet ($ in Thousands)

Net Receivables 23	8437	0	66	221	468	2145	3959	8704	14128	35675	57780	268644	1600022
Inventories 24	3668	0	49	324	1225	1617	3816	8869	10113	26299	61630	105297	457267
Net Property, Plant and Equipment 25	4097	0	5	132	229	592	2679	5497	9100	26343	83810	110123	725570
Total Assets 26	55263	0	149	741	2372	7207	15761	34747	71438	168325	347181	1342070	12263896
Notes and Loans Payable 27	9212	0	44	164	771	1749	3528	10201	13161	24626	50330	381714	1600357
All Other Liabilities 28	10728	0	57	130	804	2457	4380	13233	19811	61413	88927	277422	2127428
Net Worth 29	35323	0	47	447	797	3000	7853	11312	38467	82287	207924	682934	8906112

Selected Financial Ratios (Times to 1)

Current Ratio 30	1.2	•	1.6	3.3	2.4	1.6	2.0	1.7	2.5	1.8	2.1	1.6	1.0
Quick Ratio 31	0.8	•	0.9	2.0	1.0	0.9	1.1	0.9	1.4	1.0	1.2	1.1	0.6
Net Sales to Working Capital 32	11.4	•	8.7	4.7	3.5	8.0	4.1	7.1	3.5	5.3	4.9	3.8	•
Coverage Ratio 33	2.6	36.0	3.1	9.9	1.6	7.7	5.1	2.3	7.3	3.2	8.4	1.9	2.4
Total Asset Turnover 34	0.6	•	2.8	2.5	1.7	2.2	1.5	1.7	1.0	1.2	1.3	0.5	0.5
Inventory Turnover 35	6.8	•	6.1	3.2	2.3	6.8	4.2	5.1	5.0	5.1	5.1	4.6	10.2
Receivables Turnover 36	4.7	•	7.2	6.9	7.5	9.6	5.6	6.7	5.7	6.2	5.5	3.1	4.7
Total Liabilities to Net Worth 37	0.6	•	2.1	0.7	2.0	1.4	1.0	2.1	0.9	1.0	0.7	1.0	0.4
Current Assets to Working Capital 38	5.1	•	2.5	1.4	1.7	2.6	2.0	2.4	1.7	2.3	1.9	2.5	•
Current Liabilities to Working Capital 39	4.1	•	1.5	0.4	0.7	1.6	1.0	1.4	0.7	1.3	0.9	1.5	•
Working Capital to Net Sales 40	0.1	•	0.1	0.2	0.3	0.1	0.2	0.1	0.3	0.2	0.2	0.3	•
Inventory to Working Capital 41	1.3	•	1.1	0.5	0.9	1.0	0.8	1.0	0.6	0.7	0.6	0.7	•
Total Receipts to Cash Flow 42	7.9	8.1	14.5	6.5	9.4	7.5	9.3	11.9	5.9	7.9	7.3	8.9	7.6
Cost of Goods to Cash Flow 43	5.5	4.9	10.4	3.7	6.5	5.1	6.4	9.1	4.1	5.2	5.1	6.0	5.4
Cash Flow to Total Debt 44	0.2	•	0.3	1.0	0.3	0.5	0.3	0.2	0.4	0.3	0.4	0.1	0.2

Selected Financial Factors (in Percentages)

Debt Ratio 45	36.1	•	68.1	39.7	66.4	58.4	50.2	67.4	46.2	51.1	40.1	49.1	29.5
Return on Total Assets 46	4.8	•	5.0	25.2	4.7	13.1	5.5	8.8	8.5	5.7	7.5	2.6	4.8
Return on Equity Before Income Taxes 47	4.6	•	10.6	37.6	5.2	27.4	8.8	15.5	13.7	8.0	11.0	2.5	4.0
Return on Equity After Income Taxes 48	2.6	•	7.9	35.9	2.6	25.5	4.9	11.0	11.0	4.9	6.7	0.8	2.1
Profit Margin (Before Income Tax) 49	4.5	5.0	1.2	9.0	1.0	5.1	2.9	2.9	7.1	3.2	5.1	2.3	5.4
Profit Margin (After Income Tax) 50	2.6	4.6	0.9	8.6	0.5	4.7	1.6	2.1	5.8	2.0	3.1	0.7	2.8

149

Table II
Corporations with Net Income

ELECTRICAL EQUIPMENT

MONEY AMOUNTS AND SIZE OF ASSETS IN THOUSANDS OF DOLLARS

Item Description for Accounting Period 7/06 Through 6/07	Total	Zero Assets	Under 500	500 to 1,000	1,000 to 5,000	5,000 to 10,000	10,000 to 25,000	25,000 to 50,000	50,000 to 100,000	100,000 to 250,000	250,000 to 500,000	500,000 to 2,500,000	2,500,000 and over
Number of Enterprises **1**	567	3	•	134	159	97	27	15	•	•	•	•	•
Revenues ($ in Thousands)													
Net Sales **2**	38468942	701790	•	286684	783236	1548682	911412	747112	•	•	•	•	•
Interest **3**	729336	29	•	177	282	266	1857	395	•	•	•	•	•
Rents **4**	69591	0	•	0	0	0	278	0	•	•	•	•	•
Royalties **5**	294693	0	•	0	0	0	0	0	•	•	•	•	•
Other Portfolio Income **6**	245049	26794	•	23846	2850	174	548	5257	•	•	•	•	•
Other Receipts **7**	410086	-12	•	4	255	6494	3979	5152	•	•	•	•	•
Total Receipts **8**	40217697	728601	•	310711	786623	1555616	918074	757916	•	•	•	•	•
Average Total Receipts **9**	70931	242867	•	2319	4947	16037	34003	50528	•	•	•	•	•
Operating Costs/Operating Income (%)													
Cost of Operations **10**	68.3	60.1	•	56.0	69.3	55.3	67.9	72.9	•	•	•	•	•
Salaries and Wages **11**	7.3	26.2	•	5.7	7.3	7.3	4.7	5.2	•	•	•	•	•
Taxes Paid **12**	1.7	1.3	•	3.0	1.2	2.1	2.9	1.6	•	•	•	•	•
Interest Paid **13**	3.2	0.1	•	1.2	1.7	0.6	0.7	1.5	•	•	•	•	•
Depreciation **14**	1.5	0.8	•	0.9	0.6	0.6	1.2	1.0	•	•	•	•	•
Amortization and Depletion **15**	1.0	0.5	•	0.2	0.0	0.0	0.0	0.4	•	•	•	•	•
Pensions and Other Deferred Comp. **16**	1.2	0.2	•	0.2	0.4	1.0	0.8	0.5	•	•	•	•	•
Employee Benefits **17**	1.9	0.5	•	1.6	0.3	1.4	2.3	1.5	•	•	•	•	•
Advertising **18**	0.5	1.5	•	0.4	0.6	0.5	0.2	0.7	•	•	•	•	•
Other Expenses **19**	8.7	7.4	•	16.0	9.7	10.8	7.9	7.0	•	•	•	•	•
Officers' Compensation **20**	1.2	0.1	•	12.2	2.9	5.2	3.1	1.6	•	•	•	•	•
Operating Margin **21**	3.4	1.3	•	2.6	6.0	15.2	8.2	6.2	•	•	•	•	•
Operating Margin Before Officers' Comp. **22**	4.6	1.4	•	14.8	8.9	20.4	11.2	7.8	•	•	•	•	•

Selected Average Balance Sheet ($ in Thousands)

Net Receivables 23	14805	0	•	280	425	2032	5008	8170
Inventories 24	6769	0	•	448	1685	1927	5678	6554
Net Property, Plant and Equipment 25	7927	0	•	85	234	364	2288	3644
Total Assets 26	105925	0	•	796	2410	6772	17039	31530
Notes and Loans Payable 27	14911	0	•	229	1084	1526	3278	4808
All Other Liabilities 28	17181	0	•	158	740	1351	4344	11962
Net Worth 29	73833	0	•	410	587	3895	9417	14759

Selected Financial Ratios (Times to 1)

Current Ratio 30	1.2	•	•	3.2	2.6	2.3	2.2	2.0
Quick Ratio 31	0.7	•	•	1.8	0.8	1.3	1.1	1.2
Net Sales to Working Capital 32	18.5	•	•	4.5	4.2	5.0	4.6	5.6
Coverage Ratio 33	3.8	36.0	•	9.9	4.7	27.1	13.5	6.3
Total Asset Turnover 34	0.6	•	•	2.7	2.0	2.4	2.0	1.6
Inventory Turnover 35	6.8	•	•	2.7	2.0	4.6	4.0	5.5
Receivables Turnover 36	4.7	•	•	5.9	8.2	8.3	5.8	6.5
Total Liabilities to Net Worth 37	0.4	•	•	0.9	3.1	0.7	0.8	1.1
Current Assets to Working Capital 38	6.9	•	•	1.5	1.6	1.8	1.9	2.0
Current Liabilities to Working Capital 39	5.9	•	•	0.5	0.6	0.8	0.9	1.0
Working Capital to Net Sales 40	0.1	•	•	0.2	0.2	0.2	0.2	0.2
Inventory to Working Capital 41	1.9	•	•	0.6	1.1	0.7	0.8	0.8
Total Receipts to Cash Flow 42	6.6	8.1	•	6.2	6.8	4.1	6.5	7.4
Cost of Goods to Cash Flow 43	4.5	4.9	•	3.5	4.7	2.3	4.4	5.4
Cash Flow to Total Debt 44	0.3	•	•	0.9	0.4	1.3	0.7	0.4

Selected Financial Factors (in Percentages)

Debt Ratio 45	30.3	•	•	48.5	75.7	42.5	44.7	53.2
Return on Total Assets 46	7.6	•	•	32.8	16.7	38.2	19.0	14.6
Return on Equity Before Income Taxes 47	8.1	•	•	57.2	53.9	64.0	31.8	26.3
Return on Equity After Income Taxes 48	5.8	•	•	54.7	47.4	61.6	25.8	21.5
Profit Margin (Before Income Tax) 49	8.8	5.0	•	11.0	6.4	15.6	8.9	7.8
Profit Margin (After Income Tax) 50	6.3	4.6	•	10.5	5.6	15.0	7.2	6.4

Table I

Corporations with and without Net Income

Other Electrical Equipment and Component

Money Amounts and Size of Assets in Thousands of Dollars

Item Description for Accounting Period 7/06 Through 6/07	Total	Zero Assets	Under 500	500 to 1,000	1,000 to 5,000	5,000 to 10,000	10,000 to 25,000	25,000 to 50,000	50,000 to 100,000	100,000 to 250,000	250,000 to 500,000	500,000 to 2,500,000	2,500,000 and over
Number of Enterprises **1**	3673	524	819	882	710	333	190	95	48	32	17	18	4
Revenues ($ in Thousands)													
Net Sales **2**	59162816	701244	629547	1943141	3349109	3770956	5296480	4424492	4339832	5508104	4658985	13210181	11330744
Interest **3**	683961	978	0	134	3136	3834	7938	24019	14599	40392	72891	261176	254863
Rents **4**	27271	0	0	148	24	1003	464	3	362	647	1592	6692	16337
Royalties **5**	216250	0	0	0	691	0	2364	12314	4328	28289	19676	23211	125376
Other Portfolio Income **6**	778898	34035	0	0	33246	2976	31457	36785	64129	29255	15639	479088	52284
Other Receipts **7**	772046	11608	2534	40808	14926	13189	27393	30263	80212	49751	58781	97996	344590
Total Receipts **8**	61641242	747865	632081	1984231	3401132	3791958	5366096	4527876	4503462	5656438	4827564	14078344	12124194
Average Total Receipts **9**	16782	1427	772	2250	4790	11387	28243	47662	93822	176764	283974	782130	3031048
Operating Costs/Operating Income (%)													
Cost of Operations **10**	67.6	79.5	51.8	64.4	60.8	67.6	70.1	71.7	73.2	65.3	70.3	67.2	66.1
Salaries and Wages **11**	9.9	9.7	10.0	16.0	16.1	10.8	8.3	9.2	8.8	10.1	8.6	8.9	10.1
Taxes Paid **12**	1.8	2.0	2.5	2.6	2.5	2.7	1.8	1.9	1.7	1.6	1.4	1.4	1.6
Interest Paid **13**	2.7	3.2	0.1	2.2	1.7	2.0	0.9	1.2	1.0	1.5	3.5	3.9	4.5
Depreciation **14**	1.8	1.1	0.3	0.9	1.8	1.3	1.4	2.0	2.0	1.7	2.5	2.0	1.9
Amortization and Depletion **15**	0.9	1.6	•	0.1	0.6	0.5	0.6	0.3	0.4	0.6	1.4	1.6	1.3
Pensions and Other Deferred Comp. **16**	0.7	0.4	0.0	0.2	0.2	0.1	0.4	0.8	0.7	0.6	0.4	1.1	0.9
Employee Benefits **17**	1.6	1.4	0.0	0.7	1.4	1.3	1.3	1.9	1.8	1.7	2.0	2.4	1.0
Advertising **18**	1.0	0.4	0.5	0.6	0.5	0.8	0.4	0.5	0.5	1.0	0.5	0.9	2.6
Other Expenses **19**	9.8	12.9	26.7	14.5	11.6	6.6	7.0	10.5	6.2	10.9	12.0	9.9	9.4
Officers' Compensation **20**	1.8	4.2	7.2	2.2	6.4	3.9	2.6	1.6	1.8	1.6	0.7	0.9	0.4
Operating Margin **21**	0.2	•	0.8	•	•	2.3	5.2	•	2.0	3.5	•	•	0.3
Operating Margin Before Officers' Comp. **22**	2.0	8.0	•	•	2.8	6.2	7.8	0.2	3.8	5.0	•	0.8	0.7

Selected Average Balance Sheet ($ in Thousands)

Net Receivables 23	2458	0	119	210	655	1323	4529	8452	17211	34085	66725	104453	311261
Inventories 24	2070	0	34	219	664	2847	4358	7589	14806	23584	38705	76917	226622
Net Property, Plant and Equipment 25	1810	0	6	34	415	1151	2562	6312	12190	21536	47930	95365	260622
Total Assets 26	18228	0	232	623	2159	6661	16475	34645	66686	157458	343722	971321	6118232
Notes and Loans Payable 27	4452	0	26	1111	820	2366	4132	8549	12370	34301	127646	244847	1028846
All Other Liabilities 28	5194	0	110	245	846	1683	4447	9110	17963	37457	92096	218575	2085040
Net Worth 29	8582	0	96	-732	493	2611	7896	16987	36352	85700	123980	507899	3004347

Selected Financial Ratios (Times to 1)

Current Ratio 30	2.0	•	1.5	1.7	1.4	1.6	2.0	1.8	2.1	2.3	1.7	2.2	2.6
Quick Ratio 31	1.1	•	1.3	0.9	0.9	0.7	1.1	1.0	1.2	1.3	1.2	1.3	0.9
Net Sales to Working Capital 32	4.3	•	10.7	9.9	10.9	6.3	4.8	4.7	3.9	3.4	4.4	3.9	3.5
Coverage Ratio 33	2.7	•	9.3	0.0	•	2.5	7.9	1.8	6.5	4.9	1.1	2.8	2.7
Total Asset Turnover 34	0.9	•	3.3	3.5	2.2	1.7	1.7	1.3	1.4	1.1	0.8	0.8	0.5
Inventory Turnover 35	5.3	•	11.7	6.5	4.3	2.7	4.5	4.4	4.5	4.8	5.0	6.4	8.3
Receivables Turnover 36	6.2	•	7.4	12.3	6.7	5.3	6.2	5.7	5.2	5.8	3.6	6.0	9.0
Total Liabilities to Net Worth 37	1.1	•	1.4	•	3.4	1.6	1.1	1.0	0.8	0.8	1.8	0.9	1.0
Current Assets to Working Capital 38	2.0	•	2.8	2.5	3.5	2.6	2.0	2.3	1.9	1.8	2.4	1.8	1.6
Current Liabilities to Working Capital 39	1.0	•	1.8	1.5	2.5	1.6	1.0	1.3	0.9	0.8	1.4	0.8	0.6
Working Capital to Net Sales 40	0.2	•	0.1	0.1	0.1	0.2	0.2	0.2	0.3	0.3	0.2	0.3	0.3
Inventory to Working Capital 41	0.6	•	0.5	1.1	1.2	1.3	0.8	0.8	0.6	0.5	0.6	0.4	0.3
Total Receipts to Cash Flow 42	8.7	•	5.2	11.0	17.8	12.9	8.5	10.6	10.4	6.4	9.4	8.3	7.0
Cost of Goods to Cash Flow 43	5.9	•	2.7	7.1	10.8	8.7	5.9	7.6	7.6	4.2	6.6	5.5	4.6
Cash Flow to Total Debt 44	0.2	•	1.1	0.1	0.2	0.2	0.4	0.2	0.3	0.4	0.1	0.2	0.1

Selected Financial Factors (in Percentages)

Debt Ratio 45	52.9	•	58.7	217.5	77.2	60.8	52.1	51.0	45.5	45.6	63.9	47.7	50.9
Return on Total Assets 46	6.5	•	4.5	0.2	•	8.3	12.6	2.9	9.2	8.3	3.0	8.0	5.7
Return on Equity Before Income Taxes 47	8.6	•	9.7	6.5	•	12.6	23.0	2.6	14.3	12.2	0.6	9.8	7.4
Return on Equity After Income Taxes 48	6.1	•	8.7	6.6	•	10.0	20.4	1.2	11.8	7.8	•	7.8	5.2
Profit Margin (Before Income Tax) 49	4.6	•	1.2	•	•	2.9	6.5	0.9	5.7	6.1	0.3	6.8	7.8
Profit Margin (After Income Tax) 50	3.3	•	1.1	•	•	2.3	5.8	0.4	4.7	3.9	•	5.4	5.5

Table II

Corporations with Net Income

OTHER ELECTRICAL EQUIPMENT AND COMPONENT

MONEY AMOUNTS AND SIZE OF ASSETS IN THOUSANDS OF DOLLARS

Item Description for Accounting Period 7/06 Through 6/07		Total	Zero Assets	Under 500	500 to 1000	251 to 500	501 to 1,000	1,001 to 5,000	5,001 to 10,000	10,001 to 25,000	25,001 to 50,000	50,001 to 100,000	100,001 to 250,000	250,001 and over
Number of Enterprises	1	2101	62	•	325	372	230	153	55	35	25	8	15	•
Revenues ($ in Thousands)														
Net Sales	2	46423550	303108	•	846305	1943544	2980235	4237868	3144216	3319591	5062489	2936300	11375444	•
Interest	3	557467	681	•	1	1505	2777	2584	4255	9170	28227	43034	230133	•
Rents	4	20774	0	•	0	24	950	133	3	199	533	1111	1484	•
Royalties	5	154635	0	•	0	0	0	2364	1495	1619	27988	76	21467	•
Other Portfolio Income	6	566373	32508	•	0	15166	1492	15169	18121	31194	28577	3571	368452	•
Other Receipts	7	577640	6741	•	701	4846	4389	22318	16959	53314	45168	49719	36323	•
Total Receipts	8	48300439	343038	•	847007	1965085	2989843	4280436	3185049	3415087	5192982	3033811	12033303	•
Average Total Receipts	9	22989	5533	•	2606	5282	12999	27977	57910	97574	207719	379226	802220	•
Operating Costs/Operating Income (%)														
Cost of Operations	10	66.7	66.6	•	76.0	60.9	66.4	66.9	70.6	71.5	64.5	65.8	66.2	•
Salaries and Wages	11	9.2	11.1	•	7.1	11.0	9.4	7.6	7.5	8.0	9.5	8.0	9.2	•
Taxes Paid	12	1.8	2.2	•	2.7	2.2	2.6	1.9	1.9	1.8	1.5	1.9	1.5	•
Interest Paid	13	2.2	4.4	•	0.5	0.8	1.5	1.0	1.1	1.0	1.3	3.5	3.6	•
Depreciation	14	1.7	1.1	•	0.7	1.8	1.3	1.5	1.9	1.8	1.4	2.0	1.7	•
Amortization and Depletion	15	0.6	3.7	•	•	0.1	0.3	0.2	0.3	0.3	0.4	0.6	1.0	•
Pensions and Other Deferred Comp.	16	0.6	0.4	•	0.4	0.2	0.1	0.4	0.4	0.4	0.6	0.4	0.8	•
Employee Benefits	17	1.6	1.7	•	1.4	1.7	1.3	1.2	1.7	1.6	1.6	1.8	2.4	•
Advertising	18	1.1	0.6	•	0.0	0.6	0.9	0.5	0.4	0.4	1.0	0.6	0.9	•
Other Expenses	19	8.3	8.9	•	6.4	6.3	5.9	7.3	7.4	5.4	9.8	11.5	9.0	•
Officers' Compensation	20	1.6	0.9	•	3.7	6.4	3.5	2.6	1.1	1.7	1.5	0.5	1.0	•
Operating Margin	21	4.6	•	•	1.0	8.0	6.6	8.8	5.8	6.0	6.9	3.3	2.7	•
Operating Margin Before Officers' Comp.	22	6.2	•	•	4.7	14.4	10.2	11.5	6.8	7.7	8.4	3.8	3.7	•

Selected Average Balance Sheet ($ in Thousands)

Net Receivables 23	3297	0	•	334	666	1421	4611	9253	17371	38562	93593	112002	•
Inventories 24	2660	0	•	198	740	3045	4436	9908	16593	25993	53378	73054	•
Net Property, Plant and Equipment 25	2369	0	•	25	356	1198	2812	7046	12095	22249	63978	89436	•
Total Assets 26	24605	0	•	703	2107	6834	15699	34571	67191	158579	344412	948309	•
Notes and Loans Payable 27	4620	0	•	181	404	2491	3895	8384	12697	29163	163812	231129	•
All Other Liabilities 28	7350	0	•	180	645	1279	3981	8245	18255	41257	89093	245225	•
Net Worth 29	12636	0	•	342	1058	3064	7824	17942	36240	88159	91507	471955	•

Selected Financial Ratios (Times to 1)

Current Ratio 30	2.2	•	•	1.9	2.0	2.1	2.2	1.5	2.1	2.4	1.4	2.8	•
Quick Ratio 31	1.2	•	•	1.2	1.2	0.9	1.2	0.8	1.2	1.4	0.9	1.7	•
Net Sales to Working Capital 32	4.0	•	•	7.9	6.6	5.2	4.7	7.0	4.2	3.5	7.3	3.1	•
Coverage Ratio 33	5.1	3.7	•	3.2	12.3	5.6	11.1	7.3	10.3	8.0	2.9	3.5	•
Total Asset Turnover 34	0.9	•	•	3.7	2.5	1.9	1.8	1.7	1.4	1.3	1.1	0.8	•
Inventory Turnover 35	5.5	•	•	10.0	4.3	2.8	4.2	4.1	4.1	5.0	4.5	6.9	•
Receivables Turnover 36	6.5	•	•	12.1	6.3	5.2	6.4	5.8	5.0	6.3	•	6.4	•
Total Liabilities to Net Worth 37	0.9	•	•	1.1	1.0	1.2	1.0	0.9	0.9	0.8	2.8	1.0	•
Current Assets to Working Capital 38	1.8	•	•	2.1	2.0	1.9	1.9	2.8	1.9	1.7	3.3	1.5	•
Current Liabilities to Working Capital 39	0.8	•	•	1.1	1.0	0.9	0.9	1.8	0.9	0.7	2.3	0.5	•
Working Capital to Net Sales 40	0.2	•	•	0.1	0.2	0.2	0.2	0.1	0.2	0.3	0.1	0.3	•
Inventory to Working Capital 41	0.5	•	•	0.8	0.7	1.0	0.8	1.1	0.7	0.6	1.1	0.3	•
Total Receipts to Cash Flow 42	6.8	11.5	•	15.6	7.6	8.9	6.3	7.6	8.0	5.6	5.9	7.2	•
Cost of Goods to Cash Flow 43	4.6	7.7	•	11.9	4.7	5.9	4.2	5.4	5.7	3.6	3.9	4.8	•
Cash Flow to Total Debt 44	0.3	•	•	0.5	0.7	0.4	0.6	0.5	0.4	0.5	0.2	0.2	•

Selected Financial Factors (in Percentages)

Debt Ratio 45	48.6	•	•	51.4	49.8	55.2	50.2	48.1	46.1	44.4	73.4	50.2	•
Return on Total Assets 46	9.9	•	•	6.0	24.8	16.0	19.1	13.5	13.8	13.7	10.7	9.9	•
Return on Equity Before Income Taxes 47	15.4	•	•	8.5	45.3	29.4	34.9	22.5	23.2	21.6	26.4	14.2	•
Return on Equity After Income Taxes 48	12.5	•	•	7.9	40.9	26.2	31.6	20.2	19.8	16.1	19.7	11.6	•
Profit Margin (Before Income Tax) 49	8.8	11.7	•	1.1	9.2	6.9	9.9	7.1	8.9	9.4	6.6	8.8	•
Profit Margin (After Income Tax) 50	7.2	9.0	•	1.0	8.3	6.2	8.9	6.3	7.6	7.0	4.9	7.2	•

Table I

Corporations with and without Net Income

MOTOR VEHICLES AND PARTS

MONEY AMOUNTS AND SIZE OF ASSETS IN THOUSANDS OF DOLLARS

Item Description for Accounting Period 7/06 Through 6/07		Total	Zero Assets	Under 500	500 to 1,000	1,000 to 5,000	5,000 to 10,000	10,000 to 25,000	25,000 to 50,000	50,000 to 100,000	100,000 to 250,000	250,000 to 500,000	500,000 to 2,500,000	2,500,000 and over
Number of Enterprises	1	4587	572	1922	367	876	144	241	135	110	101	45	51	22
Revenues ($ in Thousands)														
Net Sales	2	641885178	715932	3123882	716729	6569302	1655991	7830712	8893003	13440365	26190118	26207285	67861515	478680343
Interest	3	42165029	2353	263	9	3276	1250	6751	19765	26095	69089	220936	645868	41169375
Rents	4	20647636	273	0	0	465	0	1304	4952	1480	11389	12179	11705	20603887
Royalties	5	12801911	5999	0	0	371	0	1062	8436	6893	4657	31675	302852	12439966
Other Portfolio Income	6	11069350	24728	0	0	8608	4010	14707	25204	15647	38688	272592	380564	10284603
Other Receipts	7	26503182	9371	1181	96	66644	20272	42807	90018	95451	229141	757640	613552	24577009
Total Receipts	8	755072286	758656	3125326	716834	6648666	1681523	7897343	9041378	13585931	26543082	27502307	69816056	587755183
Average Total Receipts	9	164611	1326	1626	1953	7590	11677	32769	66973	123508	262803	611162	1368942	26716145
Operating Costs/Operating Income (%)														
Cost of Operations	10	81.9	69.1	71.2	59.7	73.2	73.3	77.0	79.4	82.3	83.1	82.4	79.8	82.5
Salaries and Wages	11	3.7	5.9	13.9	9.2	8.3	4.5	4.8	4.9	3.5	3.8	3.3	4.6	3.4
Taxes Paid	12	0.9	2.0	2.2	1.8	2.1	2.2	1.9	1.7	1.4	1.5	1.2	1.3	0.7
Interest Paid	13	6.7	2.1	0.2	1.4	1.1	1.7	1.1	1.0	1.5	1.3	2.9	2.8	8.3
Depreciation	14	6.5	2.7	0.7	2.8	1.6	2.3	1.8	2.8	3.1	2.6	2.8	2.4	7.9
Amortization and Depletion	15	0.9	1.5	0.0	0.0	0.2	0.1	0.3	0.2	0.3	0.3	0.5	0.5	1.1
Pensions and Other Deferred Comp.	16	0.9	0.2	•	0.2	0.5	0.3	0.3	0.3	0.3	0.3	0.4	0.9	1.1
Employee Benefits	17	1.6	2.0	0.5	0.1	1.0	2.1	1.5	1.5	1.7	1.8	1.5	2.4	1.5
Advertising	18	1.6	0.4	0.5	0.3	0.9	0.2	0.8	0.3	0.4	0.2	0.2	0.3	2.1
Other Expenses	19	12.6	17.4	9.6	15.8	7.9	7.9	7.6	7.7	5.1	4.8	7.2	6.8	14.5
Officers' Compensation	20	0.2	0.9	2.8	3.1	2.5	1.4	2.1	0.8	0.5	0.4	0.4	0.3	0.1
Operating Margin	21	•	•	•	5.3	0.8	4.2	0.7	•	•	•	•	•	•
Operating Margin Before Officers' Comp.	22	•	•	1.2	8.4	3.3	5.6	2.8	0.2	0.4	0.4	0.3	•	•

Selected Average Balance Sheet ($ in Thousands)

Net Receivables 23 71673	0	12	173	645	1332	3700	9170	16990	33201	75150	182953	13993557
Inventories 24 9511	0	94	273	879	2872	4579	7393	12969	25051	54560	119229	1253075
Net Property, Plant and Equipment 25 42029	0	26	166	514	1761	3834	12424	24734	46815	100870	218924	7555244
Total Assets 26 239433	0	151	745	2612	6207	15577	35562	72112	155151	362944	1047754	45118527
Notes and Loans Payable 27 80845	0	129	385	1272	2919	5727	11429	28956	51806	121144	394299	15091405
All Other Liabilities 28 118440	0	225	104	1616	1571	5440	10718	22412	51198	124202	362897	23030905
Net Worth 29 40148	0	-204	256	-277	1717	4410	13416	20744	52147	117599	290558	6996217

Selected Financial Ratios (Times to 1)

Current Ratio 30 1.2	•	0.4	3.5	1.3	1.6	1.2	1.4	1.2	1.2	1.4	1.0	1.2
Quick Ratio 31 0.8	•	0.1	1.7	0.6	0.8	0.6	0.9	0.7	0.6	0.8	0.6	0.9
Net Sales to Working Capital 32 6.9	•	•	5.4	16.5	7.5	18.9	11.8	18.3	22.4	12.3	99.5	5.5
Coverage Ratio 33 1.1	1.6	•	4.8	2.8	4.3	2.4	2.1	1.6	2.0	1.8	1.3	1.0
Total Asset Turnover 34 0.6	•	10.8	2.6	2.9	1.9	2.1	1.9	1.7	1.7	1.6	1.3	0.5
Inventory Turnover 35 12.0	•	12.4	4.3	6.2	5.5	5.5	7.8	7.8	8.6	8.8	8.9	14.3
Receivables Turnover 36 1.7	•	150.9	14.0	11.5	5.6	8.6	6.7	7.3	8.4	8.2	6.9	1.3
Total Liabilities to Net Worth 37 5.0	•	•	1.9	•	2.6	2.5	1.7	2.5	2.0	2.1	2.6	5.4
Current Assets to Working Capital 38 5.7	•	•	1.4	4.1	2.6	5.8	3.6	5.6	6.7	3.6	30.8	5.6
Current Liabilities to Working Capital 39 4.7	•	•	0.4	3.1	1.6	4.8	2.6	4.6	5.7	2.6	29.8	4.6
Working Capital to Net Sales 40 0.1	•	•	0.2	0.1	0.1	0.1	0.1	0.1	0.0	0.1	0.0	0.2
Inventory to Working Capital 41 0.5	•	•	0.7	1.9	1.2	2.8	1.2	2.0	2.4	1.3	9.3	0.3
Total Receipts to Cash Flow 42 8.7	6.7	17.5	5.7	14.8	8.9	13.7	15.3	21.4	19.9	12.6	15.8	7.5
Cost of Goods to Cash Flow 43 7.1	4.6	12.5	3.4	10.8	6.5	10.5	12.1	17.6	16.6	10.4	12.6	6.2
Cash Flow to Total Debt 44 0.1	•	0.3	0.7	0.2	0.3	0.2	0.1	0.1	0.2	0.1	0.1	0.1

Selected Financial Factors (in Percentages)

Debt Ratio 45 83.2	•	234.9	65.6	110.6	72.3	71.7	62.3	71.2	66.4	67.6	72.3	84.5
Return on Total Assets 46 4.2	•	•	17.5	9.1	13.9	5.6	4.0	4.0	4.3	8.3	4.8	4.0
Return on Equity Before Income Taxes 47 1.4	•	•	12.9	40.4	38.5	11.7	5.7	5.3	6.6	11.4	4.4	0.2
Return on Equity After Income Taxes 48 •	•	•	•	39.5	36.9	7.2	2.2	1.7	2.4	6.6	0.5	•
Profit Margin (Before Income Tax) 49 0.4	1.4	•	•	5.3	2.0	5.7	1.6	0.9	1.3	2.3	1.0	0.1
Profit Margin (After Income Tax) 50 •	1.2	•	•	5.2	1.7	5.5	1.0	0.3	0.5	1.3	0.5	0.1

Table II
Corporations with Net Income

MOTOR VEHICLES AND PARTS

MONEY AMOUNTS AND SIZE OF ASSETS IN THOUSANDS OF DOLLARS

Item Description for Accounting Period 7/06 Through 6/07	Total	Zero Assets	Under 500	500 to 1,000	1,000 to 5,000	5,000 to 10,000	10,000 to 25,000	25,000 to 50,000	50,000 to 100,000	100,000 to 250,000	250,000 to 500,000	500,000 to 2,500,000	2,500,000 and over
Number of Enterprises **1**	2311	146	605	•	624	125	145	90	•	66	32	25	•
Revenues ($ in Thousands)													
Net Sales **2**	232767665	103392	2334997	•	4890965	1498248	4630776	6219348	•	18566279	19687940	38819596	•
Interest **3**	4048532	1460	0	•	1804	1248	4684	14722	•	43814	86717	160699	•
Rents **4**	3326451	0	0	•	369	0	818	3459	•	9652	4811	8337	•
Royalties **5**	959425	54	0	•	371	0	1062	5335	•	4086	31167	193026	•
Other Portfolio Income **6**	3144461	21492	0	•	8491	3990	14034	14713	•	27438	264113	256970	•
Other Receipts **7**	3671378	628	108	•	58358	19530	30021	52491	•	172613	176372	421416	•
Total Receipts **8**	247917912	127026	2335105	•	4960358	1523016	4681395	6310068	•	18822882	20251120	39860044	•
Average Total Receipts **9**	107277	870	3860	•	7949	12184	32285	70112	•	285195	632848	1594402	•
Operating Costs/Operating Income (%)													
Cost of Operations **10**	78.6	62.7	69.1	•	73.4	72.6	73.0	77.3	•	83.3	80.8	79.4	•
Salaries and Wages **11**	3.3	6.9	17.0	•	7.9	4.6	4.2	4.5	•	3.2	3.6	4.4	•
Taxes Paid **12**	1.1	2.5	1.9	•	2.1	2.2	1.8	1.5	•	1.3	1.2	1.0	•
Interest Paid **13**	2.4	2.5	0.1	•	0.7	1.2	0.6	0.9	•	0.7	1.4	1.0	•
Depreciation **14**	5.0	2.2	0.4	•	1.3	1.7	1.7	2.2	•	2.5	2.4	2.0	•
Amortization and Depletion **15**	0.2	0.5	•	•	0.1	0.0	0.0	0.1	•	0.2	0.3	0.2	•
Pensions and Other Deferred Comp. **16**	0.5	0.7	•	•	0.6	0.3	0.3	0.4	•	0.3	0.4	0.6	•
Employee Benefits **17**	1.2	2.4	•	•	1.0	2.0	1.4	1.4	•	1.7	1.4	2.0	•
Advertising **18**	1.2	0.2	0.3	•	0.3	0.2	1.0	0.3	•	0.2	0.2	0.2	•
Other Expenses **19**	7.1	8.3	7.9	•	7.1	7.7	6.7	6.1	•	3.3	5.3	5.7	•
Officers' Compensation **20**	0.4	0.3	2.5	•	2.6	1.5	2.7	0.8	•	0.4	0.4	0.2	•
Operating Margin **21**	•	10.7	0.7	•	2.9	6.0	6.6	4.5	•	2.9	2.6	3.3	•
Operating Margin Before Officers' Comp. **22**	•	11.0	3.3	•	5.4	7.5	9.3	5.4	•	3.3	2.9	3.5	•

Selected Average Balance Sheet ($ in Thousands)

Net Receivables 23	31612	0	2	•	679	1382	3548	9153	•	33553	78590	180633	•
Inventories 24	10616	0	113	•	933	2363	4804	7887	•	24994	54869	142344	•
Net Property, Plant and Equipment 25	20466	0	69	•	506	1521	3925	11285	•	48899	89428	243861	•
Total Assets 26	88591	0	198	•	2818	6020	15786	35029	•	153027	361910	1082761	•
Notes and Loans Payable 27	32746	0	139	•	771	2128	3654	8657	•	39475	85841	217428	•
All Other Liabilities 28	24587	0	163	•	726	1667	4126	9725	•	44292	126287	373555	•
Net Worth 29	31258	0	-104	•	1321	2225	8006	16647	•	69260	149781	491779	•

Selected Financial Ratios (Times to 1)

Current Ratio 30	1.6	•	0.7	•	1.8	1.7	1.8	1.7	•	1.4	1.6	1.2	•
Quick Ratio 31	1.1	•	0.3	•	0.8	0.8	0.9	1.0	•	0.8	0.9	0.7	•
Net Sales to Working Capital 32	5.5	•	•	•	8.9	7.6	7.1	8.3	•	11.7	8.9	18.8	•
Coverage Ratio 33	3.4	14.3	6.8	•	7.0	7.4	13.9	7.9	•	7.1	4.7	7.2	•
Total Asset Turnover 34	1.1	•	19.4	•	2.8	2.0	2.0	2.0	•	1.8	1.7	1.4	•
Inventory Turnover 35	7.5	•	23.6	•	6.2	3.7	4.9	6.8	•	9.4	9.1	8.7	•
Receivables Turnover 36	1.3	•	353.3	•	12.0	6.8	8.0	6.8	•	8.7	8.5	7.1	•
Total Liabilities to Net Worth 37	1.8	•	•	•	1.1	1.7	1.0	1.1	•	1.2	1.4	1.2	•
Current Assets to Working Capital 38	2.8	•	•	•	2.3	2.5	2.2	2.5	•	3.2	2.7	5.6	•
Current Liabilities to Working Capital 39	1.8	•	•	•	1.3	1.5	1.2	1.5	•	2.2	1.7	4.6	•
Working Capital to Net Sales 40	0.2	•	•	•	0.1	0.1	0.1	0.1	•	0.1	0.1	0.1	•
Inventory to Working Capital 41	0.5	•	•	•	1.1	1.2	1.1	0.9	•	1.1	0.9	1.8	•
Total Receipts to Cash Flow 42	8.7	2.9	14.0	•	11.9	7.7	8.1	9.5	•	14.8	11.2	9.3	•
Cost of Goods to Cash Flow 43	6.8	1.8	9.6	•	8.7	5.6	5.9	7.3	•	12.3	9.1	7.4	•
Cash Flow to Total Debt 44	0.2	•	0.9	•	0.4	0.4	0.5	0.4	•	0.2	0.3	0.3	•

Selected Financial Factors (in Percentages)

Debt Ratio 45	64.7	•	152.3	•	53.1	63.0	49.3	52.5	•	54.7	58.6	54.6	•
Return on Total Assets 46	9.2	•	16.8	•	13.9	17.7	16.8	13.6	•	9.1	11.4	10.1	•
Return on Equity Before Income Taxes 47	18.5	•	•	•	25.4	41.4	30.7	25.0	•	17.3	21.7	19.2	•
Return on Equity After Income Taxes 48	13.6	•	•	•	22.7	40.0	26.6	20.8	•	12.5	16.4	14.5	•
Profit Margin (Before Income Tax) 49	5.8	33.6	0.7	•	4.3	7.7	7.7	6.0	•	4.3	5.3	6.1	•
Profit Margin (After Income Tax) 50	4.2	32.3	0.7	•	3.8	7.4	6.7	5.0	•	3.1	4.0	4.6	•

Table I

Corporations with and without Net Income

AEROSPACE PRODUCT AND PARTS

MONEY AMOUNTS AND SIZE OF ASSETS IN THOUSANDS OF DOLLARS

Item Description for Accounting Period 7/06 Through 6/07	Total	Zero Assets	Under 500	500 to 1,000	1,000 to 5,000	5,000 to 10,000	10,000 to 25,000	25,000 to 50,000	50,000 to 100,000	100,000 to 250,000	250,000 to 500,000	500,000 to 2,500,000	2,500,000 and over
Number of Enterprises **1**	1345	19	783	121	123	77	95	46	20	19	9	20	13
Revenues ($ in Thousands)													
Net Sales **2**	257035330	1214275	594841	97755	892628	893722	2038896	1762268	1227109	2424467	3229448	17450029	225209891
Interest **3**	3993205	10610	544	4	355	21	3890	6767	7478	7203	50715	170582	3735037
Rents **4**	1436125	79	0	0	0	0	2320	1542	226	3150	40	44485	1384282
Royalties **5**	2484896	2894	0	0	0	0	277	0	60	3671	64	21722	2456208
Other Portfolio Income **6**	1442452	113852	0	0	301	7	23785	11166	1858	1960	3293	119441	1166788
Other Receipts **7**	4533886	7860	588	0	985	3242	14293	10776	65458	34150	53309	68749	4274478
Total Receipts **8**	270925894	1349570	595973	97759	894269	896992	2083461	1792519	1302189	2474601	3336869	17875008	238226684
Average Total Receipts **9**	201432	71030	761	808	7270	11649	21931	38968	65109	130242	370763	893750	18325130
Operating Costs/Operating Income (%)													
Cost of Operations **10**	73.7	69.3	44.4	58.2	72.9	62.4	63.6	68.0	64.0	68.4	67.5	72.0	74.3
Salaries and Wages **11**	4.6	12.8	24.5	•	5.6	8.5	5.5	7.3	13.1	8.5	6.4	7.6	4.1
Taxes Paid **12**	1.2	3.4	2.9	1.7	2.9	1.1	2.7	2.9	2.7	1.7	2.5	1.7	1.1
Interest Paid **13**	2.7	7.1	2.1	1.5	1.3	0.8	1.0	1.9	2.3	3.7	4.3	4.5	2.5
Depreciation **14**	2.1	1.8	0.7	2.4	1.6	3.2	2.8	3.1	2.4	2.4	2.1	2.5	2.1
Amortization and Depletion **15**	0.7	3.2	0.1	•	0.1	0.0	0.2	0.2	0.7	1.1	1.6	1.2	0.6
Pensions and Other Deferred Comp. **16**	1.3	1.4	•	2.7	0.3	0.2	0.6	0.6	0.7	0.4	0.6	0.8	1.4
Employee Benefits **17**	3.1	3.2	0.5	•	3.3	0.3	2.5	2.1	3.2	1.3	2.8	2.4	3.1
Advertising **18**	0.2	0.6	1.9	0.4	0.1	0.3	0.3	0.4	0.3	0.4	0.3	0.2	0.2
Other Expenses **19**	10.8	4.8	17.6	16.7	9.8	13.1	10.5	9.1	11.7	9.7	7.0	6.6	11.2
Officers' Compensation **20**	0.4	0.5	6.8	13.1	3.4	1.7	3.1	3.0	1.4	1.4	1.1	0.9	0.3
Operating Margin **21**	•	•	•	3.4	•	8.3	7.2	1.4	•	1.0	3.9	•	0.6
Operating Margin Before Officers' Comp. **22**	•	•	5.3	16.5	2.0	10.0	10.3	4.4	•	2.4	5.0	•	0.6

Selected Average Balance Sheet ($ in Thousands)

Net Receivables 23	27759	0	51	76	993	1421	2947	7011	16221	18354	61674	143758	2488379
Inventories 24	24075	0	19	393	967	4288	4931	9671	16454	35435	56626	176831	1993361
Net Property, Plant and Equipment 25	28611	0	34	16	538	1364	2767	7216	10057	23969	60139	175191	2537374
Total Assets 26	212228	0	142	782	3398	7528	14682	34086	73710	133085	371290	1240704	19163304
Notes and Loans Payable 27	58103	0	150	535	1977	2713	4466	9835	17490	58932	179773	454078	4959180
All Other Liabilities 28	96510	0	48	40	528	1123	2912	8858	20304	65252	72372	418214	9097454
Net Worth 29	57615	0	-56	206	893	3692	7305	15393	35917	8900	119145	368413	5106671

Selected Financial Ratios (Times to 1)

Current Ratio 30	1.2	•	1.5	16.3	4.8	2.8	2.2	1.8	1.8	2.1	2.2	1.5	1.1
Quick Ratio 31	0.6	•	1.2	6.6	2.2	0.8	1.0	0.9	1.1	0.8	1.2	0.8	0.6
Net Sales to Working Capital 32	16.7	•	23.0	1.3	3.1	3.5	3.9	4.0	2.8	3.4	3.2	5.6	26.5
Coverage Ratio 33	2.9	1.7	0.4	3.3	0.1	11.9	10.8	2.6	2.7	1.8	2.7	1.5	3.1
Total Asset Turnover 34	0.9	•	5.4	1.0	2.1	1.5	1.5	1.1	0.8	1.0	1.0	0.7	0.9
Inventory Turnover 35	5.9	•	18.0	1.2	5.5	1.7	2.8	2.7	2.4	2.5	4.3	3.6	6.5
Receivables Turnover 36	7.2	•	10.8	•	10.9	6.3	7.1	5.1	4.8	8.1	7.5	5.7	7.4
Total Liabilities to Net Worth 37	2.7	•	2.8	2.8	2.8	1.0	1.0	1.2	1.1	14.0	2.1	2.4	2.8
Current Assets to Working Capital 38	6.6	•	3.1	1.1	1.3	1.6	1.8	2.3	2.2	1.9	1.8	2.8	10.1
Current Liabilities to Working Capital 39	5.6	•	2.1	0.1	0.3	0.6	0.8	1.3	1.2	0.9	0.8	1.8	9.1
Working Capital to Net Sales 40	0.1	•	0.0	0.8	0.3	0.3	0.3	0.2	0.4	0.3	0.3	0.2	0.0
Inventory to Working Capital 41	2.2	•	0.6	0.6	0.6	1.1	0.9	1.0	0.8	1.1	0.7	1.2	3.2
Total Receipts to Cash Flow 42	7.4	43.6	11.6	5.6	17.7	5.2	6.0	10.7	7.6	10.7	7.8	14.2	7.1
Cost of Goods to Cash Flow 43	5.5	30.2	5.1	3.3	12.9	3.3	3.8	7.3	4.9	7.3	5.3	10.3	5.3
Cash Flow to Total Debt 44	0.2	•	0.3	0.3	0.2	0.6	0.5	0.2	0.2	0.1	0.2	0.1	0.2

Selected Financial Factors (in Percentages)

Debt Ratio 45	72.9	•	139.2	73.6	73.7	51.0	50.2	54.8	51.3	93.3	67.9	70.3	73.4
Return on Total Assets 46	6.9	•	4.1	5.0	0.2	14.6	15.1	5.6	5.0	6.5	11.1	4.7	7.0
Return on Equity Before Income Taxes 47	16.7	•	18.2	13.3	•	27.2	27.6	7.7	6.4	43.1	21.6	5.2	17.8
Return on Equity After Income Taxes 48	11.3	•	18.2	4.2	•	26.9	22.5	4.6	3.8	33.7	15.7	3.3	12.0
Profit Margin (Before Income Tax) 49	5.0	5.2	•	3.4	•	8.6	9.4	3.1	3.8	3.0	7.2	2.2	5.3
Profit Margin (After Income Tax) 50	3.4	2.8	•	1.1	•	8.6	7.7	1.8	2.2	2.3	5.2	1.4	3.5

Table II
Corporations with Net Income

AEROSPACE PRODUCT AND PARTS

MONEY AMOUNTS AND SIZE OF ASSETS IN THOUSANDS OF DOLLARS

Item Description for Accounting Period 7/06 Through 6/07	Total	Zero Assets	Under 500	500 to 1,000	1,000 to 5,000	5,000 to 10,000	10,000 to 25,000	25,000 to 50,000	50,000 to 100,000	100,000 to 250,000	250,000 to 500,000	500,000 to 2,500,000	2,500,000 and over
Number of Enterprises **1**	469	•	•	•	74	64	80	33	17	11	•	13	•
Revenues ($ in Thousands)													
Net Sales **2**	244634622	•	•	•	502842	833930	1870095	1271916	1131559	1874231	•	10481766	•
Interest **3**	3851504	•	•	•	352	15	3655	3952	3384	4202	•	71135	•
Rents **4**	1412366	•	•	•	0	0	2320	306	212	2540	•	23574	•
Royalties **5**	2482458	•	•	•	0	0	277	0	60	1932	•	21024	•
Other Portfolio Income **6**	1382991	•	•	•	301	7	20948	7595	1858	1584	•	69344	•
Other Receipts **7**	4507022	•	•	•	611	3219	8526	8731	52983	51828	•	52044	•
Total Receipts **8**	258270963	•	•	•	504106	837171	1905821	1292500	1190056	1936317	•	10718887	•
Average Total Receipts **9**	550684	•	•	•	6812	13081	23823	39167	70003	176029	•	824530	•
Operating Costs/Operating Income (%)													
Cost of Operations **10**	73.6	•	•	•	73.5	61.2	62.3	63.2	62.3	66.6	•	70.7	•
Salaries and Wages **11**	4.4	•	•	•	3.5	8.2	5.0	5.3	10.2	5.7	•	7.4	•
Taxes Paid **12**	1.2	•	•	•	0.8	1.1	2.4	2.6	2.4	1.5	•	1.8	•
Interest Paid **13**	2.6	•	•	•	1.0	0.5	1.0	1.8	2.4	1.6	•	4.6	•
Depreciation **14**	2.1	•	•	•	1.7	3.3	2.2	3.3	2.0	1.9	•	2.2	•
Amortization and Depletion **15**	0.6	•	•	•	0.3	0.0	0.2	0.3	0.5	0.4	•	1.1	•
Pensions and Other Deferred Comp. **16**	1.4	•	•	•	0.5	0.2	0.4	0.8	0.7	0.4	•	1.0	•
Employee Benefits **17**	3.1	•	•	•	0.6	0.3	2.5	2.3	2.6	0.8	•	2.7	•
Advertising **18**	0.2	•	•	•	0.1	0.3	0.3	0.3	0.2	0.3	•	0.2	•
Other Expenses **19**	10.9	•	•	•	5.8	13.0	9.4	6.4	9.6	8.6	•	4.3	•
Officers' Compensation **20**	0.4	•	•	•	5.9	1.6	3.3	3.7	1.5	1.7	•	1.0	•
Operating Margin **21**	•	•	•	•	6.4	10.4	10.9	10.0	5.6	10.6	•	3.0	•
Operating Margin Before Officers' Comp. **22**	•	•	•	•	12.3	12.0	14.2	13.7	7.0	12.3	•	4.0	•

Selected Average Balance Sheet ($ in Thousands)

Net Receivables 23	75835	851	1494	3143	7240	18152	19222	134642
Inventories 24	64114	1048	3460	5087	9488	15156	39346	172331
Net Property, Plant and Equipment 25	75738	606	1555	2639	7769	9758	23244	127915
Total Assets 26	576738	2756	7410	14796	33447	73397	128483	1190887
Notes and Loans Payable 27	154300	908	1574	3054	8831	16536	40118	475159
All Other Liabilities 28	261213	609	1058	2869	6780	19571	27706	262353
Net Worth 29	161225	1240	4778	8873	17836	37290	60659	453374

Selected Financial Ratios (Times to 1)

Current Ratio 30	1.2	3.0	3.6	2.7	2.1	1.7	2.9	2.1
Quick Ratio 31	0.6	1.6	1.0	1.3	1.0	1.0	1.0	1.1
Net Sales to Working Capital 32	18.1	4.4	3.2	3.5	3.6	3.6	3.3	3.5
Coverage Ratio 33	3.2	7.7	22.1	13.9	7.5	5.6	9.9	2.2
Total Asset Turnover 34	0.9	2.5	1.8	1.6	1.2	0.9	1.3	0.7
Inventory Turnover 35	6.0	4.8	2.3	2.9	2.6	2.7	2.9	3.3
Receivables Turnover 36	7.2	•	8.7	7.3	5.1	5.2	10.3	1.6
Total Liabilities to Net Worth 37	2.6	1.2	0.6	0.7	0.9	1.0	1.1	1.6
Current Assets to Working Capital 38	7.1	1.5	1.4	1.6	1.9	2.4	1.5	1.9
Current Liabilities to Working Capital 39	6.1	0.5	0.4	0.6	0.9	1.4	0.5	0.9
Working Capital to Net Sales 40	0.1	0.2	0.3	0.3	0.3	0.3	0.3	0.3
Inventory to Working Capital 41	2.3	0.7	1.0	0.8	0.9	0.9	0.9	0.8
Total Receipts to Cash Flow 42	7.1	8.8	4.8	5.3	6.5	5.5	4.7	12.5
Cost of Goods to Cash Flow 43	5.2	6.5	2.9	3.3	4.1	3.4	3.1	8.8
Cash Flow to Total Debt 44	0.2	0.5	1.0	0.7	0.4	0.3	0.5	0.1

Selected Financial Factors (in Percentages)

Debt Ratio 45	72.0	55.0	35.5	40.0	46.7	49.2	52.8	61.9
Return on Total Assets 46	7.4	18.9	19.8	21.8	15.4	12.0	20.5	6.8
Return on Equity Before Income Taxes 47	18.0	36.7	29.3	33.7	25.0	19.4	39.1	9.6
Return on Equity After Income Taxes 48	12.5	33.2	29.1	28.8	21.3	16.4	36.7	7.2
Profit Margin (Before Income Tax) 49	5.6	6.7	10.8	12.8	11.6	10.9	13.9	5.4
Profit Margin (After Income Tax) 50	3.9	6.1	10.7	10.9	9.9	9.2	13.1	4.1

Table I

Corporations with and without Net Income

SHIP AND BOAT BUILDING

MONEY AMOUNTS AND SIZE OF ASSETS IN THOUSANDS OF DOLLARS

Item Description for Accounting Period 7/06 Through 6/07	Total	Zero Assets	Under 500	500 to 1,000	1,000 to 5,000	5,000 to 10,000	10,000 to 25,000	25,000 to 50,000	50,000 to 100,000	100,000 to 250,000	250,000 to 500,000	500,000 to 2,500,000	2,500,000 and over
Number of Enterprises 1	1848	418	807	93	331	78	61	31	15	9	5	0	0
Revenues ($ in Thousands)													
Net Sales 2	34759527	111782	1178203	100371	2520756	1180605	1648592	1871950	1982977	1857709	22306582	0	0
Interest 3	54786	661	85	0	1749	16	952	2245	573	5315	43191	0	0
Rents 4	39921	0	0	0	5189	38	308	0	30	2596	31760	0	0
Royalties 5	14958	0	0	0	0	0	0	3394	0	0	11564	0	0
Other Portfolio Income 6	318045	3038	0	0	1917	7947	1330	3519	907	12694	286692	0	0
Other Receipts 7	153013	3352	482	0	11489	6710	3050	16465	12030	13997	85439	0	0
Total Receipts 8	35340250	118833	1178770	100371	2541100	1195316	1654232	1897573	1996517	1892311	22765228	0	0
Average Total Receipts 9	19124	284	1461	1079	7677	15325	27119	61212	133101	210257	4553046	•	•
Operating Costs/Operating Income (%)													
Cost of Operations 10	75.9	91.4	51.0	62.8	76.1	69.3	78.2	73.5	76.0	81.6	77.1	•	•
Salaries and Wages 11	3.5	7.7	13.7	6.5	3.0	11.1	4.2	4.0	3.1	3.8	2.5	•	•
Taxes Paid 12	2.0	2.6	2.9	2.4	1.6	1.9	0.8	1.2	1.8	1.7	2.2	•	•
Interest Paid 13	0.8	6.7	0.3	0.2	1.1	0.6	1.2	0.9	0.9	1.9	0.6	•	•
Depreciation 14	1.3	3.1	0.8	2.3	1.3	1.2	2.0	1.7	2.3	2.3	1.0	•	•
Amortization and Depletion 15	0.7	•	0.0	•	0.0	0.0	0.1	0.2	0.1	0.2	1.0	•	•
Pensions and Other Deferred Comp. 16	0.5	0.5	0.1	0.5	0.2	0.2	0.3	0.5	0.7	0.3	0.5	•	•
Employee Benefits 17	2.1	4.4	4.5	0.0	0.8	2.4	0.7	0.9	2.1	0.9	2.4	•	•
Advertising 18	0.5	0.0	0.6	0.3	1.3	1.2	1.0	1.5	0.9	0.7	0.2	•	•
Other Expenses 19	5.7	16.4	10.2	38.2	8.4	6.0	7.9	10.6	7.0	3.3	4.4	•	•
Officers' Compensation 20	1.4	•	3.9	5.2	5.0	2.8	1.5	1.3	1.3	0.8	0.8	•	•
Operating Margin 21	5.7	•	11.9	•	1.4	3.4	2.1	3.8	4.0	2.5	7.2	•	•
Operating Margin Before Officers' Comp. 22	7.1	•	15.8	•	6.3	6.2	3.6	5.1	5.2	3.3	8.0	•	•

Selected Average Balance Sheet ($ in Thousands)

	•	•	•	•	•	•	•	•	•	•
Net Receivables 23	1491	0	94	249	253	1096	2122	4710	11082	21374	370698
Inventories 24	2342	0	24	0	1705	1833	3640	6818	15151	13283	563992
Net Property, Plant and Equipment 25	2000	0	77	192	527	1013	4714	8840	24018	32346	429842
Total Assets 26	14789	0	301	919	3182	6428	16622	30475	64933	150442	4232064
Notes and Loans Payable 27	2816	0	249	851	1219	2591	9340	8371	13275	44680	577471
All Other Liabilities 28	5286	0	18	292	1035	2127	5638	11145	24247	47857	1546805
Net Worth 29	6688	0	34	-224	928	1710	1644	10959	27412	57905	2107789

Selected Financial Ratios (Times to 1)

	•	•	•	•	•	•	•	•	•	•
Current Ratio 30	1.4	•	5.1	0.6	1.9	1.9	1.3	1.5	1.4	1.5	1.4
Quick Ratio 31	0.5	•	4.6	0.5	0.3	0.7	0.5	0.7	0.6	0.6	0.5
Net Sales to Working Capital 32	10.2	•	8.3	•	6.5	6.5	12.8	11.1	12.9	8.4	10.9
Coverage Ratio 33	10.7	•	42.3	•	3.0	9.2	3.1	6.9	6.2	3.2	16.2
Total Asset Turnover 34	1.3	•	4.8	1.2	2.4	2.4	1.6	2.0	2.0	1.4	1.1
Inventory Turnover 35	6.1	•	30.9	•	3.4	5.7	5.8	6.5	6.6	12.7	6.1
Receivables Turnover 36	13.1	•	12.0	8.7	20.0	22.2	13.5	13.9	12.4	12.1	12.5
Total Liabilities to Net Worth 37	1.2	•	7.8	•	2.4	2.8	9.1	1.8	1.4	1.6	1.0
Current Assets to Working Capital 38	3.3	•	1.2	•	2.2	2.1	4.0	3.0	3.5	2.9	3.8
Current Liabilities to Working Capital 39	2.3	•	0.2	•	1.2	1.1	3.0	2.0	2.5	1.9	2.8
Working Capital to Net Sales 40	0.1	•	0.1	•	0.2	0.2	0.1	0.1	0.1	0.1	0.1
Inventory to Working Capital 41	1.4	•	0.1	•	1.4	1.3	1.7	1.2	1.5	0.7	1.6
Total Receipts to Cash Flow 42	9.1	•	5.4	•	11.8	11.1	11.8	7.8	9.5	18.6	8.6
Cost of Goods to Cash Flow 43	6.9	•	2.8	•	9.0	7.7	9.2	5.7	7.2	15.2	6.6
Cash Flow to Total Debt 44	0.3	•	1.0	•	0.3	0.3	0.2	0.4	0.4	0.1	0.2

Selected Financial Factors (in Percentages)

	•	•	•	•	•	•	•	•	•	•
Debt Ratio 45	54.8	•	88.7	124.4	70.8	73.4	90.1	64.0	57.8	61.5	50.2
Return on Total Assets 46	10.7	•	59.3	•	7.7	12.2	5.8	11.9	11.3	8.5	10.8
Return on Equity Before Income Taxes 47	21.5	•	511.2	88.6	17.8	40.9	39.8	28.3	22.4	15.3	20.4
Return on Equity After Income Taxes 48	14.9	•	509.0	91.1	13.9	38.7	28.5	23.9	20.9	11.4	13.3
Profit Margin (Before Income Tax) 49	7.6	•	11.9	•	2.2	4.6	2.4	5.1	4.6	4.3	9.6
Profit Margin (After Income Tax) 50	5.3	•	11.9	•	1.7	4.4	1.7	4.3	4.3	3.2	6.3

Table II
Corporations with Net Income

SHIP AND BOAT BUILDING

MONEY AMOUNTS AND SIZE OF ASSETS IN THOUSANDS OF DOLLARS

Item Description for Accounting Period 7/06 Through 6/07	Total	Zero Assets	Under 500	500 to 1,000	1,000 to 5,000	5,000 to 10,000	10,000 to 25,000	25,000 to 50,000	50,000 to 100,000	100,000 to 250,000	250,000 to 500,000	500,000 to 2,500,000	2,500,000 and over
Number of Enterprises **1**	1250	•	•	62	230	63	39	26	•	•	•	0	0

Revenues ($ in Thousands)

Item Description for Accounting Period 7/06 Through 6/07	Total	Zero Assets	Under 500	500 to 1,000	1,000 to 5,000	5,000 to 10,000	10,000 to 25,000	25,000 to 50,000	50,000 to 100,000	100,000 to 250,000	250,000 to 500,000	500,000 to 2,500,000	2,500,000 and over
Net Sales **2**	32462042	•	•	60707	2294709	1071488	1349039	1635022	•	•	•	0	0
Interest **3**	50799	•	•	0	1749	16	819	1577	•	•	•	0	0
Rents **4**	39124	•	•	0	5181	38	115	0	•	•	•	0	0
Royalties **5**	14938	•	•	0	0	0	0	3394	•	•	•	0	0
Other Portfolio Income **6**	305867	•	•	0	1913	243	1265	3304	•	•	•	0	0
Other Receipts **7**	138437	•	•	0	10671	5861	5441	13960	•	•	•	0	0
Total Receipts **8**	33011207	•	•	60707	2314223	1077646	1356679	1657257	•	•	•	0	0
Average Total Receipts **9**	26409	•	•	979	10062	17105	34787	63741	•	•	•	•	•

Operating Costs/Operating Income (%)

Item Description for Accounting Period 7/06 Through 6/07	Total	Zero Assets	Under 500	500 to 1,000	1,000 to 5,000	5,000 to 10,000	10,000 to 25,000	25,000 to 50,000	50,000 to 100,000	100,000 to 250,000	250,000 to 500,000	500,000 to 2,500,000	2,500,000 and over
Cost of Operations **10**	75.6	•	•	35.3	77.2	66.2	75.3	71.0	•	•	•	•	•
Salaries and Wages **11**	3.4	•	•	9.7	2.8	12.0	4.4	4.3	•	•	•	•	•
Taxes Paid **12**	2.0	•	•	3.9	1.4	1.9	0.8	1.4	•	•	•	•	•
Interest Paid **13**	0.7	•	•	0.4	0.6	0.5	1.0	0.8	•	•	•	•	•
Depreciation **14**	1.2	•	•	3.9	1.3	1.2	1.8	1.6	•	•	•	•	•
Amortization and Depletion **15**	0.7	•	•	•	0.0	0.0	0.1	0.2	•	•	•	•	•
Pensions and Other Deferred Comp. **16**	0.5	•	•	0.8	0.1	0.2	0.4	0.5	•	•	•	•	•
Employee Benefits **17**	2.2	•	•	0.1	0.9	2.6	0.8	0.9	•	•	•	•	•
Advertising **18**	0.4	•	•	0.5	1.3	0.9	1.1	1.0	•	•	•	•	•
Other Expenses **19**	5.0	•	•	31.5	6.8	4.3	7.6	11.3	•	•	•	•	•
Officers' Compensation **20**	1.3	•	•	8.5	4.9	1.6	1.5	1.3	•	•	•	•	•
Operating Margin **21**	6.9	•	•	5.5	2.7	8.5	5.3	5.7	•	•	•	•	•
Operating Margin Before Officers' Comp. **22**	8.2	•	•	14.0	7.5	10.1	6.9	7.0	•	•	•	•	•

Selected Average Balance Sheet ($ in Thousands)

Net Receivables 23	2076	16	271	1357	2864	4525
Inventories 24	3050	0	1731	2791	3342	5557
Net Property, Plant and Equipment 25	2722	287	717	1200	5284	8641
Total Assets 26	20496	937	3294	6156	16304	30370
Notes and Loans Payable 27	3407	821	987	1418	5433	6240
All Other Liabilities 28	7201	87	899	2140	4728	11372
Net Worth 29	9888	28	1409	2597	6143	12759

Selected Financial Ratios (Times to 1)

Current Ratio 30	1.5	1.9	1.8	2.2	1.6	1.8
Quick Ratio 31	0.5	0.7	0.3	0.8	0.7	0.8
Net Sales to Working Capital 32	9.7	15.9	9.4	6.5	9.5	8.7
Coverage Ratio 33	13.4	14.8	6.4	18.9	7.0	9.4
Total Asset Turnover 34	1.3	1.0	3.0	2.8	2.1	2.1
Inventory Turnover 35	6.4	•	4.4	4.0	7.8	8.0
Receivables Turnover 36	13.2	121.8	22.1	•	14.4	15.8
Total Liabilities to Net Worth 37	1.1	32.4	1.3	1.4	1.7	1.4
Current Assets to Working Capital 38	3.1	2.2	2.3	1.9	2.6	2.2
Current Liabilities to Working Capital 39	2.1	1.2	1.3	0.9	1.6	1.2
Working Capital to Net Sales 40	0.1	0.1	0.1	0.2	0.1	0.1
Inventory to Working Capital 41	1.3	•	1.3	1.1	1.0	0.8
Total Receipts to Cash Flow 42	8.7	3.9	12.1	8.6	8.6	6.7
Cost of Goods to Cash Flow 43	6.6	1.4	9.3	5.7	6.5	4.7
Cash Flow to Total Debt 44	0.3	0.3	0.4	0.6	0.4	0.5

Selected Financial Factors (in Percentages)

Debt Ratio 45	51.8	97.0	57.2	57.8	62.3	58.0
Return on Total Assets 46	12.1	6.2	12.6	26.5	14.6	16.2
Return on Equity Before Income Taxes 47	23.2	192.2	24.8	59.4	33.2	34.5
Return on Equity After Income Taxes 48	16.6	161.8	21.1	57.6	28.5	30.0
Profit Margin (Before Income Tax) 49	8.8	5.5	3.5	9.1	5.9	7.0
Profit Margin (After Income Tax) 50	6.3	4.6	3.0	8.8	5.1	6.1

Table I

Corporations with and without Net Income

OTHER TRANSPORTATION EQUIPMENT AND RAILROAD ROLLING STOCK

MONEY AMOUNTS AND SIZE OF ASSETS IN THOUSANDS OF DOLLARS

Item Description for Accounting Period 7/06 Through 6/07	Total	Zero Assets	Under 500	500 to 1,000	1,000 to 5,000	5,000 to 10,000	10,000 to 25,000	25,000 to 50,000	50,000 to 100,000	100,000 to 250,000	250,000 to 500,000	500,000 to 2,500,000	2,500,000 and over
Number of Enterprises 1	1335	6	756	123	275	58	56	21	12	11	7	9	0
Revenues ($ in Thousands)													
Net Sales 2	29983590	110748	128381	409466	1308311	737822	1800745	1831411	1016903	3082383	4577468	14879952	0
Interest 3	705159	0	2	42	2136	17	3770	3685	1608	6872	7818	679210	0
Rents 4	70644	0	0	0	0	2091	0	0	148	14	617	67774	0
Royalties 5	70506	0	0	0	0	0	30	595	590	5373	15	63902	0
Other Portfolio Income 6	147424	2064	0	351	0	0	5430	19195	1091	2243	1480	115571	0
Other Receipts 7	204030	0	578	15	2491	431	7622	2638	6202	14963	50510	118580	0
Total Receipts 8	31081353	112812	128961	409874	1312938	740361	1817597	1857524	1026542	3111848	4637908	15924989	0
Average Total Receipts 9	23282	18802	171	3332	4774	12765	32457	88454	85545	282895	662558	1769443	•
Operating Costs/Operating Income (%)													
Cost of Operations 10	72.0	79.9	62.5	75.1	82.7	69.5	77.4	78.8	75.3	83.7	80.9	64.2	•
Salaries and Wages 11	5.6	2.6	1.2	0.9	2.9	11.0	5.6	4.3	6.4	3.2	3.4	7.1	•
Taxes Paid 12	1.5	2.1	1.0	1.5	1.4	1.9	1.9	2.2	1.7	0.9	1.0	1.6	•
Interest Paid 13	2.1	0.4	6.4	1.0	1.1	0.9	0.8	1.3	2.1	0.9	0.5	3.3	•
Depreciation 14	2.2	0.6	2.2	1.8	2.1	1.8	1.4	0.9	1.4	1.3	1.8	2.8	•
Amortization and Depletion 15	0.6	•	0.1	0.0	0.1	0.0	0.1	0.3	1.0	0.3	0.1	0.9	•
Pensions and Other Deferred Comp. 16	0.4	0.3	0.0	0.1	0.1	0.1	0.1	0.1	0.7	0.1	0.3	0.6	•
Employee Benefits 17	1.6	2.3	0.9	1.7	0.4	3.1	1.0	0.9	1.2	0.8	1.1	2.2	•
Advertising 18	0.8	0.1	3.8	0.5	0.4	0.1	0.5	0.8	0.5	1.6	0.9	0.8	•
Other Expenses 19	8.5	•	23.1	8.9	4.3	7.3	7.3	7.1	12.5	4.1	4.2	11.2	•
Officers' Compensation 20	0.9	0.2	4.7	4.8	4.5	1.1	1.4	2.1	1.4	0.3	0.5	0.3	•
Operating Margin 21	3.9	12.1	•	3.8	•	3.3	2.6	1.4	•	2.8	5.2	5.1	•
Operating Margin Before Officers' Comp. 22	4.7	12.2	•	8.6	4.3	4.4	4.0	3.5	•	3.1	5.8	5.4	•

Selected Average Balance Sheet ($ in Thousands)

Net Receivables 23	4055	0	22	157	886	1485	4080	7618	11378	30609	53113	423801	•
Inventories 24	3668	0	29	128	682	4335	3582	12555	13052	34262	88048	214455	•
Net Property, Plant and Equipment 25	3608	0	36	133	304	1452	2868	5521	7254	26780	73515	381325	•
Total Assets 26	16895	0	104	859	2550	8452	15781	32016	66237	163596	351646	1618521	•
Notes and Loans Payable 27	5172	0	138	337	1292	1600	3545	11804	22621	22284	45006	559167	•
All Other Liabilities 28	6673	0	7	346	5237	3801	4452	10822	20017	80332	146881	507894	•
Net Worth 29	5050	0	-41	176	-3980	3051	7783	9390	23599	60980	159758	551460	•

Selected Financial Ratios (Times to 1)

Current Ratio 30	1.5	•	1.0	2.4	1.9	1.8	1.9	1.4	1.4	1.4	1.6	1.5	•
Quick Ratio 31	0.8	•	0.4	1.0	1.3	0.4	1.0	0.6	0.5	0.5	0.9	0.8	•
Net Sales to Working Capital 32	6.2	•	•	8.6	4.6	4.2	6.6	15.3	8.8	9.8	7.4	5.2	•
Coverage Ratio 33	4.7	36.1	0.1	5.0	1.1	5.1	5.3	3.0	•	5.2	13.4	4.7	•
Total Asset Turnover 34	1.3	•	1.6	3.9	1.9	1.5	2.0	2.7	1.3	1.7	1.9	1.0	•
Inventory Turnover 35	4.4	•	3.7	19.5	5.8	2.0	6.9	5.5	4.9	6.8	6.0	4.9	•
Receivables Turnover 36	5.5	•	7.0	•	5.6	7.5	9.7	9.9	6.9	10.0	12.7	6.1	•
Total Liabilities to Net Worth 37	2.3	•	•	3.9	1.8	1.8	1.0	2.4	1.8	1.7	1.2	1.9	•
Current Assets to Working Capital 38	2.8	•	•	1.7	2.1	2.3	2.1	3.8	3.5	3.8	2.6	2.9	•
Current Liabilities to Working Capital 39	1.8	•	•	0.7	1.1	1.3	1.1	2.8	2.5	2.8	1.6	1.9	•
Working Capital to Net Sales 40	0.2	•	•	0.1	0.2	0.2	0.2	0.1	0.1	0.1	0.1	0.2	•
Inventory to Working Capital 41	1.0	•	•	0.3	0.6	1.8	0.7	1.9	1.9	1.3	1.1	0.8	•
Total Receipts to Cash Flow 42	6.9	8.3	8.4	10.3	39.3	11.6	12.1	11.2	12.3	14.2	10.1	4.8	•
Cost of Goods to Cash Flow 43	5.0	6.6	5.2	7.8	32.5	8.1	9.4	8.8	9.2	11.9	8.2	3.1	•
Cash Flow to Total Debt 44	0.3	•	0.1	0.5	0.0	0.2	0.3	0.3	0.2	0.2	0.3	0.3	•

Selected Financial Factors (in Percentages)

Debt Ratio 45	70.1	•	139.4	79.6	256.1	63.9	50.7	70.7	64.4	62.7	54.6	65.9	•
Return on Total Assets 46	13.3	•	1.3	18.8	2.2	6.9	8.9	10.4	•	7.8	13.1	15.8	•
Return on Equity Before Income Taxes 47	35.0	•	23.0	73.6	•	15.3	14.6	23.5	•	16.9	26.8	36.7	•
Return on Equity After Income Taxes 48	22.4	•	23.0	58.2	0.2	15.2	12.6	21.4	•	11.8	17.9	23.0	•
Profit Margin (Before Income Tax) 49	7.9	13.9	•	3.9	0.1	3.7	3.5	2.5	•	3.7	6.5	12.2	•
Profit Margin (After Income Tax) 50	5.1	13.9	•	3.1	•	3.7	3.1	2.3	•	2.6	4.4	7.7	•

159

Table II
Corporations with Net Income

OTHER TRANSPORTATION EQUIPMENT AND RAILROAD ROLLING STOCK

MONEY AMOUNTS AND SIZE OF ASSETS IN THOUSANDS OF DOLLARS

Item Description for Accounting Period 7/06 Through 6/07	Total	Zero Assets	Under 500	500 to 1,000	1,000 to 5,000	5,000 to 10,000	10,000 to 25,000	25,000 to 50,000	50,000 to 100,000	100,000 to 250,000	250,000 to 500,000	500,000 to 2,500,000	2,500,000 and over
Number of Enterprises **1**	462	•	98	123	108	44	39	15	9	•	•	6	0
Revenues ($ in Thousands)													
Net Sales **2**	25713153	•	60932	409466	839919	496015	1552702	1483390	838417	•	•	13281785	0
Interest **3**	677448	•	2	42	2122	0	1289	636	1344	•	•	660179	0
Rents **4**	67913	•	0	0	0	0	0	0	125	•	•	67774	0
Royalties **5**	69457	•	0	0	0	0	30	595	152	•	•	63306	0
Other Portfolio Income **6**	147074	•	0	351	0	0	5430	19145	1091	•	•	115571	0
Other Receipts **7**	185829	•	477	15	1020	370	1999	2095	1935	•	•	113194	0
Total Receipts **8**	26860874	•	61411	409874	843061	496385	1561450	1505861	843064	•	•	14301809	0
Average Total Receipts **9**	58140	•	627	3332	7806	11281	40037	100391	93674	•	•	2383635	•
Operating Costs/Operating Income (%)													
Cost of Operations **10**	70.4	•	57.7	75.1	82.3	63.8	74.4	79.8	71.6	•	•	62.6	•
Salaries and Wages **11**	5.6	•	2.6	0.9	3.3	15.1	5.7	3.3	5.8	•	•	7.2	•
Taxes Paid **12**	1.5	•	0.3	1.5	1.1	2.2	1.6	1.5	1.9	•	•	1.8	•
Interest Paid **13**	1.8	•	2.9	1.0	0.2	0.8	0.6	0.8	1.4	•	•	2.8	•
Depreciation **14**	2.1	•	3.9	1.8	0.1	1.7	1.1	0.6	1.5	•	•	3.0	•
Amortization and Depletion **15**	0.5	•	0.1	0.0	0.0	0.0	0.0	0.1	1.0	•	•	0.8	•
Pensions and Other Deferred Comp. **16**	0.4	•	0.0	0.0	0.2	0.0	0.1	0.1	0.8	•	•	0.6	•
Employee Benefits **17**	1.7	•	2.0	1.7	0.0	3.7	1.0	0.8	1.4	•	•	2.3	•
Advertising **18**	0.9	•	0.8	0.5	0.0	0.1	0.5	0.8	0.3	•	•	0.8	•
Other Expenses **19**	8.0	•	13.7	8.9	6.6	5.3	7.2	6.5	4.5	•	•	11.0	•
Officers' Compensation **20**	0.8	•	10.0	4.8	6.6	1.6	1.2	1.3	1.4	•	•	0.3	•
Operating Margin **21**	6.3	•	6.0	3.8	6.9	5.7	6.6	4.1	8.4	•	•	6.7	•
Operating Margin Before Officers' Comp. **22**	7.1	•	16.0	8.6	13.5	7.4	7.7	5.4	9.8	•	•	7.0	•

Selected Average Balance Sheet ($ in Thousands)

Item											
Net Receivables **23**	10064	•	170	157	1796	1375	5589	7031	12280	•	579559
Inventories **24**	8381	•	26	64	811	6335	3643	14045	15626	•	284002
Net Property, Plant and Equipment **25**	9226	•	47	133	43	1407	2772	4460	9188	•	556692
Total Assets **26**	38701	•	278	859	3826	9127	15987	28976	63841	•	2018871
Notes and Loans Payable **27**	10276	•	245	337	629	1483	3554	10470	14606	•	633602
All Other Liabilities **28**	14668	•	52	346	12576	4051	4745	9348	16995	•	577814
Net Worth **29**	13757	•	-19	176	-9378	3593	7688	9159	32240	•	807455

Selected Financial Ratios (Times to 1)

Item									
Current Ratio **30**	1.7	•	4.0	2.4	1.8	1.9	2.1	1.6	1.7
Quick Ratio **31**	0.9	•	3.5	1.0	1.4	0.4	1.2	0.7	0.7
Net Sales to Working Capital **32**	5.5	•	4.0	8.6	4.6	2.9	6.2	11.8	7.0
Coverage Ratio **33**	7.1	•	3.3	5.0	37.3	8.2	13.9	7.3	7.5
Total Asset Turnover **34**	1.4	•	2.2	3.9	2.0	1.2	2.5	3.4	1.5
Inventory Turnover **35**	4.7	•	13.7	38.9	7.9	1.1	8.1	5.6	4.9
Receivables Turnover **36**	5.4	•	3.3	42.2	•	•	9.7	9.9	•
Total Liabilities to Net Worth **37**	1.8	•	•	3.9	•	1.5	1.1	2.2	1.5
Current Assets to Working Capital **38**	2.4	•	1.3	1.7	2.2	2.1	1.9	2.6	2.5
Current Liabilities to Working Capital **39**	1.4	•	0.3	0.7	1.2	1.1	0.9	1.6	1.5
Working Capital to Net Sales **40**	0.2	•	0.3	0.1	0.2	0.3	0.2	0.1	0.2
Inventory to Working Capital **41**	0.7	•	0.2	0.3	0.5	1.7	0.5	1.4	0.6
Total Receipts to Cash Flow **42**	6.0	•	5.4	10.3	18.3	11.5	8.6	8.8	4.4
Cost of Goods to Cash Flow **43**	4.2	•	3.1	7.8	15.1	7.3	6.4	7.0	2.8
Cash Flow to Total Debt **44**	0.4	•	0.4	0.5	0.0	0.2	0.6	0.6	0.4

Selected Financial Factors (in Percentages)

Item											
Debt Ratio **45**	64.5	•	106.8	79.6	345.1	60.6	51.9	68.4	49.5	•	60.0
Return on Total Assets **46**	18.0	•	21.7	18.8	15.1	8.2	19.1	20.9	14.9	•	19.0
Return on Equity Before Income Taxes **47**	43.5	•	•	73.6	•	18.2	37.0	57.2	25.5	•	39.8
Return on Equity After Income Taxes **48**	30.1	•	•	58.2	•	18.1	34.0	54.3	18.2	•	25.8
Profit Margin (Before Income Tax) **49**	10.8	•	6.8	3.9	7.3	5.8	7.1	5.3	8.8	•	14.5
Profit Margin (After Income Tax) **50**	7.4	•	6.8	3.1	6.9	5.8	6.6	5.0	6.3	•	9.4

Table I

Corporations with and without Net Income

FURNITURE AND RELATED PRODUCT MANUFACTURING

MONEY AMOUNTS AND SIZE OF ASSETS IN THOUSANDS OF DOLLARS

Item Description for Accounting Period 7/06 Through 6/07	Total	Zero Assets	Under 500	500 to 1,000	1,000 to 5,000	5,000 to 10,000	10,000 to 25,000	25,000 to 50,000	50,000 to 100,000	100,000 to 250,000	250,000 to 500,000	500,000 to 2,500,000	2,500,000 and over
Number of Enterprises **1**	13155	1740	8159	1223	1441	272	176	71	25	25	7	15	0
Revenues ($ in Thousands)													
Net Sales **2**	84308759	768175	4743529	2599880	10222735	5401693	5740798	4976401	3162130	5914973	3798306	36980138	0
Interest **3**	190141	68	1403	545	7171	5102	4241	5262	3519	3920	12929	145980	0
Rents **4**	52350	0	377	0	342	1006	324	5844	618	1229	11248	31362	0
Royalties **5**	61396	0	0	0	0	0	0	706	423	16	850	59402	0
Other Portfolio Income **6**	531358	7070	24444	27568	27780	1930	8809	16607	9292	11843	19205	376811	0
Other Receipts **7**	981332	26216	67623	10200	38300	10155	32461	27840	15586	34781	17291	700878	0
Total Receipts **8**	86125336	801529	4837376	2638193	10296328	5419886	5786633	5032660	3191568	5966762	3859829	38294571	0
Average Total Receipts **9**	6547	461	593	2157	7145	19926	32879	70883	127663	238670	551404	2552971	•
Operating Costs/Operating Income (%)													
Cost of Operations **10**	66.4	58.6	60.4	63.8	66.5	67.7	70.6	70.3	74.0	72.8	62.5	64.8	•
Salaries and Wages **11**	7.6	10.2	10.6	6.8	8.7	10.7	7.0	6.8	5.9	5.1	9.1	7.0	•
Taxes Paid **12**	2.1	2.3	3.0	2.8	2.5	1.6	2.3	2.2	1.8	1.5	2.1	2.1	•
Interest Paid **13**	1.5	5.3	0.8	1.1	0.9	1.3	1.1	1.1	1.8	1.6	1.0	2.0	•
Depreciation **14**	1.4	1.6	1.2	1.4	1.4	0.8	1.5	1.6	1.2	1.6	2.0	1.5	•
Amortization and Depletion **15**	0.5	0.6	0.1	0.1	0.0	0.1	0.1	0.1	0.3	0.5	0.1	0.9	•
Pensions and Other Deferred Comp. **16**	0.6	0.0	0.1	0.2	0.9	0.3	0.7	0.4	0.4	0.4	0.6	0.7	•
Employee Benefits **17**	1.9	2.0	0.8	1.3	1.5	1.6	2.1	1.8	1.7	2.2	1.9	2.2	•
Advertising **18**	1.9	0.6	0.5	0.3	1.4	0.7	0.6	1.3	1.4	1.0	4.9	2.7	•
Other Expenses **19**	11.4	15.2	16.1	11.2	10.9	8.7	8.7	10.1	8.9	8.9	14.4	12.3	•
Officers' Compensation **20**	1.8	6.0	7.2	5.1	2.4	4.8	2.0	1.3	0.9	0.9	0.8	0.5	•
Operating Margin **21**	2.8	•	•	5.9	3.1	1.7	3.3	3.0	1.7	3.5	0.6	3.4	•
Operating Margin Before Officers' Comp. **22**	4.6	3.5	6.3	11.0	5.5	6.5	5.3	4.3	2.6	4.4	1.4	3.9	•

Selected Average Balance Sheet ($ in Thousands)

Net Receivables 23	710	0	27	256	672	1873	3675	8459	16488	31289	72912	292041	•
Inventories 24	587	0	21	130	543	2383	3612	7837	21734	28645	53070	157958	•
Net Property, Plant and Equipment 25	716	0	30	112	518	1221	3780	10249	13718	32500	89557	318405	•
Total Assets 26	3823	0	114	742	2256	7288	14983	36271	71682	130925	357245	2029762	•
Notes and Loans Payable 27	1289	0	62	342	1014	3348	4510	9547	27125	44266	60834	665278	•
All Other Liabilities 28	1082	0	46	165	942	2238	2833	8119	16769	27469	115731	579572	•
Net Worth 29	1453	0	6	235	300	1703	7640	18606	27788	59191	180681	784912	•

Selected Financial Ratios (Times to 1)

Current Ratio 30	1.6	•	1.3	2.3	1.7	2.1	2.1	1.9	1.9	1.9	1.7	1.3	•
Quick Ratio 31	0.8	•	0.9	1.5	0.9	0.9	1.1	1.0	0.9	1.0	1.0	0.7	•
Net Sales to Working Capital 32	10.4	•	39.4	6.7	10.9	6.7	6.8	6.5	6.3	6.9	8.1	15.2	•
Coverage Ratio 33	4.3	1.3	2.2	7.9	5.3	2.6	4.8	4.9	2.4	3.8	3.1	4.7	•
Total Asset Turnover 34	1.7	•	5.1	2.9	3.1	2.7	2.2	1.9	1.8	1.8	1.5	1.2	•
Inventory Turnover 35	7.3	•	17.0	10.4	8.7	5.6	6.4	6.3	4.3	6.0	6.4	10.1	•
Receivables Turnover 36	8.8	•	19.6	7.7	12.1	11.2	9.0	9.3	6.8	8.3	8.3	10.4	•
Total Liabilities to Net Worth 37	1.6	•	17.6	2.2	6.5	3.3	1.0	0.9	1.6	1.2	1.0	1.6	•
Current Assets to Working Capital 38	2.8	•	4.7	1.8	2.5	1.9	1.9	2.1	2.1	2.1	2.4	4.3	•
Current Liabilities to Working Capital 39	1.8	•	3.7	0.8	1.5	0.9	0.9	1.1	1.1	1.1	1.4	3.3	•
Working Capital to Net Sales 40	0.1	•	0.0	0.1	0.1	0.1	0.1	0.2	0.2	0.1	0.1	0.1	•
Inventory to Working Capital 41	1.0	•	1.4	0.5	1.0	0.9	0.8	0.8	1.0	0.8	0.8	1.3	•
Total Receipts to Cash Flow 42	7.3	8.1	8.7	7.4	9.3	13.7	9.2	8.0	9.9	8.5	7.8	5.8	•
Cost of Goods to Cash Flow 43	4.8	4.8	5.3	4.7	6.2	9.3	6.5	5.7	7.3	6.2	4.9	3.8	•
Cash Flow to Total Debt 44	0.4	•	0.6	0.6	0.4	0.3	0.5	0.5	0.3	0.4	0.4	0.3	•

Selected Financial Factors (in Percentages)

Debt Ratio 45	62.0	•	94.6	68.4	86.7	76.6	49.0	48.7	61.2	54.8	49.4	61.3	•
Return on Total Assets 46	11.2	•	9.5	24.2	14.7	9.0	11.4	10.2	7.8	10.7	4.6	11.3	•
Return on Equity Before Income Taxes 47	22.6	•	97.9	66.8	90.0	23.9	17.6	15.8	11.9	17.5	6.2	22.9	•
Return on Equity After Income Taxes 48	17.4	•	79.5	65.8	85.5	21.2	15.4	13.7	10.5	14.0	3.3	16.2	•
Profit Margin (Before Income Tax) 49	5.1	1.8	1.0	7.4	3.8	2.0	4.1	4.2	2.6	4.4	2.1	7.3	•
Profit Margin (After Income Tax) 50	4.0	1.5	0.8	7.3	3.6	1.8	3.6	3.6	2.3	3.5	1.1	5.2	•

Table II
Corporations with Net Income

FURNITURE AND RELATED PRODUCT MANUFACTURING

MONEY AMOUNTS AND SIZE OF ASSETS IN THOUSANDS OF DOLLARS

Item Description for Accounting Period 7/06 Through 6/07	Total	Zero Assets	Under 500	500 to 1,000	1,000 to 5,000	5,000 to 10,000	10,000 to 25,000	25,000 to 50,000	50,000 to 100,000	100,000 to 250,000	250,000 to 500,000	500,000 to 2,500,000	2,500,000 and over
Number of Enterprises **1**	8934	1457	4898	1058	1111	•	142	59	15	20	•	•	0
Revenues ($ in Thousands)													
Net Sales **2**	72378982	418855	3194261	2298276	8567589	•	4452261	4310672	2207107	4901278	•	•	0
Interest **3**	179453	45	869	478	5202	•	3740	4785	3480	3470	•	•	0
Rents **4**	48176	0	1	0	342	•	324	4813	543	1229	•	•	0
Royalties **5**	61396	0	0	0	0	•	0	706	423	16	•	•	0
Other Portfolio Income **6**	512328	4690	23891	27537	19857	•	8015	16151	8795	7791	•	•	0
Other Receipts **7**	875880	11524	26597	10200	20836	•	24150	17570	12116	31524	•	•	0
Total Receipts **8**	74056215	435114	3245619	2336491	8613826	•	4488490	4354697	2232464	4945308	•	•	0
Average Total Receipts **9**	8289	299	663	2208	7753	•	31609	73808	148831	247265	•	•	•
Operating Costs/Operating Income (%)													
Cost of Operations **10**	65.7	54.2	58.0	63.4	65.3	•	67.8	68.6	73.3	72.8	•	•	•
Salaries and Wages **11**	7.3	12.9	11.5	6.4	8.1	•	7.1	7.1	5.6	5.0	•	•	•
Taxes Paid **12**	2.1	2.6	2.7	2.6	2.3	•	2.3	2.3	1.9	1.6	•	•	•
Interest Paid **13**	1.4	0.1	0.7	1.2	0.7	•	0.8	0.8	1.2	1.2	•	•	•
Depreciation **14**	1.4	2.4	0.9	1.5	1.4	•	1.4	1.6	1.2	1.5	•	•	•
Amortization and Depletion **15**	0.4	0.1	0.1	0.1	0.0	•	0.1	0.1	0.2	0.2	•	•	•
Pensions and Other Deferred Comp. **16**	0.6	0.1	0.1	0.3	1.0	•	0.7	0.4	0.5	0.5	•	•	•
Employee Benefits **17**	1.9	1.4	0.4	1.4	1.7	•	1.7	1.7	1.8	2.2	•	•	•
Advertising **18**	1.9	0.3	0.4	0.2	1.2	•	0.6	1.4	1.4	0.8	•	•	•
Other Expenses **19**	11.4	13.8	15.7	10.7	10.8	•	9.1	10.0	6.9	8.1	•	•	•
Officers' Compensation **20**	1.5	8.0	6.4	4.8	2.5	•	1.9	1.3	1.1	1.0	•	•	•
Operating Margin **21**	4.3	4.0	3.1	7.3	5.0	•	6.3	4.9	4.8	5.2	•	•	•
Operating Margin Before Officers' Comp. **22**	5.8	12.0	9.5	12.1	7.5	•	8.3	6.2	5.9	6.2	•	•	•

Selected Average Balance Sheet ($ in Thousands)

Net Receivables 23	907	0	28	285	645	3638	9074	18380	32122
Inventories 24	694	0	13	109	429	3351	7292	23658	27851
Net Property, Plant and Equipment 25	905	0	22	106	522	3613	11021	14708	34458
Total Assets 26	4910	0	104	760	2171	14798	36013	74446	133718
Notes and Loans Payable 27	1476	0	42	355	653	3565	7511	18848	35979
All Other Liabilities 28	1370	0	34	173	719	2581	7207	14024	27501
Net Worth 29	2064	0	29	232	799	8651	21294	41574	70238

Selected Financial Ratios (Times to 1)

Current Ratio 30	1.6		1.6	2.1	1.9	2.5	2.3	2.7	2.3
Quick Ratio 31	0.9		1.3	1.5	1.1	1.3	1.2	1.3	1.2
Net Sales to Working Capital 32	10.3		25.9	7.1	10.8	5.6	5.9	5.1	5.9
Coverage Ratio 33	5.9	66.0	7.5	8.5	9.5	9.7	8.7	6.0	6.0
Total Asset Turnover 34	1.7		6.2	2.9	3.6	2.1	2.0	2.0	1.8
Inventory Turnover 35	7.7		29.4	12.6	11.7	6.3	6.9	4.6	6.4
Receivables Turnover 36	8.7		21.9	9.3	15.1	9.0	9.1	6.7	8.6
Total Liabilities to Net Worth 37	1.4		2.6	2.3	1.7	0.7	0.7	0.8	0.9
Current Assets to Working Capital 38	2.7		2.6	1.9	2.2	1.7	1.8	1.6	1.8
Current Liabilities to Working Capital 39	1.7		1.6	0.9	1.2	0.7	0.8	0.6	0.8
Working Capital to Net Sales 40	0.1		0.0	0.1	0.1	0.2	0.2	0.2	0.2
Inventory to Working Capital 41	0.9		0.4	0.5	0.8	0.7	0.7	0.7	0.7
Total Receipts to Cash Flow 42	6.5	5.8	7.1	6.8	8.1	7.1	7.0	8.8	7.9
Cost of Goods to Cash Flow 43	4.2	3.2	4.1	4.3	5.3	4.8	4.8	6.4	5.7
Cash Flow to Total Debt 44	0.4		1.2	0.6	0.7	0.7	0.7	0.5	0.5

Selected Financial Factors (in Percentages)

Debt Ratio 45	58.0		72.6	69.5	63.2	41.5	40.9	44.2	47.5
Return on Total Assets 46	13.5		33.9	29.1	22.0	16.8	13.6	14.2	13.4
Return on Equity Before Income Taxes 47	26.6		107.2	84.1	53.5	25.8	20.4	21.2	21.2
Return on Equity After Income Taxes 48	21.3		100.7	82.9	51.3	23.5	18.2	19.7	17.5
Profit Margin (Before Income Tax) 49	6.8	7.9	4.7	9.0	5.5	7.1	5.9	6.0	6.1
Profit Margin (After Income Tax) 50	5.4	7.4	4.4	8.8	5.3	6.5	5.3	5.6	5.0

Table I

Corporations with and without Net Income

MEDICAL EQUIPMENT AND SUPPLIES

MONEY AMOUNTS AND SIZE OF ASSETS IN THOUSANDS OF DOLLARS

Item Description for Accounting Period 7/06 Through 6/07	Total	Zero Assets	Under 500	500 to 1,000	1,000 to 5,000	5,000 to 10,000	10,000 to 25,000	25,000 to 50,000	50,000 to 100,000	100,000 to 250,000	250,000 to 500,000	500,000 to 2,500,000	2,500,000 and over
Number of Enterprises **1**	8906	628	5923	439	1281	131	187	114	63	52	29	46	12
Revenues ($ in Thousands)													
Net Sales **2**	112367009	651160	2258995	913731	6780239	957509	4175397	4802324	3348935	7608103	6994184	31488033	42388398
Interest **3**	2367766	23153	2737	728	8492	17191	27645	37534	42341	75396	66593	396590	1669365
Rents **4**	48508	138	0	1	22	139	156	959	226	3568	19610	20539	3149
Royalties **5**	2850527	559	0	0	4148	644	1942	60372	11483	80756	20611	240287	2429725
Other Portfolio Income **6**	3135108	8619	13185	0	10524	1118	25692	45266	40809	101363	80666	723410	2084457
Other Receipts **7**	2958711	8931	36913	551	32639	43800	35887	39923	57575	380238	114280	423374	1784602
Total Receipts **8**	123727629	692560	2311830	915011	6836064	1020401	4266719	4986378	3501369	8249424	7295944	33292233	50359696
Average Total Receipts **9**	13893	1103	390	2084	5337	7789	22817	43740	55577	158643	251584	723744	4196641
Operating Costs/Operating Income (%)													
Cost of Operations **10**	50.3	46.5	38.8	53.4	60.1	53.5	55.9	56.5	49.7	47.5	43.8	50.0	49.9
Salaries and Wages **11**	15.1	19.6	12.2	9.8	12.2	22.9	16.3	17.0	17.4	18.1	16.8	13.3	15.7
Taxes Paid **12**	1.9	2.8	3.3	3.2	2.8	4.0	1.9	2.2	2.4	1.8	2.1	1.7	1.6
Interest Paid **13**	3.1	0.8	0.8	0.9	1.0	2.1	1.6	1.1	2.2	1.2	1.7	3.0	4.7
Depreciation **14**	2.4	2.1	1.8	0.6	1.2	2.2	1.9	2.2	2.7	2.3	2.2	2.1	2.8
Amortization and Depletion **15**	1.4	1.3	0.2	0.0	0.3	0.6	0.9	0.6	1.1	1.0	1.5	1.3	1.9
Pensions and Other Deferred Comp. **16**	0.6	0.1	0.5	0.2	0.4	0.4	0.4	0.4	0.5	0.5	0.8	0.7	0.7
Employee Benefits **17**	2.6	1.8	1.9	0.6	1.4	3.5	1.7	1.5	2.5	2.3	2.1	2.4	3.4
Advertising **18**	1.1	1.6	0.5	0.2	1.5	1.8	1.3	2.2	2.6	2.2	0.8	1.0	0.8
Other Expenses **19**	18.9	28.3	22.7	22.1	16.6	29.3	19.2	19.6	22.0	18.0	21.6	18.1	18.5
Officers' Compensation **20**	1.9	4.2	12.8	6.2	4.8	6.7	3.6	2.8	2.5	2.6	1.5	1.3	0.7
Operating Margin **21**	0.8	•	4.4	2.7	•	•	•	•	•	2.5	5.0	5.0	•
Operating Margin Before Officers' Comp. **22**	2.6	•	17.2	9.0	2.7	•	•	•	•	5.1	6.5	6.3	0.0

Selected Average Balance Sheet ($ in Thousands)

Item													
Net Receivables 23	2772	0	16	229	681	1191	4030	7029	11121	28688	50556	145964	961273
Inventories 24	1581	0	13	112	461	1657	3201	5296	7148	16360	30471	78424	512953
Net Property, Plant and Equipment 25	1976	0	22	92	276	592	2178	5036	9061	20268	38423	115047	665077
Total Assets 26	21120		81	707	2017	7516	16272	33909	68786	161111	341222	1061482	8782837
Notes and Loans Payable 27	4538	0	36	196	602	1772	4101	6395	14141	22498	64135	266078	1787854
All Other Liabilities 28	4738	0	26	250	697	1700	4179	8748	15147	37748	55266	217658	2041939
Net Worth 29	11844		18	260	718	4044	7993	18766	39498	100865	221821	577746	4953044

Selected Financial Ratios (Times to 1)

Item													
Current Ratio 30	2.0	•	1.1	1.5	1.7	2.8	2.1	2.2	2.5	2.2	2.8	2.1	1.8
Quick Ratio 31	1.2	•	0.7	0.9	1.1	1.6	1.3	1.5	1.6	1.3	1.6	1.2	1.0
Net Sales to Working Capital 32	3.4	•	143.9	11.0	8.4	2.0	3.7	3.6	2.5	3.3	2.4	3.6	3.1
Coverage Ratio 33	5.0	0.4	9.5	4.1	•	•	•	•	0.6	9.8	6.7	4.9	5.5
Total Asset Turnover 34	0.6	•	4.7	2.9	2.6	1.0	1.4	1.2	0.8	0.9	0.7	0.6	0.4
Inventory Turnover 35	4.0	•	11.3	9.9	6.9	2.4	3.9	4.5	3.7	4.2	3.5	4.4	3.4
Receivables Turnover 36	4.9	•	32.7	9.0	8.3	4.5	6.1	6.6	5.0	5.2	4.6	5.9	3.8
Total Liabilities to Net Worth 37	0.8	•	3.4	1.7	1.8	0.9	1.0	0.8	0.7	0.6	0.5	0.8	0.8
Current Assets to Working Capital 38	2.0	•	16.5	3.0	2.5	1.5	1.9	1.8	1.7	1.8	1.6	1.9	2.2
Current Liabilities to Working Capital 39	1.0	•	15.5	2.0	1.5	0.5	0.9	0.8	0.7	0.8	0.6	0.9	1.2
Working Capital to Net Sales 40	0.3	•	0.0	0.1	0.1	0.5	0.3	0.3	0.4	0.3	0.4	0.3	0.3
Inventory to Working Capital 41	0.5	•	4.7	0.6	0.8	0.4	0.6	0.4	0.3	0.4	0.3	0.5	0.5
Total Receipts to Cash Flow 42	3.7	4.4	4.4	4.9	10.8	19.6	7.1	7.2	5.5	3.7	3.5	3.8	2.9
Cost of Goods to Cash Flow 43	1.9	2.0	1.7	2.6	6.5	10.5	4.0	4.0	2.7	1.8	1.5	1.9	1.4
Cash Flow to Total Debt 44	0.4	•	1.4	1.0	0.4	0.1	0.4	0.4	0.3	0.6	0.4	0.4	0.3

Selected Financial Factors (in Percentages)

Item													
Debt Ratio 45	43.9	•	77.4	63.2	64.4	46.2	50.9	44.7	42.6	37.4	35.0	45.6	43.6
Return on Total Assets 46	9.1	•	35.4	11.2	•	•	•	•	1.1	11.0	8.0	9.5	10.3
Return on Equity Before Income Taxes 47	13.0	•	140.1	22.9	•	•	•	•	•	15.8	10.4	13.9	14.9
Return on Equity After Income Taxes 48	8.8	•	136.5	21.9	•	•	•	•	•	11.2	6.9	9.7	10.5
Profit Margin (Before Income Tax) 49	12.2	•	6.7	2.9	•	•	•	•	•	10.9	9.6	11.7	20.9
Profit Margin (After Income Tax) 50	8.3	•	6.5	2.7	•	•	•	•	•	7.7	6.4	8.2	14.7

Table II
Corporations with Net Income

MEDICAL EQUIPMENT AND SUPPLIES

MONEY AMOUNTS AND SIZE OF ASSETS IN THOUSANDS OF DOLLARS

Item Description for Accounting Period 7/06 Through 6/07	Total	Zero Assets	Under 500	500 to 1,000	1,000 to 5,000	5,000 to 10,000	10,000 to 25,000	25,000 to 50,000	50,000 to 100,000	100,000 to 250,000	250,000 to 500,000	500,000 to 2,500,000	2,500,000 and over
Number of Enterprises 1	6116	282	4124	372	973	56	114	54	37	40	20	35	9
Revenues ($ in Thousands)													
Net Sales 2	95304935	322161	1873497	911840	5211312	593609	3256145	3436938	2467859	6528708	5457903	26284071	38960893
Interest 3	2017665	20354	842	207	2053	4818	5544	6982	19996	55763	60570	293668	1546869
Rents 4	47957	138	0	1	5	26	5	928	182	3568	19610	20346	3149
Royalties 5	2769976	559	0	0	35	0	1150	57699	9450	80707	19199	197099	2404078
Other Portfolio Income 6	3029877	8572	13185	0	1646	429	20982	23607	34462	96223	76105	711024	2043643
Other Receipts 7	2665928	1471	36908	23	16695	35244	29588	19002	54565	378758	78689	330012	1684971
Total Receipts 8	105836338	353255	1924432	912071	5231746	634126	3313414	3545156	2586514	7143727	5712076	27836220	46643603
Average Total Receipts 9	17305	1253	467	2452	5377	11324	29065	65651	69906	178593	285604	795321	5182623
Operating Costs/Operating Income (%)													
Cost of Operations 10	50.4	47.8	39.5	53.5	56.2	49.5	57.0	58.9	48.9	49.5	44.0	49.1	50.7
Salaries and Wages 11	14.1	18.2	10.7	9.0	10.2	12.3	11.6	11.9	13.5	16.7	15.1	13.1	15.3
Taxes Paid 12	1.8	2.2	3.2	3.1	2.6	2.6	1.6	1.8	2.0	1.8	2.1	1.7	1.5
Interest Paid 13	2.7	0.5	0.6	0.8	0.5	0.6	0.9	0.4	1.9	1.2	1.3	2.2	4.5
Depreciation 14	2.3	1.4	1.5	0.6	0.8	1.5	1.4	1.7	2.4	2.2	2.3	2.2	2.7
Amortization and Depletion 15	1.2	1.2	0.2	0.0	0.1	0.1	0.3	0.3	0.8	0.9	0.7	1.0	1.8
Pensions and Other Deferred Comp. 16	0.6	0.0	0.5	0.2	0.3	0.3	0.5	0.5	0.6	0.5	0.9	0.6	0.7
Employee Benefits 17	2.6	2.2	2.0	0.5	1.0	1.3	1.3	1.0	2.3	2.3	1.8	2.4	3.4
Advertising 18	1.0	1.0	0.5	0.2	1.7	0.8	1.2	1.4	2.6	2.1	0.7	1.0	0.7
Other Expenses 19	16.8	18.6	20.8	19.1	13.0	12.8	13.6	12.7	17.8	14.9	20.1	16.7	17.6
Officers' Compensation 20	1.6	2.6	12.6	6.1	4.6	4.4	2.7	2.4	1.7	2.4	1.6	1.2	0.4
Operating Margin 21	5.0	4.4	7.8	6.9	9.0	13.7	7.9	7.0	5.6	5.5	9.4	8.8	0.6
Operating Margin Before Officers' Comp. 22	6.6	6.9	20.4	13.0	13.6	18.1	10.5	9.3	7.3	7.9	11.0	10.0	1.0

Selected Average Balance Sheet ($ in Thousands)

Net Receivables 23	3466	0	23	269	689	1554	5202	10257	13052	30839	54667	160864	1184726
Inventories 24	1981	0	15	103	458	2164	3710	6189	8334	17163	36669	84280	668575
Net Property, Plant and Equipment 25	2449	0	24	107	252	575	2546	6536	10111	22772	45672	130371	794988
Total Assets 26	25050	0	94	733	1872	7226	16355	35151	67130	165516	348345	1055440	10393743
Notes and Loans Payable 27	5283	0	37	195	373	71	3667	3486	12569	24817	45674	226899	2311165
All Other Liabilities 28	5151	0	27	241	559	1257	3633	11023	13300	38816	59861	224532	2064442
Net Worth 29	14615	0	30	298	940	5898	9055	20642	41261	101884	242810	604009	6018136

Selected Financial Ratios (Times to 1)

Current Ratio 30	2.2	•	1.1	1.6	2.2	5.0	2.2	2.0	2.8	2.1	2.7	2.4	2.2
Quick Ratio 31	1.3	•	0.8	0.9	1.4	2.1	1.4	1.3	1.7	1.3	1.7	1.4	1.1
Net Sales to Working Capital 32	3.2	•	75.5	11.1	6.8	2.1	4.2	5.8	3.0	3.7	2.5	3.2	2.7
Coverage Ratio 33	7.4	36.0	18.0	10.2	19.2	37.2	11.3	24.7	6.7	13.5	12.1	8.2	6.2
Total Asset Turnover 34	0.6	•	4.8	3.3	2.9	1.5	1.7	1.8	1.0	1.0	0.8	0.7	0.4
Inventory Turnover 35	4.0	•	12.2	12.8	6.6	2.4	4.4	6.1	3.9	4.7	3.3	4.4	3.3
Receivables Turnover 36	4.8	•	27.7	10.3	8.3	6.0	6.4	7.2	5.7	5.5	4.4	6.0	3.6
Total Liabilities to Net Worth 37	0.7	•	2.2	1.5	1.0	0.2	0.8	0.7	0.6	0.6	0.4	0.7	0.7
Current Assets to Working Capital 38	1.8	•	9.0	2.6	1.9	1.2	1.8	2.0	1.6	1.9	1.6	1.7	1.9
Current Liabilities to Working Capital 39	0.8	•	8.0	1.6	0.9	0.2	0.8	1.0	0.6	0.9	0.6	0.7	0.9
Working Capital to Net Sales 40	0.3	•	0.0	0.1	0.1	0.5	0.2	0.2	0.3	0.3	0.4	0.3	0.4
Inventory to Working Capital 41	0.4	•	2.6	0.6	0.6	0.4	0.6	0.5	0.4	0.4	0.3	0.4	0.4
Total Receipts to Cash Flow 42	3.3	3.4	3.9	4.5	5.4	3.3	4.8	5.0	3.9	3.6	3.1	3.5	2.8
Cost of Goods to Cash Flow 43	1.6	1.6	1.5	2.4	3.0	1.6	2.7	2.9	1.9	1.8	1.4	1.7	1.4
Cash Flow to Total Debt 44	0.5	•	1.8	1.2	1.1	2.4	0.8	0.9	0.7	0.7	0.8	0.5	0.4

Selected Financial Factors (in Percentages)

Debt Ratio 45	41.7	•	68.5	59.4	49.8	18.4	44.6	41.3	38.5	38.4	30.3	42.8	42.1
Return on Total Assets 46	12.6	•	54.0	25.7	28.4	30.9	18.4	19.0	12.5	15.9	12.2	12.7	11.5
Return on Equity Before Income Taxes 47	18.7	•	161.6	57.2	53.5	36.8	30.3	17.3	17.3	24.0	16.1	19.4	16.6
Return on Equity After Income Taxes 48	13.8	•	158.5	56.2	52.3	32.4	27.1	26.5	14.6	18.1	11.5	14.1	11.8
Profit Margin (Before Income Tax) 49	17.6	18.6	10.6	6.9	9.4	20.5	9.6	10.1	10.7	15.0	14.3	15.6	23.1
Profit Margin (After Income Tax) 50	13.0	13.3	10.4	6.8	9.2	18.0	8.6	8.6	9.1	11.3	10.2	11.4	16.4

Table I

Corporations with and without Net Income

OTHER MISCELLANEOUS MANUFACTURING

MONEY AMOUNTS AND SIZE OF ASSETS IN THOUSANDS OF DOLLARS

Item Description for Accounting Period 7/06 Through 6/07	Total	Zero Assets	Under 500	500 to 1,000	1,000 to 5,000	5,000 to 10,000	10,000 to 25,000	25,000 to 50,000	50,000 to 100,000	100,000 to 250,000	250,000 to 500,000	500,000 to 2,500,000	2,500,000 and over
Number of Enterprises 1	23105	1013	16541	2336	2009	380	458	174	84	54	31	22	3
Revenues ($ in Thousands)													
Net Sales 2	109633348	1632501	6813420	3364352	12264562	4544084	11007997	8790656	7802955	10606287	10059415	23668102	9079018
Interest 3	903595	17397	1523	2773	10730	6623	14681	30519	19162	28025	74120	199282	498760
Rents 4	43108	111	0	1617	2815	538	7999	1125	637	3904	21014	3322	26
Royalties 5	632085	15388	62	0	0	0	2049	14837	19509	23199	26810	134677	395555
Other Portfolio Income 6	1004142	83955	36180	12510	5603	16887	56126	43078	17265	64224	45425	503617	119271
Other Receipts 7	2090402	122922	59501	57991	29588	36451	114209	107889	124001	92147	203030	545105	597566
Total Receipts 8	114306680	1872274	6910686	3439243	12313298	4604583	11203061	8988104	7983529	10817786	10429814	25054105	10690196
Average Total Receipts 9	4947	1848	418	1472	6129	12117	24461	51656	95042	200329	336446	1138823	3563399
Operating Costs/Operating Income (%)													
Cost of Operations 10	64.5	69.2	48.9	58.7	66.5	60.5	66.7	66.9	66.3	63.8	65.6	70.1	55.5
Salaries and Wages 11	8.9	9.2	12.3	6.9	7.4	12.4	8.3	9.6	8.3	9.0	9.5	6.9	11.7
Taxes Paid 12	1.8	1.6	2.5	2.8	2.4	2.1	2.0	1.8	1.6	1.5	1.7	1.2	1.9
Interest Paid 13	2.7	4.1	1.4	1.3	1.0	1.7	1.7	1.6	2.1	2.4	3.9	2.8	7.9
Depreciation 14	1.8	1.7	1.2	1.0	1.4	2.4	1.9	2.0	1.5	2.4	2.4	1.5	2.4
Amortization and Depletion 15	0.7	1.1	0.1	0.6	0.1	0.2	0.5	0.6	0.5	0.7	1.2	0.7	2.5
Pensions and Other Deferred Comp. 16	0.5	1.1	0.6	0.0	0.4	0.4	0.3	0.4	0.4	0.6	0.3	0.4	1.1
Employee Benefits 17	1.5	1.3	1.5	1.4	1.3	2.3	1.6	2.0	1.5	1.3	1.9	1.3	1.5
Advertising 18	1.7	0.8	1.5	1.5	1.0	0.9	1.3	1.9	2.7	2.0	2.0	1.2	3.2
Other Expenses 19	13.5	21.4	18.6	20.2	11.3	12.1	12.3	10.3	11.6	9.3	13.2	12.4	23.1
Officers' Compensation 20	2.4	1.9	10.2	5.5	4.7	2.7	2.3	1.6	1.5	2.0	1.4	0.5	0.6
Operating Margin 21	0.1	•	1.0	0.3	2.5	2.2	1.0	1.3	2.0	5.1	•	1.0	•
Operating Margin Before Officers' Comp. 22	2.5	•	11.2	5.7	7.2	4.9	3.3	2.9	3.5	7.1	•	1.6	•

Selected Average Balance Sheet ($ in Thousands)

Net Receivables 23	702	0	36	192	758	1927	3806	8180	15340	32624	70371	160545	335473
Inventories 24	650	0	30	192	854	2662	4354	8101	14481	29234	41072	127796	359386
Net Property, Plant and Equipment 25	524	0	19	72	509	1449	2570	7183	10655	27388	55358	113509	340639
Total Assets 26	3649	0	117	679	2683	7103	15316	34137	67505	159676	357491	1036731	3851054
Notes and Loans Payable 27	1374	0	89	269	893	2570	5257	14747	24187	53555	150249	373682	1367028
All Other Liabilities 28	1080	0	53	180	853	1734	4592	9717	21597	44437	101270	314601	1072768
Net Worth 29	1195	0	-25	230	936	2800	5467	9673	21721	61685	105971	348449	1411258

Selected Financial Ratios (Times to 1)

Current Ratio 30	1.6	•	1.1	2.5	2.1	1.8	1.6	1.4	1.6	1.7	1.5	1.4	1.5
Quick Ratio 31	0.8	•	0.7	1.5	1.1	0.9	0.8	0.7	0.8	0.9	0.9	0.8	0.6
Net Sales to Working Capital 32	7.3	•	44.6	4.8	5.8	5.0	6.1	7.9	6.0	6.2	6.5	9.8	7.5
Coverage Ratio 33	3.1	1.4	2.7	2.9	3.8	3.1	2.6	3.2	3.1	3.9	1.2	5.5	1.9
Total Asset Turnover 34	1.3	•	3.5	2.1	2.3	1.7	1.6	1.5	1.4	1.2	0.9	1.0	0.8
Inventory Turnover 35	4.7	•	6.8	4.4	4.8	2.7	3.7	4.2	4.3	4.3	5.2	5.9	4.7
Receivables Turnover 36	6.9	•	12.2	7.9	8.1	6.1	6.1	6.0	5.9	6.0	5.6	7.0	7.8
Total Liabilities to Net Worth 37	2.1	•	•	2.0	1.9	1.5	1.8	2.5	2.1	1.6	2.4	2.0	1.7
Current Assets to Working Capital 38	2.7	•	9.4	1.7	1.9	2.2	2.6	3.3	2.6	2.5	3.1	3.2	3.2
Current Liabilities to Working Capital 39	1.7	•	8.4	0.7	0.9	1.2	1.6	2.3	1.6	1.5	2.1	2.2	2.2
Working Capital to Net Sales 40	0.1	•	0.0	0.2	0.2	0.2	0.2	0.1	0.2	0.2	0.2	0.1	0.1
Inventory to Working Capital 41	1.0	•	3.2	0.6	0.8	1.0	1.1	1.3	1.0	1.0	0.9	1.2	0.7
Total Receipts to Cash Flow 42	6.5	4.9	6.2	5.4	9.1	8.2	8.2	8.7	8.2	7.0	8.5	5.6	3.7
Cost of Goods to Cash Flow 43	4.2	3.4	3.0	3.2	6.0	5.0	5.5	5.8	4.8	4.4	5.6	3.9	2.1
Cash Flow to Total Debt 44	0.3	•	0.5	0.6	0.4	0.3	0.3	0.2	0.3	0.3	0.2	0.3	0.3

Selected Financial Factors (in Percentages)

Debt Ratio 45	67.3	•	121.2	66.2	65.1	60.6	64.3	71.7	67.8	61.4	70.4	66.4	63.4
Return on Total Assets 46	10.8	•	13.5	8.0	9.0	8.9	7.0	7.6	8.9	11.7	4.2	16.0	11.7
Return on Equity Before Income Taxes 47	22.4	•	•	15.5	19.1	15.2	12.1	18.4	18.6	22.6	2.1	38.9	14.9
Return on Equity After Income Taxes 48	16.1	•	•	14.8	17.7	13.5	9.3	13.5	14.3	18.6	•	27.0	8.7
Profit Margin (Before Income Tax) 49	5.6	1.5	2.4	2.5	2.9	3.6	2.8	3.5	4.4	7.1	0.7	12.6	6.9
Profit Margin (After Income Tax) 50	4.0	•	2.3	2.4	2.7	3.2	2.1	2.6	3.3	5.9	•	8.7	4.0

Table II

Corporations with Net Income

OTHER MISCELLANEOUS MANUFACTURING

MONEY AMOUNTS AND SIZE OF ASSETS IN THOUSANDS OF DOLLARS

Item Description for Accounting Period 7/06 Through 6/07	Total	Zero Assets	Under 500	500 to 1,000	1,000 to 5,000	5,000 to 10,000	10,000 to 25,000	25,000 to 50,000	50,000 to 100,000	100,000 to 250,000	250,000 to 500,000	500,000 to 2,500,000	2,500,000 and over
Number of Enterprises **1**	14403	320	9987	1731	1514	256	335	123	62	39	17	18	0
Revenues ($ in Thousands)													
Net Sales **2**	79106129	1149828	4467995	2401396	10496698	3642201	8326234	6936203	6349162	8632111	6682373	20021929	0
Interest **3**	364667	16405	1219	1414	4428	3037	7063	27375	8753	23918	47011	224045	0
Rents **4**	33495	111	0	911	2815	501	3400	708	568	1469	19849	3163	0
Royalties **5**	553200	15388	62	0	0	0	1109	5175	16322	15977	25417	473750	0
Other Portfolio Income **6**	839301	66339	35038	12501	4175	16191	39313	37017	15514	64072	30587	518550	0
Other Receipts **7**	1352462	117599	2007	57485	39974	10654	94938	80832	103011	75812	108945	661207	0
Total Receipts **8**	82249254	1365670	4506321	2473707	10548090	3672584	8472057	7087310	6493330	8813359	6914182	21902644	0
Average Total Receipts **9**	5711	4268	451	1429	6967	14346	25290	57620	104731	225984	406717	1216814	•
Operating Costs/Operating Income (%)													
Cost of Operations **10**	60.8	60.4	45.0	58.0	66.7	58.8	64.6	64.7	64.3	62.3	63.5	56.3	•
Salaries and Wages **11**	9.4	8.0	13.3	4.9	7.0	11.6	8.4	9.7	8.2	8.7	9.4	10.9	•
Taxes Paid **12**	1.9	1.8	2.2	2.9	2.4	1.9	2.0	1.9	1.6	1.4	1.7	1.8	•
Interest Paid **13**	1.9	3.6	0.7	1.2	0.8	1.3	1.4	1.3	1.6	1.9	3.1	3.2	•
Depreciation **14**	1.8	1.6	1.3	1.0	1.4	2.4	1.5	1.7	1.3	2.2	2.3	2.2	•
Amortization and Depletion **15**	0.6	0.6	0.2	0.5	0.1	0.1	0.3	0.3	0.3	0.5	1.0	1.2	•
Pensions and Other Deferred Comp. **16**	0.5	1.5	0.9	0.0	0.4	0.4	0.3	0.4	0.5	0.6	0.3	0.7	•
Employee Benefits **17**	1.6	1.5	1.8	1.6	1.2	2.4	1.5	2.0	1.5	1.2	1.5	1.8	•
Advertising **18**	1.7	1.1	1.2	1.5	0.9	0.7	1.1	1.8	2.9	1.8	2.4	2.1	•
Other Expenses **19**	12.4	24.9	16.1	19.5	9.9	9.8	11.2	9.3	10.7	9.4	11.1	15.8	•
Officers' Compensation **20**	2.5	0.5	9.7	5.7	4.3	2.6	2.5	1.5	1.7	2.3	0.8	0.8	•
Operating Margin **21**	4.9	•	7.5	3.1	4.9	7.9	5.2	5.6	5.5	7.8	2.8	3.3	•
Operating Margin Before Officers' Comp. **22**	7.3	•	17.2	8.8	9.2	10.5	7.6	7.1	7.1	10.1	3.6	4.2	•

Selected Average Balance Sheet ($ in Thousands)

Net Receivables 23	838	0	31	188	849	2251	3886	8931	16929	34933	78600	190151
Inventories 24	743	0	23	217	750	2561	4263	7919	14448	33150	52268	121157
Net Property, Plant and Equipment 25	588	0	22	58	483	1705	2242	6586	10463	26835	65767	144695
Total Assets 26	4093	0	119	674	2731	7305	14894	33652	66609	156802	359074	1394870
Notes and Loans Payable 27	1294	0	52	246	717	2314	4338	12918	19191	44655	135850	429741
All Other Liabilities 28	1180	0	46	169	877	1848	4153	8296	18096	48634	111687	395730
Net Worth 29	1618	0	21	259	1137	3143	6403	12438	29322	63513	111537	569399

Selected Financial Ratios (Times to 1)

Current Ratio 30	1.7	•	1.4	2.9	2.3	1.9	1.7	1.5	2.0	1.9	1.7	1.5
Quick Ratio 31	0.9	•	1.0	1.7	1.2	1.0	0.9	0.8	1.1	1.0	1.0	0.8
Net Sales to Working Capital 32	6.3	•	18.0	4.0	5.9	5.9	5.9	7.6	4.9	5.1	5.9	7.0
Coverage Ratio 33	6.4	4.8	13.6	6.1	8.0	7.5	6.1	7.2	6.0	6.2	3.0	7.1
Total Asset Turnover 34	1.3	•	3.8	2.1	2.5	1.9	1.7	1.7	1.5	1.4	1.1	0.8
Inventory Turnover 35	4.5	•	8.9	3.7	6.2	3.3	3.8	4.6	4.6	4.2	4.8	5.2
Receivables Turnover 36	6.6	•	13.0	7.0	10.2	6.4	6.1	6.1	6.4	6.2	5.4	6.9
Total Liabilities to Net Worth 37	1.5	•	4.6	1.6	1.4	1.3	1.3	1.7	1.3	1.5	2.2	1.4
Current Assets to Working Capital 38	2.3	•	3.3	1.5	1.8	2.2	2.4	3.0	2.0	2.1	2.5	2.8
Current Liabilities to Working Capital 39	1.3	•	2.3	0.5	0.8	1.2	1.4	2.0	1.0	1.1	1.5	1.8
Working Capital to Net Sales 40	0.2	•	0.1	0.2	0.2	0.2	0.2	0.1	0.2	0.2	0.2	0.1
Inventory to Working Capital 41	0.9	•	1.0	0.6	0.8	0.9	1.0	1.1	0.8	0.8	0.7	0.9
Total Receipts to Cash Flow 42	5.3	2.7	5.2	4.6	8.0	6.5	6.5	6.8	6.0	5.8	6.5	3.8
Cost of Goods to Cash Flow 43	3.2	1.6	2.3	2.7	5.4	3.8	4.2	4.4	3.9	3.6	4.1	2.1
Cash Flow to Total Debt 44	0.4	•	0.9	0.7	0.5	0.5	0.4	0.4	0.5	0.4	0.2	0.4

Selected Financial Factors (in Percentages)

Debt Ratio 45	60.5	•	82.3	61.5	58.4	57.0	57.0	63.0	56.0	59.5	68.9	59.2
Return on Total Assets 46	16.8	•	34.0	15.1	15.8	19.7	13.7	15.1	14.3	16.7	10.4	18.1
Return on Equity Before Income Taxes 47	35.9	•	177.4	32.8	33.2	39.7	26.7	35.2	27.1	34.6	22.6	38.1
Return on Equity After Income Taxes 48	28.4	•	174.3	31.9	31.6	37.5	23.4	29.8	22.7	29.3	17.0	26.6
Profit Margin (Before Income Tax) 49	10.6	13.5	8.4	6.1	5.4	8.8	6.9	7.8	7.8	9.9	6.4	19.5
Profit Margin (After Income Tax) 50	8.4	10.3	8.2	6.0	5.2	8.3	6.0	6.6	6.5	8.4	4.8	13.6

Table I

Corporations with and without Net Income

MOTOR VEHICLE AND MOTOR VEHICLE PARTS AND SUPPLIES

MONEY AMOUNTS AND SIZE OF ASSETS IN THOUSANDS OF DOLLARS

Item Description for Accounting Period 7/06 Through 6/07	Total	Zero Assets	Under 500	500 to 1,000	1,000 to 5,000	5,000 to 10,000	10,000 to 25,000	25,000 to 50,000	50,000 to 100,000	100,000 to 250,000	250,000 to 500,000	500,000 to 2,500,000	2,500,000 and over
Number of Enterprises **1**	17685	1610	9687	2768	2517	481	382	122	46	33	13	20	6
Revenues ($ in Thousands)													
Net Sales **2**	273651472	1661462	9116185	5962936	13662669	10138781	14101284	9849551	7498102	8714993	12812854	48651815	131480839
Interest **3**	2574423	9516	2330	4876	12109	9240	11870	11001	9216	21792	38142	207441	2236890
Rents **4**	609230	752	0	2471	4455	1257	10874	1409	1865	6083	6931	49728	523404
Royalties **5**	34453	396	0	0	0	0	124	0	0	0	1952	11846	20135
Other Portfolio Income **6**	1032707	3175	53928	1517	6203	10411	15155	20546	21820	15851	13037	175955	695111
Other Receipts **7**	2417494	-1154	9037	28423	75757	60826	97187	49511	54636	52043	25182	442435	1523613
Total Receipts **8**	280319779	1674147	9181480	6000223	13761193	10220515	14236494	9932018	7585639	8810762	12898098	49539220	136479992
Average Total Receipts **9**	15851	1040	948	2168	5467	21248	37268	81410	164905	266993	992161	2476961	22746665
Operating Costs/Operating Income (%)													
Cost of Operations **10**	81.6	76.5	83.0	78.8	75.1	82.1	78.9	78.2	81.3	78.6	85.8	84.4	81.5
Salaries and Wages **11**	3.8	4.6	3.9	7.3	6.5	5.4	7.5	6.6	6.0	5.7	3.3	3.5	2.6
Taxes Paid **12**	0.8	1.0	1.3	1.4	1.5	1.0	1.2	1.2	1.3	0.9	0.6	0.8	0.5
Interest Paid **13**	1.1	2.1	0.6	0.5	0.6	0.8	1.0	1.0	0.8	1.2	0.8	0.9	1.4
Depreciation **14**	2.9	0.9	0.3	0.4	0.6	0.4	0.8	1.1	1.2	1.1	0.7	1.3	5.0
Amortization and Depletion **15**	0.1	0.9	0.1	0.0	0.0	0.0	0.1	0.1	0.2	0.2	0.2	0.2	0.1
Pensions and Other Deferred Comp. **16**	0.2	0.1	0.1	0.1	0.2	0.2	0.2	0.2	0.2	0.2	0.1	0.1	0.3
Employee Benefits **17**	0.5	0.6	0.4	0.7	0.5	0.5	0.6	0.9	0.5	0.7	0.5	0.5	0.3
Advertising **18**	2.7	2.0	0.2	0.5	0.7	0.4	0.5	0.4	0.5	0.8	1.5	2.3	4.2
Other Expenses **19**	5.2	11.3	8.4	8.0	9.5	4.9	6.6	6.3	5.5	7.6	3.7	5.8	3.9
Officers' Compensation **20**	0.7	2.4	2.4	2.4	3.2	2.0	1.6	1.7	0.7	0.7	0.4	0.2	0.1
Operating Margin **21**	0.5	•	•	•	1.5	2.5	1.1	2.4	1.6	2.3	2.3	•	0.1
Operating Margin Before Officers' Comp. **22**	1.2	1.7	2.3	2.3	4.6	4.4	2.7	4.1	2.3	3.0	2.7	•	0.1

Selected Average Balance Sheet ($ in Thousands)

Net Receivables 23	2503	0	22	190	452	1918	3945	9060	15145	31897	62073	214902	5334110
Inventories 24	1715	0	54	254	804	3341	6244	12754	26243	52986	108891	355400	1674764
Net Property, Plant and Equipment 25	2303	0	13	66	227	656	1910	5950	9051	20376	48318	180828	5455887
Total Assets 26	9234	0	136	658	1882	6824	14986	34633	72001	153727	327589	1190019	17625056
Notes and Loans Payable 27	2938	0	66	201	447	1961	5478	13466	25982	46951	101735	377962	5554618
All Other Liabilities 28	3953	0	42	230	622	2407	5140	9826	21985	54266	92597	485812	8209467
Net Worth 29	2343	0	28	227	813	2456	4367	11340	24034	52510	133257	326246	3860970

Selected Financial Ratios (Times to 1)

Current Ratio 30	1.3	•	2.2	2.0	1.9	1.9	1.4	1.7	1.5	1.5	1.6	1.2	1.2
Quick Ratio 31	0.7	•	1.0	1.0	0.8	0.8	0.6	0.7	0.6	0.6	0.6	0.5	0.8
Net Sales to Working Capital 32	11.3	•	16.4	7.9	7.9	8.0	10.8	7.6	10.2	7.6	13.0	17.7	11.3
Coverage Ratio 33	3.6	0.2	1.0	2.1	4.4	5.1	3.1	4.2	4.5	3.9	4.7	2.8	3.8
Total Asset Turnover 34	1.7	•	6.9	3.3	2.9	3.1	2.5	2.3	2.3	1.7	3.0	2.0	1.2
Inventory Turnover 35	7.4	•	14.4	6.7	5.1	5.2	4.7	4.9	5.0	3.9	7.8	5.8	10.7
Receivables Turnover 36	6.4	•	42.4	13.2	11.6	10.5	9.6	9.1	10.0	8.5	15.5	11.6	4.3
Total Liabilities to Net Worth 37	2.9	•	3.9	1.9	1.3	1.8	2.4	2.1	2.0	1.9	1.5	2.6	3.6
Current Assets to Working Capital 38	4.1	•	1.9	2.1	2.2	2.2	3.5	2.5	3.2	2.9	2.7	5.4	5.0
Current Liabilities to Working Capital 39	3.1	•	0.9	1.1	1.2	1.2	2.5	1.5	2.2	1.9	1.7	4.4	4.0
Working Capital to Net Sales 40	0.1	•	0.1	0.1	0.1	0.1	0.1	0.1	0.1	0.1	0.1	0.1	0.1
Inventory to Working Capital 41	1.3	•	0.9	0.9	1.1	1.2	1.9	1.3	1.6	1.6	1.5	2.8	0.9
Total Receipts to Cash Flow 42	14.1	14.6	15.3	18.8	15.3	10.6	15.3	14.3	12.8	14.7	17.4	15.2	13.9
Cost of Goods to Cash Flow 43	11.5	11.2	15.6	12.0	15.6	8.0	12.6	11.3	10.0	11.9	8.2	14.9	12.9
Cash Flow to Total Debt 44	0.2	•	0.5	0.3	0.5	0.3	0.3	0.2	0.2	0.2	0.3	0.2	0.1

Selected Financial Factors (in Percentages)

Debt Ratio 45	74.6	•	79.5	65.5	56.8	64.0	70.9	67.3	66.6	65.8	59.3	72.6	78.1
Return on Total Assets 46	6.8	•	4.2	3.3	8.1	12.6	7.5	9.8	8.1	7.8	11.2	5.4	6.5
Return on Equity Before Income Taxes 47	19.4	•	0.6	5.1	14.6	28.2	17.4	22.8	18.8	17.0	21.7	12.8	21.9
Return on Equity After Income Taxes 48	13.7	•	•	2.8	13.0	26.1	14.6	20.9	15.6	13.4	18.3	7.1	14.8
Profit Margin (Before Income Tax) 49	2.9	•	0.0	0.5	2.2	3.3	2.1	3.2	2.8	3.4	2.9	1.7	3.9
Profit Margin (After Income Tax) 50	2.1	•	•	0.3	2.0	3.0	1.7	2.9	2.3	2.7	2.5	0.9	2.6

Table II

Corporations with Net Income

MOTOR VEHICLE AND MOTOR VEHICLE PARTS AND SUPPLIES

MONEY AMOUNTS AND SIZE OF ASSETS IN THOUSANDS OF DOLLARS

Item Description for Accounting Period 7/06 Through 6/07	Total	Zero Assets	Under 500	500 to 1,000	1,000 to 5,000	5,000 to 10,000	10,000 to 25,000	25,000 to 50,000	50,000 to 100,000	100,000 to 250,000	250,000 to 500,000	500,000 to 2,500,000	2,500,000 and over
Number of Enterprises **1**	12344	1090	6210	2063	2051	414	309	111	39	27	10	14	6
Revenues ($ in Thousands)													
Net Sales **2**	249261788	1161583	7619127	4346130	12039551	9320596	12004060	9298415	6680989	7523890	11468232	36318378	131480839
Interest **3**	2546945	6416	883	2170	9695	7458	9926	10001	8713	18288	34884	201622	2236890
Rents **4**	606004	447	0	2299	4214	1197	10860	1271	1359	5220	6931	48801	523404
Royalties **5**	34436	379	0	0	0	0	124	0	0	0	1952	11846	20135
Other Portfolio Income **6**	990920	3076	52725	176	6052	10098	10118	16042	20545	12822	12969	151188	695111
Other Receipts **7**	2301614	-2643	10413	24179	68428	57840	78795	41007	36686	35688	37132	390472	1523613
Total Receipts **8**	255741707	1169258	7683148	4374954	12127940	9397189	12113883	9366736	6748292	7595908	11562100	37122307	136479992
Average Total Receipts **9**	20718	1073	1237	2121	5913	22699	39204	84385	173033	281330	1156210	2651593	22746665
Operating Costs/Operating Income (%)													
Cost of Operations **10**	81.7	83.0	86.0	75.8	74.4	82.9	79.3	77.5	81.4	80.1	86.1	84.8	81.5
Salaries and Wages **11**	3.7	2.8	2.8	8.0	6.5	5.2	7.3	6.7	5.8	5.1	3.4	3.4	2.6
Taxes Paid **12**	0.7	0.5	0.8	1.7	1.5	0.9	1.1	1.2	1.4	0.9	0.6	0.9	0.5
Interest Paid **13**	1.1	0.5	0.3	0.3	0.6	0.8	1.0	0.9	0.7	0.8	0.6	0.8	1.4
Depreciation **14**	3.1	0.7	0.3	0.4	0.6	0.3	0.8	1.0	1.2	1.0	0.5	1.4	5.0
Amortization and Depletion **15**	0.1	0.1	0.1	0.0	0.0	0.0	0.1	0.1	0.1	0.1	0.2	0.1	0.1
Pensions and Other Deferred Comp. **16**	0.2	0.1	0.1	0.1	0.2	0.2	0.2	0.2	0.1	0.1	0.1	0.1	0.3
Employee Benefits **17**	0.4	0.2	0.2	0.7	0.5	0.5	0.7	0.9	0.5	0.7	0.4	0.5	0.3
Advertising **18**	2.7	1.2	0.2	0.4	0.7	0.4	0.4	0.4	0.6	0.6	1.5	2.0	4.2
Other Expenses **19**	4.7	7.5	5.7	8.5	9.3	4.4	5.5	6.2	5.1	6.6	3.3	4.8	3.9
Officers' Compensation **20**	0.6	1.9	2.3	2.5	3.2	1.5	1.7	1.8	0.7	0.5	0.4	0.2	0.1
Operating Margin **21**	1.0	1.6	1.1	1.5	2.4	2.8	2.1	3.2	2.4	3.4	2.7	0.9	0.1
Operating Margin Before Officers' Comp. **22**	1.6	3.5	3.4	4.1	5.6	4.4	3.7	4.9	3.1	3.8	3.2	1.2	0.1

Selected Average Balance Sheet ($ in Thousands)

Net Receivables 23	3408	0	25	232	467	2056	3734	8872	14528	33716	65464	238914	5334110
Inventories 24	2176	0	60	217	777	3430	6230	13204	27692	53965	119786	415153	1674764
Net Property, Plant and Equipment 25	3166	0	15	46	261	658	1703	5719	9595	20182	39925	204986	5455887
Total Assets 26	12251	0	149	659	1886	6803	14802	34707	71484	147223	318784	1295003	17625056
Notes and Loans Payable 27	3810	0	52	126	456	2173	5169	12301	23180	39179	86222	392575	5554618
All Other Liabilities 28	5299	0	31	250	632	2438	4859	9498	22527	53224	94545	522891	8209467
Net Worth 29	3143	0	66	282	799	2192	4775	12908	25777	54821	138018	379538	3860970

Selected Financial Ratios (Times to 1)

Current Ratio 30	1.3	•	3.1	1.9	1.8	1.8	1.5	1.7	1.4	1.5	1.8	1.3	1.2
Quick Ratio 31	0.7	•	1.5	1.2	0.8	0.8	0.6	0.7	0.6	0.6	0.7	0.5	0.8
Net Sales to Working Capital 32	11.1	•	15.6	7.4	8.7	9.0	9.7	7.4	11.2	8.6	11.5	15.2	11.3
Coverage Ratio 33	4.3	5.3	7.5	7.9	5.9	5.6	4.2	5.4	6.0	6.6	6.6	4.8	3.8
Total Asset Turnover 34	1.6	•	8.2	3.2	3.1	3.3	2.6	2.4	2.4	1.9	3.6	2.0	1.2
Inventory Turnover 35	7.6	•	17.5	7.3	5.6	5.4	4.9	4.9	5.0	4.1	8.2	5.3	10.7
Receivables Turnover 36	6.1	•	48.3	•	12.2	10.3	10.9	9.9	10.5	8.6	•	11.5	4.3
Total Liabilities to Net Worth 37	2.9	•	1.3	1.3	1.4	2.1	2.1	1.7	1.8	1.7	1.3	2.4	3.6
Current Assets to Working Capital 38	4.1	•	1.5	2.1	2.2	2.3	3.0	2.4	3.4	3.2	2.2	4.9	5.0
Current Liabilities to Working Capital 39	3.1	•	0.5	1.1	1.2	1.3	2.0	1.4	2.4	2.2	1.2	3.9	4.0
Working Capital to Net Sales 40	0.1	•	0.1	0.1	0.1	0.1	0.1	0.1	0.1	0.1	0.1	0.1	0.1
Inventory to Working Capital 41	1.3	•	0.8	0.8	1.2	1.2	1.7	1.3	1.7	1.7	1.2	2.6	0.9
Total Receipts to Cash Flow 42	13.7	12.7	19.9	11.6	9.8	15.3	14.4	11.8	14.3	10.4	16.7	14.2	13.9
Cost of Goods to Cash Flow 43	11.2	10.5	17.1	8.8	7.3	12.7	11.4	9.2	11.6	8.3	14.4	12.0	11.3
Cash Flow to Total Debt 44	0.2	•	0.7	0.5	0.6	0.3	0.3	0.3	0.3	0.3	0.4	0.2	0.1

Selected Financial Factors (in Percentages)

Debt Ratio 45	74.3	•	55.8	57.2	57.6	67.8	67.7	62.8	63.9	62.8	56.7	70.7	78.1
Return on Total Assets 46	7.6	•	18.3	8.1	11.7	14.7	10.4	11.5	9.7	9.6	15.1	7.9	6.5
Return on Equity Before Income Taxes 47	22.9	•	35.9	16.5	23.0	37.5	24.5	25.2	22.3	21.9	29.6	21.3	21.9
Return on Equity After Income Taxes 48	16.9	•	33.7	14.0	21.0	34.8	21.3	23.4	18.8	17.7	25.4	14.3	14.8
Profit Margin (Before Income Tax) 49	3.6	2.2	1.9	2.2	3.1	3.6	3.0	3.9	3.4	4.3	3.6	3.1	3.9
Profit Margin (After Income Tax) 50	2.6	2.0	1.8	1.9	2.9	3.4	2.6	3.6	2.8	3.5	3.1	2.1	2.6

Table I

Corporations with and without Net Income

LUMBER AND OTHER CONSTRUCTION MATERIALS

MONEY AMOUNTS AND SIZE OF ASSETS IN THOUSANDS OF DOLLARS

Item Description for Accounting Period 7/06 Through 6/07	Total	Zero Assets	Under 500	500 to 1,000	1,000 to 5,000	5,000 to 10,000	10,000 to 25,000	25,000 to 50,000	50,000 to 100,000	100,000 to 250,000	250,000 to 500,000	500,000 to 2,500,000	2,500,000 and over
Number of Enterprises **1**	14911	3511	4930	1056	3612	1125	448	132	57	26	5	10	0
Revenues ($ in Thousands)													
Net Sales **2**	144636675	3692458	4285195	3486592	29675909	25304117	21269244	14682469	11458845	12137300	4043863	14600683	0
Interest **3**	134763	298	6155	4197	28457	12787	8893	10332	8889	8861	24296	21598	0
Rents **4**	40207	56	0	5991	4410	3414	16961	1921	2358	945	2082	2068	0
Royalties **5**	13491	0	0	0	0	43	0	0	0	0	0	13448	0
Other Portfolio Income **6**	174580	14871	104	2408	28451	40707	33410	7751	4360	7503	3396	31619	0
Other Receipts **7**	887894	4140	5463	2814	93043	182116	106568	70497	60563	71965	25799	264928	0
Total Receipts **8**	145887610	3711823	4296917	3502002	29830270	25543184	21435076	14772970	11535015	12226574	4099436	14934344	0
Average Total Receipts **9**	9784	1057	872	3316	8259	22705	47846	111916	202369	470253	819887	1493434	•
Operating Costs/Operating Income (%)													
Cost of Operations **10**	80.3	82.7	62.5	82.4	77.3	81.6	80.8	84.7	80.3	83.1	76.4	81.6	•
Salaries and Wages **11**	5.9	3.4	7.0	2.9	6.3	5.6	6.3	5.4	6.4	5.6	6.9	6.1	•
Taxes Paid **12**	1.1	2.3	1.6	1.2	1.1	1.1	1.0	0.9	1.0	0.8	1.4	1.1	•
Interest Paid **13**	0.8	0.4	0.3	0.4	0.6	0.7	0.7	0.9	0.8	0.9	1.6	1.5	•
Depreciation **14**	0.8	0.2	0.6	0.7	0.7	0.6	0.8	0.6	0.8	0.9	1.2	1.9	•
Amortization and Depletion **15**	0.1	0.0	0.0	0.0	0.0	0.0	0.0	0.0	0.1	0.1	0.1	0.4	•
Pensions and Other Deferred Comp. **16**	0.3	0.0	1.1	0.5	0.3	0.2	0.3	0.2	0.2	0.2	0.4	0.3	•
Employee Benefits **17**	0.6	0.2	0.7	0.4	0.5	0.5	0.6	0.4	0.5	0.5	0.6	0.9	•
Advertising **18**	0.3	0.4	0.6	0.3	0.3	0.2	0.2	0.3	0.3	0.2	0.3	0.2	•
Other Expenses **19**	6.1	8.6	15.7	5.9	7.3	5.6	4.9	4.5	5.6	4.8	5.6	5.6	•
Officers' Compensation **20**	1.7	2.2	4.5	4.3	2.6	1.5	1.5	1.0	1.0	0.6	3.0	0.4	•
Operating Margin **21**	2.1	•	5.3	0.9	2.8	2.2	2.8	1.0	3.0	2.2	2.6	0.0	•
Operating Margin Before Officers' Comp. **22**	3.8	1.7	9.8	5.2	5.4	3.7	4.3	2.0	4.0	2.8	5.5	0.5	•

Selected Average Balance Sheet ($ in Thousands)

Net Receivables 23	978	0	10	311	869	2340	4799	11600	21196	53690	84379	173046	•
Inventories 24	897	0	43	227	758	2431	4836	11803	24088	37143	59532	108763	•
Net Property, Plant and Equipment 25	670	0	15	63	296	1133	2627	4635	12064	22254	114017	388610	•
Total Assets 26	3533	0	130	743	2371	6856	15429	34331	69295	149290	346364	1396628	•
Notes and Loans Payable 27	1234	0	63	129	641	2154	4591	14780	20884	48007	143344	606133	•
All Other Liabilities 28	945	0	40	183	748	1555	3845	8737	20206	56115	90420	331083	•
Net Worth 29	1353	0	27	431	983	3147	6993	10814	28205	45168	112599	459412	•

Selected Financial Ratios (Times to 1)

Current Ratio 30	1.8	•	1.7	2.6	2.0	2.1	1.8	1.7	1.7	1.5	1.1	1.7	•
Quick Ratio 31	1.0	•	0.8	1.7	1.2	1.1	0.9	0.8	0.8	0.8	0.7	0.7	•
Net Sales to Working Capital 32	9.5	•	26.5	8.6	8.4	8.0	8.9	10.2	9.6	12.3	44.2	7.9	•
Coverage Ratio 33	4.7	1.1	18.7	4.7	6.2	5.2	5.9	2.7	5.3	4.4	3.5	2.7	•
Total Asset Turnover 34	2.7	•	6.7	4.4	3.5	3.3	3.1	3.2	2.9	3.1	2.3	1.0	•
Inventory Turnover 35	8.7	•	12.5	12.0	8.4	7.6	7.9	8.0	6.7	10.4	10.4	10.9	•
Receivables Turnover 36	9.5	•	51.5	9.8	9.5	9.0	9.9	8.2	9.4	9.9	7.3	7.9	•
Total Liabilities to Net Worth 37	1.6	•	3.8	0.7	1.4	1.2	1.2	2.2	1.5	2.3	2.1	2.0	•
Current Assets to Working Capital 38	2.2	•	2.5	1.6	2.0	1.9	2.2	2.4	2.4	2.9	8.0	2.4	•
Current Liabilities to Working Capital 39	1.2	•	1.5	0.6	1.0	0.9	1.2	1.4	1.4	1.9	7.0	1.4	•
Working Capital to Net Sales 40	0.1	•	0.0	0.1	0.1	0.1	0.1	0.1	0.1	0.1	0.0	0.1	•
Inventory to Working Capital 41	0.9	•	1.1	0.4	0.7	0.9	1.0	1.1	1.1	1.2	2.2	0.6	•
Total Receipts to Cash Flow 42	13.4	14.8	6.0	18.1	11.5	13.6	14.4	20.6	13.3	15.3	12.4	15.0	•
Cost of Goods to Cash Flow 43	10.8	12.3	3.7	14.9	8.9	11.1	11.6	17.5	10.7	12.7	9.5	12.2	•
Cash Flow to Total Debt 44	0.3	•	1.4	0.6	0.5	0.4	0.4	0.2	0.4	0.3	0.3	0.1	•

Selected Financial Factors (in Percentages)

Debt Ratio 45	61.7	•	79.0	42.0	58.5	54.1	54.7	68.5	59.3	69.7	67.5	67.1	•
Return on Total Assets 46	10.5	•	39.5	7.6	13.5	12.6	13.1	8.0	13.0	12.0	12.9	4.3	•
Return on Equity Before Income Taxes 47	21.5	•	178.1	10.3	27.4	22.2	24.0	16.2	26.0	30.6	28.2	8.2	•
Return on Equity After Income Taxes 48	19.1	•	172.9	7.5	25.8	20.6	22.5	12.7	24.4	25.9	19.1	5.3	•
Profit Margin (Before Income Tax) 49	3.0	0.0	5.6	1.3	3.3	3.1	3.5	1.6	3.6	3.0	3.9	2.6	•
Profit Margin (After Income Tax) 50	2.7	•	5.4	1.0	3.1	2.9	3.3	1.2	3.4	2.5	2.7	1.7	•

Table II
Corporations with Net Income

LUMBER AND OTHER CONSTRUCTION MATERIALS

MONEY AMOUNTS AND SIZE OF ASSETS IN THOUSANDS OF DOLLARS

Item Description for Accounting Period 7/06 Through 6/07	Total	Zero Assets	Under 500	500 to 1,000	1,000 to 5,000	5,000 to 10,000	10,000 to 25,000	25,000 to 50,000	50,000 to 100,000	100,000 to 250,000	250,000 to 500,000	500,000 to 2,500,000	2,500,000 and over
Number of Enterprises **1**	10050	1108	3404	900	3091	980	384	101	•	22	•	7	0
Revenues ($ in Thousands)													
Net Sales **2**	126715762	3022774	3382061	3162116	26646312	23287297	17989738	11873996	•	9298809	•	14036434	0
Interest **3**	112494	28	3001	2997	25098	10192	8007	9203	•	8564	•	15861	0
Rents **4**	37664	0	0	5989	4336	2786	16398	1921	•	530	•	2068	0
Royalties **5**	13448	0	0	0	0	0	0	0	•	0	•	13448	0
Other Portfolio Income **6**	154050	14778	104	2163	27529	28409	33294	5711	•	7449	•	26957	0
Other Receipts **7**	608311	2889	4275	2652	68466	177325	102947	59361	•	66514	•	46706	0
Total Receipts **8**	127641729	3040469	3389441	3175917	26771741	23506009	18150384	11950192	•	9381866	•	14141474	0
Average Total Receipts **9**	12701	2744	996	3529	8661	23986	47267	118319	•	426448	•	2020211	•
Operating Costs/Operating Income (%)													
Cost of Operations **10**	80.0	80.9	60.2	82.3	76.9	81.6	79.3	84.8	•	82.5	•	83.5	•
Salaries and Wages **11**	5.8	3.8	6.0	3.1	6.2	5.5	6.7	5.1	•	5.5	•	5.5	•
Taxes Paid **12**	1.0	2.2	1.2	1.1	1.1	1.1	1.0	0.8	•	0.8	•	0.9	•
Interest Paid **13**	0.7	0.4	0.3	0.3	0.6	0.7	0.6	0.8	•	0.9	•	0.9	•
Depreciation **14**	0.8	0.2	0.6	0.6	0.7	0.6	0.8	0.6	•	0.9	•	1.6	•
Amortization and Depletion **15**	0.1	0.0	0.0	0.0	0.0	0.0	0.0	0.0	•	0.1	•	0.3	•
Pensions and Other Deferred Comp. **16**	0.3	0.0	1.3	0.5	0.3	0.2	0.3	0.2	•	0.3	•	0.3	•
Employee Benefits **17**	0.5	0.2	0.4	0.4	0.5	0.5	0.7	0.3	•	0.5	•	0.8	•
Advertising **18**	0.3	0.4	0.6	0.3	0.3	0.2	0.3	0.4	•	0.2	•	0.1	•
Other Expenses **19**	5.8	7.6	17.5	5.7	7.2	5.5	5.1	4.2	•	4.7	•	3.9	•
Officers' Compensation **20**	1.7	1.5	4.1	4.3	2.6	1.5	1.6	0.8	•	0.7	•	0.4	•
Operating Margin **21**	3.0	2.9	7.8	1.3	3.6	2.7	3.5	2.0	•	3.1	•	1.7	•
Operating Margin Before Officers' Comp. **22**	4.7	4.3	11.9	5.6	6.1	4.2	5.1	2.8	•	3.8	•	2.1	•

Selected Average Balance Sheet ($ in Thousands)

Item											
Net Receivables 23	1244	0	8	328	894	2379	4901	12624	53050	191139	•
Inventories 24	1149	0	45	237	763	2395	4783	12544	35562	159671	•
Net Property, Plant and Equipment 25	729	0	12	51	302	1073	2647	4696	23046	300867	•
Total Assets 26	3952	0	137	742	2411	6927	15671	34913	143517	969548	•
Notes and Loans Payable 27	1149	0	54	92	590	2103	4311	14216	46414	247543	•
All Other Liabilities 28	1095	0	49	195	757	1549	3664	8565	51023	290410	•
Net Worth 29	1708	0	34	455	1064	3274	7696	12131	46081	431596	•

Selected Financial Ratios (Times to 1)

Item											
Current Ratio 30	1.9	•	1.9	2.5	2.1	2.1	2.0	1.7	1.6	1.8	•
Quick Ratio 31	1.0	•	1.0	1.7	1.3	1.1	1.1	0.9	0.9	0.9	•
Net Sales to Working Capital 32	9.6	•	23.0	9.4	8.4	8.2	7.9	10.4	11.5	10.9	•
Coverage Ratio 33	6.2	9.2	28.6	7.4	7.7	6.2	8.4	4.2	5.5	4.0	•
Total Asset Turnover 34	3.2	•	7.3	4.7	3.6	3.4	3.0	3.4	2.9	2.1	•
Inventory Turnover 35	8.8	•	13.4	12.2	8.7	8.1	7.8	8.0	9.8	10.5	•
Receivables Turnover 36	9.5	•	60.4	9.8	9.8	9.6	9.4	7.5	8.3	•	•
Total Liabilities to Net Worth 37	1.3	•	3.0	0.6	1.3	1.1	1.0	1.9	2.1	1.2	•
Current Assets to Working Capital 38	2.1	•	2.1	1.7	1.9	1.9	2.0	2.4	2.8	2.2	•
Current Liabilities to Working Capital 39	1.1	•	1.1	0.7	0.9	0.9	1.0	1.4	1.8	1.2	•
Working Capital to Net Sales 40	0.1	•	0.0	0.1	0.1	0.1	0.1	0.1	0.1	0.1	•
Inventory to Working Capital 41	0.9	•	1.0	0.4	0.7	0.9	0.8	1.0	1.0	0.9	•
Total Receipts to Cash Flow 42	12.5	10.9	4.9	17.2	10.6	12.8	12.6	17.8	13.6	19.1	•
Cost of Goods to Cash Flow 43	10.0	8.8	2.9	14.2	8.1	10.4	10.0	15.1	11.2	16.0	•
Cash Flow to Total Debt 44	0.4	•	2.0	0.7	0.6	0.5	0.5	0.3	0.3	0.2	•

Selected Financial Factors (in Percentages)

Item											
Debt Ratio 45	56.8	•	75.3	38.7	55.8	52.7	50.9	65.3	67.9	55.5	•
Return on Total Assets 46	14.4	•	60.3	9.6	16.6	14.8	14.9	11.4	14.3	7.6	•
Return on Equity Before Income Taxes 47	27.9	•	235.4	13.6	32.6	26.2	26.8	25.1	36.3	12.7	•
Return on Equity After Income Taxes 48	25.0	•	229.4	10.5	31.0	24.5	25.2	21.0	31.0	8.3	•
Profit Margin (Before Income Tax) 49	3.8	3.5	8.0	1.8	4.0	3.6	4.4	2.6	4.0	2.7	•
Profit Margin (After Income Tax) 50	3.4	3.3	7.8	1.4	3.8	3.4	4.1	2.2	3.4	1.8	•

Table I
Corporations with and without Net Income

PROFESSIONAL AND COMMERCIAL EQUIPMENT AND SUPPLIES

MONEY AMOUNTS AND SIZE OF ASSETS IN THOUSANDS OF DOLLARS

Item Description for Accounting Period 7/06 Through 6/07	Total	Zero Assets	Under 500	500 to 1,000	1,000 to 5,000	5,000 to 10,000	10,000 to 25,000	25,000 to 50,000	50,000 to 100,000	100,000 to 250,000	250,000 to 500,000	500,000 to 2,500,000	2,500,000 and over
Number of Enterprises **1**	33191	5785	19609	3178	3482	484	371	134	47	55	16	21	8
Revenues ($ in Thousands)													
Net Sales **2**	199745695	3072719	11803861	6643948	21212309	15272209	16643209	9828102	6804104	17570616	9847081	33907143	47140394
Interest **3**	988792	5597	1467	5242	15669	10751	16822	19391	17509	40101	53032	293569	509643
Rents **4**	392207	28739	705	386	6098	4285	2146	27	823	3049	34945	31969	279036
Royalties **5**	90609	0	0	0	245	0	15004	356	853	40337	785	8672	24358
Other Portfolio Income **6**	657975	16926	160	1365	49547	2305	8042	26616	30442	13975	37491	384377	86729
Other Receipts **7**	1837716	169033	60585	183546	189575	181415	79765	61963	34635	135877	69265	425198	246856
Total Receipts **8**	203712994	3293014	11866778	6834487	21473443	15470965	16764988	9936455	6888366	17803955	10042599	35050928	48287016
Average Total Receipts **9**	6138	569	605	2151	6167	31965	45189	74153	146561	323708	627662	1669092	6035877
Operating Costs/Operating Income (%)													
Cost of Operations **10**	76.3	66.9	62.5	62.7	70.2	82.3	77.7	76.6	75.2	81.0	80.7	78.1	78.8
Salaries and Wages **11**	8.1	10.1	7.2	10.6	9.8	8.5	8.2	9.7	8.9	6.1	6.3	8.6	7.3
Taxes Paid **12**	1.0	1.7	1.5	1.3	1.5	0.8	1.0	1.1	1.0	0.8	0.8	0.9	0.8
Interest Paid **13**	1.0	1.1	0.6	0.8	0.7	0.2	0.5	0.9	0.9	0.7	1.1	1.3	1.6
Depreciation **14**	1.0	1.0	0.5	0.5	0.9	0.6	0.6	1.0	0.8	0.6	0.7	1.5	1.3
Amortization and Depletion **15**	0.3	0.2	0.0	0.0	0.1	0.1	0.1	0.6	0.3	0.2	0.7	0.5	0.5
Pensions and Other Deferred Comp. **16**	0.3	0.0	0.4	0.3	0.2	0.2	0.2	0.2	0.3	0.2	0.2	0.3	0.3
Employee Benefits **17**	0.8	0.4	0.4	0.5	0.9	0.6	0.5	0.7	0.9	0.6	0.5	1.1	1.0
Advertising **18**	0.8	0.7	0.5	1.1	0.8	0.3	0.6	0.4	1.0	0.6	1.5	1.0	0.7
Other Expenses **19**	8.0	17.7	14.5	14.7	9.8	5.7	7.9	6.9	7.9	6.4	6.6	5.8	7.5
Officers' Compensation **20**	1.6	3.1	7.8	5.5	4.0	1.0	1.7	1.4	1.0	0.6	0.4	0.4	0.2
Operating Margin **21**	0.8	*	4.1	1.9	1.2	*	0.9	0.4	1.6	2.3	0.5	0.6	0.0
Operating Margin Before Officers' Comp. **22**	2.5	0.2	11.9	7.4	5.2	0.7	2.6	1.8	2.6	2.9	0.8	1.0	0.2

Selected Average Balance Sheet ($ in Thousands)

Net Receivables 23	858	0	28	237	830	2677	6112	11436	22993	48646	96664	279067	1003991
Inventories 24	479	0	26	164	442	2549	3794	7130	19079	27811	61094	137916	430588
Net Property, Plant and Equipment 25	233	0	14	76	274	615	1496	4146	6711	10361	14422	85655	244400
Total Assets 26	3553	0	103	734	2112	7343	15331	35050	73133	143288	347787	1123611	6476166
Notes and Loans Payable 27	816	0	65	189	700	1833	3550	7487	17072	38456	89764	285697	1149525
All Other Liabilities 28	1255	0	36	289	944	3345	6976	15135	29494	52215	139898	386160	1986790
Net Worth 29	1482	0	1	256	468	2164	4806	12428	26567	52617	118126	451754	3339851

Selected Financial Ratios (Times to 1)

Current Ratio 30	1.5	•	1.9	2.0	1.4	1.5	1.5	1.4	1.6	1.6	1.2	1.7	1.2
Quick Ratio 31	0.9	•	1.2	1.3	1.0	0.8	1.0	0.8	0.9	1.0	0.7	1.0	0.8
Net Sales to Working Capital 32	10.8	•	16.2	6.9	12.3	15.0	10.6	11.1	7.3	8.0	19.4	6.6	17.1
Coverage Ratio 33	3.9	4.9	8.5	7.2	4.6	5.2	4.3	2.6	4.3	6.4	3.3	4.2	2.6
Total Asset Turnover 34	1.7	•	5.9	2.8	2.9	4.3	2.9	2.1	2.0	2.2	1.8	1.4	0.9
Inventory Turnover 35	9.6	•	14.4	8.0	9.7	10.2	9.2	7.9	5.7	9.3	8.1	9.1	10.8
Receivables Turnover 36	7.5	•	21.2	9.8	7.7	12.2	7.6	7.7	5.9	7.6	6.0	6.2	6.3
Total Liabilities to Net Worth 37	1.4	•	72.3	1.9	3.5	2.4	2.2	1.8	1.8	1.7	1.9	1.5	0.9
Current Assets to Working Capital 38	3.2	•	2.2	2.0	3.3	2.9	2.9	3.6	2.6	2.6	6.4	2.5	5.4
Current Liabilities to Working Capital 39	2.2	•	1.2	1.0	2.3	1.9	1.9	2.6	1.6	1.6	5.4	1.5	4.4
Working Capital to Net Sales 40	0.1	•	0.1	0.1	0.1	0.1	0.1	0.1	0.1	0.1	0.1	0.2	0.1
Inventory to Working Capital 41	0.9	•	0.6	0.5	1.0	1.2	1.0	1.3	1.0	0.8	1.7	0.6	1.4
Total Receipts to Cash Flow 42	11.0	5.7	6.4	5.9	10.1	17.6	12.1	14.6	11.1	11.0	12.6	13.3	11.3
Cost of Goods to Cash Flow 43	8.4	3.8	4.0	3.7	7.1	14.4	9.4	11.2	8.4	8.9	10.1	10.4	8.9
Cash Flow to Total Debt 44	0.3	•	0.9	0.7	0.4	0.3	0.4	0.2	0.3	0.3	0.2	0.2	0.2

Selected Financial Factors (in Percentages)

Debt Ratio 45	58.3	•	98.6	65.1	77.9	70.5	68.7	64.5	63.7	63.3	66.0	59.8	48.4
Return on Total Assets 46	6.5	•	30.5	15.7	9.0	5.2	6.1	5.0	7.8	9.7	6.3	7.6	3.8
Return on Equity Before Income Taxes 47	11.6	•	1976.2	38.8	31.9	14.3	14.9	8.6	16.6	22.2	12.9	14.5	4.4
Return on Equity After Income Taxes 48	8.9	•	1942.2	37.5	28.3	11.1	11.3	5.7	12.9	16.8	10.6	9.9	2.8
Profit Margin (Before Income Tax) 49	2.9	4.3	4.6	4.7	2.4	1.0	1.6	1.5	3.0	3.7	2.5	4.1	2.5
Profit Margin (After Income Tax) 50	2.2	3.6	4.5	4.6	2.2	0.8	1.2	1.0	2.4	2.8	2.0	2.8	1.6

Table II
Corporations with Net Income

PROFESSIONAL AND COMMERCIAL EQUIPMENT AND SUPPLIES

MONEY AMOUNTS AND SIZE OF ASSETS IN THOUSANDS OF DOLLARS

Item Description for Accounting Period 7/06 Through 6/07	Total	Zero Assets	Under 500	500 to 1,000	1,000 to 5,000	5,000 to 10,000	10,000 to 25,000	25,000 to 50,000	50,000 to 100,000	100,000 to 250,000	250,000 to 500,000	500,000 to 2,500,000	2,500,000 and over
Number of Enterprises **1**	20853	2827	11889	2612	2605	402	302	97	•	43	•	17	5

Revenues ($ in Thousands)

	Total	Zero Assets	Under 500	500 to 1,000	1,000 to 5,000	5,000 to 10,000	10,000 to 25,000	25,000 to 50,000	50,000 to 100,000	100,000 to 250,000	250,000 to 500,000	500,000 to 2,500,000	2,500,000 and over
Net Sales **2**	169841739	2864410	9391512	6295650	17933229	14073309	14586758	8179293	•	15072363	•	29712771	37183891
Interest **3**	645642	5570	784	4155	10258	8509	13086	10409	•	27300	•	232408	276791
Rents **4**	383037	28739	705	0	4659	3389	1649	27	•	1244	•	28706	278306
Royalties **5**	60197	0	0	0	245	0	14752	0	•	40322	•	3220	21
Other Portfolio Income **6**	625020	16926	0	673	38447	2299	7675	26545	•	9440	•	383471	72840
Other Receipts **7**	1446608	168990	34971	183227	159748	100731	63605	55260	•	132870	•	229417	194287
Total Receipts **8**	173002243	3084635	9427972	6483705	18146586	14188237	14687525	8271534	•	15283539	•	30589993	38006136
Average Total Receipts **9**	8296	1091	793	2482	6966	35294	48634	85274	•	355431	•	1799411	7601227

Operating Costs/Operating Income (%)

	Total	Zero Assets	Under 500	500 to 1,000	1,000 to 5,000	5,000 to 10,000	10,000 to 25,000	25,000 to 50,000	50,000 to 100,000	100,000 to 250,000	250,000 to 500,000	500,000 to 2,500,000	2,500,000 and over
Cost of Operations **10**	77.3	66.0	63.3	63.0	69.9	82.5	77.8	78.0	•	80.7	•	78.6	82.7
Salaries and Wages **11**	7.4	9.8	5.4	10.2	9.5	8.1	8.1	8.5	•	6.0	•	8.3	5.2
Taxes Paid **12**	1.0	1.8	1.2	1.3	1.5	0.7	1.0	1.0	•	0.8	•	0.9	0.8
Interest Paid **13**	0.7	1.0	0.5	0.7	0.5	0.2	0.3	0.6	•	0.5	•	0.8	0.8
Depreciation **14**	0.9	1.1	0.4	0.4	0.9	0.5	0.5	0.9	•	0.5	•	1.6	1.1
Amortization and Depletion **15**	0.2	0.1	0.0	0.0	0.0	0.0	0.1	0.2	•	0.1	•	0.4	0.1
Pensions and Other Deferred Comp. **16**	0.2	0.0	0.3	0.3	0.2	0.1	0.2	0.2	•	0.2	•	0.2	0.2
Employee Benefits **17**	0.7	0.4	0.3	0.4	1.0	0.6	0.5	0.7	•	0.5	•	1.1	0.6
Advertising **18**	0.7	0.7	0.5	1.2	0.6	0.3	0.6	0.4	•	0.7	•	1.0	0.7
Other Expenses **19**	7.1	16.5	12.9	14.1	8.8	4.5	6.7	5.5	•	6.4	•	5.1	6.4
Officers' Compensation **20**	1.6	3.0	7.7	5.4	3.9	1.0	1.7	1.2	•	0.6	•	0.3	0.2
Operating Margin **21**	2.3	•	7.3	3.1	3.3	1.5	2.6	2.8	•	3.2	•	1.7	1.3
Operating Margin Before Officers' Comp. **22**	3.9	2.8	15.0	8.5	7.2	2.5	4.3	4.0	•	3.7	•	2.0	1.5

Selected Average Balance Sheet ($ in Thousands)

Net Receivables 23	1070	0	27	274	881	2800	6490	13022	51959	277277	1102566
Inventories 24	621	0	21	157	477	2548	3702	7630	30027	150917	541965
Net Property, Plant and Equipment 25	272	0	17	82	304	652	1478	4507	10822	98496	132994
Total Assets 26	3641	0	109	753	2171	7301	15486	34254	144723	1145851	4539709
Notes and Loans Payable 27	789	0	51	203	567	1672	2868	6145	33660	219865	899792
All Other Liabilities 28	1324	0	34	269	921	2928	6672	15416	56617	403030	1429162
Net Worth 29	1528	0	24	282	684	2701	5945	12693	54445	522957	2210755

Selected Financial Ratios (Times to 1)

Current Ratio 30	1.5	•	2.1	2.2	1.6	1.7	1.6	1.5	1.7	1.7	1.1
Quick Ratio 31	0.9	•	1.4	1.3	1.1	0.9	1.0	0.9	1.0	1.0	0.7
Net Sales to Working Capital 32	11.6	•	17.6	7.1	11.2	14.2	9.9	10.0	7.7	6.5	60.2
Coverage Ratio 33	7.4	8.5	17.2	9.7	9.8	11.5	11.1	7.7	10.5	6.7	5.2
Total Asset Turnover 34	2.2	•	7.3	3.2	3.2	4.8	3.1	2.5	2.4	1.5	1.6
Inventory Turnover 35	10.1	•	23.5	9.7	10.1	11.3	10.1	8.6	9.4	9.1	11.3
Receivables Turnover 36	7.8	•	30.8	10.2	7.9	13.2	8.0	8.3	7.9	6.5	6.0
Total Liabilities to Net Worth 37	1.4	•	3.5	1.7	2.2	1.7	1.6	1.7	1.7	1.2	1.1
Current Assets to Working Capital 38	3.2	•	1.9	1.9	2.8	2.5	2.6	3.1	2.4	2.4	15.5
Current Liabilities to Working Capital 39	2.2	•	0.9	0.9	1.8	1.5	1.6	2.1	1.4	1.4	14.5
Working Capital to Net Sales 40	0.1	•	0.1	0.1	0.1	0.1	0.1	0.1	0.1	0.2	0.0
Inventory to Working Capital 41	0.9	•	0.4	0.5	0.8	1.0	0.8	1.1	0.8	0.6	4.0
Total Receipts to Cash Flow 42	10.4	5.0	5.6	5.7	9.2	16.8	11.4	12.3	10.0	13.5	11.4
Cost of Goods to Cash Flow 43	8.0	3.3	3.6	3.6	6.4	13.9	8.8	9.6	8.1	10.6	9.4
Cash Flow to Total Debt 44	0.4	•	1.7	0.9	0.5	0.5	0.4	0.3	0.4	0.2	0.3

Selected Financial Factors (in Percentages)

Debt Ratio 45	58.0	•	77.9	62.6	68.5	63.0	61.6	62.9	62.4	54.4	51.3
Return on Total Assets 46	10.9	•	59.5	21.7	15.8	12.3	11.1	11.2	12.2	8.6	7.0
Return on Equity Before Income Taxes 47	22.5	•	253.5	52.1	45.2	30.4	26.3	26.3	29.3	16.0	11.6
Return on Equity After Income Taxes 48	18.2	•	250.2	50.7	41.8	27.2	22.8	22.4	22.7	11.1	7.6
Profit Margin (Before Income Tax) 49	4.2	7.5	7.7	6.1	4.5	2.3	3.2	4.0	4.5	4.8	3.5
Profit Margin (After Income Tax) 50	3.4	6.7	7.6	5.9	4.2	2.1	2.8	3.4	3.5	3.3	2.3

Table I

Corporations with and without Net Income

METAL AND MINERAL (EXCEPT PETROLEUM)

MONEY AMOUNTS AND SIZE OF ASSETS IN THOUSANDS OF DOLLARS

Item Description for Accounting Period 7/06 Through 6/07	Total	Zero Assets	Under 500	500 to 1,000	1,000 to 5,000	5,000 to 10,000	10,000 to 25,000	25,000 to 50,000	50,000 to 100,000	100,000 to 250,000	250,000 to 500,000	500,000 to 2,500,000	2,500,000 and over
Number of Enterprises **1**	5556	449	3111	154	964	404	240	95	61	43	16	15	4
Revenues ($ in Thousands)													
Net Sales **2**	142947163	1477218	2919080	303845	6660830	9620768	11326968	9141508	11579077	16799679	13253097	38573755	21291338
Interest **3**	461548	2333	2243	1434	6031	8825	5633	16786	7162	25674	42462	92566	250398
Rents **4**	92052	0	0	0	1861	105	1264	951	663	1621	12981	20581	52025
Royalties **5**	976	0	0	0	0	0	0	0	0	515	0	2	459
Other Portfolio Income **6**	513913	23179	2919	75	51671	2195	2642	3916	4187	11544	74393	137304	199888
Other Receipts **7**	1125399	102	6314	793	68935	27526	56689	75359	47371	103824	131099	205240	402150
Total Receipts **8**	145141051	1502832	2930556	306147	6789328	9659419	11393196	9238520	11638460	16942857	13514032	39029448	22196258
Average Total Receipts **9**	26123	3347	942	1988	7043	23909	47472	97248	190794	394020	844627	2601963	5549064
Operating Costs/Operating Income (%)													
Cost of Operations **10**	88.5	89.4	77.5	72.5	76.2	86.3	87.0	87.9	87.6	88.4	90.7	91.4	90.1
Salaries and Wages **11**	2.8	3.8	1.4	4.8	5.6	3.1	3.3	2.7	2.6	2.0	1.9	2.6	3.5
Taxes Paid **12**	0.6	0.5	1.1	1.2	1.1	0.6	0.6	0.6	0.6	0.7	0.6	0.4	0.6
Interest Paid **13**	1.0	0.6	0.2	0.2	0.4	0.6	0.5	0.8	0.7	0.9	0.4	0.9	2.5
Depreciation **14**	0.4	0.1	0.6	0.9	0.5	0.3	0.3	0.5	0.5	0.3	0.4	0.3	0.7
Amortization and Depletion **15**	0.1	0.1	0.0	0.2	0.0	0.0	0.0	0.0	0.0	0.1	0.1	0.1	0.3
Pensions and Other Deferred Comp. **16**	0.2	0.1	0.6	1.4	0.4	0.2	0.2	0.1	0.1	0.3	0.2	0.1	0.1
Employee Benefits **17**	0.4	0.4	0.6	1.1	0.7	0.4	0.4	0.3	0.4	0.3	0.3	0.5	0.3
Advertising **18**	0.1	0.0	0.2	0.4	0.2	0.1	0.0	0.1	0.1	0.0	0.0	0.0	0.0
Other Expenses **19**	2.9	2.9	6.2	8.3	6.5	3.2	3.2	2.7	2.6	2.5	2.9	2.2	3.0
Officers' Compensation **20**	0.9	0.9	7.5	7.0	3.7	1.2	1.2	1.2	0.9	0.4	0.2	0.3	0.4
Operating Margin **21**	2.1	1.2	4.0	1.9	4.8	4.0	3.4	3.2	3.9	4.1	2.3	1.2	•
Operating Margin Before Officers' Comp. **22**	3.0	2.2	11.6	9.0	8.5	5.1	4.6	4.4	4.8	4.5	2.5	1.4	•

Selected Average Balance Sheet ($ in Thousands)

Net Receivables 23	3107	0	28	197	681	2442	5422	11596	20906	51914	96669	231254	1143954
Inventories 24	2962	0	20	368	759	2194	5437	13559	28661	60873	97001	286922	475848
Net Property, Plant and Equipment 25	1615	0	13	40	134	459	1219	3062	7110	13224	30910	98533	1262616
Total Assets 26	12009	0	163	761	2457	6833	14842	36668	68117	165626	363357	896966	5843916
Notes and Loans Payable 27	3687	0	32	81	371	1577	3546	12022	20426	53678	71230	365800	1801519
All Other Liabilities 28	5240	0	22	212	762	2531	5389	14644	22427	58155	141449	289197	3525192
Net Worth 29	3082	0	110	468	1324	2725	5907	10003	25264	53793	150677	241969	517205

Selected Financial Ratios (Times to 1)

Current Ratio 30	1.6	•	3.3	2.4	1.7	1.7	1.6	1.6	1.7	1.6	1.8	1.8	1.3
Quick Ratio 31	0.8	•	2.3	1.4	0.9	0.9	0.7	0.7	0.7	0.7	0.8	0.8	0.6
Net Sales to Working Capital 32	8.6	•	11.1	5.8	9.6	9.0	7.9	8.2	8.2	7.6	7.5	9.1	10.0
Coverage Ratio 33	4.9	5.9	26.1	14.3	17.9	7.8	9.5	6.4	7.5	6.7	11.3	3.8	2.1
Total Asset Turnover 34	2.1	•	5.7	2.6	2.8	3.5	3.2	2.6	2.8	2.4	2.3	2.9	0.9
Inventory Turnover 35	7.7	•	36.2	3.9	6.9	9.4	7.5	6.2	5.8	5.7	7.7	8.2	10.1
Receivables Turnover 36	9.3	•	38.5	8.7	10.0	10.1	9.7	8.2	8.9	8.6	9.3	11.3	6.5
Total Liabilities to Net Worth 37	2.9	•	0.5	0.6	0.9	1.5	1.5	2.7	1.7	2.1	1.4	2.7	10.3
Current Assets to Working Capital 38	2.6	•	1.4	1.8	1.7	2.4	2.5	2.6	2.5	2.6	2.3	2.2	4.7
Current Liabilities to Working Capital 39	1.6	•	0.4	0.8	0.7	1.4	1.5	1.6	1.5	1.6	1.3	1.2	3.7
Working Capital to Net Sales 40	0.1	•	0.1	0.2	0.2	0.1	0.1	0.1	0.1	0.1	0.1	0.1	0.1
Inventory to Working Capital 41	1.1	•	0.3	0.6	1.0	1.1	1.1	1.3	1.3	1.3	1.0	1.1	1.2
Total Receipts to Cash Flow 42	17.6	21.3	10.7	10.5	14.6	15.7	16.0	15.8	16.2	14.4	16.2	27.8	22.2
Cost of Goods to Cash Flow 43	15.6	19.1	8.3	7.6	12.6	13.6	14.1	13.8	13.6	12.7	14.7	25.4	20.0
Cash Flow to Total Debt 44	0.2	•	1.6	0.7	0.4	0.3	0.2	0.3	0.2	0.2	0.2	0.1	0.0

Selected Financial Factors (in Percentages)

Debt Ratio 45	74.3	•	32.9	38.5	46.1	60.1	60.2	72.7	62.9	67.5	58.5	73.0	91.1
Return on Total Assets 46	10.0	•	25.8	7.5	20.0	17.4	14.1	13.3	14.3	13.6	10.6	9.3	4.7
Return on Equity Before Income Taxes 47	30.9	•	37.0	11.4	34.9	38.0	31.6	41.0	33.4	35.7	23.3	25.5	27.7
Return on Equity After Income Taxes 48	23.8	•	36.3	9.1	33.5	33.7	27.5	34.2	26.9	25.3	17.3	18.0	15.8
Profit Margin (Before Income Tax) 49	3.7	3.0	4.3	2.7	6.7	4.3	4.0	4.3	4.4	4.9	4.2	2.4	2.7
Profit Margin (After Income Tax) 50	2.9	2.6	4.2	2.2	6.4	3.4	3.6	3.6	3.6	3.5	3.2	1.7	1.5

Table II

Corporations with Net Income

METAL AND MINERAL (EXCEPT PETROLEUM)

MONEY AMOUNTS AND SIZE OF ASSETS IN THOUSANDS OF DOLLARS

Item Description for Accounting Period 7/06 Through 6/07		Total	Zero Assets	Under 500	500 to 1,000	1,000 to 5,000	5,000 to 10,000	10,000 to 25,000	25,000 to 50,000	50,000 to 100,000	100,000 to 250,000	250,000 to 500,000	500,000 to 2,500,000	2,500,000 and over
Number of Enterprises	1	4631	43	2755	•	867	386	223	80	53	38	16	•	•
Revenues ($ in Thousands)														
Net Sales	2	135130732	1272046	2508218	•	6035772	9459467	10823195	7753345	10439912	15752079	13253097	•	•
Interest	3	415725	2333	1895	•	4761	7843	5633	15992	7038	22439	42462	•	•
Rents	4	91571	0	0	•	1500	105	1264	951	663	1509	12981	•	•
Royalties	5	61	0	0	•	0	0	0	0	0	0	0	•	•
Other Portfolio Income	6	462760	23179	2873	•	51640	2195	2609	3583	3711	4503	74393	•	•
Other Receipts	7	953396	102	6295	•	62797	27517	55089	74207	44447	96723	131099	•	•
Total Receipts	8	137054245	1297660	2519281	•	6156470	9497127	10887790	7848078	10495771	15877253	13514032	•	•
Average Total Receipts	9	29595	30178	914	•	7101	24604	48824	98101	198033	417822	844627	•	•
Operating Costs/Operating Income (%)														
Cost of Operations	10	88.2	92.1	77.0	•	75.3	86.4	86.8	87.6	86.9	88.1	90.7	•	•
Salaries and Wages	11	2.8	3.1	1.2	•	5.9	2.9	3.4	2.7	2.7	2.1	1.9	•	•
Taxes Paid	12	0.6	0.5	1.1	•	1.2	0.6	0.7	0.6	0.6	0.6	0.6	•	•
Interest Paid	13	0.9	0.4	0.2	•	0.3	0.6	0.4	0.7	0.6	0.8	0.4	•	•
Depreciation	14	0.4	0.1	0.6	•	0.5	0.3	0.3	0.4	0.4	0.3	0.4	•	•
Amortization and Depletion	15	0.1	0.0	0.0	•	0.0	0.0	0.0	0.0	0.0	0.1	0.1	•	•
Pensions and Other Deferred Comp.	16	0.2	0.1	0.7	•	0.4	0.2	0.2	0.1	0.1	0.3	0.2	•	•
Employee Benefits	17	0.4	0.2	0.6	•	0.7	0.4	0.4	0.3	0.4	0.3	0.3	•	•
Advertising	18	0.0	0.0	0.2	•	0.1	0.1	0.0	0.0	0.1	0.0	0.0	•	•
Other Expenses	19	2.8	1.1	6.1	•	6.0	3.0	2.9	2.3	2.7	2.5	2.9	•	•
Officers' Compensation	20	0.8	0.5	7.5	•	3.8	1.2	1.2	1.2	0.9	0.4	0.2	•	•
Operating Margin	21	2.8	1.8	4.7	•	5.8	4.3	3.7	4.1	4.6	4.5	2.3	•	•
Operating Margin Before Officers' Comp.	22	3.7	2.3	12.2	•	9.6	5.5	4.9	5.3	5.5	5.0	2.5	•	•

Selected Average Balance Sheet ($ in Thousands)

Net Receivables 23	3394	0	15	674	2486	5715	11695	22088	49007	96669
Inventories 24	3292	0	21	741	2194	5536	14435	30451	65528	112683
Net Property, Plant and Equipment 25	1022	0	12	130	477	1190	2478	6582	12360	30910
Total Assets 26	12147	0	153	2508	6893	14937	36547	68783	167225	363357
Notes and Loans Payable 27	4135	0	26	365	1569	3318	11061	19596	50340	71230
All Other Liabilities 28	4129	0	13	704	2607	5433	14802	22325	58339	141449
Net Worth 29	3883	0	113	1439	2717	6186	10683	26863	58547	150677

Selected Financial Ratios (Times to 1)

Current Ratio 30	1.7	•	4.1	2.7	1.7	1.7	1.7	1.8	1.6	1.8
Quick Ratio 31	0.8	•	2.7	1.5	0.9	0.9	0.8	0.8	0.7	0.8
Net Sales to Working Capital 32	8.1	•	11.1	5.3	9.9	8.7	7.8	7.7	7.9	7.5
Coverage Ratio 33	5.9	9.7	26.3	27.6	8.5	10.8	8.3	9.4	7.6	11.3
Total Asset Turnover 34	2.4	•	6.0	2.8	3.6	3.2	2.7	2.9	2.5	2.3
Inventory Turnover 35	7.8	•	33.4	7.1	9.6	7.6	5.9	5.6	5.6	6.7
Receivables Turnover 36	9.7	•	56.6	10.5	10.3	9.7	7.7	9.0	9.3	•
Total Liabilities to Net Worth 37	2.1	•	0.4	0.7	1.5	1.4	2.4	1.6	1.9	1.4
Current Assets to Working Capital 38	2.4	•	1.3	1.6	2.5	2.4	2.5	2.3	2.6	2.3
Current Liabilities to Working Capital 39	1.4	•	0.3	0.6	1.5	1.4	1.5	1.3	1.6	1.3
Working Capital to Net Sales 40	0.1	•	0.1	0.2	0.1	0.1	0.1	0.1	0.1	0.1
Inventory to Working Capital 41	1.0	•	0.4	0.6	1.0	1.0	1.2	1.2	1.4	1.0
Total Receipts to Cash Flow 42	16.1	26.4	9.9	8.5	14.3	15.6	14.5	14.0	13.6	16.2
Cost of Goods to Cash Flow 43	14.2	24.3	7.6	6.4	12.4	13.6	12.7	12.2	12.0	14.7
Cash Flow to Total Debt 44	0.2	•	2.3	0.8	0.4	0.4	0.3	0.3	0.3	0.2

Selected Financial Factors (in Percentages)

Debt Ratio 45	68.0	•	26.0	42.6	60.6	58.6	70.8	60.9	65.0	58.5
Return on Total Assets 46	12.3	•	31.3	22.4	18.7	15.4	15.9	16.5	15.2	10.6
Return on Equity Before Income Taxes 47	32.0	•	40.8	37.7	41.9	33.7	47.8	37.7	37.6	23.3
Return on Equity After Income Taxes 48	25.3	•	40.0	36.2	37.5	29.6	40.2	30.7	26.8	17.3
Profit Margin (Before Income Tax) 49	4.3	3.8	5.1	7.8	4.7	4.3	5.3	5.1	5.3	4.2
Profit Margin (After Income Tax) 50	3.4	3.3	5.0	7.5	4.2	3.8	4.4	4.2	3.8	3.2

Table I

Corporations with and without Net Income

ELECTRICAL GOODS

MONEY AMOUNTS AND SIZE OF ASSETS IN THOUSANDS OF DOLLARS

Item Description for Accounting Period 7/06 Through 6/07		Total	Zero Assets	Under 500	500 to 1,000	1,000 to 5,000	5,000 to 10,000	10,000 to 25,000	25,000 to 50,000	50,000 to 100,000	100,000 to 250,000	250,000 to 500,000	500,000 to 2,500,000	2,500,000 and over
Number of Enterprises	1	24771	3922	12361	3478	3382	784	435	175	110	63	25	26	10
Revenues ($ in Thousands)														
Net Sales	2	305795421	2844515	8325197	7641100	22848575	13725731	19620742	15393240	18227112	25990680	23643411	54876993	92658127
Interest	3	1038750	3030	4211	5880	18555	7050	17031	30784	41392	61366	29759	324092	495600
Rents	4	158360	63	0	0	1592	2332	2742	1575	1072	19466	2845	33574	93100
Royalties	5	700690	189	0	0	0	0	546	0	11957	5958	8812	22707	650521
Other Portfolio Income	6	351154	9132	22960	11461	14887	28315	23129	29846	11778	16037	43072	70076	70460
Other Receipts	7	4206133	32223	47195	32761	140648	94001	69274	212209	85573	276123	458909	440321	2316895
Total Receipts	8	312250508	2889152	8399563	7691202	23024257	13857429	19733464	15667654	18378884	26369630	24186808	55767763	96284703
Average Total Receipts	9	12605	737	680	2211	6808	17675	45364	89529	167081	418566	967472	2144914	9628470
Operating Costs/Operating Income (%)														
Cost of Operations	10	81.4	82.9	63.8	77.4	73.9	76.0	83.0	79.2	80.5	85.7	88.9	86.8	79.9
Salaries and Wages	11	6.0	8.3	10.2	6.7	8.2	9.2	6.2	7.4	6.7	4.4	4.5	5.3	5.1
Taxes Paid	12	0.8	0.7	1.7	1.2	1.3	1.1	0.8	0.8	0.8	0.7	0.5	0.7	0.5
Interest Paid	13	0.7	0.3	0.7	0.5	0.4	1.0	0.5	0.5	0.9	0.5	0.4	1.0	0.9
Depreciation	14	0.6	0.3	0.4	0.6	0.4	0.4	0.4	0.4	0.5	0.4	0.5	0.6	0.9
Amortization and Depletion	15	1.3	0.2	0.0	0.0	0.0	0.1	0.0	0.1	0.2	0.1	0.2	0.2	4.1
Pensions and Other Deferred Comp.	16	0.3	0.0	0.9	0.2	0.4	0.2	0.2	0.3	0.4	0.2	0.2	0.3	0.2
Employee Benefits	17	0.5	0.6	0.9	0.3	0.7	0.8	0.5	0.5	0.6	0.4	0.4	0.6	0.5
Advertising	18	1.3	0.3	0.5	0.6	0.5	0.4	0.3	0.6	0.5	0.9	0.7	0.7	2.9
Other Expenses	19	6.5	10.8	13.8	8.4	8.0	8.8	5.0	6.7	5.5	5.8	4.0	3.9	7.5
Officers' Compensation	20	0.9	0.6	6.9	3.8	3.1	1.9	1.0	1.0	0.9	0.3	0.4	0.2	0.1
Operating Margin	21	•	•	0.2	0.3	3.0	0.1	2.1	2.5	2.4	0.4	•	•	•
Operating Margin Before Officers' Comp.	22	0.6	•	7.0	4.1	6.1	2.1	3.1	3.5	3.3	0.8	•	•	•

Selected Average Balance Sheet ($ in Thousands)

Net Receivables 23	1815	0	36	174	828	2562	6147	13436	25504	71803	117709	306596	1583450
Inventories 24	1185	0	34	180	718	2725	4737	10668	19231	33514	81496	200788	834127
Net Property, Plant and Equipment 25	415	0	15	119	189	451	1026	2359	5871	10055	22518	83451	380629
Total Assets 26	5743	0	126	689	2280	7442	14933	35574	69814	166372	383764	1075116	5633880
Notes and Loans Payable 27	1167	0	109	248	629	2351	3166	6706	17946	32303	35808	148786	1140174
All Other Liabilities 28	2537	0	55	232	834	3197	8237	14095	28885	85773	220940	424148	2484679
Net Worth 29	2039	0	-38	208	817	1894	3530	14773	22983	48296	127015	502182	2009027

Selected Financial Ratios (Times to 1)

Current Ratio 30	1.5	•	1.5	1.9	1.9	1.6	1.3	1.9	1.5	1.6	1.1	1.5	1.5
Quick Ratio 31	0.8	•	1.1	1.1	1.0	0.9	0.8	1.2	0.9	1.0	0.6	0.9	0.7
Net Sales to Working Capital 32	8.9	•	21.4	8.4	7.3	7.3	13.9	6.2	8.5	8.2	43.9	9.1	7.6
Coverage Ratio 33	3.5	•	2.4	2.7	9.4	2.1	6.2	8.9	4.6	5.1	4.7	2.5	2.4
Total Asset Turnover 34	2.1	•	5.4	3.2	3.0	2.4	3.0	2.5	2.4	2.5	2.5	2.0	1.6
Inventory Turnover 35	8.5	•	12.8	9.4	7.0	4.9	7.9	6.5	6.9	10.5	10.3	9.1	8.9
Receivables Turnover 36	7.2	•	17.8	13.0	7.9	6.8	7.7	6.6	7.0	6.8	8.4	6.4	6.7
Total Liabilities to Net Worth 37	1.8	•	•	2.3	1.8	2.9	3.2	1.4	2.0	2.4	2.0	1.1	1.8
Current Assets to Working Capital 38	3.0	•	3.1	2.1	2.2	2.7	4.0	2.1	2.9	2.8	11.8	2.9	3.1
Current Liabilities to Working Capital 39	2.0	•	2.1	1.1	1.2	1.7	3.0	1.1	1.9	1.8	10.8	1.9	2.1
Working Capital to Net Sales 40	0.1	•	0.0	0.1	0.1	0.1	0.1	0.2	0.1	0.1	0.0	0.1	0.1
Inventory to Working Capital 41	0.9	•	0.8	0.8	0.8	1.1	1.5	0.7	1.1	0.8	4.2	0.8	0.8
Total Receipts to Cash Flow 42	14.1	17.6	9.3	13.9	9.9	12.2	14.9	10.6	13.0	14.3	21.1	22.6	12.9
Cost of Goods to Cash Flow 43	11.4	14.6	5.9	10.7	7.3	9.2	12.4	8.4	10.5	12.3	18.7	19.6	10.3
Cash Flow to Total Debt 44	0.2	•	0.4	0.3	0.5	0.3	0.4	0.3	0.3	0.2	0.2	0.2	0.2

Selected Financial Factors (in Percentages)

Debt Ratio 45	64.5	•	130.3	69.7	64.2	74.5	76.4	58.5	67.1	71.0	66.9	53.3	64.3
Return on Total Assets 46	5.5	•	9.5	4.7	12.4	4.8	9.5	12.0	9.8	6.0	5.0	4.7	3.4
Return on Equity Before Income Taxes 47	11.1	•	•	9.7	30.9	9.9	33.8	25.6	23.3	16.6	12.0	6.0	5.6
Return on Equity After Income Taxes 48	8.5	•	•	7.7	27.9	8.4	28.5	22.2	19.3	12.7	9.6	3.4	3.6
Profit Margin (Before Income Tax) 49	1.8	•	1.0	0.9	3.7	1.1	2.6	4.3	3.2	1.9	1.6	1.4	1.2
Profit Margin (After Income Tax) 50	1.4	•	0.9	0.7	3.4	0.9	3.7	2.7	2.7	1.5	1.3	0.8	0.8

Table II

Corporations with Net Income

ELECTRICAL GOODS

MONEY AMOUNTS AND SIZE OF ASSETS IN THOUSANDS OF DOLLARS

Item Description for Accounting Period 7/06 Through 6/07	Total	Zero Assets	Under 500	500 to 1,000	1,000 to 5,000	5,000 to 10,000	10,000 to 25,000	25,000 to 50,000	50,000 to 100,000	100,000 to 250,000	250,000 to 500,000	500,000 to 2,500,000	2,500,000 and over
Number of Enterprises 1	17092	2628	7698	2547	2879	633	368	146	•	48	20	23	•

Revenues ($ in Thousands)

Item Description for Accounting Period 7/06 Through 6/07	Total	Zero Assets	Under 500	500 to 1,000	1,000 to 5,000	5,000 to 10,000	10,000 to 25,000	25,000 to 50,000	50,000 to 100,000	100,000 to 250,000	250,000 to 500,000	500,000 to 2,500,000	2,500,000 and over
Net Sales 2	253193022	1970072	6911362	6570124	20249932	12838024	17417958	13458662	•	20761165	17882224	49945046	•
Interest 3	684930	663	3661	3445	17649	5049	13214	21270	•	41262	26567	293714	•
Rents 4	84491	40	0	0	1133	1846	2239	1575	•	19190	2293	26683	•
Royalties 5	98466	0	0	0	0	0	546	0	•	927	8628	16384	•
Other Portfolio Income 6	314953	8594	22676	11036	14887	26709	20277	28926	•	13225	36967	53211	•
Other Receipts 7	3360558	20105	45094	25560	107073	59841	46805	151332	•	243894	43447	406066	•
Total Receipts 8	257736420	1999474	6982793	6610165	20390674	12931469	17501039	13661765	•	21079663	18000126	50741104	•
Average Total Receipts 9	15079	761	907	2595	7083	20429	47557	93574	•	439160	900006	2206135	•

Operating Costs/Operating Income (%)

Item Description for Accounting Period 7/06 Through 6/07	Total	Zero Assets	Under 500	500 to 1,000	1,000 to 5,000	5,000 to 10,000	10,000 to 25,000	25,000 to 50,000	50,000 to 100,000	100,000 to 250,000	250,000 to 500,000	500,000 to 2,500,000	2,500,000 and over
Cost of Operations 10	82.4	82.5	64.0	77.5	73.8	76.3	83.0	78.3	•	85.6	88.2	85.7	•
Salaries and Wages 11	5.9	4.9	9.3	6.0	7.9	8.6	5.9	7.4	•	4.6	4.3	5.3	•
Taxes Paid 12	0.7	0.4	1.6	1.1	1.2	1.1	0.8	0.8	•	0.8	0.6	0.7	•
Interest Paid 13	0.6	0.1	0.2	0.4	0.4	0.9	0.4	0.5	•	0.3	0.4	0.9	•
Depreciation 14	0.5	0.1	0.4	0.6	0.4	0.4	0.3	0.4	•	0.4	0.4	0.6	•
Amortization and Depletion 15	0.1	0.1	0.0	0.0	0.0	0.0	0.0	0.0	•	0.1	0.2	0.1	•
Pensions and Other Deferred Comp. 16	0.3	0.0	0.9	0.2	0.4	0.2	0.2	0.3	•	0.3	0.1	0.3	•
Employee Benefits 17	0.5	0.3	0.9	0.3	0.7	0.7	0.5	0.6	•	0.4	0.4	0.5	•
Advertising 18	0.7	0.2	0.3	0.7	0.5	0.3	0.3	0.4	•	0.7	0.2	0.6	•
Other Expenses 19	5.8	7.7	11.0	7.3	7.6	7.8	4.4	6.2	•	5.0	3.1	3.6	•
Officers' Compensation 20	0.9	0.7	6.9	3.3	3.1	1.7	1.1	1.0	•	0.3	0.3	0.1	•
Operating Margin 21	1.4	3.0	4.4	2.7	3.9	2.0	3.2	4.1	•	1.6	1.7	1.4	•
Operating Margin Before Officers' Comp. 22	2.3	3.7	11.3	6.0	7.0	3.7	4.3	5.1	•	1.9	2.0	1.6	•

Selected Average Balance Sheet ($ in Thousands)

Net Receivables 23	2223	0	39	189	855	2920	6109	14085	•	68386	121383	309444
Inventories 24	1405	0	36	176	737	2463	4857	10674	•	33780	74080	201324
Net Property, Plant and Equipment 25	444	0	13	130	156	460	922	2461	•	9841	22821	88402
Total Assets 26	6259	0	144	684	2303	7507	14584	35657	•	159965	381394	1068326
Notes and Loans Payable 27	1084	0	56	222	568	2554	2576	7000	•	24021	33309	148571
All Other Liabilities 28	2599	0	59	235	854	3170	6601	13470	•	79645	217766	390988
Net Worth 29	2576	0	29	227	882	1783	5408	15187	•	56299	130318	528766

Selected Financial Ratios (Times to 1)

Current Ratio 30	1.7	•	1.9	2.0	1.9	1.5	1.6	2.0	•	1.6	1.1	1.6
Quick Ratio 31	1.0	•	1.4	1.2	1.0	0.8	0.9	1.2	•	1.0	0.6	1.0
Net Sales to Working Capital 32	8.0	•	16.1	9.7	7.3	9.2	10.0	6.0	•	8.6	35.7	9.0
Coverage Ratio 33	6.3	54.8	28.7	8.5	11.4	4.2	9.6	12.8	•	10.2	6.8	4.4
Total Asset Turnover 34	2.4	•	6.2	3.8	3.1	2.7	3.2	2.6	•	2.7	2.3	2.0
Inventory Turnover 35	8.7	•	15.9	11.4	7.0	6.3	8.1	6.8	•	11.0	10.6	9.2
Receivables Turnover 36	7.0	•	22.3	14.4	8.0	7.1	8.0	6.8	•	7.3	9.2	6.8
Total Liabilities to Net Worth 37	1.4	•	4.0	2.0	1.6	3.2	1.7	1.3	•	1.8	1.9	1.0
Current Assets to Working Capital 38	2.5	•	2.1	2.0	2.2	3.0	2.7	2.0	•	2.7	10.4	2.8
Current Liabilities to Working Capital 39	1.5	•	1.1	1.0	1.2	2.0	1.7	1.0	•	1.7	9.4	1.8
Working Capital to Net Sales 40	0.1	•	0.1	0.1	0.1	0.1	0.1	0.2	•	0.1	0.0	0.1
Inventory to Working Capital 41	0.8	•	0.5	0.8	0.8	1.2	1.0	0.7	•	0.8	3.8	0.8
Total Receipts to Cash Flow 42	12.6	9.2	7.9	11.6	9.5	11.1	14.1	9.7	•	13.5	21.6	17.1
Cost of Goods to Cash Flow 43	10.4	7.6	5.0	9.0	7.0	8.4	11.7	7.6	•	11.6	19.0	14.7
Cash Flow to Total Debt 44	0.3	•	1.0	0.5	0.5	0.3	0.4	0.5	•	0.3	0.2	0.2

Selected Financial Factors (in Percentages)

Debt Ratio 45	58.8	•	80.1	66.8	61.7	76.2	62.9	57.4	•	64.8	65.8	50.5
Return on Total Assets 46	9.1	•	35.2	14.2	15.5	9.7	13.3	15.7	•	9.5	7.0	7.9
Return on Equity Before Income Taxes 47	18.5	•	170.7	37.8	36.9	31.0	32.2	33.9	•	24.3	17.5	12.4
Return on Equity After Income Taxes 48	15.5	•	165.1	35.3	33.6	29.1	28.1	30.0	•	19.9	14.7	9.7
Profit Margin (Before Income Tax) 49	3.2	4.5	5.4	3.3	4.6	2.7	3.7	5.6	•	3.2	2.6	3.0
Profit Margin (After Income Tax) 50	2.7	4.3	5.3	3.1	4.2	2.6	3.2	4.9	•	2.6	2.1	2.4

Table I
Corporations with and without Net Income

HARDWARE, PLUMBING, HEATING EQUIPMENT, AND SUPPLIES

MONEY AMOUNTS AND SIZE OF ASSETS IN THOUSANDS OF DOLLARS

Item Description for Accounting Period 7/06 Through 6/07		Total	Zero Assets	Under 500	500 to 1,000	1,000 to 5,000	5,000 to 10,000	10,000 to 25,000	25,000 to 50,000	50,000 to 100,000	100,000 to 250,000	250,000 to 500,000	500,000 to 2,500,000	2,500,000 and over
Number of Enterprises	1	15236	534	9158	1844	2688	505	327	103	49	16	4	8	0
Revenues ($ in Thousands)														
Net Sales	2	99417091	242006	3989594	5347758	15388643	9883486	14546820	9039978	8083061	5982507	2312622	24600616	0
Interest	3	183306	916	705	3794	18347	4920	10792	9341	8063	1610	2133	122684	0
Rents	4	17069	61	333	0	3218	1183	2191	1143	5215	1047	1543	1134	0
Royalties	5	23480	4	0	0	0	4	0	8814	487	0	10284	3888	0
Other Portfolio Income	6	152019	8180	15096	3717	16575	4999	34279	4096	14208	9187	17968	23717	0
Other Receipts	7	1440759	3894	6652	28547	459703	66314	69097	53961	86074	46430	33810	586276	0
Total Receipts	8	101233724	255061	4012380	5383816	15886486	9960906	14663179	9117333	8197108	6040781	2378360	25338315	0
Average Total Receipts	9	6644	478	438	2920	5910	19725	44842	88518	167288	377549	594590	3167289	•
Operating Costs/Operating Income (%)														
Cost of Operations	10	73.3	71.7	60.5	64.9	73.1	71.4	75.2	76.6	74.7	75.8	71.5	74.8	•
Salaries and Wages	11	9.5	7.1	9.4	10.5	8.8	10.4	9.7	8.0	9.1	8.2	9.3	10.5	•
Taxes Paid	12	1.3	1.3	2.2	1.6	1.4	1.5	1.1	1.2	1.2	1.2	1.4	1.3	•
Interest Paid	13	0.9	1.9	0.8	0.5	0.6	0.7	0.6	0.7	0.8	0.8	1.8	1.6	•
Depreciation	14	0.6	0.8	0.7	0.3	0.8	0.4	0.4	0.5	0.7	0.6	1.1	0.7	•
Amortization and Depletion	15	0.1	1.1	0.2	0.0	0.1	0.0	0.0	0.1	0.0	0.2	0.1	0.4	•
Pensions and Other Deferred Comp.	16	0.5	0.3	0.6	0.9	0.7	0.4	0.3	0.4	0.4	0.3	0.7	0.5	•
Employee Benefits	17	0.9	0.6	0.5	0.8	0.8	1.0	0.6	0.7	1.0	0.8	1.3	1.3	•
Advertising	18	0.5	0.5	1.3	0.3	0.4	0.8	0.4	0.8	0.4	0.6	1.1	0.2	•
Other Expenses	19	7.7	14.2	14.8	8.5	8.7	7.5	5.3	6.4	6.8	7.2	8.1	7.8	•
Officers' Compensation	20	2.3	1.0	7.6	8.2	4.5	2.6	2.2	1.1	1.0	0.8	0.4	0.1	•
Operating Margin	21	2.3	•	1.4	3.6	0.1	3.4	4.2	3.6	4.0	3.7	3.2	0.7	•
Operating Margin Before Officers' Comp.	22	4.6	0.7	9.0	11.8	4.6	6.0	6.3	4.7	4.9	4.4	3.6	0.8	•

Selected Average Balance Sheet ($ in Thousands)

Net Receivables 23	879	0	31	286	681	2454	4761	11007	21339	44104	66961	600477	•
Inventories 24	874	0	19	188	767	2988	6478	12473	24008	74940	95768	407970	•
Net Property, Plant and Equipment 25	278	0	10	51	172	617	1056	3181	9039	19863	86036	187194	•
Total Assets 26	2882	0	88	687	2239	7000	15209	34104	67923	165225	289497	2083683	•
Notes and Loans Payable 27	952	0	85	187	439	1789	3510	9741	17160	42570	139916	883587	•
All Other Liabilities 28	869	0	48	286	789	2178	4399	8498	19075	57613	74210	573693	•
Net Worth 29	1060	0	-46	215	1012	3033	7300	15865	31688	65042	75372	626403	•

Selected Financial Ratios (Times to 1)

Current Ratio 30	2.1	•	1.2	1.7	2.1	2.0	2.1	2.1	2.2	1.8	1.5	2.3	•
Quick Ratio 31	1.1	•	0.9	1.1	1.1	0.9	1.0	1.0	1.0	0.7	0.6	1.4	•
Net Sales to Working Capital 32	6.2	•	43.0	11.9	6.1	6.3	6.4	6.1	5.6	7.1	9.7	4.8	•
Coverage Ratio 33	5.5	3.7	3.5	9.4	6.7	6.9	9.1	7.0	8.0	7.0	4.4	3.3	•
Total Asset Turnover 34	2.3	•	5.0	4.2	2.6	2.8	2.9	2.6	2.4	2.3	2.0	1.5	•
Inventory Turnover 35	5.5	•	14.2	10.0	5.5	4.7	5.2	5.4	5.1	3.8	4.3	5.6	•
Receivables Turnover 36	7.8	•	13.5	10.2	8.6	8.0	9.2	8.6	8.0	6.7	17.3	5.9	•
Total Liabilities to Net Worth 37	1.7	•	•	2.2	1.2	1.3	1.1	1.1	1.1	1.5	2.8	2.3	•
Current Assets to Working Capital 38	1.9	•	6.4	2.5	1.9	2.0	1.9	2.0	1.8	2.3	3.1	1.7	•
Current Liabilities to Working Capital 39	0.9	•	5.4	1.5	0.9	1.0	0.9	1.0	0.8	1.3	2.1	0.7	•
Working Capital to Net Sales 40	0.2	•	0.0	0.1	0.2	0.2	0.2	0.2	0.2	0.1	0.1	0.2	•
Inventory to Working Capital 41	0.8	•	1.7	0.8	0.8	1.0	0.9	0.9	0.9	1.3	1.6	0.7	•
Total Receipts to Cash Flow 42	10.3	6.0	7.6	9.7	10.3	10.7	12.1	11.2	9.7	10.0	8.7	10.4	•
Cost of Goods to Cash Flow 43	7.6	4.3	4.6	6.3	7.5	7.6	9.1	8.6	7.3	7.6	6.2	7.8	•
Cash Flow to Total Debt 44	0.3	•	0.4	0.5	0.5	0.5	0.5	0.4	0.5	0.4	0.3	0.2	•

Selected Financial Factors (in Percentages)

Debt Ratio 45	63.2	•	152.1	68.7	54.8	56.7	52.0	53.5	53.3	60.6	74.0	69.9	•
Return on Total Assets 46	11.5	•	13.8	20.0	10.0	13.7	16.5	13.2	14.9	12.3	15.7	7.8	•
Return on Equity Before Income Taxes 47	25.5	•	•	57.0	18.8	27.0	30.6	24.4	28.0	26.7	46.6	17.9	•
Return on Equity After Income Taxes 48	21.5	•	•	52.2	16.1	25.3	27.4	20.6	24.3	22.3	34.3	12.9	•
Profit Margin (Before Income Tax) 49	4.1	5.2	2.0	4.2	3.3	4.2	5.0	4.4	5.4	4.6	6.1	3.7	•
Profit Margin (After Income Tax) 50	3.5	3.3	1.9	3.9	2.8	3.9	4.5	3.7	4.7	3.9	4.5	2.6	•

Table II

Corporations with Net Income

HARDWARE, PLUMBING, HEATING EQUIPMENT, AND SUPPLIES

MONEY AMOUNTS AND SIZE OF ASSETS IN THOUSANDS OF DOLLARS

Item Description for Accounting Period 7/06 Through 6/07	Total	Zero Assets	Under 500	500 to 1,000	1,000 to 5,000	5,000 to 10,000	10,000 to 25,000	25,000 to 50,000	50,000 to 100,000	100,000 to 250,000	250,000 to 500,000	500,000 to 2,500,000	2,500,000 and over
Number of Enterprises 1	10528	467	5342	1753	2003	488	308	96	•	13	4	•	0

Revenues ($ in Thousands)

Net Sales 2	88577302	170134	2438396	5195087	12631976	9744172	14056664	8386328	•	5298209	2312622	•	0
Interest 3	173039	723	680	3189	18137	4891	10018	7672	•	1443	2133	•	0
Rents 4	15025	61	333	0	3003	1183	2191	944	•	63	1543	•	0
Royalties 5	20097	4	0	0	0	4	0	8814	•	0	10284	•	0
Other Portfolio Income 6	144401	5904	13896	2892	16297	4980	31297	4096	•	9186	17968	•	0
Other Receipts 7	994433	3818	5375	27611	448343	62973	68729	52438	•	46209	33810	•	0
Total Receipts 8	89924297	180644	2458680	5228779	13117756	9818203	14168899	8460292	•	5355110	2378360	•	0
Average Total Receipts 9	8541	387	460	2983	6549	20119	46003	88128	•	411932	594590	•	•

Operating Costs/Operating Income (%)

Cost of Operations 10	72.9	60.2	58.4	64.5	73.3	71.4	75.2	76.7	•	74.5	71.5	•	•
Salaries and Wages 11	9.7	4.7	9.4	10.5	8.5	10.4	9.9	8.0	•	8.6	9.3	•	•
Taxes Paid 12	1.3	1.1	2.4	1.6	1.3	1.5	1.1	1.1	•	1.2	1.4	•	•
Interest Paid 13	0.9	1.3	0.5	0.4	0.4	0.6	0.6	0.7	•	0.6	1.8	•	•
Depreciation 14	0.6	0.9	0.7	0.3	0.8	0.4	0.4	0.4	•	0.6	1.1	•	•
Amortization and Depletion 15	0.1	0.0	0.1	0.0	0.0	0.0	0.0	0.0	•	0.2	0.1	•	•
Pensions and Other Deferred Comp. 16	0.5	0.2	0.6	0.9	0.8	0.4	0.3	0.5	•	0.3	0.7	•	•
Employee Benefits 17	0.9	0.6	0.4	0.8	0.8	0.9	0.6	0.7	•	0.8	1.3	•	•
Advertising 18	0.5	0.1	1.7	0.3	0.4	0.8	0.4	0.8	•	0.4	1.1	•	•
Other Expenses 19	7.0	14.3	15.2	8.4	7.9	7.4	4.9	5.9	•	7.4	8.1	•	•
Officers' Compensation 20	2.2	1.0	5.6	8.3	4.7	2.6	2.1	1.1	•	0.8	0.4	•	•
Operating Margin 21	3.5	15.7	5.0	3.9	1.0	3.6	4.4	4.0	•	4.5	3.2	•	•
Operating Margin Before Officers' Comp. 22	5.7	16.7	10.5	12.3	5.7	6.2	6.5	5.2	•	5.3	3.6	•	•

Selected Average Balance Sheet ($ in Thousands)

Item											
Net Receivables 23	1159	0	31	294	738	2523	4872	10995	•	42479	66961
Inventories 24	1127	0	15	174	842	2873	6592	12407	•	64695	95768
Net Property, Plant and Equipment 25	345	0	12	45	190	598	1077	3103	•	19775	86036
Total Assets 26	3687	0	82	689	2247	6966	15421	33649	•	164743	289497
Notes and Loans Payable 27	1167	0	71	157	321	1664	3442	9358	•	43264	139916
All Other Liabilities 28	1056	0	35	292	743	2132	4347	8060	•	50839	74210
Net Worth 29	1464	0	-25	241	1183	3170	7632	16231	•	70641	75372

Selected Financial Ratios (Times to 1)

Item											
Current Ratio 30	2.2	•	1.6	1.7	2.3	2.1	2.2	2.1	•	1.7	1.5
Quick Ratio 31	1.2	•	1.2	1.1	1.3	1.0	1.0	1.0	•	0.7	0.6
Net Sales to Working Capital 32	5.9	•	18.8	11.8	6.0	6.3	6.0	6.0	•	8.2	9.7
Coverage Ratio 33	6.8	17.9	11.9	11.3	13.0	7.9	9.7	8.2	•	9.8	4.4
Total Asset Turnover 34	2.3	•	5.6	4.3	2.8	2.9	3.0	2.6	•	2.5	2.0
Inventory Turnover 35	5.4	•	17.5	11.0	5.5	5.0	5.2	5.4	•	4.7	4.3
Receivables Turnover 36	7.6	•	11.4	11.2	8.5	8.2	9.3	8.5	•	•	17.3
Total Liabilities to Net Worth 37	1.5	•	•	1.9	0.9	1.2	1.0	1.1	•	1.3	2.8
Current Assets to Working Capital 38	1.9	•	2.7	2.4	1.8	1.9	1.8	1.9	•	2.4	3.1
Current Liabilities to Working Capital 39	0.9	•	1.7	1.4	0.8	0.9	0.8	0.9	•	1.4	2.1
Working Capital to Net Sales 40	0.2	•	0.1	0.1	0.2	0.2	0.2	0.2	•	0.1	0.1
Inventory to Working Capital 41	0.8	•	0.6	0.7	0.7	0.9	0.9	0.9	•	1.3	1.6
Total Receipts to Cash Flow 42	10.1	2.9	5.7	9.4	9.4	10.6	12.3	11.1	•	9.0	8.7
Cost of Goods to Cash Flow 43	7.4	1.7	3.4	6.1	6.9	7.6	9.3	8.5	•	6.7	6.2
Cash Flow to Total Debt 44	0.4	•	0.8	0.7	0.6	0.5	0.5	0.5	•	0.5	0.3

Selected Financial Factors (in Percentages)

Item											
Debt Ratio 45	60.3	•	130.1	65.0	47.3	54.5	50.5	51.8	•	57.1	74.0
Return on Total Assets 46	13.3	35.4	21.5	14.8	14.3	17.2	14.5	•	15.3	15.7	
Return on Equity Before Income Taxes 47	28.5	•	56.2	25.9	27.5	31.2	26.4	•	32.1	46.6	
Return on Equity After Income Taxes 48	24.3	•	51.6	22.8	25.8	28.0	22.5	•	27.2	34.3	
Profit Margin (Before Income Tax) 49	5.0	21.8	5.8	4.6	4.9	4.4	5.2	4.9	•	5.6	6.1
Profit Margin (After Income Tax) 50	4.2	19.1	5.6	4.2	4.3	4.1	4.7	4.2	•	4.7	4.5

Table I

Corporations with and without Net Income

MACHINERY, EQUIPMENT, AND SUPPLIES

MONEY AMOUNTS AND SIZE OF ASSETS IN THOUSANDS OF DOLLARS

Item Description for Accounting Period 7/06 Through 6/07		Total	Zero Assets	Under 500	500 to 1,000	1,000 to 5,000	5,000 to 10,000	10,000 to 25,000	25,000 to 50,000	50,000 to 100,000	100,000 to 250,000	250,000 to 500,000	500,000 to 2,500,000	2,500,000 and over
Number of Enterprises	1	50764	3485	29673	5377	9060	1654	951	315	116	79	30	21	3
Revenues ($ in Thousands)														
Net Sales	2	248002711	5981371	14619414	10779585	50091650	28503417	31046280	21140513	13515537	18536016	12593258	28546187	12649485
Interest	3	473895	8606	10683	11833	39282	17307	28199	45339	33970	55502	44958	89701	88514
Rents	4	267674	1303	45638	6572	20297	19431	14755	9987	22617	43173	54950	15196	13755
Royalties	5	29688	0	2	0	27	1	16	437	3013	16672	3681	5557	281
Other Portfolio Income	6	1418428	54926	21251	36227	118348	56939	227148	209768	164048	136118	157245	209721	26688
Other Receipts	7	2912059	19421	384265	112664	305666	260549	401166	207052	130045	361572	327174	246866	155620
Total Receipts	8	253104455	6065627	15081253	10946881	50575270	28857644	31717564	21613096	13869230	19149053	13181266	29113228	12934343
Average Total Receipts	9	4986	1740	508	2036	5582	17447	33352	68613	119562	242393	439376	1386344	4311448
Operating Costs/Operating Income (%)														
Cost of Operations	10	75.0	87.8	66.0	71.2	71.9	76.7	77.1	76.8	77.8	77.3	72.2	77.7	73.3
Salaries and Wages	11	7.3	4.7	6.6	6.0	8.2	7.3	8.0	7.2	7.1	6.6	7.9	5.8	8.3
Taxes Paid	12	1.2	0.4	1.9	1.6	1.4	1.3	1.1	1.1	1.1	1.1	1.0	0.9	1.5
Interest Paid	13	1.0	0.2	0.5	0.8	0.9	0.8	1.1	1.0	1.2	1.4	1.9	1.0	0.9
Depreciation	14	1.6	0.2	0.8	1.0	1.1	0.8	1.6	1.7	2.3	2.6	4.4	2.1	1.1
Amortization and Depletion	15	0.1	0.1	0.0	0.1	0.1	0.1	0.1	0.1	0.1	0.2	0.3	0.1	0.1
Pensions and Other Deferred Comp.	16	0.4	0.2	1.3	0.2	0.5	0.3	0.3	0.3	0.3	0.3	0.3	0.6	1.0
Employee Benefits	17	0.9	0.2	0.8	0.8	0.8	0.8	0.8	0.8	0.8	1.4	1.6	1.1	1.0
Advertising	18	0.5	0.1	0.6	0.5	0.4	0.4	0.4	0.5	0.4	0.5	0.4	0.5	1.2
Other Expenses	19	7.4	4.1	14.4	10.3	8.6	5.7	6.7	7.0	7.0	6.5	7.8	5.6	5.7
Officers' Compensation	20	2.3	1.3	7.4	5.2	3.5	2.7	1.6	1.4	1.0	0.7	0.6	0.5	0.5
Operating Margin	21	2.3	0.7	•	2.3	2.6	3.2	1.2	1.9	0.9	1.4	1.7	4.2	5.4
Operating Margin Before Officers' Comp.	22	4.6	1.9	7.2	7.5	6.1	5.9	2.9	3.4	1.9	2.1	2.3	4.7	5.9

Selected Average Balance Sheet ($ in Thousands)

Item													
Net Receivables 23	633	0	33	224	572	1848	3797	9524	17133	39826	66800	236127	993070
Inventories 24	812	0	31	245	832	3008	5923	12331	23078	54461	122494	222885	544547
Net Property, Plant and Equipment 25	364	0	17	79	287	794	2145	5074	12061	28083	63287	162430	359490
Total Assets 26	2484	0	114	749	2230	6984	14889	34969	69032	171511	347256	979465	3071309
Notes and Loans Payable 27	806	0	59	224	800	1918	5061	11537	24683	57675	124185	282895	670776
All Other Liabilities 28	811	0	32	239	671	2541	5350	12469	20316	59264	99317	350164	753155
Net Worth 29	867	0	23	286	759	2525	4477	10963	24033	54572	123753	346406	1647377

Selected Financial Ratios (Times to 1)

Item													
Current Ratio 30	1.6	•	2.3	2.3	1.8	1.6	1.5	1.5	1.5	1.6	1.5	1.8	1.9
Quick Ratio 31	0.7	•	1.4	1.2	0.8	0.7	0.6	0.7	0.7	0.5	0.8	0.8	1.0
Net Sales to Working Capital 32	6.9	•	10.2	5.8	7.2	8.7	7.8	7.3	6.2	6.4	6.3	5.1	4.4
Coverage Ratio 33	5.4	13.7	6.8	5.7	5.1	6.4	4.1	5.2	3.8	4.4	4.4	7.1	9.4
Total Asset Turnover 34	2.0	•	4.3	2.7	2.5	2.2	2.2	1.9	1.7	1.4	1.2	1.4	1.4
Inventory Turnover 35	4.5	•	10.5	5.8	4.8	4.4	4.3	3.9	3.3	2.5	2.5	4.7	5.7
Receivables Turnover 36	8.2	•	13.9	10.1	9.5	9.0	9.3	7.6	6.9	6.4	6.5	7.2	4.5
Total Liabilities to Net Worth 37	1.9	•	3.9	1.6	1.9	1.8	2.3	2.2	1.9	2.1	1.8	1.8	0.9
Current Assets to Working Capital 38	2.5	•	1.8	1.8	2.3	2.6	3.2	2.9	2.6	3.2	3.1	2.3	2.1
Current Liabilities to Working Capital 39	1.5	•	0.8	0.8	1.3	1.6	2.2	1.9	1.6	2.2	2.1	1.3	1.1
Working Capital to Net Sales 40	0.1	•	0.1	0.2	0.1	0.1	0.1	0.1	0.2	0.2	0.2	0.2	0.2
Inventory to Working Capital 41	1.2	•	0.6	0.7	1.1	1.5	1.7	1.5	1.3	1.6	1.8	1.0	0.6
Total Receipts to Cash Flow 42	9.9	19.0	7.6	8.3	9.7	11.3	11.6	10.2	11.7	10.3	8.2	9.5	8.2
Cost of Goods to Cash Flow 43	7.4	16.7	5.0	5.9	7.0	8.7	8.9	7.8	9.1	8.0	5.9	7.4	6.0
Cash Flow to Total Debt 44	0.3	•	0.7	0.5	0.4	0.3	0.3	0.3	0.2	0.2	0.2	0.2	0.4

Selected Financial Factors (in Percentages)

Item													
Debt Ratio 45	65.1	•	79.6	61.8	66.0	63.8	69.9	68.6	65.2	64.4	68.2	64.6	46.4
Return on Total Assets 46	10.5	•	15.2	12.5	11.1	12.9	9.8	9.9	7.9	9.9	8.3	10.0	11.6
Return on Equity Before Income Taxes 47	24.6	•	63.3	27.0	26.3	30.2	24.8	25.6	16.7	21.6	20.2	24.4	19.3
Return on Equity After Income Taxes 48	20.3	•	60.7	25.0	24.2	27.6	22.0	21.0	13.0	16.7	16.1	17.2	12.6
Profit Margin (Before Income Tax) 49	4.4	2.1	3.0	3.9	3.6	4.4	3.4	4.2	3.5	6.4	4.7	6.2	7.5
Profit Margin (After Income Tax) 50	3.6	1.9	2.9	3.6	3.3	4.0	3.0	3.4	2.7	4.9	4.9	4.4	4.9

Table II
Corporations with Net Income

MACHINERY, EQUIPMENT, AND SUPPLIES

MONEY AMOUNTS AND SIZE OF ASSETS IN THOUSANDS OF DOLLARS

Item Description for Accounting Period 7/06 Through 6/07	Total	Zero Assets	Under 500	500 to 1,000	1,000 to 5,000	5,000 to 10,000	10,000 to 25,000	25,000 to 50,000	50,000 to 100,000	100,000 to 250,000	250,000 to 500,000	500,000 to 2,500,000	2,500,000 and over
Number of Enterprises **1**	32346	1887	16614	4160	6838	1528	825	282	93	68	•	•	3
Revenues ($ in Thousands)													
Net Sales **2**	220747413	5075927	11260634	9713359	40376061	26767496	27498478	19490344	11404305	16740711	•	•	12649485
Interest **3**	433382	7911	4923	9693	31179	15344	25783	44019	25850	49249	•	•	88514
Rents **4**	249901	1303	45638	586	18692	16595	13541	9776	19265	40852	•	•	13755
Royalties **5**	29686	0	0	0	27	1	16	437	3013	16672	•	•	281
Other Portfolio Income **6**	1314813	53710	14989	35077	103528	52624	203738	173443	158820	125233	•	•	26688
Other Receipts **7**	2710212	15449	371736	109618	259088	229493	383802	197016	117329	357476	•	•	155620
Total Receipts **8**	225485407	5154300	11697920	9868333	40788575	27081553	28125358	19915035	11728582	17330193	•	•	12934343
Average Total Receipts **9**	6971	2731	704	2372	5965	17724	34091	70621	126114	254856		•	4311448
Operating Costs/Operating Income (%)													
Cost of Operations **10**	74.6	90.2	64.1	71.6	70.3	76.4	76.8	76.9	76.7	77.0	•	•	73.3
Salaries and Wages **11**	7.1	3.5	6.4	5.6	8.0	7.3	8.1	7.0	7.1	6.5	•	•	8.3
Taxes Paid **12**	1.2	0.4	1.9	1.6	1.4	1.3	1.1	1.1	1.1	1.1	•	•	1.5
Interest Paid **13**	0.9	0.1	0.4	0.7	0.8	0.8	1.0	1.0	1.1	1.3	•	•	0.9
Depreciation **14**	1.6	0.2	0.6	1.0	1.0	0.7	1.5	1.7	2.2	2.5	•	•	1.1
Amortization and Depletion **15**	0.1	0.0	0.0	0.1	0.1	0.1	0.1	0.1	0.1	0.2	•	•	0.1
Pensions and Other Deferred Comp. **16**	0.5	0.2	1.6	0.2	0.5	0.3	0.3	0.4	0.3	0.4	•	•	1.0
Employee Benefits **17**	0.9	0.1	0.8	0.7	0.8	0.8	0.8	0.8	0.8	1.3	•	•	1.0
Advertising **18**	0.5	0.1	0.5	0.5	0.4	0.3	0.4	0.5	0.4	0.5	•	•	1.2
Other Expenses **19**	7.1	2.6	13.6	9.5	8.6	5.5	6.4	6.6	6.8	6.4	•	•	5.7
Officers' Compensation **20**	2.2	1.2	7.2	5.2	3.8	2.8	1.6	1.5	1.0	0.7	•	•	0.5
Operating Margin **21**	3.3	1.5	2.9	3.4	4.2	3.7	2.0	2.6	2.3	2.2	•	•	5.4
Operating Margin Before Officers' Comp. **22**	5.5	2.7	10.1	8.6	8.0	6.5	3.6	4.1	3.4	2.9	•	•	5.9

Selected Average Balance Sheet ($ in Thousands)

Net Receivables 23	877	0	43	250	580	1903	3659	9480	16793	41490	• 993070
Inventories 24	1110	0	36	248	845	2831	5960	12402	24734	58576	• 544547
Net Property, Plant and Equipment 25	492	0	20	88	264	788	2014	4845	12101	25538	• 359490
Total Assets 26	3390	0	127	760	2206	6984	14715	34784	69747	171790	• 3071309
Notes and Loans Payable 27	1026	0	48	197	692	1867	4576	11269	24254	55547	• 670776
All Other Liabilities 28	1092	0	36	240	632	2441	5221	11913	19558	59483	• 753155
Net Worth 29	1273	0	43	323	882	2677	4919	11602	25935	56760	• 1647377

Selected Financial Ratios (Times to 1)

Current Ratio 30	1.7	•	2.4	2.3	1.9	1.7	1.5	1.5	1.7	1.5	• 1.9
Quick Ratio 31	0.8	•	1.6	1.3	0.9	0.7	0.6	0.7	0.7	0.6	• 1.0
Net Sales to Working Capital 32	6.8	•	11.5	6.5	7.0	7.5	8.0	7.4	6.1	6.0	• 4.4
Coverage Ratio 33	7.0	46.2	20.1	8.6	7.4	7.4	5.3	6.0	5.6	5.5	• 9.4
Total Asset Turnover 34	2.0	•	5.4	3.1	2.7	2.5	2.3	2.0	1.8	1.4	• 1.4
Inventory Turnover 35	4.6	•	12.2	6.7	4.9	4.7	4.3	4.3	3.8	3.2	• 5.7
Receivables Turnover 36	8.3	•	13.6	11.2	9.9	9.5	9.7	7.9	7.2	6.3	• 4.5
Total Liabilities to Net Worth 37	1.7	•	1.9	1.4	1.5	1.6	2.0	2.0	1.7	2.0	• 0.9
Current Assets to Working Capital 38	2.5	•	1.7	1.8	2.1	2.5	2.9	3.0	2.5	3.0	• 2.1
Current Liabilities to Working Capital 39	1.5	•	0.7	0.8	1.1	1.5	1.9	2.0	1.5	2.0	• 1.1
Working Capital to Net Sales 40	0.1	•	0.1	0.2	0.1	0.1	0.1	0.1	0.2	0.2	• 0.2
Inventory to Working Capital 41	1.2	•	0.5	0.7	1.0	1.4	1.5	1.5	1.3	1.5	• 0.6
Total Receipts to Cash Flow 42	9.1	19.2	6.2	8.0	8.3	10.9	10.8	9.9	10.0	9.4	• 8.2
Cost of Goods to Cash Flow 43	6.8	17.3	3.9	5.7	5.8	8.3	8.3	7.6	7.7	7.3	• 6.0
Cash Flow to Total Debt 44	0.4	•	1.3	0.7	0.5	0.4	0.3	0.3	0.3	0.2	• 0.4

Selected Financial Factors (in Percentages)

Debt Ratio 45	62.5	•	65.9	57.5	60.0	61.7	66.6	66.6	62.8	67.0	• 46.4
Return on Total Assets 46	12.9	•	38.5	17.3	16.2	14.3	11.9	11.4	11.0	9.9	• 11.6
Return on Equity Before Income Taxes 47	29.3	•	107.3	36.0	35.1	32.2	29.0	28.6	24.3	24.7	• 19.3
Return on Equity After Income Taxes 48	24.8	•	104.9	33.7	32.7	29.6	26.0	23.8	20.4	20.1	• 12.6
Profit Margin (Before Income Tax) 49	5.5	3.0	6.8	5.0	5.2	4.9	4.3	4.8	5.1	5.7	• 7.5
Profit Margin (After Income Tax) 50	4.6	2.9	6.7	4.7	4.9	4.5	3.8	4.0	4.3	4.6	• 4.9

180

Table I

Corporations with and without Net Income

FURNITURE, SPORTS, TOYS, JEWELRY, OTHER DURABLE GOODS

MONEY AMOUNTS AND SIZE OF ASSETS IN THOUSANDS OF DOLLARS

Item Description for Accounting Period 7/06 Through 6/07	Total	Zero Assets	Under 500	500 to 1,000	1,000 to 5,000	5,000 to 10,000	10,000 to 25,000	25,000 to 50,000	50,000 to 100,000	100,000 to 250,000	250,000 to 500,000	500,000 to 2,500,000	2,500,000 and over
Number of Enterprises 1	70453	7842	46512	6654	6428	1546	941	273	136	75	27	16	3
Revenues ($ in Thousands)													
Net Sales 2	257156252	4514702	18764982	13236898	39297174	22388580	35079547	20543338	18485094	23232223	16205172	31495674	13912870
Interest 3	568433	31992	5965	14587	24911	17588	36552	21583	26134	75556	70336	141381	101847
Rents 4	103398	4008	625	2195	9532	5567	4165	5192	5271	9740	3410	23648	30045
Royalties 5	444526	2294	6698	3000	504	3085	5009	35216	29722	8460	74385	42617	233536
Other Portfolio Income 6	546991	21577	9279	42745	32909	52889	26137	26161	31858	70679	99352	84526	48882
Other Receipts 7	2690509	63947	252061	-225986	330473	65403	295099	127713	182026	177918	633697	632758	155397
Total Receipts 8	261510109	4638520	19039610	13073439	39695503	22533112	35446509	20759203	18760105	23574576	17086352	32420604	14482577
Average Total Receipts 9	3712	591	409	1965	6175	14575	37669	76041	137942	314328	632828	2026288	4827526
Operating Costs/Operating Income (%)													
Cost of Operations 10	77.3	76.5	66.2	73.0	72.6	73.3	79.3	80.4	76.9	81.8	85.4	81.0	82.0
Salaries and Wages 11	6.1	4.4	6.8	6.0	6.7	8.0	6.0	5.2	5.7	4.8	5.1	5.2	7.7
Taxes Paid 12	1.1	1.4	1.5	1.2	1.4	1.4	1.0	0.9	1.1	0.9	0.8	1.0	0.6
Interest Paid 13	0.9	1.8	0.6	0.5	0.7	0.9	0.9	1.0	1.0	1.5	1.2	0.9	0.7
Depreciation 14	0.7	0.5	0.7	0.7	0.7	0.6	0.5	0.6	0.7	0.7	0.8	0.8	0.8
Amortization and Depletion 15	0.2	0.6	0.1	0.1	0.0	0.1	0.1	0.2	0.2	0.3	0.4	0.2	1.2
Pensions and Other Deferred Comp. 16	0.2	0.4	0.5	0.1	0.3	0.2	0.2	0.2	0.2	0.2	0.1	0.2	0.4
Employee Benefits 17	0.5	0.8	0.4	0.4	0.3	0.5	0.4	0.4	0.5	0.7	0.8	0.4	0.4
Advertising 18	1.3	2.1	0.9	0.8	0.7	1.1	0.8	1.6	1.3	1.4	1.9	1.6	2.9
Other Expenses 19	8.7	14.4	17.5	12.3	10.1	8.6	7.2	7.0	8.5	6.5	6.2	5.6	7.6
Officers' Compensation 20	2.0	2.4	5.5	2.9	3.7	2.8	1.5	0.9	1.1	0.6	1.4	0.7	0.4
Operating Margin 21	1.1	•	•	2.1	2.7	2.6	2.1	1.6	2.8	0.8	•	2.5	•
Operating Margin Before Officers' Comp. 22	3.1	•	4.9	5.0	6.5	5.4	3.6	2.5	3.9	1.4	•	3.2	•

Selected Average Balance Sheet ($ in Thousands)

Net Receivables 23	437	0	17	167	593	2069	5162	11635	19722	44483	96943	215418	601644
Inventories 24	457	0	35	275	849	2495	5517	11978	20215	37022	54632	178394	370968
Net Property, Plant and Equipment 25	161	0	14	101	292	642	1228	3190	7357	13451	30773	101066	231632
Total Assets 26	1637	0	103	707	2286	6787	15279	35068	68602	154061	361190	995457	3367132
Notes and Loans Payable 27	465	0	53	265	561	1781	4550	11416	18916	49469	81762	187424	1094830
All Other Liabilities 28	616	0	35	311	801	2763	6160	13570	22320	56205	143901	384953	1155173
Net Worth 29	556	0	15	131	923	2243	4569	10082	27366	48388	135527	423080	1117128

Selected Financial Ratios (Times to 1)

Current Ratio 30	1.5	•	1.7	1.5	1.8	1.6	1.5	1.5	1.8	1.6	1.5	1.5	1.0
Quick Ratio 31	0.7	•	0.9	0.7	0.9	0.7	0.8	0.7	0.9	0.8	0.9	0.6	0.4
Net Sales to Working Capital 32	9.0	•	11.8	10.3	7.5	6.6	8.8	8.3	6.0	8.5	8.1	10.3	•
Coverage Ratio 33	4.1	•	2.4	2.8	6.5	4.4	4.6	3.5	5.3	2.6	2.4	7.4	0.4
Total Asset Turnover 34	2.2	•	3.9	2.8	2.7	2.1	2.4	2.1	2.0	2.0	1.7	2.0	1.4
Inventory Turnover 35	6.2	•	7.7	5.3	5.2	4.3	5.4	5.1	5.2	6.8	9.4	8.9	10.2
Receivables Turnover 36	8.6	•	26.3	11.5	9.2	7.7	7.2	6.5	7.5	7.4	7.7	9.3	8.3
Total Liabilities to Net Worth 37	1.9	•	5.9	4.4	1.5	2.0	2.3	2.5	1.5	2.2	1.7	1.4	2.0
Current Assets to Working Capital 38	2.9	•	2.3	2.8	2.2	2.6	3.0	3.1	2.3	2.7	3.0	3.1	•
Current Liabilities to Working Capital 39	1.9	•	1.3	1.8	1.2	1.6	2.0	2.1	1.3	1.7	2.0	2.1	•
Working Capital to Net Sales 40	0.1	•	0.1	0.1	0.1	0.2	0.1	0.1	0.2	0.1	0.1	0.1	•
Inventory to Working Capital 41	1.2	•	1.1	1.5	1.0	1.2	1.3	1.4	1.0	1.1	0.7	1.0	•
Total Receipts to Cash Flow 42	11.0	27.3	7.8	10.1	9.5	10.8	11.6	12.3	8.8	14.2	15.1	10.3	18.3
Cost of Goods to Cash Flow 43	8.5	20.9	5.1	7.3	6.9	7.9	9.2	9.9	6.8	11.6	12.9	8.3	15.0
Cash Flow to Total Debt 44	0.3	•	0.6	0.3	0.5	0.3	0.3	0.2	0.4	0.2	0.2	0.3	0.1

Selected Financial Factors (in Percentages)

Debt Ratio 45	66.0	•	85.5	81.4	59.6	67.0	70.1	71.2	60.1	68.6	62.5	57.5	66.8
Return on Total Assets 46	8.3	•	5.4	3.8	11.8	8.9	9.8	7.8	10.3	7.6	4.6	12.6	0.4
Return on Equity Before Income Taxes 47	18.5	•	21.5	13.0	24.7	20.8	25.6	19.4	20.9	14.7	7.2	25.7	•
Return on Equity After Income Taxes 48	15.1	•	17.9	11.0	22.9	19.0	23.0	16.5	17.5	10.2	4.0	18.8	•
Profit Margin (Before Income Tax) 49	2.8	•	0.8	0.9	3.7	3.2	3.1	2.6	4.2	2.3	1.6	5.5	•
Profit Margin (After Income Tax) 50	2.3	•	0.7	0.7	3.5	2.9	2.8	2.2	3.5	1.6	0.9	4.0	•

181

Table II

Corporations with Net Income

FURNITURE, SPORTS, TOYS, JEWELRY, OTHER DURABLE GOODS

MONEY AMOUNTS AND SIZE OF ASSETS IN THOUSANDS OF DOLLARS

Item Description for Accounting Period 7/06 Through 6/07		Total	Zero Assets	Under 500	500 to 1,000	1,000 to 5,000	5,000 to 10,000	10,000 to 25,000	25,000 to 50,000	50,000 to 100,000	100,000 to 250,000	250,000 to 500,000	500,000 to 2,500,000	2,500,000 and over
Number of Enterprises	1	40974	3855	25145	3987	5486	1287	798	222	•	51	14	•	0
Revenues ($ in Thousands)														
Net Sales	2	208702929	3564771	11947041	10363869	35825469	19101381	30818433	17749012	•	14858708	11174249	•	0
Interest	3	452883	29488	3808	10729	21042	15441	28356	15464	•	47893	38965	•	0
Rents	4	80925	4008	0	191	9476	5158	4132	4364	•	5870	2957	•	0
Royalties	5	269748	2043	0	3000	483	0	4623	35143	•	4717	46473	•	0
Other Portfolio Income	6	443290	21577	8930	37601	26843	52149	10161	24384	•	36538	96527	•	0
Other Receipts	7	2052904	14902	247306	-243279	318616	47885	252790	108837	•	133457	279762	•	0
Total Receipts	8	212002679	3636789	12207085	10172111	36201929	19222014	31118495	17937204	•	15087183	11638933	•	0
Average Total Receipts	9	5174	943	485	2551	6599	14936	38996	80798	•	295827	831352	•	•
Operating Costs/Operating Income (%)														
Cost of Operations	10	77.3	81.4	64.2	73.9	72.5	74.0	79.7	80.6	•	79.0	88.7	•	•
Salaries and Wages	11	5.8	3.4	7.3	5.2	6.8	7.2	5.4	4.9	•	5.1	3.0	•	•
Taxes Paid	12	1.1	1.3	1.5	1.0	1.4	1.3	1.0	0.9	•	0.9	0.6	•	•
Interest Paid	13	0.8	0.9	0.4	0.3	0.6	0.8	0.7	1.0	•	1.1	0.4	•	•
Depreciation	14	0.6	0.4	0.6	0.6	0.7	0.6	0.4	0.5	•	0.8	0.6	•	•
Amortization and Depletion	15	0.2	0.1	0.1	0.0	0.0	0.1	0.1	0.2	•	0.2	0.1	•	•
Pensions and Other Deferred Comp.	16	0.2	0.5	0.3	0.1	0.3	0.2	0.2	0.2	•	0.2	0.1	•	•
Employee Benefits	17	0.4	0.6	0.4	0.2	0.3	0.3	0.4	0.3	•	0.7	0.6	•	•
Advertising	18	1.1	0.3	0.8	0.6	0.5	0.9	0.6	1.4	•	1.5	1.8	•	•
Other Expenses	19	7.3	5.2	15.3	10.5	9.4	7.5	6.4	6.2	•	6.2	3.3	•	•
Officers' Compensation	20	1.9	2.0	5.1	2.1	3.8	2.9	1.5	0.9	•	0.7	0.3	•	•
Operating Margin	21	3.2	3.9	4.0	5.3	3.7	4.2	3.5	3.0	•	3.6	0.5	•	•
Operating Margin Before Officers' Comp.	22	5.2	5.8	9.1	7.4	7.4	7.1	5.0	3.9	•	4.3	0.8	•	•

Selected Average Balance Sheet ($ in Thousands)

Net Receivables 23	612	0	20	213	597	2195	5430	11742	47384	105739
Inventories 24	624	0	36	282	842	2411	5571	12307	37820	69130
Net Property, Plant and Equipment 25	210	0	14	76	290	645	1226	2646	14704	36549
Total Assets 26	2198	0	112	711	2354	6744	15482	35315	149634	348175
Notes and Loans Payable 27	517	0	39	201	506	1753	3902	10820	35977	62786
All Other Liabilities 28	815	0	33	367	772	2680	6054	13316	54380	147636
Net Worth 29	866	0	39	144	1076	2310	5526	11179	59277	137754

Selected Financial Ratios (Times to 1)

Current Ratio 30	1.7	•	2.0	1.5	2.0	1.7	1.6	1.6	1.7	1.4
Quick Ratio 31	0.8	•	1.1	0.8	1.0	0.8	0.8	0.8	0.9	0.9
Net Sales to Working Capital 32	8.1	•	10.7	13.1	7.1	6.4	7.9	7.5	6.9	11.6
Coverage Ratio 33	7.5	7.4	18.1	11.7	8.8	6.7	7.1	5.2	5.7	12.4
Total Asset Turnover 34	2.3	•	4.3	3.7	2.8	2.2	2.5	2.3	1.9	2.3
Inventory Turnover 35	6.3	•	8.4	6.8	5.6	4.6	5.5	5.2	6.1	10.2
Receivables Turnover 36	8.4	•	25.1	11.6	9.7	7.4	7.1	6.7	•	9.7
Total Liabilities to Net Worth 37	1.5	•	1.8	4.0	1.2	1.9	1.8	2.2	1.5	1.5
Current Assets to Working Capital 38	2.5	•	2.0	2.9	2.0	2.5	2.6	2.7	2.4	3.4
Current Liabilities to Working Capital 39	1.5	•	1.0	1.9	1.0	1.5	1.6	1.7	1.4	2.4
Working Capital to Net Sales 40	0.1	•	0.1	0.1	0.1	0.2	0.1	0.1	0.1	0.1
Inventory to Working Capital 41	1.0	•	0.9	1.3	0.9	1.1	1.1	1.2	0.9	1.0
Total Receipts to Cash Flow 42	9.9	9.9	6.3	8.6	8.9	10.1	10.8	11.2	10.6	14.2
Cost of Goods to Cash Flow 43	7.6	8.0	4.1	6.4	6.4	7.4	8.6	9.0	8.4	12.6
Cash Flow to Total Debt 44	0.4	•	1.0	0.5	0.6	0.3	0.4	0.3	0.3	0.3

Selected Financial Factors (in Percentages)

Debt Ratio 45	60.6	•	64.9	79.8	54.3	65.7	64.3	68.3	60.4	60.4
Return on Total Assets 46	13.0	•	27.6	13.7	14.8	12.3	12.8	11.4	12.2	11.9
Return on Equity Before Income Taxes 47	28.5	•	74.2	62.2	28.7	30.6	30.9	29.1	25.3	27.6
Return on Equity After Income Taxes 48	24.7	•	71.7	59.2	26.9	28.5	28.3	25.8	19.9	21.5
Profit Margin (Before Income Tax) 49	4.8	5.9	6.1	3.4	4.7	4.8	4.4	4.1	5.1	4.8
Profit Margin (After Income Tax) 50	4.2	5.5	5.9	3.3	4.4	4.4	4.0	3.6	4.0	3.7

Table I

Corporations with and without Net Income

PAPER AND PAPER PRODUCT

MONEY AMOUNTS AND SIZE OF ASSETS IN THOUSANDS OF DOLLARS

Item Description for Accounting Period 7/06 Through 6/07	Total	Zero Assets	Under 500	500 to 1,000	1,000 to 5,000	5,000 to 10,000	10,000 to 25,000	25,000 to 50,000	50,000 to 100,000	100,000 to 250,000	250,000 to 500,000	500,000 to 2,500,000	2,500,000 and over
Number of Enterprises **1**	10073	1332	6892	781	766	115	96	47	20	13	5	5	0
Revenues ($ in Thousands)													
Net Sales **2**	52534942	423351	3635964	1994203	5557133	3224919	5722567	5632699	4886412	7020672	2055263	12381759	0
Interest **3**	38897	18	438	2130	2317	2481	5015	538	479	2488	3657	19338	0
Rents **4**	7884	0	0	0	3074	8	69	269	719	189	0	3556	0
Royalties **5**	16789	0	0	0	3782	0	0	0	371	0	4765	7871	0
Other Portfolio Income **6**	64987	1186	403	279	15903	1578	3912	597	1484	321	37200	2125	0
Other Receipts **7**	349666	83395	24463	3061	54531	11185	39985	20503	25845	53417	-142	33420	0
Total Receipts **8**	53013165	507950	3661268	1999673	5636740	3240171	5771548	5654606	4915310	7077087	2100743	12448069	0
Average Total Receipts **9**	5263	381	531	2560	7359	28175	60120	120311	245766	544391	420149	2489614	•
Operating Costs/Operating Income (%)													
Cost of Operations **10**	82.5	89.1	71.3	57.6	72.6	81.6	84.2	85.3	83.8	88.9	85.1	87.6	•
Salaries and Wages **11**	5.4	8.3	4.6	6.0	9.3	5.6	5.3	5.8	5.6	4.1	4.2	4.3	•
Taxes Paid **12**	0.8	1.2	1.3	2.7	1.4	1.3	0.7	0.7	0.6	0.4	0.5	0.5	•
Interest Paid **13**	0.8	2.1	0.5	0.7	0.6	0.3	0.4	0.6	0.7	0.8	3.0	1.3	•
Depreciation **14**	0.4	0.9	0.4	0.8	0.5	0.2	0.2	0.3	0.3	0.3	0.6	0.4	•
Amortization and Depletion **15**	0.2	0.5	0.1	0.1	0.1	•	0.1	0.1	0.1	0.2	1.0	0.5	•
Pensions and Other Deferred Comp. **16**	0.2	0.0	0.0	0.9	0.5	0.4	0.2	0.2	0.2	0.1	0.2	0.2	•
Employee Benefits **17**	0.4	0.7	0.3	0.2	0.5	0.6	0.4	0.6	0.5	0.3	0.5	0.3	•
Advertising **18**	0.3	1.1	0.6	0.3	0.1	0.1	1.2	0.1	0.1	0.0	0.1	0.1	•
Other Expenses **19**	6.3	21.9	12.8	18.0	9.9	3.9	4.8	4.2	6.8	4.5	5.6	3.3	•
Officers' Compensation **20**	1.5	0.5	5.8	5.4	3.7	2.4	1.3	0.8	0.8	0.3	0.3	0.1	•
Operating Margin **21**	1.2	•	2.3	7.3	0.9	3.7	1.2	1.4	0.6	0.0	•	1.5	•
Operating Margin Before Officers' Comp. **22**	2.7	•	8.1	12.7	4.6	6.1	2.5	2.2	1.4	0.3	•	1.6	•

Selected Average Balance Sheet ($ in Thousands)

	•	•	•	•	•	•	•	•	•	•	•
Net Receivables 23	595	0	24	246	1007	2611	6672	15335	24836	74530	46433	301336
Inventories 24	349	0	13	208	641	1747	4053	9578	18052	35689	25932	154601
Net Property, Plant and Equipment 25	135	0	15	72	133	635	1135	2030	7541	21356	11674	67074
Total Assets 26	1603	0	88	698	2164	6745	15450	32936	68075	160777	335132	880554
Notes and Loans Payable 27	584	0	56	258	681	1793	3935	11414	18775	65124	181109	304296
All Other Liabilities 28	654	0	45	198	916	2136	6058	13094	28464	74812	88538	399103
Net Worth 29	365	0	-13	242	566	2815	5457	8427	20836	20840	65486	177155

Selected Financial Ratios (Times to 1)

	•	•	•	•	•	•	•	•	•	•	•
Current Ratio 30	1.4	•	1.0	2.7	1.5	1.9	1.6	1.5	1.7	1.4	1.4	1.1
Quick Ratio 31	0.9	•	0.7	1.8	1.0	1.1	1.1	0.9	0.9	1.0	0.7	0.7
Net Sales to Working Capital 32	15.6	•	2781.9	6.7	11.7	9.7	11.7	12.9	10.5	15.9	9.3	57.0
Coverage Ratio 33	3.5	•	7.2	11.7	5.1	14.2	6.2	4.1	2.8	2.0	1.5	2.6
Total Asset Turnover 34	3.3	•	6.0	3.7	3.4	4.2	3.9	3.6	3.6	3.4	1.2	2.8
Inventory Turnover 35	12.3	•	28.7	7.1	8.2	13.1	12.4	10.7	11.3	13.5	13.5	14.0
Receivables Turnover 36	8.7	•	21.2	10.1	7.2	14.7	8.7	7.5	10.1	6.7	6.3	8.7
Total Liabilities to Net Worth 37	3.4	•	•	1.9	2.8	1.4	1.8	2.9	2.3	6.7	4.1	4.0
Current Assets to Working Capital 38	3.4	•	282.5	1.6	2.9	2.1	2.6	3.0	2.4	3.5	3.4	11.4
Current Liabilities to Working Capital 39	2.4	•	281.5	0.6	1.9	1.1	1.6	2.0	1.4	2.5	2.4	10.4
Working Capital to Net Sales 40	0.1	•	0.0	0.1	0.1	0.1	0.1	0.1	0.1	0.1	0.1	0.0
Inventory to Working Capital 41	1.0	•	71.4	0.4	0.9	0.7	0.8	1.0	0.9	1.0	0.6	3.6
Total Receipts to Cash Flow 42	14.7	23.4	7.9	4.2	10.2	15.2	16.9	20.3	15.4	23.7	18.1	23.6
Cost of Goods to Cash Flow 43	12.1	20.8	5.7	2.4	7.4	12.4	14.2	17.4	12.9	21.1	15.4	20.6
Cash Flow to Total Debt 44	0.3	•	0.7	1.3	0.4	0.5	0.4	0.2	0.3	0.2	0.1	0.1

Selected Financial Factors (in Percentages)

	•	•	•	•	•	•	•	•	•	•	•
Debt Ratio 45	77.2	•	114.6	65.4	73.8	58.3	64.7	74.4	69.4	87.0	80.5	79.9
Return on Total Assets 46	9.6	•	21.1	30.3	9.8	18.6	9.6	8.4	6.5	5.4	5.5	9.2
Return on Equity Before Income Taxes 47	30.1	•	•	80.2	30.0	41.4	22.8	24.8	13.7	21.2	9.4	27.9
Return on Equity After Income Taxes 48	26.5	•	•	79.8	28.3	40.2	19.3	22.7	13.0	17.8	4.7	20.3
Profit Margin (Before Income Tax) 49	2.1	•	3.0	7.6	2.3	4.2	2.1	1.7	1.2	0.8	1.5	2.0
Profit Margin (After Income Tax) 50	1.9	•	3.0	7.6	2.2	4.0	1.8	1.6	1.1	0.7	0.8	1.4

Table II
Corporations with Net Income

PAPER AND PAPER PRODUCT

MONEY AMOUNTS AND SIZE OF ASSETS IN THOUSANDS OF DOLLARS

Item Description for Accounting Period 7/06 Through 6/07	Total	Zero Assets	Under 500	500 to 1,000	1,000 to 5,000	5,000 to 10,000	10,000 to 25,000	25,000 to 50,000	50,000 to 100,000	100,000 to 250,000	250,000 to 500,000	500,000 to 2,500,000	2,500,000 and over
Number of Enterprises **1**	6130	909	3727	721	501	107	86	43	•	•	•	•	0
Revenues ($ in Thousands)													
Net Sales **2**	44122709	182632	2875524	1846137	4623561	3176548	5146364	5204078	•	•	•	•	0
Interest **3**	27588	15	398	1773	1212	1313	3406	538	•	•	•	•	0
Rents **4**	1569	0	0	0	314	8	69	269	•	•	•	•	0
Royalties **5**	8198	0	0	0	3782	0	0	0	•	•	•	•	0
Other Portfolio Income **6**	61120	1186	403	0	15497	148	3363	597	•	•	•	•	0
Other Receipts **7**	221474	-1	19774	2850	52244	9953	29963	14098	•	•	•	•	0
Total Receipts **8**	44442658	183832	2896099	1850760	4696610	3187970	5183165	5219580	•	•	•	•	0
Average Total Receipts **9**	7250	202	777	2567	9374	29794	60269	121386	•	•	•	•	•
Operating Costs/Operating Income (%)													
Cost of Operations **10**	82.1	60.3	71.6	56.9	73.0	82.0	83.6	85.2	•	•	•	•	•
Salaries and Wages **11**	5.5	18.1	4.7	6.2	9.5	5.4	5.6	5.7	•	•	•	•	•
Taxes Paid **12**	0.8	1.6	1.2	2.8	1.4	1.2	0.8	0.6	•	•	•	•	•
Interest Paid **13**	0.7	0.2	0.3	0.8	0.5	0.3	0.3	0.6	•	•	•	•	•
Depreciation **14**	0.3	0.5	0.3	0.4	0.5	0.2	0.2	0.3	•	•	•	•	•
Amortization and Depletion **15**	0.1	•	0.1	0.1	0.1	•	0.0	0.1	•	•	•	•	•
Pensions and Other Deferred Comp. **16**	0.3	0.0	0.0	0.9	0.6	0.4	0.2	0.2	•	•	•	•	•
Employee Benefits **17**	0.4	0.0	0.3	0.2	0.4	0.6	0.4	0.6	•	•	•	•	•
Advertising **18**	0.3	0.6	0.7	0.3	0.1	0.0	1.3	0.1	•	•	•	•	•
Other Expenses **19**	5.8	13.7	11.2	18.5	9.2	3.5	4.2	3.9	•	•	•	•	•
Officers' Compensation **20**	1.5	0.5	4.9	5.1	3.1	2.4	1.4	0.8	•	•	•	•	•
Operating Margin **21**	2.2	4.5	4.7	7.9	1.8	3.9	2.1	1.8	•	•	•	•	•
Operating Margin Before Officers' Comp. **22**	3.7	5.0	9.6	13.0	4.9	6.3	3.5	2.6	•	•	•	•	•

Selected Average Balance Sheet ($ in Thousands)

Net Receivables 23	818	0	35	254	1332	2804	6423	15474
Inventories 24	422	0	18	113	549	2309	4185	8250
Net Property, Plant and Equipment 25	175	0	22	69	156	621	1148	2151
Total Assets 26	2150	0	131	688	2455	6800	15309	33142
Notes and Loans Payable 27	639	0	18	267	637	1916	2865	11057
All Other Liabilities 28	916	0	58	183	1167	2181	6352	13148
Net Worth 29	595	0	55	239	652	2704	6092	8937

Selected Financial Ratios (Times to 1)

Current Ratio 30	1.4	•	1.1	2.9	1.4	1.9	1.7	1.5
Quick Ratio 31	0.9	•	0.9	1.9	1.1	1.1	1.1	0.9
Net Sales to Working Capital 32	17.2	•	95.4	6.6	14.6	10.4	11.5	12.8
Coverage Ratio 33	5.3	25.0	20.8	11.7	7.3	14.2	11.1	4.6
Total Asset Turnover 34	3.3	•	5.9	3.7	3.8	4.4	3.9	3.7
Inventory Turnover 35	14.0	•	30.8	12.9	12.3	10.5	11.9	12.5
Receivables Turnover 36	9.0	•	21.0	13.1	6.7	•	8.6	8.5
Total Liabilities to Net Worth 37	2.6	•	1.4	1.9	2.8	1.5	1.5	2.7
Current Assets to Working Capital 38	3.7	•	9.6	1.5	3.3	2.1	2.5	3.0
Current Liabilities to Working Capital 39	2.7	•	8.6	0.5	2.3	1.1	1.5	2.0
Working Capital to Net Sales 40	0.1	•	0.0	0.2	0.1	0.1	0.1	0.1
Inventory to Working Capital 41	1.1	•	2.0	0.4	0.7	0.8	0.7	1.0
Total Receipts to Cash Flow 42	13.6	7.3	7.4	4.0	9.3	16.0	16.7	19.8
Cost of Goods to Cash Flow 43	11.1	4.4	5.3	2.3	6.8	13.1	13.9	16.9
Cash Flow to Total Debt 44	0.3	•	1.4	1.4	0.5	0.5	0.4	0.3

Selected Financial Factors (in Percentages)

Debt Ratio 45	72.3	•	57.8	65.3	73.4	60.2	60.2	73.0
Return on Total Assets 46	12.2	•	33.2	33.3	14.6	19.8	12.1	9.8
Return on Equity Before Income Taxes 47	35.9	•	74.9	87.8	47.5	46.4	27.6	28.4
Return on Equity After Income Taxes 48	32.2	•	74.4	87.4	45.2	45.0	24.2	26.2
Profit Margin (Before Income Tax) 49	3.0	5.2	5.4	8.2	3.4	4.2	2.8	2.1
Profit Margin (After Income Tax) 50	2.7	5.2	5.3	8.2	3.2	4.1	2.5	1.9

Table I

Corporations with and without Net Income

DRUGS AND DRUGGISTS' SUNDRIES

MONEY AMOUNTS AND SIZE OF ASSETS IN THOUSANDS OF DOLLARS

Item Description for Accounting Period 7/06 Through 6/07		Total	Zero Assets	Under 500	500 to 1,000	1,000 to 5,000	5,000 to 10,000	10,000 to 25,000	25,000 to 50,000	50,000 to 100,000	100,000 to 250,000	250,000 to 500,000	500,000 to 2,500,000	2,500,000 and over
Number of Enterprises	1	5473	442	3166	401	974	200	129	53	35	30	15	17	12
Revenues ($ in Thousands)														
Net Sales	2	410368195	9399526	1114923	952210	6258995	2695059	4623427	3939475	4772823	9547581	14094840	23531300	329438034
Interest	3	1658798	24811	123	1862	1709	3722	9305	6336	32334	33201	17971	225641	1301783
Rents	4	548077	0	0	0	121	0	0	731	525	185	484	5489	540541
Royalties	5	2333248	0	0	11565	0	0	3132	0	23250	32822	1468	425013	1835999
Other Portfolio Income	6	1352237	3668	4596	0	9271	25977	13001	9294	14922	190708	13094	295125	772582
Other Receipts	7	4972076	330388	12192	753	24703	38169	48266	55956	85515	25346	34098	360971	3955719
Total Receipts	8	421232631	9758393	1131834	966390	6294799	2762927	4697131	4011792	4929369	9829843	14161955	24843539	337844658
Average Total Receipts	9	76966	22078	357	2410	6463	13815	36412	75694	140839	327661	944130	1461385	28153722
Operating Costs/Operating Income (%)														
Cost of Operations	10	87.0	86.3	58.6	70.4	68.0	73.1	65.2	79.8	75.0	74.3	82.4	44.7	91.8
Salaries and Wages	11	3.2	3.8	8.3	6.9	6.9	6.9	9.7	5.6	7.6	7.6	3.3	8.7	2.3
Taxes Paid	12	0.4	0.5	1.5	2.7	1.1	1.4	1.9	0.6	0.8	0.8	0.6	1.0	0.3
Interest Paid	13	0.6	0.1	0.4	0.6	1.7	0.2	0.5	0.6	1.4	1.0	0.9	1.9	0.5
Depreciation	14	0.3	0.4	0.5	0.4	1.1	0.4	0.4	0.5	0.5	0.5	0.3	0.6	0.3
Amortization and Depletion	15	0.2	0.2	0.2	0.0	0.1	0.1	0.3	0.3	0.6	0.7	0.2	0.8	0.1
Pensions and Other Deferred Comp.	16	0.1	0.0	•	0.6	0.0	0.3	0.2	0.1	0.1	0.1	0.1	0.3	0.1
Employee Benefits	17	0.4	0.2	0.1	0.5	0.3	0.7	0.6	0.8	0.6	0.6	0.2	1.6	0.3
Advertising	18	0.7	0.5	1.0	2.0	1.8	0.3	1.9	0.9	2.9	1.8	0.4	3.2	0.4
Other Expenses	19	5.8	7.9	25.1	14.4	15.3	8.5	12.9	7.4	11.4	10.1	8.4	27.8	3.4
Officers' Compensation	20	0.4	0.6	5.4	5.2	4.0	3.3	2.2	1.6	1.1	0.5	0.2	0.5	0.2
Operating Margin	21	0.9	•	•	•	•	4.7	4.1	1.8	•	1.9	3.0	8.9	0.2
Operating Margin Before Officers' Comp.	22	1.3	0.0	4.3	1.5	3.8	8.0	6.4	3.4	•	2.4	3.2	9.4	0.5

Selected Average Balance Sheet ($ in Thousands)

Item													
Net Receivables 23	6711	0	17	154	528	1164	5040	9584	14360	33911	96005	150685	2432502
Inventories 24	5414	0	40	206	704	2045	4861	7224	14486	30018	82267	131896	1869192
Net Property, Plant and Equipment 25	1679	0	8	83	152	285	939	2346	6215	15668	22539	77130	528644
Total Assets 26	32866	0	128	751	2346	6813	15502	32977	69853	157650	337591	1076268	11770017
Notes and Loans Payable 27	5798	0	39	431	1554	1286	2464	8000	14874	47940	111249	249070	1755331
All Other Liabilities 28	13634	0	60	405	1096	1728	7731	12433	23711	57478	137938	360856	5036720
Net Worth 29	13434	0	29	-85	-304	3798	5306	12543	31267	52232	88405	466342	4977966

Selected Financial Ratios (Times to 1)

Item													
Current Ratio 30	1.4	•	3.0	0.9	1.4	2.0	1.5	2.0	1.6	1.4	1.8	1.7	1.3
Quick Ratio 31	0.8	•	1.0	0.5	0.7	1.1	0.9	1.3	0.9	0.8	0.9	0.9	0.8
Net Sales to Working Capital 32	15.5	•	5.9	•	12.7	5.2	8.2	5.8	8.8	9.6	9.3	6.2	19.1
Coverage Ratio 33	6.7	26.7	2.1	•	1.2	47.1	11.7	7.2	2.0	5.7	4.7	8.6	6.7
Total Asset Turnover 34	2.3	•	2.7	3.2	2.7	2.0	2.3	2.3	2.0	2.0	2.8	1.3	2.3
Inventory Turnover 35	12.1	•	5.1	8.1	6.2	4.8	4.8	8.2	7.1	7.9	9.4	4.7	13.5
Receivables Turnover 36	10.8	•	14.2	13.7	11.5	13.1	6.9	8.2	9.5	9.9	10.4	7.5	11.0
Total Liabilities to Net Worth 37	1.4	•	3.4	•	0.8	1.9	1.6	1.2	2.0	2.8	1.3	1.4	1.4
Current Assets to Working Capital 38	3.6	•	1.5	•	3.7	2.0	3.0	2.0	2.8	3.3	2.3	2.5	4.2
Current Liabilities to Working Capital 39	2.6	•	0.5	•	2.7	1.0	2.0	1.0	1.8	2.3	1.3	1.5	3.2
Working Capital to Net Sales 40	0.1	•	0.2	•	0.1	0.2	0.1	0.2	0.1	0.1	0.1	0.2	0.1
Inventory to Working Capital 41	1.1	•	0.9	•	1.3	0.7	1.0	0.5	1.0	1.0	0.9	0.6	1.3
Total Receipts to Cash Flow 42	11.6	9.5	5.8	11.1	7.5	7.5	6.0	10.1	8.9	8.0	8.7	2.5	17.5
Cost of Goods to Cash Flow 43	10.1	8.2	3.4	7.8	5.1	5.5	3.9	8.1	6.7	6.0	7.2	1.1	16.0
Cash Flow to Total Debt 44	0.3	•	0.6	0.3	0.3	0.6	0.6	0.4	0.4	0.4	0.4	0.9	0.2

Selected Financial Factors (in Percentages)

Item													
Debt Ratio 45	59.1	•	77.1	111.3	113.0	44.2	65.8	62.0	55.2	66.9	73.8	56.7	57.7
Return on Total Assets 46	9.5	•	2.2	•	5.4	14.5	14.4	9.5	5.5	11.7	12.5	21.2	7.7
Return on Equity Before Income Taxes 47	19.9	•	5.0	61.0	•	25.4	38.5	21.5	6.1	29.2	37.6	43.3	15.5
Return on Equity After Income Taxes 48	13.5	•	4.8	64.3	0.9	22.3	35.5	17.2	2.2	22.4	28.4	28.7	10.4
Profit Margin (Before Income Tax) 49	3.6	3.2	0.4	•	0.3	7.2	5.7	3.6	1.4	4.8	3.5	14.6	2.8
Profit Margin (After Income Tax) 50	2.4	1.9	0.4	•	•	6.3	5.3	2.9	0.5	3.7	2.7	9.7	1.9

Table II
Corporations with Net Income

DRUGS AND DRUGGISTS' SUNDRIES

MONEY AMOUNTS AND SIZE OF ASSETS IN THOUSANDS OF DOLLARS

Item Description for Accounting Period 7/06 Through 6/07	Total	Zero Assets	Under 500	500 to 1,000	1,000 to 5,000	5,000 to 10,000	10,000 to 25,000	25,000 to 50,000	50,000 to 100,000	100,000 to 250,000	250,000 to 500,000	500,000 to 2,500,000	2,500,000 and over
Number of Enterprises **1**	3237	313	1652	152	701	174	114	42	•	24	•	17	12
Revenues ($ in Thousands)													
Net Sales **2**	402178982	9162401	848803	334409	5171107	2570301	4222936	3860556	•	8886905	•	23531300	329438034
Interest **3**	1640020	24350	4	1493	848	3444	8132	5699	•	24532	•	225641	1301783
Rents **4**	547938	0	0	0	121	0	0	671	•	106	•	5489	540541
Royalties **5**	2308790	0	0	0	0	0	3132	0	•	32386	•	425013	1835999
Other Portfolio Income **6**	1343398	3545	4485	0	7431	25977	12828	7364	•	186409	•	295125	772582
Other Receipts **7**	4882278	324239	10144	271	21493	32813	38302	37095	•	23777	•	360971	3955719
Total Receipts **8**	412901406	9514535	863436	336173	5201000	2632535	4285330	3911385	•	9154115	•	24843539	337844658
Average Total Receipts **9**	127557	30398	523	2212	7419	15130	37591	93128	•	381421	•	1461385	28153722
Operating Costs/Operating Income (%)													
Cost of Operations **10**	87.4	87.5	64.1	64.7	75.2	73.5	66.1	79.7	•	76.6	•	44.7	91.8
Salaries and Wages **11**	3.0	3.5	9.0	1.6	5.8	6.3	8.9	5.3	•	6.8	•	8.7	2.3
Taxes Paid **12**	0.4	0.4	1.1	1.0	1.0	1.4	1.9	0.5	•	0.7	•	1.0	0.3
Interest Paid **13**	0.6	0.0	0.2	0.1	1.2	0.2	0.5	0.5	•	0.8	•	1.9	0.5
Depreciation **14**	0.3	0.4	0.1	0.2	0.6	0.4	0.4	0.4	•	0.3	•	0.6	0.3
Amortization and Depletion **15**	0.2	0.1	0.0	•	0.0	0.1	0.2	0.2	•	0.4	•	0.8	0.1
Pensions and Other Deferred Comp. **16**	0.1	0.0	•	1.5	0.0	0.3	0.2	0.1	•	0.1	•	0.3	0.1
Employee Benefits **17**	0.3	0.2	0.0	0.2	0.2	0.6	0.5	0.7	•	0.5	•	1.6	0.3
Advertising **18**	0.6	0.1	0.3	0.8	0.5	0.3	1.9	0.9	•	1.4	•	3.2	0.4
Other Expenses **19**	5.5	7.1	14.8	16.5	9.2	7.5	11.4	6.6	•	8.6	•	27.8	3.4
Officers' Compensation **20**	0.4	0.3	3.4	6.6	3.3	3.4	2.3	1.6	•	0.5	•	0.5	0.2
Operating Margin **21**	1.1	0.3	6.9	6.8	3.0	6.0	5.7	3.5	•	3.3	•	8.9	0.2
Operating Margin Before Officers' Comp. **22**	1.5	0.6	10.3	13.4	6.2	9.4	8.0	5.0	•	3.7	•	9.4	0.5

Selected Average Balance Sheet ($ in Thousands)

Net Receivables 23	11092	0	17	54	504	1220	5007	11690	38635	•	150685	2432502
Inventories 24	7710	0	56	185	745	2006	4854	8121	33713	•	112344	1904205
Net Property, Plant and Equipment 25	2691	0	7	53	176	258	912	2375	11529	•	77130	528644
Total Assets 26	54163	0	158	798	2228	6747	15274	32544	161890	•	1076268	11770017
Notes and Loans Payable 27	9023	0	24	65	749	497	2052	5455	41538	•	249070	1755331
All Other Liabilities 28	22537	0	28	637	943	1798	7232	14566	69658	•	360856	5036720
Net Worth 29	22603	0	106	95	536	4453	5989	12522	50694	•	466342	4977966

Selected Financial Ratios (Times to 1)

Current Ratio 30	1.4	•	3.6	0.7	2.0	2.7	1.6	1.9	1.6	•	1.7	1.3
Quick Ratio 31	0.8	•	1.0	0.4	1.1	1.6	0.9	1.2	0.9	•	0.9	0.8
Net Sales to Working Capital 32	15.3	•	6.9	•	7.8	4.3	7.4	7.6	8.0	•	6.2	19.1
Coverage Ratio 33	7.3	135.4	54.2	81.3	4.1	52.9	15.7	10.5	8.4	•	8.6	6.7
Total Asset Turnover 34	2.3	•	3.3	2.8	3.3	2.2	2.4	2.8	2.3	•	1.3	2.3
Inventory Turnover 35	14.1	•	5.9	7.7	7.4	5.4	5.0	9.0	8.4	•	5.5	13.2
Receivables Turnover 36	13.9	•	16.9	17.7	14.8	14.3	7.5	•	10.8	•	9.0	•
Total Liabilities to Net Worth 37	1.4	•	0.5	7.4	3.2	0.5	1.6	1.6	2.2	•	1.3	1.4
Current Assets to Working Capital 38	3.6	•	1.4	•	2.0	1.6	2.7	2.1	2.7	•	2.5	4.2
Current Liabilities to Working Capital 39	2.6	•	0.4	•	1.0	0.6	1.7	1.1	1.7	•	1.5	3.2
Working Capital to Net Sales 40	0.1	•	0.1	•	0.1	0.2	0.1	0.1	0.1	•	0.2	0.1
Inventory to Working Capital 41	1.1	•	1.0	•	0.7	0.5	0.9	0.7	0.8	•	0.6	1.3
Total Receipts to Cash Flow 42	11.6	9.4	6.0	5.2	9.4	7.4	6.1	9.7	8.1	•	2.5	17.5
Cost of Goods to Cash Flow 43	10.2	8.2	3.9	3.4	7.1	5.4	4.0	7.7	6.2	•	1.1	16.0
Cash Flow to Total Debt 44	0.3	•	1.6	0.6	0.5	0.9	0.7	0.5	0.4	•	0.9	0.2

Selected Financial Factors (in Percentages)

Debt Ratio 45	58.3	•	33.0	88.1	75.9	34.0	60.8	61.5	68.7	•	56.7	57.7
Return on Total Assets 46	10.1	•	28.5	20.4	15.6	18.7	18.5	14.9	16.2	•	21.2	7.7
Return on Equity Before Income Taxes 47	21.0	•	41.8	169.1	48.8	27.8	44.2	35.0	45.6	•	43.3	15.5
Return on Equity After Income Taxes 48	14.6	•	41.7	161.2	42.9	24.8	41.2	29.5	36.9	•	28.7	10.4
Profit Margin (Before Income Tax) 49	3.8	4.1	8.6	7.3	3.5	8.4	7.1	4.8	6.2	•	14.6	2.8
Profit Margin (After Income Tax) 50	2.7	2.7	8.6	7.0	3.1	7.5	6.7	4.0	5.0	•	9.7	1.9

Table I

Corporations with and without Net Income

APPAREL, PIECE GOODS, AND NOTIONS

MONEY AMOUNTS AND SIZE OF ASSETS IN THOUSANDS OF DOLLARS

Item Description for Accounting Period 7/06 Through 6/07		Total	Zero Assets	Under 500	500 to 1,000	1,000 to 5,000	5,000 to 10,000	10,000 to 25,000	25,000 to 50,000	50,000 to 100,000	100,000 to 250,000	250,000 to 500,000	500,000 to 2,500,000	2,500,000 and over
Number of Enterprises	1	26256	4014	17821	2010	1576	431	223	85	39	30	14	13	0
Revenues ($ in Thousands)														
Net Sales	2	93764959	761472	12985844	7805973	9620988	7508698	7282857	6698012	4974641	6582147	7027804	22516523	0
Interest	3	210321	452	4223	1551	8050	3701	7618	3218	13936	27516	25522	114535	0
Rents	4	36884	0	0	257	1378	205	352	1164	4991	20426	6419	1692	0
Royalties	5	992649	347	0	0	3504	3029	379	2606	20647	24852	54640	882646	0
Other Portfolio Income	6	550198	98	5995	167	865	14063	1922	9871	16269	32534	133439	334976	0
Other Receipts	7	1797894	17080	30243	650786	22876	53111	187700	68090	51551	35287	63111	618055	0
Total Receipts	8	97352905	779449	13026305	8458734	9657661	7582807	7480828	6782961	5082035	6722762	7310935	24468427	0
Average Total Receipts	9	3708	194	731	4208	6128	17594	33546	79800	130309	224092	522210	1882187	•
Operating Costs/Operating Income (%)														
Cost of Operations	10	67.4	76.2	70.9	69.7	76.6	68.8	74.1	74.3	67.1	62.4	61.0	59.2	•
Salaries and Wages	11	9.0	6.4	5.2	10.3	5.4	8.0	8.6	6.1	8.7	8.6	11.1	13.1	•
Taxes Paid	12	2.5	2.0	3.3	1.7	1.4	3.1	2.4	3.4	2.2	3.3	2.6	2.3	•
Interest Paid	13	1.1	0.8	0.3	0.5	0.7	0.9	1.4	0.8	1.6	1.9	1.8	1.6	•
Depreciation	14	0.7	0.4	0.3	0.2	0.3	0.2	0.4	0.3	0.8	0.9	1.1	1.5	•
Amortization and Depletion	15	0.2	0.0	0.1	0.1	0.1	0.2	0.0	0.1	0.3	0.1	0.1	0.5	•
Pensions and Other Deferred Comp.	16	0.2	1.1	0.1	0.3	0.2	0.1	0.2	0.2	0.5	0.2	0.1	0.3	•
Employee Benefits	17	0.5	0.3	0.4	0.5	0.2	0.6	0.5	0.3	0.6	1.0	0.9	0.6	•
Advertising	18	2.1	0.5	0.7	1.5	0.9	0.6	1.0	1.2	1.7	2.7	3.8	4.1	•
Other Expenses	19	12.6	14.6	14.2	12.2	9.1	11.7	10.5	7.0	12.2	12.3	13.7	15.9	•
Officers' Compensation	20	2.9	4.6	4.3	11.8	2.4	2.3	1.7	1.6	1.8	1.5	1.4	1.2	•
Operating Margin	21	0.6	•	0.1	•	2.7	3.6	•	4.5	2.5	5.0	2.4	•	•
Operating Margin Before Officers' Comp.	22	3.5	•	4.4	3.1	5.1	5.9	1.0	6.1	4.3	6.4	3.9	0.8	•

Selected Average Balance Sheet ($ in Thousands)

Net Receivables 23	400	0	17	179	569	2229	4029	9795	16958	32291	55345	295378	•
Inventories 24	457	0	33	260	662	2464	6203	13485	19250	40957	73229	248677	•
Net Property, Plant and Equipment 25	212	0	13	40	125	538	1080	1834	5904	17132	51635	228538	•
Total Assets 26	2070	0	122	747	2117	7118	15008	33751	67789	155666	337024	2000891	•
Notes and Loans Payable 27	509	0	55	292	587	1909	4481	7575	20800	41919	83929	397120	•
All Other Liabilities 28	615	0	36	344	862	2797	6615	12223	20858	36890	100162	492600	•
Net Worth 29	946	0	31	112	667	2411	3911	13953	26131	76858	152933	1111171	•

Selected Financial Ratios (Times to 1)

Current Ratio 30	1.7	•	2.2	1.4	1.5	1.7	1.5	1.9	1.7	2.2	1.8	1.6
Quick Ratio 31	0.8	•	1.2	0.7	0.8	0.8	0.7	0.8	0.7	1.0	0.7	0.9
Net Sales to Working Capital 32	7.3	•	14.5	22.7	11.7	6.7	7.5	5.8	6.2	4.1	5.6	5.9
Coverage Ratio 33	5.3	•	2.3	0.3	5.4	6.1	2.4	7.9	4.1	4.7	4.5	7.4
Total Asset Turnover 34	1.7	•	6.0	5.2	2.9	2.4	2.2	2.3	1.9	1.4	1.5	0.9
Inventory Turnover 35	5.3	•	15.6	10.4	7.1	4.9	3.9	4.3	4.4	3.3	4.2	4.1
Receivables Turnover 36	8.5	•	39.5	23.8	8.8	9.1	6.8	6.9	7.7	7.0	9.3	5.6
Total Liabilities to Net Worth 37	1.2	•	3.0	5.7	2.2	2.0	2.8	1.4	1.6	1.0	1.2	0.8
Current Assets to Working Capital 38	2.4	•	1.9	3.7	3.0	2.4	2.9	2.2	2.5	1.8	2.2	2.6
Current Liabilities to Working Capital 39	1.4	•	0.9	2.7	2.0	1.4	1.9	1.2	1.5	0.8	1.2	1.6
Working Capital to Net Sales 40	0.1	•	0.1	0.0	0.1	0.1	0.1	0.2	0.2	0.2	0.2	0.2
Inventory to Working Capital 41	1.0	•	0.7	1.6	1.1	1.0	1.4	0.9	1.0	0.8	1.0	0.9
Total Receipts to Cash Flow 42	7.2	15.1	10.1	10.4	9.9	7.0	9.7	9.1	7.2	6.4	6.4	4.9
Cost of Goods to Cash Flow 43	4.8	11.5	7.2	7.3	7.6	4.8	7.2	6.8	4.8	4.0	3.9	2.9
Cash Flow to Total Debt 44	0.4	•	0.8	0.6	0.4	0.5	0.3	0.4	0.4	0.4	0.4	0.4

Selected Financial Factors (in Percentages)

Debt Ratio 45	54.3	•	74.7	85.1	68.5	66.1	73.9	58.7	61.5	50.6	54.6	44.5
Return on Total Assets 46	10.5	•	4.2	0.7	10.9	13.3	7.2	15.5	12.0	12.7	12.3	10.3
Return on Equity Before Income Taxes 47	18.7	•	9.5	•	28.3	32.9	16.4	32.8	23.5	20.2	21.2	16.0
Return on Equity After Income Taxes 48	13.9	•	8.7	•	26.0	31.2	14.6	30.0	19.3	14.8	15.8	10.4
Profit Margin (Before Income Tax) 49	4.9	•	0.4	•	3.1	4.6	2.0	5.8	4.8	7.1	6.5	10.3
Profit Margin (After Income Tax) 50	3.7	•	0.4	•	2.8	4.3	1.7	5.3	3.9	5.2	4.8	6.7

Table II
Corporations with Net Income

APPAREL, PIECE GOODS, AND NOTIONS

MONEY AMOUNTS AND SIZE OF ASSETS IN THOUSANDS OF DOLLARS

Item Description for Accounting Period 7/06 Through 6/07		Total	Zero Assets	Under 500	500 to 1,000	1,000 to 5,000	5,000 to 10,000	10,000 to 25,000	25,000 to 50,000	50,000 to 100,000	100,000 to 250,000	250,000 to 500,000	500,000 to 2,500,000	2,500,000 and over
Number of Enterprises	1	16756	1640	11493	1578	1356	375	156	79	•	27	•	10	0
Revenues ($ in Thousands)														
Net Sales	2	80774483	417314	10192974	6255992	8988761	6484726	5792279	6591798	•	6293107	•	19036430	0
Interest	3	157645	24	1674	1036	7768	3006	6244	2779	•	19284	•	91880	0
Rents	4	29275	0	0	257	1378	0	352	1160	•	20426	•	920	0
Royalties	5	825202	347	0	0	3504	0	189	2391	•	13923	•	736821	0
Other Portfolio Income	6	525342	98	167	167	865	14041	1822	9871	•	15329	•	334813	0
Other Receipts	7	1514754	945	13769	574350	20696	33729	182913	68077	•	34058	•	479113	0
Total Receipts	8	83826701	418728	10208584	6831802	9022972	6535502	5983799	6676076	•	6396127	•	20679977	0
Average Total Receipts	9	5003	255	888	4329	6654	17428	38358	84507	•	236894	•	2067998	•
Operating Costs/Operating Income (%)														
Cost of Operations	10	66.3	70.1	72.0	66.8	76.1	68.0	73.0	74.5	•	62.2	•	56.4	•
Salaries and Wages	11	8.9	5.0	4.3	10.3	5.5	7.8	8.1	6.0	•	8.4	•	13.7	•
Taxes Paid	12	2.6	1.5	3.6	1.7	1.4	3.1	2.5	3.4	•	3.2	•	2.5	•
Interest Paid	13	0.9	0.2	0.1	0.2	0.6	0.9	0.9	0.8	•	1.9	•	1.2	•
Depreciation	14	0.7	0.5	0.3	0.1	0.3	0.2	0.3	0.3	•	0.9	•	1.7	•
Amortization and Depletion	15	0.2	•	0.1	0.0	0.0	0.2	0.0	0.1	•	0.3	•	0.4	•
Pensions and Other Deferred Comp.	16	0.2	0.7	0.2	0.4	0.2	0.1	0.2	0.2	•	0.2	•	0.3	•
Employee Benefits	17	0.5	0.5	0.3	0.5	0.2	0.6	0.5	0.3	•	0.9	•	0.6	•
Advertising	18	2.2	0.4	0.5	1.6	1.0	0.6	0.8	1.2	•	2.4	•	4.6	•
Other Expenses	19	11.9	11.3	12.0	10.9	8.8	11.3	9.6	6.8	•	12.0	•	16.1	•
Officers' Compensation	20	2.9	3.2	3.6	14.1	2.4	2.5	1.9	1.6	•	1.4	•	1.1	•
Operating Margin	21	2.6	6.5	3.1	•	4.8	4.8	2.2	4.8	•	6.1	•	1.6	•
Operating Margin Before Officers' Comp.	22	5.5	9.7	6.7	7.3	5.9	7.3	4.1	6.4	•	7.6	•	2.6	•

Selected Average Balance Sheet ($ in Thousands)

Net Receivables 23	496	0	14	171	598	2225	4275	9837	•	31106	•	268295
Inventories 24	596	0	32	283	610	2277	5960	12978	•	38201	•	280548
Net Property, Plant and Equipment 25	299	0	11	41	132	541	1006	1528	•	18634	•	282650
Total Assets 26	2743	0	123	764	2092	7163	15178	34207	•	159571	•	2235936
Notes and Loans Payable 27	577	0	30	146	542	1996	2796	7308	•	44029	•	396518
All Other Liabilities 28	731	0	28	274	856	2673	5239	12097	•	35926	•	464769
Net Worth 29	1434	0	66	343	695	2494	7143	14802	•	79617	•	1374650

Selected Financial Ratios (Times to 1)

Current Ratio 30	1.8	•	3.2	2.0	1.5	1.8	1.9	1.9	•	2.4	•	1.7
Quick Ratio 31	0.9	•	2.0	1.1	0.8	0.8	0.8	0.8	•	1.1	•	0.9
Net Sales to Working Capital 32	7.0	•	14.0	12.3	12.9	6.4	6.0	5.9	•	4.0	•	6.0
Coverage Ratio 33	8.4	30.8	29.0	11.9	7.7	7.3	7.1	8.2	•	5.1	•	11.6
Total Asset Turnover 34	1.8	•	7.2	5.2	3.2	2.4	2.4	2.4	•	1.5	•	0.9
Inventory Turnover 35	5.4	•	19.7	9.4	8.3	5.2	4.6	4.8	•	3.8	•	3.8
Receivables Turnover 36	9.2	•	51.1	24.8	9.4	8.9	•	7.6	•	8.4	•	•
Total Liabilities to Net Worth 37	0.9	•	0.9	1.2	2.0	1.9	1.1	1.3	•	1.0	•	0.6
Current Assets to Working Capital 38	2.2	•	1.5	2.0	3.0	2.3	2.1	2.1	•	1.7	•	2.4
Current Liabilities to Working Capital 39	1.2	•	0.5	1.0	2.0	1.3	1.1	1.1	•	0.7	•	1.4
Working Capital to Net Sales 40	0.1	•	0.1	0.1	0.1	0.2	0.2	0.2	•	0.3	•	0.2
Inventory to Working Capital 41	0.9	•	0.4	0.9	1.0	1.0	1.0	0.9	•	0.7	•	0.9
Total Receipts to Cash Flow 42	6.5	6.2	8.5	9.0	9.2	6.6	7.4	8.9	•	6.1	•	4.4
Cost of Goods to Cash Flow 43	4.3	4.4	6.1	6.0	7.0	4.5	5.4	6.7	•	3.8	•	2.5
Cash Flow to Total Debt 44	0.6	•	1.8	1.1	0.5	0.6	0.6	0.5	•	0.5	•	0.5

Selected Financial Factors (in Percentages)

Debt Ratio 45	47.7	•	46.5	55.1	66.8	65.2	52.9	56.7	•	50.1	•	38.5
Return on Total Assets 46	13.8	•	24.4	13.6	14.3	15.7	15.6	16.9	•	14.1	•	11.6
Return on Equity Before Income Taxes 47	23.2	•	44.1	27.8	37.4	38.8	28.5	34.3	•	22.7	•	17.3
Return on Equity After Income Taxes 48	18.2	•	43.5	27.1	34.8	37.0	27.0	31.4	•	16.9	•	11.4
Profit Margin (Before Income Tax) 49	6.9	6.8	3.3	2.4	3.9	5.6	5.5	6.1	•	7.8	•	12.5
Profit Margin (After Income Tax) 50	5.4	6.6	3.2	2.3	3.6	5.3	5.2	5.6	•	5.8	•	8.2

Table I

Corporations with and without Net Income

GROCERY AND RELATED PRODUCT

MONEY AMOUNTS AND SIZE OF ASSETS IN THOUSANDS OF DOLLARS

Item Description for Accounting Period 7/06 Through 6/07	Total	Zero Assets	Under 500	500 to 1,000	1,000 to 5,000	5,000 to 10,000	10,000 to 25,000	25,000 to 50,000	50,000 to 100,000	100,000 to 250,000	250,000 to 500,000	500,000 to 2,500,000	2,500,000 and over
Number of Enterprises **1**	33863	5337	18929	2148	5589	942	540	194	91	54	16	19	3
Revenues ($ in Thousands)													
Net Sales **2**	507809535	2971871	18389997	8601183	57161032	30469312	36992641	27295789	24288231	26918423	27300630	88298383	159122043
Interest **3**	6701761	4571	7680	1801	21561	13073	24429	15237	15888	28452	10023	181998	6377049
Rents **4**	1353817	268	1047	2862	19935	6363	8463	8833	3304	28863	10058	93495	1170327
Royalties **5**	801139	0	0	0	0	0	12169	0	206	1616	67	6401	780679
Other Portfolio Income **6**	3745948	3171	3169	10127	49241	15958	15233	7346	9691	29883	19129	117505	3465494
Other Receipts **7**	5649276	51006	100157	46582	342176	81065	301348	133198	205362	228754	198127	1005535	2955966
Total Receipts **8**	526061476	3030887	18502050	8662555	57593945	30585771	37354283	27460403	24522682	27235991	27538034	89703317	173871558
Average Total Receipts **9**	15535	568	977	4033	10305	32469	69175	141548	269480	504370	1721127	4721227	57957186
Operating Costs/Operating Income (%)													
Cost of Operations **10**	82.4	81.9	80.9	79.2	84.7	87.9	85.0	85.0	88.5	85.4	86.2	87.3	74.9
Salaries and Wages **11**	5.4	5.1	3.7	5.4	4.0	3.2	5.3	4.9	3.6	4.6	4.4	4.4	7.6
Taxes Paid **12**	1.3	0.8	1.0	0.8	1.0	0.7	0.9	0.9	0.7	1.5	0.7	0.6	2.2
Interest Paid **13**	1.2	0.6	0.2	0.4	0.3	0.5	0.4	0.5	0.6	0.8	0.3	0.5	2.8
Depreciation **14**	0.9	0.4	0.6	0.9	0.5	0.2	0.4	0.5	0.5	0.6	0.8	0.5	1.7
Amortization and Depletion **15**	0.2	0.2	0.1	0.1	0.1	0.1	0.0	0.0	0.1	0.2	0.1	0.1	0.4
Pensions and Other Deferred Comp. **16**	0.3	0.2	0.1	0.0	0.3	0.1	0.2	0.2	0.1	0.1	0.2	0.2	0.7
Employee Benefits **17**	0.6	0.6	0.3	0.3	0.3	0.3	0.5	0.5	0.4	0.6	0.6	0.6	1.0
Advertising **18**	0.5	0.6	0.2	0.3	0.3	0.2	0.3	0.3	0.6	1.4	0.3	0.7	0.7
Other Expenses **19**	6.0	8.0	8.6	9.2	5.9	4.7	5.3	5.3	4.1	4.6	5.6	6.1	6.6
Officers' Compensation **20**	0.9	1.6	3.1	3.9	2.0	1.1	1.1	0.6	0.6	0.7	0.2	0.1	0.6
Operating Margin **21**	0.4	0.1	1.3	•	0.7	1.0	0.5	1.3	0.3	•	0.6	•	0.8
Operating Margin Before Officers' Comp. **22**	1.3	1.7	4.4	3.4	2.7	2.1	1.7	1.9	0.9	0.3	0.8	•	1.4

Selected Average Balance Sheet ($ in Thousands)

Net Receivables 23	1180	0	35	227	746	2884	5446	10777	20639	30939	107313	130777	6382265
Inventories 24	774	0	17	168	412	1919	4154	9445	19305	40639	94196	202034	2680743
Net Property, Plant and Equipment 25	1528	0	24	170	306	589	2157	5546	10604	24672	91916	225889	12785646
Total Assets 26	14286		127	690	2050	6862	15610	33692	69069	141707	401182	1091677	135301620
Notes and Loans Payable 27	1651	0	47	340	621	2357	4184	10651	24480	51695	71942	279720	10931338
All Other Liabilities 28	3788	0	34	308	754	2613	5967	11857	21081	48976	197273	433014	32942948
Net Worth 29	8847	0	46	42	676	1892	5459	11184	23508	41036	131967	378942	91427333

Selected Financial Ratios (Times to 1)

Current Ratio 30	1.2	•	2.2	1.3	1.7	1.4	1.5	1.4	1.6	1.4	1.6	1.3	1.0
Quick Ratio 31	0.9	•	1.5	0.9	1.2	0.9	0.9	0.8	0.8	0.6	0.8	0.4	0.9
Net Sales to Working Capital 32	27.6	•	21.6	40.6	15.4	20.5	18.2	19.4	13.7	18.8	18.5	34.5	108.3
Coverage Ratio 33	4.4	4.6	8.9	1.6	5.5	3.7	4.9	4.7	3.0	1.9	6.2	2.1	4.7
Total Asset Turnover 34	1.0	•	7.6	5.8	5.0	4.7	4.4	4.2	3.9	3.5	4.3	4.3	0.4
Inventory Turnover 35	16.0	•	45.2	18.9	21.0	14.8	14.0	12.7	12.2	10.5	15.6	20.1	14.8
Receivables Turnover 36	13.4	•	29.6	18.1	14.1	11.1	12.2	13.5	14.0	16.3	16.9	36.0	9.1
Total Liabilities to Net Worth 37	0.6	•	1.7	15.4	2.0	2.6	1.9	2.0	1.9	2.5	2.0	1.9	0.5
Current Assets to Working Capital 38	6.9	•	1.9	4.6	2.3	3.5	3.1	3.5	2.6	3.3	2.7	4.0	51.9
Current Liabilities to Working Capital 39	5.9	•	0.9	3.6	1.3	2.5	2.1	2.5	1.6	2.3	1.7	3.0	50.9
Working Capital to Net Sales 40	0.0	•	0.0	0.0	0.1	0.0	0.1	0.1	0.1	0.1	0.1	0.0	0.0
Inventory to Working Capital 41	1.5	•	0.4	1.2	0.6	1.2	1.0	1.4	1.1	1.6	1.2	1.6	6.4
Total Receipts to Cash Flow 42	12.2	11.4	11.9	13.4	16.9	19.4	18.2	17.0	22.1	24.3	17.2	18.8	7.2
Cost of Goods to Cash Flow 43	10.0	9.3	9.6	10.6	14.3	17.0	15.4	14.5	19.5	20.7	14.8	16.4	5.4
Cash Flow to Total Debt 44	0.2	•	1.0	0.5	0.4	0.3	0.4	0.4	0.3	0.2	0.4	0.3	0.2

Selected Financial Factors (in Percentages)

Debt Ratio 45	38.1	•	63.4	93.9	67.0	72.4	65.0	66.8	66.0	71.0	67.1	65.3	32.4
Return on Total Assets 46	5.5	•	16.9	3.5	9.1	9.2	8.4	10.0	6.9	5.5	7.3	4.3	5.1
Return on Equity Before Income Taxes 47	6.8	•	40.9	21.5	22.6	24.4	19.1	23.8	13.5	9.0	18.7	6.5	5.9
Return on Equity After Income Taxes 48	4.9	•	40.7	19.8	21.3	22.5	17.4	21.2	12.0	5.3	12.9	4.1	4.0
Profit Margin (Before Income Tax) 49	4.0	2.1	2.0	0.2	1.5	1.4	1.5	1.9	1.2	0.7	1.4	0.5	10.2
Profit Margin (After Income Tax) 50	2.9	1.7	1.9	0.2	1.4	1.3	1.4	1.7	1.1	0.4	1.0	0.3	7.0

Table II
Corporations with Net Income

GROCERY AND RELATED PRODUCT

MONEY AMOUNTS AND SIZE OF ASSETS IN THOUSANDS OF DOLLARS

Item Description for Accounting Period 7/06 Through 6/07	Total	Zero Assets	Under 500	500 to 1,000	1,000 to 5,000	5,000 to 10,000	10,000 to 25,000	25,000 to 50,000	50,000 to 100,000	100,000 to 250,000	250,000 to 500,000	500,000 to 2,500,000	2,500,000 and over
Number of Enterprises 1	21355	2706	11519	1433	4127	828	428	170	•	36	•	14	3
Revenues ($ in Thousands)													
Net Sales 2	433899371	2004276	14799062	6233887	44162565	26521986	30860649	23937555	•	19094035	•	61018311	159122043
Interest 3	6553511	3223	4944	1504	17600	9908	18388	11425	•	22371	•	67292	6377049
Rents 4	1291312	73	0	2387	16900	6239	8327	8406	•	11140	•	54763	1170327
Royalties 5	785754	0	0	0	0	0	3599	0	•	350	•	853	780679
Other Portfolio Income 6	3664837	1230	1753	5814	16549	15046	4238	6424	•	29333	•	91104	3465494
Other Receipts 7	5252216	42577	90949	33090	293094	75336	170812	123751	•	197964	•	945475	2955966
Total Receipts 8	451447001	2051379	14896708	6276682	44506708	26628515	31066013	24087561	•	19355193	•	62177798	173871558
Average Total Receipts 9	21140	758	1293	4380	10784	32160	72584	141692	•	537644	•	4441271	57957186
Operating Costs/Operating Income (%)													
Cost of Operations 10	81.7	80.5	82.4	80.9	84.5	87.7	84.6	84.0	•	85.2	•	87.3	74.9
Salaries and Wages 11	5.5	3.9	2.3	4.3	3.4	3.1	5.1	5.2	•	4.3	•	5.4	7.6
Taxes Paid 12	1.3	0.7	0.9	0.6	0.8	0.7	0.9	0.9	•	1.8	•	0.7	2.2
Interest Paid 13	1.3	0.3	0.2	0.2	0.3	0.5	0.3	0.5	•	0.7	•	0.5	2.8
Depreciation 14	1.0	0.2	0.5	0.7	0.5	0.2	0.4	0.5	•	0.5	•	0.6	1.7
Amortization and Depletion 15	0.2	0.2	0.0	0.1	0.0	0.1	0.0	0.0	•	0.1	•	0.2	0.4
Pensions and Other Deferred Comp. 16	0.4	0.2	0.1	0.0	0.3	0.1	0.2	0.2	•	0.2	•	0.3	0.7
Employee Benefits 17	0.7	0.5	0.2	0.4	0.4	0.3	0.5	0.6	•	0.5	•	0.6	1.0
Advertising 18	0.5	0.2	0.1	0.3	0.2	0.2	0.2	0.3	•	1.6	•	0.5	0.7
Other Expenses 19	5.6	6.8	7.6	6.3	5.9	4.5	5.0	5.3	•	3.9	•	4.7	6.6
Officers' Compensation 20	0.9	1.5	2.9	4.6	2.1	1.0	1.2	0.7	•	0.8	•	0.1	0.6
Operating Margin 21	0.9	5.1	2.8	1.5	1.7	1.6	1.5	1.8	•	0.5	•	•	0.8
Operating Margin Before Officers' Comp. 22	1.8	6.6	5.8	6.1	3.8	2.7	2.7	2.5	•	1.2	•	•	1.4

Selected Average Balance Sheet ($ in Thousands)

Net Receivables 23	1681	0	45	250	762	2916	5379	10843	• 30651	• 133379	6382265
Inventories 24	1081	0	15	160	426	1837	4364	9344	• 44917	• 237564	3151259
Net Property, Plant and Equipment 25	2288	0	26	127	332	612	1992	5613	• 26611	• 229994	12785646
Total Assets 26	21786	0	143	687	1992	6875	15427	33592	• 143481	• 999379	135301620
Notes and Loans Payable 27	2307	0	44	240	493	2298	3465	10632	• 51247	• 256002	10931338
All Other Liabilities 28	5650	0	42	305	662	2569	5974	11048	• 45715	• 402354	32942948
Net Worth 29	13828	0	58	143	836	2008	5988	11912	• 46519	• 341023	91427333

Selected Financial Ratios (Times to 1)

Current Ratio 30	1.2	•	1.9	1.4	2.0	1.4	1.6	1.4	• 1.5	• 1.3	1.0
Quick Ratio 31	0.9	•	1.5	1.0	1.3	0.9	0.9	0.8	• 0.6	• 0.4	0.9
Net Sales to Working Capital 32	28.4	•	29.4	32.7	14.4	20.0	16.4	18.5	• 18.8	• 41.5	108.3
Coverage Ratio 33	4.9	26.2	17.8	10.0	10.1	4.9	8.2	5.8	• 3.7	• 3.0	4.7
Total Asset Turnover 34	0.9	•	9.0	6.3	5.4	4.7	4.7	4.2	• 3.7	• 4.4	0.4
Inventory Turnover 35	15.4	•	72.2	22.0	21.2	15.3	14.0	12.7	• 10.1	• 16.0	12.6
Receivables Turnover 36	12.8	•	31.5	21.1	13.8	11.7	12.8	13.3	• 15.9	• 33.0	•
Total Liabilities to Net Worth 37	0.6	•	1.5	3.8	1.4	2.4	1.6	1.8	• 2.1	• 1.9	0.5
Current Assets to Working Capital 38	7.6	•	2.1	3.7	2.0	3.5	2.7	3.2	• 3.2	• 4.6	51.9
Current Liabilities to Working Capital 39	6.6	•	1.1	2.7	1.0	2.5	1.7	2.2	• 2.2	• 3.6	50.9
Working Capital to Net Sales 40	0.0	•	0.0	0.0	0.1	0.1	0.1	0.1	• 0.1	• 0.0	0.0
Inventory to Working Capital 41	1.6	•	0.3	0.8	0.6	1.1	0.9	1.3	• 1.6	• 2.5	6.4
Total Receipts to Cash Flow 42	11.4	7.6	11.0	14.9	14.4	17.8	16.9	15.8	• 21.9	• 23.9	7.2
Cost of Goods to Cash Flow 43	9.3	6.1	9.1	12.1	12.2	15.6	14.3	13.3	• 18.6	• 20.9	5.4
Cash Flow to Total Debt 44	0.2	•	1.4	0.5	0.6	0.4	0.5	0.4	• 0.3	• 0.3	0.2

Selected Financial Factors (in Percentages)

Debt Ratio 45	36.5	•	59.6	79.3	58.0	70.8	61.2	64.5	• 67.6	• 65.9	32.4
Return on Total Assets 46	5.9	•	33.2	15.6	15.0	11.9	11.7	12.2	• 9.2	• 6.2	5.1
Return on Equity Before Income Taxes 47	7.3	•	77.4	67.5	32.2	32.6	26.5	28.4	• 20.8	• 12.1	5.9
Return on Equity After Income Taxes 48	5.4	•	77.0	66.8	30.7	30.5	24.5	25.6	• 15.8	• 8.6	4.0
Profit Margin (Before Income Tax) 49	5.0	7.4	3.5	2.2	2.5	2.0	2.2	2.4	• 1.8	• 0.9	10.2
Profit Margin (After Income Tax) 50	3.7	7.2	3.5	2.2	2.4	1.9	2.0	2.2	• 1.4	• 0.7	7.0

Table I

Corporations with and without Net Income

FARM PRODUCT RAW MATERIAL

MONEY AMOUNTS AND SIZE OF ASSETS IN THOUSANDS OF DOLLARS

Item Description for Accounting Period 7/06 Through 6/07	Total	Zero Assets	Under 500	500 to 1,000	1,000 to 5,000	5,000 to 10,000	10,000 to 25,000	25,000 to 50,000	50,000 to 100,000	100,000 to 250,000	250,000 to 500,000	500,000 to 2,500,000	2,500,000 and over
Number of Enterprises **1**	5114	952	2053	409	1167	302	158	33	17	9	7	6	0
Revenues ($ in Thousands)													
Net Sales **2**	110692273	749949	5429081	1635478	11346736	6823244	8378281	2833833	3629367	3706322	14496590	51663393	0
Interest **3**	1184544	3265	3514	4647	15149	4915	10285	2220	3583	6932	112720	1017315	0
Rents **4**	68167	54	815	329	13143	513	1498	2546	5378	258	1391	42241	0
Royalties **5**	68791	0	0	0	0	1182	149	0	0	0	0	67460	0
Other Portfolio Income **6**	420925	241	3104	18686	13431	3724	48638	2103	6217	1224	43931	279626	0
Other Receipts **7**	2267785	5004	31398	99357	226884	49798	75357	32571	28479	20918	216928	1481090	0
Total Receipts **8**	114702485	758513	5467912	1758497	11615343	6883376	8514208	2873273	3673024	3735654	14871560	54551125	0
Average Total Receipts **9**	22429	797	2663	4300	9953	22793	53887	87069	216060	415073	2124509	9091854	•
Operating Costs/Operating Income (%)													
Cost of Operations **10**	91.6	88.2	92.7	95.7	83.4	89.0	92.1	90.3	92.4	95.3	96.6	91.8	•
Salaries and Wages **11**	2.6	2.9	1.2	2.3	5.7	2.2	2.3	3.6	2.3	1.1	1.0	2.6	•
Taxes Paid **12**	0.5	0.5	0.5	0.5	0.7	0.5	0.5	0.5	0.3	0.2	0.1	0.7	•
Interest Paid **13**	1.7	1.0	0.1	0.3	1.0	0.6	0.6	1.0	1.1	1.2	1.0	2.6	•
Depreciation **14**	0.4	0.5	0.2	0.8	0.5	0.6	0.6	1.0	0.7	0.2	0.2	0.3	•
Amortization and Depletion **15**	0.0	0.1	0.0	•	0.0	0.0	0.0	0.0	0.0	0.0	0.0	0.1	•
Pensions and Other Deferred Comp. **16**	0.1	0.0	0.1	0.0	0.4	0.3	0.1	0.1	0.1	0.1	0.1	0.1	•
Employee Benefits **17**	0.3	0.0	0.2	0.1	0.4	0.1	0.2	0.3	0.2	0.1	0.1	0.5	•
Advertising **18**	0.1	0.1	0.1	0.1	0.1	0.1	0.1	0.1	0.1	0.0	0.1	0.1	•
Other Expenses **19**	3.3	8.9	3.2	4.7	4.9	3.5	3.3	3.4	3.2	1.7	1.3	3.4	•
Officers' Compensation **20**	1.0	0.1	1.4	2.0	3.2	1.1	0.5	0.5	0.4	0.4	0.4	0.8	•
Operating Margin **21**	•	•	0.2	•	•	1.8	•	•	•	•	•	•	•
Operating Margin Before Officers' Comp. **22**	•	•	1.7	•	2.9	2.9	0.1	•	•	•	•	•	•

Selected Average Balance Sheet ($ in Thousands)

Net Receivables 23	1915	0	52	89	656	1701	4699	10935	20759	37059	77809	1005589	•
Inventories 24	2108	0	9	107	382	1459	3552	9842	22699	61164	85225	666752	•
Net Property, Plant and Equipment 25	1311	0	47	125	521	1321	2599	6189	15156	7006	37765	724981	•
Total Assets 26	12144	0	203	726	2603	6863	15433	34917	76031	152087	302355	7985778	•
Notes and Loans Payable 27	4718	0	150	195	1275	1964	4926	13568	26621	59759	91143	3133724	•
All Other Liabilities 28	2955	0	100	99	735	2862	6181	12285	28552	48472	127829	1657393	•
Net Worth 29	4472	0	-48	433	593	2037	4326	9065	20858	43855	83382	3194661	•

Selected Financial Ratios (Times to 1)

Current Ratio 30	1.4	•	1.1	1.7	1.5	1.6	1.1	1.2	1.2	1.6	1.2	1.5	•
Quick Ratio 31	0.6	•	1.0	1.4	0.7	0.8	0.7	0.6	0.6	0.6	0.5	0.5	•
Net Sales to Working Capital 32	11.8	•	192.5	20.9	18.5	12.0	37.1	19.7	28.1	9.2	48.4	7.5	•
Coverage Ratio 33	2.4	•	7.6	4.5	3.2	5.1	3.0	1.5	1.4	1.3	2.6	2.2	•
Total Asset Turnover 34	1.8	•	13.0	5.5	3.7	3.3	3.4	2.5	2.8	2.7	6.8	1.1	•
Inventory Turnover 35	9.4	•	285.8	35.8	21.2	13.8	13.7	7.9	8.7	6.4	23.5	11.9	•
Receivables Turnover 36	7.8	•	48.6	20.5	15.1	11.4	12.4	7.4	12.0	8.8	31.2	15.2	•
Total Liabilities to Net Worth 37	1.7	•	•	0.7	3.4	2.4	2.6	2.9	2.6	2.5	2.6	1.5	•
Current Assets to Working Capital 38	3.2	•	9.6	2.4	3.2	2.8	7.9	6.0	6.7	2.6	5.5	2.9	•
Current Liabilities to Working Capital 39	2.2	•	8.6	1.4	2.2	1.8	6.9	5.0	5.7	1.6	4.5	1.9	•
Working Capital to Net Sales 40	0.1	•	0.0	0.0	0.1	0.1	0.0	0.1	0.0	0.1	0.0	0.1	•
Inventory to Working Capital 41	1.1	•	1.0	0.4	0.9	0.9	2.9	2.8	3.0	1.4	2.3	0.9	•
Total Receipts to Cash Flow 42	23.7	21.3	27.0	26.5	16.8	17.6	26.8	32.1	33.9	54.4	40.9	21.7	•
Cost of Goods to Cash Flow 43	21.7	18.8	25.0	25.4	14.0	15.6	24.7	29.0	31.4	51.8	39.5	19.9	•
Cash Flow to Total Debt 44	0.1	•	0.4	0.5	0.3	0.3	0.2	0.1	0.1	0.1	0.2	0.1	•

Selected Financial Factors (in Percentages)

Debt Ratio 45	63.2	•	123.7	40.4	77.2	70.3	72.0	74.0	72.6	71.2	72.4	60.0	•
Return on Total Assets 46	7.0	•	14.5	7.3	11.3	10.8	6.5	3.9	4.2	4.3	18.3	6.2	•
Return on Equity Before Income Taxes 47	10.9	•	•	9.6	33.8	29.4	15.4	5.0	4.6	3.3	41.4	8.5	•
Return on Equity After Income Taxes 48	7.7	•	•	8.3	30.6	27.4	12.6	3.4	2.0	1.3	27.3	5.6	•
Profit Margin (Before Income Tax) 49	2.3	•	1.0	1.0	2.1	2.6	1.3	0.5	0.4	0.4	1.7	3.1	•
Profit Margin (After Income Tax) 50	1.6	•	0.9	0.9	1.9	2.5	1.0	0.4	0.2	0.1	1.1	2.1	•

191

Table II

Corporations with Net Income

FARM PRODUCT RAW MATERIAL

MONEY AMOUNTS AND SIZE OF ASSETS IN THOUSANDS OF DOLLARS

Item Description for Accounting Period 7/06 Through 6/07	Total	Zero Assets	Under 500	500 to 1,000	1,000 to 5,000	5,000 to 10,000	10,000 to 25,000	25,000 to 50,000	50,000 to 100,000	100,000 to 250,000	250,000 to 500,000	500,000 to 2,500,000	2,500,000 and over
Number of Enterprises 1	2645	17	964	314	915	269	119	•	10	6	•	•	0

Revenues ($ in Thousands)

	Total	Zero Assets	Under 500	500 to 1,000	1,000 to 5,000	5,000 to 10,000	10,000 to 25,000	25,000 to 50,000	50,000 to 100,000	100,000 to 250,000	250,000 to 500,000	500,000 to 2,500,000	2,500,000 and over
Net Sales 2	9858116	415474	4958893	454331	9101169	6475889	6398582	•	1936464	2082034	•	•	0
Interest 3	1173351	3155	3496	2916	13282	3540	9526	•	3117	3919	•	•	0
Rents 4	60149	0	815	207	8469	513	1439	•	2277	258	•	•	0
Royalties 5	67609	0	0	0	0	0	149		0	0			0
Other Portfolio Income 6	405611	234	3104	18686	12175	3357	39325	•	3495	652	•	•	0
Other Receipts 7	2144819	3667	31329	45709	212834	39324	72589	•	15745	18697	•	•	0
Total Receipts 8	102436655	422530	4997637	521849	9347929	6522623	6521610	•	1961098	2105560	•	•	0
Average Total Receipts 9	38728	24855	5184	1662	10216	24248	54803	•	196110	350927	•	•	•

Operating Costs/Operating Income (%)

	Total	Zero Assets	Under 500	500 to 1,000	1,000 to 5,000	5,000 to 10,000	10,000 to 25,000	25,000 to 50,000	50,000 to 100,000	100,000 to 250,000	250,000 to 500,000	500,000 to 2,500,000	2,500,000 and over
Cost of Operations 10	91.4	99.3	92.7	87.5	81.1	89.1	91.7	•	91.7	94.8	•	•	•
Salaries and Wages 11	2.6	0.2	1.3	3.4	6.4	2.2	2.3	•	2.2	1.1	•	•	•
Taxes Paid 12	0.6	0.1	0.5	1.2	0.8	0.4	0.5	•	0.4	0.2	•	•	•
Interest Paid 13	1.7	0.7	0.1	1.0	0.8	0.5	0.6	•	1.0	0.9	•	•	•
Depreciation 14	0.4	0.0	0.1	2.2	0.5	0.5	0.6	•	0.6	0.4	•	•	•
Amortization and Depletion 15	0.0	•	0.0	•	•	0.0	0.0	•	0.0	0.0	•	•	•
Pensions and Other Deferred Comp. 16	0.1	•	0.1	•	0.4	0.3	0.2	•	0.0	0.1	•	•	•
Employee Benefits 17	0.3	0.0	0.2	0.2	0.4	0.1	0.2	•	0.1	0.1	•	•	•
Advertising 18	0.1	0.0	0.1	0.3	0.1	0.2	0.1	•	0.1	0.0	•	•	•
Other Expenses 19	3.2	2.3	2.3	12.2	5.4	3.3	3.2	•	2.5	1.5	•	•	•
Officers' Compensation 20	1.0	0.4	1.4	2.4	3.6	1.1	0.6	•	0.3	0.4	•	•	•
Operating Margin 21	•	•	1.1	•	0.4	2.3	•	•	1.0	0.7	•	•	•
Operating Margin Before Officers' Comp. 22	•	•	2.5	•	4.0	3.4	0.6	•	1.4	1.1	•	•	•

Selected Average Balance Sheet ($ in Thousands)

Net Receivables **23**	3265	0	98	80	545	1824	4239	•	20274	32258
Inventories **24**	3556	0	17	127	417	1543	3824	•	17138	57858
Net Property, Plant and Equipment **25**	2274	0	58	135	454	1026	2676	•	16766	8919
Total Assets **26**	21883	0	281	735	2610	6800	15097	•	75684	140591
Notes and Loans Payable **27**	8288	0	98	241	1093	1708	4234	•	24083	44976
All Other Liabilities **28**	5204	0	71	110	672	3105	6429	•	26753	48527
Net Worth **29**	8371	0	111	383	846	1988	4433	•	24849	47088

Selected Financial Ratios (Times to 1)

Current Ratio **30**	1.5	•	1.8	1.3	1.6	1.6	1.2	•	1.2	1.4
Quick Ratio **31**	0.5	•	1.5	1.0	0.7	0.8	0.6	•	0.6	0.5
Net Sales to Working Capital **32**	11.2	•	70.2	13.1	14.2	11.9	27.1	•	26.1	12.6
Coverage Ratio **33**	2.6	2.3	14.9	5.3	4.9	7.3	4.2	•	3.3	3.1
Total Asset Turnover **34**	1.7	•	18.3	2.0	3.8	3.5	3.6	•	2.6	2.5
Inventory Turnover **35**	9.6	•	280.7	10.0	19.4	13.9	12.9	•	10.4	5.7
Receivables Turnover **36**	7.7	•	47.0	9.7	17.9	11.4	12.7	•	•	
Total Liabilities to Net Worth **37**	1.6	•	1.5	0.9	2.1	2.4	2.4	•	2.0	2.0
Current Assets to Working Capital **38**	3.1	•	2.3	3.9	2.6	2.7	5.4	•	6.0	3.9
Current Liabilities to Working Capital **39**	2.1	•	1.3	2.9	1.6	1.7	4.4	•	5.0	2.9
Working Capital to Net Sales **40**	0.1	•	0.0	0.1	0.1	0.1	0.0	•	0.0	0.1
Inventory to Working Capital **41**	1.0	•	0.4	0.9	0.8	0.9	2.3	•	2.3	2.1
Total Receipts to Cash Flow **42**	21.8	85.8	26.1	8.8	13.6	17.0	23.5	•	24.5	32.5
Cost of Goods to Cash Flow **43**	20.0	85.3	24.2	7.7	11.0	15.2	21.6	•	22.5	30.8
Cash Flow to Total Debt **44**	0.1	•	1.2	0.5	0.4	0.3	0.2	•	0.2	0.1

Selected Financial Factors (in Percentages)

Debt Ratio **45**	61.7	•	60.3	47.8	67.6	70.8	70.6	•	67.2	66.5
Return on Total Assets **46**	7.6	•	37.2	10.9	14.7	12.2	8.8	•	8.5	6.5
Return on Equity Before Income Taxes **47**	12.2	•	87.4	16.9	36.1	36.0	22.9	•	18.0	13.2
Return on Equity After Income Taxes **48**	8.9	•	85.0	15.0	33.3	33.7	19.3	•	14.3	10.4
Profit Margin (Before Income Tax) **49**	2.7	0.9	1.9	4.5	3.1	3.0	1.9	•	2.3	1.8
Profit Margin (After Income Tax) **50**	2.0	0.6	1.8	4.0	2.8	2.8	1.6	•	1.8	1.4

Table I

Corporations with and without Net Income

CHEMICAL AND ALLIED PRODUCTS

MONEY AMOUNTS AND SIZE OF ASSETS IN THOUSANDS OF DOLLARS

Item Description for Accounting Period 7/06 Through 6/07	Total	Zero Assets	Under 500	500 to 1,000	1,000 to 5,000	5,000 to 10,000	10,000 to 25,000	25,000 to 50,000	50,000 to 100,000	100,000 to 250,000	250,000 to 500,000	500,000 to 2,500,000	2,500,000 and over
Number of Enterprises **1**	8410	1236	4479	807	1324	218	185	90	33	19	8	11	0
Revenues ($ in Thousands)													
Net Sales **2**	71202313	683752	2234166	3339490	8985864	6369383	7338211	8035933	6144845	5418324	3651046	19001300	0
Interest **3**	217650	928	179	620	6598	5745	8193	7726	10955	13839	52259	110608	0
Rents **4**	26684	235	0	0	1117	850	1556	521	6548	5980	756	9122	0
Royalties **5**	96466	0	0	0	0	0	0	944	487	528	3065	91442	0
Other Portfolio Income **6**	304260	1797	0	1605	103274	2789	8105	10088	4686	12785	34002	125129	0
Other Receipts **7**	656976	16063	8583	5879	17723	25827	73177	93622	23135	9580	31797	351589	0
Total Receipts **8**	72504349	702775	2242928	3347594	9114576	6404594	7429242	8148834	6190656	5461036	3772925	19689190	0
Average Total Receipts **9**	8621	569	501	4148	6884	29379	40158	90543	187596	287423	471616	1789926	•
Operating Costs/Operating Income (%)													
Cost of Operations **10**	78.4	71.3	65.9	37.0	69.9	86.7	81.6	82.5	88.4	90.5	80.1	78.6	•
Salaries and Wages **11**	6.5	4.9	5.6	31.5	8.0	3.5	5.0	5.4	3.2	2.2	5.3	6.2	•
Taxes Paid **12**	1.0	1.0	1.3	1.1	1.3	0.6	1.0	0.9	0.6	0.5	0.7	1.2	•
Interest Paid **13**	1.3	0.1	1.2	0.5	1.1	0.2	0.7	0.5	0.8	0.6	1.7	2.6	•
Depreciation **14**	1.1	0.4	0.7	0.5	0.9	0.4	0.6	0.8	0.4	0.6	1.4	2.2	•
Amortization and Depletion **15**	0.2	0.0	0.0	0.0	0.2	0.0	0.1	0.0	0.1	0.1	0.4	0.5	•
Pensions and Other Deferred Comp. **16**	0.3	0.3	•	0.6	0.4	0.2	0.3	0.5	0.1	0.2	0.3	0.3	•
Employee Benefits **17**	0.8	0.0	0.8	0.9	0.9	0.2	0.5	0.7	0.6	0.3	0.6	1.5	•
Advertising **18**	0.2	0.1	0.8	0.5	0.5	0.1	0.2	0.2	0.1	0.1	0.3	0.1	•
Other Expenses **19**	7.2	11.2	17.0	19.5	9.8	4.4	6.0	5.2	3.4	3.2	7.1	7.3	•
Officers' Compensation **20**	1.5	1.1	5.0	5.2	3.3	1.6	1.7	1.2	0.6	0.5	0.5	0.5	•
Operating Margin **21**	1.5	9.5	1.7	2.6	3.7	2.1	2.4	2.1	1.5	1.3	1.6	•	•
Operating Margin Before Officers' Comp. **22**	3.0	10.6	6.7	7.9	6.9	3.6	4.2	3.3	2.1	1.7	2.1	•	•

Selected Average Balance Sheet ($ in Thousands)

	•	•	•	•	•	•	•	•	•	•	•	•
Net Receivables 23	984	0	23	392	728	3297	5226	11028	22660	39953	75552	191118
Inventories 24	711	0	17	92	390	1345	5158	7285	15950	37195	36098	171676
Net Property, Plant and Equipment 25	745	0	12	49	293	688	1841	5375	7453	14719	60255	345178
Total Assets 26	4605	0	87	699	2056	7295	14921	35855	69459	149661	338843	1784491
Notes and Loans Payable 27	1204	0	84	253	606	1865	4143	7858	20846	26313	104786	439831
All Other Liabilities 28	1721	0	39	382	652	2971	5393	12537	27219	72821	86782	670475
Net Worth 29	1680	0	-36	64	797	2458	5385	15460	21393	50527	147275	674185

Selected Financial Ratios (Times to 1)

	•	•	•	•	•	•	•	•	•	•	•	•
Current Ratio 30	1.4	•	1.0	1.5	1.9	1.7	1.5	1.6	1.5	1.2	1.7	1.2
Quick Ratio 31	0.7	•	0.8	1.1	1.4	1.2	0.8	0.9	0.8	0.7	1.1	0.5
Net Sales to Working Capital 32	12.1	•	444.4	19.9	9.2	12.4	10.2	9.9	11.8	17.7	8.1	13.7
Coverage Ratio 33	3.7	83.9	2.7	6.6	5.5	11.9	6.1	7.9	3.9	4.8	3.9	2.1
Total Asset Turnover 34	1.8	•	5.7	5.9	3.3	4.0	2.7	2.5	2.7	1.9	1.3	1.0
Inventory Turnover 35	9.3	•	19.4	16.6	12.1	18.8	6.3	10.1	10.3	6.9	10.1	7.9
Receivables Turnover 36	8.7	•	17.2	14.6	8.6	9.8	6.7	9.0	9.5	6.3	6.1	9.2
Total Liabilities to Net Worth 37	1.7	•	•	10.0	1.6	2.0	1.8	1.3	2.2	2.0	1.3	1.6
Current Assets to Working Capital 38	3.4	•	63.6	3.0	2.1	2.5	3.0	2.8	3.1	5.4	2.4	5.1
Current Liabilities to Working Capital 39	2.4	•	62.6	2.0	1.1	1.5	2.0	1.8	2.1	4.4	1.4	4.1
Working Capital to Net Sales 40	0.1	•	0.0	0.1	0.1	0.1	0.1	0.1	0.1	0.1	0.1	0.1
Inventory to Working Capital 41	1.0	•	13.4	0.5	0.4	0.6	1.2	1.0	1.1	2.1	0.8	1.4
Total Receipts to Cash Flow 42	11.2	4.8	6.5	4.8	7.9	15.9	11.8	13.1	20.2	21.4	9.4	13.1
Cost of Goods to Cash Flow 43	8.8	3.4	4.3	1.8	5.5	13.8	9.7	10.8	17.9	19.4	7.6	10.3
Cash Flow to Total Debt 44	0.3	•	0.6	1.4	0.7	0.4	0.4	0.3	0.2	0.1	0.3	0.1

Selected Financial Factors (in Percentages)

	•	•	•	•	•	•	•	•	•	•	•	•
Debt Ratio 45	63.5	•	141.8	90.9	61.2	66.3	63.9	56.9	69.2	66.2	56.5	62.2
Return on Total Assets 46	8.4	•	18.8	19.9	20.5	11.4	11.8	10.1	8.1	5.2	9.1	5.2
Return on Equity Before Income Taxes 47	16.8	•	•	185.5	43.3	31.0	27.3	20.5	19.6	12.1	15.5	7.2
Return on Equity After Income Taxes 48	14.1	•	•	163.9	41.5	28.1	24.2	18.5	14.8	8.2	12.1	5.2
Profit Margin (Before Income Tax) 49	3.3	12.3	2.1	2.9	5.1	2.6	3.7	3.5	2.3	2.1	5.0	2.8
Profit Margin (After Income Tax) 50	2.8	10.6	1.8	2.5	4.9	2.4	3.3	3.2	1.7	1.5	3.9	2.0

Table II

Corporations with Net Income

CHEMICAL AND ALLIED PRODUCTS

MONEY AMOUNTS AND SIZE OF ASSETS IN THOUSANDS OF DOLLARS

Item Description for Accounting Period 7/06 Through 6/07		Total	Zero Assets	Under 500	500 to 1,000	1,000 to 5,000	5,000 to 10,000	10,000 to 25,000	25,000 to 50,000	50,000 to 100,000	100,000 to 250,000	250,000 to 500,000	500,000 to 2,500,000	2,500,000 and over
Number of Enterprises	1	5541	805	2494	591	1148	202	166	77	28	16	•	•	0
Revenues ($ in Thousands)														
Net Sales	2	62957082	679009	1637166	2703207	8188253	5640709	6748404	7752229	5615885	3139983	•	•	0
Interest	3	194062	928	179	603	5845	5508	7968	2902	10357	8150	•	•	0
Rents	4	26304	235	0	0	1010	768	1556	416	6480	5962	•	•	0
Royalties	5	95522	0	0	0	0	0	0	0	487	528	•	•	0
Other Portfolio Income	6	302111	1797	0	1115	103137	1548	8085	9944	4622	12733	•	•	0
Other Receipts	7	638161	15980	8587	3560	17176	16974	70874	89372	22409	8228	•	•	0
Total Receipts	8	64213242	697949	1645932	2708485	8315421	5665507	6836887	7854863	5660240	3175584	•	•	0
Average Total Receipts	9	11589	867	660	4583	7243	28047	41186	102011	202151	198474	•	•	•
Operating Costs/Operating Income (%)														
Cost of Operations	10	77.2	71.1	68.4	27.9	68.2	85.1	81.2	82.6	88.6	83.7	•	•	•
Salaries and Wages	11	6.9	4.9	4.2	38.0	8.4	4.0	5.1	5.2	3.1	3.8	•	•	•
Taxes Paid	12	1.0	1.0	1.1	1.2	1.4	0.6	1.0	0.9	0.6	0.9	•	•	•
Interest Paid	13	1.2	0.1	0.5	0.4	1.1	0.3	0.6	0.5	0.6	0.9	•	•	•
Depreciation	14	1.1	0.4	0.5	0.5	0.9	0.4	0.6	0.7	0.4	1.0	•	•	•
Amortization and Depletion	15	0.2	0.0	0.0	0.0	0.2	0.0	0.1	0.0	0.1	0.2	•	•	•
Pensions and Other Deferred Comp.	16	0.3	0.3	•	0.7	0.5	0.2	0.3	0.5	0.1	0.3	•	•	•
Employee Benefits	17	0.9	0.0	0.6	0.9	0.9	0.2	0.4	0.7	0.6	0.5	•	•	•
Advertising	18	0.2	0.1	0.9	0.7	0.6	0.1	0.2	0.1	0.1	0.1	•	•	•
Other Expenses	19	7.1	11.0	13.5	20.6	10.2	4.5	5.9	4.8	3.1	4.6	•	•	•
Officers' Compensation	20	1.6	1.1	4.6	5.2	3.5	1.7	1.7	1.1	0.7	0.8	•	•	•
Operating Margin	21	2.2	9.8	5.8	4.1	4.3	2.8	2.8	3.0	2.0	3.3	•	•	•
Operating Margin Before Officers' Comp.	22	3.8	10.9	10.4	9.3	7.8	4.6	4.5	4.1	2.7	4.1	•	•	•

Selected Average Balance Sheet ($ in Thousands)

Net Receivables 23	1268	0	28	427	774	3395	5386	12226	23716	31281
Inventories 24	944	0	18	84	391	1438	5255	7528	16512	38866
Net Property, Plant and Equipment 25	1026	0	16	62	319	644	1967	4462	7754	16184
Total Assets 26	5993	0	105	721	2039	7126	15143	35750	70068	139864
Notes and Loans Payable 27	1419	0	39	275	615	1136	3792	8230	18574	26913
All Other Liabilities 28	2194	0	36	403	682	2937	5541	12452	27794	43096
Net Worth 29	2381	0	30	43	742	3053	5810	15068	23700	69856

Selected Financial Ratios (Times to 1)

Current Ratio 30	1.4	•	1.5	1.4	1.8	1.6	1.5	1.6	1.5	1.5
Quick Ratio 31	0.7	•	1.1	1.1	1.3	1.1	0.8	0.9	0.8	0.7
Net Sales to Working Capital 32	12.1	•	23.7	25.2	10.7	12.2	10.2	10.8	12.3	7.5
Coverage Ratio 33	4.7	85.3	14.2	12.6	6.3	14.0	7.3	10.3	5.6	6.2
Total Asset Turnover 34	1.9	•	6.3	6.3	3.5	3.9	2.7	2.8	2.9	1.4
Inventory Turnover 35	9.3	•	24.9	15.1	12.4	16.5	6.3	11.0	10.8	4.2
Receivables Turnover 36	8.8	•	18.4	16.5	9.0	•	6.7	9.6	10.0	4.9
Total Liabilities to Net Worth 37	1.5	•	2.5	15.8	1.7	1.3	1.6	1.4	2.0	1.0
Current Assets to Working Capital 38	3.3	•	3.0	3.4	2.3	2.6	3.0	2.7	3.1	2.9
Current Liabilities to Working Capital 39	2.3	•	2.0	2.4	1.3	1.6	2.0	1.7	2.1	1.9
Working Capital to Net Sales 40	0.1	•	0.0	0.0	0.1	0.1	0.1	0.1	0.1	0.1
Inventory to Working Capital 41	1.0	•	0.6	0.7	0.5	0.6	1.2	1.0	1.1	1.2
Total Receipts to Cash Flow 42	10.3	4.7	6.2	4.3	7.3	14.3	11.4	12.4	18.7	12.4
Cost of Goods to Cash Flow 43	8.0	3.4	4.2	1.2	5.0	12.2	9.3	10.3	16.5	10.3
Cash Flow to Total Debt 44	0.3	•	1.4	1.6	0.8	0.5	0.4	0.4	0.2	0.2

Selected Financial Factors (in Percentages)

Debt Ratio 45	60.3	•	71.7	94.1	63.6	57.2	61.6	57.9	66.2	50.1
Return on Total Assets 46	10.3	•	42.6	29.4	24.3	13.8	12.7	13.5	9.8	7.6
Return on Equity Before Income Taxes 47	20.4	•	139.6	454.2	56.4	29.9	28.7	28.9	23.9	12.8
Return on Equity After Income Taxes 48	17.5	•	132.0	410.5	54.1	27.3	25.6	26.5	18.8	9.5
Profit Margin (Before Income Tax) 49	4.3	12.6	6.3	4.3	5.9	3.3	4.1	4.3	2.8	4.6
Profit Margin (After Income Tax) 50	3.7	10.9	6.0	3.9	5.6	3.0	3.7	4.0	2.2	3.4

194

Table I

Corporations with and without Net Income

PETROLEUM AND PETROLEUM PRODUCTS

MONEY AMOUNTS AND SIZE OF ASSETS IN THOUSANDS OF DOLLARS

Item Description for Accounting Period 7/06 Through 6/07		Total	Zero Assets	Under 500	500 to 1,000	1,000 to 5,000	5,000 to 10,000	10,000 to 25,000	25,000 to 50,000	50,000 to 100,000	100,000 to 250,000	250,000 to 500,000	500,000 to 2,500,000	2,500,000 and over
Number of Enterprises	1	8519	727	3730	678	2060	680	392	151	43	30	13	10	5
Revenues ($ in Thousands)														
Net Sales	2	46482656	81004024	3072392	3949121	37299921	45418802	44493104	34285488	19206443	40627502	35755895	52168851	67544713
Interest	3	351114	24497	2891	2631	17325	12190	31459	10793	24810	13384	53963	20009	137162
Rents	4	265643	24244	0	368	39498	22097	42962	14947	8795	11543	12797	80301	8092
Royalties	5	72553	0	0	0	168	816	46	0	611	1267	690	866	68090
Other Portfolio Income	6	4617655	14594	179	3401	72072	36520	49275	43307	9805	13856	110279	61842	4202527
Other Receipts	7	1453569	6210	319	4118	152883	94178	186714	135385	82601	142621	166051	166051	321382
Total Receipts	8	471586790	81073569	3075781	3959639	37581867	45584603	44803560	34489920	19333065	40810173	36094727	52497920	72281966
Average Total Receipts	9	55357	111518	825	5840	18244	67036	114295	228410	449606	1360339	2776517	5249792	14456393
Operating Costs/Operating Income (%)														
Cost of Operations	10	93.1	98.5	77.0	89.8	91.2	94.8	93.4	94.0	95.0	97.0	96.9	96.4	79.5
Salaries and Wages	11	1.5	0.3	7.3	2.2	2.5	1.6	1.8	1.7	1.2	0.8	0.8	0.8	3.2
Taxes Paid	12	0.4	0.1	1.7	1.5	0.5	0.3	1.0	0.4	0.2	0.4	0.2	0.2	0.9
Interest Paid	13	0.5	0.3	0.7	0.3	0.2	0.2	0.3	0.3	0.4	0.2	0.2	0.3	2.1
Depreciation	14	0.6	0.0	1.1	1.0	0.5	0.3	0.5	0.5	0.5	0.2	0.2	0.3	2.2
Amortization and Depletion	15	0.2	0.0	0.1	0.0	0.1	0.0	0.0	0.0	0.0	0.0	0.1	0.0	0.9
Pensions and Other Deferred Comp.	16	0.1	0.0	0.2	0.0	0.1	0.0	0.0	0.0	0.0	0.0	0.0	0.0	0.2
Employee Benefits	17	0.1	0.0	0.2	0.2	0.2	0.1	0.1	0.1	0.1	0.1	0.1	0.1	0.5
Advertising	18	0.1	0.0	0.1	0.1	0.1	0.0	0.1	0.0	0.1	0.0	0.0	0.0	0.5
Other Expenses	19	2.7	0.2	8.4	3.0	3.9	2.1	2.4	2.5	1.6	0.9	1.3	1.0	8.8
Officers' Compensation	20	0.3	0.0	2.7	1.6	0.9	0.3	0.3	0.3	0.6	0.1	0.2	0.5	0.1
Operating Margin	21	0.3	0.6	0.4	0.3	•	0.2	0.1	0.0	0.0	0.2	0.1	0.2	1.0
Operating Margin Before Officers' Comp.	22	0.6	0.6	3.1	1.9	0.7	0.6	0.4	0.3	0.7	0.3	0.3	0.7	1.1

Selected Average Balance Sheet ($ in Thousands)

Net Receivables 23	2372	0	47	258	817	2811	4837	9544	25710	65916	148474	202084	1178345
Inventories 24	1233	0	28	88	397	706	1728	3994	7275	33170	42903	285583	608528
Net Property, Plant and Equipment 25	8486	0	32	150	484	1542	4286	10956	17460	27111	62452	146398	12570645
Total Assets 26	15843	0	185	732	2389	6921	14922	34681	67039	164274	356051	902483	18320003
Notes and Loans Payable 27	4630	0	101	199	710	2179	4181	10357	18028	44899	47845	276062	5455821
All Other Liabilities 28	6294	0	26	253	834	2587	5938	14054	31009	84956	167298	388795	7095370
Net Worth 29	4919	0	59	280	845	2154	4802	10270	18002	34419	140908	237626	5768812

Selected Financial Ratios (Times to 1)

Current Ratio 30	0.9	•	4.0	1.6	1.7	1.4	1.3	1.2	1.3	1.2	1.4	1.3	0.5
Quick Ratio 31	0.5	•	3.1	1.2	1.2	1.1	0.9	0.8	0.9	0.8	1.0	0.6	0.3
Net Sales to Working Capital 32	•	•	8.3	32.8	26.0	52.3	62.5	93.0	47.6	60.2	37.9	42.9	•
Coverage Ratio 33	4.9	3.5	1.7	3.2	3.4	3.7	3.8	2.9	2.8	3.7	6.0	3.6	6.0
Total Asset Turnover 34	3.4	•	4.4	8.0	7.6	9.7	7.6	6.5	6.7	8.2	7.7	5.8	0.7
Inventory Turnover 35	41.2	•	22.8	59.1	41.6	89.6	61.4	53.4	58.4	39.6	62.1	17.6	17.7
Receivables Turnover 36	22.1	•	20.1	21.7	19.9	25.5	23.8	22.5	20.0	19.0	24.9	14.6	12.1
Total Liabilities to Net Worth 37	2.2	•	2.1	1.6	1.8	2.2	2.1	2.4	2.7	3.8	1.5	2.8	2.2
Current Assets to Working Capital 38	•	•	1.3	2.7	2.4	3.7	5.0	7.4	4.4	5.5	3.3	4.5	•
Current Liabilities to Working Capital 39	•	•	0.3	1.7	1.4	2.7	4.0	6.4	3.4	4.5	2.3	3.5	•
Working Capital to Net Sales 40	•	•	0.1	0.0	0.0	0.0	0.0	0.0	0.0	0.0	0.0	0.0	•
Inventory to Working Capital 41	•	•	0.3	0.6	0.6	0.6	1.0	1.6	0.9	1.5	0.9	2.0	•
Total Receipts to Cash Flow 42	26.8	123.3	13.2	32.4	31.1	47.8	39.6	44.9	51.3	81.4	56.9	70.9	6.7
Cost of Goods to Cash Flow 43	25.0	121.5	10.2	29.1	28.3	45.3	37.0	42.2	48.7	79.0	55.1	68.3	5.4
Cash Flow to Total Debt 44	0.2	•	0.5	0.4	0.4	0.3	0.3	0.2	0.2	0.1	0.2	0.1	0.2

Selected Financial Factors (in Percentages)

Debt Ratio 45	68.9	•	68.1	61.7	64.6	68.9	67.8	70.4	73.1	79.0	60.4	73.7	68.5
Return on Total Assets 46	9.1	•	5.7	6.3	6.4	7.7	8.1	5.9	7.9	7.4	9.7	6.8	9.1
Return on Equity Before Income Taxes 47	23.3	•	7.6	11.3	12.8	18.2	18.4	13.2	19.0	25.7	20.3	18.6	23.9
Return on Equity After Income Taxes 48	16.0	•	5.6	9.0	11.3	16.8	16.4	11.8	14.3	22.0	16.7	12.0	15.4
Profit Margin (Before Income Tax) 49	2.1	0.7	0.5	0.5	0.6	0.6	0.8	0.6	0.8	0.7	0.7	0.8	10.2
Profit Margin (After Income Tax) 50	1.4	0.4	0.4	0.4	0.5	0.5	0.7	0.5	0.6	0.6	0.9	0.5	6.6

Table II
Corporations with Net Income

PETROLEUM AND PETROLEUM PRODUCTS

MONEY AMOUNTS AND SIZE OF ASSETS IN THOUSANDS OF DOLLARS

Item Description for Accounting Period 7/06 Through 6/07		Total	Zero Assets	Under 500	500 to 1,000	1,000 to 5,000	5,000 to 10,000	10,000 to 25,000	25,000 to 50,000	50,000 to 100,000	100,000 to 250,000	250,000 to 500,000	500,000 to 2,500,000	2,500,000 and over
Number of Enterprises	1	5721	386	2319	628	1351	537	318	105	32	24	•	5	•
Revenues ($ in Thousands)														
Net Sales	2	369377882	74941379	2424293	3352344	28055169	33559676	38242664	22394946	14825823	31122344	•	28057212	•
Interest	3	290434	24140	1821	2287	12992	8534	24481	10176	4252	11779	•	12159	•
Rents	4	154317	0	0	368	33666	20200	41872	11262	4229	11543	•	10289	•
Royalties	5	71054	0	0	0	168	174	46	0	611	1267	•	8	•
Other Portfolio Income	6	4569340	12798	179	3202	53632	27399	48302	37477	8847	8692	•	56714	•
Other Receipts	7	1233142	9781	172	4117	109468	78143	151499	115723	58857	104062	•	156472	•
Total Receipts	8	375698169	74988098	2426465	3362318	28265095	33694126	38508864	22569584	14902619	31259687	•	28292854	•
Average Total Receipts	9	65670	194270	1046	5354	20922	62745	121097	214948	465707	1302487	•	5658571	•
Operating Costs/Operating Income (%)														
Cost of Operations	10	92.4	98.4	76.3	89.1	90.6	94.3	93.3	93.9	95.5	96.5	•	96.6	•
Salaries and Wages	11	1.6	0.3	8.3	2.2	2.4	1.6	1.8	1.7	1.1	0.8	•	0.7	•
Taxes Paid	12	0.5	0.0	1.7	1.6	0.6	0.3	1.1	0.4	0.2	0.5	•	0.1	•
Interest Paid	13	0.5	0.2	0.2	0.2	0.2	0.2	0.2	0.3	0.3	0.2	•	0.2	•
Depreciation	14	0.6	0.0	0.2	1.1	0.4	0.3	0.5	0.5	0.5	0.2	•	0.1	•
Amortization and Depletion	15	0.2	0.0	0.1	0.0	0.0	0.0	0.0	0.0	0.0	0.0	•	0.0	•
Pensions and Other Deferred Comp.	16	0.1	0.0	0.2	0.0	0.1	0.0	0.0	0.1	0.0	0.0	•	0.0	•
Employee Benefits	17	0.2	0.0	0.1	0.1	0.2	0.1	0.1	0.1	0.1	0.1	•	0.0	•
Advertising	18	0.1	0.0	0.1	0.1	0.1	0.0	0.1	0.1	0.0	0.0	•	0.0	•
Other Expenses	19	2.8	0.1	5.4	3.1	4.3	2.2	2.3	2.2	1.5	0.9	•	0.4	•
Officers' Compensation	20	0.3	0.0	3.1	1.7	0.8	0.4	0.3	0.3	0.2	0.1	•	0.7	•
Operating Margin	21	0.8	0.9	4.3	0.5	0.3	0.6	0.3	0.4	0.6	0.6	•	1.2	•
Operating Margin Before Officers' Comp.	22	1.0	0.9	7.4	2.3	1.1	1.0	0.7	0.7	0.8	0.7	•	1.9	•

Selected Average Balance Sheet ($ in Thousands)

Net Receivables 23	2859	0	65	257	919	2841	5127	9336	28865	70945	156763
Inventories 24	1505	0	37	69	483	757	1705	4577	8314	35486	406846
Net Property, Plant and Equipment 25	11482	0	14	145	423	1341	4342	9737	16724	26877	48769
Total Assets 26	20704	0	212	715	2342	6755	15191	33908	66419	165909	875757
Notes and Loans Payable 27	5980	0	46	170	570	1623	3992	9042	16969	38283	163928
All Other Liabilities 28	8006	0	30	231	963	2516	6123	12032	28710	84107	358057
Net Worth 29	6718	0	136	314	808	2616	5076	12835	20739	43519	353773

Selected Financial Ratios (Times to 1)

Current Ratio 30	0.8	•	5.9	1.7	1.7	1.5	1.2	1.3	1.3	1.3	1.3
Quick Ratio 31	0.5	•	4.6	1.3	1.2	1.2	0.9	0.9	1.0	0.9	0.5
Net Sales to Working Capital 32	•	•	6.7	29.1	29.6	41.2	67.0	51.1	43.3	40.4	50.0
Coverage Ratio 33	6.4	5.8	22.0	4.5	6.5	6.7	5.0	4.6	5.2	6.3	11.0
Total Asset Turnover 34	3.1	•	4.9	7.5	8.9	9.3	7.9	6.3	7.0	7.8	6.4
Inventory Turnover 35	39.7	•	21.7	69.0	38.9	77.8	65.8	43.7	53.2	35.3	13.3
Receivables Turnover 36	20.7	•	23.5	21.8	18.7	23.8	24.0	18.5	16.7		11.0
Total Liabilities to Net Worth 37	2.1	•	0.6	1.3	1.9	1.6	2.0	1.6	2.2	2.8	1.5
Current Assets to Working Capital 38	•	•	1.2	2.5	2.5	3.1	5.1	4.4	4.1	4.0	5.0
Current Liabilities to Working Capital 39	•	•	0.2	1.5	1.5	2.1	4.1	3.4	3.1	3.0	4.0
Working Capital to Net Sales 40	•	•	0.1	0.0	0.0	0.0	0.0	0.0	0.0	0.0	0.0
Inventory to Working Capital 41	•	•	0.3	0.4	0.6	0.5	1.0	0.9	0.8	1.1	2.5
Total Receipts to Cash Flow 42	22.0	95.6	11.4	29.9	24.8	39.4	37.4	34.8	45.2	62.9	48.7
Cost of Goods to Cash Flow 43	20.3	94.1	8.7	26.7	22.5	37.2	34.9	32.7	43.2	60.7	47.0
Cash Flow to Total Debt 44	0.2	•	1.2	0.4	0.5	0.4	0.3	0.3	0.2	0.2	0.2

Selected Financial Factors (in Percentages)

Debt Ratio 45	67.6	•	35.9	56.1	65.5	61.3	66.6	62.1	68.8	73.8	59.6
Return on Total Assets 46	10.6	•	22.8	8.1	11.5	11.0	9.9	9.4	9.5	9.6	14.2
Return on Equity Before Income Taxes 47	27.6	•	34.0	14.4	28.1	24.1	23.8	19.4	24.7	30.9	32.1
Return on Equity After Income Taxes 48	19.6	•	32.6	12.2	25.7	22.7	21.4	17.8	19.1	27.1	23.4
Profit Margin (Before Income Tax) 49	2.9	1.0	4.4	0.8	1.1	1.0	1.0	1.2	1.1	1.0	2.0
Profit Margin (After Income Tax) 50	2.0	0.7	4.2	0.7	1.0	0.9	0.9	1.1	0.9	0.9	1.5

Table I

Corporations with and without Net Income

BEER, WINE, AND DISTILLED ALCOHOLIC BEVERAGE

MONEY AMOUNTS AND SIZE OF ASSETS IN THOUSANDS OF DOLLARS

Item Description for Accounting Period 7/06 Through 6/07		Total	Zero Assets	Under 500	500 to 1,000	1,000 to 5,000	5,000 to 10,000	10,000 to 25,000	25,000 to 50,000	50,000 to 100,000	100,000 to 250,000	250,000 to 500,000	500,000 to 2,500,000	2,500,000 and over
Number of Enterprises	1	3958	952	1008	263	930	381	257	78	46	28	3	12	0
Revenues ($ in Thousands)														
Net Sales	2	78506665	1710002	591695	590961	9678725	8172695	10686818	7371093	6822611	10618711	2829245	19434110	0
Interest	3	187347	16740	60	666	3633	3238	1191	4966	5675	3857	1532	145789	0
Rents	4	79575	0	0	416	0	681	0	98	556	10668	12803	54353	0
Royalties	5	181278	0	0	142	1784	21	1095	0	152	2326	175759	0	0
Other Portfolio Income	6	2351375	63003	6552	0	18793	19927	17115	7428	20318	48670	3	2149567	0
Other Receipts	7	934143	41518	9167	27694	93084	69475	74521	98903	118444	177895	23424	200017	0
Total Receipts	8	82240383	1831263	607474	619879	9796019	8266037	10780740	7482488	6967756	10859801	2869333	22159595	0
Average Total Receipts	9	20778	1924	603	2357	10533	21696	41948	95929	151473	387850	956444	1846633	•
Operating Costs/Operating Income (%)														
Cost of Operations	10	75.5	73.3	63.0	70.0	76.2	74.8	74.3	74.1	75.8	73.3	85.4	77.0	•
Salaries and Wages	11	8.0	9.7	0.2	9.2	9.3	8.3	8.1	8.3	8.5	7.0	5.3	7.8	•
Taxes Paid	12	3.2	1.9	1.4	5.4	2.6	1.9	3.7	3.0	1.8	3.7	0.7	4.7	•
Interest Paid	13	1.1	2.0	0.1	0.4	0.4	0.5	1.1	0.6	0.8	0.8	1.1	2.0	•
Depreciation	14	0.5	0.4	0.3	2.2	0.4	0.5	0.6	0.5	0.9	0.5	0.3	0.5	•
Amortization and Depletion	15	0.5	0.1	0.1	0.0	0.1	0.2	0.6	0.5	0.5	0.5	0.7	0.7	•
Pensions and Other Deferred Comp.	16	0.5	0.6	1.3	0.0	0.5	0.8	0.3	0.5	0.3	0.3	0.7	0.5	•
Employee Benefits	17	0.8	0.8	0.1	0.3	1.2	0.7	0.8	0.8	0.9	0.7	1.1	0.7	•
Advertising	18	1.2	0.5	0.5	0.6	0.5	0.6	0.7	1.2	1.5	2.0	1.9	1.6	•
Other Expenses	19	6.0	10.2	16.4	10.1	5.3	6.6	5.6	7.6	5.8	6.6	3.1	5.2	•
Officers' Compensation	20	1.2	3.7	8.8	1.9	2.5	1.8	1.2	1.0	0.7	1.1	0.4	0.3	•
Operating Margin	21	1.5	•	7.8	0.0	1.1	3.4	3.0	1.8	2.3	3.6	•	•	•
Operating Margin Before Officers' Comp.	22	2.7	0.5	16.6	1.9	3.6	5.1	4.1	2.9	3.0	4.7	•	•	•

Selected Average Balance Sheet ($ in Thousands)

Net Receivables 23	1455	0	34	112	522	990	2014	5802	12336	32553	61312	183167	•
Inventories 24	1811	0	16	392	659	1627	2822	7341	14739	32357	111706	216556	•
Net Property, Plant and Equipment 25	1061	0	9	78	334	960	2268	4298	10196	18092	20683	128057	•
Total Assets 26	8412	0	136	792	2315	7018	15219	33213	69169	155993	336627	1088510	•
Notes and Loans Payable 27	2636	0	58	365	452	1423	5965	9695	19433	47467	148147	363193	•
All Other Liabilities 28	1364	0	78	277	887	1535	2818	8480	16022	44652	178266	-5873	•
Net Worth 29	4413	0	1	150	976	4060	6437	15039	33713	63875	10214	731190	•

Selected Financial Ratios (Times to 1)

Current Ratio 30	1.7	•	0.9	1.5	1.7	2.3	1.8	1.7	1.6	1.8	0.7	1.8	•
Quick Ratio 31	0.8	•	0.7	0.6	0.8	1.3	0.9	0.8	0.8	1.0	0.3	0.7	•
Net Sales to Working Capital 32	10.5	•	•	10.0	16.0	9.1	13.8	13.4	10.3	9.7	•	6.4	•
Coverage Ratio 33	6.9	2.9	124.5	14.9	6.9	9.9	4.6	6.4	6.2	8.7	1.6	7.6	•
Total Asset Turnover 34	2.4	•	4.3	2.8	4.5	3.1	2.7	2.8	2.1	2.4	2.8	1.5	•
Inventory Turnover 35	8.3	•	23.4	4.0	12.0	9.9	10.9	9.5	7.6	8.6	7.2	5.8	•
Receivables Turnover 36	10.6	•	20.8	17.9	21.2	21.7	22.7	15.5	12.4	12.8	13.4	4.9	•
Total Liabilities to Net Worth 37	0.9	•	123.3	4.3	1.4	0.7	1.4	1.2	1.1	1.4	32.0	0.5	•
Current Assets to Working Capital 38	2.4	•	•	3.0	2.5	1.8	2.2	2.5	2.6	2.2	•	2.3	•
Current Liabilities to Working Capital 39	1.4	•	•	2.0	1.5	0.8	1.2	1.5	1.6	1.2	•	1.3	•
Working Capital to Net Sales 40	0.1	•	•	0.1	0.1	0.1	0.1	0.1	0.1	0.1	•	0.2	•
Inventory to Working Capital 41	1.0	•	•	1.5	1.2	0.7	1.1	1.0	1.0	0.9	•	0.8	•
Total Receipts to Cash Flow 42	12.2	11.3	4.1	7.6	16.7	10.3	12.7	10.7	11.2	8.7	31.2	15.4	•
Cost of Goods to Cash Flow 43	9.2	8.3	2.6	5.3	12.7	7.7	9.4	8.0	8.5	6.3	26.6	11.8	•
Cash Flow to Total Debt 44	0.4	•	1.1	0.5	0.5	0.7	0.4	0.5	0.4	0.5	0.1	0.3	•

Selected Financial Factors (in Percentages)

Debt Ratio 45	47.5	•	99.2	81.1	57.9	42.2	57.7	54.7	51.3	59.1	97.0	32.8	•
Return on Total Assets 46	17.2	•	45.5	14.9	12.2	15.2	13.3	11.2	11.2	16.0	5.0	22.6	•
Return on Equity Before Income Taxes 47	28.1	•	5615.5	73.4	24.7	23.7	24.7	20.9	19.2	34.7	64.6	29.2	•
Return on Equity After Income Taxes 48	22.3	•	5595.4	57.2	21.9	22.7	24.0	18.9	17.7	32.3	0.6	19.7	•
Profit Margin (Before Income Tax) 49	6.2	3.9	10.5	4.9	2.3	4.5	3.8	3.3	4.4	5.8	0.7	13.2	•
Profit Margin (After Income Tax) 50	5.0	3.7	10.5	3.8	2.0	4.3	3.7	3.0	4.0	5.4	0.0	8.9	•

Table II
Corporations with Net Income

BEER, WINE, AND DISTILLED ALCOHOLIC BEVERAGE

MONEY AMOUNTS AND SIZE OF ASSETS IN THOUSANDS OF DOLLARS

Item Description for Accounting Period 7/06 Through 6/07	Total	Zero Assets	Under 500	500 to 1,000	1,000 to 5,000	5,000 to 10,000	10,000 to 25,000	25,000 to 50,000	50,000 to 100,000	100,000 to 250,000	250,000 to 500,000	500,000 to 2,500,000	2,500,000 and over
Number of Enterprises **1**	2176	44	399	165	852	357	217	71	34	•	0	•	0
Revenues ($ in Thousands)													
Net Sales **2**	70909824	1470689	312467	379014	8733766	7719325	9486299	6753512	5484220	•	0	•	0
Interest **3**	148584	16664	60	666	3295	3136	1160	4871	3603	•	0	•	0
Rents **4**	65827	0	0	0	0	152	0	98	556	•	0	•	0
Royalties **5**	178931	0	0	142	1784	0	1095	0	152	•	0	•	0
Other Portfolio Income **6**	2318323	43735	0	0	18793	19927	17027	5288	15384	•	0	•	0
Other Receipts **7**	894243	41446	303	27466	92228	66664	72910	98848	100999	•	0	•	0
Total Receipts **8**	74515732	1572534	312830	407288	8849866	7809204	9578491	6862617	5604914	•	0	•	0
Average Total Receipts **9**	34244	35739	784	2468	10387	21875	44141	96657	164850	•	•	•	•
Operating Costs/Operating Income (%)													
Cost of Operations **10**	75.5	73.3	45.2	69.2	74.4	74.5	74.8	74.4	76.3	•	•	•	•
Salaries and Wages **11**	8.0	9.3	0.1	7.7	10.0	8.4	8.0	8.1	7.9	•	•	•	•
Taxes Paid **12**	3.2	1.3	1.3	7.3	2.8	1.9	3.1	3.2	1.6	•	•	•	•
Interest Paid **13**	1.0	1.7	0.1	0.3	0.4	0.4	1.0	0.6	0.7	•	•	•	•
Depreciation **14**	0.5	0.4	0.3	1.5	0.5	0.5	0.6	0.5	0.8	•	•	•	•
Amortization and Depletion **15**	0.5	0.1	0.1	0.0	0.1	0.2	0.6	0.5	0.5	•	•	•	•
Pensions and Other Deferred Comp. **16**	0.4	0.5	2.5	0.0	0.4	0.8	0.3	0.5	0.4	•	•	•	•
Employee Benefits **17**	0.8	0.6	0.1	0.3	1.3	0.7	0.7	0.8	0.8	•	•	•	•
Advertising **18**	1.2	0.5	0.7	0.8	0.5	0.6	0.6	1.0	1.7	•	•	•	•
Other Expenses **19**	5.6	9.3	10.7	11.0	5.3	6.5	5.6	7.1	4.8	•	•	•	•
Officers' Compensation **20**	1.1	4.3	14.2	1.5	2.6	1.7	1.1	1.0	0.6	•	•	•	•
Operating Margin **21**	2.2	•	24.8	0.4	1.8	3.8	3.6	2.5	3.9	•	•	•	•
Operating Margin Before Officers' Comp. **22**	3.3	3.0	39.0	2.0	4.4	5.6	4.7	3.5	4.6	•	•	•	•

Selected Average Balance Sheet ($ in Thousands)

Net Receivables 23	2334	0	0	97	456	962	2003	6036	11660
Inventories 24	3089	0	15	458	687	1643	2984	7340	17386
Net Property, Plant and Equipment 25	1806	0	19	100	363	973	2442	4210	10574
Total Assets 26	13502	0	90	783	2323	7038	15040	32780	69571
Notes and Loans Payable 27	4016	0	3	267	425	1305	6033	9030	17718
All Other Liabilities 28	1945	0	27	274	832	1499	2877	8521	14565
Net Worth 29	7541	0	60	242	1065	4234	6131	15229	37288

Selected Financial Ratios (Times to 1)

Current Ratio 30	1.8	•	0.8	2.1	1.7	2.3	1.9	1.7	1.8
Quick Ratio 31	0.8	•	0.5	1.2	0.8	1.3	0.9	0.8	1.0
Net Sales to Working Capital 32	9.6	•	•	7.2	15.0	9.1	13.5	13.5	9.5
Coverage Ratio 33	8.3	4.3	325.2	30.9	8.5	12.7	5.5	7.6	10.2
Total Asset Turnover 34	2.4	•	8.7	2.9	4.4	3.1	2.9	2.9	2.3
Inventory Turnover 35	8.0	•	23.9	3.5	11.1	9.8	11.0	9.6	7.1
Receivables Turnover 36	10.4	•	12018.0	14.5	24.1	21.9	23.4	15.6	12.1
Total Liabilities to Net Worth 37	0.8	•	0.5	2.2	1.2	0.7	1.5	1.2	0.9
Current Assets to Working Capital 38	2.2	•	•	1.9	2.3	1.8	2.2	2.5	2.2
Current Liabilities to Working Capital 39	1.2	•	•	0.9	1.3	0.8	1.2	1.5	1.2
Working Capital to Net Sales 40	0.1	•	•	0.1	0.1	0.1	0.1	0.1	0.1
Inventory to Working Capital 41	0.9	•	•	0.6	1.3	0.7	1.0	1.0	0.9
Total Receipts to Cash Flow 42	11.6	9.3	2.9	5.9	14.9	10.0	11.6	10.5	10.2
Cost of Goods to Cash Flow 43	8.8	6.9	1.3	4.1	11.1	7.4	8.7	7.8	7.8
Cash Flow to Total Debt 44	0.5	•	8.7	0.7	0.5	0.8	0.4	0.5	0.5

Selected Financial Factors (in Percentages)

Debt Ratio 45	44.1	•	33.9	69.1	54.1	39.8	59.2	53.5	46.4
Return on Total Assets 46	20.1	•	216.8	24.0	15.7	16.6	16.3	13.7	15.7
Return on Equity Before Income Taxes 47	31.6	•	327.1	75.1	30.1	25.5	32.6	25.6	26.4
Return on Equity After Income Taxes 48	25.5	•	326.2	59.1	27.3	24.5	31.7	23.4	24.9
Profit Margin (Before Income Tax) 49	7.3	5.7	24.9	7.9	3.1	5.0	4.6	4.1	6.1
Profit Margin (After Income Tax) 50	5.9	5.5	24.8	6.2	2.8	4.8	4.4	3.7	5.8

Table I
Corporations with and without Net Income

MISCELLANEOUS NONDURABLE GOODS

MONEY AMOUNTS AND SIZE OF ASSETS IN THOUSANDS OF DOLLARS

Item Description for Accounting Period 7/06 Through 6/07	Total	Zero Assets	Under 500	500 to 1,000	1,000 to 5,000	5,000 to 10,000	10,000 to 25,000	25,000 to 50,000	50,000 to 100,000	100,000 to 250,000	250,000 to 500,000	500,000 to 2,500,000	2,500,000 and over
1 Number of Enterprises	32582	6208	19604	2886	2704	671	292	109	54	31	9	14	0
Revenues ($ in Thousands)													
2 Net Sales	133493721	1895366	16356124	6434884	17681401	18026751	14410416	11579732	9063105	8828403	3603351	25614189	0
3 Interest	254379	3425	4045	4412	23308	13657	19376	12571	6914	29945	14700	122028	0
4 Rents	31516	0	3539	1997	9750	1228	2200	1163	1321	2973	2381	4963	0
5 Royalties	25944	101	0	0	583	3	532	10876	3839	5905	3838	266	0
6 Other Portfolio Income	404212	29464	13443	13586	22223	30994	12267	3753	19811	41707	10080	206882	0
7 Other Receipts	1446049	11012	52605	36410	112332	64443	308899	85636	91780	172694	192901	317338	0
8 Total Receipts	135655821	1939368	16429756	6491289	17849597	18137076	14753690	11693731	9186770	9081627	3827251	26265666	0
9 Average Total Receipts	4164	312	838	2249	6601	27030	50526	107282	170125	292956	425250	1876119	•
Operating Costs/Operating Income (%)													
10 Cost of Operations	80.1	74.3	81.2	72.9	79.8	83.9	82.3	84.8	83.8	71.2	77.1	77.9	•
11 Salaries and Wages	5.8	6.5	4.4	7.9	5.6	4.3	5.6	4.9	5.6	8.7	8.0	6.7	•
12 Taxes Paid	1.5	1.4	0.9	2.2	1.9	2.1	2.4	1.0	0.8	1.3	1.2	1.1	•
13 Interest Paid	0.8	0.6	0.2	0.4	0.6	0.6	0.6	0.6	0.9	1.1	1.4	1.4	•
14 Depreciation	0.7	0.5	0.5	0.9	0.4	0.3	0.6	0.6	0.7	0.9	0.6	1.1	•
15 Amortization and Depletion	0.1	0.1	0.1	0.0	0.0	0.0	0.0	0.1	0.2	0.2	0.7	0.4	•
16 Pensions and Other Deferred Comp.	0.2	0.1	0.2	0.3	0.3	0.1	0.2	0.2	0.2	0.2	0.2	0.3	•
17 Employee Benefits	0.4	0.7	0.2	0.5	0.3	0.2	0.5	0.4	0.5	0.9	1.0	0.6	•
18 Advertising	0.6	1.2	0.2	0.3	0.4	0.4	0.9	0.3	0.5	2.3	0.2	0.5	•
19 Other Expenses	7.8	15.5	9.7	12.7	7.4	5.7	6.3	5.2	5.5	9.9	8.4	8.7	•
20 Officers' Compensation	1.3	2.0	2.1	3.1	2.5	1.0	1.3	0.9	0.9	0.7	0.6	0.3	•
21 Operating Margin	0.6	•	0.3	•	0.7	1.3	•	1.0	0.4	2.5	0.7	0.9	•
22 Operating Margin Before Officers' Comp.	1.9	•	2.4	1.9	3.2	2.3	0.7	1.9	1.3	3.2	1.4	1.2	•

Selected Average Balance Sheet ($ in Thousands)

Net Receivables 23	406	0	23	228	595	2502	5285	11790	18095	38010	65190	232916	•
Inventories 24	408	0	33	286	645	1977	4690	9859	20505	39234	63638	174834	•
Net Property, Plant and Equipment 25	208	0	17	85	167	478	2111	4817	8388	29564	16059	198113	•
Total Assets 26	1577	0	106	758	2091	6833	15328	34112	68436	170522	310479	1208041	•
Notes and Loans Payable 27	495	0	62	243	520	1988	4612	8676	24345	75300	83670	340842	•
All Other Liabilities 28	614	0	36	283	982	2776	6015	12973	24417	72047	76214	466735	•
Net Worth 29	469	0	8	231	589	2070	4701	12464	19674	23175	150594	400464	•

Selected Financial Ratios (Times to 1)

Current Ratio 30	1.4	•	2.0	1.8	1.5	1.6	1.4	1.5	1.5	1.2	1.5	1.4
Quick Ratio 31	0.8	•	1.1	0.9	0.8	0.8	0.8	0.9	0.7	0.6	0.7	0.7
Net Sales to Working Capital 32	12.8	•	21.3	8.8	11.8	12.7	15.1	12.0	10.6	15.2	8.0	11.4
Coverage Ratio 33	4.0	0.2	5.3	0.4	3.8	4.1	4.2	4.2	2.8	5.8	6.1	3.8
Total Asset Turnover 34	2.6	•	7.9	2.9	3.1	3.9	3.2	3.1	2.5	1.7	1.3	1.5
Inventory Turnover 35	8.0	•	20.4	5.7	8.1	11.4	8.7	9.1	6.9	5.2	4.9	8.2
Receivables Turnover 36	9.3	•	36.8	8.0	10.1	11.2	9.5	9.0	9.2	6.7	6.0	9.6
Total Liabilities to Net Worth 37	2.4	•	12.8	2.3	2.5	2.3	2.3	1.7	2.5	6.4	1.1	2.0
Current Assets to Working Capital 38	3.2	•	2.0	2.3	3.0	2.7	3.7	2.9	3.2	5.8	3.2	3.7
Current Liabilities to Working Capital 39	2.2	•	1.0	1.3	2.0	1.7	2.7	1.9	2.2	4.8	2.2	2.7
Working Capital to Net Sales 40	0.1	•	0.0	0.1	0.1	0.1	0.1	0.1	0.1	0.1	0.1	0.1
Inventory to Working Capital 41	1.2	•	0.8	1.0	1.2	1.0	1.3	1.1	1.3	2.1	1.3	1.3
Total Receipts to Cash Flow 42	12.0	8.0	11.9	9.8	13.5	16.4	14.7	16.1	16.7	7.4	7.4	10.3
Cost of Goods to Cash Flow 43	9.6	5.9	9.7	7.1	10.8	13.8	12.1	13.7	14.0	5.2	5.7	8.0
Cash Flow to Total Debt 44	0.3	•	0.7	0.4	0.3	0.3	0.3	0.3	0.2	0.3	0.3	0.2

Selected Financial Factors (in Percentages)

Debt Ratio 45	70.3	•	92.8	69.5	71.8	69.7	69.3	63.5	71.3	86.4	51.5	66.9
Return on Total Assets 46	8.1	•	7.4	0.5	7.1	9.7	7.7	8.3	6.6	10.9	10.6	8.3
Return on Equity Before Income Taxes 47	20.6	•	82.6	•	18.5	24.2	19.0	17.3	14.9	66.3	18.2	18.5
Return on Equity After Income Taxes 48	16.3	•	77.1	•	17.1	22.7	15.9	14.5	12.2	54.2	15.0	12.1
Profit Margin (Before Income Tax) 49	2.4	•	0.8	•	1.7	1.9	1.8	2.0	1.7	5.4	6.8	4.0
Profit Margin (After Income Tax) 50	1.9	•	0.7	•	1.5	1.7	1.5	1.7	1.4	4.4	5.6	2.7

Table II

Corporations with Net Income

MISCELLANEOUS NONDURABLE GOODS

MONEY AMOUNTS AND SIZE OF ASSETS IN THOUSANDS OF DOLLARS

Item Description for Accounting Period 7/06 Through 6/07	Total	Zero Assets	Under 500	500 to 1,000	1,000 to 5,000	5,000 to 10,000	10,000 to 25,000	25,000 to 50,000	50,000 to 100,000	100,000 to 250,000	250,000 to 500,000	500,000 to 2,500,000	2,500,000 and over
Number of Enterprises **1**	16808	2927	9104	1944	1893	524	236	91	45	24	•	•	0
Revenues ($ in Thousands)													
Net Sales **2**	110238614	871391	12580916	4392047	14478660	13185269	11519744	10646086	7552188	7489507	•	•	0
Interest **3**	211924	1223	1285	3749	17281	6936	13932	8008	6488	18425	•	•	0
Rents **4**	23269	0	3	235	8325	423	1830	904	1231	2973	•	•	0
Royalties **5**	22334	0	0	0	0	0	532	9284	3839	4830	•	•	0
Other Portfolio Income **6**	370719	27109	11059	13513	21927	29187	11424	2732	17505	19903	•	•	0
Other Receipts **7**	1262375	10075	42168	19739	79242	61175	238799	85026	97247	151146	•	•	0
Total Receipts **8**	112129235	909798	12635431	4429283	14605435	13282990	11786261	10752040	7678498	7686784	•	•	0
Average Total Receipts **9**	6671	311	1388	2278	7715	25349	49942	118154	170633	320283	•	•	•
Operating Costs/Operating Income (%)													
Cost of Operations **10**	79.9	71.0	82.3	71.6	79.4	81.5	82.2	85.3	83.6	70.8	•	•	•
Salaries and Wages **11**	5.7	8.9	3.9	7.2	5.2	4.5	5.4	4.8	5.6	7.9	•	•	•
Taxes Paid **12**	1.5	1.7	0.8	2.6	1.9	2.5	2.3	0.9	0.8	1.3	•	•	•
Interest Paid **13**	0.7	0.6	0.1	0.4	0.4	0.6	0.6	0.5	0.8	1.0	•	•	•
Depreciation **14**	0.7	0.5	0.3	0.6	0.4	0.3	0.5	0.5	0.6	0.9	•	•	•
Amortization and Depletion **15**	0.1	0.2	0.0	0.0	0.0	0.0	0.0	0.1	0.1	0.2	•	•	•
Pensions and Other Deferred Comp. **16**	0.2	0.1	0.2	0.3	0.3	0.1	0.2	0.1	0.3	0.2	•	•	•
Employee Benefits **17**	0.4	0.5	0.2	0.6	0.3	0.2	0.4	0.4	0.4	0.9	•	•	•
Advertising **18**	0.5	0.6	0.2	0.3	0.4	0.4	0.5	0.3	0.6	2.5	•	•	•
Other Expenses **19**	6.9	10.6	7.2	9.8	6.6	6.3	5.4	4.4	5.1	8.3	•	•	•
Officers' Compensation **20**	1.3	1.0	2.1	3.6	2.7	1.1	1.4	0.9	1.0	0.7	•	•	•
Operating Margin **21**	2.0	4.3	2.6	2.9	2.4	2.3	1.0	1.7	1.2	5.3	•	•	•
Operating Margin Before Officers' Comp. **22**	3.3	5.3	4.7	6.5	5.1	3.4	2.4	2.6	2.2	5.9	•	•	•

Selected Average Balance Sheet ($ in Thousands)

Net Receivables 23	656	0	33	261	611	2533	5204	12222	18054	41218
Inventories 24	663	0	44	315	728	1831	4939	9732	19707	43970
Net Property, Plant and Equipment 25	323	0	20	64	152	344	1965	4434	7845	25060
Total Assets 26	2455	0	133	753	2110	6966	15158	33547	66348	173054
Notes and Loans Payable 27	703	0	66	209	401	1943	4455	7533	22687	80626
All Other Liabilities 28	914	0	39	206	755	3002	5251	12821	21646	71922
Net Worth 29	839	0	28	338	955	2021	5453	13193	22015	20505

Selected Financial Ratios (Times to 1)

Current Ratio 30	1.5	•	1.9	2.8	1.9	1.5	1.5	1.6	1.6	1.3
Quick Ratio 31	0.8	•	1.3	1.6	1.1	0.8	0.8	0.9	0.8	0.7
Net Sales to Working Capital 32	11.2	•	28.1	5.5	9.1	11.8	12.1	12.0	9.0	12.8
Coverage Ratio 33	6.5	14.9	22.3	11.6	8.5	5.8	6.8	6.7	4.5	8.5
Total Asset Turnover 34	2.7	•	10.4	3.0	3.6	3.6	3.2	3.5	2.5	1.8
Inventory Turnover 35	7.9	•	25.7	5.1	8.3	11.2	8.1	10.3	7.1	5.0
Receivables Turnover 36	9.0	•	39.9	7.3	10.7	10.0	9.2	9.7	9.3	6.7
Total Liabilities to Net Worth 37	1.9	•	3.8	1.2	1.2	2.4	1.8	1.5	2.0	7.4
Current Assets to Working Capital 38	2.8	•	2.1	1.5	2.1	2.8	2.9	2.7	2.6	4.7
Current Liabilities to Working Capital 39	1.8	•	1.1	0.5	1.1	1.8	1.9	1.7	1.6	3.7
Working Capital to Net Sales 40	0.1	•	0.0	0.2	0.1	0.1	0.1	0.1	0.1	0.1
Inventory to Working Capital 41	1.1	•	0.7	0.7	0.8	1.0	1.1	1.0	1.1	1.8
Total Receipts to Cash Flow 42	11.1	5.9	11.1	8.9	11.9	12.6	13.1	15.9	14.7	6.8
Cost of Goods to Cash Flow 43	8.9	4.2	9.2	6.4	9.5	10.3	10.8	13.6	12.3	4.8
Cash Flow to Total Debt 44	0.4	•	1.2	0.6	0.6	0.4	0.4	0.4	0.3	0.3

Selected Financial Factors (in Percentages)

Debt Ratio 45	65.8	•	79.3	55.1	54.8	71.0	64.0	60.7	66.8	88.2
Return on Total Assets 46	12.3	•	33.1	12.2	13.4	13.4	12.4	11.2	9.3	16.1
Return on Equity Before Income Taxes 47	30.4	•	153.0	24.8	26.1	38.2	29.5	24.2	21.8	120.1
Return on Equity After Income Taxes 48	25.7	•	149.7	24.0	24.8	36.2	26.1	21.0	19.0	102.4
Profit Margin (Before Income Tax) 49	3.9	8.7	3.0	3.7	3.3	3.1	3.3	2.7	2.9	7.9
Profit Margin (After Income Tax) 50	3.3	8.4	3.0	3.6	3.1	2.9	2.9	2.4	2.5	6.7

Table I

Corporations with and without Net Income

WHOLESALE ELECTRONIC MARKETS AND AGENTS AND BROKERS

MONEY AMOUNTS AND SIZE OF ASSETS IN THOUSANDS OF DOLLARS

Item Description for Accounting Period 7/06 Through 6/07	Total	Zero Assets	Under 500	500 to 1,000	1,000 to 5,000	5,000 to 10,000	10,000 to 25,000	25,000 to 50,000	50,000 to 100,000	100,000 to 250,000	250,000 to 500,000	500,000 to 2,500,000	2,500,000 and over
Number of Enterprises 1	15705	3565	11675	157	279	10	10	5	0	0	3	0	0
Revenues ($ in Thousands)													
Net Sales 2	5882024	303436	3277753	227964	285325	37546	66457	347039	0	0	1336504	0	0
Interest 3	145147	28725	1239	2027	446	0	0	559	0	0	112152	0	0
Rents 4	3894	250	0	0	0	0	0	2850	0	0	794	0	0
Royalties 5	15154	3570	0	0	0	0	0	323	0	0	11261	0	0
Other Portfolio Income 6	62362	32772	1427	0	0	0	0	369	0	0	27795	0	0
Other Receipts 7	128047	317	69026	0	44320	0	547	3136	0	0	10699	0	0
Total Receipts 8	6236628	369070	3349445	229991	330091	37546	67004	354276	0	0	1499205	0	0
Average Total Receipts 9	397	104	287	1465	1183	3755	6700	70855	•	•	499735	•	•
Operating Costs/Operating Income (%)													
Cost of Operations 10	0.0	•	0.0	•	•	•	•	•	•	•	•	•	•
Salaries and Wages 11	24.5	12.4	13.6	15.4	53.7	31.1	13.6	55.3	•	•	41.8	•	•
Taxes Paid 12	3.4	3.5	2.8	2.5	4.8	5.0	2.0	5.9	•	•	4.3	•	•
Interest Paid 13	3.5	9.3	0.5	0.6	1.8	7.0	7.9	1.2	•	•	10.6	•	•
Depreciation 14	1.2	3.7	0.5	0.1	0.3	1.5	2.0	1.2	•	•	2.7	•	•
Amortization and Depletion 15	1.1	2.3	0.2	•	1.2	•	3.5	1.2	•	•	2.9	•	•
Pensions and Other Deferred Comp. 16	1.2	2.2	1.0	2.1	1.5	4.0	0.0	3.7	•	•	0.5	•	•
Employee Benefits 17	2.5	3.3	2.0	2.4	2.4	5.0	1.5	4.4	•	•	3.1	•	•
Advertising 18	1.2	2.4	0.9	•	0.2	0.0	17.2	0.3	•	•	1.5	•	•
Other Expenses 19	39.2	62.8	43.1	36.2	21.2	32.8	45.3	23.6	•	•	32.5	•	•
Officers' Compensation 20	16.6	11.5	22.6	32.1	17.6	14.9	2.9	1.5	•	•	4.8	•	•
Operating Margin 21	5.7	•	12.9	8.6	•	•	4.1	1.9	•	•	•	•	•
Operating Margin Before Officers' Comp. 22	22.3	•	35.5	40.7	12.9	13.6	7.0	3.4	•	•	0.1	•	•

Selected Average Balance Sheet ($ in Thousands)

Net Receivables 23	47	0	2	1	126	4536	5863	27643	•	147096
Inventories 24	1	0	0	0	1	0	874	1	•	2385
Net Property, Plant and Equipment 25	44	0	6	3	162	2823	10797	•	•	178061
Total Assets 26	312	0	63	597	1588	9071	13327	83638	•	993937
Notes and Loans Payable 27	188	0	32	333	588	1805	5985	40512	•	698246
All Other Liabilities 28	57	0	7	124	283	6323	8996	21738	•	150874
Net Worth 29	66	0	24	141	717	943	-1654	21388	•	144817

Selected Financial Ratios (Times to 1)

Current Ratio 30	1.4	•	1.6	3.0	3.6	0.6	0.9	1.1	•	1.3
Quick Ratio 31	1.0	•	1.6	3.0	3.5	0.6	0.7	0.8	•	0.7
Net Sales to Working Capital 32	9.7	•	26.4	3.7	1.3	•	•	28.5	•	5.5
Coverage Ratio 33	4.5	2.4	30.7	17.6	7.0	0.8	1.6	4.4	•	1.8
Total Asset Turnover 34	1.2	•	4.4	2.4	0.6	0.4	0.5	0.8	•	0.4
Inventory Turnover 35	0.0	•	0.0	•	•	•	•	•	•	•
Receivables Turnover 36	8.5	•	105.9	5427.7	9.0	1.7	1.3	3.6	•	6.1
Total Liabilities to Net Worth 37	3.7	•	1.6	3.2	1.2	8.6	2.9	•	•	5.9
Current Assets to Working Capital 38	3.7	•	2.6	1.5	1.4	•	•	17.5	•	5.0
Current Liabilities to Working Capital 39	2.7	•	1.6	0.5	0.4	•	•	16.5	•	4.0
Working Capital to Net Sales 40	0.1	•	0.0	0.3	0.7	•	•	0.0	•	0.2
Inventory to Working Capital 41	0.0	•	•	0.0	0.0	•	•	0.0	•	0.0
Total Receipts to Cash Flow 42	2.2	1.6	1.9	2.3	3.5	3.6	2.3	4.5	•	2.8
Cost of Goods to Cash Flow 43	0.0	•	0.0	•	•	•	•	•	•	•
Cash Flow to Total Debt 44	0.7	•	3.9	1.4	0.3	0.1	0.2	0.2	•	0.2

Selected Financial Factors (in Percentages)

Debt Ratio 45	78.7	•	61.4	76.5	54.9	89.6	112.4	74.4	•	85.4
Return on Total Assets 46	18.7	•	69.0	24.4	8.3	2.3	6.4	4.3	•	8.4
Return on Equity Before Income Taxes 47	68.2	•	173.1	97.7	15.8	•	•	13.0	•	25.0
Return on Equity After Income Taxes 48	59.8	•	171.9	94.7	15.6	•	•	8.8	•	9.8
Profit Margin (Before Income Tax) 49	12.1	12.7	15.0	9.5	11.1	•	4.9	4.0	•	8.1
Profit Margin (After Income Tax) 50	10.6	8.5	14.9	9.2	11.0	•	4.8	2.7	•	3.2

Table II
Corporations with Net Income

WHOLESALE ELECTRONIC MARKETS AND AGENTS AND BROKERS

MONEY AMOUNTS AND SIZE OF ASSETS IN THOUSANDS OF DOLLARS

Item Description for Accounting Period 7/06 Through 6/07		Total	Zero Assets	Under 500	500 to 1000	251 to 500	501 to 1,000	1,001 to 5,000	5,001 to 10,000	10,001 to 25,000	25,001 to 50,000	50,001 to 100,000	100,001 to 250,000	250,001 and over
Number of Enterprises	1	11877	2576	8957	•	172	0	10	•	0	3	0	0	0
Revenues ($ in Thousands)														
Net Sales	2	4827677	298451	3141975	•	281473	0	66457	•	0	807951	0	0	0
Interest	3	143299	28725	58	•	446	0	0	•	0	112005	0	0	0
Rents	4	3894	250	0	•	0	0	0	•	0	3643	0	0	0
Royalties	5	15154	3570	0	•	0	0	0	•	0	11584	0	0	0
Other Portfolio Income	6	61480	32772	1425	•	0	0	0	•	0	27283	0	0	0
Other Receipts	7	114344	317	68505	•	44320	0	547	•	0	539	0	0	0
Total Receipts	8	5165848	364085	3211963	•	326239	0	67004	•	0	963005	0	0	0
Average Total Receipts	9	435	141	359	•	1897	•	6700	•	•	321002	•	•	•
Operating Costs/Operating Income (%)														
Cost of Operations	10	0.0	•	0.0	•	•	•	•	•	•	•	•	•	•
Salaries and Wages	11	20.0	11.7	13.9	•	54.4	•	13.6	•	•	36.6	•	•	•
Taxes Paid	12	3.4	3.5	2.8	•	4.7	•	2.0	•	•	5.5	•	•	•
Interest Paid	13	2.8	9.5	0.5	•	1.9	•	7.9	•	•	9.8	•	•	•
Depreciation	14	1.3	3.6	0.4	•	0.3	•	2.0	•	•	4.2	•	•	•
Amortization and Depletion	15	0.9	2.3	0.1	•	1.3	•	3.5	•	•	3.3	•	•	•
Pensions and Other Deferred Comp.	16	1.3	2.2	1.0	•	1.5	•	0.0	•	•	1.7	•	•	•
Employee Benefits	17	2.2	2.0	2.0	•	2.4	•	1.5	•	•	2.7	•	•	•
Advertising	18	1.4	2.4	0.9	•	0.2	•	17.2	•	•	2.6	•	•	•
Other Expenses	19	38.0	51.7	40.9	•	21.4	•	45.3	•	•	27.7	•	•	•
Officers' Compensation	20	18.4	11.7	23.0	•	16.3	•	2.9	•	•	1.1	•	•	•
Operating Margin	21	10.4	•	14.4	•	•	•	4.1	•	•	4.8	•	•	•
Operating Margin Before Officers' Comp.	22	28.8	11.2	37.4	•	12.0	•	7.0	•	•	5.9	•	•	•

Selected Average Balance Sheet ($ in Thousands)

Line Item							
Net Receivables 23	46	0	1		204	5863	142951
Inventories 24	1	0	0		2	874	2387
Net Property, Plant and Equipment 25	55	0	7		4	2823	185554
Total Assets 26	326	0	62		1816	13327	892382
Notes and Loans Payable 27	145	0	34		953	5985	368853
All Other Liabilities 28	47	0	8		455	8996	98211
Net Worth 29	134	0	20		408	-1654	425318

Selected Financial Ratios (Times to 1)

Line Item							
Current Ratio 30	1.5		1.7		3.4	0.9	1.3
Quick Ratio 31	1.1		1.7		3.3	0.7	0.7
Net Sales to Working Capital 32	7.5		29.4		1.4		2.9
Coverage Ratio 33	7.3	3.8	32.6		7.3	1.6	3.6
Total Asset Turnover 34	1.2		5.7		0.9	0.5	0.3
Inventory Turnover 35	0.0		0.0		0.0		
Receivables Turnover 36	8.4		227.2		11.8		
Total Liabilities to Net Worth 37	1.4		2.1		3.4		1.1
Current Assets to Working Capital 38	3.0		2.4		1.4		4.2
Current Liabilities to Working Capital 39	2.0		1.4		0.4		3.2
Working Capital to Net Sales 40	0.1		0.0		0.7		0.3
Inventory to Working Capital 41	0.0				0.0		0.0
Total Receipts to Cash Flow 42	2.0	1.5	1.9		3.4	2.3	2.2
Cost of Goods to Cash Flow 43	0.0		0.0		0.0		
Cash Flow to Total Debt 44	1.1		4.4		0.3	0.2	0.3

Selected Financial Factors (in Percentages)

Line Item							
Debt Ratio 45	58.8		68.2		77.5	112.4	52.3
Return on Total Assets 46	25.8		97.7		12.2	6.4	10.5
Return on Equity Before Income Taxes 47	53.9		297.3		46.6		15.9
Return on Equity After Income Taxes 48	48.4		295.4		46.2		10.4
Profit Margin (Before Income Tax) 49	17.8	26.1	16.6		11.6	4.9	25.1
Profit Margin (After Income Tax) 50	16.0	21.8	16.5		11.5	4.8	16.4

Table I

Corporations with and without Net Income

NEW AND USED CAR DEALERS

MONEY AMOUNTS AND SIZE OF ASSETS IN THOUSANDS OF DOLLARS

Item Description for Accounting Period 7/06 Through 6/07		Total	Zero Assets	Under 500	500 to 1,000	1,000 to 5,000	5,000 to 10,000	10,000 to 25,000	25,000 to 50,000	50,000 to 100,000	100,000 to 250,000	250,000 to 500,000	500,000 to 2,500,000	2,500,000 and over
Number of Enterprises	1	50905	6625	20353	4892	8789	5659	3512	816	187	50	11	8	3
Revenues ($ in Thousands)														
Net Sales	2	724101575	3654342	24278269	13978315	86643052	162954045	208439211	98409922	40549735	19450968	8373539	24388677	32981500
Interest	3	1042492	1525	5815	27318	114287	139195	165656	109982	50050	66400	53377	254403	54485
Rents	4	307963	96	30	683	14517	22089	19229	19258	25662	21466	48476	21485	114972
Royalties	5	6843	0	0	0	1282	0	0	1	0	3982	0	1579	0
Other Portfolio Income	6	798198	68615	40922	36178	108088	75569	92202	63390	85454	59904	38668	121839	7362
Other Receipts	7	12670795	49577	177811	116622	1463282	2946277	3949709	1753093	780127	510365	149406	552539	221991
Total Receipts	8	738927866	3774155	24502847	14159116	88344508	166137175	212666007	100355646	41491028	20113085	8663466	25340522	33380310
Average Total Receipts	9	14516	570	1204	2894	10052	29358	60554	122985	221877	402262	787588	3167565	11126770
Operating Costs/Operating Income (%)														
Cost of Operations	10	87.8	81.3	85.6	86.6	87.2	88.3	88.6	88.7	87.6	85.9	87.8	87.3	84.7
Salaries and Wages	11	4.9	4.7	2.6	4.1	4.9	4.9	4.8	4.8	5.3	5.9	5.0	6.6	6.2
Taxes Paid	12	0.9	1.3	1.6	1.6	1.0	0.8	0.8	0.7	0.8	0.8	0.8	1.0	0.9
Interest Paid	13	0.9	0.5	0.6	0.7	1.2	0.9	0.8	0.8	1.0	1.1	1.4	1.3	1.4
Depreciation	14	0.3	0.3	0.2	0.3	0.2	0.2	0.3	0.4	0.6	1.0	1.8	0.4	0.4
Amortization and Depletion	15	0.1	0.0	0.0	0.0	0.0	0.0	0.1	0.1	0.1	0.1	0.1	0.3	0.6
Pensions and Other Deferred Comp.	16	0.1	0.0	0.0	0.1	0.1	0.1	0.1	0.1	0.1	0.1	0.1	0.1	0.0
Employee Benefits	17	0.4	0.2	0.1	0.2	0.5	0.5	0.4	0.4	0.4	0.5	0.5	0.4	0.4
Advertising	18	1.1	1.3	0.8	0.5	1.1	1.3	1.1	1.0	1.0	1.1	0.8	0.8	1.0
Other Expenses	19	4.0	14.6	7.3	4.7	4.6	3.6	3.7	3.3	3.6	5.3	3.7	3.4	4.0
Officers' Compensation	20	0.7	1.7	1.2	1.3	1.1	0.8	0.6	0.5	0.5	0.5	0.5	0.1	0.1
Operating Margin	21	•	•	•	•	•	•	•	•	•	•	•	•	0.3
Operating Margin Before Officers' Comp.	22	•	1.2	1.2	1.0	•	•	•	•	•	•	•	•	0.4

Selected Average Balance Sheet ($ in Thousands)

	1	2	3	4	5	6	7	8	9	10	11	12	13
Net Receivables 23	457	0	32	145	348	788	1693	3860	9414	20506	42342	79433	466745
Inventories 24	2075	0	88	356	1726	4412	8997	16782	29628	58511	95290	373702	1393718
Net Property, Plant and Equipment 25	430	0	14	48	166	512	1402	4360	10484	26934	98397	231089	766426
Total Assets 26	3887		165	692	2611	7147	14993	33304	66916	142215	317438	1303530	4779373
Notes and Loans Payable 27	2519	0	98	360	1771	5070	10862	22520	43591	87604	216579	440799	1753880
All Other Liabilities 28	522	0	35	164	403	762	1523	3197	8572	16666	37414	352563	1186549
Net Worth 29	846	0	32	168	437	1315	2609	7587	14753	37945	63444	510169	1838943

Selected Financial Ratios (Times to 1)

	1	2	3	4	5	6	7	8	9	10	11	12	13
Current Ratio 30	1.3	•	2.6	2.4	1.4	1.3	1.2	1.2	1.3	1.2	1.0	1.2	1.1
Quick Ratio 31	0.3	•	1.0	0.9	0.3	0.4	0.3	0.4	0.4	0.4	0.4	0.3	0.3
Net Sales to Working Capital 32	22.2	•	13.8	8.0	16.0	21.7	23.6	21.1	22.7	95.2	32.7	44.5	
Coverage Ratio 33	1.9	•	2.5	2.4	1.2	1.5	2.0	2.5	2.1	1.8	2.7	2.1	
Total Asset Turnover 34	3.7	•	7.2	4.1	3.8	4.0	3.6	3.2	2.7	2.4	2.3	2.3	
Inventory Turnover 35	6.0	•	11.6	7.0	5.0	5.8	6.4	6.4	5.7	7.0	7.1	6.7	
Receivables Turnover 36	31.9	•	44.3	21.4	28.2	39.6	32.1	24.8	20.5	19.2	37.6	20.4	
Total Liabilities to Net Worth 37	3.6	•	4.1	3.1	5.0	4.4	3.4	3.5	2.7	4.0	1.6	1.6	
Current Assets to Working Capital 38	4.7	•	1.6	1.7	3.8	4.7	5.0	4.8	5.7	22.2	6.3	7.8	
Current Liabilities to Working Capital 39	3.7	•	0.6	0.7	2.8	3.7	4.0	3.8	4.7	21.2	5.3	6.8	
Working Capital to Net Sales 40	0.0	•	0.1	0.1	0.0	0.0	0.0	0.0	0.0	0.0	0.0	0.0	
Inventory to Working Capital 41	3.3	•	1.0	1.1	2.7	3.4	3.4	3.0	3.3	13.6	4.2	5.3	
Total Receipts to Cash Flow 42	27.7	13.5	23.3	27.6	32.9	29.8	27.7	26.2	23.4	27.3	23.7	24.3	
Cost of Goods to Cash Flow 43	24.3	11.0	20.1	24.1	29.1	26.4	24.6	23.0	20.1	24.0	20.7	20.6	
Cash Flow to Total Debt 44	0.2	•	0.6	0.2	0.2	0.2	0.2	0.2	0.2	0.1	0.2	0.2	

Selected Financial Factors (in Percentages)

	1	2	3	4	5	6	7	8	9	10	11	12	13
Debt Ratio 45	78.2	•	80.5	75.7	83.3	81.6	82.6	77.2	78.0	73.3	80.0	60.9	61.5
Return on Total Assets 46	6.5	•	10.3	7.0	5.5	5.7	6.2	7.4	7.8	6.4	5.9	8.1	6.7
Return on Equity Before Income Taxes 47	14.0	•	31.7	16.7	6.4	10.8	17.4	19.3	21.5	12.3	12.7	13.2	9.1
Return on Equity After Income Taxes 48	12.5	•	31.4	14.6	5.8	10.3	16.7	18.3	19.6	10.7	8.6	9.2	5.9
Profit Margin (Before Income Tax) 49	0.8	•	0.9	1.0	0.3	0.5	0.8	1.2	1.5	1.2	1.1	2.2	1.5
Profit Margin (After Income Tax) 50	0.7	•	0.8	0.9	0.3	0.5	0.7	1.2	1.3	1.0	0.7	1.5	1.0

Table II

Corporations with Net Income

NEW AND USED CAR DEALERS

MONEY AMOUNTS AND SIZE OF ASSETS IN THOUSANDS OF DOLLARS

Item Description for Accounting Period 7/06 Through 6/07	Total	Zero Assets	Under 500	500 to 1,000	1,000 to 5,000	5,000 to 10,000	10,000 to 25,000	25,000 to 50,000	50,000 to 100,000	100,000 to 250,000	250,000 to 500,000	500,000 to 2,500,000	2,500,000 and over
Number of Enterprises 1	24582	1040	9460	2833	4564	3442	2387	629	167	42	•	•	3

Revenues ($ in Thousands)

Item	Total	Zero Assets	Under 500	500 to 1,000	1,000 to 5,000	5,000 to 10,000	10,000 to 25,000	25,000 to 50,000	50,000 to 100,000	100,000 to 250,000	250,000 to 500,000	500,000 to 2,500,000	2,500,000 and over
Net Sales 2	520676782	1340012	13099067	9650168	49278936	105310313	149937202	75031333	37786864	16766749	•	•	32981500
Interest 3	861578	1049	4486	17375	71237	89416	123332	93963	43949	61200	•	•	54485
Rents 4	278021	13	30	683	10710	8961	16206	18491	20820	18182	•	•	114972
Royalties 5	6843	0	0	0	1282	0	0	0	0	3982	•	•	0
Other Portfolio Income 6	570513	32849	23044	31817	59832	59176	60675	44506	76592	18310	•	•	7362
Other Receipts 7	9609503	14060	107297	53922	985141	2004290	2968901	1457562	724837	370218	•	•	221991
Total Receipts 8	532003240	1387983	13233924	9753965	50407138	107472156	153106316	76645855	38653062	17238641	•	•	33380310
Average Total Receipts 9	21642	1335	1399	3443	11045	31224	64142	121854	231455	410444	•	•	11126770

Operating Costs/Operating Income (%)

Item	Total	Zero Assets	Under 500	500 to 1,000	1,000 to 5,000	5,000 to 10,000	10,000 to 25,000	25,000 to 50,000	50,000 to 100,000	100,000 to 250,000	250,000 to 500,000	500,000 to 2,500,000	2,500,000 and over
Cost of Operations 10	87.4	78.3	81.7	85.6	86.5	88.1	88.1	87.9	87.6	87.5	•	•	84.7
Salaries and Wages 11	5.0	4.6	3.2	3.7	5.0	4.7	4.9	5.1	5.3	5.5	•	•	6.2
Taxes Paid 12	0.9	2.2	2.2	1.4	1.0	0.8	0.8	0.7	0.8	0.8	•	•	0.9
Interest Paid 13	0.8	0.4	0.5	0.6	0.9	0.8	0.7	0.8	0.9	1.1	•	•	1.4
Depreciation 14	0.3	0.3	0.1	0.2	0.2	0.2	0.3	0.4	0.5	0.5	•	•	0.4
Amortization and Depletion 15	0.1	0.0	0.0	0.0	0.0	0.0	0.0	0.1	0.1	0.1	•	•	0.6
Pensions and Other Deferred Comp. 16	0.1	0.0	0.1	0.2	0.1	0.1	0.1	0.1	0.1	0.0	•	•	0.0
Employee Benefits 17	0.4	0.2	0.1	0.1	0.4	0.4	0.4	0.4	0.4	0.4	•	•	0.4
Advertising 18	1.1	2.3	0.7	0.5	1.0	1.2	1.1	1.1	1.0	1.1	•	•	1.0
Other Expenses 19	3.7	8.3	6.3	4.2	4.4	3.4	3.6	3.3	3.4	3.8	•	•	4.0
Officers' Compensation 20	0.7	2.9	1.2	1.7	0.9	1.1	0.7	0.5	0.5	0.5	•	•	0.1
Operating Margin 21	•	0.5	4.0	1.8	•	•	•	•	•	•	•	•	0.3
Operating Margin Before Officers' Comp. 22	0.2	3.4	5.2	3.5	0.5	0.4	0.0	0.2	•	•	•	•	0.4

Selected Average Balance Sheet ($ in Thousands)

Item												
Net Receivables 23	702	0	33	151	413	868	1829	3890	8947	22079	•	466745
Inventories 24	3028	0	124	410	1823	4415	9441	17091	29810	63468	•	1311726
Net Property, Plant and Equipment 25	654	0	8	36	184	523	1362	4254	10447	24022	•	766426
Total Assets 26	5773	0	207	662	2635	7256	15206	33153	66913	142400	•	4779373
Notes and Loans Payable 27	3413	0	88	276	1502	4688	10453	21525	43041	87258	•	1753880
All Other Liabilities 28	801	0	18	114	378	813	1538	3303	8759	19122	•	1186549
Net Worth 29	1560	0	102	272	755	1755	3215	8325	15113	36020	•	1838943

Selected Financial Ratios (Times to 1)

Item												
Current Ratio 30	1.3	•	5.1	3.4	1.6	1.4	1.3	1.3	1.3	1.2	•	1.1
Quick Ratio 31	0.4	•	1.7	1.3	0.4	0.4	0.3	0.4	0.4	0.5	•	0.3
Net Sales to Working Capital 32	19.2	•	9.7	7.9	12.4	17.7	23.4	19.8	21.8	20.7	•	44.5
Coverage Ratio 33	3.1	10.4	11.2	6.0	2.9	2.9	3.2	3.2	2.9	2.4	•	2.1
Total Asset Turnover 34	3.7	•	6.7	5.1	4.1	4.2	4.1	3.6	3.4	2.8	•	2.3
Inventory Turnover 35	6.1	•	9.1	7.1	5.1	6.1	5.9	6.1	6.6	5.5	•	7.1
Receivables Turnover 36	30.7	•	39.1	21.3	23.6	40.1	33.7	31.3	26.7	19.1	•	•
Total Liabilities to Net Worth 37	2.7	•	1.0	1.4	2.5	3.1	3.7	3.0	3.4	3.0	•	1.6
Current Assets to Working Capital 38	4.0	•	1.2	1.4	2.7	3.7	4.8	4.4	4.8	5.2	•	7.8
Current Liabilities to Working Capital 39	3.0	•	0.2	0.4	1.7	2.7	3.8	3.4	3.8	4.2	•	6.8
Working Capital to Net Sales 40	0.1	•	0.1	0.1	0.1	0.1	0.0	0.1	0.0	0.0	•	0.0
Inventory to Working Capital 41	2.7	•	0.8	0.9	1.9	2.6	3.3	2.9	3.1	3.0	•	5.3
Total Receipts to Cash Flow 42	23.4	15.8	10.3	18.2	20.4	26.1	25.2	24.0	25.0	23.5	•	24.3
Cost of Goods to Cash Flow 43	20.5	12.4	8.4	15.6	17.6	22.9	22.2	21.1	21.9	20.6	•	20.6
Cash Flow to Total Debt 44	0.2	•	1.3	0.5	0.3	0.2	0.2	0.2	0.2	0.2	•	0.2

Selected Financial Factors (in Percentages)

Item												
Debt Ratio 45	73.0	•	50.9	58.9	71.3	75.8	78.9	74.9	77.4	74.7	•	61.5
Return on Total Assets 46	9.4	•	36.9	17.7	11.0	9.5	8.9	9.3	8.9	7.3	•	6.7
Return on Equity Before Income Taxes 47	23.4	•	68.5	35.9	24.9	25.8	28.7	25.4	25.7	16.7	•	9.1
Return on Equity After Income Taxes 48	21.7	•	68.2	33.7	24.2	25.1	27.8	24.3	23.7	14.7	•	5.9
Profit Margin (Before Income Tax) 49	1.7	4.1	5.0	2.9	1.7	1.5	1.5	1.8	1.7	1.5	•	1.5
Profit Margin (After Income Tax) 50	1.6	3.8	5.0	2.7	1.7	1.4	1.4	1.7	1.6	1.3	•	1.0

Table I

Corporations with and without Net Income

OTHER MOTOR VEHICLE AND PARTS DEALERS

MONEY AMOUNTS AND SIZE OF ASSETS IN THOUSANDS OF DOLLARS

Item Description for Accounting Period 7/06 Through 6/07	Total	Zero Assets	Under 500	500 to 1,000	1,000 to 5,000	5,000 to 10,000	10,000 to 25,000	25,000 to 50,000	50,000 to 100,000	100,000 to 250,000	250,000 to 500,000	500,000 to 2,500,000	2,500,000 and over
Number of Enterprises 1	43090	5823	22447	5063	7692	1376	460	139	44	29	5	11	0
Revenues ($ in Thousands)													
Net Sales 2	158803997	1101784	14646252	9049011	46768256	19864373	15299033	11907914	7713082	7751916	2181237	22521139	0
Interest 3	175317	821	3581	7491	31420	21129	18958	15487	9750	12222	3088	51370	0
Rents 4	102080	0	4633	4377	12447	9396	8555	8204	21032	1362	3338	28737	0
Royalties 5	28586	0	0	0	196	4178	0	17	81	5	0	24109	0
Other Portfolio Income 6	442646	11937	119778	10371	60229	37978	44616	14526	31022	28957	25553	57678	0
Other Receipts 7	1857668	10030	32584	91724	437173	348615	284643	101241	113602	71362	14511	352182	0
Total Receipts 8	161410294	1124572	14806828	9162974	47309721	20285669	15665805	12047389	7888569	7865824	2227727	23035215	0
Average Total Receipts 9	3746	193	660	1810	6151	14742	34034	86672	179286	271235	445545	2094110	•
Operating Costs/Operating Income (%)													
Cost of Operations 10	72.6	69.9	68.0	68.0	75.0	77.9	81.0	80.1	80.2	76.0	77.3	53.8	•
Salaries and Wages 11	9.2	8.3	9.2	8.8	8.1	7.7	6.4	7.4	7.7	8.1	6.6	16.9	•
Taxes Paid 12	1.8	2.7	2.5	2.6	1.6	1.4	1.1	1.1	1.2	1.3	0.8	2.7	•
Interest Paid 13	1.4	1.4	0.9	1.1	1.4	1.5	1.7	1.2	1.4	1.1	2.5	1.6	•
Depreciation 14	1.2	2.3	0.8	0.9	0.6	0.9	1.3	1.2	1.2	2.8	5.7	1.8	•
Amortization and Depletion 15	0.1	0.0	0.1	0.1	0.0	0.2	0.0	0.0	0.1	0.1	0.4	0.3	•
Pensions and Other Deferred Comp. 16	0.2	0.0	0.1	0.2	0.1	0.1	0.2	0.2	0.2	0.5	0.2	0.2	•
Employee Benefits 17	0.7	0.5	0.4	0.8	0.5	0.5	0.6	0.6	0.7	0.9	0.8	1.5	•
Advertising 18	1.3	1.4	1.1	1.2	1.3	1.5	1.0	0.8	0.6	1.2	0.6	2.0	•
Other Expenses 19	9.0	19.6	12.5	11.9	8.1	7.3	6.4	6.0	6.8	6.1	5.4	13.9	•
Officers' Compensation 20	1.7	4.9	5.3	3.5	2.2	1.0	0.9	0.7	0.4	0.5	0.5	0.3	•
Operating Margin 21	1.0	•	•	1.1	1.0	1.0	•	0.7	•	1.6	•	5.2	•
Operating Margin Before Officers' Comp. 22	2.7	•	4.4	4.6	3.2	1.0	0.3	1.4	•	2.1	•	5.5	•

Selected Average Balance Sheet ($ in Thousands)

	•	•	•	•	•	•	•	•	•	•	•	•
Net Receivables 23	158	0	15	79	187	648	1487	3865	11059	22365	35233	110046
Inventories 24	838	0	67	371	1522	3899	8891	16413	38332	44827	103916	524201
Net Property, Plant and Equipment 25	286	0	26	125	252	1002	2193	6084	11623	35362	84926	362754
Total Assets 26	1693	0	150	714	2331	7042	15277	34109	70064	143870	384564	1581513
Notes and Loans Payable 27	718	0	90	298	883	2789	8764	19847	38848	66406	197150	490542
All Other Liabilities 28	514	0	35	141	839	2633	3833	6874	18610	32788	75478	518132
Net Worth 29	460	0	25	275	609	1619	2680	7388	12606	44676	111935	572839

Selected Financial Ratios (Times to 1)

Current Ratio 30	1.4	•	2.0	2.6	1.6	1.4	1.3	1.3	1.2	1.3	1.2	1.0
Quick Ratio 31	0.3	•	0.6	0.6	0.3	0.3	0.2	0.3	0.3	0.5	0.3	0.2
Net Sales to Working Capital 32	11.4	•	12.2	5.4	8.2	9.5	12.0	13.3	21.8	12.3	17.7	•
Coverage Ratio 33	2.9	•	1.1	3.1	2.6	2.4	2.0	2.5	2.2	4.0	1.6	5.8
Total Asset Turnover 34	2.2	•	4.4	2.5	2.6	2.1	2.2	2.5	2.5	1.9	1.1	1.3
Inventory Turnover 35	3.2	•	6.6	3.3	3.0	2.9	3.0	4.2	3.7	4.5	3.2	2.1
Receivables Turnover 36	23.6	•	38.8	23.6	33.5	25.7	21.9	21.1	16.4	13.2	10.6	17.6
Total Liabilities to Net Worth 37	2.7	•	4.9	1.6	2.8	3.3	4.7	3.6	4.6	2.2	2.4	1.8
Current Assets to Working Capital 38	3.6	•	2.0	1.6	2.7	3.6	4.4	4.0	6.7	4.0	6.0	•
Current Liabilities to Working Capital 39	2.6	•	1.0	0.6	1.7	2.6	3.4	3.0	5.7	3.0	5.0	•
Working Capital to Net Sales 40	0.1	•	0.1	0.2	0.1	0.1	0.1	0.1	0.0	0.1	0.1	•
Inventory to Working Capital 41	2.8	•	1.3	1.2	2.2	2.8	3.4	2.9	4.8	2.4	3.8	•
Total Receipts to Cash Flow 42	11.4	25.5	12.1	9.8	12.6	14.0	16.0	16.6	15.7	13.2	17.8	6.1
Cost of Goods to Cash Flow 43	8.3	17.8	8.2	6.7	9.4	10.9	13.0	13.3	12.6	10.0	13.7	3.3
Cash Flow to Total Debt 44	0.3	•	0.4	0.4	0.3	0.2	0.2	0.2	0.2	0.2	0.1	0.3

Selected Financial Factors (in Percentages)

Debt Ratio 45	72.8	•	83.2	61.5	73.9	77.0	82.5	78.3	82.0	68.9	70.9	63.8
Return on Total Assets 46	8.7	•	4.5	8.7	9.3	7.4	7.3	7.7	7.9	8.3	4.5	11.8
Return on Equity Before Income Taxes 47	21.0	•	3.1	15.3	21.7	18.5	21.0	21.7	24.1	20.1	5.6	26.9
Return on Equity After Income Taxes 48	16.9	•	1.3	14.4	20.2	17.1	18.6	19.6	21.7	16.5	4.8	17.9
Profit Margin (Before Income Tax) 49	2.6	•	0.1	2.3	2.2	2.1	1.7	1.9	1.7	3.4	1.4	7.5
Profit Margin (After Income Tax) 50	2.1	•	0.1	2.2	2.0	1.9	1.5	1.7	1.6	2.8	1.2	5.0

Table II
Corporations with Net Income

OTHER MOTOR VEHICLE AND PARTS DEALERS

MONEY AMOUNTS AND SIZE OF ASSETS IN THOUSANDS OF DOLLARS

Item Description for Accounting Period 7/06 Through 6/07	Total	Zero Assets	Under 500	500 to 1,000	1,000 to 5,000	5,000 to 10,000	10,000 to 25,000	25,000 to 50,000	50,000 to 100,000	100,000 to 250,000	250,000 to 500,000	500,000 to 2,500,000	2,500,000 and over
Number of Enterprises **1**	25573	2650	11751	3758	5772	1121	336	111	38	24	•	•	0
Revenues ($ in Thousands)													
Net Sales **2**	129104332	576933	8805127	6932593	38245947	16285618	12084353	10227615	6800513	7325469	•	•	0
Interest **3**	146544	9	3196	6264	26252	10891	15050	14943	9036	11795	•	•	0
Rents **4**	81054	0	4277	1728	11802	1012	2322	7905	20208	1362	•	•	0
Royalties **5**	28586	0	0	0	196	4178	0	17	81	5	•	•	0
Other Portfolio Income **6**	306144	8923	39620	4455	51870	37188	39688	12716	28777	21309	•	•	0
Other Receipts **7**	1454759	9198	15244	90504	355928	225676	176961	77685	96683	50882	•	•	0
Total Receipts **8**	131121419	595063	8867464	7035544	38691995	16564563	12318374	10340881	6955298	7410822	•	•	0
Average Total Receipts **9**	5127	225	755	1872	6703	14777	36662	93161	183034	308784	•	•	•
Operating Costs/Operating Income (%)													
Cost of Operations **10**	72.4	69.0	65.9	67.6	74.6	77.1	81.4	80.6	80.6	76.9	•	•	•
Salaries and Wages **11**	9.0	5.0	8.5	8.4	8.1	7.5	6.2	6.9	7.3	8.0	•	•	•
Taxes Paid **12**	1.7	2.6	2.4	2.5	1.7	1.2	1.1	1.0	1.1	1.3	•	•	•
Interest Paid **13**	1.2	0.9	0.8	1.1	1.1	1.4	1.5	1.1	1.3	0.9	•	•	•
Depreciation **14**	1.1	1.1	0.9	0.8	0.6	1.0	1.0	1.3	1.1	1.8	•	•	•
Amortization and Depletion **15**	0.1	0.0	0.1	0.1	0.0	0.2	0.0	0.0	0.1	0.0	•	•	•
Pensions and Other Deferred Comp. **16**	0.2	•	0.2	0.2	0.2	0.2	0.2	0.2	0.2	0.5	•	•	•
Employee Benefits **17**	0.7	0.3	0.3	0.8	0.5	0.4	0.6	0.7	0.7	0.9	•	•	•
Advertising **18**	1.2	0.6	1.2	1.2	1.2	1.5	1.0	0.8	0.6	0.8	•	•	•
Other Expenses **19**	8.5	11.1	11.8	11.3	7.9	6.6	5.3	5.3	6.6	5.9	•	•	•
Officers' Compensation **20**	1.5	6.6	4.6	3.6	2.0	1.1	1.0	0.6	0.4	0.5	•	•	•
Operating Margin **21**	2.5	2.7	3.4	2.4	2.0	1.8	0.7	1.6	•	2.5	•	•	•
Operating Margin Before Officers' Comp. **22**	4.0	9.4	8.0	6.0	4.0	2.8	1.7	2.2	0.3	2.9	•	•	•

Selected Average Balance Sheet ($ in Thousands)

Net Receivables 23	233	0	18	86	220	734	1657	4015	11308	25803
Inventories 24	1116	0	67	338	1615	3486	9631	16661	39093	47777
Net Property, Plant and Equipment 25	362	0	16	138	256	1116	1730	6121	11932	28434
Total Assets 26	2247	0	151	729	2415	6989	15206	34452	70270	145844
Notes and Loans Payable 27	871	0	58	262	849	2530	8372	18856	38885	63379
All Other Liabilities 28	697	0	43	149	862	2686	3807	7071	17322	36196
Net Worth 29	679	0	51	318	703	1773	3027	8526	14063	46269

Selected Financial Ratios (Times to 1)

Current Ratio 30	1.4	•	2.2	2.6	1.6	1.4	1.3	1.4	1.2	1.4
Quick Ratio 31	0.3	•	0.8	0.7	0.3	0.3	0.3	0.3	0.3	0.5
Net Sales to Working Capital 32	11.6	•	12.3	5.4	8.2	9.0	11.9	13.5	19.2	10.6
Coverage Ratio 33	4.3	7.4	6.3	4.5	3.8	3.5	2.8	3.4	2.6	5.6
Total Asset Turnover 34	2.2	•	4.9	2.5	2.7	2.1	2.4	2.7	2.5	2.1
Inventory Turnover 35	3.3	•	7.4	3.7	3.1	3.2	3.0	4.5	3.7	4.9
Receivables Turnover 36	22.0	•	33.0	22.2	31.6	24.2	20.5	21.7	16.0	14.0
Total Liabilities to Net Worth 37	2.3	•	2.0	1.3	2.4	2.9	4.0	3.0	4.0	2.2
Current Assets to Working Capital 38	3.6	•	1.8	1.6	2.6	3.2	4.2	3.8	5.7	3.4
Current Liabilities to Working Capital 39	2.6	•	0.8	0.6	1.6	2.2	3.2	2.8	4.7	2.4
Working Capital to Net Sales 40	0.1	•	0.1	0.2	0.1	0.1	0.1	0.1	0.1	0.1
Inventory to Working Capital 41	2.7	•	1.1	1.2	2.0	2.5	3.2	2.8	4.0	2.1
Total Receipts to Cash Flow 42	10.2	7.2	8.0	9.1	11.4	12.5	15.9	15.8	14.8	12.4
Cost of Goods to Cash Flow 43	7.4	5.0	5.3	6.2	8.5	9.7	12.9	12.7	11.9	9.5
Cash Flow to Total Debt 44	0.3	•	0.9	0.5	0.3	0.2	0.2	0.2	0.2	0.2

Selected Financial Factors (in Percentages)

Debt Ratio 45	69.8	•	66.3	56.4	70.9	74.6	80.1	75.3	80.0	68.3
Return on Total Assets 46	11.9	•	24.2	12.6	11.8	10.2	9.8	10.2	8.9	10.1
Return on Equity Before Income Taxes 47	30.1	•	60.3	22.5	29.8	28.6	31.7	29.1	27.2	26.0
Return on Equity After Income Taxes 48	25.5	•	58.7	21.5	28.1	27.0	28.8	26.9	24.8	21.8
Profit Margin (Before Income Tax) 49	4.1	5.8	4.1	3.9	3.2	3.5	2.7	2.7	2.1	3.9
Profit Margin (After Income Tax) 50	3.4	5.8	4.0	3.7	3.0	3.3	2.4	2.5	1.9	3.3

Table I
Corporations with and without Net Income

FURNITURE AND HOME FURNISHINGS STORES

MONEY AMOUNTS AND SIZE OF ASSETS IN THOUSANDS OF DOLLARS

Item Description for Accounting Period 7/06 Through 6/07	Total	Zero Assets	Under 500	500 to 1,000	1,000 to 5,000	5,000 to 10,000	10,000 to 25,000	25,000 to 50,000	50,000 to 100,000	100,000 to 250,000	250,000 to 500,000	500,000 to 2,500,000	2,500,000 and over
Number of Enterprises 1	39554	5887	26821	3587	2667	334	163	36	22	23	5	10	0
Revenues ($ in Thousands)													
Net Sales 2	92761314	1054012	16779212	7523877	14065135	7850494	7863829	2629768	3984887	6843410	2840019	21326671	0
Interest 3	281655	17	3889	8233	56159	6002	8817	17729	373	59173	60307	60955	0
Rents 4	44714	0	1103	807	7930	6602	1349	1634	208	4089	2294	18698	0
Royalties 5	9544	0	0	0	0	177	0	0	0	5108	1465	2795	0
Other Portfolio Income 6	157964	0	7695	8206	42075	31520	2019	834	1459	9273	20670	34212	0
Other Receipts 7	904298	44964	84875	32657	79956	78408	125151	46079	97855	140538	41048	132768	0
Total Receipts 8	94159489	1098993	16876774	7573780	14251255	7973203	8001165	2696044	4084782	7061591	2965803	21576099	2157610
Average Total Receipts 9	2381	187	629	2111	5344	23872	49087	74890	185672	307026	593161	2157610	•
Operating Costs/Operating Income (%)													
Cost of Operations 10	58.1	55.9	59.0	64.7	60.3	62.0	64.3	59.5	56.3	52.9	56.9	52.0	•
Salaries and Wages 11	12.2	3.8	8.7	10.9	11.0	12.9	13.2	14.8	14.6	15.9	13.7	13.9	•
Taxes Paid 12	2.4	3.2	2.4	3.2	1.8	1.8	1.6	1.9	2.2	2.7	3.5	2.7	•
Interest Paid 13	0.8	0.4	0.6	0.7	0.8	0.5	0.7	0.8	0.8	1.0	1.0	1.0	•
Depreciation 14	1.1	0.5	0.7	0.6	0.7	0.7	0.7	0.8	1.2	1.4	1.4	1.9	•
Amortization and Depletion 15	0.2	0.2	0.2	0.0	0.1	0.2	0.2	0.0	0.0	0.4	0.3	0.2	•
Pensions and Other Deferred Comp. 16	0.2	0.0	0.1	0.3	0.2	0.2	0.2	0.5	0.2	0.2	0.1	0.1	•
Employee Benefits 17	0.9	0.1	0.5	0.8	0.5	0.9	0.8	1.1	1.2	0.8	1.1	1.3	•
Advertising 18	4.8	2.7	3.2	2.9	7.4	3.8	3.5	3.3	4.3	5.5	7.2	5.6	•
Other Expenses 19	16.2	46.9	19.8	13.1	13.3	13.9	12.7	15.0	18.1	20.9	15.3	15.3	•
Officers' Compensation 20	2.3	0.9	4.9	4.1	3.0	3.2	1.7	1.0	0.7	0.5	0.7	0.4	•
Operating Margin 21	1.0	•	0.1	•	0.9	0.1	0.3	1.3	0.3	•	•	5.5	•
Operating Margin Before Officers' Comp. 22	3.3	•	5.0	2.8	3.9	3.2	1.9	2.3	1.0	•	•	6.0	•

Selected Average Balance Sheet ($ in Thousands)

Net Receivables 23	131	0	21	141	328	1069	3234	8740	4704	26129	79947	92751	•
Inventories 24	389	0	58	367	1006	3940	6420	9726	28042	39709	110825	502272	•
Net Property, Plant and Equipment 25	271	0	32	131	327	1324	2854	4360	22667	45767	80705	548602	•
Total Assets 26	1065	0	153	715	2010	6749	15826	31571	74530	164360	347515	1694763	•
Notes and Loans Payable 27	324	0	87	322	698	2599	4015	9347	16003	47031	95251	367339	•
All Other Liabilities 28	410	0	47	211	746	3871	7225	9424	29271	62769	102694	677250	•
Net Worth 29	331	0	19	182	566	279	4586	12801	29255	54560	149570	650174	•

Selected Financial Ratios (Times to 1)

Current Ratio 30	1.5	•	2.0	2.2	1.8	1.0	1.4	1.7	1.5	1.3	1.6	1.4	•
Quick Ratio 31	0.5	•	0.9	0.8	0.6	0.3	0.5	0.8	0.3	0.5	0.7	0.3	•
Net Sales to Working Capital 32	10.7	•	11.9	7.3	8.0	•	15.5	7.4	12.3	14.3	6.6	8.7	•
Coverage Ratio 33	4.2	•	2.2	0.1	4.0	4.0	3.9	5.9	4.6	1.9	4.4	7.7	•
Total Asset Turnover 34	2.2	•	4.1	2.9	2.6	3.5	3.0	2.3	2.4	1.8	1.6	1.3	•
Inventory Turnover 35	3.5	•	6.3	3.7	3.2	3.7	4.8	4.5	3.6	4.0	2.9	2.2	•
Receivables Turnover 36	18.2	•	30.1	17.3	13.5	24.5	15.3	9.3	36.8	11.8	7.7	24.3	•
Total Liabilities to Net Worth 37	2.2	•	7.2	2.9	2.6	23.2	2.5	1.5	1.5	2.0	1.3	1.6	•
Current Assets to Working Capital 38	3.0	•	2.0	1.9	2.3	•	3.8	2.3	2.9	4.1	2.5	3.6	•
Current Liabilities to Working Capital 39	2.0	•	1.0	0.9	1.3	•	2.8	1.3	1.9	3.1	1.5	2.6	•
Working Capital to Net Sales 40	0.1	•	0.1	0.1	0.1	•	0.1	0.1	0.1	0.1	0.2	0.1	•
Inventory to Working Capital 41	1.7	•	1.1	1.1	1.4	•	2.1	0.9	2.1	2.0	1.3	2.1	•
Total Receipts to Cash Flow 42	8.0	4.4	7.1	12.5	9.4	10.6	10.7	7.2	7.0	7.1	7.4	6.9	•
Cost of Goods to Cash Flow 43	4.7	2.4	4.2	8.1	5.7	6.6	6.9	4.3	3.9	3.8	4.2	3.6	•
Cash Flow to Total Debt 44	0.4	•	0.6	0.3	0.4	0.3	0.4	0.5	0.6	0.4	0.4	0.3	•

Selected Financial Factors (in Percentages)

Debt Ratio 45	68.9	•	87.8	74.6	71.9	95.9	71.0	59.5	60.7	66.8	57.0	61.6	•
Return on Total Assets 46	7.2	•	5.3	0.1	7.9	7.6	8.1	10.7	9.1	3.3	7.0	9.5	•
Return on Equity Before Income Taxes 47	17.8	•	23.4	•	21.1	137.3	20.9	21.9	18.2	4.6	12.6	21.5	•
Return on Equity After Income Taxes 48	12.7	•	22.2	•	19.6	119.2	19.1	19.3	17.0	2.7	10.6	13.4	•
Profit Margin (Before Income Tax) 49	2.5	•	0.7	•	2.3	1.6	2.0	3.8	2.9	0.8	3.3	6.6	•
Profit Margin (After Income Tax) 50	1.8	•	0.7	•	2.1	1.4	1.8	3.4	2.7	0.5	2.8	4.1	•

Table II
Corporations with Net Income

FURNITURE AND HOME FURNISHINGS STORES

MONEY AMOUNTS AND SIZE OF ASSETS IN THOUSANDS OF DOLLARS

Item Description for Accounting Period 7/06 Through 6/07	Total	Zero Assets	Under 500	500 to 1,000	1,000 to 5,000	5,000 to 10,000	10,000 to 25,000	25,000 to 50,000	50,000 to 100,000	100,000 to 250,000	250,000 to 500,000	500,000 to 2,500,000	2,500,000 and over
Number of Enterprises **1**	20725	1063	16114	•	1730	288	115	•	16	14	5	7	0
Revenues ($ in Thousands)													
Net Sales **2**	68125994	227336	11427973	•	10038556	7260774	6296245	•	3214663	4513005	2840019	16308831	0
Interest **3**	235184	13	2995	•	43809	4202	4195	•	95	57993	60307	41048	0
Rents **4**	29712	0	0	•	2433	6040	726	•	184	3660	2294	12352	0
Royalties **5**	3269	0	0	•	0	177	0	•	0	0	1465	1628	0
Other Portfolio Income **6**	147479	0	7677	•	41488	31401	2019	•	1237	9273	20670	24684	0
Other Receipts **7**	682571	21280	40828	•	33828	59828	107554	•	89309	126393	41048	90141	0
Total Receipts **8**	69224209	248629	11479473	•	10160114	7362422	6410739	•	3305488	4710324	2965803	16478684	0
Average Total Receipts **9**	3340	234	712	•	5873	25564	55746	•	206593	336452	593161	2354098	•
Operating Costs/Operating Income (%)													
Cost of Operations **10**	57.1	39.6	55.8	•	59.7	61.7	65.7	•	54.8	53.9	56.9	50.1	•
Salaries and Wages **11**	12.4	1.6	8.7	•	12.1	12.9	13.3	•	14.8	15.9	13.7	13.7	•
Taxes Paid **12**	2.3	6.0	2.3	•	1.9	1.7	1.5	•	2.2	2.6	3.5	2.8	•
Interest Paid **13**	0.6	0.2	0.3	•	0.7	0.5	0.5	•	0.8	0.8	1.0	0.7	•
Depreciation **14**	1.1	0.8	0.6	•	0.7	0.6	0.6	•	1.0	1.3	1.4	2.0	•
Amortization and Depletion **15**	0.1	•	0.1	•	0.0	0.0	0.0	•	0.0	0.1	0.3	0.2	•
Pensions and Other Deferred Comp. **16**	0.2	•	0.1	•	0.2	0.2	0.2	•	0.2	0.2	0.1	0.1	•
Employee Benefits **17**	0.8	•	0.4	•	0.6	0.8	0.9	•	1.4	0.8	1.1	1.1	•
Advertising **18**	4.2	2.6	3.4	•	3.9	3.8	3.0	•	4.7	5.4	7.2	5.5	•
Other Expenses **19**	15.1	18.9	18.9	•	13.4	13.7	10.5	•	18.2	19.2	15.3	14.7	•
Officers' Compensation **20**	2.2	0.7	5.0	•	3.0	3.1	1.9	•	0.7	0.5	0.7	0.5	•
Operating Margin **21**	3.8	4.4	•	•	3.6	0.9	1.8	•	1.2	•	•	8.7	•
Operating Margin Before Officers' Comp. **22**	6.1	9.4	•	•	6.6	3.9	3.7	•	2.0	•	•	9.2	•

Selected Average Balance Sheet ($ in Thousands)

Net Receivables 23	194	0	19	•	379	906	4053	•	5557	38217	79947	106389	•
Inventories 24	539	0	51	•	1138	3636	6291	•	30972	41313	108473	552427	•
Net Property, Plant and Equipment 25	405	0	33	•	403	1330	3198	•	21323	51744	80705	649177	•
Total Assets 26	1497	0	145	•	2194	6843	16534	•	75216	176277	347515	1936695	•
Notes and Loans Payable 27	362	0	47	•	565	2248	3694	•	15177	50852	95251	384792	•
All Other Liabilities 28	569	0	39	•	784	3994	7245	•	31642	54685	102694	788069	•
Net Worth 29	566	0	58	•	845	601	5596	•	28396	70740	149570	763835	•

Selected Financial Ratios (Times to 1)

Current Ratio 30	1.5	•	2.4	•	1.8	0.9	1.4	•	1.7	1.6	1.6	1.3	•
Quick Ratio 31	0.5	•	1.2	•	0.7	0.2	0.6	•	0.3	0.8	0.7	0.3	•
Net Sales to Working Capital 32	11.1	•	11.7	•	7.9	•	16.8	•	10.6	9.3	6.6	10.0	•
Coverage Ratio 33	9.8	19.7	15.1	•	7.7	5.8	7.5	•	6.2	5.3	4.4	15.1	•
Total Asset Turnover 34	2.2	•	4.9	•	2.6	3.7	3.3	•	2.7	1.8	1.6	1.2	•
Inventory Turnover 35	3.5	•	7.7	•	3.0	4.3	5.7	•	3.6	4.2	3.0	2.1	•
Receivables Turnover 36	17.4	•	36.1	•	13.2	30.2	14.6	•	34.2	9.1	•	1.5	•
Total Liabilities to Net Worth 37	1.6	•	1.5	•	1.6	10.4	2.0	•	1.6	1.5	1.3	1.5	•
Current Assets to Working Capital 38	3.1	•	1.7	•	2.3	•	3.8	•	2.5	2.8	2.5	4.3	•
Current Liabilities to Working Capital 39	2.1	•	0.7	•	1.3	•	2.8	•	1.5	1.8	1.5	3.3	•
Working Capital to Net Sales 40	0.1	•	0.1	•	0.1	•	0.1	•	0.1	0.1	0.2	0.1	•
Inventory to Working Capital 41	1.7	•	0.8	•	1.3	•	1.9	•	1.7	1.0	1.3	2.4	•
Total Receipts to Cash Flow 42	6.6	2.0	5.6	•	7.6	10.2	10.5	•	6.2	6.1	7.4	5.4	•
Cost of Goods to Cash Flow 43	3.8	0.8	3.1	•	4.5	6.3	6.9	•	3.4	3.3	4.2	2.7	•
Cash Flow to Total Debt 44	0.5	•	1.5	•	0.6	0.4	0.5	•	0.7	0.5	0.4	0.4	•

Selected Financial Factors (in Percentages)

Debt Ratio 45	62.2	•	59.6	•	61.5	91.2	66.2	•	62.2	59.9	57.0	60.6	•
Return on Total Assets 46	13.3	•	25.4	•	14.7	10.1	13.6	•	13.4	7.9	7.0	12.4	•
Return on Equity Before Income Taxes 47	31.5	•	58.8	•	33.2	95.6	34.7	•	29.9	15.9	12.6	29.4	•
Return on Equity After Income Taxes 48	25.9	•	58.2	•	31.7	85.8	32.7	•	28.1	13.5	10.6	19.4	•
Profit Margin (Before Income Tax) 49	5.4	2.8	4.8	•	4.8	2.3	3.6	•	4.2	3.5	3.3	9.6	•
Profit Margin (After Income Tax) 50	4.5	2.8	4.8	•	4.6	2.0	3.3	•	4.0	3.0	2.8	6.4	•

Table I

Corporations with and without Net Income

ELECTRONICS AND APPLIANCE STORES

MONEY AMOUNTS AND SIZE OF ASSETS IN THOUSANDS OF DOLLARS

Item Description for Accounting Period 7/06 Through 6/07	Total	Zero Assets	Under 500	500 to 1,000	1,000 to 5,000	5,000 to 10,000	10,000 to 25,000	25,000 to 50,000	50,000 to 100,000	100,000 to 250,000	250,000 to 500,000	500,000 to 2,500,000	2,500,000 and over
Number of Enterprises **1**	32062	2464	25192	1849	2140	213	94	46	26	14	10	14	0
Revenues ($ in Thousands)													
Net Sales **2**	121882040	637305	13506021	5756407	12774819	3518839	3250412	4166744	4002222	4069605	4876290	65323376	0
Interest **3**	407986	1780	8617	4848	7824	6340	8122	6372	8050	7397	138795	209840	0
Rents **4**	66604	524	3216	1208	2594	93	1010	80	257	66	4239	53319	0
Royalties **5**	39593	0	0	0	0	0	8729	0	0	103	0	30760	0
Other Portfolio Income **6**	298193	3520	11153	22051	20632	7141	1089	32930	17742	6584	9747	165606	0
Other Receipts **7**	1956191	2770	166662	20623	101415	26450	104408	40316	40147	72219	49027	1332152	0
Total Receipts **8**	124650607	645899	13695669	5805137	12907284	3558863	3373770	4246442	4068418	4155974	5078098	67115053	0
Average Total Receipts **9**	3888	262	544	3140	6031	16708	35891	92314	156478	296855	507810	4793932	•
Operating Costs/Operating Income (%)													
Cost of Operations **10**	69.2	63.2	55.8	52.6	69.1	55.5	63.6	73.9	67.2	74.6	62.0	74.6	•
Salaries and Wages **11**	11.3	9.1	12.8	20.2	12.1	19.9	10.9	10.1	13.1	11.4	14.1	9.4	•
Taxes Paid **12**	1.8	3.2	3.1	2.3	1.8	2.3	1.3	1.3	1.4	1.4	1.8	1.6	•
Interest Paid **13**	0.6	1.3	0.7	0.4	0.7	0.5	0.7	0.4	0.5	0.4	1.7	0.5	•
Depreciation **14**	0.9	1.0	1.0	0.5	0.8	0.7	1.3	0.8	1.9	0.7	1.1	0.8	•
Amortization and Depletion **15**	0.2	0.2	0.1	0.2	0.1	0.1	0.2	0.0	0.2	0.2	1.0	0.1	•
Pensions and Other Deferred Comp. **16**	0.1	•	0.2	0.4	0.3	0.4	0.2	0.1	0.2	0.1	0.2	0.1	•
Employee Benefits **17**	0.6	0.4	0.8	1.2	0.6	1.6	0.5	0.6	0.8	0.8	1.4	0.4	•
Advertising **18**	2.1	3.6	1.6	1.2	1.8	2.0	7.5	1.2	0.9	0.9	2.9	2.3	•
Other Expenses **19**	10.4	28.8	17.2	14.5	8.3	10.7	12.6	8.7	9.4	7.2	13.4	8.9	•
Officers' Compensation **20**	1.8	7.6	6.2	5.1	3.4	4.0	1.4	1.0	1.2	2.4	0.6	0.3	•
Operating Margin **21**	0.9	•	0.5	1.4	1.0	2.4	•	1.9	3.1	•	1.1	1.1	•
Operating Margin Before Officers' Comp. **22**	2.7	•	6.7	6.5	4.4	6.4	1.1	2.8	4.4	2.2	0.5	1.3	•

Selected Average Balance Sheet ($ in Thousands)

Net Receivables 23	207	0	16	148	386	1571	3416	13720	16680	43344	42404	170104	•
Inventories 24	355	0	32	159	701	1035	3318	5937	11188	18418	59142	315198	•
Net Property, Plant and Equipment 25	236	0	20	63	384	633	1756	3480	10707	12325	39278	344597	•
Total Assets 26	1532	0	120	686	1792	6339	15459	33403	73150	151868	318516	2103797	•
Notes and Loans Payable 27	290	0	63	236	526	1310	3775	4304	14724	10567	42459	312484	•
All Other Liabilities 28	664	0	57	294	689	3641	7855	19835	26066	74421	105324	901201	•
Net Worth 29	579	0	0	156	576	1387	3829	9263	32360	66880	170734	890112	•

Selected Financial Ratios (Times to 1)

Current Ratio 30	1.4	•	1.3	1.9	1.6	1.2	1.2	1.3	1.3	1.4	1.7	1.4	•
Quick Ratio 31	0.6	•	0.7	1.2	0.8	0.9	0.8	0.9	0.9	1.0	0.8	0.4	•
Net Sales to Working Capital 32	14.2	•	31.0	15.2	13.2	17.4	17.3	21.1	17.0	10.5	6.7	13.4	•
Coverage Ratio 33	6.4	•	3.9	6.2	3.9	8.3	6.1	10.1	10.3	5.5	3.4	8.5	•
Total Asset Turnover 34	2.5	•	4.5	4.5	3.3	2.6	2.2	2.7	2.1	1.9	1.5	2.2	•
Inventory Turnover 35	7.4	•	9.4	10.3	5.9	8.9	6.6	11.3	9.2	11.8	5.1	11.0	•
Receivables Turnover 36	18.3	•	42.2	21.5	13.3	10.3	7.4	6.1	10.4	6.4	7.4	38.6	•
Total Liabilities to Net Worth 37	1.6	•	304.6	3.4	2.1	3.6	3.0	2.6	1.3	1.3	0.9	1.4	•
Current Assets to Working Capital 38	3.4	•	4.7	2.2	2.7	5.0	5.3	6.2	4.3	3.3	2.4	3.4	•
Current Liabilities to Working Capital 39	2.4	•	3.7	1.2	1.7	4.0	4.3	5.2	3.3	2.3	1.4	2.4	•
Working Capital to Net Sales 40	0.1	•	0.0	0.1	0.1	0.1	0.1	0.0	0.1	0.1	0.1	0.1	•
Inventory to Working Capital 41	1.3	•	2.1	0.7	1.1	1.1	1.2	1.4	1.1	0.7	0.6	1.5	•
Total Receipts to Cash Flow 42	9.7	19.6	7.0	7.4	12.4	8.5	7.0	9.8	8.9	13.5	7.0	10.8	•
Cost of Goods to Cash Flow 43	6.7	12.4	3.9	3.9	8.6	4.7	4.5	7.3	6.0	10.1	4.3	8.0	•
Cash Flow to Total Debt 44	0.4	•	0.6	0.8	0.4	0.4	0.4	0.4	0.4	0.3	0.5	0.4	•

Selected Financial Factors (in Percentages)

Debt Ratio 45	62.2	•	99.7	77.3	67.8	78.1	75.2	72.3	55.8	56.0	46.4	57.7	•
Return on Total Assets 46	9.2	•	11.5	12.0	9.1	10.3	9.3	11.3	11.1	4.7	8.6	9.4	•
Return on Equity Before Income Taxes 47	20.6	•	2627.1	44.4	21.0	41.5	31.4	36.9	22.7	8.8	11.3	19.5	•
Return on Equity After Income Taxes 48	15.3	•	2527.5	42.0	19.1	37.2	28.1	29.7	20.6	8.1	8.3	13.0	•
Profit Margin (Before Income Tax) 49	3.1	•	1.9	2.2	2.0	3.5	3.5	3.8	4.8	2.0	4.0	3.7	•
Profit Margin (After Income Tax) 50	2.3	•	1.9	2.1	1.8	3.1	3.1	3.0	4.3	1.9	2.9	2.5	•

ELECTRONICS AND APPLIANCE STORES

Table II

Corporations with Net Income

MONEY AMOUNTS AND SIZE OF ASSETS IN THOUSANDS OF DOLLARS

Item Description for Accounting Period 7/06 Through 6/07		Total	Zero Assets	Under 500	500 to 1,000	1,000 to 5,000	5,000 to 10,000	10,000 to 25,000	25,000 to 50,000	50,000 to 100,000	100,000 to 250,000	250,000 to 500,000	500,000 to 2,500,000	2,500,000 and over
Number of Enterprises	1	17791	1450	13292	1347	1343	190	77	43	20	10	7	11	0
Revenues ($ in Thousands)														
Net Sales	2	109292308	220688	10500568	4120996	10527830	3137880	2527602	3972604	3594777	3478854	3675839	63534670	0
Interest	3	333689	1255	7814	3371	5353	3244	6692	6273	6230	4504	132620	156334	0
Rents	4	62284	0	3216	0	1732	93	1010	80	257	66	2511	53319	0
Royalties	5	27203	0	0	0	0	0	8729	0	0	0	0	18474	0
Other Portfolio Income	6	266771	0	9224	10649	19182	2140	912	32912	16779	1174	9520	164282	0
Other Receipts	7	1638904	2457	162385	13880	91400	23417	23397	39856	39842	69433	37917	1134916	0
Total Receipts	8	111621159	224400	10683207	4148896	10645497	3166774	2568342	4051725	3657885	3554031	3858407	65061995	0
Average Total Receipts	9	6274	155	804	3080	7927	16667	33355	94226	182894	355403	551201	5914727	•
Operating Costs/Operating Income (%)														
Cost of Operations	10	70.1	32.1	57.9	43.7	71.1	52.7	57.9	73.7	69.1	73.6	65.8	75.1	•
Salaries and Wages	11	10.6	5.5	12.1	23.6	10.9	20.5	11.5	10.2	11.3	11.8	12.2	8.8	•
Taxes Paid	12	1.7	1.6	2.9	2.5	1.5	2.3	1.4	1.3	1.3	1.4	1.8	1.6	•
Interest Paid	13	0.5	0.0	0.6	0.3	0.6	0.5	0.6	0.4	0.5	0.4	1.5	0.4	•
Depreciation	14	0.8	1.4	0.8	0.5	0.7	0.7	1.5	0.7	1.9	0.7	1.1	0.8	•
Amortization and Depletion	15	0.2	•	0.1	0.2	0.1	0.1	0.2	0.0	0.2	0.2	0.7	0.1	•
Pensions and Other Deferred Comp.	16	0.1	•	0.2	0.6	0.3	0.5	0.2	0.1	0.1	0.1	0.1	0.1	•
Employee Benefits	17	0.5	0.1	0.7	1.2	0.5	1.6	0.5	0.6	0.7	0.8	0.6	0.4	•
Advertising	18	2.1	1.4	1.3	0.9	1.9	2.1	9.4	1.1	0.9	1.0	2.8	2.2	•
Other Expenses	19	9.5	27.1	14.6	16.0	7.5	10.3	11.0	8.6	8.7	7.7	12.4	8.5	•
Officers' Compensation	20	1.5	13.4	5.9	5.9	2.8	4.1	1.5	1.0	0.7	0.8	0.6	0.2	•
Operating Margin	21	2.3	17.4	2.9	4.5	2.1	4.7	4.2	2.3	4.6	1.4	0.6	1.8	•
Operating Margin Before Officers' Comp.	22	3.7	30.9	8.9	10.4	4.9	8.8	5.7	3.3	5.3	2.1	1.2	2.0	•

Selected Average Balance Sheet ($ in Thousands)

Net Receivables 23	307	0	24	160	435	1569	2159	14244	17360	45302	34411	202435	•
Inventories 24	570	0	32	143	922	1109	3948	5468	14192	24389	48954	615824	•
Net Property, Plant and Equipment 25	375	0	26	46	345	678	1850	3053	12632	16745	40733	426655	•
Total Assets 26	2281	0	156	664	2052	6313	14865	33509	71266	157987	319094	2347422	•
Notes and Loans Payable 27	337	0	57	157	632	1204	2949	4152	17530	14471	25535	260819	•
All Other Liabilities 28	1007	0	66	222	767	3780	7342	19785	25146	78898	110452	1045629	•
Net Worth 29	937	0	34	286	653	1330	4574	9572	28590	64618	183108	1040974	•

Selected Financial Ratios (Times to 1)

Current Ratio 30	1.4	•	1.5	2.2	1.8	1.2	1.3	1.2	1.4	1.4	1.7	1.4	•
Quick Ratio 31	0.6	•	0.9	1.7	0.9	0.8	0.7	0.9	0.9	0.9	0.8	0.4	•
Net Sales to Working Capital 32	14.6	•	21.4	13.7	11.6	23.2	14.4	19.1	15.5	13.1	6.6	15.1	•
Coverage Ratio 33	10.1	740.9	9.0	17.0	6.6	13.1	10.3	11.8	13.3	8.9	4.8	11.4	•
Total Asset Turnover 34	2.7	•	5.1	4.6	3.8	2.6	2.2	2.8	2.5	2.2	1.6	2.5	•
Inventory Turnover 35	7.6	•	14.1	9.4	6.0	7.8	4.8	12.5	8.8	10.5	7.1	7.0	•
Receivables Turnover 36	20.1	•	42.9	20.7	15.2	10.0	7.6	6.9	11.7	7.2	•	•	•
Total Liabilities to Net Worth 37	1.4	•	3.6	1.3	2.1	3.7	2.3	2.5	1.5	1.4	0.7	1.3	•
Current Assets to Working Capital 38	3.3	•	3.0	1.9	2.2	6.5	4.3	5.5	3.7	3.9	2.3	3.5	•
Current Liabilities to Working Capital 39	2.3	•	2.0	0.9	1.2	5.5	3.3	4.5	2.7	2.9	1.3	2.5	•
Working Capital to Net Sales 40	0.1	•	0.0	0.1	0.1	0.0	0.1	0.1	0.1	0.1	0.2	0.1	•
Inventory to Working Capital 41	1.3	•	1.1	0.3	1.0	1.6	1.3	1.2	1.1	0.9	0.6	1.6	•
Total Receipts to Cash Flow 42	9.3	2.5	6.7	5.5	11.7	7.6	6.8	9.3	8.4	10.8	6.5	10.7	•
Cost of Goods to Cash Flow 43	6.5	0.8	3.9	2.4	8.3	4.0	4.0	6.9	5.8	7.9	4.3	8.0	•
Cash Flow to Total Debt 44	0.5	•	1.0	1.5	0.5	0.4	0.5	0.4	0.5	0.3	0.6	0.4	•

Selected Financial Factors (in Percentages)

Debt Ratio 45	58.9	•	78.4	57.0	68.2	78.9	69.2	71.4	59.9	59.1	42.6	55.7	•
Return on Total Assets 46	12.9	•	26.6	25.2	14.4	15.6	14.1	12.9	17.3	8.7	11.5	11.0	•
Return on Equity Before Income Taxes 47	28.3	•	109.5	55.2	38.3	68.5	41.4	41.4	39.8	18.9	15.8	22.7	•
Return on Equity After Income Taxes 48	22.4	•	107.3	53.4	35.6	63.5	38.0	34.0	36.7	17.9	11.8	15.6	•
Profit Margin (Before Income Tax) 49	4.3	19.1	4.7	5.2	3.2	5.5	5.8	4.3	6.3	3.5	5.5	4.1	•
Profit Margin (After Income Tax) 50	3.4	18.7	4.6	5.0	3.0	5.1	5.3	3.5	5.8	3.3	4.1	2.8	•

Table I

Corporations with and without Net Income

HOMES CENTERS; PAINT AND WALLPAPER STORES

MONEY AMOUNTS AND SIZE OF ASSETS IN THOUSANDS OF DOLLARS

Item Description for Accounting Period 7/06 Through 6/07	Total	Zero Assets	Under 500	500 to 1,000	1,000 to 5,000	5,000 to 10,000	10,000 to 25,000	25,000 to 50,000	50,000 to 100,000	100,000 to 250,000	250,000 to 500,000	500,000 to 2,500,000	2,500,000 and over
Number of Enterprises 1	3340	421	1780	438	570	50	65	7	4	3	0	0	3

Revenues ($ in Thousands)

	Total	Zero Assets	Under 500	500 to 1,000	1,000 to 5,000	5,000 to 10,000	10,000 to 25,000	25,000 to 50,000	50,000 to 100,000	100,000 to 250,000	250,000 to 500,000	500,000 to 2,500,000	2,500,000 and over
Net Sales 2	145130076	274271	1707936	643261	3597530	931733	1989664	595081	584806	658839	0	0	134146955
Interest 3	106023	0	370	1275	4809	1810	1245	439	293	0	0	0	95781
Rents 4	429002	1184	0	25	1710	3122	815	0	0	0	0	0	422146
Royalties 5	226383	0	0	0	0	0	0	0	0	0	0	0	226383
Other Portfolio Income 6	40624	645	338	228	3800	433	2111	228	477	658	0	0	31708
Other Receipts 7	2121305	668	594	11603	25269	1120	26818	9751	6105	5212	0	0	2034165
Total Receipts 8	148053413	276768	1709238	656392	3633118	938218	2020653	605499	591681	664709	0	0	136957138
Average Total Receipts 9	44327	657	960	1499	6374	18764	31087	86500	147920	221570	•	•	45652379

Operating Costs/Operating Income (%)

	Total	Zero Assets	Under 500	500 to 1,000	1,000 to 5,000	5,000 to 10,000	10,000 to 25,000	25,000 to 50,000	50,000 to 100,000	100,000 to 250,000	250,000 to 500,000	500,000 to 2,500,000	2,500,000 and over
Cost of Operations 10	66.8	78.3	67.0	66.0	71.2	69.1	70.2	70.7	73.2	71.7	•	•	66.5
Salaries and Wages 11	11.3	6.5	11.9	5.5	10.4	12.9	11.3	13.8	11.1	10.9	•	•	11.3
Taxes Paid 12	2.0	0.9	6.6	1.1	2.5	2.0	1.7	1.6	1.4	1.5	•	•	2.0
Interest Paid 13	0.6	0.6	0.6	3.0	0.7	1.0	1.0	0.6	1.1	1.0	•	•	0.5
Depreciation 14	2.0	1.1	0.4	2.3	0.7	0.9	0.9	1.5	1.7	1.9	•	•	2.0
Amortization and Depletion 15	0.1	•	0.0	0.0	0.0	0.0	0.2	0.1	0.0	0.0	•	•	0.1
Pensions and Other Deferred Comp. 16	0.1	•	0.0	0.3	0.3	0.4	0.2	0.3	0.1	1.0	•	•	0.1
Employee Benefits 17	1.0	•	0.3	0.3	0.7	1.0	1.0	0.8	1.3	0.9	•	•	1.0
Advertising 18	1.6	0.2	1.1	1.3	0.4	1.2	1.1	0.7	0.5	1.8	•	•	1.7
Other Expenses 19	6.5	8.4	10.2	10.4	6.7	7.1	9.0	6.4	8.7	6.3	•	•	6.4
Officers' Compensation 20	0.3	2.4	3.0	6.9	3.6	2.6	1.5	0.9	1.3	0.1	•	•	0.1
Operating Margin 21	7.7	1.7	•	2.9	2.8	1.9	1.9	2.6	•	2.7	•	•	8.2
Operating Margin Before Officers' Comp. 22	8.0	4.0	1.9	9.8	6.4	4.6	3.4	3.5	0.9	2.8	•	•	8.3

Selected Average Balance Sheet ($ in Thousands)

Net Receivables 23	5518	0	45	71	564	796	3525	7300	13813	15570	•	5858111
Inventories 24	5986	0	107	257	785	2560	3292	12261	28975	61367	•	6171580
Net Property, Plant and Equipment 25	11288	0	18	425	202	1242	2509	8906	15702	41272	•	12298578
Total Assets 26	39717	0	197	844	2297	7208	13381	31323	59632	112555	•	42866647
Notes and Loans Payable 27	15056	0	96	554	588	1857	4251	7481	20595	36554	•	16308796
All Other Liabilities 28	11906	0	106	146	479	1994	3445	7562	8388	22179	•	12921023
Net Worth 29	12755	0	-4	145	1230	3357	5685	16280	30648	53823	•	13636827

Selected Financial Ratios (Times to 1)

Current Ratio 30	1.1	•	1.6	2.0	3.4	1.8	2.2	2.2	4.4	2.7	•	1.1
Quick Ratio 31	0.5	•	0.6	0.5	1.8	0.5	1.1	0.9	1.7	0.8	•	0.5
Net Sales to Working Capital 32	26.9	•	13.8	7.5	4.7	8.2	6.3	8.2	4.5	5.7	•	36.7
Coverage Ratio 33	18.0	5.0	•	2.6	6.6	3.6	4.6	8.2	1.7	4.6	•	19.9
Total Asset Turnover 34	1.1	•	4.9	1.7	2.7	2.6	2.3	2.7	2.5	2.0	•	1.0
Inventory Turnover 35	4.8	•	6.0	3.8	5.7	5.0	6.5	4.9	3.7	2.6	•	4.8
Receivables Turnover 36	8.4	•	23.7	21.0	11.6	17.3	9.7	11.1	8.4	3.0	•	8.2
Total Liabilities to Net Worth 37	2.1	•	•	4.8	0.9	1.1	1.4	0.9	0.9	1.1	•	2.1
Current Assets to Working Capital 38	7.8	•	2.6	2.0	1.4	2.2	1.9	1.8	1.3	1.6	•	10.7
Current Liabilities to Working Capital 39	6.8	•	1.6	1.0	0.4	1.2	0.9	0.8	0.3	0.6	•	9.7
Working Capital to Net Sales 40	0.0	•	0.1	0.1	0.2	0.1	0.2	0.1	0.2	0.2	•	0.0
Inventory to Working Capital 41	3.8	•	1.7	1.4	0.6	1.5	0.7	1.0	0.8	1.1	•	5.1
Total Receipts to Cash Flow 42	7.1	11.0	17.5	7.7	11.1	14.6	9.9	10.7	13.8	12.3	•	6.8
Cost of Goods to Cash Flow 43	4.7	8.6	11.7	5.1	7.9	10.1	6.9	7.5	10.1	8.8	•	4.6
Cash Flow to Total Debt 44	0.2	•	0.3	0.3	0.5	0.3	0.4	0.5	0.4	0.3	•	0.2

Selected Financial Factors (in Percentages)

Debt Ratio 45	67.9	•	102.2	82.9	46.4	53.4	57.5	48.0	48.6	52.2	•	68.2
Return on Total Assets 46	11.3	•	•	13.9	12.3	9.3	10.1	13.4	4.6	8.9	•	11.3
Return on Equity Before Income Taxes 47	33.1	•	215.8	50.4	19.5	14.4	18.6	22.6	3.7	14.6	•	33.7
Return on Equity After Income Taxes 48	22.4	•	238.1	42.9	18.3	11.1	17.1	22.2	3.7	14.6	•	22.6
Profit Margin (Before Income Tax) 49	9.7	2.6	•	5.0	3.8	2.6	3.5	4.3	0.8	3.6	•	10.3
Profit Margin (After Income Tax) 50	6.6	1.5	•	4.2	3.6	2.0	3.2	4.3	0.8	3.6	•	6.9

Table II
Corporations with Net Income

HOMES CENTERS; PAINT AND WALLPAPER STORES

MONEY AMOUNTS AND SIZE OF ASSETS IN THOUSANDS OF DOLLARS

Item Description for Accounting Period 7/06 Through 6/07	Total	Zero Assets	Under 500	500 to 1,000	1,000 to 5,000	5,000 to 10,000	10,000 to 25,000	25,000 to 50,000	50,000 to 100,000	100,000 to 250,000	250,000 to 500,000	500,000 to 2,500,000	2,500,000 and over
Number of Enterprises **1**	1951	417	540	•	444	40	57	7	•	3	0	0	3
Revenues ($ in Thousands)													
Net Sales **2**	142959125	269009	480475	•	3146265	710442	1874256	595081	•	658839	0	0	13146955
Interest **3**	105420	0	369	•	4649	1794	1122	439	•	0	0	0	95781
Rents **4**	425793	1184	0	•	1623	0	815	0	•	0	0	0	422146
Royalties **5**	226383	0	0	•	0	0	0	0	•	0	0	0	226383
Other Portfolio Income **6**	39489	0	338	•	3800	433	2002	228	•	658	0	0	31708
Other Receipts **7**	2112082	662	528	•	23925	1118	19110	9751	•	5212	0	0	2034165
Total Receipts **8**	145868292	270855	481710	•	3180262	713787	1897305	605499	•	664709	0	0	136957138
Average Total Receipts **9**	74766	650	892	•	7163	17845	33286	86500	•	221570	•	•	45652379
Operating Costs/Operating Income (%)													
Cost of Operations **10**	66.7	76.3	62.6	•	70.6	66.0	69.5	70.7	•	71.7	•	•	66.5
Salaries and Wages **11**	11.3	6.6	6.9	•	10.5	13.9	11.3	13.8	•	10.9	•	•	11.3
Taxes Paid **12**	2.0	0.9	4.0	•	2.5	2.1	1.7	1.6	•	1.5	•	•	2.0
Interest Paid **13**	0.6	0.7	0.2	•	0.6	1.0	0.9	0.6	•	1.0	•	•	0.5
Depreciation **14**	2.0	1.1	0.5	•	0.7	1.0	0.9	1.5	•	1.9	•	•	2.0
Amortization and Depletion **15**	0.1	•	0.0	•	0.0	•	0.2	0.1	•	0.0	•	•	0.1
Pensions and Other Deferred Comp. **16**	0.1	•	0.0	•	0.3	0.4	0.2	0.3	•	1.0	•	•	0.1
Employee Benefits **17**	1.0	•	1.0	•	0.8	1.1	1.0	0.8	•	0.9	•	•	1.0
Advertising **18**	1.6	0.2	1.6	•	0.4	0.9	1.1	0.7	•	1.8	•	•	1.7
Other Expenses **19**	6.5	8.6	14.4	•	6.3	7.3	9.0	6.4	•	6.3	•	•	6.4
Officers' Compensation **20**	0.2	2.4	6.4	•	3.9	3.2	1.4	0.9	•	0.1	•	•	0.1
Operating Margin **21**	7.9	3.3	2.4	•	3.4	3.2	2.7	2.6	•	2.7	•	•	8.2
Operating Margin Before Officers' Comp. **22**	8.1	5.7	8.8	•	7.3	6.4	4.1	3.5	•	2.8	•	•	8.3

Selected Average Balance Sheet ($ in Thousands)

Net Receivables 23	9390	0	57	•	658	920	3770	7300	15570	•	5858111
Inventories 24	10096	0	163	•	748	2568	3615	10401	61367	•	6171580
Net Property, Plant and Equipment 25	19269	0	29	•	218	1125	2195	8906	41272	•	12298578
Total Assets 26	67672	0	256	•	2496	7152	13725	31323	112555	•	42866647
Notes and Loans Payable 27	25604	0	26	•	496	1662	4626	7481	36554	•	16308796
All Other Liabilities 28	20265	0	99	•	538	2091	3348	7562	22179	•	12921023
Net Worth 29	21803	0	132	•	1461	3399	5751	16280	53823	•	13636827

Selected Financial Ratios (Times to 1)

Current Ratio 30	1.1	•	2.2	•	4.1	2.0	2.3	2.2	2.7	•	1.1
Quick Ratio 31	0.5	•	0.8	•	2.4	0.7	1.2	0.9	0.8	•	0.5
Net Sales to Working Capital 32	27.3	•	7.3	•	4.4	7.3	6.0	8.2	5.7	•	36.7
Coverage Ratio 33	18.5	7.1	13.6	•	9.2	4.7	5.1	8.2	4.6	•	19.9
Total Asset Turnover 34	1.1	•	3.5	•	2.8	2.5	2.4	2.7	2.0	•	1.0
Inventory Turnover 35	4.8	•	3.4	•	6.7	4.6	6.3	5.8	2.6	•	4.8
Receivables Turnover 36	8.3	•	10.3	•	11.2	13.5	9.5	•	3.0	•	8.2
Total Liabilities to Net Worth 37	2.1	•	0.9	•	0.7	1.1	1.4	0.9	1.1	•	2.1
Current Assets to Working Capital 38	7.9	•	1.9	•	1.3	2.0	1.7	1.8	1.6	•	10.7
Current Liabilities to Working Capital 39	6.9	•	0.9	•	0.3	1.0	0.7	0.8	0.6	•	9.7
Working Capital to Net Sales 40	0.0	•	0.1	•	0.2	0.1	0.2	0.1	0.2	•	0.0
Inventory to Working Capital 41	3.8	•	1.1	•	0.5	1.2	0.7	1.0	1.1	•	5.1
Total Receipts to Cash Flow 42	7.0	9.4	7.6	•	10.6	12.8	9.6	10.7	12.3	•	6.8
Cost of Goods to Cash Flow 43	4.7	7.2	4.8	•	7.5	8.4	6.7	7.5	8.8	•	4.6
Cash Flow to Total Debt 44	0.2	•	0.9	•	0.6	0.4	0.4	0.5	0.3	•	0.2

Selected Financial Factors (in Percentages)

Debt Ratio 45	67.8	•	48.6	•	41.4	52.5	58.1	48.0	52.2	•	68.2
Return on Total Assets 46	11.3	•	10.1	•	14.4	11.5	11.5	13.4	8.9	•	11.3
Return on Equity Before Income Taxes 47	33.3	•	18.2	•	21.9	19.0	22.1	22.6	14.6	•	33.7
Return on Equity After Income Taxes 48	22.5	•	15.7	•	20.6	14.9	20.4	22.2	14.6	•	22.6
Profit Margin (Before Income Tax) 49	9.9	4.0	2.7	•	4.5	3.6	3.9	4.3	3.6	•	10.3
Profit Margin (After Income Tax) 50	6.7	2.9	2.3	•	4.2	2.9	3.6	4.3	3.6	•	6.9

Table I

Corporations with and without Net Income

HARDWARE STORES

MONEY AMOUNTS AND SIZE OF ASSETS IN THOUSANDS OF DOLLARS

Item Description for Accounting Period 7/06 Through 6/07	Total	Zero Assets	Under 500	500 to 1,000	1,000 to 5,000	5,000 to 10,000	10,000 to 25,000	25,000 to 50,000	50,000 to 100,000	100,000 to 250,000	250,000 to 500,000	500,000 to 2,500,000	2,500,000 and over
Number of Enterprises **1**	8218	6	3528	2358	2135	144	23	20	4	0	0	0	0
Revenues ($ in Thousands)													
Net Sales **2**	21840292	5426	2790725	4241046	8788820	2165661	1164735	1323262	1360618	0	0	0	0
Interest **3**	25322	0	1738	4584	13693	1229	928	2203	946	0	0	0	0
Rents **4**	23519	0	6221	5499	6085	0	3749	834	1131	0	0	0	0
Royalties **5**	36	0	0	35	1	0	0	0	0	0	0	0	0
Other Portfolio Income **6**	51615	0	8620	8087	21200	1763	11631	303	13	0	0	0	0
Other Receipts **7**	252061	22	48858	65110	84688	23767	14306	11799	3508	0	0	0	0
Total Receipts **8**	22192845	5448	2856162	4324361	8914487	2192420	1195349	1338401	1366216	0	0	0	0
Average Total Receipts **9**	2701	908	810	1834	4175	15225	51972	66920	341554	•	•	•	•
Operating Costs/Operating Income (%)													
Cost of Operations **10**	64.3	73.8	61.7	67.3	64.5	61.8	65.1	67.2	58.7	•	•	•	•
Salaries and Wages **11**	12.6	8.9	10.9	10.5	13.1	15.2	14.8	13.0	13.5	•	•	•	•
Taxes Paid **12**	2.3	1.7	2.6	2.3	2.2	2.2	2.0	2.4	2.6	•	•	•	•
Interest Paid **13**	1.0	0.3	0.8	0.6	1.1	0.2	0.8	1.0	2.8	•	•	•	•
Depreciation **14**	1.3	0.7	0.6	1.1	1.6	1.2	0.9	1.1	1.2	•	•	•	•
Amortization and Depletion **15**	0.1	•	0.0	0.0	0.1	0.0	0.0	0.2	0.2	•	•	•	•
Pensions and Other Deferred Comp. **16**	0.3	•	0.1	0.3	0.4	0.3	0.3	0.2	0.2	•	•	•	•
Employee Benefits **17**	1.0	1.2	1.2	0.6	1.0	0.8	1.6	1.0	1.5	•	•	•	•
Advertising **18**	1.5	0.5	1.1	1.5	1.2	1.4	1.6	1.5	3.5	•	•	•	•
Other Expenses **19**	11.0	6.2	15.2	10.8	10.7	9.0	9.8	9.0	10.8	•	•	•	•
Officers' Compensation **20**	3.4	6.0	7.8	4.8	2.8	1.7	1.2	0.7	0.7	•	•	•	•
Operating Margin **21**	1.5	0.8	•	0.1	1.5	6.0	1.9	2.7	4.5	•	•	•	•
Operating Margin Before Officers' Comp. **22**	4.9	6.9	5.8	4.9	4.2	7.8	3.1	3.4	5.2	•	•	•	•

Selected Average Balance Sheet ($ in Thousands)

Net Receivables 23	132	0	35	87	247	556	2485	3223	7941
Inventories 24	435	0	138	269	741	1883	10548	10450	74346
Net Property, Plant and Equipment 25	283	0	21	88	368	4298	4326	10577	82276
Total Assets 26	1201	0	263	713	1822	8362	17592	29982	291284
Notes and Loans Payable 27	427	0	141	207	710	607	4701	13144	137804
All Other Liabilities 28	218	0	77	121	304	925	4345	5873	59426
Net Worth 29	556	0	45	385	808	6830	8545	10965	94055

Selected Financial Ratios (Times to 1)

Current Ratio 30	2.5	•	2.1	3.7	2.8	2.3	2.4	1.7	1.1
Quick Ratio 31	0.8	•	0.5	1.4	1.0	0.7	0.6	0.4	0.1
Net Sales to Working Capital 32	5.9	•	7.1	4.6	4.9	7.9	7.7	9.0	68.8
Coverage Ratio 33	4.2	5.2	1.3	4.5	3.6	34.4	7.0	4.7	2.8
Total Asset Turnover 34	2.2	•	3.0	2.5	2.3	1.8	2.9	2.2	1.2
Inventory Turnover 35	3.9	•	3.5	4.5	3.6	4.9	3.1	4.3	2.7
Receivables Turnover 36	21.8	•	22.7	26.1	17.9	29.5	13.0	28.4	85.7
Total Liabilities to Net Worth 37	1.2	•	4.8	0.9	1.3	0.2	1.1	1.7	2.1
Current Assets to Working Capital 38	1.7	•	1.9	1.4	1.5	1.7	1.7	2.3	18.3
Current Liabilities to Working Capital 39	0.7	•	0.9	0.4	0.5	0.7	0.7	1.3	17.3
Working Capital to Net Sales 40	0.2	•	0.1	0.2	0.2	0.1	0.1	0.1	0.0
Inventory to Working Capital 41	1.1	•	1.3	0.8	1.0	1.0	1.2	1.7	15.0
Total Receipts to Cash Flow 42	10.2	17.2	9.7	12.0	10.3	7.4	11.7	10.7	11.2
Cost of Goods to Cash Flow 43	6.6	12.7	6.0	8.1	6.6	4.6	7.6	7.2	6.6
Cash Flow to Total Debt 44	0.4	•	0.4	0.5	0.4	1.3	0.5	0.3	0.2

Selected Financial Factors (in Percentages)

Debt Ratio 45	53.7	•	82.8	46.0	55.6	18.3	51.4	63.4	67.7
Return on Total Assets 46	8.9	•	3.2	6.6	9.0	13.4	15.1	10.9	9.0
Return on Equity Before Income Taxes 47	14.8	•	4.7	9.5	14.7	15.9	26.7	23.4	17.8
Return on Equity After Income Taxes 48	13.1	•	3.4	9.1	13.1	15.7	22.4	20.8	11.2
Profit Margin (Before Income Tax) 49	3.1	1.3	0.3	2.0	2.9	7.2	4.5	3.9	4.9
Profit Margin (After Income Tax) 50	2.7	1.3	0.2	1.9	2.6	7.2	3.8	3.4	3.1

Table II

Corporations with Net Income

HARDWARE STORES

MONEY AMOUNTS AND SIZE OF ASSETS IN THOUSANDS OF DOLLARS

Item Description for Accounting Period 7/06 Through 6/07	Total	Zero Assets	Under 500	500 to 1,000	1,000 to 5,000	5,000 to 10,000	10,000 to 25,000	25,000 to 50,000	50,000 to 100,000	100,000 to 250,000	250,000 to 500,000	500,000 to 2,500,000	2,500,000 and over
Number of Enterprises 1	5100	•	1665	1633	1618	135	23	•	•	0	0	0	0

Revenues ($ in Thousands)

Item Description for Accounting Period 7/06 Through 6/07	Total	Zero Assets	Under 500	500 to 1,000	1,000 to 5,000	5,000 to 10,000	10,000 to 25,000	25,000 to 50,000	50,000 to 100,000	100,000 to 250,000	250,000 to 500,000	500,000 to 2,500,000	2,500,000 and over
Net Sales 2	18655049	•	2060859	3402891	7560129	2016525	1164735	•	•	0	0	0	0
Interest 3	21970	•	956	4031	12766	455	928	•	•	0	0	0	0
Rents 4	16710	•	259	4809	5945	0	3749	•	•	0	0	0	0
Royalties 5	36	•	0	35	1	0	0	•	•	0	0	0	0
Other Portfolio Income 6	39491	•	133	5082	20604	1741	11631	•	•	0	0	0	0
Other Receipts 7	229965	•	42112	56443	78863	23349	14306	•	•	0	0	0	0
Total Receipts 8	18963221	•	2104319	3473291	7678308	2042070	1195349	•	•	0	0	0	0
Average Total Receipts 9	3718	•	1264	2127	4746	15126	51972	•	•	•	•	•	•

Operating Costs/Operating Income (%)

Item Description for Accounting Period 7/06 Through 6/07	Total	Zero Assets	Under 500	500 to 1,000	1,000 to 5,000	5,000 to 10,000	10,000 to 25,000	25,000 to 50,000	50,000 to 100,000	100,000 to 250,000	250,000 to 500,000	500,000 to 2,500,000	2,500,000 and over
Cost of Operations 10	64.7	•	61.8	69.6	64.6	61.6	65.1	•	•	•	•	•	•
Salaries and Wages 11	12.1	•	10.1	9.3	12.5	15.0	14.8	•	•	•	•	•	•
Taxes Paid 12	2.2	•	2.2	1.8	2.2	2.2	2.0	•	•	•	•	•	•
Interest Paid 13	0.8	•	0.6	0.3	1.0	0.2	0.8	•	•	•	•	•	•
Depreciation 14	1.2	•	0.6	0.8	1.5	1.2	0.9	•	•	•	•	•	•
Amortization and Depletion 15	0.1	•	•	0.0	0.1	0.0	0.0	•	•	•	•	•	•
Pensions and Other Deferred Comp. 16	0.3	•	0.2	0.3	0.4	0.2	0.3	•	•	•	•	•	•
Employee Benefits 17	0.9	•	1.0	0.7	1.0	0.5	1.6	•	•	•	•	•	•
Advertising 18	1.4	•	1.3	1.2	1.1	1.4	1.6	•	•	•	•	•	•
Other Expenses 19	10.4	•	14.4	9.5	10.4	9.1	9.8	•	•	•	•	•	•
Officers' Compensation 20	3.1	•	6.3	4.7	3.0	1.8	1.2	•	•	•	•	•	•
Operating Margin 21	2.8	•	1.7	1.8	2.2	6.6	1.9	•	•	•	•	•	•
Operating Margin Before Officers' Comp. 22	5.9	•	8.0	6.5	5.1	8.4	3.1	•	•	•	•	•	•

Selected Average Balance Sheet ($ in Thousands)

Net Receivables 23	181	•	51	92	290	541	2485
Inventories 24	550	•	182	276	768	2057	10548
Net Property, Plant and Equipment 25	389	•	23	68	397	4369	4326
Total Assets 26	1608	•	355	724	2003	8428	17592
Notes and Loans Payable 27	496	•	163	114	697	572	4701
All Other Liabilities 28	290	•	117	130	329	839	4345
Net Worth 29	822	•	75	480	977	7017	8545

Selected Financial Ratios (Times to 1)

Current Ratio 30	2.5	•	2.0	4.4	2.8	2.4	2.4
Quick Ratio 31	0.8	•	0.5	1.7	1.0	0.6	0.6
Net Sales to Working Capital 32	6.3	•	9.0	4.9	5.1	7.7	7.7
Coverage Ratio 33	6.3	•	7.8	15.7	4.8	39.3	7.0
Total Asset Turnover 34	2.3	•	3.5	2.9	2.3	1.8	2.9
Inventory Turnover 35	4.3	•	4.2	5.3	3.9	4.5	3.1
Receivables Turnover 36	22.1	•	25.6	31.3	17.3	•	13.0
Total Liabilities to Net Worth 37	1.0	•	3.8	0.5	1.0	0.2	1.1
Current Assets to Working Capital 38	1.7	•	2.0	1.3	1.5	1.7	1.7
Current Liabilities to Working Capital 39	0.7	•	1.0	0.3	0.5	0.7	0.7
Working Capital to Net Sales 40	0.2	•	0.1	0.2	0.2	0.1	0.1
Inventory to Working Capital 41	1.1	•	1.4	0.8	0.9	1.1	1.2
Total Receipts to Cash Flow 42	9.3	•	7.8	11.0	9.4	7.1	11.7
Cost of Goods to Cash Flow 43	6.0	•	4.8	7.7	6.1	4.3	7.6
Cash Flow to Total Debt 44	0.5	•	0.6	0.8	0.5	1.5	0.5

Selected Financial Factors (in Percentages)

Debt Ratio 45	48.9	•	79.0	33.7	51.2	16.7	51.4
Return on Total Assets 46	12.0	•	15.1	12.0	11.0	14.2	15.1
Return on Equity Before Income Taxes 47	19.7	•	62.5	16.9	17.8	16.6	26.7
Return on Equity After Income Taxes 48	17.9	•	60.7	16.4	16.0	16.4	22.4
Profit Margin (Before Income Tax) 49	4.4	•	3.8	3.9	3.7	7.8	4.5
Profit Margin (After Income Tax) 50	4.0	•	3.7	3.8	3.3	7.7	3.8

Table I

Corporations with and without Net Income

OTHER BUILDING MATERIAL DEALERS

MONEY AMOUNTS AND SIZE OF ASSETS IN THOUSANDS OF DOLLARS

Item Description for Accounting Period 7/06 Through 6/07	Total	Zero Assets	Under 500	500 to 1,000	1,000 to 5,000	5,000 to 10,000	10,000 to 25,000	25,000 to 50,000	50,000 to 100,000	100,000 to 250,000	250,000 to 500,000	500,000 to 2,500,000	2,500,000 and over
Number of Enterprises **1**	19043	1068	11292	2290	3561	519	222	56	20	9	0	5	0
Revenues ($ in Thousands)													
Net Sales **2**	80362426	431026	6777765	6163518	22823210	10971751	8767058	4068447	3837279	3387781	0	13134589	0
Interest **3**	107656	749	778	7486	23582	7858	12386	8486	3992	22436	0	19903	0
Rents **4**	25776	0	2339	1694	5947	58	3519	9582	1198	856	0	583	0
Royalties **5**	8249	0	0	0	0	0	6587	273	0	1390	0	0	0
Other Portfolio Income **6**	176633	77749	22314	4202	17318	2920	14335	16848	2158	13897	0	4892	0
Other Receipts **7**	581707	197	5990	68005	171283	28787	58370	32801	56467	28992	0	130815	0
Total Receipts **8**	81262447	509721	6809186	6244905	23041340	11011374	8862255	4136437	3901094	3455352	0	13290782	0
Average Total Receipts **9**	4267	477	603	2727	6470	21217	39920	73865	195055	383928	•	2658156	•
Operating Costs/Operating Income (%)													
Cost of Operations **10**	73.5	69.3	67.3	71.6	72.5	75.4	76.4	74.7	77.0	75.8	•	73.8	•
Salaries and Wages **11**	8.8	11.6	6.2	8.9	8.8	9.6	8.5	9.3	8.8	10.3	•	9.2	•
Taxes Paid **12**	1.5	2.8	1.6	2.2	1.7	1.9	1.3	1.5	1.1	1.6	•	0.9	•
Interest Paid **13**	0.7	0.9	0.6	0.3	0.5	0.5	0.6	1.0	0.7	1.0	•	1.5	•
Depreciation **14**	0.9	1.0	1.6	0.5	0.8	0.6	0.9	0.9	0.9	1.1	•	1.2	•
Amortization and Depletion **15**	0.1	0.2	0.1	0.0	0.0	0.0	0.0	0.1	0.1	0.1	•	0.4	•
Pensions and Other Deferred Comp. **16**	0.4	2.5	0.1	0.3	0.3	0.2	0.4	0.4	0.4	0.3	•	0.7	•
Employee Benefits **17**	0.9	2.0	0.2	0.7	0.9	0.7	0.7	0.9	0.6	1.0	•	1.6	•
Advertising **18**	0.7	0.9	1.4	0.5	0.8	0.4	0.5	0.8	1.4	0.4	•	0.2	•
Other Expenses **19**	7.6	16.2	14.4	8.4	7.7	6.3	5.9	7.7	6.3	5.8	•	6.2	•
Officers' Compensation **20**	2.2	2.0	5.4	4.1	2.9	1.5	1.3	1.0	0.8	0.7	•	0.5	•
Operating Margin **21**	2.7	•	1.2	2.4	3.0	2.9	3.4	1.8	1.9	1.8	•	3.7	•
Operating Margin Before Officers' Comp. **22**	4.9	•	6.6	6.5	5.9	4.4	4.7	2.9	2.7	2.6	•	4.3	•

Selected Average Balance Sheet ($ in Thousands)

Net Receivables 23	386	0	25	200	566	2170	4247	7290	19324	34216	•	283852
Inventories 24	427	0	53	273	674	2030	4900	8960	18059	47133	•	218767
Net Property, Plant and Equipment 25	280	0	40	68	287	881	2726	6011	17443	57786	•	286919
Total Assets 26	1575	0	138	742	2078	7244	15046	35951	69687	174231	•	1449645
Notes and Loans Payable 27	439	0	75	135	468	1706	3737	9147	18670	24088	•	543476
All Other Liabilities 28	390	0	36	178	536	1635	3340	8531	19575	29750	•	395985
Net Worth 29	746	0	28	429	1074	3903	7969	18273	31442	120393	•	510184

Selected Financial Ratios (Times to 1)

Current Ratio 30	2.2	•	1.8	3.1	2.6	2.0	2.3	1.9	1.9	2.2	•	2.0
Quick Ratio 31	1.2	•	0.8	1.6	1.4	1.1	1.1	0.9	1.0	1.1	•	1.1
Net Sales to Working Capital 32	7.3	•	14.1	6.3	6.4	7.0	6.3	6.4	8.5	8.4	•	8.1
Coverage Ratio 33	6.2	10.5	3.7	14.8	8.8	7.0	9.1	4.5	6.0	4.9	•	4.2
Total Asset Turnover 34	2.7	•	4.3	3.6	3.1	2.9	2.6	2.0	2.8	2.2	•	1.8
Inventory Turnover 35	7.3	•	7.7	7.1	6.9	7.8	6.2	6.1	8.2	6.1	•	8.9
Receivables Turnover 36	11.0	•	21.1	15.0	11.2	11.4	8.8	7.2	10.3	7.6	•	11.0
Total Liabilities to Net Worth 37	1.1	•	4.0	0.7	0.9	0.9	0.9	1.0	1.2	0.4	•	1.8
Current Assets to Working Capital 38	1.8	•	2.2	1.5	1.6	2.0	1.8	2.1	2.1	1.8	•	2.0
Current Liabilities to Working Capital 39	0.8	•	1.2	0.5	0.6	1.0	0.8	1.1	1.1	0.8	•	1.0
Working Capital to Net Sales 40	0.1	•	0.1	0.2	0.2	0.1	0.2	0.2	0.1	0.1	•	0.1
Inventory to Working Capital 41	0.8	•	1.1	0.7	0.7	0.8	0.8	0.8	0.9	0.8	•	0.8
Total Receipts to Cash Flow 42	11.1	72.9	8.4	9.5	11.0	14.1	11.6	10.7	12.4	12.4	•	11.0
Cost of Goods to Cash Flow 43	8.2	50.6	5.7	6.8	7.9	10.7	8.9	8.0	9.5	9.4	•	8.1
Cash Flow to Total Debt 44	0.5	•	0.6	0.9	0.6	0.4	0.5	0.4	0.4	0.6	•	0.3

Selected Financial Factors (in Percentages)

Debt Ratio 45	52.6	•	80.0	42.3	48.3	46.1	47.0	49.2	54.9	30.9	•	64.8
Return on Total Assets 46	12.2	•	9.8	14.5	13.6	11.1	13.3	9.0	11.7	10.4	•	11.6
Return on Equity Before Income Taxes 47	21.6	•	35.8	23.4	23.3	17.7	22.4	13.8	21.6	12.0	•	25.1
Return on Equity After Income Taxes 48	19.1	•	33.9	22.1	22.0	16.0	20.1	11.5	18.7	9.2	•	20.0
Profit Margin (Before Income Tax) 49	3.8	8.8	1.7	3.7	3.9	3.3	4.5	3.5	3.5	3.8	•	4.9
Profit Margin (After Income Tax) 50	3.4	5.8	1.6	3.5	3.7	3.0	4.0	2.9	3.1	2.9	•	3.9

Table II

Corporations with Net Income

OTHER BUILDING MATERIAL DEALERS

MONEY AMOUNTS AND SIZE OF ASSETS IN THOUSANDS OF DOLLARS

Item Description for Accounting Period 7/06 Through 6/07		Total	Zero Assets	Under 500	500 to 1,000	1,000 to 5,000	5,000 to 10,000	10,000 to 25,000	25,000 to 50,000	50,000 to 100,000	100,000 to 250,000	250,000 to 500,000	500,000 to 2,500,000	2,500,000 and over
Number of Enterprises	1	12000	660	5687	1909	2991	488	190	44	17	9	0	5	0
Revenues ($ in Thousands)														
Net Sales	2	71853477	398455	4861590	5495603	20558010	10413565	7710033	3482177	2411675	3387781	0	13134589	0
Interest	3	98169	749	685	6738	19861	6641	9826	8071	3259	22436	0	19903	0
Rents	4	21786	0	2339	1693	3617	58	3404	8039	1198	856	0	583	0
Royalties	5	8249	0	0	0	0	0	6587	273	0	1390	0	0	0
Other Portfolio Income	6	152236	77749	21084	3438	6664	2622	9969	10426	1494	13897	0	4892	0
Other Receipts	7	504976	197	5454	67130	141142	25654	53768	27006	24816	28992	0	130815	0
Total Receipts	8	72638893	477150	4891152	5574602	20729294	10448540	7793587	3535992	2442442	3455352	0	13290782	0
Average Total Receipts	9	6053	723	860	2920	6931	21411	41019	80363	143673	383928	•	2658156	•
Operating Costs/Operating Income (%)														
Cost of Operations	10	73.3	67.3	68.2	72.3	72.5	74.9	76.7	74.2	68.4	75.8	•	73.8	•
Salaries and Wages	11	8.8	12.6	5.0	8.1	8.6	9.7	8.2	9.5	11.3	10.3	•	9.2	•
Taxes Paid	12	1.5	3.0	1.4	2.2	1.6	2.0	1.2	1.5	1.5	1.6	•	0.9	•
Interest Paid	13	0.7	1.0	0.4	0.2	0.4	0.5	0.5	0.8	0.7	1.0	•	1.5	•
Depreciation	14	0.9	1.1	1.5	0.5	0.8	0.6	0.9	0.8	1.2	1.1	•	1.2	•
Amortization and Depletion	15	0.1	0.3	0.0	0.0	0.0	0.0	0.0	0.1	0.1	0.1	•	0.4	•
Pensions and Other Deferred Comp.	16	0.4	2.7	0.0	0.3	0.3	0.0	0.3	0.3	0.5	0.3	•	0.7	•
Employee Benefits	17	0.9	2.2	0.2	0.5	0.9	0.7	0.7	0.9	0.9	1.0	•	1.6	•
Advertising	18	0.6	1.0	1.2	0.4	0.9	0.3	0.3	0.7	2.1	0.4	•	0.2	•
Other Expenses	19	7.2	16.9	12.8	8.2	7.3	6.2	5.6	7.2	8.0	5.8	•	6.2	•
Officers' Compensation	20	2.1	2.2	5.1	4.1	2.9	1.5	1.3	1.0	1.0	0.7	•	0.5	•
Operating Margin	21	3.5	•	4.1	3.1	3.8	3.3	4.3	3.0	4.4	1.8	•	3.7	•
Operating Margin Before Officers' Comp.	22	5.6	•	9.3	7.2	6.7	4.8	5.5	4.0	5.5	2.6	•	4.3	•

Selected Average Balance Sheet ($ in Thousands)

Net Receivables 23	552	0	36	213	591	2179	4293	8352	15850	34216	•	283852
Inventories 24	608	0	64	260	720	2057	5302	9473	20703	47133	•	248658
Net Property, Plant and Equipment 25	395	0	49	73	299	871	2578	6146	17052	57786	•	286919
Total Assets 26	2244	0	184	760	2186	7280	14921	34906	67772	174231	•	1449645
Notes and Loans Payable 27	591	0	77	141	438	1616	3722	8282	16508	24088	•	543476
All Other Liabilities 28	532	0	36	168	524	1574	3255	8068	17426	29750	•	395985
Net Worth 29	1121	0	71	451	1224	4090	7945	18556	33838	120393	•	510184

Selected Financial Ratios (Times to 1)

Current Ratio 30	2.4	•	2.5	3.3	2.9	2.2	2.4	1.7	2.1	2.2	•	2.0
Quick Ratio 31	1.3	•	1.4	1.8	1.6	1.2	1.2	0.8	1.0	1.1	•	1.1
Net Sales to Working Capital 32	6.9	•	11.5	6.3	6.1	6.6	6.2	8.3	6.0	8.4	•	8.1
Coverage Ratio 33	7.7	10.7	12.2	19.3	12.2	8.3	11.4	6.6	9.2	4.9	•	4.2
Total Asset Turnover 34	2.7	•	4.6	3.8	3.1	2.9	2.7	2.3	2.1	2.2	•	1.8
Inventory Turnover 35	7.2	•	9.1	8.0	6.9	7.8	5.9	6.2	4.7	6.1	•	7.8
Receivables Turnover 36	10.8	•	22.9	15.2	11.1	11.6	8.5	6.8	•	7.6	•	•
Total Liabilities to Net Worth 37	1.0	•	1.6	0.7	0.8	0.8	0.9	0.9	1.0	0.4	•	1.8
Current Assets to Working Capital 38	1.7	•	1.7	1.4	1.5	1.9	1.7	2.3	1.9	1.8	•	2.0
Current Liabilities to Working Capital 39	0.7	•	0.7	0.4	0.5	0.9	0.7	1.3	0.9	0.8	•	1.0
Working Capital to Net Sales 40	0.1	•	0.1	0.2	0.2	0.2	0.2	0.1	0.2	0.1	•	0.1
Inventory to Working Capital 41	0.7	•	0.6	0.6	0.6	0.8	0.8	0.9	0.9	0.8	•	0.8
Total Receipts to Cash Flow 42	10.5	73.6	7.1	9.0	10.5	13.5	10.8	10.0	9.0	12.4	•	11.0
Cost of Goods to Cash Flow 43	7.7	49.5	4.8	6.5	7.6	10.1	8.3	7.4	6.2	9.4	•	8.1
Cash Flow to Total Debt 44	0.5	•	1.1	1.0	0.7	0.5	0.5	0.5	0.5	0.6	•	0.3

Selected Financial Factors (in Percentages)

Debt Ratio 45	50.0	•	61.7	40.6	44.0	43.8	46.8	46.8	50.1	30.9	•	64.8
Return on Total Assets 46	14.2	•	24.0	18.3	15.8	12.2	15.9	12.2	13.3	10.4	•	11.6
Return on Equity Before Income Taxes 47	24.7	•	57.5	29.2	25.9	19.1	27.3	19.5	23.8	12.0	•	25.1
Return on Equity After Income Taxes 48	22.1	•	56.0	27.8	24.5	17.5	24.6	16.7	20.6	9.2	•	20.0
Profit Margin (Before Income Tax) 49	4.6	9.7	4.7	4.6	4.6	3.7	5.3	4.6	5.7	3.8	•	4.9
Profit Margin (After Income Tax) 50	4.1	6.5	4.6	4.4	4.4	3.3	4.8	3.9	4.9	2.9	•	3.9

Table I

Corporations with and without Net Income

LAWN AND GARDEN EQUIPMENT AND SUPPLIES STORES

MONEY AMOUNTS AND SIZE OF ASSETS IN THOUSANDS OF DOLLARS

Item Description for Accounting Period 7/06 Through 6/07	Total	Zero Assets	Under 500	500 to 1,000	1,000 to 5,000	5,000 to 10,000	10,000 to 25,000	25,000 to 50,000	50,000 to 100,000	100,000 to 250,000	250,000 to 500,000	500,000 to 2,500,000	2,500,000 and over
Number of Enterprises 1	9386	1712	4361	2039	1084	133	44	10	0	3	0	0	0
Revenues ($ in Thousands)													
Net Sales 2	17572616	853723	1987046	4061250	5123957	2055071	1614795	695851	0	1180922	0	0	0
Interest 3	23716	73	980	1520	9895	3562	1018	664	0	6004	0	0	0
Rents 4	15546	0	0	1692	7587	0	6268	0	0	0	0	0	0
Royalties 5	11103	0	0	0	0	0	0	0	0	11103	0	0	0
Other Portfolio Income 6	24567	1488	472	3810	7053	101	775	10867	0	0	0	0	0
Other Receipts 7	115199	828	3035	6384	26911	25771	11167	6043	0	35062	0	0	0
Total Receipts 8	17762747	856112	1991533	4074656	5175403	2084505	1634023	713425	0	1233091	0	0	0
Average Total Receipts 9	1892	500	457	1998	4774	15673	37137	71342	•	411030	•	•	•
Operating Costs/Operating Income (%)													
Cost of Operations 10	72.0	73.5	68.9	67.1	72.4	79.6	69.6	73.2	•	80.0	•	•	•
Salaries and Wages 11	9.0	10.6	7.0	10.6	9.5	5.9	10.6	7.3	•	8.7	•	•	•
Taxes Paid 12	1.9	1.4	2.4	2.7	1.7	1.6	1.5	1.8	•	1.1	•	•	•
Interest Paid 13	1.1	0.8	0.8	0.9	1.0	1.3	1.3	1.6	•	1.8	•	•	•
Depreciation 14	1.3	1.1	1.3	1.1	1.2	0.6	1.5	5.5	•	0.4	•	•	•
Amortization and Depletion 15	0.1	0.0	0.0	0.0	0.0	0.0	0.1	0.0	•	0.4	•	•	•
Pensions and Other Deferred Comp. 16	0.1	0.0	•	0.2	0.1	0.1	0.3	0.2	•	0.1	•	•	•
Employee Benefits 17	0.7	0.4	0.2	0.8	0.9	0.7	0.4	0.5	•	1.0	•	•	•
Advertising 18	1.0	0.6	1.1	0.9	1.1	1.3	1.0	0.6	•	0.4	•	•	•
Other Expenses 19	10.3	8.3	13.1	9.9	9.7	10.2	11.0	8.2	•	11.6	•	•	•
Officers' Compensation 20	2.6	1.4	5.5	3.9	2.3	1.0	1.2	2.4	•	0.2	•	•	•
Operating Margin 21	•	1.9	•	1.7	0.2	•	1.5	•	•	•	•	•	•
Operating Margin Before Officers' Comp. 22	2.6	3.3	5.3	5.7	2.4	•	2.7	1.2	•	•	•	•	•

Selected Average Balance Sheet ($ in Thousands)

Net Receivables 23	101	0	17	77	250	1185	2848	7414	•	•	•	30027
Inventories 24	319	0	65	273	990	4709	6070	10129	•	•	•	57240
Net Property, Plant and Equipment 25	144	0	35	163	459	317	3543	14876	•	•	•	9572
Total Assets 26	762	0	136	703	2239	6641	16197	37921	•	•	•	241847
Notes and Loans Payable 27	314	0	64	239	827	2541	7198	16816	•	•	•	151653
All Other Liabilities 28	233	0	35	187	613	2794	4822	10554	•	•	•	99239
Net Worth 29	216	0	37	277	799	1306	4177	10550	•	•	•	-9044

Selected Financial Ratios (Times to 1)

Current Ratio 30	1.6	•	2.3	2.4	1.7	1.5	1.2	•	•	•	•	0.7
Quick Ratio 31	0.5	•	0.9	0.9	0.4	0.4	0.5	•	•	•	•	0.3
Net Sales to Working Capital 32	8.6	•	8.6	6.4	6.7	9.3	22.9	•	•	•	•	•
Coverage Ratio 33	2.0	3.7	1.0	3.2	2.2	3.1	1.8	•	•	•	•	0.3
Total Asset Turnover 34	2.5	•	3.3	2.8	2.1	2.3	1.8	•	•	•	•	1.6
Inventory Turnover 35	4.2	•	4.8	4.9	3.5	4.2	5.0	•	•	•	•	5.5
Receivables Turnover 36	22.8	•	22.1	27.7	23.4	16.1	11.7	•	•	•	•	26.2
Total Liabilities to Net Worth 37	2.5	•	2.7	1.5	1.8	4.1	2.9	2.6	•	•	•	0.7
Current Assets to Working Capital 38	2.5	•	1.8	1.7	2.4	2.5	3.0	7.5	•	•	•	•
Current Liabilities to Working Capital 39	1.5	•	0.8	0.7	1.4	1.5	2.0	6.5	•	•	•	•
Working Capital to Net Sales 40	0.1	•	0.1	0.2	0.1	0.2	0.1	0.0	•	•	•	•
Inventory to Working Capital 41	1.7	•	1.0	1.1	1.6	1.9	2.1	4.3	•	•	•	•
Total Receipts to Cash Flow 42	11.8	12.3	11.0	11.9	12.2	13.7	8.8	14.3	•	•	•	12.7
Cost of Goods to Cash Flow 43	8.5	9.1	7.6	8.0	8.8	10.9	6.1	10.4	•	•	•	10.1
Cash Flow to Total Debt 44	0.3	•	0.4	0.4	0.3	0.2	0.3	0.2	•	•	•	0.1

Selected Financial Factors (in Percentages)

Debt Ratio 45	71.7	•	73.1	60.6	64.3	80.3	74.2	72.2	•	•	•	103.7
Return on Total Assets 46	5.3	2.5	•	8.5	4.7	1.1	9.1	5.3	•	•	•	0.8
Return on Equity Before Income Taxes 47	9.1	•	•	14.9	7.1	•	23.6	8.5	•	•	•	56.9
Return on Equity After Income Taxes 48	8.1	•	14.3	6.2	•	23.1	8.3	•	•	•	•	71.9
Profit Margin (Before Income Tax) 49	1.0	2.2	•	2.1	1.2	•	2.7	1.3	•	•	•	1.3
Profit Margin (After Income Tax) 50	0.9	2.2	•	2.0	1.1	•	2.6	1.3	•	•	•	1.3

217

Table II

Corporations with Net Income

LAWN AND GARDEN EQUIPMENT AND SUPPLIES STORES

MONEY AMOUNTS AND SIZE OF ASSETS IN THOUSANDS OF DOLLARS

Item Description for Accounting Period 7/06 Through 6/07		Total	Zero Assets	Under 500	500 to 1,000	1,000 to 5,000	5,000 to 10,000	10,000 to 25,000	25,000 to 50,000	50,000 to 100,000	100,000 to 250,000	250,000 to 500,000	500,000 to 2,500,000	2,500,000 and over
Number of Enterprises	1	6732	•	3074	•	866	56	36	0	0	0	0	0	0
Revenues ($ in Thousands)														
Net Sales	2	13600595	•	1799538	•	4232814	997573	1369716	0	0	0	0	0	0
Interest	3	13512	•	980	•	7361	2627	782	0	0	0	0	0	0
Rents	4	7937	•	0	•	5848	0	397	0	0	0	0	0	0
Royalties	5	0	•	0	•	0	0	0	0	0	0	0	0	0
Other Portfolio Income	6	10695	•	472	•	6725	4	713	0	0	0	0	0	0
Other Receipts	7	57521	•	3026	•	17909	11659	12140	0	0	0	0	0	0
Total Receipts	8	13690260	•	1804016	•	4270657	1011863	1383748	0	0	0	0	0	0
Average Total Receipts	9	2034	•	587	•	4931	18069	38437	•	•	•	•	•	•
Operating Costs/Operating Income (%)														
Cost of Operations	10	70.9	•	69.1	•	71.7	78.8	68.6	•	•	•	•	•	•
Salaries and Wages	11	8.9	•	6.5	•	9.4	5.5	11.1	•	•	•	•	•	•
Taxes Paid	12	2.0	•	2.4	•	1.5	2.4	1.6	•	•	•	•	•	•
Interest Paid	13	0.9	•	0.8	•	0.8	1.2	1.2	•	•	•	•	•	•
Depreciation	14	1.2	•	1.1	•	1.3	0.5	1.0	•	•	•	•	•	•
Amortization and Depletion	15	0.0	•	0.0	•	0.0	•	0.1	•	•	•	•	•	•
Pensions and Other Deferred Comp.	16	0.2	•	•	•	0.1	0.2	0.4	•	•	•	•	•	•
Employee Benefits	17	0.7	•	0.3	•	0.9	0.6	0.5	•	•	•	•	•	•
Advertising	18	0.8	•	0.8	•	1.1	0.5	0.9	•	•	•	•	•	•
Other Expenses	19	9.6	•	11.1	•	10.0	8.1	11.3	•	•	•	•	•	•
Officers' Compensation	20	2.8	•	5.8	•	2.3	1.2	1.2	•	•	•	•	•	•
Operating Margin	21	2.1	•	2.1	•	1.0	1.1	2.2	•	•	•	•	•	•
Operating Margin Before Officers' Comp.	22	4.9	•	7.9	•	3.3	2.3	3.5	•	•	•	•	•	•

Selected Average Balance Sheet ($ in Thousands)

Net Receivables 23	98	13	240	918	2352
Inventories 24	321	70	867	4607	6268
Net Property, Plant and Equipment 25	144	44	493	320	2822
Total Assets 26	725	155	2057	6594	15948
Notes and Loans Payable 27	234	69	538	2293	6912
All Other Liabilities 28	222	41	705	2259	4520
Net Worth 29	269	45	814	2042	4516

Selected Financial Ratios (Times to 1)

Current Ratio 30	1.8	2.2	1.7	1.5	1.4
Quick Ratio 31	0.6	0.8	0.5	0.3	0.3
Net Sales to Working Capital 32	8.4	10.5	7.7	8.6	11.1
Coverage Ratio 33	4.2	4.1	3.5	3.2	3.7
Total Asset Turnover 34	2.8	3.8	2.4	2.7	2.4
Inventory Turnover 35	4.5	5.8	4.0	3.0	4.2
Receivables Turnover 36	23.2	31.4	25.0		17.3
Total Liabilities to Net Worth 37	1.7	2.5	1.5	2.2	2.5
Current Assets to Working Capital 38	2.2	1.9	2.4	2.9	3.3
Current Liabilities to Working Capital 39	1.2	0.9	1.4	1.9	2.3
Working Capital to Net Sales 40	0.1	0.1	0.1	0.1	0.1
Inventory to Working Capital 41	1.4	1.1	1.4	2.2	2.4
Total Receipts to Cash Flow 42	10.5	9.8	10.8	12.2	8.1
Cost of Goods to Cash Flow 43	7.4	6.8	7.7	9.7	5.6
Cash Flow to Total Debt 44	0.4	0.5	0.4	0.3	0.4

Selected Financial Factors (in Percentages)

Debt Ratio 45	62.9	71.2	60.4	69.0	71.7
Return on Total Assets 46	10.0	11.9	6.3	10.0	10.6
Return on Equity Before Income Taxes 47	20.4	31.3	11.5	22.1	27.5
Return on Equity After Income Taxes 48	19.4	30.6	10.4	20.9	26.9
Profit Margin (Before Income Tax) 49	2.7	2.4	1.9	2.5	3.3
Profit Margin (After Income Tax) 50	2.6	2.3	1.7	2.4	3.2

Table I

Corporations with and without Net Income

FOOD AND BEVERAGE STORES

MONEY AMOUNTS AND SIZE OF ASSETS IN THOUSANDS OF DOLLARS

Item Description for Accounting Period 7/06 Through 6/07	Total	Zero Assets	Under 500	500 to 1,000	1,000 to 5,000	5,000 to 10,000	10,000 to 25,000	25,000 to 50,000	50,000 to 100,000	100,000 to 250,000	250,000 to 500,000	500,000 to 2,500,000	2,500,000 and over
Number of Enterprises 1	74603	8692	56145	4943	3927	498	196	74	50	29	13	27	7
Revenues ($ in Thousands)													
Net Sales 2	460450735	3164331	36385167	14226918	30831231	18145608	15097552	10182679	14057123	15223395	9872993	100659494	192604243
Interest 3	854467	609	3681	6236	16215	5974	6488	6245	6701	14270	8211	193251	586586
Rents 4	710232	4486	3656	10151	29407	18597	34700	13663	14747	13526	20320	223363	323616
Royalties 5	1511482	0	0	83	0	0	0	0	0	28898	9245	49995	1426262
Other Portfolio Income 6	1017839	92645	117329	5770	109040	12204	13082	20739	8096	26321	77233	458447	76937
Other Receipts 7	4493702	43127	397502	175511	291811	223272	207789	100998	163428	139521	162461	1043352	1544925
Total Receipts 8	469041457	3305198	36907335	14424669	31277704	18405655	15359611	10324324	14250095	15445931	10150463	102627902	196562569
Average Total Receipts 9	6287	380	657	2918	7965	36959	78365	139518	285002	532618	780805	3801033	28080367
Operating Costs/Operating Income (%)													
Cost of Operations 10	74.2	75.5	72.7	74.9	74.9	79.5	78.6	77.9	73.7	72.1	74.4	72.7	74.2
Salaries and Wages 11	9.6	6.7	7.6	8.0	8.8	8.7	8.5	8.2	10.7	11.6	9.7	11.1	9.4
Taxes Paid 12	1.5	1.6	2.4	1.5	1.5	1.2	1.3	1.5	2.4	1.7	1.5	1.5	1.4
Interest Paid 13	0.7	0.6	0.5	0.5	0.6	0.4	0.4	0.5	0.5	0.8	0.8	0.6	0.9
Depreciation 14	1.4	0.9	0.9	0.8	0.9	0.7	0.9	1.1	1.2	1.4	1.4	1.5	1.7
Amortization and Depletion 15	0.1	0.5	0.2	0.2	0.1	0.1	0.1	0.1	0.1	0.1	0.1	0.1	0.1
Pensions and Other Deferred Comp. 16	0.3	0.2	0.0	0.0	0.1	0.1	0.2	0.2	0.3	0.3	0.4	0.4	0.4
Employee Benefits 17	1.2	0.7	0.3	0.3	0.6	0.9	1.0	1.0	1.4	1.5	1.8	1.6	1.4
Advertising 18	0.7	0.6	0.5	0.6	1.1	0.6	0.8	0.7	0.8	1.0	0.7	0.8	0.6
Other Expenses 19	9.4	15.5	12.9	10.8	10.2	7.5	8.3	8.7	8.4	8.7	9.6	9.1	8.9
Officers' Compensation 20	0.5	2.6	2.6	1.9	1.1	0.6	0.6	0.5	0.4	0.4	0.3	0.1	0.0
Operating Margin 21	0.4	•	•	0.6	0.0	•	•	•	0.4	0.4	•	0.4	0.9
Operating Margin Before Officers' Comp. 22	0.9	•	1.9	2.4	1.1	0.4	0.1	0.2	0.7	0.8	•	0.5	1.0

Selected Average Balance Sheet ($ in Thousands)

Net Receivables 23	162	0	5	42	152	476	1549	2155	4976	8187	20471	51186	1161296
Inventories 24	345	0	36	158	401	1397	3592	7258	12694	23265	35802	193713	1772817
Net Property, Plant and Equipment 25	892	0	38	186	748	2443	5801	13271	28086	72266	153074	579925	5151997
Total Assets 26	2161	0	126	692	1940	6584	15771	33063	69498	155127	364148	1185402	12792585
Notes and Loans Payable 27	594	0	81	340	793	2456	5142	9511	20029	50495	66975	289806	2977465
All Other Liabilities 28	852	0	19	127	405	1706	5367	9168	20307	54121	134572	386106	6140930
Net Worth 29	714	0	26	225	741	2422	5261	14384	29162	50511	162600	509489	3674191

Selected Financial Ratios (Times to 1)

Current Ratio 30	1.0	•	3.0	2.2	1.9	1.5	1.2	1.3	1.2	1.1	1.0	1.4	0.7
Quick Ratio 31	0.4	•	1.1	1.0	0.9	0.8	0.5	0.5	0.4	0.4		0.5	0.3
Net Sales to Working Capital 32	•	•	15.7	17.1	17.9	31.9	54.4	42.7	81.1	172.0	271.2	32.7	•
Coverage Ratio 33	4.2	•	2.4	4.6	3.5	4.3	4.1	3.1	4.5	3.3	3.6	4.9	4.3
Total Asset Turnover 34	2.9	•	5.1	4.2	4.0	5.5	4.9	4.2	4.0	3.4	2.1	3.1	2.2
Inventory Turnover 35	13.3	•	13.0	14.7	20.7	16.8	14.8	16.3	16.3	15.8		14.0	11.5
Receivables Turnover 36	37.3	•	127.8	77.6	53.2	78.4	55.8	50.7	59.9	63.9	45.7	71.4	22.7
Total Liabilities to Net Worth 37	2.0	•	3.8	2.1	1.6	1.7	1.3	2.0	1.4	2.1	1.2	1.3	2.5
Current Assets to Working Capital 38	•	•	1.5	1.9	2.1	2.9	4.0	5.7	7.5	15.7	36.1	3.7	•
Current Liabilities to Working Capital 39	•	•	0.5	0.9	1.1	1.9	3.0	4.7	6.5	14.7	35.1	2.7	•
Working Capital to Net Sales 40	•	•	0.1	0.1	0.0	0.0	0.0	0.0	0.0	0.0	0.0	0.0	•
Inventory to Working Capital 41	•	•	0.8	0.9	0.9	1.3	2.0	2.6	3.7	7.6	16.1	1.8	•
Total Receipts to Cash Flow 42	11.7	17.6	11.9	10.7	12.2	16.8	15.1	14.2	14.4	14.1	12.8	11.8	10.7
Cost of Goods to Cash Flow 43	8.7	13.3	8.6	8.0	9.2	13.3	11.9	11.1	10.6	10.2	9.5	8.6	7.9
Cash Flow to Total Debt 44	0.4	•	0.5	0.6	0.5	0.5	0.5	0.5	0.4	0.4	0.3	0.5	0.3

Selected Financial Factors (in Percentages)

Debt Ratio 45	66.9	•	79.3	67.5	61.8	63.2	66.6	56.5	58.0	67.4	55.3	57.0	71.3
Return on Total Assets 46	8.4	•	6.4	10.4	8.3	8.4	7.8	6.6	9.0	8.8	6.0	9.4	8.3
Return on Equity Before Income Taxes 47	19.4	•	18.1	25.1	15.5	17.6	17.7	10.2	16.8	18.8	9.7	17.4	22.3
Return on Equity After Income Taxes 48	14.0	•	16.5	24.7	14.1	16.1	16.1	8.3	14.0	15.9	7.9	12.6	14.7
Profit Margin (Before Income Tax) 49	2.2	•	0.7	2.0	1.5	1.2	1.2	1.1	1.7	1.8	2.1	2.4	3.0
Profit Margin (After Income Tax) 50	1.6	•	0.7	1.9	1.3	1.1	0.9	1.5	1.7	1.5		1.7	2.0

219

Table II
Corporations with Net Income

FOOD AND BEVERAGE STORES

MONEY AMOUNTS AND SIZE OF ASSETS IN THOUSANDS OF DOLLARS

Item Description for Accounting Period 7/06 Through 6/07	Total	Zero Assets	Under 500	500 to 1,000	1,000 to 5,000	5,000 to 10,000	10,000 to 25,000	25,000 to 50,000	50,000 to 100,000	100,000 to 250,000	250,000 to 500,000	500,000 to 2,500,000	2,500,000 and over
Number of Enterprises 1	40184	•	29359	3516	2766	357	124	62	•	24	10	23	•
Revenues ($ in Thousands)													
Net Sales 2	348176913	•	24231417	12770257	21238034	10485279	10882905	8847411	•	13629368	7249016	80387436	•
Interest 3	790777	•	3140	4184	12551	5465	4783	6076	•	7743	7606	177645	•
Rents 4	373753	•	609	492	22660	13549	9888	13497	•	9257	18324	183863	•
Royalties 5	1232540	•	0	83	0	0	0	0	•	0	9245	49995	•
Other Portfolio Income 6	807394	•	114371	4311	108809	12024	11926	17840	•	7751	71849	283357	•
Other Receipts 7	3792241	•	274843	165455	235133	64101	162125	90954	•	110664	128174	876579	•
Total Receipts 8	355173618	•	24624380	12944782	21617187	10580418	11071627	8975778	•	13764783	7484214	81958875	•
Average Total Receipts 9	8839	•	839	3682	7815	29637	89287	144771	•	573533	748421	3563429	•
Operating Costs/Operating Income (%)													
Cost of Operations 10	73.4	•	73.6	75.1	74.5	76.5	78.6	77.9	•	72.8	73.3	71.7	•
Salaries and Wages 11	9.6	•	7.0	8.0	8.5	8.9	8.4	8.0	•	11.2	10.0	11.4	•
Taxes Paid 12	1.6	•	2.2	1.4	1.4	1.3	1.2	1.6	•	1.6	1.5	1.5	•
Interest Paid 13	0.6	•	0.4	0.4	0.5	0.3	0.3	0.5	•	0.5	0.7	0.6	•
Depreciation 14	1.4	•	0.7	0.7	0.9	0.7	0.7	1.1	•	1.3	1.5	1.6	•
Amortization and Depletion 15	0.1	•	0.2	0.1	0.1	0.1	0.0	0.1	•	0.1	0.1	0.1	•
Pensions and Other Deferred Comp. 16	0.4	•	0.1	0.0	0.1	0.1	0.1	0.2	•	0.3	0.3	0.4	•
Employee Benefits 17	1.3	•	0.4	0.3	0.5	1.2	0.8	0.9	•	1.5	1.7	1.8	•
Advertising 18	0.7	•	0.4	0.5	1.2	0.9	0.7	0.7	•	0.8	0.7	0.8	•
Other Expenses 19	9.0	•	10.8	10.2	9.6	7.4	7.7	8.5	•	8.3	9.8	8.6	•
Officers' Compensation 20	0.5	•	2.5	1.9	0.9	0.8	0.6	0.4	•	0.4	0.3	0.2	•
Operating Margin 21	1.4	•	1.8	1.3	1.6	1.7	0.6	0.3	•	1.3	0.1	1.2	•
Operating Margin Before Officers' Comp. 22	1.9	•	4.4	3.2	2.6	2.6	1.2	0.7	•	1.7	0.4	1.3	•

Selected Average Balance Sheet ($ in Thousands)

Net Receivables 23	232	•	6	36	141	576	1816	2001	•	8375	10638	44538
Inventories 24	548	•	46	192	390	1518	3826	6727	•	23192	39394	193487
Net Property, Plant and Equipment 25	1312	•	30	160	702	1816	4722	13898	•	78312	143913	607686
Total Assets 26	3144	•	138	705	1885	6299	15612	32844	•	155796	359449	1174793
Notes and Loans Payable 27	779	•	57	273	666	1455	3068	9305	•	39727	56765	269514
All Other Liabilities 28	1191	•	17	118	345	1596	5282	8913	•	49357	130963	378601
Net Worth 29	1174	•	64	315	874	3248	7262	14625	•	66713	171720	526679

Selected Financial Ratios (Times to 1)

Current Ratio 30	1.0	•	4.8	2.6	2.3	1.8	1.4	1.4	•	1.1	0.9	1.3
Quick Ratio 31	0.4	•	1.9	1.1	1.1	0.9	0.7	0.6	•	0.4	0.3	0.5
Net Sales to Working Capital 32	•	•	12.9	16.5	15.2	19.7	35.8	39.2	•	115.7	•	36.8
Coverage Ratio 33	6.6	•	10.0	7.6	7.6	8.8	9.9	4.7	•	5.8	6.1	6.2
Total Asset Turnover 34	2.8	•	6.0	5.1	4.1	4.7	5.6	4.3	•	3.6	2.0	3.0
Inventory Turnover 35	11.6	•	13.1	14.2	14.7	14.8	18.0	16.5	•	17.8	13.5	12.9
Receivables Turnover 36	32.7	•	135.7	101.6	50.2	52.1	•	•	•	67.6	•	•
Total Liabilities to Net Worth 37	1.7	•	1.2	1.2	0.9	1.1	1.1	1.2	•	1.3	1.1	1.2
Current Assets to Working Capital 38	•	•	1.3	1.6	1.8	2.3	3.5	3.6	•	9.8	•	4.3
Current Liabilities to Working Capital 39	•	•	0.3	0.6	0.8	1.3	2.5	2.6	•	8.8	•	3.3
Working Capital to Net Sales 40	•	•	0.1	0.1	0.1	0.1	0.0	0.0	•	0.0	•	0.0
Inventory to Working Capital 41	•	•	0.7	0.8	0.7	1.0	1.6	1.8	•	4.8	•	2.0
Total Receipts to Cash Flow 42	10.5	•	10.2	10.3	10.5	13.2	13.4	13.3	•	13.4	11.1	11.0
Cost of Goods to Cash Flow 43	7.7	•	7.8	7.8	7.8	10.1	10.6	10.4	•	9.8	8.1	7.9
Cash Flow to Total Debt 44	0.4	•	1.1	0.9	0.7	0.7	0.8	0.6	•	0.5	0.3	0.5

Selected Financial Factors (in Percentages)

Debt Ratio 45	62.7	•	53.8	55.4	53.6	48.4	53.5	55.5	•	57.2	52.2	55.2
Return on Total Assets 46	11.0	•	23.0	15.9	16.0	13.8	14.9	9.6	•	10.0	8.1	11.2
Return on Equity Before Income Taxes 47	25.1	•	44.7	31.0	30.0	23.7	28.7	16.9	•	19.2	14.1	20.9
Return on Equity After Income Taxes 48	19.0	•	43.5	30.5	28.4	22.5	26.9	14.6	•	16.6	11.8	15.4
Profit Margin (Before Income Tax) 49	3.4	•	3.5	2.7	3.4	2.6	2.4	1.7	•	2.3	3.3	3.1
Profit Margin (After Income Tax) 50	2.6	•	3.4	2.6	2.5	2.2	2.2	1.5	•	1.9	2.8	2.3

Table I

Corporations with and without Net Income

BEER, WINE, AND LIQUOR STORES

MONEY AMOUNTS AND SIZE OF ASSETS IN THOUSANDS OF DOLLARS

Item Description for Accounting Period 7/06 Through 6/07	Total	Zero Assets	Under 500	500 to 1,000	1,000 to 5,000	5,000 to 10,000	10,000 to 25,000	25,000 to 50,000	50,000 to 100,000	100,000 to 250,000	250,000 to 500,000	500,000 to 2,500,000	2,500,000 and over
Number of Enterprises **1**	19163	1221	15246	1936	700	44	3	6	6	0	0	0	0
Revenues ($ in Thousands)													
Net Sales **2**	21116403	185290	10912688	4282189	3028845	611535	46512	477669	1571674	0	0	0	0
Interest **3**	6845	353	2297	885	2316	170	1	0	823	0	0	0	0
Rents **4**	741	0	0	0	0	0	0	0	741	0	0	0	0
Royalties **5**	0	0	0	0	0	0	0	0	0	0	0	0	0
Other Portfolio Income **6**	47974	0	26373	21004	111	9	0	37	440	0	0	0	0
Other Receipts **7**	368189	8769	283648	26802	15102	4075	24019	267	5509	0	0	0	0
Total Receipts **8**	21540152	194412	11225006	4330880	3046374	615789	70532	477973	1579187	0	0	0	0
Average Total Receipts **9**	1124	159	736	2237	4352	13995	23511	79662	263198	•	•	•	•
Operating Costs/Operating Income (%)													
Cost of Operations **10**	78.0	90.1	76.8	78.8	79.1	88.7	83.4	78.2	76.2	•	•	•	•
Salaries and Wages **11**	5.6	2.7	5.8	4.5	5.5	4.3	12.3	6.0	8.0	•	•	•	•
Taxes Paid **12**	2.3	3.9	2.8	2.6	1.0	0.4	5.3	1.2	1.3	•	•	•	•
Interest Paid **13**	0.7	0.0	0.8	0.6	0.7	0.4	1.6	0.7	0.5	•	•	•	•
Depreciation **14**	0.6	0.2	0.6	0.6	0.4	0.2	0.6	0.2	1.0	•	•	•	•
Amortization and Depletion **15**	0.3	4.5	0.3	0.4	0.2	0.1	0.0	0.0	0.2	•	•	•	•
Pensions and Other Deferred Comp. **16**	0.1	•	0.1	0.0	0.2	0.2	•	0.0	0.1	•	•	•	•
Employee Benefits **17**	0.3	0.3	0.2	0.2	0.3	•	0.0	0.2	0.8	•	•	•	•
Advertising **18**	0.5	0.6	0.3	0.7	0.6	0.1	1.8	0.7	1.3	•	•	•	•
Other Expenses **19**	9.0	8.9	10.2	8.0	7.9	2.8	29.1	7.2	8.4	•	•	•	•
Officers' Compensation **20**	2.9	1.7	3.4	2.8	2.8	0.8	5.2	3.3	0.8	•	•	•	•
Operating Margin **21**	•	•	•	0.8	1.2	2.0	•	2.3	1.6	•	•	•	•
Operating Margin Before Officers' Comp. **22**	2.6	•	2.1	3.6	4.0	2.8	•	5.6	2.4	•	•	•	•

Selected Average Balance Sheet ($ in Thousands)

Net Receivables 23	14	0	2	17	70	2172	1549	1350	7079
Inventories 24	150	0	84	292	804	2824	27927	16666	28148
Net Property, Plant and Equipment 25	58	0	39	94	129	966	103	1138	32771
Total Assets 26	338	0	194	669	1597	7067	17247	29569	94258
Notes and Loans Payable 27	173	0	119	336	648	3174	11081	4801	31387
All Other Liabilities 28	69	0	32	165	282	1582	4442	15328	25824
Net Worth 29	96	0	43	167	668	2311	1723	9440	37047

Selected Financial Ratios (Times to 1)

Current Ratio 30	2.6	•	3.0	3.1	2.6	1.7	1.1	1.6	1.8
Quick Ratio 31	0.8	•	0.8	1.1	0.7	1.1	0.1	0.2	0.4
Net Sales to Working Capital 32	8.1	•	8.9	7.7	5.9	5.8	7.3	7.9	11.2
Coverage Ratio 33	3.3	•	2.9	4.2	3.4	7.3	8.7	4.2	5.4
Total Asset Turnover 34	3.3	•	3.7	3.3	2.7	2.0	0.9	2.7	2.8
Inventory Turnover 35	5.7	•	6.6	6.0	4.3	4.4	0.5	3.7	7.1
Receivables Turnover 36	61.4	•	334.0	153.4	41.9	3.7	5.7	53.4	57.5
Total Liabilities to Net Worth 37	2.5	•	3.5	3.0	1.4	2.1	9.0	2.1	1.5
Current Assets to Working Capital 38	1.6	•	1.5	1.5	1.6	2.5	7.9	2.8	2.2
Current Liabilities to Working Capital 39	0.6	•	0.5	0.5	0.6	1.5	6.9	1.8	1.2
Working Capital to Net Sales 40	0.1	•	0.1	0.1	0.2	0.2	0.1	0.1	0.1
Inventory to Working Capital 41	1.1	•	1.0	0.9	1.1	0.8	1.1	2.0	1.6
Total Receipts to Cash Flow 42	14.4	•	13.5	14.8	16.2	21.2	2.7	14.0	15.9
Cost of Goods to Cash Flow 43	11.3	•	10.3	11.7	12.8	18.8	2.2	10.9	12.1
Cash Flow to Total Debt 44	0.3	•	0.4	0.3	0.3	0.1	0.4	0.3	0.3

Selected Financial Factors (in Percentages)

Debt Ratio 45	71.6	•	77.6	75.0	58.2	67.3	90.0	68.1	60.7
Return on Total Assets 46	7.8	•	8.8	8.2	6.7	6.0	12.6	8.3	6.9
Return on Equity Before Income Taxes 47	19.3	•	25.8	25.0	11.3	15.9	111.8	19.8	14.4
Return on Equity After Income Taxes 48	17.3	•	23.9	22.0	9.5	15.2	73.8	19.8	12.6
Profit Margin (Before Income Tax) 49	1.7	•	1.6	1.9	1.7	2.6	12.4	2.3	2.0
Profit Margin (After Income Tax) 50	1.5	•	1.5	1.7	1.5	2.5	8.2	2.3	1.8

Table II

Corporations with Net Income

BEER, WINE, AND LIQUOR STORES

MONEY AMOUNTS AND SIZE OF ASSETS IN THOUSANDS OF DOLLARS

Item Description for Accounting Period 7/06 Through 6/07	Total	Zero Assets	Under 500	500 to 1,000	1,000 to 5,000	5,000 to 10,000	10,000 to 25,000	25,000 to 50,000	50,000 to 100,000	100,000 to 250,000	250,000 to 500,000	500,000 to 2,500,000	2,500,000 and over
Number of Enterprises 1	12501	•	10799	•	544	44	3	6	•	0	0	0	0

Revenues ($ in Thousands)

	Total	Zero Assets	Under 500	500 to 1,000	1,000 to 5,000	5,000 to 10,000	10,000 to 25,000	25,000 to 50,000	50,000 to 100,000	100,000 to 250,000	250,000 to 500,000	500,000 to 2,500,000	2,500,000 and over
Net Sales 2	16631984	•	8479503	•	2641112	611535	46512	477669	•	0	0	0	0
Interest 3	5739	•	1578	•	2316	170	1	0	•	0	0	0	0
Rents 4	741	•	0	•	0	0	0	0	•	0	0	0	0
Royalties 5	0	•	0	•	0	0	0	0	•	0	0	0	0
Other Portfolio Income 6	44447	•	22847	•	111	9	0	37	•	0	0	0	0
Other Receipts 7	271856	•	216875	•	13694	4075	24019	267	•	0	0	0	0
Total Receipts 8	16954767	•	8720803	•	2657233	615789	70532	477973	•	0	0	0	0
Average Total Receipts 9	1356	•	808	•	4885	13995	23511	79662	•	•	•	•	•

Operating Costs/Operating Income (%)

	Total	Zero Assets	Under 500	500 to 1,000	1,000 to 5,000	5,000 to 10,000	10,000 to 25,000	25,000 to 50,000	50,000 to 100,000	100,000 to 250,000	250,000 to 500,000	500,000 to 2,500,000	2,500,000 and over
Cost of Operations 10	77.7	•	76.6	•	79.0	88.7	83.4	78.2	•	•	•	•	•
Salaries and Wages 11	5.3	•	5.1	•	5.7	4.3	12.3	6.0	•	•	•	•	•
Taxes Paid 12	1.7	•	2.3	•	1.0	0.4	5.3	1.2	•	•	•	•	•
Interest Paid 13	0.5	•	0.6	•	0.5	0.4	1.6	0.7	•	•	•	•	•
Depreciation 14	0.6	•	0.6	•	0.4	0.2	0.6	0.2	•	•	•	•	•
Amortization and Depletion 15	0.2	•	0.2	•	0.3	0.1	0.0	0.0	•	•	•	•	•
Pensions and Other Deferred Comp. 16	0.1	•	0.1	•	0.3	0.2	0.0	0.0	•	•	•	•	•
Employee Benefits 17	0.3	•	0.2	•	0.3	•	0.0	0.2	•	•	•	•	•
Advertising 18	0.5	•	0.3	•	0.6	0.1	1.8	0.7	•	•	•	•	•
Other Expenses 19	8.5	•	9.5	•	7.5	2.8	29.1	7.2	•	•	•	•	•
Officers' Compensation 20	3.0	•	3.6	•	3.0	0.8	5.2	3.3	•	•	•	•	•
Operating Margin 21	1.5	•	0.8	•	1.6	2.0	•	2.3	•	•	•	•	•
Operating Margin Before Officers' Comp. 22	4.6	•	4.5	•	4.6	2.8	•	5.6	•	•	•	•	•

Selected Average Balance Sheet ($ in Thousands)

Net Receivables 23	18	1	87	2172	1549	1350
Inventories 24	186	86	897	2824	2394	20082
Net Property, Plant and Equipment 25	57	32	134	966	103	1138
Total Assets 26	399	211	1693	7067	17247	29569
Notes and Loans Payable 27	159	96	589	3174	11081	4801
All Other Liabilities 28	83	32	334	1582	4442	15328
Net Worth 29	158	82	770	2311	1723	9440

Selected Financial Ratios (Times to 1)

Current Ratio 30	2.8	4.1	2.4	1.7	1.1	1.6
Quick Ratio 31	0.9	1.2	0.7	1.1	0.1	0.2
Net Sales to Working Capital 32	7.0	7.3	5.9	5.8	7.3	7.9
Coverage Ratio 33	7.9	7.4	5.2	7.3	8.7	4.2
Total Asset Turnover 34	3.3	3.7	2.9	2.0	0.9	2.7
Inventory Turnover 35	5.6	7.0	4.3	4.4	5.4	3.1
Receivables Turnover 36	53.5	609.8	36.8	3.7		3.1
Total Liabilities to Net Worth 37	1.5	1.6	1.2	2.1	9.0	2.1
Current Assets to Working Capital 38	1.5	1.3	1.7	2.5	7.9	2.8
Current Liabilities to Working Capital 39	0.5	0.3	0.7	1.5	6.9	1.8
Working Capital to Net Sales 40	0.1	0.1	0.2	0.2	0.1	0.1
Inventory to Working Capital 41	1.0	0.9	1.1	0.8	1.1	2.0
Total Receipts to Cash Flow 42	12.1	11.1	15.5	21.2	2.7	14.0
Cost of Goods to Cash Flow 43	9.4	8.5	12.2	18.8	2.2	10.9
Cash Flow to Total Debt 44	0.5	0.6	0.3	0.1	0.4	0.3

Selected Financial Factors (in Percentages)

Debt Ratio 45	60.5	61.0	54.5	67.3	90.0	68.1
Return on Total Assets 46	13.2	15.9	7.9	6.0	12.6	8.3
Return on Equity Before Income Taxes 47	29.2	35.3	14.0	15.9	111.8	19.8
Return on Equity After Income Taxes 48	27.3	33.9	12.0	15.2	73.8	19.8
Profit Margin (Before Income Tax) 49	3.5	3.7	2.2	2.6	12.4	2.3
Profit Margin (After Income Tax) 50	3.2	3.5	1.9	2.5	8.2	2.3

Table I

Corporations with and without Net Income

HEALTH AND PERSONAL CARE STORES

MONEY AMOUNTS AND SIZE OF ASSETS IN THOUSANDS OF DOLLARS

Item Description for Accounting Period 7/06 Through 6/07	Total	Zero Assets	Under 500	500 to 1,000	1,000 to 5,000	5,000 to 10,000	10,000 to 25,000	25,000 to 50,000	50,000 to 100,000	100,000 to 250,000	250,000 to 500,000	500,000 to 2,500,000	2,500,000 and over
Number of Enterprises 1	40975	4164	30204	3430	2929	134	45	25	12	16	7	3	7
Revenues ($ in Thousands)													
Net Sales 2	229958928	1386820	27153669	12090216	17141875	3323480	1250963	1825607	2202111	6663211	3582914	6780414	146197647
Interest 3	288048	2111	2534	5107	9853	2953	5689	1233	949	11239	6966	11264	228149
Rents 4	105379	15	629	3445	2888	3588	314	1230	1003	348	2459	4234	85226
Royalties 5	98604	7570	0	0	2	0	0	114	1223	248	1629	34812	53005
Other Portfolio Income 6	264012	24362	1685	5336	5793	846	557	1774	172	16574	3067	1085	202761
Other Receipts 7	2560843	12480	27028	162620	80109	7065	48131	76792	17511	98148	12329	79242	1939391
Total Receipts 8	232915814	1433358	27185545	12266724	17240520	3337932	1305654	1906750	2222969	6789768	3609364	6911051	148706179
Average Total Receipts 9	5684	344	900	3576	5886	24910	29015	76270	185247	424360	515623	2303684	21243740
Operating Costs/Operating Income (%)													
Cost of Operations 10	71.9	58.0	69.9	76.0	70.0	55.0	66.1	64.3	70.9	69.2	58.6	66.9	73.4
Salaries and Wages 11	10.9	10.4	7.3	7.5	11.4	20.5	17.5	13.5	13.0	13.0	9.2	13.3	11.2
Taxes Paid 12	1.3	2.1	1.5	1.4	1.4	1.2	1.6	2.0	1.6	1.5	2.2	1.9	1.1
Interest Paid 13	0.8	5.9	0.3	0.2	0.5	0.3	0.5	2.5	2.2	1.6	2.9	1.5	0.8
Depreciation 14	0.9	0.9	0.5	0.5	0.6	0.6	1.0	1.2	0.8	0.8	1.9	1.3	1.0
Amortization and Depletion 15	0.3	0.7	0.1	0.0	0.2	0.2	0.1	0.2	0.2	0.3	0.6	0.7	0.4
Pensions and Other Deferred Comp. 16	0.3	0.1	0.2	0.6	0.3	0.3	0.7	0.2	0.2	0.2	0.2	0.3	0.3
Employee Benefits 17	0.6	0.5	0.5	0.4	0.5	0.7	1.8	0.6	1.0	1.4	1.0	1.0	0.6
Advertising 18	1.1	3.6	1.0	0.4	1.0	2.6	1.8	4.3	0.8	1.1	1.3	1.3	1.0
Other Expenses 19	8.8	23.7	10.4	6.4	8.5	14.9	14.5	13.6	7.4	10.8	18.4	11.0	7.9
Officers' Compensation 20	1.4	5.9	5.7	5.4	3.4	0.9	2.0	0.9	0.8	0.5	0.9	0.6	0.1
Operating Margin 21	1.8	•	2.7	1.3	2.1	2.9	•	•	1.1	•	2.8	0.3	2.1
Operating Margin Before Officers' Comp. 22	3.2	•	8.4	6.7	5.5	3.8	•	•	1.8	0.2	3.7	0.8	2.1

Selected Average Balance Sheet ($ in Thousands)

Net Receivables 23	343	0	17	92	388	1997	3539	7407	16629	26765	23646	113855	1479964
Inventories 24	575	0	60	247	358	1674	3280	7732	17889	41508	70217	240566	2458003
Net Property, Plant and Equipment 25	441	0	22	74	218	851	1478	7721	14596	24615	83836	290165	2015645
Total Assets 26	2479	0	150	727	1692	7351	14659	33979	78096	152073	362165	1158330	11102831
Notes and Loans Payable 27	600	0	69	122	515	1360	2336	23961	43996	67170	114815	490886	2259335
All Other Liabilities 28	732	0	45	164	452	2828	23361	14381	26675	48473	99795	373394	3148937
Net Worth 29	1146	0	35	440	725	3163	-11038	-4363	7425	36429	147554	294050	5694559

Selected Financial Ratios (Times to 1)

Current Ratio 30	1.7	•	2.2	3.1	2.4	1.9	0.4	1.1	1.5	1.6	1.7	2.1	1.6
Quick Ratio 31	0.7	•	0.9	1.5	1.5	1.3	0.2	0.5	0.6	0.7	0.4	0.5	0.7
Net Sales to Working Capital 32	11.8	•	14.7	9.3	8.1	8.8	•	49.4	13.3	12.3	12.4	7.2	11.7
Coverage Ratio 33	5.1	•	12.2	17.2	6.7	13.9	1.4	1.4	1.9	2.0	2.2	2.5	5.7
Total Asset Turnover 34	2.3	•	6.0	4.8	3.5	3.4	1.9	2.1	2.3	2.7	1.4	2.0	1.9
Inventory Turnover 35	7.0	•	10.5	10.8	11.5	8.2	5.6	6.1	7.3	6.9	4.3	6.3	6.2
Receivables Turnover 36	18.2	•	56.1	36.3	17.5	12.9	7.8	10.3	11.3	20.8	12.8	25.5	16.0
Total Liabilities to Net Worth 37	1.2	•	3.2	0.7	1.3	1.3	•	•	9.5	3.2	1.5	2.9	0.9
Current Assets to Working Capital 38	2.4	•	1.8	1.5	1.7	2.1	•	14.1	3.1	2.7	2.5	1.9	2.6
Current Liabilities to Working Capital 39	1.4	•	0.8	0.5	0.7	1.1	•	13.1	2.1	1.7	1.5	0.9	1.6
Working Capital to Net Sales 40	0.1	•	0.1	0.1	0.1	0.1	•	0.0	0.1	0.1	0.1	0.1	0.1
Inventory to Working Capital 41	1.3	•	1.0	0.6	0.6	0.7	•	5.3	1.3	1.4	1.6	0.8	1.4
Total Receipts to Cash Flow 42	11.8	19.0	10.8	15.0	11.3	6.2	12.0	9.1	14.0	11.5	6.8	11.9	12.2
Cost of Goods to Cash Flow 43	8.4	11.0	7.5	11.4	7.9	3.4	7.9	5.8	9.9	8.0	4.0	7.9	9.0
Cash Flow to Total Debt 44	0.4	•	0.7	0.8	0.5	1.0	0.1	0.2	0.2	0.3	0.3	0.2	0.3

Selected Financial Factors (in Percentages)

Debt Ratio 45	53.8	•	76.4	39.4	57.1	57.0	175.3	112.8	90.5	76.0	59.3	74.6	48.7
Return on Total Assets 46	9.3	•	18.4	14.2	11.0	12.2	•	7.7	9.9	8.7	9.0	7.2	8.7
Return on Equity Before Income Taxes 47	16.1	•	71.8	22.0	21.8	26.2	8.3	•	49.4	18.6	12.1	16.9	14.1
Return on Equity After Income Taxes 48	11.5	•	70.9	21.3	20.2	22.7	9.0	•	44.5	12.4	9.3	9.9	9.2
Profit Margin (Before Income Tax) 49	3.3	•	2.8	2.8	2.7	3.3	•	1.0	2.0	1.6	3.5	2.2	3.8
Profit Margin (After Income Tax) 50	2.4	•	2.8	2.7	2.5	2.9	•	0.9	1.8	1.1	2.7	1.3	2.5

Table II
Corporations with Net Income

HEALTH AND PERSONAL CARE STORES

MONEY AMOUNTS AND SIZE OF ASSETS IN THOUSANDS OF DOLLARS

Item Description for Accounting Period 7/06 Through 6/07	Total	Zero Assets	Under 500	500 to 1,000	1,000 to 5,000	5,000 to 10,000	10,000 to 25,000	25,000 to 50,000	50,000 to 100,000	100,000 to 250,000	250,000 to 500,000	500,000 to 2,500,000	2,500,000 and over
Number of Enterprises **1**	27697	2001	20470	2687	2362	112	16	•	8	11	•	0	7
Revenues ($ in Thousands)													
Net Sales **2**	214847172	854228	21935408	10447179	14152567	3142444	448022	•	1491895	5447254	•	0	146197647
Interest **3**	269043	901	1115	3867	5751	2312	752	•	376	7975	•	0	228149
Rents **4**	102901	0	629	3445	1426	3588	314	•	1003	348	•	0	85226
Royalties **5**	89623	0	0	0	0	0	0	•	0	177	•	0	53005
Other Portfolio Income **6**	250175	24362	373	2017	3826	788	334	•	128	11147	•	0	202761
Other Receipts **7**	2429903	5880	22080	139028	74999	3732	43521	•	11530	48391	•	0	1939391
Total Receipts **8**	217998817	885371	21959605	10595536	14238569	3152864	492943	•	1504932	5515292	•	0	148706179
Average Total Receipts **9**	7870	442	1073	3943	6028	28151	30809	•	188116	501390	•	•	21243740
Operating Costs/Operating Income (%)													
Cost of Operations **10**	72.1	57.4	70.0	77.2	69.2	55.7	61.3	•	71.7	72.4	•	•	73.4
Salaries and Wages **11**	10.7	6.1	6.7	6.6	11.0	21.1	18.6	•	11.7	11.1	•	•	11.2
Taxes Paid **12**	1.2	1.9	1.4	1.3	1.4	1.1	2.1	•	1.3	1.4	•	•	1.1
Interest Paid **13**	0.7	2.2	0.2	0.2	0.4	0.2	0.4	•	0.7	1.4	•	•	0.8
Depreciation **14**	0.9	0.6	0.4	0.4	0.6	0.4	0.6	•	0.8	0.6	•	•	1.0
Amortization and Depletion **15**	0.3	0.5	0.1	0.0	0.2	0.1	0.1	•	0.2	0.2	•	•	0.4
Pensions and Other Deferred Comp. **16**	0.3	0.1	0.2	0.6	0.4	0.3	1.5	•	0.2	0.2	•	•	0.3
Employee Benefits **17**	0.6	0.1	0.4	0.3	0.5	0.6	3.1	•	1.0	1.3	•	•	0.6
Advertising **18**	1.0	2.5	0.9	0.3	1.0	2.4	0.2	•	0.5	1.1	•	•	1.0
Other Expenses **19**	8.3	15.9	9.2	5.5	7.9	12.3	9.0	•	5.3	8.5	•	•	7.9
Officers' Compensation **20**	1.2	4.7	5.5	3.3	3.3	0.8	4.3	•	0.7	0.3	•	•	0.1
Operating Margin **21**	2.6	7.9	4.9	2.1	4.2	5.0	•	•	5.9	1.4	•	•	2.1
Operating Margin Before Officers' Comp. **22**	3.7	12.6	10.4	7.7	7.5	5.8	3.2	•	6.7	1.7	•	•	2.1

Table I
Corporations with and without Net Income

GASOLINE STATIONS

MONEY AMOUNTS AND SIZE OF ASSETS IN THOUSANDS OF DOLLARS

Item Description for Accounting Period 7/06 Through 6/07	Total	Zero Assets	Under 500	500 to 1,000	1,000 to 5,000	5,000 to 10,000	10,000 to 25,000	25,000 to 50,000	50,000 to 100,000	100,000 to 250,000	250,000 to 500,000	500,000 to 2,500,000	2,500,000 and over
Number of Enterprises **1**	39423	4973	23266	5788	4790	318	149	71	35	17	4	12	0
Revenues ($ in Thousands)													
Net Sales **2**	275461036	6869171	46636124	22401271	52517216	13540085	16159419	19166515	11972222	11753366	7637087	66808560	0
Interest **3**	94198	1075	1767	1966	8753	5657	3000	7210	3054	1902	4951	54863	0
Rents **4**	136328	797	7958	3585	26768	3307	5012	6183	19900	2892	3132	56795	0
Royalties **5**	21943	444	0	466	0	0	0	2	0	0	1363	19668	0
Other Portfolio Income **6**	483351	22031	84169	24710	46448	34092	32829	9754	11208	20896	13046	184166	0
Other Receipts **7**	1445846	65564	388417	83282	215812	46210	116029	73611	64333	170732	29952	191907	0
Total Receipts **8**	277642702	6959082	47118435	22515280	52814997	13629351	16316289	19263275	12070717	11949788	7689531	67315959	0
Average Total Receipts **9**	7043	1399	2025	3890	11026	42860	109505	271314	344878	702929	1922383	5609663	•
Operating Costs/Operating Income (%)													
Cost of Operations **10**	89.9	88.3	88.1	89.5	91.3	88.7	89.4	92.7	92.6	87.2	91.7	89.9	•
Salaries and Wages **11**	3.1	7.1	3.1	2.2	2.7	3.4	4.2	2.4	2.3	4.2	3.2	3.2	•
Taxes Paid **12**	0.9	1.0	1.0	1.6	0.9	1.8	0.7	0.7	0.5	1.9	0.4	0.5	•
Interest Paid **13**	0.5	0.5	0.3	0.6	0.6	0.4	0.5	0.3	0.4	0.5	0.2	0.4	•
Depreciation **14**	0.8	0.4	0.4	1.0	0.7	0.6	0.7	0.5	0.8	1.1	0.6	1.3	•
Amortization and Depletion **15**	0.1	0.1	0.1	0.1	0.1	0.1	0.1	0.0	0.1	0.1	0.0	0.1	•
Pensions and Other Deferred Comp. **16**	0.0	0.0	0.0	0.0	0.0	0.0	0.0	0.0	0.0	0.1	0.2	0.1	•
Employee Benefits **17**	0.2	0.1	0.1	0.0	0.1	0.2	0.1	0.1	0.2	0.3	0.3	0.3	•
Advertising **18**	0.1	0.1	0.1	0.0	0.1	0.1	0.2	0.1	0.1	0.2	0.1	0.1	•
Other Expenses **19**	4.1	6.1	6.1	4.4	3.7	4.6	4.5	3.0	3.4	4.0	2.7	3.1	•
Officers' Compensation **20**	0.4	1.3	0.9	0.8	0.5	0.4	0.2	0.2	0.2	0.2	0.1	0.1	•
Operating Margin **21**	•	•	•	•	•	•	•	•	•	0.2	0.5	0.9	•
Operating Margin Before Officers' Comp. **22**	0.3	0.7	0.7	0.4	0.3	0.3	0.2	0.2	•	0.4	0.6	1.0	•

Selected Average Balance Sheet ($ in Thousands)

Net Receivables **23**	107	0	11	33	147	556	1468	3710	7758	12005	97538	127457	•
Inventories **24**	126	0	53	74	153	811	1990	3511	5512	15127	29268	102156	•
Net Property, Plant and Equipment **25**	572	0	61	402	1070	2475	7276	15493	32679	71822	98048	662162	•
Total Assets **26**	1159	0	201	732	1789	6769	15101	35440	69191	143302	319039	1261671	•
Notes and Loans Payable **27**	520	0	121	448	1305	2490	7430	12813	23636	51583	44598	345434	•
All Other Liabilities **28**	312	0	32	73	298	1511	4634	11299	19907	45866	162719	467302	•
Net Worth **29**	327	0	48	212	186	2768	3036	11327	25648	45852	111722	448934	•

Selected Financial Ratios (Times to 1)

Current Ratio **30**	1.4	•	2.6	2.9	1.6	1.4	1.0	1.2	1.2	0.9	1.0	1.2	•
Quick Ratio **31**	0.8	•	1.1	1.6	0.9	0.9	0.6	0.6	0.7	0.5	0.7	0.7	•
Net Sales to Working Capital **32**	62.9	•	33.6	28.1	54.2	62.3	477.4	102.5	94.1	•	85.2	•	•
Coverage Ratio **33**	2.4	•	3.6	1.3	1.0	2.5	1.6	2.9	1.5	4.5	7.0	4.6	•
Total Asset Turnover **34**	6.0	•	10.0	5.3	6.1	6.3	7.2	7.6	4.9	4.8	6.0	4.4	•
Inventory Turnover **35**	49.7	•	33.6	46.6	65.5	46.6	48.7	71.3	57.5	39.9	59.8	49.0	•
Receivables Turnover **36**	68.7	•	157.6	112.5	84.9	51.5	65.2	66.1	50.3	57.2	29.6	48.0	•
Total Liabilities to Net Worth **37**	2.5	•	3.2	2.5	8.6	1.4	4.0	2.1	1.7	2.1	1.9	1.8	•
Current Assets to Working Capital **38**	3.5	•	1.6	1.5	2.6	3.5	23.4	5.8	6.7	•	•	6.0	•
Current Liabilities to Working Capital **39**	2.5	•	0.6	0.5	1.6	2.5	22.4	4.8	5.7	•	•	5.0	•
Working Capital to Net Sales **40**	0.0	•	0.0	0.0	0.0	0.0	0.0	0.0	0.0	•	•	0.0	•
Inventory to Working Capital **41**	1.2	•	0.9	0.5	0.9	1.1	8.4	1.4	1.7	•	•	1.7	•
Total Receipts to Cash Flow **42**	30.5	140.9	23.5	30.9	42.6	29.1	29.5	37.8	40.3	22.2	33.3	27.2	•
Cost of Goods to Cash Flow **43**	27.4	124.3	20.7	27.6	38.9	25.8	26.4	35.0	37.3	19.3	30.6	24.4	•
Cash Flow to Total Debt **44**	0.3	•	0.6	0.2	0.2	0.4	0.3	0.3	0.2	0.3	0.3	0.3	•

Selected Financial Factors (in Percentages)

Debt Ratio **45**	71.8	•	76.0	71.1	89.6	59.1	79.9	68.0	62.9	68.0	65.0	64.4	•
Return on Total Assets **46**	6.7	•	11.3	4.1	3.6	6.0	5.8	5.8	3.1	11.8	8.5	9.0	•
Return on Equity Before Income Taxes **47**	13.9	•	34.1	3.1	•	8.8	10.5	11.9	2.6	28.6	20.8	19.8	•
Return on Equity After Income Taxes **48**	11.5	•	33.0	2.8	•	8.3	8.4	10.9	0.5	25.6	16.3	16.1	•
Profit Margin (Before Income Tax) **49**	0.7	•	0.8	0.2	•	0.6	0.3	0.5	0.2	1.9	1.2	1.6	•
Profit Margin (After Income Tax) **50**	0.5	•	0.8	0.2	•	0.5	0.2	0.5	0.0	1.7	1.0	1.3	•

Table II
Corporations with Net Income

GASOLINE STATIONS

MONEY AMOUNTS AND SIZE OF ASSETS IN THOUSANDS OF DOLLARS

Item Description for Accounting Period 7/06 Through 6/07		Total	Zero Assets	Under 500	500 to 1,000	1,000 to 5,000	5,000 to 10,000	10,000 to 25,000	25,000 to 50,000	50,000 to 100,000	100,000 to 250,000	250,000 to 500,000	500,000 to 2,500,000	2,500,000 and over
Number of Enterprises	1	23788	2718	14410	•	2375	221	93	55	19	14	4	•	0
Revenues ($ in Thousands)														
Net Sales	2	207781787	1262942	31502550	•	36091996	9876338	11007838	15721832	7509629	9093283	7637087	•	0
Interest	3	81817	198	640	•	6163	3675	2134	4227	2328	1902	4951	•	0
Rents	4	107917	0	2111	•	20569	2923	3374	5253	8473	2892	3132	•	0
Royalties	5	21497	0	0	•	0	0	0	0	0	0	1363	•	0
Other Portfolio Income	6	459450	21584	80348	•	43537	31196	29947	9495	4897	20701	13046	•	0
Other Receipts	7	1154221	16334	327802	•	163607	44917	53962	58708	30428	153754	29952	•	0
Total Receipts	8	209606689	1301058	31913451	•	36325872	9959049	11097255	15799515	7555755	9272532	7689531	•	0
Average Total Receipts	9	8811	479	2215	•	15295	45064	119325	287264	397671	662324	1922383	•	•
Operating Costs/Operating Income (%)														
Cost of Operations	10	90.2	84.7	87.3	•	92.2	90.2	89.8	93.0	91.8	88.1	91.7	•	•
Salaries and Wages	11	2.8	3.1	3.0	•	2.2	2.5	3.4	2.3	2.5	3.5	3.2	•	•
Taxes Paid	12	0.9	1.7	0.8	•	0.8	2.2	0.6	0.6	0.5	2.2	0.4	•	•
Interest Paid	13	0.4	0.6	0.2	•	0.4	0.4	0.3	0.2	0.3	0.5	0.2	•	•
Depreciation	14	0.8	0.7	0.3	•	0.5	0.5	0.6	0.5	0.7	1.1	0.6	•	•
Amortization and Depletion	15	0.1	0.3	0.2	•	0.0	0.0	0.0	0.0	0.0	0.0	0.0	•	•
Pensions and Other Deferred Comp.	16	0.0	0.0	0.0	•	0.0	0.0	0.0	0.0	0.0	0.1	0.2	•	•
Employee Benefits	17	0.2	0.0	0.1	•	0.1	0.2	0.1	0.1	0.2	0.2	0.3	•	•
Advertising	18	0.1	0.1	0.1	•	0.1	0.0	0.2	0.1	0.1	0.1	0.1	•	•
Other Expenses	19	3.8	6.1	6.2	•	3.3	3.2	4.6	2.8	3.3	3.4	2.7	•	•
Officers' Compensation	20	0.4	1.2	1.0	•	0.3	0.4	0.3	0.2	0.2	0.2	0.1	•	•
Operating Margin	21	0.6	1.5	0.9	•	0.2	0.3	•	0.2	0.5	0.6	0.5	•	•
Operating Margin Before Officers' Comp.	22	0.9	2.7	1.9	•	0.6	0.7	0.2	0.4	0.6	0.8	0.6	•	•

Selected Average Balance Sheet ($ in Thousands)

Net Receivables 23	142	0	9	•	185	563	1387	4504	6688	11640	97538
Inventories 24	160	0	55	•	184	863	2391	3680	7781	13705	29268
Net Property, Plant and Equipment 25	676	0	54	•	911	3108	7005	13972	33616	68917	98048
Total Assets 26	1412	0	205	•	1708	6833	15128	34905	68069	140059	319039
Notes and Loans Payable 27	496	0	94	•	940	2719	5576	10103	17397	44335	44598
All Other Liabilities 28	414	0	31	•	271	1478	5179	11339	19612	42648	162719
Net Worth 29	502	0	80	•	497	2636	4373	13463	31060	53077	111722

Selected Financial Ratios (Times to 1)

Current Ratio 30	1.4	•	2.6	•	2.1	1.9	1.1	1.3	1.3	0.9	1.0
Quick Ratio 31	0.8	•	1.1	•	1.2	1.2	0.6	0.6	0.8	0.5	0.7
Net Sales to Working Capital 32	55.9	•	33.1	•	46.0	34.4	181.4	82.1	67.9	•	•
Coverage Ratio 33	5.0	8.5	11.5	•	3.5	4.1	3.2	4.6	4.9	6.2	7.0
Total Asset Turnover 34	6.2	•	10.7	•	8.9	6.5	7.8	8.2	5.8	4.6	6.0
Inventory Turnover 35	49.2	•	34.5	•	76.1	46.7	44.5	72.2	46.6	41.8	59.8
Receivables Turnover 36	63.6	•	201.2	•	89.5	49.0	67.8	60.6	52.8	53.2	29.6
Total Liabilities to Net Worth 37	1.8	•	1.6	•	2.4	1.6	2.5	1.6	1.2	1.6	1.9
Current Assets to Working Capital 38	3.3	•	1.6	•	1.9	2.1	9.5	4.8	4.5	•	•
Current Liabilities to Working Capital 39	2.3	•	0.6	•	0.9	1.1	8.5	3.8	3.5	•	•
Working Capital to Net Sales 40	0.0	•	0.0	•	0.0	0.0	0.0	0.0	0.0	•	•
Inventory to Working Capital 41	1.0	•	0.9	•	0.6	0.7	3.3	1.1	1.4	•	•
Total Receipts to Cash Flow 42	26.4	11.2	18.0	•	35.8	30.4	26.6	37.8	31.0	21.1	33.3
Cost of Goods to Cash Flow 43	23.8	9.5	15.7	•	33.0	27.4	23.9	35.2	28.5	18.6	30.6
Cash Flow to Total Debt 44	0.4	•	1.0	•	0.4	0.4	0.4	0.4	0.3	0.4	0.3

Selected Financial Factors (in Percentages)

Debt Ratio 45	64.4	•	61.1	•	70.9	61.4	71.1	61.4	54.4	62.1	65.0
Return on Total Assets 46	11.1	•	25.8	•	11.1	10.1	8.7	7.3	7.8	14.1	8.5
Return on Equity Before Income Taxes 47	25.0	•	60.4	•	27.2	19.7	20.5	14.9	13.6	31.2	20.8
Return on Equity After Income Taxes 48	22.5	•	59.3	•	26.5	18.9	18.2	13.8	11.6	28.1	16.3
Profit Margin (Before Income Tax) 49	1.4	4.5	2.2	•	0.9	1.2	0.8	0.7	1.1	2.6	1.2
Profit Margin (After Income Tax) 50	1.3	4.5	2.2	•	0.9	1.1	0.7	0.7	0.9	2.3	1.0

Table I

Corporations with and without Net Income

CLOTHING AND CLOTHING ACCESSORIES STORES

MONEY AMOUNTS AND SIZE OF ASSETS IN THOUSANDS OF DOLLARS

Item Description for Accounting Period 7/06 Through 6/07	Total	Zero Assets	Under 500	500 to 1,000	1,000 to 5,000	5,000 to 10,000	10,000 to 25,000	25,000 to 50,000	50,000 to 100,000	100,000 to 250,000	250,000 to 500,000	500,000 to 2,500,000	2,500,000 and over
Number of Enterprises **1**	51364	9369	34029	4793	2490	380	129	44	36	33	21	30	9
Revenues ($ in Thousands)													
Net Sales **2**	184827125	1650571	12517493	5942027	8102253	5263866	4202088	2283733	4432165	10106792	14223121	53240466	62862551
Interest **3**	1006220	3621	3454	5186	10880	4780	14593	3991	2502	19690	75396	197047	665079
Rents **4**	173682	238	0	56	3208	312	15179	1661	23	4964	34891	22969	90180
Royalties **5**	797842	124	0	0	0	0	3489	0	6676	17149	11269	477068	282067
Other Portfolio Income **6**	501507	729	14924	1205	13441	378	823	1952	4232	16591	48406	262459	136370
Other Receipts **7**	2673548	35052	134994	25501	76743	63327	35841	33241	118331	101363	172482	808984	1067686
Total Receipts **8**	189979924	1690335	12670865	5973975	8206525	5332663	4272013	2324578	4563929	10266549	14565565	55008993	65103933
Average Total Receipts **9**	3699	180	372	1246	3296	14033	33116	52831	126776	311108	693598	1833633	7233770
Operating Costs/Operating Income (%)													
Cost of Operations **10**	53.5	48.6	52.8	56.7	59.1	59.5	55.7	61.0	49.9	52.1	51.9	53.2	53.0
Salaries and Wages **11**	13.7	11.1	8.2	13.9	12.3	10.8	14.9	12.6	15.9	15.5	16.0	13.7	14.3
Taxes Paid **12**	2.2	3.2	2.5	2.4	2.0	2.1	2.7	2.0	2.7	2.5	2.3	2.1	2.1
Interest Paid **13**	0.9	1.2	0.8	1.0	1.0	0.9	0.8	1.0	1.3	1.0	1.0	0.6	1.1
Depreciation **14**	1.8	1.5	0.7	0.9	0.7	0.8	1.0	1.1	1.8	1.4	2.1	2.2	2.0
Amortization and Depletion **15**	0.3	0.3	0.2	0.1	0.0	0.2	0.2	0.2	0.1	0.3	0.1	0.2	0.6
Pensions and Other Deferred Comp. **16**	0.3	0.1	0.1	0.1	0.5	0.2	0.1	0.1	0.1	0.2	0.2	0.2	0.5
Employee Benefits **17**	1.1	1.1	0.4	0.6	0.7	0.4	0.8	0.8	1.2	1.0	1.0	1.2	1.3
Advertising **18**	2.8	2.6	2.4	3.1	3.6	2.7	2.2	2.9	3.8	1.7	2.2	2.8	2.9
Other Expenses **19**	18.3	33.7	21.4	14.9	15.0	17.5	19.2	14.8	20.8	22.2	19.6	18.4	16.8
Officers' Compensation **20**	1.8	4.6	10.5	4.9	4.7	2.2	2.4	1.2	1.5	1.2	0.6	0.7	0.4
Operating Margin **21**	3.4	•	0.1	1.4	0.3	2.7	2.4	2.5	0.9	0.8	3.1	4.5	4.9
Operating Margin Before Officers' Comp. **22**	5.1	•	10.6	6.2	5.0	4.9	2.4	3.7	2.4	2.1	3.7	5.3	5.3

Selected Average Balance Sheet ($ in Thousands)

Net Receivables 23	109	0	3	29	89	567	1667	2805	5425	7502	10160	41925	297406
Inventories 24	646	0	75	372	1107	3008	6930	15302	27575	62098	110792	293607	1021226
Net Property, Plant and Equipment 25	512	0	13	112	234	946	3051	6141	17408	37922	120780	287484	1185759
Total Assets 26	2151	0	131	676	1823	6601	15969	34679	68573	164325	362754	1035029	5065127
Notes and Loans Payable 27	385	0	58	261	689	2295	5229	5696	15100	39142	32760	121642	758899
All Other Liabilities 28	914	0	39	164	473	2237	6604	12269	28240	59345	156398	358519	2710793
Net Worth 29	852	0	34	251	661	2068	4135	16714	25234	65838	173596	554868	1595435

Selected Financial Ratios (Times to 1)

Current Ratio 30	1.8	•	2.3	2.6	2.1	1.5	1.4	1.7	1.5	1.5	1.9	1.9	1.6
Quick Ratio 31	0.5	•	0.5	0.6	0.4	0.3	0.4	0.4	0.4	0.3	0.5	0.7	0.6
Net Sales to Working Capital 32	7.2	•	6.2	3.9	4.3	8.3	9.7	5.5	8.0	10.2	7.1	6.8	8.4
Coverage Ratio 33	7.9	•	2.6	3.0	2.5	5.3	3.0	5.4	4.1	3.3	6.1	13.4	9.3
Total Asset Turnover 34	1.7	•	2.8	1.8	1.8	2.1	2.0	1.5	1.8	1.9	1.9	1.7	1.4
Inventory Turnover 35	3.0	•	2.6	1.9	1.7	2.7	2.6	2.1	2.2	2.6	3.2	3.2	3.6
Receivables Turnover 36	34.4	•	133.1	42.1	35.7	31.3	19.8	14.5	23.6	38.6	57.7	41.1	26.4
Total Liabilities to Net Worth 37	1.5	•	2.9	1.7	1.8	2.2	2.9	1.1	1.7	1.5	1.1	0.9	2.2
Current Assets to Working Capital 38	2.3	•	1.8	1.6	1.9	3.1	3.5	2.4	2.9	3.2	2.1	2.1	2.6
Current Liabilities to Working Capital 39	1.3	•	0.8	0.6	0.9	2.1	2.5	1.4	1.9	2.2	1.1	1.1	1.6
Working Capital to Net Sales 40	0.1	•	0.2	0.3	0.2	0.1	0.1	0.2	0.1	0.1	0.1	0.1	0.1
Inventory to Working Capital 41	1.3	•	1.3	1.2	1.4	2.2	2.1	1.6	1.8	2.1	1.3	1.1	1.4
Total Receipts to Cash Flow 42	6.3	7.4	7.5	9.1	9.4	7.1	8.2	7.7	6.7	7.1	7.3	5.9	5.6
Cost of Goods to Cash Flow 43	3.4	3.6	4.0	5.1	5.6	4.2	4.6	4.7	3.4	3.7	3.8	3.2	3.0
Cash Flow to Total Debt 44	0.4	•	0.5	0.3	0.3	0.4	0.3	0.4	0.4	0.5	0.5	0.6	0.4

Selected Financial Factors (in Percentages)

Debt Ratio 45	60.4	•	74.5	62.8	63.7	68.7	74.1	51.8	63.2	59.9	52.1	46.4	68.5
Return on Total Assets 46	12.0	•	5.8	5.3	4.7	10.3	5.0	7.8	9.3	6.3	11.9	14.6	13.7
Return on Equity Before Income Taxes 47	26.5	•	14.0	9.5	7.9	26.6	12.9	13.2	19.0	11.0	20.9	25.2	38.7
Return on Equity After Income Taxes 48	18.1	•	13.1	8.8	6.5	25.4	9.7	11.6	14.8	8.2	13.5	16.5	26.1
Profit Margin (Before Income Tax) 49	6.3	•	1.3	1.9	1.6	4.0	1.6	4.3	3.9	2.4	5.3	7.9	8.9
Profit Margin (After Income Tax) 50	4.3	•	1.2	1.8	1.3	3.8	1.2	3.7	3.0	1.8	3.5	5.2	6.0

Table II

Corporations with Net Income

CLOTHING AND CLOTHING ACCESSORIES STORES

MONEY AMOUNTS AND SIZE OF ASSETS IN THOUSANDS OF DOLLARS

Item Description for Accounting Period 7/06 Through 6/07		Total	Zero Assets	Under 500	500 to 1,000	1,000 to 5,000	5,000 to 10,000	10,000 to 25,000	25,000 to 50,000	50,000 to 100,000	100,000 to 250,000	250,000 to 500,000	500,000 to 2,500,000	2,500,000 and over
Number of Enterprises	1	28371	4200	18008	•	2011	322	94	35	30	23	17	•	9
Revenues ($ in Thousands)														
Net Sales	2	169277751	732105	7975156	•	6604037	4557662	3450071	1926094	3958850	7222489	13019614	•	62862551
Interest	3	971360	279	2511		7884	1464	14172	2016	1628	13107	61755	•	665079
Rents	4	151510	30	0		3030	15	15166	1589	0	4964	15356	•	90180
Royalties	5	782425	0	0		0	0	1167	0	6676	15537	11269	•	282067
Other Portfolio Income	6	495462	452	14685		13220	377	791	929	4227	15284	48114	•	136370
Other Receipts	7	2313452	14061	27697		63432	48165	28402	31983	95075	32570	82593	•	1067686
Total Receipts	8	173991960	746927	8020049		6691603	4607683	3509769	1962611	4066456	7303951	13238701	•	65103933
Average Total Receipts	9	6133	178	445		3328	14310	37338	56075	135549	317563	778747	•	7233770
Operating Costs/Operating Income (%)														
Cost of Operations	10	53.5	46.9	53.5	•	59.4	58.8	55.4	61.9	49.6	50.9	51.2	•	53.0
Salaries and Wages	11	13.7	8.6	8.8		11.5	10.1	14.3	11.2	15.6	14.8	15.6	•	14.3
Taxes Paid	12	2.2	2.4	2.3		2.1	2.0	2.7	2.1	2.6	2.4	2.3	•	2.1
Interest Paid	13	0.8	1.2	0.5		0.8	0.8	0.6	0.8	1.2	0.7	0.9	•	1.1
Depreciation	14	1.8	0.7	0.7		0.7	0.7	0.9	0.9	1.5	1.4	2.0	•	2.0
Amortization and Depletion	15	0.3	0.0	0.1		0.0	0.2	0.1	0.2	0.1	0.2	0.1	•	0.6
Pensions and Other Deferred Comp.	16	0.3	0.1	0.1		0.5	0.2	0.2	0.1	0.1	0.1	0.2	•	0.5
Employee Benefits	17	1.1	0.5	0.3		0.6	0.4	0.7	0.6	1.2	0.8	0.9	•	1.3
Advertising	18	2.8	2.3	2.6		3.8	2.9	2.0	2.4	3.4	1.5	2.2	•	2.9
Other Expenses	19	17.5	29.3	19.8		13.1	16.6	17.3	13.7	20.5	22.0	18.6	•	16.8
Officers' Compensation	20	1.3	2.7	5.5		5.1	2.2	2.4	1.2	1.5	1.3	0.6	•	0.4
Operating Margin	21	4.8	5.4	5.7		2.4	5.0	3.5	4.9	2.7	4.0	5.3	•	4.9
Operating Margin Before Officers' Comp.	22	6.0	8.1	11.1		7.5	7.2	5.9	6.1	4.2	5.4	5.9	•	5.3

Selected Average Balance Sheet ($ in Thousands)

Item														
Net Receivables 23	297406	•	7870	6329	5560	3181	1787	574	91	•	4	0	•	182
Inventories 24	1021226	•	105154	61564	29135	15332	7067	3750	1120	•	82	0	•	1028
Net Property, Plant and Equipment 25	1185759	•	127221	40471	16717	5124	3389	814	240	•	14	0	•	868
Total Assets 26	5065127	•	369020	165328	69174	35673	16394	6524	1801	•	152	0	•	3588
Notes and Loans Payable 27	758899	•	28192	28847	13467	5054	5180	1995	576	•	51	0	•	566
All Other Liabilities 28	2710793	•	152288	56197	28300	12696	5986	1947	474	•	40	0	•	1534
Net Worth 29	1595435	•	188540	80284	27406	17923	5228	2582	750	•	62	0	•	1488

Selected Financial Ratios (Times to 1)

Item														
Current Ratio 30	1.6	•	1.9	1.5	1.7	1.7	1.5	1.7	2.2	•	2.7	•	•	1.8
Quick Ratio 31	0.6	•	0.5	0.4	0.4	0.4	0.4	0.3	0.4	•	0.7	•	•	0.6
Net Sales to Working Capital 32	8.4	•	7.8	9.4	7.2	5.5	9.9	6.8	4.2	•	5.6	•	•	7.0
Coverage Ratio 33	9.3	•	8.7	8.4	5.5	9.4	9.0	8.6	5.4	7.2	12.3	•	•	10.1
Total Asset Turnover 34	1.4	•	2.1	1.9	1.9	1.5	2.2	2.2	1.8	•	2.9	•	•	1.7
Inventory Turnover 35	3.6	•	3.7	2.6	2.2	2.2	2.9	2.2	1.7	•	2.9	•	•	3.1
Receivables Turnover 36	26.4	•	68.8	38.2	27.8	17.0	19.3	•	34.2	•	115.5	•	•	34.1
Total Liabilities to Net Worth 37	2.2	•	1.0	1.1	1.5	1.0	2.1	1.5	1.4	•	1.5	•	•	1.4
Current Assets to Working Capital 38	2.6	•	2.1	2.9	2.5	2.4	3.1	2.5	1.9	•	1.6	•	•	2.2
Current Liabilities to Working Capital 39	1.6	•	1.1	1.9	1.5	1.4	2.1	1.5	0.9	•	0.6	•	•	1.2
Working Capital to Net Sales 40	0.1	•	0.1	0.1	0.1	0.2	0.1	0.1	0.2	•	0.2	•	•	0.1
Inventory to Working Capital 41	1.4	•	1.2	1.8	1.6	1.5	1.9	1.8	1.4	•	1.1	•	•	1.3
Total Receipts to Cash Flow 42	5.6	•	7.0	5.8	5.9	6.6	6.6	6.2	8.5	4.5	5.9	•	•	6.0
Cost of Goods to Cash Flow 43	3.0	•	3.6	3.0	2.9	4.1	3.6	3.7	5.1	2.1	3.2	•	•	3.2
Cash Flow to Total Debt 44	0.4	•	0.6	0.6	0.5	0.5	0.5	0.6	0.4	•	0.8	•	•	0.5

Selected Financial Factors (in Percentages)

Item														
Debt Ratio 45	68.5	•	48.9	51.4	60.4	49.8	68.1	58.3	60.4	•	59.4	•	•	58.5
Return on Total Assets 46	13.7	•	16.2	10.9	12.6	11.6	13.0	8.4	14.9	•	19.8	•	•	14.2
Return on Equity Before Income Taxes 47	38.7	•	28.0	19.7	26.0	20.7	36.4	16.5	33.3	•	44.8	•	•	30.8
Return on Equity After Income Taxes 48	26.1	•	19.7	16.5	21.3	18.8	32.9	15.0	32.1	•	43.9	•	•	22.0
Profit Margin (Before Income Tax) 49	8.9	•	6.9	5.0	5.4	6.7	6.1	3.8	6.1	7.4	6.2	•	•	7.7
Profit Margin (After Income Tax) 50	6.0	•	4.8	4.2	4.4	6.1	5.9	3.4	4.7	6.6	6.1	•	•	5.5

Table I
Corporations with and without Net Income

SPORTING GOODS, HOBBY, BOOK, AND MUSIC STORES

MONEY AMOUNTS AND SIZE OF ASSETS IN THOUSANDS OF DOLLARS

Item Description for Accounting Period 7/06 Through 6/07	Total	Zero Assets	Under 500	500 to 1,000	1,000 to 5,000	5,000 to 10,000	10,000 to 25,000	25,000 to 50,000	50,000 to 100,000	100,000 to 250,000	250,000 to 500,000	500,000 to 2,500,000	2,500,000 and over
Number of Enterprises 1	31776	4009	22616	2924	1898	180	77	15	11	19	9	19	0
Revenues ($ in Thousands)													
Net Sales 2	89726480	1586572	13673918	4304335	8260935	2338377	2353396	706452	1503822	5241011	5792127	43965534	0
Interest 3	117171	2699	8649	2067	10867	7036	3413	2105	3992	17048	5920	53376	0
Rents 4	72467	597	655	509	1901	134	0	3495	240	1359	348	63226	0
Royalties 5	253133	1014	0	0	87	0	0	0	0	23191	16680	212162	0
Other Portfolio Income 6	441895	125	11066	36	2228	319	3616	493	0	25995	4723	393295	0
Other Receipts 7	1432654	98336	76636	36565	49164	77211	23160	21861	11179	45679	38991	953874	0
Total Receipts 8	92043800	1689343	13770924	4343512	8325182	2423077	2383585	734406	1519233	5354283	5858789	45641467	0
Average Total Receipts 9	2897	421	609	1485	4386	13462	30956	48960	138112	281804	650977	2402182	•
Operating Costs/Operating Income (%)													
Cost of Operations 10	62.3	65.0	64.0	60.3	65.3	63.3	65.1	64.0	57.2	61.9	61.7	61.4	•
Salaries and Wages 11	12.2	13.4	10.2	13.2	10.6	14.8	12.5	8.5	15.1	13.2	11.9	12.7	•
Taxes Paid 12	2.1	1.8	1.9	2.1	1.9	1.4	1.5	1.4	2.5	2.2	1.8	2.2	•
Interest Paid 13	1.6	1.0	0.7	0.8	1.0	0.8	0.8	1.1	1.5	1.3	1.3	2.2	•
Depreciation 14	1.5	1.4	0.7	0.9	0.8	0.8	0.6	1.1	1.4	1.3	1.6	2.0	•
Amortization and Depletion 15	0.2	0.1	0.1	0.1	0.1	0.1	0.2	0.8	0.3	0.3	0.3	0.2	•
Pensions and Other Deferred Comp. 16	0.2	0.1	0.1	0.1	0.4	0.0	0.1	0.2	0.2	0.1	0.1	0.3	•
Employee Benefits 17	0.6	0.8	0.6	0.5	0.4	0.3	0.7	0.6	0.8	0.7	0.9	0.7	•
Advertising 18	2.3	2.9	1.1	2.2	2.1	2.7	2.6	6.6	3.2	3.3	3.0	2.4	•
Other Expenses 19	15.3	21.4	14.6	16.3	13.2	13.7	17.2	15.7	16.6	14.1	15.5	15.6	•
Officers' Compensation 20	2.0	1.9	6.0	2.9	3.3	1.5	2.8	1.4	0.9	0.8	0.4	0.8	•
Operating Margin 21	•	•	0.1	0.5	1.0	0.6	•	•	0.2	0.8	1.3	•	•
Operating Margin Before Officers' Comp. 22	1.8	•	6.1	3.5	4.3	2.1	•	0.0	1.1	1.6	1.6	0.5	•

Selected Average Balance Sheet ($ in Thousands)

Net Receivables 23	94	0	3	32	157	643	1947	3260	4888	19608	35830	77293	•
Inventories 24	643	0	76	390	1036	3042	6537	16076	36928	58658	196471	475196	•
Net Property, Plant and Equipment 25	377	0	27	86	271	683	1662	4274	10723	33538	75701	466036	•
Total Assets 26	1559	0	137	677	2021	7498	14005	34174	70322	171256	354876	1603330	•
Notes and Loans Payable 27	663	0	88	222	767	1651	3008	8496	17892	58814	121523	732826	•
All Other Liabilities 28	589	0	41	186	489	1923	7428	9609	30359	58146	124950	667733	•
Net Worth 29	307	0	8	269	765	3924	3569	16070	22071	54296	108402	202771	•

Selected Financial Ratios (Times to 1)

Current Ratio 30	1.5	•	1.8	2.9	2.3	1.8	1.4	1.7	1.4	1.5	1.6	1.3	•
Quick Ratio 31	0.3	•	0.4	0.6	0.7	0.6	0.4	0.5	0.2	0.4	0.5	0.3	•
Net Sales to Working Capital 32	8.8	•	13.5	4.3	5.0	6.5	10.7	5.0	10.5	7.1	7.7	10.7	•
Coverage Ratio 33	2.6	•	2.1	2.8	2.8	6.1	•	3.2	1.8	2.8	3.2	2.8	•
Total Asset Turnover 34	1.8	•	4.4	2.2	2.2	1.7	2.2	1.4	1.9	1.6	1.8	1.4	•
Inventory Turnover 35	2.7	•	5.1	2.3	2.7	2.7	3.0	1.9	2.1	2.9	2.0	3.0	•
Receivables Turnover 36	28.5	•	157.3	30.8	32.3	17.6	16.0	10.5	16.5	16.1	9.2	43.3	•
Total Liabilities to Net Worth 37	4.1	•	15.9	1.5	1.6	0.9	2.9	1.1	2.2	2.2	2.3	6.9	•
Current Assets to Working Capital 38	2.9	•	2.2	1.5	1.8	2.2	3.7	2.3	3.6	3.1	2.7	3.9	•
Current Liabilities to Working Capital 39	1.9	•	1.2	0.5	0.8	1.2	2.7	1.3	2.6	2.1	1.7	2.9	•
Working Capital to Net Sales 40	0.1	•	0.1	0.2	0.2	0.2	0.1	0.2	0.1	0.1	0.1	0.1	•
Inventory to Working Capital 41	2.0	•	1.7	1.2	1.2	1.2	2.3	1.2	2.4	2.0	2.0	2.7	•
Total Receipts to Cash Flow 42	9.1	7.9	10.3	8.0	10.5	9.1	23.5	7.0	9.6	9.9	8.7	8.5	•
Cost of Goods to Cash Flow 43	5.7	5.1	6.6	4.8	6.8	5.8	15.3	4.5	5.5	6.1	5.4	5.2	•
Cash Flow to Total Debt 44	0.2	•	0.5	0.4	0.3	0.4	0.1	0.4	0.3	0.2	0.3	0.2	•

Selected Financial Factors (in Percentages)

Debt Ratio 45	80.3	•	94.1	60.3	62.2	47.7	74.5	53.0	68.6	68.3	69.5	87.4	•
Return on Total Assets 46	7.4	•	6.5	4.9	5.9	8.7	•	5.1	5.3	6.8	6.7	8.6	•
Return on Equity Before Income Taxes 47	23.5	•	57.3	8.0	10.0	13.9	•	7.4	7.7	14.8	14.2	43.4	•
Return on Equity After Income Taxes 48	17.3	•	55.6	7.5	9.2	12.6	•	5.2	4.0	10.6	9.3	32.0	•
Profit Margin (Before Income Tax) 49	2.6	•	0.8	1.5	1.7	4.2	•	2.5	1.2	2.9	2.4	3.8	•
Profit Margin (After Income Tax) 50	1.9	•	0.7	1.4	1.6	3.8	•	1.8	0.6	2.1	1.6	2.8	•

Table II
Corporations with Net Income

SPORTING GOODS, HOBBY, BOOK, AND MUSIC STORES

MONEY AMOUNTS AND SIZE OF ASSETS IN THOUSANDS OF DOLLARS

Item Description for Accounting Period 7/06 Through 6/07	Total	Zero Assets	Under 500	500 to 1,000	1,000 to 5,000	5,000 to 10,000	10,000 to 25,000	25,000 to 50,000	50,000 to 100,000	100,000 to 250,000	250,000 to 500,000	500,000 to 2,500,000	2,500,000 and over
Number of Enterprises **1**	16584	1771	11862	1273	1427	141	57	11	8	13	6	15	0
Revenues ($ in Thousands)													
Net Sales **2**	74484592	1106197	10525533	2390675	6342394	1940615	1860079	606733	1164700	4180030	3801077	40566560	0
Interest **3**	92987	2240	1936	1286	7336	4465	1343	1524	1012	16193	2937	52717	0
Rents **4**	69961	105	0	509	1901	0	0	3419	240	1359	348	62078	0
Royalties **5**	249208	1014	0	0	0	0	0	0	0	23191	14656	210348	0
Other Portfolio Income **6**	432612	0	7816	0	2179	319	3599	493	0	24657	1221	392327	0
Other Receipts **7**	1216545	61729	58118	4907	21473	52125	3881	21160	10144	25435	37294	920279	0
Total Receipts **8**	76545905	1171285	10593403	2397377	6375283	1997524	1868902	633329	1176096	4270865	3857533	42204309	0
Average Total Receipts **9**	4616	661	893	1883	4468	14167	32788	57575	147012	328528	642922	2813621	•
Operating Costs/Operating Income (%)													
Cost of Operations **10**	62.4	58.1	65.5	60.8	64.4	63.1	65.0	65.3	57.9	63.0	60.1	61.6	•
Salaries and Wages **11**	12.0	10.7	10.1	12.3	10.2	13.8	11.8	9.2	15.1	12.4	12.4	12.6	•
Taxes Paid **12**	2.0	1.7	1.6	1.9	2.1	1.2	1.6	1.5	2.6	2.0	2.1	2.2	•
Interest Paid **13**	1.5	1.1	0.6	0.3	0.7	0.7	0.6	0.5	1.4	1.3	0.4	2.2	•
Depreciation **14**	1.5	1.4	0.5	0.7	0.8	0.5	0.5	1.1	1.1	1.3	1.8	1.9	•
Amortization and Depletion **15**	0.2	0.0	0.1	0.0	0.1	0.1	0.1	0.7	0.1	0.2	0.5	0.1	•
Pensions and Other Deferred Comp. **16**	0.2	0.2	0.0	0.2	0.5	0.0	0.1	0.2	0.2	0.1	0.2	0.3	•
Employee Benefits **17**	0.6	0.7	0.4	0.5	0.4	0.3	0.7	0.7	0.8	0.6	1.1	0.7	•
Advertising **18**	2.2	1.5	0.6	2.0	1.9	2.9	2.2	6.9	2.4	3.0	3.8	2.3	•
Other Expenses **19**	14.0	18.5	11.7	12.1	11.4	11.0	12.3	13.3	15.2	12.9	13.7	15.3	•
Officers' Compensation **20**	2.0	1.9	6.4	3.7	3.7	1.4	2.0	1.6	0.9	0.8	0.4	0.8	•
Operating Margin **21**	1.4	4.0	2.5	5.6	3.9	4.9	3.0	•	2.3	2.6	3.5	•	•
Operating Margin Before Officers' Comp. **22**	3.4	5.9	8.9	9.3	7.6	6.3	5.0	0.6	3.2	3.4	4.0	0.7	•

Selected Average Balance Sheet ($ in Thousands)

Net Receivables 23	149	0	3	28	172	704	1979	1511	5962	21518	31942	93771	•
Inventories 24	933	0	85	558	884	2398	7320	16669	38346	74028	187511	633024	•
Net Property, Plant and Equipment 25	602	0	35	84	287	589	1496	5090	10953	33054	75158	524302	•
Total Assets 26	2391	0	159	758	1975	7709	13880	33445	71655	159882	339169	1803138	•
Notes and Loans Payable 27	1000	0	69	120	577	1362	2694	3437	17487	61241	46314	879626	•
All Other Liabilities 28	905	0	43	226	455	1549	5929	8664	30577	47921	118808	754698	•
Net Worth 29	485	0	46	413	944	4799	5257	21344	23591	50720	174047	168815	•

Selected Financial Ratios (Times to 1)

Current Ratio 30	1.5	•	1.9	2.8	2.9	2.3	1.5	2.4	1.3	1.5	1.9	1.3	•
Quick Ratio 31	0.4	•	0.4	0.6	1.0	0.9	0.4	0.7	0.2	0.5	0.5	0.3	•
Net Sales to Working Capital 32	9.4	•	17.1	4.4	4.6	5.7	9.5	4.3	12.5	8.2	5.7	11.9	•
Coverage Ratio 33	3.8	10.0	6.4	20.7	7.5	12.4	6.7	7.4	3.4	4.8	14.1	2.9	•
Total Asset Turnover 34	1.9	•	5.6	2.5	2.2	1.8	2.4	1.6	2.0	2.0	1.9	1.5	•
Inventory Turnover 35	3.0	•	6.8	2.0	3.2	3.6	2.9	2.2	2.2	2.7	2.0	2.6	•
Receivables Turnover 36	29.5	•	193.5	29.2	33.1	19.4	19.1	13.1	14.6	•	7.7	•	•
Total Liabilities to Net Worth 37	3.9	•	2.5	0.8	1.1	0.6	1.6	0.6	2.0	2.2	0.9	9.7	•
Current Assets to Working Capital 38	2.9	•	2.1	1.6	1.5	1.8	3.1	1.7	4.1	3.0	2.1	4.1	•
Current Liabilities to Working Capital 39	1.9	•	1.1	0.6	0.5	0.8	2.1	0.7	3.1	2.0	1.1	3.1	•
Working Capital to Net Sales 40	0.1	•	0.1	0.2	0.2	0.2	0.1	0.2	0.1	0.1	0.2	0.1	•
Inventory to Working Capital 41	2.0	•	1.6	1.2	1.0	1.0	2.1	0.9	3.3	1.9	1.4	2.8	•
Total Receipts to Cash Flow 42	8.4	3.8	9.7	7.2	8.6	7.4	10.6	8.1	8.7	9.2	8.3	8.3	•
Cost of Goods to Cash Flow 43	5.2	2.2	6.3	4.4	5.5	4.7	6.9	5.3	5.8	5.0	5.0	5.1	•
Cash Flow to Total Debt 44	0.3	•	0.8	0.8	0.5	0.6	0.4	0.6	0.3	0.3	0.5	0.2	•

Selected Financial Factors (in Percentages)

Debt Ratio 45	79.7	•	71.2	45.5	52.2	37.8	62.1	36.2	67.1	68.3	48.7	90.6	•
Return on Total Assets 46	11.0	•	20.6	15.3	11.5	15.2	9.7	6.4	9.4	12.1	10.0	9.6	•
Return on Equity Before Income Taxes 47	40.1	•	60.5	26.8	20.9	22.4	21.7	8.6	20.1	30.2	18.2	67.2	•
Return on Equity After Income Taxes 48	32.6	•	59.9	26.0	20.0	21.1	21.0	6.4	15.3	23.6	13.6	50.0	•
Profit Margin (Before Income Tax) 49	4.3	9.9	3.1	5.9	4.4	7.8	3.5	3.3	3.3	4.8	5.0	4.2	•
Profit Margin (After Income Tax) 50	3.5	7.0	3.1	5.7	4.3	7.4	3.4	2.5	3.7	3.7	5.0	3.1	•

Table I

Corporations with and without Net Income

GENERAL MERCHANDISE STORES

MONEY AMOUNTS AND SIZE OF ASSETS IN THOUSANDS OF DOLLARS

Item Description for Accounting Period 7/06 Through 6/07	Total	Zero Assets	Under 500	500 to 1,000	1,000 to 5,000	5,000 to 10,000	10,000 to 25,000	25,000 to 50,000	50,000 to 100,000	100,000 to 250,000	250,000 to 500,000	500,000 to 2,500,000	2,500,000 and over
Number of Enterprises **1**	10993	1562	8244	694	377	28	36	11	10	5	5	8	13
Revenues ($ in Thousands)													
Net Sales **2**	585338007	16411094	4016081	981631	2205305	762572	1294020	765846	1294175	1702726	3000236	26048139	526906182
Interest **3**	3738849	108503	3117	1395	1802	588	1295	84	18979	32	12049	119690	3471315
Rents **4**	930386	232	0	0	1817	122	0	9	10936	2270	1383	17522	896095
Royalties **5**	2782754	0	0	0	122	0	0	0	0	0	0	119100	2663532
Other Portfolio Income **6**	3532881	345585	8	1269	7944	347	6975	446	133	5032	309	66116	3098719
Other Receipts **7**	17750078	48766	61402	17714	24950	714	41287	6511	16349	32376	35845	432125	17032038
Total Receipts **8**	614122955	16914180	4080608	1002009	2241940	764343	1343577	772896	1340572	1742436	3049822	26802692	554067881
Average Total Receipts **9**	55865	10829	495	1444	5947	27298	37322	70263	134057	348487	609964	3350336	42620606
Operating Costs/Operating Income (%)													
Cost of Operations **10**	73.4	62.1	70.7	71.7	61.5	60.5	71.5	73.9	67.2	62.4	64.8	72.7	74.0
Salaries and Wages **11**	11.0	12.9	6.3	9.2	13.3	15.2	10.9	11.4	13.0	13.4	13.8	10.0	10.9
Taxes Paid **12**	1.8	3.0	1.5	1.5	2.2	2.6	1.5	1.4	1.6	2.0	1.8	1.6	1.8
Interest Paid **13**	1.3	1.3	0.6	1.1	0.6	0.0	1.1	0.9	0.4	0.7	0.7	1.3	1.3
Depreciation **14**	1.5	2.9	0.6	0.3	0.7	0.5	0.5	0.8	1.0	1.5	1.6	1.4	1.5
Amortization and Depletion **15**	0.0	0.1	0.0	0.2	0.0	0.0	0.0	0.1	0.0	0.1	0.1	0.1	0.0
Pensions and Other Deferred Comp. **16**	0.4	•	0.1	•	1.4	0.3	0.1	0.1	0.2	0.2	0.2	0.2	0.5
Employee Benefits **17**	0.7	0.0	0.1	0.4	0.9	1.2	0.6	0.8	1.0	0.7	2.1	1.1	0.7
Advertising **18**	1.5	1.7	0.3	1.4	1.5	1.6	1.8	1.3	2.3	2.0	2.1	1.8	1.8
Other Expenses **19**	7.5	9.9	15.2	9.7	13.1	13.9	8.7	9.4	14.8	14.3	8.5	9.9	7.2
Officers' Compensation **20**	0.1	0.3	3.4	2.3	3.4	1.1	1.7	0.5	0.4	2.2	0.7	0.4	0.1
Operating Margin **21**	0.6	5.7	1.3	2.2	1.5	3.0	1.5	•	•	0.5	3.8	•	0.5
Operating Margin Before Officers' Comp. **22**	0.7	6.0	4.7	4.5	4.8	4.1	3.2	•	•	2.7	4.5	•	0.5

Selected Average Balance Sheet ($ in Thousands)

Net Receivables 23	993	0	4	37	110	86	1558	1220	8863	18140	55337		774634
Inventories 24	6441	0	63	217	1421	2508	6485	14969	19669	87246	154117	512194	4894781
Net Property, Plant and Equipment 25	8724	0	26	30	266	1972	2015	5380	13385	37525	87994	331028	7074335
Total Assets 26	27006	0	135	626	2010	7545	16834	36458	68010	147751	360047	1176853	21593320
Notes and Loans Payable 27	6344	0	67	264	424	160	4473	6182	9748	23198	50060	276762	5072046
All Other Liabilities 28	9549	0	21	69	511	21552	3805	12417	106952	59110	102934	445326	7556980
Net Worth 29	11112	0	47	292	1075	-14166	8555	17860	-48690	65443	207053	454765	8964294

Selected Financial Ratios (Times to 1)

Current Ratio 30	1.1	•	3.6	4.0	3.4	1.8	2.7	6.8	0.4	1.7	1.5	1.6	1.0
Quick Ratio 31	0.2	•	1.0	0.8	0.6	0.7	0.6	0.7	0.2	0.3	0.2	0.3	0.2
Net Sales to Working Capital 32	113.4	•	6.9	4.5	5.4	11.6	4.9	3.3	•	9.2	10.9	12.3	370.9
Coverage Ratio 33	5.5	7.6	6.2	5.0	6.5	89.4	6.0	1.3	5.0	5.0	9.2	2.9	5.5
Total Asset Turnover 34	2.0	•	3.6	2.3	2.9	3.6	2.1	1.9	1.9	2.3	1.7	2.8	1.9
Inventory Turnover 35	6.1	•	5.4	4.7	2.5	6.6	4.0	3.4	4.4	2.4	2.5	4.6	6.1
Receivables Turnover 36	37.1	•	116.1	42.8	61.6	131.8	26.7	16.5	16.4	21.3	28.2	52.8	35.6
Total Liabilities to Net Worth 37	1.4	•	1.9	1.1	0.9	•	1.0	1.0	•	1.3	0.7	1.6	1.4
Current Assets to Working Capital 38	20.4	•	1.4	1.3	1.4	2.3	1.6	1.2	•	2.5	2.9	2.6	67.4
Current Liabilities to Working Capital 39	19.4	•	0.4	0.3	0.4	1.3	0.6	0.2	•	1.5	1.9	1.6	66.4
Working Capital to Net Sales 40	0.0	•	0.1	0.2	0.2	0.1	0.2	0.3	•	0.1	0.1	0.1	0.0
Inventory to Working Capital 41	13.5	•	0.9	0.8	1.1	1.2	1.2	0.6	•	1.9	2.3	1.9	44.3
Total Receipts to Cash Flow 42	10.0	9.7	9.5	10.1	9.4	9.6	9.6	16.5	9.5	8.3	9.3	12.7	10.0
Cost of Goods to Cash Flow 43	7.4	6.0	6.7	7.3	5.8	5.8	6.9	12.2	6.4	5.2	6.0	9.3	7.4
Cash Flow to Total Debt 44	0.3	•	0.6	0.4	0.7	0.1	0.5	0.2	0.1	0.5	0.4	0.4	0.3

Selected Financial Factors (in Percentages)

Debt Ratio 45	58.9	•	65.0	53.3	46.5	287.7	49.2	51.0	171.6	55.7	42.5	61.4	58.5
Return on Total Assets 46	13.7	•	12.4	12.0	10.7	11.9	13.8	2.1	3.9	8.3	10.1	10.2	13.4
Return on Equity Before Income Taxes 47	27.3	•	29.8	20.6	16.9	•	22.6	0.9	•	15.0	15.7	17.3	26.4
Return on Equity After Income Taxes 48	18.4	•	29.7	20.6	14.4	•	22.5	0.4	•	12.3	12.7	11.3	17.3
Profit Margin (Before Income Tax) 49	5.7	8.8	2.9	4.3	3.1	3.3	5.4	0.2	1.6	2.9	5.4	2.4	5.8
Profit Margin (After Income Tax) 50	3.8	8.8	2.9	4.2	2.6	3.0	5.3	0.1	1.0	2.4	4.4	1.6	3.8

Table II

Corporations with Net Income

GENERAL MERCHANDISE STORES

MONEY AMOUNTS AND SIZE OF ASSETS IN THOUSANDS OF DOLLARS

Item Description for Accounting Period 7/06 Through 6/07	Total	Zero Assets	Under 500	500 to 1,000	1,000 to 5,000	5,000 to 10,000	10,000 to 25,000	25,000 to 50,000	50,000 to 100,000	100,000 to 250,000	250,000 to 500,000	500,000 to 2,500,000	2,500,000 and over
Number of Enterprises **1**	5880	406	4318	•	366	24	30	6	7	5	5	•	13
Revenues ($ in Thousands)													
Net Sales **2**	582231155	16366975	3442186	•	2126853	630292	1146422	640405	1032281	1702726	3000236	•	526906182
Interest **3**	3729734	108503	584	•	1783	476	0	84	15839	32	12049	•	3471315
Rents **4**	927371	228	0	•	1796	122	0	9	7945	2270	1383	•	896095
Royalties **5**	2782754	0	0	•	122	0	0	0	0	0	0	•	2663532
Other Portfolio Income **6**	3529977	345455	8	•	7835	323	4346	446	120	5032	309	•	3098719
Other Receipts **7**	17712108	48556	57554	•	24931	132	23078	1834	14106	32376	35845	•	17032038
Total Receipts **8**	610913099	16869717	3500332	•	2163320	631345	1173846	642778	1070291	1742436	3049822	•	554067881
Average Total Receipts **9**	103897	41551	811	•	5911	26306	39128	107130	152899	348487	609964	•	42620606
Operating Costs/Operating Income (%)													
Cost of Operations **10**	73.5	62.1	71.5	•	61.1	58.2	70.8	75.5	66.1	62.4	64.8	•	74.0
Salaries and Wages **11**	11.0	12.9	5.9	•	13.3	16.6	9.4	10.9	13.5	13.4	13.8	•	10.9
Taxes Paid **12**	1.8	3.0	1.3	•	2.2	2.6	1.3	1.4	1.7	2.0	1.8	•	1.8
Interest Paid **13**	1.3	1.3	0.4	•	0.6	0.0	0.9	0.6	0.5	0.7	0.7	•	1.3
Depreciation **14**	1.5	2.9	0.6	•	0.7	0.5	0.4	0.7	0.9	1.5	1.6	•	1.5
Amortization and Depletion **15**	0.0	0.1	0.0	•	0.0	0.0	0.0	0.2	0.0	0.1	0.1	•	0.0
Pensions and Other Deferred Comp. **16**	0.4	•	•	•	1.4	0.0	0.1	0.1	0.2	0.2	0.2	•	0.5
Employee Benefits **17**	0.7	0.0	0.1	•	0.8	1.0	0.5	0.7	1.1	0.7	2.1	•	0.7
Advertising **18**	1.5	1.7	0.3	•	1.5	1.7	1.5	1.2	2.1	2.0	2.1	•	1.5
Other Expenses **19**	7.5	9.8	12.7	•	13.3	14.0	7.1	6.2	13.1	14.3	8.5	•	7.2
Officers' Compensation **20**	0.1	0.1	2.9	•	3.4	1.2	1.8	0.6	0.5	2.2	0.7	•	0.1
Operating Margin **21**	0.7	6.0	4.3	•	1.6	4.0	6.3	2.0	0.2	0.5	3.8	•	0.5
Operating Margin Before Officers' Comp. **22**	0.8	6.1	7.2	•	4.9	5.1	8.0	2.6	0.7	2.7	4.5	•	0.5

Selected Average Balance Sheet ($ in Thousands)

Item													
Net Receivables 23	1830	0	3	•	94	100	1758	2193	12233	10669	18140	•	774634
Inventories 24	11849	0	78	•	1331	2660	6779	20834	25415	63417	154117	•	4837570
Net Property, Plant and Equipment 25	16252	0	36	•	265	1877	1114	5878	13477	37525	87994	•	7074335
Total Assets 26	50205	0	180	•	1998	7100	16756	34138	69535	147751	360047	•	21593320
Notes and Loans Payable 27	11719	0	68	•	422	166	3623	7790	11777	23198	50060	•	5072046
All Other Liabilities 28	17499	0	33	•	506	3583	3930	5848	10018	59110	102934	•	7556980
Net Worth 29	20987	0	79	•	1069	3351	9203	20501	47739	65443	207053	•	8964294

Selected Financial Ratios (Times to 1)

Item													
Current Ratio 30	1.1	•	3.3	•	3.5	1.6	2.6	4.3	4.2	1.7	1.5	•	1.0
Quick Ratio 31	0.2	•	0.9	•	0.6	0.7	0.6	0.8	1.4	0.3	0.2	•	0.2
Net Sales to Working Capital 32	106.7	•	8.7	•	5.4	13.8	5.2	5.2	3.9	9.2	10.9	•	370.9
Coverage Ratio 33	5.5	7.8	15.4	•	6.7	100.3	11.0	5.2	8.8	5.0	9.2	•	5.5
Total Asset Turnover 34	2.0	•	4.4	•	2.9	3.7	2.3	3.1	2.1	2.3	1.7	•	1.9
Inventory Turnover 35	6.1	•	7.3	•	2.7	5.7	4.0	3.9	3.8	3.4	2.5	•	6.2
Receivables Turnover 36	42.0	•	212.3	•	70.5	•	26.9	17.9	•	30.2	28.2	•	•
Total Liabilities to Net Worth 37	1.4	•	1.3	•	0.9	1.1	0.8	0.7	0.5	1.3	0.7	•	1.4
Current Assets to Working Capital 38	19.1	•	1.4	•	1.4	2.6	1.6	1.3	1.3	2.5	2.9	•	67.4
Current Liabilities to Working Capital 39	18.1	•	0.4	•	0.4	1.6	0.6	0.3	0.3	1.5	1.9	•	66.4
Working Capital to Net Sales 40	0.0	•	0.1	•	0.2	0.1	0.2	0.2	0.3	0.1	0.1	•	0.0
Inventory to Working Capital 41	12.7	•	0.9	•	1.1	1.4	1.2	1.0	0.7	1.9	2.3	•	44.3
Total Receipts to Cash Flow 42	10.0	9.4	7.9	•	9.2	8.4	7.9	17.3	8.8	8.3	9.3	•	10.0
Cost of Goods to Cash Flow 43	7.4	5.9	5.7	•	5.6	4.9	5.6	13.1	5.8	5.2	6.0	•	7.4
Cash Flow to Total Debt 44	0.3	•	1.0	•	0.7	0.8	0.6	0.5	0.8	0.5	0.4	•	0.3

Selected Financial Factors (in Percentages)

Item													
Debt Ratio 45	58.2	•	56.4	•	46.5	52.8	45.1	39.9	31.3	55.7	42.5	•	58.5
Return on Total Assets 46	13.9	•	28.3	•	11.2	15.5	21.7	9.1	9.2	8.3	10.1	•	13.4
Return on Equity Before Income Taxes 47	27.2	•	60.6	•	17.8	32.6	35.9	12.2	11.9	15.0	15.7	•	26.4
Return on Equity After Income Taxes 48	18.4	•	60.5	•	15.2	30.5	35.8	11.3	9.4	12.3	12.7	•	17.3
Profit Margin (Before Income Tax) 49	5.8	9.1	6.0	•	3.3	4.2	8.6	2.3	3.8	2.9	5.4	•	5.8
Profit Margin (After Income Tax) 50	3.9	9.1	6.0	•	2.8	3.9	8.6	2.2	3.1	2.4	4.4	•	3.8

Table I

Corporations with and without Net Income

MISCELLANEOUS STORE RETAILERS

Money Amounts and Size of Assets in Thousands of Dollars

Item Description for Accounting Period 7/06 Through 6/07	Total	Zero Assets	Under 500	500 to 1,000	1,000 to 5,000	5,000 to 10,000	10,000 to 25,000	25,000 to 50,000	50,000 to 100,000	100,000 to 250,000	250,000 to 500,000	500,000 to 2,500,000	2,500,000 and over
Number of Enterprises 1	89929	16090	63035	5829	4322	322	199	72	21	21	5	9	4
Revenues ($ in Thousands)													
Net Sales 2	135725557	1565486	30073668	10508449	18475841	3844142	5360933	3897325	2459676	5291442	2198320	14863189	37187086
Interest 3	492133	231	7158	4645	39594	14046	4189	6644	4580	22631	11741	97463	279211
Rents 4	163175	0	792	3944	18349	3327	1492	957	7801	2429	565	104605	18913
Royalties 5	165104	0	0	0	111	3143	40791	37244	678	0	4983	12939	65216
Other Portfolio Income 6	472779	10664	19510	38932	42735	21945	38734	19097	13123	75304	2811	18495	171427
Other Receipts 7	1388865	34771	259167	38896	219599	46436	82384	84758	42516	94320	23438	400002	62479
Total Receipts 8	138407613	1611152	30360295	10594966	18796229	3933039	5528523	4046025	2528374	5486126	2241858	15549693	37784332
Average Total Receipts 9	1539	100	482	1818	4349	12214	27782	56195	120399	261244	448372	1721855	9446083
Operating Costs/Operating Income (%)													
Cost of Operations 10	63.7	52.6	58.1	62.6	68.8	69.2	68.6	60.7	59.8	60.0	56.6	59.7	68.2
Salaries and Wages 11	10.9	9.3	10.1	11.5	9.4	11.0	11.4	11.0	13.4	11.8	13.1	14.8	10.2
Taxes Paid 12	1.9	2.7	2.4	2.2	1.9	1.4	1.7	1.6	1.9	2.0	1.3	2.4	1.5
Interest Paid 13	1.2	3.3	0.7	0.9	1.2	1.1	1.4	1.4	1.5	2.1	2.5	1.3	1.1
Depreciation 14	1.3	1.7	0.9	1.1	1.0	0.9	1.8	1.9	1.5	1.6	1.6	2.1	1.2
Amortization and Depletion 15	0.2	0.1	0.2	0.1	0.0	0.1	0.1	0.1	0.2	0.1	0.6	0.4	0.3
Pensions and Other Deferred Comp. 16	0.3	0.0	0.1	0.2	0.2	0.6	0.3	0.3	0.2	0.1	•	0.3	0.4
Employee Benefits 17	0.9	0.2	0.5	0.4	0.7	0.7	0.9	1.0	0.9	1.2	2.6	1.8	0.9
Advertising 18	1.8	1.6	1.7	1.5	1.0	0.8	1.3	4.7	2.5	2.6	3.1	1.1	2.5
Other Expenses 19	14.3	38.8	20.2	14.4	11.6	11.3	10.2	14.4	16.6	14.6	17.0	13.5	10.8
Officers' Compensation 20	2.3	4.4	4.8	3.8	3.6	2.4	2.2	1.9	1.5	0.7	1.1	0.4	0.2
Operating Margin 21	1.3	•	0.3	1.4	0.6	0.5	0.0	1.1	•	3.2	0.5	2.2	2.8
Operating Margin Before Officers' Comp. 22	3.5	•	5.1	5.2	4.1	2.9	2.3	2.9	1.4	3.9	1.6	2.6	3.0

Selected Average Balance Sheet ($ in Thousands)

	1	2	3	4	5	6	7	8	9	10	11	12	13
Net Receivables **23**	111	0	13	82	336	1391	1887	6724	7113	13575	31030	244136	796731
Inventories **24**	207	0	43	270	835	2675	4881	11222	28698	64748	108171	244670	920985
Net Property, Plant and Equipment **25**	132	0	22	122	391	590	2975	3849	14668	27562	52149	298342	790836
Total Assets **26**	753	0	115	679	2051	6263	13781	35117	72282	169236	359139	1388476	5234368
Notes and Loans Payable **27**	257	0	63	314	851	1986	4669	9067	24755	84871	129644	379752	1270288
All Other Liabilities **28**	266	0	30	163	483	2324	4524	14019	22113	49729	71643	427659	2665875
Net Worth **29**	229	0	22	202	716	1953	4589	12031	25414	34635	157853	581065	1313206

Selected Financial Ratios (Times to 1)

	1	2	3	4	5	6	7	8	9	10	11	12	13
Current Ratio **30**	1.4	•	2.1	1.9	1.7	1.5	1.6	1.4	1.5	2.2	1.4		0.9
Quick Ratio **31**	0.6	•	0.9	0.7	0.7	0.5	0.7	0.4	0.4	0.8	0.8		0.4
Net Sales to Working Capital **32**	11.7	•	11.5	6.3	5.5	9.2	6.1	9.1	7.4	4.5	9.6		•
Coverage Ratio **33**	3.9	•	2.7	3.4	2.9	3.7	4.4	2.8	4.7	2.0	6.2		5.2
Total Asset Turnover **34**	2.0	•	4.1	2.7	2.1	1.9	2.0	1.5	1.6	1.5	1.2	1.2	1.8
Inventory Turnover **35**	4.6	•	6.5	4.2	3.5	3.8	2.9	2.4	2.3	2.3	4.0		6.9
Receivables Turnover **36**	14.4	•	36.9	22.6	12.3	17.3	9.1	11.8	18.8	28.3	8.4		12.0
Total Liabilities to Net Worth **37**	2.3	•	4.1	2.4	1.9	2.0	1.9	1.8	3.9	1.3	1.4		3.0
Current Assets to Working Capital **38**	3.3	•	1.9	1.7	2.1	3.1	2.8	3.5	2.9	1.8	3.6		•
Current Liabilities to Working Capital **39**	2.3	•	0.9	0.7	1.1	1.4	2.1	2.5	1.9	0.8	2.6		•
Working Capital to Net Sales **40**	0.1	•	0.1	0.2	0.2	0.1	0.2	0.1	0.1	0.2	0.1		•
Inventory to Working Capital **41**	1.6	•	1.0	1.0	1.2	1.1	1.4	1.8	1.8	1.1	1.4		•
Total Receipts to Cash Flow **42**	8.1	11.5	7.6	8.5	9.6	11.3	6.2	7.3	6.9	8.0	6.5		8.7
Cost of Goods to Cash Flow **43**	5.2	6.0	4.4	5.3	6.6	7.8	3.7	4.4	4.1	4.5	3.9		5.9
Cash Flow to Total Debt **44**	0.4	•	0.7	0.4	0.3	0.3	0.4	0.3	0.3	0.3	0.3		0.3

Selected Financial Factors (in Percentages)

	1	2	3	4	5	6	7	8	9	10	11	12	13
Debt Ratio **45**	69.5	•	80.5	70.2	65.1	68.8	66.7	65.7	64.8	79.5	56.0	58.2	74.9
Return on Total Assets **46**	9.1	•	8.3	8.3	7.4	8.9	9.7	6.7	6.7	14.4	6.0	9.5	10.2
Return on Equity Before Income Taxes **47**	22.1	•	26.5	19.6	13.8	17.2	18.5	21.9	12.3	55.2	6.7	19.0	32.9
Return on Equity After Income Taxes **48**	16.4	•	25.5	18.6	12.3	13.7	16.8	19.0	10.1	44.2	3.8	12.9	21.6
Profit Margin (Before Income Tax) **49**	3.4	•	1.3	2.2	2.3	2.8	3.2	4.9	2.7	7.6	2.4	6.7	4.6
Profit Margin (After Income Tax) **50**	2.5	•	1.2	2.1	2.1	2.2	2.9	4.2	2.2	6.1	1.4	4.5	3.0

Table II
Corporations with Net Income

MISCELLANEOUS STORE RETAILERS

MONEY AMOUNTS AND SIZE OF ASSETS IN THOUSANDS OF DOLLARS

Item Description for Accounting Period 7/06 Through 6/07	Total	Zero Assets	Under 500	500 to 1,000	1,000 to 5,000	5,000 to 10,000	10,000 to 25,000	25,000 to 50,000	50,000 to 100,000	100,000 to 250,000	250,000 to 500,000	500,000 to 2,500,000	2,500,000 and over
Number of Enterprises 1	47746	5568	35407	3222	3050	260	138	57	16	15	•	•	4

Revenues ($ in Thousands)

	Total	Zero Assets	Under 500	500 to 1,000	1,000 to 5,000	5,000 to 10,000	10,000 to 25,000	25,000 to 50,000	50,000 to 100,000	100,000 to 250,000	250,000 to 500,000	500,000 to 2,500,000	2,500,000 and over
Net Sales 2	110094602	404678	20324077	6484921	15326279	3388546	4230036	3408576	1954895	4748250	•	•	37187086
Interest 3	457412	120	6613	2649	32584	10447	4124	5425	3307	21772	•	•	279211
Rents 4	85023	0	792	3944	14231	3327	122	957	2166	2429	•	•	18913
Royalties 5	164426	0	0	0	111	3143	40791	37244	0	0	•	•	65216
Other Portfolio Income 6	458491	10598	17728	38772	37476	20402	35797	19089	12278	74507	•	•	171427
Other Receipts 7	1178386	10085	168864	21131	203099	45473	77446	83075	40354	70250	•	•	62479
Total Receipts 8	113338340	425481	20518074	6551417	15613780	3469338	4388316	3554366	2013000	4917208	•	•	37784332
Average Total Receipts 9	2374	76	579	2033	5119	13344	31799	62357	125812	327814	•	•	9446083

Operating Costs/Operating Income (%)

	Total	Zero Assets	Under 500	500 to 1,000	1,000 to 5,000	5,000 to 10,000	10,000 to 25,000	25,000 to 50,000	50,000 to 100,000	100,000 to 250,000	250,000 to 500,000	500,000 to 2,500,000	2,500,000 and over
Cost of Operations 10	64.2	46.8	58.0	62.7	68.6	70.7	68.1	61.3	63.7	59.3	•	•	68.2
Salaries and Wages 11	10.5	6.6	8.7	11.8	8.9	10.3	11.6	9.8	11.1	12.5	•	•	10.2
Taxes Paid 12	1.8	2.1	2.1	2.0	1.9	1.4	1.7	1.5	1.7	2.1	•	•	1.5
Interest Paid 13	1.0	0.5	0.6	0.8	1.0	0.9	1.2	1.4	0.8	2.0	•	•	1.1
Depreciation 14	1.2	1.0	0.8	0.9	0.9	0.7	1.7	1.8	1.3	1.6	•	•	1.2
Amortization and Depletion 15	0.2	0.1	0.1	0.1	0.0	0.0	0.0	0.1	0.1	0.1	•	•	0.3
Pensions and Other Deferred Comp. 16	0.3	•	0.1	0.2	0.2	0.4	0.3	0.3	0.2	0.1	•	•	0.4
Employee Benefits 17	0.9	•	0.5	0.5	0.7	0.7	0.8	0.9	0.8	1.3	•	•	0.9
Advertising 18	1.8	1.0	1.7	1.3	1.0	0.5	1.2	4.7	2.1	2.8	•	•	2.5
Other Expenses 19	12.8	24.2	18.6	11.2	11.1	9.2	9.5	13.4	13.9	13.1	•	•	10.8
Officers' Compensation 20	1.9	6.8	4.4	3.9	3.5	2.4	2.4	2.1	1.8	0.6	•	•	0.2
Operating Margin 21	3.3	11.0	4.4	4.7	2.2	2.8	1.5	2.7	2.4	4.5	•	•	2.8
Operating Margin Before Officers' Comp. 22	5.2	17.8	8.8	8.5	5.7	5.2	3.9	4.8	4.2	5.2	•	•	3.0

Selected Average Balance Sheet ($ in Thousands)

Net Receivables 23	183	0	16	114	411	1570	2131	7943	7334	14009	•	796731
Inventories 24	293	0	44	259	925	2934	4627	10369	26509	75096	•	963210
Net Property, Plant and Equipment 25	184	0	24	94	304	462	2471	3803	11350	27741	•	790836
Total Assets 26	1121	0	131	685	2141	6111	13969	34816	73857	174444	•	5234368
Notes and Loans Payable 27	320	0	50	214	753	1659	4042	9395	16957	90088	•	1270288
All Other Liabilities 28	411	0	26	153	540	2162	4766	12359	23831	49468	•	2650875
Net Worth 29	390	0	55	319	847	2291	5161	13062	33070	34888	•	1313206

Selected Financial Ratios (Times to 1)

Current Ratio 30	1.4	•	2.7	2.6	2.0	1.8	1.6	1.6	1.7	1.5	•	0.9
Quick Ratio 31	0.6	•	1.3	1.3	0.7	0.8	0.6	0.8	0.5	0.4	•	0.4
Net Sales to Working Capital 32	11.9	•	9.7	6.2	6.2	5.8	8.8	6.0	6.0	9.3	•	•
Coverage Ratio 33	6.5	36.8	10.0	8.5	5.2	6.8	5.4	6.0	7.4	5.5	•	5.2
Total Asset Turnover 34	2.1	•	4.4	2.9	2.3	2.1	2.2	1.7	1.7	1.8	•	1.8
Inventory Turnover 35	5.1	•	7.5	4.9	3.7	3.1	4.5	3.5	2.9	2.5	•	6.6
Receivables Turnover 36	13.6	•	37.6	17.2	12.2	8.1	17.6	9.0	13.4	28.8	•	6.6
Total Liabilities to Net Worth 37	1.9	•	1.4	1.1	1.5	1.7	1.7	1.7	1.2	4.0	•	3.0
Current Assets to Working Capital 38	3.3	•	1.6	1.6	2.0	2.3	2.6	2.6	2.5	3.0	•	•
Current Liabilities to Working Capital 39	2.3	•	0.6	0.6	1.0	1.3	1.8	1.6	1.5	2.0	•	•
Working Capital to Net Sales 40	0.1	•	0.1	0.2	0.2	0.2	0.1	0.2	0.2	0.1	•	•
Inventory to Working Capital 41	1.5	•	0.8	0.8	1.1	1.2	1.6	1.2	1.3	2.1	•	•
Total Receipts to Cash Flow 42	7.4	3.3	6.1	7.5	8.4	8.7	9.5	5.6	6.4	7.3	•	8.7
Cost of Goods to Cash Flow 43	4.7	1.5	3.5	4.7	5.8	6.2	6.5	3.4	4.1	4.3	•	5.9
Cash Flow to Total Debt 44	0.4	•	1.2	0.7	0.5	0.4	0.4	0.5	0.5	0.3	•	0.3

Selected Financial Factors (in Percentages)

Debt Ratio 45	65.2	•	58.2	53.5	60.4	62.5	63.1	62.5	55.2	80.0	•	74.9
Return on Total Assets 46	13.6	•	25.9	18.9	11.9	13.0	14.1	14.3	10.3	19.6	•	10.2
Return on Equity Before Income Taxes 47	33.1	•	55.8	36.0	24.2	29.7	31.0	31.7	19.9	80.3	•	32.9
Return on Equity After Income Taxes 48	26.9	•	55.0	34.7	22.5	26.0	28.7	28.3	17.8	64.9	•	21.6
Profit Margin (Before Income Tax) 49	5.6	16.2	5.3	5.7	4.1	5.2	5.2	6.9	5.4	8.8	•	4.6
Profit Margin (After Income Tax) 50	4.5	15.1	5.3	5.5	3.8	4.6	4.8	6.2	4.8	7.2	•	3.0

Table I

Corporations with and without Net Income

NONSTORE RETAILERS

MONEY AMOUNTS AND SIZE OF ASSETS IN THOUSANDS OF DOLLARS

Item Description for Accounting Period 7/06 Through 6/07		Total	Zero Assets	Under 500	500 to 1,000	1,000 to 5,000	5,000 to 10,000	10,000 to 25,000	25,000 to 50,000	50,000 to 100,000	100,000 to 250,000	250,000 to 500,000	500,000 to 2,500,000	2,500,000 and over
Number of Enterprises	1	51103	14008	31475	2395	2426	441	173	74	42	33	11	17	7
Revenues ($ in Thousands)														
Net Sales	2	141256457	807904	15300664	7170157	15515047	9949325	9490626	4861620	5315828	14204045	8846207	22473546	27321487
Interest	3	1381487	1793	4442	6148	22186	6439	9998	17495	12331	25736	142162	207061	925697
Rents	4	89669	0	4527	6757	3483	3603	2482	6620	530	4956	699	55039	974
Royalties	5	585206	0	2075	0	19194	1506	0	3358	744	149	3595	94158	460426
Other Portfolio Income	6	726156	56340	48495	4294	118636	6643	65136	19551	9472	3588	8038	135140	250823
Other Receipts	7	3403866	13132	83125	17439	74783	119517	96342	45158	73470	182087	89584	518611	2090617
Total Receipts	8	147442841	879169	15443328	7204795	15753329	10087033	9664584	4953802	5412375	14420561	9090285	23483555	31050024
Average Total Receipts	9	2885	63	491	3008	6494	22873	55865	66943	128866	436987	826390	1381386	4435718
Operating Costs/Operating Income (%)														
Cost of Operations	10	66.4	45.3	61.3	70.0	71.8	70.9	72.8	61.5	62.4	73.5	67.0	68.9	57.7
Salaries and Wages	11	8.6	5.9	7.6	7.8	7.9	7.8	8.7	9.5	7.6	7.0	6.3	8.1	12.1
Taxes Paid	12	1.4	1.8	1.9	2.0	1.3	1.5	1.3	1.2	1.2	0.9	0.8	1.2	1.6
Interest Paid	13	1.9	1.8	0.5	0.5	0.8	0.6	0.6	1.2	1.1	0.9	0.6	1.6	5.9
Depreciation	14	1.3	2.2	1.1	1.6	1.6	1.6	1.0	1.6	1.4	0.7	0.9	0.9	1.8
Amortization and Depletion	15	0.3	0.3	0.1	0.1	0.2	0.1	0.2	0.7	0.6	0.3	0.4	0.4	0.6
Pensions and Other Deferred Comp.	16	0.2	0.1	0.2	0.4	0.2	0.2	0.2	0.2	0.2	0.2	0.1	0.3	0.1
Employee Benefits	17	0.8	0.4	0.3	1.1	0.8	0.7	0.8	1.1	0.7	0.7	0.6	0.8	1.2
Advertising	18	3.1	7.1	1.6	2.6	1.2	2.3	2.6	3.8	6.1	4.4	5.4	2.8	3.3
Other Expenses	19	14.6	41.3	19.7	8.3	11.8	12.4	11.4	18.8	15.3	10.0	14.6	10.5	20.8
Officers' Compensation	20	1.6	4.1	4.7	4.6	2.6	1.9	1.0	1.0	1.0	0.6	0.6	0.5	0.6
Operating Margin	21	•	•	1.2	1.0	•	0.1	•	•	2.6	0.9	2.7	4.1	•
Operating Margin Before Officers' Comp.	22	1.5	•	5.9	5.6	2.3	1.9	0.5	0.3	3.5	1.5	3.3	4.5	•

Selected Average Balance Sheet ($ in Thousands)

Net Receivables 23	254	0	12	143	356	1214	3715	6314	15900	33256	99742	147804	627920
Inventories 24	160	0	17	135	298	1101	3208	7983	8656	38543	81415	84728	143755
Net Property, Plant and Equipment 25	189	0	18	190	425	1716	3337	4181	7488	17703	33527	103513	420928
Total Assets 26	2773		79	722	2048	6664	16825	33205	69949	164882	360302	1165670	13152468
Notes and Loans Payable 27	593	0	45	281	674	2045	4479	8734	16802	45507	52247	259031	2439452
All Other Liabilities 28	886	0	25	203	681	2348	7021	13716	20650	61442	130425	308179	4218706
Net Worth 29	1294	0	9	238	693	2271	5325	10755	32497	57933	177631	598460	6494311

Selected Financial Ratios (Times to 1)

Current Ratio 30	1.1	•	1.6	1.8	1.5	1.5	1.4	1.4	1.7	1.5	1.8	1.6	0.7
Quick Ratio 31	0.6	•	0.9	1.1	1.0	0.8	0.8	0.8	1.0	0.8	1.0	1.0	0.4
Net Sales to Working Capital 32	37.4	•	22.6	14.6	14.9	16.5	16.9	10.4	8.4	11.3	7.2	8.7	•
Coverage Ratio 33	3.4	0.1	5.7	4.3	2.5	3.4	3.3	2.0	4.9	3.8	9.5	6.4	2.4
Total Asset Turnover 34	1.0	•	6.1	4.1	3.1	3.4	3.3	2.0	1.8	2.6	2.2	1.1	0.3
Inventory Turnover 35	11.5	•	17.9	15.6	15.4	14.5	12.4	5.1	9.1	8.2	6.6	10.7	15.7
Receivables Turnover 36	11.5	•	33.7	16.6	15.4	19.4	15.4	8.9	9.7	12.3	9.0	10.2	7.1
Total Liabilities to Net Worth 37	1.1	•	7.7	2.0	2.0	1.9	2.2	2.1	1.2	1.8	1.0	0.9	1.0
Current Assets to Working Capital 38	11.1	•	2.6	2.3	2.9	3.0	3.6	3.2	2.5	2.8	2.2	2.8	•
Current Liabilities to Working Capital 39	10.1	•	1.6	1.3	1.9	2.0	2.6	2.2	1.5	1.8	1.2	1.8	•
Working Capital to Net Sales 40	0.0	•	0.0	0.1	0.1	0.1	0.1	0.1	0.1	0.1	0.1	0.1	•
Inventory to Working Capital 41	2.4	•	0.9	0.6	0.7	1.0	1.0	1.2	0.7	1.1	0.7	0.6	•
Total Receipts to Cash Flow 42	5.9	3.3	5.3	12.3	9.0	8.2	9.3	5.5	5.5	8.9	5.3	5.8	3.7
Cost of Goods to Cash Flow 43	3.9	1.5	3.2	8.6	6.5	5.8	6.8	3.4	3.4	6.5	3.6	4.0	2.2
Cash Flow to Total Debt 44	0.3	•	1.3	0.5	0.5	0.6	0.5	0.5	0.6	0.5	0.8	0.4	0.2

Selected Financial Factors (in Percentages)

Debt Ratio 45	53.3	•	88.5	67.1	66.1	65.9	68.3	67.6	53.5	64.9	50.7	48.7	50.6
Return on Total Assets 46	6.2	•	15.8	8.1	6.6	7.0	6.1	4.9	9.9	8.6	13.6	11.3	4.2
Return on Equity Before Income Taxes 47	9.4	•	113.3	19.0	11.8	14.4	13.5	7.6	16.9	18.0	24.7	18.6	5.0
Return on Equity After Income Taxes 48	7.3	•	111.7	18.3	9.6	12.8	10.3	4.9	11.7	14.4	21.8	12.3	4.1
Profit Margin (Before Income Tax) 49	4.4	•	2.1	1.5	1.3	1.5	1.3	1.2	4.4	2.4	5.4	8.4	8.4
Profit Margin (After Income Tax) 50	3.4	•	2.1	1.5	1.0	1.3	1.0	0.8	3.0	1.9	4.8	5.6	6.8

Table II

Corporations with Net Income

NONSTORE RETAILERS

MONEY AMOUNTS AND SIZE OF ASSETS IN THOUSANDS OF DOLLARS

Item Description for Accounting Period 7/06 Through 6/07		Total	Zero Assets	Under 500	500 to 1,000	1,000 to 5,000	5,000 to 10,000	10,000 to 25,000	25,000 to 50,000	50,000 to 100,000	100,000 to 250,000	250,000 to 500,000	500,000 to 2,500,000	2,500,000 and over
Number of Enterprises	1	24514	4253	16991	1414	1311	291	120	43	33	28	•	•	14
Revenues ($ in Thousands)														
Net Sales	2	118664652	443132	11637887	4912478	9395176	7709490	7270070	3408324	4453076	12859300	•	21529723	•
Interest	3	1283069	872	1843	2365	16451	5868	6845	13767	8631	21228	•	137702	•
Rents	4	48199	0	3273	6757	2099	3521	2423	6107	530	4316	•	18096	•
Royalties	5	489831	0	0	0	0	0	0	3263	164	149	•	22554	•
Other Portfolio Income	6	643590	56158	46119	2821	75522	6643	64791	14961	8544	3588	•	133852	•
Other Receipts	7	3133951	9427	45499	14367	18330	61107	71822	23131	71222	149822	•	536441	•
Total Receipts	8	124263292	509589	11734621	4938788	9507578	7786629	7415951	3469553	4542167	13038403	•	22378368	•
Average Total Receipts	9	5069	120	691	3493	7252	26758	61800	80687	137641	465657	•	1598455	•
Operating Costs/Operating Income (%)														
Cost of Operations	10	66.6	38.8	58.5	70.9	71.8	74.3	74.7	61.0	60.2	75.1	•	69.7	•
Salaries and Wages	11	8.1	4.6	7.6	6.7	6.1	7.3	6.4	8.0	7.2	7.0	•	7.8	•
Taxes Paid	12	1.3	1.8	1.8	1.7	1.2	1.1	1.2	0.9	1.1	0.9	•	1.2	•
Interest Paid	13	1.8	0.7	0.3	0.2	0.4	0.5	0.4	0.5	1.0	0.8	•	0.9	•
Depreciation	14	1.0	2.3	0.7	0.8	0.7	1.2	0.8	1.5	0.7	0.7	•	0.8	•
Amortization and Depletion	15	0.3	0.0	0.1	0.1	0.1	0.1	0.1	0.2	0.5	0.2	•	0.3	•
Pensions and Other Deferred Comp.	16	0.2	0.0	0.2	0.5	0.2	0.2	0.2	0.2	0.2	0.2	•	0.3	•
Employee Benefits	17	0.7	0.4	0.2	1.0	0.6	0.6	0.8	1.1	0.6	0.6	•	0.8	•
Advertising	18	2.9	0.5	1.9	2.6	1.5	0.9	2.5	3.2	6.5	3.5	•	2.9	•
Other Expenses	19	13.6	39.4	19.0	6.9	10.4	9.0	10.0	18.1	15.4	8.8	•	9.2	•
Officers' Compensation	20	1.4	3.1	4.9	4.6	2.7	1.9	0.9	0.8	0.9	0.4	•	0.5	•
Operating Margin	21	2.1	8.3	4.9	3.9	4.2	3.1	2.1	4.4	5.8	1.7	•	5.7	•
Operating Margin Before Officers' Comp.	22	3.5	11.4	9.8	8.5	6.9	5.0	3.0	5.2	6.7	2.2	•	6.2	•

Selected Average Balance Sheet ($ in Thousands)

Net Receivables 23	174306	34683	17726	6887	4212	1397	478	196	13	0	473
Inventories 24	100772	44016	9570	9423	2867	1034	369	108	25	0	263
Net Property, Plant and Equipment 25	113681	18785	4887	3948	2736	1467	271	103	19	0	284
Total Assets 26	1176089	169149	68760	33954	16496	6832	2156	734	102	0	5061
Notes and Loans Payable 27	233229	49934	15407	6202	3434	1611	427	127	34	0	962
All Other Liabilities 28	330010	59780	22631	11716	6743	2172	546	229	28	0	1662
Net Worth 29	612851	59435	30723	16036	6320	3049	1184	378	40	0	2436

Selected Financial Ratios (Times to 1)

Current Ratio 30	1.6	1.6	1.6	1.7	1.5	1.7	2.1	2.1	2.3	•	1.1
Quick Ratio 31	1.1	0.8	1.0	0.8	1.0	0.9	1.4	1.6	1.2	•	0.7
Net Sales to Working Capital 32	8.2	11.4	8.5	8.9	16.3	15.8	8.9	12.1	15.9	•	64.8
Coverage Ratio 33	11.5	4.8	8.8	12.8	10.3	9.6	15.8	22.0	23.0	32.8	4.9
Total Asset Turnover 34	1.3	2.7	2.0	2.3	3.7	3.9	3.3	4.7	6.7	•	1.0
Inventory Turnover 35	10.6	7.8	8.5	5.1	15.8	19.0	13.9	22.7	16.1	•	12.3
Receivables Turnover 36	•	•	9.2	8.2	15.3	20.3	11.6	14.7	40.2	•	11.2
Total Liabilities to Net Worth 37	0.9	1.8	1.2	1.1	1.6	1.2	0.8	0.9	1.6	•	1.1
Current Assets to Working Capital 38	2.6	2.8	2.6	2.5	3.0	2.5	1.9	1.9	1.8	•	19.3
Current Liabilities to Working Capital 39	1.6	1.8	1.6	1.5	2.0	1.5	0.9	0.9	0.8	•	18.3
Working Capital to Net Sales 40	0.1	0.1	0.1	0.1	0.1	0.1	0.1	0.1	0.1	•	0.0
Inventory to Working Capital 41	0.5	1.1	0.7	1.0	0.7	0.7	0.5	0.4	0.7	•	4.0
Total Receipts to Cash Flow 42	5.8	9.3	4.6	4.3	8.2	8.6	7.2	9.9	4.5	1.8	5.3
Cost of Goods to Cash Flow 43	4.0	7.0	2.7	2.7	6.2	6.4	5.2	7.0	2.7	0.7	3.5
Cash Flow to Total Debt 44	0.5	0.5	0.8	1.0	0.7	0.8	1.0	1.0	2.4	•	0.3

Selected Financial Factors (in Percentages)

Debt Ratio 45	47.9	64.9	55.3	52.8	61.7	55.4	45.1	48.5	61.0	•	51.9
Return on Total Assets 46	13.7	10.8	17.1	15.8	16.5	17.7	19.2	22.2	40.5	•	8.3
Return on Equity Before Income Taxes 47	23.9	24.2	33.9	30.8	38.9	35.6	32.7	41.1	99.1	•	13.7
Return on Equity After Income Taxes 48	16.5	20.1	26.9	27.7	35.0	33.7	30.3	40.4	98.4	•	11.4
Profit Margin (Before Income Tax) 49	9.5	3.1	7.7	6.2	4.1	4.1	5.4	4.5	5.8	23.3	6.9
Profit Margin (After Income Tax) 50	6.6	2.6	6.1	5.6	3.7	3.9	5.0	4.4	5.7	23.1	5.7

Table I

Corporations with and without Net Income

AIR TRANSPORTATION

MONEY AMOUNTS AND SIZE OF ASSETS IN THOUSANDS OF DOLLARS

Item Description for Accounting Period 7/06 Through 6/07	Total	Zero Assets	Under 500	500 to 1,000	1,000 to 5,000	5,000 to 10,000	10,000 to 25,000	25,000 to 50,000	50,000 to 100,000	100,000 to 250,000	250,000 to 500,000	500,000 to 2,500,000	2,500,000 and over
Number of Enterprises **1**	8083	1667	4157	679	1068	235	160	52	16	16	8	14	10

Revenues ($ in Thousands)

Item	Total	Zero Assets	Under 500	500 to 1,000	1,000 to 5,000	5,000 to 10,000	10,000 to 25,000	25,000 to 50,000	50,000 to 100,000	100,000 to 250,000	250,000 to 500,000	500,000 to 2,500,000	2,500,000 and over
Net Sales **2**	130679646	782709	441429	691855	891936	1882032	3029001	2068495	1890567	3659952	3138960	14715178	97487534
Interest **3**	1433757	2924	0	987	1890	1242	2548	4674	6914	21428	18927	165058	1207164
Rents **4**	308297	0	0	0	0	4607	337	334	59	0	141	17607	284607
Royalties **5**	58	0	0	0	0	0	0	0	13	0	45	0	0
Other Portfolio Income **6**	1095010	126757	22528	0	55626	25495	31889	2789	18212	68803	39548	157814	545550
Other Receipts **7**	20155280	232665	700	19542	5365	6787	-1246	17539	27537	189913	27674	103073	19525731
Total Receipts **8**	153672048	1145055	464657	712384	955421	1920163	3062529	2093831	1943302	3940096	3225295	15158730	119050586
Average Total Receipts **9**	19012	687	112	1049	895	8171	19141	40266	121456	246256	403162	1082766	11905059

Operating Costs/Operating Income (%)

Item	Total	Zero Assets	Under 500	500 to 1,000	1,000 to 5,000	5,000 to 10,000	10,000 to 25,000	25,000 to 50,000	50,000 to 100,000	100,000 to 250,000	250,000 to 500,000	500,000 to 2,500,000	2,500,000 and over
Cost of Operations **10**	28.1	69.9	33.3	79.9	48.2	44.0	54.3	57.6	40.8	39.0	31.7	28.6	24.7
Salaries and Wages **11**	19.3	5.0	0.0	7.1	9.6	9.1	9.7	6.3	10.4	16.0	15.0	16.3	21.3
Taxes Paid **12**	2.6	0.7	2.1	0.8	2.4	2.3	1.2	1.5	1.9	1.8	1.5	2.5	2.8
Interest Paid **13**	3.7	2.1	5.9	0.1	4.7	3.3	1.6	1.7	1.3	1.8	3.0	3.3	4.0
Depreciation **14**	7.0	6.0	13.4	15.9	19.3	3.9	6.3	4.9	3.6	3.9	2.9	6.7	7.2
Amortization and Depletion **15**	0.5	1.2	0.2	•	0.2	0.1	0.1	0.5	0.3	•	1.3	1.3	0.4
Pensions and Other Deferred Comp. **16**	2.8	0.0	13.5	•	0.2	0.0	0.2	0.1	0.3	0.5	0.2	0.8	3.5
Employee Benefits **17**	2.6	0.7	2.1	0.1	0.2	1.1	1.3	1.3	1.2	2.2	1.4	1.4	3.0
Advertising **18**	1.1	0.1	0.3	0.0	0.2	0.3	0.2	1.7	0.8	0.7	0.1	0.5	1.3
Other Expenses **19**	50.9	63.0	47.8	19.8	36.9	35.0	28.3	33.3	42.1	39.2	42.5	40.9	54.9
Officers' Compensation **20**	0.3	3.6	0.0	•	1.3	1.3	0.9	0.4	0.7	0.6	1.0	0.7	0.2
Operating Margin **21**	•	•	•	•	•	•	•	•	•	•	•	•	•
Operating Margin Before Officers' Comp. **22**	•	•	•	•	•	0.8	•	•	•	•	0.5	•	•

Selected Average Balance Sheet ($ in Thousands)

Net Receivables 23	996	14	0	94	195	1585	2696	3973	12107	15865	38006	74406	491204
Inventories 24	394	19	0	0	28	99	299	650	3478	7145	13201	21114	243871
Net Property, Plant and Equipment 25	11482	66	0	280	1061	956	9307	16688	18244	58736	103380	566933	7863286
Total Assets 26	20150	109	0	685	2085	6558	15156	35292	61685	168258	344448	1093505	13218473
Notes and Loans Payable 27	10067	138	0	899	1846	4057	7608	14508	27496	67029	186978	489458	6543231
All Other Liabilities 28	10417	58	0	60	330	1219	2771	14077	22693	100083	109047	279908	7534965
Net Worth 29	-334	-86	0	-273	-91	1282	4776	6707	11496	1146	48423	324139	-859724

Selected Financial Ratios (Times to 1)

Current Ratio 30	1.1	0.8	•	5.7	5.3	1.5	1.5	0.7	1.5	0.8	1.3	1.6	1.0
Quick Ratio 31	0.7	0.4	•	5.7	4.2	1.2	1.2	0.5	1.0	0.5	0.8	1.2	0.6
Net Sales to Working Capital 32	41.6	•	•	3.1	2.5	12.9	2.2	•	10.6	•	9.8	9.1	•
Coverage Ratio 33	0.6	•	•	•	1.5	•	1.5	•	0.5	2.7	1.7	1.0	0.7
Total Asset Turnover 34	0.8	1.0	•	1.5	0.4	1.2	1.2	1.1	1.9	1.4	1.1	1.0	0.7
Inventory Turnover 35	11.6	1.9	•	•	14.5	35.6	34.3	35.2	13.9	12.5	9.4	14.2	9.9
Receivables Turnover 36	17.1	4.8	•	11.0	4.7	5.5	9.1	12.9	9.8	12.5	12.7	15.7	20.4
Total Liabilities to Net Worth 37	•	•	•	•	•	4.1	2.2	4.3	4.4	145.8	6.1	2.4	•
Current Assets to Working Capital 38	15.4	•	•	1.2	1.2	3.2	3.2	•	3.2	4.0	2.6	•	•
Current Liabilities to Working Capital 39	14.4	•	•	0.2	0.2	2.2	2.2	•	2.2	3.0	1.6	•	•
Working Capital to Net Sales 40	0.0	0.3	•	0.4	0.4	0.1	0.1	•	0.1	0.1	0.1	•	•
Inventory to Working Capital 41	1.3	•	•	0.0	0.0	0.2	0.2	•	0.4	0.5	0.2	•	•
Total Receipts to Cash Flow 42	2.9	5.8	2.0	16.0	16.0	5.8	5.8	14.4	3.2	4.4	4.6	4.4	2.6
Cost of Goods to Cash Flow 43	0.8	1.9	1.4	7.7	7.7	3.1	2.8	8.3	1.3	1.7	1.5	1.2	0.6
Cash Flow to Total Debt 44	0.3	0.1	•	0.0	0.0	0.3	0.2	0.1	0.7	0.3	0.3	0.3	0.3

Selected Financial Factors (in Percentages)

Debt Ratio 45	101.7	178.9	•	139.9	104.4	80.4	68.5	81.0	81.4	99.3	85.9	70.4	106.5
Return on Total Assets 46	1.9	•	•	•	5.9	•	•	•	1.2	6.7	5.9	3.2	2.0
Return on Equity Before Income Taxes 47	64.4	13.7	•	77.5	148.7	9.9	•	•	•	627.1	17.7	0.2	15.2
Return on Equity After Income Taxes 48	72.4	13.7	•	77.5	157.2	5.9	•	•	•	548.5	10.4	•	15.9
Profit Margin (Before Income Tax) 49	•	•	•	•	1.6	•	•	•	3.1	•	2.2	0.1	•
Profit Margin (After Income Tax) 50	•	•	•	•	0.9	•	•	•	2.7	•	1.3	•	•

Table II
Corporations with Net Income

AIR TRANSPORTATION

MONEY AMOUNTS AND SIZE OF ASSETS IN THOUSANDS OF DOLLARS

Item Description for Accounting Period 7/06 Through 6/07	Total	Zero Assets	Under 500	500 to 1,000	1,000 to 5,000	5,000 to 10,000	10,000 to 25,000	25,000 to 50,000	50,000 to 100,000	100,000 to 250,000	250,000 to 500,000	500,000 to 2,500,000	2,500,000 and over
Number of Enterprises **1**	2243	499	1138	65	346	110	41	13	8	•	•	5	6
Revenues ($ in Thousands)													
Net Sales **2**	67338325	9100	223533	578732	748173	1607804	2138837	635939	1032489	•	•	6050480	50653360
Interest **3**	726527	0	0	987	1802	769	2468	1231	4312	•	•	65125	631843
Rents **4**	231996	0	0	0	604	0	337	0	59	•	•	385	230610
Royalties **5**	13	0	0	0	0	0	0	0	13	•	•	0	0
Other Portfolio Income **6**	736211	126735	22528	0	55626	25482	30044	5	14886	•	•	106893	306026
Other Receipts **7**	18964048	289	699	0	4646	5722	9456	14312	15823	•	•	81448	18644640
Total Receipts **8**	87997120	136124	246760	579719	810851	1639777	2181142	651487	1067582	•	•	6304331	70466479
Average Total Receipts **9**	39232	273	217	8919	2344	14907	53199	50114	133448	•	•	1260866	11744413
Operating Costs/Operating Income (%)													
Cost of Operations **10**	18.0	43.4	13.1	94.3	57.4	51.4	62.5	44.1	38.5	•	•	28.2	10.4
Salaries and Wages **11**	20.4	20.8	•	3.4	9.8	7.1	7.2	10.5	8.4	•	•	19.1	22.8
Taxes Paid **12**	2.6	3.4	0.5	0.3	1.6	2.1	1.0	1.5	2.1	•	•	2.9	2.8
Interest Paid **13**	3.5	1.9	4.3	•	1.9	0.5	0.4	1.4	1.1	•	•	1.8	4.3
Depreciation **14**	6.8	38.1	1.5	0.1	9.0	1.1	0.9	5.4	3.0	•	•	4.9	7.8
Amortization and Depletion **15**	0.3	0.2	•	•	0.1	0.0	0.1	0.2	0.0	•	•	1.2	0.3
Pensions and Other Deferred Comp. **16**	2.2	0.4	0.0	•	0.3	0.0	0.2	0.1	0.4	•	•	1.0	2.7
Employee Benefits **17**	2.6	7.0	0.0	•	0.2	1.0	1.0	0.2	1.3	•	•	2.3	3.0
Advertising **18**	1.6	0.0	0.5	0.0	0.2	0.1	0.1	0.5	0.6	•	•	0.1	2.0
Other Expenses **19**	67.7	73.0	34.8	1.6	18.0	28.6	23.6	34.1	37.4	•	•	38.6	79.1
Officers' Compensation **20**	0.4	5.3	0.0	•	1.2	1.0	1.1	0.8	0.6	•	•	0.7	0.3
Operating Margin **21**	•	•	45.2	0.4	0.5	7.1	1.9	1.2	6.5	•	•	•	•
Operating Margin Before Officers' Comp. **22**	•	•	45.2	0.4	1.7	8.1	2.9	2.0	7.0	•	•	•	•

Selected Average Balance Sheet ($ in Thousands)

Net Receivables 23	1897	0	0	225	71	1742	4893	5929	12906	•	99767	477546
Inventories 24	454	0	0	0	19	383	780	644	7516	•	37385	164297
Net Property, Plant and Equipment 25	20070	0	1	18	878	868	3945	17823	18857	•	351275	6900427
Total Assets 26	35444	0	23	802	1578	6938	15619	31493	64912	•	894881	11517347
Notes and Loans Payable 27	18459	0	22	0	816	1225	3283	13458	12427	•	324324	6248197
All Other Liabilities 28	21301	0	0	567	172	1975	6875	9702	26049	•	259372	7378786
Net Worth 29	-4317	0	1	235	590	3738	5462	8333	26435	•	311185	-2109636

Selected Financial Ratios (Times to 1)

Current Ratio 30	1.1	•	549.7	1.4	2.1	2.3	1.3	0.7	1.7	•	1.7	1.1
Quick Ratio 31	0.8	•	544.3	1.4	1.1	2.1	1.0	0.5	1.2	•	1.1	0.8
Net Sales to Working Capital 32	27.4	•	9.3	40.9	9.4	5.1	23.0	•	8.0	•	8.6	41.1
Coverage Ratio 33	2.3	702.3	13.8	•	5.7	20.9	10.3	3.6	9.9	•	3.3	1.8
Total Asset Turnover 34	0.8	•	8.6	11.1	1.4	2.1	3.3	1.6	2.0	•	1.4	0.7
Inventory Turnover 35	11.9	•	562.7	•	66.9	19.6	41.8	33.5	6.6	•	9.1	5.3
Receivables Turnover 36	21.4	•	3.7	32.8	•	10.3	11.9	9.3	•	•	9.8	•
Total Liabilities to Net Worth 37	•	•	25.0	2.4	1.7	0.9	1.9	2.8	1.5	•	1.9	•
Current Assets to Working Capital 38	10.7	•	1.0	3.6	1.9	1.7	4.1	•	2.5	•	2.4	17.5
Current Liabilities to Working Capital 39	9.7	•	0.0	2.6	0.9	0.7	3.1	•	1.5	•	1.4	16.5
Working Capital to Net Sales 40	0.0	•	0.1	0.0	0.1	0.2	0.0	•	0.1	•	0.1	0.0
Inventory to Working Capital 41	0.6	•	0.0	•	0.1	0.1	0.3	•	0.5	•	0.2	0.8
Total Receipts to Cash Flow 42	1.8	0.1	1.4	53.0	5.0	5.0	5.3	3.5	2.6	•	4.9	1.5
Cost of Goods to Cash Flow 43	0.3	0.0	0.2	49.9	2.9	2.6	3.3	1.5	1.0	•	1.4	0.2
Cash Flow to Total Debt 44	0.4	•	6.4	0.3	0.4	0.9	1.0	0.6	1.3	•	0.4	0.4

Selected Financial Factors (in Percentages)

Debt Ratio 45	112.2	•	96.1	70.7	62.6	46.1	65.0	73.5	59.3	•	65.2	118.3
Return on Total Assets 46	6.9	•	517.5	6.6	14.8	20.1	14.2	7.9	21.8	•	7.9	5.8
Return on Equity Before Income Taxes 47	•	•	12455.8	22.5	32.6	35.6	36.7	21.5	48.2	•	15.8	•
Return on Equity After Income Taxes 48	•	•	12454.8	22.5	28.6	32.6	31.7	20.3	42.5	•	11.4	•
Profit Margin (Before Income Tax) 49	4.6	1302.5	55.6	0.6	8.9	9.1	3.8	3.7	9.9	•	4.1	3.6
Profit Margin (After Income Tax) 50	4.3	1301.5	55.6	0.6	7.8	8.3	3.3	3.5	8.7	•	2.9	3.5

238

Table I

Corporations with and without Net Income

RAIL TRANSPORTATION

MONEY AMOUNTS AND SIZE OF ASSETS IN THOUSANDS OF DOLLARS

Item Description for Accounting Period 7/06 Through 6/07	Total	Zero Assets	Under 500	500 to 1,000	1,000 to 5,000	5,000 to 10,000	10,000 to 25,000	25,000 to 50,000	50,000 to 100,000	100,000 to 250,000	250,000 to 500,000	500,000 to 2,500,000	2,500,000 and over
Number of Enterprises 1	425	17	211	30	91	17	19	10	7	10	0	6	7
Revenues ($ in Thousands)													
Net Sales 2	59763812	0	78654	11208	494024	116960	194808	287088	185258	1103036	0	2499033	54793742
Interest 3	1567821	0	1512	781	320	2973	807	804	2169	2492	0	91921	1464042
Rents 4	526587	0	5260	0	3525	0	1409	1661	1841	9668	0	69181	434044
Royalties 5	34361	0	3	0	280	0	0	0	0	1870	0	0	32207
Other Portfolio Income 6	512550	0	637	18351	23168	0	3627	1631	6814	7404	0	107090	343828
Other Receipts 7	2004983	-10470	-17	-1	5608	39	3965	28038	5202	14093	0	218323	1740204
Total Receipts 8	64410114	-10470	86049	30339	526925	119972	204616	319222	201284	1138563	0	2985548	58808067
Average Total Receipts 9	151553	-616	408	1011	5790	7057	10769	31922	28755	113856	•	497591	8401152
Operating Costs/Operating Income (%)													
Cost of Operations 10	27.8	•	5.8	•	5.8	0.2	21.8	48.6	10.1	34.3	•	3.1	29.1
Salaries and Wages 11	20.8	•	10.8	•	3.1	20.8	7.6	9.7	23.0	13.0	•	20.8	21.2
Taxes Paid 12	5.5	•	10.0	0.2	1.7	4.4	5.1	3.1	4.5	3.8	•	5.9	5.6
Interest Paid 13	6.2	•	5.8	•	0.6	1.2	1.5	2.7	2.7	2.3	•	6.9	6.4
Depreciation 14	7.5	•	7.1	0.5	2.4	2.3	5.4	8.5	11.8	8.3	•	9.7	7.5
Amortization and Depletion 15	0.2	•	•	•	0.0	•	0.0	0.1	0.2	0.2	•	0.5	0.2
Pensions and Other Deferred Comp. 16	0.9	•	•	•	0.3	1.0	0.0	0.2	2.4	0.6	•	1.3	0.9
Employee Benefits 17	4.8	•	0.0	•	0.6	4.0	1.3	1.6	5.4	1.3	•	4.8	4.9
Advertising 18	0.1	•	0.0	•	0.0	0.2	0.2	0.1	0.1	0.0	•	0.0	0.1
Other Expenses 19	21.1	•	40.3	41.6	88.7	50.2	27.1	21.5	31.0	30.1	•	54.7	18.6
Officers' Compensation 20	0.8	•	•	•	1.6	1.4	2.0	0.9	1.3	0.8	•	1.0	0.8
Operating Margin 21	4.3	•	20.1	57.7	•	14.4	28.0	3.0	7.5	5.2	•	•	4.8
Operating Margin Before Officers' Comp. 22	5.1	•	20.1	57.7	•	15.8	29.9	3.8	8.7	6.0	•	•	5.6

Selected Average Balance Sheet ($ in Thousands)

Net Receivables 23	14747	0	22	0	531	280	1815	4984	7574	16966	134844	727682
Inventories 24	2701	0	1	0	0	5	238	394	636	3329	3388	154445
Net Property, Plant and Equipment 25	299189	0	179	4	1111	1408	7248	24179	41557	142870	756778	17193228
Total Assets 26	386828	0	309	498	2624	6655	16019	38041	65323	190866	1293126	21880036
Notes and Loans Payable 27	83343	0	0	0	734	261	1340	15110	11527	63584	275829	4685951
All Other Liabilities 28	167451	0	-182	0	700	2088	4670	14918	21387	53529	419561	9666537
Net Worth 29	136033	0	491	498	1190	4306	10008	8012	32410	73752	597736	7527548

Selected Financial Ratios (Times to 1)

Current Ratio 30	0.7	•	3.7	•	1.4	2.3	1.8	0.6	2.0	0.8	•	1.0	0.7
Quick Ratio 31	0.5	•	3.4	•	1.2	2.2	1.7	0.5	1.7	0.6	•	0.8	0.5
Net Sales to Working Capital 32	•	•	3.9	0.8	22.7	3.1	5.1	•	2.8	•	•	134.5	•
Coverage Ratio 33	3.0	•	6.1	4.4	15.7	23.0	7.0	6.2	4.7	•	4.3	2.9	
Total Asset Turnover 34	0.4	•	1.2	0.7	2.1	1.0	0.6	0.8	0.4	0.6	0.3	0.4	
Inventory Turnover 35	14.5	•	17.6	•	2.4	9.4	35.5	4.2	11.4	3.8	14.7		
Receivables Turnover 36	9.8	•	8.6	•	11.8	8.3	4.8	4.6	4.4	7.5	3.2	11.0	
Total Liabilities to Net Worth 37	1.8	•	•	•	1.2	0.5	0.6	3.7	1.0	1.6	1.2	1.9	
Current Assets to Working Capital 38	•	•	1.4	1.0	3.4	1.8	2.2	•	2.1	•	•	66.4	
Current Liabilities to Working Capital 39	•	•	0.4	•	2.4	0.8	1.2	•	1.1	•	•	65.4	
Working Capital to Net Sales 40	•	•	0.3	1.3	0.0	0.3	0.2	•	0.4	•	•	0.0	
Inventory to Working Capital 41	•	•	0.0	•	0.0	0.1	0.1	•	•	•	•	1.8	
Total Receipts to Cash Flow 42	4.2	•	1.6	0.4	2.2	2.3	2.0	3.3	2.6	3.1	2.1	4.5	
Cost of Goods to Cash Flow 43	1.2	•	0.1	•	0.1	0.0	0.4	1.6	0.3	1.1	0.1	1.3	
Cash Flow to Total Debt 44	0.1	•	•	•	1.7	1.3	0.8	0.3	0.3	0.3	0.3	0.1	

Selected Financial Factors (in Percentages)

Debt Ratio 45	64.8	•	•	54.7	35.3	37.5	78.9	50.4	61.4	•	53.8	65.6
Return on Total Assets 46	6.9	42.7	171.2	5.1	18.7	22.1	12.7	7.6	6.2	•	9.6	6.7
Return on Equity Before Income Taxes 47	13.1	22.4	171.2	8.7	27.1	33.8	50.7	13.2	12.6	•	16.0	12.7
Return on Equity After Income Taxes 48	8.4	15.0	155.7	•	27.1	33.2	35.3	11.4	9.6	•	11.1	8.0
Profit Margin (Before Income Tax) 49	12.6	29.5	228.4	1.9	17.0	33.0	14.2	16.1	8.4	•	23.0	12.2
Profit Margin (After Income Tax) 50	8.1	19.8	207.7	•	17.0	32.4	9.9	14.0	6.4	•	16.0	7.7

Table II

Corporations with Net Income

RAIL TRANSPORTATION

MONEY AMOUNTS AND SIZE OF ASSETS IN THOUSANDS OF DOLLARS

Item Description for Accounting Period 7/06 Through 6/07	Total	Zero Assets	Under 500	500 to 1,000	1,000 to 5,000	5,000 to 10,000	10,000 to 25,000	25,000 to 50,000	50,000 to 100,000	100,000 to 250,000	250,000 to 500,000	500,000 to 2,500,000	2,500,000 and over
Number of Enterprises **1**	356	0	211	30	61	6	15	•	•	7	0	0	6
Revenues ($ in Thousands)													
Net Sales **2**	56766006	0	78654	11208	165243	116960	194808	•	•	668998	0	0	2499033
Interest **3**	1471848	0	1512	781	32	0	629	•	•	2438	0	0	91921
Rents **4**	466669	0	5260	0	3522	0	1409	•	•	4572	0	0	69181
Royalties **5**	33595	0	3	0	0	0	0	•	•	1870	0	0	0
Other Portfolio Income **6**	498248	0	637	18351	20552	0	3627	•	•	4575	0	0	107090
Other Receipts **7**	948623	0	-17	-1	3880	39	3966	•	•	11010	0	0	218323
Total Receipts **8**	60184989	0	86049	30339	193229	116999	204439	•	•	693463	0	0	2985548
Average Total Receipts **9**	169059	•	408	1011	3168	19500	13629	•	•	99066	•	•	497591
Operating Costs/Operating Income (%)													
Cost of Operations **10**	28.1	•	5.8	•	17.2	0.2	21.8	•	•	42.4	•	•	3.1
Salaries and Wages **11**	19.7	•	10.8	•	9.2	20.2	7.6	•	•	9.1	•	•	20.8
Taxes Paid **12**	5.3	•	10.0	0.2	5.0	4.4	5.0	•	•	2.8	•	•	5.9
Interest Paid **13**	6.1	•	5.8	•	0.9	1.2	1.5	•	•	1.0	•	•	6.9
Depreciation **14**	7.3	•	7.1	0.5	7.0	2.3	5.4	•	•	7.8	•	•	9.7
Amortization and Depletion **15**	0.2	•	•	•	•	•	0.0	•	•	0.0	•	•	0.5
Pensions and Other Deferred Comp. **16**	0.9	•	•	•	1.0	•	0.0	•	•	0.5	•	•	1.3
Employee Benefits **17**	4.5	•	0.0	•	1.7	3.9	1.3	•	•	1.5	•	•	4.8
Advertising **18**	0.0	•	0.0	•	0.1	0.2	0.2	•	•	0.0	•	•	0.0
Other Expenses **19**	19.6	•	40.3	41.6	53.5	47.5	26.3	•	•	18.4	•	•	54.7
Officers' Compensation **20**	0.8	•	•	•	4.7	1.4	2.0	•	•	0.9	•	•	1.0
Operating Margin **21**	7.5	•	20.1	57.7	•	18.8	28.8	•	•	15.5	•	•	•
Operating Margin Before Officers' Comp. **22**	8.3	•	20.1	57.7	4.5	20.2	30.7	•	•	16.4	•	•	•

Selected Average Balance Sheet ($ in Thousands)

Item								
Net Receivables 23	16352	22	0	276	794	2299	12707	134844
Inventories 24	2829	1	0	14	196	•	2670	5584
Net Property, Plant and Equipment 25	328974	179	4	792	3968	•	131834	756778
Total Assets 26	422276	309	498	1878	8766	•	178200	1293126
Notes and Loans Payable 27	86416	0	0	423	740	•	38061	275829
All Other Liabilities 28	189860	-182	172	3510	5219	•	51703	419561
Net Worth 29	146000	491	498	4515	9823	•	88436	597736

Selected Financial Ratios (Times to 1)

Item								
Current Ratio 30	0.7	3.7	•	2.3	0.3	1.8	1.2	1.0
Quick Ratio 31	0.5	3.4	•	1.7	0.2	1.6	0.9	0.8
Net Sales to Working Capital 32	•	3.9	0.8	8.4	•	5.7	14.6	134.5
Coverage Ratio 33	3.3	6.1	•	20.5	17.2	23.5	20.3	4.3
Total Asset Turnover 34	0.4	1.2	0.7	1.4	2.2	0.8	0.5	0.3
Inventory Turnover 35	15.9	17.6	•	•	2.4	14.5	15.2	2.3
Receivables Turnover 36	9.9	8.6	•	•	30.6	7.1	•	•
Total Liabilities to Net Worth 37	1.9	•	•	0.5	0.9	0.7	1.0	1.2
Current Assets to Working Capital 38	•	1.4	1.0	1.7	•	2.3	5.2	66.4
Current Liabilities to Working Capital 39	•	0.4	0.7	0.7	•	1.3	4.2	65.4
Working Capital to Net Sales 40	•	0.3	1.3	0.1	•	0.2	0.1	0.0
Inventory to Working Capital 41	•	0.0	•	0.0	•	0.1	0.4	1.8
Total Receipts to Cash Flow 42	4.1	1.6	0.4	1.9	2.3	2.0	3.2	2.1
Cost of Goods to Cash Flow 43	1.2	0.1	•	0.3	0.0	0.4	1.3	0.1
Cash Flow to Total Debt 44	0.1	•	•	2.4	2.0	0.9	0.3	0.3

Selected Financial Factors (in Percentages)

Item								
Debt Ratio 45	65.4	•	41.3	48.5	31.7	•	50.4	53.8
Return on Total Assets 46	7.6	42.7	27.3	44.4	25.4	•	10.8	9.6
Return on Equity Before Income Taxes 47	15.4	22.4	171.2	35.4	81.2	44.6	20.7	16.0
Return on Equity After Income Taxes 48	10.2	15.0	155.7	23.4	81.2	43.8	17.2	11.1
Profit Margin (Before Income Tax) 49	14.1	29.5	228.4	16.8	18.8	33.7	19.1	23.0
Profit Margin (After Income Tax) 50	9.3	19.8	207.7	11.1	18.8	33.1	15.9	16.0

Table I

Corporations with and without Net Income

WATER TRANSPORTATION

MONEY AMOUNTS AND SIZE OF ASSETS IN THOUSANDS OF DOLLARS

Item Description for Accounting Period 7/06 Through 6/07	Total	Zero Assets	Under 500	500 to 1,000	1,000 to 5,000	5,000 to 10,000	10,000 to 25,000	25,000 to 50,000	50,000 to 100,000	100,000 to 250,000	250,000 to 500,000	500,000 to 2,500,000	2,500,000 and over
Number of Enterprises **1**	5555	1001	2516	850	828	187	79	31	18	23	7	14	0
Revenues ($ in Thousands)													
Net Sales **2**	27619317	2346139	520256	1193037	1343435	3220933	1245775	732854	1011826	2306608	1063326	12635129	0
Interest **3**	193416	5158	1227	0	2808	859	4434	494	2667	8442	19238	148089	0
Rents **4**	117811	446	0	0	2890	511	611	1301	2828	477	0	108747	0
Royalties **5**	479	475	0	0	0	0	0	0	0	4	0	0	0
Other Portfolio Income **6**	374704	2340	67221	0	7551	19645	19390	3555	7162	38989	18924	189926	0
Other Receipts **7**	281334	-395742	130148	2200	1322	40826	10906	5956	9212	12287	301261	162959	0
Total Receipts **8**	28587061	1958816	718852	1195237	1358006	3282774	1281116	744160	1033695	2366807	1402749	13244850	0
Average Total Receipts **9**	5146	1957	286	1406	1640	17555	16217	24005	57428	102905	200393	946061	•
Operating Costs/Operating Income (%)													
Cost of Operations **10**	36.9	18.1	10.8	1.8	32.1	60.0	32.5	31.6	28.5	44.6	47.2	38.5	•
Salaries and Wages **11**	9.5	5.0	23.0	11.6	15.3	6.8	14.0	16.8	6.4	9.0	7.1	9.4	•
Taxes Paid **12**	1.8	0.4	5.8	1.6	4.0	1.1	2.5	3.9	1.9	2.0	1.1	1.6	•
Interest Paid **13**	2.4	1.0	3.4	2.3	3.0	1.8	1.6	4.0	3.3	3.4	3.8	2.4	•
Depreciation **14**	6.2	2.7	10.7	6.9	10.0	3.5	3.5	8.8	5.7	9.3	6.7	6.4	•
Amortization and Depletion **15**	0.2	0.1	0.0	0.0	0.0	0.0	0.0	0.0	0.0	0.2	0.6	0.2	•
Pensions and Other Deferred Comp. **16**	0.5	0.1	3.1	0.1	0.2	0.2	0.3	0.5	0.4	0.6	0.7	0.6	•
Employee Benefits **17**	1.7	0.5	0.2	0.7	1.4	0.8	1.5	3.2	1.0	2.1	1.1	2.3	•
Advertising **18**	0.6	1.9	0.1	0.3	2.0	0.1	0.1	1.9	0.1	0.1	0.0	0.5	•
Other Expenses **19**	36.8	56.0	48.1	69.0	22.7	22.5	36.5	26.8	44.9	23.4	47.4	36.4	•
Officers' Compensation **20**	1.5	0.4	13.3	1.9	4.2	1.6	3.0	0.8	1.2	1.0	2.7	0.8	•
Operating Margin **21**	2.0	13.9	•	3.8	5.2	1.6	4.4	1.8	6.6	4.1	•	0.9	•
Operating Margin Before Officers' Comp. **22**	3.5	14.3	•	5.7	9.4	3.2	7.5	2.6	7.8	5.2	•	1.7	•

Selected Average Balance Sheet ($ in Thousands)

Net Receivables 23	585	0	10	0	196	1122	3134	3476	8957	20078	54644	106711	•
Inventories 24	58	0	0	0	2	18	29	227	710	536	6423	17183	•
Net Property, Plant and Equipment 25	3072	0	2	389	1128	4686	4840	18588	35348	92116	116638	742145	•
Total Assets 26	5859	0	52	689	2371	7630	14085	30313	72551	152230	326573	1378092	•
Notes and Loans Payable 27	2198	0	27	540	1386	1421	4330	17259	28825	64035	102903	477323	•
All Other Liabilities 28	1359	0	6	23	188	3188	4411	5982	19305	30315	88058	326448	•
Net Worth 29	2301	0	20	126	797	3022	5344	7072	24422	57880	135613	574321	•

Selected Financial Ratios (Times to 1)

Current Ratio 30	1.3	•	1.3	1.0	1.2	0.8	1.4	1.1	1.2	1.2	1.8	1.4	•
Quick Ratio 31	1.0	•	0.9	0.7	0.7	0.6	1.2	0.8	0.8	1.0	1.5	1.1	•
Net Sales to Working Capital 32	14.9	•	32.6	369.5	15.6	•	8.2	36.0	17.9	18.4	3.5	10.1	•
Coverage Ratio 33	3.3	•	6.9	2.8	3.1	3.0	5.5	1.8	3.7	2.9	4.6	3.6	•
Total Asset Turnover 34	0.8	•	4.0	2.0	0.7	2.3	1.1	0.8	0.8	0.7	0.5	0.7	•
Inventory Turnover 35	31.4	•	•	•	275.5	584.0	175.0	32.9	22.5	83.3	11.2	20.2	•
Receivables Turnover 36	9.2	•	33.5	•	12.1	17.7	4.4	5.7	4.9	6.4	2.9	9.3	•
Total Liabilities to Net Worth 37	1.5	•	1.6	4.5	2.0	1.5	1.6	3.3	2.0	1.6	1.4	1.4	•
Current Assets to Working Capital 38	4.5	•	4.7	45.2	6.9	•	3.6	13.2	7.5	7.0	2.3	3.3	•
Current Liabilities to Working Capital 39	3.5	•	3.7	44.2	5.9	•	2.6	12.2	6.5	6.0	1.3	2.3	•
Working Capital to Net Sales 40	0.1	•	0.0	0.0	0.1	•	0.1	0.0	0.1	0.1	0.3	0.1	•
Inventory to Working Capital 41	0.2	•	•	•	0.0	•	0.0	0.4	0.3	0.1	0.1	0.2	•
Total Receipts to Cash Flow 42	3.0	2.3	1.9	2.1	5.1	7.5	3.2	4.3	2.2	3.8	1.9	2.8	•
Cost of Goods to Cash Flow 43	1.1	0.4	0.2	0.0	1.6	4.5	1.0	0.6	0.6	1.7	0.9	1.1	•
Cash Flow to Total Debt 44	0.5	•	3.3	1.2	0.2	0.5	0.6	0.2	0.5	0.3	0.4	0.4	•

Selected Financial Factors (in Percentages)

Debt Ratio 45	60.7	•	61.9	81.8	66.4	60.4	62.1	76.7	66.3	62.0	58.5	58.3	•
Return on Total Assets 46	6.9	•	91.6	12.8	6.3	12.0	9.9	5.7	9.2	6.7	8.1	5.6	•
Return on Equity Before Income Taxes 47	12.3	•	205.4	44.6	12.7	20.2	21.5	11.2	19.9	11.6	15.2	9.7	•
Return on Equity After Income Taxes 48	9.7	•	203.8	42.5	12.3	19.9	16.4	10.4	18.4	10.6	12.8	6.8	•
Profit Margin (Before Income Tax) 49	5.7	•	19.8	4.0	6.2	3.5	7.3	3.4	8.7	6.7	13.6	6.2	•
Profit Margin (After Income Tax) 50	4.5	•	19.6	3.8	6.0	3.5	5.6	3.1	8.0	6.1	11.5	4.3	•

Table II

Corporations with Net Income

WATER TRANSPORTATION

MONEY AMOUNTS AND SIZE OF ASSETS IN THOUSANDS OF DOLLARS

Item Description for Accounting Period 7/06 Through 6/07	Total	Zero Assets	Under 500	500 to 1,000	1,000 to 5,000	5,000 to 10,000	10,000 to 25,000	25,000 to 50,000	50,000 to 100,000	100,000 to 250,000	250,000 to 500,000	500,000 to 2,500,000	2,500,000 and over
Number of Enterprises **1**	3218	35	1690	720	520	131	51	•	•	18	•	11	0
Revenues ($ in Thousands)													
Net Sales **2**	20351072	929727	226116	1050783	1186224	1835054	848436	•	•	2032532	•	10209150	0
Interest **3**	141067	1371	179	0	2549	859	3768	•	•	6758	•	118192	0
Rents **4**	115075	0	0	0	2890	511	611	•	•	434	•	108704	0
Royalties **5**	475	475	0	0	0	0	0	•	•	0	•	0	0
Other Portfolio Income **6**	343601	2332	67221	0	1855	19645	18920	•	•	36581	•	176034	0
Other Receipts **7**	616879	2980	130149	0	265	39885	10056	•	•	11434	•	112403	0
Total Receipts **8**	21568169	936885	423665	1050783	1193783	1895954	881791	•	•	2087739	•	10724483	0
Average Total Receipts **9**	6702	26768	251	1459	2296	14473	17290	•	•	115986	•	974953	•
Operating Costs/Operating Income (%)													
Cost of Operations **10**	39.5	32.3	24.8	2.1	26.2	56.7	46.9	•	•	47.1	•	40.7	•
Salaries and Wages **11**	8.4	2.4	4.3	11.0	17.2	9.7	11.1	•	•	9.2	•	7.7	•
Taxes Paid **12**	1.9	0.2	3.4	1.6	4.3	1.5	1.8	•	•	2.0	•	1.8	•
Interest Paid **13**	1.9	1.3	0.5	2.3	1.2	0.8	1.2	•	•	2.3	•	2.0	•
Depreciation **14**	5.8	4.0	5.5	7.2	7.7	4.7	4.2	•	•	7.0	•	5.4	•
Amortization and Depletion **15**	0.1	0.1	0.0	0.0	0.0	0.0	0.0	•	•	0.2	•	0.2	•
Pensions and Other Deferred Comp. **16**	0.6	0.1	7.1	0.1	0.1	0.2	0.4	•	•	0.6	•	0.7	•
Employee Benefits **17**	1.5	0.1	0.6	0.8	1.5	1.0	1.3	•	•	2.2	•	1.6	•
Advertising **18**	0.3	0.6	0.1	0.3	1.6	0.0	0.1	•	•	0.1	•	0.2	•
Other Expenses **19**	32.8	45.4	52.5	66.3	19.7	16.2	21.4	•	•	22.2	•	34.1	•
Officers' Compensation **20**	1.8	0.1	25.1	2.2	4.6	2.6	3.7	•	•	1.0	•	0.8	•
Operating Margin **21**	5.3	13.2	•	6.1	15.9	6.6	7.9	•	•	6.0	•	4.8	•
Operating Margin Before Officers' Comp. **22**	7.1	13.3	1.1	8.3	20.6	9.2	11.6	•	•	7.1	•	5.6	•

Selected Average Balance Sheet ($ in Thousands)

Net Receivables 23	867	0	0	307	1334	4284	•	21838	•	116646
Inventories 24	84	0	0	3	25	45	•	483	•	20154
Net Property, Plant and Equipment 25	3910	0	0	886	4306	4676	•	89644	•	717867
Total Assets 26	7562	0	36	2368	7133	14417	•	155761	•	1355520
Notes and Loans Payable 27	2313	0	2	1042	1835	4275	•	58661	•	355823
All Other Liabilities 28	1596	0	0	252	1848	4542	•	34420	•	288810
Net Worth 29	3653	0	34	1074	3451	5599	•	62680	•	710888

Selected Financial Ratios (Times to 1)

Current Ratio 30	1.6	•	130.8	1.1	1.5	1.1	1.5	•	1.1	•	2.0
Quick Ratio 31	1.4	•	128.5	0.8	1.4	1.1	1.4	•	0.9	•	1.6
Net Sales to Working Capital 32	7.8	•	8.4	82.9	10.4	60.0	6.4	•	28.2	•	5.7
Coverage Ratio 33	7.0	11.5	135.0	3.7	15.1	13.6	11.1	•	4.7	•	6.1
Total Asset Turnover 34	0.8	•	3.7	2.2	1.0	2.0	1.2	•	0.7	•	0.7
Inventory Turnover 35	29.8	•	•	198.4	314.2	171.8	•	•	110.1	•	18.7
Receivables Turnover 36	7.7	•	356.9	•	10.8	14.2	3.7	•	•	•	•
Total Liabilities to Net Worth 37	1.1	•	0.1	0.0	3.5	1.2	1.1	•	1.5	•	0.9
Current Assets to Working Capital 38	2.6	•	1.0	10.2	3.0	10.9	3.0	•	10.3	•	2.0
Current Liabilities to Working Capital 39	1.6	•	0.0	9.2	2.0	9.9	2.0	•	9.3	•	1.0
Working Capital to Net Sales 40	0.1	•	0.1	0.0	0.1	0.0	0.0	•	0.1	•	0.2
Inventory to Working Capital 41	0.1	•	•	•	0.0	0.1	0.0	•	0.1	•	0.1
Total Receipts to Cash Flow 42	2.7	1.7	0.9	2.0	3.7	4.1	2.0	•	3.8	•	2.6
Cost of Goods to Cash Flow 43	1.1	0.5	0.2	0.0	1.0	2.3	0.0	•	1.8	•	1.1
Cash Flow to Total Debt 44	0.6	•	56.7	1.4	0.5	0.9	0.5	•	0.3	•	0.4

Selected Financial Factors (in Percentages)

Debt Ratio 45	51.7	•	7.2	78.0	54.6	51.6	61.2	•	59.8	•	47.6
Return on Total Assets 46	11.2	•	235.1	18.2	17.1	21.0	15.0	•	8.0	•	8.3
Return on Equity Before Income Taxes 47	19.9	•	251.5	60.3	35.2	40.3	35.2	•	15.7	•	13.2
Return on Equity After Income Taxes 48	17.2	•	250.1	58.1	34.7	39.9	27.7	•	14.5	•	10.2
Profit Margin (Before Income Tax) 49	11.5	14.0	63.4	6.1	16.6	9.9	11.8	•	8.7	•	10.1
Profit Margin (After Income Tax) 50	9.9	13.3	63.0	5.9	16.3	9.8	9.3	•	8.1	•	7.8

Table I

Corporations with and without Net Income

TRUCK TRANSPORTATION

Money Amounts and Size of Assets in Thousands of Dollars

Item Description for Accounting Period 7/06 Through 6/07	Total	Zero Assets	Under 500	500 to 1,000	1,000 to 5,000	5,000 to 10,000	10,000 to 25,000	25,000 to 50,000	50,000 to 100,000	100,000 to 250,000	250,000 to 500,000	500,000 to 2,500,000	2,500,000 and over
Number of Enterprises **1**	106826	26767	66097	6163	5798	1215	494	135	61	49	22	25	0
Revenues ($ in Thousands)													
Net Sales **2**	235132284	6386909	36696091	20384525	37869474	19624939	18099063	11507763	8420277	11495073	11721818	52926353	0
Interest **3**	511556	3329	4906	7405	27718	17791	15842	10614	5356	21435	12100	385061	0
Rents **4**	417850	1479	902	1560	43583	5076	25594	42648	25584	53032	29438	188954	0
Royalties **5**	221414	0	0	0	353	0	46794	26	0	0	0	174241	0
Other Portfolio Income **6**	2377059	218248	252903	114277	281533	124463	160102	114095	72171	85573	115829	837862	0
Other Receipts **7**	2868764	80184	327856	260961	542114	159060	159714	135843	45228	271219	298013	588574	0
Total Receipts **8**	241528927	6690149	37282658	20768728	38764775	19931329	18507109	11810989	8568616	11926332	12177198	55510045	0
Average Total Receipts **9**	2261	250	564	3370	6686	16404	37464	87489	140469	243395	553509	2204042	•
Operating Costs/Operating Income (%)													
Cost of Operations **10**	34.8	27.2	30.6	42.8	41.2	38.5	43.7	44.8	29.4	27.1	19.7	30.1	•
Salaries and Wages **11**	16.4	16.2	11.5	13.6	11.6	18.5	15.1	11.7	22.6	19.2	22.0	22.2	•
Taxes Paid **12**	3.5	2.1	3.0	4.1	3.0	3.2	4.4	2.8	4.2	3.3	3.8	4.1	•
Interest Paid **13**	1.2	0.8	0.9	0.9	1.2	1.1	1.2	1.1	1.8	1.8	1.7	1.4	•
Depreciation **14**	4.8	4.0	3.8	3.9	4.8	4.7	5.3	4.5	6.4	6.2	8.1	4.7	•
Amortization and Depletion **15**	0.1	0.1	0.0	0.0	0.1	0.0	0.1	0.1	0.2	0.3	0.4	0.2	•
Pensions and Other Deferred Comp. **16**	0.4	0.0	0.1	0.2	0.2	0.4	0.2	0.2	0.2	0.5	0.8	0.8	•
Employee Benefits **17**	2.4	1.4	0.9	1.4	1.6	1.2	2.1	1.6	2.3	2.7	3.1	5.1	•
Advertising **18**	0.2	0.2	0.3	0.2	0.3	0.3	0.3	0.2	0.2	0.3	0.3	0.2	•
Other Expenses **19**	34.0	35.8	43.7	30.3	34.1	28.7	26.6	32.2	32.1	40.3	41.6	30.4	•
Officers' Compensation **20**	2.0	12.8	3.7	2.7	2.2	1.5	1.6	1.1	0.7	0.7	0.5	0.4	•
Operating Margin **21**	0.2	•	1.5	•	•	1.8	•	0.8	•	•	•	0.5	•
Operating Margin Before Officers' Comp. **22**	2.1	12.0	5.2	2.6	2.0	3.4	0.9	0.8	0.6	•	•	0.9	•

Selected Average Balance Sheet ($ in Thousands)

Net Receivables 23	202	0	10	102	497	1829	3719	9162	14723	34396	60128	329737
Inventories 24	10	0	1	13	22	65	295	391	1596	1325	1267	13133
Net Property, Plant and Equipment 25	416	0	51	377	959	2968	7049	16216	38277	74486	202309	539134
Total Assets 26	949	0	89	700	2064	6938	14970	33292	71061	154872	361919	1562457
Notes and Loans Payable 27	388	0	71	391	1161	2868	7123	13986	35412	67271	126298	420609
All Other Liabilities 28	275	0	16	137	349	1721	3261	8463	17143	39853	110130	604791
Net Worth 29	287	0	2	172	555	2349	4586	10843	18506	47748	125491	537057

Selected Financial Ratios (Times to 1)

Current Ratio 30	1.2	•	1.1	1.0	1.3	1.4	1.1	1.3	1.1	1.1	1.1	1.1
Quick Ratio 31	0.9	•	0.9	0.9	1.1	1.2	0.9	1.1	0.8	0.9	0.8	0.8
Net Sales to Working Capital 32	44.5	•	260.4	•	30.2	17.4	48.9	23.4	70.4	66.3	57.5	36.2
Coverage Ratio 33	3.3	5.7	4.3	2.9	2.9	4.0	2.2	3.1	1.9	1.8	2.1	4.3
Total Asset Turnover 34	2.3	•	6.3	4.7	3.2	2.3	2.4	2.6	1.9	1.5	1.5	1.4
Inventory Turnover 35	75.5	•	136.3	110.5	124.4	95.9	54.2	97.7	25.4	48.0	82.8	48.5
Receivables Turnover 36	11.0	•	52.5	28.9	12.3	10.3	9.3	9.3	8.7	6.8	8.7	6.8
Total Liabilities to Net Worth 37	2.3	•	55.8	3.1	2.7	2.0	2.3	2.1	2.8	2.2	1.9	1.9
Current Assets to Working Capital 38	7.1	•	13.1	•	4.0	3.7	8.0	4.0	13.2	14.1	10.1	9.8
Current Liabilities to Working Capital 39	6.1	•	12.1	•	3.0	2.7	7.0	3.0	12.2	13.1	9.1	8.8
Working Capital to Net Sales 40	0.0	•	0.0	•	0.0	0.1	0.0	0.0	0.0	0.0	0.0	0.0
Inventory to Working Capital 41	0.2	•	0.3	•	0.1	0.1	0.4	0.1	0.9	0.3	0.1	0.3
Total Receipts to Cash Flow 42	3.4	3.1	2.8	3.9	3.5	4.2	4.7	4.7	3.8	3.2	3.0	3.3
Cost of Goods to Cash Flow 43	1.2	0.8	0.8	1.7	1.4	1.6	2.1	2.1	1.1	0.9	0.6	1.0
Cash Flow to Total Debt 44	1.0	•	2.3	1.6	1.3	0.8	0.7	0.8	0.7	0.7	0.7	0.6

Selected Financial Factors (in Percentages)

Debt Ratio 45	69.8	•	98.2	75.4	73.1	66.1	69.4	67.4	74.0	69.2	65.3	65.6
Return on Total Assets 46	9.5	•	25.2	12.3	10.9	10.6	6.8	8.8	6.8	4.9	5.2	8.1
Return on Equity Before Income Taxes 47	22.0	•	1103.3	32.8	26.2	23.4	12.2	18.5	12.6	6.9	7.7	18.0
Return on Equity After Income Taxes 48	17.9	•	1070.4	31.8	23.2	20.9	9.8	16.0	11.0	4.6	6.2	12.0
Profit Margin (Before Income Tax) 49	2.9	4.0	3.1	1.7	2.2	3.4	1.5	2.4	1.7	1.4	1.8	4.6
Profit Margin (After Income Tax) 50	2.3	3.8	3.0	1.7	2.0	3.0	1.2	2.0	1.5	0.9	1.5	3.0

Table II

Corporations with Net Income

TRUCK TRANSPORTATION

MONEY AMOUNTS AND SIZE OF ASSETS IN THOUSANDS OF DOLLARS

Item Description for Accounting Period 7/06 Through 6/07		Total	Zero Assets	Under 500	500 to 1,000	1,000 to 5,000	5,000 to 10,000	10,000 to 25,000	25,000 to 50,000	50,000 to 100,000	100,000 to 250,000	250,000 to 500,000	500,000 to 2,500,000	2,500,000 and over
Number of Enterprises	1	64843	14216	41834	3828	3630	895	252	83	39	32	14	21	0
Revenues ($ in Thousands)														
Net Sales	2	171718213	3353712	25395705	12270601	24946256	15347411	10876289	7640004	5830328	8247446	7647745	50162716	0
Interest	3	478731	289	4141	6872	23818	15875	10618	6304	3521	18799	3922	384571	0
Rents	4	358326	1479	665	1560	42533	2986	5202	21839	21866	41847	29396	188954	0
Royalties	5	221414	0	0	0	353	0	46794	26	0	0	0	174241	0
Other Portfolio Income	6	1949058	211109	227244	31566	218000	106911	93849	78953	51220	63591	40154	826459	0
Other Receipts	7	2345743	8419	292052	14185	541726	124054	125667	66474	35467	222857	201376	586468	0
Total Receipts	8	177071485	3575008	25919807	12451784	25772686	15597237	11158419	7813600	5942402	8594540	7922593	52323409	0
Average Total Receipts	9	2731	251	620	3253	7100	17427	44279	94140	152369	268579	565900	2491591	•
Operating Costs/Operating Income (%)														
Cost of Operations	10	33.8	27.9	33.8	30.8	38.6	36.0	44.8	45.5	33.6	27.5	25.5	30.0	•
Salaries and Wages	11	16.7	5.6	10.5	16.4	12.2	19.9	14.8	11.0	19.2	17.8	18.4	22.4	•
Taxes Paid	12	3.5	2.3	2.9	3.2	3.1	3.3	5.2	2.5	3.8	2.8	3.8	4.2	•
Interest Paid	13	1.1	1.1	0.8	1.1	1.0	0.9	0.9	0.6	1.4	1.4	1.2	1.4	•
Depreciation	14	4.4	4.0	3.0	4.5	4.2	4.1	3.8	3.8	5.1	5.4	7.9	4.6	•
Amortization and Depletion	15	0.1	0.1	0.0	0.0	0.1	0.0	0.1	0.1	0.1	0.1	0.1	0.1	•
Pensions and Other Deferred Comp.	16	0.4	0.0	0.1	0.4	0.3	0.4	0.2	0.2	0.2	0.4	0.6	0.8	•
Employee Benefits	17	2.7	1.0	1.1	2.0	1.8	1.3	1.9	1.7	2.3	2.3	2.2	5.2	•
Advertising	18	0.2	0.3	0.1	0.2	0.3	0.3	0.3	0.3	0.2	0.3	0.4	0.2	•
Other Expenses	19	32.9	30.9	39.0	35.0	34.2	28.7	24.4	30.9	31.7	41.8	38.9	30.0	•
Officers' Compensation	20	2.1	21.5	3.8	3.5	2.8	1.6	1.8	0.9	0.7	0.7	0.5	0.4	•
Operating Margin	21	2.0	5.3	4.8	2.9	1.5	3.4	1.8	2.5	1.8	•	0.5	0.7	•
Operating Margin Before Officers' Comp.	22	4.2	26.8	8.6	6.4	4.2	5.0	3.6	3.4	2.5	0.2	1.1	1.1	•

Selected Average Balance Sheet ($ in Thousands)

	1	2	3	4	5	6	7	8	9	10	11	12
Net Receivables 23	262	0	9	112	594	1949	4353	9086	16817	36402	63332	368818
Inventories 24	13	0	2	13	21	70	393	429	2191	1539	1107	23683
Net Property, Plant and Equipment 25	485	0	46	389	890	2871	6396	15346	31920	73680	216512	606005
Total Assets 26	1148	0	88	697	2221	6769	15832	32781	70452	151921	347596	1657830
Notes and Loans Payable 27	381	0	59	426	1063	2413	6158	10123	29662	58096	90841	378169
All Other Liabilities 28	352	0	16	126	375	1564	3932	8825	17825	37357	94061	664467
Net Worth 29	416	0	14	145	784	2791	5742	13833	22965	56468	162695	615195

Selected Financial Ratios (Times to 1)

	1	2	3	4	5	6	7	8	9	10	11	12
Current Ratio 30	1.2	•	1.2	0.9	1.9	1.5	1.3	1.5	1.3	1.1	1.2	1.1
Quick Ratio 31	1.0	•	1.0	0.8	1.5	1.3	1.0	1.3	0.9	0.9	0.9	0.8
Net Sales to Working Capital 32	29.9	•	104.9	•	13.5	16.2	29.3	19.2	23.0	40.6	34.2	37.0
Coverage Ratio 33	5.7	12.0	9.6	4.9	5.9	6.6	6.0	8.5	3.7	3.6	4.5	4.7
Total Asset Turnover 34	2.3	•	6.9	4.6	3.1	2.5	2.7	2.8	2.1	1.7	1.6	1.4
Inventory Turnover 35	66.6	•	125.0	77.1	125.6	88.1	49.3	97.6	22.9	46.1	125.9	30.2
Receivables Turnover 36	9.6	•	64.8	27.9	10.0	9.6	7.9	8.2	7.5	6.4	•	•
Total Liabilities to Net Worth 37	1.8	•	5.5	3.8	1.8	1.4	1.8	1.4	2.1	1.7	1.1	1.7
Current Assets to Working Capital 38	5.2	•	5.3	•	2.1	3.1	5.0	3.1	4.6	8.2	5.5	10.1
Current Liabilities to Working Capital 39	4.2	•	4.3	•	1.1	2.1	4.0	2.1	3.6	7.2	4.5	9.1
Working Capital to Net Sales 40	0.0	•	0.0	•	0.1	0.1	0.0	0.1	0.0	0.0	0.0	0.0
Inventory to Working Capital 41	0.2	•	0.2	•	0.1	0.1	0.3	0.1	0.4	0.2	0.1	0.4
Total Receipts to Cash Flow 42	3.3	2.8	2.8	3.2	3.2	4.0	4.5	4.4	3.6	2.9	3.2	3.3
Cost of Goods to Cash Flow 43	1.1	0.8	0.9	1.0	1.2	1.5	2.0	2.0	1.2	0.8	0.8	1.0
Cash Flow to Total Debt 44	1.1	•	3.0	1.8	1.5	1.1	1.0	1.1	0.9	0.9	0.9	0.7

Selected Financial Factors (in Percentages)

	1	2	3	4	5	6	7	8	9	10	11	12
Debt Ratio 45	63.8	•	84.6	79.2	64.7	58.8	63.7	57.8	67.4	62.8	53.2	62.9
Return on Total Assets 46	14.3	•	52.7	25.2	17.9	15.0	14.3	15.2	10.8	8.7	8.3	9.1
Return on Equity Before Income Taxes 47	32.7	•	307.3	96.6	42.1	30.8	32.8	31.9	24.1	16.8	13.9	19.3
Return on Equity After Income Taxes 48	28.1	•	301.3	94.5	38.7	28.0	29.0	28.7	22.1	13.9	12.1	13.1
Profit Margin (Before Income Tax) 49	5.1	11.9	6.8	4.4	4.8	5.0	4.4	4.8	3.7	3.7	4.1	5.0
Profit Margin (After Income Tax) 50	4.4	11.5	6.7	4.3	4.4	4.6	3.9	4.3	3.4	3.0	3.6	3.4

Table I

Corporations with and without Net Income

TRANSIT AND GROUND PASSENGER TRANSPORTATION

MONEY AMOUNTS AND SIZE OF ASSETS IN THOUSANDS OF DOLLARS

Item Description for Accounting Period 7/06 Through 6/07	Total	Zero Assets	Under 500	500 to 1,000	1,000 to 5,000	5,000 to 10,000	10,000 to 25,000	25,000 to 50,000	50,000 to 100,000	100,000 to 250,000	250,000 to 500,000	500,000 to 2,500,000	2,500,000 and over
Number of Enterprises **1**	26911	6266	17307	1850	1202	183	72	14	7	4	6	0	0
Revenues ($ in Thousands)													
Net Sales **2**	22778294	455170	3244771	1229890	5898385	2398162	1726567	324837	540806	1076317	5883388	0	0
Interest **3**	48173	147	1862	74	3931	1336	3790	4109	1093	2216	29615	0	0
Rents **4**	44826	951	12	1167	4197	1322	5501	3878	565	4951	22282	0	0
Royalties **5**	0	0	0	0	0	0	0	0	0	0	0	0	0
Other Portfolio Income **6**	433851	21238	14379	11	31850	162797	45651	1674	1416	12557	142278	0	0
Other Receipts **7**	1050943	949	880237	12254	40833	6375	52541	23945	4546	1899	27366	0	0
Total Receipts **8**	24356087	478455	4141261	1243396	5979196	2569992	1834050	358443	548426	1097940	6104929	0	0
Average Total Receipts **9**	905	76	239	672	4974	14044	25473	25603	78347	274485	1017488	•	•
Operating Costs/Operating Income (%)													
Cost of Operations **10**	34.5	22.0	12.6	43.9	40.3	53.9	53.7	14.5	57.7	41.4	24.1	•	•
Salaries and Wages **11**	22.9	4.8	51.5	15.5	14.4	8.2	10.8	29.7	12.7	23.7	28.8	•	•
Taxes Paid **12**	4.5	2.0	5.4	3.0	3.2	5.2	3.5	6.9	3.5	5.8	5.6	•	•
Interest Paid **13**	2.8	0.7	2.7	4.6	1.4	2.4	1.4	2.7	2.1	5.3	4.2	•	•
Depreciation **14**	6.0	5.9	4.8	3.6	4.9	10.3	6.7	5.6	5.2	3.1	6.8	•	•
Amortization and Depletion **15**	0.7	0.0	1.0	1.5	0.2	0.0	0.1	0.3	0.6	0.3	1.4	•	•
Pensions and Other Deferred Comp. **16**	0.3	0.0	•	0.1	0.4	0.5	0.6	0.1	0.7	0.8	0.3	•	•
Employee Benefits **17**	1.9	0.4	0.3	0.9	0.9	1.6	2.6	2.1	1.7	7.7	2.8	•	•
Advertising **18**	0.6	1.6	0.7	0.3	0.8	0.2	0.6	1.0	0.6	0.1	0.5	•	•
Other Expenses **19**	27.9	60.9	40.3	24.2	28.3	20.4	17.6	39.7	13.2	13.5	28.2	•	•
Officers' Compensation **20**	2.3	4.8	5.0	2.4	3.9	1.1	1.5	1.2	1.1	0.5	0.1	•	•
Operating Margin **21**	•	•	•	0.1	1.4	•	0.9	•	1.0	•	•	•	•
Operating Margin Before Officers' Comp. **22**	•	1.7	•	2.5	5.3	•	2.4	•	2.0	•	•	•	•

Selected Average Balance Sheet ($ in Thousands)

Net Receivables 23	69	0	7	39	321	1489	2454	5904	7537	33400	94068
Inventories 24	4	0	0	2	5	63	120	71	2736	2560	11409
Net Property, Plant and Equipment 25	227	0	32	152	1005	4654	6424	6960	20899	57612	380847
Total Assets 26	557	100	640	2070	7301	14365	32020	61776	180034	935967	
Notes and Loans Payable 27	292	0	73	540	1424	5728	4626	12798	28170	97286	288076
All Other Liabilities 28	99	0	14	65	290	642	3222	5237	10103	47158	214869
Net Worth 29	166	0	14	35	356	931	6517	13985	23503	35589	433021

Selected Financial Ratios (Times to 1)

Current Ratio 30	1.2	•	1.1	0.4	1.4	0.8	1.4	2.2	1.4	2.1	1.2
Quick Ratio 31	0.8	•	0.6	0.3	1.0	0.7	1.1	1.3	1.1	1.6	0.7
Net Sales to Working Capital 32	33.1	•	93.5	•	23.6	•	14.8	2.2	11.7	9.1	25.1
Coverage Ratio 33	1.9	4.0	2.1	1.3	2.9	2.4	6.1	3.4	2.1	1.1	1.3
Total Asset Turnover 34	1.5	•	1.9	1.0	2.4	1.8	1.7	0.7	1.3	1.5	1.0
Inventory Turnover 35	65.5	•	1221.3	165.6	381.1	112.9	107.4	47.1	16.3	43.5	20.7
Receivables Turnover 36	12.2	•	22.2	13.6	15.2	9.6	7.9	4.4	12.9	6.2	20.8
Total Liabilities to Net Worth 37	2.4	•	6.3	17.0	4.8	6.8	1.2	1.3	1.6	4.1	1.2
Current Assets to Working Capital 38	6.7	•	10.8	•	3.6	•	3.5	1.9	3.3	1.9	7.5
Current Liabilities to Working Capital 39	5.7	•	9.8	•	2.6	•	2.5	0.9	2.3	0.9	6.5
Working Capital to Net Sales 40	0.0	•	0.0	•	0.0	•	0.1	0.4	0.1	0.1	0.0
Inventory to Working Capital 41	0.2	•	0.0	•	0.0	•	0.1	0.0	0.4	0.1	0.3
Total Receipts to Cash Flow 42	4.4	2.0	2.8	5.6	4.7	7.1	5.2	2.7	9.1	11.3	4.1
Cost of Goods to Cash Flow 43	1.5	0.4	0.4	2.5	1.9	3.9	2.8	0.4	5.2	4.7	1.0
Cash Flow to Total Debt 44	0.5	•	0.8	0.2	0.6	0.3	0.6	0.5	0.2	0.2	0.5

Selected Financial Factors (in Percentages)

Debt Ratio 45	70.2	•	86.3	94.5	82.8	87.2	54.6	56.3	62.0	80.2	53.7
Return on Total Assets 46	8.2	•	10.9	6.0	9.8	10.3	14.1	6.7	5.5	8.4	5.6
Return on Equity Before Income Taxes 47	13.1	•	42.0	21.8	37.6	46.8	25.9	10.7	7.4	2.6	2.5
Return on Equity After Income Taxes 48	11.2	•	40.1	18.7	34.3	39.7	18.7	9.1	6.0	•	2.2
Profit Margin (Before Income Tax) 49	2.6	2.0	3.1	1.2	2.7	3.3	7.0	6.5	2.3	0.3	1.1
Profit Margin (After Income Tax) 50	2.2	2.0	2.9	1.0	2.5	2.8	5.1	5.5	1.8	•	1.0

Table II
Corporations with Net Income

TRANSIT AND GROUND PASSENGER TRANSPORTATION

MONEY AMOUNTS AND SIZE OF ASSETS IN THOUSANDS OF DOLLARS

Item Description for Accounting Period 7/06 Through 6/07		Total	Zero Assets	Under 500	500 to 1,000	1,000 to 5,000	5,000 to 10,000	10,000 to 25,000	25,000 to 50,000	50,000 to 100,000	100,000 to 250,000	250,000 to 500,000	500,000 to 2,500,000	2,500,000 and over
Number of Enterprises	1	14238	2479	9306	1264	987	115	67	•	•	4	0	0	0

Revenues ($ in Thousands)

Net Sales	2	16554947	210694	2270124	704420	5435304	1697996	1686517	•	•	3955764	0	0	0
Interest	3	37913	147	1861	70	2883	474	3647	•	•	25012	0	0	0
Rents	4	39547	951	12	0	1203	1322	5501	•	•	26363	0	0	0
Royalties	5	0	0	0	0	0	0	0	•	•	0	0	0	0
Other Portfolio Income	6	372023	21238	1694	3	31195	142548	36661	•	•	136155	0	0	0
Other Receipts	7	1034340	948	877114	12094	39534	5478	51694	•	•	19560	0	0	0
Total Receipts	8	18038770	233978	3150805	716587	5510119	1847818	1784020	•	•	4162854	0	0	0
Average Total Receipts	9	1267	94	339	567	5583	16068	26627	•	•	1040714	•	•	•

Operating Costs/Operating Income (%)

Cost of Operations	10	31.2	2.9	16.4	20.5	42.9	48.0	54.5	•	•	9.8	•	•	•
Salaries and Wages	11	26.9	5.6	65.9	23.4	13.4	10.2	10.7	•	•	39.4	•	•	•
Taxes Paid	12	4.5	2.1	5.8	4.1	3.1	6.2	3.4	•	•	5.6	•	•	•
Interest Paid	13	2.0	0.6	1.9	5.1	1.1	1.2	1.2	•	•	3.4	•	•	•
Depreciation	14	5.5	9.1	3.8	4.7	4.5	9.5	5.7	•	•	5.7	•	•	•
Amortization and Depletion	15	0.2	0.1	0.3	0.0	0.1	0.0	0.1	•	•	0.3	•	•	•
Pensions and Other Deferred Comp.	16	0.3	0.0	•	0.0	0.4	0.5	0.6	•	•	0.4	•	•	•
Employee Benefits	17	1.4	0.8	0.1	1.0	0.8	1.6	2.6	•	•	2.3	•	•	•
Advertising	18	0.6	2.8	0.8	0.4	0.7	0.2	0.4	•	•	0.6	•	•	•
Other Expenses	19	28.5	63.3	31.3	34.9	26.5	24.7	17.1	•	•	33.5	•	•	•
Officers' Compensation	20	2.5	5.8	4.8	3.6	4.1	0.5	1.4	•	•	0.3	•	•	•
Operating Margin	21	•	6.9	•	2.3	2.4	•	2.2	•	•	•	•	•	•
Operating Margin Before Officers' Comp.	22	•	12.8	•	5.9	6.5	•	3.7	•	•	•	•	•	•

Selected Average Balance Sheet ($ in Thousands)

Net Receivables 23	87	0	7	21	364	1887	2589	•	•	•	80704
Inventories 24	4	0	0	2	4	50	102	•	•	•	5245
Net Property, Plant and Equipment 25	277	0	25	192	1007	4175	5844	•	•	•	361533
Total Assets 26	659	0	106	626	2032	7259	14215	•	•	•	797166
Notes and Loans Payable 27	312	0	65	518	1213	5143	4258	•	•	•	212359
All Other Liabilities 28	137	0	13	43	294	719	3358	•	•	•	270122
Net Worth 29	210	0	28	64	524	1397	6599	•	•	•	314685

Selected Financial Ratios (Times to 1)

Current Ratio 30	1.2	•	2.1	0.5	1.6	0.8	1.6	•	•	•	1.1
Quick Ratio 31	0.8	•	0.9	0.3	1.2	0.7	1.3	•	•	•	0.6
Net Sales to Working Capital 32	25.9	•	15.7	•	17.7	•	11.3	•	•	•	63.5
Coverage Ratio 33	3.7	28.7	5.1	1.8	4.4	6.5	7.6	•	•	•	2.2
Total Asset Turnover 34	1.8	•	2.3	0.9	2.7	2.0	1.8	•	•	•	1.2
Inventory Turnover 35	87.2	•	1138.3	48.8	650.8	142.8	134.0	•	•	•	18.5
Receivables Turnover 36	13.9	•	24.3	40.0	16.6	7.7	8.4	•	•	•	16.3
Total Liabilities to Net Worth 37	2.1	•	2.8	8.7	2.9	4.2	1.2	•	•	•	1.5
Current Assets to Working Capital 38	5.4	•	1.9	•	2.6	•	2.6	•	•	•	20.9
Current Liabilities to Working Capital 39	4.4	•	0.9	•	1.6	•	1.6	•	•	•	19.9
Working Capital to Net Sales 40	0.0	•	0.1	•	0.1	•	0.1	•	•	•	0.0
Inventory to Working Capital 41	0.1	•	0.0	•	0.0	•	0.0	•	•	•	0.6
Total Receipts to Cash Flow 42	3.9	1.5	3.2	3.7	4.8	5.1	5.1	•	•	•	3.2
Cost of Goods to Cash Flow 43	1.2	0.0	0.5	0.8	2.1	2.4	2.8	•	•	•	0.3
Cash Flow to Total Debt 44	0.7	•	1.0	0.3	0.8	0.5	0.7	•	•	•	0.6

Selected Financial Factors (in Percentages)

Debt Ratio 45	68.1	•	73.7	89.7	74.2	80.7	53.6	•	•	•	60.5
Return on Total Assets 46	13.0	•	22.0	8.1	13.2	15.4	16.1	•	•	•	9.5
Return on Equity Before Income Taxes 47	29.9	•	67.3	35.0	39.4	67.8	30.2	•	•	•	13.2
Return on Equity After Income Taxes 48	27.1	•	65.5	32.5	36.7	60.3	22.4	•	•	•	12.2
Profit Margin (Before Income Tax) 49	5.4	18.0	7.7	4.0	3.8	6.4	7.9	•	•	•	4.2
Profit Margin (After Income Tax) 50	4.9	17.9	7.5	3.8	3.5	5.7	5.9	•	•	•	3.9

Table I

Corporations with and without Net Income

PIPELINE TRANSPORTATION

MONEY AMOUNTS AND SIZE OF ASSETS IN THOUSANDS OF DOLLARS

Item Description for Accounting Period 7/06 Through 6/07	Total	Zero Assets	Under 500	500 to 1,000	1,000 to 5,000	5,000 to 10,000	10,000 to 25,000	25,000 to 50,000	50,000 to 100,000	100,000 to 250,000	250,000 to 500,000	500,000 to 2,500,000	2,500,000 and over
Number of Enterprises 1	325	13	0	0	241	20	19	10	4	6	7	5	0
Revenues ($ in Thousands)													
Net Sales 2	9902446	139746	0	0	797615	111183	475939	267272	251209	2380423	646148	4832910	0
Interest 3	298405	564	0	0	1011	864	1418	4406	4564	2762	3210	279607	0
Rents 4	12572	158	0	0	0	0	9	110	0	5765	1304	5227	0
Royalties 5	907	0	0	0	907	0	0	0	0	0	0	0	0
Other Portfolio Income 6	34063	467	0	0	0	587	737	334	435	200	25834	5470	0
Other Receipts 7	215502	2597	0	0	59867	12526	16817	5929	2036	10779	54062	50887	0
Total Receipts 8	10463895	143532	0	0	859400	125160	494920	278051	258244	2399929	730558	5174101	0
Average Total Receipts 9	32197	11041	•	•	3566	6258	26048	27805	64561	399988	104365	1034820	•
Operating Costs/Operating Income (%)													
Cost of Operations 10	69.2	76.1	•	•	53.2	12.0	74.3	28.3	57.9	87.3	5.8	74.8	•
Salaries and Wages 11	3.4	2.8	•	•	13.4	5.2	2.5	4.1	6.3	3.4	2.9	1.8	•
Taxes Paid 12	1.8	0.8	•	•	1.9	6.0	1.6	6.1	4.5	0.7	3.8	1.5	•
Interest Paid 13	7.8	1.9	•	•	0.1	0.3	2.9	2.8	3.2	0.9	8.1	13.8	•
Depreciation 14	4.1	8.4	•	•	2.3	3.8	1.4	7.9	3.5	1.1	15.5	4.4	•
Amortization and Depletion 15	0.6	0.5	•	•	2.0	•	1.0	1.3	0.0	0.0	1.0	0.5	•
Pensions and Other Deferred Comp. 16	0.3	0.1	•	•	•	0.1	0.0	0.4	0.3	0.0	0.5	0.4	•
Employee Benefits 17	0.4	0.4	•	•	0.1	1.4	0.3	1.1	1.2	0.7	0.5	0.2	•
Advertising 18	0.0	0.1	•	•	0.3	0.1	0.0	•	0.9	0.0	0.0	0.0	•
Other Expenses 19	13.8	6.2	•	•	13.7	31.9	9.7	20.9	15.2	4.7	54.6	12.6	•
Officers' Compensation 20	0.4	1.1	•	•	2.0	0.6	0.8	0.5	0.4	•	0.3	0.3	•
Operating Margin 21	•	1.7	•	•	10.9	38.8	5.4	26.7	6.4	1.2	6.9	•	•
Operating Margin Before Officers' Comp. 22	•	2.7	•	•	12.9	39.4	6.2	27.2	6.8	1.2	7.1	•	•

Selected Average Balance Sheet ($ in Thousands)

	•		•		•		•		•	•
Net Receivables 23	4783	0	611	456	2292	3032	5974	20290	54972	158738
Inventories 24	700	0	84	83	242	3082	196	1480	1276	30342
Net Property, Plant and Equipment 25	15406	0	602	3906	6569	26366	25102	58273	164040	559426
Total Assets 26	41064	0	2756	7663	15392	40290	63170	152623	308798	1700617
Notes and Loans Payable 27	20219	0	863	175	6300	10600	35349	52700	99230	996367
All Other Liabilities 28	-2042	0	639	1398	3195	7448	19383	47798	146122	-473569
Net Worth 29	22887	0	1254	6090	5897	22242	8438	52125	63446	1177819

Selected Financial Ratios (Times to 1)

	•		•		•		•		•	•
Current Ratio 30	0.8	•	5.0	3.2	1.1	1.8	3.8	1.3	0.5	0.7
Quick Ratio 31	0.7	•	4.2	3.0	0.9	1.6	3.6	0.6	0.5	0.6
Net Sales to Working Capital 32	•	•	3.5	2.6	73.3	6.2	2.4	32.4	•	•
Coverage Ratio 33	1.5	3.3	125.9	179.6	4.2	12.0	3.8	3.3	3.4	0.8
Total Asset Turnover 34	0.7	•	1.2	0.7	1.6	0.7	1.0	2.6	0.3	0.6
Inventory Turnover 35	30.1	•	20.9	8.1	77.0	2.5	186.1	234.1	4.2	23.8
Receivables Turnover 36	5.8	•	5.7	7.7	16.3	3.2	7.7	31.8	1.8	4.9
Total Liabilities to Net Worth 37	0.8	•	1.2	0.3	1.6	0.8	6.5	1.9	3.9	0.4
Current Assets to Working Capital 38	•	•	1.3	1.5	10.4	2.3	1.4	4.3	•	•
Current Liabilities to Working Capital 39	•	•	0.3	0.5	9.4	1.3	0.4	3.3	•	•
Working Capital to Net Sales 40	•	•	0.3	0.4	0.0	0.2	0.4	0.0	•	•
Inventory to Working Capital 41	•	•	0.1	0.1	0.9	0.1	0.0	0.2	•	•
Total Receipts to Cash Flow 42	6.2	10.0	3.3	1.3	5.4	2.1	4.3	17.4	1.4	12.5
Cost of Goods to Cash Flow 43	4.3	7.6	1.7	0.2	4.0	0.6	2.5	15.2	0.1	9.3
Cash Flow to Total Debt 44	0.3	•	0.7	2.8	0.5	0.7	0.3	0.2	0.3	0.1

Selected Financial Factors (in Percentages)

	•		•		•		•		•	•
Debt Ratio 45	44.3	•	54.5	20.5	61.7	44.8	86.6	65.8	79.5	30.7
Return on Total Assets 46	8.6	•	22.6	37.1	20.1	22.2	12.4	7.7	8.3	6.0
Return on Equity Before Income Taxes 47	5.1	•	49.3	46.5	40.0	36.9	68.6	15.6	28.8	•
Return on Equity After Income Taxes 48	1.8	•	48.5	37.9	20.9	21.5	30.7	11.3	18.2	•
Profit Margin (Before Income Tax) 49	3.9	4.4	18.7	50.9	9.4	30.7	9.2	2.0	19.8	•
Profit Margin (After Income Tax) 50	1.4	2.0	18.4	41.5	17.9	4.1	1.5	12.5	•	•

Table II
Corporations with Net Income

PIPELINE TRANSPORTATION

MONEY AMOUNTS AND SIZE OF ASSETS IN THOUSANDS OF DOLLARS

Item Description for Accounting Period 7/06 Through 6/07	Total	Zero Assets	Under 500	500 to 1,000	1,000 to 5,000	5,000 to 10,000	10,000 to 25,000	25,000 to 50,000	50,000 to 100,000	100,000 to 250,000	250,000 to 500,000	500,000 to 2,500,000	2,500,000 and over
Number of Enterprises **1**	300	4	0	0	241	20	12	•	•	6	0	0	0

Revenues ($ in Thousands)

	Total	Zero Assets	Under 500	500 to 1,000	1,000 to 5,000	5,000 to 10,000	10,000 to 25,000	25,000 to 50,000	50,000 to 100,000	100,000 to 250,000	250,000 to 500,000	500,000 to 2,500,000	2,500,000 and over
Net Sales **2**	5821967	133133	0	0	797615	111183	465201	•	•	2380423	0	0	0
Interest **3**	24050	564	0	0	1011	864	1282	•	•	2762	0	0	0
Rents **4**	6624	158	0	0	0	0	9	•	•	5765	0	0	0
Royalties **5**	907	0	0	0	907	0	0	•	•	0	0	0	0
Other Portfolio Income **6**	28526	467	0	0	0	587	661	•	•	200	0	0	0
Other Receipts **7**	166304	2597	0	0	59867	12526	16375	•	•	10779	0	0	0
Total Receipts **8**	6048378	136919	0	0	859400	125160	483528	•	•	2399929	0	0	0
Average Total Receipts **9**	20161	34230	•	•	3566	6258	40294	•	•	399988	•	•	•

Operating Costs/Operating Income (%)

	Total	Zero Assets	Under 500	500 to 1,000	1,000 to 5,000	5,000 to 10,000	10,000 to 25,000	25,000 to 50,000	50,000 to 100,000	100,000 to 250,000	250,000 to 500,000	500,000 to 2,500,000	2,500,000 and over
Cost of Operations **10**	55.2	79.9	•	•	53.2	12.0	74.5	•	•	87.3	•	•	•
Salaries and Wages **11**	5.1	3.0	•	•	13.4	5.2	1.9	•	•	3.4	•	•	•
Taxes Paid **12**	2.6	0.8	•	•	1.9	6.0	1.3	•	•	0.7	•	•	•
Interest Paid **13**	3.7	2.0	•	•	0.1	0.3	0.5	•	•	0.9	•	•	•
Depreciation **14**	4.0	1.2	•	•	2.3	3.8	1.3	•	•	1.1	•	•	•
Amortization and Depletion **15**	0.7	0.5	•	•	2.0	•	1.0	•	•	0.0	•	•	•
Pensions and Other Deferred Comp. **16**	0.4	0.1	•	•	•	0.1	0.0	•	•	0.0	•	•	•
Employee Benefits **17**	0.7	0.4	•	•	0.1	1.4	0.3	•	•	0.7	•	•	•
Advertising **18**	0.0	0.1	•	•	0.3	0.1	0.0	•	•	0.0	•	•	•
Other Expenses **19**	15.4	6.5	•	•	13.7	31.9	8.3	•	•	4.7	•	•	•
Officers' Compensation **20**	0.6	1.1	•	•	2.0	0.6	•	•	•	•	•	•	•
Operating Margin **21**	11.6	4.6	•	•	10.9	38.8	10.9	•	•	1.2	•	•	•
Operating Margin Before Officers' Comp. **22**	12.1	5.7	•	•	12.9	39.4	10.9	•	•	1.2	•	•	•

Selected Average Balance Sheet ($ in Thousands)

Net Receivables 23	1794	0	611	456	3580	•	20290
Inventories 24	248	0	84	74	275	•	2700
Net Property, Plant and Equipment 25	11727	0	602	3906	7560	•	58273
Total Assets 26	20894	0	2756	7663	15908	•	152623
Notes and Loans Payable 27	9578	0	863	175	3365	•	52700
All Other Liabilities 28	6200	0	639	1398	4391	•	47798
Net Worth 29	5116	0	1254	6090	8152	•	52125

Selected Financial Ratios (Times to 1)

Current Ratio 30	0.9	•	5.0	3.2	1.4	•	1.3
Quick Ratio 31	0.7	•	4.2	3.0	1.2	•	0.6
Net Sales to Working Capital 32	•	•	3.5	2.6	24.7	•	32.4
Coverage Ratio 33	5.2	4.7	125.9	179.6	28.6	•	3.3
Total Asset Turnover 34	0.9	•	1.2	0.7	2.4	•	2.6
Inventory Turnover 35	43.3	•	20.9	9.0	105.2	•	128.3
Receivables Turnover 36	9.9	•	5.7	11.1	16.8	•	•
Total Liabilities to Net Worth 37	3.1	•	1.2	0.3	1.0	•	1.9
Current Assets to Working Capital 38	•	•	1.3	1.5	3.3	•	4.3
Current Liabilities to Working Capital 39	•	•	0.3	0.5	2.3	•	3.3
Working Capital to Net Sales 40	•	•	0.3	0.4	0.0	•	0.0
Inventory to Working Capital 41	•	•	0.1	0.1	0.2	•	0.2
Total Receipts to Cash Flow 42	3.5	7.6	3.3	1.3	4.4	•	17.4
Cost of Goods to Cash Flow 43	1.9	6.1	1.7	0.2	3.3	•	15.2
Cash Flow to Total Debt 44	0.4	•	0.7	2.8	1.1	•	0.2

Selected Financial Factors (in Percentages)

Debt Ratio 45	75.5	•	54.5	20.5	48.8	•	65.8
Return on Total Assets 46	17.8	•	22.6	37.1	37.4	•	7.7
Return on Equity Before Income Taxes 47	58.7	•	49.3	46.5	70.4	•	15.6
Return on Equity After Income Taxes 48	42.7	•	48.5	37.9	48.5	•	11.3
Profit Margin (Before Income Tax) 49	15.5	7.4	18.7	50.9	14.8	•	2.0
Profit Margin (After Income Tax) 50	11.3	4.9	18.4	41.5	10.2	•	1.5

Table I

Corporations with and without Net Income

OTHER TRANSPORTATION AND SUPPORT ACTIVITIES

MONEY AMOUNTS AND SIZE OF ASSETS IN THOUSANDS OF DOLLARS

Item Description for Accounting Period 7/06 Through 6/07		Total	Zero Assets	Under 500	500 to 1,000	1,000 to 5,000	5,000 to 10,000	10,000 to 25,000	25,000 to 50,000	50,000 to 100,000	100,000 to 250,000	250,000 to 500,000	500,000 to 2,500,000	2,500,000 and over
Number of Enterprises	1	44463	10435	28054	2686	2567	293	253	60	49	33	11	16	4
Revenues ($ in Thousands)														
Net Sales	2	207502315	1713903	16174809	12512459	20808011	5834062	11304540	4443405	6898847	6643781	3067219	16370506	101730773
Interest	3	901139	7286	1817	3620	12642	5276	4189	20379	11353	26246	22907	259114	526309
Rents	4	243636	22	2	7994	135	5808	2263	3721	13317	28247	17033	38614	126481
Royalties	5	2002160	0	0	0	0	0	0	583	950	0	57229	5050	1938347
Other Portfolio Income	6	741482	223350	76637	14074	17979	9646	29253	20328	22946	16385	8002	162474	140406
Other Receipts	7	1951345	75378	86332	20724	93855	59565	138916	101714	58580	125991	772160	-28179	446312
Total Receipts	8	213342077	2019939	16339597	12558871	20932622	5914357	11479161	4590130	7005993	6840650	3944550	16807579	104908628
Average Total Receipts	9	4798	194	582	4676	8155	20186	45372	76502	142979	207292	358595	1050474	26227157
Operating Costs/Operating Income (%)														
Cost of Operations	10	39.7	46.0	44.5	63.3	64.5	70.9	61.3	68.9	64.1	50.7	50.7	44.7	21.8
Salaries and Wages	11	17.1	9.3	13.0	5.2	13.3	10.4	10.8	12.9	10.3	14.4	28.0	16.8	21.8
Taxes Paid	12	2.7	3.1	2.6	3.1	1.6	1.6	1.7	2.1	4.1	2.9	3.3	2.4	3.0
Interest Paid	13	0.9	1.6	0.7	0.3	0.6	0.5	0.9	0.8	0.8	2.2	2.0	2.3	0.9
Depreciation	14	2.8	2.1	1.6	1.0	1.3	1.2	1.6	1.7	1.7	3.2	2.5	2.3	3.9
Amortization and Depletion	15	0.3	0.1	0.1	0.0	0.2	0.2	0.1	0.2	0.3	0.7	0.8	0.6	0.3
Pensions and Other Deferred Comp.	16	1.5	0.0	0.2	0.3	0.1	0.9	0.6	0.3	0.1	0.2	1.5	0.6	2.8
Employee Benefits	17	3.2	2.4	0.5	0.5	0.8	1.5	1.2	2.4	1.5	2.4	3.7	3.0	5.1
Advertising	18	0.5	0.3	0.4	0.2	0.3	0.2	0.2	0.2	0.2	0.2	1.2	0.2	0.6
Other Expenses	19	28.0	56.3	28.7	20.9	13.2	9.9	18.5	10.5	13.5	23.1	30.6	25.3	35.8
Officers' Compensation	20	1.3	3.5	5.2	2.9	2.2	1.6	1.3	1.0	0.9	1.4	1.2	0.7	0.3
Operating Margin	21	2.1	•	2.5	2.3	1.9	1.2	1.9	•	2.5	•	•	1.1	3.8
Operating Margin Before Officers' Comp.	22	3.3	•	7.7	5.2	4.1	2.8	3.1	•	3.3	0.1	•	1.8	4.1

Selected Average Balance Sheet ($ in Thousands)

Net Receivables 23	574	0	25	153	862	2264	5688	10227	23000	26586	78847	264257	3097799
Inventories 24	41	0	3	51	80	488	273	1507	1621	4241	2023	20784	130532
Net Property, Plant and Equipment 25	894	0	38	127	495	1962	5524	9244	20839	46294	65379	184334	7085611
Total Assets 26	2564	0	112	665	2178	6726	16640	35059	69193	161764	313132	975606	16860958
Notes and Loans Payable 27	568	0	60	236	939	2302	5564	10100	17731	58674	79315	156836	2913592
All Other Liabilities 28	916	0	34	172	581	2551	6172	13076	24734	54447	131030	469088	5687294
Net Worth 29	1081	0	18	258	657	1873	4904	11883	26729	48843	102788	349682	8260071

Selected Financial Ratios (Times to 1)

Current Ratio 30	1.2	•	1.7	1.9	1.7	1.6	1.1	1.3	1.4	0.9	1.4	1.2	1.1
Quick Ratio 31	1.0	•	1.5	1.4	1.5	1.3	0.9	1.0	1.1	0.6	1.1	1.0	0.9
Net Sales to Working Capital 32	31.9	•	23.5	22.4	15.4	13.0	45.9	17.7	13.3	•	7.5	17.8	73.8
Coverage Ratio 33	6.2	•	6.2	9.4	5.3	6.3	4.9	3.9	5.8	1.7	2.7	2.8	9.2
Total Asset Turnover 34	1.8	•	5.2	7.0	3.7	3.0	2.7	2.1	2.0	1.2	0.9	1.0	1.5
Inventory Turnover 35	45.1	•	81.7	58.2	65.8	28.9	100.4	33.9	55.6	24.1	69.8	22.0	42.5
Receivables Turnover 36	8.5	•	26.5	26.9	10.3	8.3	9.1	7.2	6.7	6.8	3.4	4.3	8.5
Total Liabilities to Net Worth 37	1.4	•	5.4	1.6	2.3	2.6	2.4	2.0	1.6	2.3	2.0	1.8	1.0
Current Assets to Working Capital 38	6.3	•	2.4	2.2	2.4	2.7	9.3	4.5	3.5	•	3.8	6.9	13.5
Current Liabilities to Working Capital 39	5.3	•	1.4	1.2	1.4	1.7	8.3	3.5	2.5	•	2.8	5.9	12.5
Working Capital to Net Sales 40	0.0	•	0.0	0.0	0.1	0.1	0.0	0.1	0.1	•	0.1	0.1	0.0
Inventory to Working Capital 41	0.3	•	0.1	0.2	0.2	0.3	0.4	0.3	0.2	•	0.0	0.3	0.5
Total Receipts to Cash Flow 42	3.7	3.6	4.0	5.0	7.8	9.8	5.6	10.6	8.6	5.5	3.7	4.2	2.7
Cost of Goods to Cash Flow 43	1.5	1.7	1.8	3.2	5.0	6.9	3.4	7.3	5.5	2.8	1.9	1.9	0.6
Cash Flow to Total Debt 44	0.9	•	1.5	2.3	0.7	0.4	0.7	0.3	0.4	0.3	0.4	0.4	1.1

Selected Financial Factors (in Percentages)

Debt Ratio 45	57.9	•	84.3	61.3	69.8	72.1	70.5	66.1	61.4	69.9	67.2	64.2	51.0
Return on Total Assets 46	10.7	•	21.6	21.1	11.6	9.1	11.6	6.9	9.8	4.8	4.8	6.6	11.9
Return on Equity Before Income Taxes 47	21.3	•	115.3	48.7	31.2	27.4	31.5	15.0	21.1	6.9	9.1	11.7	21.6
Return on Equity After Income Taxes 48	13.7	•	112.0	47.6	28.1	24.5	27.4	8.6	16.2	3.2	3.9	6.4	12.8
Profit Margin (Before Income Tax) 49	4.9	•	3.5	2.7	2.5	2.6	3.5	2.4	4.0	1.7	3.4	4.0	7.0
Profit Margin (After Income Tax) 50	3.2	•	3.4	2.6	2.3	2.3	3.0	1.4	3.1	0.8	1.5	2.2	4.1

Table II
Corporations with Net Income

OTHER TRANSPORTATION AND SUPPORT ACTIVITIES

MONEY AMOUNTS AND SIZE OF ASSETS IN THOUSANDS OF DOLLARS

Item Description for Accounting Period 7/06 Through 6/07	Total	Zero Assets	Under 500	500 to 1,000	1,000 to 5,000	5,000 to 10,000	10,000 to 25,000	25,000 to 50,000	50,000 to 100,000	100,000 to 250,000	250,000 to 500,000	500,000 to 2,500,000	2,500,000 and over
Number of Enterprises **1**	23707	4447	14685	2063	1947	267	180	40	38	17	•	•	•
Revenues ($ in Thousands)													
Net Sales **2**	176539857	599368	11290858	9055192	17894859	5152935	9281314	3254760	5856486	4124867	•	•	•
Interest **3**	748788	6823	1063	3154	9586	4831	2962	9188	8307	22080	•	•	•
Rents **4**	222424	22	2	7994	135	5808	2048	3303	12422	24826	•	•	•
Royalties **5**	1989021	0	0	0	0	0	0	583	941	0			
Other Portfolio Income **6**	682820	214100	68142	14074	16713	9190	26934	19681	21206	15292	•	•	•
Other Receipts **7**	1960165	66441	85399	20120	79049	44569	80294	96229	55714	107339	•	•	•
Total Receipts **8**	182143075	886754	11445464	9100534	18000342	5217333	9393552	3383744	5955076	4294404	•	•	•
Average Total Receipts **9**	7683	199	779	4411	9245	19541	52186	84594	156713	252612	•	•	•
Operating Costs/Operating Income (%)													
Cost of Operations **10**	39.1	39.4	45.3	57.7	68.2	68.2	62.7	70.7	67.3	57.2	•	•	•
Salaries and Wages **11**	17.4	7.7	11.6	6.6	13.1	11.0	11.0	12.2	9.2	8.6	•	•	•
Taxes Paid **12**	2.8	5.2	2.6	4.1	1.4	1.8	1.6	1.7	3.6	3.1	•	•	•
Interest Paid **13**	0.7	2.5	0.5	0.3	0.3	0.5	0.7	0.8	0.6	1.2	•	•	•
Depreciation **14**	2.9	2.3	1.5	1.1	1.0	1.2	1.3	1.6	1.2	3.4	•	•	•
Amortization and Depletion **15**	0.2	0.0	0.1	0.0	0.0	0.0	0.1	0.1	0.3	0.4	•	•	•
Pensions and Other Deferred Comp. **16**	1.8	0.1	0.2	0.3	0.1	0.9	0.6	0.2	0.1	0.2	•	•	•
Employee Benefits **17**	3.4	0.1	0.4	0.6	0.8	1.6	1.2	1.1	1.4	2.3	•	•	•
Advertising **18**	0.5	0.1	0.3	0.2	0.2	0.2	0.1	0.2	0.2	0.2	•	•	•
Other Expenses **19**	25.9	35.0	26.3	21.6	9.2	10.4	15.2	9.0	11.6	18.9	•	•	•
Officers' Compensation **20**	1.1	4.8	4.7	3.7	2.0	1.7	1.4	0.9	0.7	1.2	•	•	•
Operating Margin **21**	4.3	2.8	6.4	3.8	3.5	2.3	3.9	1.6	3.8	3.4	•	•	•
Operating Margin Before Officers' Comp. **22**	5.4	7.7	11.1	7.5	5.5	4.0	5.4	2.5	4.5	4.6	•	•	•

Selected Average Balance Sheet ($ in Thousands)

Net Receivables 23	895	0	27	147	945	2179	6102	10967	24262	28088
Inventories 24	55	0	3	54	80	472	334	1066	1687	2287
Net Property, Plant and Equipment 25	1496	0	35	116	432	1887	4568	10870	17625	52340
Total Assets 26	3936	0	124	659	2132	6773	17099	34387	68298	159914
Notes and Loans Payable 27	692	0	52	191	647	2000	5241	9297	16011	38021
All Other Liabilities 28	1403	0	29	145	562	2672	5856	13779	22940	43692
Net Worth 29	1842	0	42	323	923	2101	6002	11311	29347	78202

Selected Financial Ratios (Times to 1)

Current Ratio 30	1.2	•	2.0	2.6	1.9	1.8	1.3	1.3	1.5	1.4
Quick Ratio 31	1.0	•	1.7	2.0	1.8	1.5	1.0	1.1	1.3	1.0
Net Sales to Working Capital 32	31.5	•	23.8	15.8	13.6	10.7	23.8	21.8	12.0	15.6
Coverage Ratio 33	11.4	21.3	16.0	14.3	13.1	8.1	8.9	8.0	9.6	7.3
Total Asset Turnover 34	1.9	•	6.2	6.7	4.3	2.8	3.0	2.4	2.3	1.5
Inventory Turnover 35	52.7	•	100.7	47.3	78.1	27.9	96.8	54.0	61.4	60.7
Receivables Turnover 36	8.5	•	31.2	24.2	11.1	8.1	9.6	•	6.8	6.4
Total Liabilities to Net Worth 37	1.1	•	2.0	1.0	1.3	2.2	1.8	2.0	1.3	1.0
Current Assets to Working Capital 38	6.1	•	2.0	1.6	2.1	2.3	4.7	4.9	2.9	3.6
Current Liabilities to Working Capital 39	5.1	•	1.0	0.6	1.1	1.3	3.7	3.9	1.9	2.6
Working Capital to Net Sales 40	0.0	•	0.0	0.1	0.1	0.1	0.0	0.0	0.1	0.1
Inventory to Working Capital 41	0.3	•	0.0	0.2	0.1	0.3	0.2	0.3	0.2	0.2
Total Receipts to Cash Flow 42	3.6	2.7	3.5	4.7	9.3	8.5	6.1	8.4	9.2	5.0
Cost of Goods to Cash Flow 43	1.4	1.1	1.6	2.7	6.3	5.8	3.8	6.0	6.2	2.9
Cash Flow to Total Debt 44	1.0	2.7	2.7	2.8	0.8	0.5	0.8	0.4	0.4	0.6

Selected Financial Factors (in Percentages)

Debt Ratio 45	53.2	•	66.1	51.0	56.7	69.0	64.9	67.1	57.0	51.1
Return on Total Assets 46	15.6	•	51.7	30.6	18.9	11.5	17.6	15.7	13.7	13.1
Return on Equity Before Income Taxes 47	30.4	•	143.1	58.1	40.4	32.4	44.6	41.7	28.6	23.0
Return on Equity After Income Taxes 48	22.0	•	140.5	56.9	37.5	29.6	39.9	31.7	22.9	18.6
Profit Margin (Before Income Tax) 49	7.5	50.8	7.8	4.3	4.1	3.5	5.2	5.8	5.5	7.4
Profit Margin (After Income Tax) 50	5.5	39.6	7.7	4.2	3.8	3.2	4.6	4.4	4.4	6.0

WAREHOUSING AND STORAGE

Table I

Corporations with and without Net Income

MONEY AMOUNTS AND SIZE OF ASSETS IN THOUSANDS OF DOLLARS

Item Description for Accounting Period 7/06 Through 6/07	Total	Zero Assets	Under 500	500 to 1,000	1,000 to 5,000	5,000 to 10,000	10,000 to 25,000	25,000 to 50,000	50,000 to 100,000	100,000 to 250,000	250,000 to 500,000	500,000 to 2,500,000	2,500,000 and over
Number of Enterprises **1**	7324	1126	4019	640	1097	177	185	39	14	16	7	4	0
Revenues ($ in Thousands)													
Net Sales **2**	19028534	517207	1788831	741090	3655762	1165595	3172151	747697	989077	1998760	1639679	2612684	0
Interest **3**	144856	46	255	2683	6032	2327	4850	4589	3049	27898	14307	78820	0
Rents **4**	45853	257	0	16	11612	643	1277	1820	717	1429	8993	19090	0
Royalties **5**	746	0	0	0	0	0	185	0	167	10	384	0	0
Other Portfolio Income **6**	135842	9328	111	15	12393	5607	33554	3199	1817	18232	5452	46133	0
Other Receipts **7**	872418	53276	3994	5902	136662	51217	23474	23818	9854	107159	61595	395470	0
Total Receipts **8**	20228249	580114	1793191	749706	3822461	1225389	3235491	781123	1004681	2153488	1730410	3152197	0
Average Total Receipts **9**	2762	515	446	1171	3484	6923	17489	20029	71763	134593	247201	788049	•
Operating Costs/Operating Income (%)													
Cost of Operations **10**	33.5	36.9	40.3	43.8	46.3	42.9	34.0	17.9	37.9	29.5	33.7	8.2	•
Salaries and Wages **11**	20.0	12.1	13.8	14.7	19.1	12.9	15.9	22.6	16.4	22.8	21.6	33.9	•
Taxes Paid **12**	3.7	2.1	2.2	5.0	3.5	3.3	3.8	4.7	3.2	3.8	3.5	5.2	•
Interest Paid **13**	3.4	1.7	0.6	2.6	1.4	2.4	2.4	4.2	2.9	2.7	4.1	10.2	•
Depreciation **14**	4.3	1.2	1.1	3.9	3.0	2.8	4.2	7.3	3.6	3.3	7.6	8.1	•
Amortization and Depletion **15**	0.8	0.9	0.2	0.5	0.1	0.1	0.1	0.5	0.9	0.3	0.6	4.1	•
Pensions and Other Deferred Comp. **16**	0.6	0.0	0.0	0.1	0.4	0.5	1.0	1.0	0.6	0.8	1.3	0.4	•
Employee Benefits **17**	2.0	1.3	1.1	2.7	0.8	1.5	2.1	2.8	2.8	3.1	3.4	2.3	•
Advertising **18**	0.3	0.1	0.2	2.0	0.2	0.1	0.3	0.2	0.1	0.1	0.1	0.6	•
Other Expenses **19**	30.4	43.5	33.0	33.3	24.8	27.9	30.8	33.8	27.4	29.8	27.0	36.4	•
Officers' Compensation **20**	1.9	7.8	1.9	3.7	1.9	4.2	2.5	3.2	1.2	0.9	0.5	0.2	•
Operating Margin **21**	•	•	5.6	•	•	1.4	2.9	1.8	3.0	2.8	•	•	•
Operating Margin Before Officers' Comp. **22**	1.0	0.2	7.4	•	0.5	5.6	5.4	4.9	4.1	3.7	•	•	•

Selected Average Balance Sheet ($ in Thousands)

Line	Item												
23	Net Receivables	386	0	17	126	417	583	2221	12249	33205	23555	184766	•
24	Inventories	48	0	3	22	77	101	268	5740	2950	1309	2537	•
25	Net Property, Plant and Equipment	1195	0	77	427	900	3072	21492	35556	51992	183953	497710	•
26	Total Assets	3555	0	135	719	1927	7172	37567	72996	151472	325936	2885817	•
27	Notes and Loans Payable	1399	0	83	575	781	2417	17515	29711	46379	133758	1095814	•
28	All Other Liabilities	601	0	12	148	412	964	5671	12674	31392	60426	470498	•
29	Net Worth	1554	0	40	-3	734	3791	14381	30611	73701	131753	1319505	•

Selected Financial Ratios (Times to 1)

Line	Item												
30	Current Ratio	1.4	•	2.6	0.9	1.8	1.7	1.0	1.9	1.6	1.0	0.9	•
31	Quick Ratio	1.1	•	2.0	0.8	1.4	1.3	0.6	1.1	1.3	0.7	0.8	•
32	Net Sales to Working Capital	11.8	•	17.7	•	7.8	7.9	112.7	5.6	5.5	•	•	•
33	Coverage Ratio	2.6	3.7	10.7	•	3.3	3.7	2.5	2.5	4.9	1.5	2.1	•
34	Total Asset Turnover	0.7	•	3.3	1.6	1.7	0.9	0.5	1.0	0.8	0.7	0.2	•
35	Inventory Turnover	18.3	•	71.5	23.0	19.9	28.1	12.8	4.7	12.5	60.4	21.2	•
36	Receivables Turnover	7.6	•	25.0	5.9	8.3	10.8	7.5	5.6	4.1	7.3	6.4	•
37	Total Liabilities to Net Worth	1.3	•	2.4	•	1.6	0.9	1.6	1.4	1.1	1.5	1.2	•
38	Current Assets to Working Capital	3.3	•	1.6	•	2.2	2.4	43.3	2.1	2.6	•	•	•
39	Current Liabilities to Working Capital	2.3	•	0.6	•	1.2	1.4	42.3	1.1	1.6	•	•	•
40	Working Capital to Net Sales	0.1	•	0.1	•	0.1	0.1	0.0	0.2	0.2	•	•	•
41	Inventory to Working Capital	0.2	•	0.1	•	0.3	0.2	0.8	0.5	0.1	•	•	•
42	Total Receipts to Cash Flow	4.2	3.4	6.6	7.9	5.1	5.7	3.1	4.5	3.0	4.3	3.0	•
43	Cost of Goods to Cash Flow	1.4	1.3	2.6	3.4	2.4	1.5	0.6	1.7	0.9	1.5	0.2	•
44	Cash Flow to Total Debt	0.3	•	0.7	0.2	0.5	0.3	0.3	0.4	0.5	0.3	0.1	•

Selected Financial Factors (in Percentages)

Line	Item													
45	Debt Ratio	56.3	•	70.2	100.5	61.9	47.1	52.7	61.7	58.1	51.3	59.6	54.3	•
46	Return on Total Assets	6.4	•	21.1	•	7.9	8.3	7.9	5.3	7.2	11.0	4.5	4.8	•
47	Return on Equity Before Income Taxes	8.9	•	64.0	3741.9	14.3	11.4	11.2	8.2	10.4	18.0	3.8	5.5	•
48	Return on Equity After Income Taxes	7.5	•	60.0	3759.9	12.3	10.0	9.6	6.2	8.3	13.0	2.3	5.2	•
49	Profit Margin (Before Income Tax)	5.3	4.5	5.8	•	3.2	6.6	4.9	6.1	4.5	10.6	2.1	11.0	•
50	Profit Margin (After Income Tax)	4.5	4.5	5.4	•	2.7	5.8	4.2	4.7	3.6	7.7	1.3	10.6	•

251

Table II
Corporations with Net Income

WAREHOUSING AND STORAGE

MONEY AMOUNTS AND SIZE OF ASSETS IN THOUSANDS OF DOLLARS

Item Description for Accounting Period 7/06 Through 6/07	Total	Zero Assets	Under 100	100 to 250	251 to 500	501 to 1,000	1,001 to 5,000	5,001 to 10,000	10,001 to 25,000	25,001 to 50,000	50,001 to 100,000	100,001 to 250,000	250,001 and over
Number of Enterprises **1**	4157	262	2748	186	634	157	117	20	9	•	•	•	0
Revenues ($ in Thousands)													
Net Sales **2**	13434036	185102	1454267	243200	1908136	1043021	1933728	587190	849528	•	•	•	0
Interest **3**	141294	0	14	2680	5742	2160	4334	4263	2007	•	•	•	0
Rents **4**	26153	0	0	0	8647	507	959	1766	287	•	•	•	0
Royalties **5**	746	0	0	0	0	0	185	0	167	•	•	•	0
Other Portfolio Income **6**	130528	9258	60	1	12234	4721	32534	1548	1317	•	•	•	0
Other Receipts **7**	577900	52161	3994	4774	57003	46929	18142	22952	7042	•	•	•	0
Total Receipts **8**	14310657	246521	1458335	250655	1991762	1097338	1989882	617719	860348	•	•	•	0
Average Total Receipts **9**	3443	941	531	1348	3142	6989	17008	30886	95594	•	•	•	•
Operating Costs/Operating Income (%)													
Cost of Operations **10**	27.5	8.0	45.9	23.9	30.1	41.7	26.0	22.0	39.8	•	•	•	•
Salaries and Wages **11**	20.4	19.7	9.0	11.4	19.6	12.4	16.4	22.0	15.6	•	•	•	•
Taxes Paid **12**	3.7	1.5	1.5	2.1	4.6	3.0	4.0	4.6	3.1	•	•	•	•
Interest Paid **13**	3.5	0.6	0.7	1.1	1.1	2.3	2.1	2.3	2.0	•	•	•	•
Depreciation **14**	4.2	0.7	1.1	1.4	3.3	2.6	4.2	5.6	3.1	•	•	•	•
Amortization and Depletion **15**	0.8	0.0	0.3	•	0.1	0.1	0.0	0.2	0.1	•	•	•	•
Pensions and Other Deferred Comp. **16**	0.6	0.0	0.0	•	0.5	0.5	0.6	0.6	0.6	•	•	•	•
Employee Benefits **17**	2.2	1.3	0.2	0.4	1.4	1.4	2.1	3.3	2.9	•	•	•	•
Advertising **18**	0.3	0.0	0.1	3.6	0.1	0.1	0.3	0.2	0.1	•	•	•	•
Other Expenses **19**	31.7	63.9	32.4	52.3	32.0	28.7	34.4	28.8	26.9	•	•	•	•
Officers' Compensation **20**	1.6	0.3	1.0	4.8	2.4	4.6	2.2	3.6	1.3	•	•	•	•
Operating Margin **21**	3.6	4.0	8.0	•	4.8	2.7	7.7	6.6	4.4	•	•	•	•
Operating Margin Before Officers' Comp. **22**	5.2	4.3	9.0	3.8	7.2	7.3	9.8	10.2	5.7	•	•	•	•

Selected Average Balance Sheet ($ in Thousands)

Net Receivables 23	523	0	16	251	395	512	2331	3414	16033
Inventories 24	60	0	4	19	53	112	309	522	9134
Net Property, Plant and Equipment 25	1494	0	106	240	809	3024	7102	17299	38010
Total Assets 26	5039	0	174	784	1850	7056	15354	39599	76964
Notes and Loans Payable 27	1781	0	106	404	581	2299	5314	9730	20503
All Other Liabilities 28	821	0	10	124	278	663	2263	9557	15554
Net Worth 29	2438	0	57	256	991	4094	7778	20312	40907

Selected Financial Ratios (Times to 1)

Current Ratio 30	1.6	•	4.3	1.7	3.3	2.4	2.1	1.2	1.8
Quick Ratio 31	1.3	•	3.0	1.7	3.0	1.7	1.8	0.7	0.9
Net Sales to Working Capital 32	8.8	•	14.8	8.8	4.7	5.7	5.7	13.9	6.1
Coverage Ratio 33	3.9	65.8	13.8	2.9	9.4	4.4	5.9	6.1	3.9
Total Asset Turnover 34	0.6	•	3.0	1.7	1.6	0.9	1.1	0.7	1.2
Inventory Turnover 35	15.0	•	67.1	16.8	17.0	24.8	13.9	12.4	4.1
Receivables Turnover 36	6.7	•	28.8	2.6	6.4	12.3	7.9	7.6	•
Total Liabilities to Net Worth 37	1.1	•	2.0	2.1	0.9	0.7	1.0	0.9	0.9
Current Assets to Working Capital 38	2.7	•	1.3	2.4	1.4	1.7	1.9	5.5	2.2
Current Liabilities to Working Capital 39	1.7	•	0.3	1.4	0.4	0.7	0.9	4.5	1.2
Working Capital to Net Sales 40	0.1	•	0.1	0.1	0.2	0.2	0.2	0.1	0.2
Inventory to Working Capital 41	0.2	•	0.1	0.0	0.1	0.2	0.1	0.1	0.6
Total Receipts to Cash Flow 42	3.5	1.1	7.1	2.2	3.3	5.3	3.3	3.1	4.2
Cost of Goods to Cash Flow 43	1.0	0.1	3.3	0.5	1.0	2.2	0.9	0.7	1.7
Cash Flow to Total Debt 44	0.4	•	0.6	1.1	1.1	0.4	0.7	0.5	0.6

Selected Financial Factors (in Percentages)

Debt Ratio 45	51.6	•	66.9	67.4	46.4	42.0	49.3	48.7	46.8
Return on Total Assets 46	8.7	•	27.3	5.2	16.7	9.6	13.5	10.4	9.4
Return on Equity Before Income Taxes 47	13.3	•	76.7	10.5	27.8	12.9	22.2	17.0	13.0
Return on Equity After Income Taxes 48	11.8	•	72.5	9.7	25.2	11.4	19.8	14.3	10.6
Profit Margin (Before Income Tax) 49	10.1	37.0	8.3	2.1	9.2	7.9	10.4	11.8	5.6
Profit Margin (After Income Tax) 50	8.9	37.0	7.9	1.9	8.3	7.0	9.3	9.9	4.6

Table I

Corporations with and without Net Income

NEWSPAPER PUBLISHERS

MONEY AMOUNTS AND SIZE OF ASSETS IN THOUSANDS OF DOLLARS

Item Description for Accounting Period 7/06 Through 6/07		Total	Zero Assets	Under 500	500 to 1,000	1,000 to 5,000	5,000 to 10,000	10,000 to 25,000	25,000 to 50,000	50,000 to 100,000	100,000 to 250,000	250,000 to 500,000	500,000 to 2,500,000	2,500,000 and over
Number of Enterprises	1	6876	302	5323	502	481	44	101	47	26	13	11	11	14
Revenues ($ in Thousands)														
Net Sales	2	56967272	1398970	3140697	819406	1922974	214570	1727896	1803308	1387649	1619824	2692058	5737715	34502205
Interest	3	411370	1468	379	1195	448	932	9479	6195	8155	6952	16730	13611	345826
Rents	4	176783	1216	9	4673	0	917	1015	1331	3702	5383	12725	12171	133642
Royalties	5	328896	0	0	0	0	0	2	3021	105	0	669	162	324936
Other Portfolio Income	6	3645456	59161	13	212	1413	16380	15520	4583	12118	23457	107153	154924	3250521
Other Receipts	7	2423095	52573	36050	646	31571	27278	-3126	106475	164378	20058	28996	142129	1816067
Total Receipts	8	63952872	1513388	3177148	826132	1956406	260077	1750786	1924913	1576107	1675674	2858331	6060712	40373197
Average Total Receipts	9	9301	5011	597	1646	4067	5911	17335	40956	60620	128898	259848	550974	2883800
Operating Costs/Operating Income (%)														
Cost of Operations	10	24.8	15.7	32.0	41.1	29.2	35.7	35.6	24.5	31.0	33.6	14.4	25.2	23.4
Salaries and Wages	11	23.4	33.1	19.1	11.8	26.7	21.9	21.6	30.7	24.3	20.8	29.2	21.3	23.2
Taxes Paid	12	3.7	3.8	2.3	3.7	4.1	3.3	3.6	3.9	3.4	3.5	3.9	3.7	3.8
Interest Paid	13	3.6	4.8	0.5	1.5	2.4	4.0	1.1	1.6	3.6	2.1	3.5	6.9	3.7
Depreciation	14	3.1	2.1	0.7	1.5	3.5	2.3	2.9	3.2	4.2	4.3	5.5	4.0	3.0
Amortization and Depletion	15	3.4	1.5	0.3	1.4	0.9	0.5	0.4	1.4	1.1	2.8	3.0	5.5	4.1
Pensions and Other Deferred Comp.	16	1.3	3.6	0.3	0.5	0.3	1.0	0.9	1.3	1.8	0.9	1.7	0.9	1.4
Employee Benefits	17	2.7	3.7	1.2	2.6	2.6	3.5	2.7	4.0	3.1	3.2	3.6	2.8	2.6
Advertising	18	1.9	0.3	2.9	0.5	1.4	4.6	0.8	1.4	1.2	1.7	1.3	1.4	2.3
Other Expenses	19	27.5	25.9	38.3	22.4	27.8	19.5	20.9	30.0	27.8	23.1	29.6	27.6	26.9
Officers' Compensation	20	1.7	3.9	3.3	4.9	4.2	3.0	3.2	2.0	2.4	1.6	1.8	1.3	1.2
Operating Margin	21	2.8	1.5	•	8.0	•	0.6	6.3	•	•	2.3	2.5	•	4.5
Operating Margin Before Officers' Comp.	22	4.5	5.5	2.4	12.9	1.2	3.6	9.5	•	•	3.9	4.2	0.6	5.7

Selected Average Balance Sheet ($ in Thousands)

Net Receivables 23	1402	0	44	139	434	670	1869	6254	8178	20375	25839	55243	517412
Inventories 24	104	0	0	11	23	114	228	469	988	2953	3290	11761	30115
Net Property, Plant and Equipment 25	2519	0	17	179	1141	961	4063	10254	19135	47439	107044	194398	802072
Total Assets 26	17190	0	110	701	2754	7333	16830	37149	67304	163125	362860	1069838	6609711
Notes and Loans Payable 27	4463	0	112	204	1269	3157	2584	13122	25050	55680	127681	517438	1420840
All Other Liabilities 28	4258	0	134	40	546	1663	2982	9031	12552	43468	91122	297512	1593824
Net Worth 29	8469	0	-136	457	940	2513	11264	14996	29702	63978	144056	254888	3595047

Selected Financial Ratios (Times to 1)

Current Ratio 30	1.1	•	0.5	3.7	1.2	3.7	3.2	1.5	1.8	1.7	1.6	1.2	1.0
Quick Ratio 31	0.7	•	0.5	3.5	1.1	1.2	2.2	1.2	1.4	1.2	0.9	0.9	0.6
Net Sales to Working Capital 32	34.4	•	•	8.1	29.6	1.6	3.8	9.2	6.2	6.8	9.6	24.5	855.7
Coverage Ratio 33	5.2	3.0	1.5	6.9	0.5	6.4	7.5	2.6	3.7	3.4	3.4	1.7	6.8
Total Asset Turnover 34	0.5	•	5.4	2.3	1.5	0.7	1.0	1.0	0.8	0.8	0.7	0.5	0.4
Inventory Turnover 35	19.7	•	3298.0	63.4	15.3	49.7	26.7	20.0	16.7	14.2	10.7	11.2	19.2
Receivables Turnover 36	5.8	•	17.5	11.6	9.6	4.1	9.4	6.7	7.2	6.6	10.6	6.0	4.8
Total Liabilities to Net Worth 37	1.0	•	•	0.5	0.5	1.9	0.5	1.5	1.3	1.5	1.5	3.2	0.8
Current Assets to Working Capital 38	11.7	•	•	1.4	1.4	5.4	1.5	3.0	2.2	2.4	2.7	5.9	346.0
Current Liabilities to Working Capital 39	10.7	•	•	0.4	0.4	0.4	0.5	2.0	1.2	1.4	1.7	4.9	345.0
Working Capital to Net Sales 40	0.0	•	•	0.1	0.0	0.6	0.3	0.1	0.2	0.1	0.1	0.0	0.0
Inventory to Working Capital 41	0.4	•	•	0.1	0.2	0.0	0.1	0.1	0.1	0.2	0.2	0.4	11.5
Total Receipts to Cash Flow 42	2.9	3.5	2.9	3.7	3.3	4.3	3.9	3.3	3.0	4.1	3.1	3.5	2.7
Cost of Goods to Cash Flow 43	0.7	0.5	0.9	1.5	1.2	1.3	1.4	0.8	0.9	1.4	0.4	0.9	0.6
Cash Flow to Total Debt 44	0.3	•	1.8	0.5	0.3	0.8	0.3	0.5	0.5	0.3	0.4	0.2	0.3

Selected Financial Factors (in Percentages)

Debt Ratio 45	50.7	•	224.2	34.8	65.9	65.7	33.1	59.6	55.9	60.8	60.3	76.2	45.6
Return on Total Assets 46	9.0	•	4.4	23.9	1.7	17.2	8.6	4.4	10.4	6.0	8.2	5.8	9.5
Return on Equity Before Income Taxes 47	14.8	•	•	•	31.4	42.3	11.1	6.7	17.1	11.1	14.5	10.1	14.9
Return on Equity After Income Taxes 48	10.0	•	•	0.1	30.2	34.9	9.8	4.8	13.7	9.1	10.3	5.5	9.9
Profit Margin (Before Income Tax) 49	15.1	9.7	0.3	8.8	21.8	7.3	2.6	9.5	5.7	8.6	5.0	21.7	
Profit Margin (After Income Tax) 50	10.2	6.4	•	8.5	18.0	6.4	1.9	7.6	4.7	6.1	2.7	14.5	

Table II

Corporations with Net Income

NEWSPAPER PUBLISHERS

MONEY AMOUNTS AND SIZE OF ASSETS IN THOUSANDS OF DOLLARS

Item Description for Accounting Period 7/06 Through 6/07	Total	Zero Assets	Under 500	500 to 1,000	1,000 to 5,000	5,000 to 10,000	10,000 to 25,000	25,000 to 50,000	50,000 to 100,000	100,000 to 250,000	250,000 to 500,000	500,000 to 2,500,000	2,500,000 and over
Number of Enterprises 1	4892	•	3841	439	119	40	61	34	18	•	8	8	8
Revenues ($ in Thousands)													
Net Sales 2	50662936	•	2168435	794208	538977	182519	1219268	1364386	1127099	•	1919855	4326407	•
Interest 3	351163	•	377	1195	22	554	5879	2696	7924	•	15435	11499	•
Rents 4	170781	•	9	4673	0	532	666	1331	3670	•	7507	12153	•
Royalties 5	328894	•	0	0	0	0	0	3021	105	•	669	162	•
Other Portfolio Income 6	3594604	•	9	212	1196	16380	12424	4582	11499	•	105412	109752	•
Other Receipts 7	2242670	•	35795	646	16354	27256	11731	7655	167057	•	26739	68437	•
Total Receipts 8	57351048	•	2204625	800934	556549	227241	1249968	1383671	1317354	•	2075617	4528410	•
Average Total Receipts 9	11723	•	574	1824	4677	5681	20491	40696	73186	•	259452	566051	•
Operating Costs/Operating Income (%)													
Cost of Operations 10	24.3	•	34.5	40.9	38.4	38.0	36.6	27.8	32.6	•	12.6	22.1	•
Salaries and Wages 11	23.1	•	15.6	11.3	13.3	23.4	19.2	24.7	23.1	•	29.5	23.0	•
Taxes Paid 12	3.7	•	2.5	3.7	3.7	3.3	3.3	3.6	3.4	•	4.1	4.0	•
Interest Paid 13	3.3	•	0.8	1.5	1.7	3.2	0.6	1.8	2.2	•	3.3	3.5	•
Depreciation 14	3.0	•	0.8	1.5	2.4	2.5	2.6	2.8	3.1	•	4.5	4.3	•
Amortization and Depletion 15	3.4	•	0.0	1.0	0.2	0.6	0.2	1.4	0.8	•	3.3	3.4	•
Pensions and Other Deferred Comp. 16	1.3	•	0.4	0.5	0.1	1.2	0.7	1.1	2.1	•	1.2	1.0	•
Employee Benefits 17	2.6	•	0.9	2.7	2.6	3.8	2.0	3.4	3.2	•	2.8	2.4	•
Advertising 18	1.9	•	0.9	0.5	1.6	4.2	0.6	1.7	1.2	•	1.1	1.4	•
Other Expenses 19	26.9	•	34.7	22.8	20.4	17.0	19.6	25.5	28.9	•	29.4	28.4	•
Officers' Compensation 20	1.6	•	4.4	5.1	3.2	1.6	2.8	1.9	2.5	•	1.9	1.4	•
Operating Margin 21	5.0	•	4.5	8.4	12.6	1.2	11.5	4.3	•	•	6.3	5.2	•
Operating Margin Before Officers' Comp. 22	6.6	•	8.9	13.5	15.7	2.8	14.4	6.2	•	•	8.2	6.6	•

Selected Average Balance Sheet ($ in Thousands)

Net Receivables 23	1467	•	40	141	541	429	2208	5697	9372	24411	61698
Inventories 24	123	•	0	12	71	58	319	478	1210	3514	11688
Net Property, Plant and Equipment 25	3140	•	19	202	628	980	4266	10704	18018	99192	214277
Total Assets 26	21719	•	100	709	3402	7242	17685	37632	68346	377340	842586
Notes and Loans Payable 27	4958	•	29	178	1033	2227	9579	17773		112995	224709
All Other Liabilities 28	4899	•	53	40	534	1458	3138	9279	14056	81910	266370
Net Worth 29	11861	•	18	491	1835	3557	12844	18774	36518	182435	351507

Selected Financial Ratios (Times to 1)

Current Ratio 30	1.2	•	2.4	4.1	1.8	6.0	4.1	1.5	2.2	1.6	1.4
Quick Ratio 31	0.7	•	2.4	3.8	1.6	1.6	3.0	1.1	1.7	0.7	0.9
Net Sales to Working Capital 32	22.0	•	15.1	8.0	9.2	1.3	3.3	10.4	5.0	9.2	15.2
Coverage Ratio 33	6.5	•	9.1	7.2	10.5	8.9	22.5	4.1	7.2	5.4	3.8
Total Asset Turnover 34	0.5	•	5.6	2.6	1.3	0.6	1.1	1.1	0.9	0.6	0.6
Inventory Turnover 35	20.5	•	2484.9	61.1	24.6	30.1	22.9	23.3	16.9	8.6	10.2
Receivables Turnover 36	6.3	•	17.0	12.3	4.5	17.9	8.0	6.6	6.9	•	5.5
Total Liabilities to Net Worth 37	0.8	•	4.5	0.4	0.9	1.0	0.4	1.0	0.9	1.1	1.4
Current Assets to Working Capital 38	7.0	•	1.7	1.3	2.3	1.2	1.3	3.2	1.8	2.7	3.8
Current Liabilities to Working Capital 39	6.0	•	0.7	0.3	1.3	0.2	0.3	2.2	0.8	1.7	2.8
Working Capital to Net Sales 40	0.0	•	0.1	0.1	0.1	0.8	0.3	0.1	0.2	0.1	0.1
Inventory to Working Capital 41	0.3	•	0.0	0.1	0.1	0.0	0.1	0.1	0.1	0.1	0.3
Total Receipts to Cash Flow 42	2.8	•	2.7	3.6	3.1	3.1	3.2	3.4	2.6	2.7	2.9
Cost of Goods to Cash Flow 43	0.7	•	0.9	1.5	1.2	1.2	1.2	1.0	0.8	0.3	0.7
Cash Flow to Total Debt 44	0.4	•	2.5	2.3	0.9	0.4	1.3	0.6	0.8	0.5	0.4

Selected Financial Factors (in Percentages)

Debt Ratio 45	45.4	•	81.9	30.8	46.1	50.9	27.4	50.1	46.6	51.7	58.3
Return on Total Assets 46	10.3	•	38.8	27.4	23.3	18.2	16.3	8.0	14.3	11.2	8.5
Return on Equity Before Income Taxes 47	16.0	•	190.4	34.1	39.1	33.0	21.4	12.0	23.1	18.9	15.0
Return on Equity After Income Taxes 48	11.1	•	177.2	32.8	38.9	27.3	19.5	9.9	19.1	14.3	10.4
Profit Margin (Before Income Tax) 49	18.3	•	6.1	9.2	15.8	25.7	13.8	5.6	13.5	14.4	9.8
Profit Margin (After Income Tax) 50	12.7	•	5.7	8.9	15.8	21.3	12.5	4.6	11.1	10.9	6.8

Table I

Corporations with and without Net Income

PERIODICAL PUBLISHERS

MONEY AMOUNTS AND SIZE OF ASSETS IN THOUSANDS OF DOLLARS

Item Description for Accounting Period 7/06 Through 6/07	Total	Zero Assets	Under 500	500 to 1,000	1,000 to 5,000	5,000 to 10,000	10,000 to 25,000	25,000 to 50,000	50,000 to 100,000	100,000 to 250,000	250,000 to 500,000	500,000 to 2,500,000	2,500,000 and over
Number of Enterprises **1**	8966	1293	5963	763	722	68	66	37	18	14	11	9	3
Revenues ($ in Thousands)													
Net Sales **2**	28690165	463795	2266726	727049	4368436	954756	1858580	1528304	1413397	1658489	2178475	5775061	5496096
Interest **3**	600822	1528	867	1598	1280	2273	4969	6044	3959	10369	15716	178444	373775
Rents **4**	64836	635	0	86	0	600	1504	13071	2189	686	20969	12090	13005
Royalties **5**	556130	186	0	0	0	2104	0	0	759	76296	77300	287498	111987
Other Portfolio Income **6**	596199	9799	58208	0	788	1393	8106	26506	55506	7618	117359	159653	151265
Other Receipts **7**	454397	11562	4013	35832	16238	19589	21196	15607	51294	49440	27823	127658	74145
Total Receipts **8**	30962549	487505	2330814	764565	4386742	980715	1894355	1589532	1527104	1802898	2437642	6540404	6220273
Average Total Receipts **9**	3453	377	391	1002	6076	14422	28702	42960	84839	128778	221604	726712	2073424
Operating Costs/Operating Income (%)													
Cost of Operations **10**	39.9	26.4	22.6	31.2	59.5	33.0	50.1	45.2	43.0	39.0	29.1	38.5	35.4
Salaries and Wages **11**	17.6	16.2	13.6	18.6	11.1	22.5	15.7	15.7	17.3	17.9	26.4	16.8	21.9
Taxes Paid **12**	2.3	2.1	2.4	2.7	2.3	2.4	2.9	2.4	2.7	2.0	3.4	1.6	2.5
Interest Paid **13**	6.8	22.5	0.9	0.9	0.5	1.1	1.0	0.9	3.0	4.9	4.7	10.0	17.4
Depreciation **14**	1.5	0.9	0.5	1.0	0.6	1.3	2.0	1.7	1.1	1.6	2.9	1.6	2.1
Amortization and Depletion **15**	3.6	4.9	0.1	1.9	0.9	0.4	1.1	0.5	1.7	3.3	4.6	5.7	7.5
Pensions and Other Deferred Comp. **16**	0.9	0.4	0.3	1.3	0.3	1.3	0.6	0.4	1.2	1.4	1.5	0.9	1.5
Employee Benefits **17**	1.9	1.9	1.1	2.4	1.4	1.9	2.5	1.6	2.0	2.0	2.8	1.5	2.2
Advertising **18**	2.0	2.5	2.6	0.1	1.6	0.5	1.5	1.4	2.7	3.3	3.5	1.8	1.8
Other Expenses **19**	25.9	41.5	36.6	33.7	21.8	29.5	19.7	28.1	26.1	26.5	23.1	31.6	17.9
Officers' Compensation **20**	3.3	4.0	13.4	9.7	3.6	4.1	2.6	2.7	2.1	3.1	3.3	1.2	0.7
Operating Margin **21**	•	•	5.8	•	•	2.0	0.4	•	•	•	•	•	•
Operating Margin Before Officers' Comp. **22**	•	•	19.2	6.2	0.1	6.2	3.0	2.0	•	•	•	•	•

Selected Average Balance Sheet ($ in Thousands)

Net Receivables 23	475	0	19	79	380	2122	3884	•	21078	32753	•	1479964
Inventories 24	772	0	60	269	369	1820	3303	•	18281	51962	•	2554546
Net Property, Plant and Equipment 25	624	0	21	67	217	555	1751	•	15969	26602	•	2015645
Total Assets 26	3450	0	161	735	1642	7360	15401	•	75094	148758	•	11102831
Notes and Loans Payable 27	745	0	40	105	396	830	2348	•	20804	68011	•	2259335
All Other Liabilities 28	987	0	48	165	426	3142	2819	•	20259	58853	•	3148937
Net Worth 29	1719	0	73	464	820	3388	10235	•	34031	21895	•	5694559

Selected Financial Ratios (Times to 1)

Current Ratio 30	1.8	•	2.4	3.4	2.5	2.2	2.5	•	1.8	1.8	•	1.6
Quick Ratio 31	0.7	•	1.1	1.6	1.5	1.5	1.6	•	1.0	0.7	•	0.7
Net Sales to Working Capital 32	11.2	•	15.4	9.5	8.4	8.2	4.9	•	10.2	10.5	•	11.7
Coverage Ratio 33	6.5	6.2	23.3	22.5	12.3	30.4	20.6	•	10.3	2.8	•	5.7
Total Asset Turnover 34	2.2	•	6.7	5.3	3.6	3.8	1.8	•	2.5	3.3	•	1.9
Inventory Turnover 35	7.2	•	12.4	11.1	11.2	8.6	5.2	•	7.3	6.9	•	6.0
Receivables Turnover 36	18.1	•	58.4	39.0	18.1	13.2	6.5	•	9.2	20.1	•	•
Total Liabilities to Net Worth 37	1.0	•	1.2	0.6	1.0	1.2	0.5	•	1.2	5.8	•	0.9
Current Assets to Working Capital 38	2.3	•	1.7	1.4	1.7	1.8	1.7	•	2.3	2.2	•	2.6
Current Liabilities to Working Capital 39	1.3	•	0.7	0.4	0.7	0.8	0.7	•	1.3	1.2	•	1.6
Working Capital to Net Sales 40	0.1	•	0.1	0.1	0.1	0.1	0.2	•	0.1	0.1	•	0.1
Inventory to Working Capital 41	1.2	•	0.9	0.6	0.5	0.6	0.4	•	0.9	1.2	•	1.4
Total Receipts to Cash Flow 42	11.3	5.1	9.4	14.6	9.6	6.4	6.9	•	9.2	12.1	•	12.2
Cost of Goods to Cash Flow 43	8.1	2.9	6.6	11.3	6.6	3.6	4.2	•	6.6	8.8	•	9.0
Cash Flow to Total Debt 44	0.4	•	1.3	1.0	0.8	1.1	0.8	•	0.5	0.3	•	0.3

Selected Financial Factors (in Percentages)

Debt Ratio 45	50.2	•	54.7	36.8	50.1	54.0	33.5	•	54.7	85.3	•	48.7
Return on Total Assets 46	10.7	•	34.9	19.6	18.9	20.9	16.8	•	18.7	13.4	•	8.7
Return on Equity Before Income Taxes 47	18.3	•	73.7	29.7	34.8	43.9	24.1	•	37.3	59.0	•	14.1
Return on Equity After Income Taxes 48	13.8	•	73.0	28.7	33.1	39.9	21.9	•	35.7	44.0	•	9.2
Profit Margin (Before Income Tax) 49	4.0	11.6	5.0	3.5	4.8	5.3	8.8	•	6.8	2.6	•	3.8
Profit Margin (After Income Tax) 50	3.0	10.9	5.0	3.4	4.5	4.8	8.0	•	6.5	1.9	•	2.5

224

Selected Average Balance Sheet ($ in Thousands)

Net Receivables **23**	458	0	12	188	1125	1934	2966	8039	13265	18936	33899	89577	257974
Inventories **24**	100	0	4	14	35	156	1037	976	2401	4037	2111	43092	141284
Net Property, Plant and Equipment **25**	250	0	13	41	142	1006	4426	7315	7794	13048	16556	52080	142633
Total Assets **26**	4667	73	746	2387	7162	16565	35213	66672	178181	335300		1052197	6461373
Notes and Loans Payable **27**	2555	40	74	646	3199	3920	7263	17269	80566	148122		464971	4714376
All Other Liabilities **28**	1528	28	568	1734	3111	9207	16758	31650	47487	91634		561967	1037225
Net Worth **29**	584	5	104	7	851	3439	11192	17753	50128	95543		25258	709772

Selected Financial Ratios (Times to 1)

Current Ratio **30**	1.0	•	1.6	1.0	1.3	1.4	1.2	1.6	1.0	1.0	1.5	0.6	1.0
Quick Ratio **31**	0.7	•	1.3	0.7	1.1	1.2	0.7	1.3	0.8	0.7	1.3	0.4	0.4
Net Sales to Working Capital **32**	•	•	17.2	•	18.0	10.5	28.7	4.6	•	373.0	5.9	•	•
Coverage Ratio **33**	1.3	0.2	10.2	2.8	•	5.3	3.3	3.9	2.7	1.7	2.3	1.2	1.2
Total Asset Turnover **34**	0.7	•	5.2	1.3	2.5	2.0	1.7	1.2	1.2	0.7	0.6	0.6	0.3
Inventory Turnover **35**	12.8	•	23.8	21.2	103.9	29.8	13.6	19.1	14.1	11.4	27.3	5.7	4.6
Receivables Turnover **36**	7.2	•	29.5	4.9	5.3	11.4	9.4	6.7	5.8	6.9	6.1	4.8	14.2
Total Liabilities to Net Worth **37**	7.0	•	14.9	6.2	352.3	7.4	3.8	2.1	2.8	2.6	2.5	40.7	8.1
Current Assets to Working Capital **38**	•	•	2.6	•	4.7	3.2	7.3	2.6	•	149.9	3.0	•	•
Current Liabilities to Working Capital **39**	•	•	1.6	•	3.7	2.2	6.3	1.6	•	148.9	2.0	•	•
Working Capital to Net Sales **40**	•	•	0.1	•	0.1	0.1	0.0	0.2	•	0.0	0.2	•	•
Inventory to Working Capital **41**	•	•	0.1	•	0.0	0.2	1.2	0.1	•	13.5	0.1	•	•
Total Receipts to Cash Flow **42**	4.3	4.9	2.5	3.3	6.4	3.3	5.1	4.0	3.9	3.8	4.7	3.5	6.6
Cost of Goods to Cash Flow **43**	1.7	1.3	0.6	1.0	3.8	1.1	2.5	1.8	1.7	1.5	1.4	1.4	2.3
Cash Flow to Total Debt **44**	0.2	•	2.2	0.4	0.4	0.7	0.4	0.4	0.4	0.2	0.2	0.2	0.0

Selected Financial Factors (in Percentages)

Debt Ratio **45**	87.5	•	93.7	86.0	99.7	88.1	79.2	68.2	73.4	71.9	71.5	97.6	89.0
Return on Total Assets **46**	6.3	•	49.6	3.3	•	11.3	5.6	4.3	9.3	5.7	6.5	7.3	5.8
Return on Equity Before Income Taxes **47**	12.7	•	710.8	15.2	•	77.2	18.7	10.1	21.8	8.5	13.1	50.4	7.8
Return on Equity After Income Taxes **48**	8.4	•	684.5	14.1	•	76.9	15.6	4.1	14.6	7.0	7.2	17.1	7.8
Profit Margin (Before Income Tax) **49**	2.3	•	8.6	1.7	•	4.7	2.3	2.7	4.9	3.6	6.3	2.0	3.0
Profit Margin (After Income Tax) **50**	1.5	•	8.3	1.5	•	4.7	1.9	1.1	3.3	3.0	3.5	0.7	3.0

Table II
Corporations with Net Income

PERIODICAL PUBLISHERS

MONEY AMOUNTS AND SIZE OF ASSETS IN THOUSANDS OF DOLLARS

Item Description for Accounting Period 7/06 Through 6/07	Total	Zero Assets	Under 500	500 to 1,000	1,000 to 5,000	5,000 to 10,000	10,000 to 25,000	25,000 to 50,000	50,000 to 100,000	100,000 to 250,000	250,000 to 500,000	500,000 to 2,500,000	2,500,000 and over
Number of Enterprises **1**	5407	420	3969	739	136	46	33	27	15	8	5	6	3
Revenues ($ in Thousands)													
Net Sales **2**	19574186	133309	1683474	674261	753036	814523	1001823	1222458	1268722	1254791	1286867	3984825	5499096
Interest **3**	586362	272	34	1584	735	1896	4643	4566	3627	10259	13118	171854	373775
Rents **4**	36945	0	0	0	0	600	1504	13071	2189	686	3535	2354	13005
Royalties **5**	463460	0	0	0	0	2104	0	0	566	75721	20215	252866	111987
Other Portfolio Income **6**	523174	9798	49418	0	433	1215	4327	19319	43014	6451	117126	120809	151265
Other Receipts **7**	302144	7508	4009	35358	28	19590	10486	13427	46264	43721	16442	31167	74145
Total Receipts **8**	21486271	150887	1736935	711203	754232	839928	1022783	1272841	1364382	1391629	1457303	4563875	6220273
Average Total Receipts **9**	3974	359	438	962	5546	18259	30993	47142	90959	173954	291461	760646	2073424
Operating Costs/Operating Income (%)													
Cost of Operations **10**	34.9	48.6	19.7	29.8	22.9	27.4	53.0	48.5	40.6	39.3	27.9	35.0	35.4
Salaries and Wages **11**	18.5	18.4	12.3	16.9	24.6	22.0	10.5	13.7	16.9	17.9	24.6	16.8	21.9
Taxes Paid **12**	2.4	2.3	2.1	2.6	3.1	2.4	3.0	2.3	2.1	2.0	4.1	1.9	2.5
Interest Paid **13**	7.0	0.1	1.0	0.2	0.0	0.4	1.1	0.7	0.9	0.8	0.9	8.4	17.4
Depreciation **14**	1.6	0.4	0.5	1.0	1.2	1.3	2.2	1.8	1.0	1.6	1.0	1.8	2.1
Amortization and Depletion **15**	3.7	•	0.2	1.8	0.4	0.3	1.4	0.4	1.3	0.9	1.9	5.5	7.5
Pensions and Other Deferred Comp. **16**	1.2	0.3	0.1	1.4	0.6	1.4	0.5	0.5	1.0	1.8	2.4	1.1	1.5
Employee Benefits **17**	2.0	0.5	0.7	2.2	1.6	2.0	3.7	1.7	1.9	1.9	3.2	1.4	2.2
Advertising **18**	1.9	3.9	1.0	0.0	2.3	0.6	1.9	1.1	3.0	3.3	2.2	2.4	1.8
Other Expenses **19**	24.6	9.6	33.0	31.8	22.1	31.8	12.2	18.3	26.0	29.5	25.1	31.8	17.9
Officers' Compensation **20**	3.2	3.6	14.2	10.0	4.1	4.9	3.2	2.4	1.7	3.9	3.9	0.7	0.7
Operating Margin **21**	•	12.3	15.3	2.2	17.2	5.5	7.3	8.6	3.5	•	2.8	•	•
Operating Margin Before Officers' Comp. **22**	2.3	15.9	29.5	12.2	21.2	10.3	10.5	11.0	5.3	0.9	6.7	•	•

Selected Average Balance Sheet ($ in Thousands)

Net Receivables 23	511	0	15	188	692	2486	3650	7714	15334	24305	41581	103996	257974
Inventories 24	131	0	0	13	35	230	1554	1063	2392	6425	1501	15524	141284
Net Property, Plant and Equipment 25	308	0	10	38	311	1438	5143	7722	5958	19352	14466	60892	142633
Total Assets 26	6003	0	67	744	3084	7476	18550	37148	62480	161751	349630	983772	6461373
Notes and Loans Payable 27	3260	0	29	25	456	1646	4909	6244	9001	24230	35718	395457	4714376
All Other Liabilities 28	1689	0	9	471	2104	3854	7634	17996	33532	61416	118577	474187	1037225
Net Worth 29	1055	0	29	247	523	1975	6008	12907	19948	76105	195336	114129	709772

Selected Financial Ratios (Times to 1)

Current Ratio 30	1.1	•	3.1	1.0	1.7	1.4	1.3	1.6	1.1	1.5	1.7	0.7	1.0
Quick Ratio 31	0.7	•	2.8	0.8	1.3	1.1	0.9	1.3	0.8	1.2	1.6	0.6	0.4
Net Sales to Working Capital 32	28.4	•	11.7	158.0	7.8	13.4	16.1	4.5	26.1	6.4	3.7	•	•
Coverage Ratio 33	2.3	519.5	20.1	42.0	806.4	22.5	9.8	18.7	12.6	10.4	18.6	1.9	1.2
Total Asset Turnover 34	0.6	•	6.4	1.2	1.8	2.4	1.6	1.2	1.4	1.0	0.7	0.7	0.3
Inventory Turnover 35	9.6	•	4659.6	20.9	35.8	21.1	10.4	20.6	14.4	9.6	47.8	15.0	4.6
Receivables Turnover 36	7.1	•	29.8	4.9	2.8	11.5	7.5	7.6	5.7	7.7	•	•	14.2
Total Liabilities to Net Worth 37	4.7	•	1.3	2.0	4.9	2.8	2.1	1.9	2.1	1.1	0.8	7.6	8.1
Current Assets to Working Capital 38	10.9	•	1.5	60.0	2.5	3.8	4.1	2.5	9.7	2.9	2.4	•	•
Current Liabilities to Working Capital 39	9.9	•	0.5	59.0	1.5	2.8	3.1	1.5	8.7	1.9	1.4	•	•
Working Capital to Net Sales 40	0.0	•	0.1	0.0	0.1	0.1	0.1	0.2	0.0	0.2	0.3	•	•
Inventory to Working Capital 41	1.1	•	0.0	2.1	•	0.3	0.9	0.1	0.8	0.3	0.0	•	•
Total Receipts to Cash Flow 42	3.5	3.0	2.2	2.9	2.8	2.8	5.0	3.6	3.1	3.0	3.2	3.0	6.6
Cost of Goods to Cash Flow 43	1.2	1.4	0.4	0.9	0.6	0.8	2.7	1.7	1.3	1.2	0.9	1.0	2.3
Cash Flow to Total Debt 44	0.2	•	5.1	0.6	0.8	1.2	0.5	0.5	0.6	0.6	0.5	0.3	0.0

Selected Financial Factors (in Percentages)

Debt Ratio 45	82.4	•	57.0	66.7	83.0	73.6	67.6	65.3	68.1	52.9	44.1	88.4	89.0
Return on Total Assets 46	9.6	•	123.8	9.7	31.1	21.0	17.0	15.5	15.9	8.4	12.2	10.8	5.8
Return on Equity Before Income Taxes 47	30.6	•	273.4	28.3	183.3	76.1	47.2	42.1	45.8	16.1	20.6	44.4	7.8
Return on Equity After Income Taxes 48	26.7	•	267.0	27.8	178.1	75.9	43.8	35.0	38.1	14.3	14.3	33.4	7.8
Profit Margin (Before Income Tax) 49	8.9	•	28.4	18.5	7.7	17.3	9.3	12.0	10.8	7.8	15.6	7.6	3.0
Profit Margin (After Income Tax) 50	7.8	•	20.7	18.0	7.5	16.8	8.7	10.0	9.0	6.9	10.8	5.7	3.0

Table I

Corporations with and without Net Income

BOOK PUBLISHERS

MONEY AMOUNTS AND SIZE OF ASSETS IN THOUSANDS OF DOLLARS

Item Description for Accounting Period 7/06 Through 6/07	Total	Zero Assets	Under 500	500 to 1,000	1,000 to 5,000	5,000 to 10,000	10,000 to 25,000	25,000 to 50,000	50,000 to 100,000	100,000 to 250,000	250,000 to 500,000	500,000 to 2,500,000	2,500,000 and over
Number of Enterprises **1**	6014	997	4203	375	261	85	37	28	4	9	3	8	5
Revenues ($ in Thousands)													
Net Sales **2**	28156562	24087	612857	313115	949671	1132797	491345	1171610	288037	1002072	935414	3500631	17734926
Interest **3**	1191721	41	868	3296	568	2407	364	2979	717	13566	2833	40506	1123577
Rents **4**	64744	0	0	0	245	0	359	2708	941	63	4102	3	56323
Royalties **5**	384143	171	0	0	0	0	0	5444	5432	4800	701	63598	303996
Other Portfolio Income **6**	889938	0	1755	0	100	34077	2083	7294	652	1567	3	47600	794807
Other Receipts **7**	570289	149	21303	4	1016	3470	5329	34918	1886	59824	49245	177478	215668
Total Receipts **8**	31257397	24448	636783	316415	951600	1172751	499480	1224953	297665	1081892	992298	3829816	20229297
Average Total Receipts **9**	5197	25	152	844	3646	13797	13499	43748	74416	120210	330766	478727	4045859
Operating Costs/Operating Income (%)													
Cost of Operations **10**	33.0	35.5	54.2	41.5	35.6	16.5	45.6	36.1	26.6	44.4	19.2	38.8	31.4
Salaries and Wages **11**	21.2	28.7	9.1	8.1	7.4	39.6	10.7	16.0	26.7	19.8	20.7	18.5	22.6
Taxes Paid **12**	2.7	4.0	1.9	1.2	1.1	4.3	2.4	2.0	2.2	2.2	1.8	2.2	3.0
Interest Paid **13**	9.0	21.7	0.3	15.9	1.5	1.1	1.3	2.4	1.2	6.2	6.8	12.2	10.4
Depreciation **14**	3.0	3.0	0.9	0.0	0.7	1.4	2.1	2.2	2.4	0.6	1.0	2.2	3.9
Amortization and Depletion **15**	2.9	17.9	*	1.3	0.0	0.0	0.3	1.7	0.5	5.3	6.7	6.5	2.5
Pensions and Other Deferred Comp. **16**	1.1	0.6	1.2	0.0	1.7	1.3	0.8	0.4	0.7	1.0	0.4	0.9	1.1
Employee Benefits **17**	2.4	6.2	1.9	0.5	0.7	4.7	1.8	1.6	2.5	1.9	2.3	3.8	2.2
Advertising **18**	2.6	1.2	2.5	0.4	0.6	1.6	3.0	11.5	3.9	3.4	0.1	4.8	1.9
Other Expenses **19**	23.3	94.9	18.1	38.6	18.7	23.0	20.8	23.9	27.7	18.1	49.7	21.9	22.5
Officers' Compensation **20**	2.4	9.1	9.9	10.2	13.2	3.1	3.4	2.5	2.6	2.4	1.3	4.6	1.0
Operating Margin **21**	*	*	0.1	*	18.9	3.4	7.8	*	3.0	*	*	*	*
Operating Margin Before Officers' Comp. **22**	*	*	10.0	*	32.1	6.5	11.2	2.2	5.5	*	*	*	*

Selected Average Balance Sheet ($ in Thousands)

Net Receivables 23	1036	9	217	369	3102	1557	6468	16904	28769	57114	131844	792264
Inventories 24	556	0	333	476	807	3337	10584	20799	18812	17233	77021	325655
Net Property, Plant and Equipment 25	420	0	1	249	885	2460	3790	12204	3996	21421	53622	308153
Total Assets 26	8479	62	804	2257	7422	15037	38467	74019	157549	374259	1388564	6729563
Notes and Loans Payable 27	3736	26	1494	664	1766	2669	17957	80153	84459	327865	848977	2403661
All Other Liabilities 28	2792	24	349	320	2432	3396	10599	43888	44150	105304	442070	2284584
Net Worth 29	1951	12	-1039	1273	3224	8972	9911	-50022	28939	-58910	95517	2041319

Selected Financial Ratios (Times to 1)

Current Ratio 30	1.2	•	1.1	3.4	1.8	2.2	1.6	1.6	0.9	1.1	0.9	1.2
Quick Ratio 31	0.5	•	0.5	2.1	1.3	1.0	0.5	0.9	0.5	0.8	0.4	0.4
Net Sales to Working Capital 32	11.2	•	11.7	4.1	5.8	2.6	4.2	4.4	•	22.7	•	9.2
Coverage Ratio 33	1.8	•	•	14.0	7.1	8.2	2.7	6.3	1.4	0.4	0.4	2.1
Total Asset Turnover 34	0.6	•	1.0	1.6	1.8	0.9	1.1	1.0	0.7	0.8	0.3	0.5
Inventory Turnover 35	2.8	•	1.0	2.7	2.7	1.8	1.4	0.9	2.6	3.5	2.2	3.4
Receivables Turnover 36	5.2	•	5.4	8.8	4.4	5.7	6.8	4.0	3.3	7.4	3.8	5.4
Total Liabilities to Net Worth 37	3.3	•	•	0.8	1.3	0.7	2.9	•	4.4	•	13.5	2.3
Current Assets to Working Capital 38	7.5	•	8.8	1.4	2.2	1.8	2.7	2.6	•	8.9	•	6.5
Current Liabilities to Working Capital 39	6.5	•	7.8	0.4	1.2	0.8	1.7	1.6	•	7.9	•	5.5
Working Capital to Net Sales 40	0.1	•	0.1	0.2	0.2	0.4	0.2	0.2	•	0.0	0.1	0.1
Inventory to Working Capital 41	1.4	•	4.7	0.4	0.3	0.8	1.1	0.8	•	1.2	0.9	0.9
Total Receipts to Cash Flow 42	4.0	•	5.1	2.9	4.6	3.5	4.0	3.3	5.5	2.3	8.6	3.7
Cost of Goods to Cash Flow 43	1.3	•	2.1	1.0	0.8	1.6	1.4	0.9	2.5	0.4	3.3	1.2
Cash Flow to Total Debt 44	0.2	•	0.1	1.3	0.7	0.6	0.4	0.2	0.2	0.3	0.0	0.2

Selected Financial Factors (in Percentages)

Debt Ratio 45	77.0	•	229.2	43.6	56.6	40.3	74.2	167.6	81.6	115.7	93.1	69.7
Return on Total Assets 46	9.1	•	•	33.1	14.4	9.2	7.1	7.3	6.2	2.2	1.7	11.6
Return on Equity Before Income Taxes 47	18.1	•	13.5	54.6	28.5	13.5	17.5	•	9.9	21.6	•	20.2
Return on Equity After Income Taxes 48	13.6	•	13.6	54.4	26.9	12.1	11.3	•	1.5	21.6	•	16.2
Profit Margin (Before Income Tax) 49	7.6	•	•	19.1	6.9	9.2	4.1	6.3	2.6	•	•	11.6
Profit Margin (After Income Tax) 50	5.7	•	•	19.0	6.5	8.2	2.7	5.1	0.4	•	•	9.3

Table II
Corporations with Net Income

BOOK PUBLISHERS

MONEY AMOUNTS AND SIZE OF ASSETS IN THOUSANDS OF DOLLARS

Item Description for Accounting Period 7/06 Through 6/07	Total	Zero Assets	Under 500	500 to 1,000	1,000 to 5,000	5,000 to 10,000	10,000 to 25,000	25,000 to 50,000	50,000 to 100,000	100,000 to 250,000	250,000 to 500,000	500,000 to 2,500,000	2,500,000 and over
Number of Enterprises **1**	3275	464	2332	128	226	58	29	20	•	•	0	3	5
Revenues ($ in Thousands)													
Net Sales **2**	23918441	4221	601696	200943	949339	915632	394989	769267	•	•	0	1422431	17734926
Interest **3**	1177244	0	868	2011	568	1138	364	2427	•	•	0	28186	1123577
Rents **4**	59683	0	0	0	245	0	359	1815	•	•	0	0	56323
Royalties **5**	351411	0	0	0	0	0	0	5359	•	•	0	39987	303996
Other Portfolio Income **6**	889878	0	1755	0	100	34077	2083	7294	•	•	0	47553	794807
Other Receipts **7**	441205	0	21289	0	1015	1382	4079	9205	•	•	0	131232	215668
Total Receipts **8**	26831862	4221	625608	202954	951267	952229	401874	795367	•	•	0	1669389	20229297
Average Total Receipts **9**	8193	9	268	1586	4209	16418	13858	39768	•	•	•	556463	4045859
Operating Costs/Operating Income (%)													
Cost of Operations **10**	33.3	24.0	54.0	44.1	35.6	6.5	43.4	36.8	•	•	•	48.4	31.4
Salaries and Wages **11**	21.8	•	9.2	6.3	7.4	45.9	10.7	19.1	•	•	•	19.1	22.6
Taxes Paid **12**	2.9	1.2	1.8	1.4	1.1	5.1	2.6	2.8	•	•	•	2.3	3.0
Interest Paid **13**	8.4	•	0.3	1.5	1.5	1.0	1.0	2.0	•	•	•	6.3	10.4
Depreciation **14**	3.3	•	0.9	•	0.7	1.7	2.6	2.9	•	•	•	1.7	3.9
Amortization and Depletion **15**	2.2	•	•	•	0.0	0.0	0.2	2.1	•	•	•	3.8	2.5
Pensions and Other Deferred Comp. **16**	1.1	•	1.3	0.1	1.7	1.6	1.0	0.5	•	•	•	0.4	1.1
Employee Benefits **17**	2.2	25.3	1.9	0.8	0.7	5.3	1.9	1.8	•	•	•	2.6	2.2
Advertising **18**	2.1	•	2.5	0.7	0.6	1.0	2.3	3.4	•	•	•	3.9	1.9
Other Expenses **19**	21.1	27.0	17.6	28.0	18.6	23.1	20.1	19.2	•	•	•	10.1	22.5
Officers' Compensation **20**	2.2	•	10.1	15.9	13.2	3.6	3.4	3.2	•	•	•	2.1	1.0
Operating Margin **21**	•	22.5	0.5	1.3	18.9	5.2	10.8	6.0	•	•	•	•	•
Operating Margin Before Officers' Comp. **22**	1.6	22.5	10.6	17.2	32.1	8.9	14.2	9.2	•	•	•	1.5	•

Selected Average Balance Sheet ($ in Thousands)

Net Receivables 23	1555	0	16	388	426	4135	1386	5852	•	84004	792264
Inventories 24	777	0	15	5	475	812	3395	9752	•	96100	325655
Net Property, Plant and Equipment 25	622	0	14	0	288	1248	3104	4710	•	25578	308153
Total Assets 26	12694		86	754	2442	7905	14189	38015	•	1424326	6729563
Notes and Loans Payable 27	4607	0	9	605	759	2094	2954	12725	•	640407	2403661
All Other Liabilities 28	4125	0	29	29	357	2411	2404	7956	•	395069	2284584
Net Worth 29	3962	0	48	120	1326	3400	8831	17334	•	388851	2041319

Selected Financial Ratios (Times to 1)

Current Ratio 30	1.2	•	2.4	0.7	3.4	1.9	2.8	1.9	•	0.8	1.2
Quick Ratio 31	0.5	•	1.4	0.7	2.2	1.5	1.4	0.6	•	0.4	0.4
Net Sales to Working Capital 32	8.2	•	6.2	•	4.3	5.9	2.3	3.2	•	•	9.2
Coverage Ratio 33	2.4	•	17.9	2.5	14.1	10.0	12.6	5.7	•	3.7	2.1
Total Asset Turnover 34	0.6	•	3.0	2.1	1.7	2.0	1.0	1.0	•	0.3	0.5
Inventory Turnover 35	3.1	•	9.5	144.4	3.1	1.3	1.7	1.5	•	2.4	3.4
Receivables Turnover 36	5.4	•	33.0	4.8	9.2	3.7	6.5	6.8	•	4.6	5.4
Total Liabilities to Net Worth 37	2.2	•	0.8	5.3	0.8	1.3	0.6	1.2	•	2.7	2.3
Current Assets to Working Capital 38	5.4	•	1.7	•	1.4	2.1	1.6	2.1	•	•	6.5
Current Liabilities to Working Capital 39	4.4	•	0.7	•	0.4	1.1	0.6	1.1	•	•	5.5
Working Capital to Net Sales 40	0.1	•	0.2	•	0.2	0.2	0.4	0.3	•	•	0.1
Inventory to Working Capital 41	0.9	•	0.7	•	0.5	0.2	0.6	0.9	•	•	0.9
Total Receipts to Cash Flow 42	3.8	2.1	5.0	3.4	2.9	4.4	3.2	4.0	•	4.5	3.7
Cost of Goods to Cash Flow 43	1.2	0.5	2.7	1.5	1.0	0.3	1.4	1.5	•	2.2	1.2
Cash Flow to Total Debt 44	0.2	•	1.3	0.7	1.3	0.8	0.8	0.5	•	0.1	0.2

Selected Financial Factors (in Percentages)

Debt Ratio 45	68.8	•	44.6	84.1	45.7	57.0	37.8	54.4	•	72.7	69.7
Return on Total Assets 46	11.6	•	14.1	7.9	35.4	20.5	12.7	11.5	•	7.8	11.6
Return on Equity Before Income Taxes 47	21.7	•	24.1	29.6	60.6	42.8	18.8	20.7	•	20.9	20.2
Return on Equity After Income Taxes 48	17.6	•	22.7	26.4	60.3	40.7	16.9	15.8	•	14.7	16.2
Profit Margin (Before Income Tax) 49	11.8	22.5	4.4	2.3	19.1	9.2	12.2	9.3	•	17.1	11.6
Profit Margin (After Income Tax) 50	9.5	20.6	4.2	2.0	19.1	8.8	11.0	7.1	•	12.1	9.3

Table I

Corporations with and without Net Income

DATABASE, DIRECTORY, AND OTHER PUBLISHERS

MONEY AMOUNTS AND SIZE OF ASSETS IN THOUSANDS OF DOLLARS

Item Description for Accounting Period 7/06 Through 6/07		Total	Zero Assets	Under 500	500 to 1,000	1,000 to 5,000	5,000 to 10,000	10,000 to 25,000	25,000 to 50,000	50,000 to 100,000	100,000 to 250,000	250,000 to 500,000	500,000 to 2,500,000	2,500,000 and over
Number of Enterprises	**1**	5813	1606	3242	564	244	86	27	15	6	13	0	4	5
Revenues ($ in Thousands)														
Net Sales	**2**	21912842	370737	1591225	1049556	1626603	1429552	418727	612608	203097	1440111	0	2643351	10527276
Interest	**3**	589105	684	1583	1467	1430	1499	1254	3660	3433	5965	0	9520	558612
Rents	**4**	63199	0	0	0	0	0	0	2034	64	0	0	59	61043
Royalties	**5**	100873	246	0	0	0	0	0	5	0	15668	0	0	84954
Other Portfolio Income	**6**	85093	45760	510	0	3171	987	73	2765	1100	4014	0	2583	24133
Other Receipts	**7**	402347	8104	19247	225	1037	3153	8780	3666	9759	26629	0	139024	182718
Total Receipts	**8**	23153459	425531	1612565	1051248	1632241	1435191	428834	624738	217453	1492387	0	2794537	11438736
Average Total Receipts	**9**	3983	265	497	1864	6690	16688	15883	41649	36242	114799	•	698634	2287747
Operating Costs/Operating Income (%)														
Cost of Operations	**10**	25.1	32.5	8.1	12.8	28.8	47.7	45.1	13.4	52.4	31.8	•	22.0	24.3
Salaries and Wages	**11**	20.5	28.1	14.5	25.3	23.3	25.3	12.8	25.3	11.4	19.7	•	28.2	18.0
Taxes Paid	**12**	2.8	2.7	1.5	3.1	2.8	3.4	2.8	3.6	2.5	2.3	•	2.7	3.0
Interest Paid	**13**	9.2	8.2	0.0	0.2	0.1	0.6	2.0	1.5	8.7	3.4	•	4.8	16.8
Depreciation	**14**	1.1	1.7	0.2	0.9	1.7	1.0	1.1	1.2	4.0	1.9	•	1.7	0.9
Amortization and Depletion	**15**	5.6	4.4	0.0	0.0	0.1	0.4	0.3	0.7	3.4	3.3	•	1.6	10.4
Pensions and Other Deferred Comp.	**16**	0.5	0.0	0.0	1.3	0.3	0.4	0.1	1.1	0.0	0.4	•	0.7	0.6
Employee Benefits	**17**	2.0	2.5	1.0	0.7	1.2	2.1	0.6	2.2	1.6	2.7	•	3.5	2.0
Advertising	**18**	2.3	1.1	0.2	0.2	1.7	0.7	2.9	5.3	0.3	3.9	•	2.5	2.8
Other Expenses	**19**	31.0	25.2	69.5	43.8	12.3	13.5	16.4	24.6	20.6	30.5	•	29.0	31.0
Officers' Compensation	**20**	3.7	1.0	8.9	11.1	22.2	3.6	2.4	4.9	2.1	1.8	•	0.7	0.4
Operating Margin	**21**	•	•	•	0.6	5.5	1.4	13.4	16.3	•	•	•	2.5	0.4
Operating Margin Before Officers' Comp.	**22**	•	•	4.9	11.6	27.7	5.0	15.8	21.2	•	0.4	•	•	3.2

Selected Average Balance Sheet ($ in Thousands)

Net Receivables 23	934	0	3	237	997	4492	4628	7998	6209	28323	•	213944	630227
Inventories 24	254	0	3	61	23	408	1035	539	649	3720	•	5420	260008
Net Property, Plant and Equipment 25	329	0	2	52	355	581	350	2848	5452	9915	•	85006	237807
Total Assets 26	7394	0	44	711	2548	7509	14433	32801	75667	168761	•	875654	6827247
Notes and Loans Payable 27	5060	0	43	70	67	900	5311	3859	28046	57125	•	2399750	3686077
All Other Liabilities 28	2084	0	13	473	985	5084	6886	16830	15222	50227	•	555982	1544157
Net Worth 29	250	0	-12	168	1496	1526	2235	12112	32398	61409	•	-2080078	1597013

Selected Financial Ratios (Times to 1)

Current Ratio 30	1.1	•	2.2	1.1	1.8	1.2	1.8	1.7	1.0	1.3	•	0.8	1.0
Quick Ratio 31	0.7	•	1.6	0.7	1.3	1.0	1.4	1.5	0.8	0.8	•	0.7	0.6
Net Sales to Working Capital 32	26.8	•	30.7	26.1	7.3	16.4	4.3	5.9	•	6.9	•	•	36.7
Coverage Ratio 33	1.2	1.9	•	4.7	42.6	4.2	8.9	13.0	1.0	1.7	•	2.7	0.9
Total Asset Turnover 34	0.5	•	11.1	2.6	2.6	2.2	1.1	1.2	0.4	0.7	•	0.8	0.3
Inventory Turnover 35	3.7	•	14.4	3.9	82.5	19.4	6.8	10.1	27.3	9.5	•	26.9	2.0
Receivables Turnover 36	4.6	•	377.1	8.5	7.5	3.7	3.9	6.1	2.6	5.1	•	4.0	3.9
Total Liabilities to Net Worth 37	28.6	•	•	3.2	0.7	3.9	5.5	1.7	1.3	1.7	•	•	3.3
Current Assets to Working Capital 38	13.2	•	1.8	8.0	2.2	5.8	2.3	2.5	•	3.9	•	•	23.3
Current Liabilities to Working Capital 39	12.2	•	0.8	7.0	1.2	4.8	1.3	1.5	•	2.9	•	•	22.3
Working Capital to Net Sales 40	0.0	•	0.0	0.0	0.1	0.1	0.2	0.2	0.1	0.1	•	•	0.0
Inventory to Working Capital 41	1.2	•	0.2	0.9	0.0	0.5	0.2	0.0	•	0.3	•	•	2.8
Total Receipts to Cash Flow 42	4.1	5.9	1.5	7.0	7.1	9.1	3.3	2.5	6.7	3.3	•	3.0	5.3
Cost of Goods to Cash Flow 43	1.0	1.9	0.1	0.9	2.0	4.3	1.5	0.3	3.5	1.1	•	0.7	1.3
Cash Flow to Total Debt 44	0.1	•	5.7	0.5	0.9	0.3	0.4	0.8	0.1	0.3	•	0.1	0.1

Selected Financial Factors (in Percentages)

Debt Ratio 45	96.6	•	127.0	76.4	41.3	79.7	84.5	63.1	57.2	63.6	•	337.5	76.6
Return on Total Assets 46	5.7	•	•	2.4	15.7	5.2	19.2	24.1	3.9	3.7	•	9.7	4.8
Return on Equity Before Income Taxes 47	28.5	•	110.7	8.0	26.1	19.5	109.8	60.1	0.1	4.0	•	•	•
Return on Equity After Income Taxes 48	13.2	•	110.8	7.6	23.2	16.8	78.1	48.9	2.3	•	•	•	•
Profit Margin (Before Income Tax) 49	1.9	7.4	•	0.7	5.9	1.8	15.8	17.8	0.1	2.2	•	8.1	•
Profit Margin (After Income Tax) 50	0.9	4.2	•	0.7	5.2	1.5	11.2	14.5	•	1.3	•	5.3	•

Table II

Corporations with Net Income

DATABASE, DIRECTORY, AND OTHER PUBLISHERS

MONEY AMOUNTS AND SIZE OF ASSETS IN THOUSANDS OF DOLLARS

Item Description for Accounting Period 7/06 Through 6/07	Total	Zero Assets	Under 500	500 to 1,000	1,000 to 5,000	5,000 to 10,000	10,000 to 25,000	25,000 to 50,000	50,000 to 100,000	100,000 to 250,000	250,000 to 500,000	500,000 to 2,500,000	2,500,000 and over
Number of Enterprises **1**	2867	383	1885	288	192	71	23	10	•	6	0	•	•
Revenues ($ in Thousands)													
Net Sales **2**	11882961	79293	1479127	257922	1317152	1370887	370388	479819	•	604818	0	•	•
Interest **3**	224050	250	1352	1279	1336	19	1254	3428	•	3787	0	•	•
Rents **4**	3757	0	0	0	0	0	0	2034	•	0	0	•	•
Royalties **5**	75659	246	0	0	0	0	0	0	•	15405	0	•	•
Other Portfolio Income **6**	77775	45760	510	0	2975	987	73	2765	•	1563	0	•	•
Other Receipts **7**	118855	169	1	162	440	527	8779	1565	•	11631	0	•	•
Total Receipts **8**	12383057	125718	1480990	259363	1321903	1372420	380494	489611	•	637204	0	•	•
Average Total Receipts **9**	4319	328	786	901	6885	19330	16543	48961	•	106201	•	•	•
Operating Costs/Operating Income (%)													
Cost of Operations **10**	27.4	39.8	6.0	50.9	31.8	47.6	42.9	6.0	•	24.0	•	•	•
Salaries and Wages **11**	20.1	19.7	12.3	1.9	22.0	23.9	14.3	26.4	•	22.6	•	•	•
Taxes Paid **12**	2.8	4.6	1.3	1.9	2.6	3.2	2.6	3.3	•	2.9	•	•	•
Interest Paid **13**	5.9	1.0	0.0	0.1	0.1	0.6	2.2	0.6	•	3.6	•	•	•
Depreciation **14**	1.2	0.7	0.1	0.4	1.5	0.8	1.1	1.4	•	1.9	•	•	•
Amortization and Depletion **15**	2.4	•	•	0.0	0.1	0.2	0.4	0.1	•	3.9	•	•	•
Pensions and Other Deferred Comp. **16**	0.5	0.1	•	3.6	0.3	0.4	0.2	1.4	•	0.0	•	•	•
Employee Benefits **17**	1.9	0.8	0.9	0.7	0.6	2.1	0.7	2.2	•	3.9	•	•	•
Advertising **18**	2.1	2.1	0.0	0.4	2.0	0.3	3.0	6.5	•	1.4	•	•	•
Other Expenses **19**	25.9	20.3	69.5	9.9	8.7	13.3	14.1	20.4	•	22.9	•	•	•
Officers' Compensation **20**	5.2	1.8	9.5	16.8	22.3	3.2	2.7	5.6	•	2.1	•	•	•
Operating Margin **21**	4.7	9.2	0.3	13.4	8.0	4.5	15.9	26.2	•	10.6	•	•	•
Operating Margin Before Officers' Comp. **22**	9.8	11.0	9.7	30.2	30.3	7.7	18.6	31.8	•	12.8	•	•	•

Selected Average Balance Sheet ($ in Thousands)

Net Receivables 23	1221	0	0	90	1053	5169	4207	3972	•	19303
Inventories 24	388	0	0	120	9	493	1199	808	•	2058
Net Property, Plant and Equipment 25	301	0	1	17	372	541	411	4015	•	12327
Total Assets 26	6744	0	43	605	2369	7655	15086	33873	•	157591
Notes and Loans Payable 27	5872	0	0	24	64	984	3198	3745	•	68242
All Other Liabilities 28	1712	0	0	105	973	5376	7269	11992	•	31452
Net Worth 29	-840	0	43	475	1332	1295	4619	18135	•	57898

Selected Financial Ratios (Times to 1)

Current Ratio 30	1.3	•	187.3	3.4	1.9	1.2	1.6	3.9	•	1.1
Quick Ratio 31	0.8	•	151.9	1.9	1.5	1.0	1.4	3.3	•	0.6
Net Sales to Working Capital 32	7.0	•	25.4	2.9	7.8	15.8	5.2	3.9	•	25.3
Coverage Ratio 33	2.6	70.6	122.5	261.5	68.3	9.3	9.5	48.1	•	5.4
Total Asset Turnover 34	0.6	•	18.1	1.5	2.9	2.5	1.1	1.4	•	0.6
Inventory Turnover 35	2.9	•	•	3.8	234.8	18.6	5.8	3.6	•	11.7
Receivables Turnover 36	3.3	•	•	3.7	6.9	3.7	4.1	8.4	•	•
Total Liabilities to Net Worth 37	•	•	0.0	0.3	0.8	4.9	2.3	0.9	•	1.7
Current Assets to Working Capital 38	4.0	•	1.0	1.4	2.1	5.3	2.6	1.3	•	11.2
Current Liabilities to Working Capital 39	3.0	•	0.0	0.4	1.1	4.3	1.6	0.3	•	10.2
Working Capital to Net Sales 40	0.1	•	0.0	0.3	0.1	0.1	0.2	0.3	•	0.0
Inventory to Working Capital 41	0.2	•	•	0.4	0.0	0.5	0.3	0.0	•	0.5
Total Receipts to Cash Flow 42	3.2	3.6	1.4	4.9	6.4	7.1	3.2	2.1	•	2.7
Cost of Goods to Cash Flow 43	0.9	1.4	0.1	2.5	2.0	3.4	1.4	0.1	•	0.7
Cash Flow to Total Debt 44	0.2	•	1436.2	1.4	1.0	0.4	0.5	1.4	•	0.4

Selected Financial Factors (in Percentages)

Debt Ratio 45	112.5	•	0.9	21.4	43.8	83.1	69.4	46.5	•	63.3
Return on Total Assets 46	9.2	•	7.2	20.7	24.5	13.1	22.2	40.0	•	12.6
Return on Equity Before Income Taxes 47	•	•	7.2	26.3	42.9	69.3	65.0	73.2	•	27.9
Return on Equity After Income Taxes 48	•	•	7.2	26.0	38.8	65.4	47.0	62.0	•	23.8
Profit Margin (Before Income Tax) 49	9.2	67.7	0.4	13.9	8.3	4.6	18.6	27.7	•	16.0
Profit Margin (After Income Tax) 50	7.3	54.6	0.4	13.8	7.5	4.4	13.5	23.4	•	13.7

Table I

Corporations with and without Net Income

SOFTWARE PUBLISHERS

MONEY AMOUNTS AND SIZE OF ASSETS IN THOUSANDS OF DOLLARS

Item Description for Accounting Period 7/06 Through 6/07

	Total	Zero Assets	Under 500	500 to 1,000	1,000 to 5,000	5,000 to 10,000	10,000 to 25,000	25,000 to 50,000	50,000 to 100,000	100,000 to 250,000	250,000 to 500,000	500,000 to 2,500,000	2,500,000 and over
Number of Enterprises **1**	9836	1251	6539	565	757	259	199	89	51	54	25	35	13
Revenues ($ in Thousands)													
Net Sales **2**	97888141	1600633	1251590	1594877	2258130	2115069	2771500	2533817	2327380	4734757	4196927	18020596	54482864
Interest **3**	2911606	28228	2667	6799	24791	22812	40604	43319	39528	90720	110520	442634	2058982
Rents **4**	167388	420	0	0	0	1121	0	0	995	1625	9343	36845	117039
Royalties **5**	7374041	75996	0	19263	716	3697	32675	55863	119456	69138	121938	1862184	5013117
Other Portfolio Income **6**	1561804	22087	33	29197	34870	3840	7533	55614	5534	32544	51815	285867	1032869
Other Receipts **7**	24513585	21778	29075	2145	25069	79189	114408	31516	117976	99531	10301	431515	23551084
Total Receipts **8**	134416565	1749142	1283365	1652281	2343576	2225728	2966720	2720129	2610869	5028315	4500844	21079641	86255955
Average Total Receipts **9**	13666	1398	196	2924	3096	8594	14908	30563	51194	93117	180034	602275	6635073
Operating Costs/Operating Income (%)													
Cost of Operations **10**	27.8	35.1	4.5	6.8	19.8	25.3	10.1	28.2	21.2	17.6	20.9	33.3	30.0
Salaries and Wages **11**	36.4	32.2	34.2	52.0	48.1	45.5	52.1	34.2	37.7	33.3	34.8	34.3	35.6
Taxes Paid **12**	3.4	4.6	5.6	4.5	5.4	5.7	4.2	4.1	4.3	4.3	8.1	2.1	3.0
Interest Paid **13**	3.8	4.4	4.3	0.7	3.1	1.4	1.6	1.6	1.8	1.8	1.7	2.4	5.1
Depreciation **14**	2.5	1.2	3.0	0.5	3.1	2.1	3.2	1.8	1.9	2.2	1.7	2.3	2.7
Amortization and Depletion **15**	1.8	1.3	1.0	0.4	1.7	1.4	1.0	1.3	1.7	3.7	2.1	2.4	1.5
Pensions and Other Deferred Comp. **16**	0.4	0.1	0.1	2.9	0.5	0.2	0.4	0.5	0.8	0.3	0.7	0.7	0.3
Employee Benefits **17**	3.4	3.4	3.3	2.9	4.5	2.8	3.7	2.5	2.7	2.5	3.9	3.6	3.4
Advertising **18**	5.5	2.3	2.1	0.5	3.1	2.6	3.6	2.1	2.2	2.0	1.6	3.9	7.5
Other Expenses **19**	32.8	31.4	38.7	21.4	44.3	32.0	42.9	30.9	33.0	33.0	27.6	29.1	33.7
Officers' Compensation **20**	2.5	5.3	18.6	12.3	9.7	5.9	5.6	5.8	2.9	2.8	1.7	1.5	1.4
Operating Margin **21**	•	•	•	•	•	•	•	•	•	•	•	•	•
Operating Margin Before Officers' Comp. **22**	3.2	•	3.2	7.2	•	•	•	•	•	•	•	•	•

Selected Average Balance Sheet ($ in Thousands)

Net Receivables 23	2793	0	5	60	594	1823	3900	8811	13343	28325	72860	167375	1156396
Inventories 24	231	0	2	39	44	66	265	323	398	974	457	21733	96890
Net Property, Plant and Equipment 25	1115	0	6	71	196	581	1023	1796	3328	6033	14102	49751	587050
Total Assets 26	23706	0	70	680	2408	6876	15813	34247	69474	147457	364684	1215826	12258604
Notes and Loans Payable 27	4526	0	104	452	1560	3315	4958	13857	22948	45298	172530		2445666
All Other Liabilities 28	12187	0	119	301	1320	5448	9596	17550	32984	46944	103816	445638	6971638
Net Worth 29	6993	0	-153	-73	-473	-92	2902	11738	22633	77565	215569	597658	2841300

Selected Financial Ratios (Times to 1)

Current Ratio 30	0.6	•	1.5	1.2	1.0	1.7	1.3	1.1	1.8	1.9	1.7	0.4	
Quick Ratio 31	0.4	0.5	1.2	1.0	0.9	1.5	1.1	0.9	1.4	1.5	1.2	0.2	
Net Sales to Working Capital 32	•	•	19.3	12.3	•	3.0	5.6	12.2	2.7	2.2	2.5	•	
Coverage Ratio 33	5.7	•	•	•	•	•	•	2.1	2.6	2.3	1.7	8.0	
Total Asset Turnover 34	0.4	2.8	4.1	1.2	1.2	0.9	0.8	0.7	0.6	0.5	0.4	0.3	
Inventory Turnover 35	12.0	3.9	4.9	13.3	31.2	5.3	24.8	24.2	15.9	76.8	7.9	13.0	
Receivables Turnover 36	2.9	35.9	23.9	5.5	4.7	3.7	3.3	3.4	3.4	2.1	1.0	2.5	
Total Liabilities to Net Worth 37	2.4	•	•	4.4	1.9	2.1	0.9	0.7	1.0	3.3			
Current Assets to Working Capital 38	•	•	3.2	7.3	•	2.4	4.5	9.0	2.3	2.1	2.4	•	
Current Liabilities to Working Capital 39	•	•	2.2	6.3	•	1.4	3.5	8.0	1.3	1.1	1.4	•	
Working Capital to Net Sales 40	•	•	0.1	0.1	•	0.3	0.2	0.1	0.4	0.5	0.4	•	
Inventory to Working Capital 41	•	0.1	0.1	0.2	•	0.1	0.1	0.1	0.0	0.0	0.1	•	
Total Receipts to Cash Flow 42	2.2	6.2	4.4	6.2	11.5	6.0	5.1	3.2	3.2	4.0	3.7	1.6	
Cost of Goods to Cash Flow 43	0.6	2.2	0.2	0.4	2.9	0.6	1.4	0.7	0.6	0.8	1.2	0.5	
Cash Flow to Total Debt 44	0.3	•	0.2	0.6	0.1	0.2	0.3	0.4	0.3	0.2	0.3		

Selected Financial Factors (in Percentages)

Debt Ratio 45	70.5	319.6	110.8	119.6	101.3	81.6	65.7	67.4	47.4	40.9	50.8	76.8	
Return on Total Assets 46	9.2	•	•	•	•	•	2.5	2.7	1.9	1.7	14.0		
Return on Equity Before Income Taxes 47	25.7	16.1	57.7	249.9	1745.8	•	3.9	3.2	1.8	1.4	52.8		
Return on Equity After Income Taxes 48	15.7	16.4	57.8	254.9	1795.8	•	0.1	1.7	0.4	0.3	35.7		
Profit Margin (Before Income Tax) 49	18.0	•	•	•	•	•	1.9	2.8	2.3	1.6	35.8		
Profit Margin (After Income Tax) 50	11.0	•	•	•	•	•	0.1	1.5	0.5	0.4	24.2		

Table II
Corporations with Net Income

SOFTWARE PUBLISHERS

MONEY AMOUNTS AND SIZE OF ASSETS IN THOUSANDS OF DOLLARS

Item Description for Accounting Period 7/06 Through 6/07	Total	Zero Assets	Under 500	500 to 1,000	1,000 to 5,000	5,000 to 10,000	10,000 to 25,000	25,000 to 50,000	50,000 to 100,000	100,000 to 250,000	250,000 to 500,000	500,000 to 2,500,000	2,500,000 and over
Number of Enterprises **1**	3343	•	2473	290	279	95	55	30	26	34	14	•	•
Revenues ($ in Thousands)													
Net Sales **2**	81775341	•	1000035	1279007	1123443	1146289	1157585	1238416	1450442	3366624	3171004	•	•
Interest **3**	2604970	•	2067	4302	4026	5774	10966	20320	20851	56893	47788	•	•
Rents **4**	146715	•	0	0	0	725	0	0	850	1614	9343	•	•
Royalties **5**	6430096	•	0	0	0	0	32585	0	100333	17692	71557	•	•
Other Portfolio Income **6**	1468217	•	0	27638	24502	459	39	54336	985	6926	32155	•	•
Other Receipts **7**	24062611	•	24826	3	19326	58361	27800	6976	39559	29151	-7050	•	•
Total Receipts **8**	116487950	•	1026928	1310950	1171297	1211608	1228975	1320048	1613020	3478900	3324797	•	•
Average Total Receipts **9**	34845	•	415	4521	4198	12754	22345	44002	62039	102321	237486	•	•
Operating Costs/Operating Income (%)													
Cost of Operations **10**	25.5	•	3.1	0.1	23.5	23.9	4.5	40.8	21.4	16.3	19.2	•	•
Salaries and Wages **11**	35.7	•	28.1	52.2	19.3	30.6	38.5	23.0	34.4	32.5	30.5	•	•
Taxes Paid **12**	3.4	•	4.7	4.1	3.4	5.1	2.9	3.0	3.8	4.6	9.5	•	•
Interest Paid **13**	4.1	•	4.2	0.1	0.5	0.6	1.3	1.2	0.8	2.1	1.2	•	•
Depreciation **14**	2.5	•	1.3	0.2	1.8	1.6	1.9	1.2	2.0	2.0	1.4	•	•
Amortization and Depletion **15**	1.6	•	0.0	0.0	0.5	0.1	0.4	0.9	0.7	2.1	1.4	•	•
Pensions and Other Deferred Comp. **16**	0.5	•	•	3.5	0.9	0.2	0.6	0.9	0.9	0.4	1.0	•	•
Employee Benefits **17**	3.4	•	2.5	2.6	2.8	1.7	2.4	1.5	2.6	2.4	3.3	•	•
Advertising **18**	5.7	•	1.4	0.2	2.2	2.4	2.7	0.9	1.9	1.8	1.1	•	•
Other Expenses **19**	31.3	•	26.5	16.0	25.9	22.5	35.5	17.7	24.0	27.6	23.0	•	•
Officers' Compensation **20**	2.1	•	20.0	13.6	5.7	4.9	3.1	2.6	2.8	1.9	1.6	•	•
Operating Margin **21**	•	•	8.2	7.4	13.5	6.3	6.2	6.4	4.7	6.3	6.8	•	•
Operating Margin Before Officers' Comp. **22**	•	•	28.2	21.0	19.2	11.2	9.4	9.0	7.5	8.2	8.4	•	•

Selected Average Balance Sheet ($ in Thousands)

Net Receivables 23	6970	•	10	0	754	2509	5017	10484	15045	27752	81298	•	•
Inventories 24	488	•	5	63	76	82	477	367	406	488	714	•	•
Net Property, Plant and Equipment 25	2976	•	4	103	146	808	1207	2414	4264	6743	19513	•	•
Total Assets 26	61904	•	100	614	2141	7161	15882	36880	65103	146220	390264	•	•
Notes and Loans Payable 27	10845	•	122	228	1198	769	3691	5911	9407	25524	45512	•	•
All Other Liabilities 28	32486	•	221	169	760	5250	7562	16186	33587	43243	127106	•	•
Net Worth 29	18573	•	-243	217	183	1142	4629	14783	22109	77453	217646	•	•

Selected Financial Ratios (Times to 1)

Current Ratio 30	0.6	•	1.5	3.0	2.3	1.2	1.6	1.1	1.4	1.7	1.6	•	•
Quick Ratio 31	0.4	•	1.2	2.6	1.8	1.0	1.5	1.0	1.1	1.4	1.4	•	•
Net Sales to Working Capital 32	•	•	13.4	13.3	4.1	11.7	5.3	15.6	5.1	3.4	3.7	•	•
Coverage Ratio 33	7.9	•	3.6	81.4	37.3	19.5	10.8	11.7	21.4	5.7	10.3	•	•
Total Asset Turnover 34	0.4	•	4.1	7.2	1.9	1.7	1.3	1.1	0.9	0.7	0.6	•	•
Inventory Turnover 35	12.8	•	2.5	0.0	12.4	35.2	2.0	46.0	29.4	33.0	60.9	•	•
Receivables Turnover 36	2.9	•	78.9	28.9	5.2	6.3	3.5	3.3	4.1	•	2.3	•	•
Total Liabilities to Net Worth 37	2.3	•	1.8	10.7	5.3	2.4	1.5	1.9	0.8	0.9	0.8	•	•
Current Assets to Working Capital 38	•	•	3.1	1.5	1.8	5.4	2.6	7.8	3.5	2.5	2.8	•	•
Current Liabilities to Working Capital 39	•	•	2.1	0.5	0.8	4.4	1.6	6.8	2.5	1.5	1.8	•	•
Working Capital to Net Sales 40	•	•	0.1	0.1	0.2	0.1	0.2	0.1	0.2	0.3	0.3	•	•
Inventory to Working Capital 41	•	•	0.2	•	0.1	0.1	0.0	0.0	0.1	0.0	0.0	•	•
Total Receipts to Cash Flow 42	1.9	•	2.8	4.4	2.5	3.1	2.3	4.3	2.7	2.9	3.3	•	•
Cost of Goods to Cash Flow 43	0.5	•	0.1	0.0	0.6	0.7	0.1	1.7	0.6	0.5	0.6	•	•
Cash Flow to Total Debt 44	0.3	•	0.4	2.5	0.8	0.7	0.8	0.4	0.5	0.5	0.4	•	•

Selected Financial Factors (in Percentages)

Debt Ratio 45	70.0	•	344.2	64.6	91.5	84.1	70.9	59.9	66.0	47.0	44.2	•	•
Return on Total Assets 46	12.7	•	61.3	72.0	34.3	21.2	18.1	15.9	14.3	7.9	7.5	•	•
Return on Equity Before Income Taxes 47	36.9	•	•	201.1	391.1	126.3	56.4	36.3	40.1	12.3	12.1	•	•
Return on Equity After Income Taxes 48	25.8	•	•	201.0	356.2	115.3	48.4	31.7	32.5	10.0	9.6	•	•
Profit Margin (Before Income Tax) 49	28.0	•	10.9	9.9	17.8	12.0	12.4	13.0	15.9	9.6	11.6	•	•
Profit Margin (After Income Tax) 50	19.6	•	10.6	9.9	16.2	10.9	10.7	11.3	12.9	7.8	9.2	•	•

Table I

Corporations with and without Net Income

MOTION PICTURE AND VIDEO INDUSTRIES (EXCEPT VIDEO RENTAL)

MONEY AMOUNTS AND SIZE OF ASSETS IN THOUSANDS OF DOLLARS

Item Description for Accounting Period 7/06 Through 6/07	Total	Zero Assets	Under 500	500 to 1,000	1,000 to 5,000	5,000 to 10,000	10,000 to 25,000	25,000 to 50,000	50,000 to 100,000	100,000 to 250,000	250,000 to 500,000	500,000 to 2,500,000	2,500,000 and over
Number of Enterprises 1	26868	4889	19660	1058	934	99	122	47	18	13	6	13	8
Revenues ($ in Thousands)													
Net Sales 2	61743384	499217	5710869	1899801	4500637	969974	2259756	1140481	821908	969805	1606732	5855815	35508388
Interest 3	9298725	1796	7085	589	11685	636	2898	10310	5864	14708	9810	104062	9129283
Rents 4	163432	0	0	0	0	29	25	265	281	3116	2671	2902	154142
Royalties 5	606823	62971	10342	534	3165	0	0	0	0	5694	3536	114684	405898
Other Portfolio Income 6	733195	12793	179	137	7647	2163	50490	3319	25381	13030	27619	44343	546093
Other Receipts 7	2102238	52826	-23804	332	3518	47454	82166	6215	-2334	56120	18383	273940	1587423
Total Receipts 8	74647797	629603	5704671	1901393	4526652	1020256	2395335	1160590	851100	1062473	1668751	6395746	47331227
Average Total Receipts 9	2778	129	290	1797	4847	10306	19634	24693	47283	81729	278125	491980	5916403
Operating Costs/Operating Income (%)													
Cost of Operations 10	31.4	20.0	31.6	13.3	45.2	39.3	35.3	58.0	30.0	37.5	43.0	26.7	29.5
Salaries and Wages 11	10.1	6.8	4.7	29.9	9.4	12.1	13.2	9.2	13.8	5.9	11.3	11.3	9.7
Taxes Paid 12	2.7	2.9	1.8	3.1	1.4	1.6	3.1	3.7	2.7	1.8	1.8	3.5	2.8
Interest Paid 13	17.9	0.2	0.7	2.3	1.1	2.0	1.7	3.2	4.7	5.9	2.8	4.2	29.4
Depreciation 14	7.0	2.8	1.6	3.5	1.7	1.0	3.0	3.2	3.1	2.3	2.8	7.4	9.7
Amortization and Depletion 15	7.5	0.1	1.1	1.3	0.3	1.9	8.7	1.1	10.5	21.6	1.8	6.5	10.1
Pensions and Other Deferred Comp. 16	0.4	2.3	2.1	1.7	0.3	0.3	0.2	0.2	0.1	0.0	0.0	0.1	0.1
Employee Benefits 17	1.0	0.0	1.4	1.9	0.3	0.9	1.0	1.0	1.0	0.6	1.5	1.0	1.1
Advertising 18	4.3	0.2	0.2	1.0	2.5	0.5	1.4	0.5	4.0	1.4	0.7	1.8	6.5
Other Expenses 19	27.0	80.7	28.5	32.6	25.4	19.1	22.7	19.4	30.4	32.4	20.4	43.1	24.1
Officers' Compensation 20	5.0	12.7	26.3	8.1	11.3	12.1	8.6	2.2	8.3	1.7	10.0	1.1	0.6
Operating Margin 21	•	•	•	1.3	1.0	9.4	1.2	•	•	•	3.9	•	•
Operating Margin Before Officers' Comp. 22	•	26.2	•	9.4	12.3	21.5	9.8	0.5	•	13.9	•	•	•

Selected Average Balance Sheet ($ in Thousands)

Net Receivables 23	482	0	5	88	322	818	3710	4882	6301	18792	45459	45591	1310936
Inventories 24	161	0	2	38	123	11	908	988	5909	1816	16661	8512	428879
Net Property, Plant and Equipment 25	613	0	10	326	545	1218	4020	5625	17226	23567	96615	281005	1211996
Total Assets 26	19877	0	52	737	2293	7220	14708	35057	69272	141753	381393	1118815	63255146
Notes and Loans Payable 27	6344	0	154	587	1091	2515	8109	16444	25933	53829	199650	320254	19656118
All Other Liabilities 28	1498	0	27	150	689	1659	4704	13983	23107	42903	112192	196702	4164107
Net Worth 29	12035	0	-129	0	513	3046	1895	4630	20233	45021	69551	601859	39434921

Selected Financial Ratios (Times to 1)

Current Ratio 30	1.0	•	1.1	1.4	1.7	1.2	1.2	1.0	1.3	1.9	1.3	1.7	1.0
Quick Ratio 31	0.6	•	0.9	0.9	1.1	1.0	0.9	0.8	0.9	0.8	0.7	0.8	0.6
Net Sales to Working Capital 32	60.7	88.6	21.4	9.3	22.8	17.1	•	•	11.6	2.3	8.8	4.7	•
Coverage Ratio 33	1.4	•	0.7	1.6	2.4	8.1	5.2	0.7	•	0.7	3.7	1.5	1.3
Total Asset Turnover 34	0.1	•	5.6	2.4	2.1	1.4	1.3	0.7	0.7	0.5	0.7	0.4	0.1
Inventory Turnover 35	4.5	•	60.5	6.3	17.8	336.7	7.2	14.2	2.3	1.5	6.9	14.1	3.1
Receivables Turnover 36	5.9	•	69.1	24.7	18.8	9.4	7.6	6.4	6.0	3.0	7.1	5.6	4.5
Total Liabilities to Net Worth 37	0.7	•	3494.6		3.5	1.4	6.8	6.6	2.4	2.1	4.5	0.9	0.6
Current Assets to Working Capital 38	45.2	•	8.7	3.6	2.5	7.2	6.7	•	5.0	2.1	4.0	2.4	0.6
Current Liabilities to Working Capital 39	44.2	•	7.7	2.6	1.5	6.2	5.7	•	4.0	1.1	3.0	1.4	•
Working Capital to Net Sales 40	0.0	•	0.0	0.0	0.0	0.0	0.1	•	0.1	0.4	0.1	0.2	•
Inventory to Working Capital 41	4.9	•	0.5	0.4	0.2	0.0	0.7	•	0.6	0.6	0.2	0.1	•
Total Receipts to Cash Flow 42	4.0	1.6	4.1	3.6	4.3	3.3	5.1	8.6	8.5	4.6	5.3	5.7	3.7
Cost of Goods to Cash Flow 43	1.3	0.3	1.3	0.5	1.9	1.3	1.8	5.0	2.6	1.7	2.3	1.5	1.1
Cash Flow to Total Debt 44	0.1	•	0.4	0.7	0.6	0.7	0.3	0.1	0.1	0.2	0.2	0.2	0.1

Selected Financial Factors (in Percentages)

Debt Ratio 45	39.5	•	348.7	100.0	77.6	57.8	87.1	86.8	70.8	68.2	81.8	46.2	37.7
Return on Total Assets 46	2.8	•	2.9	8.9	22.3	5.7	11.1	2.4	•	2.3	7.2	2.5	2.8
Return on Equity Before Income Taxes 47	1.3	•	0.5	11712.1	14.7	46.3	69.7	1.1	•	•	28.6	1.5	1.1
Return on Equity After Income Taxes 48	1.0	•	0.6	11650.7	12.3	46.2	69.0	0.8	•	•	22.7	0.6	0.9
Profit Margin (Before Income Tax) 49	6.7	•	•	1.4	1.6	14.4	7.1	0.2	•	•	7.4	2.1	10.0
Profit Margin (After Income Tax) 50	5.0	•	•	1.4	1.3	14.3	7.1	0.1	•	•	5.9	0.8	7.6

Table II

Corporations with Net Income

MOTION PICTURE AND VIDEO INDUSTRIES (EXCEPT VIDEO RENTAL)

MONEY AMOUNTS AND SIZE OF ASSETS IN THOUSANDS OF DOLLARS

Item Description for Accounting Period 7/06 Through 6/07	Total	Zero Assets	Under 500	500 to 1,000	1,000 to 5,000	5,000 to 10,000	10,000 to 25,000	25,000 to 50,000	50,000 to 100,000	100,000 to 250,000	250,000 to 500,000	500,000 to 2,500,000	2,500,000 and over
Number of Enterprises 1	12262	1956	9199	•	430	51	71	20	9	6	3	3	•
Revenues ($ in Thousands)													
Net Sales 2	52644349	362782	4131527	•	2531880	787360	1937114	833924	475571	447652	1118363	3534154	•
Interest 3	9186074	91	5071	•	10047	530	508	5662	1085	12736	3601	32049	•
Rents 4	157283	0	0	•	0	0	0	253	281	3116	304	0	•
Royalties 5	200313	0	0	•	3065	0	0	0	0	0	0	53759	•
Other Portfolio Income 6	696289	12793	31	•	6709	1949	49242	2049	25187	12473	27161	13073	•
Other Receipts 7	1845017	231	11583	•	9807	43887	78156	5956	4216	20618	16145	167173	•
Total Receipts 8	64729325	375897	4148212	•	2561508	833726	2065020	847844	506340	496595	1165574	3800208	•
Average Total Receipts 9	5279	192	451	•	5957	16348	29085	42392	56260	82766	388525	1266736	•
Operating Costs/Operating Income (%)													
Cost of Operations 10	28.4	15.7	24.6	•	27.6	44.3	37.6	49.6	25.7	19.0	45.5	16.1	•
Salaries and Wages 11	10.1	6.8	4.4	•	11.7	11.1	12.1	9.5	12.1	6.5	6.7	9.5	•
Taxes Paid 12	2.7	2.4	1.7	•	1.6	1.4	3.1	4.0	3.5	3.2	2.2	3.5	•
Interest Paid 13	19.9	•	0.5	•	0.4	2.0	1.2	2.2	2.8	5.8	2.4	4.9	•
Depreciation 14	6.2	1.0	1.4	•	1.0	0.2	2.5	3.4	4.3	4.3	2.6	3.8	•
Amortization and Depletion 15	7.6	0.1	1.5	•	0.4	1.9	1.0	0.3	0.8	4.7	0.7	8.3	•
Pensions and Other Deferred Comp. 16	0.4	2.4	2.5	•	0.5	0.3	0.2	0.3	0.1	0.0	0.1	0.0	•
Employee Benefits 17	0.9	0.0	1.0	•	0.2	0.7	0.9	1.0	1.2	1.0	0.4	0.4	•
Advertising 18	4.5	0.1	0.2	•	4.0	0.6	1.0	0.5	1.2	0.9	0.7	1.5	•
Other Expenses 19	26.2	29.0	24.2	•	25.0	9.4	19.8	22.9	26.8	53.3	13.2	51.6	•
Officers' Compensation 20	5.0	13.1	30.0	•	17.8	14.7	9.6	2.3	10.1	1.0	13.6	0.8	•
Operating Margin 21	•	29.2	8.2	•	9.9	13.4	10.9	4.1	11.3	0.3	12.0	•	•
Operating Margin Before Officers' Comp. 22	•	42.4	38.2	•	27.8	28.1	20.5	6.4	21.3	1.3	25.6	0.3	•

Selected Average Balance Sheet ($ in Thousands)

Net Receivables **23**	925	0	8	•	317	1079	5109	7747	4169	21890	18807	67095
Inventories **24**	302	0	1	•	79	2	246	1765	6239	7754	10993	15802
Net Property, Plant and Equipment **25**	861	0	12	•	321	737	5109	10101	29925	47804	167875	631446
Total Assets **26**	41714	0	54	•	2245	6684	15150	35034	71268	153382	391452	1491317
Notes and Loans Payable **27**	12959	0	36	•	456	1475	4238	15931	19673	39943	232478	977495
All Other Liabilities **28**	2817	0	15	•	617	2276	4881	15425	10803	49295	72888	428938
Net Worth **29**	25939	0	2	•	1173	2933	6030	3678	40792	64145	86085	84884

Selected Financial Ratios (Times to 1)

Current Ratio **30**	1.1	•	1.7	2.3	1.2	1.0	0.9	2.3	1.3	1.1
Quick Ratio **31**	0.7	•	1.6	1.9	1.1	0.9	0.8	1.2	0.4	0.5
Net Sales to Working Capital **32**	17.5	•	32.9	6.3	18.2	•	•	1.9	14.1	35.9
Coverage Ratio **33**	1.6	•	19.4	26.0	15.9	3.7	7.3	2.9	7.5	2.4
Total Asset Turnover **34**	0.1	•	8.3	2.6	1.8	1.2	0.7	0.5	1.0	0.8
Inventory Turnover **35**	4.0	•	79.0	20.6	41.7	11.7	2.2	1.8	15.4	12.0
Receivables Turnover **36**	5.8	•	70.2	20.1	8.0	7.9	9.6	2.6	•	5.1
Total Liabilities to Net Worth **37**	0.6	•	22.5	0.9	1.5	8.5	0.7	1.4	3.5	16.6
Current Assets to Working Capital **38**	13.4	•	2.5	1.7	5.4	•	•	1.8	4.3	8.9
Current Liabilities to Working Capital **39**	12.4	•	1.5	0.7	4.4	•	•	0.8	3.3	7.9
Working Capital to Net Sales **40**	0.1	•	0.0	0.2	0.1	•	•	0.5	0.1	0.0
Inventory to Working Capital **41**	1.4	•	0.0	0.1	0.1	•	•	0.0	0.4	0.5
Total Receipts to Cash Flow **42**	3.5	1.7	3.4	3.0	3.7	5.4	3.6	2.2	4.5	4.9
Cost of Goods to Cash Flow **43**	1.0	0.3	0.8	0.8	1.4	2.7	0.9	0.4	2.1	0.8
Cash Flow to Total Debt **44**	0.1	•	2.6	1.8	0.8	0.2	0.5	0.4	0.3	0.2

Selected Financial Factors (in Percentages)

Debt Ratio **45**	37.8	•	95.7	47.8	56.1	60.2	89.5	42.8	58.2	78.0	94.3
Return on Total Assets **46**	3.2	•	75.8	30.2	48.7	33.5	9.6	15.2	8.3	17.3	9.4
Return on Equity Before Income Taxes **47**	1.8	•	1686.5	55.7	100.3	78.9	66.9	23.0	12.9	68.1	96.1
Return on Equity After Income Taxes **48**	1.5	•	1664.1	53.3	100.1	78.5	66.1	20.6	10.4	58.6	68.5
Profit Margin (Before Income Tax) **49**	11.1	32.9	8.6	11.1	19.1	17.4	5.9	17.7	11.1	15.7	6.9
Profit Margin (After Income Tax) **50**	9.2	32.6	8.5	10.6	19.0	17.4	5.8	15.9	9.0	13.5	4.9

Table I

Corporations with and without Net Income

SOUND RECORDING INDUSTRIES

MONEY AMOUNTS AND SIZE OF ASSETS IN THOUSANDS OF DOLLARS

Item Description for Accounting Period 7/06 Through 6/07	Total	Zero Assets	Under 500	500 to 1,000	1,000 to 5,000	5,000 to 10,000	10,000 to 25,000	25,000 to 50,000	50,000 to 100,000	100,000 to 250,000	250,000 to 500,000	500,000 to 2,500,000	2,500,000 and over
Number of Enterprises 1	7651	2717	4478	0	307	101	31	8	6	0	0	3	0
Revenues ($ in Thousands)													
Net Sales 2	7963524	98844	824577	0	398312	190279	362856	199725	258277	0	0	5630653	0
Interest 3	130892	0	33	0	2110	2536	6772	2732	767	0	0	115942	0
Rents 4	615	0	0	0	0	0	0	615	0	0	0	0	0
Royalties 5	2748671	0	0	0	28290	0	90	91779	0	0	0	2628512	0
Other Portfolio Income 6	799532	0	4304	0	0	0	5883	21092	0	0	0	768252	0
Other Receipts 7	530402	9479	49944	0	75751	0	24717	14805	447	0	0	355261	0
Total Receipts 8	12173636	108323	878858	0	504463	192815	400318	330748	259491	0	0	9498620	0
Average Total Receipts 9	1591	40	196	•	1643	1909	12913	41344	43248	•	•	3166207	•
Operating Costs/Operating Income (%)													
Cost of Operations 10	38.3	29.0	18.2	•	15.5	30.4	32.1	36.5	58.1	•	•	42.9	•
Salaries and Wages 11	15.0	4.8	11.7	•	12.9	7.3	12.3	29.4	10.4	•	•	15.9	•
Taxes Paid 12	1.9	1.5	3.0	•	2.2	1.8	1.0	2.7	1.4	•	•	1.8	•
Interest Paid 13	10.6	•	0.4	•	4.9	2.6	1.6	3.2	5.3	•	•	14.0	•
Depreciation 14	6.6	2.3	1.3	•	1.9	4.0	0.4	2.7	0.6	•	•	8.7	•
Amortization and Depletion 15	3.3	•	0.1	•	0.3	2.1	2.0	3.3	3.2	•	•	4.2	•
Pensions and Other Deferred Comp. 16	1.0	•	1.2	•	1.2	•	1.2	0.8	0.3	•	•	1.0	•
Employee Benefits 17	1.7	•	1.5	•	0.3	•	2.0	5.1	0.9	•	•	1.8	•
Advertising 18	4.4	2.2	0.2	•	0.7	0.2	12.5	1.7	4.4	•	•	5.0	•
Other Expenses 19	56.4	86.6	31.4	•	35.8	44.6	32.2	56.5	18.1	•	•	64.7	•
Officers' Compensation 20	2.8	4.6	16.4	•	5.2	•	4.7	7.4	2.3	•	•	0.5	•
Operating Margin 21	•	•	14.8	•	19.1	7.1	•	•	•	•	•	•	•
Operating Margin Before Officers' Comp. 22	•	•	31.1	•	24.4	7.1	2.6	•	•	•	•	•	•

Selected Average Balance Sheet ($ in Thousands)

Net Receivables 23	1800	0	2	•	147	70	2715	3350	7607	•	4517887
Inventories 24	73	0	0	•	0	103	736	2396	6854	•	152237
Net Property, Plant and Equipment 25	87	0	13	•	85	1863	358	5560	1919	•	109234
Total Assets 26	6743	0	55	•	1694	6466	17687	37720	81791	•	16277172
Notes and Loans Payable 27	554	0	16	•	673	4090	6242	9538	45360	•	1003543
All Other Liabilities 28	3754	0	6	•	179	481	11035	13062	19563	•	9341858
Net Worth 29	2435	0	33	•	842	1895	410	15120	16868	•	5931771

Selected Financial Ratios (Times to 1)

Current Ratio 30	0.6	•	3.5	•	6.8	9.0	0.7	1.7	1.1	•	0.5
Quick Ratio 31	0.5	•	3.3	•	6.0	1.7	0.5	0.7	0.6	•	0.5
Net Sales to Working Capital 32	•	•	8.0	•	1.6	0.5	•	2.9	37.9	•	•
Coverage Ratio 33	2.1	•	54.5	•	10.3	4.2	6.2	6.5	0.1	•	1.7
Total Asset Turnover 34	0.2	•	3.4	•	0.8	0.3	0.7	0.7	0.5	•	0.1
Inventory Turnover 35	5.5	•	191.5	•	•	5.5	5.1	3.8	3.7	•	5.3
Receivables Turnover 36	0.9	•	88.9	•	9.5	10.5	6.8	7.6	5.1	•	0.7
Total Liabilities to Net Worth 37	1.8	•	0.7	•	1.0	2.4	42.2	1.5	3.8	•	1.7
Current Assets to Working Capital 38	•	•	1.4	•	1.2	1.1	2.4	2.4	18.1	•	•
Current Liabilities to Working Capital 39	•	•	0.4	•	0.2	0.1	1.4	1.4	17.1	•	•
Working Capital to Net Sales 40	•	•	0.1	•	0.6	2.1	0.3	0.3	0.0	•	•
Inventory to Working Capital 41	•	•	0.0	•	•	0.0	0.3	0.3	8.0	•	•
Total Receipts to Cash Flow 42	1.7	1.7	2.6	•	1.4	2.0	2.7	1.7	8.8	•	1.6
Cost of Goods to Cash Flow 43	0.7	0.5	0.5	•	0.2	0.6	0.9	0.6	5.1	•	0.7
Cash Flow to Total Debt 44	0.1	•	3.3	•	1.1	0.2	0.3	0.6	0.1	•	0.1

Selected Financial Factors (in Percentages)

Debt Ratio 45	63.9	•	39.6	•	50.3	70.7	97.7	59.9	79.4	•	63.6
Return on Total Assets 46	3.5	•	73.3	•	38.8	3.2	6.5	13.8	0.3	•	2.8
Return on Equity Before Income Taxes 47	5.2	•	119.2	•	70.6	8.4	236.7	29.0	3.2	•	3.2
Return on Equity After Income Taxes 48	5.1	•	117.1	•	69.5	7.0	193.7	20.5	3.2	•	3.2
Profit Margin (Before Income Tax) 49	12.2	•	21.3	•	45.8	8.5	8.3	17.6	10.0	•	10.0
Profit Margin (After Income Tax) 50	11.9	•	21.0	•	45.1	7.0	6.8	12.4	10.0	•	10.0

Table II
Corporations with Net Income

SOUND RECORDING INDUSTRIES

MONEY AMOUNTS AND SIZE OF ASSETS IN THOUSANDS OF DOLLARS

Item Description for Accounting Period 7/06 Through 6/07	Total	Zero Assets	Under 500	500 to 1,000	1,000 to 5,000	5,000 to 10,000	10,000 to 25,000	25,000 to 50,000	50,000 to 100,000	100,000 to 250,000	250,000 to 500,000	500,000 to 2,500,000	2,500,000 and over
Number of Enterprises **1**	4069	818	2870	0	298	58	14	8	3	0	0	0	0
Revenues ($ in Thousands)													
Net Sales **2**	5516259	30226	719879	0	318928	186597	324874	199725	3736030	0	0	0	0
Interest **3**	59586	0	33	0	1462	2536	6771	2732	46052	0	0	0	0
Rents **4**	615	0	0	0	0	0	0	615	0	0	0	0	0
Royalties **5**	1612279	0	0	0	17141	0	0	91779	1503359	0	0	0	0
Other Portfolio Income **6**	750199	0	4304	0	0	0	5883	21092	718918	0	0	0	0
Other Receipts **7**	238142	0	49669	0	75627	0	4886	14805	93157	0	0	0	0
Total Receipts **8**	8177080	30226	773885	0	413158	189133	342414	330748	6097516	0	0	0	0
Average Total Receipts **9**	2010	37	270	•	1386	3261	24458	41344	2032505	•	•	•	•
Operating Costs/Operating Income (%)													
Cost of Operations **10**	35.9	3.7	17.1	•	•	31.0	33.4	36.5	43.3	•	•	•	•
Salaries and Wages **11**	12.7	•	12.2	•	14.1	7.4	7.2	29.4	12.6	•	•	•	•
Taxes Paid **12**	1.3	1.4	3.0	•	1.4	1.5	0.2	2.7	0.9	•	•	•	•
Interest Paid **13**	10.8	•	0.4	•	2.9	2.7	0.7	3.2	15.3	•	•	•	•
Depreciation **14**	1.2	0.9	1.4	•	2.3	3.1	0.2	2.7	1.0	•	•	•	•
Amortization and Depletion **15**	1.8	•	0.1	•	•	2.1	1.0	3.3	2.3	•	•	•	•
Pensions and Other Deferred Comp. **16**	1.4	•	1.2	•	1.5	•	1.0	0.8	1.6	•	•	•	•
Employee Benefits **17**	1.8	•	1.7	•	0.3	•	1.7	5.1	1.9	•	•	•	•
Advertising **18**	3.0	1.5	0.1	•	0.1	0.2	13.3	1.7	3.2	•	•	•	•
Other Expenses **19**	55.0	19.6	30.0	•	33.5	44.7	29.8	56.5	64.6	•	•	•	•
Officers' Compensation **20**	2.8	15.0	14.7	•	4.7	•	2.8	7.4	0.1	•	•	•	•
Operating Margin **21**	•	57.9	18.0	•	39.3	7.3	8.7	•	•	•	•	•	•
Operating Margin Before Officers' Comp. **22**	•	72.9	32.7	•	44.0	7.3	11.5	•	•	•	•	•	•

Selected Average Balance Sheet ($ in Thousands)

Net Receivables 23	2683	0	1	•	146	122	2475	3350	3600500
Inventories 24	122	0	0	•	0	239	472	2238	152233
Net Property, Plant and Equipment 25	105	0	16	•	83	2311	316	5560	58468
Total Assets 26	10614	0	77	•	1644	6086	18676	37720	13853857
Notes and Loans Payable 27	176	0	13	•	643	1797	7460	9538	66749
All Other Liabilities 28	6105	0	9	•	125	838	4164	13062	8188326
Net Worth 29	4333	0	54	•	875	3451	7052	15120	5598782

Selected Financial Ratios (Times to 1)

Current Ratio 30	0.5	•	3.3	•	14.1	4.3	0.9	1.7	0.5
Quick Ratio 31	0.5	•	3.2	•	12.7	1.6	0.6	0.7	0.5
Net Sales to Working Capital 32	•	•	7.7	•	1.3	1.2	•	2.9	•
Coverage Ratio 33	3.1	•	60.4	•	24.4	4.2	21.4	6.5	2.2
Total Asset Turnover 34	0.1	•	3.3	•	0.7	0.5	1.2	0.7	0.1
Inventory Turnover 35	4.0	•	193.9	•	•	4.2	16.4	4.1	3.5
Receivables Turnover 36	0.9	•	120.4	•	7.8	20.8	13.2	9.3	0.6
Total Liabilities to Net Worth 37	1.4	•	0.4	•	0.9	0.8	1.6	1.5	1.5
Current Assets to Working Capital 38	•	•	1.4	•	1.1	1.3	•	2.4	•
Current Liabilities to Working Capital 39	•	•	0.4	•	0.1	0.3	•	1.4	•
Working Capital to Net Sales 40	•	•	0.1	•	0.8	0.9	•	0.3	•
Inventory to Working Capital 41	•	•	0.0	•	•	0.1	•	0.3	•
Total Receipts to Cash Flow 42	1.5	1.5	2.4	•	1.1	1.9	2.4	1.7	1.4
Cost of Goods to Cash Flow 43	0.6	0.1	0.4	•	•	0.6	0.8	0.6	0.6
Cash Flow to Total Debt 44	0.1	•	4.8	•	1.3	0.6	0.8	0.6	0.1

Selected Financial Factors (in Percentages)

Debt Ratio 45	59.2	•	29.1	•	46.8	43.3	62.2	59.9	59.6
Return on Total Assets 46	4.2	•	85.0	•	46.7	6.0	18.5	13.8	3.1
Return on Equity Before Income Taxes 47	6.9	•	117.9	•	84.1	8.0	46.6	29.0	4.2
Return on Equity After Income Taxes 48	6.8	•	115.9	•	83.1	6.7	41.1	20.5	4.2
Profit Margin (Before Income Tax) 49	22.2	57.9	25.5	•	68.8	8.6	14.2	17.6	18.9
Profit Margin (After Income Tax) 50	21.8	57.9	25.1	•	67.9	7.2	12.5	12.4	18.9

Table I

Corporations with and without Net Income

BROADCASTING (EXCEPT INTERNET)

MONEY AMOUNTS AND SIZE OF ASSETS IN THOUSANDS OF DOLLARS

Item Description for Accounting Period 7/06 Through 6/07		Total	Zero Assets	Under 500	500 to 1,000	1,000 to 5,000	5,000 to 10,000	10,000 to 25,000	25,000 to 50,000	50,000 to 100,000	100,000 to 250,000	250,000 to 500,000	500,000 to 2,500,000	2,500,000 and over
Number of Enterprises	1	6958	2154	2732	563	1106	143	99	40	30	33	17	28	12
Revenues ($ in Thousands)														
Net Sales	2	102716338	666370	362386	1074368	2230260	608504	1095976	496660	1288655	1588085	3981849	8395548	80927678
Interest	3	3314562	5006	122	2112	4473	9316	7530	5548	4363	18115	44781	437084	2776114
Rents	4	377565	811	546	7	3802	824	233	673	899	15029	8883	11883	333975
Royalties	5	4105472	0	0	0	48491	0	0	0	0	433	31447	33137	3991963
Other Portfolio Income	6	2258041	583075	11882	0	147773	1973	76867	18534	26596	54708	49270	339652	947712
Other Receipts	7	4291748	-173736	2008	3382	38577	2861	42248	14366	50779	89440	50443	169293	4002084
Total Receipts	8	117063726	1081526	376944	1079869	2473376	623478	1222854	535781	1371292	1765810	4166673	9386597	92979526
Average Total Receipts	9	16824	502	138	1918	2236	4360	12352	13395	45710	53509	245098	335236	7748294
Operating Costs/Operating Income (%)														
Cost of Operations	10	20.0	13.1	•	20.3	17.5	34.0	31.1	24.1	6.8	16.0	49.4	13.1	19.5
Salaries and Wages	11	14.4	47.7	36.2	32.3	23.9	17.3	19.1	24.8	19.9	21.0	11.4	23.1	12.4
Taxes Paid	12	2.7	12.6	6.9	4.4	4.4	2.5	4.8	3.8	4.8	2.9	2.5	4.1	2.3
Interest Paid	13	8.1	25.6	1.7	3.7	4.6	3.2	3.2	7.1	7.2	12.7	8.0	15.1	7.4
Depreciation	14	4.7	3.6	2.8	1.2	4.6	3.8	3.6	6.1	4.2	7.0	6.4	5.5	4.5
Amortization and Depletion	15	6.5	11.0	1.6	0.8	2.1	5.5	7.0	6.5	5.6	6.4	4.3	14.7	6.0
Pensions and Other Deferred Comp.	16	0.6	0.8	0.4	0.0	0.2	0.0	0.5	0.8	0.2	0.7	0.3	0.4	0.7
Employee Benefits	17	2.5	2.0	1.8	2.5	2.6	1.4	1.1	2.4	1.4	1.6	1.4	1.4	2.8
Advertising	18	2.7	1.0	3.1	1.8	0.8	1.8	2.8	3.2	3.2	3.4	0.8	3.2	2.8
Other Expenses	19	43.9	56.6	34.9	19.3	49.5	38.7	25.1	34.0	30.7	37.3	18.7	54.2	44.9
Officers' Compensation	20	1.6	15.5	22.5	9.3	4.0	3.7	2.0	3.9	14.6	3.1	1.0	2.0	0.9
Operating Margin	21	•	•	•	4.4	•	•	•	•	1.5	•	•	•	•
Operating Margin Before Officers' Comp.	22	•	•	10.6	13.6	•	•	1.6	•	16.1	•	•	•	•

Selected Average Balance Sheet ($ in Thousands)

Net Receivables 23	3054	0	7	196	267	618	1581	2996	6704	15187	52185	66688	1416921
Inventories 24	370	0	0	2	28	9	489	286	424	331	1347	990	200752
Net Property, Plant and Equipment 25	5032	0	24	150	525	881	2563	3969	12639	20198	82362	101313	2371888
Total Assets 26	42680	0	69	738	2124	7447	14924	37254	71863	147160	372825	1320167	19972328
Notes and Loans Payable 27	16566	0	92	727	2043	4387	3594	13810	35858	84126	219783	545656	7329004
All Other Liabilities 28	10399	0	13	392	710	1242	3371	2128	14776	39914	90273	525568	4392180
Net Worth 29	15715	0	-35	-380	-629	1818	7959	21316	21229	23120	62769	248943	8251145

Selected Financial Ratios (Times to 1)

Current Ratio 30	0.9	•	1.7	0.6	1.0	2.6	1.7	2.6	1.3	1.0	1.0	1.4	0.9
Quick Ratio 31	0.7	•	1.5	0.6	0.8	2.5	1.3	1.9	1.0	0.8	0.8	0.9	0.6
Net Sales to Working Capital 32	•	•	13.7	•	•	1.9	4.4	2.4	11.8	37.7	75.8	5.1	•
Coverage Ratio 33	1.8	•	•	2.3	0.3	•	4.5	•	1.9	0.9	1.0	•	2.4
Total Asset Turnover 34	0.3	•	1.9	2.6	0.9	0.6	0.7	0.3	0.6	0.3	0.6	0.2	0.3
Inventory Turnover 35	8.0	•	•	249.3	12.8	154.2	7.0	10.4	6.8	23.3	85.8	39.8	6.5
Receivables Turnover 36	4.5	•	12.1	13.6	5.2	5.5	6.1	4.3	6.3	2.8	5.7	3.2	4.5
Total Liabilities to Net Worth 37	1.7	•	•	•	•	3.1	0.9	0.7	2.4	5.4	4.9	4.3	1.4
Current Assets to Working Capital 38	•	•	2.4	•	•	1.6	2.5	1.6	4.0	26.3	29.4	3.6	•
Current Liabilities to Working Capital 39	•	•	1.4	•	•	0.6	1.5	0.6	3.0	25.3	28.4	2.6	•
Working Capital to Net Sales 40	0.1	•	•	0.1	•	0.5	0.2	0.4	0.1	0.0	0.0	0.2	•
Inventory to Working Capital 41	•	•	•	•	•	0.0	0.0	0.0	0.1	0.0	0.5	0.0	•
Total Receipts to Cash Flow 42	2.2	•	5.5	2.4	5.5	3.7	3.8	5.4	2.8	3.4	6.2	4.2	1.9
Cost of Goods to Cash Flow 43	0.4	•	•	0.4	1.1	1.3	1.2	1.3	0.2	0.5	3.1	0.6	0.4
Cash Flow to Total Debt 44	0.3	•	0.2	0.3	0.3	0.2	0.4	0.1	0.3	0.1	0.1	0.1	0.3

Selected Financial Factors (in Percentages)

Debt Ratio 45	63.2	•	150.6	151.5	129.6	75.6	46.7	42.8	70.5	84.3	83.2	81.1	58.7
Return on Total Assets 46	5.0	•	•	22.2	1.4	•	10.7	•	8.3	3.9	5.2	•	6.1
Return on Equity Before Income Taxes 47	5.9	•	29.9	•	10.1	•	15.6	•	13.4	•	1.0	•	8.8
Return on Equity After Income Taxes 48	3.1	•	31.7	•	10.8	•	11.0	•	10.9	•	•	•	6.0
Profit Margin (Before Income Tax) 49	6.3	•	•	4.9	•	•	11.2	•	6.6	0.3	0.3	•	10.7
Profit Margin (After Income Tax) 50	3.3	•	•	4.8	•	•	7.9	•	5.4	•	•	•	7.4

Table II

Corporations with Net Income

BROADCASTING (EXCEPT INTERNET)

MONEY AMOUNTS AND SIZE OF ASSETS IN THOUSANDS OF DOLLARS

Item Description for Accounting Period 7/06 Through 6/07	Total	Zero Assets	Under 500	500 to 1,000	1,000 to 5,000	5,000 to 10,000	10,000 to 25,000	25,000 to 50,000	50,000 to 100,000	100,000 to 250,000	250,000 to 500,000	500,000 to 2,500,000	2,500,000 and over
Number of Enterprises **1**	3400	1505	847	•	664	29	62	17	15	18	7	9	•
Revenues ($ in Thousands)													
Net Sales **2**	86233533	304165	208387	•	1598781	206715	881059	375514	948566	1071177	1469921	3065480	•
Interest **3**	2754623	3715	49	•	988	4765	5463	3564	1648	11420	21279	17164	•
Rents **4**	361297	811	546	•	1561	579	233	384	448	14423	8172	156	•
Royalties **5**	4071922	0	0	•	48491	0	0	0	0	20	31447	0	•
Other Portfolio Income **6**	2065461	582620	11882	•	124019	1098	76521	16668	8070	10373	28772	258814	•
Other Receipts **7**	4073375	71499	2392	•	5706	5	39890	13599	42045	77405	36680	83879	•
Total Receipts **8**	99560211	962810	223256	•	1779546	213162	1003166	409729	1000777	1184818	1596271	3425493	•
Average Total Receipts **9**	29282	640	264	•	2680	7350	16180	24102	66718	65823	228039	380610	•
Operating Costs/Operating Income (%)													
Cost of Operations **10**	20.6	14.4	•	•	16.0	16.1	36.6	27.0	8.9	22.3	17.8	14.2	•
Salaries and Wages **11**	13.1	16.8	29.2	•	20.4	11.8	17.2	16.6	16.7	17.3	19.2	21.4	•
Taxes Paid **12**	2.6	14.6	5.0	•	2.9	2.9	5.2	2.9	3.0	2.9	4.2	4.2	•
Interest Paid **13**	6.2	5.2	2.9	•	2.0	2.3	2.4	2.9	1.6	4.4	8.2	6.6	•
Depreciation **14**	3.6	3.4	1.7	•	3.0	0.9	2.8	6.0	1.8	6.2	9.9	3.5	•
Amortization and Depletion **15**	5.8	6.1	1.1	•	0.1	2.5	1.7	1.8	2.7	3.1	4.2	9.1	•
Pensions and Other Deferred Comp. **16**	0.7	1.7	0.0	•	0.2	0.0	0.2	1.0	0.3	0.7	0.4	0.5	•
Employee Benefits **17**	2.7	2.3	1.1	•	3.3	0.3	1.0	1.2	1.0	1.2	2.5	1.5	•
Advertising **18**	2.9	1.8	2.7	•	0.7	2.3	2.5	1.4	3.7	3.6	1.4	5.1	•
Other Expenses **19**	42.9	52.1	28.2	•	49.9	45.4	18.8	25.4	25.9	30.2	28.9	23.4	•
Officers' Compensation **20**	1.5	10.0	18.4	•	4.6	3.4	1.6	2.4	19.4	2.8	2.3	1.1	•
Operating Margin **21**	•	•	9.6	•	•	12.2	10.1	11.6	15.1	5.3	1.1	9.5	•
Operating Margin Before Officers' Comp. **22**	•	•	28.0	•	1.6	15.6	11.7	13.9	34.5	8.1	3.3	10.6	•

Selected Average Balance Sheet ($ in Thousands)

	•	•	•	•	•	•	•	•	•	•	•
Net Receivables 23	5480	0	6	325	347	1914	3935	9051	17054	61968	68931
Inventories 24	718	0	0	21	6	42	112	781	396	2558	233
Net Property, Plant and Equipment 25	7829	0	19	558	325	2631	7493	11546	22965	118932	66639
Total Assets 26	73066	0	64	2059	8659	13628	38114	71327	159651	350744	1308108
Notes and Loans Payable 27	23492	0	30	1241	3893	2812	10475	15397	73112	223210	334223
All Other Liabilities 28	15883	0	26	823	857	1714	3581	20578	43699	53241	206301
Net Worth 29	33691	0	9	-5	3910	9102	24059	35352	42840	74293	767584

Selected Financial Ratios (Times to 1)

	•	•	•	•	•	•	•	•	•	•	•
Current Ratio 30	1.1	•	1.3	1.6	2.1	3.3	2.1	1.5	1.2	2.2	1.9
Quick Ratio 31	0.8	•	1.1	1.4	2.0	3.0	1.9	1.0	0.8	1.9	1.4
Net Sales to Working Capital 32	48.4	•	35.8	5.6	3.8	3.1	4.1	9.4	9.0	3.9	2.9
Coverage Ratio 33	3.1	37.2	6.7	5.2	7.6	11.0	8.2	14.0	4.7	2.1	4.1
Total Asset Turnover 34	0.3	•	3.8	1.2	0.8	1.0	0.6	0.9	0.4	0.6	0.3
Inventory Turnover 35	7.3	•	18.5	18.5	177.5	124.7	53.4	7.2	33.6	14.6	207.7
Receivables Turnover 36	4.7	11.0	7.1	2.9	7.3	4.8	7.4	3.5	4.2	•	3.2
Total Liabilities to Net Worth 37	1.2	6.4	•	1.2	0.5	0.6	1.0	2.7	3.7	•	0.7
Current Assets to Working Capital 38	20.6	4.6	2.6	2.0	1.4	1.9	3.2	5.6	1.8	•	2.1
Current Liabilities to Working Capital 39	19.6	3.6	1.6	1.0	0.4	0.9	2.2	4.6	0.8	•	1.1
Working Capital to Net Sales 40	0.0	0.0	0.2	0.3	0.2	0.3	0.1	0.1	0.3	•	0.3
Inventory to Working Capital 41	0.8	•	0.0	•	0.0	0.0	0.1	0.0	0.1	•	0.0
Total Receipts to Cash Flow 42	1.9	3.0	1.8	1.7	3.1	2.4	2.3	2.4	2.9	•	2.6
Cost of Goods to Cash Flow 43	0.4	0.2	0.3	0.3	1.1	0.7	0.2	0.5	0.5	•	0.4
Cash Flow to Total Debt 44	0.3	1.5	0.6	0.9	1.0	0.6	0.8	0.2	0.3	•	0.2

Selected Financial Factors (in Percentages)

	•	•	•	•	•	•	•	•	•	•	•
Debt Ratio 45	53.9	86.6	100.2	54.8	33.2	36.9	50.4	73.2	78.8	•	41.3
Return on Total Assets 46	6.7	75.7	12.0	14.5	27.5	13.6	19.6	7.7	10.1	•	7.1
Return on Equity Before Income Taxes 47	9.9	479.6	•	27.9	37.4	18.9	36.8	22.7	24.6	•	9.1
Return on Equity After Income Taxes 48	7.2	455.3	•	23.4	30.9	16.6	33.7	18.4	17.9	•	7.6
Profit Margin (Before Income Tax) 49	13.2	188.2	16.7	8.3	15.3	24.0	20.6	20.6	16.3	8.7	20.5
Profit Margin (After Income Tax) 50	9.6	140.9	15.9	8.0	12.8	19.8	18.1	18.8	13.3	6.3	17.1

268

INTERNET PUBLISHING AND BROADCASTING

Table I

Corporations with and without Net Income

MONEY AMOUNTS AND SIZE OF ASSETS IN THOUSANDS OF DOLLARS

Item Description for Accounting Period 7/06 Through 6/07		Total	Zero Assets	Under 500	500 to 1,000	1,000 to 5,000	5,000 to 10,000	10,000 to 25,000	25,000 to 50,000	50,000 to 100,000	100,000 to 250,000	250,000 to 500,000	500,000 to 2,500,000	2,500,000 and over
Number of Enterprises	1	6026	2265	3494	27	123	45	37	12	8	9	5	0	0
Revenues ($ in Thousands)														
Net Sales	2	12243242	113485	383842	37559	324632	544083	442192	499789	496511	569272	8831877	0	0
Interest	3	68810	1338	282	2183	1702	5209	6416	4886	3124	11531	32139	0	0
Rents	4	40921	0	0	0	0	0	0	0	145	0	40776	0	0
Royalties	5	323682	0	0	0	0	0	2604	0	0	0	321078	0	0
Other Portfolio Income	6	76757	0	0	0	0	331	337	16347	105	31	59606	0	0
Other Receipts	7	178155	291	1396	227	40	110	127	3878	828	101613	69645	0	0
Total Receipts	8	12931567	115114	385520	39969	326374	549733	451676	524900	500713	682447	9355121	0	0
Average Total Receipts	9	2146	51	110	1480	2653	12216	12207	43742	62589	75827	1871024	•	•
Operating Costs/Operating Income (%)														
Cost of Operations	10	25.7	•	6.2	9.7	16.1	29.2	34.2	26.9	7.2	18.8	28.1	•	•
Salaries and Wages	11	20.6	24.0	22.8	34.9	48.1	31.2	38.2	26.7	25.9	37.5	16.1	•	•
Taxes Paid	12	2.2	4.1	3.9	3.3	5.7	2.0	2.5	1.8	2.7	4.0	1.9	•	•
Interest Paid	13	6.6	0.1	3.8	1.8	1.2	0.3	2.6	0.3	4.7	0.5	8.5	•	•
Depreciation	14	4.8	1.5	3.1	1.5	2.6	1.7	3.3	1.0	2.7	5.1	5.7	•	•
Amortization and Depletion	15	3.0	7.2	0.0	1.3	3.0	0.9	1.9	0.6	2.4	3.2	3.4	•	•
Pensions and Other Deferred Comp.	16	0.4	•	•	•	0.2	0.0	0.5	0.6	0.1	0.1	0.4	•	•
Employee Benefits	17	1.5	0.8	1.6	2.3	4.1	4.4	1.7	0.7	1.6	2.2	1.2	•	•
Advertising	18	1.5	1.4	1.1	1.2	2.4	3.3	3.4	1.7	10.2	5.9	0.5	•	•
Other Expenses	19	33.7	44.4	68.0	85.3	40.4	29.7	24.0	30.7	44.0	32.9	32.0	•	•
Officers' Compensation	20	2.6	9.9	6.9	6.8	10.5	5.3	6.0	3.1	4.8	2.9	1.5	•	•
Operating Margin	21	•	6.6	•	•	•	•	•	6.0	•	•	0.7	•	•
Operating Margin Before Officers' Comp.	22	•	16.4	•	•	•	•	•	9.1	•	•	2.2	•	•

Selected Average Balance Sheet ($ in Thousands)

Net Receivables 23	342	0	5	7	479	1118	2775	8583	11180	13502	303684
Inventories 24	46	0	0	35	48	651	0	0	3795	1	48385
Net Property, Plant and Equipment 25	294	0	10	56	136	651	1576	715	4474	13883	292734
Total Assets 26	3279	0	31	678	2667	6726	13176	38605	66694	149851	3233556
Notes and Loans Payable 27	146	0	27	585	929	407	3901	0	20734	8329	51264
All Other Liabilities 28	2189	0	58	164	1567	3092	5872	12444	19620	42415	2349258
Net Worth 29	944	0	-53	-72	171	3227	3403	26162	26340	99108	833035

Selected Financial Ratios (Times to 1)

Current Ratio 30	1.3	•	0.6	0.8	0.9	2.1	2.0	1.9	2.4	1.7	1.1
Quick Ratio 31	1.0	•	0.5	0.6	0.7	1.8	1.9	1.6	1.7	1.4	0.8
Net Sales to Working Capital 32	12.8	•	•	•	•	4.8	2.3	3.9	3.1	2.6	48.6
Coverage Ratio 33	1.4	62.0	•	•	•	•	•	40.8	•	14.0	1.8
Total Asset Turnover 34	0.6	•	3.5	2.1	1.0	1.8	0.9	1.1	0.9	0.4	0.5
Inventory Turnover 35	11.3	•	•	3.8	8.8	•	•	•	1.2	17858.2	10.2
Receivables Turnover 36	6.0	•	21.5	10.2	7.5	8.2	6.8	5.8	3.4	2.9	6.2
Total Liabilities to Net Worth 37	2.5	•	•	•	14.6	1.1	2.9	0.5	1.5	0.5	2.9
Current Assets to Working Capital 38	4.8	•	•	•	•	2.0	2.0	2.1	1.7	2.5	14.8
Current Liabilities to Working Capital 39	3.8	•	•	•	•	1.0	1.0	1.1	0.7	1.5	13.8
Working Capital to Net Sales 40	0.1	•	•	•	•	0.2	0.4	0.3	0.3	0.4	0.0
Inventory to Working Capital 41	0.3	•	•	•	•	•	•	•	0.4	•	1.3
Total Receipts to Cash Flow 42	3.0	2.1	2.2	3.2	196.9	5.0	16.9	2.6	2.8	2.8	2.8
Cost of Goods to Cash Flow 43	0.8	•	0.1	0.3	31.8	1.4	5.8	0.7	0.2	0.5	0.8
Cash Flow to Total Debt 44	0.3	•	0.6	0.6	0.0	0.7	0.1	1.3	0.6	0.5	0.3

Selected Financial Factors (in Percentages)

Debt Ratio 45	71.2	•	270.8	110.6	93.6	52.0	74.2	32.2	60.5	33.9	74.2
Return on Total Assets 46	5.9	•	•	•	•	•	•	11.9	•	3.1	8.2
Return on Equity Before Income Taxes 47	6.2	•	35.2	803.1	•	•	•	17.1	•	4.4	13.9
Return on Equity After Income Taxes 48	1.8	•	35.2	803.1	•	•	•	9.6	•	2.9	9.1
Profit Margin (Before Income Tax) 49	2.9	8.0	•	•	•	•	•	10.7	•	6.8	6.6
Profit Margin (After Income Tax) 50	0.8	8.0	•	•	•	•	•	6.1	•	4.5	4.3

Table II
Corporations with Net Income

INTERNET PUBLISHING AND BROADCASTING

MONEY AMOUNTS AND SIZE OF ASSETS IN THOUSANDS OF DOLLARS

Item Description for Accounting Period 7/06 Through 6/07	Total	Zero Assets	Under 500	500 to 1,000	1,000 to 5,000	5,000 to 10,000	10,000 to 25,000	25,000 to 50,000	50,000 to 100,000	100,000 to 250,000	250,000 to 500,000	500,000 to 2,500,000	2,500,000 and over
Number of Enterprises **1**	2217	924	1223	•	16	7	9	9	3	3	•	0	0
Revenues ($ in Thousands)													
Net Sales **2**	10437247	58182	130909	•	120112	227700	164514	427805	134968	351963	•	0	0
Interest **3**	50003	0	0	•	0	1051	1102	4886	2136	8032	0	0	0
Rents **4**	40776	0	0	•	0	0	0	0	0	0	0	0	0
Royalties **5**	321078	0	0	•	0	0	0	0	0	0	0	0	0
Other Portfolio Income **6**	60249	0	0	•	0	329	310	4	0	0	0	0	0
Other Receipts **7**	75446	0	0	•	19	63	75	3878	101	1805	0	0	0
Total Receipts **8**	10984799	58182	130909	•	120131	229143	166001	436573	137205	361800	0	0	0
Average Total Receipts **9**	4955	63	107	•	7508	32735	18445	48508	45735	120600	•	•	•
Operating Costs/Operating Income (%)													
Cost of Operations **10**	26.8	•	0.1	•	•	39.1	15.9	25.3	5.6	24.4	•	•	•
Salaries and Wages **11**	16.7	5.3	16.4	•	45.0	5.1	26.3	16.2	31.5	23.2	•	•	•
Taxes Paid **12**	2.0	2.2	2.1	•	5.1	1.2	2.4	1.4	3.4	4.6	•	•	•
Interest Paid **13**	7.3	•	5.6	•	•	•	4.6	0.0	3.4	0.3	•	•	•
Depreciation **14**	4.6	•	1.9	•	1.5	0.5	0.6	1.2	1.6	2.4	•	•	•
Amortization and Depletion **15**	3.0	•	0.0	•	0.0	0.0	2.0	0.2	4.4	3.2	•	•	•
Pensions and Other Deferred Comp. **16**	0.4	•	•	•	•	0.0	1.2	0.5	0.1	0.1	•	•	•
Employee Benefits **17**	1.2	•	3.2	•	1.0	0.4	1.2	0.6	1.7	1.6	•	•	•
Advertising **18**	0.6	2.3	•	•	0.4	0.8	2.4	1.9	2.2	0.1	•	•	•
Other Expenses **19**	31.2	42.2	47.9	•	30.3	14.6	13.7	32.5	33.0	21.9	•	•	•
Officers' Compensation **20**	2.1	16.1	3.1	•	5.4	5.0	8.8	3.5	11.9	1.8	•	•	•
Operating Margin **21**	4.0	32.0	19.7	•	11.4	33.2	20.9	16.6	1.2	16.4	•	•	•
Operating Margin Before Officers' Comp. **22**	6.1	48.1	22.8	•	16.8	38.2	29.7	20.1	13.1	18.2	•	•	•

Selected Average Balance Sheet ($ in Thousands)

	1	2	3	4	5	6	7	8	9
Net Receivables **23**	783	0	13	708	998	4397	11444	6474	13779
Inventories **24**	110	0	0	0	0	0	0	98	40994
Net Property, Plant and Equipment **25**	602	0	19	127	489	505	953	2573	6179
Total Assets **26**	7661	0	42	4275	6741	12775	32018	60955	118204
Notes and Loans Payable **27**	154	0	54	0	7	9948	0	21769	11089
All Other Liabilities **28**	5464	0	12	4155	2976	5618	15827	16810	20041
Net Worth **29**	2043	0	-24	121	3758	-2791	16190	22376	87074

Selected Financial Ratios (Times to 1)

	1	2	3	4	5	6	7	8	9
Current Ratio **30**	1.2	0.7	•	0.8	1.6	5.1	1.9	1.9	3.9
Quick Ratio **31**	0.9	0.5	•	0.3	1.4	4.5	1.7	1.7	3.2
Net Sales to Working Capital **32**	16.9	•	•	•	17.1	2.3	3.5	3.6	1.7
Coverage Ratio **33**	2.3	4.5	•	•	•	5.8	1697.7	1.8	55.9
Total Asset Turnover **34**	0.6	2.5	•	1.8	4.8	1.4	1.5	0.7	1.0
Inventory Turnover **35**	11.5	•	•	•	•	•	•	25.6	0.7
Receivables Turnover **36**	6.1	8.7	•	7.3	10.9	5.0	5.2	3.7	0.5
Total Liabilities to Net Worth **37**	2.7	•	•	34.4	0.8	•	1.0	1.7	0.4
Current Assets to Working Capital **38**	5.6	•	•	•	2.6	1.2	2.1	2.2	1.3
Current Liabilities to Working Capital **39**	4.6	•	•	•	1.6	0.2	1.1	1.2	0.3
Working Capital to Net Sales **40**	0.1	•	•	•	0.1	0.4	0.3	0.3	0.6
Inventory to Working Capital **41**	0.4	•	•	•	•	•	•	0.0	•
Total Receipts to Cash Flow **42**	2.7	1.5	•	2.8	2.1	2.9	2.1	3.0	2.5
Cost of Goods to Cash Flow **43**	0.7	0.0	•	0.8	•	0.5	0.5	0.2	0.6
Cash Flow to Total Debt **44**	0.3	1.0	•	0.7	5.2	0.4	1.4	0.4	1.5

Selected Financial Factors (in Percentages)

	1	2	3	4	5	6	7	8	9
Debt Ratio **45**	73.3	158.2	•	972	121.8	49.4	44.3	63.3	26.3
Return on Total Assets **46**	10.2	64.4	•	20.1	37.8	27.7	163.2	4.7	19.4
Return on Equity Before Income Taxes **47**	21.3	•	•	710.9	54.7	292.7	•	5.8	25.8
Return on Equity After Income Taxes **48**	15.6	•	•	703.3	38.7	249.1	•	4.7	20.8
Profit Margin (Before Income Tax) **49**	9.2	32.0	19.7	11.4	18.6	21.8	33.8	2.9	19.2
Profit Margin (After Income Tax) **50**	6.8	32.0	19.7	11.3	13.2	19.4	28.8	2.4	15.4

Table I

Corporations with and without Net Income

TELECOMMUNICATIONS

MONEY AMOUNTS AND SIZE OF ASSETS IN THOUSANDS OF DOLLARS

Item Description for Accounting Period 7/06 Through 6/07	Total	Zero Assets	Under 500	500 to 1,000	1,000 to 5,000	5,000 to 10,000	10,000 to 25,000	25,000 to 50,000	50,000 to 100,000	100,000 to 250,000	250,000 to 500,000	500,000 to 2,500,000	2,500,000 and over
Number of Enterprises 1	17735	4122	10251	921	1199	371	337	190	143	82	39	46	34
Revenues ($ in Thousands)													
Net Sales 2	400222497	2525281	9069054	1822783	12419907	2776762	4160808	5087395	7165548	8653147	9400263	23046901	314094648
Interest 3	20651641	91304	3693	1859	18106	25498	44050	58215	128934	144764	208197	370034	19556986
Rents 4	10761991	17673	0	1814	5212	2916	4813	7953	8673	26144	10500	43317	10632977
Royalties 5	278884	0	0	0	0	14299	1304	292	6011	187118	9858	25176	34827
Other Portfolio Income 6	21347631	105496	103	5	21675	56042	532325	237055	595519	473639	234343	365276	18726150
Other Receipts 7	22024428	-416363	82706	5077	56459	91023	175342	233953	239170	210802	131561	594808	20619892
Total Receipts 8	475287072	2323391	9155556	1831538	12521359	2966540	4918642	5624863	8143855	9695614	9994722	24445512	383665480
Average Total Receipts 9	26799	564	893	1989	10443	7996	14595	29605	56950	118239	256275	531424	11284279
Operating Costs/Operating Income (%)													
Cost of Operations 10	23.1	23.3	79.0	55.1	79.1	58.0	43.4	43.9	47.2	51.5	40.3	44.4	14.8
Salaries and Wages 11	12.8	15.9	5.9	12.7	7.1	12.2	13.7	14.2	11.2	11.0	17.1	14.8	13.0
Taxes Paid 12	2.9	3.7	0.9	2.4	0.9	2.0	3.2	2.5	2.2	2.1	2.6	2.8	3.1
Interest Paid 13	8.9	15.1	0.4	3.4	0.6	1.3	2.6	3.4	3.8	3.4	6.2	6.8	10.2
Depreciation 14	9.9	9.6	0.9	1.2	1.1	5.6	7.4	7.2	8.3	7.9	12.1	11.1	10.6
Amortization and Depletion 15	1.4	2.6	0.1	1.1	0.2	0.7	1.5	1.2	1.1	0.8	2.1	3.4	1.3
Pensions and Other Deferred Comp. 16	0.9	0.5	0.6	2.1	0.2	0.4	0.4	0.3	0.3	0.3	0.3	0.6	1.1
Employee Benefits 17	1.9	2.0	0.3	0.6	0.5	1.0	1.7	1.1	1.3	1.6	2.0	1.6	2.1
Advertising 18	2.2	2.2	0.5	0.4	0.3	1.3	1.1	0.9	0.9	1.1	2.0	4.4	2.3
Other Expenses 19	42.2	31.9	11.3	19.2	9.9	22.3	30.1	30.7	27.0	26.8	26.6	23.1	47.8
Officers' Compensation 20	0.6	3.7	3.1	6.1	2.0	4.8	2.1	2.2	1.5	1.6	1.4	1.4	0.2
Operating Margin 21	•	•	•	•	•	•	•	•	•	•	•	•	•
Operating Margin Before Officers' Comp. 22	•	0.2	0.2	0.3	1.8	0.3	•	•	•	•	•	•	•

Selected Average Balance Sheet ($ in Thousands)

Net Receivables 23	7260	0	10	215	673	1346	2110	4761	6510	18582	43488	96478	3439364
Inventories 24	437	0	9	40	145	132	639	819	1756	3735	3876	16365	163964
Net Property, Plant and Equipment 25	17836	0	17	112	555	2156	5613	11007	26804	52811	127098	296265	8348774
Total Assets 26	79322	0	90	680	2444	7374	16601	34726	70524	159486	334413	1096350	38256997
Notes and Loans Payable 27	22131	0	53	1155	657	3115	6945	14266	19449	49012	126122	503668	10264850
All Other Liabilities 28	20751	0	88	681	1998	2017	1918	12041	16700	36071	90640	333738	9887745
Net Worth 29	36440	0	-52	-1155	-210	2242	7738	8420	34376	74404	117650	258943	18104402

Selected Financial Ratios (Times to 1)

Current Ratio 30	0.9	•	0.7	0.6	1.0	1.9	1.1	1.2	1.6	1.6	1.6	1.0	0.9
Quick Ratio 31	0.7	•	0.5	0.5	0.7	0.8	0.9	1.1	1.1	1.1	1.1	0.7	0.7
Net Sales to Working Capital 32	•	•	•	•	3.8	35.9	13.9	5.8	5.9	5.9	5.9	•	•
Coverage Ratio 33	2.4	•	•	•	•	5.2	1.8	3.4	2.3	•	•	•	2.6
Total Asset Turnover 34	0.3	•	9.9	2.9	4.2	1.0	0.7	0.8	0.7	0.7	0.7	0.5	0.2
Inventory Turnover 35	11.9	•	78.4	27.6	56.5	33.0	8.4	14.3	13.5	14.5	25.1	13.6	8.3
Receivables Turnover 36	3.3	•	92.3	8.5	15.8	6.8	6.0	6.2	7.4	4.8	5.6	5.2	2.9
Total Liabilities to Net Worth 37	1.2	•	•	•	•	2.3	1.1	3.1	1.1	1.1	1.8	3.2	1.1
Current Assets to Working Capital 38	•	•	•	•	•	2.1	18.2	6.7	2.6	2.7	2.8	•	1.1
Current Liabilities to Working Capital 39	•	•	•	•	•	1.1	17.2	5.7	1.6	1.7	1.8	•	•
Working Capital to Net Sales 40	•	•	•	•	•	0.3	0.0	0.1	0.2	0.2	0.2	0.2	•
Inventory to Working Capital 41	•	•	•	•	•	0.1	1.8	0.4	0.2	0.2	0.1	0.1	•
Total Receipts to Cash Flow 42	2.2	26.8	13.7	7.8	14.3	7.3	4.2	4.2	4.3	4.9	7.5	11.7	1.8
Cost of Goods to Cash Flow 43	0.5	6.2	10.8	4.3	11.3	4.2	1.8	1.8	2.0	2.5	3.0	5.2	0.3
Cash Flow to Total Debt 44	0.2	0.5	0.1	0.3	0.3	0.2	0.2	0.3	0.2	0.2	0.3	0.1	0.3

Selected Financial Factors (in Percentages)

Debt Ratio 45	54.1	•	157.7	269.8	108.6	53.4	69.6	75.8	51.3	53.3	64.8	76.4	52.7
Return on Total Assets 46	6.0	•	•	•	•	10.1	4.7	9.0	5.3	5.3	•	•	6.3
Return on Equity Before Income Taxes 47	7.5	•	34.0	6.6	41.8	17.5	8.8	12.9	6.5	5.3	•	•	8.2
Return on Equity After Income Taxes 48	5.4	•	34.5	6.8	57.1	11.5	7.9	1.5	•	•	•	•	6.2
Profit Margin (Before Income Tax) 49	12.1	•	•	•	•	11.0	2.8	•	8.9	4.6	•	•	16.0
Profit Margin (After Income Tax) 50	8.7	•	•	•	•	7.2	•	•	5.5	4.6	•	•	12.1

Table II

Corporations with Net Income

TELECOMMUNICATIONS

MONEY AMOUNTS AND SIZE OF ASSETS IN THOUSANDS OF DOLLARS

Item Description for Accounting Period 7/06 Through 6/07	Total	Zero Assets	Under 500	500 to 1,000	1,000 to 5,000	5,000 to 10,000	10,000 to 25,000	25,000 to 50,000	50,000 to 100,000	100,000 to 250,000	250,000 to 500,000	500,000 to 2,500,000	2,500,000 and over
Number of Enterprises **1**	7491	2869	2703	442	673	243	228	116	104	53	16	21	23
Revenues ($ in Thousands)													
Net Sales **2**	355105169	2055896	4138961	964244	10581826	1937405	2844836	3271022	5188010	5407750	3960608	7897244	306853365
Interest **3**	19619219	61763	1601	1253	7678	14247	35655	32199	59775	76426	89533	116860	19122229
Rents **4**	10747402	17501	0	0	4321	2916	4356	6327	7986	24584	8801	38437	10632173
Royalties **5**	250201	0	0	0	0	14299	0	292	6011	187118	7644	11	34827
Other Portfolio Income **6**	21054668	104966	97	0	19632	53049	509629	229301	519971	466193	210351	332359	18609121
Other Receipts **7**	21919872	106763	64553	2192	37934	67807	159621	203587	241286	177336	75770	353115	20429908
Total Receipts **8**	428696531	2350889	4205212	967689	10651391	2089723	3554097	3742728	6023039	6339407	4352707	8738026	375681623
Average Total Receipts **9**	57228	819	1556	2189	15827	8600	15588	32265	57914	119611	272044	416096	16333984
Operating Costs/Operating Income (%)													
Cost of Operations **10**	19.6	20.6	76.8	41.2	82.5	55.6	41.4	42.1	46.1	47.4	26.3	35.3	14.5
Salaries and Wages **11**	12.5	11.5	4.5	10.1	4.3	7.9	8.8	11.8	8.2	9.5	19.1	12.2	13.0
Taxes Paid **12**	3.0	3.8	0.6	2.4	0.7	1.8	3.2	2.3	2.3	2.4	3.1	2.5	3.1
Interest Paid **13**	9.0	12.7	0.6	0.4	0.2	0.7	1.9	1.6	2.5	2.7	4.2	7.5	9.9
Depreciation **14**	9.8	9.9	0.9	0.4	0.7	5.1	7.5	6.3	8.1	8.2	8.0	10.2	10.5
Amortization and Depletion **15**	1.2	2.4	0.0	0.0	0.1	0.4	0.4	0.5	0.8	0.7	1.3	3.6	1.3
Pensions and Other Deferred Comp. **16**	1.0	0.6	0.7	3.9	0.2	0.5	0.4	0.3	0.3	0.4	0.7	1.2	1.1
Employee Benefits **17**	2.0	2.2	0.1	0.9	0.4	0.8	1.1	0.7	1.2	1.7	2.2	2.0	2.1
Advertising **18**	2.1	1.7	0.2	0.6	0.2	0.4	1.2	0.9	0.7	1.2	1.0	1.6	2.3
Other Expenses **19**	44.3	22.2	11.3	24.2	7.0	18.5	29.6	27.5	25.9	24.8	31.5	20.6	48.1
Officers' Compensation **20**	0.3	2.1	1.9	6.5	1.1	3.7	1.5	2.3	1.0	1.1	1.8	1.1	0.1
Operating Margin **21**	•	10.2	2.3	9.3	2.7	4.6	3.0	3.7	2.9	0.0	0.8	2.2	•
Operating Margin Before Officers' Comp. **22**	•	12.3	4.3	15.9	3.8	8.3	4.4	6.0	4.0	1.1	2.6	3.3	•

Selected Average Balance Sheet ($ in Thousands)

Net Receivables 23	15749	0	19	234	805	1473	1725	4369	6385	18300	47679	78771	4868400
Inventories 24	845	0	15	77	133	105	409	859	1548	4412	2885	9409	230888
Net Property, Plant and Equipment 25	39043	0	34	119	598	2308	6280	11756	28312	58811	136242	229998	11978285
Total Assets 26	168651	0	154	651	2550	7528	16914	34365	70887	156545	347608	869887	52685871
Notes and Loans Payable 27	45771	0	124	169	458	1068	6484	7558	18035	43682	94994	404593	14144739
All Other Liabilities 28	44611	0	231	207	1087	1633	227	7199	15127	30666	101353	184360	14033064
Net Worth 29	78269	0	-201	275	1004	4827	10204	19608	37725	82197	151261	280934	24508068

Selected Financial Ratios (Times to 1)

Current Ratio 30	0.9	•	0.5	2.3	1.4	2.9	0.9	1.8	1.7	2.1	1.5	1.0	0.8
Quick Ratio 31	0.7	•	0.3	2.0	1.0	2.2	0.7	1.4	1.2	1.4	1.1	0.8	0.7
Net Sales to Working Capital 32	•	•	•	7.9	36.5	3.1	•	5.2	5.5	3.7	7.6	249.7	•
Coverage Ratio 33	2.8	2.9	7.4	23.5	17.8	18.7	16.0	12.3	8.6	7.8	3.5	2.7	2.7
Total Asset Turnover 34	0.3	•	10.0	3.4	6.2	1.1	0.7	0.8	0.7	0.7	0.7	0.4	0.3
Inventory Turnover 35	11.0	•	78.7	11.7	97.5	42.2	12.6	13.8	14.8	11.0	22.6	14.1	8.4
Receivables Turnover 36	3.3	•	101.5	7.8	20.4	6.8	6.7	7.3	8.2	5.1	5.9	4.5	3.0
Total Liabilities to Net Worth 37	1.2	•	•	1.4	1.5	0.6	0.7	0.8	0.9	0.9	1.3	2.1	1.1
Current Assets to Working Capital 38	•	•	•	1.8	3.7	1.5	•	2.3	2.5	1.9	3.2	106.2	•
Current Liabilities to Working Capital 39	•	•	•	0.8	2.7	0.5	•	1.3	1.5	0.9	2.2	105.2	•
Working Capital to Net Sales 40	•	•	•	0.1	0.0	0.3	•	0.2	0.2	0.3	0.1	0.0	•
Inventory to Working Capital 41	•	•	•	0.2	0.3	0.0	•	0.2	0.2	0.2	0.1	7.1	•
Total Receipts to Cash Flow 42	1.9	2.7	7.1	3.1	11.2	4.1	2.8	3.0	3.2	3.2	3.1	3.8	1.8
Cost of Goods to Cash Flow 43	0.4	0.6	5.5	1.3	9.2	2.3	1.2	1.3	1.5	1.5	0.8	1.4	0.3
Cash Flow to Total Debt 44	0.3	•	0.6	1.8	0.9	0.7	0.7	0.6	0.5	0.4	0.4	0.2	0.3

Selected Financial Factors (in Percentages)

Debt Ratio 45	53.6	•	231.2	57.8	60.6	35.9	39.7	42.9	46.8	47.5	56.5	67.7	53.5
Return on Total Assets 46	7.0	•	45.5	34.0	21.7	13.9	21.9	16.1	15.1	13.5	10.5	8.8	6.7
Return on Equity Before Income Taxes 47	9.7	•	•	77.1	52.0	20.5	34.0	25.9	25.0	22.4	17.4	17.1	9.0
Return on Equity After Income Taxes 48	7.4	•	•	75.6	46.3	15.3	27.3	19.2	18.8	15.5	13.3	14.2	6.9
Profit Margin (Before Income Tax) 49	16.1	24.3	3.9	9.7	3.3	12.4	27.8	18.0	18.9	18.1	10.6	12.7	16.6
Profit Margin (After Income Tax) 50	12.3	19.9	3.9	9.5	3.0	9.2	22.3	13.4	14.2	12.5	8.1	10.6	12.7

Table I
Corporations with and without Net Income

INTERNET SERVICE PROVIDERS, WEB PORTALS, AND D.P. SERVICES

MONEY AMOUNTS AND SIZE OF ASSETS IN THOUSANDS OF DOLLARS

Item Description for Accounting Period 7/06 Through 6/07	Total	Zero Assets	Under 500	500 to 1,000	1,000 to 5,000	5,000 to 10,000	10,000 to 25,000	25,000 to 50,000	50,000 to 100,000	100,000 to 250,000	250,000 to 500,000	500,000 to 2,500,000	2,500,000 and over
Number of Enterprises 1	15634	2806	11333	476	672	125	87	43	40	20	10	11	10
Revenues ($ in Thousands)													
Net Sales 2	95935155	955556	7326696	895742	2529594	906105	1640598	1999991	1996101	2017946	1827914	4576147	69262764
Interest 3	7688971	6983	2265	4858	8234	6637	14641	16338	20126	43887	44698	68937	7449368
Rents 4	674521	84	5463	0	0	0	5444	65	2151	957	0	0	659376
Royalties 5	8604797	644	0	0	0	55440	8147	2414	0	1941	5251	6710	8524251
Other Portfolio Income 6	1104141	11627	3113	255	1058	28572	1366	1677	16578	17475	74291	24154	923974
Other Receipts 7	5835076	37376	80738	11412	39259	29784	11670	35109	35928	26006	1601	14804	5511389
Total Receipts 8	119840661	1012270	7418275	912267	2578145	1026538	1681866	2055594	2070884	2108212	1954736	4690752	92331122
Average Total Receipts 9	7665	361	655	1917	3837	8212	19332	47805	51772	105411	195474	426432	9233112
Operating Costs/Operating Income (%)													
Cost of Operations 10	17.4	10.4	45.5	23.7	22.7	54.0	35.6	48.6	43.5	21.7	35.9	25.4	10.5
Salaries and Wages 11	20.6	47.2	8.7	19.3	31.4	13.1	25.9	18.0	20.0	27.7	18.7	23.9	20.8
Taxes Paid 12	2.7	3.1	1.6	2.5	2.6	4.6	3.0	2.3	3.2	3.3	3.3	2.2	2.7
Interest Paid 13	9.7	2.6	0.6	2.2	1.3	1.0	1.6	1.6	2.8	2.8	5.6	3.8	12.7
Depreciation 14	4.8	3.2	1.1	2.8	5.6	3.8	3.5	2.5	4.2	4.4	10.4	5.9	5.1
Amortization and Depletion 15	5.2	2.0	0.1	0.4	0.7	3.0	2.2	0.9	1.6	2.3	1.1	5.4	6.5
Pensions and Other Deferred Comp. 16	2.4	1.5	0.1	1.0	0.2	0.8	0.5	0.3	0.5	0.4	0.3	0.2	3.2
Employee Benefits 17	2.0	2.6	0.5	1.1	1.7	2.7	3.7	1.7	1.9	2.2	1.8	2.0	2.1
Advertising 18	4.0	0.5	3.4	0.5	2.4	1.2	3.0	1.6	1.2	2.9	0.7	7.8	4.2
Other Expenses 19	45.6	50.4	29.9	43.1	34.0	41.1	29.9	19.6	23.3	31.1	25.3	25.9	51.8
Officers' Compensation 20	2.0	6.4	6.8	5.8	5.6	5.9	2.9	3.1	2.6	2.6	2.6	0.8	1.2
Operating Margin 21	•	•	1.7	•	•	•	•	•	•	•	•	•	•
Operating Margin Before Officers' Comp. 22	8.5	•	3.3	•	•	•	•	3.1	•	1.2	•	•	•

Selected Average Balance Sheet ($ in Thousands)

Item													
Net Receivables 23	1930	0	12	120	333	791	2518	8619	9722	19735	59189	67525	2695230
Inventories 24	509	0	2	37	31	19	131	773	1222	314	2085	2402	774809
Net Property, Plant and Equipment 25	1509	0	14	113	907	630	2562	4239	8418	16596	88996	130254	1930123
Total Assets 26	24447	0	92	731	2030	6798	14708	36485	70330	160887	333698	791516	35768110
Notes and Loans Payable 27	3532	0	118	494	1705	968	4375	7801	18674	48379	134892	270114	4562687
All Other Liabilities 28	12329	0	38	603	676	1881	4468	19572	18042	54855	54096	171898	18586240
Net Worth 29	8587	0	-64	-366	-352	3949	5865	9112	33614	57654	144710	349505	12619183

Selected Financial Ratios (Times to 1)

Item													
Current Ratio 30	1.1	•	1.1	1.1	2.3	1.5	1.3	1.5	1.2	2.0	1.4		1.0
Quick Ratio 31	0.4	•	0.8	0.9	2.0	1.1	1.1	1.3	0.9	1.2	1.2		0.3
Net Sales to Working Capital 32	11.8	•	95.7	83.4	2.5	6.8	8.3	5.0	10.9	2.2	7.8		13.3
Coverage Ratio 33	2.0	•	6.3	0.7	•	2.8	1.3	0.5	2.1	1.2	0.8		2.1
Total Asset Turnover 34	0.3	•	7.0	2.6	1.9	1.1	1.3	0.7	0.6	0.5	0.5		0.2
Inventory Turnover 35	2.1	•	176.3	12.0	27.3	209.3	51.1	29.2	17.8	69.7	31.5	44.1	0.9
Receivables Turnover 36	3.0	•	54.0	22.6	10.9	10.2	7.6	7.1	5.9	4.4	3.0	5.7	2.4
Total Liabilities to Net Worth 37	1.8	•	•	•	0.7	1.5	3.0	1.1	1.8	2.0	1.3	1.3	1.8
Current Assets to Working Capital 38	17.3	•	10.0	20.1	1.8	3.2	3.9	2.9	6.5	5.5	2.0	3.7	24.9
Current Liabilities to Working Capital 39	16.3	•	9.0	19.1	0.8	2.2	2.9	1.9	5.5	1.0	1.0	2.7	23.9
Working Capital to Net Sales 40	0.1	•	0.0	0.0	0.4	0.1	0.1	0.2	0.1	0.5	0.5	0.1	0.1
Inventory to Working Capital 41	1.0	•	0.3	1.1	0.0	0.0	0.2	0.1	0.0	0.0	0.0	0.0	1.5
Total Receipts to Cash Flow 42	2.0	5.1	3.3	4.4	7.6	5.9	5.2	5.6	3.6	5.3	5.3	4.7	1.7
Cost of Goods to Cash Flow 43	0.4	0.5	1.5	1.0	4.1	2.1	2.5	2.4	0.8	1.9	1.9	1.2	0.2
Cash Flow to Total Debt 44	0.2	•	1.3	0.6	0.3	0.4	0.3	0.2	0.3	0.2	0.2	0.2	0.2

Selected Financial Factors (in Percentages)

Item													
Debt Ratio 45	64.9	•	169.3	150.0	117.3	41.9	60.1	75.0	52.2	64.2	56.6	55.8	64.7
Return on Total Assets 46	4.8	•	24.7	4.0	•	•	•	5.5	1.1	3.7	3.8	1.6	5.1
Return on Equity Before Income Taxes 47	6.8	•	•	3.5	65.7	•	•	14.0	•	5.5	1.7	•	7.5
Return on Equity After Income Taxes 48	5.3	•	3.5	3.5	69.9	•	•	6.7	•	2.4	0.0	•	6.1
Profit Margin (Before Income Tax) 49	9.5	3.0	•	•	•	•	•	2.7	•	3.1	1.4	•	13.7
Profit Margin (After Income Tax) 50	7.4	2.9	•	•	1.3	•	•	1.3	•	1.4	0.0	•	11.2

Table II
Corporations with Net Income

INTERNET SERVICE PROVIDERS, WEB PORTALS, AND D.P. SERVICES

MONEY AMOUNTS AND SIZE OF ASSETS IN THOUSANDS OF DOLLARS

Item Description for Accounting Period 7/06 Through 6/07	Total	Zero Assets	Under 500	500 to 1,000	1,000 to 5,000	5,000 to 10,000	10,000 to 25,000	25,000 to 50,000	50,000 to 100,000	100,000 to 250,000	250,000 to 500,000	500,000 to 2,500,000	2,500,000 and over
Number of Enterprises **1**	7876	1446	5678	•	258	65	39	26	20	13	5	4	•
Revenues ($ in Thousands)													
Net Sales **2**	80946032	406361	4367377	•	1919702	711863	1212812	1032972	1198633	1619908	1257555	2247033	•
Interest **3**	3055371	5460	1047	•	1349	1762	3422	9659	12728	41204	16325	16029	•
Rents **4**	473323	0	5463	•	0	0	5033	0	1077	28	0	0	•
Royalties **5**	8534061	0	0	•	0	0	8124	138	0	1941	0	389	•
Other Portfolio Income **6**	811612	11603	1586	•	733	28166	312	1674	14440	16135	60608	16142	•
Other Receipts **7**	5701013	13854	62579	•	3983	1155	8222	29359	41011	20438	97	11646	•
Total Receipts **8**	99521412	437278	4438052	•	1925767	742946	1237925	1073802	1267889	1699654	1334585	2291239	•
Average Total Receipts **9**	12636	302	782	•	7464	11430	31742	41300	63394	130743	266917	572810	•
Operating Costs/Operating Income (%)													
Cost of Operations **10**	11.7	1.1	39.3	•	22.1	60.0	37.3	33.8	44.6	16.1	43.3	18.3	•
Salaries and Wages **11**	20.5	25.7	7.9	•	25.4	2.0	17.6	19.8	17.7	27.3	17.3	23.8	•
Taxes Paid **12**	2.7	3.7	1.6	•	1.9	4.4	2.5	2.4	2.8	3.4	3.1	2.5	•
Interest Paid **13**	4.8	0.8	0.2	•	0.5	0.4	0.9	2.4	1.7	2.7	2.3	3.5	•
Depreciation **14**	3.9	2.6	1.1	•	4.5	3.5	2.4	1.7	4.5	3.7	5.8	6.3	•
Amortization and Depletion **15**	5.7	0.0	0.1	•	0.2	0.1	0.8	1.0	1.2	1.7	0.9	6.5	•
Pensions and Other Deferred Comp. **16**	2.8	3.3	0.1	•	0.2	0.7	0.3	0.5	0.7	0.5	0.4	0.3	•
Employee Benefits **17**	2.0	3.2	0.5	•	1.6	2.3	2.7	1.7	2.2	2.3	1.5	2.4	•
Advertising **18**	4.0	0.7	4.5	•	2.7	0.1	0.4	0.6	0.7	2.1	0.8	2.3	•
Other Expenses **19**	48.6	41.5	29.6	•	27.3	21.5	25.1	24.1	18.2	32.7	16.7	23.3	•
Officers' Compensation **20**	1.8	5.1	7.0	•	3.9	5.0	2.0	3.5	3.0	1.4	3.1	0.9	•
Operating Margin **21**	•	12.1	8.1	•	9.5	•	8.0	8.5	2.5	6.1	4.6	9.8	•
Operating Margin Before Officers' Comp. **22**	•	17.3	15.1	•	13.5	5.0	9.9	12.0	5.6	7.5	7.7	10.8	•

Selected Average Balance Sheet ($ in Thousands)

Item													
Net Receivables 23	2774	0	16	•	421	658	•	4122	11140	9675	18613	100604	102429
Inventories 24	981	0	1	•	10	0	•	153	236	702	117	65	3220
Net Property, Plant and Equipment 25	1888	0	11	•	782	545	•	2756	3989	11405	17101	62658	186123
Total Assets 26	37313	0	121	•	1793	6357	•	14538	34583	67300	160036	367879	860824
Notes and Loans Payable 27	5241	0	96	•	1212	541	•	3360	7929	15894	48457	78288	255370
All Other Liabilities 28	15536	0	40	•	574	764	•	4748	16911	17477	50626	112152	195887
Net Worth 29	16536	0	-16	•	6	5052	•	9743	33928	60954	177439		409568

Selected Financial Ratios (Times to 1)

Item												
Current Ratio 30	1.1	•	2.1	•	1.4	3.9	1.0	1.7	2.0	1.3	2.1	1.4
Quick Ratio 31	0.6	•	1.5	•	1.2	3.4	0.8	1.6	1.8	1.0	1.6	1.3
Net Sales to Working Capital 32	14.1	•	16.0	•	31.0	3.1	•	4.1	3.8	8.5	2.6	6.8
Coverage Ratio 33	4.2	24.2	42.0	•	19.0	10.9	12.3	6.1	5.8	5.1	5.7	4.4
Total Asset Turnover 34	0.3	•	6.4	•	4.2	1.7	2.1	1.1	0.9	0.8	0.7	0.7
Inventory Turnover 35	1.2	•	207.4	•	172.1	•	75.5	56.9	38.1	171.1	1681.2	31.9
Receivables Turnover 36	3.2	•	46.2	•	17.8	16.7	9.9	5.4	5.8	7.4	•	5.3
Total Liabilities to Net Worth 37	1.3	•	•	•	307.7	0.3	1.3	2.5	1.0	1.6	1.1	1.1
Current Assets to Working Capital 38	11.9	•	1.9	•	3.6	1.3	•	2.4	2.0	4.7	1.9	3.3
Current Liabilities to Working Capital 39	10.9	•	0.9	•	2.6	0.3	•	1.4	1.0	3.7	0.9	2.3
Working Capital to Net Sales 40	0.1	•	0.1	•	0.0	0.3	•	0.2	0.3	0.1	0.4	0.1
Inventory to Working Capital 41	1.3	•	0.0	•	0.1	•	•	0.0	0.0	0.1	0.0	0.0
Total Receipts to Cash Flow 42	1.7	2.0	2.7	•	3.0	6.5	3.1	3.0	4.3	2.7	4.8	3.1
Cost of Goods to Cash Flow 43	0.2	0.0	1.1	•	0.7	3.9	1.1	1.0	1.9	0.4	2.1	0.6
Cash Flow to Total Debt 44	0.3	•	2.1	•	1.4	1.3	1.3	0.5	0.4	0.5	0.3	0.4

Selected Financial Factors (in Percentages)

Item												
Debt Ratio 45	55.7	•	113.2	•	99.7	20.5	55.8	71.8	49.6	61.9	51.8	52.4
Return on Total Assets 46	5.5	•	63.4	•	43.0	8.3	23.4	17.1	8.8	10.7	9.1	9.9
Return on Equity Before Income Taxes 47	9.5	•	•	•	12588.8	9.5	48.6	50.6	14.5	22.6	15.6	16.1
Return on Equity After Income Taxes 48	8.0	•	•	•	11927.4	9.3	44.3	39.5	12.7	18.1	12.8	12.1
Profit Margin (Before Income Tax) 49	15.3	19.7	9.7	•	9.8	4.4	10.0	12.4	8.2	11.1	11.0	11.7
Profit Margin (After Income Tax) 50	12.9	15.2	9.5	•	9.3	4.3	9.2	9.7	7.2	8.9	9.0	8.8

Table I

Corporations with and without Net Income

OTHER INFORMATION SERVICES, NEWS SYNDICATES, LIBRARIES

MONEY AMOUNTS AND SIZE OF ASSETS IN THOUSANDS OF DOLLARS

Item Description for Accounting Period 7/06 Through 6/07	Total	Zero Assets	Under 500	500 to 1,000	1,000 to 5,000	5,000 to 10,000	10,000 to 25,000	25,000 to 50,000	50,000 to 100,000	100,000 to 250,000	250,000 to 500,000	500,000 to 2,500,000	2,500,000 and over
Number of Enterprises **1**	9966	762	8154	367	417	157	40	22	12	12	7	14	3
Revenues ($ in Thousands)													
Net Sales **2**	28973325	518132	3584028	606954	1206584	1950176	1108262	430081	751541	1585006	1208989	10623075	5400497
Interest **3**	373625	1965	1852	533	6768	6918	3783	8191	8200	21094	17613	177262	119446
Rents **4**	9448	0	0	53	677	0	0	1262	12	0	0	2550	4894
Royalties **5**	64829	0	0	0	0	0	0	9511	570	10941	7559	27437	8810
Other Portfolio Income **6**	1345521	31675	211	0	45883	68	1964	1130	1114	3342	12466	1245982	1686
Other Receipts **7**	1540532	1688	86030	3331	44341	6716	51249	11209	16899	32894	823248	438152	24775
Total Receipts **8**	32307280	553460	3672121	610871	1304253	1963878	1165258	461384	778336	1653277	2069875	12514458	5560108
Average Total Receipts **9**	3242	726	450	1664	3128	12509	29131	20972	64861	137773	295696	893890	1853369
Operating Costs/Operating Income (%)													
Cost of Operations **10**	23.1	52.5	36.3	71.1	25.1	37.6	49.4	2.8	33.3	14.7	7.8	20.6	6.4
Salaries and Wages **11**	24.7	21.8	19.5	6.9	35.9	24.3	12.0	31.4	19.9	29.5	28.4	27.1	23.8
Taxes Paid **12**	2.7	2.4	2.4	2.4	4.5	4.3	1.6	3.8	3.2	2.8	2.7	2.6	2.2
Interest Paid **13**	3.6	1.4	1.7	0.3	1.3	0.7	1.5	4.0	1.0	3.2	5.9	3.4	7.8
Depreciation **14**	2.0	1.0	0.9	0.3	2.3	1.3	2.9	5.4	1.9	3.1	3.2	2.5	1.5
Amortization and Depletion **15**	2.6	0.4	0.2	0.1	0.5	1.7	0.2	4.5	1.4	2.5	6.3	2.7	5.0
Pensions and Other Deferred Comp. **16**	0.7	0.8	1.3	0.2	0.2	1.0	0.1	0.6	0.2	0.9	1.5	0.6	0.5
Employee Benefits **17**	2.4	1.8	1.0	1.1	2.3	2.3	0.8	3.7	2.4	2.4	2.7	2.9	2.9
Advertising **18**	3.8	0.3	2.3	0.1	1.9	0.5	18.4	3.2	12.8	2.1	3.5	1.3	8.4
Other Expenses **19**	34.5	14.3	22.4	16.0	42.4	24.0	12.1	53.0	22.8	38.7	102.8	37.0	31.7
Officers' Compensation **20**	3.6	16.9	10.8	4.7	8.0	3.3	3.4	5.2	2.5	3.2	1.3	1.7	1.2
Operating Margin **21**	•	1.2	•	•	•	•	•	•	•	•	•	•	8.7
Operating Margin Before Officers' Comp. **22**	•	3.4	12.0	1.5	2.4	2.4	1.0	•	1.0	0.2	•	•	9.9

Selected Average Balance Sheet ($ in Thousands)

Item												
Net Receivables 23	534	7	31	435	2180	2864	4286	12231	19111	61099	190607	347567
Inventories 24	25	0	0	45	15	287	216	694	2065	1176	11836	1969
Net Property, Plant and Equipment 25	230	9	15	201	520	2010	3497	3745	16766	36031	68420	146887
Total Assets 26	4453	68	554	2020	7226	14152	33941	72622	167175	345152	1183182	6156721
Notes and Loans Payable 27	1240	132	322	1194	1655	3672	6717	11905	68205	91149	320973	1339086
All Other Liabilities 28	1651	33	95	1093	2435	3876	13448	25207	82408	85256	460475	2173573
Net Worth 29	1562	-97	136	-267	3136	6604	13776	35511	16562	168747	401733	2644061

Selected Financial Ratios (Times to 1)

Item												
Current Ratio 30	1.0	0.9	3.1	1.0	1.5	3.5	1.7	1.3	1.2	1.4	1.5	0.5
Quick Ratio 31	0.7	0.8	•	0.9	1.3	1.4	2.4	1.1	0.9	1.1	1.0	0.3
Net Sales to Working Capital 32	105.6	•	•	5.5	8.8	3.6	4.5	7.9	12.1	4.5	5.0	•
Coverage Ratio 33	3.2	•	•	3.2	0.7	•	2.7	3.3	1.4	1.9	5.7	2.5
Total Asset Turnover 34	0.7	6.5	3.0	1.4	1.7	2.0	0.6	0.9	0.8	0.5	0.6	0.3
Inventory Turnover 35	26.5	453.5	•	16.3	319.8	47.7	2.6	30.1	9.4	11.5	13.2	58.3
Receivables Turnover 36	5.1	51.3	20.0	6.1	6.4	9.6	4.7	6.5	5.8	2.9	5.3	2.7
Total Liabilities to Net Worth 37	1.9	•	3.1	•	1.3	1.1	1.5	1.0	9.1	1.0	1.9	1.3
Current Assets to Working Capital 38	48.4	•	1.5	•	3.1	1.4	2.4	4.4	7.4	3.5	2.8	•
Current Liabilities to Working Capital 39	47.4	•	0.5	•	2.1	0.4	1.4	3.4	6.4	2.5	1.8	•
Working Capital to Net Sales 40	0.0	•	0.2	•	0.1	0.2	0.3	0.1	0.1	0.2	0.2	•
Inventory to Working Capital 41	1.1	•	•	•	0.0	0.0	0.0	0.2	0.2	•	0.1	•
Total Receipts to Cash Flow 42	2.9	4.3	19.8	7.8	4.6	7.7	2.6	4.4	2.8	1.0	2.6	•
Cost of Goods to Cash Flow 43	0.7	1.5	14.1	2.0	1.7	3.8	0.1	1.5	0.4	0.1	0.5	0.2
Cash Flow to Total Debt 44	0.3	0.6	0.2	0.2	0.7	0.5	0.4	0.4	0.3	1.0	0.4	0.2

Selected Financial Factors (in Percentages)

Item												
Debt Ratio 45	64.9	242.7	75.3	113.2	56.6	53.3	59.4	51.1	90.1	51.1	66.0	57.1
Return on Total Assets 46	7.5	34.5	•	•	0.9	8.2	•	2.9	3.5	5.6	12.3	5.7
Return on Equity Before Income Taxes 47	14.6	•	•	178.7	•	11.1	•	4.2	10.0	5.5	30.0	7.9
Return on Equity After Income Taxes 48	11.0	•	•	185.8	•	11.0	•	•	•	1.8	24.8	6.0
Profit Margin (Before Income Tax) 49	7.9	3.7	•	•	•	2.7	•	2.4	1.3	5.4	15.9	11.6
Profit Margin (After Income Tax) 50	5.9	3.5	•	•	•	2.6	•	2.6	•	1.8	13.1	8.7

Table II
Corporations with Net Income

OTHER INFORMATION SERVICES, NEWS SYNDICATES, LIBRARIES

MONEY AMOUNTS AND SIZE OF ASSETS IN THOUSANDS OF DOLLARS

Item Description for Accounting Period 7/06 Through 6/07	Total	Zero Assets	Under 500	500 to 1,000	1,000 to 5,000	5,000 to 10,000	10,000 to 25,000	25,000 to 50,000	50,000 to 100,000	100,000 to 250,000	250,000 to 500,000	500,000 to 2,500,000	2,500,000 and over
Number of Enterprises **1**	6881	407	5805	•	141	124	22	7	9	7	•	10	3
Revenues ($ in Thousands)													
Net Sales **2**	24206560	416925	2901378	•	923004	1759196	938345	278304	670695	688210	•	8854450	5400497
Interest **3**	266604	1861	1076	•	633	4035	691	3799	7089	8658	•	103056	119446
Rents **4**	8706	0	0	•	0	0	0	1262	0	0	•	2550	4894
Royalties **5**	52209	0	0	•	0	0	0	9511	570	5017	•	20766	8810
Other Portfolio Income **6**	1326847	31417	210	•	45874	58	3	0	1106	3330	•	1231703	1686
Other Receipts **7**	1126342	1685	81935	•	36502	6698	13503	11183	16569	7249	•	112274	24775
Total Receipts **8**	26987268	451888	2984599	•	1006013	1769987	952542	304059	696029	712464	•	10324799	5560108
Average Total Receipts **9**	3922	1110	514	•	7135	14274	43297	43437	77337	101781	•	1032480	1853369
Operating Costs/Operating Income (%)													
Cost of Operations **10**	21.7	61.7	31.6	•	30.1	39.1	47.6	1.7	35.4	12.6	•	17.1	6.4
Salaries and Wages **11**	22.7	7.9	16.8	•	24.5	21.4	9.5	18.9	15.3	34.7	•	26.3	23.8
Taxes Paid **12**	2.6	1.5	2.3	•	3.1	4.2	1.5	2.8	2.7	3.3	•	2.6	2.2
Interest Paid **13**	2.8	0.0	0.2	•	1.1	0.4	0.2	1.5	1.1	1.2	•	2.3	7.8
Depreciation **14**	1.6	0.7	0.5	•	1.3	1.2	1.4	2.6	1.6	2.7	•	2.0	1.5
Amortization and Depletion **15**	2.4	0.0	0.2	•	0.1	0.4	0.0	1.4	1.1	2.0	•	2.8	5.0
Pensions and Other Deferred Comp. **16**	0.8	0.0	1.5	•	0.2	1.1	0.1	0.9	0.2	1.6	•	0.7	0.5
Employee Benefits **17**	2.2	0.5	1.0	•	1.8	2.0	0.8	2.6	1.9	2.8	•	2.7	2.9
Advertising **18**	4.0	0.3	2.8	•	0.8	0.4	21.6	3.2	12.9	2.4	•	1.0	8.4
Other Expenses **19**	33.5	8.2	21.7	•	27.0	22.5	8.7	52.7	19.8	24.0	•	38.8	31.7
Officers' Compensation **20**	3.2	16.1	12.4	•	2.4	2.8	2.3	3.9	1.8	2.3	•	1.4	1.2
Operating Margin **21**	2.5	2.9	8.9	•	7.7	4.6	6.2	7.8	6.1	10.3	•	2.3	8.7
Operating Margin Before Officers' Comp. **22**	5.7	19.0	21.3	•	10.1	7.4	8.5	11.7	7.8	12.6	•	3.7	9.9

Selected Average Balance Sheet ($ in Thousands)

Item													
Net Receivables 23	502	0	10	•	657	2185	3478	8027	14473	20120	•	126238	347567
Inventories 24	27	0	0	•	6	33	121	32	1845	157	•	16497	1969
Net Property, Plant and Equipment 25	236	0	5	•	193	532	2351	4498	4168	14628	•	69028	146887
Total Assets 26	5311	0	60	•	2059	7214	13813	32523	70609	166993	•	1229681	6156721
Notes and Loans Payable 27	1087	0	27	•	1182	1438	1482	7120	15278	19496	•	242890	1339086
All Other Liabilities 28	1829	0	25	•	1434	2256	2558	8141	27450	65794	•	415127	2173573
Net Worth 29	2396	0	7	•	-557	3520	9773	17263	27880	81703	•	571663	2644061

Selected Financial Ratios (Times to 1)

Item													
Current Ratio 30	1.0	•	1.4	•	0.8	1.4	4.7	5.2	1.4	1.4	•	1.7	0.5
Quick Ratio 31	0.7	•	1.3	•	0.7	1.3	2.7	4.4	1.2	1.1	•	1.0	0.3
Net Sales to Working Capital 32	•	•	42.4	•	•	11.2	5.5	2.5	6.7	3.3	•	5.4	•
Coverage Ratio 33	6.1	560.1	50.7	•	16.4	14.1	32.8	12.5	10.1	12.3	•	9.5	2.5
Total Asset Turnover 34	0.7	•	8.4	•	3.2	2.0	3.1	1.2	1.1	0.6	•	0.7	0.3
Inventory Turnover 35	28.1	999.9	331.5	•	170.7	168.5	21.1	14.3	78.9		•	9.2	58.3
Receivables Turnover 36	5.7	•	90.4	•	16.5	8.2	12.2	5.4	7.3	3.3	•	7.4	2.7
Total Liabilities to Net Worth 37	1.2	•	7.2	•	1.0	1.0	0.4	0.9	1.5	1.0	•	1.2	1.3
Current Assets to Working Capital 38	•	•	3.5	•	3.4	1.3	1.2	3.6	3.3		•	2.4	•
Current Liabilities to Working Capital 39	•	•	2.5	•	2.4	0.3	0.2	2.6	2.3		•	1.4	•
Working Capital to Net Sales 40	•	•	0.0	•	0.1	0.2	0.4	0.1	0.3		•	0.2	•
Inventory to Working Capital 41	•	•	0.0	•	0.0	•	0.0	0.2	0.0		•	0.1	•
Total Receipts to Cash Flow 42	2.5	8.5	3.2	•	3.3	3.9	6.8	1.5	3.6	3.2	•	2.4	2.4
Cost of Goods to Cash Flow 43	0.6	5.2	1.0	•	1.0	1.5	3.2	0.0	1.3	0.4	•	0.4	0.2
Cash Flow to Total Debt 44	0.5	•	2.9	•	0.8	1.0	1.6	1.8	0.5	0.4	•	0.6	0.2

Selected Financial Factors (in Percentages)

Item													
Debt Ratio 45	54.9	•	87.8	•	127.0	51.2	29.2	46.9	60.5	51.1	•	53.5	57.1
Return on Total Assets 46	11.3	100.3		•	56.5	11.1	24.6	22.7	11.9	8.8	•	15.6	5.7
Return on Equity Before Income Taxes 47	20.9	•	803.1	•	21.2	33.7	39.3	27.1	16.4		•	30.1	7.9
Return on Equity After Income Taxes 48	17.4	•	784.8	•	19.4	33.5	37.4	19.0	12.6		•	25.0	6.0
Profit Margin (Before Income Tax) 49	14.2	11.3	11.8	•	16.7	5.3	7.7	17.1	10.2	13.7	•	19.4	11.6
Profit Margin (After Income Tax) 50	11.9	9.8	11.5	•	15.8	4.8	7.7	16.2	7.1	10.5	•	16.1	8.7

Table I

Corporations with and without Net Income

CREDIT INTERMEDIATION

MONEY AMOUNTS AND SIZE OF ASSETS IN THOUSANDS OF DOLLARS

Item Description for Accounting Period 7/06 Through 6/07		Total	Zero Assets	Under 500	500 to 1,000	1,000 to 5,000	5,000 to 10,000	10,000 to 25,000	25,000 to 50,000	50,000 to 100,000	100,000 to 250,000	250,000 to 500,000	500,000 to 2,500,000	2,500,000 and over
Number of Enterprises	1	59634	7935	36503	4762	4791	1263	1086	764	771	833	383	400	142
Revenues ($ in Thousands)														
Net Sales	2	598137435	83208712	12125351	8783157	8443181	4680369	6587824	5105576	6245062	13680010	12346675	39497518	397434001
Interest	3	392846693	66725070	146658	34453	215693	382430	365091	931784	2132034	6298047	6259494	21027066	288328874
Rents	4	1030127	213008	0	0	4670	4954	1887	9293	12066	17057	62930	123599	580662
Royalties	5	187625	0	2082	0	133	0	0	106	6	12053	15	13356	159875
Other Portfolio Income	6	13558907	1208002	17849	5256	71713	25394	48253	149102	111315	312367	504733	1531748	9573174
Other Receipts	7	190514083	15062632	11958762	8743448	8150972	4267591	6172593	4015291	3989641	7040486	5519503	16801749	98791416
Total Receipts	8	598137435	83208712	12125351	8783157	8443181	4680369	6587824	5105576	6245062	13680010	12346675	39497518	397434001
Average Total Receipts	9	10030	10486	332	1844	1762	3706	6066	6683	8100	16423	32237	98744	2798831
Operating Costs/Operating Income (%)														
Cost of Operations	10	1.3	0.0	13.0	11.9	12.6	5.1	8.7	6.4	3.2	4.3	1.1	1.7	0.3
Salaries and Wages	11	9.3	6.4	23.4	47.5	27.1	30.3	33.5	22.3	20.5	16.1	14.4	14.7	6.3
Taxes Paid	12	1.2	1.3	3.3	1.9	3.0	2.7	3.9	2.8	2.8	2.7	2.5	2.1	0.8
Interest Paid	13	55.4	75.2	1.6	1.3	5.1	13.5	10.4	17.5	25.3	29.8	33.7	30.9	61.3
Depreciation	14	1.9	0.7	0.7	1.2	1.3	1.1	1.7	1.5	1.8	2.0	2.4	2.0	2.2
Amortization and Depletion	15	1.9	0.1	0.1	0.2	0.2	0.2	0.3	0.4	0.3	0.5	0.9	0.9	2.7
Pensions and Other Deferred Comp.	16	0.5	0.3	0.1	0.3	0.3	0.3	0.4	0.5	0.8	0.8	0.9	0.9	0.5
Employee Benefits	17	0.8	0.5	0.7	0.2	1.2	0.8	1.4	1.6	2.0	1.7	2.1	1.7	0.7
Advertising	18	1.3	0.1	1.6	1.8	2.8	3.2	3.0	3.4	1.4	1.3	1.8	2.6	1.3
Other Expenses	19	18.1	16.8	39.3	25.4	33.7	35.3	27.7	27.1	27.0	25.7	25.0	26.6	15.3
Officers' Compensation	20	1.1	0.6	7.8	3.3	4.5	5.0	5.1	4.7	6.3	3.9	3.0	2.1	0.4
Operating Margin	21	7.2	•	8.3	5.0	8.1	2.6	4.0	11.8	8.6	11.2	12.3	13.9	8.2
Operating Margin Before Officers' Comp.	22	8.3	•	16.1	8.3	12.6	7.6	9.1	16.6	14.8	15.2	15.3	16.0	8.6

Selected Average Balance Sheet ($ in Thousands)

Net Receivables 23	13306	0	20	311	626	2812	6434	15474	31237	62587	106039	276099	3793112
Inventories 24	•	•	•	•	•	•	•	•	•	•	•	•	•
Net Property, Plant and Equipment 25	915	0	12	110	209	272	704	773	1505	3127	6405	13834	275680
Total Assets 26	79882	94	699	2198	7271	16123	35695	71758	156361	351033	1004677		27961375
Notes and Loans Payable 27	45306	0	45	274	1058	3935	7126	9611	10685	20314	52637	247174	17813463
All Other Liabilities 28	28725	0	40	78	590	3851	6443	18263	50149	115385	259502	610841	8478732
Net Worth 29	5851	0	9	347	550	-516	2554	7821	10924	20662	38894	146662	1669180

Selected Financial Ratios (Times to 1)

Current Ratio 30	0.5	•	2.9	3.7	1.4	0.8	1.0	1.0	0.9	0.7	0.6	0.6	0.5
Quick Ratio 31	0.4	•	2.3	3.1	1.2	0.7	0.9	0.9	0.8	0.7	0.6	0.6	0.3
Net Sales to Working Capital 32	•	•	8.4	3.7	4.9	•	13.8	9.7	•	•	•	•	•
Coverage Ratio 33	1.1	1.0	6.0	4.7	2.6	1.2	1.4	1.6	1.3	1.4	1.3	1.4	1.1
Total Asset Turnover 34	0.1	•	3.5	2.6	0.8	0.5	0.4	0.2	0.1	0.1	0.1	0.1	0.1
Inventory Turnover 35	•	•	•	•	•	•	•	•	•	•	•	•	•
Receivables Turnover 36	•	•	•	•	•	•	•	•	•	•	•	•	•
Total Liabilities to Net Worth 37	12.7	•	9.6	1.0	3.0	3.0	5.3	3.6	5.6	6.6	8.0	5.9	15.8
Current Assets to Working Capital 38	•	•	1.5	1.4	3.6	•	21.7	33.7	•	•	•	•	•
Current Liabilities to Working Capital 39	•	•	0.5	0.4	2.6	•	20.7	32.7	•	•	•	•	•
Working Capital to Net Sales 40	•	•	0.1	0.3	0.2	•	0.1	0.1	•	•	•	•	•
Inventory to Working Capital 41	•	•	•	•	•	•	0.0	0.0	•	•	•	•	•
Total Receipts to Cash Flow 42	4.4	8.8	2.4	4.0	2.7	3.0	3.8	2.9	3.1	3.0	3.0	2.7	4.6
Cost of Goods to Cash Flow 43	0.1	0.0	0.3	0.5	0.3	0.2	0.3	0.2	0.1	0.1	0.0	0.0	0.0
Cash Flow to Total Debt 44	0.0	•	1.6	1.3	0.4	0.2	0.1	0.1	0.0	0.0	0.0	0.0	0.0

Selected Financial Factors (in Percentages)

Debt Ratio 45	92.7	•	90.5	50.4	75.0	107.1	84.2	78.1	84.8	86.8	88.9	85.4	94.0
Return on Total Assets 46	7.8	•	34.8	16.5	10.6	8.1	5.4	5.4	3.7	4.2	4.2	4.3	6.9
Return on Equity Before Income Taxes 47	11.7	•	306.4	26.1	26.0	•	9.2	9.7	5.7	8.4	9.5	8.9	13.1
Return on Equity After Income Taxes 48	7.2	•	298.4	25.3	24.5	•	7.4	8.1	4.4	6.1	6.3	5.7	8.3
Profit Margin (Before Income Tax) 49	6.8	•	8.2	4.9	8.1	2.5	3.9	11.3	7.7	10.5	11.5	13.2	7.8
Profit Margin (After Income Tax) 50	4.2	•	8.0	4.8	7.7	1.9	3.1	9.4	5.9	7.7	7.6	8.5	4.9

Table II

Corporations with Net Income

CREDIT INTERMEDIATION

MONEY AMOUNTS AND SIZE OF ASSETS IN THOUSANDS OF DOLLARS

Item Description for Accounting Period 7/06 Through 6/07	Total	Zero Assets	Under 500	500 to 1,000	1,000 to 5,000	5,000 to 10,000	10,000 to 25,000	25,000 to 50,000	50,000 to 100,000	100,000 to 250,000	250,000 to 500,000	500,000 to 2,500,000	2,500,000 and over
Number of Enterprises **1**	38641	3580	25090	2659	3047	844	768	540	602	699	347	348	115
Revenues ($ in Thousands)													
Net Sales **2**	531643055	63811552	9856581	6748165	5901420	2924214	4170578	3808242	4914810	11057655	10343131	34304733	373801972
Interest **3**	359448207	48797931	100136	25539	160295	304040	278964	707841	1601817	5287712	5682032	18753241	277748659
Rents **4**	932240	187361	0	0	4199	4194	1216	6638	11315	13946	16690	117434	569248
Royalties **5**	185407	0	0	0	0	0	0	106	6	12053	15	13356	159872
Other Portfolio Income **6**	11581680	1061448	1455	4555	66658	20294	24527	133651	91699	277285	224398	1415538	8260173
Other Receipts **7**	159495521	13764812	9754990	6718071	5670268	2595686	3865871	2960006	3209973	5466659	4419996	14005164	87064020
Total Receipts **8**	531643055	63811552	9856581	6748165	5901420	2924214	4170578	3808242	4914810	11057655	10343131	34304733	373801972
Average Total Receipts **9**	13759	17824	393	2538	1937	3465	5430	7052	8164	15819	29807	98577	3250452
Operating Costs/Operating Income (%)													
Cost of Operations **10**	1.1	0.0	13.0	15.5	15.0	6.5	9.3	6.6	3.1	1.1	1.4	1.8	0.3
Salaries and Wages **11**	8.5	5.6	25.2	50.1	22.6	31.4	27.2	18.2	18.9	15.3	15.1	14.2	6.0
Taxes Paid **12**	1.1	1.2	3.7	1.7	2.7	2.6	3.1	2.5	2.8	2.5	2.7	2.1	0.7
Interest Paid **13**	55.9	72.7	0.9	0.4	4.2	15.5	11.4	17.3	23.6	28.9	31.3	29.4	61.9
Depreciation **14**	1.1	0.8	0.6	0.5	1.2	0.9	1.2	1.0	1.8	1.7	1.9	1.7	1.1
Amortization and Depletion **15**	2.1	0.0	0.1	0.2	0.1	0.2	0.2	0.3	0.3	0.5	0.5	0.9	2.8
Pensions and Other Deferred Comp. **16**	0.5	0.2	0.1	0.4	0.3	0.1	0.5	0.6	0.8	0.8	1.1	0.8	0.5
Employee Benefits **17**	0.8	0.4	0.7	0.2	1.0	0.6	1.4	1.5	2.0	1.7	2.2	1.7	0.7
Advertising **18**	1.3	0.1	1.4	0.9	2.0	1.7	2.0	2.5	1.3	1.2	2.0	2.7	1.3
Other Expenses **19**	15.9	10.3	32.5	16.4	27.9	21.2	24.3	24.4	22.9	23.9	20.4	23.2	14.9
Officers' Compensation **20**	1.0	0.5	7.8	3.9	4.1	5.2	5.7	4.6	6.4	4.2	3.3	1.8	0.4
Operating Margin **21**	10.7	8.1	14.1	10.0	18.8	13.9	13.7	20.7	16.0	18.3	18.1	19.6	9.4
Operating Margin Before Officers' Comp. **22**	11.7	8.6	21.9	13.9	22.9	19.2	19.4	25.3	22.4	22.4	21.4	21.4	9.8

Selected Average Balance Sheet ($ in Thousands)

Net Receivables 23	16233	0	10	127	822	3299	6712	15786	32149	64189	106598	284138	3544497
Inventories 24	•	•	•	•	•	•	•	•	•	•	•	•	•
Net Property, Plant and Equipment 25	850	0	13	68	138	220	597	627	1474	3072	6470	14593	178822
Total Assets 26	111930	0	94	706	2223	7199	16099	36257	72779	157474	349761	1001371	31759447
Notes and Loans Payable 27	63548	0	22	223	812	3778	7320	9336	10432	17223	36099	205063	20311984
All Other Liabilities 28	40384	0	14	60	482	1572	5653	19387	51271	118428	270393	642590	9663207
Net Worth 29	7998	0	58	423	929	1849	3126	7533	11077	21822	43269	153718	1784256

Selected Financial Ratios (Times to 1)

Current Ratio 30	0.5	5.5	3.4	1.8	1.3	1.1	1.1	0.9	0.9	0.8	0.6	0.6	0.4
Quick Ratio 31	0.4	4.1	2.8	1.6	1.2	1.0	1.0	0.8	0.8	0.7	0.5	0.6	0.3
Net Sales to Working Capital 32	•	8.6	6.1	3.0	3.3	6.5	5.9	•	•	•	•	•	•
Coverage Ratio 33	1.2	16.5	29.1	5.5	1.9	2.2	6.5	5.9	2.2	1.6	1.5	1.6	1.1
Total Asset Turnover 34	0.1	4.2	3.6	0.9	0.5	0.3	0.2	0.2	0.1	0.1	0.1	0.1	0.1
Inventory Turnover 35	•	•	•	•	•	•	•	•	•	•	•	•	•
Receivables Turnover 36	•	•	•	•	•	•	•	•	•	•	•	•	•
Total Liabilities to Net Worth 37	13.0	0.6	0.7	1.4	2.9	4.2	3.8	5.6	6.2	7.1	7.1	5.5	16.8
Current Assets to Working Capital 38	•	1.2	1.4	2.2	4.2	11.7	20.4	•	•	•	•	•	•
Current Liabilities to Working Capital 39	•	0.2	0.4	1.2	3.2	10.7	19.4	•	•	•	•	•	•
Working Capital to Net Sales 40	•	0.1	0.2	0.3	0.3	0.2	0.2	•	•	•	•	•	•
Inventory to Working Capital 41	•	•	•	•	0.0	0.0	0.0	•	•	•	•	•	•
Total Receipts to Cash Flow 42	4.1	5.9	4.4	2.4	3.2	2.9	2.4	2.8	2.6	2.9	2.9	2.5	4.4
Cost of Goods to Cash Flow 43	0.0	0.3	0.7	0.4	0.2	0.3	0.2	0.0	0.0	0.0	0.0	0.0	0.0
Cash Flow to Total Debt 44	0.0	4.5	2.0	0.6	0.2	0.1	0.1	0.0	0.0	0.0	0.0	0.0	0.0

Selected Financial Factors (in Percentages)

Debt Ratio 45	92.9	38.3	40.1	58.2	74.3	80.6	79.2	84.8	86.1	87.6	84.6	84.6	94.4
Return on Total Assets 46	8.1	62.6	37.0	20.0	14.1	8.4	7.3	4.3	4.7	4.1	4.7	4.7	7.2
Return on Equity Before Income Taxes 47	17.5	95.4	59.6	39.3	26.0	23.5	19.0	11.1	12.6	11.9	12.6	12.1	16.3
Return on Equity After Income Taxes 48	12.5	93.6	58.4	37.9	24.2	21.4	16.6	9.5	10.1	8.7	8.7	8.6	10.7
Profit Margin (Before Income Tax) 49	10.2	14.1	9.9	18.8	13.9	13.5	20.3	15.1	17.4	17.2	18.8	18.8	8.9
Profit Margin (After Income Tax) 50	7.3	13.8	9.7	18.2	12.9	12.3	17.7	12.9	13.9	12.6	13.4	13.4	5.9

Table I

Corporations with and without Net Income

COMMERCIAL BANKING

MONEY AMOUNTS AND SIZE OF ASSETS IN THOUSANDS OF DOLLARS

Item Description for Accounting Period 7/06 Through 6/07	Total	Zero Assets	Under 500	500 to 1,000	1,000 to 5,000	5,000 to 10,000	10,000 to 25,000	25,000 to 50,000	50,000 to 100,000	100,000 to 250,000	250,000 to 500,000	500,000 to 2,500,000	2,500,000 and over
Number of Enterprises 1	1800	262	0	0	51	4	195	278	416	401	120	63	10
Revenues ($ in Thousands)													
Net Sales 2	96697359	79547830	0	0	94471	41385	299997	636075	1870547	4064278	2837872	4294079	3010825
Interest 3	75413888	64611294	0	0	2010	3919	120316	321197	1103588	2463465	1675485	2793655	2318957
Rents 4	352305	211762	0	0	2957	0	116	555	1649	4747	4454	19884	106180
Royalties 5	101	0	0	0	0	0	0	0	6	21	15	0	60
Other Portfolio Income 6	1728160	1109493	0	0	59	0	15273	46207	63888	84557	74688	113868	220127
Other Receipts 7	19202905	13615281	0	0	89445	37466	164292	268116	701416	1511488	1083230	1366672	365501
Total Receipts 8	96697359	79547830	0	0	94471	41385	299997	636075	1870547	4064278	2837872	4294079	3010825
Average Total Receipts 9	53721	303618	•	•	1852	10346	1538	2288	4497	10135	23649	68160	301082
Operating Costs/Operating Income (%)													
Cost of Operations 10	•	•	•	•	•	•	•	•	•	•	•	•	•
Salaries and Wages 11	6.9	5.7	•	•	14.6	•	16.0	12.8	13.9	14.1	12.9	13.8	7.4
Taxes Paid 12	1.5	1.3	•	•	1.7	•	2.8	2.8	2.9	2.7	2.7	2.6	2.8
Interest Paid 13	69.8	77.1	•	•	1.3	•	19.2	30.0	32.9	35.1	36.0	36.8	40.9
Depreciation 14	1.0	0.7	•	•	0.5	•	2.6	2.7	2.6	2.2	1.9	2.0	5.9
Amortization and Depletion 15	0.1	0.1	•	•	0.1	•	0.6	0.5	0.6	0.7	0.3	0.3	0.3
Pensions and Other Deferred Comp. 16	0.4	0.3	•	•	3.7	•	0.5	0.8	0.7	0.7	0.7	0.8	1.7
Employee Benefits 17	0.7	0.4	•	•	4.7	•	3.4	3.0	2.8	2.2	1.9	1.7	0.8
Advertising 18	0.3	0.1	•	•	5.9	•	0.9	1.3	1.1	1.0	0.9	0.7	0.7
Other Expenses 19	16.0	15.5	•	•	52.9	159.6	44.3	23.4	19.8	18.9	15.1	15.4	18.2
Officers' Compensation 20	1.4	0.5	•	•	7.1	•	9.9	11.5	9.0	6.1	5.4	2.5	4.2
Operating Margin 21	1.9	•	•	•	7.4	•	•	11.3	13.6	16.4	22.3	23.4	17.2
Operating Margin Before Officers' Comp. 22	3.3	•	•	•	14.5	•	9.6	22.8	22.6	22.5	27.7	26.0	21.4

Selected Average Balance Sheet ($ in Thousands)

Net Receivables 23	72059	690	0	9586	22187	43016	91187	217651	488903	1025398
Inventories 24	•	•	•	•	•	•	•	•	•	•
Net Property, Plant and Equipment 25	2124	1241	0	471	721	1409	2850	5419	13097	26306
Total Assets 26	145246	2847	7337	18340	36717	70950	150772	346991	918922	5797922
Notes and Loans Payable 27	6516	11	1970	207	626	1340	3968	14143	56834	407923
All Other Liabilities 28	122601	1614	110734	17362	29040	59938	128021	296474	768263	4844864
Net Worth 29	16130	1221	-105367	771	7051	9671	18783	36373	93825	545134

Selected Financial Ratios (Times to 1)

Current Ratio 30	0.9	1.1	0.1	1.1	1.1	1.0	1.0	0.9	0.9	0.6
Quick Ratio 31	0.9	1.1	0.1	1.1	1.1	1.0	0.9	0.9	0.9	0.6
Net Sales to Working Capital 32	1.0	14.6	•	0.8	0.7	4.3	1.4	•	•	•
Coverage Ratio 33	•	6.5	1.4	0.9	1.3	1.3	1.4	1.6	1.6	1.4
Total Asset Turnover 34	0.4	0.7	1.4	0.1	0.1	0.1	0.1	0.1	0.1	0.1
Inventory Turnover 35	•	•	•	•	•	•	•	•	•	•
Receivables Turnover 36	•	•	•	•	•	•	•	•	•	•
Total Liabilities to Net Worth 37	8.0	1.3	22.8	4.2	6.3	7.0	8.5	8.8	8.8	9.6
Current Assets to Working Capital 38	•	11.5	8.9	9.8	58.3	•	•	•	•	•
Current Liabilities to Working Capital 39	•	10.5	7.9	8.8	57.3	•	•	•	•	•
Working Capital to Net Sales 40	•	0.1	1.2	1.5	0.2	•	•	•	•	•
Inventory to Working Capital 41	•	•	•	•	•	•	•	•	•	•
Total Receipts to Cash Flow 42	6.9	1.7	2.7	3.8	3.4	3.1	2.9	2.8	2.8	3.3
Cost of Goods to Cash Flow 43	•	9.7	•	•	•	•	•	•	•	•
Cash Flow to Total Debt 44	0.1	0.7	0.0	0.0	0.0	0.0	0.0	0.0	0.0	0.0

Selected Financial Factors (in Percentages)

Debt Ratio 45	88.9	57.1	1536.1	95.8	80.8	86.4	87.5	89.5	89.8	90.6
Return on Total Assets 46	26.3	5.6	1.4	•	2.4	2.8	3.4	3.8	4.4	3.0
Return on Equity Before Income Taxes 47	4.8	11.1	5.9	•	2.9	5.4	8.0	13.2	15.9	8.8
Return on Equity After Income Taxes 48	•	8.6	5.9	•	2.1	4.1	6.2	10.2	11.6	5.9
Profit Margin (Before Income Tax) 49	1.4	7.3	•	•	8.8	11.5	14.9	20.3	21.9	16.0
Profit Margin (After Income Tax) 50	•	5.7	•	•	6.4	8.8	11.5	15.6	16.0	10.6

Table II

Corporations with Net Income

COMMERCIAL BANKING

MONEY AMOUNTS AND SIZE OF ASSETS IN THOUSANDS OF DOLLARS

Item Description for Accounting Period 7/06 Through 6/07		Total	Zero Assets	Under 500	500 to 1,000	1,000 to 5,000	5,000 to 10,000	10,000 to 25,000	25,000 to 50,000	50,000 to 100,000	100,000 to 250,000	250,000 to 500,000	500,000 to 2,500,000	2,500,000 and over
Number of Enterprises	1	1392	163	0	0	•	0	125	204	323	347	116	•	10
Revenues ($ in Thousands)														
Net Sales	2	77716131	61555943	0	0	•	0	236019	541587	1569388	3718001	2767964	•	3010825
Interest	3	57685887	47585471	0	0	•	0	80075	241693	884031	2218952	1614835	•	2318957
Rents	4	326567	186603	0	0	•	0	75	511	1379	4562	4418	•	106180
Royalties	5	101	0	0	0	•	0	0	0	6	21	15	•	60
Other Portfolio Income	6	1571282	979216	0	0	•	0	12917	43146	51376	78178	72453	•	220127
Other Receipts	7	18132294	12804653	0	0	•	0	142952	256237	632596	1416288	1076243	•	365501
Total Receipts	8	77716131	61555943	0	0	•	0	236019	541587	1569388	3718001	2767964	•	3010825
Average Total Receipts	9	55831	377644	•	•	•	•	1888	2655	4859	10715	23862	•	301082
Operating Costs/Operating Income (%)														
Cost of Operations	10	•	•	•	•	•	•	•	•	•	•	•	•	•
Salaries and Wages	11	6.8	5.5	•	•	•	•	14.4	10.6	12.7	13.2	13.0	•	7.4
Taxes Paid	12	1.5	1.1	•	•	•	•	2.7	2.7	2.9	2.7	2.7	•	2.8
Interest Paid	13	66.3	74.4	•	•	•	•	18.5	30.0	31.9	34.4	35.5	•	40.9
Depreciation	14	1.2	0.8	•	•	•	•	1.7	2.0	2.4	2.0	1.9	•	5.9
Amortization and Depletion	15	0.1	0.0	•	•	•	•	0.1	0.3	0.4	0.6	0.3	•	0.3
Pensions and Other Deferred Comp.	16	0.4	0.3	•	•	•	•	0.7	0.9	0.8	0.7	0.7	•	1.7
Employee Benefits	17	0.7	0.4	•	•	•	•	3.4	2.9	2.6	2.2	1.9	•	0.8
Advertising	18	0.3	0.1	•	•	•	•	0.6	0.8	0.9	0.9	0.9	•	0.7
Other Expenses	19	11.4	10.0	•	•	•	•	27.9	18.5	17.7	17.9	14.8	•	18.2
Officers' Compensation	20	1.4	0.5	•	•	•	•	9.0	10.0	8.5	6.0	5.2	•	4.2
Operating Margin	21	9.9	7.0	•	•	•	•	20.9	21.4	19.2	19.4	23.0	•	17.2
Operating Margin Before Officers' Comp.	22	11.3	7.4	•	•	•	•	29.9	31.4	27.8	25.4	28.3	•	21.4

Selected Average Balance Sheet ($ in Thousands)

Item								
Net Receivables 23	84941	0	10101	21669	44756	93347	218716	1025398
Inventories 24								
Net Property, Plant and Equipment 25	2354	0	227	551	1350	2803	5443	26306
Total Assets 26	173800	0	18307	37742	72412	153636	347674	5797922
Notes and Loans Payable 27	7968	0	177	802	1495	4087	13059	407923
All Other Liabilities 28	147166	0	15809	31492	62208	131077	299789	4844864
Net Worth 29	18666	0	2321	5448	8710	18473	34825	545134

Selected Financial Ratios (Times to 1)

Item								
Current Ratio 30	0.9		1.1	1.1	1.0	1.0	0.9	0.6
Quick Ratio 31	0.8		1.0	1.0	0.9	0.9	0.9	0.6
Net Sales to Working Capital 32			1.1	1.4	2.7	1.5		
Coverage Ratio 33	1.1		2.0	1.6	1.5	1.5	1.6	1.4
Total Asset Turnover 34	0.3		0.1	0.1	0.1	0.1	0.1	0.1
Inventory Turnover 35								
Receivables Turnover 36								
Total Liabilities to Net Worth 37	8.3		6.9	5.9	7.3	7.3	9.0	9.6
Current Assets to Working Capital 38	10.3		17.2	35.3				
Current Liabilities to Working Capital 39	9.3		16.2	34.3				
Working Capital to Net Sales 40	0.9		0.7	0.4				
Inventory to Working Capital 41								
Total Receipts to Cash Flow 42	5.2		2.4	3.1	3.0	2.9	2.8	3.3
Cost of Goods to Cash Flow 43	6.5							
Cash Flow to Total Debt 44	0.1		0.0	0.0	0.0	0.0	0.0	0.0

Selected Financial Factors (in Percentages)

Item								
Debt Ratio 45	89.3		87.3	85.6	88.0	88.0	90.0	90.6
Return on Total Assets 46	24.3		3.9	3.5	3.3	3.6	3.9	3.0
Return on Equity Before Income Taxes 47	27.8		15.8	9.3	9.6	10.3	14.4	8.8
Return on Equity After Income Taxes 48	21.1		13.6	7.9	7.7	8.2	11.1	5.9
Profit Margin (Before Income Tax) 49	9.3	6.7	19.4	19.1	17.1	17.8	21.0	16.0
Profit Margin (After Income Tax) 50	7.1	5.1	16.7	16.3	13.9	14.1	16.2	10.6

Table I

Corporations with and without Net Income

SAVINGS INSTITUTIONS AND OTHER DEPOSITORY CREDIT

MONEY AMOUNTS AND SIZE OF ASSETS IN THOUSANDS OF DOLLARS

Item Description for Accounting Period 7/06 Through 6/07		Total	Zero Assets	Under 500	500 to 1,000	1,000 to 5,000	5,000 to 10,000	10,000 to 25,000	25,000 to 50,000	50,000 to 100,000	100,000 to 250,000	250,000 to 500,000	500,000 to 2,500,000	2,500,000 and over
Number of Enterprises	1	1232	35	4	0	48	23	46	110	180	292	215	222	57
Revenues ($ in Thousands)														
Net Sales	2	101053423	1370538	55681	0	146596	35332	49269	263576	799806	3156023	4585601	14392165	76198834
Interest	3	70724168	790901	37595	0	68717	5151	39365	182019	655538	2400853	3745772	10550797	52247460
Rents	4	310742	622	0	0	222	3509	96	661	1657	8162	10149	69735	215929
Royalties	5	5012	0	0	0	0	0	22	22	0	0	0	4775	214
Other Portfolio Income	6	4997215	38532	0	0	6157	10595	1682	25978	22263	105429	139289	636044	4011247
Other Receipts	7	25016286	540483	18086	0	71500	16077	8126	54896	120348	641579	690391	3130814	19723984
Total Receipts	8	101053423	1370538	55681	0	146596	35332	49269	263576	799806	3156023	4585601	14392165	76198834
Average Total Receipts	9	82024	39158	13920	•	3054	1536	1071	2396	4443	10808	21328	64830	1336822
Operating Costs/Operating Income (%)														
Cost of Operations	10	0.2	•	•	•	•	•	8.7	•	0.2	0.0	•	1.1	0.0
Salaries and Wages	11	13.2	27.8	•	•	20.6	2.4	13.6	13.8	12.1	16.6	14.3	14.1	12.5
Taxes Paid	12	1.7	1.6	•	•	4.1	0.5	2.1	3.4	2.8	2.8	2.6	2.2	1.5
Interest Paid	13	46.5	41.8	21.8	•	18.4	217.4	117.3	34.5	42.9	39.4	43.3	43.2	47.8
Depreciation	14	1.6	1.3	•	•	1.4	16.6	0.8	1.9	2.0	2.0	2.0	2.7	1.3
Amortization and Depletion	15	0.8	0.3	•	•	0.1	0.5	0.0	0.1	0.1	0.2	0.2	0.4	1.0
Pensions and Other Deferred Comp.	16	1.3	0.3	•	•	1.1	0.0	1.5	2.0	1.7	1.9	1.5	1.3	1.2
Employee Benefits	17	2.0	1.5	•	•	2.0	0.3	2.2	2.8	2.5	2.3	2.6	2.1	1.9
Advertising	18	1.2	0.4	•	•	0.5	0.2	0.9	1.0	1.0	1.3	1.2	1.2	1.3
Other Expenses	19	15.5	76.8	64.5	•	43.8	33.4	21.2	18.7	17.8	19.2	14.5	15.8	14.1
Officers' Compensation	20	1.2	1.3	•	•	2.1	0.6	5.4	7.6	6.5	4.5	3.5	2.5	0.6
Operating Margin	21	14.9	•	13.7	•	5.9	•	•	14.4	10.3	9.8	14.3	13.4	16.8
Operating Margin Before Officers' Comp.	22	16.1	•	13.7	•	8.0	•	•	22.0	16.8	14.4	17.8	16.0	17.4

Selected Average Balance Sheet ($ in Thousands)

	1	2	3	4	5	6	7	8	9	10	11	12
Net Receivables 23	91923	0	0	96	2062	1513	2018	7708	19946	36605	83509	1390970
Inventories 24	•	•	•	•	•	•	•	•	•	•	•	•
Net Property, Plant and Equipment 25	12346	0	0	22	658	142	680	1375	3262	6363	14851	162240
Total Assets 26	1146591	0	206	2705	6841	16788	36935	73637	163153	352690	975871	18493163
Notes and Loans Payable 27	243301	0	27	84	1560	2180	1665	5573	13263	32017	114146	4602159
All Other Liabilities 28	847512	0	271637	12028	101552	11629	28372	57269	131278	274410	753703	13359948
Net Worth 29	55779	0	-271458	-9406	-96271	2978	6898	10795	18612	46263	108022	531057

Selected Financial Ratios (Times to 1)

	1	2	3	4	5	6	7	8	9	10	11	12
Current Ratio 30	0.2	0.1	•	6.9	0.0	0.3	0.3	0.3	0.3	0.3	0.3	0.2
Quick Ratio 31	0.2	0.1	•	6.7	0.0	0.3	0.3	0.3	0.3	0.3	0.2	0.1
Net Sales to Working Capital 32	•	•	•	2.0	•	•	•	•	•	•	•	•
Coverage Ratio 33	1.3	1.6	•	1.3	0.2	0.4	1.4	1.2	1.2	1.3	1.3	1.3
Total Asset Turnover 34	0.1	67.7	•	1.1	0.2	0.1	0.1	0.1	0.1	0.1	0.1	0.1
Inventory Turnover 35	•	•	•	•	•	•	•	•	•	•	•	•
Receivables Turnover 36	•	•	•	•	•	•	•	•	•	•	•	•
Total Liabilities to Net Worth 37	19.6	•	•	•	•	4.6	4.4	5.8	7.8	6.6	8.0	33.8
Current Assets to Working Capital 38	•	•	•	1.2	•	•	•	•	•	•	•	•
Current Liabilities to Working Capital 39	•	•	•	0.2	•	•	•	•	•	•	•	•
Working Capital to Net Sales 40	•	•	•	0.5	•	•	•	•	•	•	•	•
Inventory to Working Capital 41	•	•	•	•	•	•	•	•	•	•	•	•
Total Receipts to Cash Flow 42	3.9	5.0	1.3	2.6	•	4.1	4.0	4.0	3.9	3.8	4.0	3.9
Cost of Goods to Cash Flow 43	0.0	•	•	•	•	•	0.0	0.0	0.0	•	0.0	0.0
Cash Flow to Total Debt 44	0.0	0.0	0.0	0.1	0.0	•	0.0	0.0	0.0	0.0	0.0	0.0

Selected Financial Factors (in Percentages)

	1	2	3	4	5	6	7	8	9	10	11	12
Debt Ratio 45	95.1	132196.6	•	447.7	1507.2	82.3	81.3	85.3	88.6	86.9	88.9	97.1
Return on Total Assets 46	4.4	2401.3	•	27.5	10.2	2.8	3.1	3.1	3.2	3.4	3.7	4.6
Return on Equity Before Income Taxes 47	21.3	•	•	•	2.7	•	4.5	3.8	5.1	6.1	7.6	41.7
Return on Equity After Income Taxes 48	13.5	•	•	•	2.8	•	3.0	2.5	3.1	4.2	4.9	27.4
Profit Margin (Before Income Tax) 49	14.5	13.7	•	5.9	•	•	12.9	9.2	8.8	13.2	12.7	16.6
Profit Margin (After Income Tax) 50	9.2	13.7	•	0.9	•	•	8.6	6.0	5.3	9.1	8.2	10.9

Table II

Corporations with Net Income

SAVINGS INSTITUTIONS AND OTHER DEPOSITORY CREDIT

MONEY AMOUNTS AND SIZE OF ASSETS IN THOUSANDS OF DOLLARS

Item Description for Accounting Period 7/06 Through 6/07	Total	Zero Assets	Under 500	500 to 1,000	1,000 to 5,000	5,000 to 10,000	10,000 to 25,000	25,000 to 50,000	50,000 to 100,000	100,000 to 250,000	250,000 to 500,000	500,000 to 2,500,000	2,500,000 and over
Number of Enterprises 1	1014	11	•	0	15	10	40	72	148	257	202	•	54
Revenues ($ in Thousands)													
Net Sales 2	94928967	597790	•	0	98871	18646	42658	194595	669221	2812804	4359062	•	72943429
Interest 3	66847869	117258	•	0	68189	2901	33057	129134	548150	2124617	3558375	•	50281500
Rents 4	296985	134	•	0	222	3509	96	367	1255	7245	9728	•	205846
Royalties 5	5009	0	•	0	0	0	0	22	0	0	0	•	211
Other Portfolio Income 6	4718506	30674	•	0	6157	10508	1682	23481	19547	86542	132367	•	3834481
Other Receipts 7	23060598	449724	•	0	24303	1728	7823	41591	100269	594400	658592	•	18621391
Total Receipts 8	94928967	597790	•	0	98871	18646	42658	194595	669221	2812804	4359062	•	72943429
Average Total Receipts 9	93618	54345	•	•	6591	1865	1066	2703	4522	10945	21580	•	1350804
Operating Costs/Operating Income (%)													
Cost of Operations 10	0.2	•	•	•	•	•	10.0	•	0.3	0.0	•	•	0.0
Salaries and Wages 11	12.8	9.5	•	•	10.1	2.2	13.8	13.1	11.5	16.4	14.2	•	12.5
Taxes Paid 12	1.6	0.8	•	•	4.3	0.5	2.1	3.1	2.8	2.8	2.6	•	1.4
Interest Paid 13	46.0	26.2	•	•	27.2	9.9	42.7	31.4	42.2	38.7	42.6	•	47.4
Depreciation 14	1.4	1.1	•	•	1.8	31.3	0.8	1.8	1.9	2.0	2.0	•	1.3
Amortization and Depletion 15	0.8	0.0	•	•	0.1	•	0.0	0.0	0.1	0.1	0.2	•	0.9
Pensions and Other Deferred Comp. 16	1.3	0.2	•	•	1.6	•	1.6	1.5	1.7	1.8	1.5	•	1.3
Employee Benefits 17	2.0	0.7	•	•	•	•	2.3	2.5	2.4	2.3	2.6	•	1.9
Advertising 18	1.2	0.3	•	•	0.7	0.1	0.9	0.9	0.9	1.2	1.2	•	1.3
Other Expenses 19	13.8	11.7	•	•	31.1	4.5	10.7	17.1	15.6	16.2	14.4	•	13.5
Officers' Compensation 20	1.1	0.6	•	•	1.0	•	4.9	7.2	6.6	4.5	3.5	•	0.6
Operating Margin 21	17.6	48.9	•	•	22.1	51.6	10.3	21.4	14.2	14.2	15.2	•	17.8
Operating Margin Before Officers' Comp. 22	18.7	49.5	•	•	23.1	51.6	15.2	28.6	20.8	18.6	18.7	•	18.4

Selected Average Balance Sheet ($ in Thousands)

Net Receivables 23	108069	0	8	-14	1657	2190	7896	20635	35686	•	1447140
Inventories 24	•	•	•	•	•	•	•	•	•	•	•
Net Property, Plant and Equipment 25	14098	0	1	1457	153	594	1292	3209	6492	•	163723
Total Assets 26	1312787	0	3490	6854	16490	37414	74294	163474	351557	•	18643349
Notes and Loans Payable 27	275840	0	4	0	2460	1322	5337	13713	31748	•	4549820
All Other Liabilities 28	973222	0	325	4666	11156	29712	58336	129458	276815	•	13585335
Net Worth 29	63725	0	3160	2188	2874	6380	10621	20302	42995	•	508194

Selected Financial Ratios (Times to 1)

Current Ratio 30	0.2	•	5.0	0.1	0.3	0.3	0.3	0.3	0.3	•	0.2
Quick Ratio 31	0.2	•	4.8	0.1	0.3	0.3	0.3	0.3	0.3	•	0.1
Net Sales to Working Capital 32	•	•	5.1	•	•	•	•	•	•	•	•
Coverage Ratio 33	1.4	2.9	1.8	6.2	1.2	1.7	1.3	1.3	1.3	•	1.4
Total Asset Turnover 34	0.1	•	1.9	0.3	0.1	0.1	0.1	0.1	0.1	•	0.1
Inventory Turnover 35	•	•	•	•	•	•	•	•	•	•	•
Receivables Turnover 36	•	•	•	•	•	•	•	•	•	•	•
Total Liabilities to Net Worth 37	19.6	•	0.1	2.1	4.7	4.9	6.0	7.1	7.2	•	35.7
Current Assets to Working Capital 38	•	•	1.3	•	•	•	•	•	•	•	•
Current Liabilities to Working Capital 39	•	•	0.3	•	•	•	•	•	•	•	•
Working Capital to Net Sales 40	•	•	0.2	•	•	•	•	•	•	•	•
Inventory to Working Capital 41	•	•	•	•	•	•	•	•	•	•	•
Total Receipts to Cash Flow 42	3.7	1.7	2.3	6.1	3.7	3.7	3.7	3.7	3.7	•	3.8
Cost of Goods to Cash Flow 43	0.0	•	•	0.6	0.0	0.0	0.0	0.0	0.0	•	0.0
Cash Flow to Total Debt 44	0.0	•	8.8	0.0	0.0	0.0	0.0	0.0	0.0	•	0.0

Selected Financial Factors (in Percentages)

Debt Ratio 45	95.1	•	9.4	68.1	82.6	82.9	85.7	87.6	87.8	•	97.3
Return on Total Assets 46	4.5	•	93.1	16.7	3.4	3.7	3.4	3.5	3.5	•	4.7
Return on Equity Before Income Taxes 47	25.3	•	46.0	44.0	3.7	8.7	5.6	7.1	7.1	•	46.6
Return on Equity After Income Taxes 48	17.1	•	30.5	42.9	2.8	6.3	4.0	5.0	5.0	•	30.8
Profit Margin (Before Income Tax) 49	17.2	48.6	22.1	51.6	9.9	20.5	13.2	13.1	14.2	•	17.5
Profit Margin (After Income Tax) 50	11.6	47.0	14.6	50.4	7.4	14.8	9.4	9.2	9.9	•	11.6

Table I

Corporations with and without Net Income

CREDIT CARD ISSUING AND OTHER CONSUMER CREDIT

MONEY AMOUNTS AND SIZE OF ASSETS IN THOUSANDS OF DOLLARS

Item Description for Accounting Period 7/06 Through 6/07	Total	Zero Assets	Under 500	500 to 1,000	1,000 to 5,000	5,000 to 10,000	10,000 to 25,000	25,000 to 50,000	50,000 to 100,000	100,000 to 250,000	250,000 to 500,000	500,000 to 2,500,000	2,500,000 and over
Number of Enterprises **1**	9183	626	4760	1194	1643	466	222	106	47	42	20	40	17
Revenues ($ in Thousands)													
Net Sales **2**	83976625	364382	593800	1224052	2054897	1159734	1245741	1173915	704782	2700666	2144135	9094675	61515847
Interest **3**	26789230	240846	46827	625	75625	124921	75484	217802	42061	989199	478228	4118824	20378789
Rents **4**	31662	0	0	0	351	189	580	516	461	775	22095	2483	4212
Royalties **5**	20385	0	0	0	0	0	0	0	0	11804	0	8580	0
Other Portfolio Income **6**	1601661	1366	356	0	29064	2850	2845	43183	1952	53855	136932	198061	1131194
Other Receipts **7**	55533687	122170	546617	1223427	1949857	1031774	1166832	912414	660308	1645033	1506880	4766727	40001652
Total Receipts **8**	83976625	364382	593800	1224052	2054897	1159734	1245741	1173915	704782	2700666	2144135	9094675	61515847
Average Total Receipts **9**	9145	582	125	1025	1251	2489	5611	11075	14995	64302	107207	227367	3618579
Operating Costs/Operating Income (%)													
Cost of Operations **10**	0.4	•	•	•	•	•	0.4	0.1	1.1	0.5	0.2	0.6	0.3
Salaries and Wages **11**	9.4	22.1	14.5	26.1	13.8	17.0	19.8	16.5	16.0	12.6	14.9	12.6	7.5
Taxes Paid **12**	1.3	0.4	1.7	1.9	2.3	2.3	2.4	2.3	2.3	2.3	2.6	1.5	1.1
Interest Paid **13**	26.0	4.1	10.2	6.0	8.5	15.0	13.8	15.8	19.8	29.7	25.4	20.1	28.6
Depreciation **14**	8.0	0.0	1.9	4.2	1.3	2.7	2.8	1.7	1.9	1.1	3.0	1.5	10.3
Amortization and Depletion **15**	1.0	•	0.1	0.0	0.4	0.4	0.1	0.3	0.2	0.7	0.8	1.0	1.1
Pensions and Other Deferred Comp. **16**	0.4	0.0	•	0.0	0.4	0.2	0.9	0.7	1.0	0.1	0.2	0.2	0.5
Employee Benefits **17**	0.7	0.1	0.3	0.0	0.7	0.7	1.3	1.2	1.2	0.8	1.9	1.0	0.5
Advertising **18**	3.4	0.1	4.0	6.4	5.8	2.1	1.5	2.3	2.8	1.6	1.3	2.9	3.7
Other Expenses **19**	39.6	31.0	80.3	47.6	41.7	45.7	36.0	35.2	27.5	33.0	37.2	46.3	38.5
Officers' Compensation **20**	0.9	0.0	0.9	0.1	5.2	7.2	7.6	3.5	9.2	2.4	1.0	1.6	0.3
Operating Margin **21**	8.8	42.2	•	7.6	17.5	6.7	13.4	20.4	17.0	15.2	11.5	10.5	7.6
Operating Margin Before Officers' Comp. **22**	9.8	42.2	•	7.7	22.7	13.9	21.0	24.0	26.2	17.6	12.5	12.2	7.9

Selected Average Balance Sheet ($ in Thousands)

Net Receivables 23	33221	0	51	1054	1224	5032	11920	24164	51922	96626	211774	711243	14989453
Inventories 24	•	•	•	•	•	•	•	•	•	•	•	•	•
Net Property, Plant and Equipment 25	2793	0	14	171	51	237	909	817	1848	3526	4807	7432	1427282
Total Assets 26	56262	0	151	631	2203	7108	15274	34529	71041	161112	379528	1123956	25796418
Notes and Loans Payable 27	33433	0	107	283	1009	3863	9769	21014	41300	92903	269666	594301	15488870
All Other Liabilities 28	14775	0	27	60	258	1468	2423	4704	11204	23964	63158	305880	6955044
Net Worth 29	8053	0	18	287	937	1777	3082	8810	18537	44245	46703	223775	3348504

Selected Financial Ratios (Times to 1)

Current Ratio 30	1.7	•	4.1	7.2	2.3	2.8	2.1	2.6	2.2	2.4	1.7	1.6	1.7
Quick Ratio 31	1.6	•	2.8	6.3	2.1	2.5	2.0	2.3	2.1	2.0	1.4	1.5	1.6
Net Sales to Working Capital 32	0.6	•	1.4	0.9	1.3	0.6	0.8	0.6	0.5	0.9	1.0	0.7	0.5
Coverage Ratio 33	1.3	11.3	•	2.3	3.1	1.4	2.0	2.3	1.9	1.5	1.5	1.4	1.3
Total Asset Turnover 34	0.2	•	0.8	1.6	0.6	0.4	0.4	0.3	0.2	0.4	0.3	0.2	0.1
Inventory Turnover 35	•	•	•	•	•	•	•	•	•	•	•	•	•
Receivables Turnover 36	•	•	•	•	•	•	•	•	•	•	•	•	•
Total Liabilities to Net Worth 37	6.0	•	7.6	1.2	1.4	3.0	4.0	2.9	2.8	2.6	7.1	4.0	6.7
Current Assets to Working Capital 38	2.4	•	1.3	1.2	1.8	1.6	1.9	1.6	1.8	1.7	2.5	2.7	2.5
Current Liabilities to Working Capital 39	1.4	•	0.3	0.2	0.8	0.6	0.9	0.6	0.8	0.7	1.5	1.7	1.5
Working Capital to Net Sales 40	1.8	•	0.7	1.1	0.8	1.6	1.2	1.6	2.1	1.1	1.0	1.4	2.0
Inventory to Working Capital 41	0.0	•	•	•	•	•	0.0	0.0	•	0.0	0.0	0.0	0.0
Total Receipts to Cash Flow 42	2.2	1.4	1.6	2.2	1.8	2.1	2.2	1.9	2.3	2.3	1.8	1.8	2.2
Cost of Goods to Cash Flow 43	0.0	•	•	0.0	•	•	0.0	0.0	0.0	0.0	0.0	0.0	0.0
Cash Flow to Total Debt 44	0.1	•	0.6	1.3	0.5	0.2	0.2	0.2	0.1	0.2	0.1	0.1	0.1

Selected Financial Factors (in Percentages)

Debt Ratio 45	85.7	•	88.3	54.4	57.5	75.0	79.8	74.5	73.9	72.5	87.7	80.1	87.0
Return on Total Assets 46	5.7	•	•	22.0	14.7	7.5	10.0	11.6	7.8	17.9	10.4	5.8	5.2
Return on Equity Before Income Taxes 47	10.2	•	•	27.0	23.3	9.2	24.3	25.6	13.7	22.1	26.3	8.8	8.7
Return on Equity After Income Taxes 48	6.8	•	•	26.3	22.7	7.8	21.3	21.9	12.5	18.3	14.1	5.3	5.5
Profit Margin (Before Income Tax) 49	9.0	42.2	•	7.6	17.5	6.6	13.3	20.3	17.0	15.2	11.5	8.6	8.1
Profit Margin (After Income Tax) 50	6.0	20.3	•	7.4	17.0	5.5	11.7	17.4	15.5	12.6	6.1	5.3	5.1

Table II

Corporations with Net Income

CREDIT CARD ISSUING AND OTHER CONSUMER CREDIT

MONEY AMOUNTS AND SIZE OF ASSETS IN THOUSANDS OF DOLLARS

Item Description for Accounting Period 7/06 Through 6/07	Total	Zero Assets	Under 500	500 to 1,000	1,000 to 5,000	5,000 to 10,000	10,000 to 25,000	25,000 to 50,000	50,000 to 100,000	100,000 to 250,000	250,000 to 500,000	500,000 to 2,500,000	2,500,000 and over
Number of Enterprises **1**	4728	3	1945	686	1358	344	182	82	43	33	13	29	10
Revenues ($ in Thousands)													
Net Sales **2**	68085919	247739	443983	376187	1657839	783185	1034393	1068855	664487	2240220	1714016	6818956	51036060
Interest **3**	24014414	231215	46615	1	57027	92907	72832	197545	34174	618919	314057	3527910	18821211
Rents **4**	8700	0	0	0	319	0	207	404	461	775	44	2279	4212
Royalties **5**	20385	0	0	0	0	0	0	0	0	11804	0	8580	0
Other Portfolio Income **6**	1354278	1366	356	0	28977	2717	2845	42388	1952	53208	14490	188236	1017747
Other Receipts **7**	42688142	15158	397012	376186	1571516	687561	958509	828518	627900	1555514	1385425	3091951	3192890
Total Receipts **8**	68085919	247739	443983	376187	1657839	783185	1034393	1068855	664487	2240220	1714016	6818956	51036060
Average Total Receipts **9**	14401	82580	228	548	1221	2277	5683	13035	15453	67885	131847	235136	5103606
Operating Costs/Operating Income (%)													
Cost of Operations **10**	0.3	•	•	•	3.0	•	0.5	0.1	•	0.6	0.2	0.9	0.2
Salaries and Wages **11**	9.7	0.1	0.2	16.5	15.2	19.5	18.8	16.2	15.2	13.5	17.9	11.3	8.3
Taxes Paid **12**	1.4	0.0	0.1	3.6	2.5	2.2	2.4	2.3	2.3	2.6	3.2	1.5	1.2
Interest Paid **13**	22.9	1.8	10.6	2.0	8.0	16.8	13.6	13.5	19.7	20.6	9.6	18.3	25.4
Depreciation **14**	3.5	0.0	0.2	0.1	1.5	1.5	2.0	0.6	1.9	1.1	2.0	1.7	4.1
Amortization and Depletion **15**	1.2	•	0.0	0.1	0.3	0.5	0.1	0.3	0.2	0.7	0.6	0.9	1.3
Pensions and Other Deferred Comp. **16**	0.4	0.0	•	0.1	0.4	0.2	0.6	0.7	1.0	0.1	0.2	0.2	0.5
Employee Benefits **17**	0.7	0.0	0.0	0.1	0.7	0.7	1.1	1.3	1.2	0.8	2.4	0.7	0.6
Advertising **18**	3.9	•	0.4	1.2	2.6	1.1	1.5	2.4	3.0	1.6	1.6	3.7	4.3
Other Expenses **19**	41.9	0.1	83.3	27.7	32.2	28.4	32.6	34.9	25.2	34.5	36.4	40.6	43.7
Officers' Compensation **20**	0.9	•	0.0	0.0	6.1	6.4	8.3	2.8	8.9	2.6	1.1	1.4	0.2
Operating Margin **21**	13.2	98.0	5.3	48.5	27.3	22.8	18.6	24.8	21.5	21.2	24.7	18.8	10.1
Operating Margin Before Officers' Comp. **22**	14.2	98.0	5.3	48.5	33.5	29.2	26.9	27.7	30.4	23.8	25.8	20.2	10.3

Selected Average Balance Sheet ($ in Thousands)

Item													
Net Receivables 23	46430	0	7	390	1415	6067	12105	24749	51365	94906	206108	783642	18025579
Inventories 24	•	•	•	•	•	•	•	•	•	•	•	•	•
Net Property, Plant and Equipment 25	1623	0	2	2	34	115	830	499	1970	3680	7027	7983	686313
Total Assets 26	80088	0	152	646	2203	7224	15176	33915	71420	157644	358958	1112372	32169788
Notes and Loans Payable 27	45184	0	66	202	887	3804	9737	19872	40362	85055	155978	546986	18501536
All Other Liabilities 28	20872	0	14	46	269	1537	2135	4372	12001	24116	86682	289003	8616362
Net Worth 29	14031	0	71	398	1047	1883	3304	9671	19057	48473	116298	276383	5051890

Selected Financial Ratios (Times to 1)

Item													
Current Ratio 30	1.6	•	41.2	4.8	2.5	3.3	2.3	3.2	2.1	2.2	1.6	1.8	1.6
Quick Ratio 31	1.6	•	13.2	3.5	2.4	3.0	2.2	2.8	2.0	1.8	1.5	1.7	1.5
Net Sales to Working Capital 32	0.7	•	1.9	1.1	1.2	0.5	0.7	0.6	0.5	1.0	1.6	0.6	0.6
Coverage Ratio 33	1.6	55.5	1.5	25.0	4.4	2.3	2.4	2.8	2.1	2.0	3.6	1.9	1.4
Total Asset Turnover 34	0.2	•	1.5	0.8	0.6	0.3	0.4	0.4	0.2	0.4	0.4	0.2	0.2
Inventory Turnover 35	•	•	•	•	•	•	•	•	•	•	•	•	•
Receivables Turnover 36	•	•	•	•	•	•	•	•	•	•	•	•	•
Total Liabilities to Net Worth 37	4.7	1.1	1.1	0.6	1.1	2.8	3.6	2.5	2.7	2.3	2.1	3.0	5.4
Current Assets to Working Capital 38	2.6	1.0	1.0	1.3	1.7	1.4	1.7	1.5	1.9	1.8	2.8	2.2	2.8
Current Liabilities to Working Capital 39	1.6	0.0	0.0	0.3	0.7	0.4	0.7	0.5	0.9	0.8	1.8	1.2	1.8
Working Capital to Net Sales 40	1.5	0.5	0.5	0.9	0.9	2.1	1.4	1.6	2.0	1.0	0.6	1.7	1.6
Inventory to Working Capital 41	0.0	•	•	•	0.0	0.0	0.0	0.0	•	0.0	0.0	0.0	0.0
Total Receipts to Cash Flow 42	1.9	1.0	1.1	1.3	1.8	2.1	2.1	1.8	2.2	2.0	1.8	1.7	1.9
Cost of Goods to Cash Flow 43	0.0	•	•	•	0.0	0.0	0.0	0.0	•	0.0	0.0	0.0	0.0
Cash Flow to Total Debt 44	0.1	•	2.5	1.6	0.6	0.2	0.2	0.3	0.1	0.3	0.3	0.2	0.1

Selected Financial Factors (in Percentages)

Item													
Debt Ratio 45	82.5	•	53.2	38.4	52.5	73.9	78.2	71.5	73.3	69.3	67.6	75.2	84.3
Return on Total Assets 46	6.5	•	23.7	42.9	19.6	12.4	12.1	14.7	8.9	18.0	12.6	7.3	5.7
Return on Equity Before Income Taxes 47	13.8	•	16.8	66.8	31.9	27.3	32.0	33.3	17.4	29.7	28.0	13.9	10.8
Return on Equity After Income Taxes 48	10.0	•	15.7	65.9	31.2	25.4	28.6	29.0	16.1	25.2	20.4	10.0	7.2
Profit Margin (Before Income Tax) 49	13.4	98.0	5.2	48.5	27.3	22.6	18.6	24.7	21.4	21.2	24.7	16.3	10.7
Profit Margin (After Income Tax) 50	9.8	65.8	4.9	47.8	26.7	21.0	16.6	21.6	19.9	18.0	18.0	11.8	7.1

Table I

Corporations with and without Net Income

REAL ESTATE CREDIT INCL. MORTGAGE BANKERS AND ORIGINATORS

MONEY AMOUNTS AND SIZE OF ASSETS IN THOUSANDS OF DOLLARS

Item Description for Accounting Period 7/06 Through 6/07		Total	Zero Assets	Under 500	500 to 1,000	1,000 to 5,000	5,000 to 10,000	10,000 to 25,000	25,000 to 50,000	50,000 to 100,000	100,000 to 250,000	250,000 to 500,000	500,000 to 2,500,000	2,500,000 and over
Number of Enterprises	1	14338	1930	8282	1456	1513	502	351	149	62	40	13	28	12
Revenues ($ in Thousands)														
Net Sales	2	56211072	321557	3306581	4392931	2608477	2572321	3141687	1647265	1450173	1275730	887805	4303389	30303156
Interest	3	19169869	61765	5218	6199	30333	227224	77530	90062	206240	147229	137335	1458251	16722481
Rents	4	40408	0	0	0	639	677	946	6916	6613	303	2486	9335	12494
Royalties	5	223	0	0	0	0	0	0	0	0	223	0	0	0
Other Portfolio Income	6	1621340	7409	1273	4555	14945	10997	11668	24560	13444	54683	5070	356276	1116458
Other Receipts	7	35379232	252383	3300090	4382177	2562560	2333423	3051543	1525727	1223876	1073292	742914	2479527	12451723
Total Receipts	8	56211072	321557	3306581	4392931	2608477	2572321	3141687	1647265	1450173	1275730	887805	4303389	30303156
Average Total Receipts	9	3920	167	399	3017	1724	5124	8951	11055	23390	31893	68293	153692	2525263
Operating Costs/Operating Income (%)														
Cost of Operations	10	3.3	4.0	7.6	0.0	5.2	4.2	6.8	5.8	4.9	7.9	15.6	2.6	2.0
Salaries and Wages	11	28.2	29.6	28.3	71.0	41.3	36.1	44.4	33.2	31.5	32.3	21.1	21.1	19.0
Taxes Paid	12	2.7	5.4	5.4	1.6	3.7	2.9	5.2	3.2	3.3	3.1	2.5	2.7	2.2
Interest Paid	13	28.7	22.3	0.5	0.3	6.1	12.9	7.9	14.0	19.2	20.8	21.3	27.6	43.4
Depreciation	14	1.2	1.3	0.3	0.5	1.4	0.3	0.7	1.1	1.2	0.8	0.9	1.6	1.4
Amortization and Depletion	15	1.4	3.4	0.0	0.1	0.0	0.1	0.2	0.4	0.1	0.1	0.6	1.4	2.2
Pensions and Other Deferred Comp.	16	0.3	0.3	0.1	0.3	0.4	0.4	0.3	0.2	0.4	1.1	0.2	0.4	0.3
Employee Benefits	17	1.4	•	1.2	0.2	1.5	0.7	1.4	1.4	1.4	1.4	1.4	1.6	1.7
Advertising	18	2.1	7.5	2.3	0.8	2.7	3.8	3.7	6.8	1.8	1.8	1.9	4.3	1.3
Other Expenses	19	25.0	50.3	35.2	18.0	30.3	28.5	23.2	27.9	34.6	27.7	29.1	29.0	22.7
Officers' Compensation	20	2.2	6.1	7.4	3.3	6.0	4.2	3.1	3.2	4.1	3.2	2.0	2.8	0.6
Operating Margin	21	3.5	•	11.7	3.9	1.3	5.7	3.1	2.9	•	•	3.4	5.0	3.1
Operating Margin Before Officers' Comp.	22	5.7	•	19.1	7.2	7.4	9.9	6.2	6.1	1.7	3.0	5.4	7.8	3.7

Selected Average Balance Sheet ($ in Thousands)

Net Receivables 23	2104	0	2	32	308	1055	3543	6236	7709	36682	81278	202382	1522056
Inventories 24	•	•	•	•	•	•	•	•	•	•	•	•	•
Net Property, Plant and Equipment 25	291	0	7	57	275	317	524	728	1812	1816	4696	13390	212006
Total Assets 26	23301	80	677	2289	7474	15868	33738	71498	165664	324647	1049194		22498120
Notes and Loans Payable 27	9843	18	137	1206	4372	9786	18504	34463	92019	161510	643855		8718438
All Other Liabilities 28	11184	9	97	530	1348	3379	8976	27461	66078	129395	276635		11863424
Net Worth 29	2275	0	53	442	553	1754	2703	6258	9574	7567	33742	128704	1916258

Selected Financial Ratios (Times to 1)

Current Ratio 30	0.5	3.0	2.8	0.8	0.6	0.7	0.6	0.6	0.5	0.5	0.6	0.6	0.4
Quick Ratio 31	0.3	2.3	1.8	0.6	0.5	0.5	0.4	0.4	0.4	0.4	0.5	0.5	0.3
Net Sales to Working Capital 32	•	12.9	10.9	•	•	•	•	•	•	•	•	•	•
Coverage Ratio 33	1.1	26.5	15.0	1.2	1.4	1.4	1.2	0.9	1.0	1.2	1.2	1.2	1.1
Total Asset Turnover 34	0.2	5.0	4.5	0.8	0.7	0.6	0.3	0.3	0.3	0.2	0.2	0.1	0.1
Inventory Turnover 35	•	•	•	•	•	•	•	•	•	•	•	•	•
Receivables Turnover 36	•	•	•	•	•	•	•	•	•	•	•	•	•
Total Liabilities to Net Worth 37	9.2	0.5	0.5	3.1	3.3	4.9	4.4	6.5	20.9	8.6	7.2		10.7
Current Assets to Working Capital 38	•	1.5	1.6	•	•	•	•	•	•	•	•	•	•
Current Liabilities to Working Capital 39	•	0.5	0.6	•	•	•	•	•	•	•	•	•	•
Working Capital to Net Sales 40	•	0.1	0.1	•	•	•	•	•	•	•	•	•	•
Inventory to Working Capital 41	•	•	•	•	•	•	•	•	•	•	•	•	•
Total Receipts to Cash Flow 42	4.1	7.9	2.4	5.1	3.3	4.8	3.9	3.6	3.6	4.4	3.4		4.4
Cost of Goods to Cash Flow 43	0.1	0.3	0.2	0.0	0.1	0.3	0.2	0.2	0.3	0.4	0.6		0.1
Cash Flow to Total Debt 44	0.0	6.1	2.5	0.3	0.3	0.1	0.0	0.1	0.1	0.1	0.0		0.0

Selected Financial Factors (in Percentages)

Debt Ratio 45	90.2	33.9	34.7	75.8	76.5	83.0	81.5	86.6	95.4	89.6	87.7		91.5
Return on Total Assets 46	5.4	60.7	18.0	5.6	12.7	6.2	5.5	5.4	3.9	5.2	4.8		5.2
Return on Equity Before Income Taxes 47	6.0	88.3	25.8	4.1	16.2	10.4	5.0	•	•	6.6	5.9		4.2
Return on Equity After Income Taxes 48	2.6	87.2	24.2	3.8	14.7	9.3	4.6	•	•	5.9	0.6		0.6
Profit Margin (Before Income Tax) 49	3.5	11.7	3.8	1.3	5.5	3.1	2.8	•	•	3.3	4.9		3.2
Profit Margin (After Income Tax) 50	1.5	11.5	3.5	1.2	2.8	2.6	2.9	3.3	4.9	4.9	5.9	3.2	0.4

Table II

Corporations with Net Income

REAL ESTATE CREDIT INCL. MORTGAGE BANKERS AND ORIGINATORS

MONEY AMOUNTS AND SIZE OF ASSETS IN THOUSANDS OF DOLLARS

Item Description for Accounting Period 7/06 Through 6/07		Total	Zero Assets	Under 500	500 to 1,000	1,000 to 5,000	5,000 to 10,000	10,000 to 25,000	25,000 to 50,000	50,000 to 100,000	100,000 to 250,000	250,000 to 500,000	500,000 to 2,500,000	2,500,000 and over
Number of Enterprises	1	8646	437	5796	763	858	345	260	90	41	26	8	16	6
Revenues ($ in Thousands)														
Net Sales	2	41804193	132005	2852194	4085047	1245533	1629669	1651507	851437	871872	726515	673058	3210569	23874787
Interest	3	15173595	1268	2720	4197	15179	199344	72643	37946	92129	118757	72674	731428	13825310
Rents	4	35167	0	0	0	241	106	722	4712	6533	303	2486	8902	11162
Royalties	5	223	0	0	0	0	0	0	0	0	223	0	0	0
Other Portfolio Income	6	527235	0	1099	4555	12312	6387	4980	21110	9248	54577	5070	314030	93867
Other Receipts	7	26067973	130737	2848375	4076295	1217801	1423832	1573162	787669	763962	552655	592828	2156209	9944448
Total Receipts	8	41804193	132005	2852194	4085047	1245533	1629669	1651507	851437	871872	726515	673058	3210569	23874787
Average Total Receipts	9	4835	302	492	5354	1452	4724	6352	9460	21265	27943	84132	200661	3979131
Operating Costs/Operating Income (%)														
Cost of Operations	10	3.4	•	7.5	0.0	6.9	4.4	11.8	7.6	4.6	6.0	20.5	3.4	1.9
Salaries and Wages	11	26.1	9.0	28.4	74.2	35.4	38.6	34.5	27.6	30.7	27.1	19.4	19.9	16.6
Taxes Paid	12	2.4	2.4	5.8	1.4	3.0	3.0	3.8	2.3	3.3	2.3	2.2	2.8	1.9
Interest Paid	13	28.7	2.1	0.2	0.1	4.9	17.8	11.3	16.6	15.5	23.3	18.6	14.8	43.5
Depreciation	14	0.8	0.1	0.2	0.4	1.3	0.3	0.8	0.6	1.2	0.7	0.8	1.5	0.9
Amortization and Depletion	15	1.4	0.2	0.0	•	0.1	0.0	0.1	0.4	0.1	0.2	0.7	1.5	2.2
Pensions and Other Deferred Comp.	16	0.2	0.0	0.1	0.2	0.3	0.1	0.4	0.2	0.4	0.4	0.2	0.5	0.1
Employee Benefits	17	1.3	•	1.3	0.1	1.1	0.6	1.4	0.8	1.5	1.1	1.3	1.6	1.5
Advertising	18	1.7	1.4	1.7	0.5	3.4	1.9	1.4	6.2	1.7	0.7	2.0	4.6	1.3
Other Expenses	19	20.6	69.6	32.7	14.1	23.1	18.0	20.1	21.0	25.7	20.9	25.4	22.0	19.5
Officers' Compensation	20	2.0	1.4	5.8	2.9	4.9	4.5	4.5	3.2	4.4	3.1	1.6	2.6	0.7
Operating Margin	21	11.4	13.8	16.3	6.1	15.6	10.8	9.7	13.6	10.8	14.2	7.3	24.8	9.8
Operating Margin Before Officers' Comp.	22	13.4	15.2	22.1	9.0	20.5	15.3	14.3	16.8	15.2	17.4	8.9	27.4	10.5

Selected Average Balance Sheet ($ in Thousands)

Net Receivables 23	1784	0	2	24	240	1361	3235	4210	8875	46614	123918	263750	1119105
Inventories 24	•	•	•	•	•	•	•	•	•	•	•	•	•
Net Property, Plant and Equipment 25	327	0	7	65	222	437	617	1907	1701	6330	19261		297595
Total Assets 26	29559	0	92	654	2226	15955	34342	70539	162467	348941	985266		36198527
Notes and Loans Payable 27	11977	0	13	197	945	9974	20416	34966	79106	122918	377904		14361036
All Other Liabilities 28	14893	0	4	17	620	2957	8542	20569	65723	183263	409781		19259147
Net Worth 29	2689	0	75	439	660	1725	3024	5384	15004	17637	42760	197581	2578344

Selected Financial Ratios (Times to 1)

Current Ratio 30	0.4	•	11.8	11.2	0.9	0.6	0.5	0.5	0.7	0.6	0.7	0.8	0.3
Quick Ratio 31	0.3	•	9.8	8.9	0.6	0.5	0.3	0.3	0.4	0.6	0.6	0.7	0.2
Net Sales to Working Capital 32	•	•	10.8	11.9	•	•	•	•	•	•	•	•	•
Coverage Ratio 33	1.4	7.7	94.2	61.4	4.2	1.9	1.8	1.7	1.6	1.6	1.4	2.7	1.2
Total Asset Turnover 34	0.2	•	5.4	8.2	0.7	0.4	0.3	0.3	0.2	0.2	0.2	0.2	0.1
Inventory Turnover 35	•	•	•	•	•	•	•	•	•	•	•	•	•
Receivables Turnover 36	•	•	•	•	•	•	•	•	•	•	•	•	•
Total Liabilities to Net Worth 37	10.0	•	0.2	0.5	2.4	4.3	3.2	3.7	8.2	7.2	4.0	13.0	•
Current Assets to Working Capital 38	•	•	1.1	1.1	•	•	•	•	•	•	•	•	•
Current Liabilities to Working Capital 39	•	•	0.1	0.1	•	•	•	•	•	•	•	•	•
Working Capital to Net Sales 40	•	•	0.1	0.1	•	•	•	•	•	•	•	•	•
Inventory to Working Capital 41	•	•	•	•	•	•	•	•	•	•	•	•	•
Total Receipts to Cash Flow 42	3.5	1.2	2.3	5.4	3.0	3.8	3.3	4.1	3.3	3.1	3.3	2.3	3.8
Cost of Goods to Cash Flow 43	0.1	•	0.2	0.0	0.2	0.5	0.2	0.2	0.1	0.2	0.7	0.1	0.1
Cash Flow to Total Debt 44	0.1	13.1	4.6	13.1	0.3	0.2	0.1	0.1	0.1	0.1	0.1	0.1	0.0

Selected Financial Factors (in Percentages)

Debt Ratio 45	90.9	•	18.0	32.8	70.4	76.4	81.0	84.3	78.7	89.1	87.7	79.9	92.9
Return on Total Assets 46	6.6	•	88.4	49.7	13.4	18.5	8.4	8.3	7.8	6.4	6.2	8.0	5.9
Return on Equity Before Income Taxes 47	20.5	•	106.6	72.8	34.4	29.5	20.4	23.9	15.0	22.1	13.9	25.0	15.2
Return on Equity After Income Taxes 48	15.8	•	105.5	69.8	33.9	27.3	19.1	23.0	13.1	18.8	12.9	19.0	10.0
Profit Margin (Before Income Tax) 49	11.4	13.8	16.3	6.0	15.6	10.8	9.7	13.6	10.6	14.0	7.1	24.6	9.9
Profit Margin (After Income Tax) 50	8.8	10.7	16.1	5.7	15.4	10.0	9.1	13.1	9.2	11.9	6.6	18.7	6.5

INTL. TRADE, SECONDARY FINANCING, OTHER NONDEPOSITORY CREDIT

Table I

Corporations with and without Net Income

MONEY AMOUNTS AND SIZE OF ASSETS IN THOUSANDS OF DOLLARS

Item Description for Accounting Period 7/06 Through 6/07	Total	Zero Assets	Under 500	500 to 1,000	1,000 to 5,000	5,000 to 10,000	10,000 to 25,000	25,000 to 50,000	50,000 to 100,000	100,000 to 250,000	250,000 to 500,000	500,000 to 2,500,000	2,500,000 and over
Number of Enterprises 1	5468	815	3361	494	447	44	107	69	28	29	6	32	36
Revenues ($ in Thousands)													
Net Sales 2	215112760	1147749	1181142	108955	489446	79550	599853	595329	289878	758490	194823	3232728	206434819
Interest 3	19619892	994417	7248	13683	9264	2192	24315	92966	63502	230575	166799	1637893	192951038
Rents 4	59449	624	0	0	461	0	116	608	7	1338	1695	1418	53181
Royalties 5	2247	0	2082	0	133	0	0	3	0	5	0	0	25
Other Portfolio Income 6	2631326	15500	508	327	15701	132	5871	885	8487	4312	15081	178337	2386184
Other Receipts 7	16225846	137208	1171304	94945	463887	77226	569551	500867	217882	522260	11248	1415080	11044391
Total Receipts 8	215112760	1147749	1181142	108955	489446	79550	599853	595329	289878	758490	194823	3232728	206434819
Average Total Receipts 9	39340	1408	351	221	1095	1808	5606	8628	10353	26155	32470	101023	5734301
Operating Costs/Operating Income (%)													
Cost of Operations 10	0.2	1.0	•	•	0.3	4.2	20.5	4.2	1.9	8.1	•	9.2	•
Salaries and Wages 11	1.4	7.4	7.0	33.4	42.2	30.5	18.3	17.2	15.7	11.9	3.4	8.3	0.9
Taxes Paid 12	0.2	4.1	1.6	5.0	2.8	4.5	2.4	2.6	1.9	4.0	0.7	1.3	0.1
Interest Paid 13	81.7	50.8	3.1	12.1	8.5	16.9	8.6	23.0	24.0	29.1	75.1	31.8	84.0
Depreciation 14	0.2	0.3	0.3	2.5	2.9	2.3	2.5	0.7	0.7	1.5	1.9	0.9	0.2
Amortization and Depletion 15	3.9	0.0	0.2	0.0	0.5	0.7	0.8	0.9	0.2	0.8	1.2	0.8	4.0
Pensions and Other Deferred Comp. 16	0.2	•	•	1.5	0.1	0.6	0.2	0.4	0.1	0.3	0.1	0.3	0.2
Employee Benefits 17	0.2	0.1	0.1	0.4	0.3	1.7	1.1	1.3	1.1	0.7	0.7	0.5	0.1
Advertising 18	0.1	0.1	0.3	4.6	2.9	2.9	1.3	0.5	0.9	0.7	0.2	0.7	0.0
Other Expenses 19	5.8	13.0	86.7	61.1	33.0	48.3	28.3	26.9	39.2	25.2	11.5	15.9	4.8
Officers' Compensation 20	0.3	1.9	3.6	8.1	4.0	9.4	6.9	3.3	2.6	2.1	0.7	1.0	0.2
Operating Margin 21	5.9	21.4	•	•	2.5	•	9.1	19.1	11.8	15.6	4.6	29.2	5.4
Operating Margin Before Officers' Comp. 22	6.2	23.2	0.8	6.5	6.5	•	16.0	22.5	14.3	17.6	5.3	30.2	5.6

Selected Average Balance Sheet ($ in Thousands)

Item													
Net Receivables 23	30973	0	57	100	663	3130	5592	18205	41771	111812	146178	719132	3848094
Inventories 24	•	•	•	•	•	•	•	•	•	•	•	•	•
Net Property, Plant and Equipment 25	420	0	5	22	603	539	439	553	785	2379	3280	8846	41499
Total Assets 26	381318	131	717	2121	6552	15204	35144	70327	154129	344748		1167427	5674950
Notes and Loans Payable 27	346168	100	403	1953	5273	8838	17434	38817	98491	271236		679610	914895
All Other Liabilities 28	17794	13	65	389	1733	2419	3796	13409	25480	8616		141870	2520630
Net Worth 29	17356	17	248	-221	-454	3946	13914	18102	30159	64896		345946	2239426

Selected Financial Ratios (Times to 1)

Item													
Current Ratio 30	0.5	•	3.8	2.2	1.4	0.9	1.3	1.7	1.8	1.4	0.9	1.7	0.4
Quick Ratio 31	0.3	•	2.9	1.4	1.1	0.8	1.1	1.4	1.4	1.3	0.5	1.7	0.2
Net Sales to Working Capital 32	•	•	4.7	0.9	3.0	•	2.8	0.8	0.4	0.7	•	0.3	•
Coverage Ratio 33	1.1	1.4	0.1	•	1.3	0.3	2.1	1.8	1.5	1.5	1.1	2.0	1.1
Total Asset Turnover 34	0.1	•	2.7	0.3	0.5	0.3	0.4	0.2	0.1	0.2	0.1	0.1	0.1
Inventory Turnover 35	•	•	•	•	•	•	•	•	•	•	•	•	•
Receivables Turnover 36	•	•	•	•	•	•	•	•	•	•	•	•	•
Total Liabilities to Net Worth 37	21.0	6.7	1.9	•	•	2.9	1.5	2.9	4.1	4.3	24.2	2.4	1.5
Current Assets to Working Capital 38	•	•	1.4	1.8	3.5	4.2	2.4	2.3	3.4	1.8	•	2.4	•
Current Liabilities to Working Capital 39	•	•	0.4	0.8	2.5	3.2	1.4	1.3	2.4	0.8	•	1.4	•
Working Capital to Net Sales 40	•	1.4	0.2	1.1	0.3	0.4	1.2	2.3	1.5	1.1	0.3	3.5	•
Inventory to Working Capital 41	•	•	•	•	•	•	•	•	•	•	•	•	•
Total Receipts to Cash Flow 42	8.9	2.9	1.3	5.4	3.2	5.3	3.1	2.3	0.0	2.1	12.2	2.3	10.2
Cost of Goods to Cash Flow 43	0.0	0.0	•	0.0	0.0	0.2	0.6	0.1	0.0	•	0.0	0.2	0.0
Cash Flow to Total Debt 44	0.0	•	2.5	0.1	0.1	0.0	0.2	0.2	0.0	0.1	0.1	0.0	0.0

Selected Financial Factors (in Percentages)

Item													
Debt Ratio 45	95.4	87.0	65.4	110.4	106.9	74.0	60.4	74.3	80.4	81.2	96.0	70.4	60.4
Return on Total Assets 46	9.0	0.8	•	5.7	•	6.5	10.3	5.3	7.6	7.5	•	5.4	9.0
Return on Equity Before Income Taxes 47	11.8	•	•	•	88.0	12.9	11.8	6.7	13.4	2.3	•	9.0	12.0
Return on Equity After Income Taxes 48	7.7	•	•	95.0	•	12.0	9.0	5.7	8.5	1.3	•	6.2	7.8
Profit Margin (Before Income Tax) 49	5.2	20.7	2.5	•	2.5	9.1	19.1	11.8	15.5	4.6	•	30.9	4.7
Profit Margin (After Income Tax) 50	3.4	12.3	2.0	•	2.0	8.4	14.5	9.9	9.8	2.7	•	21.1	3.1

Table II

Corporations with Net Income

INTL. TRADE, SECONDARY FINANCING, OTHER NONDEPOSITORY CREDIT

MONEY AMOUNTS AND SIZE OF ASSETS IN THOUSANDS OF DOLLARS

Item Description for Accounting Period 7/06 Through 6/07	Total	Zero Assets	Under 500	500 to 1,000	1,000 to 5,000	5,000 to 10,000	10,000 to 25,000	25,000 to 50,000	50,000 to 100,000	100,000 to 250,000	250,000 to 500,000	500,000 to 2,500,000	2,500,000 and over
Number of Enterprises 1	3643	492	•	275	233	20	69	56	16	20	•	•	28
Revenues ($ in Thousands)													
Net Sales 2	210036880	961206	•	101551	354268	67108	315411	518799	179440	666598	•	•	3031854
Interest 3	192740578	838614	•	13283	7520	22	17562	82449	24772	176781	•	•	1400449
Rents 4	57474	624	•	0	461	0	116	608	7	1042	•	•	1418
Royalties 5	32	0	•	0	0	0	0	3	0	5	•	•	0
Other Portfolio Income 6	2606700	14504	•	0	15594	132	1020	796	8296	2367	•	•	177994
Other Receipts 7	14632096	107464	•	88268	330693	66954	296713	434943	146365	486403	•	•	1451993
Total Receipts 8	210036880	961206	•	101551	354268	67108	315411	518799	179440	666598	•	•	3031854
Average Total Receipts 9	57655	1954	•	369	1520	3355	4571	9264	11215	33330	•	•	108280
Operating Costs/Operating Income (%)													
Cost of Operations 10	0.2	0.5	•	•	•	•	0.0	1.1	3.0	9.3	•	•	9.8
Salaries and Wages 11	1.3	7.3	•	32.3	42.4	30.5	22.4	16.4	7.8	12.9	•	•	8.3
Taxes Paid 12	0.2	4.2	•	5.0	1.9	4.8	2.8	2.7	1.4	1.3	•	•	1.3
Interest Paid 13	82.0	44.7	•	1.2	3.2	11.0	11.2	19.5	20.9	22.1	•	•	29.3
Depreciation 14	0.2	0.3	•	2.0	2.7	2.6	0.6	0.7	0.2	1.6	•	•	1.0
Amortization and Depletion 15	4.0	0.0	•	0.0	0.0	0.2	1.4	0.3	0.3	0.9	•	•	0.9
Pensions and Other Deferred Comp. 16	0.2	•	•	1.6	0.1	0.7	0.3	0.4	0.1	0.3	•	•	0.2
Employee Benefits 17	0.2	0.1	•	0.1	0.4	1.9	1.5	1.5	0.8	0.7	•	•	0.4
Advertising 18	0.1	0.1	•	4.9	0.9	3.5	1.1	0.5	0.3	0.8	•	•	0.7
Other Expenses 19	5.2	12.0	•	38.9	32.2	27.5	32.7	27.6	32.5	21.5	•	•	15.4
Officers' Compensation 20	0.3	0.3	•	8.7	3.0	10.9	5.6	3.5	3.4	2.2	•	•	1.1
Operating Margin 21	6.2	30.4	•	5.3	13.3	6.3	20.4	25.8	29.2	26.5	•	•	31.5
Operating Margin Before Officers' Comp. 22	6.5	30.7	•	13.9	16.3	17.2	26.0	29.3	32.6	28.8	•	•	32.6

Selected Average Balance Sheet ($ in Thousands)

Net Receivables 23	39591	0	180	1002	4269	6197	18004	46941	118728	749501
Inventories 24	•	•	•	•	•	•	•	•	•	•
Net Property, Plant and Equipment 25	540	0	24	209	245	219	584	135	3268	9944
Total Assets 26	549888	0	653	2234	6517	15894	34900	72895	154467	1195733
Notes and Loans Payable 27	498120	0	72	1038	3915	9545	15016	37390	84372	653939
All Other Liabilities 28	25889	0	111	470	547	2682	3897	11831	28580	159906
Net Worth 29	25879	0	470	726	2055	3667	15987	23674	41515	381888

Selected Financial Ratios (Times to 1)

Current Ratio 30	0.4	•	3.5	2.0	6.7	1.4	1.8	2.3	1.5	2.0
Quick Ratio 31	0.3	•	2.6	1.5	5.5	1.2	1.5	1.9	1.3	2.0
Net Sales to Working Capital 32	•	•	0.9	1.9	0.7	1.7	0.9	0.3	0.8	0.2
Coverage Ratio 33	1.1	1.7	5.4	5.1	1.6	2.8	2.3	2.4	2.2	2.1
Total Asset Turnover 34	0.1	•	0.6	0.7	0.5	0.3	0.3	0.2	0.2	0.1
Inventory Turnover 35	•	•	•	•	•	•	•	•	•	•
Receivables Turnover 36	•	•	•	•	•	•	•	•	•	•
Total Liabilities to Net Worth 37	20.2	•	0.4	2.1	2.2	3.3	1.2	2.1	2.7	2.1
Current Assets to Working Capital 38	•	•	1.4	2.0	1.2	3.5	2.3	1.8	3.2	2.0
Current Liabilities to Working Capital 39	•	•	0.4	1.0	0.2	2.5	1.3	0.8	2.2	1.0
Working Capital to Net Sales 40	•	1.2	1.2	0.5	1.4	0.6	1.2	3.1	1.3	4.2
Inventory to Working Capital 41	•	•	•	•	•	•	•	•	0.0	0.0
Total Receipts to Cash Flow 42	9.1	2.4	3.3	2.5	3.9	2.1	2.0	1.8	2.2	2.2
Cost of Goods to Cash Flow 43	0.0	0.0	•	•	•	0.0	0.0	0.1	0.2	0.2
Cash Flow to Total Debt 44	0.0	•	0.6	0.4	0.2	0.2	0.2	0.1	0.1	0.1

Selected Financial Factors (in Percentages)

Debt Ratio 45	95.3	•	28.0	67.5	68.5	76.9	54.2	67.5	73.1	68.1
Return on Total Assets 46	9.2	•	3.7	11.2	8.9	9.1	12.0	7.7	10.5	5.7
Return on Equity Before Income Taxes 47	12.2	•	4.2	27.7	10.3	25.4	14.9	13.8	21.2	9.5
Return on Equity After Income Taxes 48	8.1	•	3.6	26.4	6.9	23.8	11.9	12.4	16.0	6.5
Profit Margin (Before Income Tax) 49	5.5	29.5	5.3	13.3	6.3	20.4	25.8	29.2	26.5	33.4
Profit Margin (After Income Tax) 50	3.6	19.5	4.6	12.6	4.2	19.1	20.5	26.2	20.0	22.9

Table I

Corporations with and without Net Income

ACTIVITIES RELATED TO CREDIT INTERMEDIATION

MONEY AMOUNTS AND SIZE OF ASSETS IN THOUSANDS OF DOLLARS

Item Description for Accounting Period 7/06 Through 6/07		Total	Zero Assets	Under 500	500 to 1,000	1,000 to 5,000	5,000 to 10,000	10,000 to 25,000	25,000 to 50,000	50,000 to 100,000	100,000 to 250,000	250,000 to 500,000	500,000 to 2,500,000	2,500,000 and over
Number of Enterprises	1	27613	4267	20096	1619	1088	225	165	52	38	28	9	15	10
Revenues ($ in Thousands)														
Net Sales	2	45086195	456656	6988146	3057220	3049293	792046	1251278	789417	1129876	1724822	1696440	4180482	19970519
Interest	3	455646	25846	49770	13946	29744	19022	28081	27737	61105	66726	55875	467645	3710148
Rents	4	235561	0	0	0	41	579	33	37	1679	1732	22051	20743	188666
Royalties	5	159657	0	0	0	0	0	0	80	0	0	0	0	159577
Other Portfolio Income	6	979205	35705	15711	374	5789	822	10911	8288	1281	9532	133670	49161	707963
Other Receipts	7	39156126	395105	6922665	3042900	3013719	771623	1212253	753275	1065811	1646832	1484844	3642933	15204165
Total Receipts	8	45086195	456656	6988146	3057220	3049293	792046	1251278	789417	1129876	1724822	1696440	4180482	19970519
Average Total Receipts	9	1633	107	348	1888	2803	3520	7584	15181	29734	61601	188493	278699	1997052
Operating Costs/Operating Income (%)														
Cost of Operations	10	10.6	0.4	19.1	34.1	28.7	15.9	18.5	26.0	9.9	23.5	•	0.8	2.1
Salaries and Wages	11	19.5	30.0	24.9	22.8	22.3	33.7	31.7	22.6	27.5	15.4	14.1	21.0	15.1
Taxes Paid	12	2.1	2.4	2.8	2.1	3.0	2.7	3.1	2.6	2.8	2.0	1.9	2.1	1.6
Interest Paid	13	7.2	0.9	1.1	0.6	1.0	4.3	7.6	7.2	11.8	7.0	15.9	9.0	10.2
Depreciation	14	1.5	1.9	0.8	0.9	0.9	0.5	2.8	1.5	1.4	3.8	4.1	1.9	1.5
Amortization and Depletion	15	1.1	0.2	0.1	0.3	0.2	0.1	0.3	0.2	0.4	0.7	3.7	2.9	1.4
Pensions and Other Deferred Comp.	16	0.7	0.0	0.1	0.4	0.1	0.2	0.2	0.5	0.6	0.3	1.2	2.3	0.8
Employee Benefits	17	1.5	0.1	0.6	0.3	1.2	1.1	1.1	1.3	1.9	1.3	1.6	2.9	1.7
Advertising	18	4.5	0.3	1.3	1.4	1.0	2.9	4.1	2.5	0.8	1.5	5.6	8.3	6.5
Other Expenses	19	38.4	49.6	29.6	25.8	30.0	34.1	26.6	19.4	32.4	40.8	54.0	37.6	45.0
Officers' Compensation	20	3.0	4.1	9.4	4.5	2.8	4.3	5.5	4.3	3.5	1.7	1.0	0.9	0.9
Operating Margin	21	9.9	9.9	10.3	6.7	8.6	0.1	•	12.0	7.0	2.0	•	10.4	13.3
Operating Margin Before Officers' Comp.	22	12.8	14.1	19.7	11.2	11.4	4.4	3.9	16.3	10.5	3.8	•	11.3	14.1

Selected Average Balance Sheet ($ in Thousands)

Net Receivables 23	1663	0	14	78	172	2187	3400	13180	18782	34862	50610	264724	3746591
Inventories 24	•	•	•	•	•	•	•	•	•	•	•	•	•
Net Property, Plant and Equipment 25	124	0	15	140	154	158	1415	1573	2787	7837	28665	30426	133394
Total Assets 26	5571	0	81	764	2044	7305	15597	36334	74067	153070	344330	1042814	11681096
Notes and Loans Payable 27	1786	0	33	351	651	3110	6356	15356	39817	36384	273220	426731	3344115
All Other Liabilities 28	1985	0	6	77	706	2881	6628	12704	21514	73492	201885	272869	4260679
Net Worth 29	1800	0	41	336	687	1314	2613	8275	12736	43195	-130774	343214	4076302

Selected Financial Ratios (Times to 1)

Current Ratio 30	1.0	•	2.3	2.6	1.3	0.8	0.8	1.2	0.8	1.1	0.9	1.4	0.9
Quick Ratio 31	0.8	•	2.1	2.3	1.2	0.7	0.6	1.0	0.7	0.9	0.6	1.1	0.7
Net Sales to Working Capital 32	•	•	13.5	5.9	9.8	•	•	3.3	•	17.4	•	2.5	•
Coverage Ratio 33	2.3	11.8	10.6	11.3	9.7	1.0	0.8	2.6	1.6	1.3	0.8	2.2	2.1
Total Asset Turnover 34	0.3	•	4.3	2.5	1.4	0.5	0.5	0.4	0.4	0.4	0.5	0.3	0.2
Inventory Turnover 35	•	•	•	•	•	•	•	•	•	•	•	•	•
Receivables Turnover 36	•	•	•	•	•	•	•	•	•	•	•	•	•
Total Liabilities to Net Worth 37	2.1	•	0.9	1.3	2.0	4.6	5.0	3.4	4.8	2.5	2.0	3.9	1.9
Current Assets to Working Capital 38	•	•	1.8	1.6	3.9	•	•	5.1	•	19.9	•	2.9	•
Current Liabilities to Working Capital 39	•	•	0.8	0.6	2.9	•	•	4.1	•	18.9	•	2.9	•
Working Capital to Net Sales 40	•	•	0.1	0.2	0.1	•	•	0.3	•	0.1	•	0.4	•
Inventory to Working Capital 41	•	•	•	•	•	•	•	0.0	•	0.1	•	0.0	•
Total Receipts to Cash Flow 42	2.2	2.2	2.9	4.0	2.9	3.4	5.2	3.5	2.8	2.6	2.1	2.3	1.8
Cost of Goods to Cash Flow 43	0.2	0.0	0.6	1.4	0.8	0.5	1.0	0.9	0.3	0.6	0.0	0.0	0.1
Cash Flow to Total Debt 44	0.2	•	3.0	1.1	0.7	0.2	0.1	0.2	0.2	0.2	0.0	0.2	0.1

Selected Financial Factors (in Percentages)

Debt Ratio 45	67.7	•	48.5	56.1	66.4	82.0	83.2	77.2	82.8	71.8	138.0	67.1	65.1
Return on Total Assets 46	4.8	•	49.2	18.1	13.2	2.1	2.9	7.7	7.5	3.7	7.3	5.3	3.7
Return on Equity Before Income Taxes 47	8.3	•	86.5	37.6	35.2	0.2	•	20.6	16.3	3.1	3.8	9.0	5.7
Return on Equity After Income Taxes 48	6.1	•	84.3	37.5	33.3	•	•	19.7	15.3	1.8	6.7	5.8	3.6
Profit Margin (Before Income Tax) 49	9.2	9.9	10.3	6.7	8.6	0.1	•	11.2	7.0	2.1	•	11.0	11.5
Profit Margin (After Income Tax) 50	6.7	9.4	10.1	6.7	8.2	•	•	10.8	6.6	1.2	•	7.2	7.3

Table II

Corporations with Net Income

ACTIVITIES RELATED TO CREDIT INTERMEDIATION

MONEY AMOUNTS AND SIZE OF ASSETS IN THOUSANDS OF DOLLARS

Item Description for Accounting Period 7/06 Through 6/07	Total	Zero Assets	Under 500	500 to 1,000	1,000 to 5,000	5,000 to 10,000	10,000 to 25,000	25,000 to 50,000	50,000 to 100,000	100,000 to 250,000	250,000 to 500,000	500,000 to 2,500,000	2,500,000 and over
Number of Enterprises 1	19218	2475	14944	936	•	126	92	36	31	15	•	•	11
Revenues ($ in Thousands)													
Net Sales 2	39070965	316869	6210390	2185380	•	425605	890591	632970	960402	893517	•	•	3882892
Interest 3	2985865	24105	6960	8059	•	8866	2797	19074	18561	29686	•	•	404462
Rents 4	207348	0	0	0	•	579	0	37	1679	20	•	•	16367
Royalties 5	159657	0	0	0	•	0	0	80	0	0	•	•	0
Other Portfolio Income 6	803679	35687	0	0	•	550	1082	2731	1281	2414	•	•	48338
Other Receipts 7	34914416	257077	6203430	2177321	•	415610	886712	611048	938881	861397	•	•	3413725
Total Receipts 8	39070965	316869	6210390	2185380	•	425605	890591	632970	960402	893517	•	•	3882892
Average Total Receipts 9	2033	128	416	2335	•	3378	9680	17582	30981	59568	•	•	352990
Operating Costs/Operating Income (%)													
Cost of Operations 10	9.9	0.6	17.1	47.7	•	28.0	20.4	28.4	11.0	0.1	•	•	0.2
Salaries and Wages 11	18.3	23.7	25.6	11.7	•	27.2	29.2	18.4	28.3	17.1	•	•	21.3
Taxes Paid 12	2.1	1.8	2.8	1.8	•	1.9	3.1	2.3	2.9	2.0	•	•	2.1
Interest Paid 13	5.7	1.3	0.4	0.5	•	5.3	5.9	7.4	7.9	5.3	•	•	7.3
Depreciation 14	1.4	2.1	0.8	0.8	•	0.5	1.4	1.2	1.5	2.1	•	•	2.0
Amortization and Depletion 15	1.1	0.0	0.1	0.4	•	0.0	0.1	0.2	0.5	0.4	•	•	2.6
Pensions and Other Deferred Comp. 16	0.7	0.1	0.1	0.5	•	0.3	0.3	0.6	0.7	0.5	•	•	0.9
Employee Benefits 17	1.5	0.0	0.5	0.3	•	0.7	1.0	1.2	2.0	1.0	•	•	3.0
Advertising 18	5.0	0.1	1.3	1.3	•	1.6	4.4	1.6	0.7	2.1	•	•	8.9
Other Expenses 19	37.4	46.8	28.8	17.8	•	20.1	19.1	15.7	30.8	51.4	•	•	38.4
Officers' Compensation 20	2.9	5.2	9.1	6.1	•	5.1	4.2	4.9	3.6	1.8	•	•	0.8
Operating Margin 21	14.2	18.1	13.2	10.9	•	9.2	11.1	18.1	10.3	16.0	•	•	12.5
Operating Margin Before Officers' Comp. 22	17.1	23.4	22.3	17.0	•	14.3	15.3	23.1	13.9	17.8	•	•	13.4

Selected Average Balance Sheet ($ in Thousands)

Net Receivables 23	1055	0	11	2	1131	3848	14721	13063	30328	304072
Inventories 24	•	•	•	•	•	•	•	•	•	•
Net Property, Plant and Equipment 25	146	0	19	133	115	1567	1502	3058	7955	38697
Total Assets 26	5960	0	89	808	6897	15312	37758	74159	148908	1201514
Notes and Loans Payable 27	1714	0	21	304	3193	5188	13194	39992	36354	422010
All Other Liabilities 28	2446	0	11	90	1683	6267	15558	19016	63376	358957
Net Worth 29	1800	0	58	413	2021	3857	9006	15151	49178	420548

Selected Financial Ratios (Times to 1)

Current Ratio 30	0.8	•	3.3	2.0	0.8	1.0	1.2	0.8	1.1	1.4
Quick Ratio 31	0.5	•	2.9	1.8	0.8	1.0	0.6	0.6	0.9	1.1
Net Sales to Working Capital 32	•	•	12.6	7.5	103.3	3.5	•	9.0	•	2.6
Coverage Ratio 33	3.3	14.8	31.3	22.7	2.7	2.9	3.5	2.3	4.0	2.8
Total Asset Turnover 34	0.3	•	4.6	2.9	0.5	0.6	0.6	0.4	0.4	0.3
Inventory Turnover 35	•	•	•	•	•	•	•	•	•	•
Receivables Turnover 36	•	•	•	•	•	•	•	•	•	•
Total Liabilities to Net Worth 37	2.3	•	0.5	1.0	2.4	3.0	3.2	3.9	2.0	1.9
Current Assets to Working Capital 38	•	•	1.4	2.0	89.6	2.0	5.4	11.2	3.7	2.0
Current Liabilities to Working Capital 39	•	•	0.4	1.0	88.6	1.0	4.4	10.2	2.7	1.0
Working Capital to Net Sales 40	•	•	0.1	0.1	0.0	0.3	•	0.1	•	0.4
Inventory to Working Capital 41	•	•	•	•	•	•	•	•	•	•
Total Receipts to Cash Flow 42	2.1	1.9	2.8	4.7	4.0	3.8	3.1	2.7	1.6	2.1
Cost of Goods to Cash Flow 43	0.2	0.0	0.5	2.2	1.1	0.8	0.9	0.3	0.0	0.0
Cash Flow to Total Debt 44	0.2	•	4.8	1.3	0.2	0.2	0.2	0.2	0.4	0.2

Selected Financial Factors (in Percentages)

Debt Ratio 45	69.8	•	35.3	48.8	70.7	74.8	76.1	79.6	67.0	65.0
Return on Total Assets 46	6.5	•	63.3	33.0	7.1	10.7	11.8	7.6	8.6	6.0
Return on Equity Before Income Taxes 47	15.1	•	94.7	61.7	15.4	27.6	35.3	21.1	19.7	11.1
Return on Equity After Income Taxes 48	11.9	•	92.6	61.6	14.8	25.2	34.2	20.0	17.6	7.6
Profit Margin (Before Income Tax) 49	13.4	18.1	13.2	10.9	9.2	11.0	18.1	10.3	16.3	13.2
Profit Margin (After Income Tax) 50	10.5	17.4	12.9	10.9	8.8	10.0	17.5	9.8	14.5	9.1

Table I

Corporations with and without Net Income

INVESTMENT BANKING AND SECURITIES DEALING

MONEY AMOUNTS AND SIZE OF ASSETS IN THOUSANDS OF DOLLARS

Item Description for Accounting Period 7/06 Through 6/07	Total	Zero Assets	Under 500	500 to 1,000	1,000 to 5,000	5,000 to 10,000	10,000 to 25,000	25,000 to 50,000	50,000 to 100,000	100,000 to 250,000	250,000 to 500,000	500,000 to 2,500,000	2,500,000 and over
Number of Enterprises **1**	3213	410	2303	167	161	38	51	20	15	14	9	11	14
Revenues ($ in Thousands)													
Net Sales **2**	249080245	641706	706827	33559	328002	255480	100928	203497	388760	436269	658489	2947097	242379632
Interest **3**	173384576	6078	65	1717	28961	3190	9497	4995	6165	13675	86750	378391	172845092
Rents **4**	557314	7052	0	0	4864	0	0	0	0	103	0	3	545292
Royalties **5**	21111	0	0	0	0	0	0	0	0	1615	0	10	19486
Other Portfolio Income **6**	8619818	16883	22470	420	224	2720	1491	18168	14158	46903	20445	656826	7819109
Other Receipts **7**	66497426	611693	684292	31422	293953	249570	89940	180334	368437	373973	551294	1911867	61150653
Total Receipts **8**	249080245	641706	706827	33559	328002	255480	100928	203497	388760	436269	658489	2947097	242379632
Average Total Receipts **9**	77523	1565	307	201	2037	6723	1979	10175	25917	31162	73165	267918	17312831
Operating Costs/Operating Income (%)													
Cost of Operations **10**	0.2	•	1.0	•	•	•	•	•	•	0.4	•	•	0.2
Salaries and Wages **11**	9.4	9.6	19.1	64.5	14.0	35.6	45.3	40.8	39.1	29.7	33.5	27.6	8.9
Taxes Paid **12**	0.8	0.3	2.7	2.1	2.0	3.9	4.2	3.5	4.1	2.9	3.5	4.4	0.7
Interest Paid **13**	67.2	74.3	0.0	2.1	7.2	2.2	7.0	1.7	2.2	4.1	11.1	17.5	68.6
Depreciation **14**	0.7	0.1	0.6	0.3	0.4	1.1	5.3	1.0	0.6	0.7	3.8	0.6	0.7
Amortization and Depletion **15**	0.2	0.0	0.0	0.3	0.3	0.1	3.1	0.0	0.4	1.6	0.1	0.1	0.2
Pensions and Other Deferred Comp. **16**	0.7	0.3	0.1	0.8	0.0	1.7	0.1	1.5	0.8	3.7	0.1	0.6	0.7
Employee Benefits **17**	0.5	0.1	5.2	0.0	0.7	2.4	3.4	2.1	1.6	0.8	1.9	1.1	0.5
Advertising **18**	0.1	0.0	0.9	•	0.1	0.1	1.2	0.6	0.1	2.7	0.3	0.2	0.1
Other Expenses **19**	9.9	14.3	47.1	36.2	54.2	29.1	47.9	42.3	22.6	35.5	34.6	18.9	9.4
Officers' Compensation **20**	1.6	2.0	6.5	5.3	10.6	31.1	4.1	1.6	8.4	3.9	3.1	1.1	1.5
Operating Margin **21**	8.8	•	16.8	•	10.5	•	•	4.8	20.0	14.2	8.0	27.9	8.6
Operating Margin Before Officers' Comp. **22**	10.4	0.9	23.2	•	21.1	23.9	•	6.5	28.3	18.0	11.1	29.0	10.1

Selected Average Balance Sheet ($ in Thousands)

Net Receivables 23	408131	0	0	•	332	110	296	1591	4183	13243	47295	61201	305840	93306965
Inventories 24	•	•	•	•	•	•	•	•	•	•	•	•	•	•
Net Property, Plant and Equipment 25	3033	•	0	14	197	283	733	2293	940	9591	7954	672781		
Total Assets 26	1418081	0	14	79	822	1848	7830	16029	33934	73218	145562	378637	1180944	323882124
Notes and Loans Payable 27	225553	0	20	104	1060	4822	2227	3532	12762	29686	74047	186766	51480826	
All Other Liabilities 28	1119659	0	16	128	686	1792	2785	3268	25075	46028	176769	360237	256459077	
Net Worth 29	72870	0	44	659	1216	9229	28923	35381	69848	127820	633940	15942220		

Selected Financial Ratios (Times to 1)

Current Ratio 30	0.9	•	1.1	0.8	3.4	2.5	2.0	9.1	1.1	1.3	1.4	1.5	0.9
Quick Ratio 31	0.5	•	1.1	0.8	2.9	1.6	1.3	4.8	0.6	1.1	0.7	1.2	0.5
Net Sales to Working Capital 32	•	196.7	•	3.5	2.6	0.4	0.7	5.2	1.8	0.9	1.1	•	
Coverage Ratio 33	1.2	1.0	878.1	2.4	•	•	3.1	9.5	4.4	1.7	2.6	1.1	
Total Asset Turnover 34	0.1	•	3.9	0.2	1.1	0.9	0.3	0.4	0.2	0.2	0.2	0.1	
Inventory Turnover 35	•	•	•	•	•	•	•	•	•	•	•	•	
Receivables Turnover 36	•	•	•	•	•	•	•	•	•	•	•	•	
Total Liabilities to Net Worth 37	18.5	0.8	25.1	1.8	5.4	0.7	0.2	1.1	1.1	2.0	0.9	19.3	
Current Assets to Working Capital 38	•	15.2	•	1.4	1.7	2.0	1.1	8.2	4.3	3.4	3.0	•	
Current Liabilities to Working Capital 39	•	14.2	•	0.4	0.7	1.0	0.1	7.2	3.3	2.4	2.0	•	
Working Capital to Net Sales 40	•	0.0	•	0.3	0.4	2.3	1.4	0.2	0.6	1.1	0.9	•	
Inventory to Working Capital 41	•	•	•	•	•	•	•	•	•	•	•	•	
Total Receipts to Cash Flow 42	6.6	11.7	1.8	4.8	1.6	6.6	7.9	2.8	2.6	2.6	2.7	4.3	6.7
Cost of Goods to Cash Flow 43	0.0	0.0	0.0	•	0.0	•	•	0.0	0.0	0.0	•	0.0	
Cash Flow to Total Debt 44	0.0	4.9	0.1	1.1	0.2	0.0	0.7	0.3	0.1	0.1	0.1	0.0	

Selected Financial Factors (in Percentages)

Debt Ratio 45	94.9	•	44.5	96.2	64.3	84.5	42.4	51.7	52.0	66.2	46.3	95.1
Return on Total Assets 46	4.2	•	64.8	•	19.6	•	1.5	7.5	3.9	3.6	10.2	4.2
Return on Equity Before Income Taxes 47	10.7	•	116.5	•	32.4	•	1.2	13.9	6.2	4.3	11.6	10.8
Return on Equity After Income Taxes 48	7.2	•	111.1	•	26.7	•	0.4	9.4	4.3	3.1	5.9	7.3
Profit Margin (Before Income Tax) 49	10.1	•	16.8	•	10.5	•	3.4	18.9	13.9	7.5	27.5	9.9
Profit Margin (After Income Tax) 50	6.8	•	16.0	•	8.7	•	1.2	12.8	9.5	5.5	14.0	6.7

Table II

Corporations with Net Income

INVESTMENT BANKING AND SECURITIES DEALING

MONEY AMOUNTS AND SIZE OF ASSETS IN THOUSANDS OF DOLLARS

Item Description for Accounting Period 7/06 Through 6/07	Total	Zero Assets	Under 500	500 to 1,000	1,000 to 5,000	5,000 to 10,000	10,000 to 25,000	25,000 to 50,000	50,000 to 100,000	100,000 to 250,000	250,000 to 500,000	500,000 to 2,500,000	2,500,000 and over
Number of Enterprises 1	1409	22	1130	60	84	27	24	•	10	8	6	7	•

Revenues ($ in Thousands)

	Total	Zero Assets	Under 500	500 to 1,000	1,000 to 5,000	5,000 to 10,000	10,000 to 25,000	25,000 to 50,000	50,000 to 100,000	100,000 to 250,000	250,000 to 500,000	500,000 to 2,500,000	2,500,000 and over
Net Sales 2	247159036	100102	562389	28220	165167	194564	69679	•	356673	389116	584648	2729654	•
Interest 3	17318101	4017	65	1641	21412	2595	7592	•	6165	8611	77575	356220	•
Rents 4	550262	0	0	0	4864	0	0	•	0	103	0	3	•
Royalties 5	19496	0	0	0	103	0	0	•	0	0	0	10	•
Other Portfolio Income 6	8595251	16883	22470	420		1453	460	•	13205	46903	19855	656579	•
Other Receipts 7	64812926	79202	539854	26159	138788	190516	61627	•	337303	333499	487218	1716842	•
Total Receipts 8	247159036	100102	562389	28220	165167	194564	69679	•	356673	389116	584648	2729654	•
Average Total Receipts 9	175415	4550	498	470	1966	7206	2903	•	35667	48640	97441	389951	•

Operating Costs/Operating Income (%)

	Total	Zero Assets	Under 500	500 to 1,000	1,000 to 5,000	5,000 to 10,000	10,000 to 25,000	25,000 to 50,000	50,000 to 100,000	100,000 to 250,000	250,000 to 500,000	500,000 to 2,500,000	2,500,000 and over
Cost of Operations 10	0.2	•	1.3	•	•	•	•	•	0.4	•	•	•	•
Salaries and Wages 11	9.2	46.7	20.6	3.9	22.8	25.1	15.6	•	41.3	28.2	35.0	26.6	•
Taxes Paid 12	0.8	1.9	2.8	1.8	3.1	3.6	2.3	•	4.1	3.0	3.7	4.0	•
Interest Paid 13	67.3	13.2	0.0	0.4	12.5	1.4	4.6	•	1.8	1.9	8.5	6.0	•
Depreciation 14	0.7	0.2	0.7	0.1	0.7	0.6	0.4	•	0.7	0.7	4.2	0.5	•
Amortization and Depletion 15	0.2	0.0	0.0	•	0.0	0.1	•	•	0.5	1.8	0.1	0.1	•
Pensions and Other Deferred Comp. 16	0.7	1.9	0.9	0.9	•	2.2	0.0	•	0.6	3.9	0.1	0.6	•
Employee Benefits 17	0.5	0.9	6.2	0.0	1.7	1.7	1.3	•	1.6	0.8	1.8	1.1	•
Advertising 18	0.1	0.0	1.1	•	0.1	0.0	0.1	•	0.1	3.0	0.2	0.1	•
Other Expenses 19	9.7	11.7	43.3	9.7	16.9	13.7	53.9	•	21.2	34.0	33.8	17.4	•
Officers' Compensation 20	1.5	1.2	1.8	6.3	15.6	36.4	6.0	•	5.4	2.5	2.9	1.1	•
Operating Margin 21	9.1	22.3	22.1	76.7	27.5	15.2	15.9	•	22.7	19.8	9.7	42.5	•
Operating Margin Before Officers' Comp. 22	10.6	23.5	23.9	83.1	43.1	51.7	21.9	•	28.1	22.2	12.5	43.6	•

Selected Average Balance Sheet ($ in Thousands)

Net Receivables 23	929283	0	1	255	35	186	3123	•	19170	39196	85794	268177
Inventories 24	•	•	•	•	•	•	•	•	•	•	•	•
Net Property, Plant and Equipment 25	6838	0	29	0	306	168	157	•	3405	1376	13894	8362
Total Assets 26	3226397	0	150	862	1986	7886	15490	•	74643	144117	388739	1272969
Notes and Loans Payable 27	512281	0	40	0	818	736	2503	•	19000	39907	107185	9809
All Other Liabilities 28	2550207	0	17	58	235	1437	5355	•	22726	37812	104037	525671
Net Worth 29	163909	0	93	805	934	5714	7631	•	32917	66399	177517	737489

Selected Financial Ratios (Times to 1)

Current Ratio 30	0.9	1.3	12.0	2.7	2.6	1.1	•	•	1.1	1.6	1.3	1.7
Quick Ratio 31	0.5	1.3	11.6	2.1	2.6	1.0	•	•	0.6	1.1	0.8	1.5
Net Sales to Working Capital 32	•	52.7	0.7	4.0	3.1	2.9	•	•	9.7	1.8	2.1	1.3
Coverage Ratio 33	1.2	2.7	920.5	182.6	3.2	11.9	4.4	•	13.1	11.0	2.1	8.0
Total Asset Turnover 34	0.1	3.3	0.5	1.0	0.9	0.2	•	•	0.5	0.3	0.3	0.3
Inventory Turnover 35	•	•	•	•	•	•	•	•	•	•	•	•
Receivables Turnover 36	•	•	•	•	•	•	•	•	•	•	•	•
Total Liabilities to Net Worth 37	18.7	0.6	0.1	1.1	0.4	1.0	•	•	1.3	1.2	•	0.7
Current Assets to Working Capital 38	•	4.1	1.1	1.6	1.6	8.5	•	•	11.5	2.7	4.5	2.3
Current Liabilities to Working Capital 39	•	3.1	0.1	0.6	0.6	7.5	•	•	10.5	1.7	3.5	1.3
Working Capital to Net Sales 40	•	0.0	1.4	0.3	0.3	0.3	•	•	0.1	0.6	0.5	0.8
Inventory to Working Capital 41	•	•	•	•	•	•	•	•	•	•	•	•
Total Receipts to Cash Flow 42	6.5	1.8	1.2	2.3	3.9	1.5	•	•	2.5	2.4	2.7	2.9
Cost of Goods to Cash Flow 43	0.0	0.0	0.0	0.0	•	0.0	•	•	0.0	0.0	•	0.0
Cash Flow to Total Debt 44	0.0	4.9	7.0	0.8	0.9	0.2	•	•	0.3	0.3	0.2	0.3

Selected Financial Factors (in Percentages)

Debt Ratio 45	94.9	•	37.8	6.7	53.0	27.5	50.7	•	55.9	53.9	54.3	42.1
Return on Total Assets 46	4.2	•	73.3	41.7	39.6	15.1	3.8	•	11.3	7.2	4.4	14.7
Return on Equity Before Income Taxes 47	11.1	•	117.7	44.4	57.9	19.1	5.9	•	23.7	14.3	5.0	22.2
Return on Equity After Income Taxes 48	7.5	•	112.6	44.4	50.2	14.0	5.0	•	16.5	10.7	3.8	14.5
Profit Margin (Before Income Tax) 49	10.4	22.0	22.1	75.9	27.5	15.5	•	•	21.9	19.5	9.2	42.0
Profit Margin (After Income Tax) 50	7.0	14.7	21.1	75.9	23.8	11.1	13.1	•	15.2	14.6	6.9	27.4

Table I

Corporations with and without Net Income

SECURITIES BROKERAGE

MONEY AMOUNTS AND SIZE OF ASSETS IN THOUSANDS OF DOLLARS

Item Description for Accounting Period 7/06 Through 6/07		Total	Zero Assets	Under 500	500 to 1,000	1,000 to 5,000	5,000 to 10,000	10,000 to 25,000	25,000 to 50,000	50,000 to 100,000	100,000 to 250,000	250,000 to 500,000	500,000 to 2,500,000	2,500,000 and over
Number of Enterprises	1	7700	1672	4271	697	713	141	89	26	16	20	7	17	31
Revenues ($ in Thousands)														
Net Sales	2	248034946	481569	1832442	1937636	2316327	329863	2155662	1341493	842134	1623413	1288957	5339644	228545806
Interest	3	147307330	83459	4110	5974	15588	4262	13542	20655	48286	186991	64757	586084	146273623
Rents	4	748904	0	0	0	0	683	1893	178	1391	2389	1477	4527	736365
Royalties	5	39787	0	0	0	0	14	7991	0	0	1814	0	818	29148
Other Portfolio Income	6	4155207	35083	2982	505	4863	31827	19125	26893	9193	29792	47119	105539	3842285
Other Receipts	7	95783718	363027	1825350	1931157	2295876	293077	2113111	1293767	783264	1402427	1175604	4642676	77664385
Total Receipts	8	248034946	481569	1832442	1937636	2316327	329863	2155662	1341493	842134	1623413	1288957	5339644	228545806
Average Total Receipts	9	32212	288	429	2780	3249	2339	24221	51596	52633	81171	184137	314097	7372445
Operating Costs/Operating Income (%)														
Cost of Operations	10	0.4	•	1.7	•	•	1.4	12.0	15.4	•	1.5	•	0.0	0.2
Salaries and Wages	11	13.5	6.6	30.6	35.2	30.8	34.4	16.1	25.8	35.8	28.7	46.8	36.4	12.0
Taxes Paid	12	1.1	1.8	2.9	1.8	3.3	3.5	1.8	2.8	4.0	3.6	3.4	3.4	0.9
Interest Paid	13	56.4	13.4	0.8	0.1	0.3	1.4	0.7	0.6	1.2	10.8	5.3	9.0	60.8
Depreciation	14	0.5	0.1	1.0	0.2	0.4	1.8	0.5	0.4	0.7	1.0	0.8	0.9	0.5
Amortization and Depletion	15	0.4	0.0	0.0	•	0.1	0.2	0.1	0.0	0.1	0.2	0.1	2.5	0.4
Pensions and Other Deferred Comp.	16	0.4	2.9	1.1	0.0	0.7	0.6	0.2	0.4	1.3	0.9	0.4	1.0	0.4
Employee Benefits	17	0.6	1.1	0.9	0.9	2.2	2.0	1.1	1.1	0.9	1.0	5.3	1.0	0.5
Advertising	18	0.3	0.0	0.8	0.1	0.1	0.3	0.2	0.3	0.2	0.8	0.2	0.6	0.3
Other Expenses	19	18.3	66.5	38.6	51.4	41.8	32.8	56.4	40.8	24.3	26.7	26.3	28.5	16.7
Officers' Compensation	20	2.2	15.2	9.5	7.0	14.4	14.8	4.4	3.9	12.8	8.2	3.2	3.2	1.8
Operating Margin	21	5.9	•	12.1	3.2	5.8	6.7	6.5	8.5	18.7	16.6	8.3	13.4	5.6
Operating Margin Before Officers' Comp.	22	8.1	7.6	21.5	10.2	20.3	21.5	10.9	12.4	31.6	24.7	11.4	16.7	7.3

Selected Average Balance Sheet ($ in Thousands)

Line Item													
Net Receivables 23	106796	0	2	116	198	520	2171	4105	15854	24814	52555	360592	26273442
Inventories 24	•	•	•	•	•	•	•	•	•	•	•	•	•
Net Property, Plant and Equipment 25	870	0	18	26	74	264	777	1109	1554	6874	6142	11502	193922
Total Assets 26	374577	•	126	681	1646	7431	16070	37374	67685	173872	366245	1256510	91939480
Notes and Loans Payable 27	69332	0	74	33	158	503	1323	1692	5789	12556	83925	104813	17111668
All Other Liabilities 28	276470	0	28	298	450	1833	7312	13741	28770	79807	174979	827436	68050252
Net Worth 29	28775	0	25	350	1039	5095	7435	21941	33126	81509	107341	324261	6777559

Selected Financial Ratios (Times to 1)

Line Item													
Current Ratio 30	1.1	•	1.6	1.9	4.8	3.8	1.5	1.9	1.4	1.4	1.0	0.9	1.1
Quick Ratio 31	0.5	•	1.2	1.2	3.5	2.7	1.2	1.3	1.1	0.9	0.6	0.7	0.5
Net Sales to Working Capital 32	1.4	•	20.4	10.4	2.9	1.0	6.9	4.5	4.1	2.6	69.3	•	1.3
Coverage Ratio 33	1.1	0.4	15.4	23.1	19.8	0.8	9.5	16.2	16.4	2.5	2.5	2.5	1.1
Total Asset Turnover 34	0.1	•	3.4	4.1	2.0	0.3	1.5	1.4	0.8	0.5	0.5	0.2	0.1
Inventory Turnover 35	•	•	•	•	•	•	•	•	•	•	•	•	•
Receivables Turnover 36	•	•	•	•	•	•	•	•	•	•	•	•	•
Total Liabilities to Net Worth 37	12.0	4.1	4.1	0.9	0.6	0.5	1.2	0.7	1.0	1.1	2.4	2.9	12.6
Current Assets to Working Capital 38	11.3	2.8	2.8	2.2	1.3	1.4	2.9	2.1	3.4	3.4	63.2	•	11.2
Current Liabilities to Working Capital 39	10.3	1.8	1.8	1.2	0.3	0.4	1.9	1.1	2.4	2.4	62.2	•	10.2
Working Capital to Net Sales 40	0.7	0.0	0.0	0.1	0.3	1.0	0.1	0.2	0.2	0.4	0.0	•	0.8
Inventory to Working Capital 41	0.0	•	•	•	•	•	•	0.0	0.1	0.2	•	•	0.0
Total Receipts to Cash Flow 42	4.5	1.9	2.2	1.9	2.3	3.1	1.6	2.3	2.5	2.6	3.5	2.7	4.9
Cost of Goods to Cash Flow 43	0.0	0.0	0.0	•	0.0	0.0	0.2	0.4	0.0	0.0	•	0.0	0.0
Cash Flow to Total Debt 44	0.0	•	1.9	4.3	2.3	0.3	1.7	1.5	0.6	0.3	0.2	0.1	0.0

Selected Financial Factors (in Percentages)

Line Item													
Debt Ratio 45	92.3	•	80.4	48.6	36.9	31.4	53.7	41.3	51.1	53.1	70.7	74.2	92.6
Return on Total Assets 46	5.4	•	43.9	13.5	12.1	0.3	10.5	12.5	14.8	12.5	6.6	5.6	5.3
Return on Equity Before Income Taxes 47	6.7	•	209.6	25.2	18.3	•	20.2	20.0	28.4	15.9	13.3	12.9	6.1
Return on Equity After Income Taxes 48	4.8	•	209.6	23.1	18.1	•	17.9	13.6	18.8	11.8	8.7	8.5	4.4
Profit Margin (Before Income Tax) 49	5.9	•	12.0	3.2	5.8	5.8	6.2	8.5	17.9	16.0	7.8	13.3	5.6
Profit Margin (After Income Tax) 50	4.3	•	12.0	2.9	5.8	5.8	5.5	5.8	11.8	11.9	5.1	8.8	4.0

Table II

Corporations with Net Income

SECURITIES BROKERAGE

MONEY AMOUNTS AND SIZE OF ASSETS IN THOUSANDS OF DOLLARS

Item Description for Accounting Period 7/06 Through 6/07		Total	Zero Assets	Under 500	500 to 1,000	1,000 to 5,000	5,000 to 10,000	10,000 to 25,000	25,000 to 50,000	50,000 to 100,000	100,000 to 250,000	250,000 to 500,000	500,000 to 2,500,000	2,500,000 and over
Number of Enterprises	1	4854	•	2967	436	496	74	68	21	11	•	•	14	31
Revenues ($ in Thousands)														
Net Sales	2	243665029	•	1103507	1515477	1434854	261529	1517871	1178067	522238	•	•	4799062	228545806
Interest	3	147203092	•	3639	5143	14154	2969	11972	15100	14451	•	•	548917	146273623
Rents	4	744647	•	0	0	0	683	1893	20	0	•	•	4525	736365
Royalties	5	37972	•	0	0	0	14	7991	0	0	•	•	818	29148
Other Portfolio Income	6	4107740	•	2402	0	3695	29851	13546	13912	3040	•	•	92929	3842285
Other Receipts	7	91571578	•	1097466	1510334	1417005	228012	1482469	1149035	504747	•	•	4151873	77664385
Total Receipts	8	243665029	•	1103507	1515477	1434854	261529	1517871	1178067	522238	•	•	4799062	228545806
Average Total Receipts	9	50199	•	372	3476	2893	3534	22322	56098	47476	•	•	342790	7372445
Operating Costs/Operating Income (%)														
Cost of Operations	10	0.3	•	1.9	•	•	1.8	13.5	16.8	•	•	•	0.1	0.2
Salaries and Wages	11	13.1	•	26.0	41.6	26.8	24.0	17.8	21.3	30.2	•	•	33.4	12.0
Taxes Paid	12	1.1	•	2.5	1.7	2.9	2.7	2.1	2.8	5.4	•	•	3.5	0.9
Interest Paid	13	57.3	•	0.7	•	0.4	0.1	0.9	0.4	0.5	•	•	9.3	60.8
Depreciation	14	0.5	•	0.0	0.1	0.4	0.4	0.5	0.3	0.6	•	•	0.9	0.5
Amortization and Depletion	15	0.4	•	0.0	•	0.1	0.2	0.1	0.0	0.0	•	•	2.7	0.4
Pensions and Other Deferred Comp.	16	0.4	•	1.8	0.0	1.1	0.5	0.3	0.4	2.2	•	•	1.1	0.4
Employee Benefits	17	0.6	•	0.7	0.9	2.0	1.2	1.3	0.9	1.2	•	•	0.9	0.5
Advertising	18	0.3	•	1.2	0.2	0.2	0.3	0.2	0.3	0.0	•	•	0.7	0.3
Other Expenses	19	17.6	•	22.7	43.6	34.7	21.3	46.9	41.2	19.5	•	•	29.1	16.7
Officers' Compensation	20	2.1	•	9.1	6.6	17.4	16.5	5.5	3.0	5.4	•	•	3.2	1.8
Operating Margin	21	6.2	•	33.2	5.2	13.9	31.1	10.8	12.5	35.1	•	•	15.2	5.6
Operating Margin Before Officers' Comp.	22	8.3	•	42.3	11.9	31.4	47.6	16.3	15.6	40.5	•	•	18.4	7.3

Selected Average Balance Sheet ($ in Thousands)

Net Receivables 23	169298	•	2	182	266	665	1330	4585	17834	•	418408	26273442
Inventories 24	•	•	•	•	•	•	•	•	•	•	•	•
Net Property, Plant and Equipment 25	1324	3	31	67	211	743	754	1027	•		12353	193922
Total Assets 26	592664	112	689	1630	7355	15378	35776	63602			1266080	91939480
Notes and Loans Payable 27	109730	27	7	227	16	1657	1063	3392	•		87073	17111668
All Other Liabilities 28	437934	29	275	368	2857	5594	12165	23034	•		896787	68050252
Net Worth 29	45001	57	407	1035	4483	8127	22548	37176	•		282220	6777559

Selected Financial Ratios (Times to 1)

Current Ratio 30	1.1	•	1.1	2.3	5.6	4.1	1.6	2.3	1.8	•	0.9	1.1
Quick Ratio 31	0.5	•	0.8	1.8	4.3	3.1	1.3	1.8	1.5	•	0.7	0.5
Net Sales to Working Capital 32	1.4	•	51.4	9.4	2.6	1.1	7.2	4.0	2.4	•	•	1.3
Coverage Ratio 33	1.1	•	45.9	•	32.0	329.9	12.6	32.8	72.3	•	2.6	1.1
Total Asset Turnover 34	0.1	•	3.3	5.0	1.8	0.5	1.5	1.6	0.7	•	0.3	0.1
Inventory Turnover 35	•	•	•	•	•	•	•	•	•	•	•	•
Receivables Turnover 36	•	•	•	•	•	•	•	•	•	•	•	•
Total Liabilities to Net Worth 37	12.2	•	1.0	0.7	0.6	0.6	0.9	0.6	0.7	•	3.5	12.6
Current Assets to Working Capital 38	11.3	•	7.7	1.7	1.2	1.3	2.8	1.8	2.2	•	•	11.2
Current Liabilities to Working Capital 39	10.3	•	6.7	0.7	0.2	0.3	1.8	0.8	1.2	•	•	10.2
Working Capital to Net Sales 40	0.7	•	0.0	0.1	0.4	0.9	0.1	0.2	0.4	•	•	0.8
Inventory to Working Capital 41	0.0	•	•	•	•	•	•	•	0.1	•	•	0.0
Total Receipts to Cash Flow 42	4.6	•	2.0	2.2	2.2	2.1	1.8	2.0	1.9	•	2.5	4.9
Cost of Goods to Cash Flow 43	0.0	•	0.0	•	0.0	0.0	0.2	0.3	0.0	•	0.0	0.0
Cash Flow to Total Debt 44	0.0	•	3.4	5.7	2.2	0.6	1.7	2.1	0.9	•	0.1	0.0

Selected Financial Factors (in Percentages)

Debt Ratio 45	92.4	•	49.5	40.9	36.5	39.1	47.2	37.0	41.5	•	77.7	92.6
Return on Total Assets 46	5.4	•	112.5	26.4	25.5	10.9	17.0	20.2	26.5	•	6.6	5.3
Return on Equity Before Income Taxes 47	7.0	•	218.2	44.6	38.9	17.8	29.6	31.1	44.7	•	18.2	6.1
Return on Equity After Income Taxes 48	5.1	•	218.1	41.8	38.7	16.3	26.8	23.4	32.2	•	12.2	4.4
Profit Margin (Before Income Tax) 49	6.3	•	33.2	5.2	13.9	22.5	10.8	12.5	35.0	•	15.0	5.6
Profit Margin (After Income Tax) 50	4.6	•	33.2	4.9	13.9	20.6	9.7	9.4	25.2	•	10.0	4.0

294

Table I

Corporations with and without Net Income

COMMODITY CONTRACTS DEALING AND BROKERAGE

MONEY AMOUNTS AND SIZE OF ASSETS IN THOUSANDS OF DOLLARS

Item Description for Accounting Period 7/06 Through 6/07		Total	Zero Assets	Under 500	500 to 1,000	1,000 to 5,000	5,000 to 10,000	10,000 to 25,000	25,000 to 50,000	50,000 to 100,000	100,000 to 250,000	250,000 to 500,000	500,000 to 2,500,000	2,500,000 and over
Number of Enterprises	1	2094	238	1540	52	109	68	36	19	8	9	6	5	4
Revenues ($ in Thousands)														
Net Sales	2	6606701	71412	209831	7741	135670	75550	111790	70040	157633	253455	232653	685105	4595822
Interest	3	3169592	5347	786	0	1385	492	2584	4484	3769	22328	18570	43048	3066798
Rents	4	8898	0	0	0	126	0	0	0	23	3	0	1	8746
Royalties	5	0	0	0	0	0	0	0	0	0	0	0	0	0
Other Portfolio Income	6	361478	1421	0	0	901	64	12226	0	433	6123	8498	183	331626
Other Receipts	7	3066733	64644	209045	7741	133258	74994	96980	65556	153408	225001	205585	641873	1188652
Total Receipts	8	6606701	71412	209831	7741	135670	75550	111790	70040	157633	253455	232653	685105	4595822
Average Total Receipts	9	3155	300	136	149	1245	1111	3105	3686	19704	28162	38776	137021	1148956
Operating Costs/Operating Income (%)														
Cost of Operations	10	0.5	•	•	•	•	•	•	•	•	1.0	11.7	•	•
Salaries and Wages	11	13.9	8.6	4.4	•	17.1	22.7	28.6	32.2	20.5	19.8	23.8	37.8	8.9
Taxes Paid	12	1.6	2.9	3.0	6.3	3.7	4.5	7.3	1.9	2.8	2.0	2.8	1.8	1.1
Interest Paid	13	44.9	9.8	3.2	7.0	10.9	0.4	7.6	8.8	4.9	7.0	12.5	10.9	60.8
Depreciation	14	0.7	0.5	0.6	26.0	1.6	0.4	1.1	0.3	0.7	0.6	0.9	0.4	0.7
Amortization and Depletion	15	1.9	1.2	•	•	4.6	•	0.9	0.2	0.7	0.9	0.1	0.1	2.5
Pensions and Other Deferred Comp.	16	0.7	0.7	1.3	•	3.7	1.0	1.7	0.7	0.8	1.0	0.9	0.7	0.5
Employee Benefits	17	0.9	1.6	0.2	•	3.5	0.9	2.6	0.6	2.5	1.5	2.2	0.8	0.7
Advertising	18	0.2	1.0	0.5	0.2	0.1	1.4	1.6	0.2	0.9	0.3	0.3	0.3	0.0
Other Expenses	19	23.7	83.6	65.7	52.8	20.5	51.8	29.8	34.5	71.0	30.6	34.6	28.2	16.8
Officers' Compensation	20	3.1	4.8	27.3	•	42.9	11.2	12.0	10.6	11.5	3.7	1.3	2.4	0.3
Operating Margin	21	7.9	•	•	7.7	•	5.7	6.7	10.2	•	31.6	8.9	16.6	7.7
Operating Margin Before Officers' Comp.	22	11.1	•	21.1	7.7	34.3	16.9	18.8	20.8	•	35.3	10.2	19.0	7.9

Selected Average Balance Sheet ($ in Thousands)

Line Item	1	2	3	4	5	6	7	8	9	10	11	12	13
Net Receivables 23	7841	0	18	37	573	345	4434	1478	16359	8798	42423	455451	3343223
Inventories 24	•	•	•	•	•	•	•	•	•	•	•	•	•
Net Property, Plant and Equipment 25	129	0	6	422	251	482	96	183	1076	1005	16158	1734	12024
Total Assets 26	30199	135	773	2323	6672	19100	34895	70786	161750	316795	1254696	12683800	
Notes and Loans Payable 27	1542	42	156	1345	1526	4716	3054	19885	16720	35305	11871	524292	
All Other Liabilities 28	26758	16	284	368	1046	11355	14081	22903	115963	248780	1190765	11632405	
Net Worth 29	1899	76	333	609	4100	3028	17761	27998	29068	32710	52059	527103	

Selected Financial Ratios (Times to 1)

Line Item	1	2	3	4	5	6	7	8	9	10	11	12	13
Current Ratio 30	0.6	4.6	0.3	1.6	5.0	1.6	1.6	0.6	0.9	0.9	0.9	0.8	0.6
Quick Ratio 31	0.5	4.1	0.3	1.1	1.1	0.8	0.8	0.6	0.5	0.5	0.6	0.5	
Net Sales to Working Capital 32	•	1.9	2.3	0.2	0.5	•	0.4	•	•	1.9	•	0.5	•
Coverage Ratio 33	1.2	•	2.1	0.2	14.2	1.9	2.2	0.1	•	5.5	1.9	2.5	1.1
Total Asset Turnover 34	0.1	1.0	•	0.2	0.5	0.2	0.2	0.1	0.3	0.2	0.1	•	0.1
Inventory Turnover 35	•	•	•	•	•	•	•	•	•	•	•	•	•
Receivables Turnover 36	•	•	•	•	•	•	•	•	•	•	•	•	•
Total Liabilities to Net Worth 37	14.9	•	0.8	1.3	2.8	0.6	5.3	1.0	1.5	4.6	8.7	23.1	23.1
Current Assets to Working Capital 38	•	1.3	•	2.6	1.2	2.6	1.6	•	•	•	•	2.6	•
Current Liabilities to Working Capital 39	•	0.3	•	1.6	0.2	1.6	0.3	•	•	•	•	•	•
Working Capital to Net Sales 40	•	0.5	•	4.0	4.0	1.8	2.8	•	•	•	•	•	•
Inventory to Working Capital 41	•	•	•	•	0.3	•	•	•	•	•	•	•	•
Total Receipts to Cash Flow 42	3.8	1.9	2.5	11.5	1.9	3.1	2.4	1.9	1.7	2.7	•	2.3	5.4
Cost of Goods to Cash Flow 43	0.0	•	•	•	•	•	•	•	0.0	0.0	•	0.3	•
Cash Flow to Total Debt 44	0.0	1.2	0.1	0.1	0.2	0.1	0.1	0.2	0.1	0.3	0.1	0.0	0.0

Selected Financial Factors (in Percentages)

Line Item	1	2	3	4	5	6	7	8	9	10	11	12	13
Debt Ratio 45	93.7	43.2	56.9	73.8	38.5	84.1	49.1	60.4	82.0	89.7	95.9	95.8	
Return on Total Assets 46	5.5	•	2.8	1.2	1.0	2.4	2.0	•	6.7	2.9	3.0	6.2	
Return on Equity Before Income Taxes 47	13.3	•	3.4	•	1.5	7.1	2.1	•	30.6	13.2	43.6	16.7	
Return on Equity After Income Taxes 48	7.7	•	2.9	•	1.5	•	2.0	•	20.4	9.4	32.5	10.3	
Profit Margin (Before Income Tax) 49	8.0	•	7.7	•	5.6	6.9	10.2	•	31.6	11.2	16.6	7.6	
Profit Margin (After Income Tax) 50	4.7	•	6.5	5.6	5.6	•	9.7	•	21.1	7.9	12.3	4.7	

Table II

Corporations with Net Income

COMMODITY CONTRACTS DEALING AND BROKERAGE

MONEY AMOUNTS AND SIZE OF ASSETS IN THOUSANDS OF DOLLARS

Item Description for Accounting Period 7/06 Through 6/07		Total	Zero Assets	Under 500	500 to 1,000	1,000 to 5,000	5,000 to 10,000	10,000 to 25,000	25,000 to 50,000	50,000 to 100,000	100,000 to 250,000	250,000 to 500,000	500,000 to 2,500,000	2,500,000 and over
Number of Enterprises	1	1480	•	1035	52	89	9	21	•	3	•	•	5	•
Revenues ($ in Thousands)														
Net Sales	2	5946713	•	217829	7741	109911	48545	128195	•	51281	•	•	685105	•
Interest	3	3034568	•	0	0	1264	0	2584	•	2180	•	•	43048	•
Rents	4	8873	•	0	0	126	0	0	•	23	•	•	1	•
Royalties	5	0	•	0	0	0	0	0	•	0	•	•	0	•
Other Portfolio Income	6	299653	•	0	0	864	0	12226	•	0	•	•	183	•
Other Receipts	7	2603619	•	217829	7741	107657	48545	113385	•	49078	•	•	641873	•
Total Receipts	8	5946713	•	217829	7741	109911	48545	128195	•	51281	•	•	685105	•
Average Total Receipts	9	4018	•	210	149	1235	5394	6105	•	17094	•	•	137021	•
Operating Costs/Operating Income (%)														
Cost of Operations	10	•	•	•	•	•	•	•	•	•	•	•	•	•
Salaries and Wages	11	14.2	•	1.8	•	17.2	15.4	22.8	•	16.5	•	•	37.8	•
Taxes Paid	12	1.5	•	2.0	6.3	3.8	5.2	4.5	•	3.8	•	•	1.8	•
Interest Paid	13	48.8	•	3.1	7.0	0.5	0.3	5.5	•	10.9	•	•	10.9	•
Depreciation	14	0.7	•	0.1	26.0	1.8	•	0.9	•	1.0	•	•	0.4	•
Amortization and Depletion	15	0.5	•	•	•	•	•	0.8	•	0.8	•	•	0.1	•
Pensions and Other Deferred Comp.	16	0.6	•	•	•	1.1	0.7	1.5	•	0.9	•	•	0.7	•
Employee Benefits	17	0.9	•	0.1	•	3.3	0.5	1.9	•	2.3	•	•	0.8	•
Advertising	18	0.1	•	0.4	0.2	0.0	0.0	0.5	•	•	•	•	0.3	•
Other Expenses	19	15.9	•	33.1	52.8	16.6	9.3	17.4	•	13.6	•	•	28.2	•
Officers' Compensation	20	2.7	•	19.5	•	47.8	6.3	9.0	•	4.7	•	•	2.4	•
Operating Margin	21	14.1	•	39.9	7.7	7.8	62.2	35.2	•	45.4	•	•	16.6	•
Operating Margin Before Officers' Comp.	22	16.8	•	59.4	7.7	55.6	68.5	44.2	•	50.2	•	•	19.0	•

Selected Average Balance Sheet ($ in Thousands)

	•	•	•	•	•	•	•	•
Net Receivables 23	7350	27	37	701	196	6185	38456	455451
Inventories 24	•	•	•	•	•	•	•	•
Net Property, Plant and Equipment 25	148	3	422	291	1	126	1176	1734
Total Assets 26	36265	163	773	1861	7704	18336	75902	1254696
Notes and Loans Payable 27	1967	63	156	610	72	7549	31697	11871
All Other Liabilities 28	32460	16	284	427	3524	6394	32616	1190765
Net Worth 29	1838	84	333	823	4108	4393	11589	52059

Selected Financial Ratios (Times to 1)

	•	•	•	•	•	•	•	•
Current Ratio 30	0.6	6.2	0.3	1.4	1.3	1.2	0.9	0.8
Quick Ratio 31	0.4	5.6	0.3	1.1	0.4	0.8	0.8	0.5
Net Sales to Working Capital 32	•	1.9	•	3.4	4.4	3.0	•	•
Coverage Ratio 33	1.3	13.8	2.1	15.8	193.4	7.4	5.2	2.5
Total Asset Turnover 34	0.1	1.3	0.2	0.7	0.7	0.3	0.2	0.1
Inventory Turnover 35	•	•	•	•	•	•	•	•
Receivables Turnover 36	•	•	•	•	•	•	•	•
Total Liabilities to Net Worth 37	18.7	0.9	1.3	0.9	0.9	3.2	5.5	23.1
Current Assets to Working Capital 38	•	1.2	•	3.8	3.9	6.5	•	•
Current Liabilities to Working Capital 39	•	0.2	•	2.8	2.9	5.5	•	•
Working Capital to Net Sales 40	•	0.5	•	0.3	0.2	0.3	•	•
Inventory to Working Capital 41	•	•	•	•	•	1.7	•	•
Total Receipts to Cash Flow 42	4.1	1.5	2.5	4.7	1.4	2.0	1.8	2.3
Cost of Goods to Cash Flow 43	•	•	•	•	•	•	•	•
Cash Flow to Total Debt 44	0.0	1.8	0.1	0.3	1.0	0.2	0.2	0.0

Selected Financial Factors (in Percentages)

	•	•	•	•	•	•	•	•
Debt Ratio 45	94.9	48.4	56.9	55.7	46.7	76.0	84.7	95.9
Return on Total Assets 46	7.0	55.6	2.8	5.6	43.8	13.6	12.7	3.0
Return on Equity Before Income Taxes 47	31.0	100.0	3.4	11.8	81.7	49.1	67.0	43.6
Return on Equity After Income Taxes 48	22.8	100.0	2.9	9.7	81.7	35.4	49.2	32.5
Profit Margin (Before Income Tax) 49	14.2	39.9	7.7	7.8	62.2	35.4	45.4	16.6
Profit Margin (After Income Tax) 50	10.4	39.9	6.5	6.5	62.2	25.5	33.4	12.3

Table I

Corporations with and without Net Income

SECURITIES & COMMODITY EXCHANGES, OTHER FINANCIAL INVESTMENT

MONEY AMOUNTS AND SIZE OF ASSETS IN THOUSANDS OF DOLLARS

Item Description for Accounting Period 7/06 Through 6/07		Total	Zero Assets	Under 500	500 to 1,000	1,000 to 5,000	5,000 to 10,000	10,000 to 25,000	25,000 to 50,000	50,000 to 100,000	100,000 to 250,000	250,000 to 500,000	500,000 to 2,500,000	2,500,000 and over
Number of Enterprises	1	40277	6744	28336	937	2757	479	468	234	130	83	29	48	31
Revenues ($ in Thousands)														
Net Sales	2	121411977	1519305	8739590	1114569	6640297	3209147	3271387	4413116	3475887	3883071	2570285	12684418	69893905
Interest	3	18501774	363804	50303	8755	55409	76975	66312	87521	92163	177416	214246	940080	16368792
Rents	4	613233	433	4508	347	474	181	2642	5410	236	56402	5003	14229	523367
Royalties	5	92152	10018	47448	0	8327	151	271	161	330	23804	1394	240	9
Other Portfolio Income	6	4371916	79861	5747	45348	167454	62729	131820	118747	87825	437080	135043	396431	2703834
Other Receipts	7	97835902	1065189	8631584	1060119	6408633	3069111	3070342	4201277	3295333	3188369	2214599	11333438	50297903
Total Receipts	8	121411977	1519305	8739590	1114569	6640297	3209147	3271387	4413116	3475887	3883071	2570285	12684418	69893905
Average Total Receipts	9	3014	225	308	1190	2409	6700	6990	18859	26738	46784	88631	264259	2254642
Operating Costs/Operating Income (%)														
Cost of Operations	10	0.7	0.4	0.4	1.1	1.0	0.2	1.1	0.3	2.4	1.7	0.1	1.0	0.6
Salaries and Wages	11	19.3	20.1	23.7	16.7	23.8	29.0	30.8	25.8	25.1	17.1	20.9	22.7	16.2
Taxes Paid	12	2.2	2.6	2.7	2.9	2.6	2.2	2.6	2.7	2.0	3.3	4.3	2.4	1.8
Interest Paid	13	12.0	18.2	0.7	0.2	1.1	1.7	3.3	3.0	3.2	4.9	10.6	6.7	17.8
Depreciation	14	1.2	1.7	0.8	0.7	1.2	1.0	2.2	1.9	1.6	2.3	1.4	0.9	1.1
Amortization and Depletion	15	0.8	3.3	0.1	0.0	0.4	0.7	0.4	0.6	0.5	0.8	1.3	2.3	0.6
Pensions and Other Deferred Comp.	16	1.3	2.5	3.2	2.0	1.7	0.6	0.8	1.0	0.7	0.6	0.7	0.8	1.2
Employee Benefits	17	1.5	1.9	1.9	1.6	1.6	1.6	1.8	1.1	1.2	1.0	1.7	1.4	1.5
Advertising	18	1.6	3.4	0.6	0.4	0.3	0.2	0.5	1.7	0.3	0.9	0.3	0.8	2.2
Other Expenses	19	32.8	34.2	32.2	20.9	29.4	37.0	27.0	27.0	29.2	19.8	34.7	37.2	33.9
Officers' Compensation	20	8.2	4.9	21.6	41.8	22.5	12.5	14.0	19.5	12.9	22.4	4.1	7.6	2.8
Operating Margin	21	18.4	6.9	12.0	11.8	14.5	13.5	15.6	15.3	20.9	25.2	19.9	16.2	20.3
Operating Margin Before Officers' Comp.	22	26.6	11.8	33.6	53.6	37.0	25.9	29.6	34.9	33.9	47.7	24.0	23.8	23.1

Selected Average Balance Sheet ($ in Thousands)

Line Item													
Net Receivables 23	2369304	136850	53677	9511	7083	5183	1131	928	277	18	9	0	2147
Inventories 24	•	•	•	•	•	•	•	•	•	•	•	•	•
Net Property, Plant and Equipment 25	251288	18955	8791	4812	4137	2673	939	358	463	26	14	0	318
Total Assets 26	14719161	1044862	339940	155384	69526	35587	15828	7161	2264	735	73	0	14063
Notes and Loans Payable 27	5787675	295791	99015	35409	16127	9014	4247	3106	736	106	24	0	5212
All Other Liabilities 28	4703115	272532	53001	26680	12225	8086	1767	1753	595	143	22	0	4225
Net Worth 29	4228371	476539	187925	93296	41173	18487	9814	2302	932	486	27	0	4626

Selected Financial Ratios (Times to 1)

Line Item													
Current Ratio 30	1.2	1.2	2.5	1.8	1.9	2.2	2.0	1.5	1.8	1.3	1.8	•	1.3
Quick Ratio 31	0.8	0.8	1.7	1.2	1.3	1.7	1.3	1.0	1.4	1.0	1.6	•	0.9
Net Sales to Working Capital 32	1.8	5.3	1.0	2.3	2.0	2.2	2.7	6.1	6.3	26.0	16.6	•	2.3
Coverage Ratio 33	2.2	3.4	2.9	6.5	7.5	6.1	5.6	8.8	14.6	48.8	17.5	1.3	2.6
Total Asset Turnover 34	0.2	0.3	0.3	0.3	0.4	0.5	0.4	0.9	1.1	1.6	4.2	•	0.2
Inventory Turnover 35	•	•	•	•	•	•	•	•	•	•	•	•	•
Receivables Turnover 36	•	•	•	•	•	•	•	•	•	•	•	•	•
Total Liabilities to Net Worth 37	2.5	1.2	0.8	0.7	0.7	0.9	0.6	2.1	1.4	0.5	1.7	•	2.0
Current Assets to Working Capital 38	5.6	6.0	1.7	2.3	2.1	1.8	2.0	2.9	2.3	4.4	2.3	•	4.9
Current Liabilities to Working Capital 39	4.6	5.0	0.7	1.3	1.1	0.8	1.0	1.9	1.3	3.4	1.3	•	3.9
Working Capital to Net Sales 40	0.6	0.2	1.0	0.4	0.5	0.5	0.4	0.2	0.2	0.0	0.1	•	0.4
Inventory to Working Capital 41	0.0	0.0	0.0	0.0	0.0	0.0	•	•	•	0.1	•	•	0.0
Total Receipts to Cash Flow 42	1.9	2.0	2.1	2.6	2.2	2.7	2.6	2.2	2.8	3.7	2.6	2.9	2.1
Cost of Goods to Cash Flow 43	0.0	0.0	0.0	0.0	0.1	0.0	0.0	0.0	0.0	0.0	0.0	0.0	0.0
Cash Flow to Total Debt 44	0.1	0.2	0.3	0.3	0.4	0.4	0.4	0.6	0.6	1.3	2.6	•	0.2

Selected Financial Factors (in Percentages)

Line Item													
Debt Ratio 45	71.3	54.4	44.7	40.0	40.8	48.1	38.0	67.9	58.8	33.9	62.9	•	67.1
Return on Total Assets 46	5.9	5.8	8.0	9.5	9.1	9.6	8.1	14.2	16.5	19.0	53.8	•	6.6
Return on Equity Before Income Taxes 47	11.0	9.0	9.5	13.4	13.4	15.5	10.8	39.2	37.2	28.1	136.9	•	12.1
Return on Equity After Income Taxes 48	7.7	4.4	6.7	10.8	12.5	13.0	9.3	34.4	35.2	24.2	133.7	•	8.8
Profit Margin (Before Income Tax) 49	20.7	16.2	20.1	26.8	20.6	15.2	15.1	13.5	14.4	11.5	12.0	6.3	18.6
Profit Margin (After Income Tax) 50	14.5	7.9	14.3	21.6	19.3	12.8	13.1	11.8	13.6	9.9	11.8	•	13.5

Table II
Corporations with Net Income

SECURITIES & COMMODITY EXCHANGES, OTHER FINANCIAL INVESTMENT

MONEY AMOUNTS AND SIZE OF ASSETS IN THOUSANDS OF DOLLARS

Item Description for Accounting Period 7/06 Through 6/07		Total	Zero Assets	Under 500	500 to 1,000	1,000 to 5,000	5,000 to 10,000	10,000 to 25,000	25,000 to 50,000	50,000 to 100,000	100,000 to 250,000	250,000 to 500,000	500,000 to 2,500,000	2,500,000 and over
Number of Enterprises	1	21560	1787	16928	740	1328	202	259	116	70	50	16	35	28
Revenues ($ in Thousands)														
Net Sales	2	107026652	1274898	5906227	1097127	5155038	2293433	2882725	3730125	2676509	2884529	1969953	11587479	65568611
Interest	3	17557060	343313	36551	8750	38952	17392	35986	38311	64599	129693	55066	900213	15888234
Rents	4	553120	0	4508	347	184	181	1026	5345	16	3162	14224	759	523367
Royalties	5	90525	10018	47448	0	8327	1	271	86	327	23798	0	240	9
Other Portfolio Income	6	4068325	72892	2994	45348	146810	62103	113244	102005	67728	398553	107565	317431	2631652
Other Receipts	7	84757622	848675	5814726	1042682	4960765	2213756	2732198	3584378	2543839	2329323	1806563	10355371	46525349
Total Receipts	8	107026652	1274898	5906227	1097127	5155038	2293433	2882725	3730125	2676509	2884529	1969953	11587479	65568611
Average Total Receipts	9	4964	713	349	1483	3882	11354	11130	32156	38236	57691	123122	331071	2341736
Operating Costs/Operating Income (%)														
Cost of Operations	10	0.4	•	0.4	•	0.7	0.2	0.8	0.2	2.4	2.2	•	1.1	0.1
Salaries and Wages	11	17.6	17.4	19.9	16.7	23.0	22.6	28.4	24.9	19.6	12.8	21.2	18.4	15.8
Taxes Paid	12	2.1	2.2	2.6	2.8	2.6	2.1	2.4	2.6	1.9	3.0	5.1	2.3	1.8
Interest Paid	13	12.5	19.8	0.4	0.1	0.8	1.1	1.7	1.5	2.5	4.7	2.3	5.3	18.3
Depreciation	14	1.1	1.5	0.7	0.6	1.1	0.4	1.3	1.1	1.0	1.1	1.5	0.8	1.1
Amortization and Depletion	15	0.8	0.5	0.1	0.0	0.5	0.2	0.2	0.3	0.3	0.9	1.3	2.4	0.6
Pensions and Other Deferred Comp.	16	1.2	0.3	2.1	2.0	1.8	0.8	0.8	0.9	0.8	0.6	0.9	0.9	1.3
Employee Benefits	17	1.5	1.1	1.5	1.7	1.6	1.4	1.4	1.1	0.8	1.0	1.9	1.3	1.5
Advertising	18	1.6	3.9	0.4	0.4	0.3	0.1	0.4	1.9	0.2	1.1	0.2	0.8	2.2
Other Expenses	19	30.1	24.3	30.6	18.4	19.2	29.9	21.4	21.7	18.7	18.6	26.5	34.9	32.4
Officers' Compensation	20	6.8	2.6	17.5	42.5	22.5	12.2	13.4	17.6	15.1	15.5	3.7	4.0	2.9
Operating Margin	21	24.4	26.2	23.8	14.8	25.8	28.9	27.9	26.2	36.7	38.7	35.2	28.0	21.9
Operating Margin Before Officers' Comp.	22	31.2	28.8	41.3	57.3	48.3	41.1	41.4	43.8	51.8	54.1	38.9	32.0	24.8

Selected Average Balance Sheet ($ in Thousands)

Net Receivables **23**	3739	0	12	11	147	1150	1141	5786	10431	7538	62459	150923	2557771
Inventories **24**	•	•	•	•	•	•	•	•	•	•	•	•	•
Net Property, Plant and Equipment **25**	478	0	18	26	602	237	858	2359	3151	5146	10789	20181	259467
Total Assets **26**	22678	90	734	2526	6923	16193	34514	68419	157292	333688		1130710	14869547
Notes and Loans Payable **27**	8748	20	112	641	1712	4339	5659	13087	38442	54751		299703	6107443
All Other Liabilities **28**	6544	16	174	598	1851	1682	8463	14449	29486	55520		283208	4457630
Net Worth **29**	7386	54	448	1286	3359	10173	20392	40883	89364	223416		547798	4304474

Selected Financial Ratios (Times to 1)

Current Ratio **30**	1.3	•	2.8	1.2	1.7	2.3	2.1	2.3	2.0	1.3	2.1	1.2	1.2
Quick Ratio **31**	0.9	•	2.6	1.0	1.4	1.7	1.5	1.9	1.4	0.9	1.5	0.9	0.9
Net Sales to Working Capital **32**	2.2	•	9.9	35.7	9.0	4.7	4.0	3.0	2.3	5.3	1.5	5.1	1.6
Coverage Ratio **33**	3.0	2.3	63.2	104.1	31.6	27.2	17.4	18.2	15.5	9.8	16.2	6.3	2.2
Total Asset Turnover **34**	0.2	•	3.9	2.0	1.5	1.6	0.7	0.9	0.6	0.4	0.4	0.3	0.2
Inventory Turnover **35**	•	•	•	•	•	•	•	•	•	•	•	•	•
Receivables Turnover **36**	•	•	•	•	•	•	•	•	•	•	•	•	•
Total Liabilities to Net Worth **37**	2.1	•	0.7	0.6	1.0	1.1	0.6	0.7	0.7	0.8	0.5	1.1	2.5
Current Assets to Working Capital **38**	4.8	•	1.5	5.4	2.4	1.7	1.9	1.8	2.0	4.2	1.9	5.0	5.2
Current Liabilities to Working Capital **39**	3.8	•	0.5	4.4	1.4	0.7	0.9	0.8	1.0	3.2	0.9	4.0	4.2
Working Capital to Net Sales **40**	0.5	•	0.1	0.0	0.1	0.2	0.3	0.3	0.4	0.2	0.6	0.2	0.6
Inventory to Working Capital **41**	0.0	•	•	0.0	•	•	•	0.0	0.0	0.0	•	0.0	0.0
Total Receipts to Cash Flow **42**	2.0	2.2	2.0	3.6	2.5	1.8	2.2	2.3	1.9	2.1	1.8	1.7	1.9
Cost of Goods to Cash Flow **43**	0.0	•	0.0	•	0.0	0.0	0.0	0.0	0.0	0.0	•	0.0	0.0
Cash Flow to Total Debt **44**	0.2	•	4.8	1.4	1.3	1.7	0.8	1.0	0.7	0.4	0.6	0.3	0.1

Selected Financial Factors (in Percentages)

Debt Ratio **45**	67.4	•	40.0	38.9	49.1	51.5	37.2	40.9	40.2	43.2	33.0	51.6	71.1
Return on Total Assets **46**	8.1	•	94.0	29.6	40.8	49.3	20.1	25.7	21.8	16.8	13.9	9.7	6.4
Return on Equity Before Income Taxes **47**	16.6	•	154.0	48.1	77.6	97.9	30.2	41.1	34.2	26.5	19.5	16.9	12.1
Return on Equity After Income Taxes **48**	12.7	•	151.4	42.6	74.6	90.2	27.7	36.6	32.7	22.1	15.4	11.4	8.6
Profit Margin (Before Income Tax) **49**	24.6	25.4	23.8	14.5	25.7	29.0	27.6	26.1	36.6	41.0	35.4	28.0	22.3
Profit Margin (After Income Tax) **50**	18.9	20.5	23.4	12.9	24.7	26.7	25.3	23.2	34.9	34.3	27.9	18.9	15.8

Table I
Corporations with and without Net Income

LIFE INSURANCE

MONEY AMOUNTS AND SIZE OF ASSETS IN THOUSANDS OF DOLLARS

Item Description for Accounting Period 7/06 Through 6/07	Total	Zero Assets	Under 500	500 to 1,000	1,000 to 5,000	5,000 to 10,000	10,000 to 25,000	25,000 to 50,000	50,000 to 100,000	100,000 to 250,000	250,000 to 500,000	500,000 to 2,500,000	2,500,000 and over
Number of Enterprises **1**	1130	49	281	108	190	71	87	55	43	44	43	70	89
Revenues ($ in Thousands)													
Net Sales **2**	946307986	27829541	56994	31632	309790	195089	1459926	1423331	1303243	2735530	4024312	19606799	887331800
Interest **3**	174414328	1788216	2871	2761	42417	15646	75858	119045	117211	249447	710762	3898515	167091579
Rents **4**	3986062	5899	81	0	88	448	2346	977	7110	9623	13735	31318	3914436
Royalties **5**	16877	0	0	0	0	0	0	0	0	659	0	208	16010
Other Portfolio Income **6**	23178632	2221318	515	520	9968	6680	34998	8675	15204	105231	41070	291503	20442948
Other Receipts **7**	745012087	23814108	53527	28351	257317	172315	1346724	1294634	1163718	2370570	3258745	15385255	695866827
Total Receipts **8**	946307986	27829541	56994	31632	309790	195089	1459926	1423331	1303243	2735530	4024312	19606799	887331800
Average Total Receipts **9**	837441	567950	203	293	1630	2748	16781	25879	30308	62171	93589	280097	9970020
Operating Costs/Operating Income (%)													
Cost of Operations **10**	56.2	84.1	27.3	20.3	10.3	22.6	32.7	69.7	52.5	42.9	46.7	53.2	55.5
Salaries and Wages **11**	2.0	0.0	•	•	•	•	0.0	0.1	1.5	0.4	0.4	0.5	2.2
Taxes Paid **12**	0.8	0.1	0.9	0.9	0.5	2.1	0.6	0.9	1.6	1.3	1.4	0.9	0.8
Interest Paid **13**	4.0	0.0	0.1	0.1	0.2	2.2	0.0	0.4	0.3	0.3	0.5	0.9	4.3
Depreciation **14**	0.7	0.0	0.1	0.1	0.0	0.2	0.1	0.1	0.4	0.2	0.3	0.3	0.7
Amortization and Depletion **15**	0.9	0.3	0.9	0.7	0.3	0.7	2.1	2.5	2.4	2.6	2.7	2.2	0.9
Pensions and Other Deferred Comp. **16**	0.4	0.0	0.2	•	0.1	0.6	0.2	0.2	1.5	0.6	0.8	0.6	0.4
Employee Benefits **17**	0.3	0.0	0.2	•	0.0	0.1	0.1	0.1	0.7	0.1	0.2	0.2	0.3
Advertising **18**	0.2	0.0	0.0	•	0.0	0.3	0.1	0.1	1.2	0.1	0.4	0.6	0.2
Other Expenses **19**	30.7	14.3	61.8	48.5	70.0	61.8	66.7	20.1	34.5	48.6	43.0	36.9	30.9
Officers' Compensation **20**	0.1	•	0.0	•	•	•	•	0.0	•	0.0	0.0	0.2	0.1
Operating Margin **21**	3.6	1.1	8.5	29.5	18.5	9.3	•	5.8	3.3	2.8	3.6	3.5	3.7
Operating Margin Before Officers' Comp. **22**	3.7	1.1	8.5	29.5	18.5	9.3	•	5.8	3.3	2.9	3.7	3.6	3.8

Selected Average Balance Sheet ($ in Thousands)

Item												
Net Receivables 23	107564	0	31	89	168	1055	779	2978	1466	1104	6519	1355977
Inventories 24	•	•	•	•	•	•	•	•	•	•	•	•
Net Property, Plant and Equipment 25	48742	0	0	3	115	129	89	288	422	1722	6532	612267
Total Assets 26	4660052	182	731	2502	6867	16965	35495	74160	163161	363709	1239033	57849408
Notes and Loans Payable 27	163773	0	0	0	235	0	146	359	846	2285	5852	2072792
All Other Liabilities 28	3785549	224	387	1434	4217	10505	24914	54319	136622	302986	1056578	46959258
Net Worth 29	710729	-42	344	1068	2414	6459	10436	19482	25694	58438	176603	8817358

Selected Financial Ratios (Times to 1)

Item												
Current Ratio 30	0.4	•	4.5	8.4	1.2	3.6	3.0	2.6	0.9	1.3	1.2	0.4
Quick Ratio 31	0.3	•	3.6	6.6	0.9	2.9	2.2	1.8	0.7	1.1	0.9	0.3
Net Sales to Working Capital 32	•	•	1.7	0.6	7.6	1.1	3.0	1.5	•	3.2	5.0	•
Coverage Ratio 33	2.0	24.5	162.8	346.1	85.9	5.2	•	10.9	8.9	7.6	4.8	2.0
Total Asset Turnover 34	0.2	•	1.1	0.4	0.7	0.4	1.0	0.4	0.4	0.3	0.2	0.2
Inventory Turnover 35	•	•	•	•	•	•	•	•	•	•	•	•
Receivables Turnover 36	•	•	•	•	•	•	•	•	•	•	•	•
Total Liabilities to Net Worth 37	5.6	•	1.1	1.3	1.8	1.6	2.4	2.8	5.4	5.2	6.0	5.6
Current Assets to Working Capital 38	•	1.3	1.1	7.6	1.4	1.5	3.2	1.6	•	4.5	6.4	•
Current Liabilities to Working Capital 39	•	0.3	0.1	6.6	0.4	0.5	2.2	0.6	•	3.5	5.4	•
Working Capital to Net Sales 40	•	0.6	1.7	0.1	0.9	0.3	0.2	0.7	0.3	0.3	0.2	•
Inventory to Working Capital 41	•	•	•	•	•	•	•	•	•	•	0.0	•
Total Receipts to Cash Flow 42	3.1	6.9	1.4	1.3	1.2	1.5	1.6	4.0	2.8	2.1	2.2	3.0
Cost of Goods to Cash Flow 43	1.7	5.8	•	0.3	0.1	0.3	0.5	2.8	1.5	0.9	1.4	1.7
Cash Flow to Total Debt 44	0.1	•	0.6	1.0	0.4	1.0	0.3	0.2	0.3	0.1	0.1	0.1

Selected Financial Factors (in Percentages)

Item												
Debt Ratio 45	84.7	123.2	53.0	57.3	64.8	61.9	70.6	73.7	84.3	83.9	85.7	84.8
Return on Total Assets 46	1.5	•	9.6	11.8	12.2	4.5	•	4.5	1.5	1.2	1.1	1.5
Return on Equity Before Income Taxes 47	4.8	•	•	25.1	28.2	10.4	•	14.3	5.1	6.6	5.8	4.8
Return on Equity After Income Taxes 48	3.2	•	•	23.1	25.1	7.6	•	11.1	3.1	1.5	3.0	3.1
Profit Margin (Before Income Tax) 49	4.1	1.1	8.5	29.5	18.4	9.2	5.8	3.3	2.7	3.0	3.3	4.2
Profit Margin (After Income Tax) 50	2.7	0.8	6.8	27.1	16.5	6.7	4.5	2.0	1.8	1.5	2.8	2.8

Table II

Corporations with Net Income

LIFE INSURANCE

MONEY AMOUNTS AND SIZE OF ASSETS IN THOUSANDS OF DOLLARS

Item Description for Accounting Period 7/06 Through 6/07	Total	Zero Assets	Under 500	500 to 1,000	1,000 to 5,000	5,000 to 10,000	10,000 to 25,000	25,000 to 50,000	50,000 to 100,000	100,000 to 250,000	250,000 to 500,000	500,000 to 2,500,000	2,500,000 and over
Number of Enterprises **1**	863	29	195	95	170	49	64	36	32	31	36	54	72
Revenues ($ in Thousands)													
Net Sales **2**	809842704	2563358	40571	26657	300392	132635	434305	1195888	937916	2035806	3367126	15596978	783211075
Interest **3**	145947821	354197	2541	2999	40519	11808	43238	88269	96543	170012	606815	2878912	141651968
Rents **4**	3152289	1694	81	0	88	127	1252	638	4393	7290	11658	29572	3095494
Royalties **5**	8728	0	0	0	0	0	0	0	0	55	0	208	8466
Other Portfolio Income **6**	20507865	91492	473	520	9610	6436	19252	7989	9424	89231	36353	230696	20006388
Other Receipts **7**	640226001	2115975	37476	23138	250175	114264	370563	1098992	827556	1769218	2712300	12457590	618448759
Total Receipts **8**	809842704	2563358	40571	26657	300392	132635	434305	1195888	937916	2035806	3367126	15596978	783211075
Average Total Receipts **9**	938404	88392	208	281	1767	2707	6786	33219	29310	65671	93531	288833	10877932
Operating Costs/Operating Income (%)													
Cost of Operations **10**	55.3	39.7	26.9	21.0	9.6	29.1	32.9	73.5	52.4	48.3	46.1	51.9	55.5
Salaries and Wages **11**	2.3	0.0	•	•	•	•	0.2	0.1	1.9	0.6	0.5	0.6	2.4
Taxes Paid **12**	0.8	0.6	1.1	0.8	0.4	1.8	1.8	0.6	1.5	1.5	1.4	1.0	0.8
Interest Paid **13**	4.3	0.0	0.0	0.1	0.2	0.3	0.1	0.2	0.1	0.4	0.6	0.8	4.5
Depreciation **14**	0.7	0.0	0.1	0.0	0.0	0.2	0.4	0.1	0.4	0.2	0.3	0.3	0.7
Amortization and Depletion **15**	0.9	2.1	1.0	0.5	0.3	0.7	1.6	2.4	2.2	2.7	2.5	2.3	0.8
Pensions and Other Deferred Comp. **16**	0.4	0.3	0.3	0.0	0.1	0.7	0.5	0.2	1.9	0.6	0.8	0.7	0.4
Employee Benefits **17**	0.3	0.0	0.1	•	0.0	0.1	0.3	0.0	0.6	0.1	0.2	0.2	0.3
Advertising **18**	0.2	0.0	0.0	0.0	0.0	0.0	0.1	0.0	0.2	0.1	0.3	0.8	0.2
Other Expenses **19**	29.7	42.6	46.0	37.3	69.7	42.3	42.0	14.0	30.9	35.6	39.9	33.4	29.5
Officers' Compensation **20**	0.1	•	•	•	•	•	•	•	•	0.1	0.1	0.2	0.1
Operating Margin **21**	4.9	14.5	24.5	40.1	19.7	24.9	20.2	8.8	7.9	9.9	7.4	7.8	4.7
Operating Margin Before Officers' Comp. **22**	5.0	14.5	24.5	40.1	19.7	24.9	20.2	8.8	7.9	9.9	7.5	8.0	4.8

Selected Average Balance Sheet ($ in Thousands)

Item	1	2	3	4	5	6	7	8	9	10	11	12	13
Net Receivables 23	133488	0	9	34	100	238	1336	1052	3356	1472	1184	7297	1589637
Inventories 24	•	•	•	•	•	•	•	•	•	•	•	•	•
Net Property, Plant and Equipment 25	59789	0	0	0	3	72	92	44	354	403	1974	7981	709171
Total Assets 26	5179454	209	855	2500	7272	16734	35560	72997	164396	362380	1269179		60800015
Notes and Loans Payable 27	198422	0	0	0	0	0	222	16	1021	2199	7584		
All Other Liabilities 28	4178717	229	344	1340	4425	9400	23306	54856	131376	296358	1063295		49032712
Net Worth 29	802316	-20	510	1160	2847	7334	12032	18126	31999	63823	198300		9396343

Selected Financial Ratios (Times to 1)

Item	1	2	3	4	5	6	7	8	9	10	11	12	13
Current Ratio 30	0.4	•	6.4	7.8	1.1	2.5	5.1	1.6	3.0	1.1	1.2	1.2	0.4
Quick Ratio 31	0.3	•	5.3	5.9	0.9	1.9	4.0	1.2	2.2	0.9	1.0	0.9	0.3
Net Sales to Working Capital 32	•	•	1.4	0.6	15.4	1.5	1.0	6.3	1.3	11.3	4.0	4.0	•
Coverage Ratio 33	2.2	1660.0	391.5	397.1	88.7	95.3	280.5	36.3	78.4	24.8	13.5	10.7	2.2
Total Asset Turnover 34	0.2	•	1.0	0.3	0.7	0.4	0.4	0.9	0.4	0.4	0.3	0.2	0.2
Inventory Turnover 35	•	•	•	•	•	•	•	•	•	•	•	•	•
Receivables Turnover 36	•	•	•	•	•	•	•	•	•	•	•	•	•
Total Liabilities to Net Worth 37	5.5	•	•	0.7	1.2	1.6	1.3	2.0	3.0	4.1	4.7	5.4	5.5
Current Assets to Working Capital 38	•	•	1.2	1.1	1.2	1.7	1.2	2.7	1.5	10.5	5.4	5.2	•
Current Liabilities to Working Capital 39	•	•	0.2	0.1	0.1	0.7	0.2	1.7	0.5	9.5	4.4	4.2	•
Working Capital to Net Sales 40	0.2	•	0.7	1.7	0.1	0.7	1.0	0.2	0.8	0.1	0.3	0.3	0.2
Inventory to Working Capital 41	•	•	•	•	•	•	•	•	•	•	•	•	0.0
Total Receipts to Cash Flow 42	3.1	2.1	1.4	1.3	1.1	1.6	1.7	4.5	2.7	2.5	2.2	2.5	3.1
Cost of Goods to Cash Flow 43	1.7	0.8	0.4	0.3	0.1	0.5	0.6	3.3	1.2	1.0	1.3	1.7	1.7
Cash Flow to Total Debt 44	0.1	•	0.6	1.2	0.4	0.4	0.2	0.3	0.2	0.1	0.1	0.1	0.1

Selected Financial Factors (in Percentages)

Item	1	2	3	4	5	6	7	8	9	10	11	12	13
Debt Ratio 45	84.5	•	109.4	40.3	53.6	60.9	56.2	66.2	75.2	80.5	82.4	84.4	84.5
Return on Total Assets 46	1.8	•	24.4	13.2	14.1	9.3	8.2	8.4	3.2	4.1	2.1	1.7	1.8
Return on Equity Before Income Taxes 47	6.3	•	•	22.1	29.9	23.4	18.6	24.3	12.7	20.0	10.9	6.1	6.3
Return on Equity After Income Taxes 48	4.4	•	•	20.4	26.8	19.9	14.7	20.0	9.8	14.1	7.8	4.2	4.4
Profit Margin (Before Income Tax) 49	5.4	14.5	24.5	40.1	19.7	24.6	20.1	8.8	7.9	9.7	7.6	5.3	5.4
Profit Margin (After Income Tax) 50	3.8	10.9	22.2	37.1	17.6	21.0	15.9	7.2	6.9	7.4	5.3	3.7	3.7

Table I

Corporations with and without Net Income

LIFE INSURANCE, STOCK COMPANIES (FORM 1120L)

MONEY AMOUNTS AND SIZE OF ASSETS IN THOUSANDS OF DOLLARS

Item Description for Accounting Period 7/06 Through 6/07		Total	Zero Assets	Under 500	500 to 1,000	1,000 to 5,000	5,000 to 10,000	10,000 to 25,000	25,000 to 50,000	50,000 to 100,000	100,000 to 250,000	250,000 to 500,000	500,000 to 2,500,000	2,500,000 and over
Number of Enterprises	1	1070	49	271	105	184	68	84	50	43	38	38	59	81
Revenues ($ in Thousands)														
Net Sales	2	847437823	27829541	55417	31545	307202	183794	1449352	1340623	1303243	2350649	3574159	16769853	792242444
Interest	3	153087398	1788216	2794	2682	41878	15183	73371	106676	117211	201229	603254	3120569	147014336
Rents	4	2981639	5899	81	0	88	448	2336	977	7110	6372	10660	18619	2929049
Royalties	5	10546	0	0	0	0	0	0	0	0	55	0	11	10480
Other Portfolio Income	6	19010603	2221318	515	520	9757	6582	34632	8048	15204	93963	36930	193357	16389778
Other Receipts	7	672347637	23814108	52027	28343	255479	161581	1339013	1224922	1163718	2049030	2923315	13437297	625898801
Total Receipts	8	847437823	27829541	55417	31545	307202	183794	1449352	1340623	1303243	2350649	3574159	16769853	792242444
Average Total Receipts	9	791998	567950	204	300	1670	2703	17254	26812	30308	61859	94057	284235	9780771
Operating Costs/Operating Income (%)														
Cost of Operations	10	57.2	84.1	27.9	20.3	10.2	23.5	32.6	70.9	52.5	41.0	46.8	54.0	56.5
Salaries and Wages	11	2.2	0.0	•	•	•	•	0.0	0.1	1.5	0.5	0.4	0.6	2.3
Taxes Paid	12	0.8	0.1	1.0	0.9	0.4	2.1	0.6	0.8	1.6	1.1	1.3	0.9	0.8
Interest Paid	13	4.3	0.0	0.1	0.1	0.2	2.3	0.0	0.5	0.3	0.4	0.6	0.8	4.6
Depreciation	14	0.7	0.0	0.1	0.1	0.0	0.2	0.1	0.1	0.4	0.2	0.3	0.3	0.7
Amortization and Depletion	15	0.9	0.3	0.9	0.7	0.3	0.7	2.0	2.5	2.4	2.5	2.5	2.1	0.8
Pensions and Other Deferred Comp.	16	0.4	0.0	0.2	•	0.1	0.6	0.2	0.1	1.5	0.5	0.6	0.5	0.4
Employee Benefits	17	0.3	0.0	0.0	•	0.0	0.0	0.1	0.1	0.7	0.1	0.1	0.2	0.3
Advertising	18	0.2	0.0	0.0	•	0.0	0.3	0.1	0.1	1.2	0.1	0.4	0.7	0.2
Other Expenses	19	29.5	14.3	60.2	48.5	69.9	60.2	66.8	18.8	34.5	50.8	42.9	36.9	29.7
Officers' Compensation	20	0.1	•	•	•	•	•	•	0.0	•	0.0	0.1	0.2	0.1
Operating Margin	21	3.5	1.1	9.6	29.4	18.8	10.0	18.8	6.0	3.3	2.8	3.9	2.8	3.5
Operating Margin Before Officers' Comp.	22	3.6	1.1	9.6	29.4	18.8	10.0	18.8	6.0	3.3	2.8	4.0	3.0	3.7

Selected Average Balance Sheet ($ in Thousands)

Item	1	2	3	4	5	6	7	8	9	10	11	12	13
Net Receivables 23	108386	0	8	32	92	173	1088	855	2978	1200	982	7437	1421662
Inventories 24	•	•	•	•	•	•	•	•	•	•	•	•	•
Net Property, Plant and Equipment 25	49447	0	0	0	3	86	132	79	288	290	1511	7129	646728
Total Assets 26	4408794	0	180	728	2505	6935	16831	34018	74160	160373	364026	1225027	57010427
Notes and Loans Payable 27	171909	0	0	0	0	246	0	160	359	979	2585	6937	2263677
All Other Liabilities 28	3541518	0	222	393	1402	4204	10281	23108	54319	131815	299609	1038923	45762137
Net Worth 29	695368	0	-42	335	1103	2486	6551	10750	19482	27579	61831	179167	8984613

Selected Financial Ratios (Times to 1)

Item	1	2	3	4	5	6	7	8	9	10	11	12	13
Current Ratio 30	0.4	•	4.3	8.4	1.2	3.5	3.6	1.4	2.6	0.9	1.4	1.2	0.3
Quick Ratio 31	0.3	•	3.4	6.6	0.9	2.8	2.7	1.1	1.8	0.7	1.2	0.9	0.3
Net Sales to Working Capital 32	•	•	1.7	0.6	7.0	1.2	2.8	8.6	1.5	•	2.4	4.2	1.9
Coverage Ratio 33	1.9	24.5	178.6	344.6	86.5	5.2	•	13.8	10.9	7.9	7.4	4.3	1.9
Total Asset Turnover 34	0.2	•	1.1	0.4	0.7	0.4	1.0	0.8	0.4	0.4	0.3	0.2	0.2
Inventory Turnover 35	•	•	•	•	•	•	•	•	•	•	•	•	•
Receivables Turnover 36	•	•	•	•	•	•	•	•	•	•	•	•	•
Total Liabilities to Net Worth 37	5.3	•	•	1.2	1.3	1.8	1.6	2.2	2.8	4.8	4.9	5.8	5.3
Current Assets to Working Capital 38	•	•	1.3	1.1	7.0	1.4	1.4	3.8	1.6	3.4	3.4	5.1	5.1
Current Liabilities to Working Capital 39	•	•	0.3	0.1	6.0	0.4	0.4	2.8	0.6	2.4	2.4	4.1	4.1
Working Capital to Net Sales 40	•	•	0.6	1.7	0.1	0.9	0.4	0.1	0.7	0.4	0.4	0.2	0.2
Inventory to Working Capital 41	•	•	•	•	•	•	•	•	•	•	•	0.0	•
Total Receipts to Cash Flow 42	3.2	6.9	1.5	1.3	1.2	1.5	1.6	4.1	2.8	2.0	2.2	2.6	3.2
Cost of Goods to Cash Flow 43	1.8	5.8	0.4	0.3	0.1	0.4	0.5	2.9	1.5	0.8	1.0	1.4	1.8
Cash Flow to Total Debt 44	0.1	•	0.6	0.6	1.0	0.4	1.0	0.3	0.2	0.2	0.1	0.1	0.1

Selected Financial Factors (in Percentages)

Item	1	2	3	4	5	6	7	8	9	10	11	12
Debt Ratio 45	84.2	123.5	54.0	56.0	64.2	61.1	68.4	73.7	82.8	83.0	85.4	84.2
Return on Total Assets 46	1.5	11.0	12.2	12.6	4.7	•	5.1	1.5	1.2	1.2	0.8	1.5
Return on Equity Before Income Taxes 47	4.5	•	26.4	28.3	10.7	•	14.9	5.1	6.0	5.9	4.4	4.5
Return on Equity After Income Taxes 48	3.0	•	24.3	25.3	7.8	•	11.6	3.1	0.6	2.9	1.6	2.9
Profit Margin (Before Income Tax) 49	4.0	9.6	29.4	18.7	9.8	•	6.0	3.3	2.7	3.9	2.8	4.1
Profit Margin (After Income Tax) 50	2.6	7.9	27.1	16.7	7.2	•	4.6	2.0	0.3	1.9	1.0	2.7

Table II

Corporations with Net Income

LIFE INSURANCE, STOCK COMPANIES (FORM 1120L)

MONEY AMOUNTS AND SIZE OF ASSETS IN THOUSANDS OF DOLLARS

Item Description for Accounting Period 7/06 Through 6/07		Total	Zero Assets	Under 100	100 to 250	251 to 500	501 to 1,000	1,001 to 5,000	5,001 to 10,000	10,001 to 25,000	25,001 to 50,000	50,001 to 100,000	100,001 to 250,000	250,001 and over
Number of Enterprises	1	826	29	189	92	170	49	64	32	32	27	32	44	66
Revenues ($ in Thousands)														
Net Sales	2	714352315	2563358	40411	25854	300392	132635	434305	1135596	937916	1738312	2983124	12866579	691193833
Interest	3	125587589	354197	2484	2390	40519	11808	43238	79811	96543	139987	518292	2145192	122153126
Rents	4	2182524	1694	81	0	88	127	1252	638	4393	5194	8583	16873	2143600
Royalties	5	8088	0	0	0	0	0	0	0	0	55	0	11	8022
Other Portfolio Income	6	16350022	91492	473	520	9610	6436	19252	7427	9424	79997	32796	132550	15960047
Other Receipts	7	570224092	2115975	37373	22944	250175	114264	370563	1047720	827556	1513079	2423453	10571953	550929038
Total Receipts	8	714352315	2563358	40411	25854	300392	132635	434305	1135596	937916	1738312	2983124	12866579	691193833
Average Total Receipts	9	864833	88392	214	281	1767	2707	6786	35487	29310	64382	93223	292422	10472634
Operating Costs/Operating Income (%)														
Cost of Operations	10	56.5	39.7	26.8	21.5	9.6	29.1	32.9	74.1	52.4	47.2	46.7	52.9	56.7
Salaries and Wages	11	2.5	0.0	•	•	•	•	0.2	0.1	1.9	0.7	0.5	0.7	2.6
Taxes Paid	12	0.8	0.6	1.1	0.8	0.4	1.8	1.8	0.5	1.5	1.3	1.3	0.9	0.8
Interest Paid	13	4.7	0.0	0.0	0.1	0.2	0.3	0.1	0.3	0.1	0.5	0.7	0.7	4.8
Depreciation	14	0.8	0.0	0.1	0.0	0.0	0.2	0.4	0.0	0.4	0.2	0.3	0.3	0.8
Amortization and Depletion	15	0.8	2.1	1.0	0.5	0.3	0.7	1.6	2.4	2.2	2.6	2.3	2.2	0.8
Pensions and Other Deferred Comp.	16	0.4	0.3	0.3	•	0.1	0.7	0.5	0.1	1.9	0.6	0.7	0.6	0.4
Employee Benefits	17	0.3	0.0	0.1	•	0.0	0.1	0.3	0.0	0.6	0.1	0.1	0.3	0.3
Advertising	18	0.3	0.0	0.0	•	0.0	0.0	0.1	0.0	0.2	0.1	0.3	0.9	0.2
Other Expenses	19	28.1	42.6	46.1	37.3	69.7	42.3	42.0	13.4	30.9	35.8	38.9	32.5	27.9
Officers' Compensation	20	0.1	•	•	•	•	•	•	•	•	0.1	0.1	0.2	0.1
Operating Margin	21	4.8	14.5	24.5	39.7	19.7	24.9	20.2	9.0	7.9	10.9	8.1	7.7	4.6
Operating Margin Before Officers' Comp.	22	4.9	14.5	24.5	39.7	19.7	24.9	20.2	9.0	7.9	10.9	8.2	7.9	4.8

Selected Average Balance Sheet ($ in Thousands)

Net Receivables 23	132732	0	9	35	100	238	1336	1180	3356	1011	1109	8576	1650486
Inventories 24	•	•	•	•	•	•	•	•	•	•	•	•	•
Net Property, Plant and Equipment 25	60258	0	0	0	3	72	92	45	354	346	1705	8963	746852
Total Assets 26	4773833	•	208	717	2500	7272	16734	34670	72997	162107	361870	1248370	58589362
Notes and Loans Payable 27	205953	•	•	0	0	0	0	250	16	1173	2474	9299	2569523
All Other Liabilities 28	3799380	•	230	338	1340	4425	9400	21472	54856	125360	292142	1034023	46613546
Net Worth 29	768500	•	-22	379	1160	2847	7334	12947	18126	35575	67253	205048	9406292

Selected Financial Ratios (Times to 1)

Current Ratio 30	0.4	•	6.2	7.6	1.1	2.5	5.1	1.5	3.0	1.2	1.4	1.4	0.4
Quick Ratio 31	0.3	•	5.1	5.7	0.9	1.9	4.0	1.2	2.2	1.0	1.2	0.9	0.3
Net Sales to Working Capital 32	6.1	•	1.5	0.6	15.4	1.5	1.0	6.9	7.8	1.3	2.5	2.9	0.3
Coverage Ratio 33	2.1	391.5	1652.0	380.7	88.7	95.3	280.5	35.3	78.4	23.6	13.0	11.5	2.1
Total Asset Turnover 34	0.2	•	1.0	0.4	0.7	0.4	0.4	1.0	0.4	0.4	0.3	0.2	0.2
Inventory Turnover 35	•	•	•	•	•	•	•	•	•	•	•	•	•
Receivables Turnover 36	•	•	•	•	•	•	•	•	•	•	•	•	•
Total Liabilities to Net Worth 37	5.2	•	0.9	1.2	1.3	1.7	1.5	3.0	3.6	4.4	5.1	5.1	5.2
Current Assets to Working Capital 38	•	1.2	1.2	14.1	2.9	1.7	1.5	6.5	3.5	3.6	4.4	3.6	5.2
Current Liabilities to Working Capital 39	•	0.2	0.2	13.1	1.9	0.7	0.5	5.5	2.5	2.5	3.5	2.6	4.2
Working Capital to Net Sales 40	•	0.7	1.7	0.1	0.7	1.0	0.8	0.1	0.4	0.4	0.4	0.4	0.1
Inventory to Working Capital 41	•	•	•	•	•	•	•	•	•	•	•	•	0.0
Total Receipts to Cash Flow 42	3.2	2.1	1.4	1.3	1.1	1.6	1.7	4.6	2.7	2.4	2.2	2.6	3.2
Cost of Goods to Cash Flow 43	1.8	0.8	0.4	0.3	0.1	0.5	0.6	3.4	1.4	1.1	1.0	1.3	1.8
Cash Flow to Total Debt 44	0.1	•	0.6	1.2	0.1	0.4	0.4	1.0	0.2	0.2	0.1	0.1	0.1

Selected Financial Factors (in Percentages)

Debt Ratio 45	83.9	•	110.4	47.2	53.6	60.9	56.2	62.7	75.2	78.1	81.4	83.6	83.9
Return on Total Assets 46	1.8	•	25.2	15.6	14.1	9.3	8.2	9.5	3.2	4.4	2.3	2.0	1.8
Return on Equity Before Income Taxes 47	6.1	•	•	29.4	29.9	23.4	18.6	24.7	12.7	19.4	11.2	10.9	5.9
Return on Equity After Income Taxes 48	4.2	•	•	27.3	26.8	19.9	14.7	20.3	9.8	13.5	8.0	7.7	4.1
Profit Margin (Before Income Tax) 49	5.4	14.5	24.5	39.7	19.7	24.6	20.1	9.0	7.9	10.7	8.1	7.7	5.3
Profit Margin (After Income Tax) 50	3.8	10.9	22.2	36.8	17.6	21.0	15.9	7.4	6.1	7.5	5.7	5.4	3.7

Table I

Corporations with and without Net Income

LIFE INSURANCE, MUTUAL COMPANIES (FORM 1120L)

MONEY AMOUNTS AND SIZE OF ASSETS IN THOUSANDS OF DOLLARS

Item Description for Accounting Period 7/06 Through 6/07	Total	Zero Assets	Under 500	500 to 1,000	1,000 to 5,000	5,000 to 10,000	10,000 to 25,000	25,000 to 50,000	50,000 to 100,000	100,000 to 250,000	250,000 to 500,000	500,000 to 2,500,000	2,500,000 and over
Number of Enterprises 1	60	0	11	3	5	3	3	5	0	6	5	11	8
Revenues ($ in Thousands)													
Net Sales 2	98870163	0	1577	87	2588	11295	10574	82709	0	384880	450153	2836945	95089355
Interest 3	21026930	0	77	79	539	463	2487	12369	0	48218	107508	777946	20077243
Rents 4	1004422	0	0	0	0	0	10	0	0	3251	3075	12700	985387
Royalties 5	6331	0	0	0	0	0	0	0	0	604	0	197	5529
Other Portfolio Income 6	4168030	0	0	0	212	98	366	628	0	11269	4141	98146	4053172
Other Receipts 7	72664450	0	1500	8	1837	10734	7711	69712	0	321538	335429	1947956	69968024
Total Receipts 8	98870163	0	1577	87	2588	11295	10574	82709	0	384880	450153	2836945	95089355
Average Total Receipts 9	1647836	•	143	29	518	3765	3525	16542	•	64147	90031	257904	11886169
Operating Costs/Operating Income (%)													
Cost of Operations 10	47.9	•	6.5	9.2	23.0	8.2	39.3	50.7	•	54.3	45.7	48.4	47.9
Salaries and Wages 11	0.8	•	•	•	•	•	•	•	•	•	0.0	0.0	0.8
Taxes Paid 12	0.9	•	0.1	2.3	3.9	2.6	2.4	1.9	•	2.5	2.0	1.3	0.9
Interest Paid 13	1.5	•	•	•	•	•	•	•	•	0.1	0.1	1.0	1.6
Depreciation 14	0.3	•	•	•	0.4	0.4	0.3	0.8	•	0.2	0.5	0.4	0.3
Amortization and Depletion 15	1.5	•	0.4	•	1.9	1.7	4.5	2.2	•	3.2	4.0	2.5	1.4
Pensions and Other Deferred Comp. 16	0.6	•	•	•	•	•	0.5	0.9	•	0.8	1.9	1.0	0.5
Employee Benefits 17	0.2	•	4.4	•	•	1.5	0.4	0.2	•	0.1	0.2	0.2	0.2
Advertising 18	0.1	•	•	•	•	•	0.1	0.0	•	0.4	0.1	0.4	0.1
Other Expenses 19	40.9	•	118.3	42.5	83.5	87.0	53.7	40.9	•	35.4	43.9	37.1	41.0
Officers' Compensation 20	0.0	•	0.2	•	•	•	•	•	•	•	•	0.1	0.0
Operating Margin 21	5.3	•	•	47.1	•	•	•	2.4	•	3.0	1.6	7.5	5.2
Operating Margin Before Officers' Comp. 22	5.3	•	•	47.1	•	•	•	2.4	•	3.0	1.6	7.5	5.3

Selected Average Balance Sheet ($ in Thousands)

Net Receivables 23	92911	0	0	63	124	18	•	3152	2037	1597	•	690921
Inventories 24	•	•	•	•	•	•	•	•	•	•	•	•
Net Property, Plant and Equipment 25	36183	0	0	776	31	186	•	1258	3330	3335	•	263341
Total Assets 26	9140810	208	2897	5318	20690	50267	•	180822	361302	1314158	•	66344092
Notes and Loans Payable 27	18684	0	0	0	0	0	•	0	0	35	•	140084
All Other Liabilities 28	8137450	245	2897	4518	16800	42975	•	167067	328849	1151269	•	59080107
Net Worth 29	984675	-37	0	800	3890	7292	•	13756	32653	162854	•	7123902

Selected Financial Ratios (Times to 1)

Current Ratio 30	0.6	148.5	6.8	0.3	6.6	0.1	2.3	•	1.2	0.6	1.0	0.6
Quick Ratio 31	0.5	145.5	•	0.3	5.7	0.1	1.3	•	1.0	0.5	0.8	0.5
Net Sales to Working Capital 32	•	0.8	0.5	•	1.0	•	1.2	•	6.1	•	•	0.5
Coverage Ratio 33	4.4	•	•	•	•	•	•	•	40.9	18.1	7.5	4.3
Total Asset Turnover 34	0.2	0.7	0.0	0.2	0.7	0.2	0.3	•	0.4	0.2	0.2	0.2
Inventory Turnover 35	•	•	•	•	•	•	•	•	•	•	•	•
Receivables Turnover 36	•	•	•	•	•	•	•	•	•	•	•	•
Total Liabilities to Net Worth 37	8.3	•	0.3	•	5.6	4.3	5.9	•	12.1	10.1	7.1	8.3
Current Assets to Working Capital 38	•	1.0	1.2	1.0	1.2	•	1.7	•	6.6	•	•	•
Current Liabilities to Working Capital 39	•	0.0	0.2	0.0	0.2	•	0.7	•	5.6	•	•	•
Working Capital to Net Sales 40	•	1.2	2.1	1.2	1.0	•	0.8	•	0.2	•	•	•
Inventory to Working Capital 41	•	•	•	•	•	•	•	•	•	•	•	•
Total Receipts to Cash Flow 42	2.3	1.1	1.5	1.1	1.2	2.0	2.4	•	3.0	2.3	2.4	2.3
Cost of Goods to Cash Flow 43	1.1	0.1	0.3	0.1	0.1	0.8	1.2	•	1.6	1.0	1.1	1.1
Cash Flow to Total Debt 44	0.1	0.5	0.1	0.1	0.7	0.1	0.2	•	0.1	0.1	0.1	0.1

Selected Financial Factors (in Percentages)

Debt Ratio 45	89.2	117.8	21.7	100.0	85.0	81.2	85.5	•	92.4	91.0	87.6	89.3
Return on Total Assets 46	1.2	•	1.6	•	•	•	0.8	•	1.1	0.4	1.5	1.2
Return on Equity Before Income Taxes 47	8.7	116.2	2.1	•	•	•	5.5	•	13.9	4.4	10.5	8.6
Return on Equity After Income Taxes 48	5.7	116.7	2.1	•	•	•	4.4	•	12.3	3.7	7.0	5.7
Profit Margin (Before Income Tax) 49	5.2	•	47.1	•	•	2.4	2.4	•	3.0	1.6	6.6	5.2
Profit Margin (After Income Tax) 50	3.4	47.1	•	•	1.9	•	1.9	•	2.6	1.4	4.4	3.4

Table II

Corporations with Net Income

LIFE INSURANCE, MUTUAL COMPANIES (FORM 1120L)

MONEY AMOUNTS AND SIZE OF ASSETS IN THOUSANDS OF DOLLARS

Item Description for Accounting Period 7/06 Through 6/07		Total	Zero Assets	Under 500	500 to 1,000	1,000 to 5,000	5,000 to 10,000	10,000 to 25,000	25,000 to 50,000	50,000 to 100,000	100,000 to 250,000	250,000 to 500,000	500,000 to 2,500,000	2,500,000 and over
Number of Enterprises	1	37	0	5	•	0	0	0	•	0	•	•	•	•
Revenues ($ in Thousands)														
Net Sales	2	95490390	0	160	•	0	0	0	•	0	•	•	•	•
Interest	3	20360232	0	56	•	0	0	0	•	0	•	•	•	•
Rents	4	969764	0	0	•	0	0	0	•	0	•	•	•	•
Royalties	5	640	0	0	•	0	0	0	•	0	•	•	•	•
Other Portfolio Income	6	4157843	0	0	•	0	0	0	•	0	•	•	•	•
Other Receipts	7	70001911	0	104	•	0	0	0	•	0	•	•	•	•
Total Receipts	8	95490390	0	160	•	0	0	0	•	0	•	•	•	•
Average Total Receipts	9	2580821	•	32	•	•	•	•	•	•	•	•	•	•
Operating Costs/Operating Income (%)														
Cost of Operations	10	46.9	•	50.6	•	•	•	•	•	•	•	•	•	•
Salaries and Wages	11	0.8	•	•	•	•	•	•	•	•	•	•	•	•
Taxes Paid	12	1.0	•	1.2	•	•	•	•	•	•	•	•	•	•
Interest Paid	13	1.6	•	•	•	•	•	•	•	•	•	•	•	•
Depreciation	14	0.3	•	•	•	•	•	•	•	•	•	•	•	•
Amortization and Depletion	15	1.5	•	•	•	•	•	•	•	•	•	•	•	•
Pensions and Other Deferred Comp.	16	0.6	•	•	•	•	•	•	•	•	•	•	•	•
Employee Benefits	17	0.2	•	•	•	•	•	•	•	•	•	•	•	•
Advertising	18	0.1	•	•	•	•	•	•	•	•	•	•	•	•
Other Expenses	19	41.5	•	17.5	•	•	•	•	•	•	•	•	•	•
Officers' Compensation	20	0.0	•	•	•	•	•	•	•	•	•	•	•	•
Operating Margin	21	5.5	•	30.0	•	•	•	•	•	•	•	•	•	•
Operating Margin Before Officers' Comp.	22	5.6	•	30.0	•	•	•	•	•	•	•	•	•	•

Selected Average Balance Sheet ($ in Thousands)

Net Receivables 23	150380
Inventories 24	
Net Property, Plant and Equipment 25	49311
Total Assets 26	14234683
Notes and Loans Payable 27	30299
All Other Liabilities 28	12647163
Net Worth 29	1557221

Values listed (right column): 0, (blank), 0, 288, 0, 234, 54

Net Receivables 23	150380	0
Inventories 24		
Net Property, Plant and Equipment 25	49311	0
Total Assets 26	14234683	288
Notes and Loans Payable 27	30299	0
All Other Liabilities 28	12647163	234
Net Worth 29	1557221	54

Selected Financial Ratios (Times to 1)

Current Ratio 30	0.6	
Quick Ratio 31	0.5	
Net Sales to Working Capital 32		0.1
Coverage Ratio 33	4.4	
Total Asset Turnover 34	0.2	0.1
Inventory Turnover 35		
Receivables Turnover 36		
Total Liabilities to Net Worth 37	8.1	4.3
Current Assets to Working Capital 38		1.0
Current Liabilities to Working Capital 39		
Working Capital to Net Sales 40		7.2
Inventory to Working Capital 41		
Total Receipts to Cash Flow 42	2.3	2.2
Cost of Goods to Cash Flow 43	1.1	1.1
Cash Flow to Total Debt 44	0.1	0.1

Selected Financial Factors (in Percentages)

Debt Ratio 45	89.1	81.3
Return on Total Assets 46	1.3	3.3
Return on Equity Before Income Taxes 47	9.0	17.8
Return on Equity After Income Taxes 48	6.0	17.0
Profit Margin (Before Income Tax) 49	5.5	30.0
Profit Margin (After Income Tax) 50	3.6	28.7

Table I

Corporations with and without Net Income

MUTUAL PROPERTY AND CASUALTY COMPANIES (FORM 1120-PC)

MONEY AMOUNTS AND SIZE OF ASSETS IN THOUSANDS OF DOLLARS

Item Description for Accounting Period 7/06 Through 6/07	Total	Zero Assets	Under 500	500 to 1,000	1,000 to 5,000	5,000 to 10,000	10,000 to 25,000	25,000 to 50,000	50,000 to 100,000	100,000 to 250,000	250,000 to 500,000	500,000 to 2,500,000	2,500,000 and over
Number of Enterprises 1	1499	5	94	52	557	127	230	134	83	69	57	66	24
Revenues ($ in Thousands)													
Net Sales 2	237368567	6595	34703	6461	516472	377350	1525651	2309746	2396363	5609144	9973362	40498720	174114001
Interest 3	14238453	600	3919	1177	46640	24614	99636	134092	168334	303354	494743	1930490	11030854
Rents 4	449682	13	0	0	1534	514	2301	1595	2451	12422	12375	70955	345521
Royalties 5	847	0	0	0	0	0	0	0	13	0	0	773	60
Other Portfolio Income 6	7470808	13	257	0	11763	8694	32273	40749	60772	165560	267151	1032009	5851568
Other Receipts 7	215208777	5969	30527	5284	456535	343528	1391441	2133310	2164793	5127808	9199093	37464493	156885998
Total Receipts 8	237368567	6595	34703	6461	516472	377350	1525651	2309746	2396363	5609144	9973362	40498720	174114001
Average Total Receipts 9	158351	1319	369	124	927	2971	6633	17237	28872	81292	174971	613617	7254750
Operating Costs/Operating Income (%)													
Cost of Operations 10	58.1	68.6	38.4	94.3	42.9	53.3	52.0	60.5	47.0	53.2	55.4	61.9	57.8
Salaries and Wages 11	12.1	0.2	16.9	0.4	14.5	10.2	9.4	10.7	16.8	16.0	14.8	13.2	11.6
Taxes Paid 12	2.4	•	1.1	3.7	2.7	3.3	2.6	2.9	3.5	2.7	2.3	2.0	2.5
Interest Paid 13	0.5	2.5	0.5	•	0.1	0.1	0.2	0.2	0.4	0.3	0.3	0.3	0.6
Depreciation 14	0.9	0.0	0.0	•	0.3	0.3	0.3	0.5	1.0	1.1	1.0	0.8	0.9
Amortization and Depletion 15	0.2	•	•	•	0.1	0.0	1.2	0.1	0.0	0.0	0.1	0.1	0.2
Pensions and Other Deferred Comp. 16	0.5	•	•	•	0.1	0.2	0.1	0.3	0.3	0.1	0.7	0.5	0.5
Employee Benefits 17	1.3	0.0	0.6	•	1.2	0.7	0.6	1.2	2.4	1.7	1.9	1.7	1.2
Advertising 18	0.4	•	0.5	•	0.3	0.2	0.2	0.3	0.6	0.4	0.2	0.3	0.4
Other Expenses 19	12.8	29.5	37.4	41.6	21.2	25.0	26.6	17.8	16.7	11.5	12.0	10.2	13.2
Officers' Compensation 20	0.3	•	1.0	•	1.9	1.2	0.7	0.9	1.0	0.6	0.7	0.3	0.2
Operating Margin 21	10.5	•	4.6	•	14.6	5.6	6.1	4.6	10.1	12.3	10.6	8.8	11.0
Operating Margin Before Officers' Comp. 22	10.8	•	4.6	•	16.6	6.7	6.8	5.4	11.1	12.9	11.2	9.1	11.1

Selected Average Balance Sheet ($ in Thousands)

Item													
Net Receivables 23	29719	0	2	13	107	265	1187	2474	5207	14620	34880	119665	1355135
Inventories 24	•	•	•	•	•	•	•	•	•	•	•	•	•
Net Property, Plant and Equipment 25	4957	0	2	57	66	97	253	758	3300	6100	21148	220806	•
Total Assets 26	371381	145	698	2632	6947	16056	35377	72187	168332	330042		1203483	17917526
Notes and Loans Payable 27	5255	22	0	22	0	92	42	320	486	1320		7504	300256
All Other Liabilities 28	227166	502	347	1037	6704	10886	24050	46628	96061	207643		732257	10942411
Net Worth 29	138960	-379	351	1572	242	5078	11285	25240	71785	121079	207643	463423	6674859

Selected Financial Ratios (Times to 1)

Item													
Current Ratio 30	0.9	•	0.2	1.8	1.9	0.9	1.0	0.9	0.9	0.9	1.0	0.9	0.9
Quick Ratio 31	0.8	•	0.2	1.2	1.7	0.8	0.8	0.8	0.7	0.8	0.9	0.8	0.8
Net Sales to Working Capital 32	•	•	•	0.5	1.1	•	•	•	•	•	•	•	•
Coverage Ratio 33	20.5	10.5	•	102.8	49.4	31.2	18.2	23.2	32.0	32.7		31.3	18.6
Total Asset Turnover 34	0.4	0.6	2.5	0.2	0.4	0.5	0.5	0.4	0.5	0.5		0.5	0.4
Inventory Turnover 35	•	•	•	•	•	•	•	•	•	•	•	•	•
Receivables Turnover 36	•	•	•	•	•	•	•	•	•	•	•	•	•
Total Liabilities to Net Worth 37	1.7	•	•	1.0	0.7	2.1	2.2	2.1	1.9	1.3	1.9	1.6	1.7
Current Assets to Working Capital 38	•	•	2.3	2.1	•	•	•	•	•	•	•	•	•
Current Liabilities to Working Capital 39	•	•	1.3	1.1	•	•	•	•	•	•	•	•	•
Working Capital to Net Sales 40	•	•	2.0	0.9	•	•	•	•	•	•	•	•	•
Inventory to Working Capital 41	•	•	•	•	•	•	•	•	•	•	•	•	•
Total Receipts to Cash Flow 42	4.7	3.5	2.4	64.6	2.9	3.4	3.2	4.8	4.0	4.6	4.8	5.9	4.5
Cost of Goods to Cash Flow 43	2.7	2.4	0.9	60.9	1.3	1.8	1.6	2.9	1.9	2.4	2.7	3.6	2.6
Cash Flow to Total Debt 44	0.1	•	0.3	0.0	0.3	0.2	0.2	0.1	0.2	0.2	0.2	0.1	0.1

Selected Financial Factors (in Percentages)

Item													
Debt Ratio 45	62.6	•	361.6	49.7	40.3	96.5	68.4	68.1	65.0	57.4	63.3	61.5	62.7
Return on Total Assets 46	4.2	•	12.8	5.0	1.9	2.3	2.1	4.0	5.6	5.2		4.1	4.1
Return on Equity Before Income Taxes 47	10.6	•	•	8.3	54.3	6.9	6.2	10.9	12.8	13.8		10.4	10.5
Return on Equity After Income Taxes 48	6.9	•	•	6.7	23.7	4.0	2.4	7.2	8.5	9.1		6.6	6.8
Profit Margin (Before Income Tax) 49	9.3	•	4.6	14.0	4.4	5.3	4.1	9.5	11.3	9.5		7.9	9.7
Profit Margin (After Income Tax) 50	6.0	•	4.0	11.4	1.9	3.1	1.6	6.3	7.5	6.3		5.0	6.3

Table II
Corporations with Net Income

MUTUAL PROPERTY AND CASUALTY COMPANIES (FORM 1120-PC)

MONEY AMOUNTS AND SIZE OF ASSETS IN THOUSANDS OF DOLLARS

Item Description for Accounting Period 7/06 Through 6/07		Total	Zero Assets	Under 500	500 to 1,000	1,000 to 5,000	5,000 to 10,000	10,000 to 25,000	25,000 to 50,000	50,000 to 100,000	100,000 to 250,000	250,000 to 500,000	500,000 to 2,500,000	2,500,000 and over
Number of Enterprises	1	1162	•	52	•	453	93	159	105	64	62	51	63	•
Revenues ($ in Thousands)														
Net Sales	2	229765538	•	17899	•	384423	268087	1126131	1883085	1856443	4959505	8240019	38032747	•
Interest	3	13655369	•	3652	•	36500	19413	66536	107564	126221	270622	437840	1772257	•
Rents	4	443790	•	0	•	778	266	1917	1552	1952	12413	10781	69094	•
Royalties	5	833	•	0	•	0	0	0	0	0	0	0	773	•
Other Portfolio Income	6	7385989	•	257	•	10460	7217	24486	33977	51874	159407	247154	1014740	•
Other Receipts	7	208279557	•	13990	•	336685	241191	1033192	1739992	1676396	4517063	7544244	35175883	•
Total Receipts	8	229765538	•	17899	•	384423	268087	1126131	1883085	1856443	4959505	8240019	38032747	•
Average Total Receipts	9	197733	•	344	•	849	2883	7083	17934	29007	79992	161569	603694	•
Operating Costs/Operating Income (%)														
Cost of Operations	10	57.5	•	3.1	•	34.7	43.1	48.4	54.3	45.5	51.4	51.9	60.1	•
Salaries and Wages	11	12.2	•	6.6	•	12.9	11.8	10.9	11.7	16.2	15.8	16.1	13.6	•
Taxes Paid	12	2.4	•	0.8	•	2.7	1.8	2.4	2.8	3.4	2.7	2.4	2.1	•
Interest Paid	13	0.5	•	•	•	0.1	0.1	0.2	0.2	0.5	0.2	0.3	0.3	•
Depreciation	14	0.9	•	•	•	0.3	0.3	0.4	0.6	1.1	1.2	1.1	0.8	•
Amortization and Depletion	15	0.2	•	•	•	0.0	0.0	0.1	0.1	0.0	0.0	0.1	0.1	•
Pensions and Other Deferred Comp.	16	0.5	•	•	•	0.1	0.3	0.2	0.3	0.4	0.1	0.6	0.5	•
Employee Benefits	17	1.3	•	0.9	•	1.2	0.8	0.6	1.3	2.8	1.8	1.8	1.7	•
Advertising	18	0.4	•	•	•	0.2	0.3	0.1	0.3	0.6	0.4	0.2	0.3	•
Other Expenses	19	12.6	•	62.3	•	21.0	23.7	22.7	14.4	13.7	11.0	11.6	9.8	•
Officers' Compensation	20	0.3	•	•	•	1.9	1.7	0.9	1.0	1.1	0.6	0.8	0.3	•
Operating Margin	21	11.3	•	26.2	•	24.8	16.0	13.1	13.1	14.7	14.7	13.1	10.5	•
Operating Margin Before Officers' Comp.	22	11.5	•	26.2	•	26.7	17.7	14.0	14.0	15.8	15.4	13.9	10.8	•

Selected Average Balance Sheet ($ in Thousands)

Net Receivables 23	37037	•	3	•	110	189	1179	2763	4211	14126	32585	121176	•
Inventories 24	•	•	•	•	•	•	•	•	•	•	•	•	•
Net Property, Plant and Equipment 25	6236	•	0	•	39	63	121	318	817	3165	5751	21302	•
Total Assets 26	463802	•	114	•	2630	7179	16386	35414	72641	169829	332938	1191359	
Notes and Loans Payable 27	6761	•	0	•	21	0	74	52	358	541	1418	7850	•
All Other Liabilities 28	280271	•	664	•	957	3325	9632	22070	44334	95886	208547	711751	•
Net Worth 29	176770	•	-551	•	1651	3854	6680	13292	27950	73403	122973	471758	•

Selected Financial Ratios (Times to 1)

Current Ratio 30	0.9	•	0.1	•	2.1	1.6	1.1	1.0	0.9	0.9	1.0	0.9	•
Quick Ratio 31	0.8	•	0.1	•	1.9	1.3	1.0	0.9	0.7	0.8	0.9	0.8	•
Net Sales to Working Capital 32	•	•	•	•	0.9	2.0	5.5	•	•	•	•	•	•
Coverage Ratio 33	21.8	•	•	•	183.6	123.5	54.8	53.8	30.7	58.3	39.0	36.3	•
Total Asset Turnover 34	0.4	•	3.0	•	0.3	0.4	0.4	0.5	0.4	0.5	0.5	0.5	•
Inventory Turnover 35	•	•	•	•	•	•	•	•	•	•	•	•	•
Receivables Turnover 36	•	•	•	•	•	•	•	•	•	•	•	•	•
Total Liabilities to Net Worth 37	1.6	•	•	•	0.6	0.9	1.5	1.7	1.6	1.3	1.7	1.5	•
Current Assets to Working Capital 38	•	•	•	•	1.9	2.8	8.1	•	•	•	•	•	•
Current Liabilities to Working Capital 39	•	•	•	•	0.9	1.8	7.1	•	•	•	•	•	•
Working Capital to Net Sales 40	•	•	•	•	1.1	0.5	0.2	•	•	•	•	•	•
Inventory to Working Capital 41	•	•	•	•	•	•	•	•	•	•	•	•	•
Total Receipts to Cash Flow 42	4.6	•	1.1	•	2.3	2.6	2.9	3.8	3.8	4.2	4.4	5.5	•
Cost of Goods to Cash Flow 43	2.6	•	0.0	•	0.8	1.1	1.4	2.1	1.7	2.2	2.3	3.3	•
Cash Flow to Total Debt 44	0.2	•	0.5	•	0.4	0.3	0.3	0.2	0.2	0.2	0.2	0.2	•

Selected Financial Factors (in Percentages)

Debt Ratio 45	61.9	•	584.8	•	37.2	46.3	59.2	62.5	61.5	56.8	63.1	60.4	•
Return on Total Assets 46	4.5	•	79.4	•	7.8	6.0	5.4	6.4	5.8	6.6	5.9	4.9	•
Return on Equity Before Income Taxes 47	11.2	•	•	•	12.4	11.0	13.0	16.9	14.5	14.9	15.7	12.1	•
Return on Equity After Income Taxes 48	7.4	•	•	•	10.6	8.4	9.8	12.8	10.3	10.2	10.6	8.2	•
Profit Margin (Before Income Tax) 49	10.0	•	26.2	•	24.2	14.8	12.3	12.5	14.0	13.7	11.9	9.5	•
Profit Margin (After Income Tax) 50	6.6	•	25.1	•	20.7	11.3	9.2	9.5	9.9	9.4	8.0	6.4	•

Table I

Corporations with and without Net Income

STOCK PROPERTY AND CASUALTY COMPANIES (FORM 1120-PC)

MONEY AMOUNTS AND SIZE OF ASSETS IN THOUSANDS OF DOLLARS

Item Description for Accounting Period 7/06 Through 6/07	Total	Zero Assets	Under 500	500 to 1,000	1,000 to 5,000	5,000 to 10,000	10,000 to 25,000	25,000 to 50,000	50,000 to 100,000	100,000 to 250,000	250,000 to 500,000	500,000 to 2,500,000	2,500,000 and over
Number of Enterprises 1	4815	139	1586	639	1064	425	298	149	145	121	68	101	80
Revenues ($ in Thousands)													
Net Sales 2	625560961	7287740	69448	39454	547004	1321599	3203909	3676109	9156997	13626579	13198295	74303936	499129889
Interest 3	34038747	210791	10144	12850	68486	81712	125072	131157	257259	511028	565609	2718433	29346205
Rents 4	736240	6994	0	0	385	2372	2975	1128	4951	16183	10303	46230	644719
Royalties 5	557410	0	0	0	203	0	9	0	0	2248	5775	9129	540046
Other Portfolio Income 6	9844851	112230	2626	6126	20179	26820	33085	43378	143978	160068	155479	815224	8325655
Other Receipts 7	580383713	6957725	56678	20478	457751	1210695	3042768	3500446	8750809	12937052	12461129	70714920	460273264
Total Receipts 8	625560961	7287740	69448	39454	547004	1321599	3203909	3676109	9156997	13626579	13198295	74303936	499129889
Average Total Receipts 9	129919	52430	44	62	514	3110	10751	24672	63152	112616	194093	735683	6239124
Operating Costs/Operating Income (%)													
Cost of Operations 10	56.6	9.3	60.4	35.9	49.8	50.8	60.4	57.8	64.6	48.8	55.0	62.5	56.5
Salaries and Wages 11	13.8	26.7	10.7	1.9	12.9	22.2	11.4	11.4	11.6	13.4	15.7	14.6	13.5
Taxes Paid 12	2.1	2.4	0.8	0.5	2.8	1.7	2.3	2.0	2.0	2.0	2.4	2.0	2.1
Interest Paid 13	1.6	1.0	0.1	1.6	0.2	0.5	0.1	0.3	0.3	0.6	0.6	0.7	1.8
Depreciation 14	0.7	1.0	0.0	•	0.1	0.2	0.4	0.3	0.4	0.5	0.7	0.8	0.7
Amortization and Depletion 15	0.3	0.4	0.1	0.1	0.2	0.1	0.0	0.1	0.1	0.2	0.2	0.2	0.3
Pensions and Other Deferred Comp. 16	0.3	0.3	•	•	0.5	0.0	0.1	0.1	0.1	0.2	0.2	0.4	0.3
Employee Benefits 17	1.1	0.1	0.3	•	0.3	0.4	0.4	0.6	0.9	5.4	1.1	1.0	1.1
Advertising 18	1.0	0.5	•	•	0.0	0.4	0.2	0.5	0.4	0.4	0.6	0.5	1.1
Other Expenses 19	13.1	55.3	6.3	18.2	17.9	13.6	18.1	20.4	13.0	20.4	16.0	11.0	12.4
Officers' Compensation 20	0.3	0.0	•	•	1.1	0.5	1.0	1.1	0.7	0.8	0.5	0.4	0.3
Operating Margin 21	9.1	2.8	21.3	41.8	14.1	9.6	5.5	5.4	6.1	7.4	7.1	5.9	9.9
Operating Margin Before Officers' Comp. 22	9.5	2.8	21.3	41.8	15.2	10.1	6.5	6.5	6.7	8.2	7.6	6.4	10.2

Selected Average Balance Sheet ($ in Thousands)

	1	2	3	4	5	6	7	8	9	10	11	12	13
Net Receivables 23	20381	0	3	18	79	374	1231	3026	6936	13309	34890	101020	1023324
Inventories 24	•	•	•	•	12	97	126	387	626	3191	6090	18608	175384
Net Property, Plant and Equipment 25	3520	0	•	•	•	•	•	•	•	•	•	•	•
Total Assets 26	353994	195	753	2403	6969	16120	35391	72675	160801	343263	1177042	•	18948493
Notes and Loans Payable 27	24578	2	5	16	101	211	497	1766	7319	19631	47090	•	1386366
All Other Liabilities 28	186026	206	493	1596	4404	11045	23923	49554	104817	218465	702528	•	9737108
Net Worth 29	143390	-13	255	791	2464	4864	10970	21354	48666	105168	427423	•	7825020

Selected Financial Ratios (Times to 1)

	1	2	3	4	5	6	7	8	9	10	11	12	13
Current Ratio 30	0.9	0.7	•	0.9	1.0	0.9	0.9	1.0	1.1	1.0	1.0	0.9	0.9
Quick Ratio 31	0.7	0.6	•	0.8	0.8	0.8	0.8	0.7	0.9	0.8	0.9	0.8	0.7
Net Sales to Working Capital 32	•	•	•	•	•	26.8	•	•	•	•	•	•	•
Coverage Ratio 33	6.9	3.3	236.6	26.1	88.7	21.4	44.9	17.8	20.3	12.7	11.6	9.6	6.5
Total Asset Turnover 34	0.4	0.2	0.2	0.1	0.1	0.4	0.7	0.7	0.9	0.7	0.6	0.6	0.3
Inventory Turnover 35	•	•	•	•	•	•	•	•	•	•	•	•	•
Receivables Turnover 36	•	•	•	•	•	•	•	•	•	•	•	•	•
Total Liabilities to Net Worth 37	1.5	•	•	2.0	2.0	1.8	2.3	2.2	2.4	2.3	2.3	1.8	1.4
Current Assets to Working Capital 38	•	•	•	•	•	19.4	•	•	•	•	•	•	•
Current Liabilities to Working Capital 39	•	•	•	•	•	18.4	•	•	•	•	•	•	•
Working Capital to Net Sales 40	•	•	•	•	•	0.0	•	•	•	•	•	•	•
Inventory to Working Capital 41	•	•	•	•	•	0.0	•	•	•	•	•	•	•
Total Receipts to Cash Flow 42	4.9	1.8	4.0	1.9	3.3	4.8	4.4	4.1	5.7	3.8	4.7	6.5	4.9
Cost of Goods to Cash Flow 43	2.8	0.2	2.4	0.7	1.7	2.4	2.7	2.4	3.7	1.9	2.6	4.0	2.8
Cash Flow to Total Debt 44	0.1	•	0.1	0.1	0.1	0.1	0.2	0.2	0.0	0.3	0.2	0.2	0.1

Selected Financial Factors (in Percentages)

	1	2	3	4	5	6	7	8	9	10	11	12	13
Debt Ratio 45	59.5	•	106.5	66.1	67.1	64.6	69.8	69.0	70.6	69.7	69.4	63.7	58.7
Return on Total Assets 46	3.9	•	4.7	3.3	3.0	4.4	3.7	3.6	5.2	5.4	4.2	4.0	3.9
Return on Equity Before Income Taxes 47	8.2	•	•	9.5	8.9	11.8	11.6	11.2	16.9	16.4	12.4	10.0	7.9
Return on Equity After Income Taxes 48	5.4	•	•	7.8	5.5	7.1	6.1	5.5	11.6	10.6	6.6	6.5	5.3
Profit Margin (Before Income Tax) 49	9.1	2.3	21.0	39.2	13.7	9.4	5.2	5.0	5.7	6.7	5.8	6.7	9.9
Profit Margin (After Income Tax) 50	6.0	1.4	18.7	32.2	8.5	5.6	2.8	2.4	3.9	4.6	3.6	3.8	6.6

307

Table II

Corporations with Net Income

STOCK PROPERTY AND CASUALTY COMPANIES (FORM 1120-PC)

MONEY AMOUNTS AND SIZE OF ASSETS IN THOUSANDS OF DOLLARS

Item Description for Accounting Period 7/06 Through 6/07	Total	Zero Assets	Under 500	500 to 1,000	1,000 to 5,000	5,000 to 10,000	10,000 to 25,000	25,000 to 50,000	50,000 to 100,000	100,000 to 250,000	250,000 to 500,000	500,000 to 2,500,000	2,500,000 and over
Number of Enterprises 1	4187	115	1409	605	945	329	232	114	117	106	58	82	75
Revenues ($ in Thousands)													
Net Sales 2	599165142	7104901	32318	27850	327608	839850	2257829	2453849	8494927	12758403	12446374	63266176	489155057
Interest 3	31141868	203743	9393	12749	64053	65467	98286	104278	207220	432359	472288	2215678	27256352
Rents 4	709716	6752	0	0	203	947	2924	806	3286	13450	9794	35586	635968
Royalties 5	556990	0	0	0	203	0	9	0	0	2248	5775	8708	540046
Other Portfolio Income 6	9610335	106003	2617	5865	16741	17574	29876	37622	128687	153625	154410	764392	8192920
Other Receipts 7	557146233	6788403	20308	9236	246408	755862	2126734	2311143	8155734	12156721	11804107	60241812	452529771
Total Receipts 8	599165142	7104901	32318	27850	327608	839850	2257829	2453849	8494927	12758403	12446374	63266176	489155057
Average Total Receipts 9	143101	61782	23	46	347	2553	9732	21525	72606	120362	214593	771539	6522067
Operating Costs/Operating Income (%)													
Cost of Operations 10	56.4	8.5	12.5	10.6	33.1	54.6	51.8	53.2	64.5	47.0	55.9	61.2	56.6
Salaries and Wages 11	13.7	27.0	2.3	2.7	11.4	9.7	11.5	12.4	11.0	13.0	13.5	15.2	13.5
Taxes Paid 12	2.1	2.4	0.7	0.1	3.5	1.6	2.5	2.4	2.0	1.9	2.4	2.0	2.1
Interest Paid 13	1.5	1.0	0.0	0.8	0.1	0.4	0.2	0.2	0.3	0.5	0.6	0.6	1.6
Depreciation 14	0.7	1.0	•	•	0.0	0.1	0.3	0.3	0.4	0.5	0.6	0.8	0.7
Amortization and Depletion 15	0.3	0.4	0.1	0.0	0.3	0.0	0.0	0.1	0.0	0.1	0.2	0.2	0.3
Pensions and Other Deferred Comp. 16	0.3	0.3	•	•	•	0.0	0.1	0.2	0.1	0.2	0.2	0.4	0.3
Employee Benefits 17	1.1	0.1	•	•	0.0	0.2	0.4	0.7	0.8	5.7	1.1	1.0	1.1
Advertising 18	1.0	0.5	•	•	0.0	0.3	0.2	0.3	0.3	0.3	0.4	0.5	1.1
Other Expenses 19	12.6	55.3	3.8	16.4	13.8	11.2	19.7	15.7	12.0	20.2	13.6	9.9	12.0
Officers' Compensation 20	0.3	0.0	•	•	•	0.4	1.1	1.5	0.7	0.8	0.5	0.4	0.3
Operating Margin 21	10.0	3.3	80.6	69.4	37.7	21.4	12.0	12.8	8.0	9.7	11.0	7.9	10.3
Operating Margin Before Officers' Comp. 22	10.3	3.4	80.6	69.4	37.7	21.7	13.1	14.4	8.7	10.4	11.5	8.3	10.6

Selected Average Balance Sheet ($ in Thousands)

Item													
Net Receivables 23	20492	0	2	19	74	374	1122	3029	7319	13575	35232	106470	958881
Inventories 24	•	•	•	•	•	•	•	•	•	•	•	•	•
Net Property, Plant and Equipment 25	3832	0	0	0	1	36	121	348	578	3315	6764	16502	183969
Total Assets 26	373505		209	758	2371	7000	16197	35608	72426	160108	343840	1184124	18776905
Notes and Loans Payable 27	24170		0	5	8	69	187	401	1343	6994	18404	47110	1269952
All Other Liabilities 28	189938		162	500	1416	4136	9851	22922	42066	100225	197073	670045	9402959
Net Worth 29	159398		48	252	947	2794	6159	12285	29017	52889	128363	466968	8103994

Selected Financial Ratios (Times to 1)

Item													
Current Ratio 30	0.9	•	0.9	0.9	1.0	1.0	1.0	1.1	1.3	1.0	1.1	1.0	0.9
Quick Ratio 31	0.7	•	0.8	0.8	0.8	0.9	0.9	0.9	1.1	0.9	1.0	0.9	0.7
Net Sales to Working Capital 32	•	•	•	•	22.5	13.5	7.0	98.5	15.3	•	•	•	•
Coverage Ratio 33	7.9	4.0	25868.0	84.5	557.6	47.8	73.6	71.1	29.7	18.0	18.7	13.2	7.3
Total Asset Turnover 34	0.4	•	0.1	0.1	0.4	0.6	0.6	1.0	0.8	0.8	0.6	0.7	0.3
Inventory Turnover 35	•	•	•	•	•	•	•	•	•	•	•	•	•
Receivables Turnover 36	•	•	•	•	•	•	•	•	•	•	•	•	•
Total Liabilities to Net Worth 37	1.3	•	3.4	2.0	1.5	1.5	1.6	1.9	1.5	2.0	1.7	1.5	1.3
Current Assets to Working Capital 38	•	•	•	•	22.1	14.3	4.5	78.4	14.1	•	•	•	•
Current Liabilities to Working Capital 39	•	•	•	•	21.1	13.3	3.5	77.4	13.1	•	•	•	•
Working Capital to Net Sales 40	•	•	0.0	0.0	0.1	0.1	0.0	0.1	0.0	0.0	0.1	0.1	•
Inventory to Working Capital 41	•	•	•	•	•	•	•	•	•	•	•	•	•
Total Receipts to Cash Flow 42	4.8	1.8	1.2	1.3	2.0	3.2	3.3	3.7	5.4	3.6	4.4	6.2	4.9
Cost of Goods to Cash Flow 43	2.7	0.2	0.2	0.1	0.7	1.8	1.7	2.0	3.5	1.7	2.4	3.8	2.8
Cash Flow to Total Debt 44	0.1	•	0.1	0.1	0.2	0.3	0.2	0.2	0.3	0.0	0.2	0.2	0.1

Selected Financial Factors (in Percentages)

Item													
Debt Ratio 45	57.3	•	77.3	66.7	60.1	60.1	62.0	65.5	59.9	67.0	62.7	60.6	56.8
Return on Total Assets 46	4.4	•	8.8	4.1	5.4	7.8	7.1	7.5	8.0	7.4	7.0	5.4	4.2
Return on Equity Before Income Taxes 47	9.0	•	38.6	12.1	13.6	19.2	18.4	21.6	19.2	21.1	17.7	12.7	8.3
Return on Equity After Income Taxes 48	6.1	•	36.3	10.3	10.4	13.7	12.9	15.0	14.4	15.1	12.1	8.9	5.6
Profit Margin (Before Income Tax) 49	10.0	2.8	80.0	66.6	37.0	21.0	11.7	12.3	7.7	9.3	10.6	7.7	10.3
Profit Margin (After Income Tax) 50	6.8	2.0	75.1	56.7	28.4	15.0	8.2	8.5	5.7	6.6	7.2	5.4	7.0

Table I

Corporations with and without Net Income

INSURANCE AGENCIES AND BROKERAGES

MONEY AMOUNTS AND SIZE OF ASSETS IN THOUSANDS OF DOLLARS

Item Description for Accounting Period 7/06 Through 6/07	Total	Zero Assets	Under 500	500 to 1,000	1,000 to 5,000	5,000 to 10,000	10,000 to 25,000	25,000 to 50,000	50,000 to 100,000	100,000 to 250,000	250,000 to 500,000	500,000 to 2,500,000	2,500,000 and over
Number of Enterprises **1**	89677	18362	61040	5572	3585	676	265	87	45	24	4	13	5
Revenues ($ in Thousands)													
Net Sales **2**	91660606	2665426	22453018	9490025	12261115	5585480	4270493	2897478	3168910	2146063	720774	8132564	17882262
Interest **3**	1296715	8162	20354	25506	38702	32153	39337	25041	24721	45158	46143	128163	863276
Rents **4**	65545	610	7294	3306	6924	10407	4558	2868	1434	3279	82	6238	18544
Royalties **5**	14617	0	0	0	0	0	488	429	0	0	0	0	13699
Other Portfolio Income **6**	2269734	30005	38153	28154	57269	28357	27206	19888	29258	9788	27308	31447	1942899
Other Receipts **7**	88013995	2613649	22387217	9433059	12158220	5514563	4198904	2849252	3113497	2087838	647241	7966716	15043844
Total Receipts **8**	91660606	2652426	22453018	9490025	12261115	5585480	4270493	2897478	3168910	2146063	720774	8132564	17882262
Average Total Receipts **9**	1022	144	368	1703	3420	8263	16115	33304	70420	89419	180194	625582	3576452
Operating Costs/Operating Income (%)													
Cost of Operations **10**	14.2	3.7	11.0	35.6	12.3	8.0	11.1	19.2	27.9	4.5	16.4	14.1	10.5
Salaries and Wages **11**	27.4	26.7	23.7	17.3	30.1	35.0	28.6	28.1	24.2	40.9	33.5	26.2	32.2
Taxes Paid **12**	2.9	3.0	3.1	2.2	2.7	3.1	2.7	2.7	2.0	3.6	2.5	2.6	3.4
Interest Paid **13**	2.0	1.4	0.6	1.1	0.6	1.3	0.9	1.1	1.3	1.8	6.2	3.0	5.7
Depreciation **14**	0.9	1.5	0.8	0.6	0.8	0.8	0.9	1.2	0.9	1.2	1.2	0.9	0.9
Amortization and Depletion **15**	1.0	0.2	0.4	1.0	0.8	0.4	0.6	0.9	0.8	1.8	0.3	3.0	1.6
Pensions and Other Deferred Comp. **16**	1.3	0.8	1.3	1.3	1.2	1.4	1.1	0.9	1.2	0.8	1.0	0.4	2.1
Employee Benefits **17**	3.0	2.1	1.7	1.5	1.8	2.1	16.5	1.7	1.8	4.1	2.5	6.3	2.3
Advertising **18**	1.1	2.9	1.8	0.9	0.9	0.9	0.9	0.6	1.6	1.7	3.4	0.6	0.5
Other Expenses **19**	25.3	25.7	25.7	18.4	25.2	21.9	22.0	26.9	27.4	27.8	26.3	29.8	25.2
Officers' Compensation **20**	9.7	6.7	16.3	12.2	12.6	13.8	9.2	8.0	5.2	3.3	3.7	3.1	2.6
Operating Margin **21**	11.0	12.8	13.6	8.0	11.1	11.1	5.4	8.6	5.7	8.5	3.0	10.0	12.9
Operating Margin Before Officers' Comp. **22**	20.8	19.5	29.9	20.2	23.7	24.9	14.6	16.6	10.9	11.8	6.7	13.1	15.5

Selected Average Balance Sheet ($ in Thousands)

Item													
Net Receivables 23	376	0	9	57	521	1244	3351	8393	18504	30046	103532	151324	4911229
Inventories 24	•	•	•	•	•	•	•	•	•	•	•	•	•
Net Property, Plant and Equipment 25	48	0	14	71	130	649	755	2220	3556	6145	7501	28547	195838
Total Assets 26	1294	•	87	741	2140	7138	14582	34006	70095	150673	352841	1144800	12843140
Notes and Loans Payable 27	231	•	32	248	513	1939	2849	6425	11865	30603	186543	226760	1584132
All Other Liabilities 28	670	•	27	215	1189	3990	8240	18421	47017	73486	157284	500151	7097944
Net Worth 29	393	•	28	277	438	1210	3494	9160	11213	46584	9015	417889	4161064

Selected Financial Ratios (Times to 1)

Item													
Current Ratio 30	1.3	•	1.7	1.2	1.3	1.1	1.2	0.9	1.1	1.0	1.0	1.0	1.4
Quick Ratio 31	1.1	•	1.5	1.1	0.9	1.0	0.9	0.8	0.9	0.4	0.7	0.4	1.3
Net Sales to Working Capital 32	6.9	•	18.2	24.8	16.5	8.4	13.6	11.1	11.9	•	37.2	•	1.9
Coverage Ratio 33	6.6	9.9	22.6	8.5	20.4	9.2	7.1	8.8	5.7	5.4	1.5	4.3	3.7
Total Asset Turnover 34	0.8	•	4.2	2.3	1.6	1.2	1.1	1.0	0.6	1.0	0.5	0.5	0.3
Inventory Turnover 35	•	•	•	•	•	•	•	•	•	•	•	•	•
Receivables Turnover 36	•	•	•	•	•	•	•	•	•	•	•	•	•
Total Liabilities to Net Worth 37	2.3	•	2.1	1.7	3.9	4.9	2.7	3.2	5.3	2.2	38.1	1.7	2.1
Current Assets to Working Capital 38	4.4	•	2.4	4.0	7.0	4.8	8.1	7.7	10.3	•	23.0	•	3.3
Current Liabilities to Working Capital 39	3.4	•	1.4	3.0	6.0	3.8	7.1	6.7	9.3	•	22.0	•	2.3
Working Capital to Net Sales 40	0.1	•	0.1	0.1	0.1	0.1	0.1	0.1	0.1	•	0.0	•	0.5
Inventory to Working Capital 41	0.0	•	•	0.1	0.0	0.1	0.1	0.0	•	•	0.0	•	•
Total Receipts to Cash Flow 42	3.3	2.5	2.9	4.5	3.1	3.5	4.2	3.2	3.3	3.1	4.4	2.7	3.7
Cost of Goods to Cash Flow 43	0.5	0.1	0.3	1.6	0.4	0.3	0.5	0.6	0.9	0.1	0.7	0.4	0.4
Cash Flow to Total Debt 44	0.3	•	2.1	0.8	0.6	0.4	0.3	0.4	•	0.3	0.1	0.3	0.1

Selected Financial Factors (in Percentages)

Item													
Debt Ratio 45	69.6	•	68.1	62.6	79.5	83.1	76.0	73.1	84.0	69.1	97.4	63.5	67.6
Return on Total Assets 46	10.7	•	59.9	20.8	18.6	14.3	6.9	9.5	6.9	6.0	4.7	7.0	5.8
Return on Equity Before Income Taxes 47	29.8	•	179.6	49.0	86.5	75.4	24.7	31.4	35.3	16.1	60.3	14.7	13.1
Return on Equity After Income Taxes 48	25.4	•	176.9	47.9	82.3	69.0	20.6	26.8	27.9	12.7	48.0	9.4	8.6
Profit Margin (Before Income Tax) 49	11.5	12.8	13.6	8.0	11.1	11.0	5.4	8.6	5.6	8.4	3.0	9.8	15.2
Profit Margin (After Income Tax) 50	9.8	12.2	13.4	7.8	10.5	10.1	4.5	7.4	4.4	6.6	2.4	6.3	10.0

Table II

Corporations with Net Income

INSURANCE AGENCIES AND BROKERAGES

MONEY AMOUNTS AND SIZE OF ASSETS IN THOUSANDS OF DOLLARS

Item Description for Accounting Period 7/06 Through 6/07	Total	Zero Assets	Under 500	500 to 1,000	1,000 to 5,000	5,000 to 10,000	10,000 to 25,000	25,000 to 50,000	50,000 to 100,000	100,000 to 250,000	250,000 to 500,000	500,000 to 2,500,000	2,500,000 and over
Number of Enterprises **1**	67561	•	47667	4621	3146	584	225	•	35	•	•	•	5
Revenues ($ in Thousands)													
Net Sales **2**	81781384	•	18924248	9088638	10445780	4550665	3713066	•	2891965	•	•	•	17882262
Interest **3**	1218374	•	18568	20950	35170	25806	33256	•	19510	•	•	•	863276
Rents **4**	58339	•	5962	2627	3654	8636	4558	•	1434	•	•	•	18544
Royalties **5**	14139	•	0	0	0	0	10	•	0	•	•	•	13699
Other Portfolio Income **6**	2214510	•	34469	24429	40937	24267	20184	•	27201	•	•	•	1942899
Other Receipts **7**	78276022	•	18865249	9040632	10366019	4491956	3655058	•	2843820	•	•	•	15043844
Total Receipts **8**	81781384	•	18924248	9088638	10445780	4550665	3713066	•	2891965	•	•	•	17882262
Average Total Receipts **9**	1210	•	397	1967	3320	7792	16503	•	82628	•	•	•	3576452
Operating Costs/Operating Income (%)													
Cost of Operations **10**	14.6	•	10.5	37.1	13.7	2.6	10.7	•	29.2	•	•	•	10.5
Salaries and Wages **11**	26.7	•	23.6	17.2	27.1	36.2	25.9	•	23.8	•	•	•	32.2
Taxes Paid **12**	2.9	•	3.0	2.1	2.7	3.3	2.4	•	1.9	•	•	•	3.4
Interest Paid **13**	2.1	•	0.5	1.1	0.5	1.6	0.7	•	1.2	•	•	•	5.7
Depreciation **14**	0.8	•	0.7	0.5	0.8	0.9	0.8	•	1.0	•	•	•	0.9
Amortization and Depletion **15**	1.0	•	0.3	0.9	0.6	0.4	0.4	•	0.5	•	•	•	1.6
Pensions and Other Deferred Comp. **16**	1.4	•	1.4	1.3	1.3	1.4	1.2	•	1.2	•	•	•	2.1
Employee Benefits **17**	3.1	•	1.5	1.5	2.0	2.0	18.4	•	1.7	•	•	•	2.3
Advertising **18**	1.0	•	1.7	0.9	0.9	0.8	0.6	•	0.5	•	•	•	0.5
Other Expenses **19**	23.1	•	22.8	16.9	22.0	21.4	19.8	•	25.0	•	•	•	25.2
Officers' Compensation **20**	9.6	•	16.0	11.6	13.8	14.0	9.3	•	5.6	•	•	•	2.6
Operating Margin **21**	13.8	•	17.9	9.0	14.6	15.5	9.8	•	8.4	•	•	•	12.9
Operating Margin Before Officers' Comp. **22**	23.3	•	33.8	20.5	28.4	29.5	19.1	•	14.0	•	•	•	15.5

Selected Average Balance Sheet ($ in Thousands)

	1	2	3	4	5	6	7	8
Net Receivables 23	484	9	67	530	1191	3453	22401	4911229
Inventories 24	•	•	•	•	•	•	•	•
Net Property, Plant and Equipment 25	56	15	76	119	697	782	4337	195838
Total Assets 26	1593	90	725	2075	7135	14479	69965	12843140
Notes and Loans Payable 27	258	27	257	315	2020	2235	10914	1584132
All Other Liabilities 28	835	27	220	1098	3912	7981	44150	7097944
Net Worth 29	499	36	248	662	1202	4263	14901	4161064

Selected Financial Ratios (Times to 1)

	1	2	3	4	5	6	7	8
Current Ratio 30	1.3	2.0	1.3	1.3	1.3	1.2	1.1	1.4
Quick Ratio 31	1.1	1.8	1.2	1.2	1.0	1.0	1.0	1.3
Net Sales to Working Capital 32	6.2	15.5	28.8	10.8	8.0	12.2	29.1	1.9
Coverage Ratio 33	7.7	34.4	9.2	27.6	10.9	14.5	8.1	3.7
Total Asset Turnover 34	0.8	4.4	2.7	1.6	1.1	1.1	1.2	0.3
Inventory Turnover 35	•	•	•	•	•	•	•	•
Receivables Turnover 36	•	•	•	•	•	•	•	•
Total Liabilities to Net Worth 37	2.2	1.5	1.9	2.1	4.9	2.4	3.7	2.1
Current Assets to Working Capital 38	4.1	2.0	4.1	4.6	4.7	7.1	16.8	3.3
Current Liabilities to Working Capital 39	3.1	1.0	3.1	3.6	3.7	6.1	15.8	2.3
Working Capital to Net Sales 40	0.2	0.1	0.0	0.1	0.1	0.1	0.0	0.5
Inventory to Working Capital 41	0.0	•	•	•	•	0.0	•	•
Total Receipts to Cash Flow 42	3.2	2.8	4.6	3.0	3.1	3.7	3.3	3.7
Cost of Goods to Cash Flow 43	0.5	0.3	1.7	0.4	0.1	0.4	1.0	0.4
Cash Flow to Total Debt 44	0.3	2.7	0.9	0.8	0.4	0.4	0.5	0.1

Selected Financial Factors (in Percentages)

	1	2	3	4	5	6	7	8
Debt Ratio 45	68.7	59.5	65.8	68.1	83.1	70.6	78.7	67.6
Return on Total Assets 46	12.4	81.5	27.3	24.2	18.7	11.9	11.3	5.8
Return on Equity Before Income Taxes 47	34.6	195.7	71.2	73.0	100.5	37.7	46.3	13.1
Return on Equity After Income Taxes 48	29.9	193.0	69.8	69.9	93.1	33.8	39.2	8.6
Profit Margin (Before Income Tax) 49	14.3	17.9	9.0	14.6	15.5	9.7	8.4	15.2
Profit Margin (After Income Tax) 50	12.3	17.6	8.8	13.9	14.4	8.7	7.1	10.0

Table I

Corporations with and without Net Income

OTHER INSURANCE RELATED ACTIVITIES

MONEY AMOUNTS AND SIZE OF ASSETS IN THOUSANDS OF DOLLARS

Item Description for Accounting Period 7/06 Through 6/07	Total	Zero Assets	Under 500	500 to 1,000	1,000 to 5,000	5,000 to 10,000	10,000 to 25,000	25,000 to 50,000	50,000 to 100,000	100,000 to 250,000	250,000 to 500,000	500,000 to 2,500,000	2,500,000 and over
Number of Enterprises **1**	15588	2533	11214	471	949	162	127	45	28	27	12	17	4
Revenues ($ in Thousands)													
Net Sales **2**	47523036	440080	3934005	519575	4809882	1726205	2022807	2616292	2716241	2992861	4308338	10741915	10694837
Interest **3**	4341067	10606	3648	3909	21568	5559	18971	25640	20280	44378	73090	283114	3830305
Rents **4**	110519	0	0	4666	9549	2404	1798	5063	1656	11083	121	4878	69302
Royalties **5**	74302	0	0	0	0	0	0	0	6339	0	0	67963	0
Other Portfolio Income **6**	888444	7962	480	0	2419	6308	8602	17747	64394	7044	332674	140972	299843
Other Receipts **7**	42108704	421512	3929877	511000	4776346	1711934	1993436	2567842	2623572	2930356	3902453	10244988	6495387
Total Receipts **8**	47523036	440080	3934005	519575	4809882	1726205	2022807	2616292	2716241	2992861	4308338	10741915	10694837
Average Total Receipts **9**	3049	174	351	1103	5068	10656	15928	58140	97009	110847	359028	631877	2673709
Operating Costs/Operating Income (%)													
Cost of Operations **10**	24.0	17.8	15.4	2.4	1.5	10.5	8.1	48.5	15.6	21.8	43.7	49.6	6.8
Salaries and Wages **11**	14.8	21.6	9.9	34.3	18.1	19.6	30.7	13.7	25.4	22.8	12.2	13.8	7.5
Taxes Paid **12**	1.9	2.7	1.8	4.2	2.5	2.1	3.6	1.5	2.8	2.7	1.2	1.6	1.5
Interest Paid **13**	8.0	1.8	0.9	•	1.1	0.6	0.8	1.0	1.4	3.0	2.0	2.6	29.4
Depreciation **14**	0.7	0.6	0.4	1.4	0.9	1.1	0.7	0.4	1.0	1.3	0.5	0.8	0.5
Amortization and Depletion **15**	0.7	0.3	0.0	•	0.1	0.1	0.3	0.4	1.4	1.4	0.2	1.7	0.4
Pensions and Other Deferred Comp. **16**	0.7	0.0	1.7	0.7	0.5	1.1	0.8	0.3	0.4	0.2	0.2	0.3	1.2
Employee Benefits **17**	1.6	3.4	1.3	4.0	1.3	1.9	1.6	1.8	1.8	6.7	0.9	1.4	0.4
Advertising **18**	0.5	1.7	0.5	2.3	0.5	0.5	0.3	0.3	0.4	0.3	0.2	0.7	0.6
Other Expenses **19**	33.8	41.8	54.9	33.7	63.7	50.0	41.0	27.2	36.9	36.0	31.7	16.9	26.4
Officers' Compensation **20**	3.4	6.5	10.8	4.2	7.2	4.3	3.7	1.7	9.5	1.2	2.4	1.4	0.3
Operating Margin **21**	9.9	2.0	2.4	12.9	2.7	8.0	8.5	3.4	3.3	2.6	4.7	9.2	24.9
Operating Margin Before Officers' Comp. **22**	13.3	8.5	13.2	17.1	9.9	12.4	12.1	5.1	12.8	3.8	7.1	10.6	25.3

Selected Average Balance Sheet ($ in Thousands)

Net Receivables **23**	176924	224754	27650	17479	6002	8711	2125	1802	697	28	5	0	461
Inventories **24**	•	•	•	•	•	•	•	•	•	•	•	•	•
Net Property, Plant and Equipment **25**	95260	38399	8433	7710	5426	1793	708	474	339	126	10	0	143
Total Assets **26**	20203824	849951	366558	158002	67166	34694	14781	7494	1874	641	62	0	7264
Notes and Loans Payable **27**	3161182	261915	96403	35077	14857	6833	2527	1324	590	0	54	0	1387
All Other Liabilities **28**	10088821	476199	140665	109905	35460	16563	7336	7030	944	178	31	0	3736
Net Worth **29**	6953821	111837	129490	13020	16849	11299	4918	-860	341	462	-23	0	2141

Selected Financial Ratios (Times to 1)

Current Ratio **30**	1.1	1.4	1.7	1.5	1.1	1.4	1.5	0.9	1.5	2.8	0.8	•	1.2
Quick Ratio **31**	0.9	1.1	0.9	1.0	1.0	1.0	1.2	0.8	1.4	1.5	0.8	•	1.0
Net Sales to Working Capital **32**	7.9	5.4	5.2	4.6	47.7	9.6	4.8	•	12.3	3.6	•	•	8.1
Coverage Ratio **33**	1.8	4.5	3.3	1.9	3.4	4.2	11.9	13.3	3.4	•	3.7	2.1	2.2
Total Asset Turnover **34**	0.1	0.7	1.0	0.7	1.4	1.7	1.1	1.4	2.7	1.7	5.7	•	0.4
Inventory Turnover **35**	•	•	•	•	•	•	•	•	•	•	•	•	•
Receivables Turnover **36**	•	•	•	•	•	•	•	•	•	•	•	•	•
Total Liabilities to Net Worth **37**	1.9	6.6	1.8	11.1	3.0	2.1	2.0	•	4.5	0.4	•	•	2.4
Current Assets to Working Capital **38**	16.6	3.5	2.4	3.0	12.9	3.8	3.0	•	3.1	1.6	•	•	6.7
Current Liabilities to Working Capital **39**	15.6	2.5	1.4	2.0	11.9	2.8	2.0	•	2.1	0.6	•	•	5.7
Working Capital to Net Sales **40**	0.1	0.2	0.2	0.2	0.0	0.1	0.2	•	0.1	0.3	•	•	0.1
Inventory to Working Capital **41**	•	0.0	0.0	0.0	0.1	0.0	0.0	•	0.0	•	•	•	0.0
Total Receipts to Cash Flow **42**	•	4.2	2.9	2.8	2.8	3.6	2.1	1.8	1.6	2.7	1.9	2.8	2.4
Cost of Goods to Cash Flow **43**	•	2.1	1.2	0.6	0.4	1.7	0.2	0.2	0.0	0.1	0.3	0.5	0.6
Cash Flow to Total Debt **44**	0.1	0.2	0.5	0.3	0.7	0.7	0.8	0.7	2.1	2.3	2.2	•	0.2

Selected Financial Factors (in Percentages)

Debt Ratio **45**	65.6	86.8	64.7	91.8	74.9	67.4	66.7	111.5	81.8	27.9	137.4	•	70.5
Return on Total Assets **46**	7.2	8.7	6.5	3.9	6.7	7.1	9.8	12.2	10.1	22.1	18.7	•	7.5
Return on Equity Before Income Taxes **47**	9.6	51.4	12.8	21.8	18.7	16.6	27.1	•	39.4	30.7	•	•	14.1
Return on Equity After Income Taxes **48**	6.3	34.6	10.4	4.7	11.6	11.4	23.5	28.9	29.4	29.4	•	•	9.7
Profit Margin (Before Income Tax) **49**	24.9	9.1	4.6	2.6	3.3	3.2	8.4	8.0	2.6	12.9	2.4	2.0	9.9
Profit Margin (After Income Tax) **50**	16.4	6.1	3.8	0.6	2.0	2.2	7.3	7.8	1.9	12.3	2.3	0.0	6.8

Table II
Corporations with Net Income

OTHER INSURANCE RELATED ACTIVITIES

MONEY AMOUNTS AND SIZE OF ASSETS IN THOUSANDS OF DOLLARS

Item Description for Accounting Period 7/06 Through 6/07	Total	Zero Assets	Under 500	500 to 1,000	1,000 to 5,000	5,000 to 10,000	10,000 to 25,000	25,000 to 50,000	50,000 to 100,000	100,000 to 250,000	250,000 to 500,000	500,000 to 2,500,000	2,500,000 and over
Number of Enterprises **1**	9508	701	7677	186	654	109	95	28	16	18	6	14	4
Revenues ($ in Thousands)													
Net Sales **2**	39666177	301444	1982333	453329	3645740	973253	1786805	1434659	1801336	2626689	3578095	10387659	10694837
Interest **3**	4239054	8309	1998	2148	15335	1228	13863	16181	11647	35153	38317	264558	3830305
Rents **4**	101137	0	0	0	9446	2404	1798	2034	1433	11083	3516	69302	0
Royalties **5**	74290	0	0	0	0	0	0	0	6339	0	67951	0	0
Other Portfolio Income **6**	869496	7843	479	0	2419	3845	7834	8629	63275	7042	332591	135694	299843
Other Receipts **7**	34382200	285292	1979856	451181	3618540	965776	1763310	1407815	1718642	2573411	3207066	9915930	6495387
Total Receipts **8**	39666177	301444	1982333	453329	3645740	973253	1786805	1434659	1801336	2626689	3578095	10387659	10694837
Average Total Receipts **9**	4172	430	258	2437	5575	8929	18808	51238	112584	145927	596349	741976	2673709
Operating Costs/Operating Income (%)													
Cost of Operations **10**	24.1	26.0	3.5	0.4	1.6	1.6	8.2	32.4	13.1	21.3	52.6	51.2	6.8
Salaries and Wages **11**	13.7	14.2	11.8	35.3	13.8	29.1	30.1	17.5	28.8	19.2	6.5	13.1	7.5
Taxes Paid **12**	1.8	2.7	2.3	3.6	1.8	3.0	3.8	2.1	3.0	2.6	0.7	1.5	1.5
Interest Paid **13**	9.0	0.2	0.4	•	0.8	0.7	0.7	0.3	1.0	2.7	0.5	2.4	29.4
Depreciation **14**	0.6	0.4	0.6	1.2	0.7	1.0	0.7	0.6	1.0	1.0	0.2	0.7	0.5
Amortization and Depletion **15**	0.6	0.0	0.0	•	0.1	0.0	0.1	0.4	0.8	1.0	0.2	1.3	0.4
Pensions and Other Deferred Comp. **16**	0.7	0.0	3.3	0.8	0.7	0.4	0.6	0.3	0.4	0.2	0.1	0.3	1.2
Employee Benefits **17**	1.5	2.9	0.8	4.1	1.3	3.0	1.6	2.5	1.5	7.0	0.2	1.3	0.4
Advertising **18**	0.5	1.8	0.6	1.1	0.3	0.4	0.3	0.2	0.5	0.4	0.0	0.7	0.6
Other Expenses **19**	30.1	20.5	41.9	32.5	64.8	33.1	41.1	30.7	27.2	36.3	30.5	16.1	26.4
Officers' Compensation **20**	3.1	2.7	15.4	3.4	7.6	7.3	2.5	2.1	13.4	0.9	1.2	1.4	0.3
Operating Margin **21**	14.2	28.6	19.4	17.6	6.6	20.4	10.4	10.9	9.3	7.5	7.2	9.9	24.9
Operating Margin Before Officers' Comp. **22**	17.4	31.3	34.8	21.0	14.2	27.7	12.8	13.0	22.8	8.4	8.4	11.3	25.3

Selected Average Balance Sheet ($ in Thousands)

Net Receivables 23	660	0	1	14	671	1991	2690	8002	5353	21886	37972	265381	176924
Inventories 24	•	•	•	•	•	•	•	•	•	•	•	•	•
Net Property, Plant and Equipment 25	181	0	11	216	434	399	639	2016	6916	9154	6774	32370	95260
Total Assets 26	10946	0	47	728	2134	7516	14737	35146	67779	164963	379198	845506	20203824
Notes and Loans Payable 27	2016	0	15	1	768	802	2289	3856	11797	43178	68878	293884	3161182
All Other Liabilities 28	5339	0	10	73	826	4551	6969	16749	35520	103638	122582	355816	10088821
Net Worth 29	3592	0	23	653	541	2164	5479	14540	20462	18147	187738	195805	6953821

Selected Financial Ratios (Times to 1)

Current Ratio 30	1.2	•	2.9	8.1	1.8	1.5	1.6	1.5	1.1	1.5	2.1	1.2	1.1
Quick Ratio 31	1.0	•	2.6	7.3	1.6	1.4	1.4	1.1	0.9	1.0	1.1	1.0	0.9
Net Sales to Working Capital 32	7.7	•	11.9	6.1	9.6	4.6	4.7	6.1	58.8	5.3	4.6	10.4	7.9
Coverage Ratio 33	2.6	173.5	55.0	•	9.6	31.5	16.1	37.3	10.1	3.7	16.4	5.0	1.8
Total Asset Turnover 34	0.4	•	5.5	3.3	2.6	1.2	1.3	1.5	1.7	0.9	1.6	0.9	0.1
Inventory Turnover 35	•	•	•	•	•	•	•	•	•	•	•	•	•
Receivables Turnover 36	•	•	•	•	•	•	•	•	•	•	•	•	•
Total Liabilities to Net Worth 37	2.0	•	1.1	0.1	2.9	2.5	1.7	1.4	2.3	8.1	1.0	3.3	1.9
Current Assets to Working Capital 38	6.9	•	1.5	1.1	2.3	3.2	2.6	3.0	14.0	2.9	1.9	5.8	16.6
Current Liabilities to Working Capital 39	5.9	•	0.5	0.1	1.3	2.2	1.6	2.0	13.0	1.9	0.9	4.8	15.6
Working Capital to Net Sales 40	0.1	•	0.1	0.2	0.1	0.2	0.2	0.2	0.0	0.2	0.2	0.1	0.1
Inventory to Working Capital 41	0.0	•	•	•	•	•	•	0.0	0.0	0.0	0.0	0.1	•
Total Receipts to Cash Flow 42	2.4	2.4	1.8	2.4	1.5	2.0	2.0	2.6	3.2	2.4	2.7	4.2	2.1
Cost of Goods to Cash Flow 43	0.6	0.6	0.1	0.0	0.0	0.0	0.2	0.8	0.4	0.5	1.4	2.2	0.1
Cash Flow to Total Debt 44	0.2	•	6.1	13.9	2.4	0.8	1.0	1.0	0.7	0.4	1.2	0.3	0.1

Selected Financial Factors (in Percentages)

Debt Ratio 45	67.2	•	51.4	10.2	74.7	71.2	62.8	58.6	69.8	89.0	50.5	76.8	65.6
Return on Total Assets 46	8.8	•	108.4	59.0	19.2	25.0	14.0	16.4	17.1	9.0	12.0	10.7	7.2
Return on Equity Before Income Taxes 47	16.5	•	219.0	65.7	67.8	84.0	35.2	38.5	51.1	59.8	22.8	37.0	9.6
Return on Equity After Income Taxes 48	12.2	•	216.3	63.4	58.1	82.5	30.9	32.0	40.8	41.4	19.5	25.3	6.3
Profit Margin (Before Income Tax) 49	14.2	28.6	19.4	17.6	6.6	20.4	10.3	10.9	9.3	7.4	7.2	9.8	24.9
Profit Margin (After Income Tax) 50	10.5	25.7	19.2	17.0	5.6	20.0	9.0	9.1	7.4	5.2	6.1	6.7	16.4

Table I
Corporations with and without Net Income

OPEN-END INVESTMENT FUNDS (FORM 1120-RIC)

MONEY AMOUNTS AND SIZE OF ASSETS IN THOUSANDS OF DOLLARS

Item Description for Accounting Period 7/06 Through 6/07		Total	Zero Assets	Under 500	500 to 1,000	1,000 to 5,000	5,000 to 10,000	10,000 to 25,000	25,000 to 50,000	50,000 to 100,000	100,000 to 250,000	250,000 to 500,000	500,000 to 2,500,000	2,500,000 and over
Number of Enterprises	1	11477	699	43	79	346	383	757	870	1335	2042	1572	2431	921
Revenues ($ in Thousands)														
Net Sales	2	409313942	4199413	34105	829	144008	87019	375527	1089340	3517418	11814247	20660599	95386588	272004848
Interest	3	193648131	1406408	3	180	114619	22507	116522	377203	1250720	4352772	7642924	36598040	141766235
Rents	4	0	0	0	0	0	0	0	0	0	0	0	0	0
Royalties	5	0	0	0	0	0	0	0	0	0	0	0	0	0
Other Portfolio Income	6	81474746	1271441	14	81	11997	23790	154714	383157	1311049	4204084	7256780	28026411	38831227
Other Receipts	7	13419065	1521564	34088	568	17392	40722	104291	328980	955649	3257391	5760895	30762137	91407386
Total Receipts	8	409313942	4199413	34105	829	144008	87019	375527	1089340	3517418	11814247	20660599	95386588	272004848
Average Total Receipts	9	35664	6008	793	10	416	227	496	1252	2635	5786	13143	39238	295336
Operating Costs/Operating Income (%)														
Cost of Operations	10	•	•	•	•	•	•	•	•	•	•	•	•	•
Salaries and Wages	11	0.0	0.0	•	3.1	0.1	0.1	0.1	0.1	0.1	0.1	0.0	0.0	0.0
Taxes Paid	12	0.2	0.3	0.0	0.7	0.1	0.2	0.3	0.2	0.2	0.3	0.2	0.2	0.2
Interest Paid	13	0.4	0.1	•	•	0.0	16.1	0.3	0.8	1.0	0.5	0.9	0.6	0.2
Depreciation	14	0.0	•	•	•	•	•	•	•	0.0	0.0	0.0	0.0	0.0
Amortization and Depletion	15	0.0	0.0	0.1	2.9	0.2	0.3	0.1	0.0	0.0	0.0	0.0	0.0	0.0
Pensions and Other Deferred Comp.	16	•	•	•	•	•	•	•	•	•	•	•	•	•
Employee Benefits	17	•	•	•	•	•	•	•	•	•	•	•	•	•
Advertising	18	0.0	•	•	•	•	•	0.0	•	•	0.0	0.0	•	0.0
Other Expenses	19	17.5	17.1	4.2	146.6	14.8	33.1	29.4	25.4	23.2	22.4	20.5	20.1	16.0
Officers' Compensation	20	0.0	0.0	•	•	•	•	0.4	0.0	0.1	0.0	0.0	0.0	0.0
Operating Margin	21	81.9	82.6	95.7	•	84.8	50.1	69.4	73.5	75.4	76.7	78.2	78.9	83.7
Operating Margin Before Officers' Comp.	22	82.0	82.6	95.7	•	84.8	50.1	69.8	73.5	75.5	76.7	78.2	78.9	83.7

Selected Average Balance Sheet ($ in Thousands)

Line Item													
Net Receivables 23	16486	0	8	6	19	258	285	779	1045	2918	4901	15923	145980
Inventories 24	•	•	•	•	•	•	•	•	•	•	•	•	•
Net Property, Plant and Equipment 25	1	0	0	0	0	0	0	0	0	0	1	1	1
Total Assets 26	1065074	679	234	2827	7598	17495	36976	73460	165226	358286	1106942		9212628
Notes and Loans Payable 27	1445	0	0	0	1	22	25	23	316	229	1907	2445	7277
All Other Liabilities 28	52872	18	43	81	228	867	1786	3999	10299	23702	78250		380697
Net Worth 29	1010758	215	636	2744	7348	16603	35168	69145	154697	332677	1026246		8824655

Selected Financial Ratios (Times to 1)

Line Item												
Current Ratio 30	2.6	2.0	2.7	0.9	4.7	3.3	3.5	3.4	3.3	2.6	2.2	2.7
Quick Ratio 31	2.3	1.9	2.3	0.3	4.3	2.9	3.2	3.1	3.0	2.3	2.0	2.4
Net Sales to Working Capital 32	0.4	44.3	3.1	•	0.2	0.2	0.3	0.3	0.2	0.3	0.4	0.5
Coverage Ratio 33	210.9	1433.7	30506.5	•	3.8	177.4	71.3	57.4	119.6	68.3	106.3	406.1
Total Asset Turnover 34	0.0	3.4	0.1	•	0.0	0.0	0.0	0.0	0.0	0.0	0.0	0.0
Inventory Turnover 35	•	•	•	•	•	•	•	•	•	•	•	•
Receivables Turnover 36	•	•	•	•	•	•	•	•	•	•	•	•
Total Liabilities to Net Worth 37	0.1	0.1	0.0	0.1	0.0	0.1	0.1	0.1	0.1	0.1	0.1	0.0
Current Assets to Working Capital 38	1.6	2.0	1.6	•	1.3	1.4	1.4	1.4	1.4	1.6	1.8	1.6
Current Liabilities to Working Capital 39	0.6	1.0	0.6	•	0.3	0.4	0.4	0.4	0.4	0.6	0.8	0.6
Working Capital to Net Sales 40	2.3	0.0	0.3	•	4.1	3.5	3.7	4.0	3.5	3.0	2.4	2.2
Inventory to Working Capital 41	•	•	•	•	•	•	•	•	•	•	•	•
Total Receipts to Cash Flow 42	1.1	1.3	1.1	1.2	1.6	1.4	1.2	1.2	1.3	1.2	1.2	1.1
Cost of Goods to Cash Flow 43	•	•	•	•	•	•	•	•	•	•	•	•
Cash Flow to Total Debt 44	0.6	43.8	4.6	0.2	0.6	0.6	0.4	0.5	0.4	0.4	0.4	0.7

Selected Financial Factors (in Percentages)

Line Item												
Debt Ratio 45	5.1	7.7	2.9	6.3	4.9	5.1	4.9	5.9	6.4	7.1	7.3	4.2
Return on Total Assets 46	2.5	324.9	12.5	•	1.9	1.6	1.9	2.1	2.0	2.3	2.4	2.5
Return on Equity Before Income Taxes 47	2.6	352.1	12.9	•	2.0	1.7	1.4	2.2	2.2	2.4	2.6	2.6
Return on Equity After Income Taxes 48	2.6	352.1	12.9	•	2.0	1.7	1.4	2.2	2.2	2.4	2.6	2.6
Profit Margin (Before Income Tax) 49	73.7	95.7	84.7	•	56.4	56.5	44.3	56.9	57.6	61.7	66.8	78.0
Profit Margin (After Income Tax) 50	73.7	95.7	84.7	•	56.4	56.5	44.3	56.8	57.6	61.7	66.8	78.0

Table II

Corporations with Net Income

OPEN-END INVESTMENT FUNDS (FORM 1120-RIC)

MONEY AMOUNTS AND SIZE OF ASSETS IN THOUSANDS OF DOLLARS

Item Description for Accounting Period 7/06 Through 6/07	Total	Zero Assets	Under 500	500 to 1,000	1,000 to 5,000	5,000 to 10,000	10,000 to 25,000	25,000 to 50,000	50,000 to 100,000	100,000 to 250,000	250,000 to 500,000	500,000 to 2,500,000	2,500,000 and over
Number of Enterprises **1**	9554	542	30	49	243	310	599	657	1073	1687	1346	2157	861
Revenues ($ in Thousands)													
Net Sales **2**	393973558	4029152	34076	599	142299	80479	336458	914551	3105825	10551750	19037929	90336567	265403872
Interest **3**	192925991	1378063	3	3	114188	22259	109215	370001	1229592	4295312	7593318	36316965	141497071
Rents **4**	0	0	0	0	0	0	0	0	0	0	0	0	0
Royalties **5**	0	0	0	0	0	0	0	0	0	0	0	0	0
Other Portfolio Income **6**	70622812	1191681	10	81	11821	20121	116510	251891	995678	3215611	6028871	24530855	34259682
Other Receipts **7**	130424755	1459408	34063	515	16290	38099	110733	292659	880555	3040827	5415740	29488747	89647119
Total Receipts **8**	393973558	4029152	34076	599	142299	80479	336458	914551	3105825	10551750	19037929	90336567	265403872
Average Total Receipts **9**	41237	7434	1136	12	586	260	562	1392	2895	6255	14144	41881	308251
Operating Costs/Operating Income (%)													
Cost of Operations **10**	•	•	•	•	•	•	•	•	•	•	•	•	•
Salaries and Wages **11**	0.0	0.0	•	•	0.0	0.1	0.1	0.0	0.1	0.1	0.1	0.0	0.0
Taxes Paid **12**	0.2	0.2	•	1.0	0.1	0.2	0.3	0.2	0.2	0.3	0.3	0.2	0.2
Interest Paid **13**	0.3	0.1	•	•	0.0	0.6	0.2	0.9	1.0	0.5	1.0	0.6	0.2
Depreciation **14**	0.0	•	•	•	•	•	0.1	0.0	0.0	0.0	0.0	0.0	0.0
Amortization and Depletion **15**	0.0	0.0	0.1	1.8	0.2	0.3	0.1	0.0	0.0	0.0	0.0	0.0	0.0
Pensions and Other Deferred Comp. **16**	•	•	•	•	•	•	•	•	•	•	•	•	•
Employee Benefits **17**	•	•	•	•	•	•	•	•	•	•	•	•	•
Advertising **18**	0.0	•	•	•	•	•	0.0	•	0.0	0.0	0.0	0.0	0.0
Other Expenses **19**	16.4	15.1	4.0	32.2	13.0	29.7	24.9	22.3	20.7	20.7	18.8	18.6	15.3
Officers' Compensation **20**	0.0	0.0	•	•	•	•	0.4	0.0	0.1	0.0	0.0	0.0	0.0
Operating Margin **21**	83.0	84.6	95.9	65.1	86.7	69.0	74.0	76.5	77.9	78.4	79.9	80.5	84.4
Operating Margin Before Officers' Comp. **22**	83.0	84.6	95.9	65.1	86.7	69.0	74.4	76.5	78.0	78.4	79.9	80.5	84.4

Selected Average Balance Sheet ($ in Thousands)

Net Receivables 23	18890	0	0	5	14	207	290	676	1068	3132	4990	16431	152386
Inventories 24	•	•	•	•	•	•	•	•	•	•	•	•	•
Net Property, Plant and Equipment 25	1	0	0	0	0	0	0	0	0	0	0	1	2
Total Assets 26	1190645	0	211	590	2810	7577	17685	36889	73689	166311	359179	1116192	9392343
Notes and Loans Payable 27	1697	0	0	1	2	28	22	30	223	302	2124	2752	7760
All Other Liabilities 28	58439	0	13	25	86	242	812	1852	3845	10498	23640	79115	385853
Net Worth 29	1130508	0	198	564	2723	7308	16851	35007	69542	155590	333415	1034324	8998730

Selected Financial Ratios (Times to 1)

Current Ratio 30	2.4	•	3.2	1.0	2.7	4.2	2.6	2.9	2.8	2.3	2.1		2.5
Quick Ratio 31	2.1	•	3.0	0.7	2.2	3.8	2.1	2.6	2.6	2.0	1.9		2.2
Net Sales to Working Capital 32	0.5	•	43.7	15.8	4.0	0.3	0.5	0.4	0.3	0.4	0.5		0.5
Coverage Ratio 33	235.6	1472.1	•	•	61653.0	114.0	375.9	75.1	68.6	130.3	71.1	126.7	427.1
Total Asset Turnover 34	0.0	•	5.4	0.0	0.2	0.0	0.0	0.0	0.0	0.0	0.0		0.0
Inventory Turnover 35	•	•	•	•	•	•	•	•	•	•	•	•	•
Receivables Turnover 36	•	•	•	•	•	•	•	•	•	•	•	•	•
Total Liabilities to Net Worth 37	0.1	•	0.1	0.0	0.0	0.0	0.1	0.1	0.1	0.1	0.1		0.0
Current Assets to Working Capital 38	1.7	•	1.5	34.2	1.6	1.3	1.7	1.5	1.6	1.8	1.9		1.7
Current Liabilities to Working Capital 39	0.7	•	0.5	33.2	0.6	0.3	0.7	0.5	0.6	0.8	0.9		0.7
Working Capital to Net Sales 40	1.9	•	0.0	0.1	0.2	3.3	1.9	2.6	3.0	2.3	2.0		1.8
Inventory to Working Capital 41	•	•	•	•	•	•	•	•	•	•	•	•	•
Total Receipts to Cash Flow 42	1.1	1.4	1.0	1.2	1.1	1.3	1.5	1.3	1.2	1.3	1.2		1.1
Cost of Goods to Cash Flow 43	•	•	•	•	•	•	•	•	•	•	•	•	•
Cash Flow to Total Debt 44	0.6	•	86.6	0.4	6.1	0.7	0.5	0.6	0.5	0.4	0.4		0.7

Selected Financial Factors (in Percentages)

Debt Ratio 45	5.1	•	6.2	4.4	3.1	3.6	4.7	5.1	5.6	6.4	7.2	7.3	4.2
Return on Total Assets 46	2.7	•	515.4	1.3	18.1	2.3	2.2	2.7	2.7	2.5	2.7	2.7	2.6
Return on Equity Before Income Taxes 47	2.8	•	549.4	1.4	18.6	2.4	2.3	2.8	2.8	2.7	2.9	2.9	2.8
Return on Equity After Income Taxes 48	2.8	•	549.4	1.4	18.6	2.4	2.3	2.8	2.8	2.7	2.9	2.9	2.8
Profit Margin (Before Income Tax) 49	77.2	81.0	95.9	65.1	86.7	66.3	70.2	70.2	67.0	66.4	68.4	71.5	80.3
Profit Margin (After Income Tax) 50	77.2	81.0	95.9	65.1	86.7	66.3	70.2	70.2	66.9	66.3	68.3	71.5	80.3

Table I

Corporations with and without Net Income

REAL ESTATE INVESTMENT TRUSTS (FORM 1120-REIT)

MONEY AMOUNTS AND SIZE OF ASSETS IN THOUSANDS OF DOLLARS

Item Description for Accounting Period 7/06 Through 6/07		Total	Zero Assets	Under 500	500 to 1,000	1,000 to 5,000	5,000 to 10,000	10,000 to 25,000	25,000 to 50,000	50,000 to 100,000	100,000 to 250,000	250,000 to 500,000	500,000 to 2,500,000	2,500,000 and over
Number of Enterprises	1	1409	131	20	10	93	68	134	102	129	185	157	230	149
Revenues ($ in Thousands)														
Net Sales	2	143346365	23481092	24424	55918	364622	143301	627018	1109930	1183150	4184379	6834888	22153248	83284394
Interest	3	56632527	440587	70	183	4325	8560	30452	282487	253390	724249	1308717	8120871	45458637
Rents	4	42271009	1756791	463	8328	32346	33861	183769	270716	624424	1932606	2723610	8489254	26214840
Royalties	5	0	0	0	0	0	0	0	0	0	0	0	0	0
Other Portfolio Income	6	32874218	21072468	24269	47407	325443	64992	289604	488960	292048	1094766	2338390	3015936	3819936
Other Receipts	7	11668611	211246	-378	0	2508	35888	123193	67767	13288	432758	464171	2527187	7790981
Total Receipts	8	143346365	23481092	24424	55918	364622	143301	627018	1109930	1183150	4184379	6834888	22153248	83284394
Average Total Receipts	9	101807	179245	1221	5592	3921	2107	4679	10882	9172	22618	43534	96318	558956
Operating Costs/Operating Income (%)														
Cost of Operations	10	•	•	•	•	•	•	•	•	•	•	•	•	•
Salaries and Wages	11	1.4	1.2	•	0.7	0.0	•	0.3	0.4	0.8	2.3	1.1	1.5	1.4
Taxes Paid	12	2.0	0.8	0.6	0.6	0.1	0.7	1.7	1.4	3.0	3.1	3.1	3.2	1.9
Interest Paid	13	17.2	3.5	0.5	1.4	0.2	1.4	4.8	12.0	15.7	14.3	10.3	13.3	23.1
Depreciation	14	5.0	1.4	0.2	2.5	0.5	1.2	2.8	1.8	6.1	6.0	5.9	6.2	5.7
Amortization and Depletion	15	0.7	0.2	•	•	0.1	0.1	0.5	0.4	0.7	0.6	0.5	0.8	0.8
Pensions and Other Deferred Comp.	16	•	•	•	•	•	•	•	•	•	•	•	•	•
Employee Benefits	17	•	•	•	•	•	•	•	•	•	•	•	•	•
Advertising	18	0.1	0.0	•	0.1	0.0	0.1	0.2	0.1	0.1	0.1	0.1	0.2	0.1
Other Expenses	19	12.2	3.0	8.3	16.1	14.1	53.6	23.9	34.7	38.0	28.1	20.8	18.9	10.7
Officers' Compensation	20	0.2	0.1	0.1	0.2	•	•	0.1	0.0	0.2	0.1	0.6	0.5	0.2
Operating Margin	21	61.2	89.9	90.5	78.5	85.0	43.0	65.7	49.3	35.4	45.5	57.6	55.5	56.1
Operating Margin Before Officers' Comp.	22	61.4	89.9	90.5	78.5	85.0	43.0	65.8	49.3	35.5	45.6	58.2	55.9	56.3

Selected Average Balance Sheet ($ in Thousands)

Net Receivables 23	44820	0	1	17	-6	330	30	1169	1580	5568	8434	24754	367480
Inventories 24	•	•	•	•	•	•	•	•	•	•	•	•	•
Net Property, Plant and Equipment 25	241902	0	80	0	656	1829	5449	9185	20801	49788	99521	316172	1602328
Total Assets 26	1064533	•	171	738	2729	7585	16636	37739	70846	170641	364040	1155513	7580117
Notes and Loans Payable 27	254267	•	187	0	408	2315	3480	5621	12787	41379	73239	233388	1896249
All Other Liabilities 28	143393	•	53	244	42	864	764	3078	1431	9234	13456	81421	1200179
Net Worth 29	666872	•	-69	494	2279	4406	12392	29040	56628	120028	277345	840704	4483690

Selected Financial Ratios (Times to 1)

Current Ratio 30	0.9	•	0.1	2.8	1.2	0.5	2.4	1.8	3.8	2.1	2.3	1.7	0.8
Quick Ratio 31	0.8	•	0.1	2.8	0.4	0.4	1.5	1.3	3.3	1.4	2.0	1.2	0.7
Net Sales to Working Capital 32	•	•	12.5	158.3	•	4.9	2.1	4.1	3.0	2.4	2.2	•	•
Coverage Ratio 33	4.6	26.9	193.2	56.6	436.5	31.7	14.8	5.1	3.2	4.2	6.6	5.2	3.4
Total Asset Turnover 34	0.1	•	7.1	7.6	1.4	0.3	0.3	0.3	0.1	0.1	0.1	0.1	0.1
Inventory Turnover 35	•	•	•	•	•	•	•	•	•	•	•	•	•
Receivables Turnover 36	•	•	•	•	•	•	•	•	•	•	•	•	•
Total Liabilities to Net Worth 37	0.6	•	0.5	0.2	0.7	0.3	1.7	0.3	0.3	0.4	0.3	0.4	0.7
Current Assets to Working Capital 38	•	•	1.5	7.4	•	0.7	1.7	2.2	1.4	1.9	1.8	2.5	•
Current Liabilities to Working Capital 39	•	•	0.5	6.4	•	0.7	0.7	1.2	0.4	0.8	0.9	1.5	•
Working Capital to Net Sales 40	•	•	0.1	0.0	•	0.2	0.7	1.2	0.5	0.4	0.3	0.4	•
Inventory to Working Capital 41	•	•	•	•	•	•	•	•	•	•	•	•	•
Total Receipts to Cash Flow 42	2.1	•	31.1	11.1	10.2	2.0	2.2	2.6	3.3	2.3	2.2	1.7	1.7
Cost of Goods to Cash Flow 43	•	•	•	•	•	•	•	•	•	•	•	•	•
Cash Flow to Total Debt 44	0.1	•	•	2.1	0.9	0.4	0.3	0.4	0.2	0.3	0.2	0.2	0.1

Selected Financial Factors (in Percentages)

Debt Ratio 45	37.4	•	140.2	33.1	16.5	41.9	25.5	23.0	20.1	29.7	23.8	27.2	40.8
Return on Total Assets 46	7.5	•	648.5	605.8	122.4	12.3	19.8	17.7	6.6	7.9	8.1	5.7	5.8
Return on Equity Before Income Taxes 47	9.3	•	•	888.9	146.3	20.5	24.8	18.5	8.6	9.0	•	6.4	7.0
Return on Equity After Income Taxes 48	9.3	•	•	888.9	146.3	20.5	24.8	18.1	8.6	9.0	5.7	6.3	7.0
Profit Margin (Before Income Tax) 49	61.2	89.9	90.5	78.5	85.0	43.0	65.7	49.3	35.4	45.5	57.6	55.5	56.1
Profit Margin (After Income Tax) 50	61.1	89.8	90.5	78.5	85.0	43.0	65.7	48.4	35.3	45.5	57.4	55.3	56.1

Table II

Corporations with Net Income

REAL ESTATE INVESTMENT TRUSTS (FORM 1120-REIT)

MONEY AMOUNTS AND SIZE OF ASSETS IN THOUSANDS OF DOLLARS

Item Description for Accounting Period 7/06 Through 6/07		Total	Zero Assets	Under 500	500 to 1,000	1,000 to 5,000	5,000 to 10,000	10,000 to 25,000	25,000 to 50,000	50,000 to 100,000	100,000 to 250,000	250,000 to 500,000	500,000 to 2,500,000	2,500,000 and over
Number of Enterprises	1	1029	98	10	3	33	37	76	70	83	138	129	207	145
Revenues ($ in Thousands)														
Net Sales	2	139860810	23253160	23847	55755	357899	116513	573748	1014634	1005422	3842535	6211390	21026374	82379533
Interest	3	56286615	432490	66	136	4095	4213	24698	277333	209786	694646	1268914	7969979	45400260
Rents	4	39062361	1542414	302	8212	24994	20938	128927	179817	484360	1567444	2171421	7567017	25366516
Royalties	5	0	0	0	0	0	0	0	0	0	0	0	0	0
Other Portfolio Income	6	32560752	21067117	24269	47407	325443	64992	286403	488566	271430	1083686	2308524	2861423	3731491
Other Receipts	7	1951082	211139	-790	0	3367	26370	133720	68918	39846	496759	462531	2627955	7881266
Total Receipts	8	139860810	23253160	23847	55755	357899	116513	573748	1014634	1005422	3842535	6211390	21026374	82379533
Average Total Receipts	9	135919	237277	2385	18585	10845	3149	7549	14495	12114	27844	48150	101577	568135
Operating Costs/Operating Income (%)														
Cost of Operations	10	•	•	•	•	•	•	•	•	•	•	•	•	•
Salaries and Wages	11	1.3	1.1	•	0.8	0.0	•	0.3	0.3	0.2	2.2	1.0	1.2	1.4
Taxes Paid	12	1.9	0.7	0.4	0.5	0.1	0.9	1.4	1.1	2.3	2.3	2.6	3.1	1.8
Interest Paid	13	16.6	2.9	0.2	1.4	0.2	1.7	2.6	11.9	8.7	9.8	8.2	12.8	22.8
Depreciation	14	4.7	1.2	0.2	2.5	0.1	1.4	2.1	1.5	4.4	4.1	4.4	5.6	5.6
Amortization and Depletion	15	0.6	0.2	•	•	0.1	0.1	0.2	0.4	0.4	0.4	0.5	0.8	0.7
Pensions and Other Deferred Comp.	16	•	•	•	•	•	•	•	•	•	•	•	•	•
Employee Benefits	17	•	•	•	•	•	•	•	•	•	•	•	•	•
Advertising	18	0.1	0.0	•	0.1	0.0	0.1	0.2	0.0	0.1	0.0	0.1	0.2	0.1
Other Expenses	19	10.8	2.6	0.3	14.1	9.7	17.4	14.0	16.6	30.7	24.9	14.5	15.5	10.6
Officers' Compensation	20	0.2	0.1	•	•	0.1	•	•	•	0.1	0.1	0.7	0.5	0.2
Operating Margin	21	63.8	91.1	99.0	80.6	89.8	78.4	79.0	68.2	53.3	56.2	68.0	60.4	56.8
Operating Margin Before Officers' Comp.	22	64.0	91.2	99.0	80.6	89.8	78.4	79.1	68.2	53.4	56.3	68.7	60.9	57.0

Selected Average Balance Sheet ($ in Thousands)

	1	2	3	4	5	6	7	8	9	10	11	12	13
Net Receivables 23	60994	0	2	0	-18	605	31	1693	2278	7078	8679	27126	377374
Inventories 24	•	•	•	•	•	•	•	•	•	•	•	•	•
Net Property, Plant and Equipment 25	298217	0	159	0	1116	2753	5270	8642	20467	40634	89523	289884	1564540
Total Assets 26	1396790	731	333	731	3386	7791	16533	37893	72461	172211	365436	1184766	7660795
Notes and Loans Payable 27	321137	0	62	0	476	3812	2341	4393	10297	30201	63779	212019	1880476
All Other Liabilities 28	193069	750	2	750	102	1396	1000	4001	738	9463	14794	86091	1221782
Net Worth 29	882584	-20	269	-20	2809	2583	13191	29500	61426	132546	286863	886656	4558537

Selected Financial Ratios (Times to 1)

	1	2	3	4	5	6	7	8	9	10	11	12	13
Current Ratio 30	0.9	•	8.6	1.0	0.6	0.5	2.3	1.7	4.0	2.4	2.3	1.8	0.8
Quick Ratio 31	0.8	•	7.7	1.0	0.3	0.5	1.4	1.4	3.4	1.6	2.0	1.3	0.7
Net Sales to Working Capital 32	•	•	184.9	•	•	•	6.6	5.4	2.3	2.8	2.4	2.0	•
Coverage Ratio 33	4.8	32.8	576.6	57.9	491.0	47.8	31.1	6.7	7.2	6.7	9.3	5.7	3.5
Total Asset Turnover 34	0.1	•	7.2	25.4	3.2	0.4	0.5	0.4	0.2	0.2	0.1	0.1	0.1
Inventory Turnover 35	•	•	•	•	•	•	•	•	•	•	•	•	•
Receivables Turnover 36	•	•	•	•	•	•	•	•	•	•	•	•	•
Total Liabilities to Net Worth 37	0.6	•	0.2	•	0.2	2.0	0.3	0.3	0.3	0.3	0.3	0.3	0.7
Current Assets to Working Capital 38	•	•	1.1	•	•	•	1.8	2.4	1.3	1.7	1.8	2.3	•
Current Liabilities to Working Capital 39	•	•	0.1	•	•	•	0.8	1.4	0.3	0.7	0.8	1.3	•
Working Capital to Net Sales 40	•	•	0.0	•	•	•	0.2	0.2	0.4	0.4	0.4	0.5	•
Inventory to Working Capital 41	•	•	•	•	•	•	•	•	•	•	•	•	•
Total Receipts to Cash Flow 42	2.0	30.1	11.4	11.7	•	2.5	2.7	1.9	2.0	2.2	1.6	•	1.6
Cost of Goods to Cash Flow 43	•	•	•	•	•	•	•	•	•	•	•	•	•
Cash Flow to Total Debt 44	0.1	•	2.2	1.6	•	0.9	0.6	0.6	0.4	0.3	0.2	0.2	0.1

Selected Financial Factors (in Percentages)

	1	2	3	4	5	6	7	8	9	10	11	12	13
Debt Ratio 45	36.8	•	19.2	102.7	17.1	66.8	22.2	20.2	15.2	23.0	21.5	25.2	40.5
Return on Total Assets 46	7.8	•	710.3	2086.0	288.2	32.4	30.6	37.3	10.4	10.7	10.0	6.3	5.9
Return on Equity Before Income Taxes 47	9.8	•	877.9	•	346.8	95.6	33.5	45.2	10.5	11.8	11.4	6.9	7.1
Return on Equity After Income Taxes 48	9.8	•	877.9	•	346.8	95.6	33.0	45.2	10.5	11.8	11.4	6.9	7.1
Profit Margin (Before Income Tax) 49	63.8	91.1	99.0	80.6	89.8	78.4	68.2	79.0	53.3	56.2	68.0	60.4	56.8
Profit Margin (After Income Tax) 50	63.7	91.1	99.0	80.6	89.8	78.4	67.2	79.0	53.3	56.2	67.9	60.3	56.8

Table I

Corporations with and without Net Income

OTHER FINANCIAL VEHICLES

MONEY AMOUNTS AND SIZE OF ASSETS IN THOUSANDS OF DOLLARS

Item Description for Accounting Period 7/06 Through 6/07	Total	Zero Assets	Under 500	500 to 1,000	1,000 to 5,000	5,000 to 10,000	10,000 to 25,000	25,000 to 50,000	50,000 to 100,000	100,000 to 250,000	250,000 to 500,000	500,000 to 2,500,000	2,500,000 and over
Number of Enterprises **1**	11364	3081	6455	222	895	181	168	71	57	49	47	87	49
Revenues ($ in Thousands)													
Net Sales **2**	23045875	805200	238123	22406	194189	124749	273569	80410	380437	610660	1042831	5324674	13948626
Interest **3**	18723302	886606	64897	11922	31245	73285	39732	41303	85126	471114	885364	4226466	11906242
Rents **4**	68354	202	4131	0	175	22450	9670	2484	2525	26706	4	6	0
Royalties **5**	11846	2602	10	0	0	0	0	0	9047	0	30	157	0
Other Portfolio Income **6**	1806271	147401	46884	476	53701	7479	60128	343	185223	39891	49379	485331	730037
Other Receipts **7**	2436102	-231611	122201	10008	109068	21535	164039	36280	98516	72949	108054	612714	1312347
Total Receipts **8**	23045875	805200	238123	22406	194189	124749	273569	80410	380437	610660	1042831	5324674	13948626
Average Total Receipts **9**	2028	261	37	101	217	689	1628	1133	6674	12462	22188	61203	284666
Operating Costs/Operating Income (%)													
Cost of Operations **10**	0.0	0.5	•	•	•	•	•	•	0.1	•	•	0.0	•
Salaries and Wages **11**	0.1	•	1.3	•	0.3	2.6	0.5	1.6	1.0	0.5	0.0	0.0	0.0
Taxes Paid **12**	0.3	2.5	2.7	1.2	3.1	2.8	2.0	4.3	1.2	0.5	0.6	0.2	0.1
Interest Paid **13**	62.2	93.9	20.2	40.6	14.9	49.5	24.6	47.2	15.6	75.2	72.2	48.9	67.8
Depreciation **14**	0.2	0.8	1.3	0.2	0.9	6.8	0.2	0.2	0.0	3.5	0.1	0.1	0.0
Amortization and Depletion **15**	0.1	0.4	0.1	•	0.5	0.0	0.4	16.3	1.1	0.5	0.0	0.1	0.0
Pensions and Other Deferred Comp. **16**	0.5	•	•	•	•	•	0.1	•	0.1	0.0	•	•	0.7
Employee Benefits **17**	0.4	•	0.7	•	0.2	•	•	0.0	0.0	0.1	0.0	0.0	0.6
Advertising **18**	0.0	•	0.1	•	0.1	•	0.0	0.1	0.1	0.0	•	•	0.0
Other Expenses **19**	10.5	30.6	68.4	59.6	70.9	39.1	62.0	15.8	52.4	14.2	11.7	9.3	5.2
Officers' Compensation **20**	0.1	0.3	5.3	2.1	1.8	•	0.0	•	0.2	0.2	0.0	0.0	0.0
Operating Margin **21**	25.5	•	•	•	7.3	•	10.2	14.7	28.0	5.2	15.4	41.5	25.5
Operating Margin Before Officers' Comp. **22**	25.6	•	5.3	•	9.1	•	10.2	14.7	28.2	5.4	15.4	41.5	25.5

Selected Average Balance Sheet ($ in Thousands)

	1	2	3	4	5	6	7	8	9	10	11	12	13
Net Receivables 23	6889	0	0	1	175	511	564	4210	1742	7774	54455	208580	1152243
Inventories 24	•	•	•	•	•	•	•	•	•	•	•	•	•
Net Property, Plant and Equipment 25	61	0	6	7	49	185	1385	825	2546	818	2103	0	0
Total Assets 26	38345	0	107	735	2334	7238	15647	36389	68719	152933	352852	1107647	6161759
Notes and Loans Payable 27	23409	0	25	17	859	1310	6358	11064	11868	53506	166985	479853	4287820
All Other Liabilities 28	4332	0	26	160	721	732	1636	3357	8914	22269	66178	161041	592155
Net Worth 29	10604	0	56	558	754	5195	7653	21968	47937	77158	119689	466753	1281784

Selected Financial Ratios (Times to 1)

	1	2	3	4	5	6	7	8	9	10	11	12	13
Current Ratio 30	0.6	•	41.2	0.7	1.4	3.2	2.3	3.9	2.0	0.8	1.1	1.2	0.5
Quick Ratio 31	0.4	•	29.3	0.7	1.2	1.8	1.4	2.6	1.3	0.5	0.9	0.8	0.4
Net Sales to Working Capital 32	•	•	1.7	•	1.1	0.5	0.8	0.1	0.6	•	3.2	1.1	•
Coverage Ratio 33	1.4	0.7	1.0	0.9	1.4	1.0	1.5	1.3	2.7	1.1	1.2	1.8	1.3
Total Asset Turnover 34	0.1	•	0.3	0.1	0.1	0.1	0.0	0.0	0.1	0.1	0.1	0.1	0.0
Inventory Turnover 35	•	•	•	•	•	•	•	•	•	•	•	•	•
Receivables Turnover 36	•	•	•	•	•	•	•	•	•	•	•	•	•
Total Liabilities to Net Worth 37	2.6	•	0.9	0.3	2.1	0.4	1.0	0.7	0.4	1.0	1.9	1.4	3.8
Current Assets to Working Capital 38	•	•	1.0	•	3.4	1.5	1.7	1.3	2.0	•	17.4	6.8	•
Current Liabilities to Working Capital 39	•	•	0.0	•	2.4	0.5	0.7	0.3	1.0	•	16.4	5.8	•
Working Capital to Net Sales 40	•	•	0.6	•	0.9	2.0	1.3	6.9	1.6	•	0.3	0.9	•
Inventory to Working Capital 41	•	•	•	•	•	•	•	•	•	•	•	•	•
Total Receipts to Cash Flow 42	3.1	•	2.2	2.0	1.8	3.0	1.8	3.3	2.8	7.4	4.0	2.3	3.3
Cost of Goods to Cash Flow 43	0.0	•	•	•	•	•	•	•	0.0	•	0.0	0.0	•
Cash Flow to Total Debt 44	0.0	•	0.3	0.3	0.1	0.1	0.1	0.0	0.1	0.0	0.0	0.0	0.0

Selected Financial Factors (in Percentages)

	1	2	3	4	5	6	7	8	9	10	11	12	13
Debt Ratio 45	72.3	•	47.6	24.0	67.7	28.2	51.1	39.6	30.2	49.5	66.1	57.9	79.2
Return on Total Assets 46	4.5	•	6.8	5.1	1.9	4.5	3.8	1.9	4.1	6.4	5.5	5.0	4.1
Return on Equity Before Income Taxes 47	4.4	•	•	•	1.5	•	2.6	0.8	3.7	0.6	2.8	5.4	4.7
Return on Equity After Income Taxes 48	2.7	•	•	•	•	•	1.0	0.3	2.8	0.4	2.0	3.5	3.1
Profit Margin (Before Income Tax) 49	22.8	•	•	5.4	•	•	12.3	14.7	26.6	3.8	15.3	41.4	21.0
Profit Margin (After Income Tax) 50	14.0	•	•	•	•	•	4.9	6.2	19.9	2.6	10.9	26.5	13.8

Table II

Corporations with Net Income

OTHER FINANCIAL VEHICLES

MONEY AMOUNTS AND SIZE OF ASSETS IN THOUSANDS OF DOLLARS

Item Description for Accounting Period 7/06 Through 6/07		Total	Zero Assets	Under 500	500 to 1,000	1,000 to 5,000	5,000 to 10,000	10,000 to 25,000	25,000 to 50,000	50,000 to 100,000	100,000 to 250,000	250,000 to 500,000	500,000 to 2,500,000	2,500,000 and over
Number of Enterprises	1	4421	424	3113	53	494	69	82	26	25	28	21	55	30
Revenues ($ in Thousands)														
Net Sales	2	15664993	571896	192675	2150	178968	119681	232515	67867	305288	466713	405167	3683729	9438343
Interest	3	11437738	369268	29731	1634	14959	68950	20196	24871	32180	329371	326128	2730493	7489956
Rents	4	53626	94	4131	0	175	22450	8111	0	100	18564	0	0	0
Royalties	5	9070	14	10	0	0	0	0	0	9047	0	0	0	0
Other Portfolio Income	6	1700981	145271	46558	476	50178	6004	56742	343	175682	35030	27579	427282	729839
Other Receipts	7	2463578	57249	112245	40	113656	22277	147466	42653	88279	83748	51460	525954	1218548
Total Receipts	8	15664993	571896	192675	2150	178968	119681	232515	67867	305288	466713	405167	3683729	9438343
Average Total Receipts	9	3543	1349	62	41	362	1735	2836	2610	12212	16668	19294	66977	314611
Operating Costs/Operating Income (%)														
Cost of Operations	10	0.0	•	•	•	•	•	•	•	0.1	•	•	•	•
Salaries and Wages	11	0.1	•	1.4	•	0.1	2.7	0.6	0.1	0.7	0.6	•	0.0	0.0
Taxes Paid	12	0.3	0.6	2.8	0.1	3.2	2.8	2.2	3.9	1.4	0.5	0.1	0.3	0.1
Interest Paid	13	46.1	43.7	7.0	•	10.3	40.4	11.5	12.2	3.6	71.1	46.2	32.4	54.4
Depreciation	14	0.2	0.0	0.5	2.6	0.2	7.1	0.2	0.1	0.0	4.6	0.0	•	0.0
Amortization and Depletion	15	0.0	0.1	0.0	•	0.0	0.0	0.2	0.2	0.0	0.0	0.0	0.1	0.0
Pensions and Other Deferred Comp.	16	0.7	•	•	•	•	•	0.1	•	0.1	0.1	•	•	1.1
Employee Benefits	17	0.6	•	0.0	•	0.2	•	•	0.0	0.0	0.1	0.0	0.0	0.9
Advertising	18	0.0	•	0.1	•	•	•	•	•	0.1	0.0	•	•	0.0
Other Expenses	19	6.5	13.6	39.6	22.7	9.9	7.4	20.6	9.8	36.7	9.8	7.1	1.6	5.6
Officers' Compensation	20	0.1	0.2	6.3	•	0.9	0.0	0.0	0.1	0.3	0.3	0.0	0.0	0.0
Operating Margin	21	45.4	41.8	42.2	74.6	75.1	39.6	64.6	73.8	56.9	12.8	46.5	65.6	37.8
Operating Margin Before Officers' Comp.	22	45.5	42.0	48.6	74.6	76.1	39.6	64.6	73.8	57.2	13.1	46.5	65.6	37.8

Selected Average Balance Sheet ($ in Thousands)

Item												
Net Receivables 23	12810	0	2	313	380	223	561	239	11813	42310	278645	1328946
Inventories 24	•	•	•	•	•	•	•	•	•	•	•	•
Net Property, Plant and Equipment 25	59	11	31	0	485	2238	7	109	210	0	0	0
Total Assets 26	60328	144	801	2237	6536	14884	34754	67388	149806	359932	1146070	6202272
Notes and Loans Payable 27	27730	11	0	512	1123	5342	11045	4462	30700	122754	311361	3360953
All Other Liabilities 28	7382	3	9	273	522	2077	6108	5482	25694	20024	153102	747637
Net Worth 29	25217	130	792	1452	4891	7465	17601	57444	93412	217154	681607	2093682

Selected Financial Ratios (Times to 1)

Item												
Current Ratio 30	0.9	2.9	5.7	5.6	1.6	3.8	3.7	1.6	1.2	1.7	2.5	0.7
Quick Ratio 31	0.7	1.6	5.1	4.0	1.0	2.6	2.4	1.0	1.0	1.6	1.8	0.6
Net Sales to Working Capital 32	•	2.4	0.5	0.8	2.2	0.4	0.7	3.5	0.5	0.2	1.7	0.7
Coverage Ratio 33	1.9	•	6.9	8.2	2.0	7.0	7.0	16.8	1.2	2.0	3.0	1.6
Total Asset Turnover 34	0.1	0.1	0.2	0.3	0.2	0.2	0.1	0.2	0.1	0.1	0.1	0.1
Inventory Turnover 35	•	•	•	•	•	•	•	•	•	•	•	•
Receivables Turnover 36	•	•	•	•	•	•	•	•	•	•	•	•
Total Liabilities to Net Worth 37	1.4	0.0	0.5	0.3	1.0	2.6	1.0	1.4	0.2	0.6	0.7	2.0
Current Assets to Working Capital 38	•	1.5	1.2	1.2	2.6	1.4	1.4	6.1	1.0	2.5	1.7	2.0
Current Liabilities to Working Capital 39	•	0.5	0.2	0.2	1.6	0.4	0.4	5.1	0.0	1.5	0.7	•
Working Capital to Net Sales 40	•	0.4	2.0	1.2	0.4	2.6	1.5	0.3	0.6	1.9	4.1	•
Inventory to Working Capital 41	•	•	•	•	•	•	•	•	•	•	•	•
Total Receipts to Cash Flow 42	2.2	1.3	1.6	2.4	1.5	1.2	2.5	5.8	1.9	1.9	1.8	2.3
Cost of Goods to Cash Flow 43	0.0	•	•	•	0.0	0.0	0.0	•	•	•	0.0	•
Cash Flow to Total Debt 44	0.0	3.4	0.3	0.4	0.3	0.1	0.5	0.1	2.3	0.1	0.0	0.0

Selected Financial Factors (in Percentages)

Item												
Debt Ratio 45	58.2	9.9	1.1	35.1	25.2	49.8	49.4	14.8	37.6	39.7	40.5	66.2
Return on Total Assets 46	5.1	20.9	3.8	13.8	21.2	15.2	6.5	11.1	9.2	5.0	5.7	4.3
Return on Equity Before Income Taxes 47	5.8	19.8	3.8	18.6	14.0	26.0	10.9	12.2	2.1	4.1	6.4	4.7
Return on Equity After Income Taxes 48	4.0	19.0	3.4	15.3	10.4	22.7	9.4	10.5	1.9	3.1	4.3	3.1
Profit Margin (Before Income Tax) 49	41.5	42.1	74.6	74.7	39.6	68.4	73.8	57.5	12.0	46.1	65.5	31.3
Profit Margin (After Income Tax) 50	28.5	40.0	65.5	61.2	29.2	59.8	63.7	49.2	10.4	34.9	44.0	20.6

Table I

Corporations with and without Net Income

LESSORS OF BUILDINGS

MONEY AMOUNTS AND SIZE OF ASSETS IN THOUSANDS OF DOLLARS

Item Description for Accounting Period 7/06 Through 6/07		Total	Zero Assets	Under 500	500 to 1,000	1,000 to 5,000	5,000 to 10,000	10,000 to 25,000	25,000 to 50,000	50,000 to 100,000	100,000 to 250,000	250,000 to 500,000	500,000 to 2,500,000	2,500,000 and over
Number of Enterprises	1	219871	27515	109697	34960	40240	4350	2208	547	219	88	29	19	0
Revenues ($ in Thousands)														
Net Sales	2	39259630	2480716	3977315	3153634	9185404	3318723	4547114	2950181	2191348	1684729	2256490	3513976	0
Interest	3	1007209	63704	50366	44975	171885	73600	92695	86159	58010	58335	62753	244727	0
Rents	4	201871	59805	23311	6799	33881	8067	27701	8980	5031	22474	2024	3798	0
Royalties	5	56919	313	19	2825	12966	384	23290	16405	353	364	0	0	0
Other Portfolio Income	6	4781710	1058483	430309	257809	666612	232398	490637	244094	151526	295247	126028	828570	0
Other Receipts	7	33211921	1298411	3473310	2841226	8300060	3004274	3912791	2594543	1976428	1308309	2065685	2436881	0
Total Receipts	8	39259630	2480716	3977315	3153634	9185404	3318723	4547114	2950181	2191348	1684729	2256490	3513976	0
Average Total Receipts	9	179	90	36	90	228	763	2059	5393	10006	19145	77810	184946	•
Operating Costs/Operating Income (%)														
Cost of Operations	10	13.1	0.5	13.8	8.6	12.8	4.7	12.0	15.2	22.1	22.5	30.0	12.3	•
Salaries and Wages	11	8.6	3.9	6.6	7.2	9.4	12.5	9.3	9.4	11.5	7.0	9.5	6.7	•
Taxes Paid	12	10.5	10.9	9.8	9.7	12.9	17.1	11.7	9.4	8.8	6.7	3.0	6.5	•
Interest Paid	13	12.4	12.9	7.4	10.2	12.1	13.3	13.4	12.3	12.4	15.0	9.9	18.5	•
Depreciation	14	7.8	8.6	5.8	7.7	8.1	9.9	9.3	7.1	7.7	7.6	4.5	8.0	•
Amortization and Depletion	15	0.7	1.0	0.2	0.4	0.5	0.5	0.6	1.1	0.6	1.0	1.2	1.4	•
Pensions and Other Deferred Comp.	16	0.4	0.0	0.1	0.2	0.5	1.0	0.5	0.5	0.3	0.3	0.1	0.2	•
Employee Benefits	17	1.1	0.6	0.6	0.9	1.3	1.8	1.2	1.5	1.2	0.7	0.6	0.4	•
Advertising	18	0.5	0.2	0.5	0.8	0.2	0.6	0.4	0.4	0.5	0.5	1.4	0.6	•
Other Expenses	19	31.5	26.9	44.9	40.2	33.1	30.1	30.8	29.4	24.4	21.2	31.2	21.3	•
Officers' Compensation	20	3.2	0.3	3.2	7.7	4.0	4.0	2.9	3.3	1.6	2.1	1.4	1.2	•
Operating Margin	21	10.4	34.2	7.2	6.6	5.1	4.8	8.1	10.5	8.9	15.3	7.3	22.9	•
Operating Margin Before Officers' Comp.	22	13.5	34.6	10.4	14.3	9.0	8.8	10.9	13.8	10.5	17.4	8.7	24.1	•

Table II

LESSORS OF BUILDINGS

Corporations with Net Income

MONEY AMOUNTS AND SIZE OF ASSETS IN THOUSANDS OF DOLLARS

Item Description for Accounting Period 7/06 Through 6/07	Total	Zero Assets	Under 500	500 to 1,000	1,000 to 5,000	5,000 to 10,000	10,000 to 25,000	25,000 to 50,000	50,000 to 100,000	100,000 to 250,000	250,000 to 500,000	500,000 to 2,500,000	2,500,000 and over
Number of Enterprises **1**	47597	5561	22103	7961	9514	1353	682	246	102	44	17	14	0
Revenues ($ in Thousands)													
Net Sales **2**	26021826	1945886	2341855	2431158	5287275	1930509	2918040	1921743	1541544	981907	1868279	2853630	0
Interest **3**	796209	46272	41233	38856	125238	54830	56275	69406	49382	40744	39491	234482	0
Rents **4**	156695	59127	13286	6331	26793	5279	21234	7082	5031	6750	1984	3798	0
Royalties **5**	14395	207	0	201	12641	384	0	254	344	364	0	0	0
Other Portfolio Income **6**	4499242	1027105	418974	249231	597539	217680	414250	219734	134362	272310	124308	823748	0
Other Receipts **7**	20555285	813175	1868362	2136539	4525064	1652336	2426281	1625267	1352425	661739	1702496	1791602	0
Total Receipts **8**	26021826	1945886	2341855	2431158	5287275	1930509	2918040	1921743	1541544	981907	1868279	2853630	0
Average Total Receipts **9**	547	350	106	305	556	1427	4279	7812	15113	22316	109899	203831	•
Operating Costs/Operating Income (%)													
Cost of Operations **10**	11.7	0.6	3.5	10.2	15.3	5.2	15.4	13.9	20.7	4.1	29.6	6.0	•
Salaries and Wages **11**	7.5	0.9	5.8	8.0	9.3	8.3	8.3	6.6	11.3	6.5	9.3	5.8	•
Taxes Paid **12**	8.1	9.3	8.8	6.4	10.6	12.0	7.0	7.5	7.4	7.3	2.5	6.6	•
Interest Paid **13**	9.4	9.2	5.1	6.0	7.1	10.8	8.6	10.9	10.3	13.7	6.9	18.3	•
Depreciation **14**	5.7	5.3	4.5	4.8	5.6	7.5	5.7	5.0	5.8	7.2	3.7	8.0	•
Amortization and Depletion **15**	0.5	0.5	0.2	0.1	0.3	0.4	0.3	0.7	0.6	0.9	1.2	0.6	•
Pensions and Other Deferred Comp. **16**	0.3	0.0	0.2	0.2	0.7	0.5	0.4	0.5	0.2	0.1	0.1	0.3	•
Employee Benefits **17**	0.8	0.1	0.6	0.8	1.1	1.0	1.0	0.8	0.9	0.5	0.6	0.3	•
Advertising **18**	0.4	0.1	0.4	1.0	0.2	0.6	0.4	0.3	0.3	0.4	1.4	0.3	•
Other Expenses **19**	25.2	14.8	36.8	35.0	22.1	24.6	25.7	24.4	21.3	21.8	29.8	20.4	•
Officers' Compensation **20**	3.3	0.1	3.2	9.4	4.3	3.8	3.3	2.7	1.5	2.6	1.3	1.1	•
Operating Margin **21**	27.1	59.1	30.9	18.1	23.2	25.2	23.7	26.7	19.6	34.9	13.6	32.3	•
Operating Margin Before Officers' Comp. **22**	30.4	59.2	34.1	27.6	27.6	29.0	27.0	29.4	21.1	37.5	14.9	33.4	•

Selected Average Balance Sheet ($ in Thousands)

Net Receivables 23	86	0	6	33	111	157	372	846	3497	4834	16893	79707
Inventories 24	•	•	•	•	•	•	•	•	•	•	•	•
Net Property, Plant and Equipment 25	1040	0	103	421	1169	4285	8985	17715	33847	79193	155795	492864
Total Assets 26	1957	0	186	717	2070	6627	15156	34427	68305	152164	391270	1109098
Notes and Loans Payable 27	1028	0	126	399	1055	3720	8658	16930	35812	68652	188655	567111
All Other Liabilities 28	227	0	11	49	229	306	1289	3824	6959	18749	49784	239841
Net Worth 29	702	0	48	268	786	2600	5209	13673	25534	64763	152831	302146

Selected Financial Ratios (Times to 1)

Current Ratio 30	1.9	•	3.6	2.8	3.1	2.4	1.8	1.4	2.1	1.4	1.5	1.2
Quick Ratio 31	1.4	•	3.1	2.2	2.3	1.7	1.3	0.9	1.6	1.1	1.0	1.0
Net Sales to Working Capital 32	2.9	•	2.9	2.6	1.7	2.3	3.2	4.9	2.0	3.4	5.9	4.5
Coverage Ratio 33	3.9	7.4	7.0	4.0	4.2	3.3	3.7	3.4	2.9	3.5	3.0	2.7
Total Asset Turnover 34	0.3	•	0.6	0.4	0.3	0.2	0.3	0.2	0.2	0.1	0.3	0.2
Inventory Turnover 35	•	•	•	•	•	•	•	•	•	•	•	•
Receivables Turnover 36	•	•	•	•	•	•	•	•	•	•	•	•
Total Liabilities to Net Worth 37	1.8	•	2.8	1.7	1.6	1.5	1.9	1.5	1.7	1.3	1.6	2.7
Current Assets to Working Capital 38	2.1	•	1.4	1.5	1.5	1.7	2.3	3.3	1.9	3.5	3.2	5.5
Current Liabilities to Working Capital 39	1.1	•	0.4	0.5	0.5	0.7	1.3	2.3	0.9	2.5	2.2	4.5
Working Capital to Net Sales 40	0.3	•	0.3	0.4	0.6	0.4	0.3	0.2	0.5	0.3	0.2	0.2
Inventory to Working Capital 41	0.0	•	•	0.0	0.0	•	0.1	0.0	0.0	0.0	0.0	0.0
Total Receipts to Cash Flow 42	3.4	4.6	2.6	3.4	3.2	3.0	2.9	2.7	3.3	3.6	5.0	4.7
Cost of Goods to Cash Flow 43	0.4	0.0	0.1	0.4	0.5	0.2	0.4	0.4	0.7	0.1	1.5	0.3
Cash Flow to Total Debt 44	0.1	•	0.3	0.2	0.1	0.1	0.1	0.1	0.1	0.1	0.1	0.1

Selected Financial Factors (in Percentages)

Debt Ratio 45	64.1	•	74.0	62.6	62.0	60.8	65.6	60.3	62.6	57.4	60.9	72.8
Return on Total Assets 46	10.2	•	20.5	10.3	8.1	7.7	9.1	8.5	6.6	7.1	5.8	9.3
Return on Equity Before Income Taxes 47	21.0	•	67.7	20.6	16.3	13.8	19.3	15.1	11.5	11.9	9.8	21.6
Return on Equity After Income Taxes 48	16.5	•	57.7	17.7	13.5	11.4	14.5	11.4	9.5	9.3	8.7	14.9
Profit Margin (Before Income Tax) 49	27.0	59.1	30.9	18.1	23.0	25.2	23.5	26.4	19.5	34.6	13.6	32.1
Profit Margin (After Income Tax) 50	21.2	43.5	26.3	15.6	19.1	20.7	17.6	19.9	16.0	26.9	12.1	22.1

Table I

Corporations with and without Net Income

LESSORS OF MINIWAREHOUSES, SELF-STORAGE, OTHER REAL ESTATE

MONEY AMOUNTS AND SIZE OF ASSETS IN THOUSANDS OF DOLLARS

Item Description for Accounting Period 7/06 Through 6/07		Total	Zero Assets	Under 500	500 to 1,000	1,000 to 5,000	5,000 to 10,000	10,000 to 25,000	25,000 to 50,000	50,000 to 100,000	100,000 to 250,000	250,000 to 500,000	500,000 to 2,500,000	2,500,000 and over
Number of Enterprises	1	78979	16273	43686	7926	8545	1583	617	175	97	48	13	15	0
Revenues ($ in Thousands)														
Net Sales	2	19659595	1289390	4029649	1007923	2867356	954043	1334324	1146688	1166842	1524524	2171209	2167646	0
Interest	3	713580	64986	24546	50382	56183	37250	57524	49097	97291	76530	30724	169067	0
Rents	4	56924	675	403	3254	4117	6656	2583	1197	3740	21512	6495	6292	0
Royalties	5	89996	545	2996	4152	16079	2623	28433	19226	11811	4131	0	0	0
Other Portfolio Income	6	3476032	594460	167809	86605	448893	144540	157407	198401	306199	494326	57669	819721	0
Other Receipts	7	15323063	628724	3833895	863530	2342084	762974	1088377	878767	747801	928025	2076321	1172566	0
Total Receipts	8	19659595	1289390	4029649	1007923	2867356	954043	1334324	1146688	1166842	1524524	2171209	2167646	0
Average Total Receipts	9	249	79	92	127	336	603	2163	6553	12029	31761	167016	144510	•
Operating Costs/Operating Income (%)														
Cost of Operations	10	10.2	0.0	22.8	1.2	7.0	0.0	11.5	31.7	0.5	6.4	5.5	6.5	•
Salaries and Wages	11	7.7	0.9	10.1	3.6	11.3	6.9	10.1	5.9	9.5	10.1	4.5	4.3	•
Taxes Paid	12	5.2	6.8	4.3	6.3	6.3	9.0	6.2	6.0	4.1	5.1	1.1	6.4	•
Interest Paid	13	8.6	5.8	3.0	8.6	8.5	18.7	9.8	8.2	11.1	11.3	3.3	18.2	•
Depreciation	14	4.5	2.9	2.1	4.5	6.6	8.3	4.3	4.1	4.7	5.7	1.4	7.5	•
Amortization and Depletion	15	0.6	0.1	0.1	0.2	0.2	0.7	0.7	0.5	0.5	1.0	1.3	1.7	•
Pensions and Other Deferred Comp.	16	0.4	0.5	0.9	•	0.5	0.7	0.5	0.2	0.2	0.3	0.1	0.4	•
Employee Benefits	17	0.7	0.2	1.2	0.4	0.4	0.4	1.6	1.4	0.6	1.0	0.1	0.6	•
Advertising	18	0.7	0.4	0.9	2.1	1.0	0.6	0.9	0.7	0.8	0.5	0.1	0.3	•
Other Expenses	19	39.3	31.0	39.0	46.1	34.4	35.5	28.6	18.6	62.1	30.8	81.4	18.9	•
Officers' Compensation	20	4.9	2.8	8.5	2.5	4.8	8.7	4.2	3.3	4.5	1.8	1.3	6.3	•
Operating Margin	21	17.1	48.6	7.1	24.4	19.0	10.6	21.7	19.5	1.5	26.0	•	29.1	•
Operating Margin Before Officers' Comp.	22	22.0	51.3	15.6	26.9	23.8	19.2	25.8	22.8	6.0	27.8	1.2	35.3	•

Selected Average Balance Sheet ($ in Thousands)

Net Receivables 23	47	0	6	33	54	398	651	2526	3684	5903	11044	32600
Inventories 24	•	•	•	•	•	•	•	•	•	•	•	•
Net Property, Plant and Equipment 25	492	0	83	394	1013	2937	5625	12018	23450	51332	144289	440157
Total Assets 26	1152	0	152	675	2025	7083	15146	36116	68995	155939	359286	1062238
Notes and Loans Payable 27	541	0	86	338	1150	3635	7189	13864	26455	67106	153017	405860
All Other Liabilities 28	148	0	21	46	274	623	2000	4530	10744	19751	78134	134881
Net Worth 29	463	0	45	291	600	2824	5957	17723	31796	69082	128135	521498

Selected Financial Ratios (Times to 1)

Current Ratio 30	2.0	•	2.2	3.2	1.6	3.5	2.5	2.7	2.5	1.7	1.7	1.0
Quick Ratio 31	1.2	•	1.4	2.4	1.0	2.3	1.4	1.7	1.5	1.2	1.0	0.6
Net Sales to Working Capital 32	2.1	•	5.0	1.4	2.3	0.5	0.9	0.9	1.2	2.8	6.2	•
Coverage Ratio 33	3.0	9.4	3.4	3.8	3.2	1.5	3.2	3.3	1.1	3.3	1.0	2.6
Total Asset Turnover 34	0.2	•	0.6	0.2	0.2	0.1	0.1	0.2	0.2	0.2	0.5	0.1
Inventory Turnover 35	•	•	•	•	•	•	•	•	•	•	•	•
Receivables Turnover 36	•	•	•	•	•	•	•	•	•	•	•	•
Total Liabilities to Net Worth 37	1.5	•	2.3	1.3	2.4	1.5	1.0	1.2	1.2	1.3	1.8	1.0
Current Assets to Working Capital 38	2.0	•	1.8	1.5	2.7	1.4	1.7	1.6	1.7	2.5	2.4	•
Current Liabilities to Working Capital 39	1.0	•	0.8	0.5	1.7	0.4	0.7	0.6	0.7	1.5	1.4	•
Working Capital to Net Sales 40	0.5	•	0.2	0.7	0.4	1.9	1.1	1.2	0.9	0.4	0.2	•
Inventory to Working Capital 41	0.0	•	•	0.0	0.0	•	0.0	0.0	0.0	0.0	0.0	•
Total Receipts to Cash Flow 42	3.6	3.0	2.8	2.0	3.0	3.4	2.7	5.5	2.9	4.3	13.7	7.0
Cost of Goods to Cash Flow 43	0.4	0.0	0.6	0.0	0.2	0.0	0.3	1.7	0.0	0.3	0.8	0.5
Cash Flow to Total Debt 44	0.1	•	0.3	0.2	0.1	0.0	0.1	0.1	0.1	0.1	0.1	0.0

Selected Financial Factors (in Percentages)

Debt Ratio 45	59.8	•	70.1	56.9	70.4	60.1	60.7	50.9	53.9	55.7	64.3	50.9
Return on Total Assets 46	5.5	•	6.1	6.2	4.5	2.3	4.4	4.9	2.1	7.6	1.5	6.5
Return on Equity Before Income Taxes 47	9.1	•	14.2	10.6	10.5	1.9	7.7	6.9	0.4	11.9	•	8.1
Return on Equity After Income Taxes 48	6.3	•	12.6	9.3	8.2	0.8	5.9	5.1	•	7.0	•	5.0
Profit Margin (Before Income Tax) 49	16.9	48.6	7.0	24.4	18.9	8.7	21.3	18.6	1.0	26.0	•	29.3
Profit Margin (After Income Tax) 50	11.8	34.3	6.2	21.2	14.7	3.8	16.3	13.9	•	15.2	•	18.0

Table II

Corporations with Net Income

LESSORS OF MINIWAREHOUSES, SELF-STORAGE, OTHER REAL ESTATE

MONEY AMOUNTS AND SIZE OF ASSETS IN THOUSANDS OF DOLLARS

Item Description for Accounting Period 7/06 Through 6/07		Total	Zero Assets	Under 500	500 to 1,000	1,000 to 5,000	5,000 to 10,000	10,000 to 25,000	25,000 to 50,000	50,000 to 100,000	100,000 to 250,000	250,000 to 500,000	500,000 to 2,500,000	2,500,000 and over
Number of Enterprises	1	28976	5877	16498	3061	2600	523	247	•	48	•	6	6	0
Revenues ($ in Thousands)														
Net Sales	2	15384325	1190614	3314003	865162	1940609	693795	1116924	•	816731	•	1964306	1266059	0
Interest	3	485412	62894	20314	17918	41347	29087	43373	•	31051	•	25894	129121	0
Rents	4	47727	667	219	682	4117	5890	1878	•	3640	•	5352	3188	0
Royalties	5	86691	545	0	4152	15785	2623	28433	•	11811	•	0	0	0
Other Portfolio Income	6	3048975	589669	160219	85058	437271	117360	130755	•	150623	•	36512	738332	0
Other Receipts	7	11715520	536839	3133251	757352	1442089	538835	912485	•	619606	•	1896548	395418	0
Total Receipts	8	15384325	1190614	3314003	865162	1940609	693795	1116924	•	816731	•	1964306	1266059	0
Average Total Receipts	9	531	203	201	283	746	1327	4522	•	17015	•	327384	211010	•
Operating Costs/Operating Income (%)														
Cost of Operations	10	10.8	•	27.7	•	6.8	•	12.0	•	0.5	•	3.0	1.6	•
Salaries and Wages	11	5.9	0.1	8.6	3.5	6.5	4.8	8.2	•	11.5	•	3.0	4.1	•
Taxes Paid	12	4.5	6.1	3.6	6.1	4.8	5.8	4.7	•	3.8	•	0.8	6.6	•
Interest Paid	13	4.5	3.0	2.2	6.1	5.1	9.6	6.2	•	6.7	•	2.6	4.3	•
Depreciation	14	3.1	1.6	1.7	4.2	6.1	5.8	3.4	•	4.2	•	0.9	1.2	•
Amortization and Depletion	15	0.5	0.1	0.1	0.2	0.2	0.4	0.7	•	0.5	•	1.4	0.7	•
Pensions and Other Deferred Comp.	16	0.4	0.5	1.1	•	0.0	0.4	0.4	•	0.1	•	0.0	0.0	•
Employee Benefits	17	0.6	0.0	1.2	0.1	0.2	0.3	1.4	•	0.7	•	0.0	0.2	•
Advertising	18	0.5	0.3	0.7	1.8	0.4	0.3	0.8	•	1.0	•	0.0	0.1	•
Other Expenses	19	29.1	20.4	27.6	29.3	17.9	23.6	21.7	•	27.6	•	83.8	5.2	•
Officers' Compensation	20	3.3	2.7	7.5	1.8	2.6	3.6	3.7	•	5.1	•	0.9	•	•
Operating Margin	21	36.8	65.1	18.1	47.0	49.3	45.2	36.8	•	38.4	•	3.6	76.2	•
Operating Margin Before Officers' Comp.	22	40.2	67.8	25.6	48.7	51.8	48.8	40.5	•	43.5	•	4.5	76.2	•

Selected Average Balance Sheet ($ in Thousands)

Item									
Net Receivables 23	43	6	8	101	126	798	2454	12316	7774
Inventories 24	•	0	0	0	0	0	0	•	•
Net Property, Plant and Equipment 25	460	82	359	804	3338	5684	21508	119855	302117
Total Assets 26	1222	160	679	2099	6900	15200	67595	349698	928701
Notes and Loans Payable 27	383	68	301	706	2800	5964	23591	101889	52452
All Other Liabilities 28	152	22	48	293	439	2243	11948	86522	22946
Net Worth 29	687	70	331	1100	3661	6992	32056	161287	853303

Selected Financial Ratios (Times to 1)

Item									
Current Ratio 30	2.6	2.4	3.3	3.2	3.9	3.5	2.4	2.0	2.4
Quick Ratio 31	1.6	2.0	2.3	2.2	2.7	2.2	1.3	1.0	1.2
Net Sales to Working Capital 32	2.9	8.6	2.6	2.1	1.8	1.4	1.6	6.6	2.1
Coverage Ratio 33	9.1	9.3	8.8	10.6	5.6	6.9	6.7	2.4	18.9
Total Asset Turnover 34	0.4	1.3	0.4	0.4	0.2	0.3	0.3	0.9	0.2
Inventory Turnover 35	22.7	•	•	•	•	•	•	•	•
Receivables Turnover 36	•	•	•	•	•	•	•	•	•
Total Liabilities to Net Worth 37	0.8	1.3	1.1	0.9	0.9	1.2	1.1	1.2	0.1
Current Assets to Working Capital 38	1.6	1.7	1.4	1.5	1.3	1.4	1.7	2.0	1.7
Current Liabilities to Working Capital 39	0.6	0.7	0.4	0.5	0.3	0.4	0.7	1.0	0.7
Working Capital to Net Sales 40	0.3	0.1	0.4	0.5	0.6	0.7	0.6	0.2	0.5
Inventory to Working Capital 41	0.0	•	0.0	0.0	•	•	0.0	•	•
Total Receipts to Cash Flow 42	2.9	2.7	1.8	2.3	2.1	2.2	2.3	15.8	3.2
Cost of Goods to Cash Flow 43	0.3	0.8	0.2	0.2	0.2	0.3	0.0	0.5	0.1
Cash Flow to Total Debt 44	0.3	0.8	0.5	0.3	0.2	0.3	0.2	0.1	0.9

Selected Financial Factors (in Percentages)

Item									
Debt Ratio 45	43.8	56.3	51.3	47.6	46.9	54.0	52.6	53.9	8.1
Return on Total Assets 46	17.9	25.3	22.1	19.3	10.4	12.7	11.2	5.8	18.3
Return on Equity Before Income Taxes 47	28.4	51.7	40.1	33.4	16.1	23.7	20.2	7.3	18.8
Return on Equity After Income Taxes 48	23.3	48.9	37.0	29.2	13.7	19.8	17.1	6.0	14.1
Profit Margin (Before Income Tax) 49	36.7	18.0	47.0	49.2	44.5	36.6	38.0	3.6	76.2
Profit Margin (After Income Tax) 50	30.2	17.0	43.3	43.0	37.7	30.6	32.3	2.9	56.9

Table I

Corporations with and without Net Income

OFFICES OF REAL ESTATE AGENTS AND BROKERS

MONEY AMOUNTS AND SIZE OF ASSETS IN THOUSANDS OF DOLLARS

Item Description for Accounting Period 7/06 Through 6/07	Total	Zero Assets	Under 500	500 to 1,000	1,000 to 5,000	5,000 to 10,000	10,000 to 25,000	25,000 to 50,000	50,000 to 100,000	100,000 to 250,000	250,000 to 500,000	500,000 to 2,500,000	2,500,000 and over
Number of Enterprises **1**	127634	31227	89674	3896	2421	234	125	20	16	13	0	5	3
Revenues ($ in Thousands)													
Net Sales **2**	70001699	3834880	36501050	8160476	7424844	507004	3371710	392166	895751	1543527	0	2504130	4866161
Interest **3**	428359	8144	22024	6899	38329	10028	4269	4409	10880	17261	0	146068	160048
Rents **4**	321313	11575	19033	15143	44908	15852	5506	586	201	35802	0	46725	125982
Royalties **5**	509373	0	0	0	51	0	0	0	0	0	0	10110	499212
Other Portfolio Income **6**	361207	34677	32100	7688	34141	35925	75604	818	1424	26134	0	45914	66779
Other Receipts **7**	6381447	3780484	36427893	8130746	7307415	445199	3286331	386353	883246	1464330	0	2255313	4014140
Total Receipts **8**	70001699	3834880	36501050	8160476	7424844	507004	3371710	392166	895751	1543527	0	2504130	4866161
Average Total Receipts **9**	548	123	407	2095	3067	2167	26974	19608	55984	118733	•	500826	1622054
Operating Costs/Operating Income (%)													
Cost of Operations **10**	16.7	2.1	15.3	32.9	8.8	7.2	33.7	47.9	27.4	46.0	•	12.6	0.5
Salaries and Wages **11**	30.4	21.4	26.9	32.5	39.9	22.2	31.3	10.7	24.3	14.2	•	39.6	48.4
Taxes Paid **12**	1.8	2.0	1.5	1.5	1.6	5.4	1.5	2.1	2.9	2.3	•	3.6	2.8
Interest Paid **13**	1.3	1.4	0.3	0.7	1.7	13.8	1.3	5.8	2.6	3.3	•	6.1	4.5
Depreciation **14**	0.9	1.1	0.7	0.7	1.0	3.2	1.3	0.6	1.4	2.2	•	1.6	1.3
Amortization and Depletion **15**	0.3	0.1	0.0	0.1	0.1	0.1	0.1	0.4	0.3	0.7	•	1.6	2.5
Pensions and Other Deferred Comp. **16**	0.8	0.1	1.3	0.5	0.4	0.5	0.2	•	0.4	0.3	•	0.0	0.5
Employee Benefits **17**	0.7	0.8	0.5	0.5	0.4	0.1	0.7	0.7	1.3	0.8	•	1.4	2.7
Advertising **18**	3.6	3.3	3.7	4.8	3.3	0.7	3.9	3.8	3.6	4.0	•	0.6	2.8
Other Expenses **19**	27.2	42.5	28.6	15.8	31.6	30.8	19.8	24.5	20.6	17.5	•	24.6	27.1
Officers' Compensation **20**	8.4	9.4	12.1	6.7	3.2	3.9	2.1	2.9	8.3	1.9	•	3.7	1.0
Operating Margin **21**	7.9	15.9	9.1	3.2	7.9	12.3	4.1	0.7	6.8	6.8	•	4.7	5.7
Operating Margin Before Officers' Comp. **22**	16.4	25.3	21.2	9.9	11.1	16.2	6.2	3.6	15.1	8.7	•	8.4	6.7

Selected Average Balance Sheet ($ in Thousands)

Item													
Net Receivables 23	30	0	3	39	172	121	1706	2526	6999	25467	•	213293	424307
Inventories 24	•	•	•	•	•	•	•	•	•	•	•	•	•
Net Property, Plant and Equipment 25	64	0	17	282	455	3946	4617	2167	11815	43887	•	70473	567366
Total Assets 26	333	0	73	727	1920	7470	16091	36427	68688	166381	•	1201203	4911599
Notes and Loans Payable 27	140	0	35	350	1176	5564	6111	19082	31133	33297	•	410930	1673638
All Other Liabilities 28	89	0	14	160	432	828	4931	5082	12881	42243	•	280541	1800759
Net Worth 29	104	0	23	217	312	1077	5049	12264	24674	90841	•	509732	1437203

Selected Financial Ratios (Times to 1)

Item													
Current Ratio 30	1.5	•	1.8	2.3	1.7	1.4	2.0	1.5	1.6	•	2.2	1.1	
Quick Ratio 31	0.9	•	1.4	1.4	0.9	0.6	0.5	0.6	1.0	•	1.5	0.5	
Net Sales to Working Capital 32	12.2	23.6	12.4	8.1	4.4	11.5	1.9	5.2	3.9	•	2.1	16.7	
Coverage Ratio 33	7.0	12.2	32.4	5.7	5.8	4.1	1.9	3.1	3.5	•	3.1	2.3	
Total Asset Turnover 34	1.6	12.2	5.6	2.9	1.6	0.3	1.7	0.5	0.8	0.7	•	0.4	0.3
Inventory Turnover 35	•	•	•	•	•	•	•	•	•	•	•	•	•
Receivables Turnover 36	•	•	•	•	•	•	•	•	•	•	•	•	•
Total Liabilities to Net Worth 37	2.2	2.1	2.3	5.2	5.9	2.2	2.0	1.8	0.8	•	1.4	2.4	
Current Assets to Working Capital 38	2.9	2.2	1.8	2.4	3.4	3.6	2.0	3.1	2.7	•	1.8	15.3	
Current Liabilities to Working Capital 39	1.9	1.2	0.8	1.4	2.4	2.6	1.0	2.1	1.7	•	0.8	14.3	
Working Capital to Net Sales 40	0.1	0.0	0.1	0.1	0.2	0.1	0.5	0.2	0.3	•	0.5	0.1	
Inventory to Working Capital 41	0.0	0.0	•	0.0	0.0	•	0.5	0.0	0.0	•	0.0	0.0	
Total Receipts to Cash Flow 42	3.3	1.8	3.0	6.7	2.9	3.2	5.2	4.7	4.5	5.1	•	3.9	3.8
Cost of Goods to Cash Flow 43	0.5	0.0	0.5	2.2	0.3	0.2	1.7	2.3	1.2	2.3	•	0.5	0.0
Cash Flow to Total Debt 44	0.7	2.7	0.6	0.7	0.1	0.5	0.2	0.3	0.3	•	0.2	0.1	

Selected Financial Factors (in Percentages)

Item													
Debt Ratio 45	68.8	•	68.2	70.1	83.8	85.6	68.6	66.3	64.1	45.4	•	57.6	70.7
Return on Total Assets 46	15.2	•	52.8	11.0	15.3	7.5	9.0	3.5	7.5	7.2	•	4.5	3.4
Return on Equity Before Income Taxes 47	42.0	•	160.7	30.4	77.8	24.6	21.7	1.2	15.1	8.9	•	4.7	6.5
Return on Equity After Income Taxes 48	39.9	•	159.6	29.6	76.2	19.9	20.5	•	14.0	7.9	•	2.0	4.0
Profit Margin (Before Income Tax) 49	7.9	16.1	9.1	3.2	7.9	12.2	4.1	0.7	6.6	6.8	•	4.8	5.8
Profit Margin (After Income Tax) 50	7.5	15.6	9.1	3.1	7.7	9.9	3.8	•	6.2	6.0	•	2.0	3.6

Table II

Corporations with Net Income

OFFICES OF REAL ESTATE AGENTS AND BROKERS

MONEY AMOUNTS AND SIZE OF ASSETS IN THOUSANDS OF DOLLARS

Item Description for Accounting Period 7/06 Through 6/07	Total	Zero Assets	Under 500	500 to 1,000	1,000 to 5,000	5,000 to 10,000	10,000 to 25,000	25,000 to 50,000	50,000 to 100,000	100,000 to 250,000	250,000 to 500,000	500,000 to 2,500,000	2,500,000 and over
Number of Enterprises **1**	87301	19428	64201	1936	1484	143	70	•	12	•	0	5	0
Revenues ($ in Thousands)													
Net Sales **2**	51717108	2668891	28039172	5329150	5496059	474221	2190036	•	743471	•	0	5120858	0
Interest **3**	217235	5558	14470	3444	25774	8448	2775	•	6642	•	0	128840	0
Rents **4**	227512	4852	1083	5520	16660	15852	2720	•	201	•	0	156413	0
Royalties **5**	192942	0	0	0	6	0	0	•	0	•	0	192936	0
Other Portfolio Income **6**	232056	26632	18483	1467	23350	35925	1098	•	1424	•	0	105209	0
Other Receipts **7**	50847363	2631849	28005136	5318719	5430269	413996	2183443	•	735204	•	0	4537460	0
Total Receipts **8**	51717108	2668891	28039172	5329150	5496059	474221	2190036	•	743471	•	0	5120858	0
Average Total Receipts **9**	592	137	437	2753	3704	3316	31286	•	61956	•	•	1024172	•
Operating Costs/Operating Income (%)													
Cost of Operations **10**	11.3	1.9	9.4	18.5	6.3	7.7	34.7	•	28.2	•	•	0.4	•
Salaries and Wages **11**	33.9	19.2	28.8	43.2	50.4	22.8	28.0	•	25.9	•	•	53.2	•
Taxes Paid **12**	1.7	1.7	1.4	1.3	1.5	5.5	1.4	•	2.6	•	•	3.3	•
Interest Paid **13**	1.0	1.1	0.3	0.5	0.9	9.6	0.8	•	2.5	•	•	4.4	•
Depreciation **14**	0.8	0.9	0.6	0.7	0.6	3.3	1.1	•	1.4	•	•	1.2	•
Amortization and Depletion **15**	0.2	0.1	0.0	0.1	0.1	0.1	0.2	•	0.1	•	•	1.1	•
Pensions and Other Deferred Comp. **16**	0.9	0.1	1.3	0.6	0.5	0.4	0.2	•	0.5	•	•	0.3	•
Employee Benefits **17**	0.7	0.7	0.4	0.5	0.3	0.1	0.8	•	1.1	•	•	2.3	•
Advertising **18**	3.4	3.5	3.6	4.5	3.8	0.7	3.9	•	4.1	•	•	0.9	•
Other Expenses **19**	23.7	29.9	27.8	13.8	18.3	29.2	17.0	•	14.5	•	•	20.6	•
Officers' Compensation **20**	8.8	10.1	12.1	7.4	3.8	3.6	2.5	•	9.5	•	•	2.4	•
Operating Margin **21**	13.6	30.7	14.3	8.9	13.6	16.8	9.4	•	9.5	•	•	10.1	•
Operating Margin Before Officers' Comp. **22**	22.5	40.8	26.4	16.2	17.4	20.5	11.9	•	19.0	•	•	12.5	•

Selected Average Balance Sheet ($ in Thousands)

Net Receivables 23	33	0	3	32	160	198	2336	8914	•	376036
Inventories 24	•	•	•	•	•	•	•	•	•	•
Net Property, Plant and Equipment 25	56	0	14	163	419	4007	2937	14898	•	306797
Total Assets 26	299	0	73	728	1935	8136	15083	64094	•	2389686
Notes and Loans Payable 27	110	0	24	194	689	5323	3741	26510	•	931175
All Other Liabilities 28	81	0	14	159	463	1226	4898	12867	•	814237
Net Worth 29	108	0	35	375	783	1588	6445	24718	•	644274

Selected Financial Ratios (Times to 1)

Current Ratio 30	1.8	•	1.9	5.6	2.3	1.6	1.5	1.5	•	1.5
Quick Ratio 31	1.1	•	1.4	3.2	1.3	0.5	0.6	0.9	•	1.0
Net Sales to Working Capital 32	10.7	•	22.0	8.6	7.0	3.7	10.8	6.7	•	4.2
Coverage Ratio 33	14.3	29.9	51.1	20.1	16.1	2.7	13.3	4.7	•	3.3
Total Asset Turnover 34	2.0	•	6.0	3.8	1.9	0.4	2.1	1.0	•	0.4
Inventory Turnover 35	•	•	•	•	•	•	•	•	•	•
Receivables Turnover 36	•	•	•	•	•	•	•	•	•	•
Total Liabilities to Net Worth 37	1.8	•	1.1	0.9	1.5	4.1	1.3	1.6	•	2.7
Current Assets to Working Capital 38	2.3	•	2.1	1.2	1.8	2.8	3.0	3.1	•	3.2
Current Liabilities to Working Capital 39	1.3	•	1.1	0.2	0.8	1.8	2.0	2.1	•	2.2
Working Capital to Net Sales 40	0.1	•	0.0	0.1	0.1	0.3	0.1	0.1	•	0.2
Inventory to Working Capital 41	0.0	•	•	•	•	•	•	0.0	•	0.0
Total Receipts to Cash Flow 42	3.0	1.8	2.6	5.1	3.6	2.9	4.5	5.5	•	3.9
Cost of Goods to Cash Flow 43	0.3	0.0	0.2	0.9	0.2	0.2	1.6	1.6	•	0.0
Cash Flow to Total Debt 44	1.0	•	4.3	1.5	0.9	0.2	0.8	0.3	•	0.2

Selected Financial Factors (in Percentages)

Debt Ratio 45	63.9	•	52.6	48.4	59.5	80.5	57.3	61.4	•	73.0
Return on Total Assets 46	29.0	•	87.2	35.2	27.8	10.8	20.9	11.4	•	6.2
Return on Equity Before Income Taxes 47	74.8	•	180.3	64.9	64.4	35.0	45.3	23.3	•	16.3
Return on Equity After Income Taxes 48	72.0	•	179.2	64.0	63.4	29.8	43.6	21.9	•	11.1
Profit Margin (Before Income Tax) 49	13.6	30.9	14.3	8.9	13.6	16.8	9.3	9.3	•	10.2
Profit Margin (After Income Tax) 50	13.1	30.3	14.2	8.7	13.4	14.2	9.0	8.7	•	7.0

Table I

Corporations with and without Net Income

OTHER REAL ESTATE ACTIVITIES

MONEY AMOUNTS AND SIZE OF ASSETS IN THOUSANDS OF DOLLARS

Item Description for Accounting Period 7/06 Through 6/07	Total	Zero Assets	Under 500	500 to 1,000	1,000 to 5,000	5,000 to 10,000	10,000 to 25,000	25,000 to 50,000	50,000 to 100,000	100,000 to 250,000	250,000 to 500,000	500,000 to 2,500,000	2,500,000 and over
Number of Enterprises **1**	177800	38369	113921	9788	12402	1393	1229	405	162	96	23	10	3
Revenues ($ in Thousands)													
Net Sales **2**	67576893	5867495	22275318	6436320	9640539	3820851	4733771	2478604	3616424	3808238	1908848	1472734	1517750
Interest **3**	1150990	34839	97634	45796	110334	61881	112591	96897	119447	100951	58089	84419	228111
Rents **4**	1614609	87397	201226	188534	142336	77141	196990	161119	99894	190138	76086	103310	90437
Royalties **5**	135915	147	844	0	1177	21129	18995	27	8956	5	0	0	84635
Other Portfolio Income **6**	3602253	278889	439716	34144	403290	145320	259456	169721	293276	423904	58337	569645	526553
Other Receipts **7**	61073126	5466223	21535898	6167846	8983402	3515380	4145739	2050840	3094851	3093240	1716336	715360	588014
Total Receipts **8**	67576893	5867495	22275318	6436320	9640539	3820851	4733771	2478604	3616424	3808238	1908848	1472734	1517750
Average Total Receipts **9**	380	153	196	658	777	2743	3852	6120	22324	39669	82993	147273	505917
Operating Costs/Operating Income (%)													
Cost of Operations **10**	14.2	32.5	6.5	9.4	25.4	5.9	17.7	24.5	24.1	8.6	11.7	3.5	0.8
Salaries and Wages **11**	25.6	31.9	22.4	45.1	22.2	37.1	16.4	12.0	19.6	32.4	9.9	20.0	32.8
Taxes Paid **12**	3.7	3.6	3.3	4.8	4.2	3.9	3.9	3.2	3.0	2.7	2.6	5.4	4.0
Interest Paid **13**	4.2	2.2	1.3	2.0	4.8	4.4	7.0	10.4	6.3	6.1	8.0	14.7	18.3
Depreciation **14**	1.8	1.0	1.0	0.8	1.7	2.6	3.3	3.7	2.2	2.5	3.3	3.9	2.7
Amortization and Depletion **15**	0.3	0.4	0.1	0.1	0.1	0.3	0.5	0.5	0.6	0.9	1.1	0.9	2.7
Pensions and Other Deferred Comp. **16**	0.7	0.5	0.9	1.9	0.4	0.5	0.3	0.2	0.3	0.2	0.5	1.2	0.5
Employee Benefits **17**	2.0	2.3	1.6	6.7	1.0	2.0	1.9	1.1	1.0	1.8	0.7	0.7	1.8
Advertising **18**	1.1	0.8	1.3	0.1	0.4	1.0	1.2	0.8	2.6	2.0	0.5	0.8	1.9
Other Expenses **19**	32.7	19.4	40.5	19.6	29.9	30.5	35.2	29.3	31.0	30.0	56.6	24.3	34.1
Officers' Compensation **20**	8.2	4.4	14.6	5.8	6.1	8.8	6.1	3.5	3.8	1.7	2.9	3.0	2.6
Operating Margin **21**	5.5	0.8	6.5	3.8	3.9	3.1	6.4	10.8	5.3	11.0	2.3	21.5	•
Operating Margin Before Officers' Comp. **22**	13.7	5.2	21.1	9.6	9.9	11.9	12.5	14.3	9.1	12.7	5.2	24.5	0.5

Selected Average Balance Sheet ($ in Thousands)

Net Receivables 23	75	0	3	55	144	525	912	2491	4819	8774	29789	118325	1418379
Inventories 24	•	•	•	•	•	•	•	•	•	•	•	•	•
Net Property, Plant and Equipment 25	221	0	21	268	683	1913	4822	10988	20324	51199	75594	156507	428855
Total Assets 26	832	0	79	705	2114	7112	14867	34573	69435	150260	353409	807787	7237474
Notes and Loans Payable 27	418	0	58	472	1223	3266	8214	18331	30906	66148	134635	428601	2378812
All Other Liabilities 28	162	0	19	113	326	1541	2533	6918	16709	28618	112791	163278	1225258
Net Worth 29	252	0	2	120	564	2305	4121	9323	21820	55494	105983	215908	3633404

Selected Financial Ratios (Times to 1)

Current Ratio 30	2.0	•	1.8	2.1	2.8	1.4	1.7	1.8	1.4	2.2	2.3	1.4	4.8
Quick Ratio 31	1.1	•	1.3	1.4	1.4	0.7	0.8	0.9	0.8	0.8	0.9	0.8	2.7
Net Sales to Working Capital 32	2.6	•	11.8	4.7	4.2	1.8	1.9	1.3	3.8	4.6	3.1	1.8	0.2
Coverage Ratio 33	2.3	1.4	6.1	2.9	1.6	1.7	2.0	1.9	1.8	2.8	1.4	2.5	0.9
Total Asset Turnover 34	0.5	•	2.5	0.9	0.4	0.4	0.3	0.2	0.3	0.3	0.3	0.2	0.1
Inventory Turnover 35	•	•	•	•	•	•	•	•	•	•	•	•	•
Receivables Turnover 36	•	•	•	•	•	•	•	•	•	•	•	•	•
Total Liabilities to Net Worth 37	2.3	39.2	4.9	2.7	2.1	2.6	2.7	2.2	3.4	1.7	2.3	2.7	1.0
Current Assets to Working Capital 38	2.0	2.3	1.9	1.5	3.3	2.4	2.3	3.4	4.2	4.3	3.2	3.2	1.3
Current Liabilities to Working Capital 39	1.0	1.3	0.9	0.5	2.3	1.4	1.3	2.4	3.2	3.3	2.2	2.2	0.3
Working Capital to Net Sales 40	0.4	0.1	0.2	0.7	0.2	0.6	0.8	0.3	0.3	0.2	0.3	0.5	4.6
Inventory to Working Capital 41	0.0	•	0.0	0.0	0.0	0.0	0.0	0.0	0.0	0.0	0.0	0.2	0.0
Total Receipts to Cash Flow 42	3.4	7.9	2.6	5.1	3.9	3.8	3.2	3.3	4.1	3.8	1.9	4.3	5.2
Cost of Goods to Cash Flow 43	0.5	2.6	0.2	0.5	1.0	0.2	0.6	0.8	1.0	0.3	0.2	0.2	0.0
Cash Flow to Total Debt 44	0.2	•	1.0	0.2	0.1	0.2	0.1	0.1	0.1	0.2	0.2	0.1	0.0

Selected Financial Factors (in Percentages)

Debt Ratio 45	69.7	•	97.5	83.0	73.3	67.6	72.3	73.0	68.6	63.1	70.0	73.3	49.8
Return on Total Assets 46	4.4	•	19.3	5.4	2.8	2.8	3.4	3.7	3.7	4.5	2.5	6.6	1.1
Return on Equity Before Income Taxes 47	8.1	•	650.2	20.8	3.8	3.5	5.8	7.0	5.3	7.7	2.2	14.6	2.2
Return on Equity After Income Taxes 48	5.9	•	622.1	18.0	2.1	1.8	3.8	5.3	2.2	5.5	•	9.5	•
Profit Margin (Before Income Tax) 49	5.4	0.8	6.5	3.8	2.8	3.0	6.2	10.7	5.2	10.8	2.9	21.4	•
Profit Margin (After Income Tax) 50	3.9	•	6.2	3.3	1.5	1.5	4.1	8.1	2.2	7.7	•	13.9	•

Table II
Corporations with Net Income

OTHER REAL ESTATE ACTIVITIES

MONEY AMOUNTS AND SIZE OF ASSETS IN THOUSANDS OF DOLLARS

Item Description for Accounting Period 7/06 Through 6/07	Total	Zero Assets	Under 500	500 to 1,000	1,000 to 5,000	5,000 to 10,000	10,000 to 25,000	25,000 to 50,000	50,000 to 100,000	100,000 to 250,000	250,000 to 500,000	500,000 to 2,500,000	2,500,000 and over
Number of Enterprises **1**	81039	15538	54830	4502	4601	666	570	187	74	49	12	10	0
Revenues ($ in Thousands)													
Net Sales **2**	47650707	4259481	16399707	5533519	5709946	2502493	3151725	1809062	1968829	2970409	1384284	1961253	0
Interest **3**	767714	24586	74909	36864	84240	33406	85565	50457	92297	56151	37379	191858	0
Rents **4**	1022933	80069	88760	63744	81352	73518	114578	104650	46852	114814	64966	189630	0
Royalties **5**	48331	0	640	0	493	21129	18247	0	7818	5	0	0	0
Other Portfolio Income **6**	2795712	234219	414716	20796	288246	123032	212809	161142	194078	392904	19756	734016	0
Other Receipts **7**	43016017	3920607	15820682	5412115	5255615	2251408	2720526	1492813	1627784	2406535	1262183	845749	0
Total Receipts **8**	47650707	4259481	16399707	5533519	5709946	2502493	3151725	1809062	1968829	2970409	1384284	1961253	0
Average Total Receipts **9**	588	274	299	1229	1241	3757	5529	9674	26606	60621	115357	196125	•
Operating Costs/Operating Income (%)													
Cost of Operations **10**	12.6	39.2	6.7	7.9	17.5	6.3	20.4	25.6	4.5	9.4	11.2	1.4	•
Salaries and Wages **11**	22.0	18.9	18.7	49.2	17.3	28.7	12.1	8.6	22.9	26.7	4.9	17.3	•
Taxes Paid **12**	3.3	3.5	2.7	4.6	3.3	4.0	3.0	3.0	3.2	2.6	2.3	4.9	•
Interest Paid **13**	2.8	1.1	0.6	0.9	3.2	2.1	4.6	5.4	4.7	4.1	3.5	21.0	•
Depreciation **14**	1.2	1.1	0.6	0.4	1.2	2.2	2.0	2.1	1.6	1.6	1.1	3.9	•
Amortization and Depletion **15**	0.3	0.2	0.0	0.1	0.1	0.5	0.2	0.3	0.7	0.8	0.8	1.6	•
Pensions and Other Deferred Comp. **16**	0.7	0.4	0.8	1.6	0.6	0.7	0.2	0.1	0.4	0.2	0.3	0.9	•
Employee Benefits **17**	1.8	0.5	1.1	7.7	1.1	2.1	1.1	0.6	0.8	1.4	0.4	0.5	•
Advertising **18**	0.9	0.4	1.3	0.1	0.2	0.3	0.5	0.7	2.6	2.4	0.1	0.6	•
Other Expenses **19**	27.8	14.7	36.3	12.0	23.6	27.1	24.9	23.1	29.2	29.7	63.2	22.1	•
Officers' Compensation **20**	7.9	3.0	14.2	5.9	6.2	8.6	4.9	1.3	5.4	1.5	1.2	4.0	•
Operating Margin **21**	18.7	17.1	16.9	9.8	25.5	17.5	26.1	29.1	23.8	19.5	10.9	21.6	•
Operating Margin Before Officers' Comp. **22**	26.6	20.0	31.1	15.7	31.8	26.1	30.9	30.4	29.3	21.0	12.1	25.6	•

Selected Average Balance Sheet ($ in Thousands)

	•	•	•	•	•	•	•	•	•	•	•
Net Receivables 23	86	3	100	155	866	1069	2319	6134	10369	22224	277822
Inventories 24	0	0	0	0	0	0	0	0	0	0	0
Net Property, Plant and Equipment 25	185	16	181	467	1751	4067	9762	15294	38372	45573	231177
Total Assets 26	885	82	701	2206	6735	14698	34603	70200	148863	326837	1818510
Notes and Loans Payable 27	347	24	368	1059	2425	6047	16674	25687	48970	115728	641711
All Other Liabilities 28	181	14	114	435	1867	2825	5111	19104	33608	82167	350936
Net Worth 29	357	44	219	712	2444	5826	12818	25408	66285	128942	825863

Selected Financial Ratios (Times to 1)

	•	•	•	•	•	•	•	•	•	•	•
Current Ratio 30	1.9	3.3	3.2	4.0	1.1	1.5	1.9	1.7	1.3	1.4	1.8
Quick Ratio 31	1.2	2.5	2.4	2.1	0.7	0.8	1.1	1.0	0.9	0.6	1.2
Net Sales to Working Capital 32	3.8	9.2	5.2	1.5	14.1	2.8	1.5	2.9	5.8	3.6	1.0
Coverage Ratio 33	7.6	28.0	11.6	8.9	9.3	6.7	6.3	6.0	5.7	4.4	2.0
Total Asset Turnover 34	0.7	3.6	1.8	0.6	0.6	0.4	0.3	0.4	0.4	0.4	0.1
Inventory Turnover 35	16.7	•	•	•	•	•	•	•	•	•	•
Receivables Turnover 36	•	•	•	•	•	•	•	•	•	•	•
Total Liabilities to Net Worth 37	1.5	0.9	2.2	2.1	1.8	1.5	1.7	1.8	1.2	1.5	1.2
Current Assets to Working Capital 38	2.1	1.4	1.4	1.3	8.6	2.9	2.1	2.5	4.4	3.7	2.3
Current Liabilities to Working Capital 39	1.1	0.4	0.4	0.3	7.6	1.9	1.1	1.5	3.4	2.7	1.3
Working Capital to Net Sales 40	0.3	0.1	0.2	0.7	0.1	0.4	0.7	0.3	0.2	0.3	1.0
Inventory to Working Capital 41	0.0	•	•	•	0.1	0.0	0.0	0.0	0.0	0.0	0.1
Total Receipts to Cash Flow 42	4.2	2.1	5.1	2.6	2.8	2.4	2.5	2.4	3.0	1.4	5.5
Cost of Goods to Cash Flow 43	1.7	0.1	0.4	0.5	0.2	0.5	0.6	0.1	0.3	0.2	0.1
Cash Flow to Total Debt 44	0.4	3.7	0.5	0.3	0.3	0.3	0.2	0.2	0.2	0.4	0.0

Selected Financial Factors (in Percentages)

	•	•	•	•	•	•	•	•	•	•	•
Debt Ratio 45	•	59.6	46.2	68.7	67.7	60.4	63.0	63.8	55.5	60.5	54.6
Return on Total Assets 46	•	14.3	63.8	18.8	16.2	10.8	9.6	10.8	9.6	5.4	4.6
Return on Equity Before Income Taxes 47	•	30.7	114.3	54.9	44.4	24.7	21.8	24.9	17.7	10.7	5.1
Return on Equity After Income Taxes 48	•	27.5	111.7	51.5	40.8	21.7	19.2	19.1	14.2	6.8	3.5
Profit Margin (Before Income Tax) 49	17.1	18.7	16.9	9.8	25.5	26.0	28.9	23.8	19.4	11.9	21.5
Profit Margin (After Income Tax) 50	15.0	16.7	16.5	9.2	23.4	22.8	25.5	18.2	15.6	7.6	14.9

Table I

Corporations with and without Net Income

AUTOMOTIVE EQUIPMENT RENTAL AND LEASING

MONEY AMOUNTS AND SIZE OF ASSETS IN THOUSANDS OF DOLLARS

Item Description for Accounting Period 7/06 Through 6/07	Total	Zero Assets	Under 500	500 to 1,000	1,000 to 5,000	5,000 to 10,000	10,000 to 25,000	25,000 to 50,000	50,000 to 100,000	100,000 to 250,000	250,000 to 500,000	500,000 to 2,500,000	2,500,000 and over
Number of Enterprises 1	7836	541	4820	984	1020	173	176	67	25	17	0	4	8
Revenues ($ in Thousands)													
Net Sales 2	61073673	107440	2047630	253589	1718895	576640	1879205	1740795	931941	1913347	0	2151850	47752341
Interest 3	1362720	25	1569	22	2151	1131	4268	4482	2983	28359	0	10055	1307676
Rents 4	183053	863	0	0	718	0	3390	29	1623	101	0	307	176023
Royalties 5	750103	0	0	0	0	0	0	0	0	0	0	0	750103
Other Portfolio Income 6	3603476	6138	32403	165	143312	47370	163918	119870	92247	153133	0	35903	2809015
Other Receipts 7	55174321	100414	2013658	253402	1572714	528139	1707629	1616414	835088	1731754	0	2105585	42709524
Total Receipts 8	61073673	107440	2047630	253589	1718895	576640	1879205	1740795	931941	1913347	0	2151850	47752341
Average Total Receipts 9	7794	199	425	258	1685	3333	10677	25982	37278	112550	•	537962	5969043
Operating Costs/Operating Income (%)													
Cost of Operations 10	18.1	0.0	10.4	20.3	13.4	15.1	24.9	37.4	26.2	35.8	•	1.4	17.6
Salaries and Wages 11	12.8	18.7	0.9	10.9	9.8	4.2	11.6	5.8	7.6	5.1	•	4.0	14.6
Taxes Paid 12	2.8	2.1	1.8	2.9	2.5	3.1	2.6	2.8	2.3	2.0	•	0.4	3.0
Interest Paid 13	6.8	7.2	1.5	6.6	5.1	6.4	6.3	7.0	8.6	5.5	•	8.5	7.1
Depreciation 14	21.4	18.0	5.8	27.2	25.9	35.4	28.1	30.8	34.3	25.3	•	70.0	18.6
Amortization and Depletion 15	0.7	•	0.0	•	0.0	0.0	0.0	0.1	0.2	0.1	•	0.2	0.9
Pensions and Other Deferred Comp. 16	0.4	•	0.0	•	0.2	0.2	0.1	0.2	0.3	0.1	•	0.1	0.5
Employee Benefits 17	1.4	2.3	0.2	0.0	0.4	0.3	0.9	0.5	0.7	0.9	•	0.4	1.7
Advertising 18	1.4	5.1	0.2	5.4	1.7	0.2	0.8	0.6	0.6	0.4	•	0.1	1.6
Other Expenses 19	29.7	28.1	78.5	25.8	29.9	19.8	18.2	11.7	14.5	19.3	•	3.9	30.7
Officers' Compensation 20	0.7	2.5	1.3	3.0	3.0	2.1	2.5	1.3	1.5	1.1	•	0.4	0.4
Operating Margin 21	3.7	15.9	•	•	8.1	13.1	4.0	1.9	3.3	4.4	•	10.6	3.3
Operating Margin Before Officers' Comp. 22	4.3	18.4	0.7	0.9	11.1	15.3	6.5	3.1	4.7	5.5	•	11.1	3.7

Selected Average Balance Sheet ($ in Thousands)

Net Receivables 23	1159	•	20	53	387	1203	1020	3589	3869	31874	49408	884402
Inventories 24	•	0	•	•	•	•	•	•	•	•	•	•
Net Property, Plant and Equipment 25	6007	0	60	414	1446	4549	10347	22152	50005	101454	760852	4348220
Total Assets 26	11110	148	799	2248	6723	15897	36354	66903	168738		1261101	8410073
Notes and Loans Payable 27	6172	168	381	1305	3905	10877	29378	50881	113962		1038534	4240694
All Other Liabilities 28	2774	3	37	147	616	1744	2483	6408	24699		120688	2486896
Net Worth 29	2164	-23	381	796	2203	3277	4493	9614	30077		101879	1682484

Selected Financial Ratios (Times to 1)

Current Ratio 30	0.6	•	1.6	2.6	1.7	3.4	0.7	0.7	0.9	0.9	0.1	0.6
Quick Ratio 31	0.5	•	1.0	2.2	1.4	2.9	0.5	0.5	0.6	0.7	0.1	0.5
Net Sales to Working Capital 32	•	•	24.7	1.2	6.9	2.6	•	•	1.8	•	•	•
Coverage Ratio 33	1.6	3.2	0.6	0.7	2.6	3.1	1.6	1.3	1.4	1.8	2.2	1.5
Total Asset Turnover 34	0.7	•	2.9	0.3	0.7	0.5	0.7	0.7	0.6	0.7	0.4	0.7
Inventory Turnover 35	•	•	•	•	•	•	•	•	•	•	•	•
Receivables Turnover 36	•	•	•	•	•	•	•	•	•	•	•	•
Total Liabilities to Net Worth 37	4.1	•	1.1	1.8	2.1	7.1	3.9	10.5	6.0	4.6	11.4	4.0
Current Assets to Working Capital 38	•	•	2.7	1.6	2.4	1.4	•	•	•	•	•	•
Current Liabilities to Working Capital 39	•	•	1.7	0.6	1.4	0.4	•	•	•	•	•	•
Working Capital to Net Sales 40	•	•	0.0	0.8	0.1	0.4	0.1	•	•	•	•	•
Inventory to Working Capital 41	•	•	0.3	•	0.2	0.0	0.2	•	•	•	•	•
Total Receipts to Cash Flow 42	4.5	2.6	7.5	5.4	4.5	10.5	6.5	10.5	10.9	5.8	7.5	4.5
Cost of Goods to Cash Flow 43	0.8	0.0	1.5	0.7	0.2	1.6	3.9	2.9	2.1	•	0.1	0.8
Cash Flow to Total Debt 44	0.2	•	1.5	0.1	0.2	0.2	0.1	0.1	0.1	•	0.1	0.2

Selected Financial Factors (in Percentages)

Debt Ratio 45	80.5	115.3	52.4	64.6	67.2	79.4	87.6	85.6	82.2	91.9	•	80.0
Return on Total Assets 46	7.4	2.5	1.5	9.7	6.3	6.9	6.6	6.6	8.2	•	•	7.5
Return on Equity Before Income Taxes 47	13.6	12.5	•	17.1	19.9	13.0	10.7	12.6	16.4	56.1	•	12.2
Return on Equity After Income Taxes 48	9.2	13.1	•	15.9	18.9	11.7	9.7	11.7	12.6	54.4	•	7.1
Profit Margin (Before Income Tax) 49	3.8	15.9	•	8.1	13.1	4.0	1.9	3.2	4.4	10.6	•	3.4
Profit Margin (After Income Tax) 50	2.6	15.5	•	7.5	12.5	3.6	1.7	3.0	3.4	10.3	•	2.0

Table II

Corporations with Net Income

AUTOMOTIVE EQUIPMENT RENTAL AND LEASING

MONEY AMOUNTS AND SIZE OF ASSETS IN THOUSANDS OF DOLLARS

Item Description for Accounting Period 7/06 Through 6/07	Total	Zero Assets	Under 500	500 to 1,000	1,000 to 5,000	5,000 to 10,000	10,000 to 25,000	25,000 to 50,000	50,000 to 100,000	100,000 to 250,000	250,000 to 500,000	500,000 to 2,500,000	2,500,000 and over
Number of Enterprises 1	3794	271	2151	463	607	106	115	44	16	•	0	•	•
Revenues ($ in Thousands)													
Net Sales 2	47072116	91505	1729747	99484	965075	474233	1373107	1066569	660459	•	0	•	•
Interest 3	1300223	25	20	22	2151	1075	2646	4117	2742	•	0	•	•
Rents 4	176880	863	0	0	718	0	1169	29	1623	•	0	•	•
Royalties 5	688626	0	0	0	0	0	0	0	0	•	0	•	•
Other Portfolio Income 6	3193042	6138	32252	165	125159	28737	119903	81496	81867	•	0	•	•
Other Receipts 7	41713345	84479	1697475	99297	837047	444421	1249389	980927	574227	•	0	•	•
Total Receipts 8	47072116	91505	1729747	99484	965075	474233	1373107	1066569	660459	•	0	•	•
Average Total Receipts 9	12407	338	804	215	1590	4474	11940	24240	41279	•	•	•	•
Operating Costs/Operating Income (%)													
Cost of Operations 10	17.4	•	0.0	0.1	20.6	17.0	23.0	34.7	26.2	•	•	•	•
Salaries and Wages 11	12.8	21.9	1.1	0.1	6.4	4.0	11.9	6.2	6.5	•	•	•	•
Taxes Paid 12	2.9	2.4	1.1	1.0	2.6	3.3	2.7	1.9	2.0	•	•	•	•
Interest Paid 13	5.9	8.5	0.7	6.6	4.1	4.0	5.4	6.2	7.7	•	•	•	•
Depreciation 14	16.8	12.3	4.4	42.8	25.6	34.7	26.0	25.6	37.1	•	•	•	•
Amortization and Depletion 15	0.8	•	•	•	0.0	0.0	0.0	0.1	0.0	•	•	•	•
Pensions and Other Deferred Comp. 16	0.5	•	0.0	•	0.3	0.2	0.1	0.3	0.4	•	•	•	•
Employee Benefits 17	1.5	2.7	0.1	0.0	0.6	0.3	0.9	0.6	0.4	•	•	•	•
Advertising 18	1.4	4.6	0.2	0.0	1.2	0.2	0.8	0.8	0.5	•	•	•	•
Other Expenses 19	32.9	28.4	87.9	20.7	16.6	16.5	19.4	15.2	11.4	•	•	•	•
Officers' Compensation 20	0.7	0.1	1.6	0.8	4.0	1.5	2.4	1.5	1.1	•	•	•	•
Operating Margin 21	6.6	19.1	2.8	27.8	17.9	18.2	7.4	6.9	6.6	•	•	•	•
Operating Margin Before Officers' Comp. 22	7.2	19.2	4.4	28.6	21.8	19.7	9.8	8.4	7.8	•	•	•	•

Selected Average Balance Sheet ($ in Thousands)

Net Receivables 23	1711	0	0	51	115	349	1065	3496	4340
Inventories 24	•	•	•	•	•	•	•	•	•
Net Property, Plant and Equipment 25	7736	0	87	448	1492	4962	9499	20553	51417
Total Assets 26	15126	0	161	862	2184	6533	15649	37086	70397
Notes and Loans Payable 27	8092	0	135	248	996	2866	10401	27482	52448
All Other Liabilities 28	3578	0	2	10	122	381	1309	2852	7638
Net Worth 29	3455	0	24	604	1065	3286	3938	6752	10310

Selected Financial Ratios (Times to 1)

Current Ratio 30	0.6	•	73.8	1.3	3.0	0.8	0.6	•	0.8
Quick Ratio 31	0.5	0.6	56.1	0.7	2.1	0.5	0.4	•	0.5
Net Sales to Working Capital 32	•	•	0.6	18.1	5.2	•	•	•	•
Coverage Ratio 33	2.1	3.3	4.9	5.2	5.3	5.5	2.4	2.1	1.9
Total Asset Turnover 34	0.8	•	5.0	0.2	0.7	0.7	0.8	0.7	0.6
Inventory Turnover 35	•	•	•	•	•	•	•	•	•
Receivables Turnover 36	•	•	•	•	•	•	•	•	•
Total Liabilities to Net Worth 37	3.4	•	5.8	0.4	1.1	1.0	3.0	4.5	5.8
Current Assets to Working Capital 38	•	•	1.0	4.4	1.5	0.5	•	•	•
Current Liabilities to Working Capital 39	•	•	0.0	3.4	0.5	0.2	•	•	•
Working Capital to Net Sales 40	•	•	1.8	0.1	0.2	0.1	•	•	•
Inventory to Working Capital 41	•	•	•	0.8	•	•	•	•	•
Total Receipts to Cash Flow 42	3.6	2.5	3.0	4.2	4.0	5.1	6.0	•	8.1
Cost of Goods to Cash Flow 43	0.6	0.0	0.0	0.9	0.7	1.2	2.1	•	2.1
Cash Flow to Total Debt 44	0.3	4.3	0.3	0.3	0.3	0.2	0.1	•	0.1

Selected Financial Factors (in Percentages)

Debt Ratio 45	77.2	•	85.4	29.9	51.2	49.7	74.8	81.8	85.4
Return on Total Assets 46	10.3	•	17.6	8.6	16.0	15.2	9.8	8.6	8.4
Return on Equity Before Income Taxes 47	23.8	•	95.8	9.9	26.6	24.7	22.4	24.9	26.4
Return on Equity After Income Taxes 48	18.2	•	94.6	9.6	25.2	23.6	20.7	23.8	25.1
Profit Margin (Before Income Tax) 49	6.6	19.1	2.8	27.8	17.9	18.2	7.4	6.9	6.6
Profit Margin (After Income Tax) 50	5.1	18.7	2.8	27.1	16.9	17.4	6.8	6.6	6.3

Table I

Corporations with and without Net Income

OTHER CONSUMER GOODS AND GENERAL RENTAL CENTERS

MONEY AMOUNTS AND SIZE OF ASSETS IN THOUSANDS OF DOLLARS

Item Description for Accounting Period 7/06 Through 6/07	Total	Zero Assets	Under 500	500 to 1,000	1,000 to 5,000	5,000 to 10,000	10,000 to 25,000	25,000 to 50,000	50,000 to 100,000	100,000 to 250,000	250,000 to 500,000	500,000 to 2,500,000	2,500,000 and over
Number of Enterprises **1**	13466	2145	9499	1117	483	147	45	17	0	3	4	5	0
Revenues ($ in Thousands)													
Net Sales **2**	21820288	441083	3241002	2024190	853064	1165181	863717	588077	0	153730	1055533	11434711	0
Interest **3**	38025	42	852	2932	616	1852	587	1220	0	2269	338	27318	0
Rents **4**	5928	0	1053	2584	0	0	0	0	0	0	2132	158	0
Royalties **5**	106868	0	0	0	0	0	0	0	0	0	0	106868	0
Other Portfolio Income **6**	147273	11054	8349	15918	10600	4174	19338	11733	0	2050	2958	61099	0
Other Receipts **7**	21522194	429987	3230748	2002756	841848	1159155	843792	575124	0	149411	1050105	11239268	0
Total Receipts **8**	21820288	441083	3241002	2024190	853064	1165181	863717	588077	0	153730	1055533	11434711	0
Average Total Receipts **9**	1620	206	341	1812	1766	7926	19194	34593	•	51243	263883	2288942	•
Operating Costs/Operating Income (%)													
Cost of Operations **10**	26.3	19.2	25.2	31.9	12.7	30.9	47.8	40.4	•	•	17.1	25.4	•
Salaries and Wages **11**	19.6	13.9	19.1	22.7	22.5	16.4	14.0	12.2	•	18.2	21.8	20.1	•
Taxes Paid **12**	3.8	5.1	4.0	4.9	7.2	3.8	2.1	3.4	•	2.1	3.9	3.4	•
Interest Paid **13**	2.8	1.9	1.4	1.4	6.4	2.0	1.8	4.9	•	9.6	7.0	2.7	•
Depreciation **14**	10.8	5.5	5.2	7.0	20.2	10.8	9.0	12.2	•	39.4	14.4	12.0	•
Amortization and Depletion **15**	1.4	0.7	0.1	•	1.9	0.2	0.2	1.1	•	0.2	10.3	1.4	•
Pensions and Other Deferred Comp. **16**	0.2	0.0	0.2	0.2	0.1	0.4	0.0	0.1	•	0.2	0.1	0.1	•
Employee Benefits **17**	1.1	0.4	1.0	0.4	0.6	2.1	0.7	1.3	•	0.8	1.4	1.3	•
Advertising **18**	2.9	4.9	1.8	2.4	2.4	2.5	1.0	1.7	•	0.2	1.9	3.6	•
Other Expenses **19**	27.3	29.3	33.3	25.8	26.8	24.0	19.0	21.2	•	24.8	17.6	28.0	•
Officers' Compensation **20**	2.3	7.6	6.0	4.8	2.1	4.4	1.9	1.8	•	2.2	1.2	0.6	•
Operating Margin **21**	1.5	11.4	2.6	•	•	2.6	2.4	•	•	2.2	3.1	1.4	•
Operating Margin Before Officers' Comp. **22**	3.8	19.0	8.7	3.4	•	7.0	4.3	1.4	•	4.4	4.4	2.0	•

Selected Average Balance Sheet ($ in Thousands)

Net Receivables 23	56	5	33	82	857	3189	1428	4945	16090	51742	•
Inventories 24	0	0	0	•	•	•	•	•	•	•	•
Net Property, Plant and Equipment 25	525	42	462	1041	2996	6847	24532	52335	175402	725160	•
Total Assets 26	1329	112	724	1501	5813	14405	38969	151558	345377	2258772	•
Notes and Loans Payable 27	576	59	529	1798	2232	7146	26176	87838	216752	703247	•
All Other Liabilities 28	469	21	79	196	688	3518	4698	7821	68089	1060100	•
Net Worth 29	283	32	116	-493	2893	3740	8095	55899	60536	495425	•

Selected Financial Ratios (Times to 1)

Current Ratio 30	0.7	1.8	2.1	1.5	3.2	1.2	0.8	•	2.5	0.5	•
Quick Ratio 31	0.4	1.3	1.2	1.1	1.5	0.8	0.4	•	2.0	0.3	•
Net Sales to Working Capital 32	•	12.8	13.9	18.1	4.3	19.1	•	•	8.3	•	•
Coverage Ratio 33	1.5	2.9	•	0.6	2.3	2.3	0.9	•	1.2	1.5	•
Total Asset Turnover 34	1.2	3.0	2.5	1.2	1.4	1.3	0.9	•	0.3	1.0	•
Inventory Turnover 35	•	•	•	•	•	•	•	•	•	•	•
Receivables Turnover 36	•	•	•	•	•	•	•	•	•	•	•
Total Liabilities to Net Worth 37	3.7	2.5	5.2	•	1.0	2.9	3.8	•	1.7	4.7	3.6
Current Assets to Working Capital 38	•	2.2	1.9	3.2	1.5	5.9	•	•	•	•	•
Current Liabilities to Working Capital 39	•	1.2	0.9	2.2	0.5	4.9	•	•	0.7	•	•
Working Capital to Net Sales 40	•	0.1	0.1	0.1	0.2	0.1	•	•	0.1	•	•
Inventory to Working Capital 41	•	0.5	0.7	0.3	0.4	1.3	•	•	•	•	•
Total Receipts to Cash Flow 42	5.8	4.7	8.4	7.4	6.0	5.8	6.9	•	4.6	8.1	5.6
Cost of Goods to Cash Flow 43	1.5	1.2	2.7	0.9	1.8	2.8	2.8	•	•	1.4	1.4
Cash Flow to Total Debt 44	0.3	0.9	0.4	0.1	0.5	0.3	0.2	•	0.1	0.1	0.2

Selected Financial Factors (in Percentages)

Debt Ratio 45	78.7	71.4	84.0	132.8	50.2	74.0	79.2	•	63.1	82.5	78.1
Return on Total Assets 46	5.2	12.3	•	4.1	6.2	5.5	4.1	•	4.0	7.8	4.2
Return on Equity Before Income Taxes 47	8.7	28.0	•	10.2	7.1	11.8	•	•	2.0	13.6	6.6
Return on Equity After Income Taxes 48	6.1	26.8	•	12.6	6.6	10.1	•	•	0.6	10.1	3.7
Profit Margin (Before Income Tax) 49	1.5	2.6	11.4	•	2.6	2.3	•	•	2.2	3.1	1.4
Profit Margin (After Income Tax) 50	1.1	2.5	11.3	2.4	2.0	•	•	•	0.6	2.3	0.8

Table II
Corporations with Net Income

OTHER CONSUMER GOODS AND GENERAL RENTAL CENTERS

MONEY AMOUNTS AND SIZE OF ASSETS IN THOUSANDS OF DOLLARS

Item Description for Accounting Period 7/06 Through 6/07	Total	Zero Assets	Under 500	500 to 1,000	1,000 to 5,000	5,000 to 10,000	10,000 to 25,000	25,000 to 50,000	50,000 to 100,000	100,000 to 250,000	250,000 to 500,000	500,000 to 2,500,000	2,500,000 and over
Number of Enterprises **1**	6407	736	5080	388	92	60	34	6	4	0	•	•	0
Revenues ($ in Thousands)													
Net Sales **2**	13361241	253629	2541867	664085	278654	424923	696723	124129	280619	0	•	•	0
Interest **3**	15780	42	762	2828	469	1204	335	221	2294	0	•	•	0
Rents **4**	4874	0	0	2584	0	0	0	0	0	0	•	•	0
Royalties **5**	39312	0	0	0	0	0	0	0	0	0	•	•	0
Other Portfolio Income **6**	113633	11054	2491	11387	1230	4068	19338	8970	3053	0	•	•	0
Other Receipts **7**	13187642	242533	2538614	647286	276955	419651	677050	114938	275272	0	•	•	0
Total Receipts **8**	13361241	253629	2541867	664085	278654	424923	696723	124129	280619	0	•	•	0
Average Total Receipts **9**	2085	345	500	1712	3029	7082	20492	20688	70155	•	•	•	•
Operating Costs/Operating Income (%)													
Cost of Operations **10**	25.0	4.9	26.1	38.4	21.4	28.1	45.2	29.5	30.1	•	•	•	•
Salaries and Wages **11**	18.9	18.0	17.0	15.4	24.8	18.2	15.2	5.0	16.0	•	•	•	•
Taxes Paid **12**	3.4	2.9	4.0	3.6	4.8	2.7	2.5	1.7	3.3	•	•	•	•
Interest Paid **13**	2.7	2.6	1.1	1.6	0.6	0.6	2.1	3.2	5.8	•	•	•	•
Depreciation **14**	13.0	7.1	4.2	7.1	6.9	4.5	11.0	16.7	13.3	•	•	•	•
Amortization and Depletion **15**	1.8	1.2	0.1	•	0.0	0.0	0.1	0.6	1.7	•	•	•	•
Pensions and Other Deferred Comp. **16**	0.2	0.0	0.2	0.0	0.1	1.2	0.0	•	0.3	•	•	•	•
Employee Benefits **17**	1.5	0.7	1.1	0.3	0.5	1.9	0.9	0.1	2.1	•	•	•	•
Advertising **18**	3.0	5.7	1.9	3.0	1.1	0.1	1.1	2.2	0.3	•	•	•	•
Other Expenses **19**	22.4	32.0	29.8	18.4	18.1	24.4	13.5	27.1	20.1	•	•	•	•
Officers' Compensation **20**	2.4	0.5	6.2	8.0	3.6	6.4	2.2	3.3	1.3	•	•	•	•
Operating Margin **21**	5.7	24.3	8.3	4.3	18.1	11.8	6.4	10.5	5.6	•	•	•	•
Operating Margin Before Officers' Comp. **22**	8.1	24.8	14.5	12.3	21.7	18.3	8.5	13.8	6.9	•	•	•	•

Selected Average Balance Sheet ($ in Thousands)

Net Receivables 23	79	0	•	5	50	250	1110	3532	823	7360
Inventories 24	•	•	•	•	•	•	•	•	•	•
Net Property, Plant and Equipment 25	697	0	•	53	433	698	1872	6583	16544	30258
Total Assets 26	1932	0	•	161	860	1686	6422	14234	28066	121442
Notes and Loans Payable 27	665	0	•	57	418	384	866	6120	10290	56772
All Other Liabilities 28	744	0	•	30	137	171	622	3272	2087	9516
Net Worth 29	523	0	•	74	304	1132	4934	4842	15688	55154

Selected Financial Ratios (Times to 1)

Current Ratio 30	0.7	•	•	2.2	2.8	3.2	4.0	1.2	0.5	1.0
Quick Ratio 31	0.5	•	•	1.5	1.7	2.6	1.7	0.9	0.4	0.7
Net Sales to Working Capital 32	•	•	•	10.1	6.9	4.6	2.1	22.1	•	1230.8
Coverage Ratio 33	3.1	10.5	•	8.5	3.8	29.4	20.0	4.0	4.3	2.0
Total Asset Turnover 34	1.1	•	•	3.1	2.0	1.8	1.1	1.4	0.7	0.6
Inventory Turnover 35	•	•	•	•	•	•	•	•	•	•
Receivables Turnover 36	•	•	•	•	•	•	•	•	•	•
Total Liabilities to Net Worth 37	2.7	•	•	1.2	1.8	0.5	1.9	0.8	•	1.2
Current Assets to Working Capital 38	•	•	•	1.9	1.6	1.5	6.5	•	•	242.0
Current Liabilities to Working Capital 39	•	•	•	0.9	0.6	0.5	5.5	•	•	241.0
Working Capital to Net Sales 40	•	•	•	0.1	0.1	0.2	0.5	0.0	•	0.0
Inventory to Working Capital 41	•	•	•	0.4	0.6	0.1	0.3	0.3	0.7	0.2
Total Receipts to Cash Flow 42	5.6	2.8	•	4.0	7.3	3.2	3.0	6.4	2.7	5.4
Cost of Goods to Cash Flow 43	1.4	0.1	•	1.0	2.8	0.7	0.9	2.9	0.8	1.6
Cash Flow to Total Debt 44	0.3	•	•	1.4	0.4	1.7	0.3	0.6	•	0.2

Selected Financial Factors (in Percentages)

Debt Ratio 45	72.9	•	•	54.1	64.6	32.9	23.2	66.0	44.1	54.6
Return on Total Assets 46	9.1	•	•	29.2	11.8	33.6	13.7	12.1	10.1	6.6
Return on Equity Before Income Taxes 47	22.7	•	•	56.2	24.4	48.4	17.0	26.5	13.9	7.1
Return on Equity After Income Taxes 48	19.8	•	•	55.3	23.9	43.0	16.3	24.8	13.0	5.7
Profit Margin (Before Income Tax) 49	5.7	24.3	•	8.3	4.3	18.1	11.8	6.3	10.5	5.6
Profit Margin (After Income Tax) 50	5.0	24.1	•	8.2	4.3	16.1	11.4	5.8	9.9	4.5

Table I

Corporations with and without Net Income

COMMERCIAL AND INDUSTRIAL MACHINERY AND EQUIPMENT RENTAL

MONEY AMOUNTS AND SIZE OF ASSETS IN THOUSANDS OF DOLLARS

Item Description for Accounting Period 7/06 Through 6/07		Total	Zero Assets	Under 500	500 to 1,000	1,000 to 5,000	5,000 to 10,000	10,000 to 25,000	25,000 to 50,000	50,000 to 100,000	100,000 to 250,000	250,000 to 500,000	500,000 to 2,500,000	2,500,000 and over
Number of Enterprises	1	29141	4652	17064	2061	4241	510	330	127	61	37	18	28	10
Revenues ($ in Thousands)														
Net Sales	2	54323981	826095	4736587	2161604	5873381	4154806	2975073	3567520	2107764	2193556	4349363	7578289	13799944
Interest	3	1255400	36318	32433	6016	15937	4002	21194	32155	39480	87962	109172	388621	482111
Rents	4	507725	4	0	0	3492	0	11217	4605	27916	4790	2974	173686	279042
Royalties	5	11971	0	0	1	0	0	0	930	0	5474	0	5236	330
Other Portfolio Income	6	3564625	120572	166250	46748	92657	185532	127769	161000	66651	196402	701030	843950	856064
Other Receipts	7	48984260	669201	4537904	2108839	5761295	3965272	2814893	3368830	1973717	1898928	3536187	6166796	12182397
Total Receipts	8	54323981	826095	4736587	2161604	5873381	4154806	2975073	3567520	2107764	2193556	4349363	7578289	13799944
Average Total Receipts	9	1864	178	278	1049	1385	8147	9015	28091	34554	59285	241631	270653	1379994
Operating Costs/Operating Income (%)														
Cost of Operations	10	30.2	24.6	36.0	40.6	29.3	37.9	36.4	47.9	25.5	32.7	34.6	22.1	22.3
Salaries and Wages	11	10.0	11.8	10.2	10.5	11.8	9.9	8.3	6.9	9.6	8.7	7.5	10.2	11.3
Taxes Paid	12	2.1	4.2	2.7	2.4	2.8	3.2	2.1	2.0	1.6	1.2	1.4	2.0	1.7
Interest Paid	13	7.3	16.6	2.9	1.7	2.5	2.3	4.8	4.0	6.9	10.7	6.1	13.1	10.6
Depreciation	14	19.3	21.9	8.2	10.4	14.7	12.4	18.1	17.4	18.9	14.6	20.6	28.5	24.5
Amortization and Depletion	15	0.6	2.3	0.0	0.0	0.1	0.0	0.1	0.3	0.4	1.0	0.6	1.1	1.1
Pensions and Other Deferred Comp.	16	0.3	0.1	0.2	0.5	0.9	0.4	0.2	0.1	0.3	0.4	0.3	0.3	0.2
Employee Benefits	17	1.4	1.2	1.5	0.9	0.9	0.7	1.3	0.8	0.9	1.2	1.3	1.5	2.0
Advertising	18	0.5	0.2	1.2	1.0	0.6	0.3	0.5	0.4	0.3	0.3	0.3	0.4	0.3
Other Expenses	19	19.8	31.2	24.4	21.6	29.1	21.3	21.3	12.4	26.7	20.6	13.2	17.2	16.9
Officers' Compensation	20	2.4	1.7	8.2	3.7	4.6	4.3	2.6	1.4	1.3	1.3	1.2	0.8	0.4
Operating Margin	21	6.2	•	4.5	6.6	2.8	7.3	4.3	6.4	7.7	7.3	13.0	2.9	8.6
Operating Margin Before Officers' Comp.	22	8.5	•	12.7	10.3	7.4	11.6	6.8	7.7	9.0	8.7	14.2	3.8	9.0

Selected Average Balance Sheet ($ in Thousands)

Net Receivables 23	707	0	15	57	264	714	1961	6369	13699	27048	74098	147923	998647
Inventories 24	•	•	•	•	•	•	•	•	•	•	•	•	•
Net Property, Plant and Equipment 25	1562	0	62	363	1057	4532	8272	16206	27590	38141	99114	357815	1722805
Total Assets 26	4121	0	137	765	1891	7443	15680	34557	67160	150914	352737	1127946	4718355
Notes and Loans Payable 27	2082	0	230	465	967	4241	7670	18197	34298	89496	167306	524005	2159204
All Other Liabilities 28	907	0	16	102	289	1055	2486	7968	10656	22408	66526	233117	1313970
Net Worth 29	1132	0	-109	198	636	2147	5523	8392	22205	39011	118905	370824	1245181

Selected Financial Ratios (Times to 1)

Current Ratio 30	1.6	•	1.8	1.4	1.7	1.1	1.5	1.2	1.4	1.7	1.9	1.7	1.5
Quick Ratio 31	1.2	•	1.6	1.0	1.2	0.7	1.1	0.7	1.1	1.0	1.2	1.4	1.2
Net Sales to Working Capital 32	4.1	•	10.3	13.3	5.7	51.2	5.6	12.1	4.9	2.4	3.5	2.5	2.7
Coverage Ratio 33	1.8	0.0	2.5	4.7	2.1	4.2	1.9	2.6	2.1	1.7	3.1	1.0	1.8
Total Asset Turnover 34	0.5	•	2.0	1.4	0.7	1.1	0.6	0.8	0.5	0.4	0.7	0.2	0.3
Inventory Turnover 35	•	•	•	•	•	•	•	•	•	•	•	•	•
Receivables Turnover 36	•	•	•	•	•	•	•	•	•	•	•	•	•
Total Liabilities to Net Worth 37	2.6	•	•	2.9	2.0	2.5	1.8	3.1	2.0	2.9	2.0	2.0	2.8
Current Assets to Working Capital 38	2.7	•	2.2	3.3	2.5	14.2	3.1	5.9	3.3	2.3	2.1	2.4	2.9
Current Liabilities to Working Capital 39	1.7	•	1.2	2.3	1.5	13.2	2.1	4.9	2.3	1.3	1.1	1.4	1.9
Working Capital to Net Sales 40	0.2	•	0.1	0.1	0.2	0.0	0.2	0.1	0.2	0.4	0.3	0.4	0.4
Inventory to Working Capital 41	0.2	•	0.1	0.5	0.2	2.5	0.4	1.3	0.5	0.3	0.4	0.2	0.1
Total Receipts to Cash Flow 42	6.3	•	19.2	4.8	5.5	4.7	6.3	7.4	4.3	6.4	8.0	9.5	6.7
Cost of Goods to Cash Flow 43	1.9	•	4.7	1.9	1.6	1.8	2.3	3.5	1.1	2.1	2.8	2.1	1.5
Cash Flow to Total Debt 44	0.1	•	0.2	0.4	0.2	0.3	0.1	0.1	0.2	0.1	0.1	0.0	0.1

Selected Financial Factors (in Percentages)

Debt Ratio 45	72.5	•	179.7	74.1	66.4	71.2	64.8	75.7	66.9	74.2	66.3	67.1	73.6
Return on Total Assets 46	5.9	•	15.0	11.3	3.9	10.5	5.2	8.5	7.5	7.1	13.0	3.2	5.6
Return on Equity Before Income Taxes 47	9.4	•	•	34.6	6.1	27.6	6.9	21.3	11.9	11.2	26.3	0.2	9.4
Return on Equity After Income Taxes 48	6.6	•	•	31.9	3.9	25.7	5.3	19.6	10.7	5.5	18.1	•	6.9
Profit Margin (Before Income Tax) 49	5.7	•	4.5	6.5	2.8	7.3	4.2	6.4	7.6	7.4	12.9	0.3	8.4
Profit Margin (After Income Tax) 50	4.0	•	4.4	6.0	1.8	6.8	3.3	5.9	6.9	3.6	8.9	•	6.2

COMMERCIAL AND INDUSTRIAL MACHINERY AND EQUIPMENT RENTAL

Table II

Corporations with Net Income

MONEY AMOUNTS AND SIZE OF ASSETS IN THOUSANDS OF DOLLARS

Item Description for Accounting Period 7/06 Through 6/07	Total	Zero Assets	Under 500	500 to 1,000	1,000 to 5,000	5,000 to 10,000	10,000 to 25,000	25,000 to 50,000	50,000 to 100,000	100,000 to 250,000	250,000 to 500,000	500,000 to 2,500,000	2,500,000 and over
Number of Enterprises **1**	14471	2097	7792	1676	2154	375	185	96	•	18	•	•	15
Revenues ($ in Thousands)													
Net Sales **2**	42336745	449923	3944086	1679131	4162109	3809070	2257825	3045322	•	1574706	•	•	3782846
Interest **3**	967972	4421	2592	4314	12581	2077	11946	26970	•	37646	•	•	267192
Rents **4**	73929	4	0	0	3490	0	11212	3325	•	4603	•	•	20406
Royalties **5**	6735	0	0	1	0	0	0	930	•	5474	•	•	0
Other Portfolio Income **6**	3104812	104209	161308	36416	61611	181253	95303	134210	•	187530	•	•	681413
Other Receipts **7**	3818297	341289	3780186	1638400	4084427	3625740	2139364	2879887	•	1339453	•	•	2813835
Total Receipts **8**	42336745	449923	3944086	1679131	4162109	3809070	2257825	3045322	•	1574706	•	•	3782846
Average Total Receipts **9**	2926	215	506	1002	1932	10158	12204	31722	•	87484	•	•	252190
Operating Costs/Operating Income (%)													
Cost of Operations **10**	30.7	19.7	38.4	40.0	19.0	38.6	37.1	48.8	•	38.5	•	•	16.9
Salaries and Wages **11**	9.4	7.3	9.4	9.1	11.4	9.1	7.8	7.1	•	8.6	•	•	6.2
Taxes Paid **12**	2.0	2.4	2.2	2.4	2.9	3.3	2.3	2.1	•	1.2	•	•	1.2
Interest Paid **13**	5.5	7.1	1.0	1.0	2.5	2.0	3.3	3.4	•	4.5	•	•	9.4
Depreciation **14**	15.9	14.5	4.9	9.3	15.0	11.0	15.2	14.1	•	10.2	•	•	20.6
Amortization and Depletion **15**	0.6	0.4	0.0	0.0	0.1	0.0	0.1	0.2	•	0.1	•	•	1.2
Pensions and Other Deferred Comp. **16**	0.4	0.1	0.1	0.7	1.3	0.4	0.2	0.1	•	0.4	•	•	0.3
Employee Benefits **17**	1.3	0.4	1.6	1.0	0.9	0.6	1.5	0.8	•	1.3	•	•	0.6
Advertising **18**	0.4	0.2	1.1	1.2	0.4	0.3	0.5	0.4	•	0.3	•	•	0.2
Other Expenses **19**	17.5	17.1	20.8	17.4	30.4	18.9	16.6	11.0	•	11.8	•	•	18.8
Officers' Compensation **20**	2.4	0.3	8.1	3.7	5.1	4.1	2.4	1.3	•	1.2	•	•	1.1
Operating Margin **21**	13.9	30.4	12.4	14.3	11.8	11.8	13.1	10.7	•	22.1	•	•	23.5
Operating Margin Before Officers' Comp. **22**	16.3	30.7	20.5	18.0	16.2	15.8	15.5	12.0	•	23.3	•	•	24.6

Selected Average Balance Sheet ($ in Thousands)

Net Receivables 23	1176	0	28	62	345	770	2083	6166	27510	177330
Inventories 24	•	•	•	•	•	•	•	•	•	•
Net Property, Plant and Equipment 25	1658	0	60	389	1036	4639	8101	14148	42119	188390
Total Assets 26	5690	0	149	754	2049	7623	15448	33778	146744	1112653
Notes and Loans Payable 27	2448	0	89	390	800	3697	6750	17122	58194	431553
All Other Liabilities 28	1349	0	23	85	244	734	2083	8566	26170	231548
Net Worth 29	1893	0	36	280	1006	3192	6614	8090	62380	449552

Selected Financial Ratios (Times to 1)

Current Ratio 30	1.7	•	2.1	1.9	2.0	1.2	1.7	1.7	1.2	2.4
Quick Ratio 31	1.3	•	1.9	1.7	1.6	0.8	1.3	1.3	0.7	2.0
Net Sales to Working Capital 32	3.6	•	12.2	9.2	4.9	27.2	5.8	11.6	4.3	1.4
Coverage Ratio 33	3.4	5.3	13.3	15.7	5.5	7.0	5.0	5.9	4.2	2.9
Total Asset Turnover 34	0.5	•	3.4	1.3	0.9	1.3	0.8	0.9	0.6	0.2
Inventory Turnover 35	•	•	•	•	•	•	•	•	•	•
Receivables Turnover 36	•	•	•	•	•	•	•	•	•	•
Total Liabilities to Net Worth 37	2.0	•	3.1	1.7	1.0	1.4	1.3	3.2	1.4	1.5
Current Assets to Working Capital 38	2.4	•	1.9	2.2	2.0	6.5	2.4	2.4	5.4	1.7
Current Liabilities to Working Capital 39	1.4	•	0.9	1.2	1.0	5.5	1.4	1.4	4.4	0.7
Working Capital to Net Sales 40	0.3	•	0.1	0.1	0.2	0.0	0.2	0.1	0.2	0.7
Inventory to Working Capital 41	0.2	•	0.1	0.0	0.1	1.2	0.3	1.4	0.3	0.1
Total Receipts to Cash Flow 42	4.6	2.8	3.7	4.2	3.9	4.3	4.6	6.0	4.6	3.4
Cost of Goods to Cash Flow 43	1.4	0.5	1.4	1.7	0.7	1.7	1.7	2.9	1.7	0.6
Cash Flow to Total Debt 44	0.2	•	1.2	0.5	0.5	0.5	0.3	0.2	0.3	0.1

Selected Financial Factors (in Percentages)

Debt Ratio 45	66.7	•	75.7	62.9	50.9	58.1	57.2	76.0	57.5	59.6
Return on Total Assets 46	9.7	•	45.8	20.2	12.9	18.3	12.9	13.2	15.9	6.3
Return on Equity Before Income Taxes 47	20.7	•	173.9	51.1	21.4	37.5	24.1	42.0	31.1	10.2
Return on Equity After Income Taxes 48	17.3	•	172.6	48.8	18.6	35.7	21.9	39.7	23.8	7.5
Profit Margin (Before Income Tax) 49	13.4	30.4	12.4	14.3	11.1	11.8	13.1	10.7	22.2	18.2
Profit Margin (After Income Tax) 50	11.2	24.2	12.3	13.6	9.7	11.2	11.8	10.1	17.0	13.3

Table I

Corporations with and without Net Income

LESSORS OF NONFINAN. INTANGIBLE ASSETS (EX. COPYRIGHTED WORKS)

MONEY AMOUNTS AND SIZE OF ASSETS IN THOUSANDS OF DOLLARS

Item Description for Accounting Period 7/06 Through 6/07	Total	Zero Assets	Under 500	500 to 1,000	1,000 to 5,000	5,000 to 10,000	10,000 to 25,000	25,000 to 50,000	50,000 to 100,000	100,000 to 250,000	250,000 to 500,000	500,000 to 2,500,000	2,500,000 and over
Number of Enterprises **1**	663	25	322	186	78	5	26	3	4	8	0	6	0
Revenues ($ in Thousands)													
Net Sales **2**	3946470	19493	236392	0	227000	488699	278338	37824	190940	465451	0	2002334	0
Interest **3**	178847	3899	194	0	1638	731	1030	1755	2105	24762	0	142732	0
Rents **4**	3458	0	26	0	0	0	0	0	0	3433	0	0	0
Royalties **5**	1157671	2588	0	0	59966	0	17508	762	6902	222374	0	847571	0
Other Portfolio Income **6**	89457	835	18465	0	27546	302	15368	6882	0	7333	0	12726	0
Other Receipts **7**	2517037	12171	217707	0	137850	487666	244432	28425	181933	207549	0	999305	0
Total Receipts **8**	3946470	19493	236392	0	227000	488699	278338	37824	190940	465451	0	2002334	0
Average Total Receipts **9**	5952	780	734	0	2910	97740	10705	12608	47735	58181	•	333722	•
Operating Costs/Operating Income (%)													
Cost of Operations **10**	9.0	•	16.6	•	1.4	•	0.0	17.5	10.6	1.1	•	13.9	•
Salaries and Wages **11**	12.5	•	5.5	•	28.1	1.7	23.5	•	0.9	7.5	•	15.3	•
Taxes Paid **12**	1.4	5.6	0.8	•	2.5	0.0	2.1	1.2	2.8	2.5	•	1.1	•
Interest Paid **13**	6.1	91.0	0.1	•	0.4	0.0	2.6	9.8	0.8	0.3	•	10.4	•
Depreciation **14**	1.3	•	0.1	•	1.5	0.0	0.9	•	0.0	0.6	•	2.2	•
Amortization and Depletion **15**	2.5	11.5	1.3	•	0.3	0.0	3.7	0.4	0.6	8.0	•	2.2	•
Pensions and Other Deferred Comp. **16**	0.3	•	•	•	2.0	0.0	1.2	0.3	0.4	0.3	•	0.1	•
Employee Benefits **17**	0.8	•	•	•	1.0	0.0	0.7	•	0.0	0.7	•	1.2	•
Advertising **18**	1.4	•	0.1	•	2.1	0.0	0.9	1.8	•	6.4	•	0.9	•
Other Expenses **19**	25.8	8.4	31.3	•	27.6	61.9	25.7	7.2	6.5	38.7	•	15.4	•
Officers' Compensation **20**	3.0	•	2.4	•	9.0	0.0	4.5	•	18.0	6.6	•	0.7	•
Operating Margin **21**	35.9	41.8	•	•	24.0	36.3	34.2	61.9	59.4	27.4	•	36.5	•
Operating Margin Before Officers' Comp. **22**	38.9	•	44.2	•	33.0	36.3	38.7	61.9	77.4	33.9	•	37.2	•

Selected Average Balance Sheet ($ in Thousands)

	Item												
23	Net Receivables	4155	0	68	1	709	205	806	0	3414	13385	•	422402
24	Inventories	•	•	•	•	•	•	•	•	•	•	•	•
25	Net Property, Plant and Equipment	1224	0	3	0	133	249	1499	0	54	7272	•	116998
26	Total Assets	23023	0	252	600	2498	7869	19371	39413	59758	198037	•	2065310
27	Notes and Loans Payable	4138	0	666	0	457	0	4743	5833	246	16778	•	369552
28	All Other Liabilities	4553	0	411	4	583	330	4758	483	28390	26935	•	397432
29	Net Worth	14331	0	-825	596	1458	7539	9870	33097	31122	154324	•	1298326

Selected Financial Ratios (Times to 1)

	Item												
30	Current Ratio	1.8	•	0.2	0.4	3.8	14.8	1.7	4.5	1.4	1.6	•	1.9
31	Quick Ratio	1.4	•	0.2	0.3	2.8	14.8	1.4	0.2	1.3	1.4	•	1.5
32	Net Sales to Working Capital	2.0	•	•	•	1.8	21.5	4.9	19.2	6.5	2.9	•	1.1
33	Coverage Ratio	6.8	0.8	831.7	•	56.4	847.2	14.4	7.3	77.7	89.1	•	4.5
34	Total Asset Turnover	0.3	•	2.9	•	1.2	12.4	0.6	0.3	0.8	0.3	•	0.2
35	Inventory Turnover	•	•	•	•	•	•	•	•	•	•	•	•
36	Receivables Turnover	•	•	•	•	•	•	•	•	•	•	•	•
37	Total Liabilities to Net Worth	0.6	•	0.0	0.0	0.7	0.0	1.0	0.2	0.9	0.3	•	0.6
38	Current Assets to Working Capital	2.2	•	0.2	•	1.4	1.1	2.3	1.3	3.8	2.6	•	2.1
39	Current Liabilities to Working Capital	1.2	•	•	•	0.4	0.1	1.3	0.3	2.8	1.6	•	1.1
40	Working Capital to Net Sales	0.5	•	•	•	0.6	0.0	0.2	0.1	0.2	0.3	•	0.9
41	Inventory to Working Capital	0.2	•	•	•	0.0	•	0.0	•	•	0.1	•	0.3
42	Total Receipts to Cash Flow	1.7	•	1.6	•	2.7	1.0	1.9	2.1	1.5	1.5	•	2.1
43	Cost of Goods to Cash Flow	0.2	•	0.3	•	0.0	0.0	0.0	0.4	0.2	0.0	•	0.3
44	Cash Flow to Total Debt	0.4	•	0.4	•	1.0	291.1	0.6	0.9	1.1	0.9	•	0.2

Selected Financial Factors (in Percentages)

	Item												
45	Debt Ratio	37.8	•	427.2	0.6	41.6	4.2	49.0	16.0	47.9	22.1	•	37.1
46	Return on Total Assets	10.8	•	121.9	•	28.4	450.0	20.3	22.9	48.1	7.7	•	7.6
47	Return on Equity Before Income Taxes	14.8	•	•	•	47.8	469.2	37.1	23.6	91.1	9.7	•	9.4
48	Return on Equity After Income Taxes	11.3	•	•	•	35.9	469.2	35.8	23.5	71.3	5.7	•	6.4
49	Profit Margin (Before Income Tax)	35.7	•	41.8	•	24.0	36.2	34.2	61.8	59.4	25.8	•	36.5
50	Profit Margin (After Income Tax)	27.1	•	39.1	•	18.0	36.2	33.0	61.8	46.5	15.2	•	24.7

Table II
Corporations with Net Income

LESSORS OF NONFINAN. INTANGIBLE ASSETS (EX. COPYRIGHTED WORKS)

MONEY AMOUNTS AND SIZE OF ASSETS IN THOUSANDS OF DOLLARS

Item Description for Accounting Period 7/06 Through 6/07	Total	Zero Assets	Under 500	500 to 1,000	1,000 to 5,000	5,000 to 10,000	10,000 to 25,000	25,000 to 50,000	50,000 to 100,000	100,000 to 250,000	250,000 to 500,000	500,000 to 2,500,000	2,500,000 and over
Number of Enterprises 1	350	12	229	0	61	5	26	3	•	•	0	•	0
Revenues ($ in Thousands)													
Net Sales 2	3358468	16904	233326	0	158880	488699	278338	37824	•	•	0	•	0
Interest 3	169797	3899	194	0	551	731	1030	1755	•	•	0	•	0
Rents 4	3433	0	0	0	0	0	0	0	•	•	0	•	0
Royalties 5	885757	0	0	0	59966	0	17508	762	•	•	0	•	0
Other Portfolio Income 6	72397	835	18465	0	27379	302	15368	6882	•	•	0	•	0
Other Receipts 7	2227084	12170	214667	0	70984	487666	244432	28425	•	•	0	•	0
Total Receipts 8	3358468	16904	233326	0	158880	488699	278338	37824	•	•	0	•	0
Average Total Receipts 9	9596	1409	1019	•	2605	97740	10705	12608	•	•	•	•	•
Operating Costs/Operating Income (%)													
Cost of Operations 10	10.4	•	16.8	•	1.4	•	0.0	17.5	•	•	•	•	•
Salaries and Wages 11	9.8	•	5.5	•	23.6	1.7	23.5	•	•	•	•	•	•
Taxes Paid 12	1.1	6.0	0.8	•	1.7	0.0	2.1	1.2	•	•	•	•	•
Interest Paid 13	2.5	0.7	0.0	•	0.5	0.0	2.6	9.8	•	•	•	•	•
Depreciation 14	1.0	•	0.1	•	2.0	0.0	0.9	•	•	•	•	•	•
Amortization and Depletion 15	1.4	•	0.4	•	0.1	0.0	3.7	0.4	•	•	•	•	•
Pensions and Other Deferred Comp. 16	0.3	•	•	•	2.4	0.0	1.2	0.3	•	•	•	•	•
Employee Benefits 17	0.5	•	•	•	0.4	0.0	0.7	•	•	•	•	•	•
Advertising 18	1.4	•	0.1	•	2.6	0.0	0.9	1.8	•	•	•	•	•
Other Expenses 19	24.3	4.6	28.9	•	24.4	61.9	25.7	7.2	•	•	•	•	•
Officers' Compensation 20	2.5	•	2.5	•	5.8	0.0	4.5	•	•	•	•	•	•
Operating Margin 21	44.8	88.7	44.9	•	35.3	36.3	34.2	61.9	•	•	•	•	•
Operating Margin Before Officers' Comp. 22	47.3	88.7	47.4	•	41.1	36.3	38.7	61.9	•	•	•	•	•

Selected Average Balance Sheet ($ in Thousands)

Net Receivables 23	7588	0	96	185	205	806	0
Inventories 24	•	•	•	•	•	•	•
Net Property, Plant and Equipment 25	1673	0	4	126	249	1499	0
Total Assets 26	21958	0	226	2311	7869	19371	39413
Notes and Loans Payable 27	2695	0	752	559	0	4743	5833
All Other Liabilities 28	5716	0	576	499	330	4758	483
Net Worth 29	13548	0	-1103	1253	7539	9870	33097

Selected Financial Ratios (Times to 1)

Current Ratio 30	2.7		0.2	4.0	14.8	1.7	4.5
Quick Ratio 31	2.1		0.2	2.6	14.8	1.4	0.2
Net Sales to Working Capital 32	1.3		•	1.7	21.5	4.9	19.2
Coverage Ratio 33	18.8	134.9	104826.0	73.6	847.2	14.4	7.3
Total Asset Turnover 34	0.4		4.5	1.1	12.4	0.6	0.3
Inventory Turnover 35	•		•	•	•	•	•
Receivables Turnover 36	•		•	•	•	•	•
Total Liabilities to Net Worth 37	0.6			0.8	0.0	1.0	0.2
Current Assets to Working Capital 38	1.6			1.3	1.1	2.3	1.3
Current Liabilities to Working Capital 39	0.6			0.3	0.1	1.3	0.3
Working Capital to Net Sales 40	0.8			0.6	0.0	0.2	0.1
Inventory to Working Capital 41	0.2			0.0	0.0		0.0
Total Receipts to Cash Flow 42	1.5	1.1	1.6	2.5	1.0	1.9	2.1
Cost of Goods to Cash Flow 43	0.2		0.3	0.0		0.0	0.4
Cash Flow to Total Debt 44	0.8		0.5	1.0	291.1	0.6	0.9

Selected Financial Factors (in Percentages)

Debt Ratio 45	38.3		589.1	45.8	4.2	49.0	16.0
Return on Total Assets 46	20.6		203.0	40.3	450.0	20.3	22.9
Return on Equity Before Income Taxes 47	31.7		•	73.4	469.2	37.1	23.6
Return on Equity After Income Taxes 48	24.5		•	55.7	469.2	35.8	23.5
Profit Margin (Before Income Tax) 49	44.7	88.7	44.9	35.3	36.2	34.2	61.8
Profit Margin (After Income Tax) 50	34.6	45.6	42.2	26.8	36.2	33.0	61.8

Selected Average Balance Sheet ($ in Thousands)

	•	•	•	•	•	•	•	•	•	•	•	•
Net Receivables 23	37	0	4	21	51	172	283	742	2885	7041	18406	64702
Inventories 24	•	•	•	•	•	•	•	•	•	•	•	•
Net Property, Plant and Equipment 25	835	0	136	510	1459	4509	10092	19275	38077	85687	154747	1024228
Total Assets 26	1279	0	187	709	2071	6839	14892	34219	67591	153493	362777	1709429
Notes and Loans Payable 27	821	0	125	499	1457	4290	9937	19226	38946	80122	189020	979691
All Other Liabilities 28	109	0	10	43	152	410	1030	3261	5866	18651	55357	260513
Net Worth 29	348	0	52	167	461	2139	3925	11731	22778	54721	118400	469226

Selected Financial Ratios (Times to 1)

	•	•	•	•	•	•	•	•	•	•	•	•
Current Ratio 30	1.8	•	2.3	2.6	1.6	2.5	1.7	1.8	2.3	1.7	1.7	1.4
Quick Ratio 31	1.2	•	1.8	1.7	1.1	1.8	1.1	1.2	1.5	1.3	1.1	0.9
Net Sales to Working Capital 32	2.0	•	2.4	1.3	2.1	1.3	2.3	2.3	1.2	1.9	2.8	2.1
Coverage Ratio 33	1.8	3.6	2.0	1.6	1.4	1.3	1.6	1.8	1.7	2.0	1.7	2.2
Total Asset Turnover 34	0.1	•	0.2	0.1	0.1	0.1	0.1	0.2	0.1	0.1	0.2	0.1
Inventory Turnover 35	•	•	•	•	•	•	•	•	•	•	•	•
Receivables Turnover 36	•	•	•	•	•	•	•	•	•	•	•	•
Total Liabilities to Net Worth 37	2.7	•	2.6	3.3	3.5	2.2	2.8	1.9	2.0	1.8	2.1	2.6
Current Assets to Working Capital 38	2.3	•	1.8	1.6	2.7	1.7	2.5	2.3	1.8	2.5	2.4	3.8
Current Liabilities to Working Capital 39	1.3	•	0.8	0.6	1.7	0.7	1.5	1.3	0.8	1.5	1.4	2.8
Working Capital to Net Sales 40	0.5	•	0.4	0.8	0.5	0.8	0.4	0.4	0.8	0.5	0.4	0.5
Inventory to Working Capital 41	0.0	•	•	0.0	0.0	0.0	0.0	0.0	0.0	0.0	0.0	0.0
Total Receipts to Cash Flow 42	4.5	6.5	3.5	3.9	4.8	4.5	4.0	3.7	4.2	5.9	5.6	5.7
Cost of Goods to Cash Flow 43	0.6	0.0	0.5	0.3	0.6	0.2	0.5	0.6	0.9	1.3	1.7	0.7
Cash Flow to Total Debt 44	0.0	•	0.1	0.0	0.0	0.0	0.0	0.1	0.1	0.0	0.1	0.0

Selected Financial Factors (in Percentages)

	•	•	•	•	•	•	•	•	•	•	•	•
Debt Ratio 45	72.8	•	72.3	76.5	77.7	68.7	73.6	65.7	66.3	64.3	67.4	72.6
Return on Total Assets 46	3.1	•	2.8	2.1	1.9	2.0	2.9	3.5	3.1	3.7	3.7	4.5
Return on Equity Before Income Taxes 47	5.2	•	5.0	3.5	2.4	1.6	4.1	4.6	3.7	5.2	4.8	9.0
Return on Equity After Income Taxes 48	3.1	•	3.1	2.4	1.3	0.7	1.7	2.6	2.6	3.1	4.0	5.8
Profit Margin (Before Income Tax) 49	10.1	34.1	7.1	6.4	4.8	4.5	7.7	10.0	8.5	15.0	7.3	22.7
Profit Margin (After Income Tax) 50	6.1	21.7	4.5	4.5	2.6	1.9	3.2	5.6	5.9	8.8	6.1	14.7

Table I

Corporations with and without Net Income

LEGAL SERVICES

MONEY AMOUNTS AND SIZE OF ASSETS IN THOUSANDS OF DOLLARS

Item Description for Accounting Period 7/06 Through 6/07	Total	Zero Assets	Under 500	500 to 1,000	1,000 to 5,000	5,000 to 10,000	10,000 to 25,000	25,000 to 50,000	50,000 to 100,000	100,000 to 250,000	250,000 to 500,000	500,000 to 2,500,000	2,500,000 and over
Number of Enterprises **1**	102278	16784	80147	2800	2191	184	116	39	11	5	0	0	0
Revenues ($ in Thousands)													
Net Sales **2**	84211558	3801912	43875185	7852460	11745705	4558557	5565064	4344678	759434	1708563	0	0	0
Interest **3**	183005	1866	45516	7934	20899	7436	10842	10168	9452	68892	0	0	0
Rents **4**	62053	0	18373	13725	16191	6681	857	3020	0	3205	0	0	0
Royalties **5**	3913	0	2795	1099	0	0	0	19	0	0	0	0	0
Other Portfolio Income **6**	131318	24	49746	23093	25214	895	4368	22337	2942	2697	0	0	0
Other Receipts **7**	3374462	184999	2021734	126481	128732	31763	209671	57134	169450	444500	0	0	0
Total Receipts **8**	87966309	3988801	46013349	8024792	11936741	4605332	5790802	4437356	941278	2227857	0	0	•
Average Total Receipts **9**	860	238	574	2866	5448	25029	49921	113778	85571	445571	•	•	•
Operating Costs/Operating Income (%)													
Cost of Operations **10**	5.2	7.3	5.5	9.8	4.0	1.0	1.7	0.0	3.3	13.9	•	•	•
Salaries and Wages **11**	30.4	9.9	24.5	25.2	34.8	45.1	52.7	51.6	59.1	45.9	•	•	•
Taxes Paid **12**	3.5	2.7	3.6	3.5	3.3	3.6	3.3	3.5	4.4	3.8	•	•	•
Interest Paid **13**	0.5	0.4	0.5	0.7	0.4	0.4	0.6	0.6	1.4	1.2	•	•	•
Depreciation **14**	0.8	0.3	0.6	0.7	0.9	1.1	1.0	1.5	2.0	2.7	•	•	•
Amortization and Depletion **15**	0.0	0.0	0.0	0.0	0.0	0.0	0.0	0.1	0.2	0.8	•	•	•
Pensions and Other Deferred Comp. **16**	2.1	2.0	1.8	1.7	2.7	2.7	2.8	3.3	3.6	0.6	•	•	•
Employee Benefits **17**	2.1	0.8	2.0	2.5	2.4	2.6	1.9	3.0	2.6	2.4	•	•	•
Advertising **18**	1.9	1.9	2.2	2.3	1.7	0.9	1.4	0.3	2.2	0.9	•	•	•
Other Expenses **19**	28.1	55.5	29.1	20.8	26.4	19.4	22.1	22.3	26.4	46.6	•	•	•
Officers' Compensation **20**	21.2	14.0	24.2	30.5	18.2	20.1	11.4	12.8	7.1	3.1	•	•	•
Operating Margin **21**	4.1	5.3	6.1	2.3	5.2	3.0	1.1	0.9	•	•	•	•	•
Operating Margin Before Officers' Comp. **22**	25.3	19.3	30.3	32.8	23.4	23.1	12.5	13.7	•	•	•	•	•

Selected Average Balance Sheet ($ in Thousands)

Net Receivables 23	10	0	3	27	135	18	583	3332	8572	27035
Inventories 24	1	0	0	1	2	0	89	4	2	11379
Net Property, Plant and Equipment 25	31	0	15	91	204	1429	3282	9402	4944	37441
Total Assets 26	182	0	82	700	1738	7017	14709	33538	60847	260447
Notes and Loans Payable 27	60	0	38	301	341	1721	4085	6464	8310	77024
All Other Liabilities 28	85	0	41	286	842	4039	6353	14538	22839	104088
Net Worth 29	37	0	3	113	555	1257	4271	12536	29699	79335

Selected Financial Ratios (Times to 1)

Current Ratio 30	1.2	•	1.1	1.1	1.5	1.3	1.3	1.3	2.0	1.0
Quick Ratio 31	0.8	•	0.8	0.6	1.1	0.8	0.6	1.1	0.9	0.7
Net Sales to Working Capital 32	41.4	•	199.0	94.7	13.2	24.7	24.8	25.5	3.1	89.1
Coverage Ratio 33	17.9	28.4	24.1	7.9	19.1	10.0	9.9	6.2	9.6	8.2
Total Asset Turnover 34	4.5	•	6.6	4.0	3.1	3.5	3.3	3.3	1.1	1.3
Inventory Turnover 35	51.8	•	244.2	413.9	101.1	1192.8	8.9	8.5	1380.7	4.2
Receivables Turnover 36	86.8	•	266.9	77.0	41.7	843.6	98.6	33.7	7.6	13.0
Total Liabilities to Net Worth 37	4.0	•	23.6	5.2	2.1	4.6	2.4	1.7	1.0	2.3
Current Assets to Working Capital 38	5.7	•	17.2	15.6	3.2	4.8	4.8	4.0	2.0	31.0
Current Liabilities to Working Capital 39	4.7	•	16.2	14.6	2.2	3.8	3.8	3.0	1.0	30.0
Working Capital to Net Sales 40	0.0	•	0.0	0.0	0.1	0.0	0.0	0.0	0.3	0.0
Inventory to Working Capital 41	0.0	•	0.1	0.0	0.0	•	0.0	•	0.0	3.2
Total Receipts to Cash Flow 42	3.3	1.7	3.0	5.1	3.7	5.8	4.7	6.0	3.2	2.0
Cost of Goods to Cash Flow 43	0.2	0.1	0.2	0.5	0.1	0.1	0.1	0.0	0.1	0.3
Cash Flow to Total Debt 44	1.7	•	2.3	0.9	1.2	0.7	1.0	0.9	0.7	0.9

Selected Financial Factors (in Percentages)

Debt Ratio 45	79.9	•	95.9	83.8	68.1	82.1	71.0	62.6	51.2	69.5
Return on Total Assets 46	41.0	•	76.4	20.7	22.2	15.8	18.7	12.0	14.9	12.6
Return on Equity Before Income Taxes 47	192.9	•	1800.1	111.8	66.0	79.2	57.8	26.8	27.4	36.4
Return on Equity After Income Taxes 48	187.9	•	1778.4	108.4	64.0	71.2	53.5	24.4	23.0	29.7
Profit Margin (Before Income Tax) 49	8.6	10.2	11.0	4.5	6.8	4.0	5.1	3.0	11.8	8.4
Profit Margin (After Income Tax) 50	8.3	10.2	10.9	4.4	6.6	3.6	4.8	2.7	9.9	6.9

Table II
Corporations with Net Income

LEGAL SERVICES

MONEY AMOUNTS AND SIZE OF ASSETS IN THOUSANDS OF DOLLARS

Item Description for Accounting Period 7/06 Through 6/07		Total	Zero Assets	Under 500	500 to 1,000	1,000 to 5,000	5,000 to 10,000	10,000 to 25,000	25,000 to 50,000	50,000 to 100,000	100,000 to 250,000	250,000 to 500,000	500,000 to 2,500,000	2,500,000 and over
Number of Enterprises	1	71330	10522	56659	2159	1688	162	97	31	11	0	0	0	0
Revenues ($ in Thousands)														
Net Sales	2	67393442	2136636	34071076	6201336	10789842	3892085	5494425	3910016	898025	0	0	0	0
Interest	3	91938	1866	36591	5169	17600	7382	9558	8393	5378	0	0	0	0
Rents	4	45614	0	11900	6465	15679	6681	857	3020	1012	0	0	0	0
Royalties	5	2006	0	1987	0	0	0	0	19	0	0	0	0	0
Other Portfolio Income	6	99792	10	49096	4439	22031	895	4307	16309	2703	0	0	0	0
Other Receipts	7	2926077	150028	1868597	34308	98137	31762	82623	55412	605213	0	0	0	0
Total Receipts	8	70558869	2288540	36039247	6251717	10943289	3938805	5591770	3993169	1512331	0	0	0	•
Average Total Receipts	9	989	218	636	2896	6483	24314	57647	128812	137485	•	•	•	•
Operating Costs/Operating Income (%)														
Cost of Operations	10	5.3	12.9	6.1	9.4	4.1	1.2	1.7	0.0	2.8	•	•	•	•
Salaries and Wages	11	30.4	14.6	23.1	25.2	35.1	42.7	53.2	51.4	38.9	•	•	•	•
Taxes Paid	12	3.4	4.0	3.4	3.4	3.3	3.6	3.3	3.6	3.9	•	•	•	•
Interest Paid	13	0.4	0.4	0.4	0.3	0.4	0.3	0.6	0.5	2.1	•	•	•	•
Depreciation	14	0.8	0.4	0.7	0.8	0.9	1.1	1.0	1.2	3.4	•	•	•	•
Amortization and Depletion	15	0.0	0.0	0.0	0.0	0.0	0.0	0.0	0.1	1.6	•	•	•	•
Pensions and Other Deferred Comp.	16	2.1	1.7	1.7	1.2	2.8	3.1	2.8	3.4	2.5	•	•	•	•
Employee Benefits	17	1.9	1.0	1.6	2.3	2.4	2.4	1.9	3.1	1.5	•	•	•	•
Advertising	18	2.1	3.3	2.4	2.8	1.8	1.1	1.4	0.3	2.5	•	•	•	•
Other Expenses	19	26.5	30.7	28.2	20.8	26.6	18.0	22.2	21.2	74.0	•	•	•	•
Officers' Compensation	20	20.0	17.6	22.5	28.4	16.2	22.7	8.3	13.6	6.8	•	•	•	•
Operating Margin	21	7.1	13.3	10.0	5.3	6.5	3.9	3.5	1.6	•	•	•	•	•
Operating Margin Before Officers' Comp.	22	27.1	30.9	32.5	33.7	22.7	26.6	11.9	15.2	•	•	•	•	•

Selected Average Balance Sheet ($ in Thousands)

Net Receivables 23	11	0	1	3	20	142	21	697	3838	13609
Inventories 24	1	0	0	0	0	5	0	107	0	124
Net Property, Plant and Equipment 25		34	0	15	102	241	1470	3013	8861	9748
Total Assets 26			196	86	710	1720	6944	14562	32424	104198
Notes and Loans Payable 27		53	0	29	262	293	1490	4532	4970	20355
All Other Liabilities 28		87	0	35	286	915	4049	6520	12066	37791
Net Worth 29		56	0	22	161	512	1405	3509	15388	46051

Selected Financial Ratios (Times to 1)

Current Ratio 30	1.3	•	1.3	1.2	1.3	1.3	1.2	1.6	1.3
Quick Ratio 31	0.9	•	0.9	0.7	1.0	0.9	0.6	1.4	0.7
Net Sales to Working Capital 32	33.1	•	56.7	28.6	22.3	20.7	29.0	19.0	5.9
Coverage Ratio 33	29.1	49.4	43.0	18.6	21.9	16.0	10.0	8.9	14.4
Total Asset Turnover 34	4.8	•	7.0	4.0	3.7	3.5	3.9	3.9	0.8
Inventory Turnover 35	67.6	•	106.5	670.1	53.8	1192.8	8.9	•	18.3
Receivables Turnover 36	84.2	•	309.4	81.0	42.7	854.0	97.6	•	•
Total Liabilities to Net Worth 37	2.5	•	3.0	3.4	2.4	3.9	3.1	1.1	1.3
Current Assets to Working Capital 38	4.4	•	4.8	5.2	4.2	4.0	5.0	2.6	3.9
Current Liabilities to Working Capital 39	3.4	•	3.8	4.2	3.2	3.0	4.0	1.6	2.9
Working Capital to Net Sales 40	0.0	•	0.0	0.0	0.0	0.0	0.0	0.1	0.2
Inventory to Working Capital 41	0.0	•	0.0	•	0.0	•	0.0	•	0.0
Total Receipts to Cash Flow 42	3.1	2.2	2.6	4.5	3.5	5.8	4.6	6.2	1.0
Cost of Goods to Cash Flow 43	0.2	0.3	0.2	0.4	0.1	0.1	0.1	0.0	0.0
Cash Flow to Total Debt 44	2.2	•	3.6	1.2	1.5	0.8	1.1	1.2	1.4

Selected Financial Factors (in Percentages)

Debt Ratio 45	71.4	•	74.7	77.3	70.2	79.8	75.9	52.5	55.8
Return on Total Assets 46	58.8	•	113.4	26.2	30.8	18.7	22.8	16.3	23.8
Return on Equity Before Income Taxes 47	198.7	437.9	109.4	98.5	86.6	85.2		30.4	50.1
Return on Equity After Income Taxes 48	194.0	•	433.1	106.4	95.9	78.4	78.8	27.9	42.1
Profit Margin (Before Income Tax) 49	11.8	20.4	15.8	6.1	7.9	5.1	5.3	3.7	28.3
Profit Margin (After Income Tax) 50	11.5	20.3	15.6	6.0	7.7	4.6	4.9	3.4	23.7

Table I

Corporations with and without Net Income

ACCOUNTING, TAX PREPARATION, BOOKKEEPING, AND PAYROLL SERVICES

MONEY AMOUNTS AND SIZE OF ASSETS IN THOUSANDS OF DOLLARS

Item Description for Accounting Period 7/06 Through 6/07		Total	Zero Assets	Under 500	500 to 1,000	1,000 to 5,000	5,000 to 10,000	10,000 to 25,000	25,000 to 50,000	50,000 to 100,000	100,000 to 250,000	250,000 to 500,000	500,000 to 2,500,000	2,500,000 and over
Number of Enterprises	1	70697	15214	52953	1475	924	54	48	12	7	6	0	3	0
Revenues ($ in Thousands)														
Net Sales	2	34803086	1240495	15556185	3753809	4277473	931437	743026	1941340	435719	775984	0	5147618	0
Interest	3	1060061	1212	15997	5565	7201	1557	1683	9362	3913	15418	0	998152	0
Rents	4	21779	0	4354	8666	2206	2619	345	322	0	0	0	3267	0
Royalties	5	766516	0	1959	0	0	0	996	0	0	12506	0	751056	0
Other Portfolio Income	6	201768	92724	37061	67	13852	331	643	11907	1799	2444	0	40940	0
Other Receipts	7	818959	96727	421070	26542	17159	19779	12954	84	18369	20752	0	185523	0
Total Receipts	8	37672169	1431158	16036626	3794649	4317891	955723	759647	1963015	459800	827104	0	7126556	0
Average Total Receipts	9	533	94	303	2573	4673	17699	15826	163585	65686	137851	•	2375519	•
Operating Costs/Operating Income (%)														
Cost of Operations	10	12.8	0.1	2.0	12.2	31.9	0.2	50.4	86.0	0.8	0.1	•	5.0	•
Salaries and Wages	11	30.5	28.7	30.5	38.2	28.6	44.2	13.0	2.0	42.1	41.3	•	35.2	•
Taxes Paid	12	4.6	4.1	4.5	5.0	4.6	3.8	5.1	3.9	3.9	3.6	•	5.3	•
Interest Paid	13	2.4	1.5	0.6	1.0	1.0	1.4	1.0	0.3	1.1	5.1	•	11.1	•
Depreciation	14	1.3	1.1	0.9	1.6	0.6	2.7	1.1	0.1	2.1	2.5	•	2.5	•
Amortization and Depletion	15	0.7	0.3	0.4	0.1	0.4	0.4	0.5	0.1	1.1	3.1	•	2.2	•
Pensions and Other Deferred Comp.	16	2.0	1.2	2.5	2.5	0.7	0.8	0.2	5.7	0.3	0.1	•	0.7	•
Employee Benefits	17	2.1	2.0	2.2	2.7	1.9	1.9	1.6	0.8	3.1	2.8	•	1.9	•
Advertising	18	1.0	1.5	0.7	0.7	0.7	0.7	0.3	0.0	0.1	1.6	•	2.7	•
Other Expenses	19	27.6	40.8	24.0	20.2	14.2	25.7	23.7	1.5	105.2	50.7	•	52.3	•
Officers' Compensation	20	14.8	17.3	24.6	12.0	10.7	15.4	1.9	0.4	5.1	0.7	•	0.2	•
Operating Margin	21	0.3	1.4	6.9	3.9	4.7	2.7	1.3	•	•	•	•	•	•
Operating Margin Before Officers' Comp.	22	15.1	18.6	31.5	15.9	18.2	15.4	3.2	•	•	•	•	•	•

Selected Average Balance Sheet ($ in Thousands)

Net Receivables 23	40	5	80	315	1413	4032	7292	13152	30272	503478	•
Inventories 24	4	0	0	0	0	71	125	30	1353	89395	•
Net Property, Plant and Equipment 25	26	10	268	174	1398	873	540	6487	13749	175710	•
Total Assets 26	348	56	710	1880	6217	15130	32284	81566	180140	5261884	•
Notes and Loans Payable 27	211	30	435	481	3529	3299	979	12171	62895	3813732	•
All Other Liabilities 28	90	12	227	724	1647	8560	25808	127507	101143	815104	•
Net Worth 29	47	14	48	675	1041	3271	5497	-58112	16103	633047	•

Selected Financial Ratios (Times to 1)

Current Ratio 30	0.5	1.3	0.8	1.2	1.2	1.4	0.8	0.4	1.1	0.3	•
Quick Ratio 31	0.4	1.2	0.5	1.1	0.9	1.0	0.8	0.3	0.6	0.2	•
Net Sales to Working Capital 32	•	49.2	•	34.7	36.5	5.2	•	•	28.0	•	•
Coverage Ratio 33	4.6	16.7	6.0	6.9	4.8	4.4	5.0	•	0.0	2.8	•
Total Asset Turnover 34	1.4	5.3	3.6	2.5	2.8	1.0	5.0	0.8	0.7	0.3	•
Inventory Turnover 35	15.7	508.5	7109.2	1087.8	•	110.2	1116.1	16.5	0.1	1.0	•
Receivables Turnover 36	14.1	68.2	33.9	15.1	13.3	4.3	36.5	4.5	4.2	4.1	•
Total Liabilities to Net Worth 37	6.5	3.0	13.8	1.8	5.0	3.6	4.9	•	10.2	7.3	•
Current Assets to Working Capital 38	•	4.0	7.1	•	6.9	3.8	•	•	16.9	•	•
Current Liabilities to Working Capital 39	•	3.0	6.1	•	5.9	2.8	•	•	15.9	•	•
Working Capital to Net Sales 40	•	0.0	0.0	0.0	0.0	0.2	•	•	0.0	•	•
Inventory to Working Capital 41	•	0.0	0.0	•	•	0.0	•	•	0.3	•	•
Total Receipts to Cash Flow 42	3.3	3.7	4.7	6.3	4.3	4.0	105.5	2.5	2.4	1.6	•
Cost of Goods to Cash Flow 43	0.4	0.1	0.6	2.0	0.0	2.0	90.7	0.0	0.0	0.1	•
Cash Flow to Total Debt 44	0.5	1.9	0.8	0.6	0.8	0.3	0.1	0.2	0.3	0.2	•

Selected Financial Factors (in Percentages)

Debt Ratio 45	86.6	75.2	93.2	64.1	83.3	78.4	83.0	171.2	91.1	88.0	•
Return on Total Assets 46	15.5	56.2	21.3	16.3	18.6	4.6	3.3	•	0.0	10.1	•
Return on Equity Before Income Taxes 47	90.8	212.5	262.0	38.9	88.2	16.4	10.6	63.6	•	53.6	•
Return on Equity After Income Taxes 48	77.7	209.5	258.0	36.0	83.8	13.8	4.6	67.4	•	35.3	•
Profit Margin (Before Income Tax) 49	8.6	16.7	10.0	4.9	5.7	5.3	3.5	0.4	•	19.8	•
Profit Margin (After Income Tax) 50	7.4	16.3	9.8	4.9	5.3	5.1	2.9	0.2	•	13.0	•

Table II

Corporations with Net Income

ACCOUNTING, TAX PREPARATION, BOOKKEEPING, AND PAYROLL SERVICES

MONEY AMOUNTS AND SIZE OF ASSETS IN THOUSANDS OF DOLLARS

Item Description for Accounting Period 7/06 Through 6/07		Total	Zero Assets	Under 500	500 to 1,000	1,000 to 5,000	5,000 to 10,000	10,000 to 25,000	25,000 to 50,000	50,000 to 100,000	100,000 to 250,000	250,000 to 500,000	500,000 to 2,500,000	2,500,000 and over
Number of Enterprises	1	51798	11594	38323	1135	658	30	41	6	4	3	0	3	0
Revenues ($ in Thousands)														
Net Sales	2	28032859	974484	11481219	3179172	3354169	686183	725915	1903074	274736	306289	0	5147618	0
Interest	3	1033669	1088	5624	5555	3115	1396	1467	1862	3310	12101	0	998152	0
Rents	4	19863	0	2616	8666	2206	2619	167	322	0	0	0	3267	0
Royalties	5	765520	0	1959	0	0	0	0	0	0	12506	0	751056	0
Other Portfolio Income	6	184120	92661	24122	67	11704	328	136	11706	9	2444	0	40940	0
Other Receipts	7	547420	70	275135	24220	13183	19727	9825	48	607	19084	0	185523	0
Total Receipts	8	30583451	1068303	11790675	3217680	3384377	710253	737510	1917012	278662	352424	0	7126556	0
Average Total Receipts	9	590	92	308	2835	5143	23675	17988	319502	69666	117475	•	2375519	•
Operating Costs/Operating Income (%)														
Cost of Operations	10	14.6	0.1	2.6	6.1	38.7	•	51.5	87.3	1.1	0.4	•	5.0	•
Salaries and Wages	11	29.3	19.0	28.3	42.9	26.5	43.2	11.5	1.0	43.2	60.3	•	35.2	•
Taxes Paid	12	4.5	3.7	4.4	5.0	4.4	3.5	4.9	3.9	3.9	1.9	•	5.3	•
Interest Paid	13	2.6	1.5	0.7	0.8	0.8	0.5	0.9	0.0	0.7	4.6	•	11.1	•
Depreciation	14	1.2	0.7	0.9	1.4	0.4	3.0	1.0	0.0	1.0	1.9	•	2.5	•
Amortization and Depletion	15	0.6	0.2	0.3	0.0	0.3	0.1	0.3	0.0	0.8	0.3	•	2.2	•
Pensions and Other Deferred Comp.	16	1.8	1.5	2.2	2.1	0.5	0.5	0.2	5.8	0.4	0.2	•	0.7	•
Employee Benefits	17	1.9	1.9	1.9	3.0	1.5	1.9	1.4	0.7	4.0	3.1	•	1.9	•
Advertising	18	1.0	1.3	0.6	0.4	0.4	0.9	0.2	0.0	0.1	3.8	•	2.7	•
Other Expenses	19	25.9	41.7	22.3	20.5	13.0	24.9	21.1	0.7	27.1	28.8	•	52.3	•
Officers' Compensation	20	13.0	16.4	23.8	12.4	6.5	14.6	1.6	0.2	1.6	0.9	•	0.2	•
Operating Margin	21	3.7	12.7	11.9	5.2	6.9	6.9	5.6	0.3	16.0	•	•	•	•
Operating Margin Before Officers' Comp.	22	16.6	29.1	35.7	17.6	13.5	21.5	7.2	0.5	17.6	•	•	•	•

Selected Average Balance Sheet ($ in Thousands)

Net Receivables 23	46	5	0	74	227	742	4240	14382	21662	24016	503478	•
Inventories 24	5	0	0	0	0	2	75	249	17	2707	16179	•
Net Property, Plant and Equipment 25	28	10	0	240	186	1807	853	484	3543	11078	175710	•
Total Assets 26	425	59	0	669	2108	6321	15667	31983	82885	159302	5261884	•
Notes and Loans Payable 27	263	27	0	431	418	3411	3494	26	6482	25902	3813732	•
All Other Liabilities 28	91	12	0	250	756	626	9409	21782	60085	88948	815104	•
Net Worth 29	71	20	0	-12	934	2284	2765	10175	16319	44453	633047	•

Selected Financial Ratios (Times to 1)

Current Ratio 30	0.5	1.5	•	0.7	1.3	2.3	1.3	1.3	1.3	1.2	0.3	•
Quick Ratio 31	0.4	1.4	•	0.4	1.2	2.1	1.0	1.3	1.1	0.4	0.2	•
Net Sales to Working Capital 32	•	32.4	•	•	20.1	14.0	6.1	43.7	6.0	7.9	•	•
Coverage Ratio 33	5.9	23.3	15.9	8.6	10.6	20.7	9.4	24.7	25.1	2.9	2.8	•
Total Asset Turnover 34	1.3	5.1	•	4.2	2.4	3.6	1.1	9.9	0.8	0.6	0.3	•
Inventory Turnover 35	14.5	595.0	•	3024.0	1034.8	•	120.7	1111.3	46.3	0.1	5.3	•
Receivables Turnover 36	13.5	62.7	•	40.4	22.0	19.1	5.7	36.1	•	3.4	7.3	•
Total Liabilities to Net Worth 37	5.0	2.0	•	•	1.3	1.8	4.7	2.1	4.1	2.6	7.3	•
Current Assets to Working Capital 38	•	2.9	•	•	3.9	1.8	4.3	4.0	4.7	7.4	•	•
Current Liabilities to Working Capital 39	•	1.9	•	•	2.9	0.8	3.3	3.0	3.7	6.4	•	•
Working Capital to Net Sales 40	•	0.0	•	•	0.0	0.1	0.2	0.0	0.2	0.1	•	•
Inventory to Working Capital 41	•	0.0	•	•	0.0	•	0.1	•	0.0	0.2	•	•
Total Receipts to Cash Flow 42	3.1	3.3	2.2	4.3	5.7	3.7	3.7	116.8	2.3	3.0	1.6	•
Cost of Goods to Cash Flow 43	0.4	0.1	0.0	0.3	2.2	•	1.9	102.0	0.0	0.0	0.1	•
Cash Flow to Total Debt 44	0.5	2.4	•	1.0	0.8	1.5	0.4	0.1	0.4	0.3	0.2	•

Selected Financial Factors (in Percentages)

Debt Ratio 45	83.2	66.4	•	101.8	55.7	63.9	82.4	68.2	80.3	72.1	88.0	•
Return on Total Assets 46	19.7	78.0	•	30.3	20.9	39.5	9.1	10.2	15.1	8.6	10.1	•
Return on Equity Before Income Taxes 47	97.2	221.9	•	42.7	104.0	45.9	73.6	30.7	73.6	20.4	53.6	•
Return on Equity After Income Taxes 48	85.6	219.0	•	39.8	100.4	42.2	49.9	24.2	49.9	14.3	35.3	•
Profit Margin (Before Income Tax) 49	12.8	14.6	22.3	6.4	7.8	10.4	7.2	1.0	17.5	8.9	19.8	•
Profit Margin (After Income Tax) 50	11.3	14.4	21.8	6.3	7.3	10.0	6.6	0.8	11.8	6.2	13.0	•

Table I

Corporations with and without Net Income

ARCHITECTURAL, ENGINEERING, AND RELATED SERVICES

MONEY AMOUNTS AND SIZE OF ASSETS IN THOUSANDS OF DOLLARS

Item Description for Accounting Period 7/06 Through 6/07	Total	Zero Assets	Under 500	500 to 1,000	1,000 to 5,000	5,000 to 10,000	10,000 to 25,000	25,000 to 50,000	50,000 to 100,000	100,000 to 250,000	250,000 to 500,000	500,000 to 2,500,000	2,500,000 and over
Number of Enterprises **1**	100061	19760	71766	3461	3763	782	271	107	60	43	22	19	6
Revenues ($ in Thousands)													
Net Sales **2**	202035189	3333746	66072050	7021277	20537192	14515335	9400261	7508954	8440251	11257297	9076181	18552815	26319831
Interest **3**	764749	21163	66742	5522	26417	25725	63817	11628	17725	105826	82974	166668	170543
Rents **4**	113176	0	4359	698	8937	1444	2373	4563	10226	7825	9657	61401	1691
Royalties **5**	184384	8200	0	0	0	1146	32	4492	157	15268	1514	37350	116224
Other Portfolio Income **6**	610807	6080	89617	40830	17473	17411	37599	18546	34723	93608	12364	219942	22613
Other Receipts **7**	1908054	27539	346303	109859	259427	81493	118792	56157	42087	88736	183136	237847	356681
Total Receipts **8**	205616359	3396728	66579071	7178186	20849446	14642554	9622874	7604340	8545169	11568560	9365826	19276023	26987583
Average Total Receipts **9**	2055	172	928	2074	5541	18724	35509	71069	142419	269036	425719	1014528	4497930
Operating Costs/Operating Income (%)													
Cost of Operations **10**	38.5	32.2	24.1	21.3	29.0	39.2	34.3	47.3	44.5	48.1	53.5	63.4	57.3
Salaries and Wages **11**	19.2	10.9	20.7	22.4	25.6	22.1	23.8	17.4	19.5	18.9	16.7	11.5	14.3
Taxes Paid **12**	2.9	3.0	3.0	3.8	4.3	3.3	3.5	3.2	2.8	2.6	2.2	2.1	1.4
Interest Paid **13**	0.8	2.5	0.4	0.8	0.7	0.7	0.7	0.8	0.7	1.4	2.2	1.7	0.7
Depreciation **14**	1.2	3.7	0.8	1.7	1.9	1.6	1.4	1.5	1.3	1.4	1.5	1.2	0.6
Amortization and Depletion **15**	0.3	1.2	0.0	0.1	0.1	0.2	0.4	0.2	0.3	0.4	1.0	0.7	0.4
Pensions and Other Deferred Comp. **16**	1.1	1.5	1.3	1.0	1.6	1.5	1.0	1.1	1.3	1.1	1.3	0.7	0.6
Employee Benefits **17**	2.3	1.6	1.6	1.8	2.1	2.5	3.1	3.2	2.7	2.4	2.6	2.8	2.7
Advertising **18**	0.3	0.3	0.4	0.6	0.5	0.3	0.4	0.4	0.2	0.2	0.3	0.1	0.1
Other Expenses **19**	22.1	31.1	26.0	37.5	21.4	18.8	22.9	16.7	20.5	20.3	12.7	14.4	21.0
Officers' Compensation **20**	8.1	7.2	16.7	8.9	8.2	5.3	5.3	3.7	3.7	1.5	1.3	1.7	0.9
Operating Margin **21**	3.2	4.8	4.8	0.2	4.6	4.5	3.3	4.6	2.5	1.6	4.8	•	0.1
Operating Margin Before Officers' Comp. **22**	11.2	12.0	21.5	9.1	12.9	9.8	8.6	8.3	6.2	3.1	6.1	1.3	1.0

Selected Average Balance Sheet ($ in Thousands)

Net Receivables 23	251	0	10	175	501	2110	6361	13994	28503	44745	100934	273296	1007136
Inventories 24	32	0	1	12	69	113	658	1382	3257	5914	11069	26464	205617
Net Property, Plant and Equipment 25	107	0	27	174	377	1731	2707	5230	9997	20555	35805	39749	178770
Total Assets 26	875	0	86	702	1883	6629	15129	32978	70084	154907	343588	977341	3669327
Notes and Loans Payable 27	238	0	50	335	669	2387	3865	7093	14156	28615	92826	309081	480564
All Other Liabilities 28	333	0	29	141	405	2431	5039	14338	32477	60498	118472	353787	1757564
Net Worth 29	304	0	8	226	810	1810	6225	11546	23451	65794	132291	314474	1431199

Selected Financial Ratios (Times to 1)

Current Ratio 30	1.4	•	1.1	1.6	2.1	1.6	1.7	1.5	1.3	1.6	1.6	1.5	1.2
Quick Ratio 31	1.0	•	1.0	1.3	1.7	1.3	1.3	1.2	1.0	1.1	1.2	1.1	0.7
Net Sales to Working Capital 32	13.6	•	172.3	14.5	8.6	12.8	8.4	9.3	12.7	7.8	6.6	6.4	12.0
Coverage Ratio 33	7.0	3.7	14.5	4.1	10.0	9.2	9.2	8.1	6.5	4.0	4.7	3.2	5.1
Total Asset Turnover 34	2.3	•	10.7	2.9	2.9	2.8	2.3	2.1	2.0	1.7	1.2	1.0	1.2
Inventory Turnover 35	24.1	•	187.8	35.0	23.0	64.7	18.1	24.0	19.2	21.3	19.9	23.4	12.2
Receivables Turnover 36	8.5	•	100.2	12.7	9.3	9.8	5.0	5.3	5.5	5.9	4.1	3.3	6.2
Total Liabilities to Net Worth 37	1.9	•	9.9	2.1	1.3	2.7	1.4	1.9	2.0	1.4	1.6	2.1	1.6
Current Assets to Working Capital 38	3.3	•	8.0	2.7	1.9	2.7	2.5	3.0	4.2	2.8	2.8	3.0	5.8
Current Liabilities to Working Capital 39	2.3	•	7.0	1.7	0.9	1.7	1.5	2.0	3.2	1.8	1.8	2.0	4.8
Working Capital to Net Sales 40	0.1	•	0.0	0.1	0.1	0.1	0.1	0.1	0.1	0.1	0.2	0.2	0.1
Inventory to Working Capital 41	0.2	•	0.2	0.1	0.1	0.1	0.2	0.2	0.3	0.2	0.2	0.1	0.5
Total Receipts to Cash Flow 42	4.3	•	3.6	2.8	4.3	4.9	4.0	5.3	5.0	4.9	5.7	6.8	4.6
Cost of Goods to Cash Flow 43	1.6	•	0.9	0.6	1.3	1.9	1.4	2.5	2.2	2.4	3.1	4.3	2.6
Cash Flow to Total Debt 44	0.8	•	3.3	1.5	1.2	0.8	1.0	0.6	0.6	0.6	0.3	0.2	0.4

Selected Financial Factors (in Percentages)

Debt Ratio 45	65.2	•	90.8	67.9	57.0	72.7	58.9	65.0	66.5	57.5	61.5	67.8	61.0
Return on Total Assets 46	13.4	•	64.2	9.4	19.8	16.9	14.2	14.3	9.0	9.6	12.1	5.5	4.3
Return on Equity Before Income Taxes 47	33.1	•	649.4	22.1	41.4	55.2	30.8	35.8	22.6	17.0	24.7	11.7	8.9
Return on Equity After Income Taxes 48	28.8	•	641.8	19.5	38.2	50.1	23.5	30.3	16.0	11.7	19.0	8.3	6.0
Profit Margin (Before Income Tax) 49	5.0	6.7	5.6	2.5	6.1	5.4	5.5	5.9	3.8	4.3	7.9	3.8	2.9
Profit Margin (After Income Tax) 50	4.3	6.2	5.5	2.2	5.7	4.9	5.0	5.5	2.7	3.0	6.1	2.7	2.0

Table II

Corporations with Net Income

ARCHITECTURAL, ENGINEERING, AND RELATED SERVICES

MONEY AMOUNTS AND SIZE OF ASSETS IN THOUSANDS OF DOLLARS

Item Description for Accounting Period 7/06 Through 6/07	Total	Zero Assets	Under 500	500 to 1,000	1,000 to 5,000	5,000 to 10,000	10,000 to 25,000	25,000 to 50,000	50,000 to 100,000	100,000 to 250,000	250,000 to 500,000	500,000 to 2,500,000	2,500,000 and over
Number of Enterprises 1	71879	12163	53975	2054	2669	562	240	96	49	34	•	15	•
Revenues ($ in Thousands)													
Net Sales 2	161514204	2696930	43530862	4978238	17154164	11671174	8657691	6982206	7347251	9953265	•	16803164	•
Interest 3	596233	11688	17854	3241	18782	18393	62936	9547	15968	33008	•	153302	•
Rents 4	94782	0	3910	698	1176	1293	2373	3632	8694	7597	•	54060	•
Royalties 5	148855	8150	0	0	0	1146	32	4492	81	15268	•	1949	•
Other Portfolio Income 6	536868	3756	87911	9949	13531	17226	37452	14242	34716	91516	•	193489	•
Other Receipts 7	1650416	22802	267590	103098	210866	76803	117574	52304	30398	72689	•	200263	•
Total Receipts 8	164541358	2743326	43908127	5095224	17398519	11788035	8878058	7066423	7437108	10173343	•	17406227	•
Average Total Receipts 9	2289	226	813	2481	6519	20972	36992	73609	151778	299216	•	1160415	•
Operating Costs/Operating Income (%)													
Cost of Operations 10	40.0	34.5	20.8	25.0	28.8	34.6	33.2	48.7	42.5	48.6	•	62.4	•
Salaries and Wages 11	18.9	9.7	20.9	23.5	25.6	23.5	23.9	16.5	19.5	18.3	•	11.6	•
Taxes Paid 12	2.9	3.1	3.4	4.0	3.7	3.7	3.5	3.1	2.9	2.6	•	2.2	•
Interest Paid 13	0.8	2.3	0.4	0.9	0.5	0.5	0.6	0.8	0.6	0.7	•	1.6	•
Depreciation 14	1.2	2.3	1.0	1.8	1.9	1.6	1.3	1.5	1.2	1.1	•	1.2	•
Amortization and Depletion 15	0.3	1.3	0.0	0.1	0.0	0.0	0.2	0.1	0.2	0.3	•	0.6	•
Pensions and Other Deferred Comp. 16	1.2	1.8	1.5	0.9	1.6	1.8	1.0	1.1	1.3	0.8	•	0.6	•
Employee Benefits 17	2.4	1.8	1.8	2.2	2.1	2.5	3.2	3.2	2.7	2.2	•	2.7	•
Advertising 18	0.3	0.3	0.5	0.6	0.4	0.3	0.4	0.3	0.2	0.2	•	0.1	•
Other Expenses 19	20.3	24.7	27.2	26.5	19.9	18.8	23.0	15.6	20.8	20.0	•	14.5	•
Officers' Compensation 20	6.4	6.7	13.9	9.3	7.6	5.7	5.3	3.3	4.0	1.3	•	1.2	•
Operating Margin 21	5.4	11.4	8.7	5.3	7.8	7.0	4.4	5.8	4.2	3.8	•	1.2	•
Operating Margin Before Officers' Comp. 22	11.8	18.1	22.6	14.5	15.4	12.7	9.7	9.1	8.2	5.1	•	2.5	•

Selected Average Balance Sheet ($ in Thousands)

Net Receivables 23	299	0	10	216	569	2133	6416	13385	29556	48049	311043	•
Inventories 24	40	0	1	21	80	105	675	1279	3221	6982	26800	•
Net Property, Plant and Equipment 25	118	0	28	211	385	1858	2799	5101	8966	21188	43908	•
Total Assets 26	977	0	88	738	1940	6770	15410	32698	69404	153734	1000491	•
Notes and Loans Payable 27	246	0	45	413	546	1399	3659	6878	12168	24821	323928	•
All Other Liabilities 28	359	0	26	194	418	2246	4946	14081	32552	59238	314463	•
Net Worth 29	372	0	17	130	977	3125	6805	11740	24684	69676	362100	•

Selected Financial Ratios (Times to 1)

Current Ratio 30	1.5	•	1.3	1.1	2.5	1.9	1.7	1.5	1.4	1.6	1.7	•
Quick Ratio 31	1.1	•	1.1	1.0	2.0	1.7	1.4	1.2	1.1	1.2	1.2	•
Net Sales to Working Capital 32	11.5	•	81.9	58.5	8.1	10.5	8.2	9.6	10.7	8.7	5.4	•
Coverage Ratio 33	10.1	6.7	22.3	9.3	21.4	18.0	13.0	9.5	9.9	9.4	4.1	•
Total Asset Turnover 34	2.3	•	9.1	3.3	3.3	3.1	2.3	2.2	2.2	1.9	1.1	•
Inventory Turnover 35	22.4	•	133.8	29.1	23.1	68.3	17.8	27.7	19.8	20.4	26.1	•
Receivables Turnover 36	8.1	•	97.8	14.4	10.2	9.8	5.5	6.2	5.4	6.1	3.5	•
Total Liabilities to Net Worth 37	1.6	•	4.3	4.7	1.0	1.2	1.3	1.8	1.8	1.2	1.8	•
Current Assets to Working Capital 38	3.0	•	4.6	9.7	1.7	2.1	2.4	3.0	3.5	2.8	2.5	•
Current Liabilities to Working Capital 39	2.0	•	3.6	8.7	0.7	1.1	1.4	2.0	2.5	1.8	1.5	•
Working Capital to Net Sales 40	0.1	•	0.0	0.0	0.1	0.1	0.1	0.1	0.1	0.1	0.2	•
Inventory to Working Capital 41	0.2	•	0.1	0.5	0.1	0.0	0.2	0.2	0.2	0.2	0.1	•
Total Receipts to Cash Flow 42	4.2	3.0	3.1	3.4	4.0	4.3	3.8	5.3	4.5	4.6	6.3	•
Cost of Goods to Cash Flow 43	1.7	1.0	0.6	0.8	1.2	1.5	1.3	2.6	1.9	2.2	3.9	•
Cash Flow to Total Debt 44	0.9	•	3.6	1.2	1.7	1.3	1.1	0.7	0.7	0.8	0.3	•

Selected Financial Factors (in Percentages)

Debt Ratio 45	61.9	•	81.3	82.3	49.7	53.8	55.8	64.1	64.4	54.7	63.8	•
Return on Total Assets 46	18.7	•	91.3	28.1	32.0	26.0	17.3	17.4	13.1	12.7	7.4	•
Return on Equity Before Income Taxes 47	44.1	•	465.5	141.7	60.5	53.3	36.1	43.4	33.1	25.0	15.4	•
Return on Equity After Income Taxes 48	39.3	•	460.6	134.2	56.8	49.2	28.6	37.4	25.5	18.7	11.7	•
Profit Margin (Before Income Tax) 49	7.3	13.1	9.5	7.6	9.2	8.0	6.8	7.0	5.5	5.9	5.0	•
Profit Margin (After Income Tax) 50	6.5	12.5	9.4	7.2	8.6	7.4	5.4	6.0	4.2	4.4	3.8	•

Table I

Corporations with and without Net Income

SPECIALIZED DESIGN SERVICES

MONEY AMOUNTS AND SIZE OF ASSETS IN THOUSANDS OF DOLLARS

Item Description for Accounting Period 7/06 Through 6/07	Total	Zero Assets	Under 500	500 to 1,000	1,000 to 5,000	5,000 to 10,000	10,000 to 25,000	25,000 to 50,000	50,000 to 100,000	100,000 to 250,000	250,000 to 500,000	500,000 to 2,500,000	2,500,000 and over
Number of Enterprises 1	38938	7954	29050	1019	756	121	23	7	5	0	3	0	0
Revenues ($ in Thousands)													
Net Sales 2	21604461	433942	11922876	2020208	2713332	1208753	550759	466681	464574	0	1823335	0	0
Interest 3	67727	276	4519	1591	3462	5917	1485	4642	3946	0	41888	0	0
Rents 4	11431	0	2628	7231	663	0	0	0	118	0	792	0	0
Royalties 5	80521	0	0	0	67726	0	2563	0	10233	0	0	0	0
Other Portfolio Income 6	50182	93	2925	486	1861	2962	19478	607	3431	0	18339	0	0
Other Receipts 7	385854	4361	92835	48851	1752	22523	34914	4285	2563	0	173770	0	0
Total Receipts 8	22200176	438672	12025783	2078367	2788796	1240155	609199	476215	484865	0	2058124	0	0
Average Total Receipts 9	570	55	414	2040	3689	10249	26487	68031	96973	•	686041	•	•
Operating Costs/Operating Income (%)													
Cost of Operations 10	47.2	21.0	43.2	64.1	62.5	60.7	38.4	83.6	60.7	•	19.6	•	•
Salaries and Wages 11	15.5	4.9	9.4	9.2	11.3	18.9	32.5	7.0	13.3	•	66.3	•	•
Taxes Paid 12	2.7	4.8	2.5	1.8	2.4	2.6	3.2	0.5	1.6	•	5.1	•	•
Interest Paid 13	0.7	1.3	0.7	0.9	0.3	0.4	1.7	0.8	1.7	•	0.9	•	•
Depreciation 14	1.3	2.6	0.8	0.8	1.0	1.4	1.1	0.5	1.5	•	5.6	•	•
Amortization and Depletion 15	0.1	0.1	0.1	0.0	0.1	0.2	0.3	•	1.9	•	0.1	•	•
Pensions and Other Deferred Comp. 16	0.7	0.3	0.7	0.8	0.8	0.6	0.6	0.6	0.3	•	0.5	•	•
Employee Benefits 17	1.2	0.4	0.7	0.8	0.9	1.1	2.3	0.9	0.6	•	5.5	•	•
Advertising 18	1.1	0.4	1.1	1.8	1.3	0.7	0.7	0.3	1.0	•	0.4	•	•
Other Expenses 19	21.6	51.4	26.3	14.3	13.8	10.4	17.4	0.9	18.9	•	17.6	•	•
Officers' Compensation 20	7.2	9.4	8.3	8.4	6.8	3.4	6.3	1.1	2.4	•	3.6	•	•
Operating Margin 21	0.8	3.4	6.2	•	•	•	•	3.7	•	•	•	•	•
Operating Margin Before Officers' Comp. 22	7.9	12.8	14.5	5.6	5.6	3.1	1.8	4.8	•	•	•	•	•

Selected Average Balance Sheet ($ in Thousands)

	1	2	3	4	5	6	7	8	9	10
Net Receivables 23	53	0	18	175	387	1396	3455	5082	17893	225812
Inventories 24	24	0	7	210	484	348	260	3869	10124	10862
Net Property, Plant and Equipment 25	36	0	15	93	351	779	1644	1489	18206	122124
Total Assets 26	237	0	80	704	2001	7311	16445	35226	92693	904647
Notes and Loans Payable 27	80	0	56	419	650	1092	1796	12320	34756	42428
All Other Liabilities 28	92	0	28	341	963	5265	8254	11673	28352	222072
Net Worth 29	65	0	-3	-56	388	955	6396	11233	29585	640148

Selected Financial Ratios (Times to 1)

	1	2	3	4	5	6	7	8	9	10
Current Ratio 30	1.4	•	1.5	1.2	1.2	0.9	1.3	1.4	1.7	2.4
Quick Ratio 31	1.0	•	1.2	0.6	0.6	0.7	0.9	0.7	0.9	2.2
Net Sales to Working Capital 32	11.6	•	20.4	25.9	12.7	•	9.5	7.2	5.5	2.1
Coverage Ratio 33	5.7	4.5	10.7	1.1	6.4	6.8	2.9	7.9	0.9	•
Total Asset Turnover 34	2.3	•	5.1	2.8	1.8	1.4	1.5	1.9	1.0	0.7
Inventory Turnover 35	11.0	•	27.0	6.1	4.6	17.4	35.4	14.4	5.6	11.0
Receivables Turnover 36	10.1	•	21.7	11.7	8.7	8.2	6.7	10.4	5.4	2.4
Total Liabilities to Net Worth 37	2.6	•	•	4.2	6.7	1.6	2.1	2.1	0.4	
Current Assets to Working Capital 38	3.3	•	2.8	6.4	5.4	5.7	4.3	3.6	2.5	1.7
Current Liabilities to Working Capital 39	2.3	•	1.8	5.4	4.4	•	3.3	2.6	1.5	0.7
Working Capital to Net Sales 40	0.1	•	0.0	0.0	0.1	•	0.1	0.1	0.2	0.5
Inventory to Working Capital 41	0.5	•	0.4	3.1	1.8	•	0.0	0.4	0.6	0.0
Total Receipts to Cash Flow 42	4.9	2.2	3.5	8.5	10.7	5.2	20.1	6.4		
Cost of Goods to Cash Flow 43	2.3	0.5	1.5	6.8	5.3	6.5	2.0	16.8	3.9	
Cash Flow to Total Debt 44	0.7	•	1.4	0.2	0.3	0.1	0.5	0.1	0.2	

Selected Financial Factors (in Percentages)

	1	2	3	4	5	6	7	8	9	10
Debt Ratio 45	72.4	•	104.3	108.0	80.6	86.9	61.1	68.1	68.1	29.2
Return on Total Assets 46	9.8	•	39.8	2.6	3.5	3.2	7.3	12.2	1.6	
Return on Equity Before Income Taxes 47	29.5	•	•	15.1	21.2	12.4	33.4			
Return on Equity After Income Taxes 48	27.0	•	8.1	8.1	12.5	11.9	8.1	28.0		
Profit Margin (Before Income Tax) 49	3.5	4.5	7.0	0.1	1.6	2.0	3.3	5.6		
Profit Margin (After Income Tax) 50	3.2	4.5	6.9	•	1.4	1.1	2.2	4.7		

Table II

Corporations with Net Income

SPECIALIZED DESIGN SERVICES

MONEY AMOUNTS AND SIZE OF ASSETS IN THOUSANDS OF DOLLARS

Item Description for Accounting Period 7/06 Through 6/07	Total	Zero Assets	Under 500	500 to 1,000	1,000 to 5,000	5,000 to 10,000	10,000 to 25,000	25,000 to 50,000	50,000 to 100,000	100,000 to 250,000	250,000 to 500,000	500,000 to 2,500,000	2,500,000 and over
Number of Enterprises 1	26097	3728	21274	446	569	54	16	7	0	3	0	0	0
Revenues ($ in Thousands)													
Net Sales 2	16261083	254207	9708881	812554	1976339	666907	463470	709260	0	1669464	0	0	0
Interest 3	16755	203	4378	1582	2203	3703	1306	1306	0	2074	0	0	0
Rents 4	3977	0	2628	0	440	0	0	118	0	792	0	0	0
Royalties 5	10233	0	0	0	0	0	0	0	0	10233	0	0	0
Other Portfolio Income 6	28073	79	2854	0	1861	181	3827	1140	0	18133	0	0	0
Other Receipts 7	202989	0	89497	39665	842	22063	12420	3383	0	35118	0	0	0
Total Receipts 8	16523110	254489	9808238	853801	1981685	692854	481023	715207	0	1735814	0	0	•
Average Total Receipts 9	633	68	461	1914	3483	12831	30064	102172	•	578605	•	•	•
Operating Costs/Operating Income (%)													
Cost of Operations 10	42.9	25.4	39.2	55.3	60.3	60.6	32.9	77.5	•	21.1	•	•	•
Salaries and Wages 11	11.9	5.2	9.2	9.0	10.8	12.6	29.6	8.4	•	27.3	•	•	•
Taxes Paid 12	2.6	1.6	2.6	2.4	2.3	2.7	3.0	0.9	•	3.8	•	•	•
Interest Paid 13	0.5	0.1	0.4	0.8	0.2	0.3	0.2	0.6	•	1.2	•	•	•
Depreciation 14	0.9	2.0	0.6	0.8	1.1	1.1	0.7	0.9	•	1.8	•	•	•
Amortization and Depletion 15	0.1	•	0.1	0.0	0.0	0.0	0.0	0.3	•	0.5	•	•	•
Pensions and Other Deferred Comp. 16	0.7	0.5	0.7	0.5	0.9	0.6	0.6	0.5	•	0.5	•	•	•
Employee Benefits 17	1.1	•	0.5	1.5	0.4	1.7	2.2	0.7	•	4.9	•	•	•
Advertising 18	1.0	0.2	1.1	0.5	1.6	0.2	0.8	0.2	•	0.4	•	•	•
Other Expenses 19	23.4	40.4	27.3	16.1	9.4	11.6	14.9	3.8	•	33.5	•	•	•
Officers' Compensation 20	7.1	6.0	8.3	10.9	6.9	4.7	7.2	1.3	•	1.5	•	•	•
Operating Margin 21	8.1	18.7	10.0	2.1	6.1	3.9	7.9	4.7	•	3.5	•	•	•
Operating Margin Before Officers' Comp. 22	15.1	24.6	18.3	13.1	13.0	8.6	15.1	6.0	•	5.0	•	•	•

Selected Average Balance Sheet ($ in Thousands)

Net Receivables 23	41	0	19	105	297	1783	4052	12533	68171
Inventories 24	24	0	6	320	422	345	372	5374	15029
Net Property, Plant and Equipment 25	32	0	13	59	381	664	1534	7956	60747
Total Assets 26	199	0	88	683	1837	6702	15935	50115	338855
Notes and Loans Payable 27	58	0	39	188	316	2074	865	6982	81733
All Other Liabilities 28	74	0	26	307	1008	3675	6750	17528	75587
Net Worth 29	68	0	23	188	513	954	8320	25605	181534

Selected Financial Ratios (Times to 1)

Current Ratio 30	1.6	•	2.0	1.3	1.3	1.1	1.6	1.7	2.0
Quick Ratio 31	1.1	•	1.7	0.6	0.7	0.8	1.5	1.2	1.4
Net Sales to Working Capital 32	12.2	•	13.6	16.4	10.5	34.2	6.9	6.7	9.0
Coverage Ratio 33	21.5	159.1	27.5	10.6	36.3	26.2	52.0	10.1	7.8
Total Asset Turnover 34	3.1	•	5.2	2.7	1.9	1.8	1.8	2.0	1.6
Inventory Turnover 35	11.2	•	27.9	3.2	5.0	21.7	25.6	14.6	7.8
Receivables Turnover 36	12.2	•	26.0	9.9	9.4	8.0	6.6	•	16.3
Total Liabilities to Net Worth 37	1.9	•	2.8	2.6	2.6	6.0	0.9	1.0	0.9
Current Assets to Working Capital 38	2.6	•	2.0	4.2	4.2	15.5	2.5	2.3	2.0
Current Liabilities to Working Capital 39	1.6	•	1.0	3.2	3.2	14.5	1.5	1.3	1.0
Working Capital to Net Sales 40	0.1	•	0.1	0.1	0.1	0.0	0.1	0.1	0.1
Inventory to Working Capital 41	0.5	•	0.2	2.1	1.4	0.9	0.0	0.4	0.2
Total Receipts to Cash Flow 42	3.5	2.2	2.9	5.7	7.6	6.7	4.5	14.5	2.8
Cost of Goods to Cash Flow 43	1.5	0.6	1.2	3.2	4.6	4.1	1.5	11.2	0.6
Cash Flow to Total Debt 44	1.4	•	2.4	0.6	0.3	0.3	0.8	0.3	1.3

Selected Financial Factors (in Percentages)

Debt Ratio 45	65.9	•	73.8	72.5	72.1	85.8	47.8	48.9	46.4
Return on Total Assets 46	31.8	•	59.2	21.2	12.5	15.0	21.7	12.4	14.9
Return on Equity Before Income Taxes 47	89.0	•	218.2	69.9	43.4	101.1	40.8	21.8	24.3
Return on Equity After Income Taxes 48	85.4	•	215.4	62.5	40.8	80.2	36.0	19.3	21.5
Profit Margin (Before Income Tax) 49	9.7	18.8	11.0	7.2	6.4	7.8	11.7	5.5	7.9
Profit Margin (After Income Tax) 50	9.3	18.8	10.9	6.4	6.0	6.2	10.3	4.9	7.0

Table I
Corporations with and without Net Income

COMPUTER SYSTEMS DESIGN AND RELATED SERVICES

MONEY AMOUNTS AND SIZE OF ASSETS IN THOUSANDS OF DOLLARS

Item Description for Accounting Period 7/06 Through 6/07	Total	Zero Assets	Under 500	500 to 1,000	1,000 to 5,000	5,000 to 10,000	10,000 to 25,000	25,000 to 50,000	50,000 to 100,000	100,000 to 250,000	250,000 to 500,000	500,000 to 2,500,000	2,500,000 and over
Number of Enterprises **1**	118944	28887	79371	4126	4773	805	541	185	96	87	32	34	5
Revenues ($ in Thousands)													
Net Sales **2**	171291666	8050774	25128656	7364663	29883781	9117743	11987780	7346627	7795204	13160694	8929608	18632139	23893999
Interest **3**	1876035	39857	16727	17115	66640	47236	79454	50543	61628	128893	85983	325052	956908
Rents **4**	64247	491	8552	0	2433	537	846	2562	3451	1691	3841	30861	8982
Royalties **5**	1881051	5447	0	1841	25942	48111	9918	5074	5421	111624	197842	899144	570688
Other Portfolio Income **6**	1266085	140453	23666	44827	64754	31640	122169	47976	67966	59051	51564	63605	548415
Other Receipts **7**	2673914	145330	348181	47244	243974	195728	77854	121987	51960	413979	108317	430360	488996
Total Receipts **8**	179052998	8382352	25525782	7475690	30287524	9440995	12278021	7574769	7985630	13875932	9377155	20381161	26467988
Average Total Receipts **9**	1505	290	322	1812	6346	11728	22695	40945	83184	159493	293036	599446	5293598
Operating Costs/Operating Income (%)													
Cost of Operations **10**	32.0	24.0	21.3	29.7	40.8	40.0	39.6	42.2	39.4	53.3	36.9	29.5	11.7
Salaries and Wages **11**	26.2	32.8	17.5	27.2	28.2	28.7	28.3	26.1	24.5	22.0	19.8	31.1	29.5
Taxes Paid **12**	3.9	3.7	3.0	3.1	3.5	3.2	3.0	3.2	6.5	2.5	2.2	3.4	7.9
Interest Paid **13**	2.1	0.6	0.7	0.5	1.0	1.3	0.9	1.4	1.5	1.7	1.6	2.1	7.9
Depreciation **14**	1.4	0.7	0.8	1.0	0.9	2.4	1.8	1.6	1.5	1.7	1.3	1.9	2.0
Amortization and Depletion **15**	1.2	0.5	0.1	0.2	0.5	1.0	1.1	1.1	1.4	1.7	2.6	1.9	2.7
Pensions and Other Deferred Comp. **16**	0.7	0.5	1.1	0.5	1.0	1.0	0.5	0.4	0.2	0.2	0.3	1.0	0.6
Employee Benefits **17**	2.5	1.2	1.5	1.7	2.0	2.6	2.2	2.1	1.8	2.3	1.8	3.6	4.5
Advertising **18**	0.9	0.5	0.8	0.5	0.9	1.0	1.7	0.9	1.0	0.9	0.4	1.3	0.3
Other Expenses **19**	26.1	32.9	33.5	26.7	16.9	22.9	23.7	21.6	20.6	17.1	33.9	26.1	35.2
Officers' Compensation **20**	5.1	7.7	14.5	9.3	6.6	4.5	3.4	2.7	1.9	1.6	1.1	1.2	0.6
Operating Margin **21**	•	•	5.3	•	•	•	•	•	•	•	•	•	•
Operating Margin Before Officers' Comp. **22**	2.9	2.6	19.8	8.7	4.3	•	•	1.6	•	•	•	•	•

Selected Average Balance Sheet ($ in Thousands)

	1	2	3	4	5	6	7	8	9	10	11	12	13
Net Receivables 23	343	0	9	187	896	2232	4524	8743	17587	32063	68413	171010	3338546
Inventories 24	16	0	2	26	44	252	390	752	1487	1957	3794	8018	30978
Net Property, Plant and Equipment 25	78	0	7	95	190	650	1211	2314	3669	8144	17029	58214	432749
Total Assets 26	1338	0	50	705	2359	7178	15142	33329	68421	156291	358776	1063716	10606092
Notes and Loans Payable 27	356	0	42	242	766	2203	2212	6915	12085	32493	76769	145350	3748508
All Other Liabilities 28	428	0	23	221	1031	3858	6991	14211	30601	44312	114658	350864	2254984
Net Worth 29	553	0	-16	242	562	1118	5939	12203	25736	79486	167350	567502	4602601

Selected Financial Ratios (Times to 1)

	1	2	3	4	5	6	7	8	9	10	11	12	13
Current Ratio 30	1.5	•	1.1	1.6	1.4	1.2	1.5	1.3	1.4	1.6	1.7	2.0	1.4
Quick Ratio 31	1.3	•	1.0	1.4	1.2	1.0	1.3	1.1	1.1	1.3	1.3	1.6	1.2
Net Sales to Working Capital 32	6.9	•	81.7	11.4	12.8	11.8	6.2	8.3	7.8	5.6	4.9	2.5	4.3
Coverage Ratio 33	2.2	•	11.4	2.9	0.1	•	•	0.8	2.4	1.3	2.9	4.2	2.0
Total Asset Turnover 34	1.1	•	6.4	2.5	2.7	1.6	1.5	1.2	1.2	1.0	0.8	0.5	0.5
Inventory Turnover 35	29.5	•	40.8	20.6	58.3	18.0	22.5	22.3	21.5	41.2	27.2	20.2	18.1
Receivables Turnover 36	4.5	•	35.4	10.6	7.9	5.0	5.5	4.7	5.1	5.1	4.2	3.4	1.5
Total Liabilities to Net Worth 37	1.4	•	•	1.9	3.2	5.4	1.5	1.7	1.7	1.0	1.1	0.9	1.3
Current Assets to Working Capital 38	3.0	•	9.2	2.7	3.4	5.3	2.9	4.0	3.5	2.7	2.5	2.0	3.7
Current Liabilities to Working Capital 39	2.0	•	8.2	1.7	2.4	4.3	1.9	3.0	2.5	1.7	1.5	1.0	2.7
Working Capital to Net Sales 40	0.1	•	0.0	0.1	0.1	0.1	0.2	0.1	0.1	0.2	0.2	0.4	0.2
Inventory to Working Capital 41	0.1	•	0.5	0.1	0.1	0.3	0.1	0.1	0.2	0.1	0.1	0.0	0.0
Total Receipts to Cash Flow 42	4.0	3.6	2.7	4.2	7.5	7.0	6.0	5.5	5.2	6.8	2.9	3.4	2.6
Cost of Goods to Cash Flow 43	1.3	0.9	0.6	1.3	3.1	2.8	2.4	2.3	2.0	3.6	1.1	1.0	0.3
Cash Flow to Total Debt 44	0.5	•	1.8	0.9	0.5	0.3	0.4	0.3	0.4	0.3	0.5	0.3	0.3

Selected Financial Factors (in Percentages)

	1	2	3	4	5	6	7	8	9	10	11	12	13
Debt Ratio 45	58.6	•	132.4	65.7	76.2	84.4	60.8	63.4	62.4	49.1	53.4	46.6	56.6
Return on Total Assets 46	4.9	•	47.9	3.5	0.1	•	•	1.4	4.3	2.1	3.7	4.5	7.3
Return on Equity Before Income Taxes 47	6.4	•	•	6.8	•	•	•	6.6	5.1	0.9	5.2	6.5	8.5
Return on Equity After Income Taxes 48	3.9	•	•	5.8	•	•	•	5.1	•	•	2.6	4.9	5.9
Profit Margin (Before Income Tax) 49	2.5	•	6.9	0.9	•	•	2.1	0.5	2.1	0.5	3.1	6.7	8.2
Profit Margin (After Income Tax) 50	1.5	•	6.8	0.8	•	•	1.6	•	1.6	•	1.6	5.1	5.7

343

Table II
Corporations with Net Income

COMPUTER SYSTEMS DESIGN AND RELATED SERVICES

MONEY AMOUNTS AND SIZE OF ASSETS IN THOUSANDS OF DOLLARS

Item Description for Accounting Period 7/06 Through 6/07	Total	Zero Assets	Under 500	500 to 1,000	1,000 to 5,000	5,000 to 10,000	10,000 to 25,000	25,000 to 50,000	50,000 to 100,000	100,000 to 250,000	250,000 to 500,000	500,000 to 2,500,000	2,500,000 and over
Number of Enterprises 1	69454	13051	49119	3166	3150	439	279	102	56	46	17	24	5
Revenues ($ in Thousands)													
Net Sales 2	137276932	20924214	23677453	6421812	5487812	6862347	8320066	5192689	6308364	9016738	5572544	15598895	23893999
Interest 3	1514058	4724	8506	11301	27175	15097	19362	25361	38169	66256	53188	288011	956908
Rents 4	47419	491	0	0	1674	106	816	737	1198	743	3014	29659	8982
Royalties 5	1764615	1791	0	0	25789	48111	60	468	3648	95206	120360	898496	570688
Other Portfolio Income 6	1094478	131705	23477	44553	18791	30417	81672	14692	67803	45208	30213	57530	548415
Other Receipts 7	1942598	187315	305005	43656	160928	152287	41030	106090	35626	62155	30378	329129	488996
Total Receipts 8	143640100	21261202	23911810	6521322	5813838	7108365	8463006	5340037	6454808	9286306	5809697	17201720	26467988
Average Total Receipts 9	2068	445	433	2060	7591	16192	30333	52353	115264	201876	341747	716738	5293598
Operating Costs/Operating Income (%)													
Cost of Operations 10	30.9	18.4	18.1	30.8	40.2	41.0	42.7	41.9	39.7	59.9	30.9	33.0	11.7
Salaries and Wages 11	23.9	33.8	15.8	23.4	25.4	23.4	22.2	23.5	21.8	15.2	15.6	30.7	29.5
Taxes Paid 12	4.0	4.2	2.8	2.7	3.2	2.8	2.7	3.2	7.3	2.0	2.1	3.4	7.9
Interest Paid 13	2.0	0.4	0.5	0.4	0.5	0.6	0.5	0.8	1.2	1.0	1.3	1.2	7.9
Depreciation 14	1.2	0.6	0.7	0.9	0.6	1.0	1.6	1.1	1.3	0.9	0.9	1.7	2.0
Amortization and Depletion 15	1.0	0.1	0.1	0.0	0.2	0.2	0.3	0.5	0.6	1.2	1.5	1.9	2.7
Pensions and Other Deferred Comp. 16	0.7	0.2	1.0	0.5	1.1	1.4	0.7	0.5	0.2	0.2	0.3	0.8	0.6
Employee Benefits 17	2.4	1.1	1.5	1.4	1.8	2.3	1.8	1.7	1.6	1.5	1.4	3.6	4.5
Advertising 18	0.7	0.4	0.6	0.4	0.6	0.5	1.3	0.8	1.0	1.0	0.3	1.4	0.3
Other Expenses 19	24.1	28.7	33.4	23.2	13.2	16.0	16.1	17.7	17.9	12.7	40.0	23.2	35.2
Officers' Compensation 20	4.8	6.0	14.3	9.2	6.4	4.1	2.7	2.2	1.5	1.2	1.2	1.2	0.6
Operating Margin 21	4.4	6.3	11.2	7.1	6.9	6.7	7.4	6.2	5.9	3.2	4.6	•	•
Operating Margin Before Officers' Comp. 22	9.2	12.3	25.5	16.3	13.3	10.7	10.1	8.3	7.4	4.4	5.8	•	•

Selected Average Balance Sheet ($ in Thousands)

Net Receivables 23	481	0	12	197	1112	3090	5899	9462	20230	30685	84081	168979	3338546
Inventories 24	15	0	2	31	33	286	409	764	1663	1454	3888	4820	29935
Net Property, Plant and Equipment 25	97	0	9	93	174	504	1389	2494	4313	5577	11513	72634	432749
Total Assets 26	1738	0	59	686	2344	7184	15494	32566	71724	158342	354630	1128884	10606092
Notes and Loans Payable 27	419	0	18	119	325	1273	1649	5338	12058	26084	83737	134081	3748508
All Other Liabilities 28	485	0	16	203	934	3201	7484	12894	36117	43946	109671	306286	2254984
Net Worth 29	833	0	25	364	1086	2711	6361	14334	23549	88312	161222	688517	4602601

Selected Financial Ratios (Times to 1)

Current Ratio 30	1.6	•	2.3	1.9	1.8	1.6	1.6	1.4	1.4	1.7	1.9	2.1	1.4
Quick Ratio 31	1.4	•	2.0	1.7	1.7	1.3	1.4	1.1	1.1	1.3	1.4	1.7	1.2
Net Sales to Working Capital 32	6.3	•	17.2	9.7	8.9	7.9	7.1	10.2	9.8	6.3	4.5	2.6	4.3
Coverage Ratio 33	5.7	35.4	28.6	23.2	18.4	19.5	20.8	12.9	7.9	7.1	7.6	8.3	2.0
Total Asset Turnover 34	1.1	•	7.2	3.0	3.2	2.2	1.9	1.6	1.6	1.2	0.9	0.6	0.5
Inventory Turnover 35	41.7	•	45.2	19.9	91.9	22.4	31.1	27.9	26.9	80.7	26.0	44.4	18.7
Receivables Turnover 36	4.9	•	36.7	12.4	7.6	5.0	5.9	5.8	•	6.1	3.8	4.3	•
Total Liabilities to Net Worth 37	1.1	•	1.4	0.9	1.2	1.7	1.4	1.3	2.0	0.8	1.2	0.6	1.3
Current Assets to Working Capital 38	2.6	•	1.8	2.1	2.2	2.8	2.7	3.8	3.5	2.5	2.2	1.9	3.7
Current Liabilities to Working Capital 39	1.6	•	0.8	1.1	1.2	1.8	1.7	2.8	2.5	1.5	1.2	0.9	2.7
Working Capital to Net Sales 40	0.2	•	0.1	0.1	0.1	0.1	0.1	0.1	0.1	0.2	0.2	0.4	0.2
Inventory to Working Capital 41	0.1	•	0.1	0.1	0.0	0.2	0.1	0.2	0.1	0.0	0.1	0.0	0.0
Total Receipts to Cash Flow 42	3.3	2.7	2.3	3.5	5.2	4.3	4.5	4.1	4.3	5.9	2.1	3.6	2.6
Cost of Goods to Cash Flow 43	1.0	0.5	0.4	1.1	2.1	1.7	1.9	1.7	1.7	3.5	0.7	1.2	0.3
Cash Flow to Total Debt 44	0.7	•	5.4	1.8	1.1	0.8	0.7	0.7	0.5	0.5	0.8	0.4	0.3

Selected Financial Factors (in Percentages)

Debt Ratio 45	52.1	•	58.1	46.9	53.7	62.3	58.9	56.0	67.2	44.2	54.5	39.0	56.6
Return on Total Assets 46	12.7	•	95.9	26.7	26.8	23.5	19.0	15.2	14.8	8.9	9.3	5.7	7.3
Return on Equity Before Income Taxes 47	21.8	•	220.6	48.0	54.7	59.2	44.0	31.8	39.4	13.8	17.8	8.2	8.5
Return on Equity After Income Taxes 48	18.9	•	218.2	47.2	51.6	51.8	38.8	27.3	36.5	11.3	12.8	6.3	5.9
Profit Margin (Before Income Tax) 49	9.2	12.4	12.8	8.6	7.9	10.3	9.4	8.9	8.2	6.2	8.7	8.7	8.2
Profit Margin (After Income Tax) 50	8.0	10.6	12.7	8.5	7.5	9.0	8.3	7.7	7.6	5.1	6.3	6.7	5.7

MANAGEMENT, SCIENTIFIC, AND TECHNICAL CONSULTING SERVICES

Table I
Corporations with and without Net Income

MONEY AMOUNTS AND SIZE OF ASSETS IN THOUSANDS OF DOLLARS

Item Description for Accounting Period 7/06 Through 6/07	Total	Zero Assets	Under 500	500 to 1,000	1,000 to 5,000	5,000 to 10,000	10,000 to 25,000	25,000 to 50,000	50,000 to 100,000	100,000 to 250,000	250,000 to 500,000	500,000 to 2,500,000	2,500,000 and over
Number of Enterprises **1**	229657	48144	169688	5447	4825	726	469	138	103	59	24	27	7
Revenues ($ in Thousands)													
Net Sales **2**	183583002	5279262	52420105	18427377	17712286	7308240	10218625	5767912	8151606	8840565	5347538	22613689	21495798
Interest **3**	1277196	10470	59344	16793	49491	18503	47756	31609	52135	66760	105933	453622	364781
Rents **4**	80426	447	747	2488	3544	199	1730	3159	3186	11897	3886	24864	24280
Royalties **5**	845228	17	698	13	42622	0	0	91	186869	10467	4550	599123	777
Other Portfolio Income **6**	804205	54044	46515	24675	112315	8098	107157	18398	51728	43593	62970	247024	27684
Other Receipts **7**	4765880	56548	990490	463237	804254	371382	420280	281216	200652	174399	130168	403741	469516
Total Receipts **8**	191355937	5400788	53517899	18934583	18724512	7706422	10795548	6102385	8646176	9147681	5655045	24342063	22382836
Average Total Receipts **9**	833	112	315	3476	3881	10615	23018	44220	83943	155045	235627	901558	3197548
Operating Costs/Operating Income (%)													
Cost of Operations **10**	29.6	19.8	20.4	69.7	28.7	21.9	39.3	33.2	35.8	35.0	37.3	16.2	25.8
Salaries and Wages **11**	24.3	19.5	19.7	10.1	24.9	28.2	23.7	25.0	23.2	24.8	29.5	41.4	27.8
Taxes Paid **12**	2.8	3.1	2.8	1.3	2.7	3.6	3.0	2.7	2.6	2.9	3.1	3.3	3.4
Interest Paid **13**	1.1	1.1	0.5	0.3	0.7	0.7	1.0	1.5	1.7	2.1	2.0	2.0	1.7
Depreciation **14**	1.0	1.1	0.8	0.4	1.1	0.9	1.2	1.2	1.8	1.3	1.4	1.3	1.2
Amortization and Depletion **15**	0.4	0.3	0.1	0.2	0.2	0.0	0.3	0.4	0.9	0.7	2.0	1.0	0.7
Pensions and Other Deferred Comp. **16**	1.4	0.9	1.8	0.6	0.9	1.2	1.3	0.9	1.2	0.9	0.5	2.1	2.0
Employee Benefits **17**	2.0	1.8	1.9	0.4	1.5	2.0	2.3	2.0	2.8	4.6	1.2	3.3	1.8
Advertising **18**	0.9	0.7	1.5	0.3	0.7	0.5	0.5	0.8	0.7	0.8	0.8	0.7	1.1
Other Expenses **19**	26.9	38.4	29.5	13.6	28.7	25.7	20.8	25.9	26.3	25.0	18.9	27.4	34.0
Officers' Compensation **20**	7.4	11.1	15.6	4.0	7.4	7.7	5.0	5.6	3.0	1.8	2.1	3.5	0.6
Operating Margin **21**	2.0	2.2	5.5	•	2.5	7.5	1.7	0.9	0.1	0.3	1.3	•	•
Operating Margin Before Officers' Comp. **22**	9.4	13.3	21.1	3.0	9.9	15.2	6.7	6.5	3.1	2.1	3.3	1.4	0.4

Selected Average Balance Sheet ($ in Thousands)

Net Receivables 23	108	0	8	149	528	1496	4751	6754	16807	40408	42777	215392	715844
Inventories 24	7	0	1	13	49	77	296	495	1158	3385	7806	13670	5386
Net Property, Plant and Equipment 25	49	0	11	102	308	642	1963	2817	8982	14941	25062	64308	192321
Total Assets 26	559	0	59	690	2128	6721	15381	35550	73934	149177	360562	1057729	4797162
Notes and Loans Payable 27	152	0	42	321	681	1761	4350	8957	22007	42457	44801	227062	889586
All Other Liabilities 28	202	0	18	222	580	2260	5154	10505	21748	49097	122573	460622	1919233
Net Worth 29	204	0	-0	147	867	2700	5877	16088	30179	57623	193188	370046	1988343

Selected Financial Ratios (Times to 1)

Current Ratio 30	1.3	•	1.6	1.7	2.1	1.2	1.5	1.1	1.6	1.5	1.5	1.2	1.0
Quick Ratio 31	1.0	•	1.4	1.4	1.6	1.0	1.3	0.8	1.3	1.1	0.9	0.8	0.7
Net Sales to Working Capital 32	13.4	•	21.6	20.3	5.7	17.9	6.9	23.5	6.3	6.3	4.8	13.3	•
Coverage Ratio 33	6.8	4.9	16.9	6.3	12.8	20.6	8.4	5.4	4.7	2.8	4.5	3.9	3.3
Total Asset Turnover 34	1.4	•	5.2	4.9	1.7	1.5	1.4	1.2	1.1	1.0	0.6	0.8	0.6
Inventory Turnover 35	32.6	•	58.3	179.0	21.4	28.7	28.9	28.0	24.5	15.5	10.6	9.9	146.9
Receivables Turnover 36	7.7	•	45.7	20.9	7.2	6.6	5.1	5.9	5.7	4.1	5.0	3.3	5.8
Total Liabilities to Net Worth 37	1.7	•	•	3.7	1.5	1.5	1.6	1.2	1.4	1.6	0.9	1.9	1.4
Current Assets to Working Capital 38	4.2	•	2.6	2.4	1.9	6.1	2.9	7.9	2.7	3.1	3.1	7.3	•
Current Liabilities to Working Capital 39	3.2	•	1.6	1.4	0.9	5.1	1.9	6.9	1.7	2.1	2.1	6.3	•
Working Capital to Net Sales 40	0.1	•	0.0	0.0	0.2	0.1	0.1	0.0	0.2	0.2	0.2	0.1	•
Inventory to Working Capital 41	0.1	•	0.0	0.1	0.1	0.2	0.1	0.4	0.1	0.2	0.3	0.2	•
Total Receipts to Cash Flow 42	3.5	2.6	3.1	7.8	3.2	2.9	4.1	3.4	3.4	3.9	4.5	3.4	2.9
Cost of Goods to Cash Flow 43	1.0	0.5	0.6	5.5	0.9	1.6	1.1	1.2	1.4	1.7	1.7	0.6	0.7
Cash Flow to Total Debt 44	0.7	•	1.6	0.8	0.9	0.8	0.6	0.6	0.5	0.4	0.3	0.4	0.4

Selected Financial Factors (in Percentages)

Debt Ratio 45	63.5	•	100.7	78.6	59.3	59.8	61.8	54.7	59.2	61.4	46.4	65.0	58.6
Return on Total Assets 46	10.4	•	41.8	10.1	15.4	20.3	11.5	9.6	8.6	5.8	5.5	6.2	3.6
Return on Equity Before Income Taxes 47	24.3	•	•	39.7	34.8	48.2	26.5	17.3	16.5	9.6	8.0	13.2	6.0
Return on Equity After Income Taxes 48	21.0	•	•	36.6	32.7	46.7	22.8	14.9	12.8	6.3	5.9	8.2	3.5
Profit Margin (Before Income Tax) 49	6.2	4.5	7.6	1.7	8.2	12.9	7.2	6.7	6.3	3.7	7.0	5.8	3.9
Profit Margin (After Income Tax) 50	5.4	3.4	7.5	1.6	7.7	12.5	6.1	5.7	4.9	2.4	5.1	3.6	2.3

Table II

Corporations with Net Income

MANAGEMENT, SCIENTIFIC, AND TECHNICAL CONSULTING SERVICES

MONEY AMOUNTS AND SIZE OF ASSETS IN THOUSANDS OF DOLLARS

Item Description for Accounting Period 7/06 Through 6/07	Total	Zero Assets	Under 500	500 to 1,000	1,000 to 5,000	5,000 to 10,000	10,000 to 25,000	25,000 to 50,000	50,000 to 100,000	100,000 to 250,000	250,000 to 500,000	500,000 to 2,500,000	2,500,000 and over
Number of Enterprises 1	135721	24981	102884	3557	3197	512	342	97	69	38	•	21	•
Revenues ($ in Thousands)													
Net Sales 2	146963457	3930304	34616356	17194749	14768102	6313187	8511023	4980640	6780354	6851270	•	18849366	•
Interest 3	1019512	5465	39281	11573	37892	7941	19243	20904	25629	55980	•	362786	•
Rents 4	57135	232	733	1380	1176	199	1517	1704	3186	4755	•	14086	•
Royalties 5	833029	0	698	13	36378	0	0	91	186869	5287	•	599123	•
Other Portfolio Income 6	639812	43835	19247	20891	91618	5304	71270	16502	46589	34372	•	203798	•
Other Receipts 7	4150844	51520	900278	490401	589411	359487	298826	279443	206542	151984	•	355793	•
Total Receipts 8	153663789	4031356	35576593	17719007	15524577	6686118	8901879	5299284	7249169	7103648	•	20384952	•
Average Total Receipts 9	1132	161	346	4981	4856	13059	26029	54632	105060	186938	•	970712	•
Operating Costs/Operating Income (%)													
Cost of Operations 10	28.9	18.3	16.3	72.1	25.9	23.9	40.2	33.9	36.2	31.2	•	14.5	•
Salaries and Wages 11	23.4	16.6	17.0	8.9	24.2	25.3	21.4	24.7	22.0	26.3	•	41.3	•
Taxes Paid 12	2.7	2.7	2.5	1.2	2.4	3.6	2.8	2.8	2.6	3.2	•	3.3	•
Interest Paid 13	0.9	0.8	0.3	0.3	0.4	0.4	0.8	1.0	1.3	1.4	•	2.0	•
Depreciation 14	0.9	0.9	0.6	0.3	0.9	0.8	1.2	1.1	1.2	0.9	•	1.3	•
Amortization and Depletion 15	0.4	0.2	0.1	0.1	0.1	0.0	0.1	0.2	0.6	0.6	•	1.1	•
Pensions and Other Deferred Comp. 16	1.5	1.0	1.8	0.6	1.1	1.1	1.4	1.0	1.4	0.7	•	2.4	•
Employee Benefits 17	1.8	1.6	0.7	0.3	1.3	1.9	2.2	2.0	3.0	5.3	•	3.6	•
Advertising 18	0.9	0.5	1.6	0.3	0.7	0.4	0.5	0.8	0.7	0.6	•	0.6	•
Other Expenses 19	25.0	27.2	28.6	11.2	27.0	22.7	18.1	23.3	25.0	24.0	•	26.1	•
Officers' Compensation 20	7.1	10.6	17.2	3.8	6.7	8.0	4.7	5.8	2.6	1.5	•	4.0	•
Operating Margin 21	6.4	19.5	13.2	0.9	9.3	11.9	6.6	3.5	3.6	4.3	•	•	•
Operating Margin Before Officers' Comp. 22	13.5	30.1	30.5	4.6	15.9	19.9	11.3	9.3	6.1	5.8	•	3.8	•

Selected Average Balance Sheet ($ in Thousands)

Net Receivables 23	153	0	7	182	617	1912	4857	7625	19049	49312	251633	•
Inventories 24	8	0	1	19	69	104	333	634	1441	1803	15821	•
Net Property, Plant and Equipment 25	58	0	9	93	270	735	2200	3100	8184	10565	67681	•
Total Assets 26	676	0	59	702	2130	6763	15528	35976	74982	144811	1041732	•
Notes and Loans Payable 27	155	0	21	294	349	1789	3866	8058	21497	32012	215010	•
All Other Liabilities 28	266	0	15	243	558	2094	4705	12532	24696	43882	485724	•
Net Worth 29	255	0	23	165	1223	2880	6957	15386	28789	68917	340997	•

Selected Financial Ratios (Times to 1)

Current Ratio 30	1.3	•	2.2	1.7	2.4	1.3	1.6	1.2	1.5	1.6	1.1	•
Quick Ratio 31	1.0	•	1.9	1.3	1.9	1.0	1.3	0.8	1.2	1.4	0.8	•
Net Sales to Working Capital 32	13.6	•	15.7	26.0	5.5	16.1	7.2	21.2	8.0	5.8	32.0	•
Coverage Ratio 33	13.1	30.3	63.7	16.0	36.3	44.6	15.4	10.6	9.5	6.5	5.0	•
Total Asset Turnover 34	1.6	•	5.7	6.9	2.2	1.8	1.6	1.4	1.3	1.2	0.9	•
Inventory Turnover 35	37.4	•	69.5	186.7	17.5	28.2	30.1	27.4	24.7	31.2	8.2	•
Receivables Turnover 36	7.8	•	47.6	22.7	8.2	6.2	5.8	6.4	6.3	4.2	3.6	•
Total Liabilities to Net Worth 37	1.6	•	1.6	3.3	0.7	1.3	1.2	1.3	1.6	1.1	2.1	•
Current Assets to Working Capital 38	4.2	•	1.8	2.5	1.7	4.9	2.7	6.8	3.0	2.5	16.9	•
Current Liabilities to Working Capital 39	3.2	•	0.8	1.5	0.7	3.9	1.7	5.8	2.0	1.5	15.9	•
Working Capital to Net Sales 40	0.1	•	0.1	0.0	0.2	0.1	0.1	0.0	0.1	0.2	0.0	•
Inventory to Working Capital 41	0.1	•	0.0	0.1	0.1	0.2	0.1	0.3	0.1	0.0	0.6	•
Total Receipts to Cash Flow 42	3.1	2.2	2.6	7.8	2.8	3.9	3.9	3.4	3.1	3.4	3.3	•
Cost of Goods to Cash Flow 43	0.9	0.4	0.4	5.6	0.7	1.6	0.7	1.1	1.1	1.1	0.5	•
Cash Flow to Total Debt 44	0.8	•	3.7	1.1	1.8	1.1	0.7	0.7	0.7	0.7	0.4	•

Selected Financial Factors (in Percentages)

Debt Ratio 45	62.3	•	61.3	76.5	42.6	57.4	55.2	57.2	61.6	52.4	67.3	•
Return on Total Assets 46	19.1	•	93.2	28.7	32.0	33.2	19.2	15.5	15.6	11.7	8.8	•
Return on Equity Before Income Taxes 47	46.7	•	237.1	114.7	54.2	76.1	40.0	32.8	36.3	20.7	21.6	•
Return on Equity After Income Taxes 48	42.2	•	235.0	110.3	52.0	74.5	35.6	29.3	30.4	16.5	14.6	•
Profit Margin (Before Income Tax) 49	11.0	22.0	16.0	3.9	14.4	17.8	11.2	9.8	10.6	7.9	8.2	•
Profit Margin (After Income Tax) 50	9.9	20.7	15.9	3.8	13.8	17.4	10.0	8.8	8.9	6.3	5.5	•

346

Table I

Corporations with and without Net Income

SCIENTIFIC RESEARCH AND DEVELOPMENT SERVICES

MONEY AMOUNTS AND SIZE OF ASSETS IN THOUSANDS OF DOLLARS

Item Description for Accounting Period 7/06 Through 6/07		Total	Zero Assets	Under 500	500 to 1,000	1,000 to 5,000	5,000 to 10,000	10,000 to 25,000	25,000 to 50,000	50,000 to 100,000	100,000 to 250,000	250,000 to 500,000	500,000 to 2,500,000	2,500,000 and over
Number of Enterprises	1	13091	972	8338	1048	1536	450	346	172	112	62	29	22	4
Revenues ($ in Thousands)														
Net Sales	2	36830438	481894	4421491	2269444	2796297	1935853	1628360	2338978	2459765	2072911	3542857	5083932	7798656
Interest	3	1537079	25616	2468	8064	42280	55996	122728	134011	213449	247005	222324	314175	148964
Rents	4	22119	0	40	0	2500	35	550	584	47	923	6629	10	10801
Royalties	5	1812098	542	0	0	62325	9099	19871	14332	49769	93785	60539	1092623	409212
Other Portfolio Income	6	1315035	26810	6984	1272	19616	11584	18805	100490	46017	37974	466156	70560	508769
Other Receipts	7	3752126	20727	175255	29721	640821	316176	173970	136538	177132	312148	97657	1232766	439214
Total Receipts	8	45268895	555589	4606238	2308501	3563839	2328743	1964284	2724933	2946179	2764746	4396162	7794066	9315616
Average Total Receipts	9	3458	572	552	2203	2320	5175	5677	15843	26305	44593	151592	354276	2328904
Operating Costs/Operating Income (%)														
Cost of Operations	10	28.6	21.3	9.5	37.3	26.9	33.0	34.4	37.4	34.7	24.8	28.2	24.6	34.7
Salaries and Wages	11	33.3	72.2	25.3	13.8	47.1	42.6	47.4	37.7	43.3	38.3	37.6	37.4	20.2
Taxes Paid	12	4.1	5.3	3.6	3.9	6.7	6.8	6.0	5.2	5.5	4.8	3.4	4.7	1.3
Interest Paid	13	3.6	4.1	0.3	1.5	2.4	3.2	4.7	2.9	3.0	4.1	3.9	5.0	5.5
Depreciation	14	4.0	4.5	0.7	1.5	4.0	4.8	5.8	5.1	4.8	6.2	4.4	6.5	2.9
Amortization and Depletion	15	3.2	5.0	0.3	0.6	2.6	1.2	2.7	4.6	3.7	8.8	3.2	3.6	4.0
Pensions and Other Deferred Comp.	16	1.8	0.2	2.5	0.8	1.3	2.1	1.3	1.0	2.2	1.8	0.5	4.6	1.0
Employee Benefits	17	3.7	4.2	1.9	1.3	6.2	5.3	5.9	3.7	5.7	4.8	4.4	5.9	0.9
Advertising	18	1.5	1.8	2.4	0.2	0.8	2.0	1.1	1.9	3.7	1.4	1.2	1.3	1.2
Other Expenses	19	54.5	123.6	45.3	41.1	63.7	59.5	94.2	69.5	78.3	80.1	56.0	53.0	28.0
Officers' Compensation	20	6.6	31.5	10.4	8.0	14.7	9.3	10.8	8.4	7.8	6.2	4.9	3.3	0.3
Operating Margin	21	•	•	•	•	•	•	•	•	•	•	•	•	•
Operating Margin Before Officers' Comp.	22	•	•	8.1	•	•	•	•	•	•	•	•	•	0.2

Selected Average Balance Sheet ($ in Thousands)

Item													
Net Receivables 23	836	0	2	135	477	1221	1401	3384	6486	7938	32032	86505	1096068
Inventories 24	172	0	0	29	40	319	393	547	1007	2424	5983	14909	256376
Net Property, Plant and Equipment 25	761	0	14	114	271	993	1657	3546	5919	15827	33724	145993	461159
Total Assets 26	7372	0	84	720	2219	6993	15645	35008	69024	152302	339857	915211	7473649
Notes and Loans Payable 27	1912	0	84	515	966	1198	3142	4804	7834	21685	115644	291219	1967118
All Other Liabilities 28	1927	0	25	254	1015	2057	3519	9093	19070	33654	74288	202851	2160708
Net Worth 29	3533	0	-25	-49	237	3738	8984	21111	42120	96963	149925	421140	3345823

Selected Financial Ratios (Times to 1)

Item													
Current Ratio 30	2.2	•	1.0	1.3	1.2	2.4	2.7	3.3	3.3	3.8	2.6	2.7	1.3
Quick Ratio 31	1.5	•	0.9	1.2	1.0	2.0	2.2	2.5	2.4	2.5	1.6	1.5	1.0
Net Sales to Working Capital 32	1.4	•	446.3	20.1	7.4	1.5	2.0	0.7	0.8	0.7	0.5	0.9	4.0
Coverage Ratio 33	•	•	6.8	•	•	•	•	•	•	•	1.7	•	5.1
Total Asset Turnover 34	0.4	•	6.3	3.0	0.8	0.6	0.3	0.4	0.3	0.2	0.4	0.3	0.3
Inventory Turnover 35	4.7	•	491.8	28.1	12.4	4.4	4.1	9.3	7.6	3.4	5.8	3.8	2.6
Receivables Turnover 36	3.6	•	172.0	12.3	3.8	4.0	3.4	4.4	3.9	3.8	3.8	3.0	2.0
Total Liabilities to Net Worth 37	1.1	•	•	8.3	0.9	0.7	0.7	0.6	0.6	1.3	1.2	1.2	1.2
Current Assets to Working Capital 38	1.8	•	37.4	4.5	6.1	1.7	1.6	1.4	1.4	1.4	0.6	1.6	4.5
Current Liabilities to Working Capital 39	0.8	•	36.4	3.5	5.1	0.7	0.6	0.4	0.4	0.4	0.6	0.6	3.5
Working Capital to Net Sales 40	0.7	•	0.0	0.0	0.1	0.7	1.3	1.2	1.4	2.0	0.9	1.1	0.3
Inventory to Working Capital 41	0.1	•	0.2	0.3	0.2	0.1	0.1	0.0	0.3	0.0	0.0	0.1	0.5
Total Receipts to Cash Flow 42	4.0	•	2.4	3.8	15.8	201.0	11354.3	0.0	0.0	4.2	6.3	2.0	2.3
Cost of Goods to Cash Flow 43	1.2	•	0.2	1.4	4.3	66.3	4247.8	•	•	1.0	1.8	0.5	0.8
Cash Flow to Total Debt 44	0.2	•	2.0	0.8	0.1	0.0	0.0	•	0.0	0.1	0.6	0.5	0.2

Selected Financial Factors (in Percentages)

Item													
Debt Ratio 45	52.1	•	130.3	106.8	89.3	46.5	42.6	39.7	39.0	36.3	55.9	54.0	55.2
Return on Total Assets 46	13.6	•	•	•	•	•	•	•	•	•	•	2.1	7.3
Return on Equity Before Income Taxes 47	•	•	•	362.6	•	•	•	•	•	•	•	1.9	13.2
Return on Equity After Income Taxes 48	•	•	•	365.0	•	•	•	•	•	•	•	•	11.5
Profit Margin (Before Income Tax) 49	1.8	•	1.8	•	•	•	•	•	•	•	•	3.4	22.6
Profit Margin (After Income Tax) 50	1.8	•	1.8	•	•	•	•	•	•	•	•	•	19.7

Table II
Corporations with Net Income

SCIENTIFIC RESEARCH AND DEVELOPMENT SERVICES

MONEY AMOUNTS AND SIZE OF ASSETS IN THOUSANDS OF DOLLARS

Item Description for Accounting Period 7/06 Through 6/07	Total	Zero Assets	Under 500	500 to 1,000	1,000 to 5,000	5,000 to 10,000	10,000 to 25,000	25,000 to 50,000	50,000 to 100,000	100,000 to 250,000	250,000 to 500,000	500,000 to 2,500,000	2,500,000 and over
Number of Enterprises **1**	6490	428	4942	268	498	185	79	29	22	11	•	12	•
Revenues ($ in Thousands)													
Net Sales **2**	25596864	25138	3921274	1123151	1392926	1574096	972810	1386280	1258103	899187	•	3083289	•
Interest **3**	416041	1114	14	965	3911	7524	19718	14731	21661	38924	•	127100	•
Rents **4**	13622	0	0	0	2228	0	303	0	0	0	•	7	•
Royalties **5**	1420693	0	0	0	53480	33	10032	7621	852	57184	•	1040553	•
Other Portfolio Income **6**	1155214	25800	0	0	13367	11083	16397	82516	43324	2375	•	52026	•
Other Receipts **7**	2756562	867	128201	18513	584403	251683	84962	64460	107785	41080	•	1019462	•
Total Receipts **8**	31358996	52919	4049489	1142629	2050315	1844419	1104222	1555608	1431725	1038750	•	5322437	•
Average Total Receipts **9**	4832	124	819	4264	4117	9970	13977	53642	65078	94432	•	443536	•
Operating Costs/Operating Income (%)													
Cost of Operations **10**	29.5	3.7	7.5	32.9	35.7	32.3	32.3	36.5	35.3	31.9	•	29.2	•
Salaries and Wages **11**	23.5	32.7	22.6	13.1	31.0	26.1	20.8	18.6	23.6	17.0	•	37.7	•
Taxes Paid **12**	3.0	4.0	3.0	2.9	4.5	4.6	3.1	3.9	3.5	2.2	•	5.3	•
Interest Paid **13**	2.6	3.7	0.1	0.7	0.7	0.6	0.7	1.1	0.3	0.9	•	4.5	•
Depreciation **14**	2.8	3.9	0.4	0.4	2.7	2.0	3.3	1.7	2.5	2.4	•	7.2	•
Amortization and Depletion **15**	1.4	0.0	0.0	0.5	0.2	0.0	0.5	0.1	0.6	1.9	•	2.9	•
Pensions and Other Deferred Comp. **16**	1.3	0.4	2.4	0.4	1.6	2.4	2.0	1.3	3.4	0.3	•	0.9	•
Employee Benefits **17**	2.6	1.5	1.8	0.4	6.2	4.5	3.1	1.9	3.8	1.4	•	5.7	•
Advertising **18**	1.1	0.3	2.6	0.1	0.3	0.9	0.3	0.3	2.9	0.2	•	0.3	•
Other Expenses **19**	31.7	73.9	40.8	33.1	34.4	24.8	27.5	22.9	19.9	22.6	•	42.9	•
Officers' Compensation **20**	3.7	2.0	8.4	5.7	12.6	4.3	4.4	3.3	2.6	2.4	•	3.3	•
Operating Margin **21**	•	•	10.4	9.8	•	•	2.1	8.3	1.4	16.8	•	•	•
Operating Margin Before Officers' Comp. **22**	0.7	•	18.7	15.5	1.8	•	6.5	11.6	4.0	19.2	•	•	•

Selected Average Balance Sheet ($ in Thousands)

Net Receivables 23	1213	0	2	227	699	1462	3044	12033	18708	23632	103530
Inventories 24	235	0	0	0	24	401	460	804	2062	4424	19909
Net Property, Plant and Equipment 25	891	0	11	50	318	894	2960	6071	7043	16970	200251
Total Assets 26	7923	0	90	634	1792	7036	16870	37258	68981	171292	968333
Notes and Loans Payable 27	1923	0	4	392	662	1133	2200	3959	2527	12555	239168
All Other Liabilities 28	2247	0	12	196	664	1991	3306	12763	24223	34904	247627
Net Worth 29	3752	0	74	46	466	3911	11365	20537	42230	123834	481537

Selected Financial Ratios (Times to 1)

Current Ratio 30	1.6	•	4.7	1.7	1.2	2.0	2.3	2.2	2.6	4.1	2.1
Quick Ratio 31	1.2	•	4.5	1.7	1.1	1.6	1.9	1.7	2.1	2.5	1.4
Net Sales to Working Capital 32	3.3	•	17.8	18.2	11.3	3.9	3.4	2.4	2.0	1.1	1.3
Coverage Ratio 33	8.8	24.0	220.6	17.9	25.9	23.8	19.5	23.6	44.4	37.3	8.2
Total Asset Turnover 34	0.5	•	8.8	6.6	1.6	1.2	1.3	0.7	0.8	0.5	0.3
Inventory Turnover 35	4.9	•	10312.8	11916.6	41.1	6.9	21.7	8.6	9.8	5.9	3.8
Receivables Turnover 36	3.6	•	232.3	13.8	5.2	5.1	4.4	5.2	4.0	3.2	•
Total Liabilities to Net Worth 37	1.1	•	0.2	12.7	2.8	0.8	0.8	0.5	0.6	0.4	1.0
Current Assets to Working Capital 38	2.5	•	1.3	2.4	5.0	2.0	1.7	1.8	1.6	1.3	1.9
Current Liabilities to Working Capital 39	1.5	•	0.3	1.4	4.0	1.0	0.7	0.8	0.6	0.3	0.9
Working Capital to Net Sales 40	0.3	•	0.1	0.1	0.1	0.3	0.3	0.4	0.5	0.9	0.8
Inventory to Working Capital 41	0.2	•	•	0.0	0.1	0.2	0.1	0.1	0.0	0.1	0.1
Total Receipts to Cash Flow 42	2.2	1.9	2.0	2.5	2.2	3.1	2.5	2.7	3.8	1.9	1.4
Cost of Goods to Cash Flow 43	0.6	0.1	0.1	0.8	0.8	1.0	0.9	0.9	1.4	0.6	0.4
Cash Flow to Total Debt 44	0.4	•	24.6	2.8	0.9	0.9	1.1	0.8	0.6	0.9	0.4

Selected Financial Factors (in Percentages)

Debt Ratio 45	52.6	•	18.0	92.7	74.0	44.4	44.9	32.6	38.8	27.7	50.3
Return on Total Assets 46	11.5	•	120.9	80.4	28.2	18.5	27.7	11.8	12.8	16.3	9.9
Return on Equity Before Income Taxes 47	21.6	•	146.7	1040.0	104.2	31.9	47.7	16.7	20.5	21.9	17.4
Return on Equity After Income Taxes 48	18.8	•	146.4	1030.1	99.1	27.4	40.5	15.1	17.6	20.0	13.8
Profit Margin (Before Income Tax) 49	20.5	84.5	13.6	11.5	17.4	14.7	20.5	15.4	15.1	33.2	32.6
Profit Margin (After Income Tax) 50	17.9	83.4	13.6	11.4	16.5	12.6	17.4	14.0	13.0	30.4	25.9

Table I

Corporations with and without Net Income

ADVERTISING AND RELATED SERVICES

MONEY AMOUNTS AND SIZE OF ASSETS IN THOUSANDS OF DOLLARS

Item Description for Accounting Period 7/06 Through 6/07		Total	Zero Assets	Under 500	500 to 1,000	1,000 to 5,000	5,000 to 10,000	10,000 to 25,000	25,000 to 50,000	50,000 to 100,000	100,000 to 250,000	250,000 to 500,000	500,000 to 2,500,000	2,500,000 and over
Number of Enterprises	1	47226	8274	35498	983	1821	357	161	55	32	22	7	10	6
Revenues ($ in Thousands)														
Net Sales	2	76710915	1215985	17785174	1401512	10205646	5451960	3967378	4075818	2911239	2652734	3234695	7160495	16648280
Interest	3	1326990	17707	5202	5047	23409	14975	21549	11810	11895	14972	4916	100240	1095268
Rents	4	74726	0	1559	1809	1080	35	0	0	384	66	0	1457	68336
Royalties	5	94772	7201	0	0	48	0	0	36107	0	76	14023	18329	18989
Other Portfolio Income	6	698453	5010	25849	41042	49607	2073	3082	30656	18378	18888	808	58623	444436
Other Receipts	7	963411	-28954	213057	8147	51169	63335	18032	33583	74580	58419	36365	87095	348582
Total Receipts	8	79869267	1216949	18030841	1457557	10330959	5532378	4010041	4187974	3016476	2745155	3290807	7426239	18623891
Average Total Receipts	9	1691	147	508	1483	5673	15497	24907	76145	94265	124780	470115	742624	3103982
Operating Costs/Operating Income (%)														
Cost of Operations	10	38.6	32.3	33.7	47.3	61.9	66.6	49.4	54.0	48.6	52.9	70.1	37.6	4.1
Salaries and Wages	11	20.5	21.0	9.2	17.1	13.6	14.2	15.5	10.6	16.7	17.0	12.3	27.1	42.9
Taxes Paid	12	2.4	1.7	2.2	2.6	1.8	1.4	1.6	1.2	1.8	2.5	1.4	2.7	4.1
Interest Paid	13	3.3	3.3	0.5	2.1	0.7	0.4	0.3	0.7	1.5	2.7	1.2	4.6	10.7
Depreciation	14	1.3	1.4	0.6	2.4	0.7	0.8	0.7	0.7	1.1	1.4	1.3	2.4	2.2
Amortization and Depletion	15	1.1	0.6	0.1	0.4	0.4	0.1	0.2	0.3	1.9	1.7	0.4	1.8	3.0
Pensions and Other Deferred Comp.	16	0.7	0.0	1.0	1.6	0.5	0.3	0.4	0.2	0.5	0.5	0.7	0.2	1.0
Employee Benefits	17	1.3	2.9	1.2	1.5	0.9	0.6	0.8	1.0	1.3	1.3	1.0	1.9	2.0
Advertising	18	4.0	14.4	5.6	6.0	0.8	0.3	14.3	13.7	2.2	6.4	0.2	4.3	0.3
Other Expenses	19	21.9	33.0	31.7	22.2	10.9	11.1	9.8	13.1	22.6	13.9	8.1	15.4	32.4
Officers' Compensation	20	4.8	2.3	9.7	9.0	6.0	2.5	3.3	1.6	1.8	2.9	1.7	1.1	3.4
Operating Margin	21	0.1	•	4.5	•	1.7	1.6	3.6	3.0	•	•	1.7	1.1	•
Operating Margin Before Officers' Comp.	22	4.8	•	14.2	•	7.8	4.2	6.9	4.6	1.7	3.4	3.4	2.2	•

Selected Average Balance Sheet ($ in Thousands)

Net Receivables 23	595	0	14	122	685	2551	6313	12865	19207	30935	118216	194176	3252854
Inventories 24	38	0	2	123	136	64	147	1729	751	1219	3836	8081	173672
Net Property, Plant and Equipment 25	128	0	15	294	191	561	1139	5050	6222	7116	35808	93830	447400
Total Assets 26	2261	0	74	821	2089	6614	15177	34708	72375	159072	307169	1001477	12472358
Notes and Loans Payable 27	388	0	43	165	521	1225	1312	5485	16912	41741	106716	306334	1580684
All Other Liabilities 28	1193	0	37	313	1100	3601	9505	18741	31364	62878	142038	332246	7030934
Net Worth 29	679	-6	0	344	468	1788	4360	10483	24099	54454	58414	362897	3860741

Selected Financial Ratios (Times to 1)

Current Ratio 30	0.9	•	1.1	1.1	1.3	1.5	1.3	1.4	0.9	1.3	0.9	1.4	0.8
Quick Ratio 31	0.7	•	0.9	0.9	1.1	1.3	1.2	1.0	0.7	1.0	0.8	1.0	0.6
Net Sales to Working Capital 32	•	•	139.7	26.6	16.3	9.5	8.8	11.2	•	7.1	•	6.7	•
Coverage Ratio 33	2.3	•	13.2	•	5.1	9.0	16.5	9.2	3.4	1.1	3.8	2.0	1.6
Total Asset Turnover 34	0.7	•	6.8	1.7	2.7	2.3	1.6	2.1	1.3	0.8	1.5	0.7	0.2
Inventory Turnover 35	16.5	•	75.8	5.5	25.5	159.6	83.1	23.1	58.9	52.4	84.4	33.3	0.7
Receivables Turnover 36	2.6	•	37.2	7.4	9.0	8.0	4.0	6.0	4.7	4.4	4.0	3.9	0.8
Total Liabilities to Net Worth 37	2.3	•	•	1.4	3.5	2.7	2.5	2.3	2.0	1.9	4.3	1.8	2.2
Current Assets to Working Capital 38	•	•	13.2	8.3	4.6	3.0	4.4	3.8	•	4.5	•	3.5	•
Current Liabilities to Working Capital 39	•	•	12.2	7.3	3.6	2.0	3.4	2.8	•	3.5	•	2.5	•
Working Capital to Net Sales 40	•	•	0.0	0.0	0.1	0.1	0.1	0.1	0.1	0.1	0.1	0.1	•
Inventory to Working Capital 41	•	•	0.6	1.0	0.5	0.0	0.0	0.2	0.0	0.0	•	0.1	•
Total Receipts to Cash Flow 42	4.6	7.6	2.9	11.8	9.2	8.4	8.2	6.1	4.4	8.2	11.2	5.9	3.3
Cost of Goods to Cash Flow 43	1.8	2.5	1.0	5.6	5.7	5.6	4.1	3.3	2.1	4.3	7.9	2.2	0.1
Cash Flow to Total Debt 44	0.2	•	2.2	0.3	0.4	0.4	0.3	0.5	0.4	0.1	0.2	0.2	0.1

Selected Financial Factors (in Percentages)

Debt Ratio 45	70.0	•	108.0	58.2	77.6	73.0	71.3	69.8	66.7	65.8	81.0	63.8	69.0
Return on Total Assets 46	5.5	•	43.2	•	9.8	8.0	8.1	13.8	6.6	2.3	7.0	6.5	3.9
Return on Equity Before Income Taxes 47	10.5	•	•	•	35.1	26.4	26.5	40.8	14.1	0.7	27.1	8.9	5.0
Return on Equity After Income Taxes 48	8.7	•	•	•	33.5	24.5	24.9	39.0	10.8	•	19.9	6.8	3.4
Profit Margin (Before Income Tax) 49	4.4	•	5.9	•	2.9	3.1	4.7	5.8	3.7	0.3	3.4	4.5	6.9
Profit Margin (After Income Tax) 50	3.7	•	5.9	•	2.8	2.9	4.4	5.5	2.9	•	2.5	3.5	4.8

Table II

Corporations with Net Income

ADVERTISING AND RELATED SERVICES

MONEY AMOUNTS AND SIZE OF ASSETS IN THOUSANDS OF DOLLARS

Item Description for Accounting Period 7/06 Through 6/07	Total	Zero Assets	Under 500	500 to 1,000	1,000 to 5,000	5,000 to 10,000	10,000 to 25,000	25,000 to 50,000	50,000 to 100,000	100,000 to 250,000	250,000 to 500,000	500,000 to 2,500,000	2,500,000 and over
Number of Enterprises 1	26866	2625	22127	332	1326	218	138	45	26	14	•	7	•

Revenues ($ in Thousands)

	Total	Zero Assets	Under 500	500 to 1,000	1,000 to 5,000	5,000 to 10,000	10,000 to 25,000	25,000 to 50,000	50,000 to 100,000	100,000 to 250,000	250,000 to 500,000	500,000 to 2,500,000	2,500,000 and over
Net Sales 2	60367500	916046	14012444	572095	8768573	4067473	3714142	3739929	2438453	1546584	4684710	•	•
Interest 3	1068211	8652	4076	4145	16821	11006	18485	6950	11263	11305	89711	•	•
Rents 4	72234	0	213	1809	0	35	0	0	384	0	1457	•	•
Royalties 5	90822	7201	0	0	48	0	0	32163	0	76	18329	•	•
Other Portfolio Income 6	617023	3572	23712	8178	47765	479	3082	29621	18378	16223	58093	•	•
Other Receipts 7	774729	1477	110475	677	30155	18258	23576	29961	74132	53943	83231	•	•
Total Receipts 8	62990519	936948	14150920	586904	8863362	4097251	3759285	3838624	2542610	1628131	4935531	•	•
Average Total Receipts 9	2345	357	640	1768	6684	18795	27241	85303	97793	116295	705076	•	•

Operating Costs/Operating Income (%)

	Total	Zero Assets	Under 500	500 to 1,000	1,000 to 5,000	5,000 to 10,000	10,000 to 25,000	25,000 to 50,000	50,000 to 100,000	100,000 to 250,000	250,000 to 500,000	500,000 to 2,500,000	2,500,000 and over
Cost of Operations 10	38.1	36.0	31.5	34.7	63.9	63.6	51.4	52.1	42.6	49.6	31.7	•	•
Salaries and Wages 11	19.4	8.8	8.7	25.5	11.7	13.3	15.7	9.8	18.6	20.4	26.3	•	•
Taxes Paid 12	2.3	1.0	2.1	2.7	1.6	1.4	1.7	1.2	1.9	2.1	2.3	•	•
Interest Paid 13	3.0	1.8	0.4	0.1	0.5	0.2	0.1	0.7	1.2	2.2	3.2	•	•
Depreciation 14	1.2	1.2	0.5	0.8	0.5	0.6	0.6	0.6	1.1	1.4	2.4	•	•
Amortization and Depletion 15	1.0	0.3	0.1	0.0	0.1	0.1	0.1	0.2	1.7	1.4	1.8	•	•
Pensions and Other Deferred Comp. 16	0.7	•	0.9	2.1	0.5	0.3	0.4	0.2	0.5	0.8	0.2	•	•
Employee Benefits 17	1.1	2.7	1.0	2.2	0.7	0.6	0.8	0.9	1.4	1.3	2.4	•	•
Advertising 18	3.2	16.3	1.7	0.0	0.3	0.3	11.5	14.8	2.6	5.3	6.6	•	•
Other Expenses 19	21.8	24.2	35.7	16.7	8.8	10.0	9.1	12.5	25.1	13.3	17.5	•	•
Officers' Compensation 20	4.6	2.0	9.0	13.3	5.5	2.4	2.9	1.4	1.9	2.6	1.5	•	•
Operating Margin 21	3.7	5.7	8.5	1.8	6.0	7.2	5.7	5.6	1.3	•	4.2	•	•
Operating Margin Before Officers' Comp. 22	8.3	7.7	17.5	15.1	11.4	9.7	8.6	7.0	3.2	2.2	5.7	•	•

Selected Average Balance Sheet ($ in Thousands)

	•	•	•	•	•	•	•	•	•	•	•
Net Receivables 23	928	0	14	210	665	3248	6986	14435	19479	29664	232614
Inventories 24	56	0	1	57	180	86	109	1726	728	295	3606
Net Property, Plant and Equipment 25	164	0	15	191	143	583	770	5885	4789	8132	78001
Total Assets 26	3149	0	79	794	1985	6771	14986	34168	71390	158517	1014658
Notes and Loans Payable 27	394	0	30	154	359	731	780	5492	13832	40071	125426
All Other Liabilities 28	1743	0	42	279	1124	4251	10158	19429	34152	70139	352372
Net Worth 29	1012	0	7	362	501	1788	4048	9247	23406	48307	536860

Selected Financial Ratios (Times to 1)

	•	•	•	•	•	•	•	•	•	•	•
Current Ratio 30	0.9	•	1.0	2.1	1.4	1.4	1.3	1.3	1.0	1.4	1.4
Quick Ratio 31	0.7	•	0.9	2.1	1.1	1.3	1.2	1.0	0.8	1.0	1.0
Net Sales to Working Capital 32	•	•	5462.9	5.7	14.3	11.5	9.6	15.7	133.8	5.3	5.0
Coverage Ratio 33	3.8	5.3	26.8	50.8	15.7	36.8	52.2	13.0	5.6	3.2	3.8
Total Asset Turnover 34	0.7	•	8.1	2.2	3.3	2.8	1.8	2.4	1.3	0.7	0.7
Inventory Turnover 35	15.2	•	256.1	10.6	23.5	138.7	126.8	25.1	54.9	185.5	58.8
Receivables Turnover 36	2.5	•	50.2	4.8	10.0	7.8	4.1	5.9	4.9	•	4.1
Total Liabilities to Net Worth 37	2.1	•	10.1	1.2	3.0	2.8	2.7	2.7	2.1	2.3	0.9
Current Assets to Working Capital 38	•	•	433.8	•	1.9	3.5	4.5	4.8	56.2	3.7	3.3
Current Liabilities to Working Capital 39	•	•	432.8	•	0.9	2.5	3.5	3.8	55.2	2.7	2.3
Working Capital to Net Sales 40	•	•	0.0	0.2	0.1	0.1	0.1	0.1	0.0	0.2	0.2
Inventory to Working Capital 41	•	•	6.5	•	•	0.5	0.0	0.2	1.1	0.0	0.0
Total Receipts to Cash Flow 42	3.9	3.9	2.4	6.2	7.6	6.5	7.3	5.5	3.6	6.3	4.3
Cost of Goods to Cash Flow 43	1.5	1.4	0.7	2.1	4.9	4.1	3.8	2.8	1.6	3.1	1.4
Cash Flow to Total Debt 44	0.3	•	3.7	0.6	0.6	0.6	0.3	0.6	0.5	0.2	0.3

Selected Financial Factors (in Percentages)

	•	•	•	•	•	•	•	•	•	•	•
Debt Ratio 45	67.9	•	91.0	54.4	74.8	73.6	73.0	72.9	67.2	69.5	47.1
Return on Total Assets 46	8.1	•	79.7	9.8	25.0	22.6	12.6	21.6	9.2	4.9	8.1
Return on Equity Before Income Taxes 47	18.5	•	851.7	21.0	92.7	83.1	45.8	73.8	23.1	10.9	11.3
Return on Equity After Income Taxes 48	16.5	•	847.5	20.2	90.7	79.9	43.9	71.4	19.0	8.9	9.3
Profit Margin (Before Income Tax) 49	8.3	7.9	9.5	4.4	7.0	8.0	6.9	8.2	5.8	4.8	9.1
Profit Margin (After Income Tax) 50	7.4	7.6	9.5	4.2	6.9	7.7	6.6	7.9	4.7	3.9	7.5

OTHER PROFESSIONAL, SCIENTIFIC, AND TECHNICAL SERVICES

Table I
Corporations with and without Net Income

MONEY AMOUNTS AND SIZE OF ASSETS IN THOUSANDS OF DOLLARS

Item Description for Accounting Period 7/06 Through 6/07	Total	Zero Assets	Under 500	500 to 1,000	1,000 to 5,000	5,000 to 10,000	10,000 to 25,000	25,000 to 50,000	50,000 to 100,000	100,000 to 250,000	250,000 to 500,000	500,000 to 2,500,000	2,500,000 and over
Number of Enterprises **1**	92375	19682	66130	3170	2688	266	280	65	38	33	13	9	0
Revenues ($ in Thousands)													
Net Sales **2**	7682966	4011677	27525321	6037877	9485261	3139571	6047937	2307902	3670152	5693526	3298550	5615192	0
Interest **3**	523746	2635	12763	2242	21935	11361	35551	19906	25433	33305	34584	324031	0
Rents **4**	24578	0	3848	0	427	0	797	1754	1403	5492	1254	9603	0
Royalties **5**	106415	0	0	0	121	0	378	0	41	23352	34969	47553	0
Other Portfolio Income **6**	373130	18980	54059	179	57849	13436	72797	9603	4772	11724	31292	98438	0
Other Receipts **7**	1692807	195250	349365	18333	207089	14642	448229	51162	68506	100088	87274	152870	0
Total Receipts **8**	79553642	4228542	27945356	6058631	9772682	3179010	6605689	2390327	3770307	5867487	3487923	6247687	0
Average Total Receipts **9**	861	215	423	1911	3636	11951	23592	36774	99219	177803	268302	694187	•
Operating Costs/Operating Income (%)													
Cost of Operations **10**	29.5	11.2	20.9	19.3	50.4	43.1	38.4	49.1	31.3	51.0	27.1	14.4	•
Salaries and Wages **11**	20.3	11.9	20.4	18.7	17.7	16.2	23.8	21.0	15.9	14.4	32.5	32.1	•
Taxes Paid **12**	3.2	2.1	3.4	3.4	2.5	2.4	3.6	3.7	1.9	2.5	3.6	4.5	•
Interest Paid **13**	1.8	0.6	0.6	1.3	1.3	0.7	1.4	1.6	1.9	1.7	3.9	10.2	•
Depreciation **14**	1.4	1.3	1.2	1.2	1.1	1.4	1.5	1.5	1.7	1.6	1.5	3.0	•
Amortization and Depletion **15**	0.9	0.8	0.2	0.6	0.6	0.3	0.6	1.0	0.6	0.9	4.1	4.1	•
Pensions and Other Deferred Comp. **16**	1.1	0.3	1.3	1.5	0.9	0.4	0.7	0.8	0.4	0.6	1.9	1.7	•
Employee Benefits **17**	1.6	1.0	1.0	1.2	1.0	4.4	2.4	2.8	1.0	2.0	4.0	2.5	•
Advertising **18**	0.8	1.1	0.9	0.8	0.7	1.1	1.1	0.4	0.9	0.4	1.1	0.7	•
Other Expenses **19**	30.1	69.1	29.9	24.4	19.9	24.1	27.5	19.8	46.9	22.8	26.4	35.6	•
Officers' Compensation **20**	7.9	5.6	11.6	22.6	5.0	6.2	3.4	3.9	1.0	1.7	1.7	3.0	•
Operating Margin **21**	1.3	•	8.7	5.2	•	•	•	•	•	0.4	•	•	•
Operating Margin Before Officers' Comp. **22**	9.2	0.5	20.3	27.7	3.9	5.9	•	•	2.1	•	•	•	•

Selected Average Balance Sheet ($ in Thousands)

Net Receivables 23	86	0	7	73	409	2712	3867	9410	20425	30709	49020	143565
Inventories 24	12	0	5	28	44	357	268	431	1056	7967	3458	6658
Net Property, Plant and Equipment 25	60	0	21	149	263	604	2011	2875	7781	16310	25109	103196
Total Assets 26	540	0	83	673	1798	6874	14733	35303	69558	164150	362873	1826027
Notes and Loans Payable 27	267	0	49	790	761	1589	3460	9026	17641	42485	104877	1274417
All Other Liabilities 28	165	0	17	136	868	2307	6116	11423	24147	55868	122846	440127
Net Worth 29	108	0	17	-253	169	2978	5157	14854	27771	65798	135150	111483

Selected Financial Ratios (Times to 1)

Current Ratio 30	1.4	•	2.0	1.8	1.2	2.0	1.4	1.8	1.5	1.2	0.8	1.2
Quick Ratio 31	1.1	•	1.6	1.4	1.1	1.7	1.1	1.3	1.1	0.9	0.5	0.8
Net Sales to Working Capital 32	15.0	•	20.8	14.8	17.8	4.4	9.0	4.4	7.9	18.6	•	13.7
Coverage Ratio 33	3.6	1.5	17.4	5.1	2.5	2.3	4.5	•	0.6	2.9	0.5	1.0
Total Asset Turnover 34	1.5	•	5.0	2.8	2.0	1.7	1.5	1.0	1.4	1.1	0.7	0.3
Inventory Turnover 35	20.1	•	18.5	13.1	40.1	14.2	31.0	40.4	28.6	11.0	19.9	13.5
Receivables Turnover 36	8.6	•	59.5	19.8	11.1	3.5	5.8	3.8	5.6	4.6	4.9	3.9
Total Liabilities to Net Worth 37	4.0	•	3.7	•	9.7	1.3	1.9	1.4	1.5	1.5	1.7	15.4
Current Assets to Working Capital 38	3.7	•	2.0	2.3	5.6	2.0	3.6	2.3	3.1	7.0	•	6.4
Current Liabilities to Working Capital 39	2.7	•	1.0	1.3	4.6	1.0	2.6	1.3	2.1	6.0	•	5.4
Working Capital to Net Sales 40	0.1	•	0.0	0.1	0.1	0.2	0.1	0.2	0.1	0.1	0.1	0.1
Inventory to Working Capital 41	0.2	•	0.3	0.3	0.3	0.2	0.1	0.1	0.1	0.8	0.7	0.1
Total Receipts to Cash Flow 42	3.4	•	3.1	4.2	5.7	4.5	3.7	7.1	2.3	4.2	4.7	3.3
Cost of Goods to Cash Flow 43	1.0	1.5	0.6	0.8	2.9	2.0	1.4	3.5	0.7	2.1	1.3	0.5
Cash Flow to Total Debt 44	0.6	•	2.1	0.5	0.4	0.7	0.6	0.2	1.0	0.4	0.2	0.1

Selected Financial Factors (in Percentages)

Debt Ratio 45	80.0	•	78.9	137.6	90.6	56.7	65.0	57.9	60.1	59.9	62.8	93.9
Return on Total Assets 46	10.3	•	54.6	19.4	6.5	3.0	9.2	•	1.5	5.3	1.4	3.5
Return on Equity Before Income Taxes 47	37.3	•	243.5	•	41.1	3.9	20.4	•	8.7	8.7	•	0.7
Return on Equity After Income Taxes 48	33.7	•	240.3	•	35.6	•	14.6	•	6.3	6.3	•	•
Profit Margin (Before Income Tax) 49	4.9	0.3	10.2	5.5	2.0	1.0	4.9	•	3.3	3.3	•	0.1
Profit Margin (After Income Tax) 50	4.4	0.0	10.1	5.3	1.7	•	3.5	•	2.4	2.4	•	•

351

Table II
Corporations with Net Income

OTHER PROFESSIONAL, SCIENTIFIC, AND TECHNICAL SERVICES

MONEY AMOUNTS AND SIZE OF ASSETS IN THOUSANDS OF DOLLARS

Item Description for Accounting Period 7/06 Through 6/07	Total	Zero Assets	Under 500	500 to 1000	251 to 500	501 to 1,000	1,001 to 5,000	5,001 to 10,000	10,001 to 25,000	25,001 to 50,000	50,001 to 100,000	100,001 to 250,000	250,001 and over
Number of Enterprises **1**	64147	10912	48398	2603	1838	135	183	34	18	17	6	4	0
Revenues ($ in Thousands)													
Net Sales **2**	55793894	1694218	23331406	5798408	7185693	2474069	5164787	1792113	1356058	2702314	1772392	2522435	0
Interest **3**	125870	2121	11610	1841	16636	4009	15722	12203	6248	23785	24677	7017	0
Rents **4**	14591	0	2328	0	427	0	96	1365	1134	3670	0	5571	0
Royalties **5**	25446	0	0	0	0	0	0	0	0	19675	984	4787	0
Other Portfolio Income **6**	265130	18605	54013	179	57722	13436	71184	7931	3670	11212	27174	3	0
Other Receipts **7**	1372949	140569	340872	30189	181004	8439	414706	34592	27533	38899	80546	75603	0
Total Receipts **8**	57597880	1855513	23740229	5830617	7441482	2499953	5666495	1848204	1394643	2799555	1905773	2615416	0
Average Total Receipts **9**	898	170	491	2240	4049	18518	30964	54359	77480	164680	317629	653854	•
Operating Costs/Operating Income (%)													
Cost of Operations **10**	28.8	14.7	20.9	19.3	51.4	43.7	38.9	47.7	36.7	34.2	20.4	16.5	•
Salaries and Wages **11**	19.3	9.8	19.5	17.6	14.6	14.0	22.4	18.2	25.2	21.0	31.6	27.8	•
Taxes Paid **12**	3.2	2.5	3.2	3.3	2.1	2.5	3.4	3.6	3.4	3.5	3.7	6.4	•
Interest Paid **13**	1.1	0.7	0.6	1.3	1.2	0.5	0.8	1.7	1.9	1.4	3.5	3.4	•
Depreciation **14**	1.2	2.2	1.1	1.1	1.0	1.1	0.9	1.3	1.5	1.7	1.4	3.0	•
Amortization and Depletion **15**	0.5	0.3	0.2	0.6	0.6	0.2	0.5	1.0	0.5	0.6	0.8	2.5	•
Pensions and Other Deferred Comp. **16**	1.2	0.7	1.3	1.5	0.9	0.4	0.7	0.9	0.4	1.1	0.6	2.9	•
Employee Benefits **17**	1.5	1.1	0.8	1.1	0.9	5.0	2.1	3.0	1.7	2.8	2.1	2.1	•
Advertising **18**	0.9	2.1	0.8	0.7	0.3	1.0	1.1	0.3	2.2	0.6	1.8	1.5	•
Other Expenses **19**	24.7	31.3	27.9	23.8	16.7	13.9	25.7	17.8	22.0	20.8	36.2	26.7	•
Officers' Compensation **20**	9.1	11.9	11.6	23.0	4.7	6.3	2.9	2.3	1.1	2.2	0.6	1.7	•
Operating Margin **21**	8.6	22.7	12.1	6.8	5.7	11.5	0.6	2.2	3.4	10.0	•	5.5	•
Operating Margin Before Officers' Comp. **22**	17.6	34.6	23.7	29.8	10.4	17.8	3.5	4.5	4.5	12.2	•	•	7.2

Selected Average Balance Sheet ($ in Thousands)

Net Receivables 23	82	0	80	480	2878	4521	11256	18843	36828	61289	219622	•
Inventories 24	10	0	27	44	459	301	369	549	1852	3151	11979	•
Net Property, Plant and Equipment 25	53	0	156	251	535	1399	3924	7150	15614	12138	110380	•
Total Assets 26	396	0	675	1749	6931	14436	36822	66610	176921	355417	1169686	•
Notes and Loans Payable 27	126	0	387	715	951	2708	11359	15631	23865	108551	322006	•
All Other Liabilities 28	132	0	140	760	2739	7066	14090	17797	58491	104553	421702	•
Net Worth 29	139	0	148	274	3241	4663	11373	33182	94565	142314	425978	•

Selected Financial Ratios (Times to 1)

Current Ratio 30	1.5	•	2.2	1.9	1.3	2.3	1.4	1.5	2.2	1.4	1.1	1.0
Quick Ratio 31	1.2	•	1.8	1.6	1.1	1.9	1.1	1.1	1.7	1.1	0.8	0.9
Net Sales to Working Capital 32	13.8	•	18.8	15.0	14.8	6.0	10.3	7.9	4.1	8.3	19.9	40.7
Coverage Ratio 33	11.9	46.1	24.1	6.9	9.0	28.8	14.2	4.3	4.4	10.7	2.2	3.7
Total Asset Turnover 34	2.2	•	5.1	3.3	2.2	2.6	2.0	1.4	1.1	0.9	0.8	0.5
Inventory Turnover 35	24.4	•	18.4	15.7	45.2	17.5	36.5	68.2	50.4	29.4	19.2	8.7
Receivables Turnover 36	9.0	•	73.5	34.5	11.6	5.6	6.7	5.2	3.6	3.1	5.4	2.1
Total Liabilities to Net Worth 37	1.9	•	1.9	3.6	5.4	1.1	2.1	2.2	1.0	0.9	1.5	1.7
Current Assets to Working Capital 38	3.0	•	1.8	2.1	4.2	1.8	3.6	3.2	1.8	3.6	7.7	22.5
Current Liabilities to Working Capital 39	2.0	•	0.8	1.1	3.2	0.8	2.6	2.2	0.8	2.6	6.7	21.5
Working Capital to Net Sales 40	0.1	•	0.1	0.1	0.1	0.2	0.1	0.1	0.2	0.1	0.1	0.0
Inventory to Working Capital 41	0.2	•	0.2	0.3	0.3	0.2	0.1	0.1	0.0	0.0	0.1	0.6
Total Receipts to Cash Flow 42	3.2	1.7	2.8	3.9	4.6	4.2	3.2	5.0	4.1	3.2	2.7	3.1
Cost of Goods to Cash Flow 43	0.9	0.3	0.6	0.8	2.4	1.9	1.2	2.4	1.5	1.1	0.6	0.5
Cash Flow to Total Debt 44	1.1	•	2.7	1.1	0.6	1.2	0.9	0.4	0.6	0.6	0.5	0.3

Selected Financial Factors (in Percentages)

Debt Ratio 45	65.0	•	65.9	78.0	84.3	53.2	67.7	69.1	50.2	46.5	60.0	63.6
Return on Total Assets 46	28.2	•	74.0	28.3	23.4	34.4	21.6	10.2	9.2	13.2	6.4	6.8
Return on Equity Before Income Taxes 47	73.9	•	208.0	110.2	132.5	70.9	62.2	25.4	14.2	22.3	8.6	13.6
Return on Equity After Income Taxes 48	69.8	•	205.6	106.4	127.6	61.1	52.3	20.1	11.3	19.1	7.9	10.7
Profit Margin (Before Income Tax) 49	11.8	32.2	13.9	7.3	9.3	12.5	10.3	5.5	11.3	13.3	4.2	9.2
Profit Margin (After Income Tax) 50	11.1	31.5	13.7	7.1	8.9	10.8	8.6	4.3	5.0	11.3	3.8	7.2

Table I

Corporations with and without Net Income

OFFICES OF BANK HOLDING COMPANIES

MONEY AMOUNTS AND SIZE OF ASSETS IN THOUSANDS OF DOLLARS

Item Description for Accounting Period 7/06 Through 6/07	Total	Zero Assets	Under 500	500 to 1,000	1,000 to 5,000	5,000 to 10,000	10,000 to 25,000	25,000 to 50,000	50,000 to 100,000	100,000 to 250,000	250,000 to 500,000	500,000 to 2,500,000	2,500,000 and over
Number of Enterprises **1**	5240	329	•	•	31	57	241	553	1009	1449	768	626	173
Revenues ($ in Thousands)													
Net Sales **2**	185903894	1681818	•	•	3637	10214	43287	387251	1551346	3574051	3748547	7891984	167007171
Interest **3**	695653227	6403175	•	•	6433	3012	148948	521615	2222114	8750809	11094528	29532356	636967571
Rents **4**	21693983	5353	•	•	0	0	199	1278	7958	33466	49061	196484	21400180
Royalties **5**	235258	3	•	•	0	0	6	12	357	227	354	5185	229113
Other Portfolio Income **6**	32204167	496826	•	•	31289	1086	10793	51863	158856	541275	716463	1448686	28746912
Other Receipts **7**	126874052	1181800	•	•	3920	2061	67161	394329	1270037	3250631	3531359	6865205	110307440
Total Receipts **8**	1062564581	9768975	•	•	45279	16373	270394	1356348	5210668	16150459	19140312	45939900	964658387
Average Total Receipts **9**	202780	29693	•	•	1461	287	1122	2453	5164	11146	24922	73386	5576060
Operating Costs/Operating Income (%)													
Cost of Operations **10**	1.5	•	•	•	•	•	•	•	0.1	0.2	1.4	0.1	1.6
Salaries and Wages **11**	64.7	66.8	•	•	153.5	7.0	73.3	44.1	42.2	59.3	72.7	86.3	63.9
Taxes Paid **12**	8.4	7.6	•	•	43.6	0.8	17.3	10.6	9.1	12.0	13.5	15.1	7.9
Interest Paid **13**	256.9	321.7	•	•	192.4	0.3	183.6	110.8	110.2	162.5	184.7	209.3	263.9
Depreciation **14**	14.5	5.3	•	•	8.0	0.1	13.2	7.4	8.2	10.9	11.1	12.9	14.9
Amortization and Depletion **15**	4.9	1.3	•	•	77.8	0.0	2.4	1.1	1.1	1.1	1.7	2.4	5.2
Pensions and Other Deferred Comp. **16**	4.5	3.5	•	•	1.6	•	8.6	4.7	3.1	3.9	4.7	5.8	4.5
Employee Benefits **17**	9.6	5.9	•	•	3.7	•	22.4	10.6	8.8	10.7	10.7	10.7	9.5
Advertising **18**	5.6	2.3	•	•	1.4	•	6.1	3.4	5.4	4.5	5.0	6.6	5.6
Other Expenses **19**	116.5	138.5	•	•	478.9	25.7	141.3	67.1	62.9	75.0	80.3	96.3	119.6
Officers' Compensation **20**	5.8	12.1	•	•	59.4	•	91.8	37.3	30.1	29.5	23.1	19.7	3.8
Operating Margin **21**	•	•	•	•	•	66.1	•	•	•	•	•	•	•
Operating Margin Before Officers' Comp. **22**	•	•	•	•	•	66.1	•	•	•	•	•	•	•

Selected Average Balance Sheet ($ in Thousands)

Line item												
Net Receivables 23	1089062	0	•	251	431	10431	22597	45885	102869	224461	608481	28572218
Inventories 24	52	0	•	0	0	0	0	1	0	1	16	1511
Net Property, Plant and Equipment 25	20503	0	•	131	0	227	579	1540	3496	7284	18966	479607
Total Assets 26	2888778	0	•	2129	7878	19173	37343	74362	162047	351197	995463	80397063
Notes and Loans Payable 27	477847	0	•	0	475	373	841	3182	7820	19106	66912	14059167
All Other Liabilities 28	1987686	0	•	64	1180	14434	31203	63436	138366	299555	836686	54198537
Net Worth 29	423245	0	•	2066	6223	4366	5298	7744	15861	32537	91865	12139358

Selected Financial Ratios (Times to 1)

Line item												
Current Ratio 30	0.8	0.7	•	28.6	2.9	1.1	1.1	1.0	1.0	1.0	0.9	0.7
Quick Ratio 31	0.7	•	•	28.4	1.9	1.0	1.0	1.0	0.9	0.9	0.9	0.6
Net Sales to Working Capital 32	•	•	1.0	0.1	0.1	0.2	0.4	0.9	•	•	•	•
Coverage Ratio 33	1.3	•	•	2.0	431.5	1.3	1.4	1.4	1.4	1.5	1.5	1.3
Total Asset Turnover 34	0.0	•	•	0.1	0.0	0.0	0.0	0.0	0.0	0.0	0.0	0.0
Inventory Turnover 35	9.9	•	•	•	•	•	2.4	2.4	11.1	56.3	0.8	10.1
Receivables Turnover 36	0.0	•	•	0.4	•	0.0	0.0	0.0	0.0	0.0	0.8	0.0
Total Liabilities to Net Worth 37	5.8	•	•	0.0	0.3	3.4	6.0	8.6	9.2	9.8	9.8	5.6
Current Assets to Working Capital 38	•	•	•	1.0	1.5	13.2	19.2	37.9	•	•	•	•
Current Liabilities to Working Capital 39	•	•	•	0.0	0.5	12.2	18.2	36.9	•	•	•	•
Working Capital to Net Sales 40	•	•	•	15.0	12.4	6.7	2.5	1.1	•	•	•	•
Inventory to Working Capital 41	•	•	•	•	0.0	0.0	0.0	0.0	•	•	•	•
Total Receipts to Cash Flow 42	0.6	0.7	•	0.6	0.7	0.5	0.9	0.9	0.7	0.6	0.5	0.6
Cost of Goods to Cash Flow 43	0.0	•	•	0.0	•	•	0.0	0.0	0.0	0.0	0.0	0.0
Cash Flow to Total Debt 44	0.0	•	•	•	0.2	0.0	0.0	0.0	0.0	0.0	0.0	0.0

Selected Financial Factors (in Percentages)

Line item												
Debt Ratio 45	85.3	•	•	3.0	21.0	77.2	85.8	89.6	90.2	90.7	90.8	84.9
Return on Total Assets 46	4.1	•	•	21.1	2.9	2.2	2.9	3.2	3.5	3.8	4.0	4.1
Return on Equity Before Income Taxes 47	6.4	•	•	10.8	3.6	2.0	5.9	9.2	11.0	13.3	14.6	6.0
Return on Equity After Income Taxes 48	4.3	•	•	8.7	2.6	1.6	4.9	7.5	8.6	10.1	10.5	4.0
Profit Margin (Before Income Tax) 49	76.1	11.4	•	190.7	126.4	48.2	44.4	46.3	70.5	88.7	106.0	75.6
Profit Margin (After Income Tax) 50	50.9	•	•	153.3	91.7	37.9	37.2	38.0	55.0	67.4	76.7	49.8

Table II
Corporations with Net Income

OFFICES OF BANK HOLDING COMPANIES

MONEY AMOUNTS AND SIZE OF ASSETS IN THOUSANDS OF DOLLARS

Item Description for Accounting Period 7/06 Through 6/07	Total	Zero Assets	Under 500	500 to 1,000	1,000 to 5,000	5,000 to 10,000	10,000 to 25,000	25,000 to 50,000	50,000 to 100,000	100,000 to 250,000	250,000 to 500,000	500,000 to 2,500,000	2,500,000 and over
Number of Enterprises 1	4505	41	•	0	3	•	179	477	913	1360	740	604	170
Revenues ($ in Thousands)													
Net Sales 2	184086559	514758	•	0	3253	•	34532	345911	1471012	3390453	3649921	7737626	166924687
Interest 3	689697177	3038078	•	0	3534	•	116595	440708	1998588	8211830	10720339	28666078	636498938
Rents 4	21674346	4101	•	0	0	•	142	766	7438	31338	45884	194865	21389811
Royalties 5	235241	3	•	0	0	•	6	12	357	210	354	5185	229113
Other Portfolio Income 6	31848255	316414	•	0	30720	•	8008	48392	146271	494893	667541	1411633	28723294
Other Receipts 7	126431853	1218732	•	0	1761	•	58871	350501	1183719	3131816	3419616	6779412	110285302
Total Receipts 8	1053973431	5092086	•	0	39268	•	218154	1186290	4807385	15260540	18503655	44794799	964051145
Average Total Receipts 9	233956	124197	•	•	13089	•	1219	2487	5265	11221	25005	74164	5670889
Operating Costs/Operating Income (%)													
Cost of Operations 10	1.5	•	•	•	•	•	•	•	0.1	0.2	1.3	0.1	1.6
Salaries and Wages 11	64.8	156.2	•	•	161.0	•	67.4	41.9	40.0	57.7	70.9	84.8	63.9
Taxes Paid 12	8.4	16.7	•	•	18.5	•	17.3	10.3	8.9	11.9	13.4	15.0	7.9
Interest Paid 13	256.8	422.2	•	•	190.8	•	178.9	105.1	105.7	160.6	182.6	207.0	263.8
Depreciation 14	14.5	12.7	•	•	7.1	•	9.9	6.5	7.7	10.8	10.9	12.7	14.9
Amortization and Depletion 15	4.9	3.5	•	•	87.0	•	0.9	0.9	0.9	1.1	1.6	2.3	5.2
Pensions and Other Deferred Comp. 16	4.5	8.1	•	•	1.8	•	9.6	4.9	3.1	3.9	4.6	5.6	4.5
Employee Benefits 17	9.6	14.6	•	•	2.2	•	21.5	10.0	8.4	10.5	10.6	10.6	9.5
Advertising 18	5.6	6.5	•	•	1.2	•	4.7	3.2	5.3	4.4	4.9	6.5	5.6
Other Expenses 19	116.4	193.4	•	•	199.4	•	102.2	59.2	57.6	71.2	78.1	94.3	119.6
Officers' Compensation 20	5.7	33.1	•	•	17.1	•	88.3	35.3	28.8	29.2	23.1	19.6	3.8
Operating Margin 21	•	•	•	•	•	•	•	•	•	•	•	•	•
Operating Margin Before Officers' Comp. 22	•	•	•	•	•	•	•	•	•	•	•	•	•

Selected Average Balance Sheet ($ in Thousands)

Net Receivables 23	1259579	0	•	398	•	11063	22765	46306	104138	226171	615049	29051783
Inventories 24	61	0	•	0	•	0	0	1	0	1	16	1110
Net Property, Plant and Equipment 25	23529	0	•	7	•	195	508	1500	3460	7229	19074	488908
Total Assets 26	3346171	0	•	1266	•	19620	37281	74756	162497	351226	1000907	81761052
Notes and Loans Payable 27	554936	0	•	0	•	439	840	3241	7795	18885	67365	14301520
All Other Liabilities 28	2300577	0	•	502	•	15476	31174	63952	138851	300099	841203	55112011
Net Worth 29	490657	0	•	764	•	3705	5267	7563	15851	32241	92339	12347521

Selected Financial Ratios (Times to 1)

Current Ratio 30	0.8	•	1.4	1.1	1.1	1.0	1.0	1.0	0.9	0.7		
Quick Ratio 31	0.7	•	1.3	1.0	1.0	1.0	0.9	0.9	0.9	0.6		
Net Sales to Working Capital 32	•	•	5.8	0.2	0.4	0.9	10.0	1.5	•	•		
Coverage Ratio 33	1.3	1.3	3.6	1.7	1.5	1.5	1.5	1.5	1.5	1.3		
Total Asset Turnover 34	0.0	•	0.9	0.0	0.0	0.0	0.0	0.0	0.0	0.0		
Inventory Turnover 35	9.9	•	•	•	•	0.9	11.1	50.0	0.8	14.0		
Receivables Turnover 36	0.0	•	•	0.0	0.0	0.0	0.0	0.0	0.0	0.0		
Total Liabilities to Net Worth 37	5.8	•	0.7	4.3	6.1	8.9	9.3	9.9	9.8	5.6		
Current Assets to Working Capital 38	•	•	3.7	15.3	17.5	35.5	562.5	35.5	•	•		
Current Liabilities to Working Capital 39	•	•	2.7	14.3	16.5	34.5	561.5	34.5	•	•		
Working Capital to Net Sales 40	•	•	0.2	5.7	2.6	1.2	0.1	0.0	•	•		
Inventory to Working Capital 41	•	•	•	0.0	0.0	0.0	0.0	0.0	•	•		
Total Receipts to Cash Flow 42	0.6	0.4	0.5	0.5	0.9	0.9	0.7	0.6	0.5	0.6		
Cost of Goods to Cash Flow 43	0.0	•	•	•	0.0	0.0	0.0	0.0	0.0	0.0		
Cash Flow to Total Debt 44	0.0	•	•	0.0	0.0	0.0	0.0	0.0	0.0	0.0		

Selected Financial Factors (in Percentages)

Debt Ratio 45	85.3	•	39.6	81.1	85.9	89.9	90.2	90.8	90.8	84.9
Return on Total Assets 46	4.1	•	591.8	2.9	3.1	3.4	3.6	3.9	4.0	4.1
Return on Equity Before Income Taxes 47	6.4	•	709.7	6.1	7.8	11.2	12.1	14.1	15.2	6.0
Return on Equity After Income Taxes 48	4.3	•	663.3	5.4	6.7	9.3	9.6	10.8	11.0	4.0
Profit Margin (Before Income Tax) 49	77.3	110.3	500.3	117.4	56.7	52.6	77.1	92.5	109.4	75.6
Profit Margin (After Income Tax) 50	51.8	73.8	467.5	104.6	48.6	43.8	60.9	70.5	79.5	49.9

Table I

Corporations with and without Net Income

OFFICES OF OTHER HOLDING COMPANIES

MONEY AMOUNTS AND SIZE OF ASSETS IN THOUSANDS OF DOLLARS

Item Description for Accounting Period 7/06 Through 6/07	Total	Zero Assets	Under 500	500 to 1,000	1,000 to 5,000	5,000 to 10,000	10,000 to 25,000	25,000 to 50,000	50,000 to 100,000	100,000 to 250,000	250,000 to 500,000	500,000 to 2,500,000	2,500,000 and over
Number of Enterprises 1	45021	8871	•	•	4415	926	984	•	249	192	84	73	25
Revenues ($ in Thousands)													
Net Sales 2	1851547	172037	•	•	19591	32636	243015	•	205587	157455	90350	654928	135285
Interest 3	7849230	284920	•	•	148483	40412	107035	•	269935	394468	679798	1945217	3639834
Rents 4	177129	4203	•	•	8047	1521	7622	•	32300	17899	15937	26697	214
Royalties 5	121890	30788	•	•	5302	10775	1971	•	6439	12148	38326	2205	0
Other Portfolio Income 6	9040138	923258	•	•	611819	412572	497223	•	686364	917148	2209229	739528	1379695
Other Receipts 7	12004642	2287033	•	•	815546	697240	756119	•	98342	1086828	817029	2425403	1564848
Total Receipts 8	31044576	3702239	•	•	1608788	1195156	1612985	•	1298967	2585946	3850669	5793978	6719876
Average Total Receipts 9	690	417	•	•	364	1291	1639	•	5217	13468	45841	79370	268795
Operating Costs/Operating Income (%)													
Cost of Operations 10	31.5	94.6	•	•	22.0	•	69.7	•	49.2	57.2	5.6	6.0	•
Salaries and Wages 11	62.2	6.2	•	•	146.8	137.3	12.6	•	45.2	79.1	102.0	30.6	280.2
Taxes Paid 12	36.1	53.8	•	•	179.1	77.9	16.7	•	22.6	41.2	51.6	28.2	25.1
Interest Paid 13	277.5	155.0	•	•	620.1	176.8	50.9	•	130.9	175.0	385.9	233.3	1353.1
Depreciation 14	8.8	2.1	•	•	78.3	25.6	4.6	•	11.0	13.4	19.3	3.9	10.0
Amortization and Depletion 15	23.1	34.6	•	•	81.4	50.5	12.1	•	5.3	31.6	15.9	2.3	147.8
Pensions and Other Deferred Comp. 16	3.3	0.6	•	•	27.8	17.2	1.2	•	4.3	2.1	12.5	1.8	5.0
Employee Benefits 17	7.1	0.3	•	•	22.3	14.8	1.1	•	4.3	17.7	12.0	2.5	14.7
Advertising 18	6.0	•	•	•	1.0	0.4	0.3	•	1.5	31.1	0.9	8.0	0.1
Other Expenses 19	367.4	790.1	•	•	2520.5	867.0	218.3	•	213.8	420.2	838.2	109.3	450.6
Officers' Compensation 20	25.8	0.5	•	•	342.2	102.6	11.2	•	16.0	31.6	19.5	14.8	66.9
Operating Margin 21	•	•	•	•	•	•	•	•	•	•	•	•	•
Operating Margin Before Officers' Comp. 22	•	•	•	•	•	•	•	•	•	•	•	•	•

Selected Average Balance Sheet ($ in Thousands)

Net Receivables 23	617		151	98	654	•	3374	7880	15955	38278	754873
Inventories 24	3		2	0	5	•	80	124	262	249	0
Net Property, Plant and Equipment 25	105		124	124	519	•	1668	5384	1224	17255	4761
Total Assets 26	8286		2295	6857	15639	•	68585	152436	346562	1095388	6563968
Notes and Loans Payable 27	1635		1515	885	4093	•	12528	27820	62554	205243	1076826
All Other Liabilities 28	1058		235	723	1870	•	6210	14171	30490	174782	890895
Net Worth 29	5594		546	5249	9676	•	49847	110445	253519	715363	4596247

Selected Financial Ratios (Times to 1)

Current Ratio 30	1.7		3.6	3.4	1.4	•	4.1	2.7	2.2	1.4	1.5
Quick Ratio 31	1.4		2.2	1.9	1.0	•	2.6	2.1	1.1	1.1	1.5
Net Sales to Working Capital 32	0.0		0.0	0.0	0.3	•	0.1	0.0	0.0	0.1	0.0
Coverage Ratio 33	4.1	7.6	7.6	13.5	6.0	•	1.8	5.6	8.5	3.0	3.1
Total Asset Turnover 34	0.0		0.0	0.0	0.0	•	0.0	0.0	0.0	0.0	0.0
Inventory Turnover 35	5.1		0.6	•	34.7	•	5.1	3.8	0.2	2.2	•
Receivables Turnover 36	0.1		0.0	•	0.4	•	0.2	0.1	0.1	0.1	0.0
Total Liabilities to Net Worth 37	0.5		3.2	0.3	0.6	•	0.4	0.4	0.4	0.5	0.4
Current Assets to Working Capital 38	2.4		1.4	1.4	3.7	•	1.3	1.6	1.8	3.4	2.8
Current Liabilities to Working Capital 39	1.4		0.4	0.4	2.7	•	0.3	0.6	0.8	2.4	1.8
Working Capital to Net Sales 40	21.0		111.0	35.5	3.7	•	14.8	20.6	36.1	6.8	128.2
Inventory to Working Capital 41	0.0		0.0	•	0.0	•	0.0	0.0	0.0	0.0	0.0
Total Receipts to Cash Flow 42	0.1	0.1	0.0	0.0		•	2.2	0.1	0.0	0.2	0.0
Cost of Goods to Cash Flow 43	0.0	0.1	0.0	•	0.2	•	1.1	0.1	0.0	0.0	•
Cash Flow to Total Debt 44	0.1		0.1	0.5	0.1	•	0.0	0.1	0.3	0.1	0.1

Selected Financial Factors (in Percentages)

Debt Ratio 45	32.5		76.2	23.5	38.1	•	27.3	27.5	26.8	34.7	30.0
Return on Total Assets 46	5.6		9.1	12.2	4.8	•	2.9	5.3	10.2	5.7	3.5
Return on Equity Before Income Taxes 47	6.3		33.1	14.8	6.5	•	1.8	6.0	12.3	5.8	3.4
Return on Equity After Income Taxes 48	4.7		27.3	13.2	4.4	•	0.2	4.5	9.9	3.7	2.6
Profit Margin (Before Income Tax) 49	860.2	1022.4	4074.7	2206.1	253.5	•	108.2	806.0	2894.9	459.1	2892.3
Profit Margin (After Income Tax) 50	639.1	779.4	3363.8	1960.6	173.7	•	10.4	610.2	2338.6	298.4	2180.4

Table II

Corporations with Net Income

OFFICES OF OTHER HOLDING COMPANIES

MONEY AMOUNTS AND SIZE OF ASSETS IN THOUSANDS OF DOLLARS

Item Description for Accounting Period 7/06 Through 6/07	Total	Zero Assets	Under 500	500 to 1,000	1,000 to 5,000	5,000 to 10,000	10,000 to 25,000	25,000 to 50,000	50,000 to 100,000	100,000 to 250,000	250,000 to 500,000	500,000 to 2,500,000	2,500,000 and over
Number of Enterprises 1	15770	2542	•	2642	2072	•	444	•	118	111	49	51	18
Revenues ($ in Thousands)													
Net Sales 2	1095867	8717	•	2594	17673	•	65742	•	151103	100628	13824	591526	7175
Interest 3	6190387	155672	•	66500	121628	•	83468	•	188782	307759	548045	1518983	2991584
Rents 4	131812	189	•	0	4094	•	5982	•	24835	2995	15187	19349	214
Royalties 5	69959	29535	•	0	4182	•	1971	•	6204	1931	0	1825	0
Other Portfolio Income 6	8505205	881992	•	90299	521274	•	438112	•	574826	890966	2175391	713704	1379695
Other Receipts 7	12963555	2573642	•	347697	942313	•	1041905	•	490873	973291	783235	2331649	1617460
Total Receipts 8	28956785	3649747	•	507090	1611164	•	1637180	•	1436623	2277570	3535682	5177036	5996128
Average Total Receipts 9	1836	1436	•	192	778	•	3687	•	12175	20519	72157	101511	333118
Operating Costs/Operating Income (%)													
Cost of Operations 10	14.2	•	•	•	24.4	•	6.1	•	42.0	69.6	8.9	2.0	•
Salaries and Wages 11	72.3	59.2	•	26.2	97.5	•	26.9	•	39.5	25.9	59.0	27.6	5204.8
Taxes Paid 12	49.9	827.7	•	197.5	159.9	•	49.6	•	24.7	52.6	290.6	28.3	456.4
Interest Paid 13	265.6	1321.7	•	1889.9	514.5	•	55.4	•	84.8	128.5	1802.0	135.7	16238.2
Depreciation 14	8.6	26.9	•	77.8	54.8	•	8.6	•	10.2	7.1	90.2	3.2	187.8
Amortization and Depletion 15	28.6	547.3	•	2.5	14.2	•	36.9	•	1.9	14.7	23.4	1.8	2783.0
Pensions and Other Deferred Comp. 16	3.5	0.1	•	•	21.1	•	0.7	•	5.5	1.1	4.1	1.8	94.7
Employee Benefits 17	6.4	4.3	•	32.0	16.8	•	1.6	•	3.1	17.5	4.3	1.7	270.0
Advertising 18	4.8	•	•	•	1.1	•	0.0	•	1.8	47.0	0.9	0.3	0.8
Other Expenses 19	214.3	2796.0	•	811.7	897.3	•	270.5	•	93.2	257.6	1560.0	84.0	4890.7
Officers' Compensation 20	29.8	1.1	•	19.3	274.9	•	28.2	•	14.5	38.9	79.5	14.9	1065.2
Operating Margin 21	•	•	•	•	•	•	•	•	•	•	•	•	•
Operating Margin Before Officers' Comp. 22	•	•	•	•	•	•	•	•	•	•	•	•	•

Selected Average Balance Sheet ($ in Thousands)

Net Receivables 23	1517	0	•	10	107	•	820	•	3768	8530	11065	48855	1016953
Inventories 24	5	0	•	0	7	•	8	•	43	62	397	357	0
Net Property, Plant and Equipment 25	133	0	•	13	114	•	557	•	1900	1312	1113	16080	6351
Total Assets 26	15749	0	•	720	2316	•	15808	•	73418	152648	352361	1128545	6783542
Notes and Loans Payable 27	2095	0	•	160	432	•	1824	•	12119	22009	63761	167623	760159
All Other Liabilities 28	2259	0	•	142	163	•	1425	•	7876	12464	17219	171543	1163829
Net Worth 29	11395	0	•	418	1721	•	12559	•	53423	118175	271381	789380	4859554

Selected Financial Ratios (Times to 1)

Current Ratio 30	2.6	•	1.6	2.6	2.8	•	4.3	4.0	1.9	2.2	2.7
Quick Ratio 31	2.3	•	1.1	1.6	2.1	•	2.8	3.1	0.9	1.8	2.6
Net Sales to Working Capital 32	0.0	•	0.0	0.0	0.1	•	0.1	0.0	0.0	0.1	0.0
Coverage Ratio 33	8.6	28.5	9.5	14.6	37.0	•	8.3	14.3	13.4	5.4	4.5
Total Asset Turnover 34	0.0	•	0.0	0.0	0.0	•	0.0	0.0	0.0	0.0	0.0
Inventory Turnover 35	2.1	•	•	0.3	1.1	•	12.6	10.1	0.1	0.7	•
Receivables Turnover 36	0.0	•	0.1	•	0.2	•	0.3	0.1	0.0	0.1	•
Total Liabilities to Net Worth 37	0.4	•	0.7	0.3	0.3	•	0.4	0.3	0.3	0.4	0.4
Current Assets to Working Capital 38	1.6	•	2.6	1.6	1.6	•	1.3	1.3	2.1	1.9	1.6
Current Liabilities to Working Capital 39	0.6	•	1.6	0.6	0.6	•	0.3	0.3	1.1	0.9	0.6
Working Capital to Net Sales 40	42.8	•	81.7	51.9	14.4	•	12.0	27.0	105.8	11.1	4185.2
Inventory to Working Capital 41	0.0	•	•	0.0	0.0	•	0.0	0.0	•	0.0	•
Total Receipts to Cash Flow 42	0.1	0.0	0.0	0.0	0.1	•	0.3	0.1	0.0	0.2	0.0
Cost of Goods to Cash Flow 43	0.0	•	0.0	0.0	0.0	•	0.1	0.1	0.0	0.0	•
Cash Flow to Total Debt 44	0.3	•	0.5	0.8	0.8	•	0.2	0.3	0.6	0.2	0.1

Selected Financial Factors (in Percentages)

Debt Ratio 45	27.6	•	42.0	25.7	20.6	•	27.2	22.6	23.0	30.1	28.4
Return on Total Assets 46	10.0	•	24.5	27.7	19.2	•	12.3	10.9	19.4	7.5	4.3
Return on Equity Before Income Taxes 47	12.2	•	37.8	34.8	23.5	•	14.9	13.1	23.3	8.7	4.7
Return on Equity After Income Taxes 48	10.0	•	36.4	30.9	20.0	•	11.7	10.7	19.5	6.1	3.6
Profit Margin (Before Income Tax) 49	2008.0	36392.5	16100.8	7015.5	1991.7	•	621.2	1706.3	22382.6	591.2	57630.9
Profit Margin (After Income Tax) 50	1635.0	31599.0	15470.4	6236.7	1699.2	•	489.1	1400.4	18754.5	413.4	44209.3

Table I

Corporations with and without Net Income

EMPLOYMENT SERVICES

MONEY AMOUNTS AND SIZE OF ASSETS IN THOUSANDS OF DOLLARS

Item Description for Accounting Period 7/06 Through 6/07	Total	Zero Assets	Under 500	500 to 1,000	1,000 to 5,000	5,000 to 10,000	10,000 to 25,000	25,000 to 50,000	50,000 to 100,000	100,000 to 250,000	250,000 to 500,000	500,000 to 2,500,000	2,500,000 and over
Number of Enterprises **1**	27346	4022	20848	861	1193	215	101	40	20	18	9	18	0
Revenues ($ in Thousands)													
Net Sales **2**	152981025	1318525	28405852	2876009	29552083	6621523	11045315	5263218	6797967	9104187	7235469	44760876	0
Interest **3**	360911	4382	6175	2387	4777	6001	5513	5604	5938	12380	13275	294479	0
Rents **4**	7539	0	0	610	265	0	1032	2277	67	1098	0	2189	0
Royalties **5**	479441	438	0	0	0	0	0	0	0	4737	31674	442592	0
Other Portfolio Income **6**	211586	771	8155	5736	9133	6007	2469	4255	11142	15628	3499	144789	0
Other Receipts **7**	1233130	59196	117518	9678	89109	30076	24414	25442	45006	32550	16871	783274	0
Total Receipts **8**	155273632	1383312	28537700	2894420	29655367	6663607	11078743	5300796	6860120	9170580	7300788	46428199	0
Average Total Receipts **9**	5678	344	1369	3362	24858	30994	109691	132520	343006	509477	811199	2579344	•
Operating Costs/Operating Income (%)													
Cost of Operations **10**	48.1	60.1	31.4	15.5	49.7	39.8	64.9	34.2	45.7	63.2	58.2	53.6	•
Salaries and Wages **11**	29.6	20.0	38.7	52.0	31.5	38.5	14.6	47.4	38.3	24.2	21.5	22.7	•
Taxes Paid **12**	6.4	6.6	5.8	4.9	6.9	7.5	7.6	6.3	6.8	5.6	5.3	6.5	•
Interest Paid **13**	0.5	0.2	0.3	0.5	0.2	0.3	0.2	0.5	0.5	0.9	1.1	0.8	•
Depreciation **14**	0.3	0.1	0.2	0.2	0.2	0.2	0.2	0.2	0.2	0.2	0.4	0.5	•
Amortization and Depletion **15**	0.3	0.0	0.4	0.0	0.0	0.1	0.1	0.0	0.2	0.6	0.8	0.6	•
Pensions and Other Deferred Comp. **16**	0.2	0.3	0.2	0.1	0.1	0.0	0.0	0.1	0.1	0.0	0.2	0.1	•
Employee Benefits **17**	2.8	1.1	3.7	3.1	3.1	3.0	3.1	1.7	4.2	1.3	1.8	2.7	•
Advertising **18**	0.4	0.4	0.6	0.4	0.2	0.9	0.3	0.3	0.2	0.2	0.2	0.4	•
Other Expenses **19**	8.6	12.9	10.8	14.6	5.9	6.8	7.2	6.1	3.5	3.9	7.8	11.1	•
Officers' Compensation **20**	1.8	4.0	5.2	3.8	0.9	1.8	0.9	3.0	0.4	0.3	0.8	0.9	•
Operating Margin **21**	1.1	•	2.7	6.3	1.2	1.1	0.8	0.1	•	•	1.8	0.3	•
Operating Margin Before Officers' Comp. **22**	2.9	•	8.0	10.0	2.1	2.9	1.7	3.1	0.3	•	2.6	1.2	•

Selected Average Balance Sheet ($ in Thousands)

Net Receivables 23	410	0	30	183	584	2593	6022	11280	19799	43387	134677	318292
Inventories 24	2	0	0	0	5	0	2	42	237	196	1587
Net Property, Plant and Equipment 25	83	0	16	41	159	456	796	2458	3224	8097	14525	59650
Total Assets 26	1393	0	116	641	2220	6958	14928	35181	66362	147690	341913	1165863
Notes and Loans Payable 27	311	0	63	145	585	5136	3007	6693	18453	51043	85940	145999
All Other Liabilities 28	488	0	39	149	900	1078	8113	14562	26041	57391	130832	387292
Net Worth 29	594	0	15	347	735	744	3808	13926	21868	39256	125141	632572

Selected Financial Ratios (Times to 1)

Current Ratio 30	1.4	•	1.0	2.2	1.4	0.9	1.5	1.3	1.1	1.3	1.5	1.5
Quick Ratio 31	1.2	•	0.9	2.0	1.2	0.7	1.2	1.0	1.0	1.1	1.4	1.3
Net Sales to Working Capital 32	31.7	•	633.2	15.4	59.9	•	30.0	28.3	90.0	26.6	12.6	16.5
Coverage Ratio 33	6.2	•	13.6	16.1	7.6	7.5	6.8	2.6	2.6	1.3	3.4	6.3
Total Asset Turnover 34	4.0	•	11.7	5.2	11.2	4.4	7.3	3.7	5.1	3.4	2.4	2.1
Inventory Turnover 35	1408.0	•	88982.2	2267.5	•	•	31733.8	1067.8	336.4	1349.2	2379.3	840.0
Receivables Turnover 36	14.5	•	48.8	11.7	39.6	9.1	22.0	13.1	15.9	12.4	6.2	9.0
Total Liabilities to Net Worth 37	1.3	•	6.9	0.8	2.0	8.4	2.9	1.5	2.0	2.8	1.7	0.8
Current Assets to Working Capital 38	3.8	•	33.8	1.8	3.4	•	2.9	4.0	7.9	4.0	2.9	3.1
Current Liabilities to Working Capital 39	2.8	•	32.8	0.8	2.4	•	1.9	3.0	6.9	3.0	1.9	2.1
Working Capital to Net Sales 40	0.0	•	0.0	0.1	0.0	0.0	0.0	0.0	0.0	0.0	0.1	0.1
Inventory to Working Capital 41	0.0	•	•	0.0	0.0	•	0.0	0.0	0.0	0.0	0.0	0.0
Total Receipts to Cash Flow 42	10.0	9.5	8.1	5.0	14.4	13.3	13.0	16.6	27.2	28.9	10.8	7.3
Cost of Goods to Cash Flow 43	4.8	5.7	2.5	0.8	7.2	5.3	8.4	5.7	12.4	18.3	6.3	3.9
Cash Flow to Total Debt 44	0.7	•	1.7	2.3	1.2	0.4	0.8	0.4	0.3	0.2	0.3	0.6

Selected Financial Factors (in Percentages)

Debt Ratio 45	57.4	•	87.4	45.9	66.9	89.3	74.5	60.4	67.0	73.4	63.4	45.7
Return on Total Assets 46	12.3	•	40.4	38.3	19.7	8.8	9.4	4.9	6.6	4.1	8.8	10.3
Return on Equity Before Income Taxes 47	24.1	•	296.6	66.4	51.8	71.7	31.5	7.7	12.3	3.4	17.0	15.9
Return on Equity After Income Taxes 48	20.1	•	292.4	65.3	49.8	67.3	27.5	4.2	11.3	0.5	15.1	11.4
Profit Margin (Before Income Tax) 49	2.6	•	3.2	6.9	1.5	1.7	1.1	0.8	0.8	0.3	2.7	4.0
Profit Margin (After Income Tax) 50	2.1	•	3.2	6.8	1.5	1.6	1.0	0.4	0.7	0.0	2.4	2.9

EMPLOYMENT SERVICES

Table II

Corporations with Net Income

MONEY AMOUNTS AND SIZE OF ASSETS IN THOUSANDS OF DOLLARS

Item Description for Accounting Period 7/06 Through 6/07	Total	Zero Assets	Under 500	500 to 1,000	1,000 to 5,000	5,000 to 10,000	10,000 to 25,000	25,000 to 50,000	50,000 to 100,000	100,000 to 250,000	250,000 to 500,000	500,000 to 2,500,000	2,500,000 and over
Number of Enterprises 1	16390	1152	13319	858	741	•	76	26	12	10	•	14	0
Revenues ($ in Thousands)													
Net Sales 2	124468682	195301	18432170	2802130	28453833	•	9699313	4662861	5328989	5069911	•	40009929	0
Interest 3	333135	4338	2909	2385	2746	•	5495	2402	5860	7971	•	281347	0
Rents 4	3757	0	0	610	265	•	1032	0	67	998	•	785	0
Royalties 5	467454	0	0	0	0	•	0	0	0	3088	•	432692	0
Other Portfolio Income 6	189453	70	3903	390	1690	•	2469	588	11140	15523	•	144789	0
Other Receipts 7	1158670	58720	92108	6703	88141	•	20134	13336	40813	23618	•	769168	0
Total Receipts 8	126821151	258429	18531090	2812218	28546675	•	9728443	4679187	5386869	5121109	•	41638710	0
Average Total Receipts 9	7738	224	1391	3278	38525	•	128006	179969	448906	512111	•	2974194	•
Operating Costs/Operating Income (%)													
Cost of Operations 10	51.2	34.7	39.2	13.6	50.6	•	65.6	37.6	40.9	58.7	•	56.2	•
Salaries and Wages 11	26.4	16.4	29.4	53.3	31.2	•	12.9	44.3	43.5	27.7	•	20.6	•
Taxes Paid 12	6.6	5.6	5.2	5.0	7.0	•	8.3	6.0	7.0	6.3	•	6.8	•
Interest Paid 13	0.5	0.8	0.3	0.4	0.2	•	0.2	0.3	0.3	0.7	•	0.8	•
Depreciation 14	0.3	0.3	0.2	0.2	0.2	•	0.2	0.2	0.2	0.3	•	0.5	•
Amortization and Depletion 15	0.2	0.1	0.1	0.4	0.0	•	0.1	0.0	0.1	0.4	•	0.5	•
Pensions and Other Deferred Comp. 16	0.1	1.8	0.3	0.2	0.1	•	0.0	0.1	0.0	0.0	•	0.1	•
Employee Benefits 17	2.5	1.4	1.4	0.3	2.9	•	3.1	1.8	4.7	1.6	•	2.8	•
Advertising 18	0.4	0.1	0.8	1.5	0.2	•	0.4	0.2	0.2	0.2	•	0.4	•
Other Expenses 19	8.2	21.9	12.2	14.7	5.3	•	7.4	4.9	2.5	3.2	•	10.0	•
Officers' Compensation 20	1.6	15.1	5.0	3.9	0.7	•	0.9	3.2	0.2	0.3	•	0.7	•
Operating Margin 21	2.0	1.8	6.1	6.7	1.6	•	1.1	1.4	0.4	0.6	•	0.6	•
Operating Margin Before Officers' Comp. 22	3.6	16.9	11.1	10.6	2.3	•	2.0	4.6	0.7	0.9	•	1.3	•

Selected Average Balance Sheet ($ in Thousands)

Net Receivables 23	529	0	28	180	508	5692	13239	21482	43074	341196
Inventories 24	2	0	0	0	0	2	65	307	365	2010
Net Property, Plant and Equipment 25	117	0	18	41	219	816	2499	3341	7904	73164
Total Assets 26	1849	0	123	639	2048	14782	33388	63093	152017	1332291
Notes and Loans Payable 27	299	0	51	140	716	2568	5522	12651	33346	125434
All Other Liabilities 28	628	0	38	116	1016	6951	12855	28374	55834	430113
Net Worth 29	922	0	34	383	316	5263	15011	22068	62837	776744

Selected Financial Ratios (Times to 1)

Current Ratio 30	1.4		1.1	2.8	1.0	1.6	1.5	1.3	1.3	1.5
Quick Ratio 31	1.3		1.0	2.5	0.8	1.1	1.3	1.2	1.2	1.3
Net Sales to Working Capital 32	28.3		192.3	12.9	4315.1	34.2	27.3	56.3	28.1	16.2
Coverage Ratio 33	9.1	42.5	26.7	19.5	10.0	7.9	7.4	6.9	3.3	7.1
Total Asset Turnover 34	4.1		11.3	5.1	18.7	8.6	5.4	7.0	3.3	2.1
Inventory Turnover 35	1751.0			76088.8	1369909.0	42676.3	1040.6	591.3	816.9	799.5
Receivables Turnover 36	15.7		48.1	13.0	62.2	25.2	13.3	16.5		10.1
Total Liabilities to Net Worth 37	1.0		2.6	0.7	5.5	1.8	1.2	1.9	1.4	0.7
Current Assets to Working Capital 38	3.3		10.3	1.5	140.8	2.8	3.0	4.2	4.0	3.0
Current Liabilities to Working Capital 39	2.3		9.3	0.5	139.8	1.8	2.0	3.2	3.0	2.0
Working Capital to Net Sales 40	0.0		0.0	0.1	0.0	0.0	0.0	0.0	0.0	0.1
Inventory to Working Capital 41	0.0			0.0	0.0	0.0	0.0		0.0	0.0
Total Receipts to Cash Flow 42	9.2	1.9	5.9	4.9	14.8	12.1	16.7	28.6	24.6	7.5
Cost of Goods to Cash Flow 43	4.7	0.7	2.3	0.7	7.5	7.9	6.3	11.7	14.4	4.2
Cash Flow to Total Debt 44	0.9		2.6	2.6	1.5	1.1	0.6	0.4	0.2	0.7

Selected Financial Factors (in Percentages)

Debt Ratio 45	50.1		72.1	40.1	84.6	64.4	55.0	65.0	58.7	41.7
Return on Total Assets 46	17.2		77.0	38.2	41.1	13.8	10.8	12.7	7.6	11.5
Return on Equity Before Income Taxes 47	30.8		266.3	60.5	239.3	33.8	20.8	30.9	12.8	17.0
Return on Equity After Income Taxes 48	26.5		263.4	59.5	232.2	30.0	15.8	29.3	9.4	12.2
Profit Margin (Before Income Tax) 49	3.7	34.2	6.6	7.1	2.0	1.4	1.7	1.5	1.6	4.6
Profit Margin (After Income Tax) 50	3.2	33.8	6.5	7.0	1.9	1.2	1.3	1.5	1.2	3.3

Table I

Corporations with and without Net Income

TRAVEL ARRANGEMENT AND RESERVATION SERVICES

MONEY AMOUNTS AND SIZE OF ASSETS IN THOUSANDS OF DOLLARS

Item Description for Accounting Period 7/06 Through 6/07	Total	Zero Assets	Under 500	500 to 1,000	1,000 to 5,000	5,000 to 10,000	10,000 to 25,000	25,000 to 50,000	50,000 to 100,000	100,000 to 250,000	250,000 to 500,000	500,000 to 2,500,000	2,500,000 and over
Number of Enterprises **1**	22103	5414	15545	458	458	46	92	25	33	15	8	9	0
Revenues ($ in Thousands)													
Net Sales **2**	36695478	947443	12723614	2106187	2388209	696055	3048353	1646401	3045684	2221681	2668756	5203094	0
Interest **3**	233849	1094	924	1194	3260	787	13842	7847	25722	8427	27777	142975	0
Rents **4**	43887	0	2552	231	0	2784	590	255	7926	749	1868	26930	0
Royalties **5**	13062	0	0	0	0	0	0	472	2429	0	0	10161	0
Other Portfolio Income **6**	436078	78	4491	6566	585	13824	36553	34800	74452	21824	27016	215889	0
Other Receipts **7**	1301817	-8967	34359	19379	4111	15042	110105	113982	104460	64004	352933	492411	0
Total Receipts **8**	38724171	939648	12765940	2133557	2396165	728492	3209443	1803757	3260673	2316685	3078350	6091460	0
Average Total Receipts **9**	1752	174	821	4658	5232	15837	34885	72150	98808	154446	384794	676829	•
Operating Costs/Operating Income (%)													
Cost of Operations **10**	56.6	65.5	76.1	59.9	55.4	70.2	56.3	20.4	58.2	48.6	72.3	10.9	•
Salaries and Wages **11**	13.9	6.0	8.5	2.6	15.3	13.4	18.9	18.7	13.2	15.1	16.9	26.6	•
Taxes Paid **12**	1.6	1.0	1.0	1.7	1.9	3.0	1.8	2.3	2.1	1.7	1.6	2.4	•
Interest Paid **13**	1.0	0.8	0.1	0.2	0.6	1.0	0.3	1.3	1.1	0.8	1.9	3.8	•
Depreciation **14**	0.8	1.0	0.2	1.3	0.8	1.1	0.8	1.1	1.0	1.8	0.8	1.4	•
Amortization and Depletion **15**	0.6	0.4	0.0	0.0	0.1	0.1	0.2	0.8	0.6	1.1	0.4	3.0	•
Pensions and Other Deferred Comp. **16**	0.6	0.1	0.3	0.5	0.5	0.2	0.4	0.4	1.3	0.4	1.1	1.4	•
Employee Benefits **17**	1.3	0.6	0.2	0.2	0.9	1.5	1.4	1.7	2.1	1.7	1.9	3.3	•
Advertising **18**	2.0	1.1	0.4	1.8	0.4	0.6	4.0	3.0	2.0	2.6	1.2	5.4	•
Other Expenses **19**	23.0	25.1	9.4	24.2	18.8	8.5	17.1	56.8	25.0	24.7	16.2	53.6	•
Officers' Compensation **20**	2.3	2.6	3.0	5.4	4.4	2.8	1.8	0.8	1.5	1.6	0.4	0.7	•
Operating Margin **21**	•	•	0.8	2.3	0.9	•	•	•	•	•	•	•	•
Operating Margin Before Officers' Comp. **22**	•	•	3.8	7.6	5.3	0.4	•	•	•	1.5	•	•	•

Selected Average Balance Sheet ($ in Thousands)

Net Receivables 23	109	0	13	78	305	2363	3747	3010	9566	18536	22954	79747	•
Inventories 24	8	0	1	14	19	147	145	141	1072	245	2446	6153	•
Net Property, Plant and Equipment 25	106	0	7	195	248	1299	1291	4578	10775	26922	19742	92025	•
Total Assets 26	1395	0	71	650	2402	7395	17620	38558	74449	160982	357436	1964115	•
Notes and Loans Payable 27	583	0	57	225	317	1943	1376	6974	17902	19557	68560	1103316	•
All Other Liabilities 28	444	0	32	135	1926	4149	11848	20936	38404	74306	133012	347185	•
Net Worth 29	368	0	-18	290	159	1303	4397	10648	18143	67119	155864	513614	•

Selected Financial Ratios (Times to 1)

Current Ratio 30	1.7	•	1.5	3.3	1.1	1.7	0.9	0.9	1.1	1.1	1.2	2.8	•
Quick Ratio 31	0.7	•	1.2	2.9	0.9	1.4	0.8	0.6	0.8	0.8	0.6	0.5	•
Net Sales to Working Capital 32	6.0	•	43.3	15.0	26.6	6.7	•	•	21.7	26.7	14.6	1.0	•
Coverage Ratio 33	2.7	•	10.9	17.3	3.0	3.2	2.7	8.2	0.2	6.1	1.3	2.2	•
Total Asset Turnover 34	1.2	•	11.5	7.1	2.2	2.0	1.7	1.9	1.2	0.9	0.9	0.3	•
Inventory Turnover 35	120.8	•	433.0	201.6	149.1	72.3	95.0	128.3	50.1	293.8	98.6	10.3	•
Receivables Turnover 36	12.0	•	96.1	75.1	19.7	6.4	14.3	8.6	10.8	9.0	14.4	3.5	•
Total Liabilities to Net Worth 37	2.8	•	•	1.2	14.1	4.7	2.6	3.0	3.1	1.4	1.3	2.8	•
Current Assets to Working Capital 38	2.5	•	3.2	1.4	10.0	2.4	•	•	7.7	13.0	6.0	1.6	•
Current Liabilities to Working Capital 39	1.5	•	2.2	0.4	9.0	1.4	•	•	6.7	12.0	5.0	0.6	•
Working Capital to Net Sales 40	0.2	•	0.0	0.1	0.0	0.1	•	•	0.0	0.0	0.1	1.0	•
Inventory to Working Capital 41	0.0	•	0.1	0.0	0.2	0.1	•	•	0.3	0.0	0.1	0.0	•
Total Receipts to Cash Flow 42	4.7	6.3	11.3	4.0	6.0	11.2	5.6	1.8	5.9	3.8	7.0	2.0	•
Cost of Goods to Cash Flow 43	2.7	4.1	8.6	2.4	3.3	7.8	3.2	0.4	3.4	1.9	5.1	0.2	•
Cash Flow to Total Debt 44	0.3	•	0.8	3.2	0.4	0.2	1.3	0.4	0.3	0.4	0.2	0.2	•

Selected Financial Factors (in Percentages)

Debt Ratio 45	73.6	•	125.0	55.4	93.4	82.4	72.4	75.0	75.6	58.3	56.4	73.9	•
Return on Total Assets 46	3.3	•	14.7	26.8	4.0	6.8	5.8	5.0	0.2	4.3	2.3	2.5	•
Return on Equity Before Income Taxes 47	7.9	•	•	56.5	40.2	26.6	13.0	17.6	•	8.7	1.2	5.2	•
Return on Equity After Income Taxes 48	5.4	•	•	53.2	33.8	13.3	9.3	14.8	•	6.7	1.0	3.0	•
Profit Margin (Before Income Tax) 49	1.7	•	1.2	3.6	1.2	2.3	2.1	2.3	•	3.9	0.5	4.6	•
Profit Margin (After Income Tax) 50	1.2	•	1.1	3.4	1.0	1.1	1.5	2.0	•	3.0	0.5	2.7	•

TRAVEL ARRANGEMENT AND RESERVATION SERVICES

Table II
Corporations with Net Income

MONEY AMOUNTS AND SIZE OF ASSETS IN THOUSANDS OF DOLLARS

Item Description for Accounting Period 7/06 Through 6/07	Total	Zero Assets	Under 500	500 to 1,000	1,000 to 5,000	5,000 to 10,000	10,000 to 25,000	25,000 to 50,000	50,000 to 100,000	100,000 to 250,000	250,000 to 500,000	500,000 to 2,500,000	2,500,000 and over
Number of Enterprises **1**	12614	1416	10329	430	262	•	77	•	23	9	•	•	0
Revenues ($ in Thousands)													
Net Sales **2**	25685443	131723	8953567	2068624	1435490	•	2493532	•	1761857	1559018	•	•	0
Interest **3**	191276	0	912	507	3164	•	13107	•	21087	4003	•	•	0
Rents **4**	43825	0	2552	231	0	•	590	•	7926	749	•	•	0
Royalties **5**	13062	0	0	0	0	•	0	•	2429	0	•	•	0
Other Portfolio Income **6**	357110	0	318	6566	585	•	36176	•	53413	18806	•	•	0
Other Receipts **7**	841791	571	27852	19379	725	•	37905	•	88966	60379	•	•	0
Total Receipts **8**	27132507	132294	8985201	2095307	1439964	•	2581310	•	1935678	1642955	•	•	0
Average Total Receipts **9**	2151	93	870	4873	5496	•	33524	•	84160	182551	•	•	•
Operating Costs/Operating Income (%)													
Cost of Operations **10**	56.3	28.7	79.5	60.0	68.7	•	60.8	•	43.4	55.2	•	•	•
Salaries and Wages **11**	12.1	1.5	6.8	2.7	9.7	•	13.4	•	17.9	13.4	•	•	•
Taxes Paid **12**	1.5	1.8	0.8	1.7	1.3	•	1.3	•	2.5	1.7	•	•	•
Interest Paid **13**	0.8	0.8	0.0	0.2	0.2	•	0.2	•	1.1	0.1	•	•	•
Depreciation **14**	0.7	2.1	0.2	1.2	0.6	•	0.8	•	1.3	1.1	•	•	•
Amortization and Depletion **15**	0.5	0.1	0.0	0.0	0.0	•	0.0	•	0.5	1.0	•	•	•
Pensions and Other Deferred Comp. **16**	0.7	0.2	0.2	0.5	0.8	•	0.4	•	1.5	0.5	•	•	•
Employee Benefits **17**	1.1	2.8	0.2	0.2	0.3	•	1.2	•	1.8	1.6	•	•	•
Advertising **18**	2.0	1.3	0.3	1.6	0.5	•	3.2	•	2.3	0.9	•	•	•
Other Expenses **19**	22.6	29.9	7.1	23.3	10.4	•	16.8	•	26.6	20.8	•	•	•
Officers' Compensation **20**	2.0	9.9	2.0	5.4	3.0	•	1.6	•	2.3	0.8	•	•	•
Operating Margin **21**	•	21.0	2.9	3.2	4.4	•	0.4	•	•	3.0	•	•	•
Operating Margin Before Officers' Comp. **22**	1.7	30.9	4.9	8.6	7.4	•	2.0	•	1.1	3.8	•	•	•

Selected Average Balance Sheet ($ in Thousands)

Net Receivables 23	123	0	4	76	435	3693	•	9173	21500
Inventories 24	10	0	•	15	34	170	•	670	245
Net Property, Plant and Equipment 25	119	0	1	6	202	252	1224	13283	17825
Total Assets 26	1219	0	65	652	2021	17102	•	73253	162865
Notes and Loans Payable 27	171	0	42	223	225	1625	•	7340	900
All Other Liabilities 28	547	0	25	127	1556	12377	•	36078	83474
Net Worth 29	502	0	-2	302	240	3100	•	29835	78491

Selected Financial Ratios (Times to 1)

Current Ratio 30	1.2	•	2.9	3.4	1.8	•	0.9	1.0	1.3
Quick Ratio 31	0.8	•	2.5	3.0	1.3	•	0.8	0.8	1.0
Net Sales to Working Capital 32	28.6	•	24.7	15.5	7.2	•	246.2	9.9
Coverage Ratio 33	7.9	26.4	67.7	26.3	23.2	19.7	8.8	87.9
Total Asset Turnover 34	1.7	•	13.4	7.4	2.7	1.9	1.0	1.1
Inventory Turnover 35	110.1	•	609.4	198.4	111.1	116.0	49.6	391.0
Receivables Turnover 36	10.8	•	257.2	77.9	16.0	9.0	9.0	•
Total Liabilities to Net Worth 37	1.4	•	•	1.2	7.4	4.5	1.5	1.1
Current Assets to Working Capital 38	7.1	•	1.5	1.4	2.3	•	97.9	4.9
Current Liabilities to Working Capital 39	6.1	•	0.5	0.4	1.3	•	96.9	3.9
Working Capital to Net Sales 40	0.0	•	0.0	0.1	0.1	•	0.0	0.1
Inventory to Working Capital 41	0.1	•	0.0	0.0	0.1	•	3.4	0.0
Total Receipts to Cash Flow 42	4.1	2.1	11.1	4.0	7.8	5.2	3.3	3.8
Cost of Goods to Cash Flow 43	2.3	0.6	8.8	2.4	5.3	3.1	1.4	2.1
Cash Flow to Total Debt 44	0.7	•	1.2	3.5	0.4	0.4	0.5	0.5

Selected Financial Factors (in Percentages)

Debt Ratio 45	58.9	•	103.6	53.6	88.1	81.9	59.3	51.8
Return on Total Assets 46	10.2	•	43.7	34.2	13.2	7.8	10.2	8.6
Return on Equity Before Income Taxes 47	21.7	•	•	71.0	106.9	40.8	22.1	17.6
Return on Equity After Income Taxes 48	18.5	•	•	67.5	99.4	36.1	16.5	14.8
Profit Margin (Before Income Tax) 49	5.3	21.4	3.2	4.5	4.7	3.9	8.6	8.0
Profit Margin (After Income Tax) 50	4.6	21.4	3.2	4.2	4.3	3.5	6.4	6.7

OTHER ADMINISTRATIVE AND SUPPORT SERVICES

Table I

Corporations with and without Net Income

MONEY AMOUNTS AND SIZE OF ASSETS IN THOUSANDS OF DOLLARS

Item Description for Accounting Period 7/06 Through 6/07		Total	Zero Assets	Under 500	500 to 1,000	1,000 to 5,000	5,000 to 10,000	10,000 to 25,000	25,000 to 50,000	50,000 to 100,000	100,000 to 250,000	250,000 to 500,000	500,000 to 2,500,000	2,500,000 and over
Number of Enterprises	1	203196	44550	145464	6478	5443	644	308	122	74	55	26	29	3

Revenues ($ in Thousands)

Net Sales	2	197939903	6526015	58526005	12910719	30342009	9858022	9728306	6450050	6698575	9182725	14945618	27779809	4992049
Interest	3	1065263	17478	50643	10540	29357	29052	27671	15607	33099	71676	139627	343892	296620
Rents	4	89394	1160	8587	12002	7194	1203	1265	6190	3452	7188	11820	17200	12132
Royalties	5	206561	9278	3174	0	50	15	3106	149	7038	445	16352	166954	0
Other Portfolio Income	6	1554484	93332	89652	10475	27845	25901	37935	22165	45587	45490	46455	1036997	72649
Other Receipts	7	3734145	227180	371746	91226	229086	196768	188147	301008	209386	347990	594494	972281	4836
Total Receipts	8	204589750	6874443	59049807	13034962	30635541	10110961	9986430	6795169	6997137	9655514	15754366	30317133	5378286
Average Total Receipts	9	1007	154	406	2012	5628	15700	32423	55698	94556	175555	605937	1045418	1792762

Operating Costs/Operating Income (%)

Cost of Operations	10	40.7	21.7	36.4	44.5	53.8	58.7	48.6	47.1	47.6	32.5	47.8	26.8	27.2
Salaries and Wages	11	19.2	24.3	16.7	15.5	14.4	14.8	21.3	18.5	19.1	27.6	22.3	25.4	27.5
Taxes Paid	12	3.7	3.0	3.4	3.4	3.0	3.4	3.7	3.4	3.5	3.2	5.1	5.0	3.4
Interest Paid	13	1.8	2.2	0.7	1.0	0.9	1.2	1.3	1.6	2.8	2.7	2.4	3.3	10.7
Depreciation	14	2.0	3.1	2.0	2.1	1.8	1.9	1.5	2.0	2.1	2.0	1.1	2.2	3.6
Amortization and Depletion	15	1.0	0.8	0.1	0.1	0.1	0.2	0.2	0.6	1.0	1.5	2.4	2.1	10.5
Pensions and Other Deferred Comp.	16	0.4	0.2	0.3	0.4	0.4	0.5	0.4	0.6	0.2	0.6	0.3	1.1	0.1
Employee Benefits	17	2.1	1.1	0.9	1.1	1.3	2.2	2.2	2.6	3.7	2.6	4.9	3.9	3.2
Advertising	18	1.3	2.3	1.4	1.1	0.6	0.3	0.4	0.6	1.1	1.2	1.2	2.4	2.0
Other Expenses	19	21.9	46.6	24.9	18.8	16.6	14.0	15.5	23.6	19.3	25.3	15.4	25.3	19.1
Officers' Compensation	20	4.2	4.8	8.0	7.6	3.6	2.5	2.5	2.0	1.6	1.6	0.5	0.9	0.6
Operating Margin	21	1.7	•	5.2	4.4	3.4	0.3	2.5	•	•	•	•	1.6	•
Operating Margin Before Officers' Comp.	22	5.9	•	13.2	12.0	7.0	2.8	4.9	•	•	1.0	•	2.6	•

Selected Average Balance Sheet ($ in Thousands)

Net Receivables 23	130	0	10	125	547	2168	5079	7838	16326	37085	49262	197984	2352003
Inventories 24	11	0	2	25	73	105	338	1093	2111	2997	4499	7446	141722
Net Property, Plant and Equipment 25	96	0	24	209	472	1689	2308	6280	10621	17339	32982	164653	704163
Total Assets 26	540	0	79	672	1978	6944	15411	35389	70116	159297	346700	1067814	5226288
Notes and Loans Payable 27	223	0	50	348	735	3041	5457	12672	31912	48391	121805	296704	3243407
All Other Liabilities 28	164	0	18	191	634	1915	5463	11412	19383	52390	90771	351778	1557959
Net Worth 29	154	0	11	132	609	1987	4491	11305	18820	58517	134124	419333	424922

Selected Financial Ratios (Times to 1)

Current Ratio 30	1.3	•	1.3	1.6	1.4	1.5	1.3	1.2	1.3	1.5	1.3	1.5	1.0
Quick Ratio 31	1.1	•	1.1	1.3	1.1	1.2	1.1	1.0	0.9	1.1	0.9	1.1	1.0
Net Sales to Working Capital 32	17.0	•	49.0	14.2	17.8	11.0	16.5	24.4	11.5	5.9	23.4	8.6	73.1
Coverage Ratio 33	3.9	•	10.3	6.5	6.1	3.4	4.9	2.7	2.1	2.7	1.7	4.3	1.0
Total Asset Turnover 34	1.8	•	5.1	3.0	2.8	2.2	2.0	1.5	1.3	1.0	1.7	0.9	0.3
Inventory Turnover 35	35.3	•	63.0	35.5	41.1	85.8	45.4	22.8	20.4	18.1	61.1	34.5	3.2
Receivables Turnover 36	8.2	•	40.6	15.7	9.4	8.6	6.5	6.3	5.8	4.7	10.6	4.8	1.1
Total Liabilities to Net Worth 37	2.5	•	6.2	4.1	2.2	2.5	2.4	2.1	2.7	1.7	1.6	1.5	11.3
Current Assets to Working Capital 38	4.2	•	4.2	2.5	3.7	2.9	4.8	7.5	4.0	2.8	4.4	3.1	112.8
Current Liabilities to Working Capital 39	3.2	•	3.2	1.5	2.7	1.9	3.8	6.5	3.0	1.8	3.4	2.1	111.8
Working Capital to Net Sales 40	0.1	•	0.0	0.1	0.1	0.1	0.1	0.0	0.1	0.2	0.0	0.1	0.0
Inventory to Working Capital 41	0.2	•	0.3	0.2	0.2	0.1	0.1	0.5	0.3	0.1	0.2	0.1	1.9
Total Receipts to Cash Flow 42	4.4	3.2	3.8	5.1	5.8	7.3	5.7	4.3	5.4	3.9	6.8	3.3	6.5
Cost of Goods to Cash Flow 43	1.8	0.7	1.4	2.3	3.1	4.3	2.8	2.0	2.6	1.2	3.3	0.9	1.8
Cash Flow to Total Debt 44	0.6	•	1.6	0.7	0.7	0.4	0.5	0.5	0.3	0.4	0.4	0.5	0.1

Selected Financial Factors (in Percentages)

Debt Ratio 45	71.4	•	86.0	80.3	69.2	71.4	70.9	68.1	73.2	63.3	61.3	60.7	91.9
Return on Total Assets 46	12.5	•	34.2	18.9	14.7	8.8	13.2	6.5	7.4	7.4	7.0	13.0	3.4
Return on Equity Before Income Taxes 47	32.5	•	221.2	81.1	39.9	21.8	36.1	12.8	14.4	12.7	7.6	25.4	•
Return on Equity After Income Taxes 48	27.6	•	218.2	80.0	37.9	19.5	33.3	11.0	10.5	10.1	4.1	16.9	•
Profit Margin (Before Income Tax) 49	5.1	•	6.1	5.4	4.4	2.8	5.1	2.7	3.0	4.4	1.8	11.1	•
Profit Margin (After Income Tax) 50	4.4	•	6.0	5.3	4.1	2.5	4.7	2.4	2.2	3.5	1.0	7.4	•

Table II

Corporations with Net Income

OTHER ADMINISTRATIVE AND SUPPORT SERVICES

MONEY AMOUNTS AND SIZE OF ASSETS IN THOUSANDS OF DOLLARS

Item Description for Accounting Period 7/06 Through 6/07	Total	Zero Assets	Under 500	500 to 1,000	1,000 to 5,000	5,000 to 10,000	10,000 to 25,000	25,000 to 50,000	50,000 to 100,000	100,000 to 250,000	250,000 to 500,000	500,000 to 2,500,000	2,500,000 and over
Number of Enterprises 1	132556	22474	99805	5105	4299	430	234	•	47	34	16	•	0
Revenues ($ in Thousands)													
Net Sales 2	150568346	2677522	40569887	10978829	23737973	7901813	8473463	•	4951107	6544415	11900011	•	0
Interest 3	835776	1436	42051	5238	21126	16945	14748	•	23879	36743	108573	•	0
Rents 4	78487	0	5180	10946	6717	243	561	•	3404	7079	11820	•	0
Royalties 5	174177	0	3174	0	50	15	3024	•	6778	78	16332	•	0
Other Portfolio Income 6	1404501	14594	77371	8431	24162	13337	33588	•	44814	32884	36123	•	0
Other Receipts 7	2967231	133970	298407	88674	172621	47839	165771	•	193581	60301	561728	•	0
Total Receipts 8	156029518	2827522	40996070	11092118	23962649	7980192	8691155	•	5223563	6681500	12634587	•	0
Average Total Receipts 9	1177	126	411	2173	5574	18559	37142	•	111140	196515	789662	•	•
Operating Costs/Operating Income (%)													
Cost of Operations 10	41.0	26.8	33.1	41.4	52.0	63.2	50.1	•	52.9	30.8	57.5	•	•
Salaries and Wages 11	18.2	11.0	16.6	15.3	14.6	11.4	19.3	•	14.3	25.4	15.6	•	•
Taxes Paid 12	3.7	2.3	3.3	3.5	2.8	2.8	3.7	•	3.2	3.4	5.0	•	•
Interest Paid 13	1.4	1.5	0.5	1.0	0.7	1.0	1.0	•	2.1	1.5	1.8	•	•
Depreciation 14	1.8	2.4	1.7	2.1	1.9	1.7	1.5	•	1.4	1.9	0.9	•	•
Amortization and Depletion 15	0.5	0.5	0.1	0.1	0.1	0.2	0.2	•	0.5	1.1	1.6	•	•
Pensions and Other Deferred Comp. 16	0.5	0.5	0.3	0.5	0.4	0.4	0.4	•	0.2	0.7	0.3	•	•
Employee Benefits 17	2.1	0.5	0.7	1.0	1.4	1.4	1.9	•	3.7	2.7	5.0	•	•
Advertising 18	1.1	0.9	1.5	1.1	0.6	0.2	0.4	•	1.3	1.3	1.4	•	•
Other Expenses 19	20.1	34.7	23.7	18.5	15.8	10.8	14.4	•	18.0	24.1	13.0	•	•
Officers' Compensation 20	4.1	4.1	8.1	8.3	3.7	2.5	2.0	•	1.7	1.0	0.5	•	•
Operating Margin 21	5.4	14.7	10.3	7.3	6.0	4.5	5.2	•	0.7	6.0	•	•	•
Operating Margin Before Officers' Comp. 22	9.5	18.8	18.4	15.6	9.7	7.0	7.2	•	2.4	7.0	7.0	•	•

Selected Average Balance Sheet ($ in Thousands)

Item												
Net Receivables 23	165	0	9	104	551	2453	5114	•	18417	39056	54254	•
Inventories 24	14	0	2	21	68	128	382	•	2931	4538	6331	•
Net Property, Plant and Equipment 25	104	0	23	241	456	1334	2544	•	9146	16435	45217	•
Total Assets 26	593	0	79	666	1941	6954	15062	•	68202	157370	338110	•
Notes and Loans Payable 27	228	0	37	350	553	2550	4826	•	28561	34480	86502	•
All Other Liabilities 28	169	0	13	125	645	1890	5347	•	23151	57225	97836	•
Net Worth 29	196	0	29	192	744	2515	4890	•	16490	65665	153772	•

Selected Financial Ratios (Times to 1)

Item												
Current Ratio 30	1.4	•	1.9	2.0	1.6	1.5	1.3	•	1.4	1.7	1.2	•
Quick Ratio 31	1.1	•	1.5	1.6	1.3	1.3	1.1	•	1.1	1.2	0.8	•
Net Sales to Working Capital 32	14.0	•	24.6	12.3	12.1	12.4	15.7	•	10.0	5.7	32.0	•
Coverage Ratio 33	7.4	14.7	23.2	9.1	10.4	6.8	8.6	•	4.1	6.2	2.9	•
Total Asset Turnover 34	1.9	•	5.1	3.2	2.8	2.6	2.4	•	1.5	1.2	2.2	•
Inventory Turnover 35	33.7	•	56.7	43.4	42.2	90.7	47.5	•	19.0	13.1	67.6	•
Receivables Turnover 36	7.9	•	42.7	17.7	9.2	8.6	7.8	•	5.6	5.3	12.6	•
Total Liabilities to Net Worth 37	2.0	•	1.7	2.5	1.6	1.8	2.1	•	3.1	1.4	1.2	•
Current Assets to Working Capital 38	3.6	•	2.2	2.0	2.6	2.9	3.9	•	3.5	2.5	5.4	•
Current Liabilities to Working Capital 39	2.6	•	1.2	1.0	1.6	1.9	2.9	•	2.5	1.5	4.4	•
Working Capital to Net Sales 40	0.1	•	0.0	0.1	0.1	0.1	0.1	•	0.1	0.2	0.0	•
Inventory to Working Capital 41	0.1	•	0.2	0.1	0.1	0.1	0.1	•	0.3	0.1	0.3	•
Total Receipts to Cash Flow 42	4.0	2.0	3.2	4.6	5.3	7.3	5.2	•	4.8	3.5	7.0	•
Cost of Goods to Cash Flow 43	1.6	0.5	1.1	1.9	2.7	4.6	2.6	•	2.5	1.1	4.0	•
Cash Flow to Total Debt 44	0.7	•	2.5	1.0	0.9	0.6	0.7	•	0.4	0.6	0.6	•

Selected Financial Factors (in Percentages)

Item												
Debt Ratio 45	67.0	•	63.2	71.2	61.7	63.8	67.5	•	75.8	58.3	54.5	•
Return on Total Assets 46	20.2	•	60.7	30.2	21.8	17.1	21.1	•	13.5	11.7	11.8	•
Return on Equity Before Income Taxes 47	52.9	•	157.7	93.1	51.4	40.3	57.4	•	42.3	23.5	17.0	•
Return on Equity After Income Taxes 48	47.0	•	156.0	92.1	49.4	37.7	54.1	•	35.3	19.7	12.0	•
Profit Margin (Before Income Tax) 49	9.1	20.3	11.4	8.3	6.9	5.5	7.8	•	6.6	8.0	3.5	•
Profit Margin (After Income Tax) 50	8.1	19.5	11.2	8.2	6.7	5.2	7.3	•	5.5	6.7	2.5	•

Table I

Corporations with and without Net Income

WASTE MANAGEMENT AND REMEDIATION SERVICES

MONEY AMOUNTS AND SIZE OF ASSETS IN THOUSANDS OF DOLLARS

Item Description for Accounting Period 7/06 Through 6/07	Total	Zero Assets	Under 500	500 to 1,000	1,000 to 5,000	5,000 to 10,000	10,000 to 25,000	25,000 to 50,000	50,000 to 100,000	100,000 to 250,000	250,000 to 500,000	500,000 to 2,500,000	2,500,000 and over
Number of Enterprises 1	14979	2052	8964	2120	1385	186	144	60	25	21	8	8	6
Revenues ($ in Thousands)													
Net Sales 2	61037592	528338	7003561	3061960	7387782	2539322	2978638	2005877	1759287	3497650	2274951	4517699	23482528
Interest 3	308856	163	816	2361	6362	1156	5275	11632	6297	8115	39595	61756	165328
Rents 4	113026	0	0	220	2482	375	1058	1095	665	956	396	1447	104333
Royalties 5	14651	0	0	0	1943	308	0	1077	0	0	10004	666	653
Other Portfolio Income 6	449037	10616	21809	109422	32004	4585	13195	27380	7113	5331	19376	1571	196636
Other Receipts 7	753043	10199	6960	8940	87387	8180	36905	48126	25785	15236	92061	35890	377369
Total Receipts 8	62676205	549316	7033146	3182903	7517960	2553926	3035071	2095187	1799147	3527288	2436383	4619029	24326847
Average Total Receipts 9	4184	268	785	1501	5428	13731	21077	34920	71966	167966	304548	577379	4054474
Operating Costs/Operating Income (%)													
Cost of Operations 10	38.6	39.1	33.3	30.2	45.2	49.6	53.4	51.5	35.5	41.8	27.3	23.0	38.8
Salaries and Wages 11	15.0	16.5	12.7	13.0	9.1	10.5	7.9	11.2	13.0	19.4	15.0	19.4	18.2
Taxes Paid 12	3.6	3.0	2.6	3.5	2.7	2.6	2.1	2.6	2.2	3.0	3.3	3.3	5.0
Interest Paid 13	3.6	2.2	0.7	2.2	1.2	1.0	1.5	2.1	2.0	2.3	6.9	6.5	5.5
Depreciation 14	5.4	1.2	2.9	6.0	3.9	2.7	4.2	3.9	3.8	3.4	6.4	5.9	7.5
Amortization and Depletion 15	1.5	0.3	0.3	0.1	0.1	0.1	0.3	0.5	0.6	0.9	3.2	3.7	2.6
Pensions and Other Deferred Comp. 16	0.4	0.0	0.3	1.1	0.5	0.2	0.4	0.5	0.9	0.5	1.7	0.4	0.3
Employee Benefits 17	1.8	1.4	1.1	0.8	1.2	1.7	1.4	2.3	2.2	2.6	3.6	2.3	2.1
Advertising 18	0.4	0.9	0.7	0.6	0.3	0.3	0.5	0.2	0.3	0.2	0.1	0.4	0.3
Other Expenses 19	31.7	27.3	35.0	33.7	27.4	25.1	22.0	19.6	35.7	19.8	36.8	35.1	35.1
Officers' Compensation 20	2.2	7.7	6.8	4.2	3.3	3.6	3.3	2.4	1.3	1.0	1.7	1.4	0.2
Operating Margin 21	•	0.4	3.5	4.6	5.2	2.7	2.9	3.2	2.4	5.2	•	•	•
Operating Margin Before Officers' Comp. 22	•	8.1	10.3	8.8	8.5	6.3	6.2	5.6	3.7	6.1	•	•	•

Selected Average Balance Sheet ($ in Thousands)

Net Receivables 23	502	0	18	55	496	2216	2728	5275	14194	29954	44570	87233	565517
Inventories 24	50	0	4	16	37	272	393	881	585	339	1656	8680	60427
Net Property, Plant and Equipment 25	1744	0	74	271	915	2094	5610	10292	19449	41985	146646	298037	2814063
Total Assets 26	4827	0	140	679	2154	6274	14987	33319	67742	164597	391826	916586	7614620
Notes and Loans Payable 27	2090	0	59	476	949	1907	5993	13396	27563	67962	201141	383725	3272817
All Other Liabilities 28	1466	0	37	132	486	2856	4071	11176	23071	43926	99232	202530	2497165
Net Worth 29	1271	0	44	71	720	1511	4922	8747	17108	52709	91453	330331	1844639

Selected Financial Ratios (Times to 1)

Current Ratio 30	1.0	•	1.0	1.5	1.7	1.4	1.6	1.3	1.1	1.2	0.8	0.7	0.9
Quick Ratio 31	0.7	•	0.9	1.0	1.4	1.2	1.3	1.0	0.8	1.0	0.7	0.4	0.6
Net Sales to Working Capital 32	•	•	438.4	13.5	12.3	12.4	9.6	11.6	41.9	24.8	•	•	•
Coverage Ratio 33	0.5	3.0	6.6	4.9	6.9	4.2	4.2	4.6	3.3	3.6	1.2	1.1	0.5
Total Asset Turnover 34	0.8	•	5.6	2.1	2.5	2.2	1.4	1.0	1.0	1.0	0.7	0.6	0.5
Inventory Turnover 35	31.4	•	61.4	27.5	65.9	24.9	28.1	19.5	42.7	205.4	46.9	15.0	25.1
Receivables Turnover 36	7.9	•	54.6	27.4	8.8	6.3	6.2	7.4	5.5	7.4	3.8	7.2	6.7
Total Liabilities to Net Worth 37	2.8	•	2.2	8.6	2.0	3.2	2.0	2.8	3.0	2.1	3.3	1.8	3.1
Current Assets to Working Capital 38	•	•	26.4	3.0	2.3	3.3	2.8	4.1	15.9	7.1	•	•	•
Current Liabilities to Working Capital 39	•	•	25.4	2.0	1.3	2.3	1.8	3.1	14.9	6.1	•	•	•
Working Capital to Net Sales 40	•	•	0.0	0.1	0.1	0.1	0.1	0.1	0.0	0.0	•	•	•
Inventory to Working Capital 41	•	•	1.0	0.2	0.1	0.2	0.1	0.5	0.3	0.1	•	•	•
Total Receipts to Cash Flow 42	4.1	3.5	2.9	3.1	3.3	4.8	4.5	4.4	2.8	4.4	3.1	3.2	5.8
Cost of Goods to Cash Flow 43	1.6	1.3	1.0	0.9	1.5	2.4	2.4	2.3	1.0	1.9	0.8	0.7	2.2
Cash Flow to Total Debt 44	0.3	•	2.8	0.8	1.1	0.6	0.5	0.3	0.5	0.3	0.3	0.3	0.1

Selected Financial Factors (in Percentages)

Debt Ratio 45	73.7	•	68.4	89.6	66.6	75.9	67.2	73.7	74.7	68.0	76.7	64.0	75.8
Return on Total Assets 46	1.7	•	25.9	23.0	20.3	9.3	8.7	9.6	6.9	8.3	6.0	4.4	•
Return on Equity Before Income Taxes 47	•	•	69.4	175.2	52.0	29.4	20.2	28.7	18.9	18.8	4.1	1.2	•
Return on Equity After Income Taxes 48	•	•	68.0	167.9	49.9	26.4	17.9	24.4	16.7	16.6	1.7	•	•
Profit Margin (Before Income Tax) 49	•	4.4	3.9	8.6	7.0	3.3	4.8	7.5	4.6	6.0	1.3	0.7	•
Profit Margin (After Income Tax) 50	•	2.1	3.9	8.2	6.7	2.9	4.2	6.4	4.1	5.3	0.6	0.3	•

Table II
Corporations with Net Income

WASTE MANAGEMENT AND REMEDIATION SERVICES

MONEY AMOUNTS AND SIZE OF ASSETS IN THOUSANDS OF DOLLARS

Item Description for Accounting Period 7/06 Through 6/07	Total	Zero Assets	Under 500	500 to 1,000	1,000 to 5,000	5,000 to 10,000	10,000 to 25,000	25,000 to 50,000	50,000 to 100,000	100,000 to 250,000	250,000 to 500,000	500,000 to 2,500,000	2,500,000 and over
Number of Enterprises **1**	9984	1047	6081	1418	1119	•	104	38	17	18	5	4	•
Revenues ($ in Thousands)													
Net Sales **2**	49592214	449101	5605328	2085753	6080770	•	2605410	1512915	1415671	3291502	1523987	2639683	•
Interest **3**	281931	163	276	2357	4718	•	4839	10585	3034	4409	36714	57308	•
Rents **4**	109374	0	0	220	1570	•	1058	952	125	956	396	0	•
Royalties **5**	12399	0	0	0	0	•	0	1077	0	0	10004	666	•
Other Portfolio Income **6**	392666	10616	18365	109300	31253	•	12244	26026	6468	4587	11460	1276	•
Other Receipts **7**	579753	10199	1461	8206	77782	•	28089	43693	8325	14478	43585	31185	•
Total Receipts **8**	50968337	470079	5625430	2205836	6196093	•	2651640	1595248	1433623	3315932	1626146	2730118	•
Average Total Receipts **9**	5105	449	925	1556	5537	•	25497	41980	84331	184218	325229	682530	•
Operating Costs/Operating Income (%)													
Cost of Operations **10**	40.0	44.1	35.1	25.5	41.8	•	52.5	48.7	37.3	43.8	18.8	21.2	•
Salaries and Wages **11**	14.0	8.9	11.8	12.5	9.0	•	7.0	11.7	12.1	18.7	18.1	19.8	•
Taxes Paid **12**	3.7	2.6	2.6	3.0	2.3	•	1.9	2.4	2.3	2.8	4.2	3.3	•
Interest Paid **13**	3.6	1.3	0.4	1.0	1.1	•	1.0	1.3	1.5	2.0	5.8	6.0	•
Depreciation **14**	5.5	1.0	2.7	4.4	3.8	•	3.6	3.2	3.4	3.1	7.5	4.9	•
Amortization and Depletion **15**	1.4	0.4	0.1	0.1	0.1	•	0.1	0.4	0.3	0.6	1.6	5.5	•
Pensions and Other Deferred Comp. **16**	0.4	0.0	0.3	1.4	0.4	•	0.4	0.6	1.1	0.5	2.5	0.2	•
Employee Benefits **17**	1.7	1.7	1.1	0.6	1.1	•	1.3	2.4	2.4	2.4	3.6	1.8	•
Advertising **18**	0.4	0.3	0.8	0.7	0.4	•	0.5	0.2	0.2	0.2	0.2	0.3	•
Other Expenses **19**	21.5	17.4	30.9	37.0	29.7	•	20.5	19.9	31.5	19.1	38.6	33.3	•
Officers' Compensation **20**	2.0	9.0	6.3	4.7	2.9	•	3.4	2.4	1.4	1.0	1.1	1.3	•
Operating Margin **21**	5.7	13.2	8.0	8.9	7.6	•	7.7	6.9	6.5	5.7	•	2.5	•
Operating Margin Before Officers' Comp. **22**	7.7	22.3	14.3	13.7	10.5	•	11.2	9.3	7.9	6.7	•	3.7	•

Selected Average Balance Sheet ($ in Thousands)

Net Receivables 23	550	0	18	65	480	•	2622	6661	17376	34481	40484	104321	•
Inventories 24	38	0	4	16	40	•	475	786	638	548	1383	5212	•
Net Property, Plant and Equipment 25	2175	0	76	201	936	•	5878	9677	20094	40443	148700	376451	•
Total Assets 26	5521	0	141	661	2152	•	15176	33212	67330	161744	385798	1118602	•
Notes and Loans Payable 27	2375	0	57	378	953	•	5740	10105	19341	66158	181905	425105	•
All Other Liabilities 28	1616	0	15	56	439	•	3171	8201	19771	41462	93562	245096	•
Net Worth 29	1531	0	69	226	761	•	6265	14906	28217	54124	110331	448401	•

Selected Financial Ratios (Times to 1)

Current Ratio 30	1.1	•	2.4	2.2	1.8	•	2.1	1.7	1.4	1.2	0.6	0.8	•
Quick Ratio 31	0.9	•	2.2	1.9	1.5	•	1.8	1.4	1.2	1.0	0.5	0.6	•
Net Sales to Working Capital 32	38.0	•	30.9	7.9	12.1	•	7.0	6.9	11.8	23.9	•	•	•
Coverage Ratio 33	3.3	14.3	20.0	15.5	9.4	•	10.4	10.5	6.2	4.1	1.8	2.0	•
Total Asset Turnover 34	0.9	•	6.5	2.2	2.5	•	1.7	1.2	1.2	1.1	0.8	0.6	•
Inventory Turnover 35	52.6	•	73.4	23.0	56.5	•	27.7	24.7	48.7	146.2	41.5	26.8	•
Receivables Turnover 36	8.6	•	63.5	21.7	10.1	•	7.3	7.1	5.6	•	3.2	•	•
Total Liabilities to Net Worth 37	2.6	•	1.1	1.9	1.8	•	1.4	1.2	1.4	2.0	2.5	1.5	•
Current Assets to Working Capital 38	8.3	•	1.7	1.8	2.2	•	1.9	2.4	3.7	7.1	•	•	•
Current Liabilities to Working Capital 39	7.3	•	0.7	0.8	1.2	•	0.9	1.4	2.7	6.1	•	•	•
Working Capital to Net Sales 40	0.0	•	0.0	0.1	0.1	•	0.1	0.1	0.1	0.0	•	•	•
Inventory to Working Capital 41	0.3	•	0.0	0.2	0.1	•	0.1	0.2	0.1	0.1	•	•	•
Total Receipts to Cash Flow 42	4.0	2.9	2.9	2.4	2.9	•	3.9	3.7	2.9	4.5	2.7	2.9	•
Cost of Goods to Cash Flow 43	1.6	1.3	1.0	0.6	1.2	•	2.0	1.8	1.1	2.0	0.5	0.6	•
Cash Flow to Total Debt 44	0.3	•	4.4	1.4	1.4	•	0.7	0.6	0.7	0.4	0.4	0.3	•

Selected Financial Factors (in Percentages)

Debt Ratio 45	72.3	•	51.3	65.7	64.6	•	58.7	55.1	58.1	66.5	71.4	59.9	•
Return on Total Assets 46	10.8	•	57.0	35.0	26.8	•	17.3	16.2	11.3	9.6	8.3	7.0	•
Return on Equity Before Income Taxes 47	27.3	•	111.3	95.4	67.8	•	37.9	32.7	22.6	21.7	13.1	8.7	•
Return on Equity After Income Taxes 48	22.8	•	109.9	92.0	65.3	•	35.4	28.8	20.6	19.2	10.0	6.2	•
Profit Margin (Before Income Tax) 49	8.4	17.9	8.3	14.7	9.5	•	9.5	12.3	7.7	6.4	4.7	5.9	•
Profit Margin (After Income Tax) 50	7.0	15.3	8.2	14.2	9.1	•	8.9	10.8	7.0	5.7	3.6	4.2	•

Table I

Corporations with and without Net Income

EDUCATIONAL SERVICES

MONEY AMOUNTS AND SIZE OF ASSETS IN THOUSANDS OF DOLLARS

Item Description for Accounting Period 7/06 Through 6/07	Total	Zero Assets	Under 500	500 to 1,000	1,000 to 5,000	5,000 to 10,000	10,000 to 25,000	25,000 to 50,000	50,000 to 100,000	100,000 to 250,000	250,000 to 500,000	500,000 to 2,500,000	2,500,000 and over
Number of Enterprises 1	47349	11541	33252	1175	1064	108	109	28	28	27	8	8	0
Revenues ($ in Thousands)													
Net Sales 2	37263167	1018540	9994115	1642202	3774258	1261146	2295176	1152053	2042413	4483568	1405082	8194613	0
Interest 3	166289	416	7208	2985	12987	2850	10351	7227	6167	25501	7678	82919	0
Rents 4	23728	0	0	0	439	378	4	615	2267	11276	612	8137	0
Royalties 5	186257	0	0	0	0	29813	0	16760	782	3383	33325	102193	0
Other Portfolio Income 6	114381	97	6908	1181	18341	98	4919	3588	3000	5964	5877	64407	0
Other Receipts 7	581727	9078	91033	17379	81676	17545	69145	32807	54279	27003	9784	172002	0
Total Receipts 8	38335549	1028131	10099264	1663747	3887701	1311830	2379595	1213050	2108908	4556695	1462358	8624271	0
Average Total Receipts 9	810	89	304	1416	3654	12147	21831	43323	75318	168766	182795	1078034	•
Operating Costs/Operating Income (%)													
Cost of Operations 10	14.3	8.4	9.6	29.2	9.4	21.5	33.2	15.7	7.2	26.2	10.3	9.4	•
Salaries and Wages 11	30.0	19.5	26.6	28.2	33.3	33.6	26.7	36.0	37.9	26.3	36.5	32.9	•
Taxes Paid 12	3.8	6.9	4.7	3.6	4.5	3.9	3.3	3.9	4.2	2.7	4.0	2.7	•
Interest Paid 13	2.1	0.1	1.1	1.8	0.8	0.7	1.2	1.0	1.7	2.5	4.5	4.3	•
Depreciation 14	2.0	1.2	1.3	2.1	1.6	1.2	2.4	2.1	3.6	2.0	2.9	2.4	•
Amortization and Depletion 15	0.9	0.3	0.3	0.1	0.3	0.5	0.4	1.6	1.6	1.4	3.8	1.3	•
Pensions and Other Deferred Comp. 16	0.5	0.1	0.8	0.5	0.4	0.5	0.4	0.5	0.7	0.4	0.4	0.2	•
Employee Benefits 17	2.1	0.8	1.8	1.9	1.7	1.2	2.0	2.7	1.7	1.2	4.4	2.9	•
Advertising 18	5.3	3.3	2.2	2.2	3.2	5.8	4.6	6.9	6.1	4.8	5.6	10.6	•
Other Expenses 19	30.1	43.2	36.7	21.1	34.5	25.6	26.4	29.3	31.1	27.7	27.7	23.5	•
Officers' Compensation 20	5.3	6.2	11.0	6.8	7.1	4.6	2.3	1.8	1.7	1.6	1.0	2.2	•
Operating Margin 21	3.7	9.9	3.9	2.5	3.2	0.9	•	•	2.6	2.9	•	7.5	•
Operating Margin Before Officers' Comp. 22	9.0	16.2	14.9	9.3	10.2	5.6	•	0.3	4.3	4.5	•	9.7	•

Selected Average Balance Sheet ($ in Thousands)

Net Receivables 23	97	0	9	66	363	2520	2523	5888	11964	25249	72702	190628
Inventories 24	7	0	2	3	14	404	230	834	1158	1780	2904	6048
Net Property, Plant and Equipment 25	125	0	23	225	704	1085	3890	6232	20890	29476	69547	187865
Total Assets 26	652	0	80	689	2031	7423	16059	35633	72147	160481	361958	1559436
Notes and Loans Payable 27	204	0	68	277	607	1885	4746	4577	21514	35727	136747	361094
All Other Liabilities 28	253	0	23	303	1116	3846	6503	12046	24858	59284	118884	619080
Net Worth 29	196	0	-11	110	308	1693	4810	19010	25776	65469	106328	579261

Selected Financial Ratios (Times to 1)

Current Ratio 30	1.1	•	1.2	1.0	1.0	1.2	1.3	1.2	1.2	1.0	1.0	1.0
Quick Ratio 31	0.9	•	1.0	0.9	0.9	1.1	1.0	0.9	1.0	0.8	0.9	0.8
Net Sales to Working Capital 32	43.2	•	45.4	•	11.3	10.8	15.1	15.1	•	144.1	•	54.7
Coverage Ratio 33	4.1	103.5	5.7	3.2	8.5	7.7	1.6	5.1	4.4	2.8	1.7	3.9
Total Asset Turnover 34	1.2	•	3.8	2.0	1.7	1.6	1.3	1.2	1.0	1.0	0.5	0.7
Inventory Turnover 35	16.0	•	13.5	140.8	23.7	6.2	30.4	7.7	4.6	24.5	6.2	15.9
Receivables Turnover 36	8.9	•	31.2	24.0	9.0	6.0	8.6	6.9	6.2	6.0	2.6	7.4
Total Liabilities to Net Worth 37	2.3	•	•	5.3	5.6	3.4	2.3	0.9	1.8	1.5	2.4	1.7
Current Assets to Working Capital 38	13.2	•	5.7	•	5.3	3.9	5.6	5.6	•	47.0	•	24.4
Current Liabilities to Working Capital 39	12.2	•	4.7	•	4.3	2.9	4.6	4.6	•	46.0	•	23.4
Working Capital to Net Sales 40	0.0	•	0.0	•	0.1	0.1	0.1	0.1	•	0.0	•	0.0
Inventory to Working Capital 41	0.4	•	0.4	•	0.5	0.3	0.3	0.3	•	1.5	•	0.4
Total Receipts to Cash Flow 42	3.5	2.3	3.1	5.4	3.3	4.2	4.7	4.8	3.6	3.7	4.2	3.5
Cost of Goods to Cash Flow 43	0.5	0.2	0.3	1.6	0.3	0.9	1.6	0.7	0.3	1.0	0.4	0.3
Cash Flow to Total Debt 44	0.5	•	1.1	0.4	0.6	0.5	0.4	0.5	0.4	0.5	0.2	0.3

Selected Financial Factors (in Percentages)

Debt Ratio 45	69.9	•	114.3	84.1	84.9	77.2	70.0	46.7	64.3	59.2	70.6	62.9
Return on Total Assets 46	10.3	•	22.8	11.4	12.2	9.0	2.6	5.6	7.5	7.2	3.6	10.9
Return on Equity Before Income Taxes 47	25.8	•	•	48.9	71.2	34.3	3.4	8.4	16.2	11.4	4.9	21.8
Return on Equity After Income Taxes 48	19.8	•	•	44.2	66.7	24.3	0.9	5.1	13.7	8.2	1.0	13.9
Profit Margin (Before Income Tax) 49	6.4	10.9	5.0	3.8	6.2	5.0	0.8	3.9	5.7	4.5	3.0	12.4
Profit Margin (After Income Tax) 50	4.9	10.7	4.8	3.5	5.8	3.5	0.2	2.4	4.8	3.2	0.6	7.9

Table II
Corporations with Net Income

EDUCATIONAL SERVICES

MONEY AMOUNTS AND SIZE OF ASSETS IN THOUSANDS OF DOLLARS

Item Description for Accounting Period 7/06 Through 6/07	Total	Zero Assets	Under 500	500 to 1,000	1,000 to 5,000	5,000 to 10,000	10,000 to 25,000	25,000 to 50,000	50,000 to 100,000	100,000 to 250,000	250,000 to 500,000	500,000 to 2,500,000	2,500,000 and over
Number of Enterprises **1**	25887	6029	18337	591	•	51	60	17	21	17	•	•	0
Revenues ($ in Thousands)													
Net Sales **2**	28132282	793438	7085950	948409	•	781570	1495471	809370	1649348	2914761	•	•	0
Interest **3**	113218	4	3573	1625	•	1907	5953	5366	5633	16635	•	•	0
Rents **4**	13324	0	0	0	•	378	0	615	833	2310	•	•	0
Royalties **5**	158092	0	0	0	•	29813	0	0	782	1123	•	•	0
Other Portfolio Income **6**	102071	0	1019	1181	•	98	2516	3588	3000	4034	•	•	0
Other Receipts **7**	471316	520	59377	29143	•	14608	61348	30260	51953	10424	•	•	0
Total Receipts **8**	28990303	793962	7149919	980358	•	828374	1565288	849199	1711549	2949287	•	•	0
Average Total Receipts **9**	1120	132	390	1659	•	16243	26088	49953	81502	173487	•	•	•
Operating Costs/Operating Income (%)													
Cost of Operations **10**	13.3	4.7	10.1	36.9	•	19.6	41.1	14.2	6.7	20.9	•	•	•
Salaries and Wages **11**	29.1	22.7	26.9	12.1	•	28.1	22.5	34.8	37.1	27.0	•	•	•
Taxes Paid **12**	3.9	7.9	5.2	2.7	•	3.6	3.0	3.6	4.4	2.7	•	•	•
Interest Paid **13**	1.8	0.0	0.8	0.5	•	0.3	0.6	0.5	1.4	1.4	•	•	•
Depreciation **14**	1.8	1.2	0.9	1.7	•	1.2	1.6	1.9	2.5	2.6	•	•	•
Amortization and Depletion **15**	0.5	0.0	0.2	0.1	•	0.7	0.0	0.7	0.9	1.1	•	•	•
Pensions and Other Deferred Comp. **16**	0.5	0.1	0.7	0.7	•	0.6	0.6	0.6	0.8	0.3	•	•	•
Employee Benefits **17**	2.1	1.0	2.0	0.3	•	1.4	1.9	2.6	1.7	1.5	•	•	•
Advertising **18**	5.3	4.2	1.4	3.3	•	8.4	2.9	7.2	6.6	4.2	•	•	•
Other Expenses **19**	27.6	35.1	30.8	21.2	•	25.0	17.4	25.3	31.4	28.2	•	•	•
Officers' Compensation **20**	4.7	4.3	10.0	7.7	•	5.1	2.2	1.3	1.6	1.6	•	•	•
Operating Margin **21**	9.3	18.9	11.1	12.7	•	5.7	6.3	7.4	5.0	8.6	•	•	•
Operating Margin Before Officers' Comp. **22**	14.1	23.1	21.1	20.4	•	10.9	8.5	8.7	6.6	10.2	•	•	•

Selected Average Balance Sheet ($ in Thousands)

Net Receivables 23	120	0	9	72	•	1439	3013	6840	13726	23735
Inventories 24	9	0	3	6	•	631	307	1280	849	1646
Net Property, Plant and Equipment 25	170	0	22	191	•	1040	4721	7368	18390	37162
Total Assets 26	831	0	93	698	•	6910	15922	35542	72184	155226
Notes and Loans Payable 27	210	0	59	122	•	1124	2994	2499	17777	29182
All Other Liabilities 28	330	0	25	320	•	2548	5729	14005	28078	58191
Net Worth 29	291	0	9	256	•	3238	7198	19039	26329	67853

Selected Financial Ratios (Times to 1)

Current Ratio 30	1.2	•	1.5	1.3	•	1.7	1.7	1.4	1.2	1.0
Quick Ratio 31	1.0	•	1.4	1.1	•	1.3	1.3	1.1	1.0	0.8
Net Sales to Working Capital 32	21.6	•	23.0	19.5	•	7.8	6.9	9.7	12.6	•
Coverage Ratio 33	7.9	7903.5	15.7	35.1	•	35.9	20.5	28.9	7.3	8.0
Total Asset Turnover 34	1.3	•	4.2	2.3	•	2.2	1.6	1.3	1.1	1.1
Inventory Turnover 35	15.4	•	13.6	102.7	•	4.8	33.4	5.3	6.2	21.8
Receivables Turnover 36	9.8	•	31.5	20.9	•	7.9	7.2	7.1	6.7	5.8
Total Liabilities to Net Worth 37	1.9	•	9.7	1.7	•	1.1	1.2	0.9	1.7	1.3
Current Assets to Working Capital 38	6.5	•	2.8	4.9	•	2.4	2.4	3.8	5.1	•
Current Liabilities to Working Capital 39	5.5	•	1.8	3.9	•	1.4	1.4	2.8	4.1	•
Working Capital to Net Sales 40	0.0	•	0.0	0.1	•	0.1	0.1	0.1	0.1	•
Inventory to Working Capital 41	0.2	•	0.2	0.1	•	0.4	0.1	0.2	0.2	•
Total Receipts to Cash Flow 42	3.1	2.2	3.0	3.3	•	3.2	4.3	3.5	3.2	3.1
Cost of Goods to Cash Flow 43	0.4	0.1	0.3	1.2	•	0.6	1.8	0.5	0.2	0.6
Cash Flow to Total Debt 44	0.6	•	1.5	1.1	•	1.3	0.7	0.8	0.5	0.6

Selected Financial Factors (in Percentages)

Debt Ratio 45	65.0	•	90.6	63.3	•	53.1	54.8	46.4	63.5	56.3
Return on Total Assets 46	18.3	•	53.5	38.1	•	26.8	18.0	17.5	10.9	12.3
Return on Equity Before Income Taxes 47	45.7	•	535.1	101.0	•	55.6	37.9	31.5	25.7	24.6
Return on Equity After Income Taxes 48	38.3	•	527.1	97.0	•	46.9	34.8	26.0	22.5	19.8
Profit Margin (Before Income Tax) 49	12.2	18.9	12.1	16.1	•	11.8	10.9	12.6	8.6	9.8
Profit Margin (After Income Tax) 50	10.3	18.7	11.9	15.5	•	9.9	10.1	10.4	7.5	7.8

Table I
Corporations with and without Net Income

OFFICES OF PHYSICIANS

MONEY AMOUNTS AND SIZE OF ASSETS IN THOUSANDS OF DOLLARS

Item Description for Accounting Period 7/06 Through 6/07	Total	Zero Assets	Under 500	500 to 1,000	1,000 to 5,000	5,000 to 10,000	10,000 to 25,000	25,000 to 50,000	50,000 to 100,000	100,000 to 250,000	250,000 to 500,000	500,000 to 2,500,000	2,500,000 and over
Number of Enterprises 1	152424	15493	130037	3517	2757	421	104	50	24	13	4	3	0
Revenues ($ in Thousands)													
Net Sales 2	224608064	4579081	131611742	16806138	34497134	11703485	5399004	5729899	2518548	2658995	975947	8128091	0
Interest 3	203377	3630	62957	12661	37366	10203	10754	14721	9406	13905	7061	20714	0
Rents 4	126404	0	58992	152	26987	9604	2420	6152	12411	8804	0	882	0
Royalties 5	14804	0	0	0	0	0	1403	0	0	13400	0	0	0
Other Portfolio Income 6	355491	12274	109949	5524	23108	10621	15924	11655	23031	12242	3821	127342	0
Other Receipts 7	7025771	979185	3753642	322048	553939	141321	156423	142449	68154	-7534	562325	353820	0
Total Receipts 8	232333911	5574170	135597282	17146523	35138534	11875234	5585928	5904876	2631550	2699812	1549154	8630849	0
Average Total Receipts 9	1524	360	1043	4875	12745	28207	53711	118098	109648	207678	387288	2876950	•
Operating Costs/Operating Income (%)													
Cost of Operations 10	4.2	16.9	3.0	3.2	5.0	2.3	8.5	16.4	11.8	9.7	12.7	0.2	•
Salaries and Wages 11	27.8	15.5	24.6	27.2	32.7	26.2	38.1	36.5	42.7	31.2	51.1	46.8	•
Taxes Paid 12	3.0	2.3	3.1	3.3	3.0	2.3	2.8	2.7	2.6	2.5	3.7	4.0	•
Interest Paid 13	0.5	1.0	0.3	0.4	0.5	0.8	0.5	0.8	0.6	1.3	3.9	1.0	•
Depreciation 14	1.0	0.8	0.7	0.9	1.6	2.9	1.4	1.2	1.6	1.8	2.4	0.3	•
Amortization and Depletion 15	0.1	0.1	0.0	0.1	0.1	0.1	0.2	0.2	0.2	0.1	1.8	0.4	•
Pensions and Other Deferred Comp. 16	3.5	1.0	3.8	3.1	3.2	1.7	2.6	2.6	2.5	1.1	2.7	6.5	•
Employee Benefits 17	2.1	2.1	1.8	1.9	2.4	1.6	2.4	3.1	3.9	1.7	3.0	5.5	•
Advertising 18	0.6	1.8	0.6	0.7	0.5	0.3	0.3	0.2	0.4	2.2	1.6	0.1	•
Other Expenses 19	32.6	52.0	30.1	31.5	28.8	51.1	40.3	36.6	34.5	48.9	68.4	36.6	•
Officers' Compensation 20	23.3	26.1	28.9	23.1	21.5	11.5	5.0	1.5	1.4	0.7	2.1	0.2	•
Operating Margin 21	1.4	•	3.1	4.6	0.7	•	•	•	•	•	•	•	•
Operating Margin Before Officers' Comp. 22	24.7	6.5	32.0	27.6	22.2	10.7	3.0	6.5	•	•	•	•	•

Selected Average Balance Sheet ($ in Thousands)

Net Receivables 23	24	2	0	35	325	736	3095	9432	16579	31383	37898	85398
Inventories 24	2	0	0	5	28	21	216	330	1015	803	2189	1801
Net Property, Plant and Equipment 25	65		29	212	709	2941	4170	10398	20553	32110	30596	39413
Total Assets 26	224		90	696	2022	7193	14366	35129	64512	140354	337971	1163555
Notes and Loans Payable 27	109		51	269	1217	4333	9455	13664	15704	34256	123458	301074
All Other Liabilities 28	88		35	254	737	2148	5256	13440	24107	50615	131738	677441
Net Worth 29	27		4	173	67	712	-345	8025	24701	55483	82776	185040

Selected Financial Ratios (Times to 1)

Current Ratio 30	1.0	•	1.0	0.9	0.9	1.0	0.9	0.9	1.4	1.6	1.4	1.4
Quick Ratio 31	0.9	•	0.8	0.8	0.6	0.8	0.7	0.7	1.2	1.4	1.2	1.2
Net Sales to Working Capital 32	790.3	•	•	•	•	•	•	•	12.5	10.6	12.1	23.0
Coverage Ratio 33	11.0	•	3.1	16.9	6.0	3.8	1.8	2.8	4.9	1.2	2.4	4.7
Total Asset Turnover 34	6.6	•	11.3	6.9	6.2	3.6	3.9	3.3	1.6	1.5	0.7	2.3
Inventory Turnover 35	40.1	•	89.4	28.7	22.2	20.5	30.2	57.1	12.2	24.7	14.2	2.8
Receivables Turnover 36	65.5	•	441.1	140.2	46.8	14.3	31.5	11.9	7.4	7.3	12.9	31.3
Total Liabilities to Net Worth 37	7.3	•	24.3	3.0	29.1	•	9.1	3.4	1.6	1.5	3.1	5.3
Current Assets to Working Capital 38	49.6	•	•	•	•	•	•	•	3.7	2.6	3.5	3.4
Current Liabilities to Working Capital 39	48.6	•	•	•	•	•	•	•	2.7	1.6	2.5	2.4
Working Capital to Net Sales 40	0.0	•	•	•	•	•	•	•	0.1	0.1	0.1	0.0
Inventory to Working Capital 41	0.8	•	•	•	•	•	•	•	0.1	0.0	0.1	0.0
Total Receipts to Cash Flow 42	3.1	2.1	3.2	3.1	3.9	2.8	2.2	2.8	3.1	2.2	1.4	2.8
Cost of Goods to Cash Flow 43	0.1	0.4	0.1	0.2	0.2	0.0	0.5	0.4	0.2	0.2	0.2	0.0
Cash Flow to Total Debt 44	2.4	3.7	3.0	1.7	1.3	2.0	1.5	0.9	1.1	0.7	1.0	

Selected Financial Factors (in Percentages)

Debt Ratio 45	87.9	•	96.0	75.1	96.7	90.1	102.4	77.2	61.7	60.5	75.5	84.1
Return on Total Assets 46	34.6	•	72.6	48.0	18.8	5.9	6.8	6.7	4.4	2.2	6.7	10.9
Return on Equity Before Income Taxes 47	260.7	•	1736.2	181.4	471.4	26.3	19.0	9.2	•	0.9	16.1	54.2
Return on Equity After Income Taxes 48	252.9	•	1714.9	180.2	460.9	22.2	13.3	•	3.9	•	9.9	39.5
Profit Margin (Before Income Tax) 49	4.8	2.1	6.1	6.6	2.5	0.7	1.4	1.3	2.2	0.2	5.5	3.7
Profit Margin (After Income Tax) 50	4.6	2.0	6.0	6.5	2.5	0.6	0.9	1.2	0.9	•	3.3	2.7

Table II
Corporations with Net Income

OFFICES OF PHYSICIANS

MONEY AMOUNTS AND SIZE OF ASSETS IN THOUSANDS OF DOLLARS

Item Description for Accounting Period 7/06 Through 6/07	Total	Zero Assets	Under 500	500 to 1,000	1,000 to 5,000	5,000 to 10,000	10,000 to 25,000	25,000 to 50,000	50,000 to 100,000	100,000 to 250,000	250,000 to 500,000	500,000 to 2,500,000	2,500,000 and over
Number of Enterprises 1	99062	7417	86617	2712	•	265	69	29	16	7	•	3	0
Revenues ($ in Thousands)													
Net Sales 2	145787721	3826173	80073073	11378130	•	8003161	4001595	3702131	1749195	1424949	•	8128091	0
Interest 3	137519	3615	33758	6164	•	6813	9082	9377	7686	9521	•	20714	0
Rents 4	49886	0	7995	0	•	9556	2285	3530	6533	2529	•	882	0
Royalties 5	14804	0	0	0	•	0	1403	0	0	13400	•	0	0
Other Portfolio Income 6	293774	12274	76138	5503	•	7146	14679	10254	16360	2655	•	127342	0
Other Receipts 7	4413792	162029	2518066	160800	•	105178	110543	59280	54404	-13802	•	353820	0
Total Receipts 8	150697496	4004091	82709030	11550597	•	8131854	4139587	3784572	1834178	1439252	•	8630849	0
Average Total Receipts 9	1521	540	955	4259	•	30686	59994	130502	114636	205607	•	2876950	•
Operating Costs/Operating Income (%)													
Cost of Operations 10	4.1	19.5	2.7	4.1	•	0.5	5.8	20.3	9.6	16.2	•	0.2	•
Salaries and Wages 11	26.6	13.8	22.8	22.3	•	25.0	36.5	37.8	40.8	38.1	•	46.8	•
Taxes Paid 12	3.0	1.7	3.0	3.2	•	2.2	2.7	2.9	3.2	3.5	•	4.0	•
Interest Paid 13	0.5	0.2	0.4	0.5	•	0.4	0.6	0.6	0.6	0.9	•	1.0	•
Depreciation 14	1.0	0.6	0.7	0.9	•	1.9	1.6	1.2	1.9	1.8	•	0.3	•
Amortization and Depletion 15	0.1	0.1	0.0	0.2	•	0.1	0.2	0.1	0.3	0.0	•	0.4	•
Pensions and Other Deferred Comp. 16	3.1	0.6	3.2	2.8	•	1.9	2.2	3.6	1.2	1.8	•	6.5	•
Employee Benefits 17	1.9	0.9	1.6	1.3	•	1.5	2.2	3.4	3.4	2.0	•	5.5	•
Advertising 18	0.7	1.9	0.9	0.8	•	0.3	0.3	0.3	0.5	3.7	•	0.1	•
Other Expenses 19	32.6	45.6	29.9	32.8	•	51.7	41.3	27.7	35.9	28.6	•	36.6	•
Officers' Compensation 20	20.8	12.0	26.8	22.4	•	13.4	6.7	1.3	1.2	0.8	•	0.2	•
Operating Margin 21	5.5	3.1	8.0	8.8	•	1.1	•	0.7	1.3	2.7	•	2.7	•
Operating Margin Before Officers' Comp. 22	26.3	15.1	34.8	31.2	•	14.5	6.6	2.1	2.5	3.5	•	3.5	•

Selected Average Balance Sheet ($ in Thousands)

Net Receivables 23	24	0	3	9	•	628	3049	10033	15639	34625	85398
Inventories 24	2	0	0	7	•	26	298	377	1222	943	1791
Net Property, Plant and Equipment 25	65	0	30	190	•	2287	4283	10265	24192	36335	39413
Total Assets 26	245	0	97	674	•	6961	14131	35022	65329	129675	1163555
Notes and Loans Payable 27	96	0	41	249	•	3189	6573	10539	14486	36852	301074
All Other Liabilities 28	81	0	31	161	•	1709	5035	13295	20367	44862	677441
Net Worth 29	68	0	26	264	•	2064	2523	11188	30476	47961	185040

Selected Financial Ratios (Times to 1)

Current Ratio 30	1.2	•	1.2	1.3	•	1.3	1.0	1.1	1.4	1.7	1.4
Quick Ratio 31	1.1	•	1.1	1.0	•	1.1	0.8	0.9	1.2	1.4	1.2
Net Sales to Working Capital 32	72.6	•	129.6	74.8	•	46.7	215.3	94.3	13.3	9.2	23.0
Coverage Ratio 33	19.4	31.9	32.3	22.1	•	7.0	6.5	5.9	10.5	4.9	4.7
Total Asset Turnover 34	6.0	•	9.5	6.2	•	4.3	4.1	3.6	1.7	1.6	2.3
Inventory Turnover 35	37.6	•	65.8	25.1	•	6.0	11.3	68.7	8.6	34.9	2.8
Receivables Turnover 36	64.9	•	358.9	303.2	•	43.3	19.6	11.3	8.6	•	
Total Liabilities to Net Worth 37	2.6	•	2.7	1.6	•	2.4	4.6	2.1	1.1	1.7	5.3
Current Assets to Working Capital 38	5.2	•	6.4	4.3	•	4.4	27.3	13.1	3.7	2.5	3.4
Current Liabilities to Working Capital 39	4.2	•	5.4	3.3	•	3.4	26.3	12.1	2.7	1.5	2.4
Working Capital to Net Sales 40	0.0	•	0.0	0.0	•	0.0	0.0	0.0	0.1	0.1	0.0
Inventory to Working Capital 41	0.1	•	0.1	0.2	•	0.0	1.4	0.1	0.0	0.0	0.0
Total Receipts to Cash Flow 42	2.8	2.1	2.8	2.7	•	2.0	2.6	3.7	2.7	3.5	2.8
Cost of Goods to Cash Flow 43	0.1	0.4	0.1	0.1	•	0.0	0.2	0.7	0.3	0.6	0.0
Cash Flow to Total Debt 44	3.0	•	4.7	3.7	•	3.0	1.9	1.5	1.2	0.7	1.0

Selected Financial Factors (in Percentages)

Debt Ratio 45	72.3	•	73.1	60.9	•	70.4	82.1	68.1	53.4	63.0	84.1
Return on Total Assets 46	55.7	•	110.7	66.9	•	13.5	16.0	12.8	11.3	7.0	10.9
Return on Equity Before Income Taxes 47	190.5	•	398.7	163.3	•	39.0	75.9	33.4	21.8	15.1	54.2
Return on Equity After Income Taxes 48	185.8	•	394.4	162.3	•	36.8	70.6	26.4	15.4	10.8	39.5
Profit Margin (Before Income Tax) 49	8.8	7.7	11.3	10.3	•	2.7	3.3	2.9	6.1	3.6	3.7
Profit Margin (After Income Tax) 50	8.6	7.6	11.2	10.2	•	2.5	3.1	2.3	4.3	2.5	2.7

Table I

Corporations with and without Net Income

OFFICES OF DENTISTS

MONEY AMOUNTS AND SIZE OF ASSETS IN THOUSANDS OF DOLLARS

Item Description for Accounting Period 7/06 Through 6/07	Total	Zero Assets	Under 500	500 to 1,000	1,000 to 5,000	5,000 to 10,000	10,000 to 25,000	25,000 to 50,000	50,000 to 100,000	100,000 to 250,000	250,000 to 500,000	500,000 to 2,500,000	2,500,000 and over
Number of Enterprises 1	71034	4080	60594	5290	1035	19	4	7	0	5	0	0	0
Revenues ($ in Thousands)													
Net Sales 2	66681703	1582371	53006474	6924851	2806589	491379	118366	245517	0	1506157	0	0	0
Interest 3	30953	1149	17865	5205	2497	0	0	20	0	4217	0	0	0
Rents 4	3640	0	3193	417	30	0	0	0	0	0	0	0	0
Royalties 5	0	0	0	0	0	0	0	0	0	0	0	0	0
Other Portfolio Income 6	295557	21284	265273	2925	1147	0	891	3082	0	956	0	0	0
Other Receipts 7	714825	469	533074	132328	27912	0	5969	5918	0	9154	0	0	0
Total Receipts 8	67726678	1605273	53825879	7065726	2838175	491379	125226	254537	0	1520484	0	0	0
Average Total Receipts 9	953	393	888	1336	2742	25862	31306	36362	•	304097	•	•	•
Operating Costs/Operating Income (%)													
Cost of Operations 10	5.8	0.7	4.7	6.3	6.8	•	•	11.1	•	45.7	•	•	•
Salaries and Wages 11	22.9	19.0	22.7	22.9	29.2	22.0	77.2	30.3	•	18.2	•	•	•
Taxes Paid 12	3.3	3.6	3.3	3.2	4.1	1.5	4.5	4.7	•	2.9	•	•	•
Interest Paid 13	1.1	2.2	0.7	2.4	1.8	0.3	•	4.3	•	5.4	•	•	•
Depreciation 14	1.6	1.7	1.3	3.6	3.1	0.8	•	4.6	•	0.9	•	•	•
Amortization and Depletion 15	0.4	0.2	0.3	1.1	0.5	•	•	1.8	•	2.5	•	•	•
Pensions and Other Deferred Comp. 16	1.9	2.5	1.9	2.4	2.0	0.3	12.1	0.4	•	0.5	•	•	•
Employee Benefits 17	1.0	0.6	1.0	1.1	0.9	•	5.4	0.9	•	2.9	•	•	•
Advertising 18	1.5	0.4	1.4	1.8	2.6	0.2	•	4.6	•	1.1	•	•	•
Other Expenses 19	36.9	40.3	38.6	30.0	25.3	74.7	6.1	35.8	•	19.4	•	•	•
Officers' Compensation 20	17.7	20.6	18.4	17.9	15.7	•	1.4	1.8	•	0.5	•	•	•
Operating Margin 21	5.9	8.1	5.8	7.5	8.0	0.3	•	•	•	0.1	•	•	•
Operating Margin Before Officers' Comp. 22	23.5	28.7	24.2	25.3	23.7	0.3	•	1.4	•	0.6	•	•	•

Selected Average Balance Sheet ($ in Thousands)

Net Receivables 23	12	0	50	3	32	1480	6539	3906	•	64910
Inventories 24	1	0	0	1	32	0	0	308	•	1341
Net Property, Plant and Equipment 25	77	0	281	53	550	1236	0	8479	•	23629
Total Assets 26	210	0	661	134	1341	5101	15912	36171	•	296054
Notes and Loans Payable 27	138	0	478	86	846	2106	0	17655	•	204115
All Other Liabilities 28	36	0	98	24	65	2667	12422	12129	•	64970
Net Worth 29	36	0	86	24	430	327	3490	6387	•	26969

Selected Financial Ratios (Times to 1)

Current Ratio 30	1.2	•	1.0	1.4	1.6	0.7	1.0	0.8	•	1.7
Quick Ratio 31	1.0	•	0.9	1.2	1.4	0.7	1.0	0.5	•	1.4
Net Sales to Working Capital 32	94.1	•	531.0	22.2	21.8	•	•	•	•	7.7
Coverage Ratio 33	7.8	5.3	11.1	4.9	6.0	2.1	•	1.8	•	1.2
Total Asset Turnover 34	4.5	•	6.5	2.0	2.0	5.1	1.9	1.0	•	1.0
Inventory Turnover 35	80.3	•	64.9	2275.5	238.1	•	•	12.6	•	102.7
Receivables Turnover 36	102.9	•	346.6	40.1	71.6	34.9	3.8	9.5	•	7.1
Total Liabilities to Net Worth 37	4.9	•	4.6	6.7	2.1	14.6	3.6	4.7	•	10.0
Current Assets to Working Capital 38	6.1	•	22.9	3.5	2.6	•	•	2.5		
Current Liabilities to Working Capital 39	5.1	•	21.9	2.5	1.6	•	•	1.5		
Working Capital to Net Sales 40	0.0	•	0.0	0.0	0.0	•	•	0.1		
Inventory to Working Capital 41	0.1	•	0.4	•	0.0	•	•	0.0		
Total Receipts to Cash Flow 42	2.6	2.4	2.5	3.0	3.4	1.3	19.2	3.2	•	9.1
Cost of Goods to Cash Flow 43	0.1	0.0	0.1	0.2	0.2	•	•	0.4	•	4.2
Cash Flow to Total Debt 44	2.1	•	3.2	0.8	0.9	4.0	0.1	0.4	•	0.1

Selected Financial Factors (in Percentages)

Debt Ratio 45	83.0	•	82.2	87.0	67.9	93.6	78.1	82.3	•	90.9
Return on Total Assets 46	37.7	•	51.4	23.6	22.1	3.0	•	7.4	•	6.6
Return on Equity Before Income Taxes 47	192.5	•	263.6	145.0	57.5	24.4	•	18.2	•	12.0
Return on Equity After Income Taxes 48	190.5	•	262.1	143.6	55.2	24.4	•	13.8	•	5.7
Profit Margin (Before Income Tax) 49	7.3	9.5	7.2	9.5	9.1	0.3	•	3.3	•	1.1
Profit Margin (After Income Tax) 50	7.3	9.4	7.1	9.4	8.8	0.3	•	2.5	•	0.5

Table II

Corporations with Net Income

OFFICES OF DENTISTS

MONEY AMOUNTS AND SIZE OF ASSETS IN THOUSANDS OF DOLLARS

Item Description for Accounting Period 7/06 Through 6/07	Total	Zero Assets	Under 500	500 to 1,000	1,000 to 5,000	5,000 to 10,000	10,000 to 25,000	25,000 to 50,000	50,000 to 100,000	100,000 to 250,000	250,000 to 500,000	500,000 to 2,500,000	2,500,000 and over
Number of Enterprises 1	53639	•	45310	4260	•	9	0	7	0	•	0	0	0
Revenues ($ in Thousands)													
Net Sales 2	44364003	•	34435979	5741695	•	41050	0	245517	0	•	0	0	0
Interest 3	24184	•	12719	5115	•	0	0	20	0	•	0	0	0
Rents 4	1097	•	650	417	•	0	0	0	0	•	0	0	0
Royalties 5	0	•	0	0	•	0	0	0	0	•	0	0	0
Other Portfolio Income 6	254694	•	227239	2787	•	0	0	3082	0	•	0	0	0
Other Receipts 7	601323	•	456072	109786	•	0	0	5918	0	•	0	0	0
Total Receipts 8	45245301	•	35132659	5859800	•	41050	0	254537	0	•	0	0	0
Average Total Receipts 9	844	•	775	1376	•	4561	•	36362	•	•	•	•	•
Operating Costs/Operating Income (%)													
Cost of Operations 10	6.1	•	5.9	7.5	•	•	•	11.1	•	•	•	•	•
Salaries and Wages 11	22.9	•	22.5	21.2	•	•	•	30.3	•	•	•	•	•
Taxes Paid 12	3.5	•	3.5	3.2	•	0.1	•	4.7	•	•	•	•	•
Interest Paid 13	1.0	•	0.7	2.3	•	3.4	•	4.3	•	•	•	•	•
Depreciation 14	1.6	•	1.3	2.6	•	9.6	•	4.6	•	•	•	•	•
Amortization and Depletion 15	0.5	•	0.3	1.2	•	•	•	1.8	•	•	•	•	•
Pensions and Other Deferred Comp. 16	2.0	•	2.0	2.1	•	•	•	0.4	•	•	•	•	•
Employee Benefits 17	1.1	•	1.0	1.0	•	•	•	0.9	•	•	•	•	•
Advertising 18	1.6	•	1.6	1.4	•	2.2	•	4.6	•	•	•	•	•
Other Expenses 19	29.5	•	29.8	27.4	•	76.5	•	35.8	•	•	•	•	•
Officers' Compensation 20	19.7	•	20.9	19.0	•	•	•	1.8	•	•	•	•	•
Operating Margin 21	10.5	•	10.3	11.1	•	8.3	•	•	•	•	•	•	•
Operating Margin Before Officers' Comp. 22	30.2	•	31.2	30.1	•	8.3	•	1.4	•	•	•	•	•

Selected Average Balance Sheet ($ in Thousands)

Net Receivables 23	9	3	56	0	3906
Inventories 24	1	1	0	0	341
Net Property, Plant and Equipment 25	69	48	235	2608	8479
Total Assets 26	206	138	662	5393	36171
Notes and Loans Payable 27	115	75	430	4447	17655
All Other Liabilities 28	33	23	104	0	12129
Net Worth 29	58	40	128	946	6387

Selected Financial Ratios (Times to 1)

Current Ratio 30	1.6	1.4	2.1	3.7	0.8
Quick Ratio 31	1.4	1.2	1.7	1.4	0.5
Net Sales to Working Capital 32	33.4	55.7	11.6	10.3	
Coverage Ratio 33	13.3	18.6	6.7	3.4	1.8
Total Asset Turnover 34	4.0	5.5	2.0	0.8	1.0
Inventory Turnover 35	70.0	58.7			11.4
Receivables Turnover 36	104.7	233.6	36.7		3.6
Total Liabilities to Net Worth 37	2.5	2.4	4.2	4.7	4.7
Current Assets to Working Capital 38	2.6	3.3	1.9	1.4	
Current Liabilities to Working Capital 39	1.6	2.3	0.9	0.4	
Working Capital to Net Sales 40	0.0	0.0	0.1	0.1	
Inventory to Working Capital 41	0.0	0.1			
Total Receipts to Cash Flow 42	2.8	2.8	2.9	1.3	3.2
Cost of Goods to Cash Flow 43	0.2	0.2	0.2		0.4
Cash Flow to Total Debt 44	2.0	2.8	0.9	0.8	0.4

Selected Financial Factors (in Percentages)

Debt Ratio 45	71.7	70.8	80.7	82.5	82.3
Return on Total Assets 46	53.8	70.7	31.5	9.9	7.4
Return on Equity Before Income Taxes 47	175.7	229.0	138.7	40.0	18.2
Return on Equity After Income Taxes 48	174.1	227.9	137.5	40.0	13.8
Profit Margin (Before Income Tax) 49	12.4	12.1	13.2	8.3	3.3
Profit Margin (After Income Tax) 50	12.3	12.1	13.0	8.3	2.5

Table I

Corporations with and without Net Income

OFFICES OF OTHER HEALTH PRACTITIONERS

MONEY AMOUNTS AND SIZE OF ASSETS IN THOUSANDS OF DOLLARS

Item Description for Accounting Period 7/06 Through 6/07		Total	Zero Assets	Under 500	500 to 1,000	1,000 to 5,000	5,000 to 10,000	10,000 to 25,000	25,000 to 50,000	50,000 to 100,000	100,000 to 250,000	250,000 to 500,000	500,000 to 2,500,000	2,500,000 and over
Number of Enterprises	1	98166	19266	76939	896	913	70	34	20	14	10	3	0	0
Revenues ($ in Thousands)														
Net Sales	2	48619868	2159744	28887188	2075842	5346470	1143692	1918000	659283	1383586	2655624	2389439	0	0
Interest	3	132843	3687	7202	288	3521	6834	5916	4889	9747	17855	72903	0	0
Rents	4	13471	7	1248	0	2445	0	72	6481	2172	1048	0	0	0
Royalties	5	149	149	0	0	0	0	0	0	0	0	0	0	0
Other Portfolio Income	6	157824	22165	28266	345	438	4891	946	1452	92905	6418	0	0	0
Other Receipts	7	799915	2087	125102	18923	44539	2134	119109	312731	48123	112023	15141	0	0
Total Receipts	8	49724070	2187839	29049006	2095398	5397413	1157551	2044043	984836	1536533	2793968	2477483	0	0
Average Total Receipts	9	507	114	378	2339	5912	16536	60119	49242	109752	279397	825828	•	•
Operating Costs/Operating Income (%)														
Cost of Operations	10	15.9	11.7	13.1	6.4	20.2	24.7	38.6	21.9	18.0	35.5	4.6	•	•
Salaries and Wages	11	21.0	13.3	19.3	35.6	23.1	30.1	9.4	32.5	23.8	29.6	21.9	•	•
Taxes Paid	12	3.3	3.7	3.7	3.9	3.7	3.2	1.2	3.6	2.3	1.6	1.5	•	•
Interest Paid	13	1.0	1.5	0.6	0.6	0.9	0.6	0.3	3.0	2.2	1.6	5.7	•	•
Depreciation	14	1.1	1.4	1.0	1.3	1.3	1.3	1.0	2.0	1.6	0.8	0.5	•	•
Amortization and Depletion	15	0.3	0.1	0.2	0.0	0.3	0.0	0.0	0.7	0.5	0.6	1.5	•	•
Pensions and Other Deferred Comp.	16	1.1	1.3	1.2	2.1	1.2	0.1	0.3	0.6	0.4	0.1	0.1	•	•
Employee Benefits	17	1.9	0.7	1.6	2.7	1.6	3.4	1.0	4.4	1.9	4.6	1.9	•	•
Advertising	18	1.7	1.4	2.3	0.7	1.1	0.4	1.0	0.2	0.9	0.5	0.8	•	•
Other Expenses	19	37.0	46.2	33.3	22.9	39.8	26.1	50.5	78.3	51.4	29.5	63.8	•	•
Officers' Compensation	20	11.1	15.1	15.6	15.1	2.8	4.6	0.5	1.4	0.6	0.3	0.4	•	•
Operating Margin	21	4.7	3.7	8.2	8.6	4.1	5.4	•	•	•	•	•	•	•
Operating Margin Before Officers' Comp.	22	15.8	18.9	23.8	23.7	6.8	10.0	•	•	•	•	•	•	•

Selected Average Balance Sheet ($ in Thousands)

Net Receivables 23	22	0	7	103	268	1369	4266	11819	11446	24948	124361
Inventories 24	3	0	2	23	16	533	722	319	1414	832	•
Net Property, Plant and Equipment 25	35	0	26	125	584	1367	2730	5574	15253	15616	39231
Total Assets 26	135	0	73	749	1642	6652	16138	35007	68844	137020	482791
Notes and Loans Payable 27	57	0	38	230	649	1610	1642	5706	21582	51483	255883
All Other Liabilities 28	40	0	13	147	231	2360	9249	18578	17664	65086	257629
Net Worth 29	39	0	22	372	762	2681	5247	10722	29598	20451	-30720

Selected Financial Ratios (Times to 1)

Current Ratio 30	1.5	•	1.8	2.3	1.9	2.2	1.2	1.2	2.3	0.9	1.2
Quick Ratio 31	1.2	•	1.5	2.1	1.4	1.3	1.0	0.8	1.9	0.5	1.0
Net Sales to Working Capital 32	22.6	•	26.3	10.7	18.2	6.7	31.9	10.5	6.0	•	20.8
Coverage Ratio 33	7.8	4.5	15.9	18.1	6.9	12.4	10.6	1.3	4.4	1.4	1.2
Total Asset Turnover 34	3.7	•	5.1	3.1	3.6	2.5	3.5	0.9	1.4	1.9	1.6
Inventory Turnover 35	27.8	•	20.8	6.4	50.9	250.3	40.8	10.0	55.8	66.6	43.9
Receivables Turnover 36	24.0	•	61.3	24.0	17.9	16.1	13.3	3.2	8.8	6.6	12.8
Total Liabilities to Net Worth 37	2.5	•	2.3	1.0	1.2	1.5	2.1	2.3	1.3	5.7	•
Current Assets to Working Capital 38	2.9	•	2.3	1.8	2.1	1.9	6.7	7.1	1.8	•	5.1
Current Liabilities to Working Capital 39	1.9	•	1.3	0.8	1.1	0.9	5.7	6.1	0.8	•	4.1
Working Capital to Net Sales 40	0.0	•	0.0	0.1	0.1	0.2	0.0	0.1	0.2	•	0.0
Inventory to Working Capital 41	0.1	•	0.2	0.1	0.1	0.0	0.3	0.3	0.0	•	0.0
Total Receipts to Cash Flow 42	2.7	2.5	3.0	3.8	2.5	3.6	2.0	1.4	2.1	3.6	1.6
Cost of Goods to Cash Flow 43	0.4	0.3	0.4	0.2	0.5	0.9	0.8	0.3	0.4	1.3	0.1
Cash Flow to Total Debt 44	1.9	•	2.4	1.6	2.7	1.1	2.6	1.0	1.2	0.6	1.0

Selected Financial Factors (in Percentages)

Debt Ratio 45	71.2	•	70.0	50.3	53.6	59.7	67.5	69.4	57.0	85.1	106.4
Return on Total Assets 46	29.1	•	47.8	31.2	21.0	17.6	10.6	3.7	13.8	4.2	11.1
Return on Equity Before Income Taxes 47	88.1	•	149.2	59.4	38.7	40.1	29.4	2.9	24.8	7.6	•
Return on Equity After Income Taxes 48	84.7	•	147.8	59.1	36.8	35.5	22.7	•	15.6	4.2	•
Profit Margin (Before Income Tax) 49	6.9	5.0	8.7	9.5	5.0	6.6	2.7	0.9	7.4	0.6	1.0
Profit Margin (After Income Tax) 50	6.7	4.5	8.6	9.5	4.8	5.8	2.1	•	4.7	0.3	0.7

Table II

Corporations with Net Income

OFFICES OF OTHER HEALTH PRACTITIONERS

MONEY AMOUNTS AND SIZE OF ASSETS IN THOUSANDS OF DOLLARS

Item Description for Accounting Period 7/06 Through 6/07	Total	Zero Assets	Under 500	500 to 1,000	1,000 to 5,000	5,000 to 10,000	10,000 to 25,000	25,000 to 50,000	50,000 to 100,000	100,000 to 250,000	250,000 to 500,000	500,000 to 2,500,000	2,500,000 and over
Number of Enterprises **1**	66845	11730	53557	688	770	50	22	10	8	7	3	0	0
Revenues ($ in Thousands)													
Net Sales **2**	36063824	1435382	21518251	1632819	3678531	593001	1190880	310516	846664	2468342	2389439	0	0
Interest **3**	114478	3677	4181	288	3097	5751	5652	529	5909	12492	72903	0	0
Rents **4**	10503	0	1248	0	2445	0	72	3817	1963	959	0	0	0
Royalties **5**	149	149	0	0	0	0	0	0	0	0	0	0	0
Other Portfolio Income **6**	141016	22165	13477	0	438	4891	757	618	92446	6223	0	0	0
Other Receipts **7**	430578	792	111470	18923	43936	3626	99632	7370	44678	85008	15141	0	0
Total Receipts **8**	36760548	1462165	21648627	1652030	3728447	607269	1296993	322850	991660	2573024	2477483	0	0
Average Total Receipts **9**	550	125	404	2401	4842	12145	58954	32285	123958	367575	825828	•	•
Operating Costs/Operating Income (%)													
Cost of Operations **10**	14.8	12.0	10.3	8.2	21.9	38.5	53.0	26.1	2.6	38.0	4.6	•	•
Salaries and Wages **11**	21.5	12.5	20.2	27.8	26.7	17.7	11.7	26.4	26.5	28.2	21.9	•	•
Taxes Paid **12**	3.3	3.5	3.7	3.3	4.5	3.4	1.5	3.3	2.8	1.2	1.5	•	•
Interest Paid **13**	1.0	1.3	0.6	0.2	1.1	0.3	0.1	2.1	1.4	0.9	5.7	•	•
Depreciation **14**	1.0	1.2	0.9	0.7	1.8	0.5	1.2	2.1	1.7	0.6	0.5	•	•
Amortization and Depletion **15**	0.3	0.0	0.1	0.0	0.4	0.0	0.0	0.6	0.4	0.5	1.5	•	•
Pensions and Other Deferred Comp. **16**	1.0	0.2	1.1	2.6	1.4	0.2	0.5	0.3	0.7	0.1	0.1	•	•
Employee Benefits **17**	1.8	0.5	1.7	1.7	1.5	1.2	0.7	3.7	2.7	4.7	1.9	•	•
Advertising **18**	1.8	1.3	2.5	0.7	1.2	0.4	0.3	0.4	0.3	0.3	0.8	•	•
Other Expenses **19**	32.6	40.7	29.8	21.9	28.6	20.4	34.5	24.7	59.7	28.0	63.8	•	•
Officers' Compensation **20**	11.0	10.3	15.5	17.7	3.8	5.1	0.5	1.2	0.5	0.2	0.4	•	•
Operating Margin **21**	9.9	16.6	13.5	15.2	7.0	12.2	•	9.2	0.7	•	•	•	•
Operating Margin Before Officers' Comp. **22**	20.9	26.9	28.9	32.9	10.8	17.3	•	10.4	1.2	•	•	•	•

Selected Average Balance Sheet ($ in Thousands)

Net Receivables 23	22	0	9		146	1464	681	10124	14724	31041	124361
Inventories 24	3	0	3	31	26	13	461	985	191	1489	832
Net Property, Plant and Equipment 25	37	0	27	67	664	1070	2818	3867	20510	8153	39231
Total Assets 26	150	0	79	724	1646	6488	16182	34267	73822	141079	482791
Notes and Loans Payable 27	54	0	31	98	656	451	732	5086	21441	48288	255883
All Other Liabilities 28	40	0	12	100	179	2641	7300	10811	12783	75053	257629
Net Worth 29	57	0	36	527	811	3396	8149	18370	39598	17739	-30720

Selected Financial Ratios (Times to 1)

Current Ratio 30	1.8	•	2.3	3.6	2.0	2.1	1.4	2.2	2.6	1.2	1.2
Quick Ratio 31	1.4	•	2.0	3.3	1.3	1.3	1.1	1.1	2.4	0.7	1.0
Net Sales to Working Capital 32	16.3	•	19.0	9.3	15.9	5.0	17.2	2.4	5.3	31.0	20.8
Coverage Ratio 33	12.6	15.8	25.0	96.6	8.6	58.3	39.1	7.3	13.4	2.7	1.2
Total Asset Turnover 34	3.6	•	5.1	3.3	2.9	1.8	3.3	0.9	1.4	2.5	1.6
Inventory Turnover 35	23.8	•	14.8	6.4	39.8	339.8	62.1	8.2	14.3	89.9	43.9
Receivables Turnover 36	26.8	•	61.0	37.7	29.3	•	21.8	•	7.4	8.7	12.8
Total Liabilities to Net Worth 37	1.6	•	1.2	0.4	1.0	0.9	1.0	0.9	0.9	7.0	•
Current Assets to Working Capital 38	2.2	•	1.8	1.4	2.0	1.9	3.5	1.8	1.6	7.4	5.1
Current Liabilities to Working Capital 39	1.2	•	0.8	0.4	1.0	0.9	2.5	0.8	0.6	6.4	4.1
Working Capital to Net Sales 40	0.1	•	0.1	0.1	0.1	0.2	0.1	0.4	0.2	0.0	0.0
Inventory to Working Capital 41	0.1	•	0.1	0.1	0.1	0.0	0.0	0.1	0.0	0.1	0.0
Total Receipts to Cash Flow 42	2.7	2.1	2.9	3.0	3.2	3.1	2.8	2.9	1.6	3.5	1.6
Cost of Goods to Cash Flow 43	0.4	0.2	0.3	0.2	0.7	1.2	1.5	0.8	0.0	1.3	0.1
Cash Flow to Total Debt 44	2.1	•	3.3	4.0	1.8	1.2	2.4	0.7	1.9	0.8	1.0

Selected Financial Factors (in Percentages)

Debt Ratio 45	62.1	•	54.1	27.3	50.7	47.7	49.6	46.4	46.4	87.4	106.4
Return on Total Assets 46	46.2	•	74.7	54.1	27.5	27.2	16.8	13.8	27.5	6.4	11.1
Return on Equity Before Income Taxes 47	112.2	•	156.3	73.6	49.3	51.1	32.6	22.3	47.5	32.0	•
Return on Equity After Income Taxes 48	108.7	•	155.1	73.4	47.2	46.1	25.9	17.0	35.4	26.4	•
Profit Margin (Before Income Tax) 49	11.9	18.5	14.1	16.3	8.4	14.6	4.9	13.2	17.8	1.6	1.0
Profit Margin (After Income Tax) 50	11.5	17.7	14.0	16.3	8.0	13.2	3.9	10.1	13.2	1.3	0.7

OUTPATIENT CARE CENTERS

Table I

Corporations with and without Net Income

MONEY AMOUNTS AND SIZE OF ASSETS IN THOUSANDS OF DOLLARS

Item Description for Accounting Period 7/06 Through 6/07	Total	Zero Assets	Under 500	500 to 1,000	1,000 to 5,000	5,000 to 10,000	10,000 to 25,000	25,000 to 50,000	50,000 to 100,000	100,000 to 250,000	250,000 to 500,000	500,000 to 2,500,000	2,500,000 and over
Number of Enterprises 1	6253	408	5211	183	351	41	14	19	9	0	8	9	0
Revenues ($ in Thousands)													
Net Sales 2	29421403	408093	3229731	483515	2753299	938316	544097	1807998	839378	0	4181988	14234988	0
Interest 3	155879	737	587	1316	5826	5212	339	10007	4254	0	34783	92818	0
Rents 4	71056	0	0	0	467	169	0	840	836	0	3503	65240	0
Royalties 5	18443	18250	0	0	0	0	0	38	0	0	0	155	0
Other Portfolio Income 6	406896	5630	0	0	76	15520	0	765	415	0	3463	381028	0
Other Receipts 7	861059	108402	39952	611	27102	-8821	3490	14824	13545	0	24330	637623	0
Total Receipts 8	30934736	541112	3270270	485442	2786770	950396	547926	1834472	858428	0	4248067	15411852	0
Average Total Receipts 9	4947	1326	628	2653	7940	23180	39138	96551	95381	•	531008	1712428	•
Operating Costs/Operating Income (%)													
Cost of Operations 10	33.6	•	14.4	29.4	19.8	1.3	53.4	60.0	12.7	•	40.2	38.9	•
Salaries and Wages 11	21.0	50.7	12.1	13.4	33.0	47.4	26.6	4.4	25.9	•	21.8	19.7	•
Taxes Paid 12	3.1	13.3	2.3	3.8	3.7	2.5	1.4	0.7	2.4	•	2.7	3.5	•
Interest Paid 13	4.4	2.6	0.8	0.8	0.4	2.0	0.4	0.0	2.9	•	1.5	8.1	•
Depreciation 14	1.6	2.6	1.0	3.0	1.0	0.6	1.1	0.3	1.5	•	1.2	2.2	•
Amortization and Depletion 15	1.8	2.8	0.0	0.1	0.1	0.6	0.3	0.0	1.3	•	1.0	3.1	•
Pensions and Other Deferred Comp. 16	0.5	0.2	0.3	0.1	1.0	4.3	0.8	0.1	0.5	•	0.2	0.3	•
Employee Benefits 17	3.4	2.3	2.0	1.7	4.9	2.7	2.0	0.6	2.0	•	5.8	3.4	•
Advertising 18	0.4	0.0	1.1	0.4	0.3	0.3	1.1	0.3	0.5	•	0.7	0.1	•
Other Expenses 19	29.5	57.9	53.5	36.2	27.2	36.3	13.8	31.0	50.0	•	20.4	24.9	•
Officers' Compensation 20	2.3	35.0	6.0	2.3	6.5	2.0	1.4	0.3	1.3	•	0.6	0.6	•
Operating Margin 21	•	•	6.3	8.8	2.0	0.1	•	2.2	•	•	4.0	•	•
Operating Margin Before Officers' Comp. 22	0.7	•	12.3	11.1	8.5	2.1	•	2.6	0.3	•	4.6	•	•

Selected Average Balance Sheet ($ in Thousands)

Net Receivables 23	534	0	4	9	515	975	2777	10316	6334	•	58538	259081
Inventories 24	67	0	1	1	178	7	1567	197	345	•	1640	16852
Net Property, Plant and Equipment 25	638	0	55	382	407	1594	3646	2092	12763	•	37444	324715
Total Assets 26	5351	0	99	826	2230	9070	14092	34223	73957	•	360783	3026177
Notes and Loans Payable 27	2419	0	165	161	435	6394	5329	1237	30799	•	74515	1428043
All Other Liabilities 28	1447	0	16	19	786	2325	5516	22704	21394	•	115941	773132
Net Worth 29	1484	0	-83	646	1009	350	3247	10281	21764	•	170327	825003

Selected Financial Ratios (Times to 1)

Current Ratio 30	1.2	•	0.3	4.1	1.5	1.1	0.8	1.6	0.7	•	1.7	1.1
Quick Ratio 31	0.8	•	0.2	4.0	1.1	0.4	0.8	1.5	0.6	•	1.4	0.6
Net Sales to Working Capital 32	26.5	•	•	8.1	16.5	50.9	•	9.8	•	•	8.6	22.1
Coverage Ratio 33	1.8	•	9.9	12.2	8.7	1.7	•	75.4	1.4	•	4.7	1.4
Total Asset Turnover 34	0.9	•	6.3	3.2	3.5	2.5	2.8	2.8	1.3	•	1.4	0.5
Inventory Turnover 35	23.4	•	62.6	534.9	8.7	42.6	13.2	289.9	34.4	•	128.3	36.5
Receivables Turnover 36	7.7	•	128.2	595.1	14.9	42.8	6.4	12.6	15.7	•	10.0	8.1
Total Liabilities to Net Worth 37	2.6	•	•	0.3	1.2	24.9	3.3	2.3	2.4	•	1.1	2.7
Current Assets to Working Capital 38	7.3	•	•	1.3	3.2	10.9	•	2.5	•	•	2.5	8.2
Current Liabilities to Working Capital 39	6.3	•	•	0.3	2.2	9.9	•	1.5	•	•	1.5	7.2
Working Capital to Net Sales 40	0.0	•	•	0.1	0.1	0.0	•	0.1	•	•	0.1	0.0
Inventory to Working Capital 41	0.4	•	•	0.0	0.5	0.0	•	0.0	•	•	0.0	0.5
Total Receipts to Cash Flow 42	3.7	5.5	2.0	2.4	3.6	3.0	10.6	3.0	2.1	•	4.1	4.7
Cost of Goods to Cash Flow 43	1.2	•	0.3	0.7	0.7	0.0	5.6	1.8	0.3	•	1.7	1.8
Cash Flow to Total Debt 44	0.3	•	1.7	6.1	1.8	0.9	0.3	1.3	0.9	•	0.7	0.2

Selected Financial Factors (in Percentages)

Debt Ratio 45	72.3	•	183.3	21.8	54.8	96.1	77.0	70.0	70.6	•	52.8	72.7
Return on Total Assets 46	7.1	•	52.4	32.0	12.9	8.3	•	10.2	5.2	•	10.1	6.1
Return on Equity Before Income Taxes 47	11.4	•	•	37.5	25.2	87.7	•	33.7	5.4	•	16.8	6.9
Return on Equity After Income Taxes 48	6.5	•	•	29.7	23.5	85.6	•	24.8	5.4	•	13.3	1.9
Profit Margin (Before Income Tax) 49	3.6	•	7.5	9.2	3.2	1.3	•	3.6	1.3	•	5.5	3.6
Profit Margin (After Income Tax) 50	2.0	•	7.4	7.3	3.0	1.3	•	2.7	1.3	•	4.3	1.0

Table II
Corporations with Net Income

OUTPATIENT CARE CENTERS

MONEY AMOUNTS AND SIZE OF ASSETS IN THOUSANDS OF DOLLARS

Item Description for Accounting Period 7/06 Through 6/07	Total	Zero Assets	Under 500	500 to 1,000	1,000 to 5,000	5,000 to 10,000	10,000 to 25,000	25,000 to 50,000	50,000 to 100,000	100,000 to 250,000	250,000 to 500,000	500,000 to 2,500,000	2,500,000 and over
Number of Enterprises **1**	4260	•	3326	120	344	29	4	14	3	0	•	•	0

Revenues ($ in Thousands)

Net Sales **2**	24822504	•	2738047	415710	2677771	861262	154700	1584286	584573	•	•	•	0
Interest **3**	114122	•	442	621	5818	5195	248	9699	3170	•	•	•	0
Rents **4**	5233	•	0	0	467	169	0	840	835	•	•	•	0
Royalties **5**	193	•	0	0	0	0	0	38	0	0	•	•	0
Other Portfolio Income **6**	391737	•	0	0	76	15520	0	765	0	0	•	•	0
Other Receipts **7**	569583	•	27457	611	26660	4148	1084	14057	1604	0	•	•	0
Total Receipts **8**	25903372	•	2765946	416942	2710792	886294	156032	1609685	590182	•	•	•	0
Average Total Receipts **9**	6081	•	832	3475	7880	30562	39008	114978	196727	•	•	•	•

Operating Costs/Operating Income (%)

Cost of Operations **10**	37.5	•	17.0	34.2	20.4	1.4	•	56.7	9.8	•	•	•	•
Salaries and Wages **11**	17.6	•	9.1	14.1	32.0	50.0	56.2	4.3	18.1	•	•	•	•
Taxes Paid **12**	2.8	•	2.0	4.2	3.7	2.5	3.2	0.7	1.9	•	•	•	•
Interest Paid **13**	3.5	•	0.7	1.0	0.4	1.7	0.6	0.1	0.5	•	•	•	•
Depreciation **14**	1.5	•	0.7	3.4	1.0	0.6	2.9	0.3	0.7	•	•	•	•
Amortization and Depletion **15**	1.4	•	0.0	0.0	0.1	0.2	0.1	0.0	0.0	•	•	•	•
Pensions and Other Deferred Comp. **16**	0.5	•	0.2	0.1	1.0	4.7	2.9	0.1	0.7	•	•	•	•
Employee Benefits **17**	3.6	•	2.2	1.9	4.9	2.8	3.7	0.6	1.3	•	•	•	•
Advertising **18**	0.3	•	1.0	0.3	0.3	0.1	0.1	0.3	0.5	•	•	•	•
Other Expenses **19**	23.6	•	46.2	23.0	26.6	32.1	27.4	32.8	59.8	•	•	•	•
Officers' Compensation **20**	2.3	•	7.1	2.3	6.7	2.0	3.7	0.3	1.2	•	•	•	•
Operating Margin **21**	5.3	•	13.8	15.5	3.0	1.9	•	3.8	5.4	•	•	•	•
Operating Margin Before Officers' Comp. **22**	7.6	•	20.9	17.8	9.7	3.9	2.9	4.1	6.6	•	•	•	•

Selected Average Balance Sheet ($ in Thousands)

Net Receivables 23	634	•	0	2	520	815	3390	8673	7637	•	•	•
Inventories 24	91	•	2	0	181	10	230	160	768	•	•	•
Net Property, Plant and Equipment 25	724	•	61	573	383	1395	5573	2800	21493	•	•	•
Total Assets 26	6649	•	104	897	2220	8922	11644	37581	64276	•	•	•
Notes and Loans Payable 27	2336	•	59	245	422	7313	3632	1314	15411	•	•	•
All Other Liabilities 28	1520	•	17	13	740	2528	4985	20891	34331	•	•	•
Net Worth 29	2793	•	27	639	1058	-918	3027	15377	14533	•	•	•

Selected Financial Ratios (Times to 1)

Current Ratio 30	1.3	•	0.4	2.1	1.6	1.2	0.8	1.8	0.6	•	•	•
Quick Ratio 31	0.9	•	0.2	2.1	1.2	0.4	0.5	1.7	0.5	•	•	•
Net Sales to Working Capital 32	15.9	•	•	21.6	14.1	27.4	•	9.8	•	•	•	•
Coverage Ratio 33	3.8	•	23.5	17.7	11.6	3.8	1.1	102.2	12.7	•	•	•
Total Asset Turnover 34	0.9	•	7.9	3.9	3.5	3.3	3.3	3.0	3.0	•	•	•
Inventory Turnover 35	23.9	•	62.4	•	8.8	42.6	•	401.5	25.0	•	•	•
Receivables Turnover 36	7.8	•	195.2	3678.8	17.5	8.3	•	51.0	•	•	•	•
Total Liabilities to Net Worth 37	1.4	•	2.8	0.4	1.1	•	2.8	1.4	3.4	•	•	•
Current Assets to Working Capital 38	4.2	•	•	1.9	2.8	5.7	•	2.3	•	•	•	•
Current Liabilities to Working Capital 39	3.2	•	•	0.9	1.8	4.7	•	1.3	•	•	•	•
Working Capital to Net Sales 40	0.1	•	0.0	0.0	0.1	0.0	•	0.1	•	•	•	•
Inventory to Working Capital 41	0.3	•	•	0.5	0.5	0.0	•	0.0	•	•	•	•
Total Receipts to Cash Flow 42	3.5	•	1.9	2.9	3.5	3.0	4.3	2.7	1.6	•	•	•
Cost of Goods to Cash Flow 43	1.3	•	0.3	1.0	0.7	0.0	•	1.5	0.2	•	•	•
Cash Flow to Total Debt 44	0.4	•	5.5	4.6	1.9	1.0	1.0	1.9	2.5	•	•	•

Selected Financial Factors (in Percentages)

Debt Ratio 45	58.0	•	73.9	28.7	52.4	110.3	74.0	59.1	77.4	•	•	•
Return on Total Assets 46	11.6	•	122.6	64.8	16.3	21.7	2.1	16.3	20.8	•	•	•
Return on Equity Before Income Taxes 47	20.2	•	449.7	85.8	31.2	•	0.6	39.4	84.7	•	•	•
Return on Equity After Income Taxes 48	16.4	•	445.1	73.7	29.5	•	0.6	31.3	84.4	•	•	•
Profit Margin (Before Income Tax) 49	9.7	•	14.8	15.8	4.2	4.8	0.0	5.4	6.3	•	•	•
Profit Margin (After Income Tax) 50	7.9	•	14.7	13.6	4.0	4.8	0.0	4.3	6.3	•	•	•

Table I

Corporations with and without Net Income

MISC. HEALTH CARE AND SOCIAL ASSISTANCE

MONEY AMOUNTS AND SIZE OF ASSETS IN THOUSANDS OF DOLLARS

Item Description for Accounting Period 7/06 Through 6/07	Total	Zero Assets	Under 500	500 to 1,000	1,000 to 5,000	5,000 to 10,000	10,000 to 25,000	25,000 to 50,000	50,000 to 100,000	100,000 to 250,000	250,000 to 500,000	500,000 to 2,500,000	2,500,000 and over
Number of Enterprises **1**	56138	10272	40859	2631	1807	272	133	54	44	36	17	12	0
Revenues ($ in Thousands)													
Net Sales **2**	83209400	1491138	22553254	5587488	6117645	5139943	4484994	3631608	3968102	4727139	6328890	19179198	0
Interest **3**	280567	4758	8185	1821	6425	12208	12672	18319	37834	49427	31285	97634	0
Rents **4**	78638	0	2740	3282	3792	592	227	1407	58562	3307	2643	2085	0
Royalties **5**	58642	0	0	0	0	0	0	250	34149	15908	8144	191	0
Other Portfolio Income **6**	556064	10014	143982	19990	30383	6651	24248	11254	19107	149646	5783	135004	0
Other Receipts **7**	1390973	-6396	162868	90874	94454	245356	79389	48931	40006	160944	104526	370024	0
Total Receipts **8**	85574284	1499514	22871029	5703455	6252699	5404750	4601530	3711769	4157760	5106371	6481271	19784136	0
Average Total Receipts **9**	1524	146	560	2168	3460	19870	34598	68736	94495	141844	381251	1648678	•
Operating Costs/Operating Income (%)													
Cost of Operations **10**	19.7	21.0	11.1	12.8	17.9	43.3	40.6	26.2	25.8	25.9	17.7	17.8	•
Salaries and Wages **11**	31.5	31.7	37.1	35.2	35.7	17.9	23.5	39.0	29.7	27.1	34.4	27.1	•
Taxes Paid **12**	4.0	5.5	4.7	4.4	5.0	1.5	3.5	4.3	4.1	3.4	4.1	3.5	•
Interest Paid **13**	2.0	1.6	0.5	1.0	1.8	0.6	1.1	1.6	2.3	4.3	4.3	3.6	•
Depreciation **14**	2.2	0.7	1.1	1.3	2.6	3.3	1.7	1.0	2.2	2.8	3.6	3.2	•
Amortization and Depletion **15**	0.9	0.9	0.2	0.4	0.1	0.1	0.3	0.6	1.2	2.4	2.6	1.5	•
Pensions and Other Deferred Comp. **16**	0.5	0.0	0.8	0.4	1.0	0.1	0.2	0.5	0.4	0.3	0.3	0.3	•
Employee Benefits **17**	2.6	2.8	1.3	1.3	2.2	1.7	1.6	3.6	6.0	2.0	3.4	4.2	•
Advertising **18**	0.6	0.8	0.9	0.4	0.7	0.2	0.5	0.4	0.7	0.4	0.4	0.4	•
Other Expenses **19**	30.6	31.8	30.5	31.8	24.7	33.9	23.8	25.7	32.0	38.1	32.5	31.2	•
Officers' Compensation **20**	4.4	7.1	9.3	10.5	5.5	0.9	1.5	1.5	2.7	1.1	0.7	0.9	•
Operating Margin **21**	0.9	•	2.6	0.4	2.8	•	1.7	•	•	•	•	6.3	•
Operating Margin Before Officers' Comp. **22**	5.3	3.2	11.8	11.0	8.3	3.2	3.2	•	•	•	•	7.3	•

Selected Average Balance Sheet ($ in Thousands)

Net Receivables 23	137	0	11	103	319	1825	3618	9963	14701	20478	55198	211166	•
Inventories 24	12	0	1	4	45	100	258	577	2201	2893	4805	13728	•
Net Property, Plant and Equipment 25	190	0	33	251	912	1519	2727	3741	10233	22528	77230	286383	•
Total Assets 26	907	0	79	671	1932	7008	15472	35040	71162	160378	376106	1770612	•
Notes and Loans Payable 27	390	0	72	906	1148	3528	4962	11714	23965	53331	158036	544667	•
All Other Liabilities 28	247	0	16	169	288	2335	5268	15398	23486	38841	99186	496182	•
Net Worth 29	270	0	-9	-405	497	1145	5242	7928	23711	67606	118883	729762	•

Selected Financial Ratios (Times to 1)

Current Ratio 30	1.5	•	1.2	1.7	1.6	1.1	1.4	1.2	1.4	1.5	2.4	1.4	•
Quick Ratio 31	1.1	•	1.1	1.4	1.3	0.9	1.1	0.9	1.0	0.9	1.5	0.9	•
Net Sales to Working Capital 32	14.8	•	88.5	20.8	11.0	56.8	13.9	22.9	8.6	8.2	4.5	12.6	•
Coverage Ratio 33	2.8	•	9.2	3.5	3.8	3.5	4.9	•	1.3	1.0	0.6	3.7	•
Total Asset Turnover 34	1.6	•	7.0	3.2	1.8	2.7	2.2	1.9	1.3	0.8	1.0	0.9	•
Inventory Turnover 35	23.9	•	45.2	67.1	13.4	82.0	53.0	30.6	10.6	11.8	13.7	20.7	•
Receivables Turnover 36	11.2	•	63.7	19.9	9.7	12.6	8.3	6.9	6.8	6.8	6.9	7.7	•
Total Liabilities to Net Worth 37	2.4	•	•	2.9	2.5	5.1	2.0	3.4	2.0	1.4	2.2	1.4	•
Current Assets to Working Capital 38	3.1	•	5.1	2.4	2.5	11.6	3.8	6.1	3.2	3.2	1.7	3.5	•
Current Liabilities to Working Capital 39	2.1	•	4.1	1.4	1.5	10.6	2.8	5.1	2.2	2.2	0.7	2.5	•
Working Capital to Net Sales 40	0.1	•	0.0	0.0	0.1	0.0	0.1	0.0	0.1	0.1	0.2	0.1	•
Inventory to Working Capital 41	0.1	•	0.2	0.0	0.1	0.3	0.1	0.1	0.2	0.2	0.1	0.1	•
Total Receipts to Cash Flow 42	3.6	5.0	3.9	3.5	4.0	3.3	4.3	5.1	4.2	3.2	4.0	2.8	•
Cost of Goods to Cash Flow 43	0.7	1.0	0.4	0.4	0.7	1.4	1.8	1.3	1.1	0.8	0.7	0.5	•
Cash Flow to Total Debt 44	0.7	•	1.6	0.6	0.6	1.0	0.8	0.5	0.4	0.4	0.4	0.5	•

Selected Financial Factors (in Percentages)

Debt Ratio 45	70.3	•	111.9	160.4	74.3	83.7	66.1	77.4	66.7	57.8	68.4	58.8	•
Return on Total Assets 46	9.4	•	31.2	11.1	12.0	6.0	11.7	•	3.7	3.7	2.7	11.7	•
Return on Equity Before Income Taxes 47	20.5	•	•	•	34.2	26.3	27.4	•	•	•	•	20.7	•
Return on Equity After Income Taxes 48	14.1	•	•	•	30.0	24.6	23.4	•	•	0.3	•	13.0	•
Profit Margin (Before Income Tax) 49	3.7	•	4.0	2.5	5.0	1.6	4.3	•	0.2	0.2	•	9.4	•
Profit Margin (After Income Tax) 50	2.6	•	3.9	2.4	4.4	1.5	3.6	•	•	•	•	5.9	•

Table II

Corporations with Net Income

MISC. HEALTH CARE AND SOCIAL ASSISTANCE

MONEY AMOUNTS AND SIZE OF ASSETS IN THOUSANDS OF DOLLARS

Item Description for Accounting Period 7/06 Through 6/07		Total	Zero Assets	Under 500	500 to 1,000	1,000 to 5,000	5,000 to 10,000	10,000 to 25,000	25,000 to 50,000	50,000 to 100,000	100,000 to 250,000	250,000 to 500,000	500,000 to 2,500,000	2,500,000 and over
Number of Enterprises	1	31347	5510	22818	1491	•	163	94	23	21	10	•	•	0
Revenues ($ in Thousands)														
Net Sales	2	58843005	1079414	14538411	4554936	•	2744717	3634901	1850900	2470069	4219636	•	•	0
Interest	3	153236	0	6959	1736	•	2895	6602	4100	8917	14838	•	•	0
Rents	4	71919	0	361	3282	•	332	89	963	57350	2468	•	•	0
Royalties	5	13071	0	0	0	•	0	0	250	10941	0	•	•	0
Other Portfolio Income	6	514674	6148	130857	19990	•	258	24160	3348	18962	4394	•	•	0
Other Receipts	7	901572	1542	71728	87516	•	60510	53683	26672	26505	79438	•	•	0
Total Receipts	8	60497477	1087104	14748316	4667460	•	2808712	3719435	1886233	2592744	4320774	•	•	0
Average Total Receipts	9	1930	197	646	3130	•	17231	39568	82010	123464	432077	•	•	•
Operating Costs/Operating Income (%)														
Cost of Operations	10	19.5	28.7	12.6	13.6	•	23.9	46.1	3.3	22.2	20.9	•	•	•
Salaries and Wages	11	29.0	25.2	33.9	34.1	•	22.5	17.6	52.8	24.0	31.2	•	•	•
Taxes Paid	12	3.7	5.7	3.9	4.8	•	2.1	3.0	5.1	3.9	3.5	•	•	•
Interest Paid	13	1.6	0.3	0.4	1.0	•	0.6	0.9	1.1	0.8	2.1	•	•	•
Depreciation	14	1.9	0.3	0.8	1.2	•	1.2	1.5	1.1	2.0	2.6	•	•	•
Amortization and Depletion	15	0.7	0.2	0.1	0.4	•	0.1	0.2	0.5	0.7	1.1	•	•	•
Pensions and Other Deferred Comp.	16	0.5	0.0	1.0	0.5	•	0.0	0.2	0.1	0.6	0.3	•	•	•
Employee Benefits	17	2.8	3.5	1.4	1.1	•	2.4	1.0	3.7	8.0	3.1	•	•	•
Advertising	18	0.5	0.8	0.9	0.3	•	0.3	0.5	0.4	0.5	0.3	•	•	•
Other Expenses	19	28.3	20.9	27.5	26.9	•	40.7	20.0	26.2	32.3	31.3	•	•	•
Officers' Compensation	20	4.3	7.1	8.4	12.4	•	1.1	1.4	1.6	2.7	0.7	•	•	•
Operating Margin	21	7.2	7.1	9.2	3.7	•	5.1	7.5	4.0	2.2	2.8	•	•	•
Operating Margin Before Officers' Comp.	22	11.5	14.3	17.6	16.1	•	6.2	8.9	5.6	5.0	3.5	•	•	•

Selected Average Balance Sheet ($ in Thousands)

Net Receivables 23	180	0	14	57	•	2688	3621	12802	17354	•	66040
Inventories 24	14	0	1	5	•	137	181	455	1441	•	6819
Net Property, Plant and Equipment 25	194	0	25	382	•	944	2369	4852	12931	•	68138
Total Assets 26	1077	0	80	723	•	6456	14554	36039	72485	•	347264
Notes and Loans Payable 27	319	0	35	377	•	2191	4572	12405	14835	•	125635
All Other Liabilities 28	281	0	13	106	•	2083	4517	13803	21645	•	71761
Net Worth 29	477	0	32	241	•	2182	5466	9832	36004	•	149868

Selected Financial Ratios (Times to 1)

Current Ratio 30	1.5	•	1.7	1.7	•	1.6	1.4	1.1	1.7	•	2.1
Quick Ratio 31	1.1	•	1.6	1.5	•	1.4	1.1	1.0	1.3	•	1.4
Net Sales to Working Capital 32	16.8	•	41.4	39.3	•	10.2	14.3	46.4	7.8	•	6.4
Coverage Ratio 33	7.2	27.3	27.9	7.1	•	13.9	12.2	6.5	9.7	•	3.5
Total Asset Turnover 34	1.7	•	8.0	4.2	•	2.6	2.7	2.2	1.6	•	1.2
Inventory Turnover 35	26.2	•	70.8	79.1	•	29.4	98.5	5.9	18.1	•	12.9
Receivables Turnover 36	10.5	•	57.1	25.4	•	7.8	9.3	6.0	•	•	7.1
Total Liabilities to Net Worth 37	1.3	•	1.5	2.0	•	2.0	1.7	2.7	1.0	•	1.3
Current Assets to Working Capital 38	3.2	•	2.4	2.4	•	2.6	3.3	11.3	2.3	•	1.9
Current Liabilities to Working Capital 39	2.2	•	1.4	1.4	•	1.6	2.3	10.3	1.3	•	0.9
Working Capital to Net Sales 40	0.1	•	0.0	0.0	•	0.1	0.1	0.0	0.1	•	0.2
Inventory to Working Capital 41	0.1	•	0.1	0.1	•	0.1	0.1	0.3	0.1	•	0.1
Total Receipts to Cash Flow 42	3.0	4.3	3.2	3.7	•	2.3	3.8	3.5	2.8	•	3.1
Cost of Goods to Cash Flow 43	0.6	1.2	0.4	0.5	•	0.6	1.8	0.1	0.6	•	0.6
Cash Flow to Total Debt 44	1.0	•	4.1	1.7	•	1.7	1.1	0.9	1.1	•	0.7

Selected Financial Factors (in Percentages)

Debt Ratio 45	55.7	•	59.9	66.7	•	66.2	62.4	72.7	50.3	•	56.8
Return on Total Assets 46	20.2	•	88.5	30.2	•	20.9	28.4	15.5	13.1	•	8.7
Return on Equity Before Income Taxes 47	39.3	•	213.1	77.9	•	57.4	69.5	48.0	23.6	•	14.5
Return on Equity After Income Taxes 48	32.8	•	209.6	76.0	•	55.9	64.1	37.2	19.6	•	9.8
Profit Margin (Before Income Tax) 49	10.0	7.8	10.7	6.1	•	7.4	9.8	5.9	7.2	•	5.1
Profit Margin (After Income Tax) 50	8.3	7.2	10.5	6.0	•	7.2	9.1	4.5	6.0	•	3.5

Table I

Corporations with and without Net Income

HOSPITALS, NURSING, AND RESIDENTIAL CARE FACILITIES

MONEY AMOUNTS AND SIZE OF ASSETS IN THOUSANDS OF DOLLARS

Item Description for Accounting Period 7/06 Through 6/07		Total	Zero Assets	Under 500	500 to 1,000	1,000 to 5,000	5,000 to 10,000	10,000 to 25,000	25,000 to 50,000	50,000 to 100,000	100,000 to 250,000	250,000 to 500,000	500,000 to 2,500,000	2,500,000 and over
Number of Enterprises	1	16576	2187	10883	1091	1817	220	201	65	40	32	9	21	9
Revenues ($ in Thousands)														
Net Sales	2	105541477	1156261	6218578	1673667	8477020	2303838	5340407	3671068	4259178	6692468	2646095	20593667	42509229
Interest	3	946041	7678	4951	128	4091	3171	9510	6852	8514	30072	23302	328275	519499
Rents	4	359874	12316	2331	0	2826	0	3185	8747	9705	12667	10106	47745	250246
Royalties	5	13722	0	0	0	0	0	0	0	0	10	4861	8851	0
Other Portfolio Income	6	1871875	237683	13596	14	11314	11603	2812	47216	10206	52966	38582	455160	990724
Other Receipts	7	3911410	108612	8845	801	447856	45304	51407	84293	79043	294249	62249	935505	1793244
Total Receipts	8	112644399	1522550	6248301	1674610	8943107	2363916	5407321	3818176	4366646	7082432	2785195	22369203	46062942
Average Total Receipts	9	6796	696	574	1535	4922	10745	26902	58741	109166	221326	309466	1065200	5118105
Operating Costs/Operating Income (%)														
Cost of Operations	10	4.3	0.3	4.2	8.4	3.8	5.5	17.8	4.1	9.1	8.0	5.9	5.2	0.9
Salaries and Wages	11	41.7	58.4	37.0	35.2	45.3	28.7	34.9	43.5	41.5	44.6	43.1	42.8	41.8
Taxes Paid	12	5.4	7.5	5.1	5.5	7.2	5.8	7.2	5.4	5.1	6.1	6.3	5.5	4.5
Interest Paid	13	3.8	12.8	1.7	1.8	1.6	2.8	2.1	2.5	2.6	2.3	4.0	4.3	4.9
Depreciation	14	2.6	2.9	1.0	1.3	1.4	1.5	1.4	1.7	1.7	1.9	2.7	2.1	3.9
Amortization and Depletion	15	0.6	0.5	0.0	0.0	0.1	0.0	0.2	0.4	0.5	0.4	0.9	1.0	0.8
Pensions and Other Deferred Comp.	16	0.6	0.1	0.1	0.1	0.1	0.1	0.4	0.2	0.3	0.3	0.1	0.3	1.1
Employee Benefits	17	4.4	2.4	1.8	2.0	3.1	2.5	4.3	3.3	3.3	4.1	4.4	4.7	5.4
Advertising	18	0.4	0.3	0.4	0.4	0.6	0.2	0.3	0.3	0.4	0.2	0.3	0.4	0.5
Other Expenses	19	37.0	46.3	37.2	43.4	36.4	49.6	31.3	38.8	36.8	35.8	39.8	37.3	36.4
Officers' Compensation	20	1.1	4.9	6.4	3.1	1.7	1.5	0.9	0.8	0.6	0.5	0.3	0.4	0.5
Operating Margin	21	•	•	5.0	•	•	1.9	•	•	•	•	•	•	•
Operating Margin Before Officers' Comp.	22	•	•	11.4	2.0	0.4	3.4	•	•	•	•	•	•	•

Selected Average Balance Sheet ($ in Thousands)

Net Receivables 23	839	10	225	443	1080	3479	6168	14685	39142	37848	131878	718849
Inventories 24	14	0	2	2	12	70	134	1305	1610	1319	2624	4079
Net Property, Plant and Equipment 25	2363	70	359	790	4167	5203	15211	27777	58626	180450	300293	2524354
Total Assets 26	6803	131	720	1983	7369	14439	33220	68994	162200	346992	1047680	7465010
Notes and Loans Payable 27	3988	214	436	1534	5390	7999	19379	42615	71196	133162	505756	4517137
All Other Liabilities 28	1696	21	222	559	2045	6056	11902	20155	73181	133736	217156	1697726
Net Worth 29	1119	-104	62	-110	-67	384	1940	6224	17823	80094	324769	1250147

Selected Financial Ratios (Times to 1)

Current Ratio 30	1.2	0.6	1.2	1.1	0.9	1.0	1.2	1.0	0.8	1.2	1.5	1.3
Quick Ratio 31	0.9	0.6	1.1	0.9	0.8	0.8	0.8	0.8	0.6	0.7	1.2	0.9
Net Sales to Working Capital 32	26.9	•	39.3	57.1	118.5	31.7	486.8	•	•	15.3	10.8	17.8
Coverage Ratio 33	2.3	0.6	0.4	3.7	2.6	2.2	1.2	1.6	•	0.4	2.1	2.6
Total Asset Turnover 34	0.9	•	2.1	2.4	1.4	1.8	1.7	1.5	1.3	0.8	0.9	0.6
Inventory Turnover 35	18.9	2012.1	73.3	74.1	47.7	67.8	17.2	7.4	10.5	13.2	19.6	11.0
Receivables Turnover 36	8.0	68.3	7.7	10.5	7.4	8.4	8.2	8.6	5.7	7.3	7.8	7.1
Total Liabilities to Net Worth 37	5.1	•	10.6	•	•	36.6	16.1	10.1	8.1	3.3	2.2	5.0
Current Assets to Working Capital 38	6.7	•	6.8	10.8	•	27.4	7.5	125.5	•	5.9	3.1	4.7
Current Liabilities to Working Capital 39	5.7	•	5.8	9.8	•	26.4	6.5	124.5	•	4.9	2.1	3.7
Working Capital to Net Sales 40	0.0	•	0.0	0.0	•	0.0	0.0	0.0	•	0.1	0.1	0.1
Inventory to Working Capital 41	0.0	•	0.0	0.0	0.3	0.1	2.5	•	•	0.1	0.0	0.0
Total Receipts to Cash Flow 42	2.9	8.0	3.1	3.1	2.0	3.9	2.7	3.2	3.1	3.7	3.0	2.7
Cost of Goods to Cash Flow 43	0.1	0.0	0.3	0.1	0.1	0.7	0.1	0.3	0.2	0.2	0.2	0.0
Cash Flow to Total Debt 44	0.4	•	0.7	0.7	0.7	0.5	0.7	0.5	0.5	0.3	0.5	0.3

Selected Financial Factors (in Percentages)

Debt Ratio 45	83.6	178.9	91.4	105.5	100.9	97.3	94.2	91.0	89.0	76.9	69.0	83.3
Return on Total Assets 46	8.1	31.4	1.5	13.7	10.2	4.5	9.3	5.0	4.8	1.2	8.3	8.0
Return on Equity Before Income Taxes 47	27.7	•	•	•	•	23.9	87.9	10.3	17.3	•	13.7	29.3
Return on Equity After Income Taxes 48	17.2	•	•	•	•	16.1	71.9	6.9	11.1	•	9.0	16.2
Profit Margin (Before Income Tax) 49	4.9	5.5	4.3	4.3	4.4	0.3	3.0	0.6	1.5	•	4.5	7.8
Profit Margin (After Income Tax) 50	3.0	5.3	4.1	4.1	4.4	0.2	2.5	0.4	0.9	•	3.0	4.3

Table II
Corporations with Net Income

HOSPITALS, NURSING, AND RESIDENTIAL CARE FACILITIES

MONEY AMOUNTS AND SIZE OF ASSETS IN THOUSANDS OF DOLLARS

Item Description for Accounting Period 7/06 Through 6/07	Total	Zero Assets	Under 500	500 to 1,000	1,000 to 5,000	5,000 to 10,000	10,000 to 25,000	25,000 to 50,000	50,000 to 100,000	100,000 to 250,000	250,000 to 500,000	500,000 to 2,500,000	2,500,000 and over
Number of Enterprises **1**	8514	500	6100	416	•	125	120	49	27	20	5	13	•
Revenues ($ in Thousands)													
Net Sales **2**	76762021	109765	3681745	723442	•	1841501	3304078	3096559	2801981	4285756	1230645	16157232	•
Interest **3**	711726	2872	923	128	•	1101	4694	5477	6668	20177	17701	199067	•
Rents **4**	256815	11901	2331	0	•	0	3110	8741	1532	4233	4044	27660	•
Royalties **5**	8851	0	0	0	•	0	0	0	0	0	0	8851	•
Other Portfolio Income **6**	1789640	236746	6579	14	•	11511	2710	47216	8956	13432	38192	442658	•
Other Receipts **7**	3305439	99907	1799	157	•	41923	41736	77526	51928	138351	64759	691147	•
Total Receipts **8**	82834492	461191	3693377	723741	•	1896036	3356328	3235519	2871065	4461949	1355341	17526615	•
Average Total Receipts **9**	9729	922	605	1740	•	15168	27969	66031	106336	223097	271068	1348201	•
Operating Costs/Operating Income (%)													
Cost of Operations **10**	3.5	3.0	4.6	17.3	•	3.9	22.2	3.0	10.8	7.2	4.9	2.4	•
Salaries and Wages **11**	41.0	70.0	29.7	37.6	•	23.5	30.6	43.5	37.1	39.7	41.6	42.7	•
Taxes Paid **12**	5.3	16.9	4.4	5.8	•	5.7	7.8	5.6	5.1	6.3	6.6	5.5	•
Interest Paid **13**	3.5	76.1	1.4	1.6	•	2.8	1.6	1.9	2.3	2.2	4.0	3.5	•
Depreciation **14**	2.6	5.9	1.0	0.9	•	1.5	1.5	1.4	1.6	2.0	3.6	1.7	•
Amortization and Depletion **15**	0.6	0.9	0.0	•	•	0.0	0.2	0.3	0.3	0.5	0.8	1.0	•
Pensions and Other Deferred Comp. **16**	0.7	0.1	0.2	0.3	•	0.1	0.3	0.2	0.3	0.3	0.1	0.3	•
Employee Benefits **17**	4.5	1.8	0.8	0.5	•	2.2	4.4	3.2	3.6	3.2	4.8	4.8	•
Advertising **18**	0.4	0.4	0.4	0.2	•	0.2	0.3	0.3	0.3	0.2	0.4	0.5	•
Other Expenses **19**	35.3	79.2	39.2	25.1	•	54.4	27.8	39.1	36.4	37.5	34.6	39.3	•
Officers' Compensation **20**	1.1	13.2	7.0	6.9	•	1.6	0.8	0.8	0.9	0.4	0.5	0.5	•
Operating Margin **21**	1.5	•	11.3	3.9	•	4.1	2.6	0.7	1.5	0.6	•	•	•
Operating Margin Before Officers' Comp. **22**	2.6	•	18.3	10.8	•	5.7	3.4	1.5	2.3	1.0	•	•	•

Selected Average Balance Sheet ($ in Thousands)

Net Receivables 23	1276	17		299	1626	3442	6896	13964	42880	52979	172297
Inventories 24	19	0	0	5	19	95	109	1599	1483	415	1212
Net Property, Plant and Equipment 25	2987	0	55	313	4192	6921	14017	26759	61241	155724	219567
Total Assets 26	9687	0	135	708	7609	15345	33177	68612	160720	326320	1120234
Notes and Loans Payable 27	5611	0	91	370	7264	8124	16670	38215	72660	78338	432451
All Other Liabilities 28	2022	0	11	135	1807	4082	13035	17647	50912	111922	298316
Net Worth 29	2054	0	33	203	-1461	3139	3473	12750	37148	136060	389467

Selected Financial Ratios (Times to 1)

Current Ratio 30	1.4	•	4.1	2.1	•	1.0	1.3	1.4	1.2	1.3	0.9	1.4
Quick Ratio 31	1.1	•	3.9	2.0	•	0.9	1.1	0.9	0.9	1.1	0.8	1.2
Net Sales to Working Capital 32	15.4	•	13.3	9.9	•	21.5	17.0	24.2	12.1	•	14.3
Coverage Ratio 33	3.7	3.0	9.2	3.4	3.6	3.7	2.7	3.1	3.1	2.8
Total Asset Turnover 34	0.9	4.5	2.5	1.9	1.8	1.9	1.5	1.3	0.8	1.1
Inventory Turnover 35	16.8	•	66.3	29.4	64.2	17.2	7.0	10.4	29.2	25.1
Receivables Turnover 36	7.5	41.6	5.1	6.6	8.0	7.9	8.5	5.1	9.3	•
Total Liabilities to Net Worth 37	3.7	3.1	2.5	3.9	8.6	4.4	3.3	1.4	1.9
Current Assets to Working Capital 38	3.8	1.3	1.9	•	•	4.5	3.8	6.3	3.9	•	3.7
Current Liabilities to Working Capital 39	2.8	0.3	0.9	3.5	2.8	5.3	2.9	2.7
Working Capital to Net Sales 40	0.1	0.1	0.1	0.0	0.1	0.0	0.1	0.1	0.1
Inventory to Working Capital 41	0.0	•	0.0	0.0	0.1	0.0	0.1	0.1	0.0
Total Receipts to Cash Flow 42	2.6	3.2	2.5	4.0	1.8	3.7	2.6	2.8	2.6	2.8	2.7
Cost of Goods to Cash Flow 43	0.1	0.1	0.1	0.7	0.1	0.8	0.3	0.2	0.1	0.1
Cash Flow to Total Debt 44	0.4	•	2.4	0.9	•	0.9	0.6	0.8	0.7	0.7	0.5	0.6

Selected Financial Factors (in Percentages)

Debt Ratio 45	78.8	•	75.4	71.3	•	119.2	79.5	89.5	81.4	76.9	58.3	65.2
Return on Total Assets 46	12.1	•	58.3	13.6	•	19.0	10.4	13.4	9.3	9.1	9.2	11.0
Return on Equity Before Income Taxes 47	41.7	•	211.4	33.7	•	36.9	93.5	31.9	27.0	14.9	20.4
Return on Equity After Income Taxes 48	30.6	•	207.6	26.9	•	35.3	81.7	29.5	22.2	10.9	14.0
Profit Margin (Before Income Tax) 49	9.5	152.7	11.6	3.9	7.1	4.2	5.1	3.9	4.7	8.2	6.4
Profit Margin (After Income Tax) 50	7.0	123.0	11.4	3.1	7.0	4.0	4.5	3.6	3.9	6.0	4.4

Table I

Corporations with and without Net Income

OTHER ARTS, ENTERTAINMENT, AND RECREATION

MONEY AMOUNTS AND SIZE OF ASSETS IN THOUSANDS OF DOLLARS

Item Description for Accounting Period 7/06 Through 6/07	Total	Zero Assets	Under 500	500 to 1,000	1,000 to 5,000	5,000 to 10,000	10,000 to 25,000	25,000 to 50,000	50,000 to 100,000	100,000 to 250,000	250,000 to 500,000	500,000 to 2,500,000	2,500,000 and over
Number of Enterprises 1	66599	17264	46482	1430	1010	214	87	39	25	28	11	10	0
Revenues ($ in Thousands)													
Net Sales 2	38150188	1167520	12326336	1504781	5119363	1466460	1038072	740335	1974074	4063982	2407758	6341507	0
Interest 3	297208	1210	14630	525	12948	2915	9824	8031	20497	30134	32479	164015	0
Rents 4	108645	235	2300	717	742	1010	861	781	279	20508	19866	61346	0
Royalties 5	124557	912	0	58	16799	0	0	0	176	82365	21035	3212	0
Other Portfolio Income 6	413169	1661	17303	2632	27011	16420	12023	7372	23406	39513	32332	233495	0
Other Receipts 7	2625115	367686	241528	33357	117779	94041	295138	210220	65203	718120	367672	114371	0
Total Receipts 8	41718882	1539224	12602097	1542070	5294642	1580846	1355918	966739	2083635	4954622	2881142	6917946	0
Average Total Receipts 9	626	89	271	1078	5242	7387	15585	24788	83345	176951	261922	691795	•
Operating Costs/Operating Income (%)													
Cost of Operations 10	18.6	14.3	8.8	21.2	14.1	6.7	17.3	16.9	38.2	16.9	33.6	33.8	•
Salaries and Wages 11	19.3	22.6	12.9	14.4	16.3	20.3	38.6	37.0	25.1	40.8	24.4	11.6	•
Taxes Paid 12	3.1	4.5	2.2	3.4	3.4	2.1	5.8	5.1	2.2	3.8	4.7	3.0	•
Interest Paid 13	1.9	0.8	0.5	0.8	0.1	4.0	1.8	1.6	1.9	2.8	4.6	4.5	•
Depreciation 14	2.3	1.6	1.8	1.8	0.9	2.3	2.1	3.4	1.3	2.9	2.7	4.4	•
Amortization and Depletion 15	1.1	0.3	0.0	0.2	0.0	0.1	0.1	0.5	0.7	4.8	1.6	2.1	•
Pensions and Other Deferred Comp. 16	2.0	0.5	3.5	4.6	1.2	0.4	0.3	1.3	0.6	2.3	1.5	0.7	•
Employee Benefits 17	1.3	4.0	0.8	0.6	0.3	0.4	1.8	3.1	0.8	2.3	3.2	1.1	•
Advertising 18	2.1	1.8	1.7	3.7	0.9	1.3	2.3	1.8	1.8	2.8	1.6	3.5	•
Other Expenses 19	36.1	71.8	39.8	33.6	24.8	49.1	42.6	56.2	19.6	34.8	30.4	33.7	•
Officers' Compensation 20	13.3	8.6	23.8	10.3	25.9	10.5	8.5	2.5	4.3	1.8	2.2	1.2	•
Operating Margin 21	•	•	4.2	5.4	12.1	2.9	•	•	3.4	•	•	0.4	•
Operating Margin Before Officers' Comp. 22	12.3	•	28.0	15.7	38.0	13.4	•	•	7.7	•	•	1.6	•

Selected Average Balance Sheet ($ in Thousands)

Net Receivables 23	34	0	2	16	165	711	2397	3467	8360	19696	16955	52652	•
Inventories 24	8	0	4	19	180	72	156	276	1049	1798	1928	3669	•
Net Property, Plant and Equipment 25	130	0	12	148	251	1145	3193	7710	14718	39970	115076	407319	•
Total Assets 26	494	0	60	667	1719	6975	15084	34577	68350	179475	381804	1232175	•
Notes and Loans Payable 27	207	0	62	312	542	3795	3435	13672	27811	64480	118114	443791	•
All Other Liabilities 28	182	0	20	83	460	5690	4141	13246	26537	80696	99058	453903	•
Net Worth 29	105	0	-22	272	717	-2511	7508	7659	14001	34299	164631	334481	•

Selected Financial Ratios (Times to 1)

Current Ratio 30	1.1	•	1.5	1.5	1.8	1.2	1.5	1.5	1.2	1.1	1.3	0.6	•
Quick Ratio 31	0.9	•	1.1	1.4	1.3	1.0	1.2	1.0	0.9	0.8	0.9	0.5	•
Net Sales to Working Capital 32	30.3	•	19.4	11.6	9.6	14.5	5.2	3.7	25.8	18.9	9.3	•	•
Coverage Ratio 33	5.4	2.2	14.7	10.9	127.2	3.6	6.2	1.7	5.6	3.1	2.9	3.2	•
Total Asset Turnover 34	1.2	•	4.4	1.6	2.9	1.0	0.8	0.5	1.2	0.8	0.6	0.5	•
Inventory Turnover 35	12.9	•	6.5	11.6	4.0	6.4	13.2	11.6	28.8	13.6	38.2	58.3	•
Receivables Turnover 36	15.4	•	116.1	51.1	28.1	9.8	4.9	4.8	10.5	8.2	11.2	8.5	•
Total Liabilities to Net Worth 37	3.7	•	•	1.5	1.4	•	1.0	3.5	3.9	4.2	1.3	2.7	•
Current Assets to Working Capital 38	8.3	2.9	3.0	2.2	6.7	3.0	2.9	7.5	8.4	4.1	•	•	•
Current Liabilities to Working Capital 39	7.3	•	1.9	2.0	1.2	5.7	2.0	1.9	6.5	7.4	3.1	•	•
Working Capital to Net Sales 40	0.0	•	0.1	0.1	0.1	0.1	0.2	0.3	0.0	0.1	0.1	•	•
Inventory to Working Capital 41	0.4	0.2	0.1	0.3	0.3	0.3	0.1	0.0	0.3	0.3	0.1	•	•
Total Receipts to Cash Flow 42	2.5	1.5	2.4	2.7	1.8	2.3	1.9	3.9	2.8	2.9	2.8	•	•
Cost of Goods to Cash Flow 43	0.5	0.2	0.2	0.4	0.1	0.4	0.1	0.3	1.5	0.5	1.0	0.9	•
Cash Flow to Total Debt 44	0.6	•	0.9	1.9	0.4	0.7	0.4	0.4	0.3	0.4	•	•	•

Selected Financial Factors (in Percentages)

Debt Ratio 45	78.8	•	135.9	59.2	58.3	136.0	50.2	77.9	79.5	80.9	56.9	72.9	•
Return on Total Assets 46	12.0	•	30.3	13.6	45.7	14.3	8.9	1.4	12.5	7.0	7.7	7.4	•
Return on Equity Before Income Taxes 47	46.1	•	•	30.4	108.7	•	15.0	2.6	50.3	24.9	11.6	18.6	•
Return on Equity After Income Taxes 48	34.3	•	•	30.2	106.4	•	13.4	•	40.1	18.9	8.5	14.1	•
Profit Margin (Before Income Tax) 49	8.4	1.0	6.4	7.9	15.4	10.5	9.4	1.1	8.9	5.9	8.8	9.8	•
Profit Margin (After Income Tax) 50	6.3	•	6.4	7.8	15.0	9.7	8.4	•	7.1	6.4	4.5	7.4	•

Table II
Corporations with Net Income

OTHER ARTS, ENTERTAINMENT, AND RECREATION

MONEY AMOUNTS AND SIZE OF ASSETS IN THOUSANDS OF DOLLARS

Item Description for Accounting Period 7/06 Through 6/07	Total	Zero Assets	Under 500	500 to 1,000	1,000 to 5,000	5,000 to 10,000	10,000 to 25,000	25,000 to 50,000	50,000 to 100,000	100,000 to 250,000	250,000 to 500,000	500,000 to 2,500,000	2,500,000 and over
Number of Enterprises 1	32758	8518	22546	695	756	112	62	19	17	20	7	7	0
Revenues ($ in Thousands)													
Net Sales 2	27792346	730880	8827891	1354983	4695157	1034371	710539	422337	1573315	3057119	1770131	3615625	0
Interest 3	218277	583	8091	131	9902	2874	6341	4184	17406	25690	15042	128033	0
Rents 4	76435	0	15	717	157	1010	861	0	279	20404	13444	39549	0
Royalties 5	96104	912	0	0	0	0	0	0	176	70769	21035	3212	0
Other Portfolio Income 6	376060	185	5288	2632	19817	16405	10470	4100	23307	38673	30941	224244	0
Other Receipts 7	2288523	422044	180178	2838	86536	69337	282490	145521	55442	558238	394710	91184	0
Total Receipts 8	30847745	1154604	9021463	1361301	4811569	1123997	1010701	576142	1669925	3770893	2245303	4101847	0
Average Total Receipts 9	942	136	400	1959	6365	10036	16302	30323	98231	188545	320758	585978	•
Operating Costs/Operating Income (%)													
Cost of Operations 10	16.0	9.2	5.7	20.3	13.4	9.4	11.6	17.3	46.3	19.2	33.6	22.0	•
Salaries and Wages 11	18.9	29.0	13.4	12.2	13.9	21.7	46.4	30.0	18.2	33.4	27.0	15.6	•
Taxes Paid 12	2.9	2.0	2.2	2.9	2.9	1.8	6.2	5.1	2.0	3.1	4.9	3.9	•
Interest Paid 13	1.6	0.1	0.3	0.7	0.1	0.4	0.6	0.6	1.5	2.4	2.3	7.1	•
Depreciation 14	2.0	0.6	0.7	1.4	0.6	1.1	1.6	2.8	1.5	3.3	2.1	6.8	•
Amortization and Depletion 15	0.8	•	0.0	0.2	0.0	0.0	0.0	0.4	0.7	3.3	2.1	2.1	•
Pensions and Other Deferred Comp. 16	1.9	0.8	3.4	0.4	1.3	0.5	0.3	1.3	0.4	2.0	1.6	0.9	•
Employee Benefits 17	1.3	6.3	0.6	0.7	0.4	0.1	1.6	1.7	0.7	2.5	3.2	1.8	•
Advertising 18	2.0	1.7	1.8	3.3	0.8	1.2	2.4	1.2	1.7	3.4	1.9	2.8	•
Other Expenses 19	31.3	58.8	34.6	29.7	22.7	31.1	38.3	43.1	12.1	37.6	28.6	30.7	•
Officers' Compensation 20	14.7	11.7	23.6	10.2	27.9	14.8	12.1	2.3	5.0	1.8	2.5	1.4	•
Operating Margin 21	6.7	•	13.7	18.0	16.0	18.0	•	•	10.0	•	•	4.9	•
Operating Margin Before Officers' Comp. 22	21.4	•	37.2	28.3	43.9	32.8	•	•	14.9	•	•	6.3	•

Selected Average Balance Sheet ($ in Thousands)

Net Receivables	23	43	0	3	20	131	418	2028	2169	9485	16596	21540	52518 •
Inventories	24	11	0	2	13	220	130	134	168	904	2474	1643	4753
Net Property, Plant and Equipment	25	192	0	12	214	164	644	2132	3312	15076	47072	94381	517338 •
Total Assets	26	680	0	74	644	1730	7629	15463	34370	68128	180580	405832	1252991 •
Notes and Loans Payable	27	232	0	29	401	465	1503	1724	3048	20552	58132	73360	562705 •
All Other Liabilities	28	193	0	27	13	492	1176	4374	10834	16941	85901	93776	292234 •
Net Worth	29	256	0	18	230	774	4950	9366	20487	30635	36546	238696	398051 •

Selected Financial Ratios (Times to 1)

Current Ratio	30	1.3	•	1.7	1.0	2.0	2.0	1.3	2.0	1.6	1.2	1.8	0.7 •
Quick Ratio	31	1.0	•	1.5	0.9	1.4	1.6	0.9	1.6	1.2	0.8	1.1	0.5 •
Net Sales to Working Capital	32	16.4	•	19.1	320.1	9.6	7.9	7.5	3.1	9.8	12.6	4.6	• •
Coverage Ratio	33	11.9	323.2	48.8	28.6	160.8	76.1	51.7	38.0	11.4	5.6	8.4	3.7 •
Total Asset Turnover	34	1.2	•	5.3	3.0	3.6	1.2	0.6	0.7	1.4	0.8	0.6	0.4 •
Inventory Turnover	35	12.0	•	9.7	30.3	3.8	6.7	22.9	9.9	11.9	47.4	51.8	23.9 •
Receivables Turnover	36	19.1	•	126.2	54.7	34.0	22.8	9.8	5.5	9.9	•	8.9	8.9 •
Total Liabilities to Net Worth	37	1.7	•	3.1	1.8	1.2	0.5	0.7	0.7	1.2	3.9	0.7	2.1 •
Current Assets to Working Capital	38	4.1	•	2.4	31.1	2.0	2.0	4.4	2.0	2.7	5.5	2.2	• •
Current Liabilities to Working Capital	39	3.1	•	1.4	30.1	1.0	1.0	3.4	1.0	1.7	4.5	1.2	• •
Working Capital to Net Sales	40	0.1	•	0.1	0.0	0.1	0.1	0.1	0.3	0.1	0.1	0.2	• •
Inventory to Working Capital	41	0.2	•	0.0	3.0	0.3	0.2	0.0	0.0	0.1	0.3	0.0	• •
Total Receipts to Cash Flow	42	2.2	1.1	2.1	2.6	2.6	1.8	1.4	1.9	4.0	2.3	2.4	2.4 •
Cost of Goods to Cash Flow	43	0.4	0.1	0.1	0.5	0.3	0.2	0.2	0.2	1.8	0.4	0.8	0.5 •
Cash Flow to Total Debt	44	0.9	•	3.3	1.8	2.5	1.9	1.1	1.0	0.6	0.5	0.6	0.3 •

Selected Financial Factors (in Percentages)

Debt Ratio	45	62.4	•	75.6	64.3	55.3	35.1	40.4	39.4	55.0	79.8	41.2	68.2 •
Return on Total Assets	46	24.1	•	85.4	58.0	66.5	32.4	20.1	16.1	23.8	11.5	11.8	10.7 •
Return on Equity Before Income Taxes	47	58.6	•	342.8	157.0	147.8	49.3	33.0	25.8	48.4	46.5	17.6	24.5 •
Return on Equity After Income Taxes	48	53.8	•	341.0	156.6	144.9	47.1	28.7	24.1	41.5	38.7	14.2	19.1 •
Profit Margin (Before Income Tax)	49	17.7	37.8	15.8	18.5	18.4	26.4	30.4	21.1	16.0	11.1	16.6	18.9 •
Profit Margin (After Income Tax)	50	16.2	32.8	15.8	18.1	18.1	25.3	26.5	19.7	13.7	9.3	13.4	14.7 •

Table I

Corporations with and without Net Income

AMUSEMENT, GAMBLING, AND RECREATION INDUSTRIES

MONEY AMOUNTS AND SIZE OF ASSETS IN THOUSANDS OF DOLLARS

Item Description for Accounting Period 7/06 Through 6/07	Total	Zero Assets	Under 500	500 to 1,000	1,000 to 5,000	5,000 to 10,000	10,000 to 25,000	25,000 to 50,000	50,000 to 100,000	100,000 to 250,000	250,000 to 500,000	500,000 to 2,500,000	2,500,000 and over
Number of Enterprises **1**	53563	7094	37092	3981	4205	579	365	151	43	23	11	14	4
Revenues ($ in Thousands)													
Net Sales **2**	47638890	418136	10090194	3203333	7922733	3055430	3250463	2644120	1309435	1855083	2931539	7223723	3734701
Interest **3**	506758	142	4204	8631	15939	9659	7747	7687	8995	9258	64456	101747	268291
Rents **4**	165307	0	3400	4004	6900	17129	6680	7206	5683	7315	11614	73673	21703
Royalties **5**	72691	0	0	0	4206	0	0	0	371	4030	1955	11461	50667
Other Portfolio Income **6**	1057967	79292	62378	130202	79498	51781	10881	33370	62508	35657	2784	332308	177310
Other Receipts **7**	3857592	4915	188720	744255	472336	125760	331647	283671	79605	101541	205160	1076094	243889
Total Receipts **8**	53299205	502485	10348896	4090425	8501612	3259759	3607418	2976054	1466597	2012884	3217508	8819006	4496561
Average Total Receipts **9**	995	71	279	1027	2022	5630	9883	19709	34107	87517	292501	629929	1124140
Operating Costs/Operating Income (%)													
Cost of Operations **10**	22.7	15.4	24.3	17.5	30.8	18.2	33.0	20.2	15.4	22.7	30.2	10.9	22.9
Salaries and Wages **11**	22.1	5.7	14.2	25.7	21.4	29.2	23.2	27.6	27.6	18.6	25.0	29.9	15.1
Taxes Paid **12**	7.9	4.9	4.5	6.9	6.2	8.5	6.9	6.9	7.9	5.2	5.5	10.9	20.2
Interest Paid **13**	5.4	2.7	1.9	2.6	3.9	3.5	3.7	2.9	6.3	6.8	6.7	8.6	17.7
Depreciation **14**	6.5	2.9	3.7	6.5	7.0	7.3	6.6	7.9	7.5	8.5	5.5	7.8	8.2
Amortization and Depletion **15**	0.7	0.0	0.2	1.9	0.5	0.5	0.6	0.5	1.3	1.2	1.2	0.6	1.9
Pensions and Other Deferred Comp. **16**	0.3	0.5	0.1	0.2	0.4	0.2	0.2	0.4	0.2	0.3	0.4	0.2	0.3
Employee Benefits **17**	1.7	1.5	0.8	1.3	1.7	0.9	2.5	2.2	1.7	1.9	1.1	2.5	2.8
Advertising **18**	2.7	5.6	2.3	2.2	2.0	2.5	2.2	3.9	2.7	3.0	2.0	3.2	4.3
Other Expenses **19**	35.8	85.3	39.1	52.7	29.8	34.2	26.9	34.5	34.7	33.7	34.7	41.4	21.2
Officers' Compensation **20**	3.3	3.9	7.0	2.6	3.5	2.6	1.4	1.5	1.2	2.4	1.3	1.0	4.2
Operating Margin **21**	•	1.8	•	•	•	•	•	•	•	•	•	•	•
Operating Margin Before Officers' Comp. **22**	•	8.9	•	•	•	•	•	•	•	•	•	•	•

Selected Average Balance Sheet ($ in Thousands)

Net Receivables **23**	82	0	3	24	98	590	874	2617	2016	8378	8137	61952	363114
Inventories **24**	32	0	4	7	92	313	444	794	1000	2418	3654	36567	17732
Net Property, Plant and Equipment **25**	658	0	57	440	1267	4515	8504	20427	37826	87047	170649	566871	956204
Total Assets **26**	1397	0	107	712	2064	7025	14925	35795	71604	167660	337019	1170524	4350958
Notes and Loans Payable **27**	882	0	84	360	1463	4243	6573	9539	31029	84805	222636	688674	3718286
All Other Liabilities **28**	263	0	18	105	298	1218	3082	5968	14932	38215	115137	313392	461988
Net Worth **29**	252	0	5	247	303	1564	5270	20288	25643	44640	-754	168458	170683

Selected Financial Ratios (Times to 1)

Current Ratio **30**	1.0	•	1.2	1.1	1.0	0.9	1.3	1.2	1.1	1.0	0.5	1.1	1.0
Quick Ratio **31**	0.7	•	0.9	1.0	0.6	0.5	0.8	0.9	0.8	0.7	0.3	0.6	0.9
Net Sales to Working Capital **32**	169.2	•	45.9	48.8	93.0	•	12.2	12.0	24.3	•	•	39.2	561.2
Coverage Ratio **33**	1.5	•	3.3	4.0	1.0	0.8	2.1	2.4	1.9	1.6	0.4	1.6	1.1
Total Asset Turnover **34**	0.6	•	2.6	1.1	0.9	0.8	0.6	0.5	0.4	0.5	0.8	0.4	0.2
Inventory Turnover **35**	6.3	•	16.2	20.1	6.3	3.1	6.6	4.4	4.7	7.6	22.0	1.5	12.1
Receivables Turnover **36**	12.8	•	93.8	47.1	19.0	7.6	11.7	8.0	14.3	9.2	35.8	7.1	5.1
Total Liabilities to Net Worth **37**	4.5	•	21.7	1.9	5.8	3.5	1.8	0.8	1.8	2.8	•	5.9	24.5
Current Assets to Working Capital **38**	50.8	•	5.1	8.3	23.0	•	4.7	5.7	10.7	•	•	17.5	286.5
Current Liabilities to Working Capital **39**	49.8	•	4.1	7.3	22.0	•	3.7	4.7	9.7	•	•	16.5	285.5
Working Capital to Net Sales **40**	0.0	•	0.0	0.0	0.0	•	0.1	0.1	0.0	•	•	0.0	0.0
Inventory to Working Capital **41**	6.1	•	0.6	0.5	4.0	•	0.5	0.6	1.2	•	•	3.0	10.7
Total Receipts to Cash Flow **42**	3.9	2.5	3.9	2.4	5.2	4.2	4.3	3.3	4.1	4.5	6.0	3.0	6.3
Cost of Goods to Cash Flow **43**	0.9	0.4	0.9	0.4	1.6	0.8	1.4	0.7	0.6	1.0	1.8	0.3	1.4
Cash Flow to Total Debt **44**	0.2	•	0.7	0.7	0.2	0.2	0.2	0.3	0.2	0.1	0.1	0.2	0.0

Selected Financial Factors (in Percentages)

Debt Ratio **45**	82.0	•	95.6	65.3	85.3	77.7	64.7	43.3	64.2	73.4	100.2	85.6	96.1
Return on Total Assets **46**	5.2	•	16.1	11.6	3.7	2.0	4.5	3.4	5.1	5.2	2.2	6.0	4.1
Return on Equity Before Income Taxes **47**	9.8	•	254.6	25.1	0.5	•	6.6	3.5	6.7	7.4	1372.3	15.2	8.3
Return on Equity After Income Taxes **48**	7.3	•	249.5	24.5	•	•	5.9	2.6	4.6	5.2	1563.9	11.8	•
Profit Margin (Before Income Tax) **49**	2.8	•	4.4	7.7	0.1	•	3.9	4.1	5.6	4.1	•	5.0	1.5
Profit Margin (After Income Tax) **50**	2.1	•	4.3	7.5	•	•	3.5	3.0	3.9	2.9	•	3.9	•

Table II
Corporations with Net Income

AMUSEMENT, GAMBLING, AND RECREATION INDUSTRIES

MONEY AMOUNTS AND SIZE OF ASSETS IN THOUSANDS OF DOLLARS

Item Description for Accounting Period 7/06 Through 6/07	Total	Zero Assets	Under 500	500 to 1,000	1,000 to 5,000	5,000 to 10,000	10,000 to 25,000	25,000 to 50,000	50,000 to 100,000	100,000 to 250,000	250,000 to 500,000	500,000 to 2,500,000	2,500,000 and over
Number of Enterprises **1**	27948	2391	20951	2026	2104	194	154	72	27	12	4	11	0
Revenues ($ in Thousands)													
Net Sales **2**	30436599	287596	6910548	2379498	5625739	1741057	1691852	1757638	988943	1041870	663918	7347940	0
Interest **3**	149113	26	2945	5137	9630	3382	3592	5046	8081	2198	12056	97020	0
Rents **4**	93375	0	11	2290	6278	11730	2201	4645	5683	6330	3445	50761	0
Royalties **5**	15317	0	0	0	4206	0	0	0	371	1	0	10738	0
Other Portfolio Income **6**	885699	78819	59489	128605	64178	50937	10297	27037	60361	19698	1310	384969	0
Other Receipts **7**	2226320	384	133753	250833	378527	38169	213081	132272	52449	73412	136226	817215	0
Total Receipts **8**	33806423	366825	7106746	2766363	6088558	1845275	1921023	1926638	1115888	1143509	816955	8708643	0
Average Total Receipts **9**	1210	153	339	1365	2894	9512	12474	26759	41329	95292	204239	791695	•
Operating Costs/Operating Income (%)													
Cost of Operations **10**	20.0	13.7	24.7	17.2	27.8	21.6	21.9	19.4	11.6	22.6	5.3	12.2	•
Salaries and Wages **11**	20.9	1.1	13.2	23.8	21.2	25.5	24.2	25.1	29.5	17.9	31.4	23.2	•
Taxes Paid **12**	9.0	3.5	4.0	5.7	6.1	9.5	7.7	6.2	7.2	5.9	8.0	18.8	•
Interest Paid **13**	3.6	1.9	1.3	1.9	2.5	1.4	2.5	1.9	4.8	4.9	9.3	7.4	•
Depreciation **14**	5.1	1.9	2.7	5.4	4.7	3.7	5.8	5.4	6.2	6.9	11.2	6.8	•
Amortization and Depletion **15**	0.7	•	0.2	2.3	0.3	0.5	0.3	0.1	0.8	0.9	1.3	1.2	•
Pensions and Other Deferred Comp. **16**	0.3	•	0.2	0.3	0.6	0.1	0.2	0.4	0.2	0.4	0.5	0.1	•
Employee Benefits **17**	1.7	1.7	0.7	0.7	1.5	0.8	2.6	1.7	1.4	2.1	1.7	3.0	•
Advertising **18**	2.3	2.5	1.7	2.2	1.9	2.5	3.1	3.1	3.1	2.7	3.0	2.6	•
Other Expenses **19**	31.9	52.8	35.7	37.7	28.0	29.8	24.9	30.8	32.8	26.0	39.4	31.2	•
Officers' Compensation **20**	3.2	5.0	6.3	2.5	4.1	2.7	1.2	1.6	1.4	1.9	1.8	1.1	•
Operating Margin **21**	1.4	16.0	9.4	0.4	1.4	2.0	5.4	4.2	1.0	7.7	•	•	•
Operating Margin Before Officers' Comp. **22**	4.5	21.1	15.6	2.9	5.5	4.7	6.6	5.8	2.4	9.6	•	•	•

Selected Average Balance Sheet ($ in Thousands)

	•	•	•	•	•	•	•	•	•	•	•	•
Net Receivables 23	69	0	5	30	129	285	886	2298	2330	10228	7549	82493
Inventories 24	32	0	3	11	76	784	465	1046	484	3086	2888	24779
Net Property, Plant and Equipment 25	614	0	41	450	1237	3618	8540	17153	39357	95038	135955	615677
Total Assets 26	1291	0	98	754	2050	7265	15105	36303	73360	174179	297632	1508640
Notes and Loans Payable 27	598	0	40	260	1068	2040	4976	8401	25449	62364	103514	862596
All Other Liabilities 28	263	0	18	108	304	1725	2634	6210	15660	45674	120778	315577
Net Worth 29	430	0	40	386	678	3500	7494	21691	32251	66142	73339	330468

Selected Financial Ratios (Times to 1)

	•	•	•	•	•	•	•	•	•	•	•	•
Current Ratio 30	1.3	•	1.6	1.3	1.3	1.3	1.2	1.2	1.4	0.9	0.9	1.3
Quick Ratio 31	0.9	•	1.3	1.1	1.0	0.4	0.9	0.8	1.1	0.7	0.3	1.0
Net Sales to Working Capital 32	18.9	•	25.1	24.4	22.5	11.9	16.4	16.0	8.1	•	•	12.9
Coverage Ratio 33	4.5	23.4	10.1	9.8	4.9	6.7	8.6	8.2	3.9	4.5	2.1	2.5
Total Asset Turnover 34	0.8	•	3.4	1.6	1.3	1.2	0.7	0.7	0.5	0.5	0.6	0.4
Inventory Turnover 35	6.9	•	26.1	19.1	9.8	2.5	5.2	4.5	8.8	6.4	3.0	3.3
Receivables Turnover 36	16.2	•	84.1	62.8	21.7	23.8	13.4	13.4	•	8.9	•	7.7
Total Liabilities to Net Worth 37	2.0	•	1.5	1.0	2.0	1.1	1.0	0.7	1.3	1.6	3.1	3.6
Current Assets to Working Capital 38	4.7	•	2.7	3.9	4.5	4.1	5.3	6.3	3.5	•	•	4.3
Current Liabilities to Working Capital 39	3.7	•	1.7	2.9	3.5	3.1	4.3	5.3	2.5	•	•	3.3
Working Capital to Net Sales 40	0.1	•	0.0	0.0	0.0	0.1	0.1	0.1	0.1	0.1	•	0.1
Inventory to Working Capital 41	0.4	•	0.2	0.3	0.8	0.7	0.5	0.9	0.1	0.1	•	0.2
Total Receipts to Cash Flow 42	3.1	1.3	3.1	2.6	3.7	3.5	2.8	2.8	3.3	2.8	3.0	3.2
Cost of Goods to Cash Flow 43	0.6	0.2	0.8	0.5	1.0	0.8	0.6	0.5	0.4	0.6	0.2	0.4
Cash Flow to Total Debt 44	0.4	•	1.9	1.2	0.5	0.7	0.5	0.6	0.3	0.3	0.2	0.2

Selected Financial Factors (in Percentages)

	•	•	•	•	•	•	•	•	•	•	•	•
Debt Ratio 45	66.7	•	59.3	48.8	66.9	51.8	50.4	40.2	56.0	62.0	75.4	78.1
Return on Total Assets 46	13.5	•	45.8	28.9	15.7	11.6	15.5	10.5	9.3	11.1	10.9	8.1
Return on Equity Before Income Taxes 47	31.5	•	101.3	50.6	37.8	20.4	27.7	15.5	15.8	22.8	23.1	22.0
Return on Equity After Income Taxes 48	28.7	•	100.2	49.9	35.8	17.9	26.6	13.6	13.2	19.9	17.7	17.3
Profit Margin (Before Income Tax) 49	12.5	43.6	12.2	16.7	9.6	8.0	18.9	13.8	13.9	17.3	10.2	10.9
Profit Margin (After Income Tax) 50	11.4	43.4	12.1	16.4	9.1	7.0	18.1	12.1	11.6	15.2	7.8	8.6

Table I

Corporations with and without Net Income

ACCOMMODATION

MONEY AMOUNTS AND SIZE OF ASSETS IN THOUSANDS OF DOLLARS

Item Description for Accounting Period 7/06 Through 6/07	Total	Zero Assets	Under 500	500 to 1,000	1,000 to 5,000	5,000 to 10,000	10,000 to 25,000	25,000 to 50,000	50,000 to 100,000	100,000 to 250,000	250,000 to 500,000	500,000 to 2,500,000	2,500,000 and over
Number of Enterprises **1**	31228	4718	14533	3435	7145	782	330	110	66	49	21	24	15
Revenues ($ in Thousands)													
Net Sales **2**	87345808	2868619	3993841	2417200	8144435	3024130	3262678	1904516	4628511	6369474	2523055	8517862	39691486
Interest **3**	2499063	21658	2537	6397	22372	7510	13025	13296	25413	88324	76819	296721	1924991
Rents **4**	555063	31460	2785	2118	7568	2471	5873	2697	10399	37008	8851	74747	369086
Royalties **5**	2011610	2533	1589	0	0	0	1070	0	72	2238	555	206160	1797393
Other Portfolio Income **6**	1961175	107143	122883	20248	133107	46112	129437	46054	157779	220777	192110	252118	533408
Other Receipts **7**	11506427	75043	38278	76343	42041	12861	218730	77780	136019	747077	200800	544312	9337143
Total Receipts **8**	105879146	3106456	4161913	2522306	8349523	3093084	3630813	2044343	4958193	7464898	3267803	9626307	53653507
Average Total Receipts **9**	3391	658	286	734	1169	3955	11002	18585	75124	152345	155610	401096	3576900
Operating Costs/Operating Income (%)													
Cost of Operations **10**	15.2	19.2	6.8	8.9	16.6	14.8	29.2	21.2	17.6	24.9	21.5	16.7	11.8
Salaries and Wages **11**	28.2	24.6	17.7	20.7	17.6	18.3	17.4	20.0	15.8	17.2	22.3	18.7	39.8
Taxes Paid **12**	7.4	8.7	8.5	6.6	6.8	6.1	5.0	6.3	3.5	4.3	6.9	9.1	8.4
Interest Paid **13**	9.1	6.3	3.2	4.4	10.5	7.7	6.1	5.8	3.3	3.4	7.5	8.4	12.3
Depreciation **14**	5.8	3.3	3.3	3.0	6.5	5.7	4.8	6.8	3.4	4.4	7.0	5.9	6.6
Amortization and Depletion **15**	0.8	0.2	0.3	0.6	0.6	0.5	0.5	0.3	0.4	0.4	0.8	1.0	1.0
Pensions and Other Deferred Comp. **16**	0.5	0.6	0.0	0.0	0.1	0.1	0.2	0.3	0.2	0.2	1.2	0.1	0.9
Employee Benefits **17**	2.7	2.7	0.5	0.8	0.9	2.7	2.0	2.6	2.7	2.0	1.2	2.2	3.7
Advertising **18**	3.4	1.6	1.7	2.7	2.1	1.4	2.0	2.9	3.3	2.9	3.6	3.6	4.3
Other Expenses **19**	40.9	42.0	64.3	45.9	34.4	36.8	41.3	37.5	54.6	50.0	32.5	41.9	37.1
Officers' Compensation **20**	1.6	0.5	2.3	2.0	3.2	1.9	1.2	1.4	0.5	0.7	2.6	1.0	1.7
Operating Margin **21**	•	•	•	4.3	0.7	4.1	•	•	•	•	•	•	•
Operating Margin Before Officers' Comp. **22**	•	•	•	6.3	3.9	6.0	•	•	•	•	•	•	•

Selected Average Balance Sheet ($ in Thousands)

Net Receivables 23	286	0	4	30	61	224	628	1181	5311	8409	23575	52048	354019
Inventories 24	86	0	3	5	16	40	104	355	1058	1370	4422	17433	116013
Net Property, Plant and Equipment 25	2960	0	104	503	1574	4626	9006	19856	35506	82428	162119	421068	3284728
Total Assets 26	7073	0	154	724	2197	6557	15136	32214	67635	170003	323886	864220	9764041
Notes and Loans Payable 27	3358	0	154	512	1905	4875	9320	20191	34178	57275	124485	463204	3956470
All Other Liabilities 28	1690	0	18	49	139	428	2385	7471	18605	33455	70232	133246	2790364
Net Worth 29	2026	0	-19	162	153	1254	3431	4551	14852	79273	129169	267771	3017208

Selected Financial Ratios (Times to 1)

Current Ratio 30	1.1	•	0.9	1.4	2.4	2.1	1.0	1.0	1.2	1.6	1.3	2.4	0.8
Quick Ratio 31	0.8	•	0.7	1.1	1.4	1.8	0.7	0.7	0.9	1.1	1.1	1.7	0.6
Net Sales to Working Capital 32	23.4	•	•	21.3	5.3	6.2	•	116.5	18.5	9.3	5.7	2.6	•
Coverage Ratio 33	1.7	0.8	•	3.0	1.3	1.8	1.3	1.4	1.6	3.0	4.0	1.5	1.7
Total Asset Turnover 34	0.4	•	1.8	1.0	0.5	0.6	0.7	0.5	1.0	0.8	0.4	0.4	0.3
Inventory Turnover 35	5.0	•	5.5	13.1	11.7	14.2	27.9	10.3	11.7	23.6	5.8	3.4	2.7
Receivables Turnover 36	7.6	•	32.3	28.5	21.0	14.5	13.6	13.5	13.1	19.0	4.1	5.2	5.4
Total Liabilities to Net Worth 37	2.5	•	•	3.5	13.3	4.2	3.4	6.1	3.6	1.1	1.5	2.2	2.2
Current Assets to Working Capital 38	8.0	•	•	3.5	1.7	1.9	•	49.0	5.2	2.8	3.9	1.7	•
Current Liabilities to Working Capital 39	7.0	•	•	2.5	0.7	0.9	•	48.0	4.2	1.8	2.9	0.7	•
Working Capital to Net Sales 40	0.0	•	•	0.0	0.2	0.2	•	0.0	0.1	0.1	0.2	0.4	•
Inventory to Working Capital 41	0.7	•	•	0.1	0.1	0.0	•	2.9	0.2	0.1	0.1	0.1	•
Total Receipts to Cash Flow 42	2.9	4.5	3.7	2.7	3.5	3.4	3.7	3.5	3.8	2.8	2.4	3.1	2.6
Cost of Goods to Cash Flow 43	0.4	0.9	0.3	0.2	0.6	0.5	1.1	0.7	0.7	0.7	0.5	0.5	0.3
Cash Flow to Total Debt 44	0.2	0.4	0.4	0.5	0.2	0.2	0.2	0.2	0.3	0.5	0.3	0.2	0.2

Selected Financial Factors (in Percentages)

Debt Ratio 45	71.4	•	112.3	77.6	93.0	80.9	77.3	85.9	78.0	53.4	60.1	69.0	69.1
Return on Total Assets 46	6.0	•	•	12.7	7.1	8.3	5.0	4.3	5.4	7.7	11.1	5.2	5.6
Return on Equity Before Income Taxes 47	8.5	•	63.0	37.6	23.7	19.8	4.5	8.8	9.1	11.0	21.0	5.7	7.4
Return on Equity After Income Taxes 48	5.6	•	65.3	36.2	21.2	18.2	2.5	5.0	5.7	7.7	14.2	4.2	4.7
Profit Margin (Before Income Tax) 49	6.1	•	•	8.7	3.2	6.4	1.5	2.3	1.9	6.7	22.6	4.3	8.5
Profit Margin (After Income Tax) 50	4.1	•	•	8.3	2.8	5.9	0.9	1.3	1.2	4.7	15.2	3.2	5.4

Table II
Corporations with Net Income

ACCOMMODATION

MONEY AMOUNTS AND SIZE OF ASSETS IN THOUSANDS OF DOLLARS

Item Description for Accounting Period 7/06 Through 6/07	Total	Zero Assets	Under 500	500 to 1,000	1,000 to 5,000	5,000 to 10,000	10,000 to 25,000	25,000 to 50,000	50,000 to 100,000	100,000 to 250,000	250,000 to 500,000	500,000 to 2,500,000	2,500,000 and over
Number of Enterprises 1	14070	1738	•	2282	4242	565	203	66	40	29	16	18	•
Revenues ($ in Thousands)													
Net Sales 2	67230412	1392897	•	1432217	5836064	2169548	2448927	1103709	1660893	3812591	1937233	6690807	•
Interest 3	2341929	14230	•	6133	20372	7338	10894	7292	19088	63298	75073	245376	•
Rents 4	488252	14318	•	2118	5653	2471	4165	2105	10015	32054	7475	48470	•
Royalties 5	1990318	2533	•	0	0	0	1070	0	5	20	206160	0	•
Other Portfolio Income 6	1875263	104095	•	15882	130580	46033	125583	41691	154555	214892	244171	176237	•
Other Receipts 7	11111317	52039	•	52951	55193	27758	217545	63971	78653	694134	193167	414790	•
Total Receipts 8	85037491	1580112	•	1509301	6047862	2253148	2808184	1218768	1923209	4816989	2663279	7575680	•
Average Total Receipts 9	6044	909	•	661	1426	3988	13833	18466	48080	166103	166455	420871	•
Operating Costs/Operating Income (%)													
Cost of Operations 10	15.0	12.2	•	3.2	15.2	18.1	32.8	16.4	22.6	25.6	26.0	17.0	•
Salaries and Wages 11	30.7	29.6	•	15.9	16.0	16.8	17.4	23.1	17.6	20.5	20.3	18.9	•
Taxes Paid 12	7.8	7.0	•	7.9	6.5	5.8	5.3	7.9	5.4	5.1	5.0	10.0	•
Interest Paid 13	9.8	4.7	•	5.0	8.2	8.4	5.6	6.4	6.0	2.8	5.9	7.4	•
Depreciation 14	5.5	3.0	•	3.9	5.6	6.4	4.3	7.4	5.5	3.5	5.7	5.8	•
Amortization and Depletion 15	0.7	0.2	•	1.0	0.5	0.3	0.2	0.2	0.6	0.4	0.6	0.7	•
Pensions and Other Deferred Comp. 16	0.6	0.2	•	0.0	0.1	0.1	0.2	0.4	0.3	0.3	1.3	0.1	•
Employee Benefits 17	2.7	4.0	•	0.8	0.8	1.5	0.9	3.4	1.4	2.6	1.2	2.1	•
Advertising 18	3.6	1.5	•	1.7	1.7	1.7	1.9	3.6	4.0	3.3	4.0	3.8	•
Other Expenses 19	37.5	33.6	•	46.3	32.0	29.0	37.0	25.8	37.7	48.2	32.4	36.9	•
Officers' Compensation 20	1.8	0.5	•	2.7	3.2	2.2	1.2	1.8	0.8	0.6	3.1	1.1	•
Operating Margin 21	•	3.4	•	11.6	10.2	9.7	•	3.6	•	•	•	•	•
Operating Margin Before Officers' Comp. 22	•	3.9	•	14.3	13.4	11.9	•	5.4	•	•	•	•	•

Selected Average Balance Sheet ($ in Thousands)

Net Receivables 23	539	0	•	24	94	213	889	539	4558	7005	29450	43158
Inventories 24	167	0	•	2	18	40	103	378	1086	1187	5379	18137
Net Property, Plant and Equipment 25	5201	0	•	534	1501	4713	9224	22237	34861	84047	128598	438585
Total Assets 26	13476	0	•	743	2200	6650	15474	32815	66413	174336	323199	889725
Notes and Loans Payable 27	5942	0	•	512	1665	4769	8778	22081	30709	53955	106871	457408
All Other Liabilities 28	3384	0	•	38	142	402	1739	6564	12207	3218	74266	131096
Net Worth 29	4150	0	•	193	394	1479	4957	4170	23497	88263	142062	301221

Selected Financial Ratios (Times to 1)

Current Ratio 30	1.1	•	•	1.7	2.3	1.7	0.8	2.0	1.5	1.4	1.4	1.9
Quick Ratio 31	0.8	•	•	1.5	2.1	1.2	0.6	1.4	1.1	1.1	1.1	1.6
Net Sales to Working Capital 32	23.3	•	•	14.3	4.6	5.7	8.6	•	4.2	9.7	4.7	3.6
Coverage Ratio 33	2.2	4.6	•	4.4	2.7	2.6	2.4	3.2	3.3	5.8	6.5	2.3
Total Asset Turnover 34	0.4	•	•	0.8	0.6	0.6	0.8	0.5	0.6	0.8	0.4	0.4
Inventory Turnover 35	4.3	•	•	12.2	11.4	17.5	38.6	7.3	8.6	28.4	5.8	3.5
Receivables Turnover 36	6.8	•	•	27.4	18.0	15.3	12.6	22.3	10.4	18.3	3.4	6.0
Total Liabilities to Net Worth 37	2.2	•	•	2.8	4.6	3.5	2.1	6.9	1.8	1.0	1.3	2.0
Current Assets to Working Capital 38	8.3	•	•	2.4	1.5	1.8	2.4	•	2.0	2.8	3.7	2.1
Current Liabilities to Working Capital 39	7.3	•	•	1.4	0.5	0.8	1.4	•	1.0	1.8	2.7	1.1
Working Capital to Net Sales 40	0.0	•	•	0.1	0.2	0.2	0.1	•	0.2	0.1	0.2	0.3
Inventory to Working Capital 41	0.7	•	•	0.0	0.0	0.0	0.1	•	0.1	0.1	0.1	0.1
Total Receipts to Cash Flow 42	2.6	3.1	•	2.3	2.6	2.8	3.3	3.1	3.0	2.5	2.0	3.0
Cost of Goods to Cash Flow 43	0.4	0.4	•	0.1	0.4	0.5	1.1	0.5	0.7	0.6	0.5	0.5
Cash Flow to Total Debt 44	0.2	•	•	0.5	0.3	0.3	0.3	0.2	0.3	0.6	0.3	0.2

Selected Financial Factors (in Percentages)

Debt Ratio 45	69.2	•	•	74.0	82.1	77.8	68.0	87.3	64.6	49.4	56.0	66.1
Return on Total Assets 46	7.5	•	•	18.6	13.8	12.7	10.4	10.3	12.5	12.2	14.2	7.0
Return on Equity Before Income Taxes 47	13.1	•	•	55.0	48.1	35.2	19.0	55.8	24.8	19.9	27.4	11.5
Return on Equity After Income Taxes 48	10.0	•	•	53.2	46.5	33.3	16.8	48.8	21.1	14.9	19.4	9.7
Profit Margin (Before Income Tax) 49	11.4	16.9	•	17.0	13.8	13.6	7.8	13.9	14.0	13.4	32.1	9.3
Profit Margin (After Income Tax) 50	8.7	14.6	•	16.4	13.3	12.8	6.9	12.2	12.0	10.0	22.7	7.9

384

Table I

Corporations with and without Net Income

FOOD SERVICES AND DRINKING PLACES

MONEY AMOUNTS AND SIZE OF ASSETS IN THOUSANDS OF DOLLARS

Item Description for Accounting Period 7/06 Through 6/07	Total	Zero Assets	Under 500	500 to 1,000	1,000 to 5,000	5,000 to 10,000	10,000 to 25,000	25,000 to 50,000	50,000 to 100,000	100,000 to 250,000	250,000 to 500,000	500,000 to 2,500,000	2,500,000 and over
Number of Enterprises **1**	257555	32993	197506	16138	9601	571	417	139	70	49	27	31	12
Revenues ($ in Thousands)													
Net Sales **2**	329650474	5292279	100017513	27612428	42624752	9418198	11120893	8097229	8679704	11027673	12838614	32113135	60808056
Interest **3**	1639870	1402	20770	11851	28141	2861	18189	12009	9824	18317	36067	332930	1147507
Rents **4**	541409	3236	15309	7606	12323	4340	8831	13416	14283	56900	54809	278914	71442
Royalties **5**	4522931	4186	6942	70	1634	966	61596	68433	57753	169817	585337	1198316	2367881
Other Portfolio Income **6**	2017794	127856	187878	38862	150405	78920	40777	42685	28790	58294	218726	242210	802390
Other Receipts **7**	9456156	75811	920270	209041	745221	78358	262800	96930	64193	174702	216595	2119214	4493024
Total Receipts **8**	347828634	5504770	101168682	27879858	43562476	9583643	11513086	8330702	8854547	11505703	13950148	36284719	69690300
Average Total Receipts **9**	1351	167	512	1728	4537	16784	27609	59933	126494	234810	516672	1170475	5807525
Operating Costs/Operating Income (%)													
Cost of Operations **10**	41.7	45.9	42.3	38.1	39.5	41.2	44.7	43.6	39.8	43.2	35.7	45.8	41.9
Salaries and Wages **11**	19.6	17.4	16.6	20.8	19.4	18.0	19.1	17.7	18.9	19.5	25.9	21.2	22.7
Taxes Paid **12**	4.1	4.4	4.4	4.2	3.9	3.6	3.7	3.8	3.5	3.8	3.8	4.6	3.8
Interest Paid **13**	1.8	1.4	0.7	1.2	1.1	1.7	1.7	2.6	1.7	3.1	3.3	3.0	3.2
Depreciation **14**	2.3	2.5	1.6	1.9	2.1	2.2	2.5	2.6	2.5	3.1	3.5	3.6	2.5
Amortization and Depletion **15**	0.5	0.6	0.3	0.5	0.4	0.5	0.5	0.3	0.4	0.9	0.6	0.5	0.7
Pensions and Other Deferred Comp. **16**	0.2	0.7	0.1	0.1	0.0	0.1	0.2	0.2	0.2	0.2	0.5	0.4	0.2
Employee Benefits **17**	1.2	0.3	0.5	0.9	0.9	0.9	1.3	1.1	1.3	1.5	1.6	1.8	2.1
Advertising **18**	2.4	2.0	1.6	2.8	3.2	3.4	3.0	3.2	2.1	2.7	2.4	3.2	2.3
Other Expenses **19**	24.8	34.9	26.2	24.4	24.9	25.0	21.9	23.1	29.2	21.7	24.5	21.6	24.4
Officers' Compensation **20**	2.5	3.5	4.6	2.9	2.7	1.3	1.5	1.4	1.1	0.9	1.1	1.1	0.7
Operating Margin **21**	•	•	1.1	2.4	1.9	2.1	•	0.4	•	•	•	•	•
Operating Margin Before Officers' Comp. **22**	1.5	•	5.7	5.3	4.6	3.4	1.2	1.8	0.4	0.3	•	•	•

Selected Average Balance Sheet ($ in Thousands)

Net Receivables **23**	52	0	3	25	86	192	980	1723	5707	10713	14823	73744	608673
Inventories **24**	22	0	7	23	51	350	580	803	1954	4108	8298	24172	122190
Net Property, Plant and Equipment **25**	293	0	55	348	897	3962	7188	17134	33518	78527	170837	450916	1488938
Total Assets **26**	757	0	115	656	1829	6866	15210	34564	66948	167634	365410	1042973	6145385
Notes and Loans Payable **27**	298	0	89	396	945	3523	7732	16233	25738	81114	182191	302636	1342562
All Other Liabilities **28**	239	0	25	109	413	1435	3845	10088	16544	50212	96257	372282	2445265
Net Worth **29**	219	0	1	152	471	1909	3633	8243	24666	36308	86962	368054	2357559

Selected Financial Ratios (Times to 1)

Current Ratio **30**	0.9	•	1.2	1.3	1.0	1.0	0.9	0.8	0.7	0.7	0.9	1.0	0.8
Quick Ratio **31**	0.7	•	0.8	0.9	0.8	0.7	0.6	0.5	0.5	0.4	0.6	0.7	0.6
Net Sales to Working Capital **32**	•	•	87.8	46.1	206.1	•	•	•	•	•	•	553.5	•
Coverage Ratio **33**	3.6	•	4.3	3.9	4.7	3.3	2.9	2.3	1.8	2.2	2.7	3.1	4.4
Total Asset Turnover **34**	1.7	•	4.4	2.6	2.4	2.4	1.8	1.7	1.9	1.3	1.3	1.0	0.8
Inventory Turnover **35**	24.8	•	31.1	28.5	34.4	19.4	20.6	31.6	25.2	23.6	20.5	19.6	17.4
Receivables Turnover **36**	23.7	•	164.1	73.7	47.7	85.1	32.3	27.1	26.1	25.8	23.2	14.1	7.9
Total Liabilities to Net Worth **37**	2.5	•	3.3	3.3	2.9	2.6	3.2	3.2	1.7	3.6	3.2	1.8	1.6
Current Assets to Working Capital **38**	•	•	5.9	4.5	22.5	•	•	•	•	•	•	101.9	•
Current Liabilities to Working Capital **39**	•	•	4.9	3.5	21.5	•	•	•	•	•	•	100.9	•
Working Capital to Net Sales **40**	•	•	0.0	0.0	0.0	•	•	•	•	•	•	0.0	•
Inventory to Working Capital **41**	•	•	1.1	0.7	2.5	•	•	•	•	•	•	12.7	•
Total Receipts to Cash Flow **42**	5.0	11.0	5.4	5.3	5.1	5.1	5.6	5.2	4.4	4.7	5.1	5.1	4.1
Cost of Goods to Cash Flow **43**	2.1	5.0	2.3	2.0	2.0	2.1	2.5	2.3	1.7	1.7	2.3	1.7	1.7
Cash Flow to Total Debt **44**	0.5	•	0.6	0.6	0.7	0.4	0.4	0.4	0.7	0.3	0.4	0.3	0.3

Selected Financial Factors (in Percentages)

Debt Ratio **45**	71.1	•	99.5	76.9	74.2	72.2	76.1	76.2	63.2	78.3	76.2	64.7	61.6
Return on Total Assets **46**	10.8	•	12.9	11.9	12.7	13.3	8.7	9.8	5.5	9.1	11.7	9.1	11.4
Return on Equity Before Income Taxes **47**	26.9	•	2144.6	38.2	38.8	33.4	24.0	22.9	6.4	22.8	30.8	17.5	23.0
Return on Equity After Income Taxes **48**	20.4	•	2075.8	36.5	36.9	31.9	21.2	20.5	4.6	17.5	21.8	11.1	14.9
Profit Margin (Before Income Tax) **49**	4.6	•	2.3	3.4	4.1	3.9	3.3	3.2	1.3	3.7	5.6	6.2	10.7
Profit Margin (After Income Tax) **50**	3.5	•	2.2	3.2	3.9	3.7	2.9	2.9	0.9	2.8	4.0	3.9	6.9

Table II

Corporations with Net Income

FOOD SERVICES AND DRINKING PLACES

MONEY AMOUNTS AND SIZE OF ASSETS IN THOUSANDS OF DOLLARS

Item Description for Accounting Period 7/06 Through 6/07	Total	Zero Assets	Under 500	500 to 1,000	1,000 to 5,000	5,000 to 10,000	10,000 to 25,000	25,000 to 50,000	50,000 to 100,000	100,000 to 250,000	250,000 to 500,000	500,000 to 2,500,000	2,500,000 and over
Number of Enterprises **1**	131221	8573	•	10225	7105	500	292	99	43	36	19	25	•
Revenues ($ in Thousands)													
Net Sales **2**	265239970	2770738	•	23282644	34482355	8546116	8797641	6328408	6373843	8576848	10921856	28491757	•
Interest **3**	1518160	1262	•	9699	20692	1569	14263	6034	4380	15573	33707	293966	•
Rents **4**	453320	403	•	6786	8112	1904	8575	7459	13254	35974	44732	274247	•
Royalties **5**	4149680	4186	•	70	1594	579	53192	40956	29689	150001	537974	1067646	•
Other Portfolio Income **6**	1860434	79553	•	36508	122841	71502	37121	30060	10795	57980	216680	225849	•
Other Receipts **7**	8402913	108862	•	160849	632971	57583	235875	62161	72152	160203	198201	1655864	•
Total Receipts **8**	281624477	2965004	•	23496556	35268565	8679253	9146667	6475078	6504113	8996579	11953150	32009329	•
Average Total Receipts **9**	2146	346	•	2298	4964	17359	31324	65405	151258	249905	629113	1280373	•
Operating Costs/Operating Income (%)													
Cost of Operations **10**	40.8	44.6	•	37.9	38.1	40.3	44.9	40.8	37.0	42.2	34.9	45.4	•
Salaries and Wages **11**	19.6	15.7	•	20.9	19.2	18.2	19.5	19.1	18.2	20.2	26.5	20.2	•
Taxes Paid **12**	4.1	4.2	•	3.9	3.9	3.7	3.7	3.6	3.2	3.9	4.0	4.8	•
Interest Paid **13**	1.7	0.9	•	0.8	1.0	1.6	1.3	2.3	1.4	2.4	2.6	2.8	•
Depreciation **14**	2.2	1.5	•	1.3	1.9	2.1	2.3	2.4	2.2	3.3	3.4	3.8	•
Amortization and Depletion **15**	0.4	0.4	•	0.2	0.4	0.4	0.4	0.5	0.3	0.7	0.6	0.5	•
Pensions and Other Deferred Comp. **16**	0.2	1.3	•	0.1	0.0	0.1	0.1	0.2	0.3	0.2	0.6	0.3	•
Employee Benefits **17**	1.3	0.6	•	0.9	0.9	0.8	1.3	1.1	1.3	1.6	1.8	1.7	•
Advertising **18**	2.5	2.3	•	2.7	3.3	3.5	2.9	3.4	2.3	3.0	2.2	3.2	•
Other Expenses **19**	23.8	25.2	•	23.0	24.0	24.2	20.3	21.7	31.4	21.2	24.7	21.1	•
Officers' Compensation **20**	2.2	2.3	•	2.9	2.6	1.4	1.6	1.5	1.1	0.9	0.9	0.7	•
Operating Margin **21**	1.3	1.0	•	5.3	4.5	3.7	1.8	3.4	1.4	0.5	•	•	•
Operating Margin Before Officers' Comp. **22**	3.5	3.3	•	8.2	7.1	5.1	3.4	4.9	2.4	1.5	•	•	•

Selected Average Balance Sheet ($ in Thousands)

	C1	C2	C3	C4	C5	C6	C7	C8	C9	C10	C11	C12	C13
Net Receivables 23	82	0	•	30	91	176	1150	1627	5155	8176	13825	46529	•
Inventories 24	33	0	•	25	52	276	632	715	2236	3848	9110	27663	•
Net Property, Plant and Equipment 25	448	0	•	301	939	3904	7304	17845	36557	82772	176245	511758	•
Total Assets 26	1193	0	•	653	1898	6757	15494	34923	68675	161255	361342	1018389	•
Notes and Loans Payable 27	393	0	•	308	819	3201	6203	15892	25514	65775	173287	333660	•
All Other Liabilities 28	372	0	•	103	433	1209	4174	7749	14623	47463	107248	268818	•
Net Worth 29	428	0	•	242	646	2347	5117	11282	28538	48017	80807	415912	•

Selected Financial Ratios (Times to 1)

	C1	C2	C3	C4	C5	C6	C7	C8	C9	C10	C11	C12	C13
Current Ratio 30	0.9	•	•	1.7	1.2	1.0	0.8	0.9	0.7	0.9	0.9		•
Quick Ratio 31	0.7	•	•	1.2	0.9	0.7	0.5	0.6	0.5	0.5	0.5		•
Net Sales to Working Capital 32	•	•	•	25.7	66.9	252.1	•	•	•	•	•		•
Coverage Ratio 33	5.4	•	10.0	9.0	7.6	5.6	3.4	3.5	3.3	3.8	3.9		•
Total Asset Turnover 34	1.7	•	•	3.5	2.6	1.9	1.8	2.2	1.5	1.6	1.1		•
Inventory Turnover 35	24.8	•	•	34.0	35.9	21.4	36.5	24.5	26.1	22.0	18.7		•
Receivables Turnover 36	23.3	•	•	87.5	46.2	32.1	33.3	28.8	29.5	45.5	22.8		•
Total Liabilities to Net Worth 37	1.8	•	•	1.7	1.9	2.0	2.1	1.4	2.4	3.5	1.4		•
Current Assets to Working Capital 38	•	•	•	2.5	7.2	39.7	•	•	•	•	•		•
Current Liabilities to Working Capital 39	•	•	•	1.5	6.2	38.7	•	•	•	•	•		•
Working Capital to Net Sales 40	•	•	•	0.0	0.0	0.0	•	•	•	•	•		•
Inventory to Working Capital 41	•	•	•	0.3	0.7	6.1	•	•	•	•	•		•
Total Receipts to Cash Flow 42	4.5	4.8	•	4.9	4.6	4.8	4.8	5.2	5.3	4.3	4.8		•
Cost of Goods to Cash Flow 43	1.8	2.1	•	1.8	1.7	1.9	2.0	2.4	2.2	1.5	2.2		•
Cash Flow to Total Debt 44	0.6	•	•	1.1	0.8	0.8	0.6	1.0	0.4	0.5	0.4		•

Selected Financial Factors (in Percentages)

	C1	C2	C3	C4	C5	C6	C7	C8	C9	C10	C11	C12	C13
Debt Ratio 45	64.1	•	•	62.9	66.0	65.3	67.7	67.0	70.2	77.6	59.2		•
Return on Total Assets 46	15.9	•	•	24.3	20.0	17.4	14.6	13.7	11.5	15.7	12.3		•
Return on Equity Before Income Taxes 47	36.3	•	•	58.3	50.9	38.5	32.1	34.1	26.9	51.5	22.3		•
Return on Equity After Income Taxes 48	29.7	•	•	56.6	49.0	37.1	29.7	31.3	21.4	37.7	15.3		•
Profit Margin (Before Income Tax) 49	7.7	8.0	•	6.2	6.8	5.3	5.7	5.8	5.4	7.2	8.1		•
Profit Margin (After Income Tax) 50	6.3	6.5	•	6.0	6.5	5.1	5.2	5.3	4.3	5.3	5.6		•

Table I

Corporations with and without Net Income

AUTOMOTIVE REPAIR AND MAINTENANCE

MONEY AMOUNTS AND SIZE OF ASSETS IN THOUSANDS OF DOLLARS

Item Description for Accounting Period 7/06 Through 6/07	Total	Zero Assets	Under 500	500 to 1,000	1,000 to 5,000	5,000 to 10,000	10,000 to 25,000	25,000 to 50,000	50,000 to 100,000	100,000 to 250,000	250,000 to 500,000	500,000 to 2,500,000	2,500,000 and over
Number of Enterprises 1	112477	13543	88496	6699	3435	211	62	11	10	4	5	0	0
Revenues ($ in Thousands)													
Net Sales 2	71501977	1833427	40700406	12118253	10755061	1362958	1010676	793444	1071371	279947	1576435	0	0
Interest 3	48786	14	14131	6590	8470	1243	4918	2860	5276	3110	2174	0	0
Rents 4	20844	0	10093	344	5957	1217	1484	597	562	61	529	0	0
Royalties 5	89409	0	0	0	0	0	0	0	1322	86178	1910	0	0
Other Portfolio Income 6	294117	68631	122644	17923	39573	1482	6851	31765	789	3247	1213	0	0
Other Receipts 7	345467	7954	104392	29689	40877	16184	16453	5673	115666	3614	4963	0	0
Total Receipts 8	72300600	1910026	40951666	12172799	10849938	1383084	1040382	834339	1194986	376157	1587224	0	0
Average Total Receipts 9	643	141	463	1817	3159	6555	16780	75849	119499	94039	317445	•	•
Operating Costs/Operating Income (%)													
Cost of Operations 10	52.0	41.4	49.2	62.6	55.2	51.3	47.2	38.8	58.7	29.0	39.8	•	•
Salaries and Wages 11	12.4	9.7	12.9	7.9	13.3	6.2	17.5	25.0	19.7	26.7	17.6	•	•
Taxes Paid 12	3.6	4.2	3.5	3.2	3.7	13.9	4.0	2.5	3.7	4.1	2.2	•	•
Interest Paid 13	1.4	0.5	0.9	1.3	2.2	1.9	1.4	2.8	2.0	9.8	5.4	•	•
Depreciation 14	1.8	2.7	1.6	1.7	2.3	1.5	3.8	4.2	2.5	3.7	2.4	•	•
Amortization and Depletion 15	0.4	0.5	0.2	0.4	0.4	0.1	0.4	1.8	0.8	6.2	2.9	•	•
Pensions and Other Deferred Comp. 16	0.2	•	0.1	0.1	0.2	0.2	0.3	0.2	0.2	0.5	0.4	•	•
Employee Benefits 17	1.1	0.3	1.0	1.2	1.0	0.7	1.1	2.2	2.6	2.2	1.8	•	•
Advertising 18	1.5	1.6	1.5	1.5	1.5	1.0	2.0	2.5	1.2	1.4	2.2	•	•
Other Expenses 19	19.1	34.2	20.6	14.3	14.6	13.4	20.1	26.8	20.2	40.6	24.5	•	•
Officers' Compensation 20	5.7	6.6	7.3	4.2	3.5	2.4	1.8	0.9	0.6	2.5	0.8	•	•
Operating Margin 21	0.9	•	1.1	1.5	2.1	7.5	0.6	•	•	•	0.0	•	•
Operating Margin Before Officers' Comp. 22	6.6	4.9	8.4	5.7	5.6	9.9	2.4	•	•	•	0.8	•	•

Selected Average Balance Sheet ($ in Thousands)

Net Receivables **23**	21	0	9	77	170	764	727	6228	14781	8348	9154
Inventories **24**	21	0	11	62	123	1343	856	2320	3037	6705	20805
Net Property, Plant and Equipment **25**	95	0	41	278	942	3182	6555	12113	17865	42833	84910
Total Assets **26**	227	0	98	678	1839	6834	17064	37948	71717	144679	360496
Notes and Loans Payable **27**	137	0	70	415	1061	2794	6561	25436	28585	50116	200076
All Other Liabilities **28**	47	0	26	107	272	2234	1010	10120	22128	57534	50211
Net Worth **29**	44	0	2	156	506	1806	9493	2392	21004	37028	110208

Selected Financial Ratios (Times to 1)

Current Ratio **30**	1.4	•	1.3	1.6	1.6	1.4	1.4	1.0	1.7	1.5	1.7
Quick Ratio **31**	0.9	•	0.9	1.0	1.1	0.5	1.0	0.6	1.2	1.0	0.4
Net Sales to Working Capital **32**	27.1	•	51.6	19.8	16.3	7.0	15.2	326.9	9.8	8.2	9.1
Coverage Ratio **33**	2.5	6.0	2.9	2.5	2.3	5.8	3.5	0.1	1.0	1.8	1.2
Total Asset Turnover **34**	2.8	•	4.7	2.7	1.7	0.9	1.0	1.9	1.5	0.5	0.9
Inventory Turnover **35**	15.8	•	20.1	18.1	14.1	2.5	9.0	12.1	20.7	3.0	6.0
Receivables Turnover **36**	32.6	•	51.6	24.5	23.2	8.9	21.8	19.4	8.3	6.6	49.7
Total Liabilities to Net Worth **37**	4.2	•	38.8	3.3	2.6	2.8	0.8	14.9	2.4	2.9	2.3
Current Assets to Working Capital **38**	3.3	•	4.3	2.7	2.7	3.6	3.8	61.6	2.5	3.1	2.4
Current Liabilities to Working Capital **39**	2.3	•	3.3	1.7	1.7	2.6	2.8	60.6	1.5	2.1	1.4
Working Capital to Net Sales **40**	0.0	•	0.0	0.1	0.1	0.1	0.1	0.0	0.1	0.1	0.1
Inventory to Working Capital **41**	0.9	•	1.1	0.7	0.7	1.8	0.6	18.7	0.3	0.2	0.7
Total Receipts to Cash Flow **42**	6.9	4.4	6.6	8.6	7.7	5.7	5.6	6.8	7.9	3.2	5.9
Cost of Goods to Cash Flow **43**	3.6	1.8	3.3	5.4	4.2	2.9	2.6	2.6	4.6	0.9	2.3
Cash Flow to Total Debt **44**	0.5	•	0.7	0.4	0.3	0.2	0.4	0.3	0.3	0.2	0.2

Selected Financial Factors (in Percentages)

Debt Ratio **45**	80.8	•	97.5	77.0	72.5	73.6	44.4	93.7	70.7	74.4	69.4
Return on Total Assets **46**	9.6	•	12.4	8.6	8.8	10.2	4.7	0.3	3.1	8.5	5.5
Return on Equity Before Income Taxes **47**	30.0	•	321.0	22.5	18.4	31.9	6.0	•	0.5	14.6	2.5
Return on Equity After Income Taxes **48**	27.8	•	307.1	21.5	16.9	29.6	5.1	•	•	14.5	•
Profit Margin (Before Income Tax) **49**	2.1	2.5	1.7	1.9	3.0	8.9	3.5	0.1	0.1	7.7	0.9
Profit Margin (After Income Tax) **50**	1.9	2.1	1.6	1.9	2.7	8.3	3.0	•	•	7.7	•

Table II

Corporations with Net Income

AUTOMOTIVE REPAIR AND MAINTENANCE

MONEY AMOUNTS AND SIZE OF ASSETS IN THOUSANDS OF DOLLARS

Item Description for Accounting Period 7/06 Through 6/07	Total	Zero Assets	Under 500	500 to 1,000	1,000 to 5,000	5,000 to 10,000	10,000 to 25,000	25,000 to 50,000	50,000 to 100,000	100,000 to 250,000	250,000 to 500,000	500,000 to 2,500,000	2,500,000 and over
Number of Enterprises 1	61772	5854	49616	4065	2061	132	31	•	3	•	0	0	0
Revenues ($ in Thousands)													
Net Sales 2	47174314	1061062	24608585	8965134	9282186	1122049	779192	•	135780	•	0	0	0
Interest 3	26406	1	7604	4448	6409	823	1483	•	419	•	0	0	0
Rents 4	12767	0	6418	0	3293	1217	831	•	5	•	0	0	0
Royalties 5	62768	0		0	0	0	0	•	0	•	0	0	0
Other Portfolio Income 6	226450	68631	60572	17667	39533	1482	6841	•	0	•	0	0	0
Other Receipts 7	232871	1582	48381	21560	31575	16184	939	•	108082	•	0	0	0
Total Receipts 8	47735576	1131276	24731560	9008809	9362996	1141755	789286	•	244286	•	0	0	0
Average Total Receipts 9	773	193	498	2216	4543	8650	25461	•	81429	•	•	•	•
Operating Costs/Operating Income (%)													
Cost of Operations 10	51.6	40.4	45.3	65.4	56.7	61.4	42.3	•	24.6	•	•	•	•
Salaries and Wages 11	11.9	8.0	12.7	8.1	12.6	5.2	18.8	•	55.8	•	•	•	•
Taxes Paid 12	3.4	3.7	3.4	3.0	3.6	3.2	4.0	•	5.7	•	•	•	•
Interest Paid 13	0.9	0.6	0.5	1.0	1.0	1.7	0.9	•	2.3	•	•	•	•
Depreciation 14	1.4	2.4	1.1	1.6	1.7	1.8	3.3	•	4.6	•	•	•	•
Amortization and Depletion 15	0.2	0.6	0.1	0.2	0.2	0.1	0.3	•	1.0	•	•	•	•
Pensions and Other Deferred Comp. 16	0.2	•	0.2	0.1	0.2	0.2	0.3	•	1.2	•	•	•	•
Employee Benefits 17	1.0	0.1	0.9	1.0	1.1	0.5	1.3	•	8.5	•	•	•	•
Advertising 18	1.3	1.9	1.5	0.6	1.3	1.0	2.2	•	0.1	•	•	•	•
Other Expenses 19	17.2	28.2	20.0	11.2	14.1	11.8	16.6	•	53.6	•	•	•	•
Officers' Compensation 20	5.8	7.1	7.9	4.2	3.4	2.3	2.2	•	0.8	•	•	•	•
Operating Margin 21	5.2	6.8	6.5	3.6	4.0	10.7	7.8	•	•	•	•	•	•
Operating Margin Before Officers' Comp. 22	11.0	14.0	14.4	7.8	7.4	13.0	10.0	•	•	•	•	•	•

Selected Average Balance Sheet ($ in Thousands)

Net Receivables 23	27	0	104	229	793	545	•	12354
Inventories 24	21	0	57	159	749	1408	•	2799
Net Property, Plant and Equipment 25	90	0	308	750	3713	9451	•	8724
Total Assets 26	223	0	696	1761	6728	16622	•	69320
Notes and Loans Payable 27	97	0	367	666	3966	5636	•	11511
All Other Liabilities 28	40	0	107	275	1130	3200	•	28680
Net Worth 29	87	0	222	820	1632	7785	•	29129

Selected Financial Ratios (Times to 1)

Current Ratio 30	1.9	•	2.0	1.9	2.0	1.8	1.2	1.6
Quick Ratio 31	1.3	•	1.6	1.3	1.4	0.9	0.9	1.4
Net Sales to Working Capital 32	18.2	•	22.6	17.4	12.7	7.4	34.7	7.2
Coverage Ratio 33	8.3	22.8	14.2	5.0	5.7	8.1	10.7	12.5
Total Asset Turnover 34	3.4	•	5.5	3.2	2.6	1.3	1.5	0.7
Inventory Turnover 35	19.1	•	23.9	25.2	16.0	7.0	7.5	4.0
Receivables Turnover 36	31.2	•	49.5	21.8	24.4	11.3	24.7	3.2
Total Liabilities to Net Worth 37	1.6	•	1.5	2.1	1.1	3.1	1.1	1.4
Current Assets to Working Capital 38	2.1	•	2.0	2.1	2.0	2.2	6.0	2.8
Current Liabilities to Working Capital 39	1.1	•	1.0	1.1	1.0	1.2	5.0	1.8
Working Capital to Net Sales 40	0.1	•	0.0	0.1	0.1	0.1	0.0	0.1
Inventory to Working Capital 41	0.5	•	0.4	0.4	0.5	0.9	1.2	0.1
Total Receipts to Cash Flow 42	5.7	3.2	5.0	8.3	7.1	5.3	5.1	1.7
Cost of Goods to Cash Flow 43	2.9	1.3	2.3	5.4	4.0	3.2	2.2	0.4
Cash Flow to Total Debt 44	1.0	•	1.8	0.6	0.7	0.3	0.6	0.6

Selected Financial Factors (in Percentages)

Debt Ratio 45	61.0	•	60.0	68.1	53.4	75.7	53.2	58.0
Return on Total Assets 46	24.8	•	41.4	16.3	15.1	17.9	15.2	19.0
Return on Equity Before Income Taxes 47	56.0	•	96.1	40.7	26.7	64.7	29.5	41.5
Return on Equity After Income Taxes 48	54.0	•	94.4	39.6	25.2	60.7	27.1	36.9
Profit Margin (Before Income Tax) 49	6.4	13.4	7.0	4.1	4.9	12.4	9.1	26.7
Profit Margin (After Income Tax) 50	6.2	12.9	6.9	4.0	4.6	11.6	8.4	23.7

Table I

Corporations with and without Net Income

OTHER REPAIR AND MAINTENANCE

MONEY AMOUNTS AND SIZE OF ASSETS IN THOUSANDS OF DOLLARS

Item Description for Accounting Period 7/06 Through 6/07		Total	Zero Assets	Under 500	500 to 1,000	1,000 to 5,000	5,000 to 10,000	10,000 to 25,000	25,000 to 50,000	50,000 to 100,000	100,000 to 250,000	250,000 to 500,000	500,000 to 2,500,000	2,500,000 and over
Number of Enterprises	1	57407	11732	42060	1759	1615	102	105	19	10	5	0	0	0
Revenues ($ in Thousands)														
Net Sales	2	41529936	903220	20418764	3478742	7765190	1516748	3567836	1502495	1136673	1240267	0	0	0
Interest	3	32196	1001	4565	1407	7674	3374	5874	1348	5099	1853	0	0	0
Rents	4	7603	229	1562	0	4601	99	811	168	0	133	0	0	0
Royalties	5	704	0	0	0	0	0	0	126	430	149	0	0	0
Other Portfolio Income	6	61899	0	34169	5471	16031	2096	2926	834	347	25	0	0	0
Other Receipts	7	205652	20564	35499	10964	54166	32773	17925	7803	16318	9642	0	0	0
Total Receipts	8	41837990	925014	20494559	3496584	7847662	1555090	3595372	1512774	1158867	1252069	0	0	0
Average Total Receipts	9	729	79	487	1988	4859	15246	34242	79620	115887	250414	•	•	•
Operating Costs/Operating Income (%)														
Cost of Operations	10	54.2	40.3	50.3	58.9	52.2	58.5	65.1	67.1	64.1	68.6	•	•	•
Salaries and Wages	11	13.0	2.9	14.1	7.4	17.1	11.2	10.0	7.1	18.5	6.3	•	•	•
Taxes Paid	12	2.7	1.9	2.6	3.5	3.3	2.3	2.2	2.6	3.1	2.6	•	•	•
Interest Paid	13	1.0	0.8	0.5	1.1	1.5	0.9	0.7	1.7	6.2	2.4	•	•	•
Depreciation	14	1.5	3.6	1.3	1.4	1.3	1.8	1.7	1.5	1.9	1.1	•	•	•
Amortization and Depletion	15	0.2	0.1	0.1	0.2	0.3	0.1	0.1	0.4	1.5	1.9	•	•	•
Pensions and Other Deferred Comp.	16	0.3	0.1	0.1	0.3	0.3	0.9	0.9	0.3	1.6	0.2	•	•	•
Employee Benefits	17	2.1	1.0	0.6	2.1	5.1	2.2	1.5	4.6	5.0	2.5	•	•	•
Advertising	18	0.7	1.3	1.0	0.6	0.4	0.6	0.4	0.3	0.3	0.2	•	•	•
Other Expenses	19	15.5	38.3	18.5	16.3	12.0	14.0	9.6	7.4	1.8	10.5	•	•	•
Officers' Compensation	20	5.4	9.0	7.3	6.1	3.5	2.9	1.9	2.1	1.3	0.9	•	•	•
Operating Margin	21	3.3	0.8	3.6	2.1	3.0	4.5	5.8	5.1	•	2.8	•	•	•
Operating Margin Before Officers' Comp.	22	8.6	9.8	10.9	8.2	6.4	7.4	7.7	7.2	•	3.7	•	•	•

Selected Average Balance Sheet ($ in Thousands)

Line Item									
Net Receivables 23	56	0	176	525	1929	4996	12722	15843	62875
Inventories 24	39	0	93	393	1351	4076	8358	15630	13578
Net Property, Plant and Equipment 25	48	0	223	393	1333	2982	5869	10989	16418
Total Assets 26	221	0	714	1956	6878	15514	35399	75033	235002
Notes and Loans Payable 27	102	0	220	931	1402	4160	13385	55471	101264
All Other Liabilities 28	61	0	156	532	2583	5139	9782	24593	65087
Net Worth 29	57	0	337	493	2892	6215	12232	-5031	68651

Selected Financial Ratios (Times to 1)

Line Item										
Current Ratio 30	1.7	•	2.0	2.1	1.8	1.8	1.8	2.8	0.7	1.7
Quick Ratio 31	1.1	•	1.4	1.1	1.2	1.0	1.7	•	0.3	1.1
Net Sales to Working Capital 32	12.5	•	21.3	9.8	6.8	6.7	4.9	•	•	5.7
Coverage Ratio 33	4.9	5.0	8.6	3.5	8.8	10.3	4.5	•	0.5	2.5
Total Asset Turnover 34	3.3	•	6.2	2.8	2.2	2.2	2.2	•	1.5	1.1
Inventory Turnover 35	10.0	•	20.4	12.5	6.4	5.4	6.4	•	4.7	12.5
Receivables Turnover 36	13.6	•	34.5	11.9	7.2	6.6	8.8	•	5.1	4.9
Total Liabilities to Net Worth 37	2.9	•	6.8	1.1	1.4	1.5	1.9	•	•	2.4
Current Assets to Working Capital 38	2.3	•	2.0	1.9	2.3	2.3	1.6	•	•	2.5
Current Liabilities to Working Capital 39	1.3	•	1.0	0.9	1.3	1.3	0.6	•	•	1.5
Working Capital to Net Sales 40	0.1	•	0.0	0.1	0.1	0.2	0.2	•	•	0.2
Inventory to Working Capital 41	0.7	•	0.5	0.5	0.6	0.8	0.5	•	•	0.4
Total Receipts to Cash Flow 42	6.2	2.9	5.4	6.5	5.7	7.6	9.7	•	•	8.3
Cost of Goods to Cash Flow 43	3.4	1.2	2.7	3.8	3.3	4.9	6.5	•	•	5.7
Cash Flow to Total Debt 44	0.7	•	1.3	0.8	0.7	0.5	0.4	•	•	0.2

Selected Financial Factors (in Percentages)

Line Item										
Debt Ratio 45	74.0	•	87.2	52.8	74.8	57.9	59.9	65.4	106.7	70.8
Return on Total Assets 46	16.6	•	27.4	10.2	13.6	17.0	15.9	16.7	4.6	6.5
Return on Equity Before Income Taxes 47	50.9	•	189.6	15.5	39.2	35.9	35.8	37.6	72.7	13.5
Return on Equity After Income Taxes 48	46.0	•	184.9	13.1	36.2	29.7	28.7	33.4	82.2	7.6
Profit Margin (Before Income Tax) 49	4.0	3.2	3.9	2.6	4.0	7.0	6.5	5.8	•	3.7
Profit Margin (After Income Tax) 50	3.6	2.7	3.8	2.2	3.7	5.8	5.3	5.2	•	2.1

Table II

Corporations with Net Income

OTHER REPAIR AND MAINTENANCE

MONEY AMOUNTS AND SIZE OF ASSETS IN THOUSANDS OF DOLLARS

Item Description for Accounting Period 7/06 Through 6/07	Total	Zero Assets	Under 500	500 to 1,000	1,000 to 5,000	5,000 to 10,000	10,000 to 25,000	25,000 to 50,000	50,000 to 100,000	100,000 to 250,000	250,000 to 500,000	500,000 to 2,500,000	2,500,000 and over
Number of Enterprises 1	32932	4576	25838	1109	1188	96	98	•	6	•	0	0	0
Revenues ($ in Thousands)													
Net Sales 2	34053555	624660	16936212	2359158	6233271	1467117	3397947	•	538485	•	0	0	0
Interest 3	22980	490	2303	1406	7301	2766	5811	•	420	•	0	0	0
Rents 4	6579	229	705	0	4601	99	811	•	0	•	0	0	0
Royalties 5	435	0	0	0	0	0	0	•	287	•	0	0	0
Other Portfolio Income 6	54712	0	34000	373	15041	2096	2260	•	197	•	0	0	0
Other Receipts 7	195316	20537	32865	10269	51194	32166	17136	•	14528	•	0	0	0
Total Receipts 8	34333577	645916	17006085	2371206	6311408	1504244	3423965	•	553917	•	0	0	0
Average Total Receipts 9	1043	141	658	2138	5313	15669	34938	•	92320	•	•	•	•
Operating Costs/Operating Income (%)													
Cost of Operations 10	53.7	47.7	50.2	55.1	48.8	58.5	65.0	•	63.8	•	•	•	•
Salaries and Wages 11	13.3	0.6	14.7	7.3	18.0	10.6	10.0	•	9.4	•	•	•	•
Taxes Paid 12	2.6	1.7	2.6	3.3	2.9	2.2	2.2	•	1.7	•	•	•	•
Interest Paid 13	0.7	0.8	0.3	0.9	1.3	0.9	0.6	•	3.0	•	•	•	•
Depreciation 14	1.3	2.1	1.0	1.7	1.4	1.6	1.6	•	2.9	•	•	•	•
Amortization and Depletion 15	0.1	0.1	0.1	0.1	0.3	0.1	0.1	•	0.6	•	•	•	•
Pensions and Other Deferred Comp. 16	0.3	0.1	0.1	0.4	0.3	1.0	0.9	•	0.3	•	•	•	•
Employee Benefits 17	2.1	1.2	0.6	2.1	5.9	2.2	1.5	•	2.9	•	•	•	•
Advertising 18	0.6	0.9	0.7	0.5	0.4	0.4	0.4	•	0.2	•	•	•	•
Other Expenses 19	14.4	25.9	16.6	15.7	12.1	13.2	9.7	•	12.5	•	•	•	•
Officers' Compensation 20	5.1	9.2	6.8	6.7	3.3	3.0	1.9	•	1.8	•	•	•	•
Operating Margin 21	5.9	9.7	6.1	6.2	5.4	6.2	6.1	•	0.9	•	•	•	•
Operating Margin Before Officers' Comp. 22	11.0	18.9	12.9	12.9	8.7	9.3	8.0	•	2.7	•	•	•	•

Selected Average Balance Sheet ($ in Thousands)

Net Receivables 23	82	0	19	208	583	1991	5009	16802
Inventories 24	51	0	11	54	433	1421	3973	13518
Net Property, Plant and Equipment 25	60	0	25	231	380	1232	2761	12450
Total Assets 26	292	0	97	703	2052	6821	15539	72982
Notes and Loans Payable 27	108	0	44	221	845	1490	3715	34854
All Other Liabilities 28	73	0	19	84	467	2132	5329	17886
Net Worth 29	112	0	34	399	739	3199	6495	20242

Selected Financial Ratios (Times to 1)

Current Ratio 30	2.2	•	2.6	3.0	2.2	1.8	1.8	1.5
Quick Ratio 31	1.4	•	1.8	2.6	1.4	1.1	1.1	0.8
Net Sales to Working Capital 32	10.0	•	18.6	8.5	6.9	6.9	6.5	7.0
Coverage Ratio 33	10.4	17.8	20.0	8.6	6.1	10.5	12.5	2.3
Total Asset Turnover 34	3.5	•	6.7	3.0	2.6	2.2	2.2	1.2
Inventory Turnover 35	10.9	•	29.5	21.6	5.9	6.3	5.7	4.2
Receivables Turnover 36	13.5	•	41.6	9.9	9.3	7.1	7.0	4.2
Total Liabilities to Net Worth 37	1.6	•	1.9	0.8	1.8	1.1	1.4	2.6
Current Assets to Working Capital 38	1.9	•	1.6	1.5	1.8	2.3	2.2	2.9
Current Liabilities to Working Capital 39	0.9	•	0.6	0.5	0.8	1.3	1.2	1.9
Working Capital to Net Sales 40	0.1	•	0.1	0.1	0.1	0.1	0.2	0.1
Inventory to Working Capital 41	0.5	•	0.4	0.1	0.6	0.6	0.8	1.1
Total Receipts to Cash Flow 42	5.5	2.8	5.0	5.4	6.2	5.4	7.4	7.5
Cost of Goods to Cash Flow 43	3.0	1.4	2.5	3.0	3.0	3.2	4.8	4.8
Cash Flow to Total Debt 44	1.0	•	2.1	1.3	0.6	0.8	0.5	0.2

Selected Financial Factors (in Percentages)

Debt Ratio 45	61.7	•	65.0	43.3	64.0	53.1	58.2	72.3
Return on Total Assets 46	26.3	•	46.3	22.9	20.2	21.6	16.7	8.3
Return on Equity Before Income Taxes 47	62.0	•	125.6	35.7	46.9	41.7	36.7	16.7
Return on Equity After Income Taxes 48	57.6	•	123.4	32.6	44.2	35.7	29.5	12.8
Profit Margin (Before Income Tax) 49	6.7	13.1	6.5	6.7	6.6	8.7	6.9	3.8
Profit Margin (After Income Tax) 50	6.2	12.4	6.4	6.1	6.2	7.5	5.5	2.9

Table I

Corporations with and without Net Income

PERSONAL AND LAUNDRY SERVICES

MONEY AMOUNTS AND SIZE OF ASSETS IN THOUSANDS OF DOLLARS

Item Description for Accounting Period 7/06 Through 6/07	Total	Zero Assets	Under 500	500 to 1,000	1,000 to 5,000	5,000 to 10,000	10,000 to 25,000	25,000 to 50,000	50,000 to 100,000	100,000 to 250,000	250,000 to 500,000	500,000 to 2,500,000	2,500,000 and over
Number of Enterprises **1**	153674	36273	105459	6928	4419	378	126	38	25	11	4	12	0
Revenues ($ in Thousands)													
Net Sales **2**	76462412	3016064	28651880	7880027	11999125	3864806	2207642	1733449	1965801	1376814	1466247	12300557	0
Interest **3**	501281	122	11714	5941	13987	5642	9081	10403	5402	3304	6439	429246	0
Rents **4**	51567	39	748	3162	3378	356	5785	616	1295	187	7769	28231	0
Royalties **5**	133751	4348	0	0	0	0	53	0	250	4080	0	125020	0
Other Portfolio Income **6**	684382	69635	186437	47651	49238	41424	5029	9912	20772	29840	62343	162098	0
Other Receipts **7**	1287770	21498	154681	328250	153331	80458	56844	22889	38179	147857	-3200	286988	0
Total Receipts **8**	79121163	3111706	29005460	8265031	12219059	3992686	2284434	1777269	2031699	1562082	1539598	13332140	0
Average Total Receipts **9**	515	86	275	1193	2765	10563	18130	46770	81268	142007	384900	1111012	•
Operating Costs/Operating Income (%)													
Cost of Operations **10**	27.9	19.9	22.4	31.6	29.1	41.3	27.6	16.8	36.4	39.4	44.0	32.0	•
Salaries and Wages **11**	20.4	13.3	20.3	21.0	20.6	17.4	25.0	26.8	20.9	21.3	21.6	20.6	•
Taxes Paid **12**	3.9	4.0	3.4	3.8	4.8	4.3	2.9	3.7	3.0	3.4	3.6	4.7	•
Interest Paid **13**	2.5	1.1	1.1	1.9	2.9	1.4	3.2	1.6	2.0	5.6	2.5	6.2	•
Depreciation **14**	3.3	3.2	2.6	4.1	2.9	5.6	4.5	2.9	3.1	4.1	5.2	3.4	•
Amortization and Depletion **15**	1.0	0.3	0.5	0.6	0.6	0.3	0.8	0.2	0.7	1.6	3.2	3.2	•
Pensions and Other Deferred Comp. **16**	0.4	0.3	0.3	0.4	0.4	0.3	0.4	0.5	0.6	0.4	0.5	0.8	•
Employee Benefits **17**	1.5	1.2	0.8	1.2	1.8	0.7	2.6	2.7	5.2	2.2	2.4	2.4	•
Advertising **18**	2.2	2.6	2.6	1.8	1.6	1.6	4.0	8.9	1.4	2.0	0.4	1.5	•
Other Expenses **19**	31.1	43.9	35.9	29.0	31.4	23.2	27.5	34.0	25.9	30.7	19.1	22.7	•
Officers' Compensation **20**	5.1	9.6	7.6	6.9	4.9	2.5	2.1	1.3	1.4	1.7	0.7	0.6	•
Operating Margin **21**	0.7	0.6	2.7	•	•	1.4	•	0.5	•	•	•	1.9	•
Operating Margin Before Officers' Comp. **22**	5.8	10.2	10.3	4.7	4.0	3.9	1.5	1.8	0.8	•	•	2.5	•

Selected Average Balance Sheet ($ in Thousands)

Net Receivables 23	28	0	3	67	206	624	3071	3086	7007	12438	30312	114956	•
Inventories 24	17	0	3	21	56	420	450	1585	5624	8370	20001	69598	•
Net Property, Plant and Equipment 25	129	0	35	338	918	2963	4531	8213	24593	36138	99679	523411	•
Total Assets 26	400	0	82	683	1942	7251	14997	32135	71550	148660	325320	2414084	•
Notes and Loans Payable 27	195	0	66	355	1087	2079	6386	9440	21119	81371	72150	1004761	•
All Other Liabilities 28	104	0	15	112	487	2194	4610	17095	23972	51999	130595	650118	•
Net Worth 29	101	0	2	216	368	2978	4001	5599	26459	15290	122575	759205	•

Selected Financial Ratios (Times to 1)

Current Ratio 30	1.3	•	1.3	1.3	1.5	1.1	1.4	1.0	1.2	1.0	1.6	1.3	•
Quick Ratio 31	0.8	•	0.9	1.0	1.1	0.8	1.0	0.5	0.7	0.7	1.1	0.6	•
Net Sales to Working Capital 32	22.3	•	44.3	27.6	14.8	41.9	9.5	66.5	24.5	•	10.9	10.9	•
Coverage Ratio 33	2.7	4.4	4.6	2.4	1.3	4.3	1.9	2.9	2.3	1.2	1.7	2.7	•
Total Asset Turnover 34	1.2	•	3.3	1.7	1.4	1.4	1.2	1.4	1.1	0.8	1.1	0.4	•
Inventory Turnover 35	8.4	•	17.5	17.2	14.0	10.0	10.8	4.8	5.1	5.9	8.1	4.7	•
Receivables Turnover 36	15.5	•	68.0	18.4	13.2	12.0	6.3	10.7	11.2	6.9	10.3	9.3	•
Total Liabilities to Net Worth 37	2.9	•	43.0	2.2	4.3	1.4	2.7	4.7	1.7	8.7	1.7	2.2	•
Current Assets to Working Capital 38	4.1	•	3.9	4.1	3.0	8.5	3.5	22.6	6.8	•	2.6	4.1	•
Current Liabilities to Working Capital 39	3.1	•	2.9	3.1	2.0	7.5	2.5	21.6	5.8	•	1.6	3.1	•
Working Capital to Net Sales 40	0.0	•	0.0	0.0	0.1	0.0	0.1	0.0	0.0	•	0.1	0.1	•
Inventory to Working Capital 41	0.7	•	0.6	0.6	0.3	1.7	0.3	2.7	1.4	•	0.6	1.1	•
Total Receipts to Cash Flow 42	4.2	2.8	3.6	4.7	6.5	5.0	4.4	4.3	5.9	5.7	6.2	4.1	•
Cost of Goods to Cash Flow 43	1.2	0.6	0.8	1.5	1.9	2.0	1.2	0.7	2.1	2.2	2.7	1.3	•
Cash Flow to Total Debt 44	0.4	•	0.9	0.5	0.3	0.5	0.4	0.4	0.3	0.2	0.3	0.2	•

Selected Financial Factors (in Percentages)

Debt Ratio 45	74.6	•	97.7	68.3	81.0	58.9	73.3	82.6	63.0	89.7	62.3	68.6	•
Return on Total Assets 46	8.4	•	16.6	7.6	5.2	8.6	7.2	6.7	5.2	5.8	4.7	7.1	•
Return on Equity Before Income Taxes 47	20.8	•	572.7	14.1	6.3	16.1	12.8	24.9	7.9	10.6	5.2	14.1	•
Return on Equity After Income Taxes 48	17.5	•	567.3	12.9	4.5	14.6	9.6	20.9	6.8	4.3	5.2	10.0	•
Profit Margin (Before Income Tax) 49	4.2	3.8	3.9	2.7	0.9	4.7	2.9	3.1	2.7	1.3	1.8	10.5	•
Profit Margin (After Income Tax) 50	3.6	3.4	3.9	2.5	0.6	4.3	2.2	2.6	2.3	0.5	1.7	7.4	•

Table II

Corporations with Net Income

PERSONAL AND LAUNDRY SERVICES

MONEY AMOUNTS AND SIZE OF ASSETS IN THOUSANDS OF DOLLARS

Item Description for Accounting Period 7/06 Through 6/07	Total	Zero Assets	Under 500	500 to 1,000	1,000 to 5,000	5,000 to 10,000	10,000 to 25,000	25,000 to 50,000	50,000 to 100,000	100,000 to 250,000	250,000 to 500,000	500,000 to 2,500,000	2,500,000 and over
Number of Enterprises **1**	82750	17939	57517	4108	2759	275	92	25	14	•	0	•	0
Revenues ($ in Thousands)													
Net Sales **2**	55959343	2267385	19573263	6140289	7750931	2815409	1707441	824483	1244142	•	0	•	0
Interest **3**	479079	6	9064	3993	9960	3265	6220	6675	4303	•	0	•	0
Rents **4**	41319	0	9	954	2836	16	5728	542	1270	•	0	•	0
Royalties **5**	125861	0	0	0	0	0	0	0	168	•	0	•	0
Other Portfolio Income **6**	557618	68549	102795	32211	47437	31546	622	6094	19689	•	0	•	0
Other Receipts **7**	1177360	39678	106712	313200	138849	67081	46186	14442	35210	•	0	•	0
Total Receipts **8**	58340580	2375618	19791843	6490647	7950013	2917317	1766197	852236	1304782	•	0	•	0
Average Total Receipts **9**	705	132	344	1580	2881	10608	19198	34089	93199	•	•	•	•
Operating Costs/Operating Income (%)													
Cost of Operations **10**	27.1	16.7	22.2	35.4	22.4	40.1	27.8	24.2	31.0	•	•	•	•
Salaries and Wages **11**	19.7	13.5	19.2	19.0	20.6	19.1	23.5	17.9	19.3	•	•	•	•
Taxes Paid **12**	3.8	3.2	3.2	3.6	4.8	4.3	2.4	2.7	3.3	•	•	•	•
Interest Paid **13**	2.4	0.9	0.7	1.2	2.9	1.3	1.7	2.1	1.3	•	•	•	•
Depreciation **14**	2.8	1.9	1.7	2.8	2.8	6.2	4.8	4.1	3.3	•	•	•	•
Amortization and Depletion **15**	1.1	0.1	0.4	0.3	0.7	0.4	0.6	0.3	0.3	•	•	•	•
Pensions and Other Deferred Comp. **16**	0.5	0.2	0.2	0.4	0.5	0.2	0.4	0.9	0.7	•	•	•	•
Employee Benefits **17**	1.5	1.1	0.6	1.0	1.6	0.6	2.8	2.6	6.1	•	•	•	•
Advertising **18**	2.0	2.1	2.7	1.8	1.1	1.5	3.7	1.7	1.4	•	•	•	•
Other Expenses **19**	29.6	36.6	33.6	25.9	34.2	20.0	24.6	35.0	30.7	•	•	•	•
Officers' Compensation **20**	4.5	9.0	6.4	6.9	5.5	2.1	2.1	2.3	1.2	•	•	•	•
Operating Margin **21**	5.1	14.8	9.1	1.6	3.0	4.3	5.8	6.1	1.4	•	•	•	•
Operating Margin Before Officers' Comp. **22**	9.6	23.7	15.5	8.4	6.4	6.4	7.8	8.4	2.6	•	•	•	•

Selected Average Balance Sheet ($ in Thousands)

Net Receivables 23	41	0	4	83	218	751	2738	3921	7621
Inventories 24	25	0	4	22	53	545	457	1772	8077
Net Property, Plant and Equipment 25	167	0	28	359	854	2753	4481	8289	26657
Total Assets 26	588	0	80	710	2056	7485	15479	32523	77349
Notes and Loans Payable 27	240	0	44	304	819	1983	5307	7950	16747
All Other Liabilities 28	153	0	12	96	598	2490	4738	13536	26330
Net Worth 29	195	0	24	310	639	3011	5433	11037	34272

Selected Financial Ratios (Times to 1)

Current Ratio 30	1.5	•	1.7	1.7	2.0	1.2	1.5	1.2	1.3
Quick Ratio 31	0.9	•	1.2	1.4	1.4	0.9	1.0	0.6	0.8
Net Sales to Working Capital 32	15.2	•	27.1	16.9	8.8	22.7	8.7	14.5	14.2
Coverage Ratio 33	4.9	23.6	15.9	6.9	2.9	7.3	6.4	5.6	5.9
Total Asset Turnover 34	1.1	•	4.2	2.1	1.4	1.4	1.2	1.0	1.1
Inventory Turnover 35	7.3	•	18.1	23.5	11.8	7.5	11.3	4.5	3.4
Receivables Turnover 36	14.3	•	72.7	19.6	12.9	11.9	7.2	•	9.3
Total Liabilities to Net Worth 37	2.0	•	2.3	1.3	2.2	1.5	1.8	1.9	1.3
Current Assets to Working Capital 38	3.1	•	2.5	2.4	2.0	5.2	3.1	6.8	4.0
Current Liabilities to Working Capital 39	2.1	•	1.5	1.4	1.0	4.2	2.1	5.8	3.0
Working Capital to Net Sales 40	0.1	•	0.0	0.1	0.1	0.0	0.1	0.1	0.1
Inventory to Working Capital 41	0.6	•	0.3	0.2	0.2	1.2	0.2	0.8	0.8
Total Receipts to Cash Flow 42	3.6	2.1	3.0	4.3	5.4	4.9	3.6	3.8	4.6
Cost of Goods to Cash Flow 43	1.0	0.4	0.7	1.5	1.2	2.0	1.0	0.9	1.4
Cash Flow to Total Debt 44	0.5	•	2.0	0.9	0.4	0.5	0.5	0.4	0.5

Selected Financial Factors (in Percentages)

Debt Ratio 45	66.8	•	69.8	56.3	68.9	59.8	64.9	66.1	55.7
Return on Total Assets 46	13.5	•	46.1	17.9	11.4	12.6	13.0	11.7	8.6
Return on Equity Before Income Taxes 47	32.4	•	143.2	35.0	23.9	27.0	31.4	28.3	16.0
Return on Equity After Income Taxes 48	29.3	•	142.4	33.6	22.3	25.3	28.1	25.3	14.5
Profit Margin (Before Income Tax) 49	9.3	19.6	10.2	7.3	5.4	7.9	9.2	9.5	6.2
Profit Margin (After Income Tax) 50	8.5	19.4	10.1	7.0	5.1	7.4	8.2	8.5	5.6

Table I

Corporations with and without Net Income

RELIGIOUS, GRANTMAKING, CIVIC AND PROFESSIONAL ORGANIZATIONS

MONEY AMOUNTS AND SIZE OF ASSETS IN THOUSANDS OF DOLLARS

Item Description for Accounting Period 7/06 Through 6/07	Total	Zero Assets	Under 500	500 to 1,000	1,000 to 5,000	5,000 to 10,000	10,000 to 25,000	25,000 to 50,000	50,000 to 100,000	100,000 to 250,000	250,000 to 500,000	500,000 to 2,500,000	2,500,000 and over
Number of Enterprises **1**	45656	5297	34615	3378	2015	247	78	15	8	3	0	0	0
Revenues ($ in Thousands)													
Net Sales **2**	12533790	349261	3803685	1967558	2254688	729228	626796	421428	1731091	650056	0	0	0
Interest **3**	257343	5416	73769	45513	90020	20318	5897	3038	3811	9561	0	0	0
Rents **4**	25396	0	6729	9171	7541	1036	488	8	87	336	0	0	0
Royalties **5**	6	0	0	0	0	0	0	6	0	0	0	0	0
Other Portfolio Income **6**	34633	0	6525	3378	4318	4916	5660	6719	1662	1457	0	0	0
Other Receipts **7**	1994225	28923	715599	293043	478551	246671	108718	40192	39818	42708	0	0	0
Total Receipts **8**	14845393	383600	4606307	2318663	2835118	1002169	747559	471391	1776469	704118	0	0	0
Average Total Receipts **9**	325	72	133	686	1407	4057	9584	31426	222059	234706	•	•	•
Operating Costs/Operating Income (%)													
Cost of Operations **10**	32.1	9.9	14.4	17.9	31.6	4.3	48.5	42.2	92.5	40.9	•	•	•
Salaries and Wages **11**	10.5	0.5	7.5	7.0	17.9	15.8	12.7	23.9	2.4	23.2	•	•	•
Taxes Paid **12**	1.8	1.3	1.5	1.3	2.9	2.3	3.0	2.2	0.3	2.4	•	•	•
Interest Paid **13**	0.6	0.6	0.5	0.4	0.5	1.8	2.7	0.2	0.1	0.1	•	•	•
Depreciation **14**	1.6	0.2	0.8	0.9	2.1	3.9	4.6	2.9	1.0	1.7	•	•	•
Amortization and Depletion **15**	0.1	0.0	0.0	0.0	0.0	0.0	0.2	0.0	0.0	1.1	•	•	•
Pensions and Other Deferred Comp. **16**	0.2	•	0.1	0.0	0.2	0.2	0.0	1.2	0.0	1.5	•	•	•
Employee Benefits **17**	1.4	0.2	0.5	0.7	1.9	8.3	1.7	1.9	0.1	3.2	•	•	•
Advertising **18**	0.5	2.6	0.4	0.0	0.5	0.4	0.2	0.3	0.1	2.1	•	•	•
Other Expenses **19**	67.0	89.7	94.5	82.2	65.3	99.5	42.6	27.6	5.7	29.1	•	•	•
Officers' Compensation **20**	1.5	4.5	0.6	5.6	0.8	0.3	0.5	0.9	0.1	2.2	•	•	•
Operating Margin **21**	•	•	•	•	•	•	•	•	•	•	•	•	•
Operating Margin Before Officers' Comp. **22**	•	•	•	•	•	•	•	•	•	•	•	•	•

Selected Average Balance Sheet ($ in Thousands)

	•	•	•	•	•	•	•	•	•	•
Net Receivables 23	23	0	3	33	115	1204	275	4627	12696	34690
Inventories 24	2	0	0	0	13	13	332	255	111	5186
Net Property, Plant and Equipment 25	79	0	9	74	460	3124	9444	8881	38236	51711
Total Assets 26	308	0	96	708	1939	7130	14660	30330	64930	192500
Notes and Loans Payable 27	34	0	9	38	173	1504	3758	1185	3753	8116
All Other Liabilities 28	76	0	19	194	451	1959	1896	11579	19776	101489
Net Worth 29	198	0	68	476	1315	3668	9007	17567	41401	82895

Selected Financial Ratios (Times to 1)

	•	•	•	•	•	•	•	•	•	•
Current Ratio 30	2.9	•	4.9	3.4	3.1	1.5	1.9	1.1	1.4	1.5
Quick Ratio 31	2.5	•	4.5	3.0	2.7	1.2	1.6	0.7	1.2	1.3
Net Sales to Working Capital 32	2.1	•	1.7	1.4	1.3	2.8	4.9	21.1	30.5	7.6
Coverage Ratio 33	3.0	1.5	0.9	5.4	5.0	1.4	1.9	52.4	5.7	8.9
Total Asset Turnover 34	0.9	•	1.2	0.8	0.6	0.4	0.5	0.9	3.3	1.1
Inventory Turnover 35	49.9	•	108.4	1586.3	27.3	9.5	11.7	46.5	1799.6	17.1
Receivables Turnover 36	13.4	•	39.1	21.8	8.9	3.9	14.4	8.3	27.4	4.3
Total Liabilities to Net Worth 37	0.6	•	0.4	0.5	0.5	0.9	0.6	0.7	0.6	1.3
Current Assets to Working Capital 38	1.5	•	1.3	1.4	1.5	3.2	2.1	8.1	3.3	3.1
Current Liabilities to Working Capital 39	0.5	•	0.3	0.4	0.5	2.2	1.1	7.1	2.3	2.1
Working Capital to Net Sales 40	0.5	•	0.6	0.7	0.8	0.4	0.2	0.0	0.0	0.1
Inventory to Working Capital 41	0.0	•	0.0	0.0	0.0	0.0	0.2	0.3	0.0	0.2
Total Receipts to Cash Flow 42	1.8	1.4	1.4	1.5	1.9	1.1	2.6	3.2	21.6	3.7
Cost of Goods to Cash Flow 43	0.6	0.1	0.2	0.3	0.6	0.0	1.3	1.4	20.0	1.5
Cash Flow to Total Debt 44	1.4	•	2.9	1.7	1.0	0.8	0.6	0.7	0.4	0.5

Selected Financial Factors (in Percentages)

	•	•	•	•	•	•	•	•	•	•
Debt Ratio 45	35.6	•	29.1	32.7	32.2	48.6	38.6	42.1	36.2	56.9
Return on Total Assets 46	1.5	0.5	0.5	1.7	1.4	1.0	2.9	7.9	1.0	0.9
Return on Equity Before Income Taxes 47	1.6	•	•	2.1	1.7	0.5	2.2	13.4	1.3	1.9
Return on Equity After Income Taxes 48	0.8	•	•	1.6	1.0	•	1.1	10.1	0.6	1.4
Profit Margin (Before Income Tax) 49	1.1	0.3	1.7	1.7	1.9	0.6	2.5	8.4	0.2	0.7
Profit Margin (After Income Tax) 50	0.6	•	•	1.3	1.2	•	1.3	6.3	0.1	0.5

Table II

Corporations with Net Income

RELIGIOUS, GRANTMAKING, CIVIC AND PROFESSIONAL ORGANIZATIONS

MONEY AMOUNTS AND SIZE OF ASSETS IN THOUSANDS OF DOLLARS

Item Description for Accounting Period 7/06 Through 6/07	Total	Zero Assets	Under 500	500 to 1,000	1,000 to 5,000	5,000 to 10,000	10,000 to 25,000	25,000 to 50,000	50,000 to 100,000	100,000 to 250,000	250,000 to 500,000	500,000 to 2,500,000	2,500,000 and over
Number of Enterprises **1**	25033	2288	•	3035	1514	•	40	•	3	3	0	0	0
Revenues ($ in Thousands)													
Net Sales **2**	7600409	155771	•	1790161	1418145	•	430468	•	86386	650056	0	0	0
Interest **3**	205676	3594	•	42356	70427	•	3096	•	1851	9561	0	0	0
Rents **4**	21617	0	•	9171	5364	•	439	•	87	336	0	0	0
Royalties **5**	6	0	•	0	0	•	0	•	0	0	0	0	0
Other Portfolio Income **6**	31075	0	•	3378	4031	•	5619	•	1662	1457	0	0	0
Other Receipts **7**	1386835	28921	•	225738	327092	•	60326	•	16989	42708	0	0	0
Total Receipts **8**	9245618	188286	•	2070804	1825059	•	499948	•	106975	704418	0	0	0
Average Total Receipts **9**	369	82	•	682	1205	•	12499	•	35658	234706	•	•	•
Operating Costs/Operating Income (%)													
Cost of Operations **10**	20.2	•	•	19.7	10.8	•	44.8	•	3.8	40.9	•	•	•
Salaries and Wages **11**	12.4	1.2	•	5.9	21.7	•	8.7	•	32.7	23.2	•	•	•
Taxes Paid **12**	2.0	1.9	•	1.0	3.5	•	1.9	•	3.5	2.4	•	•	•
Interest Paid **13**	0.6	0.0	•	0.4	0.4	•	1.7	•	0.1	0.1	•	•	•
Depreciation **14**	1.3	0.0	•	0.5	1.8	•	2.5	•	9.0	1.7	•	•	•
Amortization and Depletion **15**	0.1	0.0	•	0.0	0.1	•	0.0	•	0.0	1.1	•	•	•
Pensions and Other Deferred Comp. **16**	0.3	•	•	0.1	0.1	•	0.0	•	0.9	1.5	•	•	•
Employee Benefits **17**	1.2	•	•	0.4	1.8	•	1.3	•	2.7	3.2	•	•	•
Advertising **18**	0.6	0.2	•	0.0	0.8	•	0.2	•	1.2	2.1	•	•	•
Other Expenses **19**	75.7	98.5	•	78.7	80.9	•	46.8	•	57.9	29.1	•	•	•
Officers' Compensation **20**	2.2	0.3	•	6.1	0.5	•	0.7	•	2.3	2.2	•	•	•
Operating Margin **21**	•	•	•	•	•	•	•	•	•	•	•	•	•
Operating Margin Before Officers' Comp. **22**	•	•	•	•	•	•	•	•	•	•	•	•	•

Selected Average Balance Sheet ($ in Thousands)

Net Receivables 23	20	0	•	22	74	•	354	•	1026	34690
Inventories 24	2	0	•	0	14	•	383	•	58	5289
Net Property, Plant and Equipment 25	71	0	•	53	263	•	8205	•	34541	51711
Total Assets 26	394	0	•	703	1846	•	13725	•	60235	192500
Notes and Loans Payable 27	31	0	•	26	82	•	2689	•	231	8116
All Other Liabilities 28	100	0	•	186	494	•	2757	•	13948	101489
Net Worth 29	264	0	•	491	1270	•	8280	•	46057	82895

Selected Financial Ratios (Times to 1)

Current Ratio 30	3.2	•	•	3.2	3.4	•	1.5	•	6.1	1.5
Quick Ratio 31	2.8	•	•	2.8	3.0	•	1.2	•	2.9	1.3
Net Sales to Working Capital 32	1.6	750.9	•	1.5	1.0	•	11.4	•	1.7	7.6
Coverage Ratio 33	9.1	•	•	8.0	17.9	•	5.3	•	116.3	8.9
Total Asset Turnover 34	0.8	•	•	0.8	0.5	•	0.8	•	0.5	1.1
Inventory Turnover 35	28.2	•	•	1586.3	7.4	•	12.6	•	18.9	16.8
Receivables Turnover 36	17.0	•	•	30.4	13.0	•	11.1	•	6.6	•
Total Liabilities to Net Worth 37	0.5	•	•	0.4	0.5	•	0.7	•	0.3	1.3
Current Assets to Working Capital 38	1.5	•	•	1.5	1.4	•	3.2	•	1.2	3.1
Current Liabilities to Working Capital 39	0.5	•	•	0.5	0.4	•	2.2	•	0.2	2.1
Working Capital to Net Sales 40	0.6	•	•	0.7	1.0	•	0.1	•	0.6	0.1
Inventory to Working Capital 41	0.0	•	•	0.0	0.0	•	0.0	•	0.0	0.2
Total Receipts to Cash Flow 42	1.5	1.0	•	1.5	1.4	•	2.0	•	1.8	3.7
Cost of Goods to Cash Flow 43	0.3	•	•	0.3	0.2	•	0.9	•	0.1	1.5
Cash Flow to Total Debt 44	1.5	•	•	1.9	1.1	•	1.0	•	1.2	0.5

Selected Financial Factors (in Percentages)

Debt Ratio 45	33.1	•	•	30.2	31.2	•	39.7	•	23.5	56.9
Return on Total Assets 46	4.3	•	•	2.7	3.4	•	7.2	•	4.6	0.9
Return on Equity Before Income Taxes 47	5.7	•	•	3.4	4.7	•	9.6	•	5.9	1.9
Return on Equity After Income Taxes 48	4.7	•	•	2.9	3.8	•	7.3	•	4.2	1.4
Profit Margin (Before Income Tax) 49	5.0	18.8	•	2.8	6.4	•	7.4	•	9.5	0.7
Profit Margin (After Income Tax) 50	4.1	14.7	•	2.4	5.1	•	5.6	•	6.7	0.5

Index

Index

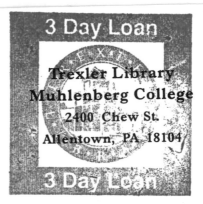